Dodgers

JOURNAL

Year by Year & Day by Day with
the Brooklyn & Los Angeles Dodgers Since 1884

Dodgers
JOURNAL

JOHN SNYDER

For further information, contact the publisher at:

Clerisy Press
1700 Madison Road
Cincinnati, OH 45206
www.clerisypress.com

Library of Congress Cataloging-in-Publication Data

Snyder, John, 1951–
    Dodgers journal : year by year and day by day with the Brooklyn and Los Angeles Dodgers since 1884 / John Snyder.
    p. cm.
    ISBN-13: 978-1-57860-333-6
    ISBN-10: 1-57860-333-1
    1. Los Angeles Dodgers (Baseball team)—History. 2. Brooklyn Dodgers (Baseball team)—History. I. Title.

GV875.L6S69 2009
796.357'646--dc22

                                    2008051295

Edited by Jack Heffron
Cover designed by Stephen Sullivan
Interior designed by Mary Barnes Clark
Distributed by Publishers Group West

Cover photo © AP Photo (ca. 1962)
Interior photos and back cover photos appear courtesy of Dennis Goldstein.
    Baseball cards appear courtesy of the Topps Company Inc.

About the Author

John Snyder has a master's degree in history from the University of Cincinnati and a passion for baseball. He has authored more than fifteen books on baseball, soccer, hockey, tennis, football, basketball, and travel and lives in Cincinnati.

Acknowledgments

This book is part of a series that takes a look at Major League Baseball teams. The first was *Redleg Journal: Year by Year and Day by Day with the Cincinnati Reds Since 1866*, the winner of the 2001 Baseball Research Award issued by *The Sporting News* and SABR. That work was followed by *Cubs Journal: Year by Year and Day by Day with the Chicago Cubs Since 1876*, *Red Sox Journal: Year by Year and Day by Day with the Boston Red Sox Since 1901*, *Indians Journal: Year by Year and Day by Day with the Cleveland Indians Since 1901*, *Cardinals Journal: Year by Year and Day by Day with the St. Louis Cardinals since 1882* and *White Sox Journal: Year by Year and Day by Day with the Chicago White Sox Since 1901*. Each of these books is filled with little-known items that have never been published in book form.

Greg Rhodes was my co-author on *Redleg Journal*, in addition to publishing the book under his company's name Road West Publishing. While Greg did not actively participate in the books about the Cubs, Red Sox, Cardinals, Indians or White Sox, he deserves considerable credit for the success of these books because they benefited from many of the creative concepts he initiated in *Redleg Journal*.

The idea for turning *Redleg Journal* into a series of books goes to Richard Hunt, president and publisher of Emmis Books and its successor company Clerisy Press, and editorial director Jeff Heffron.

I would also like to thank the staff at the Public Library of Cincinnati and Hamilton County. The vast majority of the research for this book came from contemporary newspapers and magazines. The library staff was extremely helpful with patience and understanding while retrieving the materials for me, not only for this book but for all of my other endeavors as well. Dick Miller deserves thanks for providing me with material from his personal collection of baseball books. Dick was a lifelong friend of my father, who passed away in 1999, and installed in me a love of both history and baseball.

And finally, although they should be first, thanks to my wife, Judy, and sons, Derek and Kevin, whose encouragement and support helped me through another book.

Contents

PART ONE: DODGERS DAY BY DAY

Introduction: When Does Time Begin? 8

1884–1889 10

1890–1899 40

1900–1909 86

1910–1919 129

1920–1929 177

1930–1939 230

1940–1949 289

1950–1959 361

1960–1969 448

1970–1979 523

1980–1989 593

1990–1999 660

2000–2008 727

❖ ❖ ❖

PART TWO: DODGERS BY THE NUMBERS

Dodgers All-Time Batting Leaders 1884–2008 794

Dodgers All-Time Pitching Leaders 1884–2008 796

When Does Time Begin?

Today's Dodgers have been part of the National League since 1890 and moved from Brooklyn to Los Angeles at the end of the 1957 season. From 1884 through 1889, the Brooklyn Dodgers were part of another major league organization called the American Association.

The foundations of the franchise that would become the Dodgers extend back to the years preceding the American Civil War. Brooklyn was one of the original hotbeds of baseball. As various bat-and-ball games were being refined, the rules perfected in New York City, Brooklyn and neighboring New Jersey were eventually adopted by the rest of the nation.

Many of the early baseball clubs in Brooklyn were among the best in the world. At this time, Brooklyn was a separate city, and not a borough of the New York City as it is today. It was not only a separate municipal entity, but the third-largest city in the US, with a population of nearly 300,000 in 1860 that trailed only New York and Philadelphia. From 1857 through 1865, the New York metropolitan championship was held by one team or another from Brooklyn. These early powers were known as the Atlantics, the Eckfords and the Excelsiors. The Atlantics were twice recognized as the national champions.

The first known instance of admission being charged to a baseball game came in 1858 when a team of Brooklyn All-Stars played a squad of New York stars in a series of games on Long Island. Brooklyn lost two games of the three contests. In 1862, William Cammeyer placed a fence around a playing field for the first time with the object of charging spectators for the right to see a game and to keep free loaders outside. It was known as Union Grounds and located at the corner of Lee and Rutledge in the Williamsburg section of Brooklyn just across the East River from lower Manhattan. The stands were capable of holding perhaps 1,500. Cammeyer charged an admission of 10 cents.

The first completely professional baseball team was formed in Cincinnati in 1869 and embarked on a national tour. Called the Red Stockings, the Cincinnati outfit steamed into Brooklyn on June 14, 1870 with a winning streak of 81 games. Cincinnati's opponent was the Atlantics. Despite a ticket price of 50 cents, between 12,000 and 15,000 jammed the Capitoline Grounds to witness the match. The contest went into extra innings with the teams deadlocked at 5–5. The Red Stockings scored twice in the top of the 11th, but the Atlantics roared back with three in their half to win 8–7.

The first professional league was organized in 1871 and called the National Association. There were no Brooklyn clubs in the circuit during the initial season, but that omission was rectified in 1872 with the inclusion of the Eckfords and Atlantics. The Eckfords dropped out after one year, but the Atlantics stuck through the 1875 campaign in which they posted an abysmal record of 2–42.

The National Association had fallen on hard times. Scheduling was piecemeal, contract jumping rampant, betting was openly flaunted at the ballparks, and rowdiness abounded. The NA was dissolved at the end of the 1875 season and in its place the National League was organized in 1876 with eight teams. The new NL owners agreed to a strict schedule, drawn up by the league instead of by individual teams. There were heavy fines for any club that failed to play its games. Each club would respect the contracts of the others. Open betting was prohibited, along with the sale of alcohol at the ballparks.

The New York Mutuals were among the teams granted a franchise in the inaugural National League season, and were given the territory of New York and Brooklyn. The home games were played in Brooklyn at the Union Grounds. The Mutuals were expelled from the NL after one season for failing to complete their schedule and for being accused of dumping games, leaving New York without a club in the circuit. However, the Hartford, Connecticut, franchise played its home games in Brooklyn in 1877. The Hartford-Brooklyn club folded at the end of that season due to a lack of patronage.

Even with a population that had exceeded a half-million by 1880, Brooklyn was without a professional team until 1883, the year the world famous Brooklyn Bridge opened. It was also the year the team which evolved into the present-day Dodgers was born. The franchise played in the Inter-State Association of Professional Baseball Clubs, which today is recognized as a minor league, and consisted of teams in New York, New Jersey, Pennsylvania and Delaware. In the same year, a new club from New York was admitted to the National League and were soon known as the Giants.

The owners of the new Brooklyn club were Charles Byrne, George Taylor, Joseph Doyle and Ferdinand Abell, with Byrne serving as president. Byrne was a 39-year-old New York realtor who owned a piece of a gambling house in Manhattan. Taylor, 30, was the night editor of the *New York Herald* and had noted the insatiable appetite for baseball news among the fans of the sport. Doyle was Byrne's brother-in-law and ran a gambling casino on Ann Street in Manhattan. Abell, a Rhode Island casino owner, was the chief financial backer. Byrne, who owned about 20 percent of the stock, was established as club president and was the face of the franchise until his death in 1898.

The group built a ballpark in the Park Slope neighborhood of Brooklyn at a cost of $30,000. It was located between Fourth and Fifth Avenues and Third and Fifth Streets and called Washington Park because George Washington had used the site as his headquarters during the Revolutionary War. The new Brooklyn club, which had not yet acquired the nickname of Dodgers, won the pennant in their first season.

A second major league called the American Association was formed in 1882 with six teams. The AA expanded to eight teams in 1883 and to 12 in 1884. The present-day Dodgers were one of the four teams admitted into the circuit in 1884. At the start of that season, the 12 teams were located in Baltimore, Brooklyn, Cincinnati, Columbus (Ohio), Indianapolis, Louisville, New York, Philadelphia, Pittsburgh, Toledo, St. Louis and Washington.

Our story begins with the 1884 American Association season.

THE STATE OF THE DODGERS

The Dodgers became a major league team in 1884 by joining the American Association. After a 40–64 record that first season, the club became a pennant contender by 1888 and finished the 1889 campaign in first place. Overall, the Dodgers were 410–354 during the decade, a winning percentage of .537. American Association pennant winners outside of Brooklyn during the decade were the New York Metropolitans (1884) and the St. Louis Browns (1885, 1886, 1887 and 1888).

THE BEST TEAM

The 1889 Dodgers won the American Association pennant with a 93–44 record.

THE WORST TEAM

The first club in 1884 won 40, lost 64, and finished in ninth place in a 12-team league.

THE BEST MOMENT

The St. Louis Browns (today's St. Louis Cardinals) won four straight American Association championships from 1885 through 1888, but the Dodgers ended the reign by nosing out St. Louis by two games in a thrilling pennant race.

THE WORST MOMENT

The Dodgers took an immediate dislike of new pitcher Phenomenal Smith, and intentionally made errors behind him during an 18–5 loss to St. Louis on June 17, 1885.

THE ALL-DECADE TEAM • YEARS W/DODS

Bob Clark, c	1886–90
Dave Foutz, 1b	1888–96
Bill McClellan, 2b	1885–88
George Pinckney, 3b	1885–91
Germany Smith, ss	1885–90
Darby O'Brien, lf	1888–92
Jim McTamany, cf	1886–87
Ed Swartwood, rf	1885–87
Adonis Terry, p	1884–91
Bob Caruthers, p	1888–91
Henry Porter, p	1885–87
Mickey Hughes, p	1888–90

THE DECADE LEADERS

Batting Avg:	Darby O'Brien	.290
On-Base Pct:	Darby O'Brien	.357
Slugging Pct:	Darby O'Brien	.392
Home Runs:	Germany Smith	16
RBIs:	Germany Smith	293
Runs:	George Pinckney	566
Stolen Bases:	Germany Smith	235
Wins:	Adonis Terry	95
Strikeouts:	Adonis Terry	953
ERA:	Adonis Terry	3.41
Saves:	Adonis Terry	4

THE HOME FIELD

The Dodgers played their home games in the Park Slope section of Brooklyn (then known as Red Hook) in Washington Park. The ballpark burned down on May 19, 1889. It was rebuilt quickly, and a new Washington Park opened only 11 days later.

THE GAME YOU WISHED YOU HAD SEEN

The Dodgers routed the Baltimore Orioles 25–1 at Washington Park on June 24, 1886. The game still stands as club records for most runs scored in a game and the largest margin of victory.

THE WAY THE GAME WAS PLAYED

The first all-professional team was established in Cincinnati in 1869, and the game was still very much in the evolutionary stage during the 1880s. American Association teams averaged about 11 runs per game in this period, but about half of them were unearned as rough fields made defensive play an adventure. Many players still played bare-handed when the Brooklyn franchise began play in 1884, but gloves were nearly universal by 1890, although they were fingerless and meant only to protect the palm of the hand. Also in 1884, pitchers had to throw from a position below the waist in a sidearm or underhanded motion. By the mid-1880s, the overhand delivery was legalized, giving hurlers more speed and leverage on the breaking pitches. The pitching distance was 50 feet in 1884 and 55 feet in 1887. In 1884, six balls were needed for a batter to draw a walk. The four ball-three strike count was established in 1889.

THE MANAGEMENT

The first president of the Dodgers was Charlie Byrne, with Ferdinand Abell as the main source of capital. George Taylor was another investor, and also served as the club's first field manager in 1884. Charlie Hackett started the 1885 season as manager, but Byrne took over as skipper in June of that season and held the job through the end of the 1887 campaign. Bill McGunnigle (1888–90) followed Byrne.

THE BEST PLAYER MOVE

The best move was the purchase of Bob Caruthers and Dave Foutz from St. Louis during the 1887–88 off-season.

THE WORST PLAYER MOVE

The Dodgers made no player moves during the 1880s which had a long-term negative impact on the club.

1884

LA

Season in a Sentence

In their first season as a major league team, the Dodgers finish ninth in the 12-team American Association.

Finish • Won • Lost • Pct • GB

Ninth   40   64   .385   33.5

Manager

George Taylor (40–64)

Stats

Stats	Dods	AA	Rank
Batting Avg:	.225	.240	10
On-Base Pct:	.263	.278	9
Slugging Pct:	.292	.326	10
Home Runs:	16		8
ERA:	3.79	3.24	9
Fielding Avg:	.899	.897	8
Runs Scored:	476		8
Runs Allowed:	644		9

Starting Lineup

Jack Corcoran, c
Charlie Householder, c-1b
Bill Greenwood, 2b
Fred Warner, 3b
Billy Geer, ss
Jack Remsen, lf-cf
Oscar Walker, cf
John Cassidy, rf
Ike Benners, lf
Jimmy Knowles, 1b

Pitchers

Adonis Terry, sp
Sam Kimber, sp

Attendance

65,000 (eighth in AA)

Club Leaders

Batting Avg:	Oscar Walker	.270
On-Base Pct:	Oscar Walker	.292
Slugging Pct:	Oscar Walker	.359
Home Runs:	Three	
	tied with	3
RBIs:	Not available	
Runs:	Billy Geer	68
Stolen bases:	Not available	
Wins:	Adonis Terry	20
Strikeouts:	Adonis Terry	233
ERA:	Adonis Terry	3.49
Saves:	None	

JANUARY 16   A baseball game on ice skates is played on the Dodgers' frozen home field of Washington Park. In a five-inning game, a team of professionals defeated a team of amateurs 16–8. Among the major leaguers on the Professionals were Sam Kimber, Bill Schenck, Billy Barnie, Oscar Walker, Candy Nelson and Dasher Troy. The Amateurs were selected by Henry Chadwick, who is known as "The Father of Baseball," because of his early influence on the rules and direction of the game. Chadwick also umpired the contest.

APRIL 12   The Dodgers open their pre-season exhibition schedule with a 5–2 loss at Washington Park in Brooklyn to Cleveland, a National League club.

> *Washington Park was located in the Park Slope neighborhood of Brooklyn, bounded by Third Street on the north side, Fourth Avenue on the west, Fifth Street on the south and Fifth Avenue on the west. Park Slope experienced a real estate boom following the opening of the Brooklyn Bridge in 1883. The neighborhood contained many Victorian mansions that are now part of the 24-block Park Slope Historical District. The 1890 census showed Park Slope to be the richest community in the United States. Washington Park was built in a hollow with the main entrance at Third Street and Fourth Avenue. It was constructed entirely out of wood with a single tier grandstand and a set of bleachers. The ballpark was named after George Washington, who used the Gowanus House on the site during the Battle of Long Island during the*

Revolutionary War. The house was built as a stone farmhouse in 1699. Facing 2000 English troops, the 400 soldiers under Washington's command were outflanked and forced to retreat. As a result of the devastating defeat, 259 of the 400 were killed and another 100 wounded. The Dodgers rebuilt Gowanus House as a ladies's restroom and later as a clubhouse. The house was burned and razed in 1897 and rebuilt in 1934, although about 50 yards from its original location, and still stands today.

APRIL 18   The long-standing Dodgers-Giants rivalry gets underway with an exhibition game at Washington Park. The New York Giants won the game 6–0. Future Hall of Famer Mickey Welch pitched the shutout. The Dodgers and Giants wouldn't meet during the regular season until 1890, after the Dodgers moved from the American Association to the National League.

There were three major league teams in the New York area in 1884. The Giants were in the National League, having joined that circuit in 1883. The Dodgers had a New York rival in the American Association with a club known as the Metropolitans, which won the 1884 pennant. The Metropolitans dropped in the standings in subsequent years, however, and folded after the 1887 season. The nickname was revived in 1962 when it was taken by a New York City National League expansion club and shortened to Mets.

MAY 1   The Dodgers play their first regular season game, and lose 12–0 to Washington in Washington. The shutout was thrown by John Hamill. The Brooklyn line-up for the first contest was Bill Greenwood (2b), Fred Warner (3b), John Cassidy (ss), Ike Benners (lf), Oscar Walker (cf), Charlie Householder (1b), Jack Corcoran (c), Adonis Terry (rf) and Sam Kimber (p). The contest was one of only two that Cassidy played as a shortstop during his 10-year major league career. The other one was with Troy in 1881.

The Dodgers manager in 1884 was George Taylor, who was also a part-owner of the club. Taylor was a 31-year-old night editor with the New York Herald *and had no playing experience, giving him little credibility with the players.*

MAY 2   The Dodgers win their first game as a major league club with a 7–5 decision over Washington in Washington. Adonis Terry was the winning pitcher.

William Terry acquired the nickname Adonis because of his good looks and physique, which helped attract women to the ballpark. Because of his prowess as a hitter, Terry played about one-third of his career games as an outfielder, and often batted higher than the ninth spot in the order even when pitching. He was only 19-years-old at the start of the 1884 season and played for the club from 1884 through 1891.

MAY 5   The Dodgers play a regular season game in Brooklyn for the first time and win 11–3 over Washington before a crowd of nearly 4,000 at Washington Park. The winning pitcher was Jim Conway. John Cassidy struck the first home run in Dodgers history. Contero's Ninth Regiment Band gave a 90-minute concert before the contest.

The Washington club folded in mid-season and was replaced by another team representing Richmond, Virginia.

MAY 9
The Dodgers play the present-day Pittsburgh Pirates for the first time, and lose 8–2 in Pittsburgh.

> *At the time, the Pittsburgh club went by the nickname of Alleghenies. They became known as the Pirates beginning in 1891. Pittsburgh was one of four American Association teams to eventually find their way into the National League, having transferred in 1887. The Dodgers and Cincinnati Reds moved to the NL in 1890, and the St. Louis Cardinals in 1892.*

MAY 27
The Dodgers play an extra-inning game for the first time, and lose 7–6 in 12 innings to Indianapolis at Washington Park.

MAY 29
The Dodgers play the present-day St. Louis Cardinals for the first time, and win 2–1 at Washington Park.

> *The Cardinals were then known as the Browns. The Cardinals nickname was attached to the club in 1900.*

MAY 30
On Memorial Day, the Dodgers play two games in one day for the first time by playing two different teams at Washington Park. In the morning, the Dodgers lost 10–5 to St. Louis. In the afternoon, the Dodgers downed Indianapolis 5–0 before a crowd of 8,170. Sam Kimber pitched the shutout, the first in club history. The New York Metropolitans also played St. Louis and Indianapolis on the same day at the Polo Grounds in Manhattan.

MAY 31
The Dodgers score six runs in the first inning and pummel St. Louis 16–1 at Washington Park.

JUNE 7
The Dodgers play the present-day Cincinnati Reds for the first time and win 3–2 in 10 innings at Washington Park.

JUNE 18
Two days after the first roller coaster in the United States opens at Coney Island in Brooklyn, the Dodgers play an African-American opponent for the first time during a 6–4 win over Toledo at Washington Park. The Toledo catcher was Moses Fleetwood Walker, who was the first African-American in baseball history.

> *Walker's brother Welday also played in Toledo in 1884. They were the first two African-Americans to play in the big leagues, and the only two until the arrival of Jackie Robinson in 1947.*

JUNE 19
The Dodgers score nine runs in the third inning and rout Toledo 14–7 at Washington Park.

JUNE 22
The Dodgers play on a Sunday for the first time, and get arrested in Columbus, Ohio. It was rumored that the players would be arrested if the game took place because the law in Columbus wasn't clear as to whether or not playing on the Christian Sabbath was legal. In the fifth inning, with Columbus leading 8–0, several officers made their appearance onto the field, with warrants for the rest of the men. It was decided by the police to allow the game to continue until it was completed. After Columbus closed out an 8–2 victory, six members of the home team and three Dodgers were taken into custody. Each paid a fine following a court date.

Games on Sunday weren't legal in New York or Brooklyn in 1917, although the Dodgers often tried to circumvent the law (see May 2, 1886).

JULY 21   The Dodgers play their American Associations rivals from New York for the first time, and lose 4–0 to the Metropolitans at the Polo Grounds.

AUGUST 2   Because of an illness to umpire John Valentine, Dodgers pitcher Adonis Terry takes over the officiating duties, and the Dodgers defeat Baltimore 9–7 at Washington Park. According to the wire-service reports, Terry "discharged the duty impartially."

At the time, only one umpire was assigned to the games, a situation that would exist into the early 20th century.

AUGUST 6   Sam Kimber pitches a one-hitter and beats Pittsburgh 6–0 at Pittsburgh. The only hit off Kimber was a double by Ed Colgan.

AUGUST 14   Richmond player Bill Schenk is showered with gifts from fans in the first inning of a 3–2 Dodgers loss at Washington Park. Schenk played for Brooklyn in 1883 when the club was in the Interstate League. He was presented with a basket of flowers, a gold watch and a gold medal.

AUGUST 15   The Dodgers rout Richmond 13–3 at Washington Park.

AUGUST 21   A disputed play causes a row during a 13-inning, 4–4 tie against the Metropolitans in New York. With the Metropolitans leading 4–3 in the bottom of the 13th, Brooklyn's John Cassidy tried to score on a sacrifice fly, but on his way to the plate, Metropolitan third baseman Dude Esterbrook got in Cassidy's way. Umpire E. A. Griffith declared Cassidy out, and after a lengthy argument by the Brooklyn players, changed his decision and called Cassidy safe as a result of Esterbrook's interference. Jerry Dorgan of the Dodgers tried to punch Esterbrook, but was held back by his teammates. By the time the dust settled, it was too dark to begin the 14th inning.

The Dodgers batted last in a game on the road because during the 19th century the batting order was determined by a pre-game coin flip.

SEPTEMBER 26   The Dodgers lose 17–2 to the Metropolitans in New York.

OCTOBER 4   A month before Grover Cleveland wins the Presidential election, succeeding Chester Arthur in the White House, Sam Kimber pitches a 10-inning no-hitter in a game which ends in a 0–0 tie against Toledo at Washington Park. The game was called on account of darkness. The first hit by either team was a double by Charlie Householder in the fifth inning. The Dodgers collected only four hits off Toledo's Tony Mullane. Kimber walked two, hit three with pitches and struck out six. At the time pitchers had to deliver pitches to the plate from a position below the waist. The Dodgers complained that Mullane was violating the edict by throwing above the waist, but umpire John Dyler ignored the accusations.

Kimber was a 31-year-old rookie in 1884 and had an 18–20 record with a 3.81 ERA. He pitched in only one big-league game after 1884 with Providence in the National League the following season.

OCTOBER 10   The Cincinnati Reds play a "home" game at Washington Park. The Reds and
Indianapolis squared off against each other in Brooklyn to make up a game
postponed earlier in the season in Cincinnati. Indianapolis was in New York to play
the Dodgers while the Reds were in New York for a series against the Metropolitans.
The two clubs decided it was less expensive to play the game in Brooklyn rather than
travel back to Cincinnati for the contest. The Reds won 4–3.

What is a Dodger?

For purposes of simplicity and consistency, the present-day Los Angeles franchise in the National League is called the "Dodgers" throughout this book. A fan of the club prior to 1895 would have been confused by the name "Dodgers," however, because it wasn't until that year that the nickname was coined. The nickname was originally "Trolley Dodgers" and shortened over time to simply "Dodgers." For some five decades prior to the 1930s, the franchise was known by a variety of nicknames. None was "official" until "Dodgers" was adopted by the club. "Dodgers" appeared on a team uniform for the first time in 1933.

The "Trolley Dodgers" nickname first appeared in newspapers in August 1895. That the nickname originated in a newspaper was typical of the period. Many of the most famous nicknames in baseball, such as Cubs, Reds, Yankees, Phillies, Cardinals, Giants, Braves, Pirates, Indians, Tigers and Orioles, were created not by the clubs themselves but by enterprising sportswriters. In some cases, including Dodgers, a newspaperman heard the nickname spoken by a fan, and included it in a story. The name then caught the fancy of the public and began to be used in everyday speech until it became part of the team's identity.

The editors and authors of many baseball histories have attempted retroactively to attach a single nickname to clubs from the 19th and early 20th centuries, but in fact many of these nicknames were seldom used. In other cases, and the Brooklyn franchise is a prime example, several nicknames were used simultaneously, as each newspaperman had his favorite and would use it in his stories. The nicknames usually weren't recognized by the officials of the club, and therefore weren't official. In addition, clubs of the period were often called the name of the city

instead of a nickname, for instance, the "Chicagos," the "New Yorks," the "Bostons," or the "Brooklyns."

Nicknames used to describe the Brooklyn club during their illustrious history include:

Brooklyns (1884–87)
During the early years of the franchise, the team had no nickname which was used on a frequent basis. Newspaper reports simply and unimaginatively called the aggregation the "Brooklyns," "Brooklyn club," "Brooklyn team" or "Brooklynites." Adding the letter "s" to the end of the city of origin of a particular team of the period was a common practice during the 19th century. The term "Brooklyns" continued to be used on a regular basis until at least 1918.

Bridegrooms (1888–97)
During first part of 1888, several of the Brooklyn players were married. Newspapers began calling the team the Bridegrooms around June of that year, and the nickname stuck. The name Bridegrooms was sometimes shortened to "Grooms." The Bridegrooms nickname was phased out by 1898.

Ward's Wonders (1891–92)
With John Montgomery Ward as manager in 1891 and 1892, the club was sometimes called Ward's Wonders.

Trolley Dodgers, Dodgers (1895-present)
The nickname which would eventually become identified with the franchise had its origins in 1895 (see August 30, 1895). It derived from the dangerous maze of streetcar and trolley tracks which criss-crossed Brooklyn, particularly around Eastern Park, where the club played from 1891 through 1897 (see April 27, 1891). Gradually

over the years, Trolley Dodgers was shortened to Dodgers. It would be the 1930s before Dodgers became the club's primary nickname, however.

Superbas (1899–1925)

During the 19th century, an acrobatic troupe called "Hanlon's Superbas" dazzled audiences on the vaudeville stage. When Ned Hanlon took over as manager with a strong Brooklyn club in 1899, it became known as the "Superbas," although Hanlon was not related to the acrobats. Hanlon left the team after a 104-loss season in 1905. Even after Hanlon was gone and the team was far from "superb" in many seasons, the nickname of "Superbas" lived on until 1925.

Robins (1916–31)

The Dodgers got off to a fast start in 1916 and spent most of the season in first place. In honor of manager Wilbert Robinson, then in his third season in Brooklyn, the New York-area sportswriters began calling the club the "Robins." The franchise still had no official nickname, and newspapers used "Robins," "Dodgers," and "Superbas" interchangeably. The confusion was best exemplified by the April 12, 1917, edition of the *New York Times*. In covering the previous day's Opening Day victory, the paper used "Robins" in the headline across the top of the page. The team was called the "Superbas" in another headline at the top of the column in which the story of the game appeared. The lead paragraph of the story referred to the team as the "Dodgers." The nickname Robins became irrelevant at the end of the 1931 season when Robinson stepped down as manager. Shortly thereafter, "Dodgers" became the club's exclusive nickname. It received official approval in 1933 when it appeared on the team's uniforms. However, many newspapers continued to call the team "The Flock," which derived from the phrase "a flock of Robins." New York City papers continued to periodically call the club "The Flock" through the 1950s.

Ironically, Dodgers became the primary nickname of the team at a time when the electric trolleys and streetcars, which had inspired the moniker, were being phased out of the New York public transportation system, a process which began in 1930. The unwieldy trolleys, confined to tracks, were an impediment to automobile traffic. The trolleys were being replaced on the streets by more maneuverable gas-powered buses. In addition, New Yorkers much preferred the faster-moving subways, elevated trains and commuter railroads to the old trolleys. Trolleys tracks were torn up throughout Manhattan in 1947. By 1951, the only streetcar line left in Brooklyn was the one which went to Coney Island. It was eliminated in 1955.

1885

Season in a Sentence

With only two regulars returning from the 1884 club, the Dodgers land in fifth place in the eight-team American Association with a strong finish after team president Charlie Byrne takes over as manager.

Finish • Won • Lost • Pct • GB

Fifth   53   59   .473   26.0

Managers

Charlie Hackett (15–22) and Charlie Byrne (38–37)

Stats

Stats	Dods •	AA •	Rank
Batting Avg:	.245	.246	6
On-Base Pct:	.295	.292	3
Slugging Pct:	.319	.328	6
Home Runs:	14		7
ERA:	3.46	3.24	6
Fielding Avg:	.910	.909	4
Runs Scored:	624		4
Runs Allowed:	650		5

Starting Lineup

Jackie Hayes, c
Bill Phillips, 1b
George Pinckney, 2b-3b
Bill McClellan, 3b-2b
Germany Smith, ss
Ed Swartwood, lf-rf
Pete Hotaling, cf
John Cassidy, rf
Adonis Terry, lf-p
Jimmy Peoples, c

Pitchers

Henry Porter, sp
John Harkins, sp
Adonis Terry, sp

Attendance

85,000 (fifth in AA)

Club Leaders

Batting Avg:	Bill Phillips	.302
On-Base Pct:	Bill Phillips	.364
Slugging Pct:	Bill Phillips	.422
Home Runs:	Germany Smith	4
RBIs:	Bill Phillips	63
Runs:	Bill McClellan	85
Stolen Bases:	Not available	
Wins:	Henry Porter	33
Strikeouts:	Henry Porter	197
ERA:	Henry Porter	2.78
Saves:	Adonis Terry	1

APRIL 20   Two months after the opening of the Washington Monument in the nation's capital, the Dodgers begin the season with a 7–3 win over the Orioles in Baltimore.

The Brooklyn club was almost completely made over between the 1884 and 1885 seasons. The only returning regulars were Adonis Terry and John Cassidy. Club management purchased six players from Cleveland in the National League for $9,000 after that franchise folded. The five who made the 1885 roster were Bill Phillips, Germany Smith, Pete Hotaling, John Harkins and George Pinckney. Charlie Hackett, the Cleveland manager in 1884, became the Dodgers skipper in 1885. Cleveland posted a 35–77 record in 1884, so the incoming talent was more in the realm of quantity than quality. Also, the new players did not mesh well with the holdovers, disrupting team harmony.

APRIL 24   In the first home game of the season, the Dodgers lose 6–5 to Baltimore before 3,700 at Washington Park.

The American Association reduced its membership from 12 clubs during the 1884–85 off-season, dropping Columbus, Indianapolis, Richmond and Toledo.

The returning clubs were Baltimore, Brooklyn, Cincinnati, Louisville, New York, Philadelphia, Pittsburgh and St. Louis.

APRIL 30   The Dodgers score four runs in the first inning and rout Baltimore 12–1 at Washington Park.

MAY 20   The Dodgers crush the Louisville Colonels 14–4 in Louisville.

MAY 30   During a double-header at Washington Park, the Dodgers win 14–10 and 11–4 over Louisville. In the first game, the Dodgers scored eight runs in the second inning. In the second contest, Brooklyn broke a 4–4 tie with seven runs in the ninth.

JUNE 6   The Dodgers trounce Pittsburgh 13–2 at Washington Park.

JUNE 13   The Dodgers take an 11–4 lead after five innings and outlast Cincinnati 11–9 in Brooklyn.

JUNE 14   Charlie Hackett resigns as manager, holding a 15–22 record. Players complained loudly about Hackett's tactics and said he was to blame for the slow start. Hackett was replaced by club president Charlie Byrne, who remained as manager through the end of the 1887 season.

JUNE 17   The Dodgers intentionally make errors behind new pitcher John (Phenomenal) Smith and lose 18–5 to St. Louis at Washington Park. Smith was a 20-year old from Allentown, Pennsylvania, playing in his first game with Brooklyn. He had previously appeared in two games with two different American Association teams in 1884, and lost both. Despite his lack of credentials, Smith gave himself the nickname "Phenomenal" and said that he was so good that he didn't need the help of his teammates. The Dodgers tried to prove him wrong by making 14 errors behind him, many of them on purpose. Shortstop Germany Smith (no relation) set a major league record with seven errors. Catcher Jackie Hayes was credited with five passed balls.

> *"It's an outrage the way my men treat this new player," said club president and new manager Charlie Byrne, "and I will take steps to punish them for it." Byrne fined the ring leaders of the rebellion a total of $500, and during a long and heated clubhouse lecture, threatened them with expulsion from baseball if they failed to give their best in the future. In the interest of team harmony, however, Smith was released. The pitcher appeared in three games with Detroit in the National League in 1886, then moved on to the Baltimore Orioles in 1887. Smith had the unique distinction of playing for four different teams in his first four big-league games, and five clubs in his first seven contests, over four years. He finished his big-league career in 1891 with a 54–74. Smith was a long-time minor league player-manager, and is credited with discovering Christy Mathewson.*

JUNE 18   A day after making 14 errors in an 18–5 loss, the Dodgers respond to the fines, lecture and threats of Charlie Byrne by beating St. Louis 3–1 at Washington Park without making a single error.

JUNE 20   The Dodgers continue to play well following the June 17 debacle and defeat St. Louis 10–0 at Washington Park.

JUNE 24   The Dodgers rout the Metropolitans 13–6 at Washington Park. Adonis Terry struck the first home run by a pitcher in club history.

JUNE 25   The Dodgers collect 29 hits and win a 21–14 slugfest against the Philadelphia Athletics at Washington Park. George Pinckney collected six hits, all singles, in six at-bats. He also scored five runs. Brooklyn scored 10 times in the sixth inning to take a 20–6 lead. Ten different players had at least two hits—a major league record. In addition to the six by Pinckney, Bill Phillips and John Cassidy each picked up four base hits, Bill McClellan three, along with two apiece from Pete Hotaling, Germany Smith, John Harkins, Bill Krieg and Jackie Hayes. For Philadelphia, George Strief set two major league records. He collected four triples for one record, and adding a double, set another mark with five extra base hits.

JUNE 26   The slugging prowess of the Dodgers continues with a 13–9 win over the Athletics at Washington Park. Brooklyn scored 46 runs in three consecutive games.

AUGUST 6   The Dodgers record drops to 27–45 following a 13-inning, 3–2 loss to Philadelphia at Washington Park. With two out in the 13th inning, Dodger pitcher Henry Porter allowed a single, then walked three straight batters.

               The Dodgers had a 26–14 record over the remainder of the season.

AUGUST 20   The Dodgers garner 20 hits and clobber Baltimore 16–1 at Washington Park.

SEPTEMBER 1   The Dodgers win their eighth game in a row with a 7–6 win over the Metropolitans in New York.

OCTOBER 1   Henry Porter wins his 33rd game of the season with an 8–7 decision over St. Louis at Washington Park.

               In his first season with the Dodgers, Porter had a 33–21 record with a 2.78 ERA. He completed 53 of his 54 starts and pitched 481 2/3 innings. The top hitter was first baseman Bill Phillips with a .302 average.

1886

LA

Season in a Sentence

The Dodgers bring back most of the 1885 roster and continue their rise through the American Association standings to third place with the first winnings season in franchise history.

Finish • Won • Lost • Pct • GB

Third   76   61   .555   16.0

Manager

Charlie Byrne

Stats

Stats	Dods •	AA •	Rank
Batting Avg:	.250	.243	4
On-Base Pct:	.311	.305	4
Slugging Pct:	.330	.323	4
Home Runs:	16		6 (tie)
Stolen Bases:	248		5
ERA:	3.42	3.44	4
Fielding Avg:	.900	.906	7
Runs Scored:	832		4
Runs Allowed:	832		5

Starting Lineup

Jimmy Peoples, c
Bill Phillips, 1b
Bill McClellan, 2b
George Pinckney, 3b
Germany Smith, ss
Ernie Burch, lf
Jim McTamany, cf
Ed Swartwood, rf
Adonis Terry, p-lf-cf-rf
Bob Clark, c

Pitchers

Henry Porter, sp
Adonis Terry, sp
John Harkins, sp
Hardie Henderson, sp
Steve Toole, sp

Attendance

185,000 (third in AA)

Club Leaders

Batting Avg:	Ed Swartwood	.280
On-Base Pct:	Ed Swartwood	.377
Slugging Pct:	Jim McTamany	.371
Home Runs:	Jimmy Peoples	3
	Ed Swartwood	3
RBIs:	Bill Phillips	72
	Ernie Burch	72
Runs:	Bill McClellan	131
Stolen Bases:	Bill McClellan	43
Wins:	Henry Porter	27
Strikeouts:	Henry Porter	163
ERA:	Adonis Terry	3.09
Saves:	None	

APRIL 17   The Dodgers open the season with a 4–1 loss to the Orioles in Baltimore.

APRIL 21   The Dodgers trounce the Athletics 14–2 in Philadelphia.

APRIL 22   The Dodgers win their home opener 6–3 over Baltimore before 4,000 at Washington Park.

MAY 2   With the playing of baseball on Sunday in Brooklyn illegal, the Dodgers and Philadelphia Athletics travel to Ridgewood in Queens for a game at the grounds of the Long Island Athletic Club. The club was located near the Brooklyn-Queens border. A crowd of 7,000, a huge gathering for the era, passed through the turnstiles. The game ended in a 19–19 tie when it was called because of darkness at the end of the eighth inning. The spectators encroached on the playing field, making it nearly impossible for the outfielders to move freely, contributing to the large score. Batters who hit balls into the crowd were limited to two bases, and there were 20 doubles during the contest. George Pinckney collected four hits and scored four runs. Brooklyn had a 10–0 lead before Philadelphia scored nine times in the fourth. In the eighth, the entire supply of baseballs on hand was exhausted after six were hit over the short fences. The Athletics delayed the game for 20 minutes when a practice ball, the only one at hand, was thrown into play by the umpire. Finally, the Philadelphia club consented to continue the contest after Charlie Byrne threatened to have the game forfeited in favor of the Dodgers. In the top eighth, Brooklyn scored five times for a 19–14 advantage, only to have the Athletics respond with five in their half.

The Dodgers made their first attempt to play on a Sunday a week earlier on April 25, and won 11–1 over Baltimore before 7,000 fans. The results of the contest didn't count, however, because American Association president Wheeler Wyckoff ruled the Dodgers did not have approval of the league to play the game. The Dodgers continued to play Sunday games in Ridgewood until 1889.

MAY 6   The Dodgers collect 22 hits and win a 15–13 slugfest against Baltimore at Washington Park. Trailing 13–11, the Dodgers scored a run in the eighth inning and three in the ninth to capture the victory.

MAY 11   The Dodgers score eight runs in the first inning and defeat Philadelphia 13–4 at Washington Park.

MAY 16   The Dodgers score seven runs in the second inning and win 13–7 over Philadelphia at the Dodgers Sunday grounds in Ridgewood, Queens.

MAY 19   Fans react violently to the decision of umpire Jimmie Clinton against the home team during a 7–4 loss to St. Louis at Washington Park. At the end of the game, a mob chanted "Hit him! Hit him!," and attacked Clinton as he walked to the dressing room. The Brooklyn team ran to his assistance and with their bats, kept the "roughs" at bay until the arrival of police.

MAY 23   The Dodgers edge St. Louis 13–12 in 10 innings in Ridgewood, Queens. Brooklyn held a 12–5 lead before St. Louis scored seven runs in the ninth inning.

MAY 31   The Dodgers play two teams in one day at Washington Park, beating Cincinnati 8–6 in the morning, and before a crowd of 10,000, down Louisville 9–6 in the afternoon.

JUNE 3   The Dodgers easily defeat Louisville 11–2 at Washington Park.

JUNE 4   Trailing 7–0, the Dodgers score eight runs in the eighth inning and four in the ninth to rush past Cincinnati 12–7 at Washington Park.

JUNE 5   The Dodgers achieve double figures in runs for the third day in a row against three different teams with a 15–10 victory over Philadelphia at Washington Park.

JUNE 8   The Dodgers outlast Philadelphia 11–9 at Washington Park.

JUNE 12   The Dodgers take first place with a 6–5 win over Baltimore at Washington Park.

The victory gave the Dodgers a 23–15 record. The stay in first place lasted only one day. The club was out of the pennant race by the end of July.

JUNE 24   The Dodgers collect 28 hits and trounce Baltimore 25–1 at Washington Park. Brooklyn scored a run in the first inning, five in the second, five in the third, one in the fourth, one in the fifth, two in the sixth and 10 in the seventh. The Oriole pitchers who absorbed the pounding were Matt Kilroy and Joe Sommer. Kilroy allowed 11 runs, and threw six wild pitches in just two innings. The catchers were part of the problem. Gloves in those days offered little protection, and Baltimore catcher Chris Fulmer had sore hands forcing Kilroy to take something off his fastball. Fulmer left the contest with none out in the third inning and was replaced by Ed Greer, who was normally an outfielder. Bob Clark collected five hits, including a double, in five at-bats and scored four runs. Jimmy Peoples hit a grand slam off Sommer in the seventh.

The 25 runs and 24-run margin of victory are still Dodger club records.

JUNE 26   Two days after winning 25–1, the Dodgers edge the Orioles 1–0 at Washington Park. Adonis Terry pitched a one-hit shutout. The only Baltimore hit was a single by Sadie Houck. Brooklyn collected just three base hits off Hardie Henderson.

JULY 24   Adonis Terry pitches a no-hitter and beats St. Louis 1–0 at Washington Park. He walked two and struck out three. The lone run of the game scored in the eighth inning on a triple by Bill Phillips.

JULY 27   The Dodgers score eight runs in the sixth inning and smash Cincinnati 10–2 at Washington Park.

AUGUST 3   The Dodgers suffer a terrible pounding at the hands of the Pirates in Pittsburgh and lose 18–0. Just 10 days after pitching a no-hitter, Adonis Terry gave up all 18 runs along with 19 hits.

AUGUST 10   The Dodgers produce another embarrassing defeat, dropping a 16–0 decision to the Colonels at Louisville. Henry Porter pitched the entire game.

Porter was normally effective in 1886. He had a 27–19 record and a 3.42 ERA.

AUGUST 11   The Dodgers commit 10 errors and lose 14–7 to the Colonels in Louisville.

AUGUST 12   The Dodgers' pitching problems persist with a shocking 27–11 defeat to the Colonels in Louisville. The contest was mercifully called after seven innings to allow the Dodgers to catch a train. Brooklyn surrendered 57 runs in three consecutive games.

AUGUST 15   The Dodgers miserable play continues with a 19–0 loss to the Cardinals in St. Louis. Adonis Terry allowed 18 runs in seven innings.

AUGUST 16   Down 6–1, the Dodgers erupt for nine hits and 10 runs in the eighth inning and hang on to beat the Cardinals 11–9 at St. Louis. The Dodgers were held to two hits over the first seven innings by St. Louis hurler Bob Caruthers before he was lit up in the eighth. Caruthers had a tremendous day with the bat, however, collecting two homers, a triple and a double. He was tagged out at the plate for the final out of the ninth inning trying to stretch a triple into his third home run of the game.

AUGUST 23   The Dodgers score eight runs in the fifth inning and beat the Metropolitans 16–6 at Washington Park.

AUGUST 28   Brooklyn pitcher Hardie Henderson is presented with a diamond ring containing nine stones by Baltimore players when he steps to the plate in the second inning of a 9–5 Dodgers win over the Orioles in a contest at Washington Park called at the end of the seventh because of darkness. The Dodgers acquired Henderson from Baltimore a few weeks earlier.

SEPTEMBER 9   Five days after the surrender of Geronimo, ending the last major Indian war, the Dodgers trail 11–10 before scoring runs in the ninth and 11th innings and defeat the Athletics 12–11 in Philadelphia. Ed Swartwood was credited with a home run in the 11th when his drive rolled *under* the center field fence. It was the first extra-inning home run in Dodgers history.

Swartwood was Brooklyn's top hitter in 1886. He batted .280 and led the American Association in walks with 70. Bill McClellan ranked fourth in the AA in runs with 133 and George Pinckney fifth with 119.

SEPTEMBER 16   The Dodgers outslug Cincinnati 12–10 at Washington Park. The contest was called after eight innings by darkness.

OCTOBER 5   Three weeks before the dedication of the Statue of Liberty, the Dodgers score seven runs in both the fourth and fifth innings and rout the Colonels 23–3 in Louisville. Rookie pitcher Elton (Icebox) Chamberlain gave up all 23 runs.

1887   L A

Season in a Sentence

After slipping back to sixth place, the Dodgers embark on an off-season spending spree to improve the club.

Finish • Won • Lost • Pct • GB

Sixth   60   74   .448   34.5

Manager

Charlie Byrne

Stats

Stats	Dods	AA	Rank
Batting Avg:	.261	.273	6
On-Base Pct:	.330	.337	4
Slugging Pct:	.350	.367	6
Home Runs:	25		6
Stolen Bases:	409		6
ERA:	4.47	4.29	5
Fielding Avg:	.905	.906	5
Runs Scored:	904		4
Runs Allowed:	918		6

Starting Lineup

Jimmy Peoples, c
Bill Phillips, 1b
Bill McClellan, 2b
George Pinckney, 3b
Germany Smith, ss
Ed Greer, lf
Jim McTamany, cf
Ed Swartwood, rf
Adonis Terry, rf-p
Ernie Burch, lf

Pitchers

Henry Porter, sp
Adonis Terry, sp
John Harkins, sp
Steve Toole, sp
Hardie Henderson, sp

Attendance

273,000 (first in AA)

Club Leaders

Batting Avg:	Germany Smith	.294
On-Base Pct:	Bill McClellan	.363
Slugging Pct:	Germany Smith	.439
Home Runs:	Germany Smith	4
RBIs:	Bill Phillips	101
Runs:	George Pinckney	133
Stolen Bases:	Bill McClellan	70
Wins:	Adonis Terry	16
Strikeouts:	Adonis Terry	138
ERA:	Adonis Terry	4.02
Saves:	Adonis Terry	3

APRIL 16 | The Dodgers open the season with a 14–10 win over the Metropolitans in 10 innings at Washington Park before a crowd of 7,000 on a raw and chilly day. Brooklyn tied the thrilling contest with three runs in the ninth inning before the four-run rally in the 10th. A bouquet of flowers was presented to each woman who entered the grounds. Ernie Burch hit a home run among his four hits, and scored three runs in addition to driving in three. Jim McTamany collected three base hits.

Washington Park had a new grandstand in 1887, but apparently the grading of the outfield was not yet complete. New York left fielder Darby O'Brien fell into a ditch while chasing a long drive off the bat of Brooklyn's Jack O'Brien. The new stands proved to be a hit with fans, however. Despite a fall from third place to sixth, the Dodgers led the American Association in attendance in 1887, and again in 1888 and 1889.

APRIL 25 | The Dodgers win 16–10 over Baltimore at Washington Park in a contest called by darkness after six innings. Oriole pitcher Ed Knouff set a major league record by hitting six Brooklyn batters with pitches.

The Dodgers uniforms in 1887 were white and maroon.

APRIL 26 | Down 3–0, the Dodgers score 11 runs in the second inning and defeat Baltimore 14–7 at Washington Park. Due to heavy rains, the playing field was a quagmire. According to the newspaper reports, "the players at times slipped about in a ridiculous manner."

APRIL 27 | The second inning is lucky for the Dodgers again, as the Brooklyn club scores seven times and wins 14–1 over the Athletics in Philadelphia. It marked the third consecutive game that the Dodgers reached double figures in runs. Jack O'Brien of the Dodgers, a Philadelphia native, was presented with "two handsome medals by admiring friends," then responded by knocking a home run. It was his only home run of the season and the only one he struck in the majors between 1885 and 1890.

MAY 5 | The Dodgers win 16–13 over the Metropolitans at St. George Grounds on Staten Island.

The Metropolitans played on Staten Island in 1886 and 1887. In 1886, fans could not only watch a baseball game, but view the Statue of Liberty being riveted together in New York Harbor. The play The Fall of Babylon *was staged there in 1887, and the set was located in right field. No reliable figures indicate how close the stage was to home plate, but any balls hit into the staging area were ground rule singles.*

MAY 12 | The Dodgers outlast the Cleveland Spiders 17–12 in Cleveland.

The Pittsburgh Pirates moved from the American Association to the National League during the 1886–87 off-season and were replaced by a club representing the city of Cleveland.

MAY 17 | The Dodgers score two runs in the ninth inning and beat the Reds 11–10 in Cincinnati.

MAY 25 | The Dodgers lose 27–9 to the Colonels in Louisville. Adonis Terry allowed 11 runs in the fourth inning and seven more in the fifth.

JUNE 10   The Dodgers score eight runs in the seventh inning and pummel the Reds 17–5 at Washington Park.

JUNE 11   The Dodgers clobber Louisville 14–7 at Washington Park.

JUNE 24   Trailing 3–0, St. Louis scores four runs in the fifth inning and defeats the Dodgers 4–3 at Washington Park. Yank Robinson scored the winning run when he cut in front of third base without touching the bag, an incident noticed by nearly everyone in the ballpark except umpire Charlie Mitchell. Brooklyn manager Charlie Byrne argued with the umpire to no avail, then plopped down next to Robinson on the St. Louis bench to lecture the player on proper sportsmanship.

JULY 17   Steve Toole pitches a two-hitter and beats the Reds 4–0 in Cincinnati. The only hits off Toole were a double by Hugh Nicol and a single from opposing pitcher Elmer Smith.

AUGUST 7   The Dodgers edge Baltimore 13–12 in a slugging match at Washington Park.

AUGUST 10   The Dodgers outhit Philadelphia 13–10 at Washington Park. Brooklyn broke a 2–2 tie with two runs in the fifth inning, then added five tallies in the sixth.

AUGUST 17   Bob Clark collects five hits, including a double, in five at-bats during a 15–2 thrashing of the Athletics in Philadelphia.

AUGUST 21   Trailing 6–4, the Dodgers score five runs in both the seventh and eighth innings and beat the Reds 14–9 in Cincinnati.

AUGUST 22   The Dodgers bash the Spiders 15–4 in Cleveland.

AUGUST 23   The Dodgers reach double figures in runs for the third game in a row with a 10–6 victory over the Spiders in Cleveland.

SEPTEMBER 3   The Dodgers trounce Louisville 14–9 at Washington Park.

SEPTEMBER 5   The Dodgers easily beat the squad from Louisville again, this time 14–4 at Washington Park.

SEPTEMBER 9   The Dodgers score eight times in the fourth inning and vanquish Cleveland 16–3 in a contest at Washington Park called after seven innings by darkness.

SEPTEMBER 24   The Dodgers score eight runs in the first inning to set the stage for a 21–5 rout of Philadelphia at Washington Park.

               Brooklyn's top offensive performers in 1887 were Germany Smith (.294 batting average), George Pinckney (133 runs) and Bill Phillips (101 RBIs).

OCTOBER 8   The Dodgers purchase the franchise of the New York Metropolitans for $25,000.

               Charlie Byrne originally planned to move the Metropolitans elsewhere thus eliminating part of his competition for the New York fan base. When that plan fell through, Byrne retained the best players from the defunct New York team and sold the rest. The Dodgers kept Dave Orr, Paul Radford, Darby O'Brien, Al Mays and Bill Holbert of the 1887 Mets to play in Brooklyn in 1888.

New York's place in the American Association was taken by a club representing Kansas City. Jim Donahue, Frank Hankinson, Charley Jones of the Mets and Dodgers players Bill Phillips, Jim McTamany, Henry Porter and Steve Toole were sold to Kansas City in January 1888. O'Brien and Orr were the big prizes in the deal. O'Brien was Brooklyn's starting left fielder for five seasons. During spring training in 1893, however, he was too ill to play and was sent to Colorado to recuperate. A benefit game was held in O'Brien's honor to cover his expenses. He died from typhoid fever in June at the age of 29. Orr played first base. A squat five-foot-eleven, Orr weighed 250 pounds in an era when few players topped 200. His great strength made him one of the best power hitters of the 19th century. The Dodgers kept Orr only one season, selling his contract to Columbus of the American Association in 1889. He played for Brooklyn in the Players League in 1890 and hit .371 in 107 games before suffering a career-ending stroke. Orr was a caretaker at Ebbets Field when it was built in 1913.

OCTOBER 15   Game five of the 15-game, post-season between American Association champion St. Louis and National League pennant winner Detroit is played at Washington Park in Brooklyn with St. Louis winning 6–2 before a crowd of 6,796.

OCTOBER 22   Game 12 of the St. Louis-Detroit series is played at Washington Park with St. Louis winning 5–1 before 1,138. The game was called after seven innings by darkness.

OCTOBER 30   New acquisition Dave Orr is injured defending a woman in an apartment building on East 112th Street in New York City. Orr threw the assailant down a flight of stairs, but lost his balance and fell down the steps himself. Orr fractured an elbow and a hand and sprained an ankle.

NOVEMBER 21   The Dodgers purchase Doc Bushong from St. Louis. Bushong was Brooklyn's starting catcher in 1888. He had obtained a Doctor of Dental Surgery degree from the University of Pennsylvania in 1882, and practiced dentistry after his baseball career ended in 1891.

The St. Louis club won its third straight American Association pennant in 1887, but owner Chris Von der Ahe was livid after a World Series loss to the National League champion Detroit Wolverines. Von der Ahe set out to dispense with the players he believed were responsible for the defeat, and the Dodgers were the beneficiary as Charlie Byrne and his compatriots opened their wallets to purchase some of the best St. Louis players.

NOVEMBER 26   The Dodgers purchase Bob Caruthers from St. Louis for $8,250. The deal was held up until December 13 when Caruthers agreed to a contract calling for a $5,000 salary in 1888, which made him the highest-paid player in the American Association. "We are perhaps crazy in going as far as we did in the matter," said Charlie Byrne, "but we had gone too far to stop. But we have got Caruthers, and in him the best player in the country. We will gain our money back by charging an increased price of admission and in the larger crowds the Brooklyn club will draw."

Caruthers was a four-year veteran in the majors, and had a lifetime won-lost record of 106–38 at the time he arrived in Brooklyn. In between pitching assignments, Caruthers played in the outfield. He was such a good hitter that Caruthers often batted third and fourth in the batting order even when listed as a pitcher. In 1887, he had a 29–9 record and compiled a .357 batting average in

364 at-bats. But St. Louis owner Chris Von der Ahe blamed carousing and card playing for the World Series loss to Detroit, and Caruthers, an expert at billiards and poker, was a scapegoat. He rewarded Brooklyn with four excellent seasons, winning 110 games with just 51 defeats. In 1889, he helped the Dodgers win the AA pennant with a 40–11 mark. The 40 victories is a club record which will stand for all eternity. At the end of his career, Caruthers was 218–99, a winning percentage of .688, which ranks among the best in major league history.

NOVEMBER 29   The Dodgers purchase Dave Foutz from St. Louis for a reported $6,000.

Like Bob Caruthers, Dave Foutz was a star pitcher who doubled as an outfielder. From 1884 through 1887, Foutz had a record of 114–48, but by the time he was acquired by the Dodgers, his arm was about shot. Foutz was a good enough hitter, however, to be a starter in the Brooklyn batting lineup as an outfielder and first baseman for six seasons. He was the club's player-manager from 1893 through 1896 and before being dismissed from the post just prior to dying of asthma in March 1897. With Caruthers and Foutz in the fold, the Dodgers won the American Association pennant in 1889, in a close race with St. Louis, and the National League crown in 1890.

1888   LA

Season in a Sentence

Following an off-season infusion of high-priced, star-quality talent, the Dodgers take a 6½ game lead in mid-June, but slip out of contention by the end of August.

Finish • Won • Lost • Pct • GB

Second   88   52   .629   6.5

Manager

Bill McGunnigle

Stats	Dods	AA	Rank
Batting Avg:	.242	.238	4
On-Base Pct:	.300	.297	4
Slugging Pct:	.321	.315	4
Home Runs:	25		5
Stolen Bases:	334		5
ERA:	2.33	3.06	2
Fielding Avg:	.918	.917	5
Runs Scored:	758		3
Runs Allowed:	584		2

Starting Lineup

Doc Bushong, c
Dave Orr, 1b
Jack Burdock, 2b
George Pinckney, 3b
Germany Smith, ss
Darby O'Brien, lf
Paul Radford, cf
Dave Foutz, rf
Bob Caruthers, rf-cf-p
Bill McClellan, 2b
Oyster Burns, ss

Pitchers

Bob Caruthers, sp
Mickey Hughes, sp
Adonis Terry, sp
Dave Foutz, sp
Al Mays, sp

Attendance

245,000 (first in AA)

Club Leaders

Batting Avg:	Dave Orr	.305
On-Base Pct:	Dave Orr	.330
Slugging Pct:	Dave Orr	.388
Home Runs:	Bob Caruthers	5
RBIs:	Dave Foutz	99
Runs:	George Pinckney	134
Wins:	Bob Caruthers	29
Strikeouts:	Mickey Hughes	159
ERA:	Adonis Terry	2.03
Saves:	None	

APRIL 18   The Dodgers win the season opener 10–1 over Cleveland at Washington Park. Bob Caruthers was the winning pitcher in his Brooklyn debut. Dave Orr and Dave Foutz each had three hits in their first games with the Dodgers. Germany Smith also collected three hits. There was a pre-game band concert, and Brooklyn mayor A. C. Chapin was in attendance.

The new Dodgers manager was Bill McGunnigle. Club president Charlie Byrne served as field manager from June 1885 through the end of the 1887 season, but realized he needed an experienced hand at the helm. McGunnigle was 33 years old when he took over as the Brooklyn skipper. As a minor leaguer in 1875, he is credited with being the first player to wear a glove. For a game against Harvard, McGunnigle donned a pair of bricklayer's gloves. He later pioneered the use of removable baseball spikes. McGunnigle played in the majors as a pitcher-outfielder from 1879 through 1882 and had been a successful manager in the minors. He would guide the Dodgers to pennants in the American Association in 1889 and the National League in 1890.

APRIL 19   The Dodgers clobber Cleveland 14–3 at Washington Park. The contest was called after seven innings by darkness.

MAY 12   The Dodgers score two runs in the ninth inning after two are out and win 3–2 over the Athletics in Philadelphia.

MAY 16   The Dodgers outslug the Spiders 12–9 in Cleveland.

MAY 17   The Dodgers trounce the Spiders 15–0 in Cleveland. The score was 2–0 before Brooklyn erupted for five runs in the sixth inning, four in the seventh and four in the eighth.

MAY 20   Bob Caruthers pitches a two-hitter in beating the Kansas City Cowboys 9–0 at Ridgewood, Queens. The only hits off Caruthers were singles by Sam Barkley and Jumbo Davis. Caruthers faced the minimum 27 batters as both runners were retired on the base paths.

Caruthers was 29–15 with a 2.34 ERA in 1888.

MAY 27   Adonis Terry pitches a no-hitter in defeating Louisville 4–0 at Ridgewood, Queens before a crowd of 4,782. Terry walked three and struck out eight. It was his second career no-hitter. The first was on July 24, 1886.

MAY 28   Trailing 5–1, the Dodgers score two runs in the eighth inning and three in the ninth to beat Louisville 6–5 at Washington Park.

JUNE 2   The Dodgers achieve their eighth win in a row with a 15–6 decision over the Reds in Cincinnati. Dave Orr collected five hits in five at-bats and scored four runs.

JUNE 10   The Dodgers take a 6½-game lead in the American Association pennant race with a 10–2 triumph over Cleveland at Washington Park.

The Dodgers started the season with a 33–10 record, but a stretch of 23 losses in 37 games during July and August ruined the club's chances for a pennant.

JUNE 24   The Dodgers rout Baltimore 14–5 at Ridgewood, Queens.

                 In mid-season, newspapers began calling the Brooklyn club the "Bridegrooms"
                 because several players had recently married.

JULY 6   The Dodgers defeat the Cardinals 6–2 on a festive day in St. Louis. It was the first
                 game in the city for Bob Caruthers, Dave Foutz and Doc Bushong since they were
                 sold by the St. Louis club to Brooklyn the previous November. A parade was given
                 in their honor in the morning with about 20 carriages and a brass band in line as
                 they passed through the principal streets of the city. The three returning heroes were
                 enthusiastically cheered.

JULY 8   A two-out, two-run single in the ninth inning by Dave Foutz beats the Cardinals 4–3
                 in St. Louis.

JULY 10   In St. Louis, the Cardinals break a 1–1 tie with three runs in the top of the ninth
                 inning on Ed Herr's home run, but the Dodgers score three in their half of the ninth
                 and one in the 10th for a 5–4 victory. The three ninth-inning runs crossed the plate
                 on a two-run triple by Paul Radford and an error. The winning run scored on a
                 single by Bob Caruthers. The victory gave the Dodgers a 4½-game lead over
                 St. Louis in the pennant race.

JULY 14   At Kansas City, players are used as substitute umpires, with Adonis Terry of the
                 Dodgers behind the plate and Jim Donahue of the Cowboys on the bases. Kansas
                 City scored three runs in the top of the ninth to take a 5–4 lead. With one out in
                 the bottom half, Donahue called Bill McClellan out on a pick-off play at first base.
                 During the wrangle which followed, Terry refused to umpire any further, and the
                 Dodgers walked off the field, resulting in a forfeit. Terry stated that he heard Kansas
                 City captain Sam Barkley, who was playing second base, order Donahue to call
                 McClellan out. Barkley indignantly denied the charge.

JULY 22   The Dodgers drop out of first place with a 4–3 loss to Philadelphia at Washington Park.

                 By the end of August, the Dodgers were 11½ games out of first place. St. Louis
                 won its fourth consecutive pennant despite selling their two top pitchers (Bob
                 Caruthers and Dave Foutz) and starting catcher (Doc Bushong) to the Dodgers.

AUGUST 2   Claiming illness, Dave Orr misses a team practice. Later that day, he was spotted at
                 Coney Island, and Charlie Byrne removes Orr as team captain.

                 Orr hit .305 for Brooklyn in 1888, his only season with the club. George
                 Pinckney was another offensive star with a league-leading 134 runs. Dave Foutz
                 batted .277 and hit 13 triples.

AUGUST 4   Umpire Bob Ferguson causes a commotion during a 4–4 tie between the Dodgers
                 and St. Louis at Washington Park. Weary of repeated catcalls over his decisions from
                 both clubs and the fans, Ferguson put on his hat and coat at the end of the ninth
                 inning with the game tied and walked toward the exit. Charlie Byrne confronted
                 Ferguson, and after considerable coaxing, convinced the umpire to continue.
                 Ferguson called the contest at the end of the 11th even though there was about
                 an hour of daylight remaining.

AUGUST 7   Mickey Hughes pitches a two-hitter in beating Louisville 7–0 at Washington Park. The only hits off Hughes were singles by Wally Andrews and opposing pitcher Guy Hecker.

AUGUST 10   The Dodgers purchase Oyster Burns from Baltimore.

Thomas (Oyster) Burns was a starter in the Dodgers lineup until 1894 and in the process became one of the most popular players in Brooklyn. In 1890, he led the National League in both home runs and runs-batted-in. Burns reportedly earned his nickname by selling shellfish in the off-season.

AUGUST 11   At a time when Jack the Ripper is making headlines by terrorizing London, Darby O'Brien hits a two-out, two-run single in the 11th inning to beat the Reds 6–5 in Cincinnati.

AUGUST 12   Adonis Terry shuts out the Reds 1–0 in Cincinnati.

AUGUST 15   The Dodgers score five runs in the first inning and eight in the second on the way to an 18–7 thrashing of the Colonels in Louisville.

AUGUST 22   The only Dodgers hit off Silver King of the Cardinals during a 4–2 Brooklyn loss at St. Louis is a pop fly by Darby O'Brien in the ninth inning which drops between shortstop Bill White and left fielder Tip O'Neill.

SEPTEMBER 2   After the Reds score four runs in the top of the ninth for a 4–3 lead, the Dodgers rally for two runs in the bottom half to win 5–4 at Washington Park. Jack Burdock's home run tied the score 4–4. Oyster Burns's triple provided the winning run.

The home run by Burdock was the only one he hit all year and his first since 1884. During the 1888 season, Burdock batted an abysmal .122 in 70 games and 246 at-bats with a slugging percentage of .154.

SEPTEMBER 3   Bob Caruthers pitches the Dodgers to a 1–0 win over St. Louis at Washington Park. Doc Bushong drove in the winning run with a single.

SEPTEMBER 16   Mickey Hughes pitches a two-hitter to beat Philadelphia 8–0 at Washington Park. The only hits off Hughes were a double and single by Lou Bierbauer.

Hughes was 25–13 with a 2.13 ERA in 1888.

SEPTEMBER 15   The Dodgers sell Bill McClellan to Cleveland.

SEPTEMBER 23   The Dodgers purchase Pop Corkhill from the Reds.

SEPTEMBER 30   The Dodgers purchase Hub Collins from Louisville.

A second baseman, Collins proved to be another excellent acquisition. In 1890, he led the National League in runs scored, but two years later he died at the age of 28 from typhoid fever.

OCTOBER 16   The Dodgers close the season with their 10th victory in a row by scoring five runs in the ninth inning to cap a thrilling 6–5 decision over Baltimore at Washington Park.

OCTOBER 19   Game four of the post-season series between American Association champion
               St. Louis and the New York Giants National League pennant winners is held at
               Washington Park in Brooklyn with New York winning 6–3 before 3,062.

DECEMBER 23   Seven weeks after Benjamin Harrison defeats Grover Cleveland in the Presidential
               election, the Dodgers sell Dave Orr and Al Mays to Columbus, a new club in the
               American Association. Columbus replaced the Cleveland franchise, which moved
               to the National League.

1889   L A

Season in a Sentence

The Dodgers fall 6$\frac{1}{2}$ games behind in June, rally to win an exciting pennant race over St. Louis, lose to the Giants in the World Series, then leave the American Association for the National League.

Finish • Won • Lost • Pct • GB

First   93   44   .679   +2.0

Manager

Bill McGunnigle

World Series

The Dodgers lost six games to three to the New York Giants.

Stats

Stats	Dods	AA	Rank
Batting Avg:	.263	.262	4
On-Base Pct:	.344	.333	2
Slugging Pct:	.364	.354	4
Home Runs:	47		3
Stolen Bases:	389		3
ERA:	3.61	3.84	5
Fielding Avg:	.928	.916	1
Runs Scored:	995		1
Runs Allowed:	706		2

Starting Lineup

Joe Visner, c
Dave Foutz, 1b
Hub Collins, 2b
George Pinckney, 3b
Germany Smith, ss
Darby O'Brien, lf
Pop Corkhill, cf
Oyster Burns, rf
Bob Clark, c

Pitchers

Bob Caruthers, sp
Adonis Terry, sp
Tom Lovett, sp
Mickey Hughes, sp

Attendance

353,690 (first in AA)

Club Leaders

Batting Avg:	Oyster Burns	.304
On-Base Pct:	Oyster Burns	.391
Slugging Pct:	Oyster Burns	.423
Home Runs:	Joe Visner	8
	Pop Corkhill	8
RBIs:	Dave Foutz	113
Runs:	Darby O'Brien	146
Stolen Bases:	Darby O'Brien	91
Wins:	Bob Caruthers	40
Strikeouts:	Adonis Terry	186
ERA:	Bob Caruthers	3.13
Saves:	Bob Caruthers	1

APRIL 17   The scheduled season opener against the Athletics in Philadelphia is postponed by rain.

APRIL 18   The Dodgers get the 1889 season underway with a 3–2 loss to the Athletics on
               Philadelphia.

APRIL 25   Three days after the Oklahoma land rush opens the territory to white settlement, the
                home opener ends in a 9–9 tie against Columbus before 3,500 at Washington Park.
                The contest was called after nine innings by darkness. Oyster Burns collected three
                hits and Joe Visner smacked a home run.

                *Though he was a catcher, Visner's eight home runs led the Dodgers in 1889.
                Burns batted .304, drove in 100 runs and scored 105. Darby O'Brien batted
                .300 and scored 146 runs. Hub Collins scored 139 times and Dave Foutz drove
                in 113 runs. Bob Caruthers was the leading pitcher with a league-leading, and
                club record, 40 victories along with 11 only defeats and a 3.13 ERA. Adonis
                Terry was 22–15 and had an earned run average of 3.29.*

MAY 5   The Dodgers lose a forfeit to Philadelphia before 12,614 at Ridgewood, Queens.
                By the time the game started, every seat was taken and a wall of humanity began
                to form around the field. The crowd in center field was so dense that many of the
                spectators couldn't see the players. In the sixth inning, the Athletics scored four
                runs to break a 1–1 tie. The crowd ringing the outfield began to close in toward the
                infield. Charlie Byrne led a contingent to try and push the crowd back, but to no
                avail. In a few minutes, fans had swarmed the field and the players of both teams
                went to their dressing rooms. Umpire Willard Holland declared the game a forfeit
                in favor of the Athletics.

MAY 7   The Dodgers score five runs in the first inning and crush the Colonels 13–3 in
                Louisville.

MAY 8   The Dodgers score 10 runs in the eighth inning to cap a 21–2 thrashing of the
                Colonels in Louisville.

MAY 10   The Dodgers continue to pound the Colonels pitching staff with a 10–6 win at
                Louisville.

MAY 12   The Dodgers reach double figures in runs scored for the fourth consecutive game
                with a 10–7 victory over the Reds in Cincinnati. Oyster Burns collected five hits,
                including two triples, in five at-bats.

MAY 19   With the Dodgers in St. Louis, Washington Park is almost totally destroyed by
                a fire which was discovered at 1:00 a.m. The flames started in the dressing room
                underneath the wooden grand stand on the Fifth Avenue side of the lot and
                spread with great rapidity. The cause of the blaze was never determined. Dodgers
                management immediately began work on a new stand, employing carpenters around
                the clock. The next scheduled home game was on May 30 with a double-header
                against St. Louis and the damage was sufficiently repaired to allow the use of the
                facility. The afternoon game of the May 30 contest drew a then-record 21,122 fans.

MAY 20   The two teams combine to score in 15 different half-innings during a 18–12 Dodgers
                loss to the Cowboys in Kansas City. The Cowboys scored in all nine innings, with
                Brooklyn doing so in six, failing to dent the plate only in the second, third and sixth.

MAY 21   The Dodgers and Cowboys engage in another slugging match with Brooklyn winning
                14–13 in Kansas City. The Cowboys scored five runs in the ninth inning and ended
                the contest with the tying run on third base.

MAY 22
The Dodgers heavy hitting continues with a 13–7 win over the Cowboys in Kansas City.

MAY 23
The Dodgers score nine runs in the first inning and pummel the Cowboys 17–3 in Kansas City in a contest halted by rain in the sixth inning. Brooklyn scored 55 runs in the four-game series in Kansas City.

JUNE 8
A week after the Johnstown, Pennsylvania, flood claims 2,000 lives, the Dodgers trounce Louisville 14–5 at Washington Park.

At the end of the day, Brooklyn was 24–17 and 6½ games behind a St. Louis club vying for its fifth consecutive American Association pennant.

JUNE 20
The Dodgers score 13 times in the last three innings and defeat Baltimore 14–5 at Washington Park.

JUNE 24
The Dodgers win a forfeit over Columbus at Washington Park. Regular umpire Fred Goldsmith was unavailable and William Paasch was assigned as a substitute. Columbus refused to play if Paasch officiated, and the contest was forfeited. Columbus did agree to play off a contest which had been postponed in April and won 13–7 with Paasch serving as umpire.

JUNE 30
With the playing of baseball illegal on Sunday in Philadelphia, the Dodgers and Athletics play a regular season game in Gloucester, New Jersey with Brooklyn winning 8–3.

JULY 4
The Dodgers defeat the Cardinals 12–10 in the afternoon game of a holiday double-header in St. Louis. Brooklyn scored six times in the fifth inning to take an 8–6 lead. St. Louis won the morning tilt 4–3.

JULY 6
The Dodgers beat the Cowboys 12–11 in Kansas City with a run in the ninth inning. The Cowboys scored nine runs in the third inning to take an 11–4 lead before Brooklyn rallied.

JULY 13
The Dodgers belt the Reds 15–5 in Cincinnati.

JULY 26
The Dodgers rout the Reds 20–6 at Washington Park. Brooklyn scored a run in the second inning, five in the third, two in the fourth, four in the fifth, five in the sixth and three in the eighth.

AUGUST 1
The Dodgers win a double-header 8–6 and 14–1 over Louisville at Washington Park. After heavy morning rains, the outfield turned into a marsh with small ponds settling throughout the grass.

AUGUST 3
The Dodgers score seven runs in the sixth inning and beat St. Louis 13–6 in a contest called by rain after seven innings. By the end of the game, outfielders were standing ankle deep in mud.

AUGUST 5
The Dodgers win 13–0 over the Athletics in Philadelphia. The game was scoreless until Brooklyn erupted with three runs in the sixth inning, five in the seventh and five in the eighth.

AUGUST 8   Darby O'Brien collects six hits, including three doubles, in six at-bats during a 12–11 win over Columbus in Columbus.

AUGUST 11   The Dodgers fall 2½ games in the pennant race with a 14–4 loss to the Cardinals before a crowed of 16,000 in St. Louis.

Because of the importance of the game, the American Association assigned two umpires. The overflow from the packed grandstand ringed the outfield, and a rule was adopted that any ball hit into the crowd would be a double. With one out in the seventh, St. Louis outfielder Charlie Duffee knocked a ball over the fence for a home run. The hit caused a scrap that lasted for half an hour. The Dodgers claimed that the drive should be a double because of the ground rule. The Cardinals asserted that it was a home run since it left the park. Umpire John Kerins ruled the play a home run. Fellow arbiter Bob Ferguson said it should be a double. While an argument ensued, many in the crowd surged onto the field, and it took the combined efforts of the police and the Cardinals players to clear the diamond. Ferguson and the Dodgers finally got their way, and Duffee went to second base. Later, Duffee collided with Brooklyn catcher Bob Clark, who claimed he was injured and couldn't continue. At the time, substitutions couldn't be made without the consent of the opposition and the umpires. St. Louis manager Charlie Comiskey refused to allow Clark to leave the game. Four doctors were called to examine Clark, creating another delay of approximately 30 minutes as hundreds of fans again stormed the field. Clark was compelled to stay in the game.

AUGUST 17   The Dodgers score seven runs in the eighth inning and whip the Colonels 10–0 in Louisville.

AUGUST 20   The Dodgers collect 20 hits and outslug the Colonels 18–11 at Louisville. Darby O'Brien had two triples and two doubles in six at-bats.

AUGUST 30   The Dodgers clobber Kansas City 14–4 at Washington Park.

AUGUST 31   The Dodgers move into a tie for first place with St. Louis with a double-header sweep of Kansas City by scores of 11–4 and 8–2 at Washington Park.

SEPTEMBER 1   The idle Dodgers take sole possession of first place when St. Louis loses 6–5 at Columbus.

SEPTEMBER 3   The Dodgers trounce the Reds 13–8 at Washington Park.

SEPTEMBER 4   The Dodgers slaughter the Reds 12–1 at Washington Park.

SEPTEMBER 7   In the first game of a pennant showdown series against the Cardinals at Washington Park, umpire Fred Goldsmith declares a forfeit in favor of the Dodgers.

The Cardinals led 4–2 in the ninth inning. St. Louis manager Charlie Comiskey tried convincing Goldsmith that it was too dark to continue, serving only to aggravate the umpire, who had listened to a steady stream of complaints from St. Louis players all day. Cardinals owner Chris Von der Ahe attempted to make his point about the gathering darkness by buying candles from a nearby grocery store and then lit and arranged them around the St. Louis bench like footlights, which did not improve Goldsmith's mood or that of the partisan Brooklyn fans. Some threw beer steins at the candles. They succeeded in knocking down a number of the candles, which ignited stray paper nearby and in turn created a small fire that briefly threatened to set the wooden grandstand ablaze. Fortunately, the flames were extinguished before any real damage was done. Determined to finish the game, the umpire forced the players to begin the ninth. Soon, Comiskey refused to play and ordered his men off the field. As they exited, Brooklyn fans threw bottles and a few St. Louis players were struck. Goldsmith threatened to declare a forfeit. When he did so, many of the crowd of 15,143 rioted, and broke windows of the clubhouse which housed the St. Louis players, where they huddled in fear until police arrived.

SEPTEMBER 8   The Dodgers win another forfeit against St. Louis in a contest scheduled for Brooklyn's Sunday grounds in Ridgewood, Queens.

St. Louis owner Chris Von der Ahe refused to send his players out to the field. Dodger games at Ridgewood, which had been taking place since 1886, were technically in violation of New York state law which prohibited Sunday amusements. The Queens County sheriff tacitly allowed the games to continue, but since he was violating the statute by doing so, could not send any of his officers to the grounds. With no police presence, and a large crowd of about 17,000 inflamed by the pennant race and the tensions of the September 7 game, Von der Ahe feared for the safety of his players. On September 23, a special American Association meeting reversed the forfeit of September 7 in favor of the Dodgers and awarded a 4–2 victory to the Cardinals. But the forfeit of September 8 stood.

SEPTEMBER 15   The Dodgers sweep Louisville 7–2 and 6–5 at Ridgewood, Queens. The second game went 14 innings with Dave Foutz driving in the winning run with a double.

The 1889 season was the Dodgers last at Ridgewood. In 1890, the club moved to the National League, which banned games on Sundays until 1892. Sunday baseball in Brooklyn wasn't legal until 1917.

SEPTEMBER 23   Umpire Ed Hengle causes a wrangle during a game against Columbus at Washington Park which results in a 3–2 Dodgers loss. Hengle's decisions angered players from both clubs, and Mark Baldwin of Columbus and Joe Visner of the Dodgers were ejected. With darkness approaching, Hengle ordered the start of the ninth inning with Columbus leading 3–2. The Dodgers scored a run to tie the contest, but Hengle then called the game claiming it was too dark to continue. By rule, the score went back to the last completed inning, which meant a 3–2 Columbus victory. This action enraged the crowd and a wild rush was made for the umpire. The police and players quickly surrounded Hengle, who safely reached the clubhouse.

SEPTEMBER 24   The Dodgers shut out Columbus 10–0 at Washington Park.

OCTOBER 7   The Dodgers score seven runs in the third inning and walk over the Athletics 17–0 at Washington Park.

OCTOBER 8   The Dodgers take a two-game lead in the pennant race with a 12–9 victory over the Orioles in Baltimore with five runs in the seventh inning just before the contest is called by darkness.

OCTOBER 9   The Dodgers garner 20 hits and defeat the Orioles 17–9 in Baltimore. Bob Caruthers earned his 40th victory of the season.

OCTOBER 14   The Dodgers clinch the pennant with a 6–1 win at Columbus.

The Dodgers played the National League champion New York Giants in the post-season. Even though it involved two New York-area teams, who were champions of two leagues with no franchises west of Kansas City or south of Washington, the newspapers across the nation had no hesitation in calling the Dodgers-Giants match-up the "World Series." Managed by Jim Mutrie, the Giants were 83–43 in 1889. The series was a best-of-11 affair. It was the first time that the Dodgers and Giants met in a meaningful game. Previously, the two franchises had played each other only in exhibition contests. Even in the early stages, the antagonism between the Dodgers and Giants was intense. The October 19, 1889, editions of the New York Times *reported: "The rivalry between New York and Brooklyn as regards to baseball is unparalleled in the history of the national game. It is not attached to the players or attaches of the clubs, but the patrons take part in it. Old men, middle-aged men, beardless youths, small boys, and even members of the gentler sex have the fever, and when the champions of the two teams meet, heated arguments as to the merits of the nines are sure to follow."*

OCTOBER 18   Before a crowd of 8,848 at the Polo Grounds, the Dodgers take the opening game of the 1889 World Series with a 12–10 victory over the Giants in a contest called after eight innings. Brooklyn took a 5–0 lead in the first inning, but couldn't hold the advantage. With darkness falling and the Dodgers batting in the last of the eighth with New York leading 10–8, Brooklyn scored four runs in the deepening gloom for the victory. Hub Collins drove in the tying run with a double, and scored on Darby O'Brien's single. At the conclusion of the inning, umpire Bob Ferguson declared it was too dark to continue, and the Dodgers had the victory.

OCTOBER 19   The Dodgers lose game two 6–2 to the Giants before 16,172 at Washington Park.

OCTOBER 22   The Dodgers win game three 8–7 at the Polo Grounds. As in game one, the contest was called after eight innings by darkness. Controversy swirled as Brooklyn delayed the contest at every opportunity, so that darkness would end the proceedings while the Dodgers were still in the lead. Umpire John Gaffney ended the game with one out in the Giants ninth inning and the bases loaded. "The Brooklyn boys played like schoolboys," said Giants manager Jim Mutrie. "I would rather lose a game than win as they did this afternoon."

The actions of the Dodgers also angered the New York-area fans. Attendance was sparse at the remaining games.

OCTOBER 23   In sub-40-degree temperatures and heavy winds, the Dodgers take a three-games-to-one lead over the Giants with a 10–7 victory before 3,045 at Washington Park called after six innings by darkness. At one point, the Giants threatened to leave the field in protest because of the calls by umpires Tom Lynch and John Gaffney. The Giants scored five runs in the top of the sixth to tie the game 7–7 with the sun nearly set over the horizon. The Dodgers got two men on base in the bottom half when Oyster Burns hit a drive to left field. Giants outfielder John O'Rourke couldn't see the ball because it was too dark, and the ball fell for a game-winning three-run homer.

As a result of the problems attempting to play nine innings before sunset, the start of the remaining games were moved up one hour to 2:30 p.m.

OCTOBER 24   The Dodgers lose game five 11–3 to the Giants before 2,901 at Washington Park.

OCTOBER 25   The Giants even the series at three games apiece with an 11-inning, 2–1 win at the Polo Grounds. The Dodgers led 1–0 heading into the ninth, but the Giants tied the contest when John Montgomery Ward singled with two out, stole second and third and scored on Roger Connor's single. With two away in the 11th, Ward drove in the winning run with a walk-off single.

OCTOBER 27   The Giants take game seven 11–7 over the Dodgers at the Polo Grounds. New York took a 9–0 lead with eight runs in the second inning. At the time, balls were still in play when hit into the seats. Germany Smith hit a drive into the big-league bleachers with the bases loaded, but Jim O'Rourke of the Giants jumped the fence, retrieved the ball, and fired it home, where Smith was tagged out.

OCTOBER 28   The Giants decline the Dodgers' offer to postpone the game because of a muddy field, and win game eight 16–7 before 2,584 at Washington Park. Dave Foutz hit an inside-the-park homer on a pop fly after Mike Slattery slipped on the outfield grass.

OCTOBER 29   The Giants win their fifth straight game and the world championship with a 3–2 victory over the Dodgers at the Polo Grounds. New York scored the winning run in the seventh when Mike Slattery scored from second base on a third strike to Buck Ewing that sailed over the head of Brooklyn catcher Doc Bushong.

NOVEMBER 14   A week after North Dakota, South Dakota, Montana and Washington are granted statehood, the Dodgers and the Cincinnati Reds bolt the American Association and join the National League. The owners of both franchises were disgusted with the domination of St. Louis owner Chris Von der Ahe over league affairs. Brooklyn and Cincinnati replaced Indianapolis and Washington in the National League lineup. The other National League clubs were Boston, Chicago, Cleveland, New York, Philadelphia and Pittsburgh.

DECEMBER 16   The Players League is formally organized.

The new league grew out of dissatisfaction among players over their salaries and contracts. Many of the top stars in the National League and American Association teams joined the new league. The Players League located clubs in Boston, Brooklyn, Buffalo, Chicago, Cleveland, New York, Philadelphia and Pittsburgh. The Brooklyn entry played its games in the East New York section of Brooklyn at Eastern Park. The Dodgers did not suffer the loss of players to the Players League as readily as most big-league clubs because Charlie Byrne was willing to match or exceed the salary offers of the new organization. Among the 1889 regulars, only catcher Joe Visner went to the Players League after signing a contract with Pittsburgh. The Brooklyn entry in the league, nicknamed the Wonders, fielded a strong club, however, with athletes such as future Hall of Famer John Montgomery Ward, who also served as manager, plus stars of the day like George Van Haltren, Gus Weyhing, Lou Bierbauer, Bill Joyce and Dave Orr. The Dodgers and the Wonders also had competition from a third major league club in Brooklyn when the American Association installed a team in the circuit. Nicknamed the Gladiators, the AA team played its home game at Ridgewood, Queens, the former Sunday home of the Dodgers. With the fan base split, all three franchises suffered heavy losses. The Dodgers attendance dropped from 353,690 in 1889 to 121,412 in 1890 despite finishing in first place again. The Players League entry finished second and attracted 79,272. The American Association team attracted just 37,000 and folded in August with a record of 26–72. The Players League lasted only one season. By 1891, the Dodgers were once again the only team in Brooklyn.

THE STATE OF THE DODGERS

After winning the 1889 American Association pennant, the Dodgers joined the National League and won the championship in 1890 in the team's first season in the circuit. Brooklyn closed the decade finishing first again in 1899. In between those two stellar years, the club never finished higher than third and had four losing seasons. Overall, the Dodgers compiled a record of 732–644 during the 1890s, a winning percentage of .532. Brooklyn was one of only three NL franchises to win pennants during the last decade. The others were the Boston Braves (1891, 1892, 1893, 1897 and 1898) and Baltimore Orioles (1894, 1895 and 1896).

THE BEST TEAM

The 1899 Dodgers were 101–47 and won the National League pennant by eight games. The winning percentage of .682 wouldn't be matched again until 1953.

THE WORST TEAM

The worst team preceded the 1899 champions. In 1898, the Dodgers had a 54–91 record and landed in 10th place in a 12-team league.

THE BEST MOMENT

The precise moment and person responsible is impossible to identify, but sometime in 1895, someone began calling Brooklyn's baseball team the "Trolley Dodgers." The moniker caught the fancy of the public, and after later being shortened to "Dodgers," one of sport's most enduring nicknames was born.

THE WORST MOMENT

Dodgers second baseman Hub Collins died of typhoid fever on May 21, 1892, just a week after falling ill. Death would visit the Dodgers again 13 months later in June 1893 when Darby O'Brien passed away from consumption. Dave Foutz died from asthma in March 1897 shortly after being released by the club.

THE ALL-DECADE TEAM • YEARS W/DODS

Con Daily, c	1891–95
Dan Foutz, 1b	1888–96
Tom Daly, 2b	1890–96, 1898–1901
Bill Shindle, 3b	1894–98
Tommy Corcoran, ss	1892–96
John Anderson, lf	1894–99
Mike Griffin, cf	1891–98
Oyster Burns, rf	1888–95
Brickyard Kennedy, p	1892–1901
Ed Stein, p	1892–96
Tom Lovett, p	1889–91
Jim Hughes, p	1899, 1901–02

Other outstanding players with the Dodgers during the 1890s were first basemen Candy LaChance (1893–98) and Dan Brouthers (1892–93) and pitchers Jack Dunn (1897–1900), Bob Caruthers (1888–91) and Adonis Terry (1884–91).

THE DECADE LEADERS

Batting Avg:	Mike Griffin	.305
On-Base Pct:	Mike Griffin	.399
Slugging Pct:	Oyster Burns	.444
Home Runs:	Tom Daly	37
RBIs:	Mike Griffin	477
Runs:	Mike Griffin	881
Stolen Bases:	Mike Griffin	264
Wins:	Brickyard Kennedy	154
Strikeouts:	Brickyard Kennedy	646
ERA:	Bob Caruthers	3.11
Saves:	Brickyard Kennedy	9

THE HOME FIELD

The Dodgers played at Washington Park in the Park Slope neighborhood of Brooklyn from 1883 through 1890. The team moved to Eastern Park in the East New York section in 1891, and remained there until 1897. Attendance lagged, however, because East New York was then in a relatively unpopulated part of town. The Dodgers went back to Park Slope in 1898 at a new Washington Park built across the street from the old one.

THE GAME YOU WISHED YOU HAD SEEN

In the midst of a nail-biting pennant race, the Dodgers played a triple header against Pittsburgh at Washington Park on September 1, 1890, and won all three by scores of 10–9, 3–2 and 8–4.

THE WAY THE GAME WAS PLAYED

In 1893, the pitcher was moved from 55 feet to 60 feet, six inches from home plate. The added distance put more offense in the game. League batting averages jumped from .245 in 1892 to .280 in 1893 and .309 in 1894. The decade is known for its rough, even dirty, baseball, with many managers encouraging players to bend every rule and challenge every ball. Brawling became commonplace.

THE MANAGEMENT

Charlie Byrne was the president of the Dodgers from the founding of the franchise in 1883 until his death in January 1898. Charles Ebbets succeeded Byrne as president and held the position until 1925. The largest stockholder was Ferdinand Abell from 1883 until 1907, when he was bought out by Ebbets. Field managers during the 1890s were Bill McGunnigle (1888–90), John Montgomery Ward (1891–92), Dave Foutz (1893–96), Billy Barnie (1897–98), Mike Griffin (1898), Ebbets (1898) and Ned Hanlon (1899–1905).

THE BEST PLAYER MOVE

After finishing in 10th place with a 54–91 record in 1898, the Dodgers quickly rectified the situation by purchasing the Baltimore Orioles, a club which was 96–53 that season and ended the year in second place. At the time it was legal for individuals to own more than one National League team. Many of Baltimore's best players were transferred to Brooklyn during the 1898–99 off-season including future Hall of Famers Willie Keeler, Joe Kelley and Hughie Jennings. As a result, Brooklyn won the 1899 pennant while Baltimore fell from second to fourth.

THE WORST PLAYER MOVE

The Dodgers made a monumental blunder in January 1894 by trading future Hall of Famers Willie Keeler and Dan Brouthers for Bill Shindle and George Treadway.

1890

L A

Season in a Sentence

In their first season in the National League, the Dodgers drop six games behind in July, then rally to finish in first place for the second year in a row before losing the World Series again, this time to Louisville.

Finish • Won • Lost • Pct • GB

First   86   43   .667 +6.0

Manager

Bill McGunnigle

World Series

The Dodgers played seven games against the Louisville Colonels with each team winning three and a seventh ending in a tie.

Stats

	Dods •	NL •	Rank
Batting Avg:	.264	.254	2
On-Base Pct:	.346	.329	2
Slugging Pct:	.369	.342	1
Home Runs:	43		2
Stolen Bases:	349		1
ERA:	3.06	3.56	3
Fielding Avg:	.940	.927	1
Runs Scored:	884		1
Runs Allowed:	620		2

Starting Lineup

Tom Daly, c
Dave Foutz, 1b
Hib Collins, 2b
George Pinckney, 3b
Germany Smith, ss
Adonis terry, lf-p
Darby O'Brien, cf-lf
Oyster Burns, rf
Bob Caruthers, lf
Pop Corkhill, cf

Pitchers

Tom Lovett, sp
Adonis Terry, sp
Bob Caruthers, sp
Mickey Hughes, sp

Attendance

121,412 (fourth in NL)

Club Leaders

Batting Avg:	Darby O'Brien	.314
On-Base Pct:	George Pinckney	.411
Slugging Pct:	Oyster Burns	.464
Home Runs:	Oyster Burns	13
RBIs:	Oyster Burns	128
Runs:	Hub Collins	148
Stolen Bases:	Hub Collins	85
Wins:	Tom Lovett	30
Strikeouts:	Adonis Terry	185
ERA:	Tom Lovett	2.78
Saves:	Dave Foutz	2

APRIL 19   The Dodgers open with a 15–9 loss against the Braves in Boston. Adonis Terry was hit early and often, surrendering eight runs in the third inning and four in the fourth. Oyster Burns collected three hits, including a double. Brooklyn's Players League club, nicknamed Ward's Wonders after manager John Montgomery Ward, also opened on the same day, and lost 3–2 to the Boston Red Stockings in Boston.

The April 19 contest was the Dodgers' first as a member of the National League and the franchise's first in the city of Boston. It was also the Dodgers first contest against the present-day Atlanta Braves franchise. The Braves played in Boston from 1876 through 1952, Milwaukee from 1953 through 1965, and Atlanta since 1966.

APRIL 21   After the Braves score five runs in the top of the ninth inning to tie the score 6–6, the Dodgers respond with a tally in the bottom half to win 7–6 in Boston. Darby O'Brien drove in the winning run with a double.

O'Brien hit .314 and collected 28 doubles for the Dodgers in 1890.

APRIL 28   The Dodgers play their first home game of the season and win 10–0 over the Phillies at Washington Park. It was also the first time that the Dodgers played the Phillies. Bob Caruthers pitched the shutout. The game was played on a Monday afternoon following three postponements of the scheduled home opener on the previous Thursday, Friday and Saturday. Brooklyn's Players League entry played their first home game at Eastern Park on the same day and beat Philadelphia 3–1. Eastern Park would become the home of the Dodgers from 1891 through 1897 (see April 27, 1891).

Caruthers was 23–11 with a 3.09 ERA in 1890.

MAY 1
The Dodgers and Braves play only one inning at Washington Park before rain halts play, but George Pinckney is injured when accidentally spiked by Chippy McGarr.

MAY 2
George Pinckney is unable to play during an 11–2 loss to the Braves at Washington Park, ending a streak of playing in 577 consecutive games dating back to September 21, 1885. The streak was the longest in the majors prior to 1920. Pinckney also played in every inning of every game while playing in 577 straight games. Only Cal Ripken, Jr., has played in more consecutive innings in major league history.

Pinckney played in 126 of the Dodgers 129 games in 1890, batted .309, and scored 115 runs.

MAY 3
The Dodgers play their first regular season game against the Giants and win 7–3 at Washington Park. The Dodgers and Giants met previously in exhibition games and in the 1889 World Series. Dave Foutz hit a home run which rolled to the carriages parked along the outfield fence.

During the 19th century, it was common for clubs to allow those who arrived in horse-drawn carriages to park them on the playing field just inside the outfield fences. Some fans remained in their carriages and watched the game from there. The carriages at Washington Park were in play, and occasionally, outfielders had to risk life and limb by trying to retrieve balls which landed around the hooves of skittish horses.

MAY 7
The Dodgers crush the Phillies 17–7 in Philadelphia. Brooklyn scored seven runs in the second inning for a 7–0 lead, but allow the Phils to tie the score, then broke the deadlock by exploding for nine tallies in the eighth.

MAY 18
The Dodgers belt the Pirates 18–2 at Washington Park.

MAY 20
The Dodgers score eight runs in the third inning and clobber the Reds 19–4 at Washington Park.

MAY 28
The Dodgers thrash Cleveland 14–5 at Washington Park.

The Dodgers were 17–3 against Cleveland in 1890.

MAY 29
The Dodgers play the Cubs for the first time and win 8–4 at Washington Park. Brooklyn pulled off a triple play in the fifth inning. With runners on first and second, Germany Smith caught a grounder, threw to second baseman Hub Collins, who in turn fired to first baseman Dave Foutz for the second. Tom Burns tried to score on the play and was out on a throw from Foutz to catcher Tom Daly to complete the triple play.

Foutz hit .303 and drove in 98 runs in 1890.

JUNE 3   The Dodgers score 10 runs in the second inning and rout the Giants 20–7 in New York. Oyster Burns collected five singles in five at-bats.

Burns led the NL in RBIs in 1890 with 128 and hit 13 homers along with a .284 batting average.

JUNE 5   Oyster Burns hits a grand slam in the fifth inning, but the Dodgers lose 6–5 to the Phillies in Philadelphia.

JUNE 12   The Dodgers resort to trickery during a 12–6 win over the Giants at Washington Park. In the second inning, Darby O'Brien was coaching at third base and deluded the New York fielders by running toward home plate, drawing a throw. O'Brien was ordered to the bench by the umpires and wasn't allowed to coach at third for the rest of the

First baseman Dave Foutz played nine seasons in Brooklyn, enjoying his most productive one in 1890 when he posted a .303 average.

game. In the fourth inning, New York first baseman Dude Esterbrook tried to make a throw to the plate to retire Hub Collins, but Oyster Burns wrapped his arms around Esterbrook prevented him from making the play. Collins was called out on the play because of Burns's interference.

Collins led the NL in runs scored in 1890 with 148. He had six more runs than hits. Collins also drew 85 walks, hit 32 doubles and batted .278.

JUNE 14   The Dodgers score eight runs in the second inning and slaughter the Giants 16–2 at Washington Park.

JUNE 20   The Dodgers win the eighth game in a row with a 10–3 decision over the Spiders in Cleveland.

JULY 3   On the day Idaho is admitted as the 43rd state in the Union, the Dodgers lose 9–6 to the Reds in Cincinnati.

The defeat knocked the Dodgers into third place with a record of 34–24, six games out of first place. The club won 43 of its next 55 games.

JULY 4	The Dodgers sweep the Pirates 11–10 and 5–3 in Pittsburgh. In the opener, Brooklyn led 10–2, but Bob Caruthers allowed eight runs in the fifth inning. The Dodgers scored the winning tally in the sixth.
JULY 5	After playing a holiday double-header in Pittsburgh, the Dodgers and Pirates play another twin bill the next day at Washington Park. The Dodgers won twice again, this time 14–3 and 12–11. Fans in the right-field bleachers shot off fireworks repeatedly during the games. Pittsburgh third baseman Doggie Miller got into the spirit and set one off himself on the playing field.
JULY 14	Four days after Wyoming is admitted as the 44th state in the Union, the Dodgers roll to their 11th win in a row with a 10–3 decision over the Cubs at Washington Park.
JULY 21	Tom Lovett allows 20 runs and 20 hits during a 20–11 loss to the Reds in Cincinnati.

The pounding was rare for Lovett, as he compiled a 30–11 record and a 2.78 ERA in 372^1/$_3$ innings in 1890. Lovett was 23–19 and pitched a no-hitter in 1891, then sat out the entire 1892 season in a salary dispute. He returned in 1893, but never again pitched with the same effectiveness.

JULY 22	The Dodgers break open a close game with eight runs in the fifth inning and defeat the Reds 16–5 in Cincinnati.
JULY 30	The Dodgers defeat the Cleveland Spiders 15–5 in a game played at a neutral site in Indianapolis.
AUGUST 1	The Dodgers sweep the Pirates 7–3 and 20–1 at Washington Park. Brooklyn scored 11 runs in the first inning of the second game. Oyster Burns hit for the cycle. The carnage might have worse, but the contest was called after seven innings by darkness.
AUGUST 2	The Dodgers take first place with a 9–2 win over the Pirates at Washington Park.

The Dodgers remained in first for the rest of the season.

AUGUST 3	The Dodgers rout the Pirates 16–6 at Washington Park. In the third inning, Hub Collins circled the plate on a batted ball which traveled only a few feet. The ball came to a rest right in front of the plate, but neither pitcher Robert Gibson or catcher Harry Decker made any attempt to field it. Collins sped toward first, then turned to second. Finally, Decker picked up the ball, but fired it over the head of second baseman Sam LaRoque and into center field, allowing Collins to score.

One of the worst teams in major league history, Pittsburgh had a record of 23–113 in 1890. The Dodgers won 18 of 20 meetings against the Pirates.

AUGUST 7	The Dodgers mash Boston 14–5 at Washington Park.
AUGUST 9	The Dodgers run their winning streak to nine games with a 5–0 win over the Giants in New York.
AUGUST 20	The Dodgers sweep the Phillies 13–2 and 12–7 at Washington Park. In the eighth inning of the opener, umpire Thomas Lynch was struck in the mask with a foul tip

with sufficient force to break the wire and tear a deep cut in his forehead. Dodgers catcher Doc Bushong umpired the remainder of the contest, as well as the second tilt. Adonis Terry was the starting pitcher in both games. He was relieved by Dave Foutz in the opener and hurled a complete game in the nightcap.

Terry was 26–16 with a 3.94 ERA in 370 innings in 1890.

AUGUST 22   The Dodgers lose a controversial 1–0 decision to the Cubs at Washington Park. The lone run of the game scored in the ninth inning when Bob Glenalvin scored on a sacrifice fly by Chicago pitcher Ed Stein. Glenalvin left for home a full two yards from third base, which escaped the detection of umpire Jack McQuaid. The heated appeals by the Dodgers were in vain.

AUGUST 30   Dave Foutz hits a two-run homer in the first inning for the lone runs of a 2–0 win over Cleveland at Washington Park. Tom Lovett pitched the shutout.

SEPTEMBER 1   The Dodgers play the first triple header in major league history, and sweep the Pirates 10–9, 3–2 and 8–4. Three games were played because the Dodgers scheduled the make up of a contest postponed in May to the Labor Day twin bill. There was one game played in the morning and two in the afternoon. Brooklyn led 10–0 in the opener at the end of the eighth inning with Bob Caruthers working on a three-hitter. Suddenly, Caruthers fell apart in the ninth, and the score was 10–6 with the bases loaded. Doggie Miller hit a deep drive to the outfield, scoring three runs. Miller tried for a game-tying, inside-the-park grand slam on the play, but was thrown out at home plate on a relay from center fielder Darby O'Brien to shortstop Germany Smith to catcher Bob Clark.

> *There were two other triple headers played in major league history. The second was played on September 7, 1896 with the Baltimore Orioles defeating the Louisville Colonels 4–3, 9–1 and 12–8 with the third game ending after eight innings by darkness. On October 2, 1920, the Reds and Pirates played three in Pittsburgh with Cincinnati winning 13–4 and 7–3 and losing 6–0 in a contest called by darkness after six innings. The September 1, 1890 triple header between the Dodgers and Pirates is the only one in which all three games went nine innings.*

SEPTEMBER 2   The Dodgers score three runs in the ninth inning to beat the Pirates 5–4 at Washington Park. Pitcher Bob Caruthers tripled in two runs and scored on an error. Controversy arose because of the introduction of a new ball in the ninth. At the time, a ball was used in a game until it was literally coming apart at the seams. Whenever a new ball was put in, it caused problems because it was likely to travel farther because it was more resilient and easier to see because of the gleaming white cover, and therefore favored the team at bat. A new ball was put into play just before the last Pittsburgh batter was retired. When the Pirates took the field in the bottom of the inning, Doggie Miller and Eddie Burke rubbed the ball in the dirt. Umpire George Strief replaced the muddy ball with another new one, causing a long argument form the Pirates who claimed he had no authority to do so. The Pirates protested the contest to the National League office, but the protest was denied.

SEPTEMBER 3   The Dodgers easily down Boston 13–4 at Washington Park.

SEPTEMBER 4   The Dodgers win their ninth game in a row with a 7–3 decision over the Giants at Washington Park. The victory gave Brooklyn a 77–36 record.

SEPTEMBER 26   The idle Dodgers clinch the pennant as the second-place Cubs lose 5–4 to the Phillies in Chicago.

SEPTEMBER 29   Tom Lovett wins his 30th game of the season with a 6–5 decision over the Spiders in Cleveland.

The Dodgers met the American Association champion Louisville Colonels in the World Series. Managed by Jack Chapman, Louisville was 88–44 in 1890 after making an astonishing leap from an abysmal eighth-place, 27–111, finish in 1889. The Series was scheduled as a best-of-nine affair.

OCTOBER 17   The Dodgers win the opening game of the World Series 9–0 against the Colonels before 5,563 in Louisville. Brooklyn opened the scoring with three runs in the first inning. The game was called after eight innings by darkness. Adonis Terry pitched a two-hit shutout. The only Louisville hits were singles by Phil Tomney and Farmer Weaver.

OCTOBER 18   Behind the six-hit pitching of Tom Lovett, the Dodgers win game two by a 5–3 score in Louisville. Brooklyn broke a 2–2 tie with two runs in the fourth.

OCTOBER 20   In freezing 30-degree weather in Louisville, the Dodgers and Colonels play to a 7–7 deadlock in a contest called after eight innings by darkness. Attendance was only 1,253. Louisville scored three times in the eighth to tie the game on a walk, three hits, a sacrifice fly and a passed ball with Adonis Terry on the mound.

OCTOBER 21   On another cold day in Louisville, the Colonels win their first game of the Series with a 5–4 decision over the Dodgers before a crowd of only 1,050. Louisville broke a 4–4 tie with a rally in the seventh inning.

OCTOBER 25   Following a travel day and two postponements, the Dodgers take a 3–1–1 lead in the Series with a 7–2 victory before just 1,000 fans at Washington Park. Oyster Burns smacked a two-run homer in the first inning. Tom Lovett was the winning pitcher.

OCTOBER 27   Weather fit only for polar bears keeps the game-six crowd to 600, and the Dodgers lose 9–8 to Louisville at Washington Park. The Dodgers led 5–1, then fell behind 9–5 before a three-run rally in the eighth inning fell one run short.

OCTOBER 28   Only 300 show up for game seven at Washington Park, and the Dodgers lose 6–2 to Louisville.

After seven games, Brooklyn and Louisville each had three victories with another ending in a tie. It would take at least two more games to complete the best-of-nine Series. There was little interest in continuing the 1890 World Series because of the forecast of more cold weather and dwindling attendance. Prior to the October 28 contest, Dodgers manager Bill McGunnigle and Louisville skipper Jack Chapman resolved to settle the championship in the spring, but the playoff never occurred and the title remains undecided. McGunnigle never managed another game for the Dodgers, having been fired during a tumultuous off-season.

The Players League folded after just one season. George Chauncey was the owner of the Brooklyn entry in the league, and suffered heavy financial losses, as did Dodgers owners Charlie Byrne, Ferdinand Abell and Joseph Doyle. Chauncey offered to invest in the Dodgers, and the proposal was accepted. In exchange for his cash, Chauncey insisted on a few changes. First, the Dodgers would play their home games at Eastern Park, which Chauncey built for his Players League club. Secondly, he insisted that John Montgomery Ward, who was manager of that team, also manage the Dodgers in 1891. The hiring of Ward left McGunnigle out of a job despite winning the pennant the previous two seasons, topping the American Association in 1889 and the National League in 1890. Overall, he was 267–139, a winning percentage of .658, as the Brooklyn manager. McGunnigle never had success again. He managed the Pirates during the last portion of the 1891 season, and was 24–33. The only other major league team that McGunnigle managed was a Louisville outfit in 1896, which finished in 12th place with a 36–76 won-lost ledger.

1891   LA

Season in a Sentence

After winning titles in 1889 and 1890, the Dodgers fire Bill McGunnigle as manager and sink to sixth place in a season of turmoil under new skipper John Montgomery Ward.

Finish • Won • Lost • Pct • GB

Sixth   61   76   .445   25.5

Manager

John Montgomery Ward

Stats

Stats	Dods	NL	Rank
Batting Avg:	.260	.252	2
On-Base Pct:	.330	.325	3
Slugging Pct:	.345	.342	4
Home Runs:	23		7
Stolen Bases:	337		1
ERA:	3.86	3.34	8
Fielding Avg:	.924	.928	6
Runs Scored:	765		4
Runs Allowed:	820		7

Starting Lineup

Tom Kinslow, c
Dave Foutz, 1b
Hub Collins, 2b
George Pinckney, 3b
John Montgomery Ward, ss
Darby O'Brien, lf
Mike Griffin, cf
Oyster Burns, rf
Con Daily, c
Tom Daly, c-1b

Pitchers

Tom Lovett, sp
Bob Caruthers, sp
George Hemming, sp
Adonis Terry, sp
Bert Inks, sp

Attendance

181,447 (fifth in NL)

Club Leaders

Batting Avg:	Oyster Burns	.285
On-Base Pct:	George Pinckney	.366
Slugging Pct:	Oyster Burns	.417
Home Runs:	Darby O'Brien	5
RBIs:	Oyster Burns	83
Runs:	Mike Griffin	106
Stolen Bases:	Mike Griffin	65
Wins:	Tom Lovett	23
Strikeouts:	Tom Lovett	129
ERA:	Bob Caruthers	3.12
Saves:	Three tied with	1

APRIL 22   Four months after the massacre at Wounded Knee South Dakota, the last major
            conflict between Native Americans and U.S. troops, the Dodgers open the season
            with seven runs in the first inning and beat the Phillies 14–8 in Philadelphia. Dave
            Foutz led the way with four hits. Mike Griffin and Con Daily each had three hits in
            their Dodgers debuts. George Hemming also played in first game with the club, and
            was the winning pitcher.

            *New manager John Montgomery Ward was one of the most important
            individuals in baseball during the 19th century. He was a star player as both a
            pitcher and a shortstop, a winning manager, a labor organizer and club owner.
            As an 18-year-old rookie with Providence in the National League in 1878,
            Ward won 22 games and led the circuit with a 1.51 ERA. In 1879, he won
            47 games and was victorious on 40 occasions in 1880 in addition to pitching a
            perfect game. But pitching over 500 innings in both 1879 and 1880 eventually
            ruined his arm. By 1884, Ward became an outfielder with the New York Giants
            and a year later converted to shortstop. With Ward playing a key role, the
            Giants won the NL pennant in both 1888 and 1889. During the off-season,
            he attended classes at Columbia University and earned a law degree. In 1885,
            the Brotherhood of Professional Base Ball Players was formed to protect and
            enhance the welfare and interests of the players. Ward was elected president.
            In 1890, the players revolted and formed their own league (see December 16,
            1889). After the league collapsed (see October 28, 1890), Ward became manager
            of the Dodgers. In addition to serving as manager, Ward was Brooklyn's starting
            shortstop. He hit .277 in 1891.*

APRIL 25   The Dodgers lose the home opener 3–1 to the Phillies before 4,891 at Washington
            Park.

            *This was the Dodgers "farewell" game at Washington Park, which had been the
            club's home since its inception in the Interstate League in 1883.*

APRIL 27   The Dodgers open Eastern Park by allowing two runs in the ninth inning to lose to
            the Giants 6–5 before 17,892.

            *Eastern Park, with a seating capacity of about 12,000, would be the Dodgers
            home from 1891 through 1897. The ballpark featured a double-decked wooden
            stand with a roof at each end finished with a turret topped by a conical spire.
            Bleachers extended the seating from the first base side on one side and from
            third base on the other. It was located in the East New York neighborhood of
            Brooklyn bounded on the north by Eastern Parkway (now Pitkin Avenue), the
            west by Powell Street, the south by Sutter Avenue and east by Vesta Avenue
            (now Van Sinderen Street). The site was in relatively unpopulated section of
            Brooklyn, but was well-served from all points of the city by the electric trolley
            line and elevated railroads which criss-crossed the city with little planning or
            foresight. Electrically-powered streetcars and trolleys had been introduced to
            New York in 1890. Previously, streetcars were horse-drawn. While the electric
            streetcars could handle larger loads, were more efficient, and didn't pollute the
            streets with manure and urine, they were no safer. Drivers were unfamiliar with
            the new equipment, the brakes on the cars were inadequate, and pedestrians
            were unaccustomed with the speed of the vehicles. (New York City began
            keeping track of deaths and injuries due to streetcar accidents in 1908.*

In that year alone, 444 people died and nearly 60,000 were injured). To get to Eastern Park from the nearest stops, one had to dodge trains speeding down the tracks of the New York & Manhattan Beach Railroad, which ran excursion trains from a ferry in Greenpoint to the resorts on Jamaica Bay and Coney Island. The dangerous maze of tracks and trains led to the coining of "Trolley Dodgers" as a new nickname for the club. This was later shortened to Dodgers. The name wouldn't be used in the print media until late in the 1895 season, however. In 1891, the Brooklyn franchise was known primarily as the "Bridegrooms," a name which had been in use since 1888, and sometimes as "Ward's Wonders" after manager John Montgomery Ward.

MAY 1   Oyster Burns hits a grand slam during a 13–6 win over Boston at Eastern Park.

MAY 5   On the day Carnegie Hall opens in New York City, the Dodgers defeat the Phillies 15–5 at Eastern Park.

MAY 8   The Dodgers score five runs in the second inning to take a 9–1 lead, and hang on to defeat the Phillies 12–10 at Eastern Park.

MAY 12   The Dodgers score in eight of nine innings and collect 20 hits for an 18–7 victory over the Reds in Cincinnati.

MAY 25   The Dodgers score eight runs in the third inning and defeat the Spiders 12–5 in Cleveland.

MAY 28   Bob Caruthers pitches a two-hitter, but Hub Collins makes four errors at second base in the second inning and the Dodgers lose 4–2 to the Spiders in Cleveland.

Collins was much better with a bat in his hands in 1891, hitting .276.

JUNE 2   The Dodgers belt the Pirates 15–6 at Eastern Park.

JUNE 13 The Dodgers win their eighth game in a row with an 11–1 decision over the Reds at Eastern Park.

JUNE 22 Tom Lovett pitches a no-hitter and beats the Giants 4–0 at Eastern Park. Lovett walked three and struck out four. New York went out in order in each of the last three innings.

JUNE 27 A fire ignites during the fourth inning of a 10–7 Phillies win over the Dodgers at Huntington Grounds in Philadelphia. The fire started in the left-field stands which caused an immediate evacuation of fans. The flames made considerable headway for awhile, but the blaze was finally subdued and the game resumed. One man was badly burned about the face, and another had his wrist broken.

JUNE 30 With a fantastic late surge, the Dodgers score four runs in the ninth inning and two in the 10th for an 11–9 lead in Philadelphia, then survive a Phillie rally in the bottom of the 10th for an 11–10 victory.

JULY 13 The Dodgers clobber the Spiders 19–7 in Cleveland.

JULY 16   The Dodgers lose 7–5 and win 12–8 during a double-header against the Pirates in
               Pittsburgh.

JULY 20   A serious collision between second baseman Hub Collins and right fielder Oyster
               Burns in the eighth inning mars a 5–4 loss to the Giants at the Polo Grounds. The
               two Dodger fielders came together chasing a drive off the bat of Roger Connor. Both
               fell to the ground unconscious and covered in blood with cuts in the face. Three
               spectators fainted. Burns was back in action in a week, but Collins missed nearly
               a month.

               Burns hit .285 in 1891.

JULY 25   The Dodgers walk over the Phillies 15–2 at Eastern Park.

AUGUST 25   The Dodgers lose 28–5 to the Cubs in Chicago. The debacle set a club record for
               most runs allowed in a game which still stands. The Cubs collected 28 hits and 54
               total bases on 13 singles, four doubles, five triples and four homers. Remarkably,
               George Hemming pitched a complete game for Brooklyn in what is without question
               the worst pitching performance in team history. In addition to the 28 runs and 28
               hits, he walked six and hit a batter.

               *The 1891 season was Hemming's only one as a Dodger. He was 8–15 with a
               4.96 ERA. Overall, Hemming had a 91–82 record during an eight-year career.*

SEPTEMBER 7   Just 13 days after losing 28–5 to the Cubs, the Dodgers defeat the Chicago club 21–3
               in the first game of a double-header at Eastern Park. Brooklyn scored nine runs in
               the second inning, two in the fourth, two in the fifth, three in the seventh, two in the
               eighth and three in the ninth. The Cubs won the second contest 9–8.

SEPTEMBER 16   The Dodgers win 1–0 in 10 innings over the Reds in the first game of a double-
               header at Eastern Park. Tom Lovett pitched a two-hitter. The only Cincinnati hits
               were singles by Long John Reilly and Arlie Latham. The winning run scored on a
               double by Mike Griffin and a two-base error. Lovett also started the second game,
               but was relieved after allowing six runs in the first innings of an 8–4 loss.

DECEMBER 17   The American Association folds and four AA teams are incorporated into the
               National League. The four new NL clubs were the St. Louis Cardinals, Louisville
               Colonels, Washington Senators and Baltimore Orioles. This left the National League
               as the only major league, a situation that would exist until 1901.

               *The four American Association franchises which ceased to exist were Boston,
               the 1891 AA pennant-winners, Milwaukee, Philadelphia and Columbus. This
               left a scramble for the 12 remaining clubs to sign the best players from the
               four defunct teams. The Dodgers picked up Dan Brouthers, Bill Joyce, Tommy
               Corcoran and George Haddock, each of whom became regulars in 1892.
               Brouthers was the big prize. During his Hall of Fame career, Brouthers led his
               league in batting average five times, in addition to seven in slugging percentage,
               seven in on-base percentage, four in total bases, three in hits, two in runs and
               two in runs-batted-in. He was 33 years old when acquired by the Dodgers, but
               was still a productive hitter. Had the Most Valuable Player Award existed in
               1892, Brouthers would have been a leading candidate.*

1892

L A

Season in a Sentence

Backed by the best offense in the National League, which averages nearly six runs a game, the Dodgers rebound from the disastrous 1891 season to win 95 games and finish third.

Finish • Won • Lost • Pct • GB

First   95   59   .617   9.0

Manager

John Montgomery Ward

Stats	Dods	NL	Rank
Batting Avg:	.262	.245	1
On-Base Pct:	.344	.317	1
Slugging Pct:	.350	.327	2
Home Runs:	30		9 (tie)
Stolen Bases:	409		1
ERA:	3.25	3.28	7
Fielding Avg:	.940	.928	1
Runs Scored:	935		1
Runs Allowed:	733		5

Starting Lineup

Con Daily, c
Dan Brouthers, 1b
John Montgomery Ward, 2b
Tom Daly, 3b-cf-lf
Tommy Corcoran, ss
Darby O'Brien, lf
Mike Griffin, cf
Oyster Burns, rf
Bill Joyce, 3b
Tom Kinslow, c
Dave Foutz, lf-rf-p

Pitchers

George Haddock, sp
Ed Stein, sp
Dave Foutz, sp
Brickyard Kennedy, sp
Bill Hart, sp

Attendance

183,727 (third in NL)

Club Leaders

Batting Avg:	Dan Brouthers	.335
On-Base Pct:	Dan Brouthers	.432
Slugging Pct:	Dan Brouthers	.480
Home Runs:	Bill Joyce	6
RBIs:	Dan Brouthers	124
Runs:	Dan Brouthers	121
Stolen Bases:	John Montgomery Ward	88
Wins:	George Haddock	29
Strikeouts:	Ed Stein	190
ERA:	Ed Stein	2.84
Saves:	Five tied with	1

FEBRUARY 29   Two months after the opening of the immigrant processing center on Ellis Island, the Dodgers leave for Florida and spring training from New York aboard the steamship *Algonquin*. There was a large crowd on the pier to see the players as they boarded. Many of the players feared the water journey, however, and took the train south.

The Dodgers trained in Ocala, Florida in 1892. Spring training trips to warmer climates were a recent phenomenon. Previously teams trained in their hometowns, gathering a few weeks before the opening of the season. When the spring weather prohibited playing outdoors, clubs trained in local gymnasiums.

APRIL 12   In the season opener, the Dodgers score five runs in the first inning and win 13–3 over the Orioles in Baltimore. A chilly wind blew dust in the faces of the players. Dave Foutz pitched a complete game victory.

With 12 teams and a 154-game schedule, the National League split the season into two halves. The winners of the two halves were slated to meet in a post-season series. With the exception of the strike-interrupted 1981 season, it was the only time that the major leagues had two pennant races in a season.

APRIL 22   In the home opener, the Dodgers score seven runs in the first inning and defeat the Phillies 9–5 at Eastern Park. It rained throughout the contest, which was called after eight innings. The inclement weather kept the crowd to 2,051.

APRIL 23   Scoring all of their runs in the first five innings, the Dodgers beat the Phillies 12–0 in the first game of a double-header at Eastern Park. The second tilt was called at the end of the 10th inning because of darkness with the score 2–2.

APRIL 25   The Dodgers score four runs in the first inning and rout the Orioles 13–0 at Eastern Park.

APRIL 26   The Dodgers edge the Orioles 12–10 at Eastern Park. Brooklyn broke a 9–9 tie with two runs in the eighth inning. After Oyster Burns sprained his ankle, Darby O'Brien replaced him in right field and collected a triple, double and two singles in four turns at bat.

                The Dodgers led the National League in runs scored in 1892 with 935. Dan Brouthers was the start of the lineup with a .335 batting average, 121 runs, 20 triples, and league-leading figures in hits (197), total bases (282) and RBIs (124). Oyster Burns batted .315 and drove in 96 runs. Mike Griffin scored 103 runs. John Montgomery Ward crossed the plate 109 times and stole a league-leading 88 bases.

MAY 6   Ted Breitenstein of the Cardinals carries a no-hitter into the ninth inning before settling for a two-hitter and a 14–2 win over the Dodgers in St. Louis. The only Brooklyn hits were singles by Dan Brouthers and Bill Hart.

MAY 14   Tom Daly hits the first pinch-hit home run in major league history during a 10-inning, 8–7 win over the Braves in Boston. Daly batted for Hub Collins in the ninth inning and homered off future Hall of Famer John Clarkson to tie the score 6–6.

                Collins left the game because he said he was suffering from a cold (see May 21, 1892).

MAY 17   Bill Hart narrowly misses a no-hitter and defeats the Braves 2–0 at Eastern Park. The only Boston hit during the afternoon was a ninth-inning single by Bobby Lowe.

MAY 21   Declining rapidly after leaving the May 14 game with a "cold," Hub Collins dies from typhoid fever at the age of 28. Collins's wife was called to his bedside from their hometown of Louisville, Kentucky, expecting to nurse her husband back to health, but by the time she arrived he had passed away.

MAY 23   The Dodgers defeat Washington 6–5 at Eastern Park. Players from both teams wore crepe on their left arms out of respect for the memory of Hub Collins.

MAY 24   The Dodgers drub Washington 24–4 at Eastern Park. Brooklyn scored two runs in the second inning, two in the third, nine in the fifth, five in the sixth, five in the seventh and one in the ninth. The Dodgers collected 16 hits and were helped by four Senators errors and 10 walks, four wild pitches and a hit batsman. Oyster Burns scored four runs without a base hit.

MAY 29   The Dodgers hold a benefit game at Eastern Park for the widow of Hub Collins (see May 21, 1892). There were was a crowd of 7,126 in attendance and over $3,000 was raised. The Dodgers played an amalgamated team consisting of players from the Giants, Reds and Cardinals and lost 6–1.

JUNE 8   In a drizzling rain at Eastern Park, the Dodgers score six runs in the ninth inning to cap a 17–7 win over the Pirates.

JUNE 10   John Montgomery Ward ties a major league record for second baseman with 12 assists during a 5–4 win in the first game of a double-header against the Pirates at Eastern Park. Ward also collected a homer, a double and two singles in five at-bats. Brooklyn won game two by a 4–3 score in 11 innings.

JUNE 24   After beating the Senators 13–0 in the first game of a double-header in Washington, the Dodgers lose 2–0 in the nightcap.

JULY 5   The Dodgers win both ends of a double-header against the Cubs with scores of 2–1 and 5–4 at Eastern Park. The opener went 14 innings. The contest was scoreless until both clubs crossed the plate once in the 11th. Dave Foutz pitched a complete game six-hitter.

JULY 14   The first half of the 1892 season ends (see April 12, 1892) with the Dodgers in second place holding a 51–26 record and two-and-a-2½ games behind Boston. Brooklyn was 44–33 in the second half and finished a distant third nine-and-a-half games back of Cleveland.

JULY 19   The Dodgers win 1–0 and 13–0 in a double-header sweep over the Cardinals at Eastern Park. George Haddock not only pitched a complete game in the opener, but drove in the lone run in the fifth inning off future Hall of Famer Pud Galvin, who came into the contest with 360 career victories. Catcher Tom Kinslow tripled and Haddock came to the plate with a bat which was flat on one side. Flat bats were legal at the time and used in bunting situations. Haddock crossed up the Cardinals by looping a single into left-field to score Kinslow. Ed Stein pitched a two-hitter in the nightcap. The St. Louis hits were by Perry Werden and Dick Buckley.

> *Haddock was nicknamed "Gentleman George." The Dodgers acquired him after he was 34–11 with Boston in the American Association in 1891. In his first season with the Dodgers, Haddock had a 29–13 record with a 3.14 ERA in 381⅓ innings in 1892. Arm trouble limited him to only 12 big-league victories after 1892, however. Ed Stein also starred for the Dodgers during the 1892 campaign with a 27–16 record and a 2.84 ERA in 377⅓ innings.*

AUGUST 5   Dave Foutz allows only three hits in 12 innings, but loses 2–0 to Boston at Eastern Park. After hitting a batter with a pitch, Foutz allowed a home run to left fielder Jack Stivetts. Primarily a pitcher, Stivetts occasionally made appearances in the outfield in between starts.

AUGUST 6   A day after hitting a game-winning homer, Jack Stivetts pitches a no-hitter to lead Boston to an 11–0 win over the Dodgers at Eastern Park.

AUGUST 13   The Dodgers score eight runs after two are out in the second inning and defeat the Giants 12–2 at Eastern Park.

AUGUST 22   John Montgomery Ward collects two doubles, a triple and a home run during a 17–1 win over the Pirates in Pittsburgh.

SEPTEMBER 17   The Dodgers drub Louisville 15–2 at Eastern Park.

SEPTEMBER 29   The Dodgers defeat the Orioles and the setting sun 5–4 in a contest at Eastern Park called after seven innings by darkness. Brooklyn scored four runs in the seventh inning for the win.

OCTOBER 1   The Dodgers edge the Orioles 10–9 at Eastern Park. Brooklyn led 10–0 before Baltimore scored eight runs in the fifth inning and one in the sixth. The game was called at the end of the seventh by darkness.

OCTOBER 15   Three weeks before Grover Cleveland returns to the White House after defeating Benjamin Harrison in the Presidential election, John Montgomery Ward's two-run double in the second game of a double-header provides the only two runs of a 2–0 win over the Orioles in the second game of a double-header in Baltimore on the final day of the season. George Haddock pitched the shutout. The Dodgers also won the opener 10–5.

1893

Season in a Sentence

The Dodgers end June in a tie for first place, but a sputtering offense leads to 15 losses in a 16-games stretch in July.

Finish • Won • Lost • Pct • GB

Sixth (tie)   65   63   .508   20.5

Manager

Dave Foutz

Stats

Stats	Dods	NL	Rank
Batting Avg:	.266	.280	8
On-Base Pct:	.341	.356	10
Slugging Pct:	.371	.379	7
Home Runs:	45		4
Stolen Bases:	213		8
ERA:	4.55	4.66	7
Fielding Avg:	.930	.931	7
Runs Scored:	775		8
Runs Allowed:	845		7 (tie)

Starting Lineup

Tom Kinslow, c
Dan Brouthers, 1b
Tom Daly, 2b-3b
George Shoch, 3b-rf
Tommy Corcoran, ss
Dave Foutz, lf-1b
Mike Griffin, cf
Oyster Burns, rf
Con Daily, c
Danny Richardson, 2b
Harry Stovey, cf-lf

Pitchers

Brickyard Kennedy, sp
Ed Stein, sp
George Haddock, sp
Dan Daub, sp
George Sharrott, sp
Tom Lovett, sp-rp

Attendance

235,000 (third in NL)

Club Leaders

Batting Avg:	Tom Daly	.289
On-Base Pct:	Mike Griffin	.396
Slugging Pct:	Tom Daly	.445
Home Runs:	Tom Daly	8
RBIs:	Tom Daly	70
Runs:	Tom Daly	94
Stolen Bases:	Dave Foutz	39
Wins:	Brickyard Kennedy	29
Strikeouts:	Brickyard Kennedy	107
ERA:	Brickyard Kennedy	3.72
Saves:	Three tied with	1

FEBRUARY 15   The Dodgers sell John Montgomery Ward to the Giants for $6,000.

The deal ended Ward's two-year reign as Dodgers manager. While running the Brooklyn club in 1892, Ward had won 20 shares of New York Giants stock on a bet with one of the club's shareholders on where the Giants would finish. Today, such a conflict of interest, not to mention betting on the standings, would be cause for banishment from the game. However, it was common in the 1890s for individuals, whether they be players, managers or owners, to openly bet on games. It was also common for owners to own shares in other teams, and occasionally, players and managers did the same. The Giants posted a losing record in 1892, and the National League needed a strong draw in New York. The transfer of Ward to the Manhattan-based Giants was made to bolster the franchise. Dave Foutz, who had been an outfielder, first baseman and pitcher for the Dodgers since 1888, became the new Brooklyn skipper. Foutz would manage the Dodgers until 1896. Ward managed the Giants for two years, then retired after a second-place finish with an 88–44 record and a victory in a post-season series against the first-place Orioles.

FEBRUARY 18   The Dodgers send Bill Joyce and cash to the Senators for Danny Richardson.

Richardson was expected to be the Dodgers starting second baseman, but was suspended in July for the remainder of the season because he missed several games as a result of persistent problems with alcohol abuse.

APRIL 28   In the season opener, the Dodgers lose 7–5 to the Phillies in Philadelphia.

APRIL 29   The Dodgers take a thrilling 11–10 decision in 10 innings over the Phillies in Philadelphia. Brooklyn trailed 9–4 before scoring five runs in the ninth on three singles, a double and two walks. After the Phils scored in the top of the 10th, the Dodgers rallied for two in the bottom half.

MAY 5   The Dodgers win 2–1 over the Phillies in the home opener at Eastern Park.

MAY 9   The Dodgers overcome a nine-run deficit to stun the Giants 11–10 at the Polo Grounds. Brooklyn trailed 10–1 before scoring two runs in the fifth inning, one in the sixth, five in the seventh, one in the eighth and one in the ninth. Among the crowd of 6,000 were many officers and sailors from visiting war vessels, including those of England, France, Germany and Italy.

MAY 21   The Dodgers and Giants hold a benefit game at Eastern Park for Darby O'Brien, who played for Brooklyn from 1888 through 1892. The contest was played on a Sunday, which was illegal in New York State, but the authorities looked the other way because of the non-profit element of the event. O'Brien reported to spring training in 1893, but was too ill to play and was sent to Colorado to recuperate. By May, his situation was terminal. According to the newspaper reports, the benefit was held to enable O'Brien "to pass the remaining days of his life in such comfort as can be given to a man who is in the last stage of consumption." Consumption was the term used in the 19th century for tuberculosis. The Dodgers defeated the Giants 13–7, although the two teams traded batteries with Dodger hurlers Tom Lovett, Brickyard Kennedy and Ed Stein and catchers Tom Kinslow and Con Daily playing for the

New York club. The game drew nearly 9,000 and raised about $5,000. O'Brien died on June 15 in his hometown of Peoria, Illinois.

MAY 25   The Dodgers sign Harry Stovey as a free agent following his release by the Orioles.

An outfielder and first baseman, Stovey was one of the top players in baseball during the 1880s, but by the time he arrived in Brooklyn was just about washed up. His given name was Harry Stowe, but he changed his name to Stovey so that his mother, opposed to playing baseball for a living, wouldn't see his name in the box scores.

MAY 30   Brickyard Kennedy pitches two complete games victories in one day, defeating Louisville 3–0 and 6–2 in a Memorial Day double-header at Eastern Park. Kennedy pitched a two-hitter in the opener, allowing only a pair of singles to ex-Dodger George Pinckney. Kennedy allowed six hits in the second tilt.

Kennedy had a record of 25–20 in 1893, the first of four seasons in which he won at least 20 games. He pitched for the Dodgers from 1892 through 1901 and still ranks fourth in wins (177), third in losses (149), first in complete games (279), first in walks (1,128), third in innings (2,857), fourth in games started (332) and eighth in games pitched (381) on the Dodgers all-time statistical lists. Kennedy earned his nickname from his hometown of Bellaire, Ohio, the location of a large brick manufacturer. He was also known as "Roaring Bill" because he spoke extremely loudly. Kennedy was illiterate and considered a rube by his teammates. Unable to read menus, Kennedy always ordered whatever his dining companion was having. He once missed a game against the Giants because while trying to find his way from Brooklyn to the Polo Grounds, Kennedy was misdirected by a policeman who thought he was asking him how to go home to Ohio.

JUNE 7   The Dodgers maul St. Louis 14–1 at Eastern Park.

JUNE 12   The Dodgers take first place with a 14–13 win over the Reds at Eastern Park. Brooklyn scored seven runs in the second inning for a 7–3 lead, fell behind 11–7, then scored five times in the eighth to pull ahead 12–11. Cincinnati crossed the plate twice in the top of the ninth on a home run by pitcher Tony Mullane off Brickyard Kennedy for a 13–12 advantage, but the Dodgers rallied for two in their half for the victory. Kennedy redeemed himself by driving in the tying run with a single, stealing second, advancing to third on an infield out, and scoring on Harry Stovey's single.

JUNE 15   The Dodgers beat Cleveland 14–6 at Eastern Park.

JUNE 24   Three days after Lizzie Borden is convicted of the ax murder of her parents, Dodgers chop up the Senators 8–5 and 14–10 in a double-header at Eastern Park.

JUNE 27   After the Cubs score eight runs in the first inning, the Dodgers rally to win 14–13 in Chicago. Brooklyn took a 13–8 lead with nine tallies in the fourth inning on nine singles and a triple by Mike Griffin. After each team scored once more, the Dodgers survived some anxious moments in the ninth when the Cubs added four runs.

JUNE 30   The Dodgers win a 22–16 hitting fest over the Pirates in Pittsburgh. There would have been even more scoring if the two clubs hadn't set a major league record (since tied) by leaving 30 men on base. The Dodgers stranded 16 and the Pirates 14. Brooklyn took a 9–5 lead with five runs in the fourth inning. Pittsburgh closed the gap to 10–9 in the fifth, but the Dodgers responded with 12 unanswered runs by scoring nine in the sixth, two in the seventh and one in the ninth. Four of the sixth-inning runs scored on bases-loaded-walks by Frank Killen. The Pirates closed the scoring with seven tallies in the bottom of the ninth.

JULY 1   The Dodgers drop out of first place with a 13–2 loss to the Pirates in Pittsburgh.

JULY 11   The Dodgers collect 20 hits and win an 18–13 slugging match over the Colonels in Louisville. Brooklyn scored 10 runs in the fifth inning to take a 17–6 lead.

JULY 17   Center fielder Mike Griffin tied a major-league record for outfielders with four assists, but the Dodgers lose 9–8 to the Orioles in Baltimore.

JULY 20   The Dodgers are victims of a triple play at the hands of the Orioles in a 5–3 loss at Eastern Park. It was Brooklyn's 15th defeat in a span of 16 games.

JULY 21   Trailing 8–3, the Dodgers score two runs in the eighth inning and four in the ninth to stun the Orioles 9–8 at Eastern Park. All four runs in the ninth scored before a batter was retired.

JULY 27   Willie Keeler makes his Dodgers debut during a 20–2 win over the Phillies at Eastern Park. Keeler collected a home run and two singles in four at-bats. The Dodgers scored four runs in the second inning, one in the third, one in the fifth, six in the fifth, one in the sixth, one in the seventh and five in the eighth.

              The Dodgers purchased Keeler from the Giants for $800. He played in 21 games for the Giants over two seasons and hit .325, but struggled defensively at both third base and in the outfield. Keeler was tried at third even though he threw left-handed. He also stood only five-foot-four, and Giants manager John Montgomery Ward deemed him too small to stand up to major league competition. Willie carried a 29-ounce, 30-inch bat, which is likely the smallest in big-league history. Keeler collected 14 hits in his first 26 at-bats with the Dodgers, and batted .313 in 20 games. The defensive problems continued, however, and Keeler was benched in August. In January 1894, he was packaged with Dan Brouthers in a trade to the Orioles for Billy Shindle and George Treadway. The deal proved to be one of the worst in Dodgers history. Brouthers turned 36 in 1894, but had one good year remaining. Settling in right field, Keeler was a sensation in Baltimore. Over the next five seasons, he collected 1,097 hits in 644 games and batted .388, with a high of .424 in 1897. Keeler would return to Brooklyn in another deal in 1899 (see February 7, 1899).

JULY 30   Ed Stein pitches a two-hitter to defeat the Giants 3–0 at Eastern Park. Mark Baldwin threw a three-hitter for New York. The only hits off Stein were singles by George Davis and Shorty Fuller.

AUGUST 15   Brickyard Kennedy pitches a one-hitter for a 3–0 win over the Giants at Eastern Park. The only New York hit was a single by Parke Wilson.

AUGUST 22   Brickyard Kennedy allows a run and five hits in a 2–1, 12-inning complete game victory over the Pirates at Eastern Park. Gil Hatfield drove in the winning run with a single.

AUGUST 24   The Dodgers bash the Pirates 13–7 at Eastern park.

SEPTEMBER 26   The Dodgers close a disappointing season with a 7–5 loss to the Reds in Cincinnati.

1894

Season in a Sentence

In the greatest offensive season in major league history, the Dodgers compile a .312 team batting average and average 7.6 runs per game, but are outscored by four other clubs and finish in fifth place.

Finish • Won • Lost • Pct • GB

Fifth   70   61   .534   20.5

Manager

Dave Foutz

Stats

Stats	Dods	NL	Rank
Batting Avg:	.312	.309	6
On-Base Pct:	.379	.379	6
Slugging Pct:	.440	.435	6
Home Runs:	42		8 (tie)
Stolen Bases:	282		4
ERA:	5.51	5.32	8
Fielding Avg:	.928	.927	5
Runs Scored:	1,021		5
Runs Allowed:	1,007		8

Starting Lineup

Tom Kinslow, c
Dave Foutz, 1b
Tom Daly, 2b
Billy Shindle, 3b
Tommy Corcoran, ss
George Treadway, lf
Mike Griffin, cf
Oyster Burns, rf
Candy LaChance, 1b
George Shoch, cf
Con Daily, c

Pitchers

Ed Stein, sp
Brickyard Kennedy, sp
Dan Daub, sp
Con Lucid, sp
Hank Gastright, sp

Attendance

214,000 (fifth in NL)

Club Leaders

Batting Avg:	Mike Griffin	.358
On-Base Pct:	Mike Griffin	.467
Slugging Pct:	George Treadway	.518
Home Runs:	Tom Daly	8
RBIs:	Oyster Burns	107
Runs:	Tom Daly	135
Stolen Bases:	Tom Daly	51
Wins:	Ed Stein	27
Strikeouts:	Brickyard Kennedy	107
ERA:	Ed Stein	4.54
Saves:	Brickyard Kennedy	2
	Hank Gastright	2

APRIL 19   The Dodgers open the season with a 13–2 loss to the Braves in Boston. Brickyard Kennedy pitched a complete game, and allowed 19 hits.

APRIL 21   The Dodgers lose the home opener 3–0 to Boston before 19,200 at Eastern Park. Future Hall of Famer Kid Nichols pitched the shutout. According to the newspaper reports, pre-game activities included "the usual blare of trumpets, music by the band, and marching across the field" by players of both teams, features typical of Opening Day during the 1890s and the early part of the 20th century. The march to the flagpole by players of the opposing teams to raise the American flag was a feature of Opening Days into the 1930s.

APRIL 24   The Dodgers drop to 0–4 in the young 1894 season with a 22–5 loss to the Phillies in Philadelphia. Brickyard Kennedy and Jim Korwan pitched for Brooklyn. It was Korwan's major league debut, and the only contest he played for the Dodgers. A 20-year-old native of Brooklyn, Korwan allowed 14 runs, eight of them earned, in five innings. He later appeared in five contests with the Cubs in 1897.

APRIL 26   The Dodgers lose 13–3 to the Phillies at Eastern Park, but win the protest. In the first inning, Jack Taylor pinch-hit for Phillies pitcher Gus Weyhing, but Weyhing was allowed to remain in the game. Brooklyn protested the game, and the National League ordered that it be replayed in its entirety. The replay took place on July 23, and the Dodgers won 7–3.

APRIL 28   The Dodgers score seven runs in the first inning and hang on to win 10–9 over the Senators in a contest called after six innings by darkness in Washington.

APRIL 30   The Dodgers take a 9–0 lead and outslug the Senators 15–10 in Washington.

MAY 1   The Dodgers win a forfeit in Washington when the Senators refuse to play. With the Senators leading 2–1 in the sixth, Dave Foutz was called safe by umpire on a close play at first base. The Washington players argued vehemently, and umpire Billy Stage took out his watch and gave them one minute to resume their positions. When the Senators continued the discussion of the disputed play beyond the time limit, Stage forfeited the contest to the Dodgers.

MAY 10   Ed Stein allows only two hits, but loses 7–1 to the Braves in Boston with the help of nine walks and two wild pitches along with five errors by Dodgers fielders.

            Stein was 27–14 with a 4.54 ERA in 1894.

MAY 14   The Dodgers take a 12–7 lead with six runs in the seventh inning and beat Washington 14–7 at Eastern Park.

MAY 15   The Dodgers rout Washington 16–7 at Eastern Park.

MAY 18   The Dodgers hammer the Giants 16–7 in New York.

MAY 19   Pitcher Dan Daub has to leave the game against the Giants at Eastern Park when the ball glances off his bat and strikes him in the forehead, creating a wound which requires six stitches. The contest ended in a 3–3 tie when called on account on darkness at the end of the 10th inning.

JUNE 1   Hank Gastright pitches a one-hitter and beats the Cubs 5–0 at Eastern Park. The only Chicago hit was a single by Walt Wilmot.

            The shutout was Gastright's first since 1891. He was 2–6 with a 6.39 ERA in 1894.

JUNE 2   Ed Stein pitches a six-inning no-hitter and beats the Cubs 1–0 in a contest at Eastern Park called by rain. Stein walked five and struck out none. The lone run scored with two out in the first inning on a triple by George Treadway and a single from Mike Griffin.

Griffin hit .358 and scored 122 runs in 1894.

JUNE 7 The Dodgers and Pirates play to a 13–13 tie in a game at Eastern Park called by darkness after 10 innings. Brooklyn prevented defeat with two runs in the ninth.

JUNE 9 The Dodgers win their eighth game in a row with a 14–5 decision over the Pirates at Eastern Park.

JUNE 11 The Dodgers edge the Reds 12–11 at Eastern Park for their 10th win in a row. Brooklyn survived a five-run Cincinnati rally in the ninth inning for the victory.

The win gave the Dodgers a 22–15 record. The club was 33–18 on June 29, but went 37–43 the rest of the way.

Slick-fielding shortstop Tommy Corcoran set career highs by batting .300 and driving in 92 runs in 1894.

JUNE 16 The Dodgers score six runs in the first inning and defeat Cleveland 11–7 at Eastern Park.

JUNE 18 With the help of nine Senators errors, the Dodgers win 10–6 in Washington.

JUNE 19 Two big innings highlight a 11–9 win over the Senators at Eastern Park. The Dodgers scored nine runs in the first inning, and Washington countered with eight in the third.

JUNE 20 The Dodgers reach double digits in runs for the fourth game in a row, but lose 16–12 to the Senators in Washington.

JUNE 21 The Dodgers score at least 10 runs for the fifth consecutive game in defeating the Giants 16–1 at Eastern Park. All 16 runs scored in the first five innings. According to the newspaper reports, New York outfielders Eddie Burke, Mike Tiernan and George Van Haltren were often "lost among the ragweed and spear grass beyond the bicycle track, hunting three-baggers and home runs with the avidity of three pointers beating the bushes for game." The description highlighted two features of 19th century baseball. Outfield fences were much farther from home plate than those today. A distance of 500 feet was not unusual. Since few balls traveled that far, owners saved expenses by failing to trim the grass near the fences. Batters occasionally legged out inside-the-park homers when the ball was lost amid the high grass. Some teams kept extra baseballs hidden in the grass. When the batted ball disappeared, they simply picked up another one and returned it to the infield. Also, bicycle races were the craze of the 1890s, and many teams, including the Dodgers, installed tracks around the field to host races on off days. In addition, teams installed facilities to allow those fans who rode bicycles to the game to park the vehicles. The love affair with bicycles lasted until shortly after the start of the 20th century when the automobile satisfied the craving of Americans for private transportation.

JULY 8   Catcher Con Daily hits two inside-the-park homers during a 12–5 win over the Cardinals in St. Louis. It was the Dodgers third straight game with at least 10 runs in the series in St. Louis, following a 13–12 loss on July 5 and a 10–5 victory on July 7.

JULY 9   Brickyard Kennedy gives up 19 hits and 20 runs in a 20–8 loss to the Colonels in Louisville.

JULY 10   Con Daily has to be smuggled out of Eclipse Park in Louisville ahead of a mob following a 13–7 loss to the Colonels. Future Hall of Famer Fred Clarke ran into Daily on a play at the plate in the fifth inning and knocked over the Dodgers catcher. Daily rushed at Clarke and struck him twice. According to the newspaper reports, "the crowd shouted for someone to smash Daily with a bat and made so much noise the game could not proceed." Daily put on his street clothes and sneaked out of the ball park. Many in the crowd followed a person they believed was Daily, but pursued the wrong man. Daily expressed regret for striking Clarke, but said he was "blind with rage."

JULY 14   A four-run rally with two out in the ninth inning ties the game 8–8 against the Cubs in Chicago and ends with that score when called by darkness. Pitcher Ed Stein started the rally with a double.

JULY 19   The Dodgers score seven runs in the eighth inning to cap a 19–8 win over the Orioles in Baltimore.

JULY 26   Trailing 6–2, the Dodgers score eight runs in the third inning and defeat the Braves 15–9 in Boston.

AUGUST 6   The Dodgers collect 25 hits and slaughter the Giants 21–8 in New York. Brooklyn scored a run in the first inning, four in the third, seven in the fourth, three in the fifth, two in the sixth, two in the eighth and two in the ninth.

AUGUST 7   In a double-header against the Orioles in Baltimore, the Dodgers lose 21–5 and win 18–8.

AUGUST 8   The Dodgers give 18-year-old Brooklyn amateur pitcher Andy Sommerville a chance as the starting pitcher in the second game of a double-header against the Orioles at Eastern Park. In what proved to be his only big-league appearance, Sommerville allowed six runs in a single and five walks in one-third of an inning. The Dodgers lost 13–5. Baltimore also won the opener 4–1.

AUGUST 11   The Dodgers win a thrilling 11–10 decision over Boston at Eastern Park. The lead changed hands six times. The Dodgers led at the end of the first, fifth, seventh and eighth, only to have the Braves go ahead or tie the score in the top half of the next inning. Brooklyn starter Con Lucid, a native of Dublin, Ireland, was pitching in his third big-league game and his first for the Dodgers. The Dodgers scored three times in the seventh for a 7–6 lead, but the Braves rallied for two runs in the top of the eighth on a home run by Tommy Tucker which rolled under the right-field fence. The Dodgers responded with three tallies in the bottom half. Lucid was still on the mound in the ninth inning with the 10–8 lead, but surrendered two runs. Candy LaChance won the game with an inside-the-park homer in the bottom of the ninth. LaChance stumbled and fell about six feet from home, and crawled to touch the plate just before the tag was applied.

George LaChance became known as "Candy" because he preferred peppermints to chewing tobacco.

AUGUST 13   The Dodgers score in seven of eight turns at bat, and beat Boston 13–5 at Eastern Park.

AUGUST 20   The Dodgers win 20–4 over St. Louis at Eastern Park. Dad Clarkson gave up all 20 runs. Brooklyn scored five runs in the first inning, four in the second, three in the third, one in the fourth, five in the fifth and two in the sixth. George Treadway collected two doubles, a triple and a homer in four at-bats.

Treadway set a club record with 26 triples in 1894.

AUGUST 21   The Dodgers score 20 runs for the second day in a row with a 20–11 triumph over St. Louis at Eastern Park. Ted Breitenstein gave up all 20 runs. Brooklyn scored three runs in the first inning, two in the second, three in the third, one in the fourth, five in the fifth, one in the seventh and four in the eighth. The Dodgers had 23 hits in the contest, five of them by Oyster Burns in six at-bats. Burns collected four singles and a double.

AUGUST 24   The Dodgers score four runs in each of the first three innings and defeat the Reds 15–9 at Eastern Park. Billy Shindle hit a grand slam off Chauncey Fisher in the third inning.

AUGUST 30   The Dodgers win 19–8 and lose 9–1 in a double-header against the Pirates at Eastern Park. In the opener, the Dodgers led 15–1 after four innings. The second contest was called after six innings by darkness.

SEPTEMBER 1   The Dodgers sweep Louisville 6–5 and 20–7 at Eastern Park. The Dodgers scored two runs in the ninth inning to win the opener. There were 24 Brooklyn hits in the second tilt, five by Candy LaChance in six at-bats. LaChance collected a triple, two doubles and two singles. The Dodgers scored four runs in the first inning, five in the second, one in the third, one in the fourth, five in the sixth, one in the seventh and three in the eighth before the contest was called one inning short of the regulation nine on account of darkness.

SEPTEMBER 12   The Dodgers outlast the Cubs 12–8 in Chicago.

SEPTEMBER 25   Brickyard Kennedy is ejected after striking umpire William Betts during a 10–7 loss to the Pirates in Pittsburgh. In the seventh inning, Pittsburgh's Jake Beckley was called safe on a close play at third base. This so angered Kennedy that he first hit Betts on the shoulder with his fist, and then smacked the umpire on the cheek with his open hand.

SEPTEMBER 30   On the final day of the season, the Dodgers lose 10–8 and win 12–4 in a double-header against the Colonels in Louisville. The second tilt was called by darkness after five innings. In the nightcap, Pete Browning played in the last of his 1,183 big-leagues games, and his only one with the Dodgers, and collected two singles in two at-bats.

Browning played 13 seasons in the majors. He is best remembered for helping to start the customized bat industry. In 1884, while playing for Louisville, Browning walked into J. F. Hillerich's wood shop complaining of a batting slump. Hillerich manufactured a bat to Browning's liking. Pete broke out of a slump and extolled the virtues of his personalized bat throughout baseball. In a short time, Hillerich's wood shop grew into Hillerich & Bradsby, the world's largest bat manufacturer and the maker of the Louisville slugger.

1895   L A

Season in a Sentence

A 12-game winning streak in August helps the Dodgers finish above the .500 mark for the fourth year in a row.

Finish • Won • Lost • Pct • GB

Fifth (tie)   71   60   .542   16.5

Manager

Dave Foutz

Stats

Stats	Dods	NL	Rank
Batting Avg:	.282	.296	10
On-Base Pct:	.346	.361	6
Slugging Pct:	.379	.400	10
Home Runs:	39		5
Stolen Bases:	183		11
ERA:	4.94	4.78	8
Fielding Avg:	.941	.930	2
Runs Scored:	867		6
Runs Allowed:	834		5 (tie)

Starting Lineup

John Grim, c
Candy LaChance, 1b
Tom Daly, 2b
Billy Shindle, 3b
Tommy Corcoran, ss
John Anderson, lf
Mike Griffin, cf
George Treadway, rf
George Shoch, rf-lf

Pitchers

Brickyard Kennedy, sp
Ed Stein, sp
Ad Gumbert, sp
Dan Daub, sp
Con Lucid, sp

Attendance

230,000 (seventh in NL)

Club Leaders

Batting Avg:	Mike Griffin	.333
On-Base Pct:	Mike Griffin	.444
Slugging Pct:	Mike Griffin	.457
Home Runs:	John Anderson	9
RBIs:	Candy LaChance	108
Runs:	Mike Griffin	140
Stolen Bases:	Tom Daly	37
Wins:	Brickyard Kennedy	19
Strikeouts:	Ed Stein	55
ERA:	Dan Daub	4.29
Saves:	Jack Cronin	2

JANUARY 26   The Dodgers trade Tom Kinslow to the Pirates for Ad Gumbert.

APRIL 18   The Dodgers open the season with a 7–4 win over the Giants in New York. Brickyard Kennedy was the winning pitcher and collected three hits. Tom Daly also had three hits.

Kennedy had a record of 19–12 in 1895.

APRIL 25   The Dodgers wallop the Orioles 14–6 in Baltimore. Brooklyn trailed 6–4 before scoring three runs in the seventh inning, five in the eighth and two in the ninth.

MAY 1   In the home opener, the Dodgers score two runs in the ninth inning to defeat the Orioles 7–6 before 16,000 at Eastern Park. The game-winning rally consisted of consecutive one-out singles by pitcher Ad Gumbert, Mike Griffin, Tommy Corcoran and Candy LaChance. Earlier in the contest, LaChance hit a home run.

            Griffin hit .332, collected 38 doubles and scored 140 runs in 1895.

MAY 13   The Dodgers edge the Cardinals 13–12 in St. Louis. Brooklyn took an 8–7 lead with two runs in the fifth inning.

MAY 19   Cubs pitcher, and ex-Dodger, Adonis Terry collects a homer, a double and two singles in a 14–9 win over the Dodgers in Chicago. The homer was a fluke, rolling into a hole near the outfield fence allowing him to circle the bases.

MAY 23   The Dodgers win a forfeit in Louisville because the Colonels run out of baseballs. At the start of the contest, there were only three new balls at hand. With the Dodgers leading 3–1 in the third inning, those three had been battered out of shape, and when umpire William Betts called for a new one, it was not to be had. Louisville business manager Harry Pulliam telegraphed for a dozen more and sent a messenger to retrieve them. The messenger boarded a streetcar, which proceeded to break down, preventing him from returning to the ballpark. Unwilling to wait any longer, Betts declared a forfeit to the Dodgers since it is the home team's responsibility to supply enough new baseballs to complete the game. A five-inning exhibition was played afterward to a 2–2 tie.

MAY 26   The Dodgers clobber the Colonels 11–0 at Louisville.

MAY 28   The Dodgers rout the Cubs 15–2 in Chicago.

JUNE 6   The Dodgers take a 9–1 lead after four innings and outlast Louisville 12–11 at Eastern Park.

JUNE 7   The Dodgers score two runs in the ninth inning to down the Reds 10–9 at Eastern Park. Tom Daly doubled in the tying run and scored all the way from second on a wild pitch by Billy Rhines.

JUNE 12   The Dodgers score seven runs in the third inning of a 13–8 win over St. Louis at Eastern Park. Making his major league debut, Sandy McDougal pitched the final three innings for the Dodgers. It proved to be his only game with Brooklyn in one of the most unusual careers in big-league history. McDougal didn't play in his second game in the majors for another 10 years when he appeared in five games with the Cardinals in 1905.

JUNE 22   The Dodgers score seven runs in the first inning of a 12–9 victory over the Phillies at Eastern Park.

JUNE 26   The Dodgers beat Washington 1–0 in 13 innings at Eastern Park. Ed Stein threw a complete game and allowed only five hits. Stein started the game-winning rally with a single and came around to score on singles by Mike Griffin and Tommy Corcoran.

JULY 2

Trailing 10–4 after three innings, the Dodgers rally to win 12–11 over the Giants at Eastern Park. Brooklyn started the comeback with five runs in the fourth inning, and after each team scored once, finished it with two tallies in the eighth.

JULY 6

A late comeback falls short as the Dodgers lose 16–15 to the Reds in Cincinnati. Brooklyn trailed 8–0 after two innings and 11–4 after four.

JULY 9

George Treadway hits an inside-the-fence homer during a 6–5 loss to the Reds in the first game of a double-header in Cincinnati. In center field, there was an inner fence and an outer fence, and Treadway's drive went rattling down between them. The Reds also won the nightcap, called on account of darkness after eight innings, 14–6.

JULY 14

The Dodgers score eight runs in the first inning, take a 13–0 lead in the third, and beat the Colonels 16–3 at Louisville.

JULY 25

Con Lucid gives up 20 runs and 20 hits in a 20–3 loss to the Cardinals in St. Louis.

AUGUST 1

The Dodgers slip past the Phillies 10–8 in Philadelphia.

AUGUST 2

The Dodgers topple the Giants 11–6 at the Polo Grounds in New York.

AUGUST 3

The Dodgers break a 3–3 tie with six runs in the third inning and beat the Giants 13–3 at Eastern Park. It was Brooklyn's third consecutive game with 10 or more runs.

During this period, the Dodgers and Giants often played games in both Brooklyn and Manhattan on consecutive days.

AUGUST 22

Brickyard Kennedy pitches a two-hitter and defeats the Pirates 6–0 at Eastern Park. The only Pittsburgh hits were singles by Jake Stenzel and Bill Merritt.

AUGUST 23

A two-run, walk-off triple by Tommy Corcoran beats the Pirates 7–6 at Eastern Park.

AUGUST 24

Candy LaChance hits a grand slam during an 18–4 win over the Cardinals at Eastern Park.

AUGUST 27

The Dodgers score seven runs in the sixth inning for a 12–0 lead, and beat the Cardinals 12–5 at Eastern Park.

AUGUST 28

The Dodgers score eight runs in the second inning and wallop Louisville 13–5 at Eastern Park.

AUGUST 29

The Dodgers win their 12th game in a row with an 11–6 victory over the Reds at Eastern Park. The winning streak gave Brooklyn a 59–45 record and a position in fourth place, seven games out of first.

AUGUST 30

According to the August 30 edition of the *Daily Globe* in Atchison, Kansas, "Trolley Dodgers is the new name which eastern baseball cranks have given the Brooklyn club." It is the first known reference to the Brooklyn club as the Dodgers. The new nickname appeared in two New York papers on September 3. Trolley Dodgers had been a disparaging term of Manhattanites to given to Brooklyn residents for the maze of trolley lines which criss-crossed Brooklyn. Rather than be insulted, the inhabitants of Brooklyn embraced the name. The area around Eastern Park was one of those in which "dodging" trolleys was a necessity to save life and limb (see April 27, 1891). It would take some time, however, for Dodgers to become the club's primary nickname. The team was often referred to by a variety of other nicknames into the 1930s, including the Bridegrooms (until the late 1890s), Superbas (1899–1924) and Robins (1916–31).

SEPTEMBER 2   The Dodgers pounce on the Cubs 11–3 and 15–6 in a double-header at Eastern Park.

SEPTEMBER 4   Mike Griffin sets a club record by scoring in his 17th consecutive game during a 15–5 loss to Cleveland at Eastern Park.

SEPTEMBER 5   The Dodgers shove the Pirates off the plank with a 11–1 win at Eastern Park.

SEPTEMBER 10   The Dodgers score two runs in the ninth inning to beat the Reds 2–1 at Eastern Park. Candy LaChance hit a home run to tie the score, followed by a triple from Tom Daly and single by George Shoch.

SEPTEMBER 11   The Dodgers score two runs in the ninth inning for the second day in a row for a 3–2 victory over the Orioles in Baltimore.

SEPTEMBER 14   In the eighth inning of a 14–5 loss to the Orioles in Baltimore, a foul tip shatters the mask of umpire Tim Hurst driving a wire into his forehead which strikes an artery. Amazingly, Hurst remained in the game despite the blood.

Hurst, who also worked as a boxing referee, may have been the toughest umpire in big-league history. During a Dodgers game in 1897, Hurst was struck in the temple by a foul tip, which according to the newspaper reports caused him to "fall like a log." The blow rendered him unconscious for 15 minutes, but again, he remained in the game until the finish.

SEPTEMBER 16   The Dodgers lose 16–12 and win 11–3 in a double-header against the Senators in Washington. The second contest was called after six innings by darkness.

SEPTEMBER 17   The Dodgers win 12–5 over the Senators in Washington in a contest called after eight innings on account of darkness.

SEPTEMBER 27   The Dodgers and Phillies play to a 14–14 tie in a game in Philadelphia called after nine innings by darkness. John Anderson deadlocked the contest with a ninth-inning grand slam off Deke White.

Anderson played for the Dodgers from 1894 through 1899 at the start of a 14-year major league career. He was born in Sarpsborg, Norway.

NOVEMBER 18   The Dodgers purchase Tommy McCarthy from Boston for $6,000.

1896

Season in a Sentence

Dave Foutz is let go as manager after the Dodgers compile their worst winning percentage in 12 years.

Finish • Won • Lost • Pct • GB

Ninth (tie) 58 73 .443 33.0

Manager

Dave Foutz

Stats

Stats	Dods •	NL •	Rank
Batting Avg:	.284	.290	10
On-Base Pct:	.340	.354	10
Slugging Pct:	.379	.387	10
Home Runs:	28		8 (tie)
Stolen Bases:	198		8
ERA:	4.25	4.36	5
Fielding Avg:	.945	.938	4
Runs Scored:	692		10
Runs Allowed:	764		6

Starting Lineup

John Grim, c
John Anderson, 1b-lf-rf
Tom Daly, 2b
Billy Shindle, 3b
Tommy Corcoran, ss
Tommy McCarthy, lf
Mike Griffin, cf
Fielder Jones, rf
Candy LaChance, 1b
George Shoch, 2b
Buster Burrell, c

Pitchers

Brickyard Kennedy, sp
Harley Payne, sp
Dan Daub, sp
Bert Abbey, sp
George Harper, sp
Ed Stein, sp

Attendance

201,000 (eighth in NL)

Club Leaders

Batting Avg:	Fielder Jones	.354
On-Base Pct:	Fielder Jones	.427
Slugging Pct:	Fielder Jones	.443
Home Runs:	Candy LaChance	7
RBIs:	Tommy Corcoran	73
Runs:	Mike Griffin	101
Stolen Bases:	John Anderson	37
Wins:	Brickyard Kennedy	17
Strikeouts:	Brickyard Kennedy	76
ERA:	Harley Payne	3.39
Saves:	Brickyard Kennedy	1

April 16   Three months after Utah is admitted as the 45th state in the Union, the Dodgers win the season opener by a 6–5 score over the Orioles in Baltimore. Brickyard Kennedy was the winning pitcher.

April 22   The Dodgers score six runs in the sixth inning to take a 12–8 lead just before the contest against the Senators in Washington is called on account of darkness.

April 29   The Dodgers lose the home opener 6–4 to Washington before 17,000 at Eastern Park.

May 12   Six days after the Supreme Court case *Plessy vs. Ferguson* approves racial segregation under the "separate but equal" doctrine, the Dodgers win a 9–8 battle over the Colonels at Louisville on a Candy LaChance homer in the ninth inning. Down 5–0, Brooklyn scored seven times in the third inning and took an 8–5 advantage in the sixth, but allowed Louisville to tie with three tallies in the eighth. In the absence of a regular umpire, players John Grim of the Dodgers and Bert Cunningham of the Colonels officiated.

May 9   The Dodgers collect 22 hits and wallop the Spiders 19–8 in Cleveland.

May 17   The Dodgers score nine runs in the top of the first inning, but manage to lose 16–10 to the Reds in Cincinnati. The Reds took an 11–10 lead with three runs in the fifth, then added five more in the sixth.

| MAY 20 | The Dodgers take a 22–0 lead by the end of the seventh inning and clobber the Pirates 25–6 in Pittsburgh. Brooklyn collected 25 hits, including six doubles, three triples and a home run. The Dodgers scored two runs in the first inning, two in the second, two in the third, four in the fourth, seven in the fifth, two in the sixth, three in the seventh and three in the ninth. |

| JUNE 1 | The Dodgers pummel St. Louis 15–2 at Eastern Park. |

| JUNE 12 | A walk-off single by John Grim in the ninth inning beats the Spiders 4–3 at Eastern Park. Cleveland left fielder Jesse Burkett picked up the ball Grim drove into the outfield and heaved it completely over the grandstand. |

| JUNE 18 | The Dodgers score two runs in the ninth inning and one in the 10th to beat the Giants 4–3 at Eastern Park. Tommy Corcoran drove in the winning run with a single. |

| JUNE 19 | The Dodgers win their seventh game in a row with a 3–2 decision over the Giants in New York. |

The winning streak gave the Dodgers a 27–23 record, but the club was 31–50 the rest of the way.

| JUNE 23 | In his first game back in Boston where he starred from 1892 through 1895, Dodgers outfielder Tommy McCarthy is given a rousing reception during a 9–3 loss to the Braves. McCarthy was presented with a diamond ring and a large floral horseshoe. |

| JULY 6 | After being held to no runs and one hit by Spiders pitcher Nig Cuppy through eight innings, the Dodgers score five runs in the ninth inning, but it's too late to prevent a 6–5 loss in Cleveland. |

| AUGUST 6 | The Dodgers overcome a 10–0 deficit to shock the Phillies 11–10 at Eastern Park. Philadelphia scored four runs in the first inning and six in the fifth for the lead. Brooklyn began the comeback with two in the bottom of the fifth. Two more runs were added in the sixth, three in the seventh, two in the eighth and two in the ninth. Jack Taylor pitched a complete game for the Phils. Billy Shindle smacked run-scoring triples in both the seventh and eighth innings. In the ninth, John Anderson sparked the rally with another triple. George Shoch drove him in with a single to tie the score 10–10. The bases were loaded when John Grim was hit by a pitch and relief pitcher George Harper reached on an error. Mike Griffin ended the contest with a sacrifice fly. A rookie pitching less than a month after his big-league debut, Harper hurled four hitless innings from the sixth through the ninth. |

| AUGUST 12 | Harley Payne pitches a two-hitter to defeat the Orioles 3–0 at Eastern Park. The only Baltimore hits were a single and triple from future Hall of Famer Hughie Jennings. |

| AUGUST 13 | The Orioles score 10 runs in the first inning off George Harper and Bert Abbey and beat the Dodgers 19–3 in the second game of a double-header in Baltimore. The Dodgers won the opener 5–2. |

| AUGUST 24 | Brickyard Kennedy pitches a shutout and drives in the lone run of the game with a seventh-inning single in a 1–0 victory over the Cubs at Eastern Park. The contest was called in the eighth inning by rain. |

SEPTEMBER 23   The Dodgers lose 17–16 to the Phillies in Philadelphia in a contest called after seven innings by darkness. The Dodgers trailed 15–5 before scoring seven times in the fifth. After the Phils added a run in the bottom of the fifth, the Dodgers plated a run in the sixth and three in the seventh to tie the score 16–16 and overcame a 10-run deficit against the Phillies for the second time in less than two months (see August 6, 1896). Philadelphia won this time, however, by scoring in the bottom of the seventh.

SEPTEMBER 26   The Dodgers close the 1896 season with 21 hits and a 13–10 win over the Phillies in Philadelphia.

The game is Foutz's last as a manager of the Dodgers. He had a 264–257 record in four seasons. Foutz was replaced 44-year-old Billy Barnie, who had previously managed in Baltimore (1883–91), Washington (1982) and Louisville (1893–94). Barnie lasted only 35 games into the 1898 season as Dodgers manager. A few months after being succeeded by Barnie, Foutz died from asthma on March 5, 1897, at the age of 40.

NOVEMBER 13   The Dodgers trade Tommy Corcoran to the Reds for Germany Smith, Chauncey Fisher and $1,000.

The Dodgers came out on the wrong end of this deal. Smith, who previously played for the Dodgers from 1885 through 1890, had only two years left in his career, and hit .190 in 163 games. Fisher played just one season in Brooklyn. Corcoran, on the other hand, had a 10-year run as Cincinnati's starting shortstop.

1897

Season in a Sentence

New manager Billy Barnie fails to be the antidote for the Dodgers' problems as the club, with virtually the same cast of characters as the previous season, finishes 10 games under .500.

Finish • Won • Lost • Pct • GB

Sixth (tie) 61   71   .462 32.0

Manager

Billy Barnie

Stats

Stats	Dods •	NL •	Rank
Batting Avg:	.279	.292	9
On-Base Pct:	.336	.354	11
Slugging Pct:	.366	.386	10
Home Runs:	24		9
Stolen Bases:	187		8
ERA:	4.60	4.31	9
Fielding Avg:	.936	.939	7
Runs Scored:	802		5
Runs Allowed:	845		9

Starting Lineup

John Grim, c
Candy LaChance, 1b
George Shoch, 2b
Billy Shindle, 3b
Germany Smith, ss
John Anderson, lf
Mike Griffin, cf
Fielder Jones, rf
Jim Canavan, 2b
Aleck Smith, c

Pitchers

Brickyard Kennedy, sp
Harley Payne, sp
Jack Dunn, sp
Chauncey Fisher, sp
Dan Daub, sp

Attendance

220,831 (seventh in NL)

Club Leaders

Batting Avg:	John Anderson	.325
On-Base Pct:	Mike Griffin	.416
Slugging Pct:	John Anderson	.455
Home Runs:	Three tied with	4
RBIs:	Billy Shindle	105
Runs:	Mike Griffin	136
Stolen Bases:	Fielder Jones	48
Wins:	Brickyard Kennedy	18
Strikeouts:	Harley Payne	86
ERA:	Brickyard Kennedy	3.91
Saves:	Brickyard Kennedy	1
	Chauncey Fisher	1

APRIL 22   The Dodgers open the season by scoring two runs in the ninth inning to defeat the Senators 5–4 in Washington. Harley Payne was the winning pitcher.

MAY 3   In the home opener at Eastern Park, the Dodgers and Orioles end in a 3–3 tie in a contest called after 11 innings by darkness.

MAY 17   The Dodgers break a 2–2 tie with six runs in the sixth inning and drub the Cardinals 15–5 in St. Louis.

MAY 25   Chauncey Fisher pitches eight innings of one-hit shutout relief in a 6–2 win over the Reds in Cincinnati. He relieved Harley Payne, who left after the first inning. It was Fisher's first game of the season after recovering from an illness he contracted in spring training.

JUNE 14   A team from Australia plays a combined team from members of the Dodgers and Cubs at Eastern Park. The players "from Kangarooland" beat the major leaguers 11–8 in a five-inning contest. In the regularly scheduled game, the Dodgers defeated the Cubs 15–4.

Wee Willie Keeler demonstrates the swing that made him one of the greatest hitters of his day.

JUNE 16   The Reds score 12 runs in the second inning off Harley Payne and Chauncey Fisher, and beat the Dodgers 15–6 at Eastern Park.

JUNE 19   Brickyard Kennedy pitches the Dodgers to a 1–0 win over the Reds at Eastern Park. The lone run of the contest occurred in the seventh inning when Mike Griffin singled, stole second, and crossed the plate on John Anderson's double.

               Griffin hit .316 and scored 136 runs in 1897.

JUNE 22   The Dodgers stop Boston's 17-game winning streak with a 7–4 triumph at Eastern Park.

JULY 10   St. Louis fans throw eggs at umpire Jack Sheridan during a game between the Dodgers and the Cardinals. With the score tied 2–2 in the fifth inning, Sheridan made a call that infuriated the hometown crowd. The game was halted, and Sheridan threatened the Cardinals with a forfeit unless he was granted police protection. St. Louis owner Chris Von der Ahe made the concession, and the Cardinals went on to win 4–3.

JULY 14 The Dodgers score nine runs in the sixth inning and defeat the Cubs 15–7 in Chicago.

JULY 22 The Dodgers score six runs in the ninth inning on four singles, two doubles and an error to beat the Reds 9–6 in Cincinnati. John Anderson collected both of the two base hits.

JULY 27 The Dodgers break a scoreless tie with seven runs in the fifth inning and win 14–2 over the Colonels in Louisville.

JULY 31 Brickyard Kennedy throws away a lead and the Dodgers lose 4–3 to the Giants at Eastern Park. Brooklyn led 2–0 heading into the ninth before New York scored three times on two singles, an error, a sacrifice, another single, and a sacrifice fly. With a 3–2 advantage, George Davis was the Giants runner on second base and George Van Haltren was coaching at third. At this point, stories diverge. Some newspapers, including the *New York Times,* reported that Van Haltren ran toward home imitating a base runner, and Kennedy fell for the ruse and threw plateward. There was no one to cover the plate, however, because catcher John Grim was arguing with umpire Hank O'Day. Others claimed that Kennedy deliberately threw the ball in attempt to strike O'Day, who was bending over to sweep off the plate. O'Day had angered the Dodgers because of several close calls in favor of the Giants. All agree that Kennedy's throw rolled to the grandstand, and Davis scored from second for a 4–2 New York lead. The Dodgers scored a run in the bottom of the ninth, but the rally fell a run short.

AUGUST 2 Mike Griffin scores five runs, but the Dodgers lose 9–8 to the Giants at Eastern Park. Griffin reached base on a double, a single and three walks.

AUGUST 6 The Dodgers clobber Washington 15–5 at Eastern Park.

AUGUST 9 Trailing 6–0, the Dodgers score 10 runs in the third inning and defeat the Orioles 16–9 at Eastern Park. During the 10-run outburst, Baltimore third baseman John McGraw berated pitcher Joe Corbett, who finally had enough. Corbett threw the ball away, walked to the dressing room, and refused to return.

Corbett's brother was James J. Corbett, who was heavyweight boxing champion from January 1894 through March 1897.

AUGUST 19 The Dodgers squelch St. Louis 13–5 at Eastern Park.

AUGUST 20 The Dodgers score seven runs in the first inning and defeat St. Louis 12–7 at Eastern Park.

AUGUST 25 The Dodgers defeat the Pirates 14–6 in a contest at Eastern Park called after eight innings by darkness.

SEPTEMBER 1   Brickyard Kennedy pitches a two-hitter in beating Cleveland 5–1 at Eastern Park. The only two hits off Kennedy were a double by Bobby Wallace and a single from Jack O'Connor.

SEPTEMBER 6   The Dodgers collect 20 hits, 19 of them singles, and defeat the Cubs 14–7 in the first game of a double-header at Eastern Park. Chicago turned the tables in the nightcap, winning 12–6 in a contest called after eight innings by darkness.

SEPTEMBER 17   The Dodgers score three runs in the ninth inning and defeat Washington 5–4 at Eastern Park. Billy Shindle drove in the winning run with a single.

                Shindle batted .284 and drove in 105 runs in 1897.

SEPTEMBER 21   The Dodgers score 12 runs in the first inning and win 22–5 over the Braves in the first game of a double-header in Boston. The Dodgers added five runs in the fourth, three in the fifth, and two in the eighth and collected 21 hits in the contest. Brooklyn was unable to hit in the nightcap, however, and lost 9–1 in a contest called after seven innings by darkness.

SEPTEMBER 25   The Dodgers sweep the Phillies 15–3 and 3–0 at Eastern Park.

OCTOBER 2   The Dodgers close the season with a 15–6 victory over Boston in Brooklyn. It was the Dodgers' last game at Eastern Park. In 1898, the club moved to a new Washington Park in Park Slope (see April 30, 1898). It was also the Dodgers' last game in the city of Brooklyn. On January 1, 1898, Brooklyn became a borough in New York City.

                In an oddity, the Dodgers and Washington Senators tied in the standings two years in a row. Both were 58–73 and in ninth place in 1896, and 61–71 and in sixth place in 1897.

NOVEMBER 12   The Dodgers send George Shoch and $1,000 to St. Louis for Bill Hallman.

1898

Season in a Sentence

Charles Ebbets takes over as president, moves the Dodgers into a new ball park, and even manages the team from June through the end of the season, but can't prevent a 10th-place finish.

Finish • Won • Lost • Pct • GB

| 10th | 54 | 91 | .372 | 46.0 |

Managers

Billy Barnie (15–20), Mike Griffin (1–3) and Charles Ebbets (38–68)

Stats

Stats	Dods	NL	Rank
Batting Avg:	.256	.271	10
On-Base Pct:	.309	.334	11
Slugging Pct:	.322	.347	10
Home Runs:	17		9
Stolen Bases:	130		9
ERA:	4.01	3.60	9
Fielding Avg:	.947	.942	5
Runs Scored:	638		10
Runs Allowed:	811		9

Starting Lineup

Jack Ryan, c
Candy LaChance, 1b
Bill Hallman, 2b
Billy Shindle, 3b
George Magoon, ss
Jimmy Sheckard, lf
Mike Griffin, cf
Fielder Jones, rf
Tommy Tucker, 1b
Aleck Smith, lf-c

Pitchers

Brickyard Kennedy, sp
Jack Dunn, sp
Joe Yeager, sp
Ralph Miller, sp
Kip McKenna, sp-rp

Attendance

122,514 (10th in NL)

Club Leaders

Batting Avg:	Fielder Jones	.304
On-Base Pct:	Mike Griffin	.379
Slugging Pct:	Mike Griffin	.367
Home Runs:	Candy	
	LaChance	5
RBIs:	Fielder Jones	69
Runs:	Fielder Jones	89
Stolen Bases:	Fielder Jones	36
Wins:	Brickyard	
	Kennedy	16
	Jack Dunn	16
Strikeouts:	Brickyard	
	Kennedy	73
ERA:	Brickyard	
	Kennedy	3.37
Saves:	None	

JANUARY 1   In ill health, Charlie Byrne resigns as club president, and is replaced by Charles Ebbets. Byrne died three days later.

Ebbets had been with the Dodgers since the founding of the franchise in 1883, beginning as a ticket taker at the age of 23. Ebbets impressed Charlie Byrne with his entrepreneurial spirit, and his responsibilities grew with each passing year. By 1897, Ebbets was club treasurer with ambitions of running the club himself. When elevated to the club presidency, he owned about 18 percent of the club and was one of three shareholders. Ferdinand Abell held the largest share of stock, as he had since 1883. Following his death, the stock held by Byrne passed to his estate, which was administered by his brother. Ebbets would become the majority owner in 1907, a position he held until his death in 1925. Among his innovations are the rain check and regularly scheduled batting and fielding practice. Ebbets also advanced the idea that teams should draft new players in inverse relation to their season records. His greatest legacy, however, is the building of Ebbets Field, which opened in 1913 and closed in 1957 when the Dodgers moved to Los Angeles.

MARCH 5   Three weeks after the battleship Maine explodes in Havana, killing 260 U.S. sailors, the Dodgers purchase Tommy Tucker from the Senators.

A first baseman, Tucker was nicknamed both Noisy Tom and Foghorn because as a third base coach his booming voice could be heard all over the ballpark.

APRIL 16   The Dodgers open the season with a 7–6 victory over the Phillies in Philadelphia. Brooklyn broke a 5–5 tie with two runs in the seventh. Brickyard Kennedy was the winning pitcher. Candy LaChance homered.

APRIL 30   Six days after the United States declares war on Spain over the sovereignty of Cuba, starting the Spanish-American War, the Dodgers open the new Washington Park with a 6–4 loss to the Phillies. Jimmy Sheckard homered for the Dodgers. The crowd was about 14,000, many waving small flags in the patriotic fervor attending the declaration of war.

The second Washington Park stood diagonally across the intersection of Third Street and Fourth Avenue from the first one, used by the Dodgers from 1884 through 1890 (see April 12, 1884). The new Washington Park replaced Eastern Park, which was the club's home from 1891 through 1897. Eastern Park was abandoned because the location was difficult to reach for most of Brooklyn's population in the late 19th century. The lot on which the new Washington Park was built measured 655 feet by 450 feet and was bounded by Third Avenue on the west (left field), Third Street on the south (third base), Fourth Avenue on the east (first base) and First Street on the north (right field). The new ballpark had about 18,000 seats in 1898 in a single tier grandstand covered by a truss roof. Only the portion of the stands between first and third base were covered by the roof, however. The others were open to the elements. Washington Park was built at a cost of $25,000, about half of which was supplied by the Nassau Railroad and the Brooklyn Heights Railroad. Both companies hoped to cover their investment in contributing to the construction by collecting fares from fans attending the games. By train, a fan could reach the ballpark in 18 minutes from downtown Manhattan. Although convenient, it was hardly an idyllic location because of the air pollution which wafted over the playing field. It emanated from nearby factories and the stench from the Gowanus Canal, which was a block away and curled its way around two sides of the ballpark. The stagnant water of the canal was also a breeding ground for mosquitoes. The Guinea Flats apartments overlooked the right-field fence and provided residents with a fine vista of the playing field, which provided a source of irritation for Dodgers management. A large piece of canvas was placed on top of the fence to obstruct the view of the "freeloaders." The second Washington Park would serve as the club's home through the 1912 season.

MAY 2   Trailing 9–5, the Dodgers score five runs in the eighth inning to beat the Phillies 10–9 at Washington Park.

MAY 3   Jimmy Sheckard collects a homer and two triples to lead the Dodgers to a 9–6 win over the Phillies at Washington Park.

One of the few Pennsylvania Dutch to play at the major league level, Sheckard made his major league debut at the age of 18 in 1897. He played for the Dodgers as a left fielder in 1897 and 1898 and again from 1900 through 1905. Sheckard's 76 triples with the club still ranks ninth on the all-time career lists.

MAY 6   The Dodgers score six runs in the ninth inning to beat the Senators 10–9 at Washington Park. The first three runs scored on a one-out, bases-loaded triple by Aleck Smith, who crossed the plate on a ground out. That left the Dodgers still trailing 9–8 with two out and no one on base, but Mike Griffin kept the rally alive with a single, followed by a walk to Fielder Jones. Switch hitting Candy LaChance was up next. LaChance was hitless in five previous at-bats against Washington lefty Doc Amole. LaChance went to the plate hitting left-handed, took a strike, then switched to the right side, and hit a two-run, walk-off double to win the game.

MAY 7   The Dodgers run their record to 9–4 with an 8–2 win over the Washington Senators at Washington Park.

         The victory represented the high point of the season. The Dodgers were 45–87 the rest of the way.

MAY 17   The Dodgers' only hit off Fred Lewis of the Braves in a 12–0 loss in Boston is a single by pitcher Joe Yeager in the ninth inning.

MAY 22   The Dodgers' only hit off Chick Fraser of the Colonels is a single by Fielder Jones with one out in the ninth inning of a 3–0 loss in the first game of a double-header in Louisville. It was the second time in six days that the Dodgers broke up a no-hit bid in the ninth. The Colonels also won the second tilt 7–2.

JUNE 5   Mike Griffin replaces Billy Barnie as manager of the Dodgers.

         Barnie lasted only 167 games as Dodgers manager and had a record of 76–91. Griffin, who was the club's center fielder, wanted no part of the job, and quit after four games. Club president Charles Ebbets took over the managerial duties for the rest of the season, even though he had never played the game professionally. Ebbets was 38–68 as the Brooklyn skipper. Ebbets was not only the Dodgers owner and manager, but served on New York's City Council. He was a member of the New York legislature from 1895 through 1897 and on City Council from 1897 through 1901.

JUNE 18 The Dodgers lose 7–5 and win 13–8 in a double-header against the Orioles at Washington Park. Brooklyn led the second game 11–2 in the fifth inning before hanging on for the win.

JULY 15 After entering the game as a substitute center fielder for injured Mike Griffin, Aleck Smith triples in the 12th inning and comes home with the winning run on Fielder Jones's walk-off single for a 3–2 win over St. Louis at Washington Park.

JULY 19 The Dodgers sell Tommy Tucker to St. Louis.

AUGUST 4 The Cardinals stun the Dodgers with five runs in the ninth inning to win 8–7 in St. Louis. Brickyard Kennedy provided comic relief during the rally by throwing the ball over the grandstand after center fielder Mike Griffin made an error. Umpire Bob Emslie ejected Kennedy.

AUGUST 21   Nine days after the surrender of Spain ending the Spanish-American War, Walter Thornton of the Cubs pitches a no-hitter to defeat the Dodgers 2–0 in the second game of a double-header in Chicago. The last out was recorded on a grounder by Fielder Jones to Cubs third baseman Barry McCormick. Thornton also walked three and struck out three. The Cubs also won the first game 4–3.

AUGUST 26   Held without a hit until the seventh inning by Bill Hart of the Pirates, the Dodgers collect three runs and five hits during the last three innings to win 3–2 in Pittsburgh.

AUGUST 27   Because of low attendance figures in Cleveland, the Dodgers and Spiders play a regular season game in Rochester, New York. The Spiders won 6–2 in the first of a three-game series. In the final two games in Rochester, the Dodgers beat Cleveland 7–5 on August 28, and 13–7 on August 29.

SEPTEMBER 3   The Dodgers rout the Cubs 16–8 in Chicago. In an oddity, the Dodgers collected exactly four runs in four different innings, scoring in the first, second, fifth and seventh.

SEPTEMBER 5   On Labor Day, the Dodgers lose 4–2 and win 14–3 against the Giants at Washington Park.

SEPTEMBER 18   With Sunday baseball illegal in New York, the Dodgers and Giants move across the Hudson River to play a regular season game in Weehawken, New Jersey, on the grounds of the West New York Field Club. The Giants won 7–3 before a crowd of 7,000.

SEPTEMBER 19   The Dodgers score twice in the ninth inning to defeat the Pirates 11–10 in the first game of a double-header at Washington Park. Pittsburgh won the second contest, called after five innings by darkness, 6–2.

SEPTEMBER 20   Brickyard Kennedy allows 15 runs and 20 hits in a 15–0 loss to the Pirates at Washington Park.

OCTOBER 11   The Dodgers score seven runs in the fourth inning to take a 12–0 lead, and beat the Phillies 14–2 in a contest at Washington Park called after seven innings by darkness.

OCTOBER 15   In the final game of the season, Candy LaChance hits a grand slam and Jimmy Sheckard collects three doubles and a homer during a 12–8 win over the Phillies in Philadelphia.

The Superbas

The Dodgers leaped from 10th place with a 54–91 record in 1898 to first place with 101 wins and 47 losses in 1899 in one of the most remarkable turnarounds in major league history. It was accomplished when club owners Charles Ebbets and Ferdinand Abell bought the Baltimore Orioles and transferred the Orioles' best players to Brooklyn. The move made the Orioles a virtual farm team of the Dodgers. It is a tactic that would be illegal under baseball bylaws today, but at the time there was no rule prohibiting an individual from owning stock in more than one franchise.

During the middle years of the 1890s, the Orioles were at the pinnacle of the baseball pyramid. Baltimore won the National League pennant in 1894, 1895 and 1896. Among the players were future Hall of Famers Dan Brouthers, Hughie Jennings, Willie Keeler, Joe Kelley, John McGraw and Wilbert Robinson. The manager was Ned Hanlon, another enshrinee at Cooperstown.

Hanlon played in the majors from 1880 through 1892. During his last season as a player, he became the manager of the Orioles, and the club finished dead last. Two years later, they were pennant winners. The Orioles were not only known for their winning ways, but for the way they won. Under Hanlon, the club became expert craftsmen at what then was known as "inside" or "scientific" baseball, and what today is known as "little ball," by elevating the bunt, the stolen base, the sacrifice, place hitting and the hit-and-run to an art form never before seen in the sport. The innovative Hanlon was also among the first to platoon players by matching left-handed batters against right-handed pitchers, and vice-versa. The Orioles were among the roughest and toughest players in the roughest and toughest era in baseball history. There was only one umpire on the field during the 1890s, and he could not possibly see everything. Hanlon's charges were not above cutting corners around the bases or grabbing or tripping enemy runners when the umpire was looking in the other direction. Their swagger and intimidation tactics beat many opponents before the first pitch was thrown. The club's vicious baiting of umpires won them more than their share of close calls.

The Orioles finished second to Boston in both 1897 and 1898. The Baltimore franchise was losing money despite the success on the field, however. Small markets played a part in baseball even in the 19th century, and Baltimore was among the least populated cities in the majors. The club also had the misfortune of achieving its greatest success during a period in which the country was gripped by one of the worst economic depressions in history. Although the financial crisis had improved by 1898, few clubs made money that season because the nation was distracted by the Spanish-American War. The Orioles finished ninth in attendance in a 12-team league in 1898.

While the Orioles were at the top of the National League, Brooklyn was struggling in the lower portion of the standings. Soon after the 1898 season ended, Ebbets and Abell got together with Orioles owner Harry Von der Horst. They began talking in December with the deal completed in February 1899. Each man purchased a portion of the other's ball club and would own 40 per cent each. Ebbets had a 10 percent share, as did Hanlon, who would became manager of the Dodgers. The best players on the Baltimore roster would be sent to the larger market in Brooklyn to create a super team. Among the 1898 Orioles who became Dodgers in 1899 were Keeler, Kelley, Jennings, Dan McGann, Doc McJames and Jim Hughes. The attempt to make the Dodgers even stronger was thwarted when John McGraw and Wilbert Robinson refused to move to Brooklyn because of business interests in Baltimore.

During spring training, the team drew the nickname of "Hanlon's Superbas" after a vaudeville act of the same name which created complex and extravagant comic-dramatic musical spectacles built around pantomime and gymnastics. According to author Glenn Stout, "their act was roughly akin to a small-scale Cirque du Soleil with a touch of the Marx Brothers."

The Dodgers won the National League pennant in 1899, while the Orioles finished a respectable fourth 15 games behind. But fans in Baltimore, feeling betrayed by the departure of their favorite players, stayed away from the ballpark. In March 1900, the National League eliminated four clubs to became an eight-team organization. Baltimore, with Washington, Cleveland and Louisville, was one of the four franchises eliminated.

The Dodgers won again in 1900, with the help of pitcher Joe McGinnity, another future Hall of Famer who played for the Orioles in 1899. The attendance boost expected at Washington Park failed to materialize, however. The club was fourth in attendance among 12 teams in 1899 and a shocking seventh among eight teams in 1900. Fans in Brooklyn simply failed to take to the new players from Baltimore who they had fervently rooted against when they were wearing opposition uniforms.

The American League was formed during the 1900–01 off-season, and through January

1903, began to whisk players away from National League rosters with offers of higher salaries. A new Baltimore club was admitted to the AL and signed McGinnity in 1901 and Kelley in 1902. The new Orioles moved to New York in March 1903 to establish the present-day Yankees franchise. Keeler signed with Yankees (then known as the Highlanders) in 1903. Beginning in 1904, the Dodgers experienced 11 losing seasons in a row. Hanlon was terminated after a 48–104 record in 1905.

The act of merging the two clubs was called "syndicate baseball" and was never tried again after 1900. A rule was passed in 1910 prohibiting a person from owning stock in more than one franchise.

1899
LA

Season in a Sentence

After a 10th place finish in 1898, the Dodgers purchase the Baltimore Orioles, bring that club's best players to Brooklyn, and win the National League pennant.

Finish • Won • Lost • Pct • GB

First   101   47   .682   +8.0

Manager

Ned Hanlon

Stats

	Dods	NL	Rank
Batting Avg:	.291	.282	2
On-Base Pct:	.368	.343	1
Slugging Pct:	.383	.366	3
Home Runs:	27		6 (tie)
Stolen Bases:	271		2
ERA:	3.25	3.85	1
Fielding Avg:	.948	.942	2
Runs Scored:	892		2
Runs Allowed:	658		2

Starting Lineup

Duke Farrell, c
Dan McGann, 1b
Tom Daly, 2b
Doc Casey, 3b
Bill Dahlen, ss
Joe Kelley, lf
John Anderson, cf-1b
Willie Keeler, rf
Fielder Jones, cf
Hughie Jennings, 1b

Pitchers

Jim Hughes, sp
Jack Dunn, sp
Brickyard Kennedy, sp
Doc McJames, sp

Attendance

269,641 (fourth in NL)

Club Leaders

Batting Avg:	Willie Keeler	.379
On-Base Pct:	Willie Keeler	.425
Slugging Pct:	Willie Keeler	.451
Home Runs:	Joe Kelley	6
RBIs:	Joe Kelley	93
Runs:	Willie Keeler	140
Stolen Bases:	Willie Keeler	45
Wins:	Jim Hughes	28
Strikeouts:	Doc McJames	105
ERA:	Jim Hughes	2.68
Saves:	Jack Dunn	2
	Brickyard Kennedy	2

FEBRUARY 27   The deal in which the Dodgers purchase the Baltimore Orioles is completed. Negotiations began the previous December. At the time, there was no rule which prohibited an individual from owning stock in more than one team. Under the arrangement, Harry Von der Horst, who had owned the Orioles, had a 40 percent share in both the Orioles and Dodgers. Ferdinand Abell, majority stockholder of the Dodgers, also had 40 percent of both franchises. Charles Ebbets and Ned Hanlon each held 10 percent. Hanlon, who had been manager of the Orioles from 1892 through 1898 and guided Baltimore to NL pennants in 1894, 1895 and 1896, became manager of the Dodgers. The best of the Orioles players, including future Hall of Famers Willie Keeler, Joe Kelley and Hughie Jennings, were transferred to Brooklyn.

APRIL 15   The Dodgers open the season with a 1–0 loss in 11 innings to the Braves before 20,000 at Washington Park. Both Brickyard Kennedy and Kid Nichols pitched complete games. Five of the first six hitters in the Opening Day lineup were playing in their first game as Dodgers. The quintet consisted of Joe Kelley, Willie Keeler, Hughie Jennings, Bill Dahlen and Dan McGann.

Dahlen was the only one of the five who didn't come from the Orioles in the merger of the two clubs. He was acquired in a trade with the Cubs, where he starred at shortstop from 1891 through 1898. Dahlen appeared in 2,444 games in the majors over 21 seasons. He was a Dodger player from 1899 through 1903 and managed the club from 1910 until 1913.

APRIL 25   The Dodgers send Pete Cassidy, Mike Heyden, Dan McFarlan and $2,500 to Washington for Doc Casey and Duke Farrell.

MAY 6   The Dodgers pull out a 12–10 victory in 10 innings over the Braves in Boston. Brooklyn led 10–3 when Boston plated seven runs in the ninth off Brickyard Kennedy and Joe Yeager to send the contest into extra innings.

The game was a rare lapse for Kennedy in a season in which he was 22–9 with a 2.79 ERA.

MAY 13   The Dodgers sweep the Senators 12–1 and 7–3 at Washington Park.

MAY 15   Willie Keeler hits an inside-the-park homer off Wiley Piatt in the eighth inning of an 8–5 win over the Phillies at Washington Park.

A Brooklyn native, Keeler hit .379, collected 216 hits, and scored a league-leading 140 runs in 1899. It was during that season that Keeler delivered one of the most famous quotes in baseball. When Brooklyn Eagle newspaperman Abe Yager asked Keeler to explain how he hit, Willie responded: "Keep a clear eye, and hit 'em where they ain't." Joe Kelley celebrated his first season in Brooklyn by hitting .325 with 108 runs scored. Tom Daly, who had been with the Dodgers since 1890, batted .313.

MAY 19   The Dodgers record their eighth victory in a row with a 7–5 decision over the Reds in Cincinnati.

MAY 22   The Dodgers take first place with a 5–2 victory over the Colonels in Louisville.

Brooklyn remained in first for the remainder of the season.

JUNE 2

Down 10–0, the Dodgers rally with a run in the sixth inning, two in the seventh, seven in the eighth and one in the ninth to stun the Spiders 11–10 at Washington Park.

JUNE 3

The Dodgers hammer the Spiders 13–4 at Washington Park.

JUNE 5

The Dodgers reach double digits in runs scored for the third game in a row with a 14–2 victory over the Spiders at Washington Park. It was the Dodgers' eighth victory in a row.

The Cleveland Spiders were one of the worst teams in baseball history. During the 1898–99 off-season, brothers Frank and Stanley Robison, owners of the Spiders, also bought the St. Louis Cardinals franchise. The best Cleveland players were transferred to St. Louis. As a result, the Spiders were 20–134 in 1899, the last season of their existence. In 14 meetings between the Dodgers and Spiders that season, Brooklyn won every one of them.

JUNE 7

Kip Selbach of the Reds hits a home run through an open gate at Washington Park in the fifth inning of a 6–5 Dodgers victory. The gate served as an entrance to the clubhouse.

JUNE 8

The Dodgers extend their winning streak to 11 games with five runs in the first inning for a 5–0 win over the Reds at Washington Park.

JUNE 9

The Dodgers win their 12th in a row with a 6–3 decision over the Reds at Washington Park.

JUNE 16

Five days after Butch Cassidy and the Sundance Kid rob a train of $60,000 in Wyoming, the Dodgers win a forfeit over the Giants in New York. The Giants were in a constant wrangle over the decisions of umpire Thomas Burns from the first pitch. In the bottom of the first inning, Burns ejected second baseman Kid Gleason and catcher John Warner. Parke Wilson replaced Warner as the New York catcher. Warner deliberately stepped out of the way of one of pitcher Cy Seymour's deliveries so that it would strike Burns. After the umpire shook off the blow, he forfeited the game to the Dodgers.

JUNE 18

The Dodgers score six runs in the third inning for an 8–2 lead and outlast the Reds 13–11 in Cincinnati.

JUNE 22

The Dodgers win their eighth game in a row with an 8–0 decision over the Spiders in Cleveland. The victory gave Brooklyn a 44–12 record.

JUNE 23

In Chicago, Bill Dahlen, who played for the Cubs from 1891 through 1898, is presented with a huge mass of flowers, a diamond stud, a pair of diamond cuff buttons and $500 in cash before a 3–2 Dodgers loss.

Dahlen hit .283 for the Dodgers in his first season with the club.

JULY 8

The Dodgers extend their home winning streak to a club-record 22 games with a 6–2 victory over the Phillies at Washington Park. The winning streak started on May 10.

JULY 11   The Dodgers take a 9–3 lead with five runs in the fourth inning and defeat the Cardinals 11–10 at Washington Park.

JULY 14   The Dodgers trade Dan McGann and Aleck Smith to Washington for Deacon McGuire.

McGuire became the Dodgers starting catcher and hit .298 in 202 games with the club through the 1901 season. He was already 35 years old when he arrived in Brooklyn, however, in the 15th year of a big-league career in which he played in 26 seasons, a record which wouldn't be broken until Nolan Ryan played in his 27th in 1993. The Dodgers came out on the short end of the deal because McGann was one of the better first basemen in baseball during the first decade of the 1900s. He had been one of the players bought from Baltimore following the merger with the Orioles. In 1910, two years after his sojourn in the majors ended, McGann committed suicide by shooting himself in the heart with a revolver. Earlier, McGann's brother and sister had each taken their own lives, and another brother died from an infection following an accidental shooting.

AUGUST 3   The Dodgers send Hughie Jennings back to the Orioles.

The move was roundly hooted in both Baltimore and Brooklyn because fans in both cities were assured that there would be no players transferred from one club to another after Opening Day. Jennings was the best shortstop in baseball, and one of the best players overall, when he became to Brooklyn following the merger between the Dodgers and Orioles. He had been expected to be the Dodgers' starting shortstop in 1899, but, because of a sore arm, was unable to play the position and moved to first base. Jennings would play only two seasons and 184 games with the Dodgers. In 1907, he became manager of the Detroit Tigers and won a pennant in each of his first three seasons with the club with the help of a rising young star named Ty Cobb.

AUGUST 11   The Dodgers score in an unusual manner to beat Louisville 1–0 at Washington Park. In the second inning, Bill Dahlen was hit by a pitch, moved to second base on Doc Casey's sacrifice, took third on an infield out, and crossed the plate while Duke Farrell was caught in a rundown between first and second. Brickyard Kennedy pitched the shutout.

AUGUST 16   The Dodgers vanquish Cleveland 13–2 at Washington Park.

AUGUST 17   The Dodgers rout Cleveland for the second day in a row with a 20–2 victory at Washington Park. Brooklyn scored three runs in the first inning, one in the third, eight in the fourth, one in the fifth, two in the sixth, four in the seventh and one in the eighth.

SEPTEMBER 4   The Dodgers and Giants play in two different ballparks on Labor Day, with the Dodgers taking both with late-inning comebacks. In the morning, the two Greater New York clubs met at Washington Park. The Dodgers won 3–2 by scoring two runs in the ninth. With two out and no one on base, John Anderson drew a walk as a pinch hitter, Fielder Jones and Willie Keeler singled to load the bases, Hughie Jennings contributed an infield single to tie the score, and Joe Kelley hammered home the winning run with another single. In the afternoon tilt at the Polo Grounds, the Dodgers trailed 4–1 before scoring four times in the eighth for a 5–4 victory.

SEPTEMBER 5   The Dodgers score seven runs in the fifth inning and defeat the Giants 16–5 in a contest at Washington Park called after seven innings by darkness.

SEPTEMBER 7   A 2–1 loss to Boston at Washington Park culminates in a riot. A mob of about 4,000 rushed upon the field and attacked umpire Bob Emslie after he called Brooklyn's Tom Daly out at home plate on a play which ended the game. One individual in the crowd struck Emslie in the neck. The umpire turned and dealt his assailant a hard blow to the face. Charles Ebbets and several policemen and players drove the crowd back to allow Emslie to exit safely. The police cleared the grounds, but the crowd waited outside for Emslie and Frank Dwyer, his umpiring partner. Emslie and Dwyer were led through Third Street to the elevated train station at Fifth Avenue, but the crowd followed. Stones were thrown, but none struck the umpires. At the station, Emslie and Dwyer were escorted up the stairs and the police did not allow anyone on the platform until their train had left.

SEPTEMBER 8   In the wake of the riot a day earlier, in which only three policemen were assigned to Washington Park, a squad a 50 officers are strung out in front of the grandstand and bleachers in order to quell any further trouble. Umpires Bob Emslie and Frank Dwyer, the focal points of the riot, walked onto the field just before the start of the contest and were stunned by the roar of applause that greeted their arrival. Emslie doffed his cap to the crowd. According to the wire service reports: "It was truly a day of triumph for the veteran judge of play. It showed that the better element of Brooklyn baseball patrons resented the actions of the mob the previous day." The Dodgers defeated Boston 5–0.

SEPTEMBER 9   On 9/9/99, Dodgers pitcher Doc McJames comes within one out of a no-hitter in a 4–0 win over Boston at Washington Park. The lone hit off McJames was a single by Hugh Duffy with two out in the ninth.

James McCutcheon (Doc) McJames came to the Dodgers after winning 27 games for the Orioles in 1898. He was 19–15 for the Dodgers in 1899 despite missing a few weeks after contracting malaria. McJames didn't play in 1900 to study medicine at the University of South Carolina, but after graduating returned to baseball. He was released by the Dodgers in July 1901 and returned to his hometown of Charlestown, South Carolina. Shortly thereafter, he suffered serious injuries in a runaway buggy accident and died on September 23, 1901 at the age of 28.

SEPTEMBER 13   At Washington Park, the Pirates tie the score 4–4 in the ninth inning and have the bases loaded with one out when umpire Ed Swartwood calls the game because of darkness. The score reverted back to the last completed inning, which gave the Dodgers a 4–3 victory.

SEPTEMBER 14   The Dodgers sweep the Pirates 7–5 and 7–1 at Washington Park. The second game was called on account of darkness after seven innings. The pair of victories gave the Dodgers an 88–37 record and an eight-game lead in the pennant race.

SEPTEMBER 16   Umpire Ed Swartwood calls the game between the Dodgers and Cubs at Washington Park because of darkness at the end of the seventh inning with the Dodgers leading 9–7. The Cubs believed another inning could have been played before sunset, and the umpire was surrounded by angry Chicago players. According to the newspaper reports, Swartwood was "knocked around a little" by the Cubs, and outfielder Bill Lange reached out and "tweaked" the umpire's ear.

SEPTEMBER 22   Dodgers pitcher Jack Dunn tosses a two-hitter in beating the Cardinals 2–0 at Washington Park. The only St. Louis hits were singles by Bobby Wallace and Jack O'Connor.

Dunn finished the season with a 23–13 record and a 3.60 ERA in 1899. Because of a sore arm, he won only 11 more big-league games following that season. Dunn made his greatest contribution to baseball after his playing career ended. In 1914, he was owner-manager of the Baltimore Orioles, then a minor league outfit in the International League. At Baltimore's St. Mary's Industrial Home for Boys, Dunn discovered a teenage pitching sensation named George Herman Ruth and signed him to a contract. The Orioles players resented Dunn's protective attitude toward Ruth and gave the young player the nickname "Babe." With Dunn in charge, the Orioles won seven consecutive International League pennants beginning in 1919.

SEPTEMBER 25   The Dodgers wallop the Senators 13–1 in a game at Washington Park called by darkness after 6½ innings.

OCTOBER 7   The Dodgers clinch the pennant with a 13–2 win over the Giants in a contest at Washington Park called after seven innings by darkness. The Dodgers scored five runs in the second inning and seven in the third.

OCTOBER 12   Jim Hughes wins his 28th game of the season with a 5–1 decision over the Orioles at Washington Park.

Hughes finished the season with a 28–6 record and a 2.68 ERA, following a rookie campaign in which he was 23–12 for the Orioles in 1898. Hughes didn't play the majors in 1900, preferring to pitch in the Pacific Coast League near his home in Sacramento, California. He played again for the Dodgers with records of 17–12 in 1901 and 15–10 in 1902, then went back to the PCL. Hughes won 34 games for Seattle in 1903.

OCTOBER 14   The Dodgers earn their 100th victory of the season with a forfeit against the Orioles at Washington Park. In the second inning, umpire George Hunt tossed Baltimore outfielder Jimmy Sheckard for vehemently arguing an out call on a steal attempt. When Sheckard ignored the ejection and tried to take his place in the field, Hunt ordered Orioles manager John McGraw to remove Sheckard from the game. McGraw refused, compelling Hunt to forfeit the game to the Dodgers. To placate the angry crowd, McGraw and Dodgers skipper Ned Hanlon agreed to play a makeup game for an early-season postponement. The Dodgers won 8–3 in a contest called after five innings by darkness.

The Dodgers record of 101–47 in 1899 gave the club a winning percentage of .6824, which is the best in club history. The 1953 Dodgers were 105–49, a percentage of .6818.

THE STATE OF THE DODGERS

The Dodgers won their second straight pennant in 1900, but it was almost all downhill for the rest of the decade. The creation of the American League, which took away the core of the team by offering more lucrative contracts, was the primary reason for the slide. By 1905, the club was in last place and began a long, slow climb out of the cellar. Brooklyn fans suffered through 11 consecutive losing seasons from 1904 through 1914. Overall, the Dodgers were 649–809 from 1900 through 1909, a winning percentage of .445, which was the sixth-best among the eight teams in the NL. During this period, the league was dominated by the Cubs, Pirates and Giants, three clubs that won every pennant from 1901 through 1913 and usually finished in the top three spots in the standings. Pennant winners other than the Dodgers during the 1900s were the Pirates (1901, 1902, 1903 and 1909), Giants (1904 and 1905) and Cubs (1906, 1907 and 1908).

THE BEST TEAM

The 1900 pennant winners had a record of 82–54.

THE WORST TEAM

The 1905 Dodgers were 48–104 to set a club record for defeats in a season that still stands.

THE BEST MOMENT

The pennant-winning Dodgers won a post-season series against the second-place Pirates following the 1900 season. It would be the last post-season series victory for Brooklyn until defeating the Yankees in the World Series in 1955.

THE WORST MOMENT

The 1903 season brought the double whammy of John McGraw turning the Giants into a pennant contender in his first full season with the club and the creation of a New York franchise in the American League that would be nicknamed the Yankees. For most of the next four decades, the Dodgers played third fiddle in Greater New York. From 1903 through 1938, the Dodgers had the third-best record in the Big Apple 27 times, the second-best in seven seasons and the best only in 1915 and 1916. The Dodgers were also third in attendance among the three New York teams in 31 of 35 seasons from 1904 through 1938.

THE ALL-DECADE TEAM • YEARS W/DODS

Bill Bergen, c	1904–11
Tim Jordan, 1b	1906–10
John Hummel, 2b	1905–15
Doc Casey, 3b	1899–1900, 1906–07
Bill Dahlen, ss	1899–1903, 1910–11
Jimmy Sheckard, lf	1898, 1900–05
Al Burch, cf	1907–11
Harry Lumley, rf	1904–10
Nap Rucker, p	1907–16
Doc Scanlan, p	1905–11
Jim Hughes, p	1899, 1901–02
Frank Kitson, p	1899–1901

When compiling the All-Decade Teams, only a player's years with the Dodgers are taken into consideration, which puts Sheckard and Lumley ahead of future Hall of Famers Willie Keeler (1899–1902) and Joe Kelley (1899–1901). Pitcher Harry McIntire (1905–09) was another outstanding individual on the club during the 1900s. The Dodgers had serious problems throughout most of the decade in fielding competent players at second and third base as well as center field.

THE DECADE LEADERS

Batting Avg:	Willie Keeler	.345
On-Base Pct:	Willie Keeler	.379
Slugging Pct:	Jimmy Sheckard	.425
Home Runs:	Harry Lumley	38
RBIs:	Jimmy Sheckard	342
Runs:	Jimmy Sheckard	503
Stolen Bases:	Jimmy Sheckard	199
Wins:	Doc Scanlon	53
	Frank Kitson	53
Strikeouts:	Nap Rucker	531
ERA:	Nap Rucker	2.13
Saves:	Frank Kitson	6
	Elmer Stricklett	6

THE HOME FIELD

Compared to those of the 21st century, ballparks at the beginning of the 20th century were ramshackle affairs made of wood, iron and steel. Washington Park, an 18,000-seat edifice that served as the home of the Dodgers from 1898 through 1912, was no exception. A revolution in ballpark construction took place beginning in 1909 with the building of much-larger concrete-and-steel facilities in Philadelphia (Shibe Park) and Pittsburgh (Forbes Field) and a rebuilt Sportsman's Park in St. Louis. Charles Ebbets immediately began putting together plans for a similar ballpark of his own, which would be accomplished in 1913 with the opening of Ebbets Field.

THE GAME YOU WISHED YOU HAD SEEN

Nap Rucker pitched a no-hitter and struck out 14 batters against the Boston Braves on September 5, 1908.

THE WAY THE GAME WAS PLAYED

In this decade of pitching and defense, the NL set all-time lows in ERA and batting average. The hit-and-run, base stealing and sacrifice plays dominated strategy. In part, this was the result of a 1901 rule change that for the first time counted foul balls as strikes. The merits of the foul-strike rule were hotly debated for years afterward. Offense started a gradual decline that was not reversed until the introduction of the cork-center ball in 1910.

THE MANAGEMENT

Charles Ebbets began working for the Dodgers in 1883 as a ticket taker and worked his way up to the club presidency by 1898. He achieved a lifelong dream of owning the franchise by purchasing a controlling interest in 1907. Field managers were Ned Hanlon (1899–1905), Patsy Donovan (1906–08) and Harry Lumley (1909).

THE BEST PLAYER MOVE

The Dodgers purchased Zack Wheat from Mobile in the Southern League during the summer of 1909.

THE WORST PLAYER MOVE

The Dodgers dealt Bill Dahlen to the Giants in December 1903 for Charlie Babb and Jack Cronin. Brooklyn also lost an All-Star team to the American League from 1901 through 1903 when players such as Tom Daly, Wild Bill Donovan, Fielder Jones, Willie Keeler, Joe Kelley, Frank Kitson, Joe McGinnity and Deacon McGuire signed with the new league.

1900

L A

Season in a Sentence

The Dodgers pull away to win their second consecutive pennant with an infusion of more players from the now-defunct Orioles, but outdraw only one other NL club.

Finish • Won • Lost • Pct • GB

First   82   54   .603   +4.5

Manager

Ned Hanlon

Stats

Stats	Dods	NL	Rank
Batting Avg:	.293	.279	1
On-Base Pct:	.359	.339	1
Slugging Pct:	.383	.366	1
Home Runs:	26		6 (tie)
Stolen Bases:	274		1
ERA:	3.89	3.69	6
Fielding Avg:	.948	.942	2
Runs Scored:	816		1
Runs Allowed:	722		2

Starting Lineup

Duke Farrell, c
Hughie Jennings, 1b
Tom Daly, 2b
Lave Cross, 3b
Bill Dahlen, ss
Joe Kelley, lf
Fielder Jones, cf
Willie Keeler, rf
Jimmy Sheckard, lf
Deacon McGuire, c
Gene DeMontreville, 2b

Pitchers

Joe McGinnity, sp
Brickyard Kennedy, sp
Jerry Nops, sp
Harry Howell, sp

Attendance

170,000 (seventh in NL)

Club Leaders

Batting Avg:	Willie Keeler	.362
On-Base Pct:	Willie Keeler	.402
Slugging Pct:	Joe Kelley	.485
Home Runs:	Joe Kelley	6
RBIs:	Joe Kelley	91
Runs:	Willie Keeler	106
	Fielder Jones	106
Stolen Bases:	Willie Keeler	41
Wins:	Joe McGinnity	28
Strikeouts:	Joe McGinnity	93
ERA:	Joe McGinnity	2.94
Saves:	Frank Kitson	4

MARCH 8   The National League votes to reduce its membership from 12 teams to eight, dropping Baltimore, Cleveland, Louisville and Washington. The NL roster of Boston, Brooklyn, Chicago, Cincinnati, New York, Philadelphia, Pittsburgh and St. Louis remained unchanged from 1900 until the Boston Braves moved to Milwaukee in March 1953.

The Dodgers gained considerably from the contraction of four franchises because they already owned the Baltimore franchise (see February 27, 1899). Among the 1899 Orioles who became 1900 Dodgers were Joe McGinnity, Jerry Nops, Harry Howell, Jimmy Sheckard and Gene DeMontreville. The Dodgers also inherited the contracts of John McGraw and Wilbert Robinson, but both refused to report to the club. They were sold to the Cardinals on March 23, but they initially balked at moving to St. Louis as well. McGraw and Robinson finally signed with the Cards in May.

APRIL 19   The Dodgers start the season with a 3–2 win over the Giants in New York. With Brooklyn trailing 2–0, Brickyard Kennedy drove in the first run with a single in the seventh. Bill Dahlen smacked a two-run single in the eighth for the tying and winning runs. Kennedy also pitched a complete game.

Kennedy was 20–13 with a 3.91 ERA in 1900.

APRIL 21 After the 1899 pennant is run up the flagpole in pre-game ceremonies, the Dodgers defeat the Giants 5–2 in the home opener before 15,000 at Washington Park. According to the news reports: "The stands were arrayed gorgeously in festoons of bunting and banners. Everywhere, the national colors predominated." A band played "patriotic melodies."

The Dodgers' white home uniforms in 1900 displayed a maroon Old English letter "B" on the left breast, along with maroon stockings. The road grays had "Brooklyn" written in black across the front and black stockings.

APRIL 28 Fielder Jones hits an inside-the-park grand slam off Kid Nichols in the first inning of a 10–1 win over the Braves at Washington Park.

MAY 5 Dodgers pitcher Joe McGinnity takes exception to the decisions of umpire Tommy Connolly during a 5–3 loss to the Giants at Washington Park. According to the wire service report, McGinnity "went over to the umpire in the ninth inning and elbowed him roughly around the diamond." Amazingly, McGinnity was allowed to stay in the game.

Battery mates "Iron" Joe McGinnity and "Deacon" Jim McGuire helped the Brooklyn team win the National League pennant in 1900. McGinnity won 28 of the team's 82 victories.

Joe (Iron Man) McGinnity had a record of 28–16 as a rookie with the Orioles in 1899. He followed that with a 28–8 record and a 2.94 ERA in a league-leading 343 innings for the Dodgers in 1900. It proved to be McGinnity's only season in Brooklyn. In 1901 he went back to Baltimore with a new Orioles club in the American League and later starred with the Giants from 1902 through 1908, twice winning more than 30 games. McGinnity's career ended with a 246–142 record, earning him a berth in the Hall of Fame. There is some dispute over how he acquired the nickname Iron Man. Some claim it was because of McGinnity's remarkable durability. He averaged 362 innings a season over the nine-year period from 1899 through 1907. Others assert that it derived from McGinnity's off-season job in an Oklahoma iron foundry.

MAY 7 The Dodgers outslug the Phillies 13–9 at Washington Park.

MAY 12   The Dodgers score three runs in the ninth inning to defeat the Cardinals 5–4 in St. Louis. All three runs scored with two out. Frank Kitson, pinch-hitting for Joe McGinnity, drove in the first run with a single. Willie Keeler followed with a two-run base hit on a two-strike pitch with the bases loaded.

Keeler had a batting average of .352 in four seasons with the Dodgers. The figure still ranks number one in franchise history among players with at least 2,000 plate appearances.

MAY 24   Leading 4–0, Brickyard Kennedy allows four runs in the ninth inning and one in the 10th to lose 5–4 to the Pirates in Pittsburgh.

MAY 25   Trailing 7–3, the Dodgers erupt for nine runs in the eighth inning to beat the Cubs 12–7 in Chicago.

JUNE 5   Down 4–0, the Dodgers score two runs in the eighth inning and three in the ninth to defeat the Cubs 5–4 at Washington Park. Willie Keeler broke the tie with a sacrifice fly.

The Dodgers entered the game with a 19–15 record in second place, 3¹/₂ games behind the Phillies.

JUNE 10   The Dodgers clobber the Reds 11–1 at Washington Park.

JUNE 19   The Dodgers win their ninth game in a row with a 10–4 victory over the Braves in Boston.

JUNE 21   The Dodgers take first place with five runs in the ninth inning on six hits, a walk and two wild pitches to defeat the Phillies 8–6 in Philadelphia.

The Dodgers remained in first for the remainder of the season, but the race failed to ignite the passions of the Dodgers fans. The club drew only 170,000 in 1900, a figure that ranked seventh in an eight-team league. Rumors were circulating that the Dodgers were moving to another city, with Washington at the top of the list.

JUNE 22   The umpires declare the Dodgers the victors by forfeit over the Phillies at Philadelphia with the score 20–13 in favor of Brooklyn in the 11th inning. The Dodgers scored three runs in the top of the eighth inning to lead 10–5, but the Phils countered with four in their half to pull within a run. The ninth inning was a repeat of the eighth with Brooklyn scoring three to go ahead 13–9 and Philadelphia responding with four to tie the score 13–13. There was no scoring in the 10th with darkness rapidly approaching. The Phillies prolonged the action as long as possible in the 11th in the hopes the inning would not be completed so the contest would go into the books as a 13–13 tie. Pitcher Bert Conn intentionally walked Brooklyn hitters and the Philadelphia club made no attempt to retire base runners, letting them run at their will. After the Dodgers scored seven runs, umpire Hank O'Day declared the forfeit.

JUNE 23   The Dodgers rout the Giants 12–1 in New York.

JUNE 25	The Dodgers collect 23 hits and clobber the Giants 15–2 at Washington Park.
JULY 5	Jerry Nops pitches a one-hitter in beating the Reds 2–0 in Cincinnati. The only hit off Nops was a single by ex-Dodger Tommy Corcoran in the first inning. Bill Dahlen scored both runs in the seventh and ninth.
JULY 6	Frank Kitson pitches the Dodgers' second consecutive one-hitter in defeating the Reds 10–0 in Cincinnati. The only hit off Kitson was a bunt single by Jimmy Barrett in the sixth inning. Over two days, Nops and Kitson pitched 13 consecutive hitless innings.

The gems by Nops and Kitson mark the only time in Dodgers history that one-hitters were thrown in back-to-back games.

JULY 14	Brickyard Kennedy pitches the Dodgers to a 1–0 triumph over the Giants at Washington Park. Joe Kelley drove in the lone run with a single.

Kelley hit .319 and collected 17 triples and 91 runs batted in for the Dodgers in 1900. The club's leading hitter was Willie Keeler with a .362 average and a league-leading 204 hits.

JULY 17	The Dodgers topple the Giants 13–7 at Washington Park. Christy Mathewson made his major league debut in relief of Ed Doheny.
JULY 18	The Dodgers knock out a 10–2 victory over Boston at Washington Park.
JULY 19	The Dodgers outslug the Reds 12–8 at Washington Park. It was the third straight game in which Brooklyn scored at least 10 runs, and it was accomplished against three different teams.
JULY 31	The Pirates collect 26 hits and defeat the Dodgers 17–1 at Washington Park.
AUGUST 1	The Dodgers net seven runs in the sixth inning for a 10–1 lead and beat the Pirates 10–6 at Washington Park.
AUGUST 9	The Dodgers take an 8½-game lead in the pennant race with a 7–3 win over the Cardinals in St. Louis.
AUGUST 12	The Dodgers score three runs in the ninth inning to down the Cardinals 3–2 in St. Louis.
AUGUST 22	The Dodgers succeed in defeating the Braves 16–8 in Boston.
AUGUST 30	The Dodgers explode for 10 runs in the eighth inning and defeat the Phillies 14–3 at Washington Park. Bill Dahlen hit two triples in the big inning.
AUGUST 31	Brickyard Kennedy sets a National League record by walking six batters in a row during the second inning of a 9–4 loss to the Phillies at Washington Park.
SEPTEMBER 4	A four-run rally in the ninth inning falls short as the Dodgers lose 8–7 to the Cubs at Washington Park. The game ended when Joe McGinnity was thrown out in a close play at the plate on an attempted double steal.

SEPTEMBER 13   Five days after a hurricane in Galveston, Texas, claims more than 6,000 lives, the Dodgers sweep the Reds 7–2 and 13–9 in a double-header against the Reds at Washington Park. The second game ended after 6½ innings by darkness.

SEPTEMBER 19   With the Dodgers leading the Cardinals 2–0 in the third inning at Washington Park, St. Louis catcher Wilbert Robinson objects to the decision of umpire John Gaffney. After the umpire called Brooklyn base runner Duke Farrell safe at home, Robinson jumped up and threw the ball at Gaffney, then punched him in the chest. Gaffney swung his mask at Robinson, grazing his nose, and threw him out of the game. The Cardinals refused to put in another catcher, claiming one was injured and the other was suspended. Gaffney responded by forfeiting the game to the Dodgers. Charles Ebbets issued refunds to any fans who requested one.

SEPTEMBER 21   Another row with an umpire mars a 4–3 loss to the Giants at Washington Park, with both clubs acting as perpetrators. In the eighth inning, Pink Hawley of the Giants attacked umpire Pop Snyder and was ordered off the grounds. The game ended with Snyder calling Joe McGinnity out at first base on the back end of a double play. Joe Kelley threw his glove at Snyder and McGinnity pushed the umpire around the diamond. Snyder was escorted from the grounds by the police amid the hooting of the crowd, which surged onto the field.

SEPTEMBER 25   A 2–1 loss to the Phillies at Washington Park ends in another dispute. Umpire Tim Hurst insisted on playing the ninth inning, even though it was so dark the fielders had trouble locating the ball. Even though his team won, Jack Dunn of the Phillies accused Hurst of trying to throw the game to the Dodgers. Hurst rushed at Dunn, but he was held back by Phillies outfielders Elmer Flick and Ed Delahanty. Charles Ebbets and a couple of policemen prevented further trouble.

With the defeat, the Dodgers lead over the Pirates fell to one game. The Dodgers had led by a margin of 8½ games on August 9.

SEPTEMBER 26   The Dodgers score seven runs in the fifth inning and defeat the Phillies 12–0 at Washington Park. In light of the recent troubles at the ballpark, 24 policemen surrounded the diamond.

OCTOBER 1   The Dodgers increase their lead to four games with a 4–3 and 5–0 sweep of Boston at Washington Park. The first game went 11 innings. The second contest was halted after seven innings due to darkness.

OCTOBER 6   The Dodgers clinch the pennant with an 8–6 victory over the Pirates in Pittsburgh. It was Joe McGinnity's 28th victory of the season.

The championship was the fifth in a span of seven years for Ned Hanlon. He also managed the Orioles to pennants in 1894, 1895 and 1896 and the Dodgers in 1899. The first-place Dodgers and second-place Pirates met in a post-season challenge series sponsored by the Pittsburgh Chronicle-Telegraph. *The winner would be decided in a best-of-five format for the "world championship," with all of the contests being played in Pittsburgh. The newspaper offered a silver cup to the victor.*

OCTOBER 15   In the first game of the *Chronicle-Telegraph* Cup series, the Dodgers defeat the Pirates 5–2 at Exposition Park in Pittsburgh. In a battle of future Hall of Famers,

Joe McGinnity outdueled Rube Waddell. In the eighth inning, McGinnity was caught in a rundown between third and home and, in a collision, McGinnity was kneed in the head by Waddell. The Dodger hurler shook off the blow and finished the game, although he allowed two runs in the ninth.

In the morning, the Exposition Park diamond was the site of football practice for the Duquesne University football team. Waddell joined the practice and dashed around the field for two hours.

Managers Buck Ewing of the New York Giants and Brooklyn skipper Ned Hanlon pose for a photograph. Hanlon's team finished first that year while Ewing's finished last.

OCTOBER 16   The Dodgers take game two 4–2 over the Pirates in Pittsburgh. Frank Kitson pitched a complete game four-hitter.

OCTOBER 17   In the third game of the series, the Pirates rout the Dodgers 10–0 in Pittsburgh. Deacon Philippe pitched the shutout.

OCTOBER 18   Three weeks before William McKinley wins re-election to the presidency by defeating William Jennings Bryan, the Dodgers win their series against the Pirates with a 6–1 decision over the Pirates in Pittsburgh.

The Dodgers received the silver cup donated by the Chronicle-Telegraph *the following evening in between acts of a play at Pittsburgh's Alvin Theater. Half the team was missing, however, having left the city for their off-season homes. The Dodgers wouldn't win another post-season series until 1955.*

1901

Season in a Sentence

Hampered by a rapidly aging roster and the loss of star players to the American League, the Dodgers fall to third place.

Finish • Won • Lost • Pct • GB

Third   79   57   .581   9.5

Manager

Ned Hanlon

Stats   Dods • NL • Rank

Batting Avg:	.287	.267	1
On-Base Pct:	.335	.321	3
Slugging Pct:	.387	.348	1
Home Runs:	32		3
Stolen Bases:	178		5
ERA:	3.14	3.32	4
Fielding Avg:	.950	.947	4
Runs Scored:	744		3
Runs Allowed:	600		4

Starting Lineup

Deacon McGuire, c
Joe Kelley, 1b
Tom Daly, 2b
Charlie Irwin, 3b
Bill Dahlen, ss
Jimmy Sheckard, lf
Tom McCreery, cf
Willie Keeler, rf
Duke Farrell, c
Cozy Dolan, cf
Frank Gatins, 3b

Pitchers

Wild Bill Donovan, sp
Frank Kitson, sp
Jim Hughes, sp
Doc Newton, sp
Doc McJames, sp
Brickyard Kennedy, sp-rp

Attendance

198,200 (seventh in NL)

Club Leaders

Batting Avg:	Jimmy Sheckard	.354
On-Base Pct:	Jimmy Sheckard	.407
Slugging Pct:	Jimmy Sheckard	.534
Home Runs:	Jimmy Sheckard	11
RBIs:	Jimmy Sheckard	104
Runs:	Willie Keeler	123
Stolen Bases:	Jimmy Sheckard	35
Wins:	Wild Bill Donovan	25
Strikeouts:	Wild Bill Donovan	226
ERA:	Wild Bill Donovan	2.77
Saves:	Frank Kitson	2

JANUARY 28   The American League formally organizes as a second major league with clubs in Baltimore, Boston, Chicago, Cleveland, Detroit, Milwaukee, Philadelphia and Washington. The AL also announced plans to raid National League rosters by offering more lucrative contracts.

The Dodgers lost several regulars off of the 1900 pennant-winning club. Pitchers Joe McGinnity, Harry Howell and Jerry Nops went to the Baltimore Orioles. Others making deals with American League clubs included outfielder Fielder Jones (Chicago), pitcher Joe Yeager (Detroit), outfielder-first baseman John Anderson (Milwaukee) and third baseman Lave Cross (Philadelphia). The Dodgers were also without Hughie Jennings, who was sold to the Phillies for $3,000.

APRIL 18   The Dodgers open the season with six runs in the first inning and beat the Phillies 12–7 in Philadelphia. Jimmy Sheckard contributed three triples. Joe Kelley garnered three hits. Wild Bill Donovan pitched the complete-game victory.

Sheckard is the only batter in Dodgers history to hit three triples in a single game.

APRIL 29   A crowd of 7,000 braves wintry weather to see the Dodgers beat the Phillies 10–2 in the home opener at Washington Park.

MAY 13   The Dodgers lose on a forfeit to the Giants in New York. With the score 7–7 in the ninth inning, the Dodgers protested a decision by umpire Hank O'Day, who ruled that Willie Keeler had not crossed the plate before Tom Daly was retired at third base. The entire Brooklyn team surrounded O'Day, who gave them three minutes to resume their position. When the time limit expired, O'Day declared the forfeit.

MAY 24   The Dodgers wallop the Cubs 15–7 at Washington Park.

JUNE 17   The Dodgers purchase Cozy Dolan from the Cubs.

          Dolan was a starting outfielder for the Dodgers through the end of the 1902 season, when he signed a contract with the White Sox. While playing for the Braves in 1907, Dolan died at the age of 26 from typhoid fever during spring training.

JUNE 21   Willie Keeler has five hits, including a home run and a double, and scores five runs in five at-bats during a 21–3 thrashing of the Reds at Washington Park. The Dodgers collected 26 hits in the contest. Cincinnati pitcher Doc Parker, in his first and only appearance as a member of the Reds, gave up all 21 runs. The Dodgers scored one run in the first inning, one in the second, four in the third, one in the fourth, seven in the fifth, one in the sixth, six in the seventh and four in the ninth.

          During an eight-game span from June 19 through June 26, Keeler collected 23 hits in 36 at-bats. He finished the year batting .339 with 123 runs and 202 hits. Jimmy Sheckard batted .354, scored 116 runs, 196 hits, 11 home runs, 104 runs batted in and league-leading figures in triples (19) and slugging percentage (.534). Tom Daly had a .315 batting average and 38 doubles. Joe Kelley hit .307. The best pitcher on the staff was Wild Bill Donovan. He entered the season as a 24-year-old with a 3–10 record and a 4.81 ERA over three big-league seasons. In 1901, Donovan led the league in victories (with a 25–15 record), games pitched (45) and shutouts (three). He had a 2.77 ERA and 226 strikeouts in 351 innings while completing 36 of his 38 starts. Donovan pitched one more season in Brooklyn, with a 17–15 record, before signing a contract with the Tigers. In Detroit, he pitched for pennant-winners in 1907, 1908 and 1909.

JUNE 26   The Dodgers pound out 20 hits and defeat the Pirates 16–3 at Washington Park.

JULY 8   An eighth-inning decision by umpire Hank O'Day infuriates the crowd in St. Louis. When the contest ended with a 7–6 Dodgers win, hundreds of fans rushed at O'Day, who suffered a split lip before police, with revolvers drawn, could rescue him. The crowd milled around after the contest for an hour, and O'Day needed police protection again to move from his dressing room to a waiting police carriage. While the carriage was stalled in traffic on the way to O'Day's hotel, the umpire was recognized and pelted with stones. Once again, police drew their revolvers to quell the disturbance.

          O'Day couldn't make it to the ballpark for the remaining two games of the Dodgers-Cardinals series because of the injuries he suffered at the hands of the St. Louis crowd. One player from each team served as umpires during the two contests.

JULY 16	The Dodgers purchase Charlie Irwin from the Reds.
JULY 25	Frank Kitson pitches a one-hitter to beat the Giants 5–0 at the Polo Grounds. The only New York hit was a single by Algie McBride.
AUGUST 9	Jimmy Sheckard hits a two-run, walk-off double in the ninth inning to beat the Braves 4–3 at Washington Park. The Braves took a 3–2 lead in the top of the ninth by scoring twice.
AUGUST 20	The Dodgers run their winning streak to nine games with a 4–1 and 3–2 sweep of the Phillies in a double-header in Philadelphia.
SEPTEMBER 2	The morning game of a Labor Day double-header against the Cardinals at Washington Park is postponed because the Cardinals' train is delayed by a bridge washout in Cleveland while the club was traveling from St. Louis to New York. The afternoon tilt was played as scheduled, and the Dodgers won 11–5.
SEPTEMBER 6	On the day that President William McKinley is shot by Leon Czolgosz during a reception in Buffalo, the Dodgers score seven runs in the second inning of a 13–1 drubbing of the Reds in Washington Park.
SEPTEMBER 14	The game against the Phillies in Philadelphia is postponed when news arrives of the death of President McKinley from the wounds he suffered when he was shot on September 6. Former New York Governor Theodore Roosevelt succeeded McKinley as president.
SEPTEMBER 19	All major league games are postponed on the day of the funeral of William McKinley.
SEPTEMBER 23	The Dodgers wallop the Reds 25–6 in Cincinnati. The Dodgers scored seven runs in the second inning, 11 in the fifth, five in the sixth and two in the seventh. The 25 tallies tied a club record for most runs in a game, set on May 20, 1896. There were 26 Brooklyn hits in the contest, including five by Tom Daly on three singles and two doubles in six at-bats. Joe Kelley and Jimmy Sheckard both hit inside-the-park grand slams. Kelley's slam was struck off Archie Stimmel in the second inning. Kelley also smacked a solo shot in the seventh off Jack Sutthoff. Sheckard cleared the bases with a drive off Stimmel in the fifth.
SEPTEMBER 24	The Dodgers collect 21 hits and thump the Reds 16–2 in Cincinnati. The victory gave the Dodgers 41 runs in back-to-back games. Jimmy Sheckard hit an inside-the-park grand slam for the second day in a row, connecting off Bill Phillips in the fourth inning. Pitcher Frank Kitson collected four hits, including a home run.
OCTOBER 5	The Dodgers close the season with an 8–0 and 4–2 sweep of the Giants at Washington Park. Wild Bill Donovan pitched the shutout in the opener for his 25th victory of the season. Gene Wright, in his major league debut, pitched a complete game in the nightcap.

The game proved to be only one that Wright pitched as a member of the Dodgers. A native of Cleveland, he signed a contract with the Indians during the 1901–02 off-season. Wright finished his career with a 14–26 record.

1902

L_A

Season in a Sentence

The Dodgers end the season in second place, but they finish closer to the last-place Giants (26¹/₂ games) than to the first-place Pirates (27¹/₂ games).

Finish • Won • Lost • Pct • GB

Second   75   63   .543   27.5

Manager

Ned Hanlon

Stats	Dods	NL	Rank
Batting Avg:	.256	.259	4
On-Base Pct:	.310	.312	4
Slugging Pct:	.319	.319	3
Home Runs:	19		1
Stolen Bases:	145		6
ERA:	2.69	2.78	5
Fielding Avg:	.952	.949	3
Runs Scored:	564		4
Runs Allowed:	519		4

Starting Lineup

Hugh Hearne, c
Tom McCreery, 1b
Tim Flood, 2b
Charlie Irwin, 3b
Bill Dahlen, ss
Jimmy Sheckard, lf
Cozy Dolan, cf
Willie Keeler, rf
Duke Farrell, c

Pitchers

Frank Kitson, sp
Wild Bill Donovan, sp
Doc Newton, sp
Jim Hughes, sp
Roy Evans, sp

Attendance

199,868 (sixth in NL)

Club Leaders

Batting Avg:	Willie Keeler	.333
On-Base Pct:	Willie Keeler	.365
Slugging Pct:	Willie Keeler	.386
Home Runs:	Tom McCreery	4
	Jimmy Sheckard	4
RBIs:	Bill Dahlen	74
Runs:	Willie Keeler	86
	Jimmy Sheckard	86
Wins:	Frank Kitson	19
Strikeouts:	Wild Bill Donovan	170
ERA:	Doc Newton	242
Saves:	Wild Bill Donovan	1

APRIL 17   The Dodgers win the season opener 2–1 over Boston before 10,000 at Washington Park. Wild Bill Donovan allowed just three hits in winning a duel with Vic Willis. The Brooklyn runs were driven in by second baseman Tim Flood, making his Dodgers debut, and first baseman George Hildebrand, in his first appearance in a big-league game.

The Dodgers lost more talent to the American League during the 1901–02 off-season. Joe Kelley and Jimmy Sheckard both went to the Orioles, although Sheckard returned to the Dodgers after playing just four games in Baltimore. Tom Daly signed a contract with the White Sox after playing 12 seasons in Brooklyn. Deacon McGuire cast his lot with the Tigers.

APRIL 24   Willie Keeler scores five runs during a 16–8 win over the Phillies in Philadelphia. The Dodgers took a 7–4 lead with six runs in the fourth inning.

Keeler hit .333 in 1902 and finished second in the NL in base hits with 186. Keeler had collected 200 or more hits in eight consecutive seasons from 1894 through 1901 to set a major league record that still stands. Wade Boggs came close to matching Keeler with seven straight 200-hit seasons between 1983 and 1989.

MAY 13   The Cubs collect only one hit off Wild Bill Donovan but win 2–0 in Chicago. The Cubs scored their run in the sixth inning on a walk, an error by Donovan, a sacrifice, a single from Dusty Miller and an error by third baseman Charlie Irwin.

MAY 30   The Dodgers sweep the Braves 7–1 and 10–3 in a Memorial Day double-header at Washington Park.

MAY 31   The Dodgers sweep the Braves for the second day in a row with a pair of 2–1 decisions at Washington Park. The second game went 10 innings, with John McMakin pitching a complete-game three-hitter.

McMakin pitched in only four big-league games and had a record of 2–2.

JUNE 5   The Dodgers win their eighth game in a row with a 4–0 decision over the Reds at Washington Park.

The winning streak couldn't get the Dodgers back into a pennant race dominated by the Pirates. Although ending the year in second place, the Dodgers finished 27½ games behind the Pirates' record of 103–36. One of the reasons for Pittsburgh's runaway was American League President Ban Johnson's refusal to permit any of his clubs to sign Pirates players. Johnson figured, correctly, that if the Pirates were left intact and the other seven clubs were weakened, there would be no pennant race, which would harm the box office of the NL clubs. The only AL team that was allowed by Johnson to sign NL players were the Yankees during the 1902–03 off-season. This was because Johnson desired a strong team in New York.

JUNE 16   The Dodgers score eight runs in the sixth inning and wallop the Cardinals 12–1 at Washington Park.

JUNE 28   The Dodgers score three runs in the ninth inning to beat the Braves 5–4 in the first game of a double-header in Boston. Brooklyn completed the sweep with a 4–3 victory in the second contest.

JULY 4   The Dodgers and Pirates play a double-header at Exposition Park with the outfield flooded with water. The ballpark stood on the banks of the Allegheny River near the present-day site of PNC Park. Heavy rains had caused the river to spill over its bank and the sewers to back up. Big crowds were expected for the holiday twin bill, which consisted of separate admission contests with one in the morning and one in the afternoon. In the morning game, the water in the outfield was a foot deep. Because of the flood, the umpires decreed that any ball that landed in the water would be a single. The Pirates won 3–0. By the start of the afternoon tilt, the murky flood waters had moved within 20 feet of second base. Ironically, the Dodgers' second baseman was Tim Flood. The outfielders were standing in knee-deep water and could only catch balls hit directly at them. Fortunately, the baseballs were so water-logged, that it was almost impossible to hit them as far as the outfield. The Pirates won in another shutout by a score of 4–0.

JULY 6   The Dodgers thrash the Reds 14–3 in Cincinnati.

JULY 8   John McGraw negotiates his release as manager of the Baltimore Orioles and signs a contract to manage the New York Giants.

McGraw would manage the Giants until 1932. His long tenure in New York shifted the balance of baseball power in the city, adversely affected the Dodgers for decades and intensified the rivalry between the two teams. From 1890 through 1902, the two New York teams in the National League were on about equal footing. The Dodgers had a better record in seven of those 13 years, including four in a row beginning in 1899. The Giants won more games than the Dodgers in 11 consecutive seasons beginning in 1903, and in 32 of 36 seasons from 1903 through 1938.

JULY 12   A three-run homer by Cardinals pitcher Kid Nichols off Frank Kitson in the fourth inning supplied the only three runs in a 3–0 Dodgers defeat in St. Louis.

JULY 19   The Dodgers win a 14-inning battle with Boston by a 5–4 score at Washington Park. Doc Newton, who pitched all 14 innings, started the game-winning rally with a single and scored on Jimmy Sheckard's triple.

JULY 22   In his first game with the Dodgers, Roy Evans pitches a shutout to defeat the Phillies 3–0 in the second game of a double-header at Washington Park. Evans had been acquired by the club following his release by the Giants. The Dodgers also won the opener 7–5.

JULY 25   Frank Kitson hits a solo homer and pitches a complete-game shutout to beat the Giants 2–0 in New York.

AUGUST 17   The Dodgers and Cardinals play to an 18-inning, 7–7 tie in St. Louis. Most of the scoring was done in the first two innings. The Dodgers led 5–4 at the end of the second, the Cardinals scored two in the sixth, and the Dodgers tied the game with a run in the ninth. Both clubs tallied once in the 13th. Wild Bill Donovan pitched all 18 innings for Brooklyn.

AUGUST 21   Dodgers catcher Pat Deisel makes his major league debut and collects two singles and a walk in four plate appearances during a 7–4 loss to the Reds in Cincinnati.

             Deisel was a Cincinnati-area amateur who the Dodgers pressed into service because of injuries to their catchers. In the era before farm systems, it was not unusual for clubs to use local amateurs to fill in on an emergency basis. The August 21 game proved to be Deisel's only one with the Dodgers. He played in two games with the Reds in 1903, drawing a walk in his only plate appearance, and finished his career in the majors with a batting average of .667 and an on-base percentage of .800.

AUGUST 23   The Dodgers collect a club-record five triples, four of them in the third inning, during a 9–8 win over the Pirates in Pittsburgh. Cozy Dolan hit two of the triples, with Jimmy Sheckard, Wild Bill Donovan and Jim Hughes adding the others. Normally a pitcher, Donovan played first base during the contest and batted fifth in the batting order.

SEPTEMBER 27 The Dodgers score nine runs in the sixth inning to beat the Giants 12–4 in the second game of a double-header at Washington Park. The Giants won the opener 4–0. The field resembled a swamp due to heavy rains and outfielders splashed around in several inches of water.

1903

Season in a Sentence

The American League establishes a new franchise in New York, John McGraw begins to build the Giants into a powerhouse and the Dodgers drop from second to fifth in a rebuilding year.

Finish • Won • Lost • Pct • GB

Fifth   70   66   .515   19.0

Manager

Ned Hanlon

Stats

Stats	Dods	NL	Rank
Batting Avg:	.265	.269	6
On-Base Pct:	.348	.331	1
Slugging Pct:	.339	.349	6
Home Runs:	15		5
Stolen Bases:	273		1
ERA:	3.44	3.26	6
Fielding Avg:	.951	.946	3
Runs Scored:	667		5
Runs Allowed:	682		5

Starting Lineup

Lew Ritter, c
Jack Doyle, 1b
Tim Flood, 2b
Sammy Strang, 3b
Bill Dahlen, ss
Jimmy Sheckard, lf
John Dobbs, cf
Judge McCredie, rf
Dutch Jordan, 2b
Fred Jacklitsch, 2b

Pitchers

Henry Schmidt, sp
Oscar Jones, sp
Ned Garvin, sp
Bill Reidy, sp
Roy Evans, sp

Attendance

224,170 (sixth in NL)

Club Leaders

Batting Avg:	Jimmy Sheckard	.332
On-Base Pct:	Jimmy Sheckard	.423
Slugging Pct:	Jimmy Sheckard	.476
Home Runs:	Jimmy Sheckard	9
RBIs:	Jack Doyle	91
Runs:	Sammy Strang	101
Stolen Bases:	Jimmy Sheckard	67
Wins:	Henry Schmidt	22
Strikeouts:	Ned Garvin	154
ERA:	Oscar Jones	2.94
Saves:	Henry Schmidt	2
	Ned Garvin	2

JANUARY 9   The National and American Leagues reach a peace accord at a meeting in Cincinnati. The two leagues agreed to refrain from raiding one another's rosters and set up a three-man governing body consisting of the presidents of the two leagues and Cincinnati Reds President Garry Herrmann. Another proviso was the establishment of an American League franchise in New York, a club that eventually would be known as the Yankees. This was accomplished when the Baltimore Orioles were shifted to New York in March 1903. The creation of a third big-league team in the city was staunchly opposed by both the Dodgers and Giants, but the objections were ignored. The agreement didn't come fast enough for the Dodgers to lose more players to the AL. Willie Keeler signed with the new AL team in New York. Others leaving for the American League were Duke Farrell (Boston), Cozy Dolan (Chicago), and Wild Bill Donovan and Frank Kitson (Detroit). Bill Dahlen and Jimmy Sheckard were the only two players on Brooklyn's 1900 National League champions who were on the club's roster on Opening Day in 1903 as the club was decimated by defections to the American League.

JANUARY 30   The Dodgers purchase Jack Doyle from the Senators.

              Doyle was nicknamed "Dirty Jack" because he would use any tactic, legal or illegal, to win a game. He hit .313 as a first baseman for the Dodgers in 1903.

APRIL 16   The scheduled opener between the Dodgers and Giants in New York is postponed by rain.

APRIL 17   The Dodgers lose the season opener 9–7 to the Giants before 30,000 at the Polo Grounds. Making his major league debut, Henry Schmidt was the Brooklyn starting pitcher and gave up a first-inning, leadoff home run to George Browne. Jack Doyle collected three hits off Christy Mathewson in the losing cause.

APRIL 21   The Dodgers lose the home opener 2–1 to the Giants before 16,000 at Washington Park. The game produced a National League-record 43 assists as pitchers Henry Schmidt and Christy Mathewson kept the ball on the ground. The Dodgers accounted for 24 of the 43 assists.

APRIL 25   Henry Schmidt shuts out the Phillies 8–0 at Washington Park.

APRIL 29   Henry Schmidt earns his second consecutive shutout with a 2–0 decision over the Braves at Washington Park.

APRIL 30   The new American League ballpark opens in New York with the home club beating Washington 6–2.

            The new AL club was known as the Highlanders in the early years because they played at Hilltop Park on one of the highest points in Manhattan on a lot bounded by 168th Street, Fort Washington Avenue, 165th Street and Broadway. Within a few seasons, the moniker Yankees would supplant Highlanders as the club's nickname.

MAY 4   Henry Schmidt hurls his third shutout in a row with a 5–0 victory over the Phillies at Washington Park.

            A native of Brownsville, Texas, Schmidt had one of the strangest careers in baseball history. He was 29 years old when Ned Hanlon discovered him pitching in the Pacific Coast League. Schmidt proved to be a tremendous find with a 22–13 record for Brooklyn in 1903. He returned his 1904 contract unsigned, however, with a note that simply said, "I do not like living in the East and will not report." Schmidt never pitched in the majors again, earning him the distinction as the only pitcher to win at least 20 games in his only season in the big leagues.

MAY 6   The Giants lambaste the Dodgers 20–2 at Washington Park.

MAY 7   A day after losing by 18 runs, the Dodgers score seven runs in the third inning and defeat the Braves 12–1 at Washington Park.

MAY 26   The Dodgers score six runs in the fifth inning for an 11–0 lead and beat the Cardinals 13–6 at Washington Park.

JUNE 17   After losing the first game of a double-header 3–2 to the Braves in Boston, the Dodgers turn the tables and win the second tilt 14–6.

JUNE 26   Trailing 8–2, the Dodgers score three runs in the sixth inning, two in the seventh and two in the eighth to beat the Reds 9–8 at Washington Park. Walt McCredie drew a bases-loaded walk that brought home the tying run. Jack Doyle brought home the winning run with a sacrifice fly.

McCredie hit .324 in a career that lasted just one season, 56 games and 213 at-bats.

JULY 5   The Dodgers win a 16–12 slugging match against the Reds in Cincinnati. Brooklyn took a 9–2 lead with four runs in the second inning, let the Reds pull within a run, then salted the game away with three tallies in the fifth and three more in the sixth.

JULY 6   Catcher Ed Hug, a Cincinnati area amateur, is pressed into service by the Dodgers due to injuries to the Brooklyn receivers and draws a walk in what proves to be his only big-league plate appearance. The Dodgers lost the contest, the second of a double-header, 11–3 after winning the opener 9–3.

AUGUST 17   Three weeks after H. Nelson Jackson completes history's first coast-to-coast trip by automobile, Jimmy Sheckard hits a grand slam off Clarence Currie in the second inning of a 6–3 win over the Cardinals in the first game of a double-header at Washington Park. The Dodgers completed the sweep with a 4–3 victory in the second tilt.

AUGUST 21   The Dodgers game against the Reds at Washington Park is postponed because of a conflict with the America's Cup yachting race held in New York harbor. Charles Ebbets feared low attendance because of interest in the race, and the contest was rescheduled as part of a double-header the following day.

AUGUST 27   The Dodgers outlast the Phillies 11–10 during a weird affair played in a drizzling rain at Washington Park. Two Philadelphia pitchers combined to walk 17 batters with only one strikeout. Three Brooklyn pitchers struck out six batters without issuing a single walk. The 17 walks by the Phillies hurlers tied a National League record for a nine-inning game. The Dodgers continually overcame Phillie leads. A four-run fourth tied the score 5–5. After the Phils went ahead with two in the top of the fifth, the Dodgers countered with three in their half. Once again, the Dodgers fell behind 10–8 in the seventh, but they scored

Returning to Brooklyn after a short stint in Baltimore, Jimmy Sheckard led the team with a .332 average.

three times with two out in the eighth for the victory. The first two runs scored on bases-loaded walks by Bill Duggleby to Tom McCreery and Sammy Strang. Jimmy Sheckard singled in the game-winner.

Strang scored 101 runs and hit .272 for the Dodgers in 1903.

AUGUST 31   The Dodgers pummel the Braves 14–4 at Washington Park.

SEPTEMBER 1   The Dodgers sweep Boston 8–3 and 2–0 at Washington Park. Henry Schmidt pitched a two-hitter in the second tilt. The only Boston hits were singles by Dick Cooley and Ed Abbaticchio.

SEPTEMBER 5   Giants ace Christy Mathewson pitches a five-inning no-hitter and beats the Dodgers 2–1 in a contest at Washington Park called by rain after five innings. The lone Brooklyn run scored in the fourth inning on a three-base error and a sacrifice fly by Jimmy Sheckard.

SEPTEMBER 7   The Dodgers and Giants play in both Brooklyn and New York during a Labor Day double-header. In the morning, the Giants won 6–4 at Washington Park. In the afternoon, the two teams met at the Polo Grounds with the Dodgers winning 2–0.

SEPTEMBER 9   Jimmy Sheckard hits consecutive drives over the right-field fence at Washington Park during a 4–1 win over the Braves in the second game of a double-header, called after eight innings by darkness. Both were struck off Togie Pittenger. Boston won the opener 1–0 in 11 innings.

The Dodgers hit only 15 home runs as a team in 1903, and Sheckard accounted for nine of them to lead the National League. He also scored 99 runs and batted .332.

SEPTEMBER 22 Henry Schmidt earns his 22nd win of the season with a 5–4 win in 10 innings over the Pirates in Pittsburgh.

SEPTEMBER 27 On the last day of the season, the Dodgers rout the Reds 14–7 in the first game of a double-header in Cincinnati. The Dodgers lost the second game, called after 4½ innings by darkness, 7–6.

DECEMBER 12   The Dodgers send Bill Dahlen to the Giants for Charlie Babb, Jack Cronin and $6,000.

The Dodgers made a terrible deal. Dahlen was 34 when traded, but he had five more seasons as a big-league regular and was a key player on the 1905 world champion Giants. Babb was expected to be Dahlen's replacement at shortstop, but he was a bust. Cronin lost 23 games in his only season in Brooklyn.

1904

LA

Season in a Sentence

Ned Hanlon's Superbas are far from superb in a year that results in 97 defeats, 50 more than the arch-rival Giants.

Finish • Won • Lost • Pct • GB

Sixth   56   97   .366   50.0

Manager

Ned Hanlon

Stats

Stats	Dods	AL	Rank
Batting Avg:	.232	.249	7
On-Base Pct:	.297	.306	6
Slugging Pct:	.295	.322	8
Home Runs:	15		7 (tie)
Stolen Bases:	205		3
ERA:	2.70	2.73	5
Fielding Avg:	.945	.950	7
Runs Scored:	497		7
Runs Allowed:	614		6

Starting Lineup

Bill Bergen, c
Pop Dillon, 1b
Dutch Jordan, 2b
Mike McCormick, 3b
Charlie Babb, ss
Jimmy Sheckard, lf
John Dobbs, cf
Harry Lumley, rf
Doc Gessler, cf
Sammy Strang, 2b
Lew Ritter, c

Pitchers

Oscar Jones, sp
Jack Cronin, sp
Ed Poole, sp
Ned Garvin, sp
Doc Scanlan, sp

Attendance

214,600 (sixth in AL)

Club Leaders

Batting Avg:	Harry Lumley	.279
On-Base Pct:	Charlie Babb	.345
Slugging Pct:	Harry Lumley	.428
Home Runs:	Harry Lumley	9
RBIs:	Harry Lumley	78
Runs:	Harry Lumley	79
Stolen Bases:	Charlie Babb	34
Wins:	Oscar Jones	17
Strikeouts:	Jack Cronin	110
ERA:	Ned Garvin	1.68
Saves:	Ed Poole	1
	Bill Reidy	1

JANUARY 16   A month after the Wright brothers' first successful flight, the Dodgers purchase Bill Bergen from the Reds.

Bergen played 947 games during 11 seasons in the majors, the last eight of which were spent in Brooklyn, and hit only .170 in 3,028 at-bats. His lifetime batting average is by far the worst of any major leaguer with at least 3,000 lifetime at-bats. Next worst is Billy Sullivan Sr., another deadball-era catcher, who batted .212. In addition, Bergen's career on-base percentage (.194) and slugging percentage (.201) are lower than Sullivan's batting average. In his 11 seasons, Bergen topped the .200 mark only once, with a .227 average for Cincinnati in 1903. As a Dodger, Bergen hit .162 in 2,191 at-bats, bottoming out at .139 with only three extra-base hits in a career-high 112 games in 1909. Naturally, it would take outstanding defense to keep an inept hitter like Bergen in the lineup for so long, and contemporary sources raved about his abilities behind the plate, especially in throwing out enemy base stealers.

APRIL 14   The Dodgers open with a 7–1 loss to the Giants in New York. Christy Mathewson pitched a three-hitter.

APRIL 15   The Dodgers lose the season opener 5–2 against the Giants at Washington Park.

APRIL 17   The Dodgers attempt to play a game at Washington Park on a Sunday. The New York State penal code prohibited "racing, gaming and other sports" on the Christian Sabbath. Charles Ebbets believed he found a loophole in the statute because it forbade the charging of admission. Ebbets tried to circumvent the law by refusing to charge for tickets, but fans were required to buy a scorecard at a price equal to that of a ticket to gain admission to the ballpark. The scorecards were priced differently and color-coded to allow fans entrance to the grandstand or bleachers for the same price as games played on weekdays and Saturdays, which ranged from 25 cents to one dollar. A crowd of 12,000 attended and watched the Dodgers defeat the Braves 9–1.

APRIL 24   Arrests accompany the Dodgers' second attempt to play a game at Washington Park on a Sunday. After a couple of pitches, Brooklyn's starting battery of pitcher Ed Poole and catcher Fred Jacklitsch were taken into custody along with Phillies leadoff batter Frank Roth. The two teams were notified ahead of time that the arrests would take place, and therefore Poole, Jacklitsch and Roth were "decoys" and immediately replaced by players the Dodgers and Phillies intended to use in the starting lineup. Poole was succeeded by Grant Thatcher, Jacklitsch by Lew Ritter and Roth by Hugh Duffy. The appearance by Thatcher was his only one in 1904 and the last of his big-league career Three sellers of scorecards were also arrested. All six of those arrested were quickly bailed out for $200 each. The game proceeded without further interference, and the Dodgers won 8–6.

> On May 4, a judge ruled in favor of the individuals arrested during the April 24 game, which allowed the Dodgers to continue to play on Sundays. The Kings County Sabbath Observation Association protested the judge's decision and filed an appeal.

APRIL 30   The Dodgers sell Jack Doyle to the Phillies.

MAY 5   The Dodgers belt the Phillies 13–3 in Philadelphia.

MAY 23   The Dodgers score six runs in the ninth inning and beat the Cardinals 7–4 in St. Louis. The Dodgers collected seven hits during the six-run rally, including homers by Jimmy Sheckard and Harry Lumley.

> As a rookie right fielder in 1904, Lumley hit .279 and led the NL in triples (18) and home runs (nine) and ranked second in total bases (247). He had a run of about four seasons as one of the top sluggers of the deadball era before injuries and issues with his weight diminished his effectiveness. Lumley was player-manager of the Dodgers in 1909.

MAY 29   The Dodgers play their third Sunday game of the season at Washington Park. A crowd of 20,000 watched the home team lose 7–3 to the Giants.

> The Dodgers played at home on five consecutive Sundays from May 29 through June 26.

JUNE 20   Shortstop Charlie Babb commits five errors in nine chances during a 12–7 loss to the Giants in New York. The Dodgers made nine errors as a team.

JUNE 22   Dodger pitcher Ned Garvin allows only five hits in a 13-inning complete game, but he loses 1–0 to the Phillies at Washington Park.

JUNE 23   The Dodgers score two runs in the ninth inning to defeat the Phillies 5–4 at Washington Park. Lew Ritter's sacrifice fly drove in the winning run.

JUNE 24   The Dodgers score two runs in the ninth inning for the second game in a row and beat the Phillies 4–3 at Washington Park. The tying and winning runs scored on a two-out, two-run single by John Dobbs.

JUNE 26   Just after the start of the seventh Sunday game of the 1904 season at Washington Park, pitcher Oscar Jones and catcher Fred Jacklitsch are arrested in violation of the state statutes (see April 17, 1904). Jones and Jacklitsch were replaced by Ned Garvin and Lew Ritter. The remainder of the contest went on without any more interference from legal authorities, and the Dodgers defeat the Braves 8–2.

                 Later in the week, a judge ruled that the playing of baseball games on Sundays at Washington Park was illegal. Charles Ebbets tried another maneuver to get around the law the following year (see April 30, 1905).

JULY 2   The Dodgers score eight runs in the eighth inning and beat the Phillies 13–2 in Philadelphia. Brooklyn was shut out in the opener, losing 2–0.

JULY 15   The Dodgers edge the Cardinals 1–0 in 10 innings in St. Louis. The lone run scored on an error. Ned Garvin pitched a three-hit shutout.

JULY 29   The Dodgers win 1–0 in the first game of a double-header against the Giants in the first game of a double-header at Washington Park. Christy Mathewson forced in the winning run on a bases-loaded walk to Sammy Strang. Jack Cronin pitched the shutout. New York won the second tilt 2–0.

AUGUST 11   Oscar Jones pitches a 17-inning complete game, but he loses a 4–3 decision to the Cardinals at Washington Park. St. Louis scored twice in the top of the 17th inning before Brooklyn came back with one in their half in a futile rally. Kid Nichols also pitched a complete game for the Cards. The game lasted only two hours and 25 minutes.

                 Jones was 19–14 as a rookie for the Dodgers in 1903. He was 17–25 in 1904 and 8–15 in 1905, his last year in the majors.

SEPTEMBER 15   A month before the first section of the New York subway system opens, the Dodgers win 14–7 over the Phillies in the second game of a double-header, called after seven innings by mutual agreement. Philadelphia won the opener 5–2.

                 A National League rule in effect from 1904 through 1907 allowed teams to end second games of double-headers after seven innings by pre-game mutual agreement.

1905

Season in a Sentence

The 1905 season heaps more misery on Dodgers fans as the club compiles a record of 48–104 to set a club record for defeats in Ned Hanlon's last year as manager.

Finish • Won • Lost • Pct • GB

Eighth 48 104 .316 56.5

Manager

Ned Hanlon

Stats

Stats	Dods	NL	Rank
Batting Avg:	.246	.255	6
On-Base Pct:	.297	.315	7
Slugging Pct:	.317	.332	6
Home Runs:	29		2
Stolen Bases:	186		4
ERA:	3.76	2.99	8
Fielding Avg:	.937	.954	8
Runs Scored:	506		7
Runs Allowed:	807		8

Starting Lineup

Lew Ritter, c
Doc Gessler, 1b
Charlie Malay, 2b
Emil Batch, 3b
Phil Lewis, ss
Jimmy Sheckard, lf
John Dobbs, cf
Harry Lumley, rf
Bill Bergen, c
Charlie Babb, ss
Bob Hall, lf-cf

Pitchers

Doc Scanlan, sp
Harry McIntire, sp
Elmer Stricklett, sp
Oscar Jones, sp
Mal Eason, sp

Attendance

227,924 (seventh in NL)

Club Leaders

Batting Avg:	Harry Lumley	.293
On-Base Pct:	Jimmy Sheckard	.380
Slugging Pct:	Harry Lumley	.412
Home Runs:	Harry Lumley	7
RBIs:	Harry Lumley	47
Runs:	Emil Batch	64
Stolen Bases:	Doc Gessler	26
Wins:	Doc Scanlan	14
Strikeouts:	Doc Scanlan	135
	Harry McIntire	135
ERA:	Doc Scanlan	2.92
Saves:	Three tied with	1

APRIL 14 The Dodgers open the season with a 12–8 loss to the Phillies before 10,000 at Washington Park. The Dodgers held a 4–0 lead before Philadelphia scored six times off Oscar Jones. Playing in his first game with the Dodgers, and his first in the majors since 1899, second baseman Red Owens collected four hits, including a triple, in five at-bats.

APRIL 22 The Dodgers win their first game of the season following an 0–6 start by beating the Braves 4–0 at Washington Park. Harry McIntire pitched the shutout.

Playing for the Dodgers from 1905 through 1909, McIntire had the misfortune of pitching for some of the worst clubs in franchise history and compiled a record of 46–98.

APRIL 23 The Dodgers try playing on Sundays again, using the ruse of allowing fans into the ballpark without a ticket but requiring them to purchase a scorecard for admission to the stands (see April 17, 1904). A crowd of 11,642 showed up for the contest against the Braves. There was no interference from police, but the officers took the names of the players and the sellers of the scorecards. The Dodgers won 4–0 with Mal Eason hurling the shutout.

The Dodgers played on five Sundays in 1905 before the practice was ruled illegal (see July 3, 1905).

APRIL 26   The Dodgers score two runs in the ninth inning off Joe McGinnity to defeat the Giants 3–2 at Washington Park. Pitcher Harry McIntire doubled in the tying run and scored on Harry Lumley's walk-off single.

APRIL 30   A Sunday game against the Giants draws about 30,000 to Washington Park. Around 25,000 made their way into the park, with another 5,000 left outside when Dodgers management closed the gates for safety reasons. The stands held 18,000, and the excess surrounded the playing field, covering nearly every square inch of foul territory and much of the outfield. Any fair ball hit into the crowd was a ground-rule double. The Dodgers lost the contest 5–3.

MAY 3   The Dodgers win a 13–9 battle with the Phillies at Washington Park. The Phils scored six times in the eighth for a 9–8 lead. The Dodgers, although playing at home, elected to bat first and plated five runs in the top of the ninth.

MAY 20   A bases-loaded walk-off single by Harry Lumley in the ninth inning beats the Cubs 4–3 at Washington Park.

            Lumley batted .293 for the Dodgers in 1905.

JUNE 8   Alice Roosevelt, daughter of President Theodore Roosevelt, watches the Dodgers lose 11–2 to the Reds in Cincinnati.

            Dubbed "Princess Alice" in the press, the 20-year-old beauty was probably the most popular person in the country at the time. The public couldn't get enough of the exploits of the free-spirited, outspoken young woman. "I can be President of the United States or I can control Alice," said her father. "I cannot possibly do both." Among those who attended the game with Miss Roosevelt was 35-year-old Ohio Congressman Nicholas Longworth. The two became engaged the following December and were married in a White House ceremony in February 1906.

JUNE 13   Umpire Bill Klem needs police protection to leave the field after being surrounded by a mob following a 6–1 Dodgers win over the Cardinals in St. Louis. The crowd was angry over an eighth-inning decision by Klem that led to the ejections of two Cardinals players.

JUNE 30   At Washington Park, Moonlight Graham makes his only big-league appearance as a defensive replacement for the Giants in right field late in an 11–1 Dodgers loss.

            Archibald (Moonlight) Graham later became a medical doctor in Chisholm, Minnesota, and began a blood pressure and heart test program in schools that was nationally recognized. Graham is best known as a character played by Burt Lancaster in the 1991 film Field of Dreams, *although the film erroneously states the appearance by Graham was in 1922. (See August 6, 1905 for Dodgers players of the era who became doctors).*

JULY 3   A New York Supreme Court justice rules the Dodgers' practice of selling scorecards to gain admission to Washington Park (see April 17, 1904) is illegal. According to the court decision it was "not illegal per se to play baseball on Sunday, but it may become illegal by attending circumstances. It is illegal when carried on as a public sport, as, for example, when the public is invited by advertisement in the public press or otherwise and an admission fee is charged or collected." Charles Ebbets was not finished trying to play on Sundays at Washington Park, however (see April 15, 1906).

JULY 4   Pitcher Harry McIntire breaks a 1–1 tie in the third inning with a homer, and the run holds up for a 2–1 victory over the Braves in the first game of a double-header at Washington Park. The Dodgers took the second tilt 8–0 behind the pitching of Mal Eason.

The home run was the first of two that McIntire hit during a nine-year career in which he had 615 at-bats. The other homer was struck in 1910 while playing for the Cubs.

JULY 20   The Dodgers survive five errors by shortstop Phil Lewis to beat the Reds 2–1 at Washington Park.

Jack Doscher, who pitched for the Dodgers from 1903 through 1907, was the first son of a former big-leaguer to play in the majors. Jack's father, Herm, was a third baseman with five clubs between 1872 and 1882.

JULY 24   Pitcher Harry McIntire drives in the tying run in the ninth inning with a single and scores the winning run on a walk-off double by Jimmy Sheckard to beat the Cardinals 8–7 at Washington Park.

Sheckard hit .292 for the Dodgers in 1905.

JULY 31   The Dodgers win 1–0 over the Pirates in 10 innings at Washington Park. Doc Scanlan pitched the complete-game shutout. The lone run scored on a three-base error and a walk-off single by Bill Bergen.

Bergen's brother Marty preceded Bill in the majors, playing for the Braves from 1896 through 1899. Marty's life ended tragically on January 19, 1900, when he killed his wife and two children with an axe and a razor, then took his own life.

AUGUST 6 Dodgers and Reds pitchers combine to tie a major league record for fewest walks in a double-header by issuing only one free pass in Cincinnati as Brooklyn sweeps 6–3 and 2–0. There were no walks by Cincinnati hurlers Tom Walker and Charlie Chech and Brooklyn's Doc Scanlan in the opener. In the second tilt, Harry McIntire walked one and the Reds Bob Ewing none.

The players of 100 years ago were a generally uneducated lot, and many were illiterate. Fewer than half of the U.S. population in this era graduated from high school, and it is likely this was also true of those playing professional baseball. An amazing number of players in the majors just before and after the turn of the 20th century had training in medical school, however, including three on the 1905 Dodgers. There were eight of them playing with the Dodgers from

1890 through 1909, each of them nicknamed "Doc." Albert (Doc) Bushing was a catcher in Brooklyn from 1888 through 1890. He earned his Doctor of Dental Surgery degree from the University of Pennsylvania and earned a living as a practicing dentist after his playing career ended. James (Doc) McJames, a pitcher in 1899 and 1901, graduated from the medical school at the University of South Carolina, but he died from injuries suffered in an accident before he could practice medicine (see September 9, 1899). William (Doc) Scanlan pitched for the Dodgers from 1904 through 1911. He graduated from Long Island Medical College and practiced medicine in the Park Slope section of Brooklyn for 38 years before his death in 1949. Frank (Doc) Reisling was a pitcher for the Dodgers in 1904 and 1905 who later conducted a dental practice in Tulsa, Oklahoma, from 1918 through 1946. James (Doc) Casey was a third baseman in Brooklyn in 1899 and 1900 and again in 1906 and 1907. He trained as a dentist and as a pharmacist and owned a drug store in Detroit for many years. Eustace (Doc) Newton, a pitcher with the club in 1901 and 1902, graduated from the medical school at the University of Indianapolis, but never practiced medicine. William (Doc) Marshall, a catcher for the 1909 club, practiced medicine in Clinton, Illinois, for 46 years before his death in 1959. Henry (Doc) Gessler was an outfielder-first baseman with the Dodgers from 1903 through 1906. He graduated from the medical school at John Hopkins University and practiced medicine in Oklahoma and Indiana before his death in 1924. Gessler played for the Cubs in the 1906 World Series and was one of three doctors in that series. The other two were Guy (Doc) White and Frank Owen of the White Sox.

AUGUST 10   There are nine Dodgers errors by eight different players during a 5–4 loss to the Cardinals in St. Louis.

SEPTEMBER 25   The Dodgers end a 10-game losing streak with a 2–0 victory over the Cubs in the first game of a double-header in Chicago. The Cubs won the second tilt 3–2.

SEPTEMBER 26   Mal Eason pitches the Dodgers to a 1–0 win over the Cubs in Chicago.

SEPTEMBER 27   The Dodgers break up the no-hit bid of Carl Lundgren of the Cubs with two out in the ninth inning of a 7–2 loss in Chicago. A double by Jimmy Sheckard was the first Brooklyn hit and was followed by a Doc Gessler single, a stolen base and an error for two runs.

OCTOBER 3   Doc Scanlan pitches two nine-inning, complete-game victories in one day, beating the Cardinals 4–0 and 3–2 in St. Louis. Scanlan threw a three-hitter in the opener and allowed nine hits in the nightcap.

There was trouble at the outset of the season when Charles Ebbets cut the salary of Ned Hanlon from $12,500 to $6,500 during spring training. Ebbets and Hanlon each owned 10 percent of the ball club, grew to despise one another and hoped to gain the shares of the other in a power struggle to control the franchise. In 1903, Hanlon purchased the Baltimore ballpark, organized a team in the Eastern League and wanted to move the Dodgers to Baltimore, causing further conflicts with Ebbets. Hanlon had been labeled a "genius" when winning five National League pennants in Baltimore and Brooklyn from 1894 through 1900, but the tag was severely tarnished after the Dodgers compiled a record of 48–104 in 1905, to set a still-standing franchise record for defeats *in a season. Ebbets now had the leverage to force Hanlon out of town. Hanlon took a job managing the Cincinnati Reds on December 12, 1905. Ebbets bought out Hanlon's shares of the franchise. Hanlon would manage the Reds for two seasons to a pair of sixth-place finishes. Patsy Donovan became the new manager of the Dodgers in 1906. Born in County Cork, Ireland, in 1865, Donovan was an outfielder in the majors for 17 seasons beginning in 1890. He had previously managed the Pirates (1897 and 1899), Cardinals (1901–03) and Senators without finishing higher than fourth. Donovan led the Dodgers for three seasons to a record of 184–270.*

DECEMBER 16   The Dodgers trade Jimmy Sheckard to the Cubs for Billy Maloney, Jack McCarthy, Doc Casey, Buttons Briggs and $2,000. The deal was completed while Charles Ebbets and Cubs President Charles Murphy walked across the Brooklyn Bridge.

The Cubs gave up four regulars to acquire Sheckard, who was just about the only player of value left on the Brooklyn roster. Despite the one-for-four deal, the Dodgers came out on the short end of the transaction. In Chicago, Sheckard was the starting left fielder in the 1906, 1907, 1908 and 1910 World Series. In 1911, he led the National League in runs, walks and on-base percentage.

1906   L A

Season in a Sentence

With nowhere to go but up, the Dodgers revamp the roster and finish in fifth place under new manager Patsy Donovan.

Finish • Won • Lost • Pct • GB

| Fifth | 66 | 86 | .434 | 50.0 |

Manager

Patsy Donovan

Stats

Stats	Dods	NL	Rank
Batting Avg:	.236	.244	6
On-Base Pct:	.297	.310	6
Slugging Pct:	.308	.310	4
Home Runs:	25		1
Stolen Bases:	175		4
ERA:	3.13	2.62	7
Fielding Avg:	.955	.959	7
Runs Scored:	496		6
Runs Allowed:	625		7

Starting Lineup

Bill Bergen, c
Tim Jordan, 1b
Whitey Alperman, 2b
Doc Casey, 3b
Phil Lewis, ss
Jack McCarthy, lf
Billy Maloney, cf
Harry Lumley, rf
John Hummel, 2b
Lew Ritter, c
Emil Batch, lf

Pitchers

Doc Scanlan, sp
Elmer Stricklett, sp
Harry McIntire, sp
Mal Eason, sp
Jim Pastorius, sp

Attendance

277,400 (seventh in NL)

Club Leaders

Batting Avg:	Harry Lumley	.324
On-Base Pct:	Harry Lumley	.386
Slugging Pct:	Harry Lumley	.477
Home Runs:	Tim Jordan	12
RBIs:	Tim Jordan	78
Runs:	Harry Lumley	72
Stolen Bases:	Billy Maloney	38
Wins:	Doc Scanlan	18
Strikeouts:	Harry McIntire	121
ERA:	Elmer Stricklett	2.72
Saves:	Elmer Stricklett	5

APRIL 12   The Dodgers open the season with a 2–0 loss to the Braves before 12,000 at Washington Park. Irv Young pitched a two-hit shutout in a duel with Harry McIntire. Boston's Johnny Bates hit a home run in his first major league at-bat.

APRIL 15   The Dodgers play on a Sunday at Washington Park without charging admission or selling scorecards or programs and draw 5,000 for a game against the Braves on a rainy day, although they lose 5–3. At all of the gates, contribution boxes were conspicuously placed and the majority of those who passed through voluntarily dropped into the receptacles the regular amount that was charged on weekdays for the grandstand, pavilion or bleachers seats. Any persons who did not contribute passed into the ballpark without hindrance. A few fans deposited worthless junk. After opening the box, club officials found poker chips, buttons, foreign coins and counterfeit money. The Dodgers had tried playing on Sundays in 1904 and 1905 by charging for scorecards instead of for tickets (see April 17, 1904) but the practice was ruled to be illegal (see July 3, 1905). The Dodgers played two more regular season games and an exhibition game on Sunday before being foiled again by the authorities (see June 17, 1906).

APRIL 18   On the day of the great San Francisco earthquake, which sparks a fire that destroys much of the city, the Dodgers lose 4–1 to the Giants at Washington Park to drop their record on the '06 season to 0–6. It was the second year in a row that Brooklyn opened with six consecutive defeats.

APRIL 22   On a Sunday afternoon, the Dodgers throw open the gates at Washington Park and play an intra-squad game. Fans attending dropped about $1,000 into contribution boxes, with the money being donated to the San Francisco earthquake relief fund.

APRIL 27   Trailing 8–1, the Dodgers score three runs in the fifth inning, three in the eighth and three in the ninth to win 10–9 over the Braves in Boston.

APRIL 28   The Dodgers trade Doc Gessler to the Cubs for Hub Knolls.

APRIL 29   The Dodgers play another Sunday game at Washington Park in which no admission is charged, but fans make contributions (see April 22, 1906) and the Dodgers win 1–0 over the Phillies. The lone Brooklyn run scored in the first inning when leadoff batter Harry Lumley hit the very first pitch from Bill Duggleby over the right-field fence for a home run. Elmer Stricklett pitched the shutout.

Lumley is the only player in Dodgers history to homer on the first pitch of the first inning and have it hold up for a 1–0 victory. Lumley finished the season ranked first in the NL in slugging percentage (.477), second in home runs (nine), third in batting average (.324) and third in triples (12).

MAY 1   Johnny Lush of the Phillies pitches a no-hitter to beat the Dodgers 6–0 at Washington Park. He struck out 11 and walked three. Tim Jordan made the final out on a grounder to shortstop Mickey Doolan.

As a 27-year-old rookie first baseman in 1906, Jordan ranked first in the NL in home runs (12) and third in runs batted in (78). He would lead the league in home runs in 1908 by smacking 12 again, but he injured his knees the following season, which led to a premature end to his big-league career.

MAY 31   Mal Eason pitches the Dodgers to a 1–0 win over the Braves at Washington Park.

JUNE 9   A controversial ruling by umpire Jim Johnstone results in a 2–0 loss to the Cubs at
                  Washington Park. With the bases loaded in the sixth inning, Whitey Alperman hit a
                  drive down the left field line for a triple, but after the play was over, Johnstone ruled
                  the ball landed in foul territory. There was a noisy demonstration and Johnstone was
                  threatened as he left the field, but he escaped unharmed.

JUNE 12   Doc Scanlan pitches the Dodgers to a 1–0 win over the Cubs at Washington Park.
                  The lone run scored on a single by John Hummel in the eighth inning.

                  *The Cubs had a record of 116–36 in 1906 to set a record for most victories in
                  a season, which was tied by the Mariners in 162 games in 2001.*

JUNE 17   In another test of the Sunday baseball law, there are several arrests at the start of a
                  3–0 loss to the Reds at Washington Park. Charles Ebbets was informed before the
                  contest that he, Dodgers manager Patsy Donovan, Cincinnati skipper Ned Hanlon
                  and the first pitcher and batter would be arrested. Mal Eason was the Brooklyn
                  pitcher and Chick Fraser the opposition hitter. Fraser looked upon the situation as an
                  adventure. "I've never been arrested," he explained, "although I often thought that
                  I deserved to be." After two pitches from Eason to Fraser, the five dastardly criminals
                  were hauled off to the police station and released on $200 bail.

                  *Ebbets didn't try to play on Sunday in Brooklyn again until 1917 (see July 1,
                  1917). During the 11-year interval, he tirelessly besieged the state legislature
                  to change the law.*

JUNE 26   A 4–1 win over the Braves in Boston is interrupted by a small riot. It occurred when
                  police made two arrests for alleged gambling in the first-base bleachers. The crowd
                  surged onto the field, stopping play. According to the newspaper reports, the police
                  "had to beat off many would-be rescuers on the way to the gates."

JUNE 27   The Dodgers score four runs in the first inning to spark a 10–0 win over the Phillies
                  at Washington Park. Elmer Stricklett pitched the shutout.

                  *Stricklett, who had a 35–50 record for the Dodgers from 1905 through 1907,
                  is credited with introducing the spitball to the major leagues. He was a minor
                  leaguer in 1904 when he learned the pitch from George Hildebrand, who
                  accidentally discovered the downward break of the ball caused by the application
                  of saliva. Nearly every pitcher in baseball tried out the spitball around 1905 and
                  1906, but most rejected its use because it was too difficult to control. Many,
                  including Ed Walsh, who learned to throw the pitch directly from Stricklett
                  while they were teammates with the White Sox, mastered the delivery and
                  fashioned Hall of Fame careers. The spitball remained a legal pitch until 1920.*

JULY 7   Elmer Stricklett allows 11 runs in the fourth inning of a 12–0 loss to the Phillies at
                  Washington Park.

JULY 10   Trailing 4–0, the Dodgers score five runs in the fifth inning and beat the Pirates 7–6
                  in Pittsburgh. Prior to the five-run outburst, the Dodgers had allowed 33 unanswered
                  runs over four games against the Phillies and Pirates.

JULY 19   The Dodgers score three runs in the 15th inning to defeat the Cardinals 6–3 in St. Louis. Jim Pastorius pitched all 15 innings.

JULY 20   Mal Eason pitches a no-hitter to defeat the Cardinals 2–0 in St. Louis. He walked three and struck out five. In the ninth inning, pinch-hitter Red Murray flied out to left fielder Jack McCarthy, Al Burch reached on an error by shortstop Phil Lewis, Pug Bennett fouled out to catcher Lew Ritter and Sam Mertes hit a grounder that Eason fielded and threw to first baseman Tim Jordan.

AUGUST 1   Harry McIntire does not allow a hit until the 11th inning, but winds up losing 1–0 to the Pirates at Washington Park by allowing a run in the 13th. It was the second time in less than two weeks that a Brooklyn hurler held the opposition hitless for at least the first nine innings of a game. Unlike Eason on July 20, McIntire had to extend himself beyond the ninth because Brooklyn failed to score off Lefty Leifield. McIntire faced only 31 batters in the first 10 innings. With two out in the Pittsburgh 11th, a thunderstorm stopped the game for five minutes. When play resumed, Claude Ritchey collected the first hit off McIntire with a single. The Pirates were retired in order in the 12th. McIntire finally weakened in the 13th, giving up three hits before recording an out. Bob Ganley singled, went to third on Honus Wagner's double and scored on Jim Nealon's single. In the bottom of the 13th, McIntire led off with a single and moved to second on a sacrifice, but he was left stranded. Leifield pitched all 13 innings and allowed nine hits. McIntire walked one and fanned eight.

AUGUST 9   Harry McIntire walks 11 and hits a batter during a 5–3 loss to the Cubs at Washington Park.

AUGUST 15   Trailing 10–0, the Dodgers score seven runs in the ninth inning in a futile rally and lose 10–7 to the Cubs in Chicago.

AUGUST 21   The Dodgers lose their 11th game in a row in agonizing fashion, dropping a 10-inning, 8–7 decision to the Pirates in Pittsburgh. The Dodgers led 7–1 heading into the ninth, but Elmer Stricklett gave up six runs in the frame and Harry McIntire surrendered another one in the 10th.

AUGUST 22   The Dodgers break their 11-game losing streak with a 7–4 victory over the Reds in Cincinnati.

AUGUST 24   Jake Weimer of the Reds pitches a seven-inning no-hitter to defeat the Dodgers 1–0 in the second game of a double-header in Cincinnati. The game ended by mutual agreement. The Dodgers won the opener 6–1.

SEPTEMBER 3   On Labor Day, the Dodgers hurl two shutouts at the Phillies in Philadelphia. Doc Scanlan won the opener 8–0. Harry McIntire won a 10–0 decision in the nightcap. The victory was sparked by a seven-run rally in the first inning.

SEPTEMBER 8   For the second time in six days, the Dodgers record a double-header shutout, this time against the Giants at Washington Park. Mal Eason won the opener 6–0 and Doc Scanlan the second game 1–0.

SEPTEMBER 24   Pitching in only his second major league game, Cardinals hurler Stoney McGlynn pitches a seven-inning no-hitter in the second game of a double-header against the

Dodgers at Washington Park. The game ended in a 1–1 tie when it was called on account of darkness. The Brooklyn run scored in the first inning on a walk, a stolen base and an error. The Dodgers won the first tilt 6–5 in 11 innings.

The no-hitter was the fifth involving the Dodgers in 1906 (see May 1, July 20, August 1 and August 24).

SEPTEMBER 25   Jack Pfiester of the Cubs pitches a one-hitter to defeat the Dodgers 1–0 at Washington Park. The only Brooklyn hit was a single by Bill Bergen.

OCTOBER 3   The Dodgers score six runs in the ninth inning to take a 13–0 lead, and they survive a grand slam by Johnny Bates in the bottom half to defeat the Braves 13–4 in Boston.

1907   L A

Season in a Sentence

After losing 16 of their first 17 games, the Dodgers stumble to a fifth place finish for the second year in a row.

Finish • Won • Lost • Pct • GB

Fifth   65   83   .439   40.0

Manager

Patsy Donovan

Stats

Stats	Dods	NL	Rank
Batting Avg:	.232	.243	8
On-Base Pct:	.287	.308	7
Slugging Pct:	.298	.309	7
Home Runs:	18		5
Stolen Bases:	121		7
ERA:	2.38		3
Fielding Avg:	.959	.960	6
Runs Scored:	446		7
Runs Allowed:	522		3

Starting Lineup

Lew Ritter, c
Tim Jordan, 1b
Whitey Alperman, 2b
Doc Casey, 3b
Phil Lewis, ss
Emil Batch, lf
Billy Maloney, cf
Harry Lumley, rf
John Hummel, 2b-lf

Pitchers

Nap Rucker, sp
Jim Pastorius, sp
Elmer Stricklett, sp
George Bell, sp
Harry McIntire, sp
Doc Scanlan, sp

Attendance

312,500 (sixth in NL)

Club Leaders

Batting Avg:	Tim Jordan	.274
On-Base Pct:	Tim Jordan	.371
Slugging Pct:	Harry Lumley	.425
Home Runs:	Harry Lumley	9
RBIs:	Harry Lumley	66
Runs:	Doc Casey	55
Stolen Bases:	Billy Maloney	25
Wins:	Jim Pastorius	16
Strikeouts:	Nap Rucker	131
ERA:	Nap Rucker	2.06
Saves:	George Bell	1

APRIL 11   The scheduled season opener against the Braves in Boston is postponed because of wet grounds.

APRIL 12   The Dodgers play their first game of the 1907 season and lose 1–0 to the Braves on a frigid day in Boston. The lone run scored in the first inning off Elmer Stricklett. Irv Young pitched the complete-game shutout. It was the second consecutive season in which he held Brooklyn without a run on Opening Day (see April 12, 1906).

The new road uniforms in 1907 were a daring departure. Instead of the standard plain gray, they were made from a gray cloth with a fine blue checked pattern. The jerseys evoked ridicule throughout the league, and the club went back to plain gray in 1908.

APRIL 16   The Dodgers lose the home opener 4–1 to the Giants before 18,000 at Washington Park.

APRIL 18   After starting the season with four defeats, the Dodgers collect only three hits but defeat the Giants 3–0 at Washington Park. Doc Scanlan pitched a two-hitter, allowing only singles to Bill Dahlen and opposing pitcher Dummy Taylor.

The Dodgers lost their next 12 games in a row to drop their season record to 1–16. The club was 3–20 before posting a 62–63 record the rest of the way.

MAY 11   The Dodgers break their 12-game losing streak with a 1–0 win over the Cubs in the first game of a double-header at Washington Park. Nap Rucker pitched the shutout for his first career victory. Chicago won the second tilt 2–0.

A left-handed fastball pitcher, George (Nap) Rucker spent his entire 10-year big-league career (1907–16) in Brooklyn. He might have made the Hall of Fame if he had pitched for pennant-winning clubs. Rucker was widely hailed by his contemporaries as one of the best pitchers of the period, but unfortunately, his best years were spent with dismal Dodgers teams. Rucker's earned run averages were consistently well below the league average and he ranked in the top five in strikeouts five straight seasons beginning in 1908, but he finished his big-league career with a won-lost record of 134–134. He still ranks 11th all-time among Dodgers pitchers in victories and fifth in defeats. Rucker is also second in earned run average (2.42), fifth in complete games (186), fourth in shutouts (38), eighth in innings pitched (2,375 1/3), 10th in walks (701) and 10th in strikeouts (1,217). After his baseball career ended, Rucker scouted the southern region of the United States for the Dodgers and served as mayor and water commissioner of Roswell, Georgia, where he lived in a mansion built prior to the Civil War.

MAY 14   The Dodgers defeat the Cardinals 10–0 at Washington Park. George Bell pitched the shutout.

The run-scoring outburst was highly unusual in the early part of the 1907 season. The Dodgers scored only 46 runs in the first 29 games.

MAY 30   After losing the first game of a Memorial Day double-header 4–0 to the Braves at Boston, the Dodgers win the nightcap 4–3 in 14 innings. With umpire Jim Johnstone ill, one player from each team served as umpire during the twin bill. Elmer Stricklett of the Dodgers officiated both games. For Boston, it was Patsy Flaherty in the opener and Vive Lindaman in the second tilt. In the 13th inning, Lindaman ejected Brooklyn shortstop Phil Lewis after a long wrangle.

JUNE 1   Phil Lewis collects five hits, including a triple and two doubles, in five at-bats to lead the Dodgers to a 10-inning, 7–5 win over the Giants in New York.

JUNE 5   George Bell pitches the Dodgers to a 1–0 win over the Reds in Cincinnati. Whitey Alperman drove in the lone run with a double in the eighth inning.

As a 32-year-old rookie in 1907, Bell had a 2.25 ERA, but with little offense to back him up he posted a record of 8–16.

JUNE 16   The Dodgers clobber the Cubs 11–1 in Chicago.

JUNE 18   Nap Rucker faces only 28 batters and pitches a two-hitter to defeat the Cardinals 1–0 in St. Louis. The only batter to reach base was Pug Bennett, who hit a pair of singles.

In 1907, Nap Rucker pitched the first of 10 seasons for Brooklyn, winning 134 games.

JULY 3   Elmer Stricklett pitches a shutout and drives in the winning run with a walk-off single to defeat the Giants 1–0 at Washington Park.

JULY 4   The Dodgers win their second straight 1–0 decision, this time in 12 innings over the Giants behind a complete-game shutout from Jim Pastorius in the first game of a holiday double-header at Washington Park. Harry Lumley drove in the winning run with a sacrifice fly. New York won game two 5–3.

In a period known as the "Deadball Era" for its suppressed offense, Lumley was second in home runs in the NL in 1907 with nine and his .425 slugging percentage ranked third.

JULY 5   The Dodgers purchase Al Burch from the Cardinals.

JULY 8   Cubs first baseman and player-manager Frank Chance barely escapes bodily harm during a 5–0 Dodgers loss at Washington Park.

Despite the lead, Chance spent much of the game arguing with the umpires, which agitated the throng at the ballpark. As soon as the Cubs took the field in the ninth inning, some in the crowd began throwing pop bottles at Chance. He ignored the first few volleys, but he then became angry, picked up three of the bottles and hurled them into the stands. One of these struck a child and, in an instant, a shower of bottles began descending upon Chance. Some of the fans jumped onto the field. Chance stopped to collect more bottles to throw when teammate Joe Tinker seized him by the arms while the other Cubs checked the advance of the mob. Chance was led from the field by a police escort. After the game, he had to remain in the clubhouse for three hours until officers could disperse the angry mob waiting outside. Chance left in an armored police car with three officers. He was suspended for seven days by National League president Harry Pulliam.

JULY 10   Doc Scanlan pitches the Dodgers to a 1–0 win over the Cubs at Washington Park. The lone run scored in the third inning on a triple by Whitey Alperman and a sacrifice fly from Doc Casey.

JULY 29   Harry Lumley's home run in the 10th inning gives the Dodgers a 1–0 lead over the Cubs in Chicago, but Harry McIntire gives up two runs in the bottom half to lose 2–1.

AUGUST 20   There are five home runs by the Dodgers and Reds during a 9–3 Brooklyn win at Washington Park. Whitey Alperman, Harry Lumley and John Hummel homered for the Dodgers and John Kane and Mike Mitchell homered for Cincinnati.

The Dodgers hit only 18 home runs in 153 games in 1907 and allowed 16. There were just 19 home runs, nine by the home team, in 77 games at Washington Park, so five in a single contest was highly unusual. Dimensions at the ballpark in 1907 were 376 feet down the left-field line, 415 feet to left center, 425 feet to center field, 349 to right center, and 302 feet down the right-field line. In this era of place hitting and prior to the introduction of the cork-center baseball, clearing the fence in left or center field was a nearly impossible feat. The rare balls that traveled over the walls at Washington Park went to right field.

SEPTEMBER 2   The Dodgers and Giants battle to a 13-inning, 0–0 tie in New York. The game was called because of darkness. George Bell and Red Ames each pitched complete games.

SEPTEMBER 20   Nick Maddox of the Pirates pitches a no-hitter and Elmer Stricklett allows just two base hits in a 2–1 Pittsburgh victory at Exposition Park in Pittsburgh. Maddox struck out five, walked three batters and hit one. The Dodgers took a 1–0 lead in the fourth inning on errors by Maddox and shortstop Honus Wagner. The Pirates scored in the fifth and seventh.

OCTOBER 5   Six weeks before Oklahoma is admitted to the Union as the 46th state, the Dodgers close the season with 6–5 and 11–0 losses to the Braves in Boston. In the opener, the Braves scored four times in the ninth inning for the victory. Manager Patsy Donovan, at the age of 42, put himself into the game as a substitute in right field and was hitless in one at-bat. The second tilt was stopped after seven innings by darkness.

> *During the 1907–08 off-season, Charles Ebbets achieved his dream of owning a controlling interest in the franchise by buying the stock of the estate of Harry Von der Horst, who died in 1905, and Ferdinand Abell, one of the original investors when the franchise was formed in 1883. Ebbets had to borrow heavily from Brooklyn furniture dealer Henry Medicus to swing the deal, however. Ebbets would run the Dodgers until his death in 1925.*

1908   L A

Season in a Sentence

After Charles Ebbets gains financial control of the franchise during the previous off-season, the Dodgers average only 2.4 runs per game and lose 101 times, leading to the dismissal of Patsy Donovan as manager.

Finish • Won • Lost • Pct • GB

Seventh   53   101   .344   46.0

Manager

Patsy Donovan

Stats

Stats	Dods	NL	Rank
Batting Avg:	.213	.239	8
On-Base Pct:	.266	.299	8
Slugging Pct:	.277	.306	8
Home Runs:	28		1
Stolen Bases:	113		8
ERA:	2.47	2.35	6
Fielding Avg:	.961	.961	8
Runs Scored:	377		7
Runs Allowed:	516		5

Starting Lineup

Bill Bergen, c
Tim Jordan, 1b
Harry Pattee, 2b
Tommy Sheehan, 3b
Phil Lewis, ss
Al Burch, lf-cf-rf
Billy Maloney, cf
Harry Lumley, rf
John Hummel, lf-2b
Whitey Alperman, 2b

Pitchers

Nap Rucker, sp
Kaiser Wilhelm, sp
Harry McIntire, sp
Jim Pastorius, sp
George Bell, sp

Attendance

275,600 (sixth in NL)

Club Leaders

Batting Avg:	Tim Jordan	.247
On-Base Pct:	Tim Jordan	.328
Slugging Pct:	Tim Jordan	.371
Home Runs:	Tim Jordan	12
RBIs:	Tim Jordan	60
Runs:	Tim Jordan	58
Stolen Bases:	Harry Pattee	24
Wins:	Nap Rucker	17
Strikeouts:	Nap Rucker	199
ERA:	Kaiser Wilhelm	1.87
Saves:	Harry McIntire	2

APRIL 14   Three months after the subway links Manhattan and Brooklyn, the Dodgers open the season with a 9–3 loss to the Braves before 17,500 at Washington Park. The crowd began to get unruly after the game started and many jumped the fences and rushed out and seated themselves on the grass a few yards behind the baselines. Toward the end of the game they had completely surrounded the diamond, shutting off the view of the contest from many of the spectators. Fair balls hit into the crowd were doubles. Tim Jordan provided a rare Brooklyn highlight by homering over the right-field fence.

Charles Ebbets expanded the seating capacity of Washington Park by placing seats within 15 feet of home plate.

APRIL 16   Harry McIntire pitches a two-hitter and beats the Braves 3–1 at Washington Park. The only Boston hits were singles by George Browne and Bill Dahlen.

MAY 9   Kaiser Wilhelm pitches a two-hitter, but he loses 1–0 to the Phillies in Philadelphia. The lone run scored on an RBI-single by opposing pitcher Lew Moren.

Irvin (Kaiser) Wilhelm had a 1.87 ERA in 332 innings in 1908, but he had a record of 16–22. He was one of three 20-game losers on the Dodgers in 1908. Jim Pastorius had a 4–20 record despite an earned run average of 2.44. Harry McIntire was 11–20. Nap Rucker barely escaped losing 20 with a record of 17–19. The four combined had a 2.22 earned run average in 1,177 innings, yet won only 48 while losing 81. The pitchers were betrayed by the worst offense in Dodgers history. The 1908 season was the worst for hitters in major league history, with a .239 league-wide batting average, a slugging percentage of .306 and an average of 3.3 runs per team per game. The Dodgers set club-record lows for runs (377 in 154 games), batting average (.213), on-base percentage (.266), slugging percentage (.277) and extra-base hits (198 on 110 doubles, 60 triples and 28 home runs). The .213 batting average is also the lowest of any National League club since the 60-foot, six-inch distance was established in 1893.

MAY 24   The Dodgers win 2–0 over the Reds in Cincinnati on a pair of first-inning errors. John Hummel singled and Al Burch reached on an error. Harry Lumley hit a grounder to second baseman Miller Huggins, who stepped on second to force Burch, but Huggins's throw to first sailed into foul territory. By the time the ball was retrieved, Lumley had circled the bases.

Hummel played all over the diamond for the Dodgers in 11 seasons from 1905 through 1915. He played 547 games at second base, 157 at first base, 139 in left field, 124 in right field, 74 at shortstop and 19 in center field. Hummel's 82 triples with the club ranks sixth on the all-time list.

MAY 26   Nap Rucker strikes out 12 batters in eight innings, but he loses 4–2 to the Reds in Cincinnati.

JUNE 6   Pembroke Finlayson, a 19-year-old native of Brooklyn, has a rocky major league debut by allowing five runs, all earned, and four walks in one-third of an inning of relief during an 8–2 loss to the Reds at Washington Park.

Finlayson pitched only one more big-league game. He died in 1912 at the age of 23 from peritonitis of the heart, brought on by an injury he received while pitching.

JUNE 17   The Dodgers score all five runs of a 5–0 victory over the Cardinals at Washington Park in the second inning.

JUNE 22   Nap Rucker pitches a 10-inning shutout to defeat the Phillies 1–0 at Washington Park. The lone run scored on a walk-off single by Tommy Sheehan.

JUNE 29   Trailing 4–2, the Dodgers score seven runs off Joe McGinnity in the fifth inning and beat the Giants 11–7 at Washington Park.

JULY 11   Kaiser Wilhelm pitches the Dodgers to a 1–0 victory over the Cardinals in St. Louis.

JULY 22   Tim Jordan hits the first ball over the outfield wall at Exposition Park in Pittsburgh in nine years, providing the only Brooklyn run in a 2–1 loss to the Pirates. The last player prior to Jordan to accomplish the feat was Danny Green of the Cubs in 1899.

The dimensions of Exposition Park were 380 feet down the right-field line, 400 feet down the left-field line and 515 feet to center field.

JULY 27   Tim Jordan drives two balls over the fence at Washington Park during a 6–5 win over the Cubs in the second game of a double-header. A three-run double in the eighth by Harry Lumley put the Dodgers into the lead. Chicago won the opener 3–1.

There were only 19 home runs struck in 77 games at Washington Park in 1908. Jordan led the National League in home runs with 12.

AUGUST 3   Harry McIntire pitches a one-hitter to defeat the Cardinals 1–0 at Washington Park. The only St. Louis hit was an infield single by Tom Reilly in the eighth inning.

AUGUST 6   Johnny Lush of the Cardinals pitches a six-inning no-hitter to beat the Dodgers 2–0 at Washington Park in a contest called by rain. Lush also hurled a nine-inning no-hitter against Brooklyn on May 1, 1906, while a member of the Phillies.

AUGUST 22   The Dodgers lose a 17-inning marathon 1–0 to the Pirates in Pittsburgh. Jim Pastorius pitched a complete game for Brooklyn. Irv Young hurled a 17-inning shutout for the Pirates and started the game-winning rally with a two-out single. He advanced to second on another single. A walk loaded the bases and Danny Moeller broke the scoreless tie with a single. Moeller entered the game as a first baseman in the 16th. The 17-inning contest was completed in two hours and 40 minutes.

AUGUST 23   The day after a 17-inning, 1–0 defeat, the Dodgers lose a pair of 2–0 decisions to the Cubs in a double-header in Chicago.

Over five games from August 21 through August 24, the Dodgers failed to score in 41 consecutive innings.

SEPTEMBER 2   The Dodgers lose in 17 innings for the second time in less than two weeks, this time 3–2 to the Phillies in Philadelphia. The Dodgers scored twice in the ninth to send the contest in to extra innings on a double by Whitey Alperman, a John Hummel single and a triple from Tim Jordan. Frank Corridon pitched a complete game for the Phils and drove in the winning run with a walk-off single off Nap Rucker. The contest took three hours and seven minutes to complete. It was supposed to be the first game of a double-header, but by the time the marathon tilt was completed, it was too dark to start game two.

SEPTEMBER 5   In the second game of a double-header against the Braves at Washington Park, Nap Rucker pitches a no-hitter and strikes out 14 batters for a 6–0 victory in one of the greatest pitching performances in club history. Rucker walked no one. Errors cost him a perfect game. The only three Boston base runners reached on errors by shortstop Phil Lewis in the first inning, third baseman Tommy Sheehan in the fifth and right fielder Harry Lumley in the eighth. Lumley misjudged the ball at first, then came charging after it. He got both hands on the ball, then dropped it. There was some hesitation by the official scorer, but the play was ruled an error. The first three hitters due up in the ninth were left-handed, and Braves manager Joe Kelley sent three right-handed pinch-hitters up to the plate in the ninth to face the left-handed Rucker. Claude Ritchey was the first pinch-hitter and grounded out to second baseman Whitey Alperman. Frank Bowerman also grounded out to Alperman. Rucker ended the game by striking out Harry Smith. Boston won the opener of the twin bill 4–3.

The no-hitter by Rucker broke a seven-game losing streak and was the club's only victory in a span of 17 games. A nine-game losing streak began two days later.

SEPTEMBER 7   The Dodgers lose twice by 1–0 scores to the Braves in a Labor Day double-header at Washington Park. Jim Pastorius pitched a one-hitter in the opener but lost a duel to Bill Chappelle. The only Boston hit was a single by Bill Sweeney in the fifth inning that drove in the lone run following a walk and a sacrifice.

SEPTEMBER 8   The Dodgers lose their third consecutive 1–0 decision by dropping an 11-inning decision to the Giants in New York. Christy Mathewson pitched the shutout, beating Nap Rucker, who made his first start following his September 5 no-hitter.

SEPTEMBER 9   Because of injuries to all of their catchers, the Dodgers are forced to move center fielder Billy Maloney behind the plate for a game against the Giants in New York. Maloney had caught 86 previous big-league games, but none since 1902. The Giants stole nine bases and won the game 7–3.

SEPTEMBER 26   Six weeks before William Howard Taft defeats William Jennings Bryan in the presidential election, Ed Reulbach of the Cubs hurls two complete-game, nine-inning shutouts in one day, defeating the Dodgers 5–0 and 3–0 in a double-header at Washington Park. He is the only pitcher in major league history to throw two shutouts in one day.

After the end of the 1908 season, Patsy Donovan was replaced as manager by 28-year-old Harry Lumley, the club's slugging right fielder. The hiring of Lumley cut the payroll of Charles Ebbets, who didn't have to pay a non-playing manager. It was also hoped the appointment of Lumley, who was the most popular player on the team, would distract fans from the mounting defeats. It didn't work. Lumley's weight had ballooned over the years, his injured knees continued to cause him problems and he missed a month with a broken finger suffered in the second game of the season. Lumley played only 55 games in 1909. First baseman Tim Jordan also suffered through an injury-plagued season. With a dismal offense weakened further without Lumley and Jordan in the lineup, the Dodgers had a record of 55–98 in 1909 as Lumley was booed often. He was replaced as manager by Bill Dahlen after the close of the 1909 campaign. Lumley returned as a player in 1910, but he appeared in only eight games.

1909

Season in a Sentence

Harry Lumley lasts only one season as manager when an injury-riddled lineup loses 98 games.

Finish • Won • Lost • Pct • GB

Sixth   54   98   .359   55.5

Manager

Harry Lumley

Stats

Stats	Dods	NL	Rank
Batting Avg:	.229	.244	7
On-Base Pct:	.279	.310	8
Slugging Pct:	.296	.314	7
Home Runs:	16		5
Stolen Bases:	141		7
ERA:	3.10	2.59	6
Fielding Avg:	.955	.956	4
Runs Scored:	444		7
Runs Allowed:	627		6

Starting Lineup

Bill Bergen, c
John Hummel, 1b-2b-ss
Whitey Alperman, 2b
Ed Lennox, 3b
Tommy McMillan, ss
Wally Clement, lf
Al Burch, cf
Harry Lumley, rf
Tim Jordan, 1b
Pryor McElveen, 3b

Pitchers

Nap Rucker, sp
George Bell, sp
Harry McIntire, sp
Doc Scanlan, sp
Kaiser Wilhelm, sp
George Hunter, sp
Jim Pastorius, sp

Attendance

321,300 (fifth in NL)

Club Leaders

Batting Avg:	Al Burch	.271
On-Base Pct:	Ed Lennox	.337
Slugging Pct:	Ed Lennox	.359
Home Runs:	John Hummel	4
RBIs:	John Hummel	52
Runs:	Al Burch	80
Stolen Bases:	Al Burch	38
Wins:	George Bell	16
Strikeouts:	Nap Rucker	201
ERA:	Nap Rucker	2.24
Saves:	Three tied with	1

APRIL 15   In Harry Lumley's debut as manager, the Dodgers beat the Giants 3–0 in 13 innings before 30,000 at the Polo Grounds in one of the most thrilling Opening Days in club history. John McGraw surprised nearly everyone by bypassing Christy Mathewson to start Red Ames. Lumley also made the bewildering choice of Kaiser Wilhelm over Nap Rucker. Both managers went with number two starters because they didn't want to risk using their aces on a bitterly cold day. There were few complaints once the game started as Ames and Wilhelm staged a magnificent pitching duel. Ames faced only 27 batters through the first nine innings without surrendering a base hit. Kaiser Wilhelm held New York without a hit until the eighth inning, when Admiral Schlei collected a one-out single. Art Devlin, who had walked, tried to score from

second base on Schlei's hit, but he was thrown out at the plate on a throw by center fielder Jimmy Sebring, who was playing in his first game with the Dodgers. Brooklyn collected the first hit off Ames with a double from Whitey Alperman with one out in the 10th. Ames gave up two more hits in the 11th and 12th. With darkness setting in at the start of the 13th, Lumley smacked a one-out triple. After a walk to Tim Jordan, Lumley scored on a single by Ed Lennox, who like Sebring was playing in his first game with the Dodgers. Bill Bergen singled in Jordan for a 2–0 lead. Lennox reached third on the hit and scored when Al Burch hit a slow roller down the third base line. Devlin, playing third base, waited for the ball to roll foul, but it stayed in fair territory. After holding the Dodgers hitless through nine innings, Ames gave up seven hits in the four extra frames. His magnificent performance was outdone by Wilhelm, who hurled a 13-inning shutout while giving up only three hits. After Schlei's single, Wilhelm surrendered singles to Buck Herzog in the 11th and Chief Meyers in the 13th.

> *Wilhelm won only two more games in 1909 and finished the season with a 3–13 record.*

APRIL 22   The Dodgers lose the home opener 8–5 to the Giants before 22,000 at Washington Park. The crowd overflowed the grandstand and stood two to three deep around the playing field.

APRIL 28   After being held to two hits by Bill Foxen through eight innings, the Dodgers break a 1–1 tie with five runs in the ninth to defeat the Phillies 6–1 in Philadelphia.

MAY 8   The Dodgers lose a fight-filled 8–2 decision to the Phillies at Washington Park. The row started in the fifth inning when Ed Lennox believed that Philadelphia second baseman Otto Knabe intentionally spiked him. Lennox struck Knabe on the jaw, Knabe hit back and the two clinched. Soon, thousands of fans swarmed the field. Three spectators became engaged in fisticuffs with players on the Phillies bench, but they retreated when the players threatened them with baseball bats. In the meantime, a free-for-all erupted around third base. Phillies third-base coach Kid Gleason knocked Lennox down and the mob chased Gleason into the office of Charles Ebbets. Gleason was locked into the office to prevent him from being beaten. While Ebbets was fighting his way to the gate to let the police into the ballpark, someone punched him. According to the wire service reports: "A sqaud of police ended the trouble by batting everybody in sight over the head with their clubs."

> *Charles Ebbets made a speech in 1909 in which he argued that baseball was still in its "infancy." Most of his fellow owners thought the contention was ridiculous, since the sport had been in existence for well over a half-century, and Ebbets was laughed off the podium. But Ebbets could see a more lucrative future in the sport with the construction of new ballparks built out of concrete and steel that opened in 1909 in St. Louis (a rebuilt Sportsman's Park), Philadelphia (Shibe Park) and Pittsburgh (Forbes Field). By 1915, similar ballparks had been built in Brooklyn (Ebbets Field), Boston (Fenway Park and Braves Field), Chicago (Comiskey Park and Wrigley Field), Cincinnati (Crosley Field), Cleveland (League Park), Detroit (Tiger Stadium), New York (a rebuilt Polo Grounds) and Washington (Griffith Stadium). These facilities would greatly expand interest in the sport within a decade.*

MAY 19 · George Bell pitches a two-hitter for a 2–0 win over the Pirates at Washington Park. The only Pittsburgh hits were singles by Honus Wagner and George Gibson. Ed Lennox drove in both Brooklyn runs with a double in the sixth inning.

JUNE 23 · The Dodgers break a 10-game losing streak with a 2–0 and 5–1 sweep of the Phillies in a double-header at Washington Park.

JULY 3 · Amid a nearly uncontrollable crowd during a double-header at Washington Park, the Dodgers lose 5–3 in 14 innings and 2–1 in the regulation nine to the Giants. Harry McIntire took the loss in the opener after pitching all 14 innings. Attendance was about 25,000, one of the largest ever inside the gates of the ballpark that served as the home of the Dodgers from 1898 through 1912. Much of the interest in the two closely contested games was marred by the unruly behavior of the crowd that congregated on the field in close proximity to the catchers. The number of police on hand were insufficient and seemed to be an incentive for the mob to do as it pleased. Bottles, glasses and other missiles were thrown all over the field, and for a time it appeared that the Dodgers would have to forfeit. A large number of young boys took delight in chasing after foul balls that were hit. At the time, it was illegal for fans to keep baseballs. Fans who caught balls in foul territory had to return them or face arrest. Some 50 balls were lost, and several arrests were made.

JULY 17 · The Dodgers win the first game of a double-header 1–0 over the Cubs at Washington Park. George Bell pitched the shutout. The lone run scored on a double by Doc Marshall in the seventh inning. Chicago won the second tilt 4–0.

JULY 24 · The Dodgers take a pair of 1–0 victories over the Cardinals at Washington Park. George Bell pitched the shutout in the opener. Nap Rucker was brilliant in the second contest, throwing a two-hitter with 16 strikeouts. The only St. Louis hits were singles by Rube Ellis and Ed Konetchy. The lone run scored in the sixth on a triple by Harry Lumley and a bunt from Tommy McMillan. There were only 12 hits by the two teams during the twin bill. The Dodgers had three hits in each contest, while the Cards had four in the first game and two in the second. The teams also set a record for fewest official at-bats by two teams in a double-header with 109. The Dodgers set a record for the least at-bats by one club with 52.

JULY 28 · Jim Pastorius comes within two outs of a no-hitter before settling for a one-hitter and a 4–0 defeat of the Phillies in Philadelphia. The only hit off Pastorius was a triple by pinch-hitter Doc Martel with one out in the ninth inning.

The victory was the only one of the season for Pastorius. He finished the 1909 campaign with a record of 1–9 after going 4–20 in 1908.

AUGUST 3 · Jim Pastorius walks 10 batters in seven innings of a 9–1 loss to the Pirates in Pittsburgh.

The game marked the first time that the Dodgers played at Forbes Field, which served as the home of the Pirates from 1909 through 1970.

AUGUST 4 · Harry McIntire pitches the Dodgers to a 1–0 victory over the Pirates in Pittsburgh. The lone run scored on a single by Tommy McMillan.

AUGUST 7   Nap Rucker pitches a two-hitter but loses 3–2 to the Cubs in Chicago. Wildfire
              Schulte hit a two-run homer in the first inning and Joe Tinker drove in a run with
              a single in the second.

AUGUST 9   George Bell throws a two-hitter and defeats the Cubs 2–0 in Chicago. The only hits
              off Bell were a double by Harry Steinfeldt and a single from Frank Chance.

AUGUST 21   The Dodgers defeat the Cardinals 1–0 in 13 innings in the first game of a double-
              header at Washington Park. Doc Scanlan pitched a complete game. Whitey Alperman
              drove in the lone run with a two-out, walk-off single. Brooklyn completed the sweep
              with a 6–3 triumph in the nightcap.

Bill Bergen was one of the best fielding catchers in baseball history and one
of the worst hitters. His career .170 batting average is the all-time low for
players with more than 2,500 at-bats. But in the deadball era, he saved his
Brooklyn team many runs with his strong arm and superb defense.

AUGUST 23   Bill Bergen throws out all six Cardinals runners who try to steal a base, although
              the Dodgers lose 9–1 in the second game of a double-header at Washington Park.
              Brooklyn won the opener 7–0.

SEPTEMBER 6   Bill Bergen hits his first home run in eight years during a 6–2 win over the Phillies in the first game of a double-header at Washington Park. Philadelphia won game two 3–1.

Bergen homered only twice in 11 seasons, 947 games and 3,028 at-bats. The other home run was struck with the Reds in 1901. During the 1909 season, Bergen played in 112 games with 346 at-bats, but he had a batting of only .139, an on-base percentage of .163 and a slugging percentage of .156. The home run on September 6 was one of only three extra-base hits he had all year.

SEPTEMBER 11   Zack Wheat makes his major league debut in the first game of a double-header against the Giants in New York. Wheat was hitless in four at-bats against Christy Mathewson in a 4–0 defeat. In game two, Wheat collected two hits in three official at-bats and also contributed two sacrifices during a 10–1 victory. In the opener, Wheat played in left field, a position he would play 2,328 times during his big-league career. In the second contest, Wheat was in center field, where he played on only four more occasions before his career ended in 1927.

Wheat played 18 of his 19 big-league seasons with the Dodgers in a stellar career that would land him in the Hall of Fame. He is still the all-time franchise leader in games played (2,322), at-bats (8,859), hits (2,804), doubles (464), triples (171) and total bases (4,003). Wheat is also second in runs scored (1,255), third in runs batted in (1,210), fifth in batting average (.317) and seventh in walks (632). He also holds the record for the longest hitting streak in franchise history with 29 in 1916. Wheat led the NL in slugging percentage in 1916 and won a batting title by hitting .335 in 1918. He was also one of the best defensive outfielders of his era.

SEPTEMBER 14   Nap Rucker pitches the Dodgers to a 1–0 victory over the Phillies in Philadelphia.

OCTOBER 7   Trailing 5–0 to the Giants at Washington Park on the last day of the season, the Dodgers rally to win 7–5 with a run in the third inning, another in the fourth, three in the fifth and single runs in the seventh and eighth.

The contest proved to be Harry Lumley's last as manager. Charles Ebbets had wanted Bill Dahlen to manage the club in 1909, but he was the property of the Braves, where he was the starting shortstop, and Ebbets was unable to negotiate a trade. Dahlen's skills declined during the 1909 season and he was no longer able to play effectively on a regular basis, which gave the Dodgers an opportunity to obtain his services as manager. He had previously played for the Dodgers from 1899 through 1903. Dahlen spent four seasons as Dodgers manager. His fiery temperament, which was exasperated by running losing clubs, placed him in almost constant turmoil with his players and with reporters and umpires. Charles Ebbets loved Dahlen, however, and kept him around despite the fact that the Dodgers never finished higher than sixth with him at the helm and were 251–355 overall. To his credit, Dahlen started a youth movement that included many players who would play on the 1916 National League pennant-winning club under Wilbert Robinson, who succeeded Dahlen after the end of the 1913 season.

The Washington Park Wall

The Dodgers played at Washington Park from 1898 through 1912. Few know that a piece of the left-field wall still exists along Third Avenue in Brooklyn. It is believed to be the oldest standing piece of a major league ballpark.

Washington Park was abandoned by the Dodgers when Ebbets Field opened in 1913. The Federal League started up in 1914 and established a franchise in Brooklyn, which rebuilt Washington Park. The Federal League folded after the end of the 1915 season and the site was unused until Con Edison purchased the land in 1922 to use as a truck depot and storage facility. All remnants of the ballpark were torn down except for the 20-foot high stone wall along Third Avenue that made up part of a loading dock. The small windows, high off the ground, were bricked up.

Con Edison announced plans in July 2002 that would have required demolition of the wall. The plans were blocked by the Society for American Baseball Research (SABR), which organized an e-mail campaign and brought in historians and architects to attest to the site's importance. They concluded that the wall was part of a carriage shed built in 1899 as part of an expansion of the ballpark. The shed was located behind the left-field bleachers. It is also likely that the shed was converted to house some of the first automobiles to travel the streets of New York after the turn of the century when individuals began replacing their horse-drawn carriages with gasoline-powered vehicles.

As of 2008, the future of the Washington Park wall remains unclear as conservationists continue efforts to preserve it.

THE STATE OF THE DODGERS

The Dodgers were one of the worst franchises in baseball at the start of the 1910s. The club hadn't posted a winning season since 1904, and there was little hope for the immediate future. But a youth movement began to pay dividends and, after winning 58 games in 1912, the Dodgers improved to 65 victories in 1913, 75 in 1914, 80 in 1915 and 94 and a National League pennant in 1916. The bubble burst quickly, however, and the Dodgers closed the decade with three more losing seasons. Overall, the Dodgers were 696–787 during the 1910s, a winning percentage of .469 that was the sixth-best among eight NL clubs. National League pennants outside of Brooklyn were won by the Cubs (1910 and 1918), Giants (1911, 1912, 1913 and 1917), Braves (1914), Phillies (1915) and Reds (1919).

THE BEST TEAM

The best team was naturally the pennant winner of 1916, which was 94–60 and won the National League by 2¹/₂ games in Wilbert Robinson's third year as manager.

THE WORST TEAM

The 1912 team was 58–95 with Bill Dahlen as manager and finished in seventh place, 46 games out of first.

THE BEST MOMENT

The Dodgers clinched their first National League pennant since 1900 by beating the hated Giants 9–6 on October 3, 1916.

THE WORST MOMENT

The Dodgers lost the 1916 World Series in five games to the Red Sox. The defeat was the start of Brooklyn's post-season frustrations. The club would lose again in the Fall Classic in 1920, 1941, 1947, 1949, 1952 and 1953 before finally winning a world championship in 1955.

THE ALL-DECADE TEAM • YEARS W/DODS

Otto Miller, c	1910–22
Jake Daubert, 1b	1910–18
George Cutshaw, 2b	1912–17
Red Smith, 3b	1911–14
Ivy Olson, ss	1915–24
Zack Wheat, lf	1909–26
Hy Myers, cf	1909, 1911, 1914–22
Casey Stengel, rf	1912–17
Jeff Pfeffer, p	1913–21
Nap Rucker, p	1907–16
Sherry Smith, p	1915–22
Rube Marquard, p	1915–20

Rucker was also on the 1900s All-Decade Team. With the exception of Red Smith, the eight position players were regulars on the 1916 pennant-winning team, while Pfeffer, Marquard and Sherry Smith were in the starting rotation. Wheat, Marquard and Stengel are in the Hall of Fame, although Stengel was elected as a manager.

THE DECADE LEADERS

Batting Avg:	Jake Daubert	.305
On-Base Pct:	Jake Daubert	.365
Slugging Pct:	Zack Wheat	.419
Home Runs:	Zack Wheat	51
RBIs:	Zack Wheat	636
Runs:	Jake Daubert	648
Stolen Bases:	George Cutshaw	166
Wins:	Jeff Pfeffer	96
Strikeouts:	Nap Rucker	686
ERA:	Jeff Pfeffer	2.16
Saves:	Jeff Pfeffer	23

THE HOME FIELD

The Dodgers moved into the second ballpark named Washington in 1898. Located in the Park Slope section of Brooklyn, it was largely constructed of wood and was typical of ballparks of the period. By 1910, Washington Park was woefully inadequate, however, as clubs began building much larger facilities built with steel and concrete. In 1913, the Dodgers moved into Ebbets Field, one of the many classic ballparks built between 1909 and 1915 (see May 8, 1909).

THE GAME YOU WISHED YOU HAD SEEN

The Dodgers opened Ebbets Field on April 5, 1913, with an exhibition game against the Yankees that drew 30,000 for a 3–2 victory. The first regular season game at the new Brooklyn ballpark was played four days later, but it attracted only 13,000 fans who witnessed the Dodgers lose 1–0 to the Phillies.

THE WAY THE GAME WAS PLAYED

Pitching and defense continued to dominate baseball. Offense spiked in the early years of the decade after the NL adopted the cork-centered ball in 1910, but by the mid-teens the league batting average was back around .250. Home runs were at a premium. There were more than twice as many triples as home runs and speedy outfielders were a necessity to cover playing fields much larger than those common today. NL pitchers completed 55 percent of their starts, but this was a significant drop from the 79 percent of the previous decade. During the 1910s, the strategic use of relief pitching, pinch-hitters and platooning became important aspects of the game for the first time.

THE MANAGEMENT

Charles Ebbets began his career with the Dodgers as a ticket taker in 1883, became club president in 1898 and the majority stockholder in 1907. He ran the club throughout the 1910s and would continue to do so until his death in 1925. Field managers were Bill Dahlen (1910–13) and Wilbert Robinson (1914–31).

THE BEST PLAYER MOVE

The best move was the purchase of Jeff Pfeffer from Grand Rapids of the Central League in August 1913. The best trade brought Burleigh Grimes, Al Mamaux and Chuck Ward from the Pirates for Casey Stengel and George Cutshaw in January 1918.

THE WORST PLAYER MOVE

The worst move was the sale of Fred Toney to the Reds in February 1915.

1910

L A

Season in a Sentence

Bill Dahlen is the latest Dodgers manager, but like his predecessors, he is saddled with an anemic offense and loses 90 games.

Finish • Won • Lost • Pct • GB

Sixth   64   90   .416   40.0

Manager

Bill Dahlen

Stats

Stats	Dods	NL	Rank
Batting Avg:	.229	.256	8
On-Base Pct:	.294	.328	8
Slugging Pct:	.305	.338	8
Home Runs:	25		5
Stolen Bases:	151		7
ERA:	3.07	3.02	5
Fielding Avg:	.964	.959	1
Runs Scored:	497		7
Runs Allowed:	623		4

Starting Lineup

Bill Bergen, c
Jake Daubert, 1b
John Hummel, 2b
Ed Lennox, 3b
Tony Smith, ss
Zack Wheat, lf
Bill Davidson, cf
Al Burch, rf-cf
Jack Dalton, rf
Pryor McElveen, 3b
Tex Erwin, c

Pitchers

Nap Rucker, sp
Cy Barger, rp
George Bell, sp
Doc Scanlan, sp
Elmer Knetzer, sp

Attendance

279,321 (seventh in NL)

Club Leaders

Batting Avg:	Zack Wheat	.284
On-Base Pct:	Zack Wheat	.341
Slugging Pct:	Zack Wheat	.403
Home Runs:	Jake Daubert	8
RBIs:	John Hummel	74
Runs:	Zack Wheat	78
Stolen Bases:	Bill Davidson	27
Wins:	Nap Rucker	17
Strikeouts:	Nap Rucker	147
ERA:	Nap Rucker	2.58
Saves:	Doc Scanlan	2

APRIL 7

The Dodgers visit the White House and are greeted by President William Howard Taft. The club was in Washington for an exhibition game against the Senators.

A week later, on April 14, Taft began the tradition of having the president of the United States throw out the first pitch on Opening Day in Washington.

APRIL 13

The Dodgers trade Harry McIntire to the Cubs for Bill Davidson, Tony Smith and Happy Smith.

APRIL 14

Nap Rucker pitches a two-hitter on Opening Day to defeat the Phillies 2–0 in Philadelphia. The only hits off Rucker were singles by Johnny Bates and Otto Knabe. Ed Lennox was the Dodgers batting star with two singles and a double.

APRIL 20

The Dodgers lose the home opener 6–2 to the Phillies before 16,000 at Washington Park.

Part of the Opening Day tradition of the period was a march to the flagpole by players of both teams, after which the U.S. flag was raised to the strains of "The Star-Spangled Banner." On this day, the rope broke and the flag came crashing to the ground.

APRIL 28   A seventh-inning triple play highlights a 10–3 win over the Braves at Washington Park. With Boston runners Fred Beck on first and Bill Sweeney on second, Peaches Graham hit a fly ball caught by Al Burch in right field. Burch threw to first baseman Jake Daubert to double up Beck, and Daubert shot the ball to third baseman Pryor McElveen to retire Sweeney, who attempted to advance to third on the play.

MAY 9   A 7–6 loss to the Pirates in Pittsburgh results in a chaotic finish. With one out in the bottom of the ninth and the score 6–6, Honus Wagner was the runner on third base and Dots Miller on first. Wagner was called out at the plate on an infield ground out and protested the decision. During the argument, Miller made a dash for third, and Dodgers catcher Tex Erwin threw the ball past the base, allowing Miller to score the winning run. Wagner grabbed the ball and headed for the clubhouse, but Brooklyn manager Bill Dahlen tore the ball from Wagner and threw to third, claiming that Miller hadn't touched the base. The umpires disagreed with Dahlen's contention, and the game was over.

In four years (1910–1913) as the Brooklyn skipper, Bill Dahlen had little success, compiling a 251–355 record.

MAY 10   George Bell pitches the Dodgers to a 1–0 win over the Pirates in Pittsburgh.

Bell had a 10–27 record in 1910 despite an ERA of 2.64 and four shutouts. The defeats are the most of any Dodgers pitcher in a season since the 60-foot, six-inch pitching distance was established in 1893. No Dodgers hurler since 1910 has lost more than 21 games in a single year. Bell pitched 17 career shutouts in five big-league seasons and his 2.85 ERA is the fourth best all-time among Dodgers pitchers with at least 1,000 innings, but he had a record of only 43–79.

MAY 12   The Dodgers outlast the Pirates 11–9 in 12 innings at Forbes Field. Both teams scored in the 11th inning, which ended in an 8–8 tie. Brooklyn scored three times in the top of the 12th and survived a Pittsburgh rally in the bottom half.

MAY 30   George Bell pitches a one-hitter and faces only 28 batters for a 2–0 victory over the Braves in the morning game of a Memorial Day double-header at Washington Park. The only Boston hit was a single by Bill Collins. The Dodgers completed the sweep with a 3–1 victory in the afternoon contest.

JUNE 7   The Dodgers rout the Reds 10–0 at Washington Park.

JUNE 8   In his major league debut, Dodgers reliever Frank Schneiberg allows five hits, four walks and eight runs, seven of them earned, during a 13–2 loss to the Reds in Cincinnati. Schneiberg never pitched another big-league game and finished his career with an earned run average of 63.00.

JUNE 14   Cy Barger pitches 14 innings, collects four hits, two of them doubles, and drives in the winning run for a 3–2 win over the Cubs at Washington Park. Barger's first double drove in a run in the fifth for a 2–1 lead, but the Cubs tied the contest in the sixth. Barger then pitched shutout ball over the final eight innings and drove in the game-winner with a walk-off double.

Barger's given name was Eros Bolivar Barger. His father wanted to give him an impressive-sounding Greek name and chose Eros without knowledge of its source. The middle name of Bolivar came from Simon Bolivar, who led Venezuela to their independence from Spain in 1821.

JUNE 17   Nap Rucker pitches 13 innings and allows just six hits, but he loses 1–0 to the Cubs at Washington Park. The lone run crossed the plate on Rucker's wild pitch with Harry Steinfeldt scoring from third base.

JUNE 21   Playing in only his second major league game, Dodgers right fielder Jack Dalton collects five hits off Christy Mathewson in five at-bats, although the Dodgers lose 12–1 to the Giants at Washington Park.

Dalton batted only .227 in 77 games as a rookie in 1910. He spent the next three seasons in the minors, returned to the Dodgers and batted .319 in 128 contests in 1914. He then left the club to sign with the Federal League.

JUNE 23   Giants players Larry Doyle and Art Devlin are arrested during an 8–2 New York win over the Dodgers at Washington Park. At the end of the third inning, Devlin rushed across the diamond from the third base position and struck a heckling spectator. The fan struck back, starting a spirited fight. Doyle came to Devlin's aid. Devlin and Doyle emerged from the fray under arrest. Other fans swarmed the field and someone threw a bottle that narrowly missed Devlin. Play was resumed after officers cleared the field.

Devlin was cleared of the assault charges in court, but he was suspended for five days by the National League.

JULY 7   Jake Daubert hits a three-run homer in the 11th inning to defeat the Phillies 7–4 in the first game of a double-header in Philadelphia. The Dodgers completed the sweep with a 2–0 victory in the second tilt.

Daubert was a 26-year-old rookie first baseman in 1910. He played for nine seasons in Brooklyn and won back-to-back batting titles by hitting .350 in 1913 and .329 in 1914. Daubert's 87 triples in a Dodger uniform ranks fourth in franchise history.

JULY 14   The Dodgers score three runs in the ninth inning to defeat the Cardinals 3–1 during a contentious afternoon in St. Louis. In the seventh inning, umpire Bill Klem ejected Bill Dahlen and two of his players. According to the wire service reports, "Dahlen made a gesture not to the liking of the umpire." Cardinals pitcher Frank Corridon allowed only one hit through eight innings before giving up the three ninth-inning runs. After the contest a spectator criticized Cardinals manager Roger Bresnahan and his team for blowing the game. Armed with a couple of baseball bats, Bresnahan and third baseman Mike Mowrey started after the fan, but they were prevented from doing any harm by a police officer.

JULY 23   George Bell pitches 11⅓ innings and allows only four hits, but he loses 1–0 when the Cubs score in the 12th inning at Chicago.

AUGUST 5   The Dodgers sweep the Cardinals 3–0 and 8–1 at Washington Park. Nap Rucker pitched a two-hitter in the opener, allowing only a double to Elmer Zacher and a single to Mike Mowrey.

AUGUST 13   In the second game of a double-header at Washington Park, the Dodgers and Pirates tie 8–8 before the contest is called after nine innings by darkness. In addition to runs scored, the clubs tied in eight other statistical categories. Each had 38 at-bats, 13 hits, three walks, five strikeouts, one hit batter, two errors, 12 assists and one passed ball. Pittsburgh won the opener 3–2 in 13 innings.

AUGUST 15   Going from one extreme to the other, the Dodgers lose 14–0 and win 9–1 in a double-header against the Cubs at Washington Park.

AUGUST 25   In the 12th inning at Pittsburgh, Bobby Byrne of the Pirates stretches a single into a double, then steals third and home to defeat the Dodgers 4–3.

AUGUST 26   During a 4–2 Dodgers loss to the Pirates at Forbes Field, the two clubs tie a major league record with only one putout by the outfielders. The pitchers were Elmer Knetzer of the Dodgers and Babe Adams of the Pirates. The lone outfield putout was recorded by Pittsburgh right fielder Chief Wilson. The only other big-league game in which there has been only one outfield putout was in 1884.

SEPTEMBER 15   In his first major league start, Sandy Burk of the Dodgers walks 10 batters and throws two wild pitches in eight innings of a 7–2 loss to the Reds at Washington Park.

SEPTEMBER 23   In his second major league start, Sandy Burk allows only two hits, but he walks 11 batters and hits another in a 6–2 loss to the Cardinals at Washington Park.

            Burk pitched three seasons for the Dodgers and had a 1–6 record with a 5.15 ERA and 77 walks in 85⅔ innings.

SEPTEMBER 26   The Dodgers sweep the Pirates with a pair of 4–1 victories at Washington Park. Nap Rucker pitched a two-hitter in the second tilt, allowing only singles to Bill McKechnie and Tommy Leach.

SEPTEMBER 27   The Dodgers score three runs in the ninth inning and one in the 10th to defeat the Pirates 4–3 at Washington Park. The Dodgers collected only one hit off Howie Camnitz through the first eight innings. In the ninth, Bob Coulson drove in the tying run with a single. Tex Erwin drove in the game-winner with a bases-loaded pinch-single.

SEPTEMBER 30   The Dodgers and Phillies battle to a 10-inning, 9–9 tie in a contest at Washington Park called on account of darkness. Philadelphia scored eight runs in the eighth inning to take a 9–6 lead. Bob Coulson's three-run homer in the bottom of the ninth deadlocked the game.

The home run was the only one that Coulson collected over four major league seasons in which he had 692 at-bats in 197 games.

1911   L A

Season in a Sentence

The Dodgers' offensive problems remain unsolved as the club scores 119 fewer runs than any other NL club and finishes in seventh place.

Finish • Won • Lost • Pct • GB

Seventh   64   86   .427 33.5

Manager

Bill Dahlen

Stats

Stats	Dods	NL	Rank
Batting Avg:	.237	.260	8
On-Base Pct:	.301	.335	8
Slugging Pct:	.311	.356	8
Home Runs:	28		6
Stolen Bases:	184		5
ERA:	3.39	3.39	6
Fielding Avg:	.962	.958	3
Runs Scored:	538		8
Runs Allowed:	659		4

Starting Lineup

Bill Bergen, c
Jake Daubert, 1b
John Hummel, 2b
Eddie Zimmerman, 3b
Bert Tooley, ss
Zack Wheat, lf
Bill Davidson, cf
Bob Coulson, rf
Tex Erwin, c
Dolly Stark, ss-2b

Pitchers

Nap Rucker, sp-rp
Cy Barger, sp
Elmer Knetzer, sp
Bill Schardt, sp-rp
Doc Scanlan, sp-rp
George Bell, sp-rp
Pat Ragan, rp-sp

Attendance

269,000 (seventh in NL)

Club Leaders

Batting Avg:	Jake Daubert	.307
On-Base Pct:	Jake Daubert	.366
Slugging Pct:	Zack Wheat	.412
Home Runs:	Tex Erwin	7
RBIs:	Zack Wheat	76
Runs:	Jake Daubert	89
Stolen Bases:	Jake Daubert	32
	Bob Coulson	32
Wins:	Nap Rucker	22
Strikeouts:	Nap Rucker	190
ERA:	Nap Rucker	2.74
Saves:	Nap Rucker	4
	Bill Schardt	4

APRIL 12   Three weeks after a building housing New York City's Triangle Shirtwaist Factory catches fire, causing the death of 146 people, the Dodgers lose the season opener 2–1 to the Braves in Boston. Cy Barger pitched a five-hit complete game.

APRIL 14   The Dodgers pummel the Braves 15–2 in Boston.

APRIL 21   The Dodgers lose the home opener 9–5 to the Braves before a crowd of 10,000 at Washington Park.

MAY 17   George Bell pitches the Dodgers to a 1–0 win over the Cubs at Washington Park. Al Burch drove in the lone run with a single in the seventh inning.

JUNE 21   Doc Scanlan pitches 15 innings and allows just six hits, but he loses 2–1 to the Phillies at Washington Park. Mickey Doolan drove in the winning run with two out in the 15th inning on a drive that bounced off the fingertips of center fielder Al Burch. Grover Alexander pitched all 15 innings for Philadelphia.

JUNE 23   Nap Rucker hurls a 1–0 victory over the Giants at Washington Park. The lone run scored on a walk-off single by John Hummel in the ninth inning.

Rucker was 22–18 with a 2.71 ERA and 190 strikeouts in 315²/₃ innings. He was the pitcher at the end of 37 Dodgers games in 1910, completing 23 of his 33 starts and finishing 14 of his 15 relief appearances. As a reliever, Rucker had a 5–4 record with four saves. Relief pitching took on a much greater importance beginning in the 1910s. During the 1911 season, relievers made 1,369 appearances in 1,237 games, compared to 316 appearances in 1,110 contests just 10 years earlier in 1901. Few managers employed relief specialists, however, and instead utilized staff aces like Rucker in the role in between starts. The dual role proved to be too much for Rucker. By 1914, he was a sore-armed pitcher unable to pitch without a week's rest in between pitching assignments.

JULY 8   Fans attack umpire Ralph Frary in the ninth inning of a 3–1 loss to the Pirates at Washington Park. The Dodgers players and fans objected to the calls of Frary all afternoon. In the bottom of the ninth, the umpire ordered the Dodgers bench cleared of all individuals not involved in the game. Bill Dahlen at first refused, but threatened with a forfeit, he and the six reserve players slowly marched to the clubhouse beyond the left-field wall. At that point a fusillade of hundreds of bottles and drinking glasses began to be hurled in the direction of Frary. One bounced off the turf and struck him in the face. The appearance of four policemen and two detectives in front of the stands prevented further trouble. Frary needed protection from the officers to leave the grounds safely.

Frary was fired by the National League a week later.

JULY 15   Nap Rucker strikes out 12 batters during a 2–1 win over the Cardinals at Washington Park.

JULY 22   In a tremendous pitching duel between Nap Rucker and Reds hurler Frank Smith, the Dodgers win 1–0 at Washington Park. Rucker came within one out of a no-hitter. The only Cincinnati hit was a single by Bob Bescher with two out in the ninth. Smith allowed the Dodgers only two hits, on singles by Jake Daubert in the fourth and Eddie Zimmerman in the eighth. The lone run scored in the seventh on two errors and an infield out. The two teams also tied a National League record for the fewest official at-bats for two teams in a nine-inning game with 48. Each team had 24 at-bats.

JULY 28   Tex Erwin hits a grand slam off Art Fromme in the sixth inning, but the Dodgers lose 8–6 to the Reds in Cincinnati.

JULY 29   Zack Wheat scored four runs and collects four hits during a 9–2 win over the Reds in Cincinnati.

AUGUST 2   King Cole of the Cubs pitches a complete game one-hitter and Jimmy Archer hits a walk-off homer in the 10th inning off Nap Rucker to beat the Cubs 1–0 in Chicago.

AUGUST 3   At West Side Grounds in Chicago, the Dodgers hit three home runs in the fifth inning to defeat the Cubs 5–3. The homers were struck by Eddie Zimmerman, Tex Erwin and Zack Wheat. Zimmerman circled the bases when his drive down the right-field line landed in fair territory, then veered under a pile of lumber stacked in foul ground in right field.

The August 3, 1911, game marked the first time that the Dodgers hit three home runs in an inning. It didn't happen again until 1929.

AUGUST 8   Zack Wheat scores both runs of a 2–0 win over the Cardinals in St. Louis. Elmer Knetzer pitched the shutout.

AUGUST 14   The Dodgers lead 9–1 after three innings against the Braves in Boston, but they wind up losing 13–9. The Braves broke the 9–9 tie with three tallies in the seventh.

AUGUST 15   The Dodgers blow a big lead against the Braves in Boston for the second day in a row. Brooklyn was ahead 8–1 in the fifth inning, but the game ended in a 9–9 tie when called after 12 innings on account of darkness.

AUGUST 17   The Dodgers score three runs in the ninth inning to defeat the Pirates 8–7 at Washington Park. Bob Coulson hit a two-run double to tie the score. Eddie Zimmerman drove in the winning tally with a single.

AUGUST 24   With the Dodgers trailing the Cubs 5–4 and two runners on base in the 10th inning at Washington Park, Tex Erwin smacks a drive over the left-field wall. Erwin was credited with only a triple, however, and the Dodgers garnered a 6–5 victory. According to the scoring rules of the day, the game ended when the winning run crossed the plate, so Erwin's drive accounted for only three bases. The rules were changed in 1919 to score hits such as Erwin's as home runs.

Erwin had only 218 at-bats in 1911, but he led the Dodgers in home runs with seven.

SEPTEMBER 17   In the eighth inning of a 5–0 loss to the Cubs in the second game of a double-header in Chicago, Zack Wheat hits a drive line at the head of pitcher Larry Cheney, driving his thumb into his nose and breaking both. It was Cheney's first major league start. The Dodgers were also shutout in the opener, losing 4–0.

Cheney won 26 games as a rookie in 1912. He pitched for the Dodgers from 1915 through 1919 and was an 18-game winner on the 1916 National League pennant-winners.

SEPTEMBER 19   The Dodgers scored three runs in the ninth inning to beat the Reds 7–5 in Cincinnati. Red Smith put the Dodgers into the lead with a two-run single.

SEPTEMBER 27   The Dodgers score three times in the ninth inning to down the Cardinals 4–3 in St. Louis.

OCTOBER 6   After losing the first game of a double-header 1–0 to the Braves at Washington Park, the Dodgers erupt for eight runs in the seventh inning of the second tilt and win 13–3.

OCTOBER 9   Red Smith makes four errors at third base during a 10–4 loss to the Giants at Washington Park.

OCTOBER 12   On the final day of the 1911 season, the Dodgers sweep the Giants 3–0 and 5–2. Bill Dahlen played shortstop at the age of 41 in the second game, struck out three times and made an error. It was the last of Dahlen's 2,444 big-league appearances in a playing career that began in 1891. Charlie Faust, the Giants 21-year-old mascot, pitched an inning and shutout the Dodgers on one hit. In a plate appearance, Faust was hit by a pitch and was then allowed to steal second and third without drawing a throw, before crossing the plate on an infield out.

Faust approached Giants manager John McGraw before the 1911 season and explained that a fortune teller told him that if he pitched for the Giants the club would win the pennant. Faust became a good-luck charm, traveled with the team and warmed up to pitch every game. The Giants did in fact win the pennant, their first since 1905. Faust was committed to a mental institution in 1914 and died a year later from tuberculosis.

1912
L A

Season in a Sentence

The Dodgers turn over much of the roster in a youth movement, but the result is a seventh-place finish.

Finish • Won • Lost • Pct • GB

Seventh   58   95   .379   46.0

Manager

Bill Dahlen

Stats

Stats	Dods	NL	Rank
Batting Avg:	.268	.272	6
On-Base Pct:	.336	.340	5
Slugging Pct:	.358	.369	6
Home Runs:	32		6
Stolen Bases:	179		4
ERA:	3.64	3.40	6
Fielding Avg:	.959	.960	5
Runs Scored:	651		8
Runs Allowed:	754		6

Starting Lineup

Otto Miller, c
Jake Daubert, 1b
John Hummel, 2b-rf
Red Smith, 3b
Bert Tooley, ss
Zack Wheat, lf
Herbie Moran, cf-rf
Hub Northen, rf-cf
George Cutshaw, 2b
Tom Fisher, ss
Jud Daley, lf-cf

Pitchers

Nap Rucker, sp
Pat Ragan, sp
Eddie Stack, sp-rp
Earl Yingling, sp-rp
Frank Allen, sp
Cy Barger, sp
Elmer Knetzer, rp-sp

Attendance

243,000 (seventh in NL)

Club Leaders

Batting Avg:	Jake Daubert	.308
On-Base Pct:	Jake Daubert	.369
Slugging Pct:	Zack Wheat	.450
Home Runs:	Zack Wheat	8
RBIs:	Jake Daubert	66
Runs:	Jake Daubert	81
Stolen Bases:	Jake Daubert	28
Wins:	Nap Rucker	18
Strikeouts:	Nap Rucker	151
ERA:	Nap Rucker	2.21
Saves:	Nap Rucker	4

JANUARY 2   Charles Ebbets announces plans to build a new ballpark, which would acquire the
             name Ebbets Field, in the Flatbush section of Brooklyn. The announcement was
             made by Ebbets at a dinner given for a party of sportswriters. The 4½-acre plot
             was bounded by 475 feet on Bedford Avenue, 478 feet on Sullivan Place, 637 feet
             on Cedar Place and 450 feet on Montgomery Street, with the main entrance at the
             corner of Cedar Place and Sullivan Place. Cedar Place was on the third-base side of
             the ballpark, while Sullivan Place was on the first-base side. Montgomery Street was
             behind the left-field wall and Bedford Avenue beyond right field. None of the four
             streets were parallel to each other, giving the block an awkward shape. The cost of
             the Dodgers new home was $750,000. With public funding of ballparks decades in
             the future, the entire cost was borne by the stockholders of the club, primarily Ebbets
             himself. To help finance the project, Ebbets gave a one-half interest in the club for
             $100,000 to Steve and Ed McKeever, a pair of brothers who owned the construction
             company that built it. (Cedar Place was later renamed McKeever Place in their
             honor.) Ebbets hoped to open the ballpark before the end of the 1912 season, but
             construction delays forestalled those plans until 1913.

             *Ebbets selected the site for his new ballpark in 1908. The land was owned by
             20 different individuals, and he began secretly buying the parcels through an
             agent, a process that took three years. It was located in an undeveloped part of
             Flatbush called "Pigtown" because of the preponderance of pig farms in the area
             until late in the 19th century. It had two attributes that appealed to Ebbets. First,
             it was located near the geographic center of Brooklyn and could be reached by
             12 subway or elevated lines. Secondly, land was cheap in an area the* New York
             Times *called a "howling wilderness." In fact, the streets that would surround
             Ebbets Field existed only on paper in 1912. They had yet to be built by the city.
             At the time construction began on the ballpark, the site was used as a garbage
             dump and was occupied by what the* Times *described as "several old houses
             and shanties and goats and tomato cans." The few residents were mostly Italian
             immigrant families. Beyond was a largely empty landscape. Only three houses
             were standing over a five-block expanse to the east and northeast past Bedford
             Avenue. The block beyond Sullivan Place contained no buildings at all. But
             with his political connections, Ebbets knew of a deal that would soon interlink
             the city's then-independent trolley lines and triple the track to 619 miles. This
             agreement helped Brooklyn expand well beyond its existing neighborhoods
             near the Brooklyn Bridge and into then-rural southwestern, central and eastern
             Brooklyn. The expanded transit system created a population explosion in which
             Brooklyn grew from 1.1 million residents in 1900 to 2.6 million in 1930. By
             the 1920s, the area around Ebbets Field experienced a building boom and the
             empty blocks were filled with row houses, apartments and businesses. Because
             of the ballpark's central location, there was no residence in Brooklyn more than
             six miles from Ebbets Field. Including sections of Queens and lower Manhattan,
             there were more than three million people living within that six-mile radius
             by 1930.*

APRIL 11   Two months after the admission of New Mexico and Arizona as the 47th and
             48th states, the 1912 season opener at Washington Park ends in a riot and an 18–3
             thrashing of the Dodgers at the hands of the Giants. A crowd of more than 25,000
             attended, several thousand more than the seating capacity. Fans poured onto the
             playing field and defied the combined efforts of the police, club officials and
             the players in an attempt to bring about law and order. The crowd surged onto

the field and became unmanageable, which prevented the game from starting. The fans resisted efforts of the police to push them back. Players from both teams took their bats and, forming a long line, charged the crowd, but the fans fought back and refused to give way. There was little room for them to move anyway, because the stands were jammed and the aisles were completely filled. When the game finally began, 30 minutes after the scheduled start, fans were occupying the outfield within a dozen yards of the bases. The immense throng on the field cut off the view of the action of those behind them, including those who had paid a premium for box seats. Pop flies hit into the crowd were doubles. The game evolved into a farce and, after six innings of play, it was called on account of darkness with the Giants leading 18–3. There were 14 doubles hit in the game, 10 of them by the New York club.

APRIL 20   Six days after the sinking of the Titanic, Bill Dahlen fights umpire Cy Rigler at the end a 4–3 loss to the Giants in New York. Art Wilson hit a two-run, walk-off homer into the stands to win the game. Dahlen thought the drive was foul and ran toward Rigler to protest. The Dodgers manager nudged the umpire during the argument, and Rigler responded by punching Dahlen in the face. The two men engaged in a hot fistic battle in spite of the efforts of Brooklyn catcher Tex Erwin and New York coach Wilbert Robinson to separate them. The crowd surged onto the field, and Rigler managed to escape to the safety of the clubhouse.

MAY 1   Trailing 5–1, the Dodgers score three runs in the seventh inning and seven in the eighth to defeat the Braves 11–8 in Boston.

MAY 3   The Dodgers wallop the Braves 14–3 in Boston. There were 16 runs in the final two innings. With the score 1–0, the Dodgers scored five times in the eighth inning and eight in the ninth to take a 14–0 advantage before the Braves plated three in the bottom of the ninth.

MAY 10   The Dodgers play at Redland Field in Cincinnati for the first time and lose 6–5 to the Reds.

Redland Field was renamed Crosley Field in 1934 and served as the home of the Reds from 1912 through 1970.

MAY 17   The Dodgers thrash the Cardinals 13–5 in St. Louis.

MAY 22   Jake Daubert collects five hits, including a triple and a double, in five at-bats, but the Dodgers lose 10–6 to the Cubs in Chicago.

JUNE 3   The Dodgers pull off an unusual triple play in the eighth inning of a 7–4 loss to the Reds in Cincinnati. The Reds had the bases loaded with Bob Bescher on third, Armando Marsans on second and Dick Hoblitzel on first. Mike Mitchell grounded to shortstop Tom Fisher, who threw home to force Bescher. Catcher Otto Miller turned toward first and faked a throw. Marsans was duped by Miller's action, rounded third and became caught in a rundown between third and home. By the time Marsans was tagged out, Hoblitzel had reached third and Mitchell second. Mitchell strayed too far off the bag, however, and was called out on a throw from Miller to second baseman John Hummel.

JUNE 10	Nap Rucker pitches the Dodgers to a 1–0 win over the Pirates at Washington Park. Herbie Moran drove in the lone run with a double in the second inning. The contest took only one hour and 12 minutes to complete.

> *Rucker's ERA of 2.21 was the third-best in the National League and he pitched six shutouts, but with inadequate offensive support, Nap posted a losing record of 18–21.*

JUNE 14	The Dodgers defeat the Cardinals 11–2 at Washington Park. Flag Day was celebrated with the invitation of 1,000 children from "two orphan asylums and a disciplinary school." There were three bands made up of youngsters who played "the popular airs of the day."
JUNE 15	The Dodgers take an exciting 5–4 decision in 11 innings over the Cardinals at Washington Park. St. Louis twice took leads with runs in the top of the ninth and 10th, but Brooklyn tied it up in the bottom half of both innings. Hub Northen drove in the winning run with a pinch-hit single.
JUNE 27	The Dodgers narrowly escape with a 9–8 win over the Braves in Boston. The Braves had the bases loaded with two out in the ninth when Ben Houser hit a grounder between first and second that appeared to be headed into right field for a two-run single, but the ball struck base runner John Titus to end the game just before Bill Sweeney was about to cross the plate with the tying run.
JULY 1	Jake Daubert collects seven hits, including a double, in eight at-bats during a double-header against the Phillies in Philadelphia. The Dodgers lost the first game 10–7 and won the second 14–1.
JULY 3	Giants pitcher Rube Marquard wins his 19th consecutive game, the major league record for a single season, by defeating the Dodgers 2–1 in the first game of a double-header in New York. The Giants won the second tilt 10–9 to extend their team winning streak to 16 games.
JULY 4	The Dodgers break the 16-game winning streak of the Giants with a sweep in a holiday double-header in New York by scores of 5–2 and 10–4.
JULY 6	The cornerstone is laid at Ebbets Field. During the ceremonies, letter were read from President William Howard Taft, New York Mayor William Gaynor, Pennsylvania Governor John Tener and many baseball moguls from both leagues.
AUGUST 15	Jake Daubert collects five hits, including a triple and a double, in five at-bats of a 10-inning, 7–3 victory over the Reds in the first game of a double-header in Cincinnati. The Dodgers lost the second contest 5–0.
AUGUST 20	Both umpires are injured in a bizarre sequence during a 3–2 win over the Pirates in the first game of a double-header at Forbes Field. At the time, only two umpires were assigned to big-league games. On this day, Bill Brennan was on the bases and Brick Owens behind the plate. In the first inning, Pittsburgh's Max Carey attempted a steal of second. Brennan ran toward the bag to call the play, but he stopped too quickly and slipped, breaking a leg and tearing cartilage in his knee. The players carried Brennan to the clubhouse and an ambulance was called. In the second inning,

Dots Miller of the Pirates hit a foul tip that struck Owens in the breastbone. Owens collapsed unconscious and was taken to the clubhouse and laid next to Brennan. Both umpires were taken to the hospital in the same ambulance. The game continued with players Eddie Phelps of the Dodgers and Ham Hyatt of the Pirates serving as umpires. Phelps and Hyatt also umpired in the second tilt, won by the Dodgers 9–1.

AUGUST 21   Nap Rucker pitches the Dodgers to a 1–0 win over the Pirates in Pittsburgh.

SEPTEMBER 2   The Dodgers play two extra-inning games against the Phillies in a Labor Day double-header in Philadelphia. The Dodgers won the opener 4–2 in 11 innings. Pinch-hitter Tex Erwin hit a home run with two out in the ninth inning to tie the score 2–2. Otto Miller won the contest with a two-run double in the 11th. The Phillies took the nightcap 2–1 in 13 innings.

SEPTEMBER 4   Dodgers pitcher Eddie Stack allows only three hits in a 13-inning complete game and beats the Braves 2–1 at Washington Park. Stack allowed a run in the second on a triple by John Titus and a single from Art Devlin. The only other Boston hit was a single by Titus in the 10th. Stack nearly wound up as the losing pitcher before the Dodgers tied the score 1–1 on an error with two out in the ninth. John Hummel drove in the winning run with a single.

SEPTEMBER 5   The Dodgers score two runs in the ninth inning to defeat the Braves 4–3 at Washington Park. Red Smith drove in the tying run with a double and scored on a single by John Hummel.

SEPTEMBER 7   Elmer Knetzer pitches a two-hitter to down the Braves 4–0 in the second game of a double-header in Boston. The only hits off Knetzer were a triple by Jay Kirke and a single from Vin Campbell. The Dodgers scored all four of their runs in the seventh inning. Knetzer also pitched an inning of relief in the opener, a 2–1 loss.

SEPTEMBER 17   Casey Stengel makes his major league debut and reaches base five times in five plate appearances, on four hits and a walk, to lead the Dodgers to a 7–3 win over the Pirates at Washington Park. He also stole two bases.

                 The newspapers covering Stengel's debut referred to him as Charley Stengel. He acquired the familiar nickname "Casey" later because he hailed from Kansas City (K.C.), Missouri. Stengel collected 10 hits in his first 16 big-league at-bats and hit .316 in 17 games as a rookie. Best known for managing the Yankees to 10 pennants and seven world championships in 12 years from 1949 through 1960, and for leading the woeful expansion Mets from 1962 through 1965, Stengel had an excellent playing career. He was a starter in the Dodgers outfield from the day he reported to the club in 1912 until he was traded to the Pirates in January 1918.

SEPTEMBER 21   The Dodgers clobber the Cardinals 12–0 at Washington Park.

SEPTEMBER 26   Nap Rucker pitches a shutout and collects a bases-loaded triple in the second inning of a 4–0 triumph over the Phillies in the first game of a double-header at Washington Park. Philadelphia won game two 5–4.

OCTOBER 5   The Dodgers play their final game at Washington Park and lose 1–0 to the Giants before a crowd of 10,000. When the game ended, Shannon's Military band played a few ragtime tunes along with "Auld Lang Syne."

The Dodgers moved into Ebbets Field in 1913. Washington Park wasn't through with major league baseball, however. The ballpark was rebuilt and used by Brooklyn's Federal League team in 1914 and 1915.

OCTOBER 6   A month before Woodrow Wilson is elected president in a three-way race with William Howard Taft and Theodore Roosevelt, the pitches of Nap Rucker and Walter Johnson are tested for speed at the Remington Arms Plant in Bridgeport, Connecticut. A 12-time American League leader in strikeouts while pitching for the Senators, Johnson was coming off a season in which he had a 33–12 record. It's likely that equipment used at the plant greatly underestimated the fastballs of the two pitchers. Rucker was clocked at 77 miles per hour and Johnson at 83.

1913
L A

Season in a Sentence

The Dodgers open Ebbets Field and win 19 of their first 28 games, but they end up with their 10th consecutive losing season.

Finish • Won • Lost • Pct • GB

Sixth   65   84   .436   34.5

Manager

Bill Dahlen

Stats

Stats	Dods	NL	Rank
Batting Avg:	.270	.262	3
On-Base Pct:	.321	.325	5
Slugging Pct:	.363	.354	3
Home Runs:	39		3
Stolen Bases:	188		3
ERA:	3.13	3.20	3
Fielding Avg:	.961	.962	4
Runs Scored:	595		7
Runs Allowed:	613		3

Starting Lineup

Otto Miller, c
Jake Daubert, 1b
George Cutshaw, 2b
Red Smith, 3b
Tom Fisher, ss
Zack Wheat, lf
Casey Stengel, cf
Herbie Moran, rf
John Hummel, rf-ss

Pitchers

Pat Ragan, sp
Nap Rucker, sp
Cliff Curtis, sp-rp
Earl Yingling, sp-rp
Frank Allen, sp
Ed Reulbach, sp
Eddie Stack, rp-sp

Attendance

347,000 (fourth in NL)

Club Leaders

Batting Avg:	Jake Daubert	.350
On-Base Pct:	Jake Daubert	.405
Slugging Pct:	Red Smith	.441
Home Runs:	Three tied with	7
RBIs:	George Cutshaw	80
Runs:	Jake Daubert	76
Stolen Bases:	George Cutshaw	39
Wins:	Pat Ragan	15
Strikeouts:	Nap Rucker	111
ERA:	Frank Allen	2.83
Saves:	Nap Rucker	3

MARCH 17   Six weeks after the opening of New York City's Grand Central Terminal, the Dodgers spring training field in Augusta, Georgia, is under two feet of floodwater and approachable only by boat from two blocks away. The Dodgers were forced to find another field in a drier part of town.

APRIL 5   The Dodgers open Ebbets Field and defeat the Yankees 3–2 in an exhibition game before a crowd of 30,000. Another 5,000 were left outside after the gates were closed. The first ball was tossed out by Charles Ebbets's 20-year-old daughter Genevieve. Casey Stengel hit an inside-the-park homer in the fifth and Jake Daubert did likewise in the sixth for a 2–0 lead. The Yankees scored twice in the ninth off Frank Allen to tie the score. The Dodgers broke the deadlock in the ninth on a bunt single by Zack Wheat, an error, a sacrifice by Daubert and a single from Red Smith.

There were several embarrassing incidents in the opener. It took considerable time to allow bleacher patrons into the ballpark because the key to the gate could not be found. Before the game, there was a march out to the flagpole led by Charles Ebbets that included other club officials and players from both teams. But when the parade arrived at its destination, it was discovered that no one had remembered to bring along the flag. And, the outfield grass was sparse as construction delays had forestalled plans to plant the seed. Outfielders had to traverse a barren, and often muddy, landscape at Ebbets Field until June.

First baseman Jake Daubert won the MVP Award in 1913 while leading the league in hitting. He hit over .300 in seven of his nine years as a Dodger.

APRIL 9   The Dodgers play their first regular season game at Ebbets Field and lose 1–0 to the Phillies before 10,000 on a bitterly cold day. Tom Seaton pitched the shutout. Nap Rucker threw the first pitch to Dode Paskert, who singled and later scored the lone run. Brooklyn Borough President Alfred Steers threw out the first pitch. According to the *New York Times*, "there was a brass band, a great floral horseshoe and a parade of players across the field. Jake Daubert was presented with a gold bat, and there was all the usual ceremony that is faithfully followed at every baseball opening."

The main entrance of Ebbets had a semi-circular rotunda at the entrance with a diameter of 80 feet with a tiled floor and white glazed brick side walls. The walls contained 12 gilded ticket windows. The height from the floor to the center of the dome was 27 feet. It was accentuated by a chandelier featuring facsimiles of baseball bats as part of the fixture, which suspended illuminated glass globes made to look like baseballs. For all of its magnificence, the rotunda turned out to be a tremendous bottleneck. Once inside, fans had to fight one another to get to the correct entrance and maneuver around those waiting in line for tickets. No ballpark was ever built like that again. The original stands were double-decked from the right-field corner at Bedford Avenue around to just past third base on the Cedar Place side. There they met a concrete bleacher section that extended to the left-field wall on Montgomery Street. Seating capacity in 1913 was 22,000. The field dimensions were 301 feet down the right-field line, 477 feet to dead center and 419 feet down the left-field line. In right field, there was a concrete barrier 19 feet high, the bottom half of which was cantilevered inward at a 15-degree angle, a structural feature placed inside the park to create more room for pedestrians on the sidewalk outside. Outfielders would have difficulties playing caroms off the wall for the next 44 years. The odd shape of the field, with its short porch in right and canyonesque dimensions in left and center, was due to the block on which the ballpark was built (see January 2, 1912). There was an average of only 27 home runs per year struck at Ebbets Field from 1913 through 1920. Nearly all of them went over the right-field wall or were inside-the-park homers on balls driven into the large expanse in left and center fields. One significant omission was a press box. Ebbets removed two rows of seats behind home plate and roped off the area for the writers. A permanent press box wasn't built until 1929.

APRIL 14   Trailing 2–1 with two out in the ninth inning, Jake Daubert doubles and Red Smith homers to defeat the Giants 3–2 in New York.

Daubert and Smith were the Dodgers' best players in 1913. Daubert won the batting title with an average of .350. He also finished second in the NL in hits with 178 and his .405 on-base percentage was third in the league. Smith batted .296 and his 40 doubles led the majors.

APRIL 18   The second regular season game at Ebbets Field ends with the same result as the first, with the Dodgers losing 1–0 to the Phillies (see April 9, 1913). The contest also featured the same two starting pitchers, with Tom Seaton pitching a complete-game shutout and outdueling Nap Rucker.

APRIL 19   Amazingly, the third regular season game at Ebbets Field also results in a 1–0 loss to the Phillies. Philadelphia scored the winning run in the ninth inning.

APRIL 21   The Dodgers finally score a regular season run at Ebbets Field, but they lose 2–1 to the Phillies.

The Dodgers were shutout in their first 28 regular season innings at Ebbets Field and scored only one run in the first 39 innings.

APRIL 26   After four defeats and only one run in their first four regular season games at Ebbets Field, the Dodgers finally win with a 5–2 decision over the Giants. Casey Stengel, who hit the first homer in the first exhibition game at the new ballpark, also hit the first regular season homer.

APRIL 29   After holding the Giants hitless through the first seven innings and without a run through the first 12, Nap Rucker gives up six runs in the 13th inning to lose 6–0 at Ebbets Field.

MAY 1   Casey Stengel hits two inside-the-park home runs during a 4–2 win over the Braves at Ebbets Field. Stengel homered leading off the first inning and added the other one in the second.

MAY 11   Police prevent an exhibition game from being played on a Sunday at Ebbets Field. The Dodgers had planned to play the Brooklyn Lodge of Elks for the benefit of the Brooklyn Press Club, which had recently lost its home through a fire.

MAY 19   The Dodgers win 2–1 in 11 innings over the Cardinals at Ebbets Field. Red Smith drove in the winning run with a single. Earl Yingling pitched 10⅓ innings of relief, replacing Nap Rucker, who left in the first inning when struck in the hand by a line drive.

            The victory was the high point of the 1913 season. The Dodgers had a 19–9 record and were in a virtual tie for first place with the Phillies, who were 17–7. Brooklyn still had a record of 35–28 on July 2 before going 30–56 over the remainder of the campaign.

MAY 22   The game against the Pirates at Ebbets Field develops into a farce because of umpire Bill Klem's determination to finish the game despite the heavy rain that turned the field into a morass. The Pirates took a 1–0 lead in the fifth. During the inning, part of the rain-soaked crowd invaded the field, but when Klem threatened a forfeit, the fans went back to their seats. Klem finally called the game in the bottom of the sixth when Casey Stengel attempted to steal second and slid 15 feet in the mud beyond the base and was tagged out.

MAY 30   The Dodgers score two runs in the ninth inning to defeat the Braves 2–1 in the first game of a double-header in Boston. John Hummel tripled in the tying run and scored on Red Smith's single. The Dodgers won the second game 7–6. The games were played at Fenway Park. The Braves used the ballpark as a home field on a part-time basis from 1913 through 1915.

JUNE 5   Nap Rucker pitches a two-hitter and wins 4–0 over the Reds in Cincinnati. The only hits off Rucker were singles by Joe Tinker and Johnny Kling.

JUNE 9   The Dodgers explode for six runs in the ninth inning to defeat the Pirates 10–7 in Pittsburgh. Pinch-hitter Leo Callahan pulled the Dodgers within a run with a bases-loaded walk. Jake Daubert's single tied the score and Red Smith cleared the bases with a three-run double. Brooklyn won despite six errors from six different players.

JUNE 16   The Dodgers collect 20 hits and defeat the Cardinals 10–5 in St. Louis.

JUNE 23   Zack Wheat hits a two-run homer in the 10th inning to defeat the Giants 4–2 in the first game of a double-header in New York. The Giants won the second contest 5–1.

JUNE 25   The Dodgers score seven runs in the second inning to take an 8–3 lead, but they wind up losing 11–8 to the Phillies in Philadelphia.

JUNE 26   The Dodgers score three runs in the 14th inning to defeat the Phillies 5–2 in the first game of a double-header in Philadelphia. The Dodgers completed the sweep with a 4–2 triumph in the nightcap.

JULY 2   The Dodgers score nine runs in the third inning and overwhelm the Braves 15–3 at Ebbets Field.

JULY 3   The day after winning 15–3, the Dodgers lose 17–4 to the Braves in Boston.

JULY 14   The Dodgers break a 10-game losing streak with a 9–2 victory over the Cubs at Ebbets Field.

JULY 15   Ebbets Field is formally dedicated in ceremonies prior to a 9–6 loss to the Cubs. In the evening, Charles Ebbets hosted a banquet at Brighton Beach.

JULY 21   The Dodgers outslug the Pirates 13–6 at Ebbets Field. Brooklyn trailed 6–3 before scoring five runs in the seventh inning and five more in the eighth.

AUGUST 4   George Cutshaw hits two inside-the-park homers during a 7–1 win over the Cubs in Chicago. Cutshaw homered in the first and seventh innings.

                  A defensive standout and one of the best base stealers of the 1910s, Cutshaw was the Dodgers starting second baseman from 1912 through 1917.

AUGUST 5   The Dodgers trade Eddie Stack to the Cubs for Ed Reulbach.

                  Reulbach played in four World Series for the Cubs from 1906 through 1910 and had a 135–65 career record when acquired by the Dodgers. He showed flashes of his former brilliance while with the Dodgers, but he was on the downside of his career and posted an 18–24 mark in two seasons in Brooklyn.

AUGUST 10   Ed Reulbach pitches a two-hitter to defeat the Cardinals 3–0 in St. Louis. The only hits off Reulbach were singles by Ted Cather and Ivy Wingo.

AUGUST 13   The Dodgers score two runs in the ninth inning and one in the 10th to defeat the Pirates 4–3 in the first game of a double-header at Ebbets Field. Ed Reulbach pitched six innings of hitless relief. The Dodgers completed the sweep with a 7–3 victory in the second tilt.

AUGUST 16   After losing the first game of a double-header 1–0 to the Cardinals in St. Louis, the Dodgers come back with a vengeance to win the nightcap 14–5. Shortstop Tom Fisher collected two inside-the-park homers and a triple. Rookie catcher William Fischer hit his first big league home run. Casey Stengel also homered.

AUGUST 25   Jeff Pfeffer reports to the Dodgers following his purchase from Grand Rapids of the Central League.

                  Pfeffer was 25 years old and had previously pitched two games in the majors with the St. Louis Browns in 1911. He proved to be a tremendous acquisition. From 1914 through 1916, Pfeffer had a record of 67–37 for the Dodgers and was 113–80 with the club before being traded to the Cardinals in 1921. Pfeffer's earned run average of 2.31 as a Dodger ranks as the lowest all-time in franchise history among pitchers with at least 1,000 innings pitched. He is also seventh in complete games (157) and eighth in shutouts (25).

SEPTEMBER 6   Ed Reulbach pitches a two-hitter to defeat the Giants 2–0 at the Polo Grounds. The only New York hits were singles by Red Murray and George Burns.

SEPTEMBER 19   The Dodgers score two runs in the ninth inning to defeat the Reds 2–1 in the second game of a double-header in Cincinnati. Red Smith drove in the tying run with a double and scored on Tom Fisher's double. The Reds won the opener 1–0 in 10 innings.

SEPTEMBER 23   The Dodgers sweep the Pirates 6–1 and 1–0 in Pittsburgh. Nap Rucker pitched the second-game shutout. The lone run scored on a triple by Red Smith and a single from William Fischer.

SEPTEMBER 30   The Dodgers score nine runs in the top of the first inning, but they wind up losing 10–9 to the Phillies in the first game of a double-header in Philadelphia. The Phils scored five runs in the eighth inning to tie the contest 9–9 and won it in the ninth. Nap Rucker pitched the complete game. The Dodgers took the second tilt 3–1.

After the season ended, the Dodgers went on a barnstorming trip to Cuba, where they played 17 games.

NOVEMBER 18   The Dodgers hire 50-year-old Wilbert Robinson as manager to replace Bill Dahlen.

Robinson would manage the Dodgers for the next 18 seasons, which included appearances in the World Series in 1916 and 1920. Carrying 215 pounds on a five-foot-eight-inch frame, Robinson was a catcher in the majors leagues from 1886 through 1902 and played on the National League champion Orioles in 1894, 1895 and 1896. During that period, Robinson became a business partner with John McGraw, operating a saloon, a cafe, a billiards parlor and a bowling alley in Baltimore. Robinson became a full-time coach under McGraw with the Giants in 1911. The club won three straight pennants in 1911, 1912 and 1913 and Robinson was given considerable credit for developing the pitchers on the staff. McGraw fired Robinson, however, following a spat after the 1913 World Series. The two grew to despise one another, and the mutual enmity further intensified the rivalry between the Dodgers and Giants. McGraw managed the Giants during the entire 18-year period in which Robinson ran the Dodgers. Most of the teams that Robinson managed in Brooklyn were among the oldest in baseball. He preferred to acquire hard-drinking veterans, many rejected by other teams because they were too difficult to control, as opposed to fresh-faced youngsters from the minor leagues. The plan worked occasionally, as in 1916 and 1920, but the Dodgers finished in the lower half of the NL in 12 of Robinson's 18 years at the helm. Overall, the Dodgers were 1,375–1,341 with Robinson as manager. Discipline was usually lax, but win or lose, the team was almost always entertaining. Popular with sportswriters and the fans alike, Robinson became such a beloved figure in Brooklyn that the club was often referred to as the "Robins" in his honor. His kindly nature also earned him the nickname "Uncle Robbie." The club was also called the "Daffiness Boys" because lack of discipline under Robinson led to numerous mistakes on the field.

NOVEMBER 25   The Dodgers purchase Joe Tinker from the Reds.

Tinker played shortstop in four World Series for the Cubs from 1906 through 1910 and was part of the famous "Tinker to Evers to Chance" infield for those clubs. Although near the end of his career, Tinker was still an effective player and was expected to be the Dodgers starting shortstop in 1914. He refused to report to the Dodgers, however, and signed with the Chicago Whales of the new Federal League, which announced plans during the 1913–14 off-season to became a third major league. Franchises were created in Brooklyn, Baltimore, Buffalo, Chicago, Indianapolis, Kansas City, Pittsburgh and St. Louis. The Brooklyn entry played at a rebuilt Washington Park, which had served as the home of the Dodgers from 1898 through 1912. The Federal League immediately began to lure players from the established National and American Leagues with higher salaries. The Dodgers not only had competition from another team in Brooklyn but had their payroll increased significantly. The Federal League lasted two seasons, and during that period the Dodgers lost pitcher Frank Allen late in the 1914 season and pitcher Ed Reulbach and catcher William Fischer during the 1914–15 off-season. Nicknamed the Tip Tops, the Brooklyn club in the Federal League had a record of 77–77 in 1914 and 70–82 in 1915, finishing the season in fifth place in the first season and seventh in the second.

1914

Season in a Sentence

In Wilbert Robinson's first year as manager, the Dodgers are 75–79, a modest achievement that represents the club's best record in 11 years.

Finish • Won • Lost • Pct • GB

Fifth	75	79	.487	19.5

Manager

Wilbert Robinson

Stats

Stats	Dods	NL	Rank
Batting Avg:	.269	.251	1
On-Base Pct:	.323	.317	3
Slugging Pct:	.355	.334	2
Home Runs:	31		5
Stolen Bases:	173		4
ERA:	2.82	2.78	5
Fielding Avg:	.961	.958	5
Runs Scored:	622		4
Runs Allowed:	618		5

Starting Lineup

Lew McCarthy, c
Jake Daubert, 1b
George Cutshaw, 2b
Red Smith, 3b
Dick Egan, ss
Zack Wheat, lf
Jack Dalton, cf
Casey Stengel, rf
Ollie O'Mara, ss
Hy Myers, cf
Gus Getz, 3b
John Hummel, 1b-rf

Pitchers

Jeff Pfeffer, sp
Ed Reulbach, sp-rp
Pat Ragan, sp
Raleigh Aitchison, sp-rp
Frank Allen, sp-rp
Nap Rucker, sp

Attendance

122,671 (seventh in NL)

Club Leaders

Batting Avg:	Jake Daubert	.329
On-Base Pct:	Casey Stengel	.404
Slugging Pct:	Zack Wheat	.452
Home Runs:	Zack Wheat	9
RBIs:	Zack Wheat	89
Runs:	Jake Daubert	89
Stolen Bases:	George Cutshaw	34
Wins:	Jeff Pfeffer	23
Strikeouts:	Jeff Pfeffer	135
ERA:	Jeff Pfeffer	1.97
Saves:	Jeff Pfeffer	4

FEBRUARY 14   The Dodgers sign Kid Elberfield as a free agent.

APRIL 14   In Wilbert Robinson's debut as manager, the Dodgers open the season with an 8–2 win over the Braves before 12,000 at Ebbets Field. Ed Reulbach was the winning pitcher.

MAY 9   The Dodgers rout the Phillies 14–3 in Philadelphia.

MAY 11   The Brooklyn Tip Tops of the Federal League play their first game at Washington Park and lose 2–0 to Pittsburgh before a crowd of 15,000. The Ward brothers, who were millionaire bakers, owned the Brooklyn franchise and called the club the Tip Tops after their packaged bread.

> *After drawing 243,000 in their last season at Washington Park in 1912, the Dodgers attracted an attendance of 347,000 at Ebbets Field in 1913. Competition from another major league club in Brooklyn proved costly, as the Dodgers drew only 122,671 fans in 1914.*

JUNE 1   Trailing 2–1 in the sixth inning, pitcher Frank Allen hits a three-run triple to beat the Braves 4–2 in the second game of a double-header at Ebbets Field. The Dodgers also won the opener 6–2.

JUNE 14   Ollie O'Mara mixes it up with Cardinals player-manager Miller Huggins during a 2–1 loss at Ebbets Field. Huggins tried to knock the ball out of O'Mara's hands during a tag play at second base. Umpire Bill Byron stepped between them. Neither player was ejected.

JUNE 17   Jeff Pfeffer pitches a 10-inning complete game in which he allows only three hits to defeat the Reds 2–1 at Ebbets Field.

> *Pfeffer was 23–12 with a 1.97 ERA in 1914. He completed 27 of his 34 starts and finished all nine of his relief appearances, earning four saves.*

JULY 4   Six days after the assassination of Archduke Ferdinand of Austria, an event which precipitates the start of World War I in August, the Dodgers defeat the Braves 7–5 and 4–3 in a double-header at Boston. The opener, played in the morning, went 11 innings. In the afternoon tilt, the winning run scored in the ninth. With the score 3–3, Jake Daubert reached first base on a force out and attempted to steal second. The throw from Boston catcher Hank Gowdy sailed past both second baseman Johnny Evers and center fielder Josh Devore. Daubert tried to score on the play and was safe with a hard slide, but his head struck one of Gowdy's shinguards and the Brooklyn first baseman was knocked unconscious.

> *Daubert recovered to win his second consecutive batting title, with an average of .329. He also scored 89 runs to rank third in the NL. Four of the top five finishers in Batting Avg: in 1914 were Dodgers. Jack Dalton and Zack Wheat both batted .319 and Casey Stengel hit .316. Stengel also led the National League in on-base percentage with a figure of .404. Wheat had 170 hits and 89 RBIs. The Dodgers of this period were an aggressive lot at the plate. The club's hitters ranked last or next to last in walks 10 consecutive seasons,*

*finishing eighth in the NL in 1913, 1914, 1915, 1918, 1919 and 1922, and
seventh in 1916, 1917, 1920 and 1921.*

JULY 17   Frank Allen pitches a one-hitter, but loses 3–2 to the Cubs in Chicago. Four
                 Brooklyn errors, one by Allen himself, led to two Cubs runs in the fourth to tie the
                 score 2–2. The winning run in the seventh scored on a double by Wilbur Good,
                 another error and a sacrifice fly.

AUGUST 1   The Dodgers sweep the Pirates 7–1 and 10–1 at Ebbets Field. The Dodgers scored
                 eight runs in the second inning of the second game.

AUGUST 3   Ed Konetchy of the Pirates hits the first grand slam at Ebbets Field during a 7–3 win
                 over the Dodgers. Konetchy's blast was struck in the 13th inning.

AUGUST 4   Jeff Pfeffer pitches the Dodgers to a 1–0 win over the Cardinals at Ebbets Field. The
                 lone run scored on a walk-off single from Jake Daubert with two out in the ninth.

AUGUST 10   The Dodgers sell Red Smith to the Braves.

                 *The Dodgers made a huge mistake in selling Smith. He helped the Braves win
                 the pennant in 1914 with excellent play during a stretch drive in which the club
                 leaped from a last-place predicament on July 19 to first place by winning 60 of
                 their last 77 games. Smith was Boston's starting third baseman until 1918.*

AUGUST 15   On the day of the opening of the Panama Canal, the Dodgers sweep the Phillies 4–3
                 and 13–5 at Ebbets Field. In the second game, Jake Daubert tied a major league
                 record with four sacrifices. The Dodgers scored in seven of eight innings before the
                 contest was called on account of darkness at the end of the eighth. Shortstop Gus
                 Getz, playing in his second game with the Dodgers, collected four hits in four at-bats.

AUGUST 16   Ed Reulbach holds the Reds hitless for the first seven innings of a 6–3 win over the
                 Reds in Cincinnati. The first hit off Reulbach was a single by Bert Daniels leading off
                 the eighth. Reulbach gave up three runs and three hits in the ninth.

AUGUST 27   Ed Reulbach pitches a 10-inning complete game to defeat the Pirates 1–0 in
                 Pittsburgh. Casey Stengel drove in the winning run with a single.

SEPTEMBER 21   Trailing 5–1, the Dodgers score seven runs in the sixth inning and beat the Reds
                 9–6 in the first game of a double-header at Ebbets Field. The Dodgers completed the
                 sweep with an 8–2 victory in the second tilt.

SEPTEMBER 26   The Dodgers extend their winning streak to 11 games with a 6–3 decision over
                 the Cardinals in the first game of a double-header at Ebbets Field. The streak was
                 stopped by a 3–0 defeat in the nightcap.

                 *The 11-game winning streak came too late to prevent the Dodgers from
                 recording their 11th consecutive losing season. Still, the 75–79 record of 1914
                 was the club's best since 1903.*

SEPTEMBER 28   George Cutshaw hits a grand slam off Slim Sallee in the first inning of a 7–3 win over the Cardinals at Ebbets Field. The slam was the first by a Dodger player at the historic ballpark.

OCTOBER 5   Dodgers pitcher Pat Ragan strikes out three batters on the minimum nine pitches in the eighth inning, but he gives up five runs in the ninth to lose 9–5 to the Braves in the second game of a double-header at Ebbets Field. The Dodgers lost the opener 15–2.

Ragan met his wife in unusual fashion. While a minor leaguer in Omaha, Nebraska, a newspaper took a photograph of a group of young women wearing the club's uniforms. Ragan was fascinated with the woman who donned his jersey and arranged to meet her. Soon after, the two were married.

OCTOBER 6   On the final day of the season, Jeff Pfeffer wins his 23rd game of 1914 with a 3–2 decision over the Braves at Ebbets Field. The Dodgers lost the second contest, called after seven innings by darkness, 7–3.

1915

LA

Season in a Sentence

The Dodgers are only one game out of first place on September 7 and finish the season with a winning record for the first time in 12 years.

Finish • Won • Lost • Pct • GB

Third   80   72   .526   10.0

Manager

Wilbert Robinson

Stats

Stats	Dods	NL	Rank
Batting Avg:	.248	.248	5
On-Base Pct:	.295	.309	8
Slugging Pct:	.317	.331	8
Home Runs:	14		8
Stolen Bases:	131		6
ERA:	2.66	2.74	4
Fielding Avg:	.963	.964	6
Runs Scored:	536		7
Runs Allowed:	560		4

Starting Lineup

Otto Miller, c
Jake Daubert, 1b
George Cutshaw, 2b
Gus Getz, 3b
Ollie O'Mara, ss
Zack Wheat, lf
Hy Myers, cf
Casey Stengel, rf
Lew McCarty, c

Pitchers

Jeff Pfeffer, sp
Jack Coombs, sp
Sherry Smith, sp-rp
Wheezer Dell, sp-rp
Nap Rucker, sp
Phil Douglas, sp-rp
Pete Appleton, rp

Attendance

247,766 (fourth in NL)

Club Leaders

Batting Avg:	Jake Daubert	.301
On-Base Pct:	Jake Daubert	.368
Slugging Pct:	Jake Daubert	.381
Home Runs:	Zack Wheat	5
RBIs:	Zack Wheat	66
Runs:	Ollie O'Mara	77
Wins:	Jeff Pfeffer	19
Strikeouts:	Wheezer Dell	94
ERA:	Jeff Pfeffer	2.10
Saves:	Jeff Pfeffer	3

FEBRUARY 22   The Dodgers sell Fred Toney to the Reds.

Toney had been chosen by the Dodgers in the minor-league draft the previous November. He was 26 years old and had three unimpressive seasons as a pitcher with the Cubs from 1911 through 1913. Toney balked at the salary the Dodgers were offering and made threats about signing with the Federal League. To help recoup the money spent on drafting Toney, the Dodgers sold him to the Reds. It proved to be a huge mistake and ranks as the worst player transaction made by the Dodgers during the 1910s. Toney had a 135–97 major league record after 1915 and won 24 games for the Reds in 1917 and 21 for the Giants in 1920.

MARCH 13   Wilbert Robinson attempts to catch a baseball dropped from an airplane in Daytona Beach, Florida, during spring training.

Billy Sullivan of the Cubs in 1894 and Gabby Street of the Senators in 1908 had both caught balls dropped from the window of the Washington Monument, a little over 500 feet above the ground. A former catcher, Robinson had long been intrigued by the stunts. During the Dodgers spring training encampment at Daytona Beach in 1915, female aviator Ruth Law had been dropping golf balls as a publicity gimmick for a local golf course. Airplanes were still a novelty in 1915. The Wright Brothers' first successful flight was only a little more than 11 years earlier, in December 1903. Although he was 51 years old, Robinson bragged that he could catch a baseball dropped from Law's plane. She agreed to drop the ball, but upon reaching the plane, Law realized she had forgotten to bring along the ball. At the last minute, she substituted a grapefruit from the lunch of one of her ground crew. The grapefruit was dropped from a height of about 500 feet with Robinson standing on the beach. The fruit struck Robinson in the arm and exploded all over his chest. Thinking he was covered in his own blood, Robinson cried out for help, but drew nothing but laughter from onlookers. Casey Stengel later claimed credit for exchanging the baseball with a grapefruit, but Law always insisted it was her idea.

APRIL 14   The Dodgers open the season with a 16–3 loss to the Giants in New York. Jeff Pfeffer was the starting pitcher and allowed seven runs in two innings.

APRIL 15   Giants hurler Rube Marquard pitches a no-hitter and beats the Dodgers 2–0 in New York. Marquard walked two and struck out two.

APRIL 22   The Dodgers defeat the Giants 6–4 in the home opener at Ebbets Field. Rube Marquard was the losing pitcher in his first appearance since his no-hitter.

MAY 14   Seven days after the sinking of the *Lusitania* by a German submarine, the Cubs take a 17–0 lead after five innings and wallop the Dodgers 19–4 at Ebbets Field.

MAY 15   Wheezer Dell pitches a two-hitter and defeats the Reds 7–1 at Ebbets Field. The only Cincinnati hits were singles by Fritz Mollwitz in the second inning and Tommy Griffith in the seventh.

Dell was a 29-year-old rookie in 1915 and won 11 games, but he never reached that figure again. He stood six-foot-four, which made him one of the tallest players of the period. Dell also holds the distinction of being the first individual born in Nevada to play in the majors.

JUNE 1   Zack Wheat stars in an 11-inning, 5–4 victory over the Phillies at Ebbets Field. Philadelphia scored twice in the ninth for a 4–3 lead. Wheat stepped to the plate with two out in the bottom of the inning and hit a two-strike pitch for an inside-the-park homer to left field. Wheat also drove in the game-winning with a walk-off single in the 11th.

JUNE 10   The Dodgers and Reds battle 14 innings to a 2–2 tie at Ebbets Field. The contest was called on account of darkness. Wheezer Dell of the Dodgers and Gene Dale of the Reds both pitched complete games.

JUNE 11   The day after a 14-inning tie game, the Dodgers lose 1–0 in 15 innings to the Reds in Cincinnati. Ed Appleton of the Dodgers and Rube Benton of the Reds both pitched complete games. The winning run scored on a walk-off single by Tommy Griffith.

JUNE 13   The Dodgers purchase Phil Douglas from the Reds.

JUNE 17   The Dodgers battle the Cubs for 19 innings before losing 4–3 in Chicago. Jeff Pfeffer pitched a complete game, only to wind up with the defeat. Zip Zabel was the winning pitcher, hurling 18$\frac{1}{3}$ innings in the longest relief assignment in major league history. Zabel entered the game for starter Bert Humphries, who left with two out in the first inning after being struck in the hand by a line drive off the bat off Zack Wheat. Both teams scored in the 15th inning. The winning run scored on a single by Tom Fisher, a sacrifice and a throwing error by second baseman George Cutshaw.

             Pfeffer was 19–14 with six shutouts and a 2.10 ERA in 291$\frac{1}{3}$ innings in 1915. He completed 26 of his 34 starts.

JUNE 26   The only base runner off Grover Alexander in a 4–0 loss to the Phillies in Philadelphia is Zack Wheat, who singles in the eighth inning.

JUNE 29   The Dodgers drop into last place with a 5–4 loss to the Phillies in Philadelphia. The defeat left the club with a 26–34 record and 9$\frac{1}{2}$ games behind the first-place Cubs.

JUNE 30   Jeff Pfeffer pitches a two-hitter to defeat the Giants 7–0 at Ebbets Field. The Dodgers broke open a close game in a six-run rally in the eighth inning that included seven consecutive singles from Pfeffer, Hy Myers, Ollie O'Mara, Jake Daubert, Zack Wheat, George Cutshaw and Bill Zimmerman. The only New York hits were singles by Eddie Grant and Fred Snodgrass.

             Daubert had a .301 Batting Avg: in 1915. He was the only individual on the Dodgers roster with at least 150 at-bats to hit higher than .258.

JULY 7   After the Dodgers defeat the Braves 4–3 in the first game of a double-header at Ebbets Field, the two clubs battle 16 innings to a 0–0 tie in the second tilt. Phil Douglas pitched a complete game for the Dodgers. In addition to the 16-inning shutout, he allowed only one hit through the first nine innings and just four altogether, but he didn't get credit for a victory. Bill James (five innings) and George Davis (11 innings) pitched for Boston.

             In less than a month, the Dodgers played games of 14, 15, 16 and 19 innings. They came away with two losses and two ties.

JULY 9 — Down 7–1, the Dodgers score a run in the fourth inning, four in the sixth, one in the seventh and one in the 10th for an 8–7 win over the Cubs at Ebbets Field. The winning run scored on consecutive doubles by Ollie O'Mara and Jake Daubert.

JULY 12 — The Dodgers extend their winning streak to eight games with a 3–2 decision over the Cubs at Ebbets Field.

JULY 17 — The Dodgers purchase Ivy Olson from the Reds.

When acquired by the Dodgers, Olson was a 29-year-old journeyman shortstop. He found a home in Brooklyn, however, and was the Dodgers starter at short from 1916 through 1922, a period that included two World Series appearances. Olson led the NL in hits in 1919.

JULY 19 — Less than three weeks after residing in eighth place, the Dodgers move into a tie for second with a 3–0 decision over the Pirates at Ebbets Field. The victory gave the Dodgers a 43–37 record and put them just one game behind the first place Phillies. Hy Myers extended his hitting streak to 23 games during the contest.

Myers played 1,166 games for the Dodgers in 1909, 1911 and from 1914 through 1922. His 97 triples ranks third all-time in franchise history behind Zack Wheat and Willie Davis. Myers led the National League in triples, slugging percentage and RBIs in 1919 and triples again in 1920.

JULY 22 — The Dodgers win 1–0 and lose 11–1 during a double-header against the Cardinals at Ebbets Field. Sherry Smith pitched the first game shutout.

Smith was 14–8 as a 24-year-old rookie for the Dodgers in 1915. He was 69–70 over eight seasons in Brooklyn, and his 2.91 ERA with the club is sixth best all-time among pitchers with at least 1,000 innings.

JULY 26 — Facing Slim Sallee of the Cardinals, lead-off batter Hy Myers hits the first pitch of the first inning for a home run sparking a 13–8 Dodgers victory at Ebbets Field.

The Dodgers had a record of 22–5 from June 29 through July 26.

AUGUST 7 — Cardinals manager Miller Huggins dupes Dodgers rookie pitcher Ed Appleton into an error in the seventh inning of a 6–4 loss in St. Louis. As Appleton stepped to the mound with the score tied 4–4 and Cardinal runner Dots Miller at third base, Huggins, coaching at third, called for the ball. Appleton obliged, Huggins stepped aside and Miller scored.

A change in the rules prevented such trickery in the future.

AUGUST 8 — The Dodgers sweep the Cubs 10–7 and 5–4 in Chicago. In the second game, Brooklyn scored two runs in the ninth inning and one in the 11th for the victory. Jake Daubert scored the winning run following a double and fly balls by Zack Wheat and George Cutshaw.

AUGUST 9 — George Cutshaw collects six hits in six at-bats during a 13–0 win over the Cubs in Chicago. All six hits were singles off George Pearce and Pete Standridge.

The Dodgers outhit the Cubs 23–2. Jeff Pfeffer pitched the shutout. The only Chicago hits were singles by Wilbur Good in the first inning and Jimmy Archer in the second.

AUGUST 19   The Dodgers move within two percentage points of the first-place Phillies with a 6–5 win over the Cubs at Ebbets Field.

AUGUST 20   After the Cubs score in the top of the 10th inning, the Dodgers win 6–5 on Zack Wheat's two-run, walk-off double in the bottom half.

AUGUST 21   Wheezer Dell pitches the Dodgers to a 1–0 win over the Reds in the second game of a double-header at Ebbets Field. The lone run scored in the third inning on a suicide squeeze by Ivy Olson that scored Lew McCarty from third base. Cincinnati won the opener 4–1.

AUGUST 31   The Dodgers purchase Rube Marquard from the Giants and Larry Cheney from the Cubs.

The Dodgers picked up two veteran pitchers for the stretch pennant run. It didn't help in 1915, but the Dodgers couldn't have reached the World Series in 1916 without Marquard and Cheney. Marquard had a record of 73–28 for the Giants from 1911 through 1913 while Wilbert Robinson was a coach for the team, but he fell to 12–22 in 1914 and still struggled in 1915, despite a no-hitter against the Dodgers earlier in the season (see April 15, 1915). The Dodgers manager had a knack for squeezing a few more seasons out of aging arms, and Marquard and Cheney are cases in point. Marquard's career underwent a revival after rejoining Robinson and was 13–6 for the Dodgers in 1916 and 19–12 in 1917. Marquard was still in the starting rotation for the club during the pennant-winning season of 1920. He finished his career at 201–177 and was elected to the Hall of Fame. Cheney also put together a brilliant three-year period in the majors. From 1912 through 1914, he had a record of 67–42 for the Cubs and also saved 16 games, 11 of them in 1913 to lead the league. Pitching over 300 innings a year as both a starter and a reliever was too much of a strain and, like Marquard, Cheney was struggling when acquired by the Dodgers. Cheney had one great season in Brooklyn, posting an 18–12 mark in 1916.

SEPTEMBER 2   The Dodgers play the Braves at Braves Field in Boston for the first time and score six times in the first inning to spark a 10–1 win.

Braves Field served as the home of the Boston Braves through the end of the 1952 season. The club moved to Milwaukee in March 1953.

SEPTEMBER 4   The only Dodger base runner off Braves pitcher Art Nehf during a 6–0 loss to the Braves in Boston is Otto Miller, who singles in the eighth inning. Miller's fly ball fell safely after right fielder Pete Compton lost it in the sun. Miller was retired during a double play and Nehf faced the minimum 27 batters.

SEPTEMBER 7   The Dodgers pull within one game of first place with a 7–1 win over the Phillies at Ebbets Field.

The win gave the Dodgers a record of 70–59. The club was only 10–13 over the remainder of the season, however, and finished in third place, 10 games behind Philadelphia.

SEPTEMBER 8   The Dodgers sell Phil Douglas to the Cubs.

SEPTEMBER 9   The Dodgers collect only one hit off Braves hurler Lefty Tyler, but they win 1–0 at
               Ebbets Field behind a two-hitter from Jeff Pfeffer. Brooklyn scored in the second
               inning on a walk to Hy Myers, a single from Gus Getz, a double steal and an infield
               out by Al Nixon. The only Boston hits were singles by Herbie Moran in the fourth
               inning and Dick Egan in the eighth.

SEPTEMBER 16   The Dodgers take a tough 12-inning, 1–0 loss at the hands of the Cubs in Chicago to
               fall 5½ games out of first place. Jeff Pfeffer pitched a complete game.

OCTOBER 4   The Dodgers win 3–2 over the Phillies in a contest in Philadelphia that lasts only an
               hour and three minutes.

1916

Season in a Sentence

The Dodgers stun the baseball world by winning their first National League pennant in 16 years before losing the World Series to the Red Sox.

Finish • Won • Lost • Pct • GB

First   94   60   .610   +2.0

World Series

The Dodgers lost four games to one to the Boston Red Sox.

Manager

Wilbert Robinson

Stats

Stats	Dods	NL	Rank
Batting Avg:	.261	.247	1
On-Base Pct:	.313	.303	1
Slugging Pct:	.345	.328	1
Home Runs:	28		4
Stolen Bases:	187		2
ERA:	2.12		1
Fielding Avg:	.965	.963	4
Runs Scored:	585		2
Runs Allowed:	471		2

Starting Lineup

Chief Meyers, c
Jake Daubert, 1b
George Cutshaw, 2b
Mike Mowrey, 3b
Ivy Olson, ss
Zack Wheat, lf
Hy Myers, cf
Casey Stengel, rf
Jimmy Johnston, rf-cf
Otto Miller, c

Pitchers

Jeff Pfeffer, sp
Larry Cheney, sp
Sherry Smith, sp
Jack Coombs, sp
Wheezer Dell, sp

Attendance

477,747 (fourth in NL)

Club Leaders

Batting Avg:	Jake Daubert	.316
On-Base Pct:	Jake Daubert	.371
Slugging Pct:	Zack Wheat	.461
Home Runs:	Zack Wheat	9
RBIs:	Zack Wheat	73
Runs:	Zack Wheat	76
Stolen Bases:	George Cutshaw	27
Wins:	Jeff Pfeffer	25
Strikeouts:	Larry Cheney	166
ERA:	Rube Marquard	1.58
Saves:	Rube Marquard	5

FEBRUARY 10   The Dodgers purchase Chief Meyers from the Giants.

Like nearly every other player of Native American descent during the late 19th and early 20th centuries, John Torres Meyers was nicknamed "Chief." One of the best catchers in baseball during the first half of the 1910s, Meyers hit over .300 in each of the Giants three consecutive pennant-winning seasons of 1911, 1912 and 1913. He was near the end of his career when acquired by the Dodgers, but he had enough left to help the club reach the World Series in 1916.

APRIL 12   The Dodgers open the season with a 5–1 loss to the Braves before 10,000 at Ebbets Field. Larry Cheney was the losing pitcher.

Cheney was 18–12 with a 1.97 ERA in 1916 and struck out 166 batters in 253 innings.

APRIL 21   A fistfight between rival shortstops Ivy Olson of the Dodgers and Rabbit Maranville of the Braves highlights a 10–3 Brooklyn victory in Boston. The fight occurred in the first inning after Maranville lunged at Olson after a tag play at third. Both were ejected.

The Dodgers wore unique uniforms both home and away in 1916. The shirts and pants had both vertical and horizontal blue pinstriping, creating a cross-hatched or window-pane pattern. The Dodgers wore similar uniforms in 1907. Despite winning the pennant in 1916, the club abandoned the cross-hatched design after only one season and went back to a more traditional uniform in 1917.

MAY 6   George Cutshaw hits a freak home run to close out a 3–2 win over the Phillies at Ebbets Field. With the score 2–2 in the 11th inning, Cutshaw hit a drive that landed in front of the right-field wall just inside the foul line. The ball bounced crazily off the ground, struck the bottom half of the angled wall in right and went up and over the barrier onto Bedford Avenue.

When the Dodgers leaped into first place early in the 1916 season, New York-area sportswriters began calling the club the Robins in honor of manager Wilbert Robinson. The writers also called the Brooklyn team the Superbas and the Dodgers as well. At times, two nicknames, and even all three, were used in the same newspaper stories. Club management did not recognize any of these monikers, and therefore the team had no official nickname.

MAY 17   The Dodgers play at Wrigley Field for the first time and lose 7–2 to the Cubs.

Known as Weeghman Park in its early days, Wrigley Field opened in 1914 for the Federal League Chicago Whales. The Cubs moved into the facility in 1916 after the Federal League folded.

MAY 27   The Dodgers score six runs in the ninth inning to defeat the Phillies 8–3 in the first game of a double-header in Philadelphia. Brooklyn completed the sweep with a 6–0 triumph in the nightcap.

MAY 30	The Dodgers defeat the Braves 1–0 in the second game of a double-header at Ebbets Field. Sherry Smith pitched the shutout. Chief Meyers drove in the lone run with a single in the seventh inning. Boston won the opener 5–3.
JUNE 13	Jeff Pfeffer pitches a two-hitter to defeat the Cardinals 3–1 at Ebbets Field. The only St. Louis hits were singles by Bill Long and Rogers Hornsby.

Pfeffer had an outstanding season in 1916 with a 25–11 record, six shutouts, 30 complete games in 36 starts and a 1.92 ERA on 328²/₃ innings.

JUNE 14	Left fielder Zack Wheat boots a ball into the stands for a home run during an 8–5 win over the Cardinals at Ebbets Field. In the fourth inning, Bruno Betzel hit a ball past Brooklyn third baseman Mike Mowrey. In racing over to field it, Wheat accidentally kicked the ball into the stands along the third-base line. According to the rules of the day, the hit was called a home run. The homer was the first of only two that Betzel collected during a five-year career in which he had 1,444 at-bats.

Wheat's 262 total bases led the National league in 1916. He also hit .312 and collected 32 doubles and 177 hits. Jake Daubert batted .316 and Casey Stengel had an average of .279.

JUNE 22	Jeff Pfeffer pitches his second two-hitter in 10 days to down the Phillies 5–0 in the first game of a double-header at Ebbets Field. The only Philadelphia hits were a double by Bert Niehoff and a single from Dode Paskert.
JUNE 26	The Dodgers score eight runs after two are out in the fifth inning but lose 11–8 to the Giants in the first game of a double-header at Ebbets Field. The Dodgers trailed 6–0 before breaking loose for the eight-run rally on a home run by George Cutshaw, two doubles and five singles. The Giants came back to win on a run in the sixth inning and four in the seventh. The Dodgers recovered to take the second contest 2–1 in 12 innings. The winning run scored on a suicide squeeze by pinch-hitter Lew McCarty that scored Cutshaw from third base.
JULY 16	The Dodgers and Cubs play to a 16-inning tie called by darkness in Chicago with the score 7–7. The Cubs tied the game 4–4 with three runs in the ninth. After the Dodgers plated three tallies in the 10th, the Cubs came back with three in their half.
JULY 18	The Dodgers win by forfeit when Cubs manager Joe Tinker refuses to leave the field. With the score 4–4 in the 10th inning in Chicago, umpire Bill Byron called a balk on hurler Hippo Vaughn for delaying the game after he held the ball and refused to throw a pitch. Tinker voiced a violent protest. Byron gave Tinker 60 seconds to leave the field, and when Tinker failed to vacate the premises, Byron awarded the contest to the Dodgers.
JULY 22	The Dodgers sweep the Pirates 7–1 and 3–2 in a double-header in Pittsburgh. The second game went 15 innings. Both teams scored in the 14th. The winning run scored on a sacrifice fly by Mike Mowrey. Larry Cheney (10 innings) and Rube Marquard (five innings) pitched for the Dodgers.
JULY 28	The Dodgers overcome a five-run deficit to defeat the Cardinals 9–5 at Ebbets Field. St. Louis scored five runs in the top of the second inning for a 5–0 lead, but the

Dodgers countered with five tallies in the bottom half and broke the deadlock with four runs in the eighth.

AUGUST 5   The Dodgers extend their winning streak to eight games with a 4–0 win over the Pirates in the first game of a double-header at Ebbets Field. The streak was broken with a 7–1 defeat in the second tilt.

AUGUST 9   Larry Cheney pitches a two-hitter to defeat the Cubs 6–0 at Ebbets Field. The only Chicago hits were singles by Vic Saier and Joe Kelly.

AUGUST 11   The Dodgers take a five-game lead in the National League pennant race with a 2–1 and 4–1 double-header sweep over the Cubs at Ebbets Field. The twin victories gave the Dodgers a record of 62–35.

AUGUST 19   George Cutshaw is both the hero and the goat during a double-header against the Pirates in Pittsburgh. In the opener, his throwing error in the 10th inning led to the winning run in a 2–1 defeat. In the second tilt, Cutshaw drove in the lone run of a 1–0 triumph with a sacrifice fly in the fourth inning. Rube Marquard pitched the shutout.

AUGUST 20   Jack Coombs pitches a one-hitter to defeat the Cubs 1–0 in Chicago. The only hit off Coombs was a single by Max Flack in the seventh inning. It was the Dodgers second consecutive 1–0 victory. The lone run scored in the third inning on a triple by Zack Wheat and a wild pitch.

Coombs had a 31–9 record for the Philadelphia Athletics in 1910 and won 28 games in 1912 and 21 in 1913. His career seemed over when late in the 1913 season he was stricken by typhoid fever, a disease which nearly killed him. Coombs missed nearly all of 1914 before joining the Dodgers, where he was 15–10 in 1915 and 13–8 in 1916.

AUGUST 25   The Dodgers purchase Fred Merkle from the Giants for Lew McCarty.

Merkle is best known for his base-running gaffe that cost the Giants the National League pennant in 1908, but he played in 1,583 big-league games after that season and appeared in five World Series, including one with the Dodgers in 1916. Unfortunately, Merkle was on the losing side in all five Fall Classics. The others were with the Giants in 1911, 1912 and 1913 and the Cubs in 1918.

AUGUST 27   The Dodgers score six runs in the fifth inning for an 11–3 lead and outslug the Reds 13–6 in Cincinnati.

SEPTEMBER 6 The reeling Dodgers fall out of first place behind the Phillies after splitting a double-header against the Giants in New York. The Dodgers lost 4–1 and won 2–1.

After taking a five-game lead in the National league pennant race on August 11, the Dodgers lost 16 of 28 games from August 12 through September 7.

SEPTEMBER 9 The Dodgers regain sole possession of first place with a 5–0 win over the Braves in Boston.

SEPTEMBER 14   Larry Cheney wins his own game with a walk-off double off Burleigh Grimes in the ninth inning to defeat the Pirates 3–2 at Ebbets Field.

SEPTEMBER 15   The Dodgers score eight runs in the second inning and defeat the Pirates 8–1 in a contest at Ebbets Field called after five innings by rain. The big inning was highlighted by an inside-the-park grand slam by Zack Wheat that was hit over the head of left fielder Bill Hinchman. The hit extended Wheat's hitting streak to 28 games.

SEPTEMBER 16   Zack Wheat extends his hitting streak to 29 games during a 4–3 win over the Reds in the first game of a double-header at Ebbets Field. The streak was stopped in the nightcap when he was hitless in four at-bats against Fred Toney. The contest ended in a 1–1 tie when called by darkness after 12 innings.

Wheat's hitting streak is the second-longest in Dodgers history. The only longer one was a 31-game streak by Willie Davis in 1969.

SEPTEMBER 22   The Dodgers rout the Cardinals 11–1 at Ebbets Field. In the eighth inning, Jimmy Johnston stole second, third and home. The steal of home was recorded as part of a double steal in conjunction with Jim Hickman, who swiped second.

Johnston was a popular member of the Dodgers from 1916 through 1925. Known for his versatility, Johnston played seven positions with the club, with 434 games at third base, 237 at second, 178 at shortstop, 167 in right field, 82 in center, 68 in left and 49 at first base.

SEPTEMBER 28   In the first game of a pennant-showdown series against the Phillies at Ebbets Field, the Dodgers lose 8–4. The defeat cut Brooklyn's lead to one-half game with Philadelphia one game up in the loss column. The Dodgers were 90–58 and the Phillies 88–57.

SEPTEMBER 30   After a postponement due to rain on September 29, the Dodgers and Phillies play a morning-afternoon double-header with separate admissions at Ebbets Field. The Phillies won the first game 7–2 to take over first place by one-half game. The Dodgers regained the top spot in the National League with a 6–2 victory in the second contest.

OCTOBER 2   The Dodgers take a one-game lead over the Phillies in the pennant race with a 2–0 triumph over the Giants at Ebbets Field. Jack Coombs pitched the shutout.

The Giants won a major league record 26 games in a row from September 7 through September 30.

OCTOBER 3   The Dodgers clinch the National League pennant with a 9–6 win over the Giants at Ebbets Field, while the Phillies lose both ends of a double-header to the Braves in Philadelphia by scores of 6–3 and 6–1. The Giants scored three runs in the first inning on a misplayed fly ball and three Dodgers errors, two by pitcher Sherry Smith. New York took a 4–1 lead in the top of the third, but the Dodgers responded with four tallies in the bottom half to pull ahead 5–4. After the Giants tied the game 5–5, the Dodgers scored in the fifth for a lead the club never relinquished. Jeff Pfeffer pitched six innings of relief for his 25th victory of the season. New York manager

John McGraw created controversy when he left the bench in the fifth inning and did not return. After the game, he told the press that his runners had ignored his signals and that pitcher Pol Perritt had allowed the Dodgers to steal bases by using an exaggerated motion with men on base. McGraw stopped short of saying his club threw the game. For the record, the Dodgers stole only two bases, with one caught stealing and another picked off first base, and the Giants left only four runners on base while scoring six times. Wilbert Robinson was succinct when he told reporters: "We beat the Giants 15 times in 22 games. Tell McGraw to stop pissing on my pennant."

The Dodgers played the Boston Red Sox in the World Series. Managed by Bill Carrigan, the Red Sox were 91–63 in 1916. The club was gunning for its third world championship in five years and the second in a row. The Sox defeated the Giants in the 1912 Fall Classic and the Phillies in 1915. Some of Boston's top hitters in 1916 were left-handed, which caused Wilbert Robinson to alter the Brooklyn starting rotation. In a questionable strategy, the Dodgers manager moved staff ace Jeff Pfeffer, who had a 25–11 record during the season, to the bullpen. Larry Cheney's (18–12) only appearance against the Red Sox was a three-inning relief stint. The starters in Games One and Two were southpaws Rube Marquard (13–6) and Sherry Smith (14–10). Right-hander Jack Coombs (13–8) was the starting pitcher in Game Three because of his prior experience in the post-season. Coombs had a 4–0 record for the Athletics in the 1910 and 1911 Fall Classics. Marquard, Smith and Coombs combined for a 1–3 record with a 3.82 ERA in 30²/₃ innings during the 1916 World Series.

OCTOBER 7
The Dodgers open the World Series with a 6–5 loss to the Red Sox before 36,117 at Braves Field. The Sox broke a 1–1 tie with a run in the fifth inning, then added three in the seventh and one in the eighth for a 6–1 lead. The Dodgers scored four in the ninth. The first two runs scored on two singles, a walk and an error. Fred Merkle drew a bases-loaded walk to make the score 6–4. Hy Myers's two-out single pulled Brooklyn within a run, but the game ended when shortstop Everett Scott made a great stop deep in the hole on a ground ball and threw to first to retire Jake Daubert by half a step to end the game.

The Red Sox played both the 1915 and 1916 seasons at Braves Field because it had a larger seating capacity than Fenway Park.

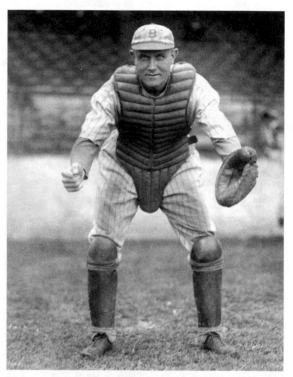

Never a great hitter, Otto Miller specialized in getting hitters out as a Dodger catcher for 13 seasons. He was a leader on the pennant-winning team of 1916.

OCTOBER 9   After an off day on Sunday, the Red Sox edge the Dodgers 2–1 in 14 innings in Boston. Babe Ruth and Sherry Smith both pitched complete games. Ruth was then 22 years old, in his second big-league season and was used exclusively a pitcher. (His conversion to an outfielder took place in 1918.) With two out in the first inning, Hy Myers hit a long drive to right-center for an inside-the-park home run. Boston answered with a run in the third on a triple by Everett Scott and a ground out from Ruth. There was no scoring from the fourth through the 13th. With darkness rapidly settling over Braves Field in the 14th, Smith gave up the winning run on a walk to Dick Hoblitzel and a double to pinch-hitter Del Gainor.

The game stood alone as the longest in World Series history for 89 years. The White Sox and Astros also played 14 innings in Game Three of the 2005 Series.

OCTOBER 10   The Dodgers win for the first time in the 1916 World Series with a 4–3 decision over the Red Sox before 21,087 in arctic weather at Ebbets Field. Brooklyn collected a run in the third inning, another in the fourth and two in the fifth for a 4–0 advantage before Boston tallied twice in the sixth and once in the seventh. Jeff Pfeffer retired all eight batters to face him after relieving Jack Coombs with one out in the seventh. Jake Daubert had a triple and two singles. The triple was struck in the sixth inning. Daubert tried to stretch the drive into an inside-the-park homer, but he started his slide too early and was thrown out at the plate.

For the World Series, the Dodgers added 4,500 temporary seats to the 23,500 permanent ones at Ebbets Field for a capacity of 28,000. A trench was dug in front of the front row to add two more rows of seating. Over 4,000 bleachers seats were built in left and right fields. There were about 7,000 empty seats at the ballpark for the Series, however, partly because of the high price of tickets. Charles Ebbets charged a premium price of $5 for 9,500 of the 28,000 seats, including some in the upper deck. Most fans thought this was exorbitant price-gouging and, as a result, many of the $5 seats went unsold. The $1 temporary bleacher seats in the outfield were packed.

OCTOBER 11   The Red Sox move within one victory of a world championship by defeating the Dodgers 6–2 before 21,662 at Ebbets Field. Nap Rucker pitched two innings of scoreless relief in his last big-league appearance. A 10-year veteran of the Dodgers, Rucker had already announced his retirement effective after the season.

The 1916 World Series also marked Casey Stengel's first appearance in the post-season. He collected four hits in 11 at-bats.

OCTOBER 12   Three weeks before Woodrow Wilson wins a second term to the presidency in an election against Charles Evans Hughes, Ernie Shore fires a three-hitter to lead the Red Sox to a world championship with a 4–1 triumph over the Dodgers before 43,620 on Columbus Day at Braves Field.

1917

LA

Season in a Sentence

Entering the season as defending National League champions, the Dodgers lose 14 of their first 19 games and experience an unexpected slide to seventh place.

Finish • Won • Lost • Pct • GB

Seventh   70   81   .464 26.5

Manager

Wilbert Robinson

Stats

Stats	Dods	NL	Rank
Batting Avg:	.247	.305	5
On-Base Pct:	.296	.305	8
Slugging Pct:	.322	.328	5
Home Runs:	25		5
Stolen Bases:	130		6
ERA:	2.78	2.70	5
Fielding Avg:	.962	.964	5

Starting Lineup

Otto Miller, c
Jake Daubert, 1b
George Cutshaw, 2b
Mike Mowrey, 3b
Ivy Olson, ss
Zack Wheat, lf
Hy Myers, cf
Casey Stengel, rf
Jim Hickman, cf
Jimmy Johnston, lf-cf
Frank O'Rourke, 3b

Pitchers

Rube Marquard, sp
Leon Cadore, sp
Jeff Pfeffer, sp
Sherry Smith, sp-rp
Larry Cheney, sp-rp
Jack Coombs, rp-sp

Attendance

366,218 (third in NL)

Club Leaders

Batting Avg:	Hy Myers	.268
On-Base Pct:	Jake Daubert	.341
Slugging Pct:	Casey Stengel	.375
Home Runs:	Jim Hickman	6
	Casey Stengel	6
RBIs:	Casey Stengel	73
Runs:	Casey Stengel	69
Stolen Bases:	George Cutshaw	22
Wins:	Rube Marquard	19
Strikeouts:	Rube Marquard	117
ERA:	Jeff Pfeffer	2.23
Saves:	Leon Cadore	3
	Sherry Smith	3

APRIL 11   Five days after the United States declares war on Germany and enters World War I, the Dodgers open the season with a 6–5 loss to the Phillies before 5,000 at Ebbets Field. Before the game, 400 cadets from the Second Naval Battalion marched on the field and raised the American flag. The Dodgers home uniforms featured an American flag on the left breast.

Other than overt displays of patriotism, the war had little effect on baseball in 1917. The changes were dramatic in 1918, however, as many players were drafted and the season ended a month early.

APRIL 17   An 8–3 loss to the Giants at Ebbets Field drops the Dodgers record to 0–4.

It was obvious early in 1917 that the Dodgers wouldn't repeat as pennant winners. By May 14, the club was 5–14, and it ended the season in seventh place. Because of the slide in the standings and the war, attendance plummeted from 447,747 in 1916 to 221,619 in 1917.

MAY 17   The Dodgers overcome a seven-run deficit to beat the Reds 13–10 at Ebbets Field. Cincinnati led 9–2 in the fifth inning and was still ahead 10–5 when the Dodgers broke loose with an eight-run rally in the eighth. The first two runs were the result of bases-loaded walks. Jim Hickman singled to make the score 10–8 before Casey

Stengel put Brooklyn into the lead with a three-run double. Hits by George Cutshaw and Ivy Olson scored two more.

JUNE 19   The Dodgers score eight runs in the fifth inning to defeat the Phillies 12–5 in Philadelphia. Jim Hickman hit a three-run homer during the big inning.

JULY 1   Charles Ebbets tries to play on a Sunday for the first time since 1906. It was still illegal in New York State to charge admission for a sporting event on the Christian Sabbath. In an attempt to circumvent the law, Ebbets sold tickets for a patriotic pre-game concert, with part of the proceeds donated to war charities. When the game against the Phillies began, the gates were thrown open and fans were admitted free of charge. About 15,000 attended. About half paid, with the other half wandering in after the music concluded. The Dodgers won the game 3–2 with a two-run rally in the ninth. Mike Mowrey drove in the tying and winning runs with a walk-off single.

Ebbets planned more Sunday games, but he canceled them after he and Wilbert Robinson were arrested and charged with violating the law following the July 1 contest. In 1917, the only three National League teams able to play home games on Sundays were the Chicago Cubs, Cincinnati Reds and St. Louis Cardinals. After a change in the New York State statutes, the Dodgers, Giants and Yankees were able to play in their home ballparks on Sundays beginning in 1919.

JULY 5   The Dodgers raise the 1916 National League pennant before a 6–3 win over the Giants at Ebbets Field.

At the time, it was customary to raise the pennant in mid-season in order to try to draw fans to the ballpark for the event. Heading into the July 5 contest, the Dodgers were in sixth place, had a record of 29–35 and were 12½ games behind the first-place Giants.

JULY 14   The Dodgers sweep the Pirates 5–3 and 1–0 at Ebbets Field. Rube Marquard pitched a two-hitter in the second tilt. The only Pittsburgh hits were a pair of singles by Frank Miller.

JULY 17   Casey Stengel hits a walk-off homer over the right field wall in the 10th inning to defeat the Cardinals 2–1 at Ebbets Field.

JULY 25   The Dodgers score two runs in the ninth inning and one in the 13th to down the Pirates 4–3 in Pittsburgh.

AUGUST 14   Casey Stengel and Giants shortstop Art Fletcher fight during a 3–1 Dodgers victory in the second game of a double-header at the Polo Grounds. The scrap hatched in the sixth inning when Stengel slid hard into Fletcher at second base. The two exchanged punches, causing both benches to empty. Stengel and Fletcher were both ejected. The Giants won the opener 5–4.

AUGUST 16   The Dodgers sell Fred Merkle to the Cubs and Chief Meyers to the Braves.

AUGUST 20   The Dodgers lose 1–0 in 10 innings to the Pirates in Pittsburgh.

AUGUST 21   The Dodgers and Pirates battle 13 innings to a 3–3 tie. The contest was called on account of darkness. Both teams scored twice in the 10th. Hy Myers collected five hits, including a triple, in six at-bats.

AUGUST 22   The Dodgers defeat the Pirates 6–5 in a 22-inning marathon at Forbes Field. It was the third consecutive extra-inning contest between the two clubs. The Dodgers raced to a 5–0 lead, but the Pirates countered with a run in the third inning, two in the sixth and two in the seventh. There was no scoring from either team from the eighth through the 21st. With one out in the 22nd, Jim Hickman walked and Frank O'Rourke singled. Otto Miller forced O'Rourke at second, with Hickman advancing to third. Pittsburgh second baseman Jake Pitler deliberated for a second about throwing to first, then held onto the ball. Hickman took advantage of Pitler's indecision and raced toward the plate, just beating Pitler's throw to score the winning run. Leon Cadore (seven innings), Larry Cheney (13 innings) and Rube Marquard (two innings) pitched for the Dodgers. Neither Cheney nor Marquard allowed a run. Wilbur Cooper (five innings) and Elmer Jacobs (17 innings) hurled for Pittsburgh. Hickman collected five hits, including a double, in nine at-bats. Hy Myers also had five hits, one of them a double, in 10 at-bats. It was Myers's second consecutive five-hit game. The Dodgers had 28 hits in all. The 22-inning fray lasted four hours and 15 minutes. It was the first game of a scheduled double-header. The two clubs started the second tilt, but it was stopped in the second inning due to darkness.

AUGUST 25   The Dodgers sweep the Cardinals 12–0 and 4–0 at Ebbets Field. Jeff Pfeffer and Rube Marquard pitched the shutouts. Pfeffer threw a two-hitter, allowing only singles to Jack Smith in the first inning and John Brock in the ninth. Casey Stengel and Jake Daubert backed Pfeffer with bases-loaded triples.

              Marquard was 19–12 with a 2.55 ERA in 1917.

SEPTEMBER 4   Jeff Pfeffer pitches a 14-inning complete game and allows only three hits, but the contest against the Phillies at Ebbets Field ends in a 0–0 tie. The only Philadelphia hits were singles by Milt Stock and Dave Bancroft and a double from Fred Luderus. Joe Oeschger also pitched a complete game for the Phils.

SEPTEMBER 10 Trailing 6–5, the Dodgers score seven runs in the eighth inning and defeat the Giants 13–6 in the first game of a double-header in New York. The Dodgers also won the opener 2–1. In between games, three Army regiments were presented with baseball equipment purchased with funds raised by fans.

OCTOBER 16   The Dodgers purchase Clarence Mitchell from the Reds.

1918

LA

Season in a Sentence

The Dodgers lose their first nine games, score fewer runs than any team in the majors and finish in fifth place in a season that ends on Labor Day because of World War I.

Finish • Won • Lost • Pct • GB

Fifth   57   69   .452   25.5

Manager

Wilbert Robinson

Stats

Stats	Dods	NL	Rank
Batting Avg:	.250	.254	4
On-Base Pct:	.291	.311	8
Slugging Pct:	.315	.328	6
Home Runs:	10		8
Stolen Bases:	113		6
ERA:	2.81	2.76	4
Fielding Avg:	.963	.965	6
Runs Scored:	360		8
Runs Allowed:	463		4

Starting Lineup

Otto Miller, c
Jake Daubert, 1b
Mickey Doolan, 2b
Ollie O'Mara, 3b
Ivy Olson, ss
Zack Wheat, lf
Hy Myers, cf
Jimmy Johnston, rf
Jim Hickman, rf
Mack Wheat, c

Pitchers

Burleigh Grimes, sp-rp
Rube Marquard, sp
Leon Cadore, sp-rp
Jack Coombs, sp
Dick Robertson, sp-rp

Attendance

83,831 (eighth in NL)

Club Leaders

Batting Avg:	Zack Wheat	.335
On-Base Pct:	Zack Wheat	.369
Slugging Pct:	Jake Daubert	.429
Home Runs:	Hy Myers	4
RBIs:	Zack Wheat	51
Runs:	Ivy Olson	63
Stolen Bases:	Jimmy Johnston	22
Wins:	Burleigh Grimes	19
Strikeouts:	Burleigh Grimes	113
ERA:	Burleigh Grimes	2.14
Saves:	Burleigh Grimes	1
	Larry Cheney	1

JANUARY 9   The Dodgers trade Casey Stengel and George Cutshaw to the Pirates for Burleigh Grimes, Al Mamaux and Chuck Ward.

The Dodgers gave up considerable talent in dealing Stengel and Cutshaw to Pittsburgh, but because of the acquisition of Grimes, the trade proved to be one of the best in club history. Mamaux was actually the pitcher the Dodgers most desired, however. He had a record of 21–8 for the Pirates in 1915 and 21–15 in 1916, but Mamaux's career took a sharp downturn in 1917 when he was 2–11. Wilbert Robinson had been a master at reviving the careers of pitchers, but Mamuax won 26 and lost 30 in six seasons in Brooklyn. At the time of the trade, Grimes was 24 and had a lifetime record of 5–18. A relentless competitor, he was an immediate sensation with the Dodgers, compiling a 19–9 mark in a 1918 season that was shortened by a month because of World War I. Grimes pitched nine seasons with the Dodgers, won 20 or more games four times and led the league three times in complete games, twice in innings pitched and once each in victories and strikeouts. His success was due in large part to mastering the spitball. The pitch was made illegal before the 1920 season, but Grimes was one of 17 major leaguers who were allowed to continue to doctor the ball (see February 9, 1920). On the all-time Dodgers lists, Grimes ranks sixth in victories

(158), eighth in defeats (121), fourth in complete games (205), fifth in innings pitched (2,425²/₃), seventh in walks (744) and 10th in games started (285). He ended his career in 1934 with a record of 270–212, earning him election to the Hall of Fame. Grimes also managed the Dodgers in 1937 and 1938.

APRIL 16   The Dodgers open the season with a 6–4 loss to the Giants in New York. Rube Marquard was the losing pitcher. The game was preceded by a parade of players and Naval reserves from Pelham Bay station. Army Major General William Mann threw out the ceremonial first pitch.

Military drafts and enlistments due to World War I drastically altered major league rosters in 1918. On Opening Day, Sherry Smith, Johnny Miljus, Duster Mails and Lew Malone were in the service. By the time the season ended, Jeff Pfeffer, Leon Cadore, Clarence Mitchell, Jim Hickman, Ray Schmandt, Ernie Krueger, Red Sheridan and Chuck Ward had donned military uniforms. Al Mamaux went to work in a Quincy, Massachusetts shipyard.

APRIL 19   Burleigh Grimes makes his debut with the Dodgers and is the losing pitcher in a 7–3 defeat at the hands of the Giants in New York.

In addition to a 19–9 record, Grimes pitched seven shutouts, struck 113 batters in 269²/₃ innings, compiled an ERA of 2.14 and appeared in a league-leading 40 games.

APRIL 24   In the home opener, the Dodgers lose 6–2 to the Giants at Ebbets Field. The loss was Brooklyn's seventh in a row at the start of the season.

APRIL 26   The Dodgers fall to 0–9 with an 11–5 loss to the Giants at Ebbets Field. The Dodgers were also nine games out of first place nine games into the 1918 season because the rival Giants were 9–0.

The nine losses at the start of the campaign is the worst in franchise history. With a combination of the miserable start, the war, and the loss of a long homestand due to the short season, the Dodgers drew an all-time low 83,831 fans in 1918, the worst figure in the major leagues.

APRIL 27   The Dodgers finally get into the win column with a 5–3 victory over the Giants at Ebbets Field.

MAY 6   Dodgers pitcher Dan Griner comes within one out of a no-hitter before nailing down a 2–0 victory over the Phillies at Ebbets Field. The only Philadelphia hit during the afternoon was a single by Gavvy Cravath with two out in the ninth inning.

The victory was Griner's only one in a Brooklyn uniform and the last of his big-league career. He had a 1–5 record as a Dodger and was 28–55 during six seasons in the majors.

MAY 7   The Braves slaughter the Dodgers 16–0 in Boston. Larry Cheney allowed 11 runs in six innings.

MAY 20 | Jack Coombs pitches the Dodgers to a 1–0 win over the Cubs in Chicago. The lone run scored in the sixth inning on a double by Ernie Krueger and a single from Ivy Olson.

Olson's given name was Ivan Massie Olson.

MAY 27 | Burleigh Grimes pitches a two-hitter to defeat the Cardinals 1–0 in St. Louis. The only hits off Grimes were singles by Doug Baird and Gene Paulette. The lone run scored in the eighth inning on a double by Jim Hickman.

MAY 30 | With two out in the ninth inning and two strikes on Ernie Krueger, Hy Myers tries to steal home and is called out at the plate, ending a 4–3 loss to the Braves in the second game of a double-header at Ebbets Field. The Dodgers also lost the opener 2–1.

JUNE 3 | The Dodgers lodge a protest after losing 15–12 to the Cardinals in 12 innings at Ebbets Field. In the sixth inning, Dave Baird of the Cardinals was the base runner on second when Walton Cruise knocked a low liner to center that Jim Hickman held momentarily and then dropped. Baird reached third and, believing the ball was caught, started back for second. After going about 20 feet, Baird realized that Hickman failed to hold onto Cruise's drive. Instead of touching third again, Baird cut across the diamond and scored. Umpire Cy Rigler counted the run despite the protests of the Dodgers. According to Rigler, Baird had already legally touched third base, and didn't need to do so again.

National League President John Tener ruled that Rigler should have called Baird out and ordered that the June 3 contest be wiped off the books and replayed in its entirety.

JUNE 4 | The Cardinals erupt for seven runs in the 13th inning to defeat the Dodgers 8–1 at Ebbets Field. Cy Rigler was again a source of controversy. With the score 1–1 and the bases loaded, Marty Kavanaugh drove a ball down the third-base line. Rigler ruled it fair, but the Dodgers made no attempt to field the ball, claiming it was foul. During the course of the argument, Kavanaugh rounded the bases for a grand slam home run. Dozens of fans rushed onto the field to get at Rigler. Players prevented the mob from reaching the umpire, with the exception of one individual who punched Rigler on the neck.

JUNE 5 | Leon Cadore, on furlough from the Army, makes his first appearance of the 1918 season and pitches a four-hit shutout to defeat the Cardinals 2–0 at Ebbets Field.

A few months later, Cadore was fighting as a lieutenant in the trenches of France.

JUNE 6 | Rube Marquard pitches the Dodgers to a 1–0 victory over the Pirates at Ebbets Field. The lone run scored in the second inning on a single by Ollie O'Mara.

JUNE 10 | Wilbur Cooper of the Pirates pitches a two-hitter, but the Dodgers win 2–0 at Ebbets Field. Burleigh Grimes not only pitched the shutout, but he drove in both runs with an eighth-inning double.

JUNE 16 | The Dodgers beat the Reds 6–0 on Bat and Ball Fund Day at Ebbets Field. The gate proceeds went to purchase baseball equipment for military personnel.

Several hundred sailors from the Brooklyn Naval Yard were in attendance along with soldiers from Camp Mills. The game was stopped for five minutes in the second inning when a pilot performed stunts overhead in his airplane. Chuck Ward and Clarence Mitchell, both on furlough from the army, played in the game.

JUNE 21   Rube Marquard pitches a two-hitter to defeat the Giants 1–0 at Ebbets Field. The only New York hits were singles by Heinie Zimmerman and Walter Holke.

JULY 1   At Braves Field in Boston, the Dodgers and Braves play the first twilight game in major league history. The contest started at 6:00 p.m. and was won by the Braves 5–3. Playing time was only 77 minutes as players rushed to complete the nine innings by sunset.

JULY 4   The Dodgers make seven errors, but they win 4–3 in 10 innings over the Giants in the first game of a double-header in New York. Jack Coombs pitched a complete game and started the game-winning rally with a triple. Coombs scored on a single by Jimmy Johnston. Brooklyn also won the nightcap 2–0.

JULY 9   Larry Cheney throws a club-record five wild pitches during a 6–4 loss to the Cardinals in St. Louis.

JULY 16   The Dodgers win 3–2 in 16 innings over the Cubs at Wrigley Field. Burleigh Grimes pitched a complete game and allowed seven hits. Hippo Vaughn also hurled all 16 innings for Chicago. The winning run scored on a single by Mickey Doolan.

            After his career ended, Doolan opened a dental practice.

JULY 18   On furlough from the Navy in Chicago, Jeff Pfeffer pitches his only game of the 1918 season and hurls a two-hit, complete game shutout to defeat the Cubs 2–0 at Wrigley Field. The only hits off Pfeffer were singles by Charlie Hollocher and Les Mann.

JULY 25   Burleigh Grimes pitches a one-hitter for a 10–0 win over the Pirates in the first game of a double-header at Ebbets Field. The lone Pittsburgh hit was a single by Billy Southworth in the seventh inning. The Dodgers won the second tilt 6–2.

JULY 27   The Dodgers go from one extreme to the other during a double-header against the Cardinals, winning the opener 2–0 before losing the nightcap 22–7. Dick Robertson pitched the first-game shutout. Harry Heitman, who was in the Navy and stationed at the Brooklyn Naval Yard, made his major league debut as a starting pitcher in the second game. He was relieved after surrendering hits to all four batters he faced, and he never pitched in the big leagues again. Jack Coombs started both games in right field and pitched the last three innings of the second game in relief, allowing 10 runs.

AUGUST 1   The National Commission, baseball's governing body, announces that the 1918 season will end on September 2 in order to comply with an order issued by the federal government requiring all men of draft age to either enter the military service or find a war-related job.

AUGUST 7   The Wheat brothers star in a 3–2 win over the Cubs at Ebbets Field. Mack Wheat accounted for all three Brooklyn runs with a three-run homer in the fourth inning. Zack Wheat extended his hitting streak to 26 games.

Zack Wheat was Mr. Consistency for the Dodgers, hitting over .300 in 12 seasons and leading the league in batting in 1918.

The homer was Mack's first as a major leaguer and the runs batted in were the first three of his career and his only three in 157 at-bats in 1918. Mack didn't homer again until 1920, when he was playing for the Phillies. Zack batted .444 during his 26-game streak. He ended the season with a league-leading .335 average, although with much less power than he exhibited for most of his career. Among his 137 hits, only 18 went for extra bases on 15 doubles and three triples. Zack's .386 slugging percentage was the second-lowest of his 19 years in the majors. The 51-point difference between his batting Average and slugging percentage was the lowest of his career.

AUGUST 10   Police quell a riot at Ebbets Field during the second game of a double-header against the Phillies. The Dodgers won the opener 4–0 before losing a contentious second tilt 3–2. Umpire Charlie Moran called a drive off the right-field wall by Philadelphia's Cy Williams a fair ball, although nearly everyone else at the ballpark believed it was foul. After the game, fans rushed the field and surrounded Moran, who needed police protection to leave the ballpark.

AUGUST 21   The Dodgers sell Jimmy Archer to the Reds.

AUGUST 30   The Dodgers lose 1–0 to the Giants in New York in a contest that lasts only 57 minutes.

SEPTEMBER 2   The Dodgers close the season with a split of a double-header against the Phillies in Philadelphia. The Dodgers lost the first game 4–2 and won the second 5–3.

NOVEMBER 1   A subway accident in Brooklyn causes the death of 97 people. Dodgers management threw open the gates of Ebbets Field for the treatment of the less seriously injured. About 50 were treated by doctors volunteering their services.

NOVEMBER 11   An armistice is signed with Germany ending World War I.

When the 1918 season came to a close, it appeared there would be no baseball in 1919 because the end of the war was nowhere in sight. But a series of victories by the Allies, led by the United States, Great Britain and France, sped the conflict to a conclusion by November 1918. Owners hastily made plans for the 1919 season, but due to a late start in preparing for the campaign and the anticipation of a poor year at the gate, baseball executives shortened the season to 140 games. It was a decision that officials came to regret, as attendance reached record levels in 1919.

1919   L A

Season in a Sentence

With few players remaining from the 1916 pennant-winning club, the Dodgers win 11 of their first 14 games but fade to a fifth-place finish.

Finish • Won • Lost • Pct • GB

Fifth   69   71   .493   27.0

Manager

Wilbert Robinson

Starting Lineup

Ernie Krueger, c
Ed Konetchy, 1b
Jimmy Johnston, 2b
Lew Malone, 3b
Ivy Olson, ss
Zack Wheat, lf
Hy Myers, cf
Tommy Griffith, rf
Lee Magee, 2b

Pitchers

Jeff Pfeffer, sp
Leon Cadore, sp
Al Mamaux, sp
Burleigh Grimes, sp
Sherry Smith, sp
Clarence Mitchell, rp-sp

Stats

Stats	Dods	NL	Rank
Batting Avg:	.263	.258	3
On-Base Pct:	.304	.311	7
Slugging Pct:	.340	.337	4
Home Runs:	25		3
Stolen Bases:	112		8
ERA:	2.73	2.91	4
Fielding Avg:	.963	.967	8
Runs Scored:	525		3
Runs Allowed:	513		5

FEBRUARY 1   The Dodgers trade Jake Daubert to the Reds for Tommy Griffith.

After the 1918 season ended a month before the scheduled closing, the owners immediately cut off the pay to the players. Daubert claimed he was still owed a month's salary, however, because he was under a multi-year contract. He sued the Dodgers for back pay, and the case was settled out of court. Although

Daubert hit .308 and led the league in triples with 15 in 1918, Charles Ebbets was livid over the first baseman's legal action and traded him to the Reds. Daubert was 35 at the time of the deal, but he still had six years remaining as a starting first baseman. He died while still an active player on October 9, 1924, from complications following an appendectomy.

APRIL 14   The Dodgers purchase Ed Konetchy from the Cardinals.

APRIL 18   The Dodgers purchase Lee Magee from the Reds.

The Dodgers purchased Magee even though the Reds suspected him of throwing games in collusion with gamblers during the 1918 season. The Dodgers had the same suspicions over the course of the 1919 campaign and released him after 45 games with the club. In 1920, Magee admitted to throwing a game on July 25, 1918, while with Cincinnati and was banned from the sport for life.

APRIL 19   The Dodgers open the season with a pair of victories in a double-header against the Braves on Patriots Day in Boston. The Dodgers won the opener 5–2 in 10 innings. Leon Cadore pitched a complete game and Tommy Griffith, in his Dodgers debut, broke the 2–2 tie with a two-run single. Brooklyn completed the sweep with a 3–2 triumph in the second tilt.

APRIL 30   The Dodgers and Phillies battle 20 innings to a 9–9 tie in Philadelphia. The game was called on account of darkness. Both Jeff Pfeffer of the Dodgers and Joe Oeschger of the Phils pitched complete games. The Dodgers tied the game 6–6 with a run in the ninth. The score stayed that way until the top of the 19th when Hy Myers hit a three-run homer, but Philadelphia responded with three runs in the bottom half. The Dodgers collected 22 hits and the Phillies 15.

MAY 2   The Dodgers win the home opener 3–0 over the Braves before 10,000 at Ebbets Field. Jeff Pfeffer pitched the shutout.

There were no advertisements for alcoholic beverages on the walls at Ebbets Field in 1919 because Prohibition began in New York State on July 1. Prohibition took effect nationally on January 16, 1920. There would be no alcoholic drinks sold at any major league ballpark until 1933, after Prohibition ended.

MAY 4   The Dodgers play their first legal home game on a Sunday and beat the Braves 6–2 before 25,000 at Ebbets Field.

Earlier in the week, a law was signed by the governor of New York allowing the Dodgers, Giants and Yankees to play at home on Sundays.

MAY 7   Down 7–0, the Dodgers score six runs in the third inning, one each in the fourth, fifth and sixth, and two in the seventh to defeat the Phillies 11–9 at Ebbets Field. Before the game, ex-Dodger Jack Coombs, now manager of the Phillies, was presented with several gifts, including a silver tea service and a gun.

MAY 14   The Dodgers run their record to 11–3 and take a one-game lead in the pennant race with a 7–0 victory over the Reds at Ebbets Field.

The euphoria over the start of the 1919 season evaporated quickly. By June 14, Brooklyn's record was 20–25.

MAY 15   In one of the strangest games in club history, the Dodgers lose 10–0 in 13 innings to the Reds at Ebbets Field. The game was a scoreless duel between Al Mamaux of the Dodgers and Hod Eller of the Reds for 12 innings before Mamaux collapsed in the 13th and allowed 10 runs. With two out, Mamaux allowed a walk and seven consecutive hits.

Mamaux spent some 20 years both during and after his playing career touring as a vaudeville singer. He was known as "The Golden Voiced Tenor." Outfielder Tommy Griffith also appeared on the stage as a singer, performing many tunes he had written himself. Griffith is also the grandfather of Matt Williams, who hit 378 home runs for three teams from 1987 through 2003.

MAY 25   Sherry Smith pitches his first game since 1917 and tosses a three-hit shutout to defeat the Pirates 5–0 at Ebbets Field. Smith missed the entire 1918 season while serving overseas in the Army. All five Brooklyn runs scored in the third inning, three of them on a bases-loaded triple by Hy Myers.

The game was highlighted by a famous incident in which ex-Dodger Casey Stengel, playing right field for Pittsburgh, released a bird from inside of his cap. The triple by Myers went through Stengel's legs, bringing hoots from the crowd. On his way to the bench in the sixth inning, Casey spotted Leon Cadore holding a sparrow in the bullpen. Stengel placed the bird in his cap, and when he came to bat in the top of the seventh, he acknowledged the crowd's boos by tipping his cap and releasing the sparrow.

MAY 31   The Dodgers score two runs in the ninth inning to defeat the Giants 3–2 at Ebbets Field. Rube Marquard drove in the winning run with a walk-off double. An unusual situation happened in the first inning when the first four Dodgers hit singles, and none scored. Ivy Olson and Lee Magee led off with singles and Magee was picked off second. Olson was thrown out at the plate on Tommy Griffith's single. Zack Wheat's single sent Griffith to third. The two attempted a double steal, but Griffith was thrown out at home.

Wheat hit .297 for the Dodgers in 1919.

JUNE 1   The Dodgers lose an 18-inning battle to the Phillies 10–9 at Ebbets Field. Brooklyn scored four runs in the eighth inning to tie the score 8–8. Both teams scored in the 16th. Fred Luderus drove in the winning run with a double. Hy Myers collected five hits, including a double, in nine at-bats. Jeff Pfeffer pitched a complete game. He also pitched a 20-inning complete game against the Phillies on April 30 in a contest that ended in a 9–9 tie.

Myers led the National League in slugging percentage (.436), runs batted in (73) and triples (14) in 1919 in addition to batting .307.

JUNE 14   The Dodgers lose their 10th game in a row by dropping a 2–1 decision to the Cardinals in St. Louis.

JUNE 15 — A two-run, pinch-hit single by Hy Myers in the ninth inning beats the Cardinals 3–2 in St. Louis.

JUNE 24 — Tommy Griffith collects five hits, including a grand slam and a double, in five at-bats during a 9–3 win over the Giants in the second game of a double-header at Ebbets Field. The slam was struck in the eighth inning off Jesse Barnes. New York won the opener 4–2.

JUNE 28 — The Dodgers sell Larry Cheney to the Braves.

JUNE 29 — Ed Konetchy collects five hits, including a triple, in five at-bats during a 9–4 win over the Phillies at Ebbets Field. The performance gave him base hits in eight consecutive at-bats. During a 6–3 win over the Phils in Brooklyn the previous day, Konetchy garnered a double and two singles in his last three at-bats.

Scrappy shortstop Ivy Olson played on the pennant-winning teams of 1916 and 1920, providing excellent defense and hustle. In 1919 he led the league in hits, though he batted only .278.

JULY 1 — Ed Konetchy collects singles in his first two-at-bats of a 6–1 loss to the Giants in New York. Combined with the games of June 28 and June 29, Konetchy extended his streak of hits in consecutive at-bats to a National League record-tying 10. The 10 hits consisted of eight singles, a double and a triple.

Konetchy is the only batter in Dodgers history with hits in 10 consecutive at-bats.

JULY 5 — The Dodgers sweep the Braves 4–2 and 15–3 in a double-header at Ebbets Field. Brooklyn scored eight runs in the first inning of the second game.

JULY 19 — Jimmy Johnston hits a two-run, bases-loaded, walk-off single in the 12th inning to beat the Reds 2–1 at Ebbets Field.

AUGUST 8 — The only Dodgers hit off Wilbur Cooper of the Pirates during a 3–0 loss at Pittsburgh is a triple by Ivy Olson leading off the first inning.

AUGUST 13 — Al Mamaux pitches a 13-inning complete game and wins his own game with a walk-off double for a 3–2 defeat of the Cubs in the second game of a double-header at Ebbets Field. Chicago won the opener 4–3.

AUGUST 15 — Burleigh Grimes pitches a complete game, collects three hits in three at-bats and drives in two runs for a 3–1 win over the Cubs at Ebbets Field.

AUGUST 24   The Dodgers collect 21 hits and beat the Cardinals 10–1 at Ebbets Field.

AUGUST 26   The Dodgers sweep the Cardinals 1–0 and 2–1 at Ebbets Field. Al Mamaux pitched
                 the first game shutout. Ivy Olson drove in the lone run with a double in the eighth
                 inning. Burleigh Grimes pitched a complete game in the nightcap and scored both
                 Brooklyn runs.

                 Olson's 164 hits led the National League in 1919.

AUGUST 31   Umpire Bill Klem clears the Dodgers bench of all reserve players during a 4–3 win
                 over the Giants at Ebbets Field. Klem ordered the players to the clubhouse after
                 repeated objections to his calls on balls and strikes.

SEPTEMBER 11   Cardinals pitcher Ferdie Schupp hits an inside-the-park, walk-off homer in the ninth
                 inning to defeat the Dodgers 4–3 in St. Louis.

SEPTEMBER 21   The Dodgers win 3–1 over the Reds in a contest in Cincinnati that lasts only
                 55 minutes.

SEPTEMBER 24   The Dodgers rout the Phillies 13–3 in Philadelphia.

THE STATE OF THE DODGERS

The Dodgers closed the 1910s with a pennant in 1916 followed by three consecutive losing seasons. The club won an unexpected National League title in 1920 with an roster of aging veterans. After three seasons around the .500 mark in 1921, 1922 and 1923, Brooklyn experienced a thrilling pennant race in 1924 before finishing second to the Giants. There was little to cheer about during the second half of the 1920s as the Dodgers fielded a succession of mediocre teams that finished in sixth place five seasons in a row. It was during this period that the Dodgers were dubbed "The Daffiness Boys" due to their bizarre behavior and erratic play. Overall, the club was 765–768 during the '20s, a winning percentage of .499 that was the sixth-best among the eight NL teams. Pennant winners outside of Brooklyn were the Giants (1921, 1922, 1923 and 1924), Pirates (1925 and 1927), Cardinals (1926 and 1928) and Cubs (1929).

THE BEST TEAM

The 1920 club produced the only pennant-winner in Brooklyn between 1916 and 1941 with a 93–61 record before losing the World Series to the Indians.

THE WORST TEAM

The 1927 Dodgers were 65–88 and finished the season in sixth place, 28¹/₂ games out of first place.

THE BEST MOMENT

The Dodgers took a two-games-to-one lead in the 1920 World Series, giving fans hope for a world championship.

THE WORST MOMENT

The Dodgers were known as the "Daffiness Boys" because of plays like the one on August 15, 1926, in which three players ended up on third base.

THE ALL-DECADE TEAM • YEARS W/DODS

Player	Years
Hank DeBerry, c	1922–30
Jack Fournier, 1b	1923–26
Jimmy Johnston, 2b	1916–25
Andy High, 3b	1922–24
Ivy Olson, ss	1915–24
Zack Wheat, lf	1909–26
Hy Myers, cf	1909, 1911, 1914–22
Babe Herman, rf	1926–31, 1945
Dazzy Vance, p	1922–32, 1935
Burleigh Grimes, p	1918–26
Leon Cadore, p	1915–23
Jesse Petty, p	1925–28

Wheat, Myers and Olson were also on the 1910s All-Decade Team. Wheat, Grimes and Vance are in the Hall of Fame. Other outstanding Dodgers of the 1920s included right fielder Tommy Griffith (1919–25), first baseman Del Bissonette (1928–31, 1933) and pitcher Dutch Ruether (1921–24).

THE DECADE LEADERS

Batting Avg:	Zack Wheat	.340
On-Base Pct:	Jack Fournier	.421
Slugging Pct:	Jack Fournier	.552
Home Runs:	Jack Fournier	82
RBIs:	Zack Wheat	570
Runs:	Zack Wheat	620
Stolen Bases:	Jimmy Johnston	93
Wins:	Dazzy Vance	147
Strikeouts:	Dazzy Vance	1,464
ERA:	Dazzy Vance	3.10
Saves:	Al Mamaux	8

THE HOME FIELD

Ebbets Field opened in 1913. The only significant change to the ballpark during the '20s was the addition of a small stand of bleachers in left field in 1920.

THE GAME YOU WISHED YOU HAD SEEN

In his first start since pitching a one-hitter, Dazzy Vance went one better with a no-hitter at Ebbets Field on September 13, 1925, to beat the Phillies 10–1.

THE WAY THE GAME WAS PLAYED

Rule changes in 1920 and the emergence of Babe Ruth as a star changed baseball from a low-scoring defensive affair into a high-scoring offensive carnival. This was the first decade in which baseball embraced the home run. Teams went from averaging 3.5 runs a game in 1917 to 5.0 runs a game in 1922 to 5.7 per game in 1930. Team batting averages in the NL ballooned from .249 in 1917 to .292 in 1922 and .303 in 1930. Not surprisingly, team ERA jumped nearly two runs. The 1928 season was the first in National League history in which there were more home runs than stolen bases. There wouldn't be another season in which the number of steals exceeded the number of homers in the NL until 1975. Pitchers completed less than half of their starts in the NL in 1922, the first time that happened, as relief pitching continued to gain importance.

THE MANAGEMENT

Charles Ebbets began his career in baseball as a ticket-taker with the Dodgers in 1883 and rose to the presidency of the club in 1898. He died on April 18, 1925, throwing ownership of the club into internal chaos that wouldn't be fully resolved until 1950, when Walter O'Malley gained control of the franchise. Ebbets's logical successor was Ed McKeever. Ed and his brother Steve had owned half of the stock in the franchise since 1912. But Ed passed away just 11 days after Ebbets. Steve served as interim president for only 26 days before being ousted. Wilbert Robinson, who had been field manager since 1914, became the compromise choice as president after the heirs of Ebbets denied Steve McKeever the top position in the organization. The Ebbets and McKeever families feuded for

years in competing 50–50 blocks in a convoluted ownership structure, and Robinson and McKeever stopped speaking to one another. Robinson continued as president until February 1930, when he was succeeded by Frank York. Robinson remained as manager until 1931, however.

THE BEST PLAYER MOVE

The best player move was the purchase of Dazzy Vance from New Orleans of the Southern Association in 1922. The best trade was the acquisition of Jack Fournier from the Cardinals for Hy Myers and Ray Schmandt in February 1923.

THE WORST PLAYER MOVE

The worst trade sent Burleigh Grimes to the Giants as part of a three-team trade that brought Butch Henline from the Phillies in January 1927.

1920

L A

Season in a Sentence

After three consecutive losing seasons and a roster full of players past the age of 30, the Dodgers produce an unexpected National League pennant before losing the World Series to the Indians

Finish • Won • Lost • Pct • GB

First   93   61   .604 +7.0

World Series

The Dodgers lost five games to two to the Cleveland Indians.

Manager

Wilbert Robinson

Stats

Stats	Dods	NL	Rank
Batting Avg:	.277	.270	3
On-Base Pct:	.324	.322	5
Slugging Pct:	.367	.357	2
Home Runs:	28		5
Stolen Bases:	70		8
ERA:	2.62	3.13	1
Fielding Avg:	.966	.966	4
Runs Scored:	660		3
Runs Allowed:	528		1

Starting Lineup

Otto Miller, c
Ed Konetchy, 1b
Pete Kilduff, 2b
Jimmy Johnston, 3b
Ivy Olson, ss
Zack Wheat, lf
Hy Myers, cf
Tommy Griffith, rf
Bernie Neis, rf

Pitchers

Burleigh Grimes, sp
Leon Cadore, sp
Jeff Pfeffer, sp
Rube Marquard, sp
Al Mamaux, rp-sp
Sherry Smith, rp-sp
Clarence Mitchell, rp-sp

Attendance

808,722 (second in NL)

Club Leaders

Batting Avg:	Zack Wheat	.328
On-Base Pct:	Zack Wheat	.385
Slugging Pct:	Zack Wheat	.463
Home Runs:	Zack Wheat	9
RBIs:	Hy Myers	80
Runs:	Zack Wheat	89
Stolen Bases:	Jimmy Johnston	19
Wins:	Burleigh Grimes	23
Strikeouts:	Burleigh Grimes	131
ERA:	Burleigh Grimes	2.22
Saves:	Al Mamaux	4

FEBRUARY 9   Baseball's rules committee adopts new regulations that usher in the era of the lively ball. The changes were spurred in part by the owners' recognition of the positive impact of Babe Ruth. Ruth clubbed a then-record 29 home runs for the Red Sox in 1919 and helped the American League set all-time attendance records. The committee adopted a more-lively ball, agreed to keep a fresh ball in play at all times and banned pitchers from using any foreign substances to deface the ball. These included paraffin, resin, powder, emery boards, files and saliva. There were 17 pitchers, however, who were allowed to continue to use the spitball for the remainder of their careers because they had come to rely heavily on the pitch. Two of the 17 were Dodger pitchers Burleigh Grimes and Clarence Mitchell.

APRIL 14   The Dodgers win the season opener 9–2 over the Phillies at Ebbets Field. Leon Cadore was the winning pitcher. Hy Myers contributed a triple and scored three runs.

Myers led the NL in triples with 22 in 1920 in addition to collecting 36 doubles, batting .304 and driving in 80 runs. The 22 triples are the second-most of any Dodger batter in a single season. George Treadway holds the record with 26 in 1894.

APRIL 20   Leon Cadore pitches an 11-inning complete-game shutout to defeat the Braves 1–0 at Ebbets Field. Rookie right fielder Wally Hood drove in the winning run with a two-out double. Joe Oeschger pitched a complete game for Boston. In the fifth inning, Hy Myers and Boston third base coach Oscar Dugey were ejected for engaging in a fist fight. Dugey made a remark that angered Myers, and the Dodgers outfielder punched Dugey in the nose.

The RBI by Hood was the first of his career and the only one he would collect in 1920. Cadore and Oeschger would hook up in a much longer game 11 days later.

APRIL 25   A game between the Dodgers and Giants at Ebbets Field ends in a Brooklyn defeat by forfeit. The Dodgers kept selling tickets long after the supply of reserved seats was exhausted. No accurate count exists of the number of fans inside the ballpark, but newspapers estimated there were between 30,000 and 35,000 in a facility with 23,000 seats. With two out in the bottom of the ninth and the Dodgers losing 5–2, much of the crowd swarmed the field and resisted all efforts to clear the diamond. Umpire Barry McCormick declared a forfeit in favor of New York.

MAY 1   In Boston, Leon Cadore of the Dodgers and Joe Oeschger of the Braves duel 26 innings to a 1–1 tie in the longest game ever played in the major leagues. The contest was called on account of darkness. Oeschger shut out the Dodgers over the last 21 innings. Cadore didn't allow a run over the final 20 frames. Oeschger gave up nine hits, all singles, and Cadore surrendered 15 in a contest that lasted three hours and 50 minutes. Cadore faced 96 batters, struck out eight and walked five. Oeschger faced 90 batters, struck out three and walked four. Over the final 13 innings, Cadore gave up only two hits, and none in the last six. Oeschger pitched the equivalent of a no-hitter by holding the Dodgers hitless over the final nine innings. The only Brooklyn base runner over the final nine frames was Wally Hood, who walked in the 22nd. The Dodger run scored in the fifth on a walk to Ernie Krueger, an infield out that advanced him to second and a single by Ivy Olson. Boston tied the contest in the sixth on a triple by Walton Cruise and Tony Boeckel's single. Boeckel was out at the plate trying to score on Rabbit Maranville's double after a fine stop by Hood, who was playing center field and had just entered the game as a replacement for Hy Myers. Oeschger was saved by a remarkable double play in the 17th. With the bases loaded and one out, Rowdy Elliott grounded to the Boston pitcher. Zack Wheat was forced at the plate, but catcher Hank Gowdy's throw to first baseman Walter Holke was low and was fumbled. Ed Konetchy tried to score from second, and Holke's throw home was wide, but Gowdy threw himself across the plate to tag Konetchy. No one kept an accurate count of the number of pitches that Cadore and Oeschger delivered. Neither starting catcher finished the contest. For the Dodgers, Krueger was replaced by Elliott in the sixth inning. Boston's Mickey O'Neil was lifted for a pinch-hitter in the ninth. Gowdy caught the final 17 innings. The umpires for the historic contest were Barry McCormick at home plate and Bob Hart on the bases.

The 26-Inning Record Breakers

The longest game in major league history was played between the Dodgers and Braves in Boston on May 1, 1920. The epic clash ended in a 1–1 tie when it was called by darkness after 26 innings. There have been two 25-inning contests in the majors. The Cardinals defeated the Mets 4–3 in New York on September 11, 1974. The other one took place over two days on May 8 and May 9, 1984, at Comiskey Park in Chicago, with the White Sox defeating the Brewers 7–6 on a walk-off home run by Harold Baines. The contest was suspended after 17 innings on May 8 and completed the following day.

The following is a list of major league records set and tied during the 26-inning clash between the Dodgers and Braves

Records set
Most at-bats without a hit in a game
11 by Charlie Pick, Boston. Chuck Ward and Leon Cadore of Brooklyn were each hitless in 10 at-bats.
Longest game without an extra-base hit
26 innings by Brooklyn.
Longest game without a home run
26 innings by both Brooklyn and Boston.
Longest game without a stolen base
26 innings by Boston.
Longest game without a double play
26 innings by Boston.
Most innings pitched in a game
26 by Joe Oeschger, Boston, and Leon Cadore, Brooklyn. Others who played all 26 innings were Boston's Walter Holke (first base), Charlie Pick (second base), Tony Boeckel (third base), Rabbit Maranville (shortstop), Les Mann (left field), Ray Powell (center field) and Walton Cruise (right field) and Brooklyn's Ed Konetchy (first base), Ivy Olson (second base), Jimmy Johnston (third base), Zack Wheat (left field) and Bernie Neis (right field).
Most batters faced in a game
96 by Leon Cadore, Brooklyn.
Most consecutive scoreless innings in a game
21 by Joe Oeschger, Boston.

Longest game without hitting a batter with a pitch
26 innings by Leon Cadore, Brooklyn, and Joe Oeschger, Boston.
Longest game without a wild pitch
26 innings by Leon Cadore.
Most putouts by a first baseman in a game
42 by Walter Holke, Boston.
Most chances accepted by a first baseman in a game
43 by Walter Holke, Boston.
Most putouts by a team in a game
78 by Boston and Brooklyn.
Most assists in a game by a team
41 by Boston.
Most chances accepted by a team in a game
119 by Boston.

Records tied
Most at-bats in a game
11 by Charlie Pick and Tony Boeckel, Boston.

Of course, the most remarkable record was the 26 innings pitched by Leon Cadore and Joe Oeschger. It is a mark that will stand for all eternity.

It had often been written that the endurance test ruined the careers of both pitchers, but that is not the case. Each had strong seasons in both 1920 and 1921. Cadore entered the 1920 season as a 29-year-old with a 28–25 record. He finished the 1920 campaign with a 15–14 mark and a 2.62 ERA in 254$^1/_2$ innings. Cadore was 13–14 in 1921, before his career went south. He ended a 10-year career in 1924 with 68 wins and 72 losses.

Oeschger began 1920 at the age of 27 with a won-lost ledger of 31–44. He was 15–13 in 1920 with a 3.46 ERA in 299 innings. Oeschger pitched 299 innings again in 1921 and won 20 while losing 14 with an earned run average of 3.52. After 1921, however, he was 16–45 with an ERA of 5.14. Oeschger ended his career in 1925 pitching in 21 games with the Dodgers. His final record was 82–116.

The game was played on a Saturday afternoon. At the time, Sunday baseball was illegal in Boston, and rather than have the Dodgers sit idle on a lucrative Sunday date, the National League scheduled a one-game series against the Phillies at Ebbets Field on May 2. This required the Dodgers to board a train for Brooklyn immediately after their 26-inning clash against the Braves, then return to Boston for a game on May 3. The Braves had a day off on May 2.

MAY 2   A day after playing a 26-inning game in Boston, the Dodgers lose 4–3 to the Phillies in 13 innings at Ebbets Field. Burleigh Grimes pitched a complete game.

MAY 3   The Dodgers return to Boston and play 19 innings against the Braves before losing 2–1. Both Sherry Smith of the Dodgers and Dana Fillingim of the Braves pitched complete games. The first 18 innings were a duplication of the 26-inning contest two days earlier, as the Dodgers scored in the fifth inning and the Braves responded with a tally in the sixth. Tony Boeckel drove in the winning run with a single in the 19th. The time of the game was three hours and five minutes.

The Dodgers played 58 innings in three games in three days while traveling from Boston to Brooklyn and back to Boston in between each of the three contests. Even more remarkable, the Dodgers did not use a single relief pitcher in any of the three marathon encounters with Leon Cadore (26 innings), Burleigh Grimes (13 innings) and Sherry Smith (19 innings) each pitching complete games. The three combined to allow only six runs in the 58 innings, but all the Dodgers had to show for it was two losses and a tie. Still, the Dodgers recovered from the struggles to win the National League pennant. Heading into the season, only the foolishly optimistic were predicting a first-place finish.

Manager Wilbert Robinson, owner Charles Ebbets and pitcher Leon Cadore pose for the camera during the pennant-winning 1920 season. Cadore, who pitched a 26-inning game on May 1, posted 15 wins that year, a career high.

MAY 7   The Dodgers lose again in extra innings, this time 7–6 to the Giants in 11 innings in New York. Brooklyn scored twice in the top of the 11th for a 6–4 lead only to have the Giants respond with three runs in their half.

MAY 9   Leon Cadore makes his first start since pitching 26 innings on May 1. Facing the Phillies at Ebbets Field, Cadore pitched four shutout innings before being relieved after surrendering four runs in the fifth. Sherry Smith, who pitched 19 innings six days earlier, threw 5²/₃ innings of scoreless relief to help the Dodgers win 5–4 in 10 innings.

MAY 14   The Dodgers score four runs in the 14th inning to defeat the Cardinals 5–1 in St. Louis. It was Brooklyn's sixth extra-inning game in the first 14 days of May.

MAY 24   Al Mamaux pitches the Dodgers to a 1–0 win over the Pirates at Pittsburgh. Ed Konetchy drove in the lone run with a double in the fourth inning.

MAY 27   The Phillies wear the Dodgers road uniforms at Ebbets Field and defeat their hosts 5–4 in 11 innings. The Phils uniforms had been placed on the wrong train in Chicago the previous day and had not yet arrived in Brooklyn at game time.

JUNE 1   The Dodgers score three runs in the eighth inning and two in the ninth to defeat the Giants 10–9 at Ebbets Field. Tommy Griffith, making his first appearance of 1920 after a prolonged holdout, started the ninth-inning rally with a single. Hy Myers ended it with another single that drove in the winning run.

JUNE 10   Umpire Cy Rigler has to be escorted from the field by police after a 9–3 Dodgers loss to the Cardinals at Ebbets Field. The crowd took exception to a call made by Rigler in the seventh inning and, when the game ended, several hundred jumped onto the field and made a rush in his direction.

JUNE 25   The Dodgers and Braves make up the 26-inning tie on May 1 as part of a double-header. The Dodgers won the first game 5–1 and lost the second 4–2.

JUNE 29   The Dodgers fall 3¹/₂ games behind in the pennant race with an 8–1 loss to the Braves in Boston. Brooklyn's record was 31–30 and the club occupied fourth place.

JULY 4   The Dodgers sweep the Phillies 10–1 and 7–0 at Ebbets Field.

JULY 5   After traveling from Brooklyn to Boston, the Dodgers sweep a double-header for the second day in a row with 9–5 and 5–2 victories over the Braves at Braves Field. In the opener, Brooklyn trailed 5–2 before scoring three runs in the ninth inning and four in the 10th. Zack Wheat hit a three-run homer in the 10th.

> *Wheat finished in the top five in the NL in batting average (.328), on-base percentage (.385) and slugging percentage (.463) in 1920.*

JULY 8   The Dodgers play at Sportsman's Park in St. Louis for the first time and defeat the Cardinals 14–2.

> *Sportsman's Park was the home of the Cardinals from 1920 through 1966. The name of the ballpark was changed to Busch Stadium in 1953.*

JULY 12   The Dodgers sweep the Cubs 13–4 and 10–2 in a double-header in Chicago.

JULY 14   The Dodgers sweep the Cubs 3–2 and 4–1 in an eventful double-header in Chicago.
                 In the sixth inning of the first game, Ivy Olson hit a dribbler down the third-base line
                 that hopped into the stands and was ruled a home run by umpire Bill Klem. At the
                 time, the rules stipulated that any ball that reached the stands at least 235 feet from
                 home plate was a homer. The Cubs maintained the ball rolled out of bounds less
                 than 235 feet from home, entitling Olson to only two bases. Klem asked for a tape
                 measure, which showed that the ball rolled out 241 feet from the plate.

JULY 17   The Dodgers take a four-game lead in the National League pennant race with a
                 3–2 win over the Reds in Cincinnati. The Dodgers won 18 of their first 21 games
                 in July in a span of 17 days.

                 *The Dodgers were an old team by 1920 standards. Among those with at
                 least 300 at-bats, Ed Konetchy and Ivy Olson were 34, Zack Wheat 32, Zack
                 Taylor and Hy Myers 31, Tommy Griffith and Jimmy Johnston 30, and Pete
                 Kilduff 27. Pitchers with at least 100 innings were Rube Marquard (age 33),
                 Jeff Pfeffer (32), Leon Cadore (29), Sherry Smith (29), Burleigh Grimes (26)
                 and Al Mamaux (26).*

AUGUST 8   Trailing the Pirates 1–0 in the eighth inning at Ebbets Field, fans shower umpire
                 Charlie Moran with bottles after a call adverse to the home team. The Dodgers
                 rallied to win 2–1 with runs in the eighth and ninth.

AUGUST 11   Umpire Ernie Quigley is the target of bottles thrown by excited Dodgers fans in the
                 seventh inning of a 4–3 loss to the Cubs in the second game of a double-header at
                 Ebbets Field. The Dodgers won the opener 9–3.

                 *After drawing just 83,831 fans in 1918 and 360,721 in 1919, attendance at Ebbets
                 Field zoomed to 808,722 in 1920, which shattered the existing team record. Prior
                 to 1920, the highest single-season attendance figure was 447,747 in 1916.*

SEPTEMBER 4   Two weeks after the passage of the 19th amendment, which grants women the right
                 to vote, Leon Cadore pitches a 12-hit shutout to defeat the Braves 10–0 in Boston.

SEPTEMBER 6   The Dodgers drop out of first place behind the Reds after losing 3–2 and 6–5 in a
                 double-header against the Phillies in Philadelphia.

SEPTEMBER 9   The Dodgers take sole possession of first place with a 4–2 triumph over the Cardinals
                 at Ebbets Field. Burleigh Grimes earned his 20th victory of the season.

                 *Grimes finished the season with a 23–11 record with 25 complete games in
                 33 starts, five shutouts and a 2.22 ERA in 303²/₃ innings.*

SEPTEMBER 10   Needing a victory to remain in first place, the Dodgers take a thrilling 9–8 decision
                 over the Cardinals in 11 innings at Ebbets Field. The Dodgers trailed 5–3 with
                 two out and two runners on base in the ninth when Ray Schmandt and Ivy Olson
                 delivered run-scoring singles to tie the score 5–5. Jeff Pfeffer gave up three runs in
                 the 11th, however, and Brooklyn trailed 8–5. A four-run rally in the bottom half
                 won the contest. The first run scored on a ground out after Otto Miller led off with

a double and Pfeffer singled him to third. With one out, Jimmy Johnston hit a sacrifice fly that narrowed the gap to a run but accounted for the second out of the inning. A St. Louis error plus singles by Bernie Neis, Zack Wheat and Hy Myers brought home the tying and winning runs.

SEPTEMBER 11   The Dodgers sweep the Cardinals 15–4 and 2–0 at Ebbets Field. Brooklyn batters collected 20 hits in the opener.

> *Just before the start of the double-header, two streetcars jammed with fans heading for the ballpark crashed into each other. One man was killed and 87 were injured.*

SEPTEMBER 13   The Dodgers win their 10th game in a row with a 7–3 decision over the Cubs at Ebbets Field. The streak gave the Dodgers a five-game lead and virtually sewed up the 1920 pennant.

SEPTEMBER 15   Sherry Smith shuts out the Cubs 1–0 at Ebbets Field. Zack Wheat drove in the winning run with a double.

SEPTEMBER 27   Eleven days after a bomb explodes on Wall Street in New York City, killing 30 people, the idle Dodgers clinch the National League pennant when the second-place Giants split a double-header against the Braves in New York.

OCTOBER 3   In the final game of the season, the Dodgers score two runs in the ninth inning and one in the 10th to defeat the Braves 4–3 at Ebbets Field. Hy Myers tripled in the winning run.

> *The Dodgers played the Cleveland Indians in the 1920 World Series. Managed by Tris Speaker, the Indians were 98–56 and won the American League pennant for the first time in franchise history after surviving a tight three-team pennant race with the White Sox and Yankees. Cleveland also weathered a tragedy to win the AL title. On August 16, shortstop Ray Chapman was killed by a pitch thrown by Carl Mays of the Yankees. The 1920 Fall Classic was a best-of-nine affair. It was one of four modern World Series in which the victor needed five wins to claim the world championship. The other three were in 1903 (the first of the modern era), 1919 and 1921. The 1919 Series, won by the Reds five games to three over the White Sox, cast a shadow over the 1920 clash between the Dodgers and Indians. During a trial in Chicago over the final week of September, eight members of the White Sox admitted to throwing the 1919 Series to Cincinnati. The eight were immediately suspended by White Sox owner Charles Comiskey with the club still in the thick of the 1920 pennant race. There were rumors swirling that the 1920 World Series was also fixed. Brooklyn District Attorney Harry E. Lewis called in 12 Dodgers players on October 1 and 2 to examine allegations suggesting that they had been approached by gamblers. The investigation proved no wrongdoing.*

OCTOBER 5   The Dodgers open the Series with a 3–1 loss to the Indians before 23,573 at Ebbets Field. Cleveland scored first with two runs in the second inning off Rube Marquard, who was the losing pitcher. It was the third time that Marquard was the loser in the opening game of the World Series. The other two were with the Giants in 1913 and the Dodgers in 1916. Stan Coveleski was the winning hurler with a five-hitter.

The 1920 clash marked the first time that brothers faced each other in World Series play. Jimmy Johnston was a third baseman for the Dodgers while his older brother Doc was the first baseman for Cleveland. Jimmy played in all 155 regular season games for Brooklyn in 1920 and appeared in the first four Series games before missing the final three with an injury. Replacing Johnston at third base was Jack Sheehan, who had played in only three games during the regular season and had just two hits in five at-bats during his major league career before making his first post-season appearance. Sheehan was two-for-11 in the three Series games he played. They were his final two hits in the majors. In 1921, Sheehan was hitless in 12 at-bats and went back to the minors. He's the only player in history to appear in fewer than 10 career regular season games but play in a World Series.

OCTOBER 6   The Dodgers even the Series with a 3–0 victory over the Indians before 22,559 at Ebbets Field. Burleigh Grimes threw a complete-game seven-hitter. The Dodgers opened the scoring with a run in the first inning and added single runs in the third and the fifth.

OCTOBER 7   The Dodgers take a two-games-to-one lead with a 2–1 triumph over the Indians before 25,088 at Ebbets Field. Sherry Smith pitched a complete-game three-hitter. The two Brooklyn runs scored in the first inning on RBI-singles by Zack Wheat and Hy Myers. Duster Mails pitched 6²/₃ inning of shutout relief for Cleveland.

Mails pitched 13 games for the Dodgers in 1915 and 1916 and had a record of 0–2. From then until August 1920, he languished in the minors until purchased by the Indians. Mails was a surprise package during the stretch run of the pennant race, posting seven victories without a defeat.

OCTOBER 9   The Indians even the Series with a 5–1 win over the Dodgers at League Park in Cleveland. Stan Coveleski pitched a complete game for his second victory over the Dodgers.

OCTOBER 10   The Indians win 8–1 over the Dodgers in a historic game in Cleveland. The contest produced the only unassisted triple play in World Series history, the first grand slam and the first home run by a pitcher. The slam was struck by Cleveland right fielder Elmer Smith in the first inning off Burleigh Grimes. In the fourth, Jim Bagby of the Indians accounted for the first-ever World Series homer by a pitcher. Grimes was again the victim. The triple play was achieved by Indians second baseman Bill Wambsganss in the fifth. Pete Kilduff led off the inning with a single and advanced to second on Otto Miller's single. On a 3–2 pitch, relief pitcher Clarence Mitchell scorched a liner toward right, but Wambsganss jumped high in the air and snared the ball in one hand, touched second and tagged a stunned Miller for the triple play. Running on the play, Miller was only a few feet from the bag. Mitchell later hit into a double play in the eighth.

Playing second base, Kilduff unwittingly contributed to the pounding that Grimes took on the mound. The Indians noticed that whenever Grimes threw a spitball, Kilduff picked up a handful of dirt to better handle the wet ball should it be hit his way.

OCTOBER 11   The Indians move within one game of the world championship with a 1–0 triumph in Cleveland in game six. Duster Mails pitched a three-hitter and outdueled Sherry Smith for the win. The run scored with two out in the sixth on a single by Tris Speaker and a double from George Burns.

Smith was the losing pitcher in the 14-inning epic against the Red Sox in Game Two in 1916 (see October 9, 1916). He made three starts in World Series play and had a 0.89 ERA in 30¹/₃ innings, but he possessed only a 1–2 record to show for it.

OCTOBER 12   Three weeks before Warren Harding wins the presidential election, the Indians close out the 1920 World Series with a 3–0 win over the Dodgers in Cleveland. Stan Coveleski pitched a shutout for his third win against Brooklyn. He also won Games One and Four and allowed only two runs in 27 innings. The Indians won the world championship five games to two. The Cleveland pitching staff allowed only two runs in the last 43 innings of the Series. Over the course of the seven games, the Dodgers were outscored 21–8.

Rube Marquard was scheduled to be the starting pitcher in Game Seven, but he had been arrested by Cleveland police prior to Game Four for scalping tickets. On only one day of rest, Burleigh Grimes started instead of Marquard. A native of Cleveland, Rube was fined just $1 plus $3.80 in court costs by a judge, but Charles Ebbets wasn't so forgiving. He ordered that Marquard never pitch another game for the Dodgers. On December 15, 1920, Marquard was traded to the Reds for Dutch Ruether.

1921   LA

Season in a Sentence

The defending champion Dodgers win 11 games in a row in April and May, but by season's end they are only two games above .500.

Finish • Won • Lost • Pct • GB

Fifth   77   75   .507   16.5

Manager

Wilbert Robinson

Stats

Stats	Dods	NL	Rank
Batting Avg:	.280	.289	7
On-Base Pct:	.325	.338	7
Slugging Pct:	.386	.397	6
Home Runs:	59		5
Stolen Bases:	91		6
ERA:	3.70	3.78	5
Fielding Avg:	.964	.967	7
Runs Scored:	667		6
Runs Allowed:	681		4 (tie)

Starting Lineup

Otto Miller, c
Ray Schmandt, 1b
Pete Kilduff, 2b
Jimmy Johnston, 3b
Ivy Olson, ss
Zack Wheat, lf
Hy Myers, cf
Tommy Griffith, rf
Bernie Neis, rf-cf
Ed Konetchy, 1b

Pitchers

Burleigh Grimes, sp
Leon Cadore, sp
Dutch Ruether, sp
Clarence Mitchell, rp-sp
Sherry Smith, rp-sp
Johnny Miljus, rp-sp

Attendance

613,245 (third in NL)

Club Leaders

Batting Avg:	Jimmy Johnston	.325
On-Base Pct:	Jimmy Johnston	.372
Slugging Pct:	Zack Wheat	.484
Home Runs:	Zack Wheat	14
RBIs:	Zack Wheat	85
Runs:	Jimmy Johnston	104
Stolen Bases:	Jimmy Johnston	28
Wins:	Burleigh Grimes	22
Strikeouts:	Burleigh Grimes	136
ERA:	Burleigh Grimes	2.83
Saves:	Sherry Smith	4

APRIL 13   The Dodgers open the season with a thrilling 5–4 win over the Braves in Boston with three runs in the eighth inning and two in the ninth. A two-run double by Zack Wheat in the eighth inning pulled Brooklyn within a run. In the ninth, Ernie Krueger double, Wally Hood was hit by a pitch and Ivy Olson singled to tie the score. Hood crossed the plate on an error.

The Dodgers lost their next five games, then won 11 in a row for a record of 12–5.

APRIL 17   The Dodgers lose the home opener 4–2 against the Braves before 15,000 on a rainy day at Ebbets Field.

The Dodgers installed temporary bleachers in left field for the 1920 World Series and kept them in place until 1930, when a larger and more permanent structure was constructed. The seats shortened the home run distance in left field from 419 feet to 383.

MAY 2   The Dodgers extend their winning streak to 11 games by scoring two runs in the ninth inning for a 4–3 decision over the Phillies. Zack Wheat singled in the tying run and scored on Ed Konetchy's walk-off triple.

During the 11-game winning streak, the Dodgers came from behind eight times, seven of them in the seventh, eighth and ninth innings.

MAY 22   Fans throw a barrage of bottles at umpire Cy Rigler after a call against the Dodgers in the seventh inning of a 6–4 loss to the Cubs at Ebbets Field.

MAY 28   The Dodgers trounce the Phillies 15–3 in Philadelphia.

JUNE 16   The Dodgers score three times in the ninth inning to tie the Pirates 5–5 in Pittsburgh, but wind up losing 6–5 in 17 innings.

JUNE 18   The Dodgers trade Jeff Pfeffer to the Cardinals for Ferdie Schupp and Hal Janvrin.

JUNE 21   Newly appointed Baseball Commissioner Kenesaw Landis helps raise the 1920 National League pennant at Ebbets Field prior to a 4–2 win over the Phillies.

JUNE 25   Solo home runs by Zack Wheat in the fourth inning and Tommy Griffith in the eighth beats the Braves 2–1 at Ebbets Field.

Wheat batted .320 with 14 home runs in 1921.

JUNE 27   Otto Miller fights Tony Boeckel of the Braves during a 5–2 win at Ebbets Field. Boeckel hit Miller with his backswing, and the Dodgers catcher made a few pointed comments about Boeckel's lack of bat control. The two were soon throwing punches and, after being separated, were ejected from the premises.

JULY 2   The Dodgers sweep the Phillies 11–9 and 5–3 in Philadelphia.

JULY 4   The Dodgers sell Ed Konetchy to the Phillies.

JULY 7	A two-out home run by first baseman Ray Schmandt beats the Giants 7–6 in New York. The Dodgers tied a club record with five triples during the contest. Otto Miller hit two of them, with Jimmy Johnston, Dutch Ruether and Hy Myers adding the rest.
JULY 11	The Dodgers score four runs in the ninth inning to defeat the Pirates 9–8 at Ebbets Field. Four straight singles by Ivy Olson, Jimmy Johnston, Bernie Neis and Zack Wheat scored two runs. Wheat stole second and Neis stole home on a double steal. Hy Myers delivered the winning run with a walk-off single.

> *Johnston played in all 152 of the Dodgers games in 1921 and hit .325 with 104 runs, 203 hits and 41 doubles. It was the second straight year that Johnston played in every regular season game, although he missed three games in the 1920 World Series with an injury.*

JULY 23	The Dodgers clobber the Cardinals 14–4 in St. Louis.
AUGUST 1	The Dodgers score five runs with two out in the ninth to stun the Cardinals 8–7 in St. Louis. A two-run double by Ivy Olson brought home the first two runs. Jimmy Johnston tied the game with another two-run two-bagger and then scored on a wild pitch.
AUGUST 3	The Dodgers score three runs with two out in the ninth inning to win 4–3 over the Reds in Cincinnati. It was the second consecutive game in which the club came from behind with a two-out in rally in the ninth. The first run scored on a two-out, two-strike single by Zack Taylor. Bernie Neis drove in the final two runs with another single.
AUGUST 6	About 7,000 veterans from the 80th Division, in Pittsburgh for a reunion, watch the Dodgers defeat the Pirates 3–2 at Forbes Field. Brooklyn pitcher Johnny Miljus, who served with the division in France during World War I, was honored before the game. Although suffering from a sore arm, Miljus was given the starting assignment and it nearly cost the Dodgers a victory. Miljus walked the first two batters, both of whom eventually scored, before being replaced. Leon Cadore hurled nine shutout innings of relief.
AUGUST 10	Leon Cadore pitches the Dodgers to a 1–0 win over the Pirates in Pittsburgh. Cadore also drove in the lone run of the game with a fifth-inning single that scored Ray Schmandt.
AUGUST 11	Zack Wheat collects seven hits in 10 at-bats during a double-header against the Giants in New York with a triple, two doubles and four singles. The Dodgers won the first game 5–3 and lost the second 6–5 in 13 innings.
AUGUST 27	The Dodgers rout the Cubs 15–5 at Ebbets Field. Brooklyn broke a 4–4 tie with four runs in the seventh inning, and then added six in the eighth.
AUGUST 29	Dutch Ruether pitches a shutout to defeat the Pirates 1–0 at Ebbets Field. The lone run scored in the ninth inning on a double by Hy Myers and a two-base error by Pittsburgh pitcher Wilbur Cooper, who dropped a throw from Charlie Grimm while covering first base.

SEPTEMBER 1   Burleigh Grimes earns his 20th win of the season with a 5–1 decision over the Giants at Ebbets Field. The Dodgers pulled off a triple play in the fifth inning with New York runners on second and third. Third baseman Jimmy Johnston caught Earl Smith's line drive, stepped on third to double up Irish Meusel and threw to shortstop Ivy Olson to retire Rawlings.

Grimes led the National League in wins (with a 22–13 record), complete games (30 in 35 starts) and strikeouts (136 in 302^2/$_3$ innings) in addition to finishing fifth in earned run average (2.83).

SEPTEMBER 28   Dutch Ruether hits a home run in the ninth inning that bounces through a hole in the scoreboard at Braves Field, capping a 9–5 win over Boston. Lead-off batter Ivy Olson sparked the victory with a home run on the first pitch of the first inning off Braves pitcher Johnny Cooney.

The Zeitgeist of the Brooklyn Dodgers Fan

The Dodgers failed to win a National League pennant from 1921 through 1940. During that period, the club finished in the top half of the NL only six times and was in contention for first place in the month of September only in 1924 and 1930. At the other end of the Brooklyn Bridge were the two most glamorous teams in baseball. The Yankees won their first American League title in 1921, establishing an enduring dynasty. The Yanks reached the World Series six times during the 1920s and five more in the 1930s. The Giants won four NL championships in the 1920s and three during the 1930s. The New York clubs met in the Fall Classic in 1921, 1922, 1923, 1936 and 1937.

The contrast between the lack of success of the Dodgers and the success of their rivals across the East River was not limited to achievement on the field. The Yankees played in imposing Yankee Stadium in the Bronx, capable of holding 70,000 fans. The stadium hosted not only the World Series but also 15 world heavyweight championship boxing bouts. Joe Louis fought there for the title seven times. Notre Dame's football team played at Yankee Stadium nearly every year from 1925 through the end of the 1940s, usually against Army. The Polo Grounds, home of the Giants, lacked the imposing architecture of Yankee Stadium or the charm of Ebbets Field, but it contained over 50,000 seats. It was also the site of big events. There were six world heavyweight boxing title fights at the Polo Grounds, as well as five National Football League championship games. The Dodgers, on the other hand, played their games at cramped Ebbets Field, which, after an expansion in 1930, held a little over 30,000.

The contrast between the Yankees, Giants and Dodgers over the 1920s and 1930s had a profound effect on the psyche of Brooklyn fans. As author Bob McGee put it in his book *The Greatest Ballpark Ever: Ebbets Field and the Story of the Brooklyn Dodgers*, it was during this period "that the ballpark itself was becoming defined as a haven for madcap zaniness and acknowledged as a comfortable home for those for whom a straitjacket was not out of the question."

The population shifts in New York during this period also helped to reshape the image of the Dodgers. During the first quarter of the 20th century, Brooklyn had grown to represent a step up the ladder for a largely working-class, immigrant population that had first settled in the teeming slums of lower Manhattan. Population leaped from 1.1 million in 1900 to 2.6 million in 1930. In 1900, the residents of the borough were largely pious descendants of Dutch and German settlers who helped establish Brooklyn's nickname of "The City of Churches." By 1930, half of the population of Brooklyn was foreign-born, largely Italian, Irish and Jewish. The borough developed into one the most ethnically diverse communities in the world, which gave it a distinctive personality.

Most of the immigrants, particularly those of the second generation, were eager to assimilate and to be stamped as Americans. And there were few institutions more American than baseball. The new residents of both Brooklyn and the United States adopted the Dodgers with a fierce passion. "It was during those years," wrote Stanley Cohen in *Dodgers!: The First 100 Years,* "that the Dodgers began to project the image that would stamp their identity and fuse a bond between a team and its fans that had no equal. The image was one of adorable losers and lovable clowns, bizarre and zany free spirits who brought each game an impromptu recklessness that appeared to leave the outcome in hands other than their own. They managed to lose with more flair than other teams could muster in victory. And the fans loved them."

Glenn Stout also wrote of the shift in the passions of the Dodgers fans beginning in the early 1920s in *The Dodgers: 120 Years of Dodgers Baseball.* "Wins and losses simply would never be as important in Brooklyn," wrote Stout, "because everyone knew in their hearts that Brooklyn had fallen behind the rest of New York. It was still a fabulous place, and much beloved by residents, but Brooklyn's aspirations as a place were as well-defined as its borders. Just as traffic on the bridge flowed in only one direction, so did expectations for the ballclub. To criticize them or hold them to the higher standard set by the Giants and Yankees was, in a sense, to admit Brooklyn's shortcomings. To ignore the final score and exalt in the character of the team and its personality was to celebrate the same about Brooklyn." Cohen added that Brooklyn "was a citizenry that had long ago learned to measure success in small doses. The Dodgers of that era were a team scaled to the same dimension as their fans. They appeared to be ill-suited for prosperity and disdainful of its gifts."

The political situation of Brooklyn also contributed to the mixture of pride and inferiority that infected the community. If it were autonomous, Brooklyn would have been the third-largest city in the United States in 1930 with its more than 2$\frac{1}{2}$ million residents. It was 40 percent more populous than Manhattan, but it was merely one of five boroughs of New York City and endured a subservient posture to its more cosmopolitan neighbor across the East River. Manhattanites tended to view anyone who lived east of the Brooklyn Bridge as uncultured bumpkins. As a consequence, constituents in Brooklyn developed a "Cinderella complex" as the unwanted stepchild of the power base located on Manhattan Island. The heated rivalry between the Giants and Dodgers extended far beyond baseball because working-class Brooklynites held seething grudges against the Giants fans who were perceived as Wall Street fat cats who lived in luxury apartments on the Upper East Side and on estates in Westchester County.

Brooklyn's second-class status was impossible for its residents to avoid internalizing. The borough had an identity all its own, and was no longer merely a place that anchored one end of a famous bridge. It evoked a boisterous, brusque, confrontational style, an off-kilter sense of humor with an edge and a chip-on-the-shoulder audacity. That attitude is best exemplified by the famous and infamous who were born or grew up in Brooklyn, including such iconoclastic figures as Barbra Streisand, Howard Cosell, Mel Brooks, Woody Allen, Neil Simon, Jerry Seinfeld, Danny Kaye, Jackie Gleason, Phil Silvers, Moe and Curly Howard, Jimmy Durante, Richard Lewis, Chris Rock, Eddie Murphy, Adam Sandler, Gilbert Gottfried, Jimmy Kimmel, Andrew "Dice" Clay, Joan Rivers, Larry David, Mickey Rooney, Buddy Hackett, Jerry Stiller, Anne Meara, Rudy Giuliani, Vince Lombardi, Red Auerbach, Mae West, Rosie Perez, Rhea Perlman, Leah Remini, Edie Falco, Spike Lee, Louis Gossett Jr., Elliott Gould, Alan Arkin, Richard Dreyfuss, Eli Wallach, Shelley Winters, Larry King, Harvey Keitel, Colin Quinn, Cyndi Lauper, Pat Benatar, Joy Behar, Judge Judy Sheindlin, Steve Buscemi, John Turturro, Marisa Tomei, Mickey Spillane, Bobby Fischer, Mike Tyson, Bugsy Siegel and Al Capone.

By the 1940s, the image of the Brooklyn Dodger fan was firmly fixed in the national consciousness. A comedian could arouse laughter by the mere mention of the word Brooklyn. It seems as though every World War II movie or novel had a likable, wisecracking, dim-witted character from Brooklyn who spoke lovingly about the Dodgers and how much he missed Ebbets Field while speaking "Brooklynese" in the district's distinctive accent, which twisted the English language. In 1941, Sidney Ascher tried to counteract the negative image by founding

The Society for the Prevention of Disparaging Remarks About Brooklyn, citing 6,457 examples in the media in which the borough was maligned in that single year. By the end of the decade, the organization had 50,000 members.

The Dodgers would win seven National League pennants from 1941 through 1956 and, despite failing to win a World Series until 1955, Brooklynites finally had a ball club they could brag about, particularly when Giants fans were in the vicinity. But pride turned to anger when Walter O'Malley moved the franchise to Los Angeles at the end of the 1957 season, leaving a void in the borough that has yet to be filled.

1922

Season in a Sentence

The Dodgers add Dazzy Vance, but the club hovers around the .500 mark all season and finishes in sixth place.

Finish • Won • Lost • Pct • GB

Sixth   76   78   .494   17.0

Manager

Wilbert Robinson

Stats	Dods	NL	Rank
Batting Avg:	.290	.292	6
On-Base Pct:	.335	.348	6
Slugging Pct:	.392	.404	6
Home Runs:	56		4
Stolen Bases:	79		5
ERA:	4.05	4.10	4
Fielding Avg:	.967	.967	5
Runs Scored:	743		6
Runs Allowed:	754		4

Starting Lineup

Hank DeBerry, c
Ray Schmandt, 1b
Ivy Olson, 2b-ss
Andy High, 3b
Jimmy Johnston, ss-2b
Zack Wheat, lf
Hy Myers, cf
Tommy Griffith, rf
Bert Griffith, rf

Pitchers

Dutch Ruether, sp
Dazzy Vance, sp
Burleigh Grimes, sp
Leon Cadore, sp
Harry Shriver, sp-rp
Al Mamaux, rp
Sherry Smith, rp-sp
Art Decatur, rp

Attendance

498,865 (fifth in NL)

Club Leaders

Batting Avg:	Zack Wheat	.335
On-Base Pct:	Zack Wheat	.388
Slugging Pct:	Zack Wheat	.503
Home Runs:	Zack Wheat	16
RBIs:	Zack Wheat	112
Runs:	Jimmy Johnston	110
Stolen Bases:	Jimmy Johnston	18
Wins:	Dutch Ruether	21
Strikeouts:	Dazzy Vance	134
ERA:	Dutch Ruether	3.53
Saves:	Al Mamaux	3

MARCH 14   The Dodgers purchase Possum Whitted from the Pirates.

APRIL 12   The Dodgers open the season with a 4–3 victory over the Giants in New York. Dutch Ruether was the winning pitcher.

APRIL 13   Dazzy Vance makes his debut with the Dodgers and loses 4–3 to the Giants in New York.

Clarence (Dazzy) Vance was acquired from New Orleans of the Southern Association the previous off-season. The player from New Orleans who

Charles Ebbets most desired was catcher Hank DeBerry. The New Orleans club refused to sell DeBerry, however, unless the Dodgers also took Vance, and Brooklyn reluctantly agreed. At the time he made his debut with Brooklyn, Vance was 31 years old and had yet to win a major league game. Appearing in nine contests in 1915 and two more in 1918 with the Pirates and the Yankees, Vance had an 0–4 record and a 4.91 ERA. Given a new lease on life, the late-blooming Vance was 18–12 with a 3.70 ERA and a league-leading 134 strikeouts in 1922. It was only the beginning. Vance would finish his career in 1935 with a record of 197–140, good enough to earn him enshrinement in the Hall of Fame. Vance topped the NL in strikeouts seven consecutive seasons from 1922 through 1928. During his 11 seasons with the Dodgers, he also led the league four times in shutouts, three seasons in ERA and twice in wins and complete games. Vance achieved his success with long arms and a high leg kick, which produced a blinding fastball and a sharp-breaking curve. He was six-foot-two and had an 83-inch reach. Dazzy also pitched with a long-sleeved undershirt with a tattered right sleeve that fluttered in the breeze to distract the hitters. The tactic was later outlawed. Among Dodger pitchers, Vance ranks third in wins (190), sixth in defeats (131), third in complete games (212), fourth in strikeouts (1,918), fourth in innings pitched (2,757²/₃), fifth in games started (326), sixth in shutouts (30), sixth in walks (764) and ninth in games pitched (378).

APRIL 15 The Giants score 11 runs in the first inning off Clarence Mitchell, Ray Gordinier and Harry Shriver and beat the Dodgers 17–10 in New York.

APRIL 16 The Dodgers win the home opener 10–2 over the Phillies. Dutch Ruether was not only the winning pitcher, but he collected four hits, including a triple, in four at-bats. Zack Wheat and Hy Myers hit home runs.

Wheat batted .335 with 16 homers, 112 RBIs and 201 hits in 1922.

APRIL 22 Trailing 3–0, the Dodgers score five runs in the seventh inning to beat the Yankees 5–3 at Ebbets Field. During the rally, Wilbert Robinson used three consecutive left-handed pinch-hitters, each of whom drew a walk from right-hander Rosy Ryan. The three pinch-hitters were Dutch Ruether (for Ray Schmandt), Tommy Griffith (for Sam Crane) and Sam Post (for Otto Miller). In addition, two of the three were lifted for pinch-runners after they reached base.

Hy Myers batted .317 in his last of 11 seasons in Brooklyn. The average was a career high, as was his total of 89 RBIs.

APRIL 26   Rookie catcher Bernie Hungling drives in six runs with a triple, double and single
                during a 10–1 win over the Braves in Boston. The Dodgers were held scoreless before
                scoring four runs in the seventh inning, four in the eighth and two in the ninth.

                *Hungling drove in only 15 runs over 51 games and 137 at-bats over a three-year
                big league career.*

MAY 1   In his first major league start, Harry Shriver pitches a three-hit shutout to defeat the
                Phillies 2–0 at Ebbets Field.

                *Shriver had a two-year career with a record of 4–6. He pitched only one more
                shutout (see September 16, 1922).*

MAY 6   The Dodgers trounce the Braves 15–2 at Ebbets Field.

MAY 25   Jimmy Johnston hits for the cycle in five at-bats during an 8–7 win in the first game
                of a double-header in Philadelphia. In the first inning, Johnston singled off Phillies
                hurler Bill Hubbell. The next batter was Zack Wheat, who hit a line drive that struck
                Hubbell in the head. Johnston collected a homer, triple and double off Jesse Winters,
                Hubbell's replacement. Johnston was also two-for-five with a double and single in
                the second contest, a 9–6 victory.

                Johnston hit .319 and scored 110 runs in 1922.

MAY 26   The Dodgers sweep the Phillies for the second day in a row with 7–5 and 7–0
                victories in Philadelphia.

MAY 27   Playing their third double-header in three days against the Phillies in Philadelphia,
                the Dodgers extend their winning streak to eight games with a 7–3 decision in the
                opening contest by scoring four runs in the 10th inning. Clarence Mitchell hit a
                three-run homer in the extra inning. He entered the game as a substitute at first base.
                The winning streak ended with a 3–2 loss in the nightcap.

                *During his 18-year career, Mitchell appeared in 390 games as a pitcher, but
                because of his abilities as a hitter, he often played in the field and as a pinch-
                hitter in between mound assignments. He appeared in 75 games as a first
                baseman and 24 in the outfield. As a pitcher, Mitchell had a lifetime record of
                125–139. His career batting average was .257 with seven home runs in 1,287
                at-bats.*

JUNE 4   An immense crowd of at least 30,000 jams Ebbets Field for a game against the
                Giants and spills onto the playing field surrounding the diamond. Ground rules were
                necessary as balls hit into the crowd were doubles. The Giants scored three runs in
                the ninth inning to defeat the Dodgers 5–4. Base umpire Bob Emslie was the target of
                bottle-throwing fans in the ninth when he made a call against the home team.

JUNE 10   The Dodgers collect 24 hits and wallop the Cubs 13–0 at Ebbets Field. Brooklyn
                scored seven runs in the fourth inning for an 11–0 advantage. Jimmy Johnston
                garnered five hits, including a triple, in five at-bats.

JUNE 16   The Dodgers clobber the Cardinals 12–2 at Ebbets Field.

JUNE 18   A special policeman attacks two disabled World War I veterans at Ebbets Field during a 2–0 loss to the Pirates that was called in the sixth inning by rain. Robert Smith, a 56-year-old retired police officer from the New York City force, was accused of knocking down and kicking Henry Straub and Frank Flower, both residents of Brooklyn. The two former soldiers were in the bleachers when patrons scurried to get out of the rain. Straub and Flower sought shelter beneath the stands, where Smith charged the pair with trying to get into the grandstand and attacked them. Smith was found guilty of third-degree assault by a jury in December 1922.

JUNE 19   The Dodgers win a thrilling 6–5 decision over the Pirates in 14 innings at Ebbets Field. Brooklyn scored four runs in the ninth inning to tie the contest. A two-run double by Jimmy Johnston put the Dodgers within a run and Tommy Griffith's two-bagger tied the contest. Zack Wheat drove in the winning run with a single.

The Dodgers employed a platoon in right field in 1922 with two players named Griffith. Tommy Griffith played in 82 games at the position, and Bert Griffith played in 69. The two were not related to one another.

JUNE 21   The Dodgers win another exciting encounter with a 15–14 triumph over the Pirates in 10 innings at Ebbets Field. The Dodgers led 10–6 before Pittsburgh scored four times in the eighth inning and two in the ninth for a 12–10 lead. Brooklyn responded with two in the bottom of the ninth to send the contest into extra innings. The Pirates scored twice in the 10th, but the Dodgers countered with three tallies in their half for the victory. The final-inning rally consisted of a double by Ivy Olson, two Pittsburgh errors and a sacrifice fly by Tommy Griffith.

JULY 1   Dutch Ruether pitches a 10-inning, complete-game shutout and drives in the lone run to defeat the Braves 1–0 in Boston. His RBI-double in the 10th followed a single by catcher Hank DeBerry. Ruether also started a double play in the ninth that choked off a Boston rally.

The July 1 victory gave Ruether a 14–3 record just 70 games into season. He finished the year with 21 wins, 12 losses, a 3.53 ERA in 267$^{1}/_{3}$ innings and 26 complete games in 35 starts.

JULY 2   Fans throw bottles at uniformed policemen during a double-header against the Braves at Ebbets Field. The deplorable incident occurred just before the start of the second game as fans in the left-field bleachers started for the grandstand seats. The policemen attempted to check the migration and were greeted with a fusillade of bottles. The officers beat a hasty retreat, but the bombardment continued for several more minutes. It was not stopped until Dodgers manager Wilbert Robinson made a personal appeal to the fans. Bottles had to be cleared from the field before the game could begin. The Dodgers won both games 8–6 and 6–3.

AUGUST 5   A walk-off homer into the left-field seats by pitcher Leon Cadore beats the Reds 3–2 in the second game of a double-header at Ebbets Field. The Dodgers also won the opener 5–0.

AUGUST 10   The Dodgers score 10 runs in the fourth inning and clobber the Cubs 16–1 at Ebbets Field.

AUGUST 25   The Dodgers score two runs in the ninth inning and defeat the Pirates 8–7 in the first game of a double-header in Pittsburgh. Hy Myers singled in the tying run, took second on a walk and scored on Andy High's single.

Andy's surname didn't match his size. High stood only five-foot-six.

SEPTEMBER 1   The Dodgers score two runs in the 10th inning to defeat the Giants 8–7 at Ebbets Field. With two out in the 10th, Tommy Griffith struck a pinch-hit double to drive in the tying run and scored on Leon Cadore's walk-off single. Cadore had given up a run in the top of the 10th to put New York ahead 7–6.

SEPTEMBER 9   A walk-off homer by Hy Myers in the 12th inning beats the Braves 6–5 at Ebbets Field. Burleigh Grimes pitched a complete game despite allowing 18 hits.

SEPTEMBER 16   The Dodgers win 1–0 in 10 innings over the Cubs in the second game of a double-header at Ebbets Field. The lone run scored on singles by Andy High, bunts from Bernie Hingling and Harry Shriver, and a single by Ivy Olson. Shriver pitched the complete-game shutout.

SEPTEMBER 18   The Dodgers sell Sherry Smith to the Indians.

SEPTEMBER 23   Dutch Ruether earns his 20th win of the season with a 9–5 decision over the Pirates in the first game of a double-header at Ebbets Field. The Dodgers completed the sweep with a 5–1 triumph in the second contest.

SEPTEMBER 24   The Dodgers come from behind to beat the Pirates 4–2 in the first game of a double-header at Ebbets Field. Zack Wheat tied the score with a two-run homer in the eighth inning. The Dodgers won the contest on a two-run walk-off home run from Andy High in the ninth. In the nightcap, Pittsburgh scored 10 runs in the sixth inning and won 11–3 in a game called after seven innings by darkness.

1923
L A

Season in a Sentence

The Giants and Yankees play each other in the World Series for the third consecutive year, and the Dodgers lose 12 of their first 16 games before stumbling to a sixth-place finish.

Finish • Won • Lost • Pct • GB

Sixth   76   78   .494   19.5

Manager

Wilbert Robinson

Stats

Stats	Dods	NL	Rank
Batting Avg:	.285	.286	6
On-Base Pct:	.340	.343	6
Slugging Pct:	.387	.395	7
Home Runs:	62		5
Stolen Bases:	71		6
ERA:	3.74	3.99	2
Fielding Avg:	.955	.966	8
Runs Scored:	753		4
Runs Allowed:	741		6

Starting Lineup

Zack Taylor, c
Jack Fournier, 1b
Ivy Olson, 2b
Andy High, 3b-ss
Jimmy Johnston, ss-2b
Zack Wheat, lf
Bernie Neis, cf
Tommy Griffith, rf
Gene Bailey, cf
Bert Griffith, lf
Hank DeBerry, c
Bill McCarren, 3b

Pitchers

Burleigh Grimes, sp
Dazzy Vance, sp
Dutch Ruether, sp
Leo Dickerman, sp-rp
Dutch Henry, sp-rp
Art Decatur, rp
George Smith, rp

Attendance

564,666 (fifth in NL)

Club Leaders

Batting Avg:	Jack Fournier	.351
On-Base Pct:	Jack Fournier	.411
Slugging Pct:	Jack Fournier	.588
Home Runs:	Jack Fournier	22
RBIs:	Jack Fournier	102
Runs:	Jimmy Johnston	111
Stolen Bases:	Jimmy Johnston	16
Wins:	Burleigh Grimes	21
Strikeouts:	Dazzy Vance	197
ERA:	Dazzy Vance	3.50
Saves:	Art Decatur	3

FEBRUARY 11   The Dodgers trade Clarence Mitchell to the Phillies for George Smith.

FEBRUARY 15   The Dodgers trade Hy Myers and Ray Schmandt to the Cardinals for Jack Fournier.

This was the best trade made by the Dodgers during the 1920s. Myers had played 11 seasons with the Dodgers, but he was near the end of his career. Fournier wasn't happy with the prospect of leaving St. Louis and threatened to retire rather than report to Brooklyn. He missed the first three weeks of the season before finally ending his holdout. He proceeded to give the Dodgers three tremendous seasons in Brooklyn before entering the decline phase of his career. Among those with at least 2,000 plate appearances with the Dodgers, Fournier still ranks second in on-base percentage (.413), third in batting average (.337) and fifth in slugging percentage (.552).

APRIL 17   The Dodgers open the season with a 14-inning, 5–5 tie against the Phillies at Ebbets Field. The game was called on account of darkness. Dutch Ruether pitched all 14 innings. Brooklyn tied the score 5–5 with three runs in the sixth. There was no scoring over the final eight innings. Zack Wheat collected four hits in seven at-bats.

APRIL 18

On the day that Yankee Stadium opens, the Dodgers score five runs in the ninth inning to stun the Phillies 6–5 at Ebbets Field. All five scored without a batter being retired. Zack Wheat started the rally with a home run. Dutch Schliebner singled, Turner Barber walked and Dutch Ruether, acting as a pinch-hitter, also walked to load the bases. The final four runs were driven home on consecutive singles by Hank DeBerry, Burleigh Grimes and Ivy Olson.

Hall of Famer Burleigh Grimes won 20 games four times in five years between 1920 and 1924.

APRIL 26

The Dodgers spoil Philadelphia's home opener by defeating the Phillies 14–4 at Baker Bowl.

MAY 2

Dazzy Vance strikes out 15 batters, but the Dodgers lose 7–6 in 11 innings to the Giants in New York. He fanned 10 batters in the first five innings, but he weakened and allowed three runs in the ninth to send the contest into extra innings. Vance put the eventual winning run on base in the 11th before being relieved.

Vance had an 18–15 record with a 3.50 ERA and led the NL in strikeouts with 197 in 280¹/₃ innings.

MAY 4

The Dodgers record falls to 4–12 with a 13-inning, 1–0 loss to the Braves in Boston. Ex-Dodger Rube Marquard pitched the complete-game shutout.

MAY 7

The Dodgers blow an 8–0 lead, but they come back to trim the Braves 12–11 in 10 innings in Boston. Brooklyn took the eight-run advantage in the fifth and was still ahead 11–5 before the Braves scored three runs in the eighth and three more in the ninth. Jack Fournier drove in the winning run with a sacrifice fly. Jimmy Johnston collected five hits in six at-bats.

Johnston hit .325, scored 111 runs and collected 203 hits in 1923.

MAY 12

Trailing 8–3, the Dodgers score a run in the seventh inning and seven in the eighth to defeat the Cubs 11–7 at Ebbets Field.

MAY 18

Specs Torporcer of the Cardinals hits a fluke homer in the sixth inning of a 3–1 St. Louis win over the Dodgers at Ebbets Field. The drive went down the right-field line, hit the fence and caromed into an alleyway at the end of the right-field stands.

MAY 19

The Dodgers score two runs with two out in the ninth inning to defeat the Cardinals 6–5 at Ebbets Field. Dutch Ruether started the rally with a single and moved to third base on a double by Bernie Neis. Jimmy Johnston followed with a two-run double. St. Louis had scored two runs in the top of the ninth off Ruether to take a 5–4 lead.

MAY 26   All five runs of a 5–0 win over the Braves at Ebbets Field are scored in the third inning.

MAY 29   In his first major league start, Dutch Henry pitches a shutout to defeat the Giants 3–0 in New York.

JUNE 9   Prior to a 2–0 win over St. Louis at Sportsman's Park, former Cardinal Jack Fournier is presented with a floral wreath and a traveling bag.

JUNE 15   The Dodgers score three runs in the ninth inning and two in the 11th to beat the Cubs 9–7 at Wrigley Field. The runs in the ninth scored after two were out on four singles and two Chicago errors. Zack Wheat broke the 7–7 tie with a double.

JUNE 17   Dazzy Vance loses a no-hitter when Sammy Bohne of the Reds singles with two out in the ninth inning in Cincinnati. Vance had to settle for a one-hitter and a 9–0 victory.

JUNE 27   Jimmy Johnston hits a homer, triple and double during a 15–5 win over the Phillies in Philadelphia. Moe Berg made his major league debut, playing at shortstop.

> *Berg played 49 games for the Dodgers in 1923 and hit only .186. After two years in the minors, he played 14 more seasons in the majors, mostly as a weak-hitting reserve catcher, with four American League teams from 1926 through 1939. He may have been the most intelligent man ever to play professional baseball. Berg read and spoke 12 languages, including Sanskrit. He held degrees from Princeton University, Columbia Law School and the Sorbonne. Berg enthralled newsmen with discourses on subjects ranging from ancient Greek history to astronomy. He appeared on the popular radio program* Information Please, *correctly answering questions on Roman mythology, French impressionism, spatial geometry and the infield fly rule. Few knew that Berg was also working as a spy for the United States government during his playing career. At the end of the 1934 season, while playing for the Indians, Berg was added at the last minute to a team of all-stars, which included Babe Ruth, on a goodwill trip to Japan. Organizers cited his fluent Japanese as the reason for including him on this roster of stars. However, instead of playing, Berg spent much of his time taking photographs. By order of the State Department, Berg was to photograph key Japanese military installations and other potential targets from the roof of a Tokyo hospital. In April 1942, Major General Jimmy Doolittle used these photos in making the first American air attack on Japan during World War II. Once the war started, Berg joined the Office of Strategic Services, the forerunner of the CIA. His primary objective was to determine Germany's nuclear potential. Berg took several dangerous missions behind enemy lines to keep track of German scientists. Some of these missions were rumored to have involved assassinations. His gift for languages served him well, and he always returned home safely.*

JUNE 29   Jack Fournier collects six hits in six at-bats during a 14–5 victory over the Phillies in Philadelphia. He hit a home run, two doubles and three singles. Fournier's home run was struck off Whitey Glazner in the third inning and was his fifth in a span of seven games. His sixth base hit of the afternoon was a single in the ninth facing Ralph Head. The Dodgers collected 25 hits in all.

Fournier hits six home runs in the next 10 games to give him 11 homers in a span of 17 contests. Playing in his first season in Brooklyn, Fournier became the first player in franchise history to hit at least 20 homers in a season. He ended the 1923 campaign with 22 homers, 102 RBIs and a .351 batting average.

JUNE 30   Jimmy Johnston picks up eight hits in nine at-bats during a double-header against the Phillies in Philadelphia. He was four-for-five in the opener, a 10–4 victory. Johnston was perfect in four at-bats in the second tilt, a 5–3 defeat. He had a double and three singles in each contest.

JULY 6   The Dodgers sell Leon Cadore to the White Sox.

Cadore married Maie Ebbets, the daughter of Charles Ebbets, in 1931. He was 40 years old while Maie was 49. The two created headlines in 1936 when they applied for relief even though she still owned stock in the Dodgers that she inherited following the death of her father in 1925.

JULY 30   The Dodgers score five runs in the top of the ninth inning to take a 6–4 lead, and then survive a Cardinals rally in the bottom half for a 6–5 victory in St. Louis. A three-run homer by Tommy Griffith was the big blow of the inning.

AUGUST 3   There are no games in Major League Baseball due to the death of President Warren Harding the previous day. All of the games on August 10, the day of Harding's funeral, were also postponed. Calvin Coolidge succeeded Harding as president.

AUGUST 10 Dazzy Vance wins his 10th game in a row by defeating the Pirates 11–3 in the first game of a double-header at Ebbets Field. The Dodgers also won the second tilt 6–0.

AUGUST 19 Dodgers pitcher Leo Dickerman walks five batters in the ninth inning, four of them in succession, to close out a 15–8 loss to the Cubs at Ebbets Field.

AUGUST 31 The Dodgers break a 10-game losing streak by defeating the Giants 5–1 at Ebbets Field.

SEPTEMBER 7 A run scores while Dodgers catcher Zack Taylor argues with umpire Hank O'Day during an 11–3 loss to the Braves in Boston. With Boston runners Stuffy McInnis on third and Hod Ford on second, Bob Smith singled both of them home. Smith took second on right fielder Tommy Griffith's throw to the plate. Taylor contended that Ford ran outside the base line and voiced his concerns to O'Day. As Taylor held the ball and argued with O'Day, Smith advanced to third base. The confab continued and Smith came home as Taylor stood near the plate with the ball in his hands.

SEPTEMBER 9 Jack Fournier hits his 20th home run of the season during a 6–3 triumph over the Giants at Ebbets Field to become the first Dodger to reach the 20-homer mark.

SEPTEMBER 15 The Dodgers score eight runs in the fourth inning and five in the ninth to down the Pirates 13–2 in the second game of a double-header at Forbes Field. Pittsburgh won the first contest 4–1.

SEPTEMBER 24   Burleigh Grimes earns his 20th win of the season with an 8–2 decision over the Cardinals in the first game of a double-header in St. Louis. The Dodgers also won the second contest by a score of 7–3.

SEPTEMBER 30   Dazzy Vance strikes out 12 batters in 12 innings, but he loses 6–4 to the Phillies at Ebbets Field. Before the game, Zack Wheat was presented with an automobile as a gift. Wheat won the car following a newspaper popularity contest by vote of Dodger fans conducted by *The New York Morning Telegraph*.

OCTOBER 13   The Notre Dame football team defeats Army 13–0 before 30,000 at Ebbets Field. The game was originally scheduled to be played at the Polo Grounds, but that facility was being used for a World Series matchup between the Giants and Yankees.

That season, Notre Dame had a record of 9–1–0, while Army was 6–2–1. The two schools played each other nearly every season from 1913 through 1947, usually on a neutral site at the Polo Grounds or Yankee Stadium, in one of the most eagerly anticipated games on the college football schedule.

1924   LA

Season in a Sentence

After falling 13½ games behind on August 9, the Dodgers storm within percentage points of the first-place Giants by September 4 with the help of a 15-game winning streak and finish second following a thrilling final month of the season.

Finish • Won • Lost • Pct • GB

Finish	Won	Lost	Pct	GB
Second	92	62	.597	1.5

Manager

Wilbert Robinson

Stats

Stats	Dods	NL	Rank
Batting Avg:	.287	.283	4
On-Base Pct:	.345	.337	2
Slugging Pct:	.391	.392	6
Home Runs:	72		3
Stolen Bases:	34		8
ERA:	3.64	3.87	4
Fielding Avg:	.968	.970	6
Runs Scored:	717		4
Runs Allowed:	675		4

Starting Lineup

Zack Taylor, c
Jack Fournier, 1b
Andy High, 2b
Milt Stock, 3b
Jimmy Johnston, ss
Zack Wheat, lf
Eddie Brown, cf
Tommy Griffith, rf
Johnny Mitchell, ss
Hank DeBerry, c
Bernie Neis, cf-rf-lf

Pitchers

Dazzy Vance, sp
Burleigh Grimes, sp
Bill Doak, sp
Dutch Ruether, sp
Tiny Osborne, sp-rp
Rube Ehrhardt, sp-rp
Art Decatur, rp

Attendance

818,883 (second in NL)

Club Leaders

Batting Avg:	Zack Wheat	.375
On-Base Pct:	Zack Wheat	.428
	Jack Fournier	.428
Slugging Pct:	Zack Wheat	.549
Home Runs:	Jack Fournier	27
RBIs:	Jack Fournier	116
Runs:	Andy High	98
Stolen Bases:	Jack Fournier	7
Wins:	Dazzy Vance	28
Strikeouts:	Dazzy Vance	262
ERA:	Dazzy Vance	2.16
Saves:	Dutch Ruether	3

APRIL 15   The Dodgers open the season with a 3–2 win over the Giants in New York behind the pitching of Dutch Ruether.

APRIL 19   Zack Wheat collects five hits in five at-bats during an 11–4 win over the Phillies in Philadelphia.

              Although he celebrated his 36th birthday in May, Wheat had the best season of his Hall of Fame career in 1924. He batted .375 with 212 hits, 41 doubles, 14 homers and 97 RBIs. Wheat ranked second in the NL in batting average, fourth in on-base percentage (.428) and third in slugging percentage (.549). He was one of only four players with at least 300 at-bats or 100 or more innings pitched on both the 1920 World Series team and the 1924 squad that nearly reached the Fall Classic again. The other three were Jimmy Johnston, Tommy Griffith and Burleigh Grimes.

APRIL 20   In the home opener, the Dodgers lose 4–1 to the Phillies in a contest at Ebbets Field called after six innings by rain.

              The home opener was played on a Sunday and sandwiched between games played in Philadelphia on Saturday and Monday. The two clubs traveled because it was illegal to play baseball in Pennsylvania on a Sunday in 1924, a situation that would continue until 1934.

APRIL 21   Hank DeBerry hits a three-run homer in the 10th inning to beat the Phillies 7–4 in Philadelphia.

APRIL 25   The Dodgers trade Mike Gonzalez to the Cardinals for Milt Stock.

APRIL 30   In his first game with the Dodgers, Milt Stock hits a two-run single in the 11th inning to beat the Braves 6–4 in Boston.

MAY 3   Zack Wheat garners two homers and two singles in four at-bats during a 7–2 win over the Phillies at Ebbets Field.

              In four games from May 3 through May 6, Wheat had 11 hits, including four homers and a double, in 17 at-bats.

MAY 17   Trailing 2–1, the Dodgers erupt for seven runs in the seventh inning and defeat the Reds 9–2 in Cincinnati.

MAY 30   Down 5–0, the Dodgers score two runs in the sixth inning, three in the ninth and one in the 12th to beat the Braves 6–5 in the first game of a double-header at Ebbets Field. Brooklyn completed the sweep with a 5–1 victory in the nightcap.

MAY 31   The Dodgers score seven runs in the first inning and six in the third for a 13–3 lead and beat the Braves 14–8 at Ebbets Field.

JUNE 9   The Dodgers score two runs in the ninth inning to defeat the Cubs 4–3 at Ebbets Field. Jack Fournier walked with the bases loaded to tie the score. Andy High drove in the winning run with a walk-off single. Dazzy Vance walked 11 batters.

Fournier led the NL in home runs in 1924 with 27. He also batted .334, had an on-base percentage of .428, a slugging percentage of .536, collected 188 hits and drove in 116 runs. High was one of several Dodgers to put together the best season of his career, which helped propel the Dodgers into pennant contention in 1924. He batted .328 and picked up 191 hits.

JUNE 13   The Dodgers trade Leo Dickerman to the Cardinals for Bill Doak.

The Dodgers made an excellent short-term deal, as Doak won 10 decisions in a row for the club during the 1924 pennant race near the end of a career in which he won 169 games. Doak and Charles Ebbets haggled over salary during the following off-season, however, and the pitcher not only sat out the 1925 season, but 1926 as well. Doak could afford to sit out because of his success off the field as the inventor of a baseball glove. Before Doak came along, fielders' mitts were little more than small leather pillows. The glove helped protect the hand but did not aid the fielder in making a catch, particularly before being broken in. Players often spent several seasons pounding out a satisfactory pocket. Some even cut out the palm of the glove to form a pocket. In 1919, Doak sketched a glove with a pocket already formed. He inserted a lace of leather strips between the thumb and the forefinger, which were previously connected with a single slab of leather. He took the sketches to the Rawlings Sporting Goods Company and, within a few years, Doak's glove was the most popular mitt on the market. It still protected the hand, but for the first time, it also helped the fielder snag the ball. Fielding improved dramatically in the 1920s after the introduction of the mitt based on Doak's prototype. He continued to receive royalties, which earned him as much as $25,000 a year, until he passed away in 1954. Doak also made a small fortune in Florida real estate.

JUNE 28   The Dodgers sweep the Phillies 9–1 and 10–1 at Ebbets Field. Eddie Brown collected three homers and two doubles in nine at-bats.

JUNE 29   After the Phillies score three runs in the top of the 10th inning, the Dodgers respond with four in their half to win 5–4 at Ebbets Field. A bases-loaded walk to Milt Stock brought home the first run. Tommy Griffith stroked a two-run single to tie the contest. Zack Taylor's walk-off single was the game-winner.

JULY 8   The Dodgers outlast the Cubs 13–11 at Wrigley Field. Brooklyn scored four runs in the first inning, but Chicago responded with seven tallies in the bottom half. The Dodgers took a 12–9 lead with six runs in the seventh.

JULY 22   Zack Wheat collects five hits, including a double, in five at-bats and scores the winning run while leading the Dodgers to a 10-inning, 4–3 win over the Pirates in Pittsburgh.

JULY 26   A walk-off inside-the-park homer by Tommy Griffith in the ninth inning beats the Reds 3–2 at Ebbets Field. The drive struck an odd angle of the center-field wall and caromed into left field.

JULY 28   After Dodgers starting pitcher Tiny Osborne gives up three runs in the first inning, Rube Ehrhardt pitches $8^{1}/_{3}$ innings of one-hit, shutout baseball, but it's not enough to prevent a 3–2 loss to the Reds at Ebbets Field.

AUGUST 1   Dazzy Vance pitches a three-hitter and strikes out 14 batters, including a streak of
            seven in a row, and beats the Cubs 14–0 at Ebbets Field. Vance started the streak
            of seven strikeouts in a row by fanning Gabby Hartnett for the last out of the first
            inning. He then struck out Barney Friberg, Denver Grisgby, and Cliff Heathcote
            in the second and Bob Barrett, Vic Aldridge and Jigger Statz in the third. Charlie
            Hollocher broke the string by drawing a walk in the fourth.

            *Vance had the best season of his career, and one of the best by any pitcher in
            franchise history. He finished the 1924 campaign with a 28–6 record. Vance not
            only led the NL in wins, but also in earned run average (2.12), strikeouts (262 in
            308$\frac{1}{3}$ innings) and complete games (30 in 34 starts). Teammate Burleigh Grimes
            was second to Vance in victories (with a 22–13 record) and strikeouts (135), tied
            Vance for the lead in complete game (30 in 36 starts) and topped the circuit in
            innings pitched (310$\frac{2}{3}$). The domination by Vance and Grimes in the strikeout
            totals in the NL was remarkable. The 262 batters fanned by Vance and the 135
            by Grimes was far ahead of third-place finisher Dolf Luque, who had just 86.
            Vance struck out 7.65 batters per nine innings in a year in which National League
            pitchers averaged 2.79 strikeouts per nine innings.*

Battery mates Hank DeBerry and Dazzy Vance pose for a picture after Vance's 13th
straight win.

AUGUST 8   The Dodgers erupt for eight runs in the fifth inning for an 11–2 lead and hang on to
            beat the Cardinals 11–9 at Ebbets Field. Jim Bottomley of the Cards hit a fluke home
            run in the ninth. Bottomley's drive glanced off the glove of Dodgers outfielder Bernie
            Neis and into the seats along the right-field foul line.

AUGUST 9   The Dodgers lose 5–1 to the Cardinals at Ebbets Field to fall 13$\frac{1}{2}$ games behind the
            first-place Giants. Brooklyn had a 56–50 record and occupied fourth place.

The Dodgers would win 29 of their next 34 games, an unexpected emergence that vaulted the club into the pennant race.

AUGUST 14   Dazzy Vance earns his 20th victory of the season with a 5–0 decision over the Reds in Cincinnati.

AUGUST 23   Dazzy Vance strikes out 15 batters during a 6–5 win over the Cubs in Chicago. Vance gave up five runs in the first two innings to fall behind 5–1, but he then pitched seven consecutive shutout innings while Dodgers batters scored five runs. The Dodgers were also the victims of a triple play in the seventh inning.

AUGUST 24   The Cardinals collect 25 hits and clobber the Dodgers 17–0 in the second game of a double-header in St. Louis. Brooklyn also lost the opener 7–6 on a walk-off homer in the ninth inning by Rogers Hornsby.

SEPTEMBER 1   The Dodgers sweep the Phillies 7–2 and 6–3 during a Labor Day double-header in Philadelphia.

SEPTEMBER 2   The Dodgers win a double-header for the second day in a row in Philadelphia with 12–9 and 4–3 triumphs over the Phillies. The first game went 10 innings. The second contest was called after five innings on account of darkness. The twin victories extended Brooklyn's winning streak to nine games and pulled the club within two games of the first-place Giants.

SEPTEMBER 3   The Dodgers win a double-header for the third day in a row at Baker Bowl in Philadelphia by defeating the Phillies 7–6 and 7–0. The pair of victories extended the Dodgers winning streak to 11 games and put the Dodgers only 1$\frac{1}{2}$ games behind the first-place Giants. Brooklyn had been 13$\frac{1}{2}$ games out on August 9.

The Dodgers were no more than 1$\frac{1}{2}$ games behind the Giants at the end of each day from September 3 through September 26, but they couldn't overtake their New York rivals. The closest the Dodgers came to first place was one percentage point at the close of the contests played on September 22. The Pirates also stayed within striking distance of the Giants during September, making it a three-team race.

SEPTEMBER 4   The Dodgers continue their incredible string of victories by sweeping their fourth consecutive double-header in four days, all on the road, by defeating the Braves 5–1 and 9–1 in Boston. Dazzy Vance was the winning pitcher in the opener by pitching a three-hitter and striking out 11. It was both his 12th win in a row and the club's 12th consecutive victory. The two wins put the Dodgers only three percentage points behind the first-place Giants.

SEPTEMBER 5   The Dodgers run their winning streak to 14 games by scoring all four runs in the third inning of a 4–0 win over the Braves in Boston. Rookie Rube Ehrhardt pitched the shutout.

SEPTEMBER 6   The Dodgers play their fifth double-header, and 11th game, in a span of six days and spilt the two games with the Braves in Boston. The Dodgers won the opener 1–0 to extend their winning streak to 15 games. Bill Doak pitched a two-hit shutout. The only Braves hits were singles by Frank Gibson and Mickey O'Neil. The 15-game winning streak ended in the second tilt with a 5–4 defeat in 10 innings. Brooklyn scored in the top of the 10th, but the Braves countered with two tallies in their half, aided by a crucial error by pitcher Art Decatur on a wild throw to second base. A victory would have put the Dodgers into sole possession of first place. At the end of the day, five percentage points separated the top three teams in the National League. The Giants were 81–53, the Pirates 78–52 and the Dodgers 82–55.

The 15-game winning streak is the longest in club history. The Dodgers had streaks of 13 games in 1947, 1953, 1962 and 1965.

SEPTEMBER 7   At Ebbets Field, some 7,000 fans force their way into a crucial game between the Dodgers and Giants. The day began with the Giants one-half game ahead of the Dodgers. Many used crowbars and a telephone pole to rip the heavy gate in left field off its hinges to get into the ballpark. Others scaled the outfield walls. Dozens were injured, including a 13-year-old boy with a fractured skull. It was estimated that 32,000 jammed into an edifice with about 24,000 seats. Some 40 police battled the crowd and had to call for 150 reinforcements to clear the streets of some 15,000 who were milling around the ballpark after the gates were secured. The overflow inside moved onto the field, causing ground rules that stipulated that fair balls hit into the crowd were doubles. Some watched the contest perched on top of the left- and center-field walls. The score was 3–3 before the Giants scored five times in the eighth inning with the help of a bases-loaded error by shortstop Johnny Mitchell. The Dodgers did not go quietly and scored a run in the eighth and three in the ninth to make the final score 8–7. The encroaching crowd stopped play for 10 minutes during Brooklyn's ninth-inning rally while police, umpires and a few players pushed back the throng.

The Dodgers set an existing attendance record in 1924 by drawing 818,883.

SEPTEMBER 8   Dazzy Vance wins his 25th game of 1924 with a 7–2 decision over the Giants in New York. Zack Wheat ran his hitting streak to 24 games. The win cut the Giants lead over the Dodgers to one-half game. The Giants would remain a step ahead of the Dodgers the rest of the season.

SEPTEMBER 14   Dazzy Vance strikes out three batters on nine pitches in the third inning of a 2–0 win over the Reds at Ebbets Field. Vance fanned Sammy Bohne, Bubbles Hargrave and Eppa Rixey.

SEPTEMBER 16   Cardinals first baseman Jim Bottomley sets a major league record (since tied) by driving in 12 runs during a 17–3 win over the Dodgers at Ebbets Field. He accomplished the feat off five different Brooklyn pitchers. In the first inning, Bottomley connected for a two-run single off Rube Ehrhardt. In the second, Bottomley had a run-scoring double against Bonnie Hollingsworth. Art Decatur gave Bottomley a grand slam homer in the fourth and a two-run homer in the sixth. A two-run single off of Tex Wilson in the seventh gave the St. Louis first sacker his 10th and 11th runs batted in. The record-breaking 12th RBI was achieved on a single off Jim Roberts in the ninth. The only other player in major league history who has collected 12 RBIs in a game is Mark Whiten of the Cardinals in 1993.

SEPTEMBER 18   Dazzy Vance wins his 15th game in a row with a 12-inning, 7–5 decision over the Cardinals in the first game of a double-header at Ebbets Field. Vance earned the victory by pitching the final four innings in relief. The Dodgers also won the opener 4–2 on Zack Wheat's two-run homer in the 12th.

The winning streak of 15 games by Vance is the all-time Dodgers record for a single season. Phil Regan won 13 in a row in 1966 and Burt Hooton 12 in 1975.

SEPTEMBER 22   The Dodgers move within one percentage point of the first-place Giants with a 2–1 win in 12 innings over the Cubs at Ebbets Field. Bill Doak pitched the complete game to earn his 10th victory in a row. At the end of the day, the Giants had a record of 89–59 (.601). The Dodgers were 90–60 (.600). The Pirates were also in the race, just 1½ games back with 86 wins and 59 losses. The Dodgers had won in the presidential election years of 1916 and 1920, and numerologists were convinced that Brooklyn was going to host a World Series again in 1924.

SEPTEMBER 23   The Dodgers fall one game behind in the pennant race with a 10-inning, 5–4 loss to the Cubs at Ebbets Field. Dazzy Vance struck out 11 batters and allowed just four hits, but three of them were home runs. Gabby Hartnett's home run in the 10th was the game-winner. The drive bounced into the left-field bleachers. The other two homers were struck by George Grantham.

SEPTEMBER 27   The Dodgers are eliminated from the pennant race with a 3–2 loss to the Braves at Ebbets Field.

SEPTEMBER 28   On the last day of the season, Dazzy Vance wins his 28th game of the season by defeating the Braves 8–1 at Ebbets Field.

The Dodgers finished the season 1½ games behind the Giants, who won their fourth consecutive National League pennant. The 22 head-to-head matchups between Brooklyn and New York in 1924 produced 14 Giants victories. Brooklyn made the pennant run with an aging club that included many players having career seasons. Among pitchers with at least 100 innings and batters with 300 or more at-bats, Zack Wheat was 36; Jack Fournier, Jimmy Johnston and Tommy Griffith, 34; Dazzy Vance and Bill Doak, 33; Eddie Brown, 32; Tiny Osborne, 31; Milt Stock, Dutch Ruether, Art Decatur and Burleigh Grimes, 30; Andy High, 26; and Zack Taylor, 25. The Dodgers would finish in sixth place each of the next five seasons.

DECEMBER 17   Six weeks after Calvin Coolidge retains residence in the White House by winning the presidential election, the Dodgers sell Dutch Ruether to the Washington Senators.

1925

L A

Season in a Sentence

Charles Ebbets and Ed McKeever die 11 days apart in April, the pitching staff falls apart and the club wins only 68 games, 24 fewer than the previous season.

Finish • Won • Lost • Pct • GB

Sixth (tie) 68   85   .444 27.0

Manager

Wilbert Robinson

Stats

Stats	Dods	NL	Rank
Batting Avg:	.296	.292	3
On-Base Pct:	.351	.348	4
Slugging Pct:	.406	.414	5
Home Runs:	64		6
Stolen Bases:	37		8
ERA:	4.77	4.27	7
Fielding Avg:	.966	.966	5
Runs Scored:	786		4
Runs Allowed:	866		7

Starting Lineup

Zack Taylor, c
Jack Fournier, 1b
Milt Stock, 2b
Jimmy Johnston, 3b
Johnny Mitchell, ss
Zack Wheat, lf
Eddie Brown, cf
Dick Cox, rf
Cotton Tierney, 3b
Hod Ford, ss

Pitchers

Dazzy Vance, sp
Burleigh Grimes, sp
Rube Ehrhardt, sp-rp
Tiny Osborne, sp-rp
Jesse Petty, sp
Bill Hubbell, rp

Attendance

659,435 (third in NL)

Club Leaders

Batting Avg:	Jack Fournier	.350
On-Base Pct:	Jack Fournier	.446
Slugging Pct:	Jack Fournier	.569
Home Runs:	Jack Fournier	22
RBIs:	Jack Fournier	130
Runs:	Zack Wheat	125
Stolen Bases:	Milt Stock	8
Wins:	Dazzy Vance	22
Strikeouts:	Dazzy Vance	221
ERA:	Dazzy Vance	3.53
Saves:	Four tied with one	

FEBRUARY 4   The Dodgers trade Bernie Neis to the Braves for Cotton Tierney.

APRIL 14   The Dodgers open the season with a 3–1 win over the Phillies before 22,000 at Ebbets Field. Dazzy Vance was the winning pitcher.

APRIL 15   A fight between Jack Fournier and Phillies coach Benny Myers mars a 6–4 win over the Phillies at Ebbets Field. The altercation followed verbal sparring between the two men. Several blows were struck before Fournier and Myers could be separated by umpires and players. Fournier was ejected and replaced at first base by Jimmy Johnston, who hit a two-run double in the eighth inning that broke the 4–4 tie.

APRIL 18   Charles Ebbets, who had played a prominent role in the franchise since its founding in 1883 and had served as club president since 1898, dies of heart disease at the age of 65.

Ebbets had been in ill health for about a year prior to his death. His passing left the ownership of the club in a muddle. The club's stock had been split since 1912, with Ebbets owning half of the club and brothers Ed and Steve McKeever holding the other half. A rift between the Ebbets and McKeever families had begun a few years earlier, when Charles Ebbets Jr. was relieved of his duties as club secretary after an argument with Steve McKeever, who was team treasurer. Charles Jr. sued the club, of which his father was president, for back pay. Ed McKeever, who had been running the day-to-day operation of the franchise during Ebbets's illness, was elevated from vice president to club president. But in a cruel twist of fate, he would serve in the capacity for only 11 days (see April 29, 1925).

APRIL 20   The Dodgers purchase Joe Oeschger from the Phillies.

APRIL 21   All National League games are postponed for the funeral of Charles Ebbets. Flags flew at half-mast at all NL ballparks for 30 days, and the Dodgers wore black arm bands for the same 30-day period.

APRIL 24   Zack Wheat collects five hits, including a home run, in five at-bats in a 10–8 win over the Phillies in Philadelphia.

APRIL 27   The Dodgers trounce the Braves 15–2 at Ebbets Field.

APRIL 29   Club president Ed McKeever dies of pneumonia at the age of 62.

McKeever had been club president for only 11 days, taking the position following the death of Charles Ebbets (see April 18, 1925). McKeever had insisted on attending Ebbets's funeral on a cold, windy and rainy day despite orders from his physician to stay home, and pneumonia developed from the exposure to the elements. Ed's brother Steve took over as interim club president until a meeting of the board of directors, scheduled for May 25 (see May 25, 1925).

MAY 3   A two-out, two-run, walk-off homer in the ninth inning by Jack Fournier beats the Phillies 2–1 at Ebbets Field.

Fournier finished fifth in the NL in batting average (.350), second in on-base percentage (.446), fifth in slugging percentage (.569), third in home runs (22), second in RBIs (130), fifth in total bases (310) and second in triples (16) in 1925.

MAY 6   The Dodgers wallop the Braves 10–0 in Boston. Dazzy Vance pitched the shutout.

MAY 10   After the Reds scored twice in the top of the 12th inning, the Dodgers rally for three runs in the bottom half to win 9–8 at Ebbets Field. Eddie Brown doubled in the first run. With two out and runners on second and third, Charlie Hargreaves drew an intentional walk, followed by pinch-hitter Zack Taylor's two-run walk-off single. The game was highlighted by an altercation between opposing pitchers Tiny Osborne of the Dodgers and Dolf Luque of Cincinnati. After being struck by a pitch thrown by Osborne, Luque was banished from the premises for throwing a bat in the direction of the mound. Osborne ducked out of the way of the flying bat in the nick of time. The nickname "Tiny" was a facetious one, since Osborne stood six-foot-four and weighed 215 pounds. He immediately charged the five-foot-seven and 160-pound Luque. Fortunately, umpire Cy Rigler intercepted Osborne and wrestled him to the ground before the Dodger hurler could tear Luque limb from limb.

On the same day, the Dodgers traded Tommy Griffith to the Cubs for Bob Barrett.

MAY 16   The Dodgers purchase Hod Ford from the Phillies.

MAY 18   The Dodgers score seven runs in the fourth inning and defeat the Pirates 12–7 at Ebbets Field.

MAY 19   The "Golden Jubilee" game is held at Ebbets Field. Each National League team in 1925 celebrated the 50th season of the National League. Before the 9–5 win over the Pirates, the Dodgers introduced several former players who had either played in Brooklyn or grew up in the area, including Oyster Burns and Bill Dahlen.

MAY 23   The Dodgers score five runs in the ninth inning to beat the Cubs 6–5 at Ebbets Field. The runs were driven in by five different players on a double from Jack Fournier, singles by Zack Wheat, Milt Stock and Hank DeBerry, and a bases-loaded walk to Charlie Hargreaves.

              At the age of 37, Wheat hit .359 with 125 runs, 221 hits, 42 doubles, 14 triples, 14 homers and 103 RBIs in 1925. The runs, hits, doubles and triples figures were career highs.

MAY 25   In a meeting of the board of directors, Wilbert Robinson is elected president of the Dodgers. Robinson had been manager of the club since November 1913. He remained as field manager in addition to his duties in the front office.

              Robinson's election was a compromise between the Ebbets family and Steve McKeever. Charles Ebbets had died on April 18 and Ed McKeever, Ebbets's successor, had passed away 11 days later. The Ebbets family owned half of the stock and Steve McKeever owned the other half of the club, but a schism had been developing for several years. Steve McKeever, who had been club treasurer and was serving as interim club president, seemed to be the logical heir apparent to his brother. The Ebbets family did not want him to be club president, however, while still holding a grudge over Charles Ebbets Jr. being relieved of his duties as team secretary some two years earlier (see April 18, 1925). The election of Robinson made him the fourth individual to serve as club president in slightly over five weeks. Robinson was enormously popular with the Dodgers fans and had directed the club to the pennant in 1916 and 1920 and nearly won another one in 1924. Robinson, who had a lax management style, was ill-suited to run the club, however. He decided that he couldn't serve as both president and manager and appointed Zack Wheat as "assistant manager" to run the team during games. But Wheat failed to possess the demeanor for the role, and the club slid in the standings. After a few weeks, Robinson returned as full-time manager in addition to his role as club president. To make matters more difficult for Robinson, the rift between the opposing factions of the Ebbets family and McKeever developed into a mutual enmity which made it nearly impossible for them to agree on the simplest of matters. The franchise was in an almost constant state of turmoil and floundered, leading to a succession of finishes in the lower half of the standings for the remainder of the 1920s and most of the 1930s.

MAY 31   Dazzy Vance strikes out 13 batters but loses 2–0 to the Giants at Ebbets Field.

JUNE 2   The Dodgers score two runs in the ninth inning and one in the 12th to beat the Giants 6–5 at Ebbets Field. The winning run scored on a bases-loaded walk to Charlie Hargreaves. It was the second time in 10 days that Hargreaves had a walk-off walk (see May 23, 1925).

JUNE 5   Zack Wheat smacks two homers and hits into a triple play during a 7–6 win over the Cubs in Chicago. The home runs were struck in the first and third innings. In the seventh, with Jimmy Johnston on first base and Hod Ford on second, Wheat lined to first baseman Bernie Friberg, who stepped on the bag before Johnston could return. Shortstop Rabbit Maranville retired Ford by touching second after taking a throw from Friberg.

JUNE 6   Trailing 4–1, the Dodgers score eight runs in the sixth inning and beat the Cubs 12–9 in Chicago.

JUNE 7   Down 9–5, the Dodgers plate five runs in the eighth inning for a 10–9 victory over the Cubs in Chicago.

              The win represented the peak of the season. The Dodgers were 27–19 and occupied second place, 4¹/₂ games out of first. The club was 41–66 the rest of the way.

JUNE 14   The Dodgers break a 2–2 tie with eight runs in the fifth inning and defeat the Reds 12–3 in Cincinnati.

JUNE 20   The Pirates collect 25 hits and overwhelm the Dodgers 21–5 in Pittsburgh.

JUNE 30   Milt Stock picks up four hits, including two doubles, in seven at-bats during a 10–9 loss in 11 innings against the Phillies in Philadelphia.

JULY 1   Milt Stock has four hits in five at-bats and scores the winning run during a 4–3 triumph over the Braves at Ebbets Field. Stock tripled in the tying run and scored on second baseman Don Padgett's wild throw to third base.

JULY 2   The Dodgers score 10 runs in the first inning and clobber the Braves 20–7 at Ebbets Field. Brooklyn added five runs in the sixth inning, one in the seventh and four in the eighth for a 20–1 lead before Boston scored six times in the ninth. Milt Stock had his third consecutive four-hit game with four singles in six at-bats.

JULY 3   Milt Stock puts together his fourth consecutive four-hit game. He had a triple and three singles in five at-bats during a 6–3 win over the Giants at Ebbets Field.

              Stock is the only player in major league history with four straight four-hit games. In the four contests from June 30 through July 3, he had 12 singles, two doubles and two triples in 25 at-bats. During the 1925 season, Stock batted .325 and had 202 hits. They were also the last 202 hits of his career. In 1926, Stock held out during spring training and, after signing his contract, reported out of shape. He then was seriously injured in a collision with Lou Gehrig during an exhibition game against the Yankees. The Dodgers released him after three games and eight hitless at-bats. Stock was later a coach for the Dodgers in 1949 and 1950 and gained infamy for sending Cal Abrams home on a play that helped cost the Dodgers the 1950 National League pennant (see October 1, 1950).

JULY 5   Burleigh Grimes is ejected in the eighth inning of a 4–2 loss in the second game of a double-header against the Braves at Ebbets Field for shoving umpire Peter McLaughlin. Players and the other two umpires had to separate Grimes and McLaughlin. Boston also won the opener 4–1.

JULY 20   Dazzy Vance strikes out 17 batters in 10 innings and defeats the Cardinals 4–3 at Ebbets Field. Vance also starred with the bat in his hands by collecting three hits in four at-bats. He hit a two-run homer in the fifth inning. In the 10th, Hank DeBerry doubled and scored on Vance's walk-off single.

Vance led the NL in wins (with a 22–9 record), shutouts (four) and strikeouts (221 in 265⅓ innings) in 1925. He completed 26 of his 31 starts and had an ERA of 3.53.

JULY 25   The day after John Scopes is convicted and fined $100 for teaching evolution following the "Monkey Trial" in Tennessee, the Dodgers sell Andy High to the Braves.

JULY 28   The Dodgers outslug the Cardinals 12–9 at Ebbets Field.

AUGUST 1   Zack Wheat has five hits, including two doubles, in five at-bats during a 7–1 win over the Cubs in Chicago.

AUGUST 2   Zack Wheat collects two hits and two walks in four plate appearances during a 4–2 win over the Cubs in Chicago. The two hits gave him a streak of nine hits in nine consecutive official at-bats over three games.

AUGUST 7   Burleigh Grimes and Pirates center fielder Max Carey come to blows in the seventh inning of a 10–9 loss to the Pirates in Pittsburgh. Carey sought to return to second base after starting for third on a fly ball and collided with the Dodgers pitcher. Grimes took a swing at Carey and was ejected.

AUGUST 23   Dazzy Vance pitches a two-hitter to defeat the Cubs 2–0 in the first game of a double-header at Ebbets Field. The only Chicago hits were a double by Mandy Brooks and a single from Pinky Pittinger. The Cubs won the second tilt 9–7.

AUGUST 24   The Dodgers score nine runs in the third inning and beat the Cubs 13–6 in the first game of a double-header at Ebbets Field. Zack Wheat hit a grand slam. Eleven Cubs were sent to the clubhouse for protesting the decisions of umpire Frank Wilson. The Cubs won the second contest 11–6.

AUGUST 27   The Dodgers score two runs in the 10th inning to beat the Cardinals 10–9 at Ebbets Field. A home run by Dick Cox tied the score. The Dodgers then loaded the bases and won the game on Hank DeBerry's walk-off single.

SEPTEMBER 5   Dazzy Vance wins his 20th game of the season with a 5–3 decision in the first game of a double-header over the Braves in Boston. Brooklyn lost the second contest 4–3.

SEPTEMBER 8   On two day's rest, Dazzy Vance pitches a one-hitter to defeat the Phillies 1–0 in the first game of a double-header at Ebbets Field. He faced only 27 batters. The lone hit was a single by Chicken Hawks with one out in the second inning. Hawks was out trying to steal second. Brooklyn also won the second game 4–3 in 10 innings.

SEPTEMBER 12   Milt Stock hits a three-run homer in the seventh inning to account for all of the Dodger runs in a 3–1 victory over the Giants in New York. It was Stock's only home run of the 1925 season, and the last one of his career.

SEPTEMBER 13   In his first start since his one-hitter on September 8, Dazzy Vance pitches a no-hitter to beat the Phillies 10–1 at Ebbets Field. During the two consecutive starts, Vance hurled 16 consecutive hitless innings. He struck out nine and walked one in the no-hitter. The lone run off Vance scored in the second inning on a three-base error by left fielder Jimmy Johnston and a sacrifice fly from Bernie Friberg. In the ninth inning, Vance got two quick strikes on pinch-hitter Lew Fonseca, who then lifted a pop-up that was dropped by Charlie Hargreaves. Normally a catcher, Hargreaves was playing first base for the first time in his major league career. Vance came back and fanned Fonseca, then struck out Wally Kimmick, another pinch-hitter, on three pitches. The game ended on a line drive by Freddie Leach that Johnston caught near the foul line. Philadelphia won the second tilt 7–3, highlighted by an altercation between Hargreaves and Phillies outfielder George Harper. The two collided near first base in the seventh inning and almost came to blows before being separated. When Harper took his position in left field, he was greeted with a shower of bottles, some of which struck him. Play had to be stopped for several minutes while the field was cleared of debris. After the eventful double-header, Hargreaves never played at first base again as a big-leaguer.

SEPTEMBER 15   Jack Fournier announces his retirement, effective at the end of the season, because of his treatment at the hands of the Brooklyn fans. "I have been 16 years in baseball," said Fournier, "and am accustomed to the fickleness of crowds, but the roasting I have received in Brooklyn has been so savage I cannot play in a Brooklyn uniform and retain my self-respect. Every vile name has been hurled at me over and over again because I made the ordinary run of errors or had not done something which foul-mouthed persons in the stands had expected me to do." Over the previous three years with the Dodgers, Fournier had hit .345 in 432 games and had averaged 24 homers and 116 RBIs per season (see September 27, 1925).

SEPTEMBER 18   In his first game since his no-hitter, Dazzy Vance gives up seven runs in the eighth inning and loses 9–5 in St. Louis. Vance surrendered 13 hits in all in 7²/₃ innings.

SEPTEMBER 22   Burleigh Grimes hits into two double plays and a triple play during a 12-inning, 3–2 loss to the Cubs in Chicago. He pitched all 12 innings. The triple play came in the eighth inning with Chuck Corgan on third base and Zack Taylor on first. Grimes grounded to shortstop Sparky Adams, whose throw to second baseman Gale Staley forced Taylor and was doubled at first on Staley's relay to first baseman Charlie Grimm. Corgan attempted to score on the play, but he was nipped at the plate on a toss from Grimm to catcher Gabby Hartnett.

Grimes was nicknamed "Old Stubblebeard" because he refused to shave on days he pitched.

SEPTEMBER 25   The Dodgers lose their 12th game in a row by dropping an 18–7 decision to the Reds in Cincinnati.

SEPTEMBER 27   In the Dodgers first home game since Jack Fournier announced his retirement on September 15, Fournier is given a loud ovation from the crowd of 15,000 at Ebbets Field. He collected three hits in five at-bats, stole a base, twice drove in the tying run and had a hand in the ninth inning rally that beat the Giants 5–4.

Three weeks later, Fournier announced that he would return to the Dodgers in 1926.

OCTOBER 6   The Dodgers trade Jimmy Johnston, Zack Taylor and Eddie Brown to the Braves for Gus Felix, Jesse Barnes and Mickey O'Neil.

OCTOBER 11   The New York Giants football team plays their first game in New York City and defeats the Providence Steam Roller 13–0 at the Polo Grounds.

NOVEMBER 9   The Dodgers purchase Rabbit Maranville from the Cubs.

When acquired by the Dodgers, Maranville had just completed the 14th season of his 23-year Hall of Fame career. He had been player-manager for the Cubs during the second half of the 1925 season, but he was fired and released, in part because of his alcoholism. Expected to be the Dodgers starting shortstop, Maranville played only 78 games for the club and hit just .235.

1926

Season in a Sentence

With the Ebbets family and Steve McKeever barely speaking to each other, and McKeever not speaking at all to manager Wilbert Robinson, a directionless team finishes sixth again after turning over most of the roster.

Finish • Won • Lost • Pct • GB

Sixth   71   82   .464   17.5

Manager

Wilbert Robinson

Stats

Stats	Dods	NL	Rank
Batting Avg:	.263	.280	8
On-Base Pct:	.328	.338	8
Slugging Pct:	.358	.386	8
Home Runs:	40		6
Stolen Bases:	76		6
ERA:	3.82	3.82	6
Fielding Avg:	.963	.968	8
Runs Scored:	623		8
Runs Allowed:	705		6

Starting Lineup

Mickey O'Neal, c
Babe Herman, 1b
Chick Fewster, 2b
William Marriott, 3b
Johnny Butler, ss
Zack Wheat, lf
Gus Felix, cf-lf
Dick Cox, rf
Merwin Jacobson, cf-rf
Jack Fournier, 1b
Rabbit Maranville, ss
Charlie Hargreaves, c

Pitchers

Jesse Petty, sp
Burleigh Grimes, sp
Doug McWeeny, sp-rp
Jesse Barnes, sp
Dazzy Vance, sp
Bob McGraw, sp
Rube Ehrhardt, rp

Attendance

650,819 (sixth in NL)

Club Leaders

Batting Avg:	Babe Herman	.319
On-Base Pct:	Babe Herman	.375
Slugging Pct:	Babe Herman	.500
Home Runs:	Babe Herman	11
	Jack Fournier	11
RBIs:	Babe Herman	81
Runs:	Zack Wheat	68
Stolen Bases:	William Marriott	12
Wins:	Jesse Petty	17
Strikeouts:	Dazzy Vance	140
ERA:	Jesse Petty	2.84
Saves:	Rube Ehrhardt	4

APRIL 13   The Dodgers open the season with a one-hitter thrown by Jesse Petty for a 3–0 win over the Giants in New York. The only New York hit was a single in the sixth inning by Frankie Frisch. Zack Wheat led the offensive attack with a double and two singles.

APRIL 18   The Dodgers win the home opener 2–1 over the Phillies in 11 innings at Ebbets Field. In his first start since his Opening Day one-hitter, Jesse Petty pitched a complete game.

> *Petty had a 9–9 record as a 30-year-old rookie in 1925. He started the 1926 season with wins in his first five starts while allowing five runs in 47 innings. Petty finished the campaign with a 17–17 mark, a 2.84 ERA in 275²/₃ innings and 23 complete games in 33 starts in 1926. He became the Dodgers number-one starter due to an off season from Dazzy Vance. Dazzy led the NL in strikeouts for the fifth consecutive season with 140 in 169 innings, but hampered by a bad case of boils, he had a won-lost record of only 9–10 after winning 50 games over the previous two seasons.*

APRIL 25   Hostilities between the Dodgers and Giants bubble to the surface during an 8–6 Brooklyn victory at Ebbets Field. Frank Snyder of the Giants took exception to remarks by Mickey O'Neil and threatened the Dodgers catcher with his bat before umpire Cy Rigler intervened.

MAY 9   The Dodgers take a 1½-game lead in the National League pennant race with a 3–1 win over the Cardinals in St. Louis.

            The May 9 victory gave Brooklyn a 15–7 record. The club dropped out of first place six days later and never came close to regaining the top spot after Memorial Day.

MAY 12   The Dodgers defeat the Cubs 2–0 in Chicago with two runs in the ninth inning. Babe Herman tripled in Zack Wheat and scored on an infield out. Doug McWeeny pitched the shutout.

            During the month of June, a feud between Wilbert Robinson and a New York newspaper developed into an irreconcilable break between the Dodgers manager and part-owner Steve McKeever. Robinson was angry over a New York Sun cartoon that intimated that again Dodgers stars Zack Wheat, Jack Fournier, Dazzy Vance and Burleigh Grimes were overpaid. Robinson berated the Sun sports editor, Keats Speed, in complaining about the cartoon. As a consequence, the paper reversed its policy on calling the team the "Robins." The Sun never used the nickname again, reverting to "Dodgers," a moniker that had been used only occasionally. In addition, the news outlet thereafter referred to Robinson as "the manager of the Dodgers" and never used his name. Other New York papers were also angry at Robinson over his snit with the Sun and reduced their coverage of the Dodgers. The incident was the last straw for McKeever. He and Robinson stopped talking to each other, and their bitter feud remained unresolved until Robinson departed at the end of the 1931 season.

JUNE 9   Dazzy Vance strikes out 14 batters in nine innings during a 10-inning, 4–3 victory over the Reds at Ebbets Field. Vance allowed two runs in the ninth to fall behind 3–1, but his teammates rallied in the bottom half to send the contest into extra innings. The game was tied on a sacrifice fly by Jerry Standaert, who pinch-hit for Vance. The winning run scored on a double by Zack Wheat, a single from Babe Herman and an error.

JUNE 21   The Dodgers score five runs in the ninth inning to tie the Braves 7–7 in the first game of a double-header in Boston, but they wind up losing 8–7 in 11 innings. The Dodgers recovered to win the second tilt 6–4.

JUNE 29   A walk-off single by Charlie Hargreaves in the 11th inning beats the Phillies 4–3 at Ebbets Field. Bill Marriott drove in the first three runs with a pair of homers. He struck a two-run blast in the fourth inning and a solo shot in the ninth.

            Marriott hit only four career home runs in 826 at-bats over six seasons. He also played seven seasons of minor league ice hockey.

JUNE 30   The Dodgers outlast the Phillies 11–9 at Ebbets Field. Brooklyn took a 7–6 advantage with a two-run fifth inning and never relinquished the lead.

JULY 5   The Dodgers score seven runs in the first inning and beat the Braves 14–5 in the first game of a double-header in Boston. The Braves won the opener 5–4.

JULY 12   The Dodgers score five runs in the fourth inning of a 5–0 win over the Cubs in Chicago.

JULY 13   Jack Fournier becomes the first Dodger batter to hit three homers in a game, but Brooklyn loses 12–10 to the Cardinals in St. Louis. Fournier's home runs were hit in consecutive at-bats and drove in five runs.

              Despite the big day, Fournier experienced a rapid decline in 1926, batting .284 with 11 home runs in 87 games. He was released at the end of the season.

AUGUST 5   Zack Wheat is injured while rounding the bases after hitting a home run in the ninth inning of an 11–9 loss to the Cardinals at Ebbets Field. As he turned past first base, Wheat pulled a muscle so severely that he was forced to stop and sit down at second base. Rabbit Maranville came out to run for him, but was waved away. Wheat rose after a few minutes and walked the remaining 180 feet to home plate.

              Wheat was limited to pinch-hitting duty for the remainder of the year, which proved to be the last of his 18 seasons as a Dodger. He was released on January 1, 1927.

AUGUST 11   Babe Herman collects hits in the first two at-bats of a 4–2 win over the Pirates at Ebbets Field to run his streak of hits in consecutive at-bats to nine. Herman was three-for-three in a 9–3 loss to Pittsburgh on August 9 and four-for-four against Pittsburgh during a 10–2 defeat on August 10. He had two homers, a double and six singles during the streak.

AUGUST 13   The Dodgers purchase Max Carey from the Pirates.

              A center fielder, Carey was in the 17th season of a 20-year Hall of Fame career when he was acquired by the Dodgers. He had played in Pittsburgh since 1910 and led the NL in stolen bases in 10 different seasons while a member of the club. Bothered by sinus trouble, Carey started slowly in 1926 and was sold to the Dodgers by Pirates owner Barney Dreyfuss in a fit of pique following a disagreement between Carey and Fred Clarke, who was serving as an adviser to Pittsburgh manager Bill McKechnie. Carey played for the Dodgers until 1929, but he was deep into the decline phase of his career and did little to help Brooklyn advance in the standings. Carey later managed the Dodgers in 1932 and 1933.

AUGUST 15   A legendary play develops during a 4–1 win over the Braves in the first game of a double-header at Ebbets Field which comes to epitomize the Dodgers of the "Daffiness Boys" era of the 1920s and 1930s. With the score tied 1–1, Babe Herman doubled with the bases loaded in the seventh inning and wound up with one run batted in, a double play and three Brooklyn runners standing on third base. Hank DeBerry was on third, Dazzy Vance on second and Chick Fewster on first, when Herman lined a pitch from George Mogridge off the right-field wall. Vance held up to make sure the ball would land safely, and Fewster likewise slowed up to make certain he wouldn't pass Vance. Herman, head down, passed Fewster between second and third. Vance, believing he couldn't score, went back to third, and he and

Herman ended up occupying the bag at the same time. Fewster, completely confused, resumed running and joined his teammates on third base. Fewster then hightailed it back toward second and ran into the outfield to avoid a tag from second baseman Doc Gautreau. Herman was called out for passing Fewster, who was called out for occupying third base illegally. Despite the embarrassment of having three men on third at the same time, the bizarre play did drive in the winning run. The Dodgers also won the second game 11–3 in a contest called after eight innings to allow both teams to catch a train.

Over the years, Herman was given the blame for the play and has occasionally been erroneously credited for tripling into a triple play, when in actuality he doubled into a double play. The play inspired a classic joke in which one man says to another: "The Dodgers have three men on base." The response was: "Which base?" Vance shouldered much of the blame, however, for failing to score from second on a double, as does third-base coach Mickey O'Neil, whose garbled shouts helped create the chaos on the base paths. Herman began the season on the bench as a 22-year-old rookie, but he won a starting job at first base in early May after an injury to Jack Fournier. Herman showed considerable promise as a hitter, batting .319 in 1926 with 11 home runs. Playing for the Dodgers from 1926 through 1931, and again for 34 games during the war year of 1945, Herman compiled a batting average of .339, which is the second-best in franchise history among players with at least 2,000 plate appearances, trailing only Willie Keeler. Herman is also third in slugging percentage (.557) and ninth in on-base percentage (.389). His batting average of .393 in 1930 is the Dodgers single-season record and his .381 average in 1929 is the second-best. During the 1930 season, Herman also set season club records for slugging percentage (.678), hits (241) and total bases (416). Despite his batting prowess, fielding deficiencies at both first base and in right field, the infamous base running gaffe of August 15, 1926, and a relatively short major league career (1,552 games) have combined to keep Herman from serious consideration for the Hall of Fame.

AUGUST 21   The Dodgers release Rabbit Maranville.

SEPTEMBER 9   The Dodgers explode for nine runs in the ninth inning to beat the Phillies 12–6 in Philadelphia. During the game, Brooklyn pinch-hitters collected five hits in five at-bats. The quintet were Zack Wheat (single), Jack Fournier (single), Jerry Standaert (double), Moose Clabaugh (double) and Dick Cox (single). Cox's pinch-hit came in the ninth. He batted once more during the inning and garnered another single. The hit by Clabaugh was the only one in his major league career in 14 at-bats.

SEPTEMBER 26   On the last day of the season, Dazzy Vance strikes out 15 batters in a 3–1 victory in the first game of a double-header against the Cubs at Ebbets Field. The Dodgers also won the second contest 6–2.

OCTOBER 10   The first National Football League game is played at Ebbets Field before a crowd of 3,000, and the Brooklyn Lions win 6–0 over the Hartford Blues.

The Lions lasted only one season in the NFL due to poor attendance figures as they posted a record of 3–8–0 (see October 12, 1930).

NOVEMBER 4   The Dodgers release Jack Fournier.

1927

Season in a Sentence

The Dodgers finish first in the National League in earned run average, but the excellent pitching is negated by an offense that scores 110 fewer runs than any other team in the circuit.

Finish • Won • Lost • Pct • GB

Sixth   65   88   .425   28.5

Manager

Wilbert Robinson

Stats

Stats	Dods	NL	Rank
Batting Avg:	.253	.282	8
On-Base Pct.	.306	.339	8
Slugging Pct.	.342	.386	8
Home Runs:	39		6
Stolen Bases:	106		2
ERA:	3.36	3.91	1
Fielding Avg:	.963	.968	8
Runs Scored:	541		8
Runs Allowed:	619		1

Starting Lineup

Hank DeBerry, c
Babe Herman, 1b
Jay Partridge, 2b
Bob Barrett, 3b
Johnny Butler, ss
Gus Felix, lf
Jigger Statz, cf
Max Carey, rf
Harvey Hendrick, lf-1b
Jake Flowers, ss

Pitchers

Dazzy Vance, sp
Jesse Petty, sp
Bill Doak, sp
Jumbo Elliott, sp
Doug McWeeny, sp
Rube Ehrhardt, rp

Attendance

637,230 (fifth in NL)

Club Leaders

Batting Avg:	Jigger Statz	.274
On-Base Pct:	Max Carey	.345
Slugging Pct:	Babe Herman	.481
Home Runs:	Babe Herman	14
RBIs:	Babe Herman	73
Runs:	Jay Partridge	72
Stolen Bases:	Max Carey	32
Wins:	Dazzy Vance	16
Strikeouts:	Dazzy Vance	184
ERA:	Dazzy Vance	2.70
Saves:	Jumbo Elliott	3

JANUARY 1   After 18 seasons in Brooklyn, the Dodgers release Zack Wheat. He played one more big-league season and hit .324 in 88 games for the Philadelphia Athletics in 1927.

JANUARY 9   In a three-team trade involving the Dodgers, Phillies and Giants, the Dodgers trade Burleigh Grimes to the Giants and receive Butch Henline from the Phillies.

> *The deal was the worst one perpetrated by the Dodgers during the 1920s. Grimes was 33 at the time of the trade, but he still had enough left to compose a record of 94–49 over the next five seasons, although he did so with four different NL clubs, moving from New York to Pittsburgh to Boston to St. Louis. Henline was nothing more than a weak-hitting backup catcher.*

APRIL 12   The Dodgers open the season with a 6–3 win over the Braves in Boston. Jesse Petty was the winning pitcher.

APRIL 17   The Dodgers lose the home opener 7–2 before 25,000 at Ebbets Field. Bill Doak was the winning pitcher in his first game since 1924. He had spent the previous two seasons in Florida dabbling in real estate.

APRIL 28	The Dodgers record falls to 2–12 with an 8–4 loss to the Phillies at Ebbets Field.
MAY 12	Dazzy Vance collects four hits, including a double, in four at-bats and pitches a four-hitter to defeat the Reds 6–3 at Ebbets Field.

Vance led the NL in strikeouts for the sixth year in a row with 184 in 273 1/3 innings. He also topped the NL in complete games with 25 in 32 starts and had a record of 16–16 along with an earned run average of 3.89.

MAY 20	During a 7–5 Cubs win over the Dodgers at Ebbets Field, Brooklyn fans shower umpire Pete McLaughlin with hundreds of bottles. One of them was a bottle of "bootleg" whiskey, a beverage outlawed during prohibition.
MAY 21	On the day that Charles Lindbergh lands in Paris after his historic flight across the Atlantic, umpires are the target of fans once more at Ebbets Field. The Cubs won both games by scores of 6–4 and 11–6. In the second game, the Cubs scored nine runs in the ninth inning off five Dodger pitchers for the victory. At the conclusion, umpire Frank Wilson was extracted from a threatening crowd with great difficulty by special police and several Brooklyn players. It was agreed beforehand that the game would be called at 5:45 p.m. to allow the Cubs to catch a train. Wilson interpreted that to mean that no inning could start after 5:45. Dodgers manager Wilbert Robinson believed that the contest would end at precisely 5:45. The ninth inning began at 5:40, took more than one-half hour to complete and turned an almost certain Brooklyn victory into a defeat. Robinson filed a protest to National League President John Heydler, but the protest was denied.
MAY 22	The Dodgers collect 20 hits and overwhelm the Phillies 20–4 at Ebbets Field. Babe Herman picked up five hits in five at-bats. Brooklyn scored five runs in the first inning, four in the second, two in the fourth, five in the fifth, three in the sixth and one in the eighth.
JUNE 11	The Dodgers win a hectic 11–10 struggle against the Pirates in Pittsburgh. Brooklyn trailed 8–3 before scoring four runs in the sixth inning to pull within a run. Still down 8–7 heading into the ninth, the Dodgers plated four tallies to take an 11–8 advantage and then survived a two-run Pittsburgh rally in the bottom half.
JUNE 12	The Dodgers win 11–10 against the Pirates for the second day in a row, this time at Ebbets Field. The two teams traveled from Pittsburgh to Brooklyn for a Sunday game because the playing of baseball on the Christian Sabbath was illegal in Pennsylvania. The Dodgers trailed 10–6, but they scored three runs in the seventh inning and two in the eighth. The Dodgers and Pirates were back in Pittsburgh for another contest the following day.
JULY 20	Hank DeBerry hits a two-run triple in the fourth inning for the only runs of a 2–1 victory over the Cardinals in the first game of a double-header at Ebbets Field. The Dodgers lost the second tilt 3–1 in 11 innings.
AUGUST 17	A two-run, walk-off single by Bob Barrett beats the Cubs 6–5 at Ebbets Field.
SEPTEMBER 3	Doc Gautreau of the Braves steals home twice during an 11-inning, 4–3 win over the Dodgers in Boston. Brooklyn won the opener 6–4.

SEPTEMBER 14   Max Carey hits a grand slam in the third inning of a 10–6 win over the Cubs in Chicago. It was Carey's only home run in 1927 and his first since 1925 when he was a member of the Pirates.

SEPTEMBER 20   Bill Doak pitches a two-hitter to defeat the Pirates 3–0 at Forbes Field. The only Pittsburgh hits were a double by Johnny Gooch in the third inning and a single from Lloyd Waner in the sixth.

OCTOBER 14   The Dodgers sign Dave Bancroft as a free agent following his release by the Braves.

Bancroft was yet another player acquired by the Dodgers near the end of a Hall of Fame career when the franchise desperately needed an infusion of youth. He was paid $40,000 in salary for the 1928 season, which made him the highest-paid player in Dodgers history up to that point, and for some years afterward. Bancroft turned 37 just after Opening Day in 1928, and while he won the starting shortstop job, he contributed next to nothing to the long-term success of the club.

1928   LA

Season in a Sentence

The Dodgers lead in NL in ERA for the second season in a row, but with only a moderate improvement in the offense, the club finishes in sixth place with a record of 77–76.

Finish • Won • Lost • Pct • GB

Sixth   77   76   .503   17.5

Manager

Wilbert Robinson

Stats

Stats	Dods	NL	Rank
Batting Avg:	.266	.281	8
On-Base Pct:	.340	.344	5
Slugging Pct:	.374	.397	6
Home Runs:	66		5
Stolen Bases:	81		3
ERA:	3.25	3.99	1
Fielding Avg:	.965	.971	8
Runs Scored:	665		5
Runs Allowed:	640		3

Starting Lineup

Hank DeBerry, c
Del Bissonette, 1b
Jake Flowers, 2b
Harvey Hendrick, 3b
Dave Bancroft, ss
Rube Bressler, lf
Max Carey, cf-rf
Babe Herman, rf
Harry Riconda, 3b
Ty Tyson, cf

Pitchers

Dazzy Vance, sp
Jesse Petty, sp
Doug McWeeny, sp
Jumbo Elliott, sp-rp
Watty Clark, rp-sp
Bill Doak, rp-sp

Attendance

664,863 (fourth in NL)

Club Leaders

Batting Avg:	Babe Herman	.340
On-Base Pct:	Harvey Hendrick	.397
Slugging Pct:	Del Bissonette	.543
Home Runs:	Del Bissonette	25
RBIs:	Del Bissonette	106
Runs:	Del Bissonette	90
Stolen Bases:	Max Carey	18
Wins:	Dazzy Vance	22
Strikeouts:	Dazzy Vance	200
ERA:	Dazzy Vance	2.09
Saves:	Watty Clark	3
	Bill Doak	3

MARCH 13	The Dodgers purchase Rube Bressler from the Reds.
APRIL 11	The Dodgers open the season with a 4–3 loss to the Phillies before a crowd of 12,000 at Ebbets Field. Harvey Hendrick hit a home run in the losing cause.

Hendrick batted .318 with 11 home runs in 1928.

APRIL 18	The Dodgers score seven runs in the third inning to take a 9–0 lead and win 10–5 over the Braves at Ebbets Field.
APRIL 24	The Dodgers score in seven different innings and defeat the Phillies 12–7 at Ebbets Field.
APRIL 25	A two-out, two-run, pinch-hit, walk-off triple by Butch Henline in the ninth inning defeats the Phillies 3–2 at Ebbets Field.
MAY 10	Jess Petty is suspended for 10 days and fined $200 for repeatedly breaking curfew. "I have never taken a dime from a player in my life and there are no managers more easygoing than I am." Robinson said. "That has been my way for years and in general it brings me good results. But I had to draw the line somewhere."
MAY 24	In the first game since the end of his 10-day suspension, Jess Petty pitches a three-hitter to beat the Giants 3–0 at Ebbets Field.
MAY 26	Dazzy Vance pitches the Dodgers to a 1–0 win over the Braves at Ebbets Field. The lone run scored in the second inning on a single by Hank DeBerry.
JUNE 3	About 100 bottles fly out of the stands during the top of the ninth inning against the Pirates at Ebbets Field after a call by umpire Charley Moran incites the crowd. Pittsburgh ended up as the victor 9–7 in 14 innings.
JUNE 7	Bill Doak pitches an 11-inning complete game to beat the Reds 1–0 at Ebbets Field. The winning run crossed the plate on an infield single by Rube Bressler that rolled down the third-base line.
JUNE 8	The Dodgers trade Charlie Hargreaves to the Pirates for Joe Harris and Johnny Gooch.
JUNE 12	Held scoreless with only one hit through the first five innings, the Dodgers erupt for four runs in the sixth inning, four in the seventh and five in the eighth to beat the Cubs 13–1 at Ebbets Field. Harvey Hendrick stole second, third and home in the eighth. The steal of home was part of a double steal in which Max Carey swiped second.
JUNE 17	Dazzy Vance strikes out 15 batters and pitches a three-hitter to defeat the Cubs 4–0 at Ebbets Field. Vance twice fanned five batters in a row.

At the age of 37, Vance led the NL in strikeouts for the seventh consecutive season in 1928, fanning 200 in 280$^{1}/_{3}$ innings. He also led the NL in shutouts (four) and ERA (2.09), compiled a record of 22–10 and completed 24 of his 32 starts.

JUNE 19   Dodgers pitcher Jumbo Elliott hits a home run in the top of the ninth inning to break
               a 9–9 tie, but he allows two runs in the bottom half to lose 11–10 to the Phillies in
               Philadelphia.

               *At six-foot-three and 235 pounds, Jumbo Jim Elliott was one of the largest
               players of the era. After his playing days ended, he was a sheriff of Vigo County
               in Indiana, which includes the city of Terre Haute, for 25 years. Elliott lost a
               re-election bid in 1968 to former basketball star Clyde Lovellette, who was
               six-foot-nine. Lovellette had played on an NCAA championship team at the
               University of Kansas in 1952 and on NBA title teams with the Celtics in 1963
               and 1964.*

JUNE 23   Watty Clark pitches a two-hitter to beat the Braves 7–0 in the second game of a
               double-header in Boston. The only hits off Clark were singles by Rogers Hornsby
               and Les Bell. The Dodgers completed the sweep with a 6–3 victory in the nightcap.

JUNE 26   The Dodgers score three runs in the ninth inning to beat the Braves 6–5 in the
               second game of a double-header in Boston. The rally consisted of a double by Dave
               Bancroft, a walk to pinch-hitter Max Carey, a pinch-hit double by Joe Harris and a
               two-run single to Jake Flowers.

JUNE 30   After losing the first game of a double-header 4–3 in 14 innings to the Phillies at
               Ebbets Field, the Dodgers rebound to win the second tilt 13–5.

JULY 3   Dodgers center fielder Ty Tyson suffers a compound fracture of the left leg just above
               the ankle after a collision with right fielder Rube Bressler during an 11-inning, 8–7
               loss to the Giants in New York. The injury was so severe that Tyson never played
               another major league game.

JULY 19   The Dodgers score three runs in the ninth inning to defeat the Pirates at Pittsburgh.
               Brooklyn broke the scoreless tie on a triple by Rube Bressler and a double from
               Del Bissonette.

               *Delphia (Del) Bissonette was a 28-year-old rookie first baseman in 1928. He hit
               .320 with 13 triples, 25 homers and 106 RBIs. Due to the late start of his career
               and subsequent injuries, Bissonette lasted only five seasons in the majors.*

JULY 25   The Dodgers score all eight of their runs in the fourth inning of an 8–1 victory over
               the Cardinals at Ebbets Field. The big blow was a triple by Babe Herman.

               Herman hit .340 with 12 homers in 1928.

AUGUST 17   Doug McWeeny throws a shutout to defeat the Cubs 1–0 in Chicago. The lone run
               scored on a single by Rube Bressler in the ninth inning.

AUGUST 26   Del Bissonette's walk-off homer with two out in the 10th inning beats the Giants
               4–3 at Ebbets Field. The game started an hour after the scheduled start because the
               Dodgers were late in arriving from Cincinnati.

SEPTEMBER 2   The Dodgers score two runs in the 11th inning to defeat the Phillies 6–5 at Ebbets
               Field. Babe Herman doubled in the tying run and scored on a two-out single from
               pinch-hitter Rube Bressler.

SEPTEMBER 4   Jake Flowers homers in the 10th inning to beat the Braves 3–2 in the first game of a double-header in Boston. The Dodgers completed the sweep with a 9–2 triumph in the nightcap.

SEPTEMBER 9   Dazzy Vance earns his 20th victory of the season with a 3–2 decision over the Giants at Ebbets Field. The winning run scored in the ninth inning. With Babe Herman on second base and one out, Jake Flowers hit a grounder straight at New York third baseman Fred Lindstrom, but the ball took a bad hop and bounced off Lindstrom's shoulder and into left field, scoring Herman.

SEPTEMBER 14   The Dodgers gallop past the Phillies 10–0 in Philadelphia. Jumbo Elliott pitched a shutout on two days' rest.

SEPTEMBER 21   Dazzy Vance pitches a two-hitter to beat the Cubs 2–1 at Ebbets Field. The only Chicago hits were singles by Hack Wilson in the first inning and Woody English in the ninth.

SEPTEMBER 30   On the final day of the season, the Dodgers win 5–1 over the Phillies at Ebbets Field to preserve a winning season with a record of 77–76. The club finished sixth in an eight-team league and, in an unusual situation, were closer to first place than seventh. The Dodgers were 17½ games behind the first-place Cardinals and 27 games ahead of the seventh-place Braves.

DECEMBER 11   Five weeks after Herbert Hoover defeats Al Smith in the presidential election, the Dodgers trade Jesse Petty and Harry Riconda to the Pirates for Glenn Wright.

                 At the time of his acquisition, Wright was one of the top shortstops in baseball. He was limited to 25 at-bats in 1929, however, because he separated his shoulder playing handball. Wright recovered and was a starter in the Brooklyn lineup for three seasons.

1929

Season in a Sentence

The franchise continues to atrophy and the club lands in sixth place for the fifth consecutive season with one of the oldest rosters in baseball.

Finish • Won • Lost • Pct • GB

Sixth   70   83   .458   28.5

Manager

Wilbert Robinson

Stats

Stats	Dods	NL	Rank
Batting Avg:	.291	.294	6
On-Base Pct:	.355	.357	5
Slugging Pct:	.427	.426	6
Home Runs:	99		5
Stolen Bases:	80		5
ERA:	4.92	4.71	6
Fielding Avg:	.968	.971	7
Runs Scored:	755		6
Runs Allowed:	888		7

Starting Lineup

Val Picinich, c
Del Bissonette, 1b
Eddie Moore, 2b-ss
Wally Gilbert, 3b
Dave Bancroft, ss
Rube Bressler, lf
Johnny Frederick, cf
Babe Herman, rf
Harvey Hendrick, lf-1b
Hank DeBerry, c
Billy Rhiel, 2b

Pitchers

Watty Clark, sp
Dazzy Vance, sp
Ray Moss, sp-rp
Clise Dudley, sp-rp
Doug McWeeny, sp-rp
Johnny Morrison, rp

Attendance

731,886 (third in NL)

Club Leaders

Batting Avg:	Babe Herman	.381	
Slugging Pct:	Babe Herman	.436	
Slugging Pct:	Babe Herman	.612	
Home Runs:	Johnny Frederick	24	
RBIs:	Babe Herman	113	
Runs:	Johnny Frederick	127	
Stolen Bases:	Babe Herman	21	
Wins:	Watty Clark	16	
Strikeouts:	Watty Clark	140	
ERA:	Watty Clark	3.74	
Saves:	Johnny Morrison	8	

APRIL 16   The Dodgers scheduled opener against the Braves in Boston is postponed by rain. The April 17 contest was also postponed.

APRIL 18   The Dodgers get under way in 1929 with a 13–12 loss to the Braves in Boston. The Braves took an 11–4 lead with five runs in the fifth inning and withstood a Brooklyn comeback. Del Bissonette and Harvey Hendrick hit home runs. Babe Herman collected four hits and drove in three runs. Dave Bancroft also had four hits. Johnny Frederick contributed two doubles in his major league debut. On the same day, the Dodgers traded Johnny Gooch and Rube Ehrhardt to the Reds for Val Picinich.

Frederick was a 27-year-old rookie center fielder in 1929. He had a tremendous start with a .328 batting average, 127 runs, 206 hits, 24 homers and a league-leading 52 doubles. The doubles figure set a Dodgers club record that still stands. With two weeks remaining in the season, however, Frederick suffered a broken ankle that affected him for the rest of his career. He lasted only six seasons in the majors.

APRIL 21   In the first home game of the season, the Dodgers lose 4–1 to the Phillies before 17,000 at Ebbets Field. The contest was called after seven innings by rain. The defeat was Brooklyn's fifth in a row and dropped the club's season record to 0–5.

APRIL 27   Clise Dudley of the Dodgers hits a home run on the first pitch thrown to him in the
            major leagues, but he is also the losing pitcher in an 8–3 decision against the Phillies
            at Ebbets Field. The victim of Dudley's homer was Claude Willoughby. Neither
            Wilbert Robinson nor Philadelphia manager Burt Shotton were in the ballpark, as
            both were suffering from colds. Max Carey was acting skipper for the Dodgers.

            *Dudley played five years in the majors, two of them in Brooklyn. He hit three
            career homers in 173 at-bats. As a pitcher, Dudley had a record of 17–33 with
            a 5.03 ERA.*

MAY 17   The Dodgers end a nine-game losing streak with a 14–13 win over the Phillies in
            Philadelphia. Brooklyn took a 10–6 lead with four runs in the fourth inning and
            never relinquished the advantage, although there were several tense moments. The
            Phils scored three runs in the ninth and had the bases loaded when the final out was
            recorded. The Dodgers managed to win despite making five errors and issuing nine
            walks.

MAY 18   The day after playing a game in which 27 runs are scored, the Dodgers and Phillies
            participate in a double-header in which 50 runs cross the plate at Baker Bowl. The
            Dodgers won the opener 20–16 and lost the second tilt 8–6. In the opener, Brooklyn
            garnered 23 hits and never trailed, scoring five runs in the first inning for a 5–0
            lead, two in the third to make the score 7–3, three in the fourth (10–6), two in the
            sixth (12–6), six in the seventh (18–6) and two in the ninth to move ahead 20–12.
            Philadelphia also scored four times in the ninth. The Dodgers pulled off a triple play
            in the fourth. With runners on first and second, first baseman Harvey Hendrick
            caught Lefty O'Doul's line drive, stepped on the bag and threw to shortstop Dave
            Bancroft for the third out. Johnny Frederick collected five hits, including two doubles
            and a homer, in five at-bats and scored five runs. Babe Herman was also five-for-six,
            with four singles and a double, and drove in five runs. Frederick was two-for-five in
            the second contest to give him seven hits in the twin bill.

MAY 25   During a 5–3 win at Ebbets Field, the Dodgers pull off their second triple play in
            eight days against the Phillies. With the bases loaded, shortstop Dave Bancroft
            caught Homer Peel's line drive off his shoe tops. Bancroft straightened up while
            still running and whipped the ball to first baseman Harvey Hendrick for the second
            out. Hendrick made a quick relay to second baseman Eddie Moore to complete the
            triple play.

MAY 26   After Cy Williams of the Phillies hit a three-run homer in the top of the ninth inning
            to give his team a 4–3 lead, the Dodgers respond with two in their half to win 5–4 at
            Ebbets Field. The rally started with a triple from Johnny Frederick and ended with a
            double by Rube Bressler.

MAY 30   Harvey Hendrick runs his hitting streak to 25 games during an 8–7 loss to the Giants
            in the first game of a double-header in New York. The streak ended in the second
            tilt, a 15–6 defeat.

JUNE 4   Babe Herman collects six hits in seven at-bats during a double-header against the
            Cardinals in St. Louis. He had two singles in four at-bats in the opener, a 3–1 loss.
            Herman contributed a triple, two doubles and a single in an 11–8 victory in the
            nightcap.

JUNE 18   Babe Herman hits a walk-off homer in the ninth inning to beat the Giants 7–6 in the second game of a double-header against the Giants at Ebbets Field. The Dodgers also won the opener 8–7.

Herman hit .381 in 1929 to finish second in the batting race to Lefty O'Doul, who had an average of .393. Herman also had 105 runs, 217 hits, 42 doubles, 13 triples, 21 homers and 113 RBIs.

JUNE 21   The Dodgers score four runs in the 15th inning to defeat the Braves 7–3 in Boston. The rally was capped by a three-run homer from Rube Bressler. The game was deadlocked at 1–1 at the end of the 11th inning. Both teams scored twice in the 12th.

JUNE 23   Hank DeBerry collects six hits in seven at-bats during a 12-inning, 9–8 victory over the Giants at Ebbets Field. All six hits were singles. The sixth one drove in the winning run for DeBerry's third RBI of the game. Oddly, he didn't score a run. The Dodgers trailed 8–4 before scoring a run in the seventh inning, two in the eighth and one in the ninth.

Two of the National League's top hitters shake hands before a game. Lefty O'Doul of the Phillies topped the circuit in 1929 with a .398 average while Brooklyn's Babe Herman finished second at .381. They played as teammates in 1931 for the Dodgers.

JUNE 25   Trailing 10–3, the Dodgers score two runs in the seventh inning, five in the ninth and two in the 10th to shock the Giants 12–10 in New York. The highlights of the amazing comeback were a two-run homer by Val Picinich in the ninth inning and a two-run triple from Harvey Hendrick in the 10th.

JULY 12   A wild ninth inning caps an 8–7 win over the Cardinals at Ebbets Field. St. Louis scored five times in the top of the ninth for a 7–2 lead, but the Dodgers rallied with six runs in their half for a stunning 8–7 victory. There were only three Brooklyn hits in the six-run inning. The Cards contributed to their own demise by making three errors and issuing four walks. Johnny Frederick's one-out bases-loaded single ended the game.

JULY 13   Trailing 8–6, the Dodgers explode for nine runs in the eighth inning to beat the Cardinals 15–8 at Ebbets Field. It was the second day in a row in which the Dodgers put together a huge rally in the late innings. The first hit of the eighth was a grand slam by Babe Herman. Rube Bressler also homered and Eddie Moore hit a triple. The 15 runs scored on only nine hits. St. Louis pitchers walked 12 and the fielders made four errors.

AUGUST 6 | The Dodgers beat the Cubs in near-riot conditions on Ladies Day at Wrigley Field. Nearly 29,000 women and at least 20,000 men overpowered the ticket-takers and turnstile keepers, leaving at last 10,000 outside. The crowd overran the playing field, stood in the aisles and sat atop the outfield fences. Some newspapers estimated that 65,000 people were inside the ballpark.

AUGUST 12 | Johnny Frederick hits a walk-off homer in the 10th inning to beat the Pirates 4–2 at Ebbets Field.

AUGUST 15 | Bottle-throwing fans mar a double-header against the Cubs at Ebbets Field. The first game, a 9–5 Dodgers defeat, ended in a barrage of bottles aimed at umpire Peter McLaughlin after an unfavorable call against Brooklyn in the ninth inning. Police checked the bombardment and escorted the umpires off the field at the intermission. Another volley of bottles marked the final exit of the arbiters following game two, in spite of the fact that the Dodgers won 5–4.

AUGUST 21 | Clise Dudley pitches the Dodgers to a 1–0 win over the Cardinals at Ebbets Field. Del Bissonette drove in the lone run with a single in the first inning.

AUGUST 22 | Trailing 5–0, the Dodgers erupt for nine runs in the third inning and defeat the Reds 13–9 at Ebbets Field.

SEPTEMBER 2 | The Dodgers sweep the Braves 6–2 and 10–0 during a double-header at Ebbets Field. Watty Clark pitched a two-hitter in the second game. The only Boston hits were singles by Joe Dugan and Lance Richbourg.

SEPTEMBER 12 | A fluke home run by Hod Ford of the Reds helps beat the Dodgers 3–2 in Cincinnati. Ford sliced a looping liner toward the right-field line. Brooklyn right fielder Babe Herman missed the ball, jackknifed over the railing in front of the box seats and landed flat on his back in the concrete aisle. Ford continued on his merry way around the base paths for an inside-the-park homer.

SEPTEMBER 17 | The Dodgers sweep the Cubs 8–7 and 9–6 in a double-header in Chicago. In the opener, the Dodgers took a 6–0 lead with six runs in the third inning, fell behind 7–6 and then scored twice in the ninth for the victory. Johnny Frederick collected his 50th double of the season during the game. In the second contest, Babe Herman hit a grand slam in the eighth inning off Sheriff Blake with Brooklyn trailing 6–5.

SEPTEMBER 22 | At Sportsman's Park, the Dodgers and Cardinals combine to set a record for the fewest walks in a double-header with one. The lone walk was issued by Jim Lindsay of the Cards in the opener. Dazzy Vance and Ray Moss pitched complete games for Brooklyn. The Dodgers won the first tilt 7–2, while St. Louis nabbed the second 4–0. The twin bill took only three hours and 12 minutes to complete.

The first radio broadcast of a major league game took place over KDKA in Pittsburgh in 1921. By the end of the 1920s, nearly every major league club was broadcasting some or all of their home games on radio. The three New York teams were an exception. The Dodgers, Giants and Yankees had an agreement which stipulated that none of their games would be carried over the radio. In addition, clubs visiting New York were not permitted to broadcast the game back to their home city. The radio blackout continued until 1939.

OCTOBER 10   The Dodgers release Dave Bancroft and Max Carey.

DECEMBER 11   Six weeks after the stock market crash starts the country on the road to the Great
                  Depression, Commissioner Kenesaw Landis tries to broker peace between the
                  warring factions of the Dodgers ownership group. The efforts were initially fruitless,
                  as the antagonism between the Ebbets family and Steve McKeever was so deep
                  that conciliation was all but impossible. Each owned half of the team. For years,
                  the Ebbets family staunchly backed club president and manager Wilbert Robinson.
                  McKeever wasn't even on speaking terms with Robinson. In February 1930,
                  National League President John Heydler and the other seven clubs in the circuit
                  imposed a compromise of sorts in which Robinson would step down as president and
                  as a member of the board of directors but would continue as manager for another
                  two years. Frank York, the club's attorney and an individual who had close ties
                  to Steve McKeever, became president. Joe Gilleaudeau, the son-in-law of the late
                  Charles Ebbets and the administrator of the Ebbets estate, replaced Robinson on the
                  board of directors. A fifth member of the board, with no stock in the club or ties to
                  either McKeever or the Ebbets family, was added to break any ties in the votes. The
                  fracture in the Dodgers ownership structure wasn't completely healed, however. The
                  quarreling continued well into the 1930s and hampered efforts to rebuild the club.

THE STATE OF THE DODGERS

The Dodgers had a record of 734–793 during the 1930s, a winning percentage of .481 which ranked sixth among the eight NL teams. It was the fourth consecutive losing decade for the club. Things began to change in January 1938 when Larry MacPhail was hired to run the Dodgers. Although he ran the Dodgers for only four years, MacPhail brought direction to the franchise which had been drifting for more than 10 years due to a fractured ownership situation in which the Ebbets and McKeever families were constantly at odds. Beginning with the 1940s, the Dodgers have had seven consecutive winning decades. National League pennant winners during the 1930s were the Cardinals (1930, 1931 and 1934), Cubs (1932, 1935 and 1938), Giants (1933, 1936 and 1937) and Reds (1939).

THE BEST TEAM

The best team was the first one. The 1930 Dodgers were 86–68, spent 76 days in first place, and ended the season in fourth place just six games behind the pennant-winning Cardinals.

THE WORST TEAM

The worst team was the one in 1937 which was 62–91 and landed in sixth place, 33½ games out of first.

THE BEST MOMENT

The best moment was on September 16, 1930, when the Dodgers held first place with 12 days left in the season.

THE WORST MOMENT

The worst moment occurred on September 17, 1935, when outfielder Len Koenecke suffered a bizarre death aboard an airplane.

THE ALL-DECADE TEAM • YEARS W/DODS

Babe Phelps, c	1935–41
Dolph Camilli, 1b	1938–43
Tony Cuccinello, 2b	1932–35
Cookie Lavagetto, 3b	1937–41, 1946–47
Lonny Frey, ss	1933–36
Lefty O'Doul, lf	1931–33
Johnny Frederick, cf	1929–34
Babe Herman, rf	1926–31, 1945
Watty Clark, p	1927–37
Luke Hamlin, p	1937–41
Van Lingle Mungo, p	1931–41
Freddie Fitzsimmons, p	1937–43

Herman was also on the 1920s All-Decade Team. Other outstanding Dodgers of the 1930s include catcher Al Lopez (1928, 1930–35), third baseman Joe Stripp (1932–37) and outfielder Danny Taylor (1932–36).

THE DECADE LEADERS

Batting Avg:	Babe Herman	.352
On-Base Pct:	Babe Herman	.409
Slugging Pct:	Babe Herman	.601
Home Runs:	Johnny Frederick	61
RBIs:	Johnny Frederick	302
Runs:	Johnny Frederick	371
Stolen Bases:	Danny Taylor	44
Wins:	Van Lingle Mungo	101
Strikeouts:	Van Lingle Mungo	1,022
ERA:	Dazzy Vance	3.38
Saves:	Jack Quinn	23

THE HOME FIELD

Ebbets Field was remodeled during the 1930–31 off-season with the addition of a double-decked stand which was erected in left field and dead center field, and a large scoreboard in right field. The new stands reduced the distance from home plate to the outfield walls by some 30 feet down the left-field line and in the left-field power alley, and about 100 feet to straightaway center. A screen was added to the top of the right-field wall in August 1930. Lights were installed in 1938, making the Dodgers the second major league team to host night games. The club finished in the top half of the National League in attendance each season during the 1930s despite the succession of losing teams. Attendance peaked at 1,097,339 in 1930 and dipped to 434,188 by 1934, but the decrease was due largely to the Great Depression. The 1934 figure was nearly 10 percent ahead of the National League average of 400,013, in a season in which the Dodgers finished in sixth place.

THE GAME YOU WISHED YOU HAD SEEN

The best day to be at Ebbets Field during the 1930s was on June 15, 1938. The game resulted in a Dodgers defeat, but those in attendance witnessed history. It was the first night game in the history of the ballpark, and Johnny Vander Meer of the Reds became the only pitcher in major league history to throw two consecutive no-hitters. The first one took place four days earlier against the Braves in Cincinnati.

THE WAY THE GAME WAS PLAYED

The offensive explosion that changed baseball during the 1920s peaked in 1930 when the National League batting average was .303, and teams averaged 5.7 runs per game. The NL moguls deadened the ball for 1931, and batting averages dipped to .277, and runs per game fell to 4.5 and 4.0 in 1933. From 1934 through 1939, batting averages were generally around .270. There were only 354 stolen bases in 1938, less than half the total of 1924.

THE MANAGEMENT

Charles Ebbets sold half of the franchise to brothers Ed and Steve McKeever in 1912. Ebbets and Ed McKeever died 11 days apart in 1925, leaving the franchise in disarray. For the remainder of the 1920s and most of the 1930s, Steve McKeever feuded with the heirs of the Ebbets estate. At the start of the 1930s, Wilbert Robinson had been manager since 1914 and both manager and club president since 1925. Robinson stepped down as president in 1930 and was replaced by Frank York. Steve McKeever succeeded York in 1932 and was president until his death in 1938. Larry MacPhail followed McKeever and held the position until 1942. Bob Quinn was the first individual in franchise history to hold the title of general manager. He had the job from 1933 until 1935 and was followed by John Gorman (1935–38) and MacPhail (1938–42). Following Robinson as field manager were Max Carey (1932–33), Casey Stengel (1934–36), Burleigh Grimes (1936–37) and Leo Durocher (1939–46). All five individuals who managed the Dodgers during the 1930s wound up in the Hall of Fame. MacPhail is also in the Hall of Fame.

THE BEST PLAYER MOVE

The best player move of the 1930s was the purchase of Pee Wee Reese from the Red Sox organization in July 1939. Reese had been playing with Louisville in the American Association. He made his debut in the majors in 1940. Just six days after acquiring Reese, the Dodgers pulled off another brilliant transaction by purchasing Dixie Walker from the Tigers.

THE WORST PLAYER MOVE

The worst move was the trade of Babe Herman, Ernie Lombardi and Wally Gilbert to the Reds for Tony Cuccinello, Joe Stripp and Clyde Sukeforth in March 1932.

1930s

1930

L A

Season in a Sentence

Following five straight sixth-place finishes from 1925 through 1929, the Dodgers take a 4½-game lead in the National League pennant race in June, and are in first place with 12 days remaining in the season before fading to fourth.

Finish • Won • Lost • Pct • GB

Fourth   86   68   .558   6.0

Manager

Wilbert Robinson

Stats

Stats	Dods	NL	Rank
Batting Avg:	.304	.303	5
On-Base Pct:	.364	.360	6
Slugging Pct:	.454	.448	5
Home Runs:	122		4
Stolen Bases:	53		6
ERA:	4.03	4.97	1
Fielding Avg:	.972	.970	4
Runs Scored:	871		6
Runs Allowed:	738		1

Starting Lineup

Al Lopez, c
Del Bissonette, 1b
Neal Finn, 2b
Wally Gilbert, 3b
Glenn Wright, ss
Rube Bressler, lf
Johnny Frederick, cf
Babe Herman, rf
Jake Flowers, 2b
Eddie Moore, 2b-lf-ss

Pitchers

Dazzy Vance, sp
Dolf Luque, sp
Watty Clark, sp-rp
Ray Phelps, sp-rp
Jumbo Elliott, sp-rp
Ray Moss, rp-sp
Sloppy Thurston, rp-sp

Attendance

1,097,329 (second in NL)

Club Leaders

Club Leaders		
Batting Avg:	Babe Herman	.393
On-Base Pct:	Babe Herman	.455
Slugging Pct:	Babe Herman	.678
Home Runs:	Babe Herman	35
RBIs:	Babe Herman	130
Runs:	Babe Herman	143
Stolen Bases:	Babe Herman	18
Wins:	Dazzy Vance	17
Strikeouts:	Dazzy Vance	173
ERA:	Dazzy Vance	2.61
Saves:	Watty Clark	6

FEBRUARY 5   The Dodgers trade Doug McWeeny to the Reds for Dolf Luque.

Luque was 39 years old when acquired by the Dodgers, but gave the club two solid seasons with a record of 21–14. A native of Cuba, Luque was also the first Latin player in Dodgers history. McWeeny failed to win a game for the Reds.

APRIL 15   The Dodgers open the season with a 1–0 loss to the Phillies before 27,000 at Ebbets Field. Les Sweetland, a pitcher who finished the 1930 campaign with a 7.71 ERA in 167 innings, hurled a three-hit shutout for Philadelphia. Sweetland retired the last 18 batters to face him. He also scored the lone run of the game. In the eighth inning, Sweetland doubled off hard-luck loser Watty Clark, and crossed the plate on a single by Chuck Klein.

APRIL 21   Del Bissonette drives in seven runs on a grand slam and a bases-loaded triple during a 15–8 victory over the Braves at Ebbets Field. The Dodgers scored eight runs in the seventh for a 15–1 lead before Boston added seven tallies during the last two innings.

APRIL 23	The Dodgers lose 16–15 to the Phillies at Baker Bowl. Brooklyn scored six runs in the seventh inning for a 15–12 lead, but Philadelphia scored twice in both the eighth and ninth for the victory. Dodgers third baseman Wally Gilbert drove in six runs.
	The Dodgers lost seven of their first nine games in 1930, then won 30 of their next 40.
APRIL 29	The Dodgers outlast the Giants 19–15 at the Polo Grounds. Brooklyn scored 11 runs in the second inning for a 13–0 advantage and led 16–2 before New York plated nine runs in the bottom of the third to make the score 16–11. By the end of the fifth, the score was 19–14. After 33 runs in the first five innings, there was only one run in the final four. The Dodgers collected 23 hits during the contest. Babe Herman drove in seven runs.
MAY 3	The Dodgers edge the Cardinals 11–10 in 10 innings at Sportsman's Park. Brooklyn scored five times in the top of the 10th, then withstood a four-run St. Louis rally in the bottom half. Johnny Frederick collected five hits in six at-bats. The Dodgers had 23 hits in all.
MAY 4	The Dodgers sweep the Cardinals 2–1 and 11–10 at Sportsman's Park. The second game was similar to the previous day's action. St. Louis scored four runs in the ninth inning to tie the contest 8–8. The Dodgers plated three runs in the top of the 13th, and the Cards countered with two in their half.
MAY 14	Glenn Wright hits a homer, two triples and a single during a 7–4 victory over the Reds in Cincinnati.
	Wright hit .321 with 22 homers and 126 RBIs in 1930.
MAY 20	Babe Herman collects five hits, including a homer, and drives in six runs during a 16–9 thrashing of the Phillies in Philadelphia.
MAY 21	The Dodgers heavy hitting continues with a 12–1 triumph over the Braves in Boston.
MAY 24	A three-run homer by Rube Bressler in the 11th inning beats the Braves 5–2 in Boston. Gordon Slade hit a home run in his first major league at-bat.
	Slade started at shortstop in place of Glenn Wright, who was out with an injured ankle. Slade had only 37 at-bats in 1930, and didn't hit another big league homer until the following season. He hit only eight home runs in 1,372 at-bats during a six-year career.
MAY 26	Dazzy Vance pitches a two-hitter to defeat the Giants 3–0 at Ebbets Field. The only New York hits were singles by Jimmie Reese in the fifth inning and Mel Ott in the seventh.
	At the age of 39, Vance was 17–15 and led the NL in ERA (2.61) and shutouts (four) in 1930. He fanned 173 batters in 258²/₃ innings.
MAY 30	The Dodgers sweep the Phillies 11–1 and 11–9 in a Memorial Day double-header at Ebbets Field. In the second game, the Dodgers scored four runs in the fifth inning

to tie the contest, then broke the deadlock with a tally in the sixth. Del Bissonette collected seven hits in nine at-bats during the double-header, including a perfect five-for-five in the nightcap. His seven base hits included a home run and two doubles, and he drove in seven runs. Bissonette should have had a second home run. In the second inning of the first game, he drove the ball over the right-field wall. Babe Herman paused between first and second base to make sure he wouldn't be caught, and Bissonette was called out for passing Herman. Instead of a homer, Del was credited with only a single.

Two of Brooklyn's top sluggers in 1930—Babe Herman and Johnny Frederick.

JUNE 1   Babe Herman and Johnny Frederick hit back-to-back homers twice during a 10–2 win over the Phillies at Ebbets Field. The pair struck in the second and fourth innings. Del Bissonette also homered.

JUNE 4   The Dodgers commit eight errors, four of them in the first inning, during a 12–6 loss to the Pirates at Ebbets Field. Pittsburgh committed five miscues.

JUNE 5   An altercation between members of the Pirates and umpire Ted McGrew mars a 6–5 Dodgers victory at Ebbets Field. The game ended with a double play on which Pittsburgh catcher Rollie Hemsley was called out at the plate trying to score from third base following a forceout at second base. Hemsley shoved McGrew, while manager Jewel Ens and coach Max Carey joined in the protest. A policeman came onto the field to escort McGrew to the dressing room.

JUNE 7   Trailing 9–8 in the seventh inning, pitcher Watty Clark hits a three-run homer and the Dodgers go on to beat the Cubs 12–9 at Ebbets Field.

The home run was the only one that Clark hit during a 12-year major league career which spanned 357 games and 598 at-bats.

JUNE 12   The Dodgers defeat the Reds 3–2 at Ebbets Field to take a 4½-game lead in the National League pennant race with a record of 32–17.

JUNE 14   A walk-off homer by Del Bissonette in the 12th inning beats the Cardinals 6–5 at Ebbets Field.

JUNE 23   The Dodgers pound out 28 hits and beat the Pirates 19–6 in Pittsburgh. Brooklyn collected 12 consecutive hits during the sixth and seventh innings. Ten of the hits in the streak occurred in the sixth. The feat was accomplished by Johnny Frederick (single), Wally Gilbert (inside-the-park homer), Babe Herman (single), Del Bissonette (single), Glenn Wright (triple), Neal Finn (double), Al Lopez (single), Jumbo Elliott (single) and Frederick (single). Frederick was the third out when he tried to stretch his single into a double. In the seventh, Gilbert led off with a single, followed by a home run from Herman.

Only 21-years-old at the start of the 1930 season, Lopez won the job as Brooklyn's starting catcher and held the position until 1935 when he was traded to the Braves. Lopez's playing career lasted until 1947, and he caught 1,918 major league games to set a record which lasted until 1987 when he was passed by Bob Boone. Lopez was elected to the Hall of Fame in 1977 based largely on his record as a manager. The Yankees won 14 AL pennants in 16 seasons from 1949 through 1964, and Lopez managed both of the teams that interrupted the streak by guiding the 1954 Indians and 1959 White Sox to the World Series. The Indians didn't reach the Fall Classic again until 1995, and the White Sox until 2005. Lopez died on October 30, 2005 at the age of 97, just four days after the White Sox won their first world championship since 1917.

JULY 1   The Cardinals score 11 runs in the third inning and trounce the Dodgers 15–7 in St. Louis.

JULY 2   Babe Herman makes out the starting lineup for the slumping Dodgers, and the club wins 6–5 over the Cardinals in St. Louis.

JULY 6   In his first game with the Dodgers, outfielder Ike Boone hits a home run and a single during a 10–4 win over the Braves at Ebbets Field.

JULY 9   The Dodgers sweep the Braves 8–0 and 6–4 at Ebbets Field. In the second game, Del Bissonette broke a 2–2 tie with a grand slam off Bill Sherdel in the seventh inning.

JULY 14   Glenn Wright drives in seven runs on two homers and two singles during a 12–8 victory over the Pirates at Ebbets Field.

JULY 15   Watty Clark pitches a one-hitter to beat the Pirates 5–0 at Ebbets Field. The only Pittsburgh hit was a single by Pie Traynor.

JULY 16   The Dodgers split a boisterous double-header with the Cubs at Ebbets Field, losing 6–4 and winning 5–3. The crowd in excess of 30,000 overflowed the stands and circled the diamond. In the first game, Del Bissonette tried to stretch a triple into an inside-the-park homer, and in sliding into home plate, knocked himself unconscious by hitting his head on the plate. Many fans blamed Cubs catcher Gabby Hartnett for Bissonette's injury and threw bottles at Hartnett. Gabby tried to charge the stands, but was held back by teammates. It wasn't the only excitement during the afternoon. Dolf Luque nearly came to blows with Chicago hurler Charlie Root after being hit by a pitch. Dodgers coach Ivy Olson had a wordy battle with umpire Bill Klem, and Klem was soon the target of bottle-throwing patrons.

JULY 21

A three-run, pinch-hit, walk-off homer by Harvey Hendrick in the ninth inning beats the Cardinals 9–8 in the first game of a double-header against the Cardinals at Ebbets Field. St. Louis won the second tilt 17–10. It was one of a record four pinch-hit homers during the double-header. In the opener, Jim Bottomley and George Puccinelli of the Cards also collected pinch-hit homers. In the nightcap, Hal Lee of the Dodgers homered in a pinch-hit role. It was the first major league hit for both Puccinelli and Lee. It was also Lee's only home run in a Brooklyn uniform.

JULY 22

Dodgers pitcher Sloppy Thurston pitches a three-hitter to defeat the Cardinals 1–0 at Ebbets Field. Rube Bressler drove in the lone run of the game with a single in the third inning.

JULY 28

Sloppy Thurston pitches a two-hitter to defeat the Braves 2–0 in Boston. The only hits off Thurston were singles by Earl Clark and opposing pitcher Ben Cantwell.

Hollis (Sloppy) Thurston was a meticulous dresser who wore the latest Jazz Age fashions. He drew his nickname from his father, a charitable restaurant owner who would dish out free soup to the poor. Thurston died tragically in 1973 at the age of 74 from a self-inflicted gunshot wound to the head.

JULY 31

Babe Herman collects five hits, including two doubles and a homer, but the Dodgers lose 12–7 to the Phillies in Philadelphia.

Herman set Dodgers single season records in 1930 in batting average (.393), slugging percentage (.678), hits (241), and total bases (416). His on-base percentage (.455) and runs scored figure (143) are the highest of any Dodgers batter since 1900. Herman's 48 doubles are the second best in club history. Babe's 130 runs-batted-in ranks fourth. His 35 home runs were the most of any Dodger prior to 1950. Herman failed to lead the NL in any major category in 1930, however, as it came in a year of unprecedented hitting. National League batters compiled an average of .303 that season, and teams averaged 5.7 runs per game. Bill Terry of the Giants won the batting title with an average of .401.

AUGUST 3

In a duel of future Hall of Famers Dazzy Vance and Carl Hubbell, the Dodgers edge the Giants 1–0 at Ebbets Field. In the ninth inning, Babe Herman led off with a double and was sacrificed to third. After intentional walks to Glenn Wright and Rube Bressler to load the bases, Hubbel walked Jake Flowers to force in the winning run.

AUGUST 5

The Dodgers take a thrilling 9–8 decision in 10 innings over the Giants at Ebbets Field. Brooklyn led 6–1, but New York scored five runs in the ninth and two in the 10th for an 8–6 advantage. The Dodgers responded with three tallies in the 10th for the victory. Jake Flowers drove in the tying run with a single. Eddie Moore accounted for the game-winner with a sacrifice fly.

AUGUST 8	Babe Herman collects two homers and two singles during an 11–5 decision over the Cardinals in St. Louis.

> *The victory gave the Dodgers a 66–41 record and a 3¹/₂-game lead in the pennant race. Brooklyn lost 15 of the next 18 contests, however, to fall to third place, 6¹/₂ games behind the first place Cubs. Heading into September, it appeared as though the Dodgers chances for reaching the World Series had disappeared.*

AUGUST 13	The Dodgers drub the Cubs 15–5 in Chicago.
AUGUST 27	While the club is on the road, the Dodgers erect a 19-foot high screen on top of the 19-foot high concrete right field wall at Ebbets Field to protect the glass store fronts across Bedford Avenue from being damaged by flying baseballs. Balls hit into the screen were home runs through the end of the 1935 season. Beginning in 1936, balls which struck the screen were in play.
AUGUST 31	The Dodgers collect 23 hits and beat the Phillies 14–3 at Ebbets Field. It was the first home game following the erection of the screen on top of the right field wall. No balls were hit into the screen. Babe Herman and Phillies first baseman Don Hurst homered over the new barrier.
SEPTEMBER 2	The Dodgers lose 6–0 to the Braves in Boston to fall into fourth place, six games back of the first place Cubs.
SEPTEMBER 6	The Dodgers collect 24 hits and pummel the Phillies 22–8 at Ebbets Field. Brooklyn scored three runs in the first inning, six in the second, three in the third, eight in the fifth, one in the sixth and one in the seventh.
SEPTEMBER 11	The Dodgers complete a three-game sweep of the first place Cubs at Ebbets Field by winning 2–1. Dazzy Vance struck out 13 batters. Glenn Wright hit a two-run homer in the first inning for the only two Brooklyn runs. The first two games of the series were won by shutouts from Ray Phelps and Dolf Luque.

> *At the end of the day, the Dodgers were in third place, one-half game behind the Cubs and one percentage point back of the second place Cardinals. The Giants were fourth, three games behind.*

SEPTEMBER 12	Al Lopez hits a long drive which bounces into the left field bleachers at Ebbets Field during a 7–3 win over the Reds. Lopez was credited with a home run under the existing rules, but this would be baseball's last bounding home run. The NL and AL changed the rule after the season, making all such hits ground rule doubles.
SEPTEMBER 14	The Dodgers extend their winning streak to 10 games and take over first place with an 8–3 decision over the Reds at Ebbets Field. Just 12 days earlier, the Dodgers were in fourth place, six games behind.
SEPTEMBER 15	The Dodgers run their winning streak to 11 games with a 13–5 victory over the Reds at Ebbets Field. Cincinnati scored three times in the first, but the Dodgers responded with six runs in the bottom half. Brooklyn scored the six runs in the opening salvo despite a base-running gaffe. With Wally Gilbert on second and Babe Herman on first, Glenn Wright bounced a drive into the left-field bleachers for an apparent home run.

But Herman held up to see if the ball would be caught, and Wright was called out for passing him on the base paths.

The win put the Dodgers one game ahead of the Cardinals, and 1½ up on the Cubs. The Cards were scheduled to visit Ebbets Field for a three-game series beginning the following day.

SEPTEMBER 16   In the first game of the pennant-showdown series against the Cardinals, the Dodgers suffer a crushing 10-inning, 1–0 loss at Ebbets Field. The defeat knocked Brooklyn out of first place, one percentage point behind the Cardinals. St. Louis hurler Wild Bill Hallahan retired the first 20 batters to face him and didn't allow a hit until the eighth inning. Dazzy Vance pitched a complete game. He allowed the lone run on a double by ex-Dodger Andy High and a single from Taylor Douthit. In the bottom of the inning, the Dodgers loaded the bases, but a double play ended the contest. The twin killing started when shortstop Sparky Adams barehanded a sizzling grounder by Al Lopez.

SEPTEMBER 17   The Dodgers fall one game behind the Cardinals with a 5–3 loss at Ebbets Field. Andy High broke a 3–3 tie with a two-run pinch-double in the ninth.

Flint Rhem was scheduled to be the starting pitcher for the Cardinals, but showed up at the ballpark, after disappearing for 48 hours, bleary-eyed and in no condition to pitch. He tried to cover his tracks with an outlandish tale. Rhem claimed he was standing in front of the Cardinals' hotel in Manhattan when two men called him over to a limousine. Flint said he walked over, and the pair pushed him into the vehicle and pointed a gun. The men drove him to New Jersey and forced him to drink raw whiskey. According to Rhem, the men were gamblers and threatened him with bodily harm if he pitched and won his start against the Dodgers. Cardinal management was skeptical, but called police. Rhem couldn't find the place in New Jersey where he was taken, however, and law enforcement officials dropped the pursuit of the "abductors."

SEPTEMBER 18   The Cardinals complete a three-game sweep of the Dodgers at Ebbets Field with a 4–3 decision. Burleigh Grimes, another former Dodger, pitched a complete game for Brooklyn.

The Dodgers never recovered from the losses to the Cardinals. Brooklyn's losing streak would reach seven games before it ended. The Dodgers went from first place to fourth during the final 12 days of the season. The Cardinals, who trailed by 12 games in August, won the NL pennant by taking 39 of their last 49 games. Overall, the Dodgers spent 76 days in first place in 1930.

SEPTEMBER 27   Dazzy Vance strikes out 12 batters during an 8–2 win over the Braves in the first game of a double-header at Ebbets Field. Boston won the second tilt 7–1.

The exciting pennant race was a boon to attendance. The Dodgers drew 1,097,339 fans, shattering the previous record of 818,883 set in 1924. The increase in patronage led to changes at Ebbets Field (see February 11, 1931). The Dodgers wouldn't attract over one-million fans into the ballpark again until 1942, however.

OCTOBER 12   The Brooklyn Dodgers football team plays it's first game at Ebbets Field, and wins 32–0 over the Newark Bears before a crowd of 7,000.

Although they shared the same nickname and home field, the Dodgers football team was not affiliated with the baseball franchise until much later (see January 6, 1948). The football Dodgers were a member of the NFL from 1930 through 1944. During the club's final season, the nickname was changed from Dodgers to Tigers, but an 0–10 record and dwindling attendance spelled an end of the NFL in Brooklyn. Professional football returned to Ebbets Field for three seasons beginning in 1946 when another club named the Brooklyn Dodgers competed in the All-American Football Conference.

OCTOBER 14   The Dodgers send Jumbo Elliott, Hal Lee, Clise Dudley and cash to the Phillies for Lefty O'Doul and Fresco Thompson.

The Dodgers pulled off a brilliant short-term deal. O'Doul broke into the majors as a pitcher with the Yankees in 1919, but had only a 1–1 record as a hurler in four seasons. He went back to the minors, became an outfielder, and was back in the big leagues in 1928. O'Doul won the NL batting title with an average of .398 with the Phillies in 1929 and batted .383 in 1930. As a Dodger, he compiled an average of .340 in 352 games over three seasons, and led the league in batting average in 1932.

1931   LA

Season in a Sentence

Wilbert Robinson's 18-year reign as manager comes to an end following the Dodgers second consecutive fourth place finish.

Finish • Won • Lost • Pct • GB

Fourth   79   73   .520   21.0

Manager

Wilbert Robinson

Stats

Stats	Dods	NL	Rank
Batting Avg:	.276	.277	5
On-Base Pct:	.331	.334	5
Slugging Pct:	.390	.387	5
Home Runs:	71		4
Stolen Bases:	45		6
ERA:	3.84	3.86	4
Fielding Avg:	.969	.971	6
Runs Scored:	681		5
Runs Allowed:	673		3

Starting Lineup

Al Lopez, c
Del Bissonette, 1b
Neal Finn, 2b
Wally Gilbert, 3b
Gordon Slade, ss
Lefty O'Doul, lf
Johnny Frederick, cf
Babe Herman, rf
Glenn Wright, ss

Pitchers

Watty Clark, sp
Dazzy Vance, sp
Joe Shaute, sp
Sloppy Thurston, sp
Ray Phelps, sp
Dolf Luque, sp
Jack Quinn, rp
Fred Heimach, rp-sp

Attendance

753,133 (third in NL)

Club Leaders

Batting Avg:	Lefty O'Doul	.336
On-Base Pct:	Lefty O'Doul	.396
Slugging Pct:	Babe Herman	.525
Home Runs:	Babe Herman	18
RBIs:	Babe Herman	97
Runs:	Babe Herman	93
Stolen Bases:	Babe Herman	17
Wins:	Watty Clark	14
Strikeouts:	Dazzy Vance	150
ERA:	Watty Clark	3.20
Saves:	Jack Quinn	15

FEBRUARY 11   The Dodgers announce an expansion of Ebbets Field. In 1930, the ballpark had a double-decked stand from the right-field corner of Bedford Avenue to about 30 feet past third base on the Cedar Place side. There they met a concrete bleacher section which extended to the left-field wall on Montgomery Street. There was also a "temporary" wooden bleacher section in left field which was erected for the 1920 World Series and left standing for 10 years. The expansion called for the elimination of the two bleacher sections. A new double-decked stand wrapped around the left-field corner and extended to the point where Montgomery met Bedford, just to the right of straightaway center field. Ebbets Field now had two levels of seats on three of the four sides of the ballpark. The expansion increased the seating capacity of Ebbets Field from about 25,000 to a little over 31,000. About half of the extra 6,000 seats were ready by Opening Day, with the rest available by the first week of May. Another addition was a 35-foot-high scoreboard in right field. The stands in left field drastically cut the home run distances. The distance down the left-field line was reduced from 384 feet to 353; left-center from 391 feet to 365; and center field from 500 feet to 399.

APRIL 14   In the season opener, the Dodgers take a 4–0 lead after three innings, but wind up losing 7–4 to the Braves in Boston. Jack Quinn, making his debut with the Dodgers, was the starting, and losing, pitcher.

> *Quinn made his big-league debut in 1909 and was 47 years old at the start of the 1931 season. His Opening Day start was his only one in a Brooklyn uniform. The rest of Quinn's 38 appearances in 1931 and all 42 in 1932 were in relief. He led the National League in saves both seasons, with 15 in 1931 and eight in 1932. Quinn's last season in the majors was 1933 when he played in 14 games with the Reds. His last appearance that season was on July 7, two days his 50th birthday. Quinn is the oldest player in major league history who was not part of a publicity stunt.*

APRIL 15   Dodgers right fielder Alta Cohen has an unusual big-league debut during a 9–3 loss to the Braves in Boston. Babe Herman started the game in right batting third in the lineup, but was taken out in the fifth inning in a double switch, with the pitcher batting third and Cohen playing right field and batting ninth. Making his first big-league plate appearance, Cohen batted in the sixth inning in Herman's old spot in the third slot in the batting order and singled. The inning was over before anyone noticed that Cohen had batted out of turn. The umpires decreed that Cohen would hit ninth for the remainder of the game, and he hit twice more with another single.

> *Cohen didn't play another big-league game for the remainder of the season before being sent to the Dodgers farm team in Hartford. He appeared in nine contests with the Dodgers in 1932 and 19 with the Phillies in 1933, and finished his brief career with a .194 batting average in 67 at-bats.*

APRIL 28   The Dodgers record falls to 2–10 with a 3–2 defeat at the hands of the Giants in New York.

MAY 6   Five days after the opening of the Empire State Building, the Dodgers edge the Giants 1–0 at Ebbets Field. Ray Phelps (seven innings) and Jack Quinn (two innings) combined on the shutout. Ernie Lombardi, pinch-hitting for Phelps in the seventh, hit a sacrifice fly to drive in the lone run.

MAY 7 — The Dodgers sell Harvey Hendrick to the Reds.

MAY 18 — The Dodgers wallop the Reds 14–4 in Cincinnati. Babe Herman hit for the cycle and scored four runs in addition to stealing a base and throwing out a base runner from the outfield. Herman started his cycle with a homer in the first inning and a triple in the second off Al Eckert.

MAY 24 — The Dodgers score two runs in the ninth inning and one in the 10th to defeat the Phillies 6–5 at Ebbets Field. In the ninth, a two-out, two-run single by Del Bissonette tied the score. With two away in the 10th, Wally Gilbert doubled and scored the winning run on Neal Finn's single. Finn entered the game in the ninth as a defensive replacement at second base.

MAY 30 — The Dodgers sweep the Giants 5–2 and 18–8 during a Memorial Day double-header before a crowd of 60,000 at the Polo Grounds. Rube Bressler tied the opener 2–2 in the ninth inning with a two-out single. Del Bissonette hit a three-run homer in the 10th. In the second game, Wally Gilbert collected six hits, including a double, in seven at-bats. Gordon Slade hit a grand slam in the fourth.

JUNE 2 — The Dodgers score three runs in the ninth inning to defeat the Cubs 7–6 in Chicago. Johnny Frederick deadlocked the contest with a two-run triple and scored the winning run on Babe Herman's sacrifice fly.

JUNE 25 — Dazzy Vance retires the first 20 batters to face him and allows only three hits, but loses 1–0 to the Cardinals at Ebbets Field. The first batter to reach base was George Watkins on a bunt single with two out in the seventh inning. Watkins took third on a single by Jim Bottomley, then stole home plate.

Vance was 40 in 1931, but was the third-oldest pitcher on the club. Dolf Luque turned 41 in August and Jack Quinn celebrated his 48th birthday in July.

JUNE 26 — The Dodgers score eight runs in the first inning and defeat the Cardinals 16–5 at Ebbets Field.

JUNE 27 — Ray Phelps pitches a two-hitter to defeat the Cardinals 7–0 in the first game of a double-header at Ebbets Field. The only St. Louis hits were singles by George Watkins and Jim Bottomley. The Dodgers completed the sweep with a 4–3 victory in the second tilt.

JUNE 29 — With the Dodgers trailing 4–1, Johnny Frederick hits a grand slam off Eppa Rixey in the fifth inning to lead the Dodgers to a 6–4 triumph over the Reds at Ebbets Field.

JULY 4 — The Dodgers sweep the Giants 4–0 and 3–0 before an overflow crowd of over 40,000 at Ebbets Field. Dazzy Vance and Watty Clark pitched the shutouts.

On July 6, the Dodgers had a record of 42–33 and occupied fourth place, 3 1/2 games behind the Cardinals. The Dodgers could pull no closer to first place over the remainder of the season.

JULY 24 — Babe Herman hits for the cycle during an 8–7 loss to the Pirates in Pittsburgh. The Dodgers scored only seven runs despite 21 hits. Lefty O'Doul was a perfect five-for-five with four singles and a double.

Herman is the only player in major league history to hit for the cycle twice in a season. The first time was on May 18. Herman finished the season with a .313 batting average, 43 doubles, 16 triples, 16 homers and 97 RBIs. O'Doul hit .336 with seven homers.

AUGUST 20   Babe Herman has a hand in all four runs of a 4–1 win over the Cubs at Ebbets Field. In the eighth inning, Herman drove in three runs with a bases-loaded double, then scored on a single from Del Bissonette.

AUGUST 23   The Dodgers win a pair of 5–4 decisions over the Pirates at Ebbets Field, both with ninth-inning rallies. In the opener, the Dodgers scored twice in the ninth. Pittsburgh hurler Heinie Meine walked two batters, then threw Neal Finn's sacrifice bunt over the head of third baseman Pie Traynor, allowing both Brooklyn runners to score. In the ninth, the Dodgers broke a 4–4 tie on two singles, a long fly ball, and a wild pitch by Larry French.

SEPTEMBER 7   In his major league debut, 20-year-old Van Lingle Mungo pitches a three-hit shutout to defeat the Braves 4–0 in the second game of a double-header at Ebbets Field. Mungo also tripled and singled in three at-bats. The Dodgers also won the opener 5–4 in 10 innings.

Mungo was a hard-drinking pitcher with an explosive temper who pitched for the Dodgers from 1931 through 1941. His peak was 1933 through 1936 when he was 68–60 on four clubs that posted losing records. Mungo twice led the NL in complete games, and once each in shutouts, innings pitched and shutouts. After hurting his arm while pitching in the 1937 All-Star Game, Mungo was never the same. He was largely forgotten after retiring from baseball in 1945, but was brought back to considerable notoriety in 1969 because of the use of his lyrical name as the title of a novelty song by Dan Frishberg. The song's lyrics consist entirely of baseball players from the 1930s, 1940s and 1950s strung together with a bossa nova beat. Mungo's name is used as a refrain.

SEPTEMBER 13   The Dodgers score three runs in the ninth inning to defeat the Pirates 6–5 at Ebbets Field. The rally was capped by a two-run double by Glenn Wright which scored Lefty O'Doul and Del Bissonette.

SEPTEMBER 24   All three New York major league teams are in the same ballpark for the first time. The occasion took place at the Polo Grounds to raise money for unemployed. A crowd of 44,000 watched the Dodgers lose 3–1 to the Giants and 5–1 to the Yankees. Another benefit for the unemployed took place on September 9, with the Yanks defeating the Giants 7–3 at Yankee Stadium. The two events raised $107,000.

OCTOBER 23   Wilbert Robinson is dismissed as manager of the Dodgers.

The Wilbert Robinson regime began when he was hired as manager in November 1913. It was a turbulent 18 years. He won National League pennants in both 1916 and 1920, but the club posted a winning record only eight times and finished in the top half of the league standings in just six seasons. The Dodgers were fourth in his last two seasons as manager, with records of 86–68 in 1930 and 79–73 in 1931. It was the first time that the club had back-to-back winning seasons since 1920 and 1921. Expectations were high heading into 1931, because the Dodgers were in first place with 12 days remaining in the 1930 campaign.

Long-dormant pennant hopes were revived, but the Dodgers finished far out of the running in 1931, which led to Robinson's removal. It was the climax of a six-year war between Steve McKeever, who owned half the club, and the heirs of Charles Ebbets, who held the other 50 percent of the stock. McKeever held an intense dislike for Robinson and stopped speaking to him in 1926 (see May 12, 1926). The Ebbets heirs steadfastly refused to remove Robinson. By 1929, Baseball Commissioner Kenesaw Landis and National League

Wilbert "Uncle Robby" Robinson managed Brooklyn from 1914 through 1931. In good years and bad, he was a fan favorite, a stout, commanding presence in the dugout.

president John Heydler were called in to broker peace between the warring factions in the club hierarchy (see December 11, 1929). Max Carey was hired to replace Robinson as manager. Carey was born Maximillian Carnarius, a name he shortened upon entering professional baseball. Carey had a Hall of Fame playing career as a center fielder for the Pirates from 1910 through 1926, and with the Dodgers from 1926 through 1929. He served as a coach in Pittsburgh in 1930 and 1931. Carey was 41 at the time he was hired as manager of the Dodgers. The club ended the 1932 season with an 81–73 record and in third place, the club's highest finish since 1924, but Carey was fired following a 65–88 mark in 1933. Robinson was 68 at the time he was relieved of his duties with the Dodgers. He was named president of the Atlanta Crackers of the Southern Association in 1933, and died the following year. In 1945, Robinson was elected to the Hall of Fame.

December 17   The board of directors of the Brooklyn baseball franchise announce they are open to the suggestion of a new nickname for the team.

Unlike most teams, the Brooklyn club had multiple nicknames for the first 50 years of its history. In 1889, the club began to be known as the Bridegrooms because several players were recently married. The nickname was in use for about 10 years. In 1895, Trolley Dodgers, later contracted to Dodgers, began to appear in the newspapers because Brooklyn residents had to frequently dodge speeding trolleys on the city streets. By 1899, Superbas had become the club's primary nickname. It was still the favorite of many newspapermen into the 1920s. The hiring of Wilbert Robinson in 1913 inspired the moniker of the Robins. For many years, Superbas, Dodgers and Robins were used interchangeably, often in a single newspaper story. None of these names were recognized officially by the club, and didn't appear on any of the uniforms, where the team was identified with the word Brooklyn or the letter B. With the dismissal of Robinson as manager (see October 23, 1931), the nickname Robins became obsolete. On January 23, 1932, the Brooklyn chapter of the Base Ball Writers' Association of America met to officially select a team nickname. Dodgers was the obvious choice since it had been in use for more than 30 years. Prominent Brooklyn sportswriter Tommy Holmes suggested "Carnaries" since new manager Max Carey's given name was Carnarius, but fortunately the idea failed to catch on. Others said the club should be known as the "Kings," since Brooklyn was located in Kings County. In the end, however, Dodgers won in a landslide. By the start of the 1932 season, most the New York-area papers called the club the Dodgers exclusively. The New York Times was a brief holdout, continuing to call the team the Robins after Opening Day, but shortly afterward the venerable institution bowed to the popular will and referred to the team as the Dodgers. In 1933, Dodgers appeared on the team jerseys for the first time.

1932

LA

Season in a Sentence

In Max Carey's first year as manager, the Dodgers leap from seventh place in July to pennant contention and second place in August, only to slip to third by season's end.

Finish • Won • Lost • Pct • GB

Third   81   73   .526   9.0

Manager

Max Carey

Stats

Stats	Dods	NL	Rank
Batting Avg:	.283	.276	2
On-Base Pct:	.334	.328	2
Slugging Pct:	.420	.396	2
Home Runs:	110		3
Stolen Bases:	61		4
ERA:	4.27	3.88	7
Fielding Avg:	.968	.971	8
Runs Scored:	752		3
Runs Allowed:	747		7

Starting Lineup

Al Lopez, c
George Kelly, 1b
Tony Cuccinello, 2b
Joe Stripp, 3b
Glenn Wright, ss
Lefty O'Doul, lf
Danny Taylor, cf
Hack Wilson, rf
Johnny Frederick, cf-rf
Gordon Slade, ss

Pitchers

Watty Clark, sp
Van Lingle Mungo, sp
Dazzy Vance, sp
Sloppy Thurston, sp
Jack Quinn, rp
Fred Heimach, rp
Joe Shaute, rp

Attendance

681,827 (second in NL)

Club Leaders

Batting Avg:	Lefty O'Doul	.368
On-Base Pct:	Lefty O'Doul	.423
Slugging Pct:	Lefty O'Doul	.555
Home Runs:	Hack Wilson	23
RBIs:	Hack Wilson	123
Runs:	Lefty O'Doul	120
Stolen Bases:	Joe Stripp	14
Wins:	Watty Clark	20
Strikeouts:	Van Lingle Mungo	107
ERA:	Watty Clark	3.49
Saves:	Joe Quinn	8

JANUARY **22**   The Dodgers release Rube Bressler and Dolf Luque.

JANUARY **23**   The Dodgers send Bob Parham and $45,000 to the Cardinals for Hack Wilson.

A future Hall of Famer, Wilson was an outfielder who packed a muscular 190 pounds on a five-foot-six-inch frame. While playing for the Cubs from 1926 through 1930, Wilson batted .331 and averaged 35 homers and 142 runs batted in per season. He led the NL in homers four times and RBIs twice. Wilson's best season was in 1930 when he hit 56 home runs, to set a National League record which stood until 1998, and drove in 191 runs, to establish a major league mark which still stands. Wilson had trouble controlling his alcohol consumption, however, and experienced an extreme downturn in 1931 when he struck only 13 home runs and drove in just 61 runs. The Cubs traded Wilson to St. Louis in December 1931, but Wilson objected to the contract offered by the Cards, which called for a 25 percent cut from his 1931 salary of $33,000. The Cardinals passed him on to the Dodgers a month after the trade with the Cubs. Wilson had somewhat of a revival in Brooklyn in 1932, by batting .297 with 23 homers and 123 runs batted in. He suffered another relapse in 1933, though, and was traded by the Dodgers to the Phillies in 1934, Hack's last season in the majors.

FEBRUARY **27**   The Dodgers sign Waite Hoyt, most recently with the Athletics, as a free agent.

A Brooklyn native, Hoyt had a lifetime record of 189–131 when acquired by the Dodgers. He had was 32 years old and had pitched in seven World Series with the Yankees and Athletics. Hoyt was the Opening Day starter for the Dodgers in 1932, but like many Brooklyn players during the period, had a fondness for alcoholic beverages and was released after only eight games. After playing for the Giants and the Pirates, Hoyt would return to the Dodgers in 1937 and 1938 at the end of his career.

MARCH **14**   Thirteen days after the kidnapping of the Lindbergh baby, the Dodgers trade Babe Herman, Ernie Lombardi and Wally Gilbert to the Reds for Tony Cuccinello, Joe Stripp and Clyde Sukeforth.

The deal with Cincinnati was one of the worst in club history. With the country suffering through the depths of the Great Depression, Herman was offered a pay cut from his 1931 salary and refused to report to spring training. Herman's flamboyant and unpredictable play was also an anathema to new manager Max Carey, a strict disciplinarian who emphasized speed, steady defense and consistency in stark contrast to laissez-faire *approach of Wilbert Robinson. Although Herman never reached the heights he achieved in 1929 and 1930 when he posted batting averages of .381 and .393, he was still a productive hitter for another five years. The Dodgers had two young catchers with bright futures in Al Lopez and Ernie Lombardi in 1932, and believing that Lopez was the better prospect, dealt Lombardi to the Reds. Lombardi went on to play 16 more seasons in the majors. At the close of his career, Lombardi had a .306 career batting average, two batting titles, an MVP award, seven All-Star Game selections, two World Series appearances, and would earn election into the Hall of Fame in 1986. Cuccinello started at second base for the Dodgers for four seasons and Stripp was a regular at third for five years, but they failed to compensate for the loss of Herman and Lombardi.*

APRIL 7   The Dodgers purchase George Kelly from the Minneapolis club in the American Association.

> *A future Hall of Famer, Kelly played first base on four consecutive World Series teams for the Giants from 1921 through 1924. He was acquired because Del Bissonette, who was the starter at first base from 1928 through 1931, injured his leg in spring training and missed the entire 1932 season. Kelly was all but through as a player, and was released in July after playing in 64 games for the Dodgers.*

APRIL 12   In Max Carey's first game as manager, the Dodgers open the season with an 8–3 loss to the Braves before 30,000 at Ebbets Field. Commissioner Kenesaw Landis was among those in attendance. Waite Hoyt was the starting, and losing, pitcher.

APRIL 16   Dazzy Vance pitches a two-hitter to defeat the Phillies 5–0 at Ebbets Field. Philadelphia was held without a hit until Don Hurst singled with one out in the seventh. The other hit was a single by Les Mallon in the ninth.

APRIL 17   Van Lingle Mungo pitches an 11-inning complete game, but loses 2–0 to the Phillies at Ebbets Field. Ed Holley pitched a three-hitter for Philadelphia. The game-time temperature was 44 degrees.

APRIL 23   Dodgers center fielder Alta Cohen commits three errors during a 7–1 loss to the Braves in Boston.

MAY 3   Trailing 7–3, the Dodgers erupt for eight runs in the ninth inning and beat the Giants 11–7 in New York. The rally started with a home run from Johnny Frederick, his fourth hit of the game in his fifth at-bat. The Dodgers tied the score on a two-run single by Glenn Wright. George Kelly drove in the go-ahead tally with another single. Frederick came up again with the bases loaded and collected hit number five with a single which brought two runs across the plate.

MAY 7   The Dodgers purchase Danny Taylor from the Cubs.

MAY 16   The Dodgers score eight runs in the ninth inning to swamp the Pirates 11–1 in Pittsburgh. Brooklyn put together a streak of seven consecutive hits, including a homer by Johnny Frederick. It was the second time in less than two weeks that the Dodgers had an eight-run rally in the ninth.

MAY 18   Watty Clark retires the first 18 batters to face him, and finishes with a four-hitter and a 4–2 victory over the Pirates in Pittsburgh.

MAY 26   Al Lopez has an eventful day when the Dodgers lose a run because he bats out of turn before scoring the winning run in a 12-inning, 3–2 decision over the Giants in New York. Lopez hit out of turn in each of his first three plate appearances, according to the lineup submitted to umpire Cy Rigler by Max Carey. Lopez struck out in his first two times up, but singled in a run in the sixth inning in his third appearance at the plate drawing a protest from the Giants. Lopez was called out and the run disallowed. Batting in the proper position, Lopez singled in the 12th and came to score the deciding run.

May 30	The Dodgers sweep the Phillies 13–4 and 5–3 at Ebbets Field. Brooklyn won the opener despite committing seven errors. Van Lingle Mungo struck out 12 batters in eight innings of game two.
June 5	The Phillies score five runs in the ninth inning to defeat the Dodgers 7–6 at Ebbets Field. The wildness of Van Lingle Mungo contributed to the loss. He walked 11 and hit a batter before being removed with none out in the ninth.
June 8	Hack Wilson drives in all five Brooklyn runs during a 5–2 win over the Cubs at Ebbets Field. He hit a grand slam off Pat Malone in the first inning and an RBI-single against Jakie May in the eighth.
June 10	A fistfight between Neal Finn of the Dodgers and Billy Jurges of the Cubs highlights a 4–3 win over the Cubs at Ebbets Field. In the first inning, Finn bumped Jurges at second base when the latter was about to try for a double play. As Finn turned away, Jurges made a remark that Finn didn't take kindly, and the two went at it. Third baseman Woody English charged into the fray with a flying tackle that carried both combatants to the ground. Members of both teams rushed up and there was some indiscriminate punching before order was restored.
June 11	Danny Taylor hits a grand slam off Jim Lindsay in the fifth inning of a 12–3 win over the Cardinals at Ebbets Field.

> *In late June, the Dodgers wore uniform numbers for the first time after the National League passed an edict requiring its clubs to assign the numerals to help fans better identify the players on the field. The first numbers were issued to Johnny Frederick (1), Neal Finn (2), Joe Stripp (3), Hack Wilson (4), Tony Cuccinello (5), Lefty O'Doul (6), Glenn Wright (7), Gordon Slade (8), Danny Taylor (9), Al Lopez (10), Clyde Sukeforth (11), Val Picinich (12), George Kelly (14), Dazzy Vance (15), Van Lingle Mungo (16), Watty Clark (17), Fred Heimach (18), Ray Phelps (19), Sloppy Thurston (20), Joe Shaute (21), Jack Quinn (22), Cy Moore (24), Max Rosenfeld (25), coach Casey Stengel (31), coach Otto Miller (32) and manager Max Carey (33). The first seven numbers corresponded to the batting order used by the club at the time.*

July 3	Dazzy Vance strikes out 12 batters in 11 innings, but winds up losing 4–3 to the Phillies at Ebbets Field.
July 8	The Dodgers score seven runs in the first inning and beat the Reds 15–5 in Cincinnati.
July 9	The Dodgers break a 2–2 tie with seven runs in the ninth inning and beat the Pirates 9–3 in Pittsburgh.
July 23	The Dodgers lose both ends of a double-header by scores of 10–2 and 16–5 to the Phillies in Philadelphia.

> *The pair of defeats dropped the Dodgers' record to 42–50. The club was in seventh place, 12 games out of first.*

JULY 26 — The Dodgers score 11 runs in the seventh inning and beat the Cardinals 12–6 in the first game of a double-header at Ebbets Field. The 11-run rally consisted of 10 hits and two walks, including two hits each by George Kelly (both doubles), Tony Cuccinello, Glenn Wright and pitcher Joe Shaute. The Dodgers also won the second game 5–4 with a run in the ninth on a triple by Al Lopez and a sacrifice fly from Johnny Frederick.

JULY 27 — The Dodgers beat the Cardinals again 5–4 with a run in the ninth inning. Neal Finn drove in the winning run with a single.

JULY 31 — First baseman Bud Clancy, in his first day with the Dodgers, collects six hits, including two doubles, in eight at-bats during a double-header against the Cubs at Ebbets Field. The Dodgers lost the first game 6–3, then won the second 5–4.

AUGUST 2 — In his third game as a Dodger, Bud Clancy is three-for-four again during a 4–2 victory over the Cubs at Ebbets Field.

Clancy was in his eighth season in the majors when acquired by the Dodgers. He hit .306 in 53 games with the club.

AUGUST 4 — Lefty O'Doul hits a walk-off homer in the 10th inning which beats the Pirates 6–5 in the second game of a double-header at Ebbets Field. It was his second home run of the game and his third of the day. O'Doul also hit a home run in the opener, a 7–4 Brooklyn victory.

O'Doul won the National League batting race with a .368 average in 1932. He also struck 21 homers, scored 120 runs, drove in 90, and collected 219 hits.

AUGUST 12 — The Dodgers hit into six double plays, but escape with a 1–0 triumph over the Giants in New York. Watty Clark pitched the shutout. The lone run scored in the fifth inning on a double by Joe Stripp, a single from Lefty O'Doul and Johnny Frederick's sacrifice fly. Frederick entered the game in right field in the third inning after Hack Wilson was ejected for arguing a called third strike.

AUGUST 13 — The Dodgers sweep the Giants 18–9 and 5–4 in New York. The opener was unusual on many levels. The Dodgers scored all 18 runs in a span of three innings with eight runs in the fourth inning, seven in the fifth and six in the sixth. Sloppy Thurston tied a modern major league record by allowing six home runs, but also starred with a bat in his hands, collecting four hits, including a double, in five at-bats. In the fourth, Thurston surrendered homers to Bill Terry, Mel Ott and Fred Lindstrom on three consecutive pitches. Thurston allowed two other homers to Terry and one more to Ott. Tony Cuccinello, Danny Taylor and Hack Wilson also struck home runs for the Dodgers. To add to the weirdness of the day, the two teams tied a major league record for fewest strikeouts in a double-header with two. Waite Hoyt of the Giants recorded both strikeouts. Hoyt was Brooklyn's Opening Day starter before being released by the club in June.

AUGUST 14 — Jack Quinn becomes the oldest pitcher in major league history to win a game with two innings of relief during a 10-inning, 2–1 decision over the Giants in the first game of a double-header at the Polo Grounds. New York won the second game 8–4.

Quinn was 40 days past his 49th birthday on August 14, 1932, when he won his last big-league game. Quinn finished his career with 247 victories and 218 defeats.

AUGUST 20   The Dodgers sweep the Reds 6–0 and 6–1 in a double-header in Cincinnati.

The Dodgers won 24 of 30 games in 28 days from July 24 through August 20, lifting the club from seventh place to second, just 1¹/₂ games behind first-place Chicago. The Cubs swept the Dodgers three straight games at Wrigley Field from August 24 through August 26, however, and Brooklyn never seriously threatened for the pennant again over the remainder of the season.

AUGUST 31   The Dodgers sweep the Reds 7–1 and 11–10 in Cincinnati. In the second game, the Dodgers fell behind 5–0 in the second inning and still trailed 10–8 before scoring three times in the eighth.

SEPTEMBER 8   Lefty O'Doul collects two homers and two singles in four at-bats during a 12–2 win over the Pirates at Ebbets Field.

SEPTEMBER 12   A two-run, pinch-hit, walk-off home run by Johnny Frederick in the ninth inning beats the Cubs 4–3 at Ebbets Field. Frederick's homer followed a double from Glenn Wright.

The homer by Frederick was his sixth in 1932 in a pinch-hit role, which set a major league record. He didn't hit his first pinch-homer until July 12. The others were struck on July 15, August 10, August 14 and September 10 before Frederick's September 12 game-winner. The previous record for pinch-hit home runs in a season was three. Frederick had nine hits in 29 pinch-hit at-bats that season, and 16 homers overall in 384 at-bats. He hit eight pinch-hit homers during his career. The other two were in 1929 and 1934. Frederick held sole possession of the major league record for pinch-hit home runs in a season for 58 years until Dave Hansen accounted for seven for the Dodgers in 2000. Craig Wilson of the Pirates also struck seven pinch-homers in 2001.

SEPTEMBER 13   The Dodgers defeat the Cardinals 6–5 in the first game of a double-header at Ebbets Field with a squeeze play in the 10th inning. The bunt by Al Lopez scored Glenn Wright from third base. The Dodgers completed the sweep with a 3–1 victory in game two.

SEPTEMBER 24   Watty Clark picks up his 20th victory of the season with a 3–2 decision over the Braves at Ebbets Field.

Clark had a 20–12 record in 1932 along with a 3.49 ERA in 273¹/₃ innings. He also led the NL in games started with 36. Clark was never quite the same after that season, however, and posted a record 28–29 over the remaining five years of his career.

SEPTEMBER 25   In the final game of the season, Joe Stripp hits a grand slam to give the Dodgers a 6–1 lead over the Braves at Ebbets Field, but Boston rallies to win 13–7.

OCTOBER 12   Steve McKeever replaces Frank York as club president.

One of Brooklyn's top pitchers—and most colorful characters throughout the 1930s—Van Lingle Mungo is now remembered mostly for a novelty jazz song named after him.

York was named as a compromise candidate as president two years earlier (see December 11, 1929). He left the club to devote more time to his law practice. McKeever was 78 years old at the time of his appointment and owned half of the stock in the club. Fifteen heirs of Charles Ebbets owned the other half. McKeever and the Ebbets family had been waging an internal feud for control of the franchise since the death of Charles Ebbets in 1925. McKeever's presidency did alleviate the turmoil in the front office, however, and the franchise struggled, with losing records in six consecutive seasons from 1933 through 1938. McKeever held his role at the top of the organization until his death in 1938.

DECEMBER 15   Six weeks after New York governor Franklin Roosevelt defeats Herbert Hoover in the Presidential election, the Dodgers trade Cy Moore, Mickey Finn and Jack Warner to the Phillies for Ray Benge.

Finn played 51 games for the Phillies in 1933 before undergoing surgery for duodenal ulcers. He died on July 6, 1933, at the age of 29 following the operation.

1933

L A

Season in a Sentence

An 8–19 record in July dooms the Dodgers to a sixth place finish, and Max Carey is dismissed as manager after only two years on the job.

Finish • Won • Lost • Pct • GB

Sixth   65   88   .425   26.5

Manager

Max Carey

Stats

Stats	Dods	NL	Rank
Batting Avg:	.263	.266	5
On-Base Pct:	.316	.317	5
Slugging Pct:	.359	.362	6
Home Runs:	62		3
Stolen Bases:	82		2
ERA:	3.68	3.33	7
Fielding Avg:	.971	.973	6
Runs Scored:	617		5
Runs Allowed:	695		7

Starting Lineup

Al Lopez, c
Sam Leslie, 1b
Tony Cuccinello, 2b
Joe Stripp, 3b
Jimmy Jordan, ss
Hack Wilson, lf
Danny Taylor, cf
Johnny Frederick, rf
Buzz Boyle, lf-cf
Jake Flowers, ss-2b

Pitchers

Van Lingle Mungo, sp-rp
Boom-Boom Beck, sp
Ownie Carroll, sp
Ray Benge, sp
Joe Shaute, rp
Sloppy Thurston, rp-sp

Attendance

526,815 (third in NL)

Club Leaders

Batting Avg:	Johnny Frederick	.308
On-Base Pct:	Johnny Frederick	.355
Slugging Pct:	Johnny Frederick	.410
Home Runs:	Three tied with	9
RBIs:	Tony Cuccinello	65
Runs:	Danny Taylor	75
Stolen Bases:	Jake Flowers	13
Wins:	Van Lingle Mungo	16
Strikeouts:	Van Lingle Mungo	110
ERA:	Van Lingle Mungo	2.72
Saves:	Sloppy Thurston	3

JANUARY 27   The Dodgers sign Joe Judge, most recently with the Senators, as a free agent.

FEBRUARY 8   The Dodgers trade Dazzy Vance and Gordon Slade to the Cardinals for Jake Flowers and Ownie Carroll.

Vance had played 10 seasons for the Dodgers and won a club record 190 games, but was 41 at the time of the trade and about finished as an effective pitcher. He would return to Brooklyn to pitch the last 20 games of his career as a Dodger in 1935.

APRIL 12   The scheduled opener between the Dodgers and Phillies in Philadelphia is postponed by rain.

APRIL 13   The Dodgers win the season opener 5–4 over the Phillies in Philadelphia. Watty Clark was the winning pitcher.

The word Dodgers *appeared on the club's uniforms for the first time in 1933. It was also the first time that a nickname was sewn onto the jerseys. Prior to 1933, the team was identified with either the word* Brooklyn *or the letter* B. *The 1933 uniforms had* Dodgers *in blue in fancy capital letters. The shirts and pants had pinstripes and a letter B was included on the left sleeve. On the road grays, Dodgers was written in blue and outlined in red. From 1934 through 1937, however, the home and road jerseys had Brooklyn splashed across the front. Dodgers would return on the home uniforms in 1938, and has been a feature ever since.*

APRIL 16   In the home opener, the Dodgers and Giants play a 14-inning, 1–1 draw before 32,000 at Ebbets Field. The game was called on account of darkness.

With the end of Prohibition, beer was sold at Ebbets Field for the first time since 1919.

APRIL 27   Dodgers pitcher Boom-Boom Beck beats the Braves 1–0 at Ebbets Field. Del Bissonette drove in the lone run with a single in the second inning.

Walter (Boom-Boom) Beck earned his unusual nickname a year later due to an incident involving Hack Wilson (see July 4, 1934). Beck led the NL in games started in 1933, but finished the season with a record of 12–20. He is the only Dodgers pitcher to lose at least 20 games in a season between 1912 and the present.

APRIL 29   The Dodgers release Jack Quinn.

MAY 12   The Dodgers score two runs in the ninth inning to defeat the Reds 7–6 at Ebbets Field. Jake Flowers drove in the winning run with a single. Lefty O'Doul collected five hits in five at-bats and accounted for five runs batted in.

MAY 14   A walk-off, grand slam, pinch-home run by Hack Wilson beats the Phillies 8–6 at Ebbets Field. Rain was pouring down heading into the bottom of the ninth with the Dodgers trailing 6–4, but umpire Cy Pfirman refused to stop play. Most of the 12,000 in attendance had either gone home or had sought shelter under the overhangs around the park. A single and two walks loaded the bases before Wilson's blast off Ad Liska, which landed in the screen above the right-field wall.

MAY 16   A two-run single by Johnny Frederick off Dizzy Dean defeats the Cardinals 6–5 in St. Louis.

MAY 18   The Dodgers score eight runs in the first inning and down the Cardinals 14–5 in St. Louis.

JUNE 7   The Dodgers trade Del Bissonette to Baltimore of the International League for Buzz Boyle.

Boyle was a starter in the Dodgers outfield for three seasons. Pete Rose was one of his nephews. Boyle was a scout with the Reds in 1960 when he signed Rose to his first professional contract.

JUNE 15   The Dodgers collect 21 hits and defeat the Phillies 9–3 in Philadelphia. Sloppy Thurston pitched a complete game and drove in four runs with a pair of doubles.

JUNE 16   The Dodgers trade Lefty O'Doul and Watty Clark to the Giants for Sam Leslie.

JUNE 20   Center fielder Danny Taylor completes an unassisted double play in the ninth inning of a 15–4 loss to the Cardinals at Ebbets Field. With St. Louis pitcher Syl Johnson on first base, Pepper Martin hit a twisting fly to right-center with Johnson running with the pitch. Taylor caught the ball, and holding an 11-run lead, Johnson made no effort to get back to the bag. Taylor doubled Johnson by stepping on first on his way to the dugout.

JUNE 23   Trailing the Pirates 4–1 in the eighth inning at Ebbets Field, Tony Cuccinello hits a grand slam off Larry French to lift the Dodgers to a 5–4 victory.

On the same day, the Dodgers sold Val Picinich to the Pirates.

JUNE 30   Joe Stripp collects five hits, including two doubles, in five at-bats during a 6–3 win over the Cubs at Ebbets Field.

JULY 2   Al Lopez steals home in the ninth inning to close out a 4–3 triumph over the Cubs in the second game of a double-header at Ebbets Field. Lopez unexpectedly broke for the plate and slid under the tag of Chicago catcher Gabby Hartnett. Lopez was immediately engulfed in a crowd of fans who raced onto the field. The Dodgers also won the opener 7–3.

Lopez batted a career high .301 in 1933.

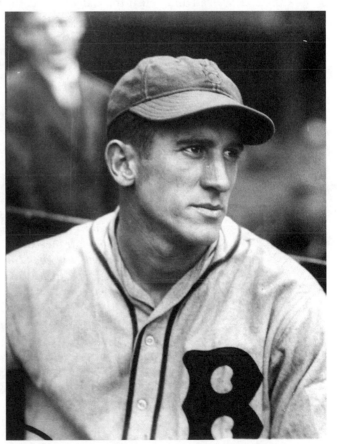

JULY 6   Dodger second baseman Tony Cuccinello participates in the first All-Star Game, which was played at Comiskey Park in Chicago. Pinch-hitting for Carl Hubbell, Cuccinello struck out in the seventh inning. The American League won the game 4–2.

JULY 29   The Dodgers sweep the Phillies 12–11 and 14–4 in Philadelphia. Brooklyn scored two runs in the ninth inning to win the opener.

AUGUST 8   Ray Benge pitches an 11-inning shutout and allows only three hits to defeat the Giants 1–0 at Ebbets Field. Hal Schumacher also pitched a complete game for New York, and collected two of the

One of the great backstops of his era and one of the great baseball minds of all time, Al Lopez played six seasons for the Dodgers.

three hits off Benge. In the 11th, the Dodgers loaded the bases with Danny Taylor the runner on third. Taylor was caught flat-footed off the bag on a throw from Giants catcher Gus Mancuso, but third baseman Johnny Vergez juggled the ball, then hit Taylor in the back with the return throw as the Dodger raced to the plate with the winning run.

AUGUST 13   The Dodgers score seven runs in the first inning and beat the Braves 11–0 in the second game of a double-header at Ebbets Field. The Dodgers lost the opener 6–2.

AUGUST 16   Danny Taylor hits two homers for the only two runs of an 11-inning, 2–1 victory over the Pirates in the first game of a double-header at Ebbets Field. Taylor homered in the sixth inning and hit a walk-off blast in the 11th, both off Larry French. Pittsburgh won the second tilt 11–7.

The Dodgers were down to three healthy infielders in late August. As a result, Hack Wilson started five games at second base and Al Lopez one. They were the only five games that Wilson played at second during his 12-year career. Lopez appeared in just four games at second base during his 19 years in the majors.

AUGUST 29   The Dodgers score six runs in the second inning and five in the third for an 11–0 lead and defeat the Cubs 13–5 in the first game of a double-header at Ebbets Field. Chicago won the second contest 6–2.

SEPTEMBER 6   The Reds score 10 runs in the sixth inning for an 18–2 lead, and beat the Dodgers 18–8 in the second game of a double-header in Cincinnati. The Dodgers won the opener 7–3.

SEPTEMBER 7   Boom Boom Beck pitches a shutout to defeat the Reds 2–0 in Cincinnati. The two Brooklyn runs crossed the plate in the eighth inning on a double by Lonny Frey, a triple from Johnny Frederick and Hack Wilson's sacrifice fly.

SEPTEMBER 19   Bob Quinn is named general manager of the Dodgers.

Quinn was the first individual in club history to hold the title of general manager by handling the business end of the franchise in addition to running the farm system, and making trades and other personnel decisions. Quinn was previously the business manager of the St. Louis Browns from 1917 through 1923, and owner of the Red Sox from 1923 through 1933. During Quinn's regime in Boston, the Sox finished last in the American League six consecutive seasons beginning in 1925. Quinn lasted only two undistinguished seasons in Brooklyn before purchasing the Boston Braves.

OCTOBER 2   Five weeks before the election of Fiorello LaGuardia as mayor of New York City, the Dodgers draft Jim Bucher from the Cardinals organization.

1934   L A

Season in a Sentence

Knocking the arch-rival Giants out of the pennant race following a sarcastic question from New York manager Bill Terry serves as a moral victory in Casey Stengel's first season as manager.

Finish • Won • Lost • Pct • GB

Sixth   71   81   .467   23.5

Manager

Casey Stengel

Stats

Stats	Dods	NL	Rank
Batting Avg:	.281	.279	4
On-Base Pct:	.350	.333	1
Slugging Pct:	.396	.394	5
Home Runs:	79		5
Stolen Bases:	55		3
ERA:	4.48	4.06	7
Fielding Avg:	.970	.972	6
Runs Scored:	748		3
Runs Allowed:	795		7

Starting Lineup

Al Lopez, c
Sam Leslie, 1b
Tony Cuccinello, 2b
Joe Stripp, 3b
Lonny Frey, ss
Danny Taylor, lf
Len Koenecke, cf
Buzz Boyle, rf
Jimmy Jordan, ss-2b
Johnny Frederick, rf

Pitchers

Van Lingle Mungo, sp
Ray Benge, sp
Johnny Babich, sp
Tom Zachary, sp-rp
Dutch Leonard, rp-sp
Les Munns, rp

Attendance

434,188 (third in NL)

Club Leaders

Batting Avg:	Sam Leslie	.332
On-Base Pct:	Len Koenecke	.411
Slugging Pct:	Len Koenecke	.509
Home Runs:	Len Koenecke	14
	Tony Cuccinello	14
RBIs:	Sam Leslie	102
Runs:	Buzz Boyle	88
Stolen Bases:	Danny Taylor	12
Wins:	Van Lingle Mungo	18
Strikeouts:	Van Lingle Mungo	184
ERA:	Van Lingle Mungo	3.37
Saves:	Dutch Leonard	5

JANUARY 25   Giants manager and star first baseman Bill Terry riles nearly everyone in Brooklyn by making a wisecrack during an interview with reporters.

The Giants had won the National League pennant and World Series in 1933, and Terry declared before a bevy of New York writers that "We should win again this year. If we don't, we won't finish lower than third. I think the Cubs, Pirates and Cardinals will give us the most trouble." Roscoe McGowan of the New York Times asked, "What about Brooklyn?" "Brooklyn?" quipped Terry. "Gee, I haven't heard a peep out of there. Is Brooklyn still in the league?"

FEBRUARY 17   The Dodgers release Glenn Wright.

FEBRUARY 21   The Dodgers release Max Carey as manager and replace him with Casey Stengel. Carey was under contract for the 1934 season, and was paid in full. At his first press conference, Stengel responded to the sarcastic comment made by Bill Terry a month earlier (see January 25, 1934). "The first thing I want to say," said Casey, "is the Dodgers are still in the league. Tell that to Terry."

When hired by the Dodgers, Stengel was far from the national icon he would become later in life as manager of the Yankees (see September 17, 1912). He was a starting outfielder for the Dodgers from 1912 through 1917 at the start of a 14-year playing career. Casey played in the World Series for Brooklyn in 1916 and as a Giant in 1922 and 1923. He was a coach for the Dodgers under Carey in 1932 and 1933. Stengel would last three years as manager of the Dodgers, and never finished a season above the .500 level.

MARCH 20   Babe Didrikson, one of the greatest female athletes in history, pitches an inning for the Philadelphia Athletics against the Dodgers in an exhibition game in Fort Myers, Florida. Didrikson hurled the first inning, and walked Danny Taylor and nicked Johnny Frederick with a pitch before Joe Stripp hit into a triple play. Shortstop Dib Williams caught Stripp's liner, and the triple killing was completed Williams to second baseman Rabbit Warstler to first baseman Jimmie Foxx.

APRIL 17   The Dodgers win the season opener 8–7 over the Braves before 30,000 at Ebbets Field. The Dodgers led 8–2 after five innings, then survived a Boston comeback which included two runs in the sixth inning and three in the ninth. Van Lingle Mungo pitched a complete game. Hack Wilson struck a three-run homer in the third. Danny Taylor homered, doubled and singled before leaving the game in the eighth after being injured in an outfield collision with Buzz Boyle.

It was an eventful afternoon. During the opening ceremonies, an enthusiastic fan in a field box set off a string of firecrackers several feet in length just as the band and the players lined up for the march to the center-field flagpole. Further adding to the excitement, a large piece of bunting on the upper stands caught fire and the blazing fragments fell into the seats below as the spectators scrambled for safety. In the confusion, home plate umpire Ernie Quigley overlooked the ceremonial first pitch, scheduled to be thrown out by Brooklyn Borough President Raymond Ingersoll. After Mungo threw a strike to Boston lead-off hitter Billy Urbanski, Quigley stopped the game and gave Ingersoll a ball. It was duly thrown to Dodgers catcher Al Lopez, and the contest resumed.

APRIL 19   The game at Ebbets Field against the Braves is called after seven innings because of fog, with the score 1–1.

APRIL 20   Len Koenecke hits two homers and two singles in four at-bats during a 5–0 win over the Phillies at Ebbets Field. Dutch Leonard pitched the shutout.

Leonard had an 18–23 record in four seasons with the Dodgers from 1933 through 1936. He led the NL in saves in 1935 with eight. After being released by Brooklyn, Leonard learned to throw a knuckleball in the minor leagues with Atlanta in the Southern Association and resurfaced in the majors with the Washington Senators in 1938. He lasted in the big leagues until 1951, won a total 191 games and was named to five All-Star teams.

APRIL 29   Trailing 6–0, the Dodgers score four runs in the fifth inning and four in the eighth and defeat the Phillies 8–7 at Baker Bowl. Four Philadelphia pitchers combined to walk 12 batters.

MAY 11   The Dodgers score seven runs in the eighth inning and wallop the Cubs 13–1 in Chicago.

MAY 30   With the jab by New York manager Bill Terry still resonating in Brooklyn (see January 25, 1934), the Dodgers play before 41,209, the largest crowd in the history of Ebbets Field, which watches the home team lose 5–2 and 8–6 to the Giants. The ballpark had about 31,000 seats. The excess sat in the runways and in the aisles. A few daring fans perched in the girders high in the stands.

JUNE 5   Buzz Boyle extends his hitting streak to 25 games during an 11–10 loss to the Phillies in the first game of a double-header at Baker Bowl. Ex-Dodger Bud Clancy, playing in his first game for Philadelphia, hit a three-run, walk-off homer in the ninth. Boyle didn't start game two, a 5–4 loss. He struck out in his only at-bat as a substitute in left field for Hack Wilson.

JUNE 7   Len Koenecke leads off the game with a home run, and it holds up for a 1–0 win over the Phillies in Philadelphia. The blow was struck off George Darrow. Dutch Leonard pitched the shutout.

A 30-year-old center fielder in his first season with the Dodgers and his second in the majors, Koenecke hit .320 with 14 homers in 1934. Koenecke would die tragically the following season (see September 17, 1935).

JUNE 12   The Dodgers purchase Tom Zachary from the Braves.

JUNE 17   The Dodgers sweep the Reds 4–2 and 9–7 at Crosley Field with a pair of ninth-inning rallies. The Dodgers scored three times in the ninth in the opener. Len Koenecke drove in the go-ahead run with a single. Brooklyn broke a 6–6 tie with three runs in the top of the ninth in game two, then survived a Cincinnati rally for the victory.

JUNE 24   Van Lingle Mungo strikes out 12 batters, but loses 5–1 to the Cubs in the first game of a double-header at Wrigley Field. Chicago also won the second game 8–0.

Mungo was 18–16 with a 3.37 ERA, 22 complete games and 184 strikeouts. He also led the NL in innings pitched (315^1/$_3$) and games started (22).

JUNE 29   The Dodgers purchase Watty Clark from the Giants.

JULY 4   Walter (Boom Boom) Beck earns his nickname in the first inning of an 11–2 loss to the Phillies in the first game of a double-header in Philadelphia. When manager Casey Stengel came out to remove Beck after the pitcher faced only eight batters, Beck reacted by heaving the ball into right field. The throw struck the tin-plated outfield wall with a loud boom. The rebound aroused Dodgers right fielder Hack Wilson, who was relaxing during the pitching change and thought the game had resumed. Wilson pursued the ball and fired a strike back to the infield. The Dodgers won the opener 8–5.

JULY 6   Sam Leslie hits an inside-the-park grand slam off Al Smith in the sixth inning of an 11–2 victory over the Giants at Ebbets Field. The drive appeared to be headed for only a single, but the ball hit a bump in the outfield and bounded over the head of center fielder George Watkins and rolled to the wall.

Leslie hit .332 and drove in 102 runs in 1934.

JULY 10   Van Lingle Mungo is the losing pitcher in a 9–7 National League defeat in the All-Star Game at the Polo Grounds in New York City. With the NL leading 4–2, Mungo gave up four runs in the fifth inning.

JULY 12   Tony Cuccinello ties a major league record for most total chances in a game by a third baseman with 13 during a 9–7 win over the Reds in the first game of a double-header at Ebbets Field. Cuccinello had four putouts and nine assists. Cincinnati won the second tilt 13–5.

JULY 19   A two-run walk-off homer by Lonny Frey beats the Pirates 4–2 at Ebbets Field.

JULY 22   On the day that John Dillinger is killed by FBI agents in Chicago, the Dodgers sweep the Pirates 3–2 and 13–10 at Ebbets Field. In the second game the Dodgers took a 10–0 lead with 10 runs in the second inning, and survived a seven-run Pittsburgh rally in the ninth. All nine Brooklyn batters scored in the second, with Tony Cuccinello crossing the plate twice. Pitcher Ray Benge contributed a double and a single during the rally.

AUGUST 2   Al Lopez hits a walk-off homer in the ninth inning to defeat the Phillies 8–7 at Ebbets Field. After the game, manager Jimmy Wilson and the Phillies and coach Otto Miller of the Dodgers engaged in a fistfight under the grandstand. The fight stemmed from an argument which started in the seventh with Joe Stripp at bat. Wilson and Miller exchanged heated words, and, after Stripp fouled out, Wilson hurled the ball past Miller's head into right field. After heaving the ball, Wilson issued a challenge to Miller for a later meeting. The scrap didn't last long before police intervened, but Miller managed to score a knockdown and Wilson inflicted a little damage to his opponent's face before they were pulled apart.

AUGUST 8   The Dodgers release Hack Wilson.

AUGUST 18   After being held to one hit through 7²/₃ innings by Burleigh Grimes, the Dodgers erupt for two runs in the eighth inning and four in the ninth to beat the Pirates 6–2 in Pittsburgh.

AUGUST 19   The Dodgers leave 16 runners on base, but beat the Pirates 2–1 in Pittsburgh.

AUGUST 31   The "daffy" Dodgers lose a 2–1 decision to the Giants at Ebbets Field in which Len Koenecke fails to run out a bunt. With Sam Leslie the base runner on first, Koenecke topped the ball and claimed it struck his foot. Believing he hit a foul ball, Koenecke limped around the plate arguing with umpire Ernie Quigley. Leslie ran for second, and New York catcher Gus Mancuso threw the ball into center field, and Leslie was safe at home on a throw from center fielder Hank Leiber to third baseman Johnny Vergez. At Casey Stengel's urging, Koenecke finally started toward first and was thrown out by a step on a throw from Vergez to first baseman Bill Terry. In the end, Koenecke was thrown out at first on a ball handled by the catcher, center fielder, third baseman and first baseman.

SEPTEMBER 6 The Giants take a seven-game lead over the second-place Cardinals in the National League pennant race with a 12-inning, 2–1 win over the Cubs in New York.

SEPTEMBER 9   The Dodgers sweep the Reds 5–0 and 3–0 in a double-header at Ebbets Field.
               Ray Benge pitched a two-hitter in the opener. The only Cincinnati hits were singles
               by Gordon Slade in the fourth inning and Sparky Adams in the sixth. Van Lingle
               Mungo hurled a three-hitter in the nightcap.

SEPTEMBER 12   The Dodgers edge the Reds 8–7 in 10 innings at Ebbets Field. In the 10th, Buzz Boyle
               tripled off Si Johnson, and after two intentional walks, Cincinnati brought in reliever
               Junie Barnes, who was making his major league debut. Barnes walked Sam Leslie to
               force in the winning run.

SEPTEMBER 19   Trailing 2–1, the Dodgers score seven runs in the seventh inning and beat the Pirates
               8–4 in the second game of a double-header at Ebbets Field. Brooklyn also won the
               opener 4–1.

SEPTEMBER 21   After Dizzy Dean pitches a three-hit shutout for a 13–0 victory in the first game of
               a double-header at Ebbets Field, his younger brother Paul pitches a no-hitter in the
               second tilt for a 3–0 Cardinals win. Dizzy had a no-hitter until Buzz Boyle beat out
               a slow roller for a single with one out in the eighth inning. The only base runner off
               Paul Dean was a walk to Len Koenecke in the first inning. After that, the St. Louis
               pitcher retired 25 batters in a row, six on strikeouts. The final out was a grounder by
               Boyle to shortstop Leo Durocher.

               *The Dodgers entered the final two days of the season with two games against
               the Giants in New York. The Giants had squandered their seven-game lead of
               September 6, and headed into the Dodgers series tied with the Cardinals for
               first place. Both the Giants and Cards had 93–58 records. The Dodgers had
               been seething all year about Bill Terry's flippant remark about Brooklyn (see
               January 25, 1934), but thus far had done little to exact revenge. On the morning
               of September 29, the Dodgers had a record of 6–14 against their New York arch
               enemies in 1934, and had lost seven of nine at the Polo Grounds on the way to
               landing in sixth place, far out of the race.*

SEPTEMBER 29   The Dodgers beat the Giants 5–1 at the Polo Grounds. The loss put the Giants one
               game behind the Cardinals. Most of the 13,774 in attendance were Dodgers fans
               who had ventured across the East River. Van Lingle Mungo pitched the complete
               game. He closed out the ninth inning by fanning Travis Jackson, George Watkins
               and Lefty O'Doul with runners on first and second. "Tell Terry we're still in the
               league," said Casey Stengel after the game. "But we're by no means still."

SEPTEMBER 30   The Dodgers finish off the pennant hopes of the Giants by winning 8–5 before
               44,055 in New York. Again, most of the crowd was rooting for Brooklyn. Many
               paraded through the stands at the Polo Grounds with signs reading: "Brooklyn
               Is Still In The League." The Dodgers trailed 4–0 at the end of the first inning, but
               battled back to tie the score 5–5 with two runs in the eighth, then plated three in the
               10th for the victory. Dutch Leonard pitched 6²/₃ innings of relief and allowed only
               one run. Johnny Babich, a 21-year-old rookie, hurled a scoreless ninth and 10th. The
               Giants used Freddie Fitzsimmons (7²/₃ innings), Hal Schumacher (1¹/₃ innings) and
               Carl Hubbell (one inning). The three combined for a 62–36 record in 1934. By the
               end of the game, the Giants were being taunted by Dodgers fans and booed by their
               own followers for blowing a sure pennant. In Cincinnati, the Cardinals defeated the
               Reds 9–0.

DECEMBER 31   The Dodgers purchase Babe Phelps from the Cubs.

"Babe" was not the only nickname for Gordon Phelps. The other one, in apparent contradiction to "Babe," was "Blimp" because he was six-foot-two and weighed 225 pounds, which was huge for the period. A catcher, Phelps was unable to crack the Chicago lineup because of the presence of Gabby Hartnett. He was a three-time All-Star in Brooklyn, while playing for the Dodgers from 1935 through 1941 and compiled a batting average of .315.

1935   L A

Season in a Sentence

After making few changes to the cast that finished in sixth place in 1934, the Dodgers win 17 of their first 26 games, suffer through the bizarre death of Len Koenecke in September, and end the season 13 games under .500.

Finish • Won • Lost • Pct • GB

Fifth   70   83   .458   29.5

Manager

Casey Stengel

Stats

Stats	Dods	NL	Rank
Batting Avg:	.277	.277	5
On-Base Pct:	.333	.331	5
Slugging Pct:	.376	.391	7
Home Runs:	59		8
Stolen Bases:	60		4
ERA:	4.22	4.02	5
Fielding Avg:	.969	.968	4
Runs Scored:	711		5
Runs Allowed:	767		5

Starting Lineup

Al Lopez, c
Sam Leslie, 1b
Jim Bucher, 2b-ss-lf
Joe Stripp, 3b
Lonny Frey, ss
Danny Taylor, lf
Frenchy Bordargaray, cf-rf
Buzz Boyle, rf
Tony Cuccinello, 2b-3b
Len Koenecke, cf
Jimmy Jordan, 2b-ss

Pitchers

Van Lingle Mungo, sp
Watty Clark, sp
George Earnshaw, sp
Johnny Babich, sp-rp
Ray Benge, sp
Tom Zachary, sp
Dutch Leonard, rp

Attendance

470,517 (fourth in NL)

Club Leaders

Batting Avg:	Sam Leslie	.308
On-Base Pct:	Sam Leslie	.379
Slugging Pct:	Lonny Frey	.437
Home Runs:	Lonny Frey	11
RBIs:	Sam Leslie	93
Runs:	Lonny Frey	88
Stolen Bases:	Frenchy Bordagaray	18
Wins:	Van Lingle Mungo	16
Strikeouts:	Van Lingle Mungo	143
ERA:	Watty Clark	3.30
Saves:	Dutch Leonard	8

APRIL 2   The Dodgers purchase Dazzy Vance from the Cardinals.

Vance won a club-record 190 games for Brooklyn from 1922 through 1932, then played two seasons with the Cardinals and Reds. By the time he came back to the Dodgers in 1935, Dazzy was 44 years old and of little use. He pitched in 20 games, all in relief, before calling it a career.

APRIL 16   The Dodgers open the 1935 season with a 12–3 win over the Phillies in Philadelphia. Van Lingle Mungo was the star of the day. Not only did he pitch a complete game, but Mungo collected three singles and drove in five runs. Danny Taylor was a perfect three-for-three. Lonny Frey hit a home run.

Frey batted .262 with 88 runs, 35 doubles, 11 triples and 11 homers in 1935.

APRIL 19   Danny Taylor hits a grand slam off Flint Rhem in the first inning to account for all of the Brooklyn runs in a 4–2 victory over the Braves in the second game of a double-header on Patriots Day in Boston. The Dodgers also won the opener by the same 4–2 score.

APRIL 23   The Dodgers open the home schedule by trouncing the Phillies 12–5 before 30,000 at Ebbets Field. Lonny Frey struck a grand slam in the fourth inning. Tony Cuccinello also homered.

APRIL 25   Johnny Babich pitches a one-hitter to defeat the Phillies 6–0 at Ebbets Field. A single by Mickey Haslin with one out in the eighth inning ruined the no-hit bid.

APRIL 26   The Dodgers defeat the Braves 5–4 at Ebbets Field to take a 1½ game lead in the National League pennant.

The April 26 victory gave the Dodgers an 8–2 record. The club was 17–9 on May 17 and still in first place before a rapid decline.

APRIL 27   During a 4–2 loss to the Braves at Ebbets Field, Ralph Onis singles in what proves to be the only at-bat of his major league career. Onis entered the game as a substitute catcher after Babe Phelps was lifted for a pinch-hitter in the seventh inning.

APRIL 30   In the first meeting against the Giants since the Dodgers knocked the New York club out of the pennant race the previous season (see September 29, 1934 and September 30, 1934), the Dodgers win 12–5 at Ebbets Field. Many in the crowd threw firecrackers at the Giants players.

MAY 15   The Dodgers purchase George Earnshaw from the White Sox.

Nicknamed "Moose" because he stood six-foot-four, Earnshaw had a record of 67–28 on three World Series teams for the Philadelphia Athletics from 1929 through 1931, but was well into the decline phase of his career by the time he arrived in Brooklyn. Earnshaw was 13–21 in two seasons with the Dodgers. He was past 40 when he volunteered for military service during World War II, and won a Bronze Star as a naval officer.

MAY 16   Tom Zachary pitches a 13-inning complete-game shutout to defeat the Pirates 2–0 in Pittsburgh. Waite Hoyt also went all the way for Pittsburgh. Zachary allowed 12 hits, walked three, and stranded 14 base runners. The Brooklyn runs scored on an RBI-single by Jim Bucher and a sacrifice fly by Lonny Frey.

MAY 21   The Dodgers score seven in the first inning and beat the Reds 9–1 at Ebbets Field.

MAY 30   A crowd of 63,943 crams into the Polo Grounds to watch the Giants beat the Dodgers 8–3 and 6–0 during a Memorial Day double-header.

JUNE 7   The Dodgers outslug the Phillies 11–9 in Philadelphia in a contest with five lead changes. Brooklyn took a 10–7 advantage with four runs in the eighth inning.

JUNE 13   Van Lingle Mungo pitches a shutout, drives in two runs, and is involved in a weird double play during a 3–0 win over the Pirates at Ebbets Field. In the eighth, Mungo was on first base when Buzz Boyle bunted down the third base line. Mungo moved to second while the Pirates waited to see if the ball would roll foul. Boyle kept on running and wound up on second base with Mungo. Both were tagged out in the ensuing rundown.

JUNE 22   The Dodgers score nine runs in the third inning and clobber the Reds 17–4 at Ebbets Field.

JUNE 26   A three-run, walk-off homer in the 10th inning by Jim Bucher beats the Cardinals 7–5 at Ebbets Field. St. Louis tied the score 4–4 by scoring three times in the ninth, and took the lead with a run in the top of the 10th.

JULY 3   The Dodgers score in seven of eight innings and beat the Braves 13–6 at Ebbets Field.

JULY 5   The Dodgers collect 21 hits and wallop the Giants 14–4 in New York. The contest was highlighted by home runs from the Cuccinello brothers. Tony Cuccinello homered for Brooklyn in the eighth inning, while younger brother Al did likewise for New York in the ninth.

JULY 6   The Dodgers score seven runs in the fifth inning to break a 2–2 tie and defeat the Giants 12–7 in New York.

JULY 10   The Dodgers play a regular-season night game for the first time, and lose 15–2 to the Reds at Crosley Field in Cincinnati. Babe Herman hit the first home run in a major league night game, connecting off Dodgers hurler Dutch Leonard.

            The Reds became the first team in big-league history to play a portion of their schedule under the lights. The first night game took place on May 24, 1935, against the Phillies. The July 10 game was the fourth of seven night games the Reds played that season.

JULY 22   The Dodgers collect 22 hits and outlast the Cubs 14–13 in 11 innings at Wrigley Field. Chicago tied the score 12–12 with a run in the ninth. Al Lopez homered in the top of the 10th, but the Cubs deadlocked the game again in the bottom half. Lonny Frey drove in the game-winner with a single. Lopez had entered the game in the fourth inning after Babe Phelps broke his thumb. Before the injury, Phelps also homered.

JULY 24   Danny Taylor hits a grand slam off Bill Lee in the eight inning for a 6–4 lead, but the Cubs rally to win 7–6 in 11 innings at Wrigley Field. Chicago also won the opener 9–3.

AUGUST 2   The Dodgers score four runs in the first inning without hitting the ball out of the infield, and beat the Phillies 8–3 at Baker Bowl. The runs scored on an infield single by Buzz Boyle, two walks, three errors by Philadelphia first baseman Dolph Camilli, and a double steal involving Boyle and Danny Taylor.

AUGUST 9   The Dodgers score four runs in the ninth inning to stun the Braves 6–5 at Ebbets Field. Pitcher Bobby Reis singled, two Brooklyn batters were retired, and Jim Bucher singled. Sam Leslie lifted a fly ball for what appeared to be the third out, but Boston center fielder Wally Berger misjudged the drive, and Leslie was awarded a two-run double. Tony Cuccinello finished the rally with a two-run, walk-off homer.

AUGUST 18   The Dodgers tie a National League record with 21 assists by the infielders during a 9–3 victory over the Pirates in the second game of a double-header at Ebbets Field. The assists were recorded by first baseman Sam Leslie (three), Jimmy Jordan (11), shortstop Lonny Frey (five) and third baseman Tony Cuccinello (two). The Dodgers also won the opener 3–0.

SEPTEMBER 1   The Dodgers score seven runs in the second inning and beat the Braves 8–4 in Boston.

SEPTEMBER 6   The Pirates score in all eight turns at bat, and shellac the Dodgers 13–0 in Pittsburgh.

SEPTEMBER 14   The Cubs take over first place with an 18–14 win over the Dodgers at Wrigley Field. The Cubs scored eight runs in the sixth inning to take a 16–4 lead, then hung on for the victory. It was Chicago's 11th win in a row in a streak which would reach 21 games and wrap up the National league pennant.

SEPTEMBER 17   Len Koenecke dies on a chartered plane over Toronto, Canada. It may be the most bizarre death ever suffered by a major league player. Koenecke was cut the previous day by the Dodgers while the club was in St. Louis because of "behavior and erratic play," despite a respectable .283 batting average. Despondent over his release, Koenecke boarded an American Airlines plane back to New York, but appearing drunk, he tried to fight several fellow passengers and knocked down stewardess Eleanor Woodward. Koenecke was ordered off the aircraft during a stopover in Detroit, then chartered a three-seater to Buffalo. The plane left at 10 p.m. In mid-air, Koenecke flew into a rage, grabbed for the controls and got into a fight with Irwin Davis, a friend of pilot William Mulqueeney and a professional parachute-jumper. The pilot joined the fray which lasted some 10 to 15 minutes. Fearing that Koenecke would bring the plane down and kill all three on board, Mulqueeny struck the ballplayer with a fire extinguisher at least three times to subdue him. With the careening, damaged and blood-splattered plane far off course, Mulqueeney landed it on a racetrack near Toronto. After attempting baseball's first skyjacking, Koenecke was pronounced dead from a brain hemorrhage. "If he's dead," Mulqueeny told law enforcement officials, "I'm the one that killed him." Mulqueeny and Davis were arraigned on a manslaughter charge, but a jury quickly exonerated the two after determining they acted in self-defense.

If the death of Koenecke wasn't strange enough, the plane was previously owned by Broadway blues singer Libby Holman, and her husband Smith Reynolds, a young tobacco heir who was found shot to death under mysterious circumstances in his Winston-Salem, North Carolina, home in 1933. The murder of Reynolds was never solved.

SEPTEMBER 21   The Dodgers score eight runs in the second inning and beat the Giants 13–6 in the second game of a double-header in New York. The Dodgers lost the opener 3–2 in 11 innings.

SEPTEMBER 25   The Dodgers sweep the Giants 10–4 and 1–0 in a double-header at Ebbets Field. In the opener, Brooklyn scored eight runs in the second inning. Van Lingle Mungo pitched the game-two shutout. Buzz Boyle drove in the lone run with a walk-off double.

SEPTEMBER 28   The Dodgers defeat the Phillies 12–2 before a "crowd" of 194 at Ebbets Field.

SEPTEMBER 29   On the final day of the season, Van Lingle Mungo strikes out 15 batters and pitches a two-hitter for a 2–0 triumph over the Phillies in the first game of a double-header at Ebbets Field. The only Philadelphia hits were a double by Johnny Moore and a single from opposing pitcher Orville Jorgens. The second tilt ended in a 4–4 tie when called on account of darkness at the end of the eighth inning.

NOVEMBER 21   Bob Quinn resigns as general manager to purchase the Boston Braves. John Gorman, who had been the Dodgers traveling secretary, took over Quinn's duties as GM.

The Braves had just completed a season in which they won only 38 games and lost 115. By 1937, Boston's National League club had a winning record, but in the end Quinn couldn't compete with Red Sox owner Tom Yawkey's millions of dollars, and he sold the Braves to a group headed by Lou Perini in 1944.

DECEMBER 12   The Dodgers trade Tony Cuccinello, Al Lopez, Ray Benge and Bobby Reis to the Braves for Ed Brandt and Randy Moore.

Cuccinello and Lopez both became valuable regulars in the Boston lineup for several seasons. In exchange, the Dodgers received next to nothing. Brandt lasted only one season as a Dodger and compiled an 11–13 record as a starting pitcher. An outfielder, Moore played only 55 games in a Brooklyn uniform and batted .218.

1936

L A

Season in a Sentence

A horrible 4–21 record in June and a powerless club that hits only 33 home runs dooms the Dodgers to a seventh place finish and brings an end to Casey Stengel's term as manager.

Finish • Won • Lost • Pct • GB

Seventh 67 87 .435 21.0

Manager

Casey Stengel

Stats

Stats	Dods	NL	Rank
Batting Avg:	.272	.278	7
On-Base Pct:	.323	.335	7
Slugging Pct:	.353	.386	8
Home Runs:	33		8
Stolen Bases:	55		4
ERA:	3.98	4.02	5
Fielding Avg:	.966	.969	7
Runs Scored:	662		7
Runs Allowed:	752		5

Starting Lineup

Babe Phelps, c
Buddy Hassett, 1b
Jimmy Jordan, 2b
Joe Stripp, 3b
Lonny Frey, ss
George Watkins, lf
Johnny Cooney, cf
Frenchy Bordagaray, rf-cf
Jim Bucher, 3b-2b-rf
Ray Berres, c

Pitchers

Van Lingle Mungo, sp
Fred Frankhouse, sp
Ed Brandt, sp
George Earnshaw, sp-rp
George Jeffcoat, rp
Max Butcher, rp-sp
Tom Baker, rp
Watty Clark, rp-sp

Attendance

489,618 (third in NL)

Club Leaders

Batting Avg:	Joe Stripp	.317
On-Base Pct:	Lonny Frey	.369
Slugging Pct:	Buddy Hassett	.405
Home Runs:	Babe Phelps	5
RBIs:	Sam Leslie	82
Runs:	Buddy Hassett	79
Stolen Bases:	Frenchy Bordagaray	12
Wins:	Van Lingle Mungo	18
Strikeouts:	Van Lingle Mungo	238
ERA:	Van Lingle Mungo	3.35
Saves:	Van Lingle Mungo	3
	George Jeffcoat	3

JANUARY 16   The Dodgers sign Fred Lindstrom, most recently with the Cubs, as a free agent.

FEBRUARY 6   The Dodgers trade Johnny Babich and Gene Moore to the Braves for Fred Frankhouse.

FEBRUARY 20   The Dodgers sell Sam Leslie to the Giants. On the same day, the Dodgers sent Johnny McCarthy, Buzz Boyle and $40,000 to the Yankees for Buddy Hassett.

MARCH 1   Frenchy Bordagaray reports to spring training in Clearwater, Florida, with a mustache.

Bordagaray grew a mustache for a bit part he had in the film Prisoner of Shark Island. *He liked the look and wore it when reporting to spring training. In the 1930s, facial hair on ballplayers was strictly forbidden, but Bordagaray kept it for about two months. He was finally ordered to shave by Casey Stengel. "If anyone is going to be a clown on this team," said Stengel, "it's going to be me." It wouldn't be until 1972, when the entire Oakland A's team grew mustaches, that another major leaguer sported facial hair.*

MARCH 23   The Dodgers announce the installation of loud speakers at Ebbets Field. The speakers were placed on top of the scoreboard. Baseball's first public-address system was located at the Polo Grounds in 1929. The Dodgers were the second-to-last major league team to have an amplifying system at their ballpark. The last holdout was the Yankees at Yankee Stadium.

APRIL 14   The Dodgers lose 8–5 to the Giants before an Opening Day crowd of 54,292 at the Polo Grounds, which included Babe Ruth, New York mayor Fiorello LaGuardia and former mayor Jimmy Walker. Ruth retired as a player in June 1935. Brooklyn led 5–2, but the Giants scored two runs in the sixth inning, one in the seventh and three in the eighth. George Earnshaw pitched a complete game.

APRIL 15   Dick Bartell of the Giants and Brooklyn pitcher Van Lingle Mungo take time out to trade punches during the second inning of a 5–3 Brooklyn loss in New York. Bartell tripped crossing first base and immediately swung at Mungo, who was covering the bag. Bartell thought that Mungo tripped him intentionally. After the fight was broken up, both were ejected.

APRIL 16   The Dodgers suffer a crushing 7–6 loss to the Giants at the Polo Grounds. Brooklyn possessed a 6–5 lead in the ninth with two out and no one on base. After Burgess Whitehead and Mel Ott singled, Hank Leiber hit an easy fly ball, but left fielder Fred Lindstrom and shortstop Jimmy Jordan collided, allowing the ball to fall safely and both runners to score.

APRIL 17   In the home opener, the Dodgers win 4–3 in 10 innings over the Phillies before 8,000 at Ebbets Field. Both teams scored three times in the third. Babe Phelps drove in the winning run with a single. The weather helped hold down the crowd. The game-time temperature was 48 degrees.

On the same day, the Dodgers released Tom Zachary.

APRIL 26   Dodgers shortstop Ben Geraghty sets a major league record (since tied) by reaching base twice on catcher's interference during a 10–7 win over the Phillies in Philadelphia. Geraghty's bat was nicked twice by Philadelphia catcher Earl Grace.

MAY 9   Fred Lindstrom has a hand in both runs of a 2–0 win over the Braves in Boston. Lindstrom drove in a run with a single in the fourth inning and scored in the sixth. Watty Clark (five innings) and Ed Brandt (four innings) combined on the shutout.

MAY 12   Casey Stengel and Cardinals shortstop Leo Durocher tangle after a 5–2 win over St. Louis at Ebbets Field. Stengel and Durocher bickered at each other across the diamond all afternoon and settled their differences under the grandstand immediately after the game. Durocher claimed that Stengel hit him with a bat, but Casey said that Leo merely thought it was a bat that hit him. The 46-year-old Stengel said that is was just a good old-fashioned right hook which flattened the 30-year-old Durocher.

MAY 16   The Dodgers sign George Watkins, most recently with the Phillies, as a free agent.

MAY 17   Reds manager Charley Dressen starts right-hander Don Brennan before switching to southpaw Al Hollingsworth after just two batters to face a Dodgers lineup loaded with left-handed batters. The ploy worked as the Reds won 3–2.

MAY 28   Trailing 9–7, the Dodgers explode for six runs in the ninth inning and beat the
           Phillies 13–10 in Philadelphia.

           The Dodgers never had a winning streak longer than three games in 1936.

JUNE 2   A three-run rally in the ninth inning falls short, and the Dodgers lose 5–4 to the
           Cardinals in St. Louis. The contest ended on a third strike to Frenchy Bordagaray,
           who was ready to fight home-plate umpire Cy Pfirman until players from both teams
           intervened.

JUNE 10   Disgruntled pitcher Van Lingle Mungo leaves the Dodgers in Pittsburgh, hoping the
           action would force a trade to another club. He called his teammates "mismanaged
           semi-pros."

           *Mungo returned to the Dodgers two days later. He finished the season with an
           18–19 record and a league-leading 238 strikeouts in 311²/₃ innings.*

JUNE 21   Van Lingle Mungo stops the Cubs' 15-game winning streak with a 6–4 victory in the
           second game of a double-header at Wrigley Field. Chicago extended their streak to
           15 with a 7–2 decision over the Dodgers in game one.

JUNE 25   Van Lingle Mungo strikes out 11 batters, but loses 5–4 to the Reds in the first game
           of a double-header at Ebbets Field. Mungo struck out seven in a row, fanning
           Billy Myers in the second inning, Alex Kampouris, Gene Schott and Kiki Cuyler in
           the third, and Lew Riggs, Ival Goodman and Lee Scarsella in the fourth. Cincinnati
           also won the second tilt 5–1.

JUNE 26   The Dodgers play host to 2,000 kids from eleven different orphanages, admitted to
           Ebbets Field for free, and lose 6–1 to the Cardinals.

JUNE 28   Buddy Hassett hits an unusual home run off Dizzy Dean during a 5–1 win over
           the Cardinals at Ebbets Field. The drive struck the screen in right field next to the
           scoreboard, and became lodged on top of the wall.

JULY 5   The Dodgers' record falls to 24–53 with a 3–1 loss to the Giants in New York.

           *The Dodgers were 6–28 from June 2 through July 5 before a 43–34 record in
           the second half.*

JULY 12   The Dodgers play a double-header in 104-degree heat in St. Louis and beat the
           Cardinals twice by scores of 6–3 and 11–4.

JULY 26   The Dodgers sweep the Pirates 1–0 and 4–3 at Ebbets Field with a pair of ninth-
           inning rallies. In the opener, a walk-off double by right fielder Eddie Wilson provided
           the lone run. Van Lingle Mungo pitched the shutout. The Dodgers scored twice in
           the ninth in game two. Frenchy Bordagaray drove in the winning run with a single.

JULY 29   The Dodgers sweep the Cardinals 22–7 and 5–4 at Ebbets Field. In the opener, the
           Dodgers scored three runs in the first inning, five in the second, one in the fourth,
           four in the fifth, four in the seventh and five in the eighth. The Dodgers received
           six runs batted in from their pitchers with Mungo accounting for two and reliever
           Tom Baker with four.

During the 1936 season, the Dodgers pitching staff had a Baker (Tom) and a Butcher (Max), but no candlestick maker.

AUGUST 26   The Dodgers score nine runs in the fifth inning and defeat the Pirates 10–3 in Pittsburgh.

SEPTEMBER 3   The Dodgers squeak by the Cubs 1–0 in 10 innings in Chicago. Van Lingle Mungo pitched the shutout. Frenchy Bordagaray drove in the lone run with a single.

SEPTEMBER 7   Van Lingle Mungo strikes out 14 batters during an 11-inning complete game and defeats the Braves 2–1 in the first game of a double-header in Boston. Johnny Cooney drove in the game-winner with a single. Brooklyn dropped the nightcap 4–1.

Cooney began his career as a pitcher, compiling a 34–44 record with the Braves from 1921 through 1930. During a stint in the minors, he became an outfielder and was the Dodgers' starting center fielder in 1936 and 1937. Cooney had a .286 lifetime batting average in 1,172 games and 3,372 at-bats in the majors, but hit only two home runs. Both were struck in consecutive games while playing for the Braves in 1939.

SEPTEMBER 9   After the Pirates score four times in the top of the ninth for a 7–5 lead, the Dodgers splurge for three in their half to win 8–7 at Ebbets Field. The winning run crossed the plate on a single by Babe Phelps.

Phelps batted .367 in 115 games in 1936.

SEPTEMBER 10   The Dodgers stage a celebration of the 60th anniversary of the National League prior to an 11–5 loss to the Pirates at Ebbets Field. The contest was preceded by a three-inning exhibition between two amateur teams wearing 1876-vintage uniforms and playing according to the rules of that period. Dozens of former players were introduced, including Babe Ruth, Honus Wagner, Zack Wheat, Burleigh Grimes and Bill Dahlen.

SEPTEMBER 29   The Dodgers select Luke Hamlin from the Cleveland Indians organization in the Rule 5 draft.

Hamlin was nicknamed "Hot Potato" because of the way he juggled the ball when getting ready to pitch. He was 32 when he made his debut with the Dodgers in 1937 and had one good year with the club, winning 20 games in 1939.

OCTOBER 4   Casey Stengel is relieved of his duties as manager of the Dodgers.

The decision to fire Stengel came as a surprise, despite the club's three consecutive losing seasons during his term as manager and a seventh place finish in 1936. Casey still had a year to go on his contract. After sitting out the 1937 season, Stengel managed the Braves for five seasons from 1938 through 1942, and finished in fifth place once and in seventh four times. After bouncing around the minors, Stengel was the stunning choice to manage the Yankees for the 1949 season. He won the world championship in his first five seasons with the Yanks, and in 12 seasons, captured 10 AL pennants and seven World Series.

The Yankees let Stengel go at the end of the 1960 season because he was 70 years old. He then became the first manager of the New York Mets in 1962, which lost a post-1900 major league record 120 games. He retired in July 1965 when the Mets were on their way to a fourth straight last place finish.

NOVEMBER 5   Two days after Franklin Roosevelt defeats Alf Landon in the Presidential election, the Dodgers hire 43-year-old Burleigh Grimes as manager.

Grimes had a 272–212 record as a pitcher from 1916 through 1934. He won 129 of those 270 contests as a Dodger from 1918 until 1926. Grimes managed in the minors for two seasons before taking the Dodgers job. Under Grimes, Louisville of the American Association finished seventh in 1936 and Burleigh was ejected from 21 games. It was a trend that would continue in Brooklyn. The Dodgers were 62–91 in 1937 and 69–80 in 1938 before he was fired. Grimes's frequent eruptions at umpires earned him the nickname "Boiling Boily."

DECEMBER 4   The Dodgers trade Ed Brandt to the Pirates for Cookie Lavagetto and Ralph Birkofer.

The Dodgers completed a terrible transaction in trading for Brandt (see December 12, 1936), but made an excellent one in dealing him to Pittsburgh. A third baseman, Lavagetto was named to four consecutive All-Star teams from 1938 through 1941 before serving four years in the military during World War II. After the war, he returned as a part-time player in 1946 and 1947. Lavagetto is best known for his walk-off double in game four of the 1947 World Series, which not only won the game but ruined a no-hit bid of Yankees pitcher Bill Bevens.

DECEMBER 5   The Dodgers trade Lonny Frey to the Cubs for Woody English and Roy Henshaw.

Frey was a solid hitter in three seasons as a starting shortstop for the Dodgers, but struggled defensively. He led NL shortstops in errors in both 1935 and 1936. After a year in Chicago, Frey was switched to second base by the Reds in 1938, and played in two World Series and three All-Star Games.

DECEMBER 8   The Dodgers sign Heinie Manush, most recently with the Red Sox, as a free agent.

A future Hall of Fame outfielder, Manush was 35 and had a .331 career batting average when acquired by the Dodgers. He gave the club one solid season, batting .333 in 132 games in 1937.

1937

L A

Season in a Sentence

Casey Stengel, one of the funniest men in baseball history, is succeeded as Dodgers manager by Burleigh Grimes, who finds nothing humorous in a season in which the club loses 91 games, including 14 in a row in September.

Finish • Won • Lost • Pct • GB

Sixth   62   91   .405   33.5

Manager

Burleigh Grimes

Stats

Stats	Dods	NL	Rank
Batting Avg:	.265	.272	6
On-Base Pct:	.327	.332	6
Slugging Pct:	.354	.382	7
Home Runs:	37		8
Stolen Bases:	69		3
ERA:	4.13	3.91	7
Fielding Avg:	.964	.971	8

Starting Lineup

Babe Phelps, c
Buddy Hassett, 1b
Cookie Lavagetto, 2b-3b
Joe Stripp, 3b
Woody English, ss
Tom Winslett, lf
Johnny Cooney, cf
Heinie Manush, rf
Jim Bucher, 2b-3b
Gibby Brack, cf-lf-rf

Pitchers

Max Butcher, sp-rp
Luke Hamlin, sp-rp
Fred Frankhouse, sp
Van Lingle Mungo, sp
Waite Hoyt, sp
Freddie Fitzsimmons, sp
Roy Henshaw, rp-sp

Attendance

482,481 (third in NL)

Club Leaders

Batting Avg:	Buddy Hassett	.304
On-Base Pct:	Heinie Manush	.389
Slugging Pct:	Heinie Manush	.442
Home Runs:	Cookie Lavagetto	8
RBIs:	Heinie Manush	73
Runs:	Buddy Hassett	71
Stolen Bases:	Buddy Hassett	13
	Cookie Lavagetto	13
Wins:	Luke Hamlin	11
	Max Butcher	11
Strikeouts:	Van Lingle Mungo	122
ERA:	Van Lingle Mungo	2.91
Saves:	Van Lingle Mungo	3

APRIL 20   The Dodgers open the season with a 4–3 loss to the Giants before a crowd of 32,387 at Ebbets Field. It didn't take long to create the first controversy of the season. Dick Bartell, the Giants lead-off batter, was arguing with umpire Beans Reardon for calling Van Lingle Mungo's first pitch a strike, when a fan fired a tomato which struck Bartell squarely in the chest and splattered all over his uniform shirt. The Dodgers staked Mungo to a 3–0 lead, but he couldn't hold it. New York broke a 3–3 tie in the ninth.

The Dodgers tried a new color combination in 1937 by abandoning the blue trim, which had been a part of the uniforms since the 19th century, for green. On both the home and road jerseys, Brooklyn was written in kelly green, and the club had green caps and stockings. Instead of the traditional gray, the road shirts and pants were also tan. The bold design lasted only one season. In 1938, the club returned to blue-trimmed uniforms and wore gray on the road.

APRIL 25   Trailing 6–1, the Dodgers score a run in the seventh inning, three in the eighth, one in the ninth and four in the 11th for a 10–6 win over the Phillies at Philadelphia. Buddy Hassett broke the 6–6 tie with a solo homer before his teammates added three insurance runs.

MAY 6   The Dodgers break a scoreless tie with seven runs in the fifth inning and beat the Pirates 9–5 at Ebbets Field.

During the game, the German dirigible Hindenburg passed over Ebbets Field. The passenger airship left Hamburg, Germany, and crossed the Atlantic in 60 hours. On the way to the Hindenburg's landing site at Lakehurst, New Jersey, it passed over several New York landmarks, including Wall Street, Times Square, Ebbets Field, and the Polo Grounds, where the Giants were playing the Reds. Thousands thronged the streets to watch the spectacle, and traffic was tied up throughout Manhattan as many left their vehicles to glance skyward. As the Hindenburg landed at 7:25 p.m. at Lakehurst, it suddenly burst into flames. Of the 97 on board, 35 were killed along with one worker on the ground.

MAY 7   The Dodgers score seven runs in the fourth inning and defeat the Cubs 12–1 at Ebbets Field. It was the second day in a row that the Dodgers scored seven runs in an inning.

MAY 22   Van Lingle Mungo is fined $1,000 and suspended three days for fighting with teammate Jim Bucher in the team hotel prior to a 4–1 win over the Cardinals in St. Louis. Witnesses said that Mungo entered Bucher's room and woke him up to engage in the fight. The battle lasted half an hour, and several pieces of furniture were smashed. Bucher emerged with an injured hand and Mungo with a black eye.

MAY 24   Max Butcher pitches the Dodgers to a 1–0 win over the Reds in Cincinnati. Joe Stripp drove in the lone run with a single in the second inning.

MAY 29   Van Lingle Mungo hits a walk-off single in the ninth inning to beat the Braves 2–1 in the first game of a double-header at Ebbets Field. Mungo also allowed only three hits, none after the third inning. Brooklyn lost the second contest 4–3 in 10 innings.

MAY 31   The Dodgers break Carl Hubbell's 24-game regular-season winning streak with a 10–3 decision over the Giants in the first game of a double-header in New York. Hubbell allowed six runs in 3⅓ innings. He had won his last 16 games in 1936 and the first eight in 1937. Fred Frankhouse was the winning pitcher. New York won the second game 5–4.

JUNE 5   The Dodgers score four runs in the ninth inning to defeat the Reds 5–4 at Ebbets Field. A single by Heinie Manush, a double from Babe Phelps, Cookie Lavagetto's triple and a single by Woody English tied the score 4–4. After a sacrifice by Roy Henshaw, an intentional walk, and a walk to pinch-hitter Paul Chervinko loaded the bases, Joe Stripp drove a pitch off the left field-wall for the game-winner.

Phelps hit .313 with seven home runs in 1937.

JUNE 6   Woody English hits the Abe Stark sign on the right-field scoreboard at Ebbets Field with a third-inning double off Johnny Vander Meer during a 9–2 loss to the Reds. Ival Goodman was the right fielder.

The Abe Stark sign offered a free suit to any batter hitting it with a batted ball on the fly during a game. Stark owned a clothing store located at 1514 Pitkin Avenue in the Brownsville section of Brooklyn. The sign was at the base of the scoreboard from 1931 until 1957 and stood three-feet high and 30-feet long. Because of the size and location, it was nearly impossible to hit, but it's prominence helped make Stark famous and fueled his business.

JUNE 11   The Dodgers trade Tom Baker to the Giants for Freddie Fitzsimmons.

Fitzsimmons was nicknamed "Fat Freddie" for his rotund figure. Despite his bulk and the fact that Fitzsimmons was 35 at the time he arrived in Brooklyn, the Dodgers pulled off a tremendous deal. He had a 16–2 record for the club in 1940.

JUNE 12   The Dodgers purchase Waite Hoyt from the Pirates.

JUNE 29   Max Butcher pitches a complete game, but loses 1–0 in 12 innings to the Braves in Boston. Lou Fette also pitched a complete game for the Braves and drove in the lone run with a walk-off single.

JUNE 30   The Dodgers lose a double-header 1–0 and 7–0 to the Braves in Boston.

The Dodgers were held scoreless in 36 consecutive innings over four games from June 29 through July 1.

JULY 4   Van Lingle Mungo allows only one hit through the first six innings, before pulling a muscle in his side and blowing a 5–0 lead by surrendering two runs in the seventh and four in the eighth to lose 6–5.

JULY 7   Because of the injury suffered in the July 4 loss to the Giants, Van Lingle Mungo is ordered by the Dodgers not to pitch in the All-Star Game at Griffith Stadium, but does so anyway, and allows two runs in two innings during an 8–3 National League loss.

JULY 9   The Dodgers collect 20 hits and breeze to a 15–2 win over the Giants at Ebbets Field.

JULY 11   Angry at Van Lingle Mungo for pitching in the All-Star Game against orders, Burleigh Grimes starts him against the Giants in the first game of a double-header at Ebbets Field. Mungo allowed four runs in four innings of a 10–4 loss. The Dodgers also lost the second tilt 5–1.

On June 27, Mungo had a 9–5 record and seemed to be on his way to his first 20-win season. Favoring the pulled muscle in his side suffered in the July 4 game, Mungo injured his shoulder and he lost his last six decisions in 1937 to finish at 9–11. He was never again the same pitcher, although he continued to play for the Dodgers until 1941 and with the Giants from 1942 through 1945. From July 1, 1937, through the end of the 1943 season, Mungo had a record of 13–31.

JULY 13   Heinie Manush hits a walk-off homer in the ninth inning to beat the Braves 2–1 at Ebbets Field.

JULY 14   Babe Phelps fights Reds pitcher Lee Grissom in the ninth inning of a 5–3 loss at Ebbets Field. Grissom slid aggressively into home plate which drew a punch from Phelps. Grissom tore into the Dodgers catcher with a flurry of rights and lefts before umpire George Magerkurth interceded as a peacemaker. Magerkurth came out of the fray with his face pushed into the dirt and the sleeve of his coat torn. Grissom and Phelps were both ejected.

JULY 16   The Dodgers score three times in the ninth inning to defeat the Reds 6–5 at Ebbets Field. Cookie Lavagetto tied the score with a single. Jim Bucher's one-base hit drove in the game-winner.

JULY 24   The Dodgers commit seven errors and lose 20–2 to the Cardinals at Ebbets Field.

JULY 25   The day after losing by 18 runs, the Dodgers win a thrilling 6–5 decision in 11 innings against the Cardinals in the first game of a double-header at Ebbets Field. St. Louis scored twice in the ninth inning to tie the score 3–3, then added two more in the 11th. Brooklyn rallied in the bottom half and won on a three-run, walk-off homer by left fielder Tom Winsett. In the nightcap, the Dodgers score two runs in the ninth to deadlock the contest 7–7. It ended with that score when called on account of darkness at the end of the 12th inning.

AUGUST 9   The Dodgers purchase Ben Cantwell from the Giants.

AUGUST 21   Johnny Cooney collects three doubles and a triple during an 8–4 win over the Braves at Ebbets Field.

AUGUST 27   Fred Frankhouse pitches an abbreviated no-hitter and beats the Reds 5–0 at Ebbets Field. Frankhouse pitched 7$\frac{2}{3}$ innings of no-hit ball before a torrential downpour struck the ballpark forcing the umpires to call the game. Frankhouse walked three and struck out six.

AUGUST 31   Burleigh Grimes angrily yanks first baseman Buddy Hassett from a 4–2 loss to the Cubs at Ebbets Field. In the eighth, Hassett committed an error which so infuriated Grimes that he ran onto the field and pulled the player from the game in the middle of the inning. Hassett and Grimes exchanged angry words in the dugout, and Johnny Cooney was summoned from center field to play first base. Cooney didn't possess a first baseman's mitt, and Hassett refused to surrender his. The game was briefly delayed while another mitt could be found.

Unable to control his temper, Grimes was ejected from 10 games by the umpires in 1937.

SEPTEMBER 2   A walk-off single by relief pitcher Max Butcher in the 11th inning beats the Cubs 4–3 at Ebbets Field.

SEPTEMBER 3   Jim Bucher hits a grand slam off Cliff Melton in the third inning of a 15–7 win over the Giants in New York.

SEPTEMBER 12   Eddie Wilson hits a grand slam off Syl Johnson in the third inning of a 9–5 win over the Phillies in the second game of a double-header at Ebbets Field. The Dodgers lost the opener 4–3 in 10 innings.

The homer struck by Wilson was his only one of 1937 and the last of four he collected during his two-year big-league career.

SEPTEMBER 23   Heinie Manush collects his 2,500th career hit during a 5–4 loss to the Cardinals in St. Louis. Manush singled as a pinch-hitter.

SEPTEMBER 27   Outfielder Tom Winsett pitches the last inning of an 11–3 loss to the Phillies in Philadelphia. Winsett allowed two runs.

SEPTEMBER 30   The Dodgers extend their losing streak to 14 games by losing both ends of a double-header 5–2 and 3–2 to the Braves in Boston.

OCTOBER 1   The Dodgers end their 14-game losing streak with a 7–4 victory over the Giants at Ebbets Field.

It was during the abysmal 1937 season that the Dodgers began to be referred to as the "Bums." Willard Mullin, a cartoonist for the New York World-Telegram, *stepped into a cab after a game, and the cab driver asked: "So how did the bums do today?" Mullin drew a caricature of a grizzled, cigar-chewing, pot-bellied bum in tattered clothing, which became the unofficial symbol and mascot of the Dodgers until the club moved to Los Angeles at the end of the 1957 season.*

OCTOBER 5   The Dodgers trade Johnny Cooney, Jim Bucher, Joe Stripp and Roy Henshaw to the Cardinals for Leo Durocher.

At the time of the trade, Durocher was 32 years old and had gained a reputation as a slick-fielding shortstop who would do anything to win. He debuted with the Yankees in 1925, but his love of the New York nightlife and brash demeanor alienated nearly everyone on the team. Because of Durocher's struggles with the bat, Babe Ruth dubbed him "The All-American Out." Leo played for the Reds from 1930 through 1933, then was traded to the Cardinals and became a member of the famous "Gas House Gang" which included such luminaries as Dizzy Dean, Joe Medwick, Frankie Frisch and Pepper Martin. In 1937, Durocher batted only .203 with a slugging percentage of .245 and argued constantly with Frisch, who was manager of the team. The Cards were anxious to get rid of Durocher and found the Dodgers to be willing participants in a trade. The deal seemed to make little sense. The Dodgers gave up four players for a weak-hitting shortstop, but it proved to be one of the best in franchise history because of Durocher's later contributions as the manager of the club (see October 12, 1938).

1938

L_A

Season in a Sentence

Larry MacPhail arrives to bring direction to a troubled franchise, although it's not immediately apparent when the Dodgers finish in seventh place.

Finish • Won • Lost • Pct • GB

Seventh   69   80   .463   18.5

Manager

Burleigh Grimes

Stats

Stats	Dods	NL	Rank
Batting Avg:	.257	.267	6
On-Base Pct:	.338	.329	2
Slugging Pct:	.367	.376	6
Home Runs:	61		6
Stolen Bases:	66		1
ERA:	4.07	3.78	7
Fielding Avg:	.973	.972	3
Runs Scored:	704		6
Runs Allowed:	710		6

Starting Lineup

Babe Phelps, c
Dolph Camilli, 1b
Johnny Hudson, 2b
Cookie Lavagetto, 3b
Leo Durocher, ss
Buddy Hassett, lf
Ernie Koy, cf-lf
Goody Rosen, rf-cf
Kiki Cuyler, rf

Pitchers

Luke Hamlin, sp-rp
Freddie Fitzsimmons, sp
Bill Posedel, sp-rp
Van Lingle Mungo, sp
Tot Presnell, rp-sp
Vito Tamulis, sp-rp
Fred Frankhouse, rp

Attendance

663,087 (fourth in NL)

Club Leaders

Batting Avg:	Ernie Koy	.299
On-Base Pct:	Dolph Camilli	.393
Slugging Pct:	Dolph Camilli	.485
Home Runs:	Dolph Camilli	24
RBIs:	Dolph Camilli	100
Runs:	Dolph Camilli	106
Stolen Bases:	Cookie Lavagetto	15
	Ernie Koy	15
Wins:	Luke Hamlin	12
	Vito Tamulis	12
Strikeouts:	Luke Hamlin	97
Saves:	Luke Hamlin	6

JANUARY 19   With the franchise in financial difficulty, the Dodgers hire Larry MacPhail as general manager.

McPhail would right the ship and helped turn the Dodgers from perennial losers to a National League pennant in 1941. MacPhail didn't enter baseball until he was 40 years old when he became president of the Columbus club in the American Association in 1930. MacPhail grew up in wealth, the son of a man who owned a chain of banks. His given name was Leland Stanford MacPhail, named after the benefactor of Stanford University. MacPhail's mother and Stanford's wife were close friends. A man of seemingless boundless, but restless, energy, MacPhail had attended four colleges, worked as an attorney in Chicago, served as a captain of an artillery outfit during World War I (during which he concocted an unsuccessful scheme to kidnap the Kaiser), and as a businessman drifting from one venture to another. MacPhail also officiated college football games. Once he took the job at Columbus, baseball became MacPhail's focus, though he rarely stayed in one place for long. In 1933, the Cincinnati Reds were bankrupt and in the hands of a bank, which hired MacPhail to run the affairs of the franchise. A few months later, he recruited Powel Crosley to purchase the team. Crosley and MacPhail introduced night baseball to the major leagues in 1935. But the two men had a falling out, and MacPhail resigned in

September 1936. Meanwhile, the Dodgers had been taking loans for years from the Brooklyn Trust Company, and were deeply in debt. The bank insisted that someone be hired to run the day-to-day operation of the club, and because of his experience in Cincinnati, MacPhail was the obvious choice. He was put in charge of the business end of the Dodgers as well as player development and procurement. MacPhail convinced the bank to loan even more money to purchase players and to vastly improve the condition of deteriorating Ebbets Field, including the installation of lights for night baseball. The ballpark was refurbished from top to bottom with brightly colored paint, the repairing of broken seats, the cleaning and replacing of the plumbing in the antiquated restrooms, the addition of new concessions stands, an improved press box, and by smoothing out the ruts and crevices on what had been one of the worst playing fields in the majors. The surly ushers, who often extorted tips from fans, were replaced by courteous individuals in natty uniforms. Although he stayed in Brooklyn only five seasons, he sent the franchise on it's way from being the "Daffiness Boys" to the "Boys of Summer."

FEBRUARY 3   The Dodgers sign Kiki Cuyler, most recently with the Reds, as a free agent.

MARCH 5   Dodgers president Stephen McKeever dies at the age of 84.

McKeever had been part-owner of the Dodgers since 1912 and president since 1932. His 50 percent stake in the club was left to his daughter, Dearie, and her husband, James Mulvey, who was president of Samuel Goldwyn Productions. General manager and executive vice-president Larry MacPhail succeeded McKeever as club president. A few weeks later, the New York City Council changed the name of Cedar Place, along the third-base side of Ebbets Field, to McKeever Place. James and Dearie Mulvey sold half of their stock in the club during 1944, but retained a 25 percent interest until their deaths during the 1970s.

MARCH 6   The Dodgers send Eddie Morgan and $45,000 to the Phillies for Dolph Camilli.

The purchase of Camilli was the first indication that MacPhail would spend the money necessary to turn the Dodgers into winners. Camilli hit .339 with 27 homers for Philadelphia in 1937, and led the NL in on-base percentage. He spent six seasons in Brooklyn as the team's starting first baseman. Camilli led the NL in home runs and RBIs during the Dodgers pennant-winning season of 1941 and won the MVP award in 1942.

APRIL 15   The Dodgers purchase Ernie Koy from the Yankees.

Of American Indian ancestry, Koy made an immediate impact with the Dodgers as a 28-year-old rookie outfielder. He homered in his first at-bat (see April 19, 1938) and hit .299 with 11 home runs. Koy never reached those numbers again, however, and was out of the majors by 1942. Both of his sons played on national collegiate football champions at the University of Texas in addition to performing in the NFL. Ernie, Jr., was a running back on the 1963 Texas squad and played pro football with the New York Giants from 1965 through 1970. Ted was on the 1969 Texas team and played tight end for the Buffalo Bills in 1971 and 1972.

APRIL 19

On Opening Day, two players homer in their first big-league at-bat during a 12–5 win over the Phillies in Philadelphia. The pair were Ernie Koy of the Dodgers and Heinie Mueller of the Phillies. It's the only time in major league history that two players homered in their first at-bat in the majors in the same game. Others homering were Chuck Klein of the Phillies and Dodger batters Dolph Camilli (in his debut with the club) and Cookie Lavagetto. Koy also doubled and singled. Lavagetto hit two doubles in addition to his home run. Johnny Hudson collected three hits. Luke Hamlin was the winning pitcher in relief of Van Lingle Mungo.

Lavagetto started the season with 11 hits in his first 16 at-bats.

APRIL 21

Dodgers pitcher Tot Pressnell hurls a shutout in his major league debut to defeat the Phillies 9–0 in Philadelphia. He allowed nine hits.

Through the first 50 years of their existence, the Dodgers experimented with numerous uniform designs, most of which lasted only a year or two. In 1938, a design debuted which would have some permanence. For the first time, Dodgers appeared in script with an underlining flourish. The uniforms have changed little from 1938 until the present. The only significant change to the home shirts over the last 70 years was the addition of a red uniform number on the front in 1952. The road uniforms have been altered little except for the name on the front. In 1938, Dodgers *was written across the jersey. In subsequent years, the front read* Brooklyn *(1939–45),* Dodgers *(1946–57),* Los Angeles *(1958–70),* Dodgers *again (1971–98) and* Los Angeles *once more (1999–present). Also, during the 1938 and 1939 seasons, the New York World's Fair logo appeared on the left sleeves of the Dodgers jerseys to help advertise the upcoming event. The World's Fair, also called* The World of Tomorrow, *attracted millions of visitors to the city in 1939 and 1940. It was located near the site on which Shea Stadium and Citi Field were later built.*

APRIL 22

The Dodgers lose the home opener 3–2 to the Giants before 31,154 at Ebbets Field.

APRIL 24

Goody Rosen's single leading off the first inning is the only Brooklyn hit off Hal Schumacher in a 1–0 loss to the Giants at Ebbets Field. Mel Ott homered off Van Lingle Mungo in the second inning for the lone run of the game.

A native of Toronto, Rosen was the first Jewish-Canadian in major league history. The second was Adam Stern, who debuted with the Red Sox in 2005.

APRIL 27

The Dodgers belt the Braves 13–2 in Boston. Brooklyn scored 12 runs in the last four innings.

MAY 8

Dodger shortstop Leo Durocher is presented with a new automobile by St. Louis fans prior to a 4–2 loss at Sportsman's Park.

MAY 15

The Dodgers release Waite Hoyt and sell Heinie Manush to the Pirates.

MAY 17

For the second time in less than a month, Goody Rosen spoils the no-hit bid of an opposing pitcher by collecting the only hit off Bill McGee during a 2–1 loss to the Cardinals at Ebbets Field. Rosen singled in the sixth inning and scored when the ball rolled through the legs of left fielder Joe Medwick for a three-base error.

MAY 22   The Dodgers announce they will spend $110,000 on a lighting system in order to play night games at Ebbets Field. Nine steel towers were erected with a total of 615 floodlights. The Dodgers were ready to host their first night game on June 15. The club played seven home games at night in 1938, which was the maximum then allowed by the National League.

The Dodgers were the second major league team to play at night, following the Reds, who began the practice in 1935. Larry MacPhail was the general manager of both teams at the time the lights were installed. By 1948, every team in the majors had lights at their ballparks with the exception of the Cubs, who didn't add them to Wrigley Field until 1988.

MAY 29   The Dodgers edge the Braves 1–0 in a spectacular 13-inning pitching duel in Boston. Freddie Fitzsimmons started for the Dodgers, and pitched 11 innings while allowing only three hits, but wound up with a no-decision. Lou Fette went all 13 innings for the Braves. In the 13th, Goody Rosen was walked, was sacrificed to second by Pete Coscarat, went to third on a single from Babe Phelps, and scored on Ernie Koy's single. Max Butcher pitched the final two innings for Brooklyn to earn the save.

JUNE 8   The Dodgers score four runs in the ninth inning to stun the Cardinals 7–6 in St. Louis. The rally consisted of singles by Leo Durocher, Woody English, Kiki Cuyler and Babe Phelps along with a hit batsman and an error.

JUNE 12   Dolph Camilli hits a grand slam off Larry French in the third inning of a 6–0 win over the Cubs in the second game of a double-header at Wrigley Field. Chicago won the opener 9–3.

Camilli hit .251 with 24 home runs, 100 RBIs, 106 runs scored and a league-leading 119 walks.

JUNE 14   The game against the Reds at Ebbets Field is postponed because the Dodgers' train was five hours late in arriving from Grand Rapids, Michigan, where the club played an exhibition game the day before.

JUNE 15   The Dodgers host their first night game at Ebbets Field and Johnny Vander Meer of the Reds becomes the only pitcher in major league history to throw back-to-back no-hitters in leading his team to a 6–0 victory. In his previous start on June 11, Vander Meer no-hit the Braves in a 3–0 victory in Cincinnati. Against the Dodgers, Vander Meer walked eight, struck out seven, and allowed only five balls to be hit out of the infield. In the ninth, partisan Dodgers fans, realizing they were witnessing history, were cheering wildly for the Cincinnati hurler. With one out, Vander Meer walked Babe Phelps, Cookie Lavagetto and Dolph Camilli to load the bases. Ernie Koy then grounded to third baseman Lew Riggs, who threw to catcher Ernie Lombardi for a forceout. The final out came on a fly ball by Leo Durocher to center fielder Harry Craft.

The official attendance figure was 38,748. An estimated 20,000 were turned away once the gates were closed. Prior to the game, the Dodgers entertained fans with a parade of color guards, marching bands, a fireworks display and a track-and-field exhibition by Jesse Owens, who two years earlier won worldwide fame with four gold medals at the Berlin Olympics. Owens raced Ernie Koy of the Dodgers and Lee Gamble of the Reds in the 100-yard dash. The ballplayers were given a 10-yard head start, and Owens beat Koy by a nose with a time of 9.7 seconds. Due to the hoopla surrounding the event, the game didn't start until 9:20 p.m. Among those in the crowd were 500 friends and relatives from Vander Meer's hometown of Midland, New Jersey. He was a farm hand in the Dodger system from 1933 through 1935.

JUNE 18   A walk-off homer by Babe Phelps in the ninth inning beats the Cubs 2–1 at Ebbets Field.

On the same day, the Dodgers signed Babe Ruth as a first base coach. It was assumed by most people, including Ruth himself, that he would soon succeed Burleigh Grimes as manager. The Ruth signing was little more than a publicity stunt concocted by Larry MacPhail, however. For a few weeks after his hiring, fans came to the ballpark early and often to watch Ruth take batting practice and cheered his every move on the field, but eventually the novelty of seeing the Babe in a Dodgers uniform wore off. Ruth was released by the club at the end of the season and never realized his ambition to manage a big-league club. Ruth also clashed with Burleigh Grimes and Leo Durocher. Ruth and Durocher had a longstanding feud that dated back to when the two were teammates with the Yankees 10 years earlier.

JUNE 23   Babe Phelps drives in six runs on a solo homer, a three-run double and a two-run single during an 8–1 win over the Pirates at Ebbets Field.

JUNE 30   Van Lingle Mungo pitches a one-hitter to defeat the Braves 5–0 at Ebbets Field. The only Boston hit was a double by Rabbit Warstler in the fifth inning. Mungo walked eight and struck out six.

JULY 4   The Dodgers are pummeled by the Giants 3–0 and 16–1 in a holiday double-header in New York.

JULY 6   Leo Durocher hits a "bunt-home run" in the seventh inning of the All-Star Game at Crosley Field in Cincinnati. Durocher laid down a sacrifice bunt off Lefty Grove with Frank McCormick, the runner on first base. Jimmy Foxx, playing third base for the American League, fielded the bunt and threw the ball into right field because second baseman Charlie Gehringer failed to cover first. Joe DiMaggio, playing right field, retrieved the ball, but overthrew the plate in an attempt to retire McCormick, allowing Durocher to circle the bases and score. The National League win 4–1.

JULY 8   The Dodgers break a 1–1 tie with five runs in the fifth inning and wallop the Phillies 13–2 at Shibe Park in Philadelphia.

It was the first time that the Dodgers played at Shibe Park. It had been the home of the Philadelphia Athletics since 1909. The Phillies moved from Baker Bowl to Shibe Park in mid-season in 1938. The Phils shared the facility with the Athletics through the 1954 season, when the A's moved to Kansas City. The name of the ballpark was subsequently changed to Connie Mack Stadium, and remained the Phillies' home until 1970.

JULY 12   After losing the first 10 meetings in 1938 to the Giants, the Dodgers finally vanquish their New York rivals with a 13–5 victory at Ebbets Field. The Dodgers exploded for eight runs in the first inning to spark the victory.

Later that evening, Dodgers fan Robert Joyce, a 33-year-old postal worker, got into an argument with William Diamond, the son of the owner of Pat Diamond's Bar and Grill at Seventh Avenue and Ninth Street in Brooklyn. Diamond, a Giants fan, had been needling Joyce about the futility of the Dodgers. After drinking heavily, Joyce left, announcing he would return with two guns "and shoot up the place." Joyce returned as promised and shot Diamond in the side, then sent a bullet into the heart of Frank Krug, a patron of the establishment. Krug died instantly and Diamond passed away three days later. Joyce was later convicted of first degree murder.

JULY 13   The Dodgers break a 3–3 tie with seven runs in the ninth inning and beat the Pirates 10–5 at Forbes Field. The victory ended Pittsburgh's 13-game winning streak on the 13th of the month.

JULY 17   A five-run splurge in the ninth inning beats the Reds 5–3 in the first game of a double-header in Cincinnati. Tuck Stainback doubled in the first run. With two out, Cookie Lavagetto struck a two-run double to tie the contest 3–3, and scored the go-ahead run on an error. Ernie Koy's double drove home the final run. The Dodgers also won the second tilt 7–4.

JULY 21   Luke Hamlin pitches a two-hitter to defeat the Cubs 1–0 in the second game of a double-header at Wrigley Field. Hamlin pitched no-hit ball until a single by Billy Jurges in the seventh inning and a double from Billy Herman in the ninth. The lone run scored on a home run by Dolph Camilli in the second inning off Charlie Root. Chicago won the opener 5–2.

JULY 26   Following the ejections of Burleigh Grimes and Leo Durocher in the seventh inning of a 10–8 loss to the Cubs, irate fans at Ebbets Field shower the umpires with bottles.

JULY 27   The Dodgers score three runs in the ninth inning to down the Cubs 3–2 at Ebbets Field. Two Chicago errors contributed to the rally. Tuck Stainback drove in the game-winner with a single.

AUGUST 2   The Dodgers and Cardinals experiment with dandelion-yellow baseballs during a 6–2 Brooklyn win in the first game of a double-header at Ebbets Field. The switch to a conventional white ball in the second tilt resulted in a 9–3 victory by the Dodgers.

The motivating force behind the yellow ball was scientist Frederick Rahr, who made an agreement with the Spalding Baseball Company to manufacture the balls. Rahr believed that its high visibility would lessen the dangers of players being hit by pitched balls. Dodgers general manager Larry MacPhail took it from there and persuaded National League president Ford Frick and the Cardinals management team of Sam Breadon and Branch Rickey to sanction the test. Player reaction was mixed, but most agreed that the ball was easier to follow. One drawback surfaced when the yellow dye came off on the hands of the pitchers. The entire side of the uniform of Dodgers hurler Freddie Fitzsimmons was stained where he wiped off the dye. The yellow balls were used in three more games involving the Dodgers in 1939 (see July 23, 1939, July 30, 1939, and September 17, 1939).

AUGUST 7   Trailing 7–0 in the second inning, the Dodgers rally to beat the Reds 11–10 in the first game of a doubler-header at Ebbets Field. Still down 10–8 heading into the bottom of the ninth, the Dodgers scored three times for the victory. Tuck Stainback hit a two-out, pinch-hit single to drive in the first run. Goody Rosen's two-run, walk-off double off the scoreboard won the game. The Dodgers completed the sweep with a 6–3 triumph in game two.

AUGUST 8   The Dodgers trade Max Butcher to the Phillies for Wayne LaMaster.

AUGUST 14   Gilly Campbell drives in the only two runs of a 2–0 win over the Braves in Boston with a single in the seventh inning. Freddie Fitzsimmons pitched the shutout.

AUGUST 19   Cookie Lavagetto's walk-off single of Lou Fette in the 11th inning beats the Braves 1–0 in Boston. Fred Frankhouse was brilliant for the Dodgers, hurling a complete game, three-hit shutout. It was his first start in two months.

                  The Dodgers were 38–39 on the road in 1938, but only 31–41 at Ebbets Field.

AUGUST 24   A drag bunt by Ernie Koy in the second inning is the only hit off Curt Davis in a 5–0 loss to the Cardinals in St. Louis. Koy beat the throw to first base by inches.

AUGUST 25   Jimmy Jordan hits into three double plays during a 5–4 loss to the Cubs in the first game of a double-header at Wrigley Field. Chicago also won the opener 3–2.

SEPTEMBER 10   The Giants overwhelm the Dodgers 20–2 in New York.

SEPTEMBER 11   The day after the Dodgers allow 20 runs in the Giants, Luke Hamlin shuts out the New York club to win 3–0 at the Polo Grounds. All of the Brooklyn runs scored in the third inning.

SEPTEMBER 21   The Dodgers are rained out at Ebbets Field for the third day in a row. Postponed were games against the Cubs on September 19 and the Pirates on September 20 and 21. The rain was part of a vicious storm that brought a hurricane to New England and Long Island and resulted in the deaths of 600 people.

SEPTEMBER 29   The Dodgers score eight runs in the second inning and hang on to beat the Braves in the second game of a double-header at Ebbets Field. The contest was called after seven innings by darkness. Boston won the opener 2–1.

                  Even though there were lights at Ebbets Field, a National League rule stipulated that they couldn't be turned on to finish a day game. The rule remained in effect until 1950.

OCTOBER 2   Making his major league debut, Sam Nahem pitches the Dodgers to a 7–3 win over the Phillies in Philadelphia. The Dodgers also won the second game 7–2 behind John Gaddy, who was pitching in his second big-league contest.

                  Nahem never pitched another game for the Dodgers and didn't appear in another big-league contest until 1941, when he played for the Cardinals.

Gaddy's career in the majors consisted of only two games, but he had a 2–0 record and an 0.69 ERA in 13 innings.

OCTOBER 10   Burleigh Grimes is fired as manager of the Dodgers. Grimes never managed another big-league club, although he was a minor league skipper for about 10 years and a major league scout with the Yankees, Athletics and Orioles as late as 1971. He was suspended for the entire 1941 season after getting into a fight with an umpire while at the helm of the Grand Rapids club in the Michigan State League.

OCTOBER 12   The Dodgers name Leo Durocher as manager.

Durocher was 33 years old and still the Dodger starting shortstop at the time of his appointment. It was one of the most important decisions in club history as the brash, cocky and argumentative Durocher helped transform the culture of the franchise from perennial losers into winners. He took over a club which had six consecutive losing seasons from 1933 through 1938 and was sneered at by the fans of the rival Giants and Yankees, and often ignored in the New York media. Durocher accomplished the turnaround by surrounding himself with players in his own image. Under Durocher's leadership, the Dodgers were a pugnacious, hard-drinking, carousing club who were mean and nasty on the field and often settled disagreements with their fists. Brooklyn rose to third place in 1939, second in 1940, and the World Series in 1941. After a close second in 1942, the club suffered through three mediocre seasons with a depleted roster during World War II. The veterans were back in 1946, and the Dodgers nearly reached the Fall Classic again before losing a playoff to the Cardinals. With his tempetuous personality, Leo was never far from controversy, however. He battled his bosses, umpires and fans alike and surrounded himself with individuals who had questionable reputations. Among them was Hollywood movie actor George Raft. Durocher's lifestyle caught up with him in 1947, when Baseball Commissioner Happy Chandler suspended him for a full season for associating with gamblers. The Dodgers won the pennant without him. Leo returned as Dodgers manager in 1948, but was fired in July and immediately hired by the rival Giants.

DECEMBER 6   Five weeks after Orson Welles fools many Americans into believing that Martians are invading New Jersey on his *Mercury Theatre on the Air* radio program, Larry MacPhail announces that all Dodgers games would be carried on radio during the 1939 season.

In 1938, 13 of the 16 big-league clubs broadcast most, if not all, of their games on radio. The exceptions were the Dodgers, Giants and Yankees. The three New York clubs had agreed not to carry any games on the medium because of the fear that providing games over the airwaves for free would hinder attendance figures. Once MacPhail broke the deadlock, the Yankees and Giants followed and carried the home half of their schedules on the radio during the 1939 season. The Yankees hired Mel Allen to announce the games. The Dodgers games were heard on WHN, with Red Barber and Al Helfer at the mike. With his Southern accent and understated, friendly, homespun, folksy style, Barber quickly became a Brooklyn institution. He was highly disciplined, and considered himself a reporter, never openly rooting for the home team. Barber originally attracted the notice of MacPhail while broadcasting Reds games in Cincinnati from 1934 through 1938. Barber would continue as the Dodgers radio, and later television, announcer until 1953 when he shifted to the Yankees. Barber became nationally known as well by covering the World Series on radio and television nearly every season for more than two decades.

DECEMBER 10   The Dodgers sign Tony Lazzeri, most recently with the Cubs, as a free agent.

DECEMBER 13   The Dodgers trade Buddy Hassett and Jimmy Outlaw to the Braves for Gene Moore and Ira Hutchinson.

1939

Season in a Sentence

In a watershed year in Dodgers history, Leo Durocher takes over as manager and brings home a third-place finish.

Finish • Won • Lost • Pct • GB

Third   84   69   .549   12.5

Manager

Leo Durocher

Stats	Dods •	NL •	Rank
Batting Avg:	.265	.272	6
On-Base Pct:	.338	.335	4
Slugging Pct:	.380	.386	6
Home Runs:	78		5
Stolen Bases:	59		1
ERA:	3.64	3.92	3
Fielding Avg:	.972	.972	4
Runs Scored:	708		4
Runs Allowed:	645		3

Starting Lineup

Babe Phelps, c
Dolph Camilli, 1b
Pete Coscarat, 2b
Cookie Lavagetto, 3b
Leo Durocher, ss
Ernie Koy, lf
Dixie Walker, cf
Gene Moore, rf
Johnny Hudson, ss-2b
Al Todd, c
Art Parks, lf-rf

Pitchers

Luke Hamlin, sp
Hugh Casey, sp-rp
Tot Presnell, sp-rp
Freddie Fitzsimmons, sp
Whit Wyatt, sp
Van Lingle Mungo, sp
Vito Tamulis, rp-sp
Ira Hutchinson, rp

Attendance

955,668 (second in NL)

Club Leaders

Batting Avg:	Cookie Lavagetto	.300
On-Base Pct:	Dolph Camilli	.409
Slugging Pct:	Dolph Camilli	.524
Home Runs:	Dolph Camilli	26
RBIs:	Dolph Camilli	104
Runs:	Dolph Camilli	105
Stolen Bases:	Cookie Lavagetto	14
Wins:	Luke Hamlin	20
Strikeouts:	Luke Hamlin	88
ERA:	Hugh Casey	2.93
Saves:	Vito Tamulis	4

FEBRUARY 16   The Dodgers release Joe Stripp.

MARCH 31   The Dodgers trade Bill Posedel to the Braves for Al Todd.

APRIL 18   The Dodgers lose 7–3 to the Giants on Opening Day before a crowd of 25,496 at Ebbets Field. The game was Leo Durocher's debut as a manager and the first Dodger game broadcast over the radio.

APRIL 20   Leo Durocher wins the first of his 2,008 games as a manager with a 5–3 decision over the Giants at Ebbets Field.

MAY 1   The day after the opening of the New York World's Fair, the Dodgers win a bizarre 13–12 decision over the Phillies at Ebbets Field. Brooklyn led 11–5 before Philadelphia scored seven times in the top of the inning. The Dodgers rebounded with two tallies in their half for the victory. Both crossed the plate on a single by Cookie Lavagetto.

Lavagetto hit an even .300 with 10 home runs in 1939.

MAY 10   Trailing 5–3, the Dodgers score seven runs in the seventh inning and defeat the Reds 10–5 at Ebbets Field.

MAY 16   The Dodgers score seven runs in the first inning and wallop the Cubs 12–2 in Chicago.

MAY 17   The Dodgers and Cubs play 19 innings to a 9–9 tie at Wrigley Field. The contest was called on account of darkness. Brooklyn scored with two out in the top of the ninth to tie the game 9–9 on a single by Ernie Koy and a double from Pete Coscarat. There was no scoring over the final 10 frames. Vito Tamulis pitched 11 shutout innings of relief for the Dodgers, and allowed only four hits. Kirby Higbe hurled the final seven innings for Chicago, and surrendered just one hit.

MAY 24   The Dodgers record falls to 11–17 with a 6–3 loss to the Pirates in Pittsburgh.

It appeared as though the Dodgers were headed for their seventh consecutive losing season, but the club was 73–52 the rest of the way in 1939. From 1939 through 1957, the Dodgers would finish above .500 in 18 of 19 seasons. The lone exception was 1944, when much of the roster wore military uniforms.

MAY 28   Cookie Lavagetto drives in seven runs during a 16–12 win over the Braves at Ebbets Field. Four of the RBIs came on a grand slam off Fred Frankhouse in the seventh inning.

MAY 29   Tot Pressnell pitches a two-hitter to defeat the Braves 1–0 at Ebbets Field. The only Boston hits were a single by Buddy Hassett and a double by Rabbit Warstler. The lone run scored on a single by Fred Sington in the eighth inning.

JUNE 1   In the 14th inning, Gene Moore triples and crosses the plate on a botched suicide squeeze to defeat the Cubs 3–2 at Ebbets Field. Moore's three-bagger was followed by intentional walks to Dolph Camilli and Babe Phelps. Leo Durocher squared to bunt for the squeeze play, but Chicago pitcher Charlie Root threw wild to the plate and catcher Mike Garbark fumbled the ball, allowing Moore to score. The Cubs had scored two runs in the ninth to tie the score 2–2. The Dodgers, who collected only five hits in the 14 innings, pulled off a triple play in the 12th. With Stan Hack as the Chicago runner on second and Billy Herman on first, Jimmy Gleeson popped a bunt into the air. Third baseman Cookie Lavagetto let it drop, and threw to first. Camilli tagged Herman for one out and stepped on first for another. Meanwhile, Hack had broken for third, and after Camilli's throw, was tagged out in a rundown involving Lavagetto and Durocher.

Camilli played in all 157 games for the Dodgers in 1939, and compiled a .290 batting average along with 26 homers, 104 RBIs, 105 runs and a league-leading 110 walks. Phelps batted .285 with six homers.

JUNE 4   The Dodgers collect a club-record nine doubles and drub the Pirates 14–1 in the second game of a double-header at Ebbets Field. The nine two-baggers were recorded by Babe Phelps (two), pitcher Hugh Casey (two), Cookie Lavagetto (two), Dolph Camilli (one), Lyn Lary (one) and Gene Moore (one). Pittsburgh won the opener 7–3.

JUNE 11   The Dodgers score two runs in the 11th inning to defeat the Reds 9–8 in the second game of a double-header at Ebbets Field. For the second time in less than two weeks, the winning run scored on a bungled suicide squeeze (see June 1, 1939). Durocher missed the bunt, and Johnny Hudson was caught in a rundown between third and home. Hudson escaped, however, when third baseman Bill Werber threw high to catcher Ernie Lombardi, allowing the Brooklyn runner to slide under the tag. Cincinnati won the opener 3–1 in 10 innings.

JUNE 17   The Dodgers score five runs in the ninth inning to defeat the Cubs 5–0 in Chicago. Whit Wyatt hit a two-run single during the rally in addition to pitching the complete game shutout.

> *Wyatt was 31 years old at the start of the season and had a 26–43 lifetime record and 5.22 ERA with three American League teams over nine seasons. With the Dodgers, Wyatt found sudden success adding a slider and gaining control of his pitches. He won his first eight decisions in 1939. Because of an arm injury, Wyatt finished the year with an 8–3 record, but recovered and posted a mark of 70–36 for Brooklyn from 1940 through 1943. Wyatt was known for his hard-nosed attitude on the mound, and for throwing at hitters. Joe DiMaggio called him "The meanest man I ever saw." Among pitchers with at least 1,000 innings in a Dodgers uniform, Wyatt ranks sixth in winning percentage (.640) and fifth in ERA (2.86).*

JUNE 21   The Dodgers defeat the Reds 2–1 in Cincinnati on solo homers by Tuck Stainback in the second inning and Dolph Camilli in the eighth.

JUNE 25   The Dodgers score three runs in the ninth inning to defeat the Pirates 6–5 in Pittsburgh. A two-out, two-run double by Cookie Lavagetto drove in the tying and winning runs.

JUNE 27   The Dodgers and Braves play 23 innings to a 2–2 tie in a contest in Boston called by darkness. The two teams nearly matched their all-time record 26-inning encounter played on May 1, 1920. The 23-inning clash lasted five hours and 15 minutes. Both Boston runs scored in the second inning. The Dodgers held the opposition scoreless over the final 21 innings and tied the contest with single runs in the third and eighth. Whit Wyatt pitched the first 16 innings for the Dodgers. The relievers were Tot Pressnell (five innings), Ira Hutchinson (one inning) and Hugh Casey (one inning).

JULY 2   A 6–4 loss to the Giants in the second game of a double-header at the Polo Grounds is marred by a fight between Leo Durocher and New York first baseman Zeke Bonura. In the fourth inning, Bonura was elbowed by Durocher on a play at first base. Bonura first threw the ball, then his glove, at Durocher's head before the pair tangled. After they were separated, both were ejected. The Dodgers won the opener 3–2.

JULY 14   The Dodgers belt the Pirates 14–4 at Ebbets Field. The victory was aided by five-run rallies in the second and eighth innings.

JULY 18   The Dodgers purchase Pee Wee Reese from the Red Sox for four players and $75,000.

Harold (Pee Wee) Reese was five days shy of his 21st birthday and was playing for the Red Sox farm team in Louisville in the American Association. Most considered Reese to be the best shortstop prospect in the minor leagues, but Boston had future Hall of Famer Joe Cronin at the position. Cronin was also manager of the team, and believed he had five years of playing time left in his career. Cronin told reporters that he didn't think it was fair to keep Reese waiting that long. There were also concerns about Reese's small stature. (Reese earned his nickname, not because he was five-foot-nine, but as a result of his expertise at shooting marbles as a child. A "pew wee" is a small marble.) Reese spent the remainder of the 1939 season in the minors, and debuted with the club in 1940. Like Cronin, Leo Durocher was the manager and the starting shortstop, but had no qualms about turning over his position to Reese. He played with the Dodgers over his entire career, which ended in 1958. Reese was also a leader in the clubhouse. He was the player the others on the ballclub went to for advice, and was the first Dodger player to accept Jackie Robinson as a teammate. Pee Wee ranked in the top 10 in the MVP voting eight times. Despite missing three seasons (1943–45) because of World War II, Reese is first all-time in club history in runs (1,338), first in walks (1,210), second in hits (2,170), second in at-bats (8,058), third in games played (2,166), fourth in doubles (330), fifth in total bases (3,038), seventh in RBIs (885), eighth in triples (80) and ninth in stolen bases (232).

JULY 23   The Cardinals sweep the Dodgers 12–0 and 8–2 at Ebbets Field. The first game was the second experiment in the use of yellow baseballs (see August 2, 1938).

JULY 24   The Dodgers purchase Dixie Walker from the Tigers.

Just six days after acquiring Pee Wee Reese, the Dodgers made another tremendous deal in purchasing Walker. He was 28 and had bounced around the American League with the Yankees, White Sox and Tigers. Walker had been a decent hitter, possessing a .295 career batting average upon his arrival in Brooklyn, but was often beset by shoulder and knee injuries. He soon regained his health and became one of the most popular players in Dodgers history, earning the nickname "The People's Choice." Walker was named to five All-Star teams with the club, and led the NL in batting average in 1944 and RBIs in 1945. On the Dodgers all-time lists, his .311 batting average currently ranks 10th.

JULY 30   The color of the baseball makes no difference as the Dodgers lose both ends of a double-header to the Cardinals in St. Louis by identical 5–2 scores. Yellow baseballs were used in the opener, and a white ones in the nightcap.

AUGUST 5   The Dodgers score five runs in the ninth inning to beat the Reds 5–0 in the first game of a double-header at Crosley Field. It was the second time in less than two months that the Dodgers won 5–0 with five runs in their final at-bat (see June 17, 1939). Cincinnati won the second tilt 8–6.

AUGUST 7   In his first game as a Dodger at Ebbets Field, Dixie Walker delivers a walk-off single to beat the Braves 7–6.

Fears that broadcasting games on radio would harm attendance proved to be unfounded (see December 6, 1938). The Dodgers drew 955,668 fans in 1939, up from 482,481 in 1937 and 663,087 in 1938. More importantly, the Dodgers outdrew the Yankees (859,785) and Giants (702,457). It was the first time the Dodgers attracted more fans than their two New York rivals since the Yankees were established in 1903.

AUGUST 14   The Dodgers purchase Lyn Lary from the Browns.

AUGUST 26   The Dodgers and Reds participate in the first major league game to be televised. Both games of the double-header at Ebbets Field were telecast with Red Barber handling the play-by-play. There was one camera at ground level behind the first-base dugout and another in the upper deck behind home plate. The game was telecast by NBC's experimental station W2XBS at a time when there were only 400 television sets in the New York area. Many were located at the New York World's Fair, where crowds gathered around the primitive TVs. Previously, NBC telecast a college baseball game between Columbia and Princeton on May 17. *Cincinnati Enquirer* sportswriter Lou Smith reported that television "gives one a splendid picture of the plate and the infield, but it is not big enough to take in the outfield play. There is still plenty of room for improvement." The Reds won the first game 5–2, and the Dodgers the second 6–1.

Later that fall, on October 22, the first televised professional football game was broadcast from Ebbets Field. The football Dodgers defeated the Philadelphia Eagles 23–14. At the time, it appeared that commercial television would become a reality within a few short years, but World War II put those plans on hold. Regular telecasts of Dodgers baseball games on New York City stations would begin in 1946.

SEPTEMBER 2   The day after Germany invades Poland, triggering a declaration of war from England and France and the start of World War II, nine different players hit home runs during a 10–6 loss to the Giants in the first game of a double-header at the Polo Grounds. New York batters connecting for home runs were Burgess Whitehead, Frank Demaree, Harry Danning, Billy Jurges and Jo-Jo Moore. The Brooklyn home runs were delivered by Dixie Walker, Dolph Camilli, Babe Phelps and Cookie Lavagetto. The Dodgers won the nightcap 7–3.

SEPTEMBER 9   Trailing 3–1, the Dodgers score seven runs in the eighth inning to beat the Giants 8–3 at Ebbets Field. During the rally, pinch-hitter Chris Hartje hit a two-run double in his first major league at-bat.

Hartje's big-league career lasted only nine games. He died in 1946 in a bus crash while playing for a Spokane, Washington, minor league team. Eight of Hartje's teammates also perished in the accident.

SEPTEMBER 17   The Dodgers and Cubs use yellow baseballs during a double-header in Chicago. The Dodgers won both ends of the twin bill 10–4 and 3–2.

SEPTEMBER 23   The Dodgers pummel the Phillies 22–4 and 8–0 in Philadelphia. In the opener, the Dodgers scored five runs in the first inning, one in the second, four in the third, three in the fourth, two in the sixth, four in the seventh and three in the eighth. Cookie Lavagetto collected six hits, on four singles and two doubles, in six at-bats. Lavagetto came to the plate in the ninth inning for a chance at a seventh hit, but walked. In all, the Dodgers accumulated 27 hits and a club-record 46 total bases on 17 singles, four doubles, three triples and three homers. In the second tilt, Carl Doyle pitched a three-hit shutout in his start with the Dodgers, and his first game in the majors in three years.

Doyle came into the game with a 2–10 lifetime record. The game on September 23, 1939, proved to be his last start and only victory as a member of the Dodgers, and his lone big-league shutout.

SEPTEMBER 24   The Dodgers sweep the Phillies for the second day in a row with 3–1 and 6–1 victories in Philadelphia.

SEPTEMBER 26   Cookie Lavagetto hits a grand slam off Carl Hubbell in the second inning, but the Dodgers lose 9–5 in the first game of a double-header against the Giants in New York. The Dodgers won the second contest, called after seven innings by darkness, 3–2.

SEPTEMBER 30   The Dodgers sweep the Phillies again, this time by scores of 14–5 and 5–1 at Ebbets Field. In the opener, Brooklyn scored in every turn at bat but the first. In the second game, Luke Hamlin earned his 20th victory of the season.

Hamlin finished the season with a 20–13 record with a 3.64 ERA in 269$^{1}/_{3}$ innings in a season in which he celebrated his 35th birthday in July. He entered the campaign with a lifetime mark of 26–31. It's the only season of Hamlin's career in which he won more than 12 games.

DECEMBER 8   The Dodgers trade Al Todd to the Cubs for Gus Mancuso.

THE STATE OF THE DODGERS

The Dodgers finished in the top half of the National League standings only seven times from 1903 through 1938, and earned notoriety as baseball's "Daffiness Boys" for their ability to lose in an entertaining manner. That reputation vanished during the 1940s, as Brooklyn won National League pennants in 1941, 1947 and 1949 and finished a close second in 1942 and 1946. Along the way, the Dodgers became the first major league team since 1884 to field African-Americans, beginning with Jackie Robinson in 1947. Overall, the club was 894–646, a winning percentage of .581 which was the third best in the majors, trailing only the Cardinals and Yankees. It was also the first winning decade for the Brooklyn franchise since the 1890s. On the downside, all three World Series appearances resulted in losses to the Yankees. NL pennant-winners outside of Brooklyn were the Reds (1940), Cardinals (1942, 1943, 1944 and 1946), Cubs (1945) and Braves (1948).

THE BEST TEAM

The 1942 squad posted the best won-lost record at 104–50, but finished in second place, two games behind the Cardinals. The 1941 pennant-winners were 100–54.

THE WORST TEAM

The only team with a losing record in the 1940s was the 1944 club. With a roster consisting of draft-exempt players, many of them teenagers or pushing 40, the Dodgers had a record of 63–91.

THE BEST MOMENT

In what is arguably the best moment in major league history, Jackie Robinson signed a contract to play for the Dodgers on October 23, 1945, an act that changed the sport forever.

THE WORST MOMENT

Catcher Mickey Owen let a High Casey pitch slip past in the ninth inning of game four of the 1941 World Series, which led to a Yankees victory.

THE ALL-DECADE TEAM • YEARS W/DODS

Mickey Owen, c	1941–45
Dolph Camilli, 1b	1938–43
Jackie Robinson, 2b	1947–56
Pee Wee Reese, ss	1940–42, 1946–58
Augie Galan, lf	1941–46
Pete Reiser, cf	1940–42, 1946–48
Dixie Walker, rf	1939–47
Whit Wyatt, p	1939–44
Ralph Branca, p	1944–53, 1956
Hugh Casey, p	1939–42, 1946–48
Curt Davis, p	1940–46

Camilli was also on the 1930 All-Decade Team. Other outstanding Dodgers during the 1940s included second basemen Eddie Stanky (1944–47) and Billy Herman (1941–43, 1946), third baseman Arky Vaughan (1942–43, 1946–47), outfielders Joe Medwick (1940–43, 1946), Carl Furillo (1946–60) and Gene Hermanski (1943, 1946–51) and pitchers Joe Hatten (1946–51) and Kirby Higbe (1941–43, 1946–47). Reese, Robinson, Herman, Medwick and Vaughan are all in the Hall of Fame.

THE DECADE LEADERS

Batting Avg:	Dixie Walker	.312
	Jackie Robinson	.312
On-Base Pct:	Dixie Walker	.388
Slugging Pct:	Dolph Camilli	.492
Home Runs:	Dolph Camilli	89
RBIs:	Dixie Walker	687
Runs:	Pee Wee Reese	609
Stolen Bases:	Pee Wee Reese	108
Wins:	Whit Wyatt	72
Strikeouts:	Whit Wyatt	488
	Kirby Higbe	488
ERA:	Whit Wyatt	2.92
Saves:	Hugh Casey	50

THE HOME FIELD

Ebbets Field was arguably the center of the baseball universe during the 1940s. Among the three New York teams, Brooklyn ranked third in attendance 31 times in 35 years from 1904 through 1938. The Dodgers led their two New York rivals in attendance figures for the first time in 1939 despite possessing a much smaller ballpark and led New York City in attendance again in 1940, 1941, 1942, 1943 and 1945. In addition, Brooklyn led the National League in attendance in eight of the ten seasons during the 1940s, missing only in 1944 and 1948, and topped all of Major League Baseball in 1941, 1942 and 1943. Overall, the Dodgers drew 12,172,291 during the 1940s, more than double the 6,072,212 figure of the 1930s. In addition to the long-standing rivalry with the Giants, the Dodgers had a new one with the Cardinals. Brooklyn and St. Louis finished one-two in the National League standings five times (1941, 1942, 1946, 1947 and 1949) during the 1940s. Four of those five pennant races with the Cardinals were decided by 2^1/$_2$ games or less.

THE GAME YOU WISHED YOU HAD SEEN

It would be hard to top the historical significance of Jackie Robinson's debut on April 15, 1947, but for sheer thrills, there have been few games better than game four of the 1947 World Series against the Yankees, played on October 3. With one swing of the bat, Cookie Lavagetto broke up Bill Bevens's bid for a no-hitter and gave the Dodgers a walk-off victory.

THE WAY THE GAME WAS PLAYED

The most significant change in the game was integration with the arrival of Jackie Robinson in 1947. League statistics and averages in 1949 looked very similar to those of 1940, although offense dipped during the war years and there was a surge in home runs at the end of the decade. Home runs in the NL jumped from 562 in 1946 to 1,100 in 1950.

THE MANAGEMENT

Larry MacPhail was hired as the general manager in 1938 with the club in financial chaos and little leadership from an ownership group that consisted of members of the Ebbets and McKeever families, who had been feuding for more than a decade. MacPhail brought immediate results and helped transform the Dodgers into winners. He was elected club president a year later. MacPhail left the club at the end of the 1942 season and was replaced by Branch Rickey, who was the force behind the signing of Jackie Robinson and put together the club that would win six NL pennants in ten years from 1947 through 1956. Rickey held the title of president-general manager until October 1950. He and Walter O'Malley bought stock in the franchise in 1944 and purchased a controlling interest a year later. At the end of the 1940s, O'Malley was listed third on the club's organization chart as vice-president-secretary. Field managers were Leo Durocher (1939–46, 1948) and Burt Shotton (1947–50) with Clyde Sukeforth (1947) and Ray Blades (1948) serving as interim managers for a game or two.

THE BEST PLAYER MOVE

Even excluding the historic change it brought to baseball, the signing of Jackie Robinson was the best player move of the 1940s. He played in six All-Star Games and won an MVP award. The club also acquired Duke Snider, Gil Hodges and Roy Campanella. The best player trade brought Preacher Roe, Billy Cox and Gene Mauch from the Pirates in December 1947 for Dixie Walker, Hal Gregg and Vic Lombardi.

THE WORST PLAYER MOVE

The worst trade sent Eddie Stanky to the Braves for Bama Rowell, Ray Sanders and $40,000 in March 1948.

1940

L A

Season in a Sentence

The Dodgers win their first nine games and hold first place into the first week of July before finishing second to the Reds.

Finish • Won • Lost • Pct • GB

Second   88   65   .575   12.0

Manager

Leo Durocher

Stats

Stats	Dods	NL	Rank
Batting Avg:	.260	.264	6
On-Base Pct:	.327	.326	6
Slugging Pct:	.383	.376	4
Home Runs:	93		2
Stolen Bases:	56		5
ERA:	3.50	3.85	2
Fielding Avg:	.970	.972	5
Runs Scored:	697		4
Runs Allowed:	621		2

Starting Lineup

Babe Phelps, c
Dolph Camilli, 1b
Pete Coscarat, 2b
Cookie Lavagetto, 3b
Pee Wee Reese, ss
Joe Medwick, lf
Dixie Walker, cf
Joe Vosmik, lf-rf
Jimmy Wasdell, rf
Pete Reiser, 3b-rf

Pitchers

Whit Wyatt, sp
Freddie Fitzsimmons, sp
Luke Hamlin, sp
Curt Davis, sp
Tex Carleton, sp
Hugh Casey, rp
Vito Tamulis, rp

Attendance

975,978 (first in NL)

Club Leaders

Batting Avg:	Dixie Walker	.308
On-Base Pct:	Dolph Camilli	.397
Slugging Pct:	Dolph Camilli	.529
Home Runs:	Dolph Camilli	23
RBIs:	Dolph Camilli	96
Runs:	Dolph Camilli	92
Stolen Bases:	Pee Wee Reese	15
Wins:	Freddie Fitzsimmons	16
Strikeouts:	Whit Wyatt	134
ERA:	Luke Hamlin	3.06
Saves:	Five tied with	2

FEBRUARY 5   The Dodgers sign Roy Cullenbine, most recently with the Tigers, as a free agent.

FEBRUARY 12   The Dodgers purchase Joe Vosmik from the Red Sox.

APRIL 16   On Opening Day, the Dodgers win 5–0 over the Braves in Boston. Whit Wyatt pitched the five-hit shutout. Dolph Camilli contributed a triple, single and three RBIs. Babe Phelps was ejected by the umpires in the second inning.

The Dodgers began the 1940 season with nine straight victories. The 9–0 start is the second best in club history. The 1955 Dodgers were 10–0.

APRIL 19   The Dodgers open the season with back-to-back shutout victories by winning the home opener 12–0 over the Giants before 24,741 at Ebbets Filed. Hugh Casey hurled a complete game. The offensive highlights were a three-run double by Cookie Lavagetto in the seventh inning and a six-run eighth.

Four of the team's first six games in 1940 were postponed by rain or cold weather.

APRIL 23   Pee Wee Reese makes his major league debut and collects a single in three at-bats during an 8–3 victory over the Braves at Ebbets Field.

APRIL 26   Cookie Lavagetto hits a grand slam off Roy Bruner in the seventh inning of a 6–0 win over the Phillies in Philadelphia. The 6–0 victory gave the Dodgers a 6–0 record.

APRIL 30   The Dodgers extend their season-opening winning streak to nine games behind a no-hitter from Tex Carleton that beats the Reds 3–0 in Cincinnati. Carleton walked two and struck out four. His teammates made three errors. Pete Coscarat gave Brooklyn the lead with a three-run homer in the fifth inning off Jim Turner. In the ninth inning, Bill Werber led off by grounding out to third baseman Cookie Lavagetto. Lonny Frey lifted a fly ball caught by right fielder Roy Cullenbine near the fence. The final out was recorded on a fly ball hit by Ival Goodman to center fielder Dixie Walker.

             The no-hitter came in Carleton's second start with the Dodgers. He had a 94–70 record with the Cubs and Cardinals from 1932 through 1938, and spent the 1939 season in the minors with Milwaukee in the American Association. The 1940 season was Carleton's last in the major leagues. He posted a 6–6 record and a 3.81 earned run average with the Dodgers.

MAY 1   The Dodgers lose for the first time in 1940 by dropping a 9–3 decision to the Reds in Cincinnati.

MAY 5   The Dodgers score four runs in the ninth inning with a pair of two-run doubles by Ernie Koy and Roy Cullenbine to defeat the Cardinals 9–6 in St. Louis. The Dodgers tied a major league record by using four catchers during the contest. The four were Gus Mancuso, Babe Phelps, Herman Franks and Tony Giuliani.

MAY 7   The Cardinals club seven home runs and demolish the Dodgers 18–2 at Ebbets Field. Johnny Mize and Eddie Lake each hit two homers, and Don Padgett, Stu Martin, and Joe Medwick added one each. Hugh Casey surrendered five of the homers, along with 13 runs, in seven innings. Max Macon gave up the other two home runs while on the mound in the eighth.

             After the game, the Dodgers traveled by air for the first time in club history, leaving Lambert Field in St. Louis bound for Chicago aboard two planes. After the series against the Cubs, the Dodgers took another plane for New York and landed at Floyd Bennett Field in Brooklyn before a delegation of about 10,000 fans. Brooklyn was the third major league team to fly. The first was the Reds in 1934 when Larry MacPhail was the club's general manager. The Red Sox also attempted air travel in 1936. Regularly scheduled flights by baseball teams didn't occur until the late-1950s, however, with the introduction of jet airplanes and the move of the Dodgers and Giants to California.

MAY 14   The Dodgers sell Goody Rosen to the Pirates.

MAY 21   A two-run, walk-off single by Dolph Camilli in the ninth inning beats the Cubs 4–3 at Ebbets Field.

             Camilli hit .287 and clubbed 23 homers in 1940.

MAY 27   The Dodgers sell Roy Cullenbine to the Browns for Joe Gallagher.

MAY 29	The Dodgers sell Gene Moore to the Braves.
MAY 30	The Dodgers lose 7–0 and 12–5 in a Memorial Day double-header against the Giants at Ebbets Field. In the opener, Carl Hubbell faced the minimum 27 batters and allowed only one Brooklyn batter to reach base. Johnny Hudson prevented Hubbell from pitching a perfect game with a single in the third inning. Hudson was erased on a double play. In the second tilt, the Giants scored eight runs in the top of the 12th.
JUNE 2	Five days after the surrender of Holland and Belgium to Germany, Jimmy Wasdell hits a two-run homer in the ninth inning to defeat the Cubs 3–2 in the first game of a double-header in Chicago. The Dodgers also won the second contest 2–1.
JUNE 7	Three days after 350,000 British troops are evacuated at Dunkirk, a two-run homer by Dolph Camilli in the 11th inning downs the Reds 4–2 at Crosley Field. The win put the Dodgers into first pace. Brooklyn was saved by an absent-minded Cincinnati grounds crew. In the ninth inning with the score 2–2, Harry Craft of the Reds hit a ball that appeared to be headed for a home run, but struck a canvas shade, measuring five feet by eight feet, atop the left-center field wall. The shade was used during night games to keep the glare of a street lamp out of the batter's eyes. It was normally taken down for day games, but was somehow overlooked on this sunny afternoon. According to the ground rules, balls striking the shade were in play and Craft was limited to a double.
JUNE 8	The Reds collect 27 hits and whip the Dodgers 23–2 in Cincinnati. Carl Doyle pitched four innings for the Dodgers and allowed 14 runs, 16 hits and two wild pitches in addition to tying a modern major league record by hitting four Reds batters with errant tosses.
	Doyle was traded to the Cardinals four days later.
JUNE 12	The Dodgers send Ernie Koy, Carl Doyle, Sam Nahem, Bert Haas and $125,000 to the Cardinals for Joe Medwick and Curt Davis.
	Medwick made six consecutive All-Star teams from 1934 through 1939, a period in which he led the league in RBIs and doubles three times each, twice in hits, and once in runs, home runs, triples, batting average and slugging percentage. The Cardinals had grown weary of Medwick's salary demands, however, and believed he was on the decline. While he was past his peak, the Dodgers made a tremendous trade as Medwick was still among the top outfielders in the game, played in three more All-Star Games in a Brooklyn uniform, and helped Brooklyn beat St. Louis for the 1941 NL pennant. Davis also aided the Dodgers by posting a combined record of 28–13 in 1941 and 1942. None of the four players the Dodgers surrendered in the deal helped the Cards in any significant way.
JUNE 14	Luke Hamlin pitches a two-hitter and defeats the Reds 2–0 at Ebbets Field. The only Cincinnati hits were singles by Junior Thompson in the third inning and Frank McCormick in the seventh.
JUNE 16	The Dodgers and Reds play another wacky game in the first contest of a twin bill at Ebbets Field, won by Cincinnati 1–0 on a freak ninth-inning home run by Lonny Frey. Frey's drive struck the top of the 19-foot concrete wall in right field, bounced straight up in the air, glanced off the screen, rolled along the top of the wall, and

disappeared down a triangular-shaped opening between the wall and the scoreboard. Frey's homer was one of only two hits the Reds collected off Whit Wyatt. The Reds also won the second game 5–2.

JUNE 18   Just six days after being traded by the Cardinals to the Dodgers, Joe Medwick is beaned by St. Louis pitcher Bob Bowman in the first inning of an 11-inning 7–5 Brooklyn loss at Ebbets Field.

Bowman denied throwing at Medwick intentionally but few believed him. Bowman had exchanged words with Medwick and Leo Durocher that morning at Manhattan's Hotel New Yorker. According to Durocher, Bowman shouted, "I'll take care of both of you guys! Wait and see!" On Medwick's first at-bat, he was hit in the temple by a fastball, which gave him a severe concussion. The next day, Durocher sought out Bowman at the hotel, and the two nearly came to blows. National League president Ford Frick spent several days accumulating testimony from nearly everyone on both clubs but absolved Bowman of any blame in the incident. Medwick was playing again in four days.

JUNE 19   With tensions high because of the beaning of Joe Medwick the previous day, Leo Durocher and Cardinals catcher Mickey Owen engage in a fistfight during an 8–3 win at Ebbets Field. Owen took exception to a remark by Durocher in the third inning and charged the Dodger manager. Players from both teams joined in the melee, which was broken up by the umpires. Less than six months later, Owen was traded to the Dodgers.

JUNE 29   Seven days after France surrenders to Germany, Dixie Walker hits a grand slam off Bill Posedel in the eighth inning of a 10–4 win over the Braves at Ebbets Field.

JULY 3   The Dodgers score six runs in the ninth inning to defeat the Giants 7–3 in New York. Joe Medwick hit the first pitch of the inning for a home run. Later, Pee Wee Reese broke a 3–3 tie with a grand slam off Hy Vandenberg.

Medwick wore uniform number 7 with the Cardinals and wanted the same number with the Dodgers, but coach Charley Dressen already wore it. The two worked out a compromise. At home, Medwick wore number 7 and Dressen number 77. The pair reversed their numbers on the road.

JULY 5   The Dodgers need 20 innings to subdue the Braves 6–2 in Boston. The struggle lasted five hours and 19 minutes. The score was 1–1 before both teams scored in the ninth. There were ten scoreless innings before Brooklyn's four-run explosion in the 20th. The first run scored on a bases-loaded walk to Dixie Walker. Another crossed the plate on an error, and Pee Wee Reese delivered a two-run single. Luke Hamlin pitched the first nine innings and Hugh Casey hurled 9⅓ innings of shutout relief.

JULY 6   The Dodgers win their seventh game in a row with a 2–0 decision over the Braves in Boston. Both runs scored in the seventh inning. Pee Wee Reese drove in the first run with a single and scored on a hit by Cookie Lavagetto. Tot Pressnell pitched the shutout.

The victory gave the Dodgers a record of 45–21 and a one-game lead over the Reds. Brooklyn was knocked from the top perch the following day, but stayed within sight of Cincinnati until mid-August.

JULY 9   Whit Wyatt pitches two shutout innings (the fifth and sixth) during a 4–0 National League win in the All-Star Game at Sportsman's Park in St. Louis.

JULY 14   Freddie Fitzsimmons earns the 200th win of his career with a 2–0 decision over the Pirates in the second game of a double-header in Pittsburgh. The Dodgers lost the opener 6–2.

                As a 38-year-old player-coach, Fitzsimmons had a remarkable season in 1940. He pitched in 134$^1/_3$ innings in 20 games, 18 of them starts, and had a 16–2 record with a 2.81 ERA. Fitzsimmons achieved 12 of his 16 victories over the Pirates and Phillies, with six against each club.

JULY 19   Fisticuffs erupt during an 11–4 loss to the Cubs in Chicago. In the eighth inning, Cubs pitcher Claude Passeau was hit in the ribs by Hugh Casey. Passeau responded by flinging his bat at the mound, sparking the fight. Passeau and Dodgers outfielder Joe Gallagher were both ejected.

JULY 24   The Dodgers and Reds brawl during a 4–3 Cincinnati win in 11 innings in the first game of a double-header at Ebbets Field. Brooklyn second baseman Pete Coscarat believed that Reds second baseman Lonny Frey came into the bag with his spikes too high to break up a double play. Coscarat jumped on Frey and began to pummel him with his fists. Pitcher Whit Wyatt joined in the fray and flailed away at Frey with his glove. The Reds also won the second game 9–3.

                Newspaper photos revealed that Frey never touched Coscarat. The Dodger infielder spiked himself when he leaped in the air to make the throw to first base.

JULY 29   The Dodgers fight again, this time against the Pirates during a 7–6 win at Ebbets Field. The Pirates scored six runs in the top of the ninth to tie the score 6–6. In the bottom half of the inning, Babe Phelps and Pittsburgh shortstop Arky Vaughan traded punches on the first base line before Pete Coscarat delivered a walk-off single.

AUGUST 4   Trailing 6–1, the Dodgers score four runs in the sixth inning, one in the ninth and one in the 11th to beat the Cubs 7–6 at Ebbets Field. A homer by Pee Wee Reese tied the score in the ninth. The game ended on Dolph Camilli's home run. Chicago won the opener 11–3.

AUGUST 7   Dolph Camilli's two-out, three-run homer in the 12th inning beats the Giants 6–3 in New York.

AUGUST 9   Whit Wyatt pitches a shutout and scores the lone run of a 1–0 win over the Braves in Boston. After singling in the eighth, Wyatt advanced to second on a single by Dolph Camilli and crossed the plate on a hit by Babe Phelps.

                Phelps hit .295 with 13 homers in 1940.

AUGUST 15   Freddie Fitzsimmons is given a new car, purchased with donations from fans, prior to a 12-inning, 2–1 loss to the Braves at Ebbets Field.

AUGUST 18   The Dodgers sweep the Braves 7–2 and 3–1 in a double-header at Ebbets Field.

The twin victories put the Dodgers 4½ games behind the first-place Reds, but the club lost the next five games to end any dreams about a pennant in Brooklyn.

AUGUST 24   The Dodgers score eight runs in the second inning and beat the Cubs 11–3 in Chicago. Right fielder Joe Gallagher collected a homer and a double in the big inning.

SEPTEMBER 6   Joe Medwick stars as the Dodgers beat the Phillies twice in a double-header in Philadelphia. He smacked a three-run homer off Kirby Higbe in the third inning of the opener to provide the only three runs of a 3–0 win. Freddie Fitzsimmons pitched the shutout. Medwick hit a grand slam in game two.

SEPTEMBER 12   Hugh Casey is the winning pitcher as both a starter and a reliever and pitches 11⅔ innings of shutout ball during a double-header against the Pirates at Ebbets Field. Casey hurled a complete game shutout in the opener to win 7–0. In the second tilt, he pitched the last 2⅔ innings of a 7–4 Brooklyn victory.

SEPTEMBER 16   On the day of the passage of the Selective Service Act, America's first peacetime draft, umpire George Magerkurth is punched by a fan after a ten-inning, 4–3 loss to the Reds at Ebbets Field. Magerkurth reversed a decision by fellow ump Bill Stewart in the tenth, drawing the ire of Leo Durocher. The Dodgers manager engaged in a long and animated argument with the umpiring crew. After the game, the six-foot-three-inch Magerkurth was attacked and punched several times on the field by 21-year-old fan Frankie Germano, who stood five-foot-five.

Germano was discovered to be a parole violator and was returned to prison. Magerkurth declined to press charges. Durocher was fined $100 and suspended five days by National League President Ford Frick "for prolonged discussion and conduct inciting to riot."

SEPTEMBER 18   Babe Phelps hits a grand slam off Lon Warneke in the first inning, but the Dodgers lose 14–7 to the Cardinals at Ebbets Field.

SEPTEMBER 23   Dolph Camilli hits a walk-off homer in the ninth inning to defeat the Giants 3–2 at Ebbets Field.

SEPTEMBER 29   Lee Grissom pitches a two-hitter and strikes out 11 to defeat the Phillies 5–0 at Shibe Park. The only Philadelphia hits were singles by Chuck Klein in the sixth inning and Bill Atwood's double in the seventh.

Grissom was 2–5 with this lone shutout in two seasons as a Dodger.

NOVEMBER 11   A week after Franklin Roosevelt wins his third term as President by defeating Wendell Willkie, the Dodgers send Vito Tamulis, Bill Crouch, Mickey Livingston and $100,000 to the Phillies for Kirby Higbe.

The deal with the Phillies was an absolute steal as Higbe paid immediate dividends with a 22–9 record in 1941, sparking the Dodgers to the franchise's first NL pennant in 21 years. He played in Brooklyn from 1941 through 1943, and after two years in the service during World War II, again in 1946 and 1947. Higbe was 70–38 as a Dodger. His winning percentage of .648 ranks fourth in club history among pitchers with at least 100 decisions.

DECEMBER 4   The Dodgers send Gus Mancuso, John Pintar and $65,000 to the Cardinals for Mickey Owen.

Although he was never able to live down the failure to catch a third strike in game four of the 1941 World Series (see October 5, 1941), the trade with the Cardinals proved to be beneficial as Owen was named to four consecutive All-Star teams with the Dodgers from 1941 through 1944.

DECEMBER 9   The Dodgers trade Pep Young to the Reds for Lew Riggs.

1941

Season in a Sentence

The Dodgers win 100 games and the National League pennant in a thrilling race with the Cardinals, before a World Series against the Yankees that turns on a passed ball.

Finish • Won • Lost • Pct • GB

First   100   54   .649   +2.5

World Series

The Dodgers lost to the New York Yankees four games to one.

Manager

Leo Durocher

Stats

Stats	Dods	AL	Rank
Batting Avg:	.272	.258	1
On-Base Pct:	.347	.326	1
Slugging Pct:	.405	.361	1
Home Runs:	101		1
Stolen Bases:	36		7 (tie)
ERA:	3.14	3.63	1
Fielding Avg:	.974	.972	3
Runs Scored:	800		1
Runs Allowed:	581		2

Starting Lineup

Mickey Owen, c
Dolph Camilli, 1b
Billy Herman, 2b
Cookie Lavagetto, 3b
Pee Wee Reese, ss
Joe Medwick, lf
Pete Reiser, cf
Dixie Walker, rf
Jimmy Wasdell, rf

Pitchers

Kirby Higbe, sp
Whit Wyatt, sp
Curt Davis, sp-rp
Luke Hamlin, sp-rp
Freddie Fitzsimmons, sp
Hugh Casey, rp-sp

Attendance

1,214,910 (first in AL)

Club Leaders

Batting Avg:	Pete Reiser	.343
On Base Pct:	Dolph Camilli	.407
Slugging Pct:	Pete Reiser	.558
Home Runs:	Dolph Camilli	34
RBIs:	Dolph Camilli	120
Runs:	Pete Reiser	117
Stolen Bases:	Pee Wee Reese	10
Wins:	Whit Wyatt	22
	Kirby Higbe	22
Strikeouts:	Whit Wyatt	176
ERA:	Whit Wyatt	2.34
Saves:	Hugh Casey	7

JANUARY 31   The Dodgers sign Paul Waner, most recently with the Pirates, as a free agent.

The Pirates released Waner after 15 seasons with the club in which he had eight years of 200 or more hits, and 2,868 hits in all. Waner began the season as Brooklyn's right fielder, with Dixie Walker on the bench. The controversial

*move prompted many Dodger fans to threaten a boycott of Ebbets Field if
the popular Walker wasn't restored to the starting line-up. The Dodgers then
released Waner on May 11 after he appeared in just 11 games. Waner returned
to play for Brooklyn again in 1943 and 1944.*

MARCH 8   The Dodgers become the first team to mandate that their players wear batting helmets.

*The announcement was made in Havana, Cuba, where the Dodgers conducted
spring training in 1941 and 1942. The devices weren't similar to the batting
helmets we know today, but were one-ounce shields that slipped inside the
caps of the batters. "Every player in the Dodgers organization will wear this
protector," said Larry MacPhail. "And I want to make a prediction that within
a year every player in the major leagues will be wearing it." Many players
resisted the idea of using batting helmets, however, and they didn't become
commonplace until the 1950s. There were mandated by the National League
in 1954 and the American League in 1958.*

MARCH 9   After raising a ruckus in Havana, Van Lingle Mungo is fined $200 by the club and
sent back to the States. Among Mungo's transgressions was a drunken rampage in
which he caused considerable damage to the fixtures at the bar in the Hotel Nacional
de Cuba.

APRIL 15   The Dodgers lose the season opener 6–4 to the Giants before 31,604 at Ebbets Field.

APRIL 19   The Dodgers sweep the Braves with a pair of 8–0 victories on Patriots Day in Boston.
Luke Hamlin and Whit Wyatt pitched the shutouts.

APRIL 22   The Dodgers purchase Mace Brown from the Pirates.

APRIL 28   Whit Wyatt pitches a complete game and delivers a walk-off single in the ninth
inning to defeat the Reds 3–2 at Ebbets Field.

APRIL 29   The Dodgers romp to a 13–2 triumph over the Reds at Ebbets Field.

APRIL 30   The Dodgers extend their winning streak to nine games with a 4–3 decision over the
Reds at Ebbets Field. The Dodgers scored three runs in the eighth inning and one in
the ninth for the victory. Mickey Owen hit a double to drive in the winning run.

*The win gave the Dodgers a 13–4 record after starting the season with three
straight losses.*

MAY 6   The Dodgers send Johnny Hudson, Charlie Gilbert and $65,000 to the Cubs for
Billy Herman. Later that day, Herman played in his first game with the Dodgers and
contributed a double, three singles and a walk in five plate appearances leading his
club to a 7–3 win over the Pirates at Ebbets Field. Dixie Walker broke a 3–3 tie with
a grand slam off Rip Sewell in the seventh inning. Walker also homered in the fourth.

*After making the deal for Herman, Larry MacPhail bragged to reporters,
"I've just bought the pennant." The Dodgers general manger proved to correct.
Herman was on the downside of his Hall of Fame career but still had enough to
start at second base and make the All-Star team in each of his first three seasons
in Brooklyn before entering the service at the end of the 1943 season.*

MAY 10   Billy Herman garners five hits, including two triples, in five at-bats during a 4–1 win over the Phillies in Philadelphia.

Herman had 14 hits in his first 24 at-bats with the Dodgers. He played 133 games with the club in 1941, and batted .291.

MAY 25   Pete Reiser hits a grand slam off Monte Pearson that breaks a 4–4 tie in the sixth inning and lifts the Dodgers to an 8–4 win over the Phillies at Ebbets Field.

Reiser was a 22-year-old outfielder in 1941 and was playing in his first full season in the majors. With his tremendous hustle and speed, Reiser made an immediate impact by leading the NL in batting average (.344), slugging percentage (.558), runs (117), doubles (39) and triples (17). He once ran a 100-yard dash in 9.8 seconds while wearing baseball spikes. Reiser's future looked limitless, but was beset by a series of crippling injuries, beginning when he ran into the wall at Sportsman's Park the following season (see July 19, 1942).

JUNE 1   The Dodgers extend their winning streak to nine games with a 3–2 decision over the Cardinals at Ebbets Field.

It was Brooklyn's second nine-game winning streak in 1941. On June 1, the Dodgers were 31–12 and in a tie for first place with the Cardinals. The fast start brought fans into Ebbets Field in unprecedented numbers. In 1940, the club drew 975,978 to lead the National League in attendance for the first time in club history. In 1941, the Dodgers attracted 1,214,910, more than any other team in baseball. The three New York City teams had the three highest attendance figures in the majors that season. The Yankees were second with 964,722 and the Giants were third with 763,098.

JUNE 13   Babe Phelps is suspended indefinitely and fined $500 for refusing to travel with the Dodgers on a road trip. He said he was ill, but had been examined by two physicians who found nothing wrong with him. Phelps sat out the remainder of the season. After a trade to Pittsburgh, he played in 95 games with the Pirates in 1942.

On the same day, Larry MacPhail refused to rent Ebbets Field for a rally to be held by the Brooklyn chapter of the American First Committee, an organization dedicated to keeping the United States out of World War II. Many prominent Americans were part of the group, among them famed pilot Charles Lindbergh, who was scheduled to be a featured speaker at the rally. MacPhail was the chairman of the Brooklyn division of the New York Chapter of the Committee to Defend America by Aiding the Allies, which supported American involvement in the war against Nazi Germany.

JUNE 14   Trailing 4–0, the Dodgers score seven runs in the sixth inning and down the Cardinals 12–5 in St. Louis.

JUNE 17   Jimmy Wasdell hits a three-run homer in the top of the tenth inning and the Dodgers withstand a two-run rally in the bottom half to beat the Cubs 7–6 in Chicago.

JUNE 22   The day after Germany's invasion of the Soviet Union, the Dodgers outlast the Reds 2–1 in 16 innings in the first game of a double-header at Crosley Field. Whit Wyatt (ten innings) and Hugh Casey (six innings) pitched for Brooklyn. Paul Derringer hurled all 16 innings for Cincinnati. The game was scoreless until Wyatt homered in the 11th, but on the 90-degree day, was relieved in the bottom of the inning. Casey gave up a run to tie the score, but followed with five shutout innings. The run in the 16th crossed the plate on a squeeze bunt by Dixie Walker, which scored Pete Reiser from third base. The Dodgers also won the second contest 3–2.

Walker hit .311 with nine home runs in 1941.

JUNE 26   The Dodgers score seven runs in the third inning and club the Braves 11–2 at Ebbets Field.

JUNE 28   A 3–2 loss to the Braves in Boston starts with players serving as umpires. Regular umpires Babe Pinelli, Al Barlick and Lee Ballanfant sent a telegram informing the two clubs that they were delayed because the boat on which they were traveling from New York City was delayed by fog. The contest began with Freddie Fitzsimmons and Johnny Cooney of the Braves as the arbiters. Cooney called balls and strikes from behind the pitcher. Pinelli, Barlick and Ballanfant arrived in the second inning with the fans greeting them with foghorn imitations.

JULY 4   The Dodgers release Joe Vosmik.

JULY 8   Billy Herman collects a double and a single in three at-bats during a 7–5 National League loss in the All-Star Game at Briggs Stadium in Detroit.

JULY 11   The Dodgers score seven runs in the first inning and hammer the Reds 12–2 at Ebbets Field.

JULY 14   The Dodgers win a dramatic 1–0 win over the Cubs at Ebbets Field. The lone run scored in the ninth inning. With the bases loaded, Leo Durocher inserted himself into the game as a pinch-hitter and laid down a perfect bunt just to the left of the mound. Cubs pitcher Vern Olsen picked up the ball, and seeing he had no chance to throw out any of the runners, threw the ball over the Ebbets Field grandstand. Kirby Higbe pitched a two-hitter. The only Chicago hits were singles by Babe Dahlgren in the second inning and Phil Cavaretta in the seventh.

JULY 15   The Dodgers sweep the Cubs 7–0 and 8–4 to take a four-game lead over the Cardinals in the NL pennant race. Brooklyn's record was 56–26.

JULY 22   The Reds score five runs in the ninth inning to defeat the Dodgers 5–4 at Crosley Field. With the score 4–1 and the bases loaded, Chuck Aleno ducked out of the way of a Hugh Casey fastball. The bat inadvertently hit the ball, which flew down the right field line for a fluke triple. Pitcher Bucky Walters drove in Aleno with a sacrifice fly.

JULY 29   The Dodgers and Cardinals battle 12 innings in St. Louis in 103-degree heat for nothing as the contest ends in a 7–7 tie when called by darkness.

JULY 30   The Dodgers fall 6–4 to the Cardinals in St. Louis to drop three games behind in the NL pennant race. After leading by four games on July 15, the Dodgers lost 10 of 13.

On the same day, the Dodgers purchased Johnny Allen from the Browns.

AUGUST 4	Mickey Owen sets a major league record (since tied) by catching three foul pop-ups in a single inning during an 11–6 win over the Giants at Ebbets Field.
AUGUST 10	The Dodgers sweep the Braves 14–4 and 4–0 at Ebbets Field. Beanballs were exchanged by the two clubs in the opener, requiring the intervention of police to avert trouble.
AUGUST 11	The Dodgers score seven runs in the first inning to spark a 15–7 win over the Giants at Ebbets Field. Pitcher Kirby Higbe collected four hits, including a double, in five at-bats.
AUGUST 17	Kirby Higbe and Whit Wyatt star in a sweep of the Braves in Boston. Kirby Higbe pitched a complete game for a 5–1 win in the opener and collected four hits, including a double, in four at-bats. It was his second consecutive four-hit game. In the second tilt, Wyatt entered the ninth inning with a perfect game intact. He struck out Paul Waner to begin the ninth and extend his streak of consecutive batters retired to 25, but Phil Masi ended the no-hit bid with a single. Wyatt set down the next two hitters to preserve a one-hit, 3–0 victory.

Higbe and Wyatt were stars all season long. Higbe was 22–9 with a 3.13 ERA in 298 innings. He also led the league in games pitched (48) and games started (39). Wyatt had a 22–10 record with a league-leading seven shutouts and a 2.34 earned run average in 288$^1/_3$ innings. He completed 23 of his 35 starts.

AUGUST 19	The Dodgers score seven innings and beat the Pirates 9–0 in the first game of a double-header at Ebbets Field. In the second tilt, the Dodgers scored five times in the eighth for a 6–2 victory.

The Dodgers had an almost completely right-handed pitching staff in 1941. Left-handers combined for only four starts, 86 innings, and two victories during the season.

AUGUST 20	The Dodgers purchase Larry French from the Cubs.
AUGUST 21	Leo Durocher is ejected twice during a 6–2 loss to the Cubs at Ebbets Field. The Dodgers manager was given the heave-ho in the third inning for continued protests of a ball called in the first. In the seventh, the umpires discovered he was still lurking in the stairway leading to the dugout, and he was told to leave the premises again.
AUGUST 24	Whit Wyatt pitches a complete game and hits a walk-off single in the ninth inning to beat the Cardinals 3–2 in the second game of a double-header at Ebbets Field. St. Louis won the opener 7–3.
AUGUST 26	The Dodgers purchase Augie Galan from the Cubs.
AUGUST 31	The Dodgers wallop the Giants 13–6 in New York.
SEPTEMBER 1	The Dodgers outlast the Braves 6–5 in 15 innings in the first game of a double-header at Ebbets Field. Both teams scored in the tenth. In the 15th, Dolph Camilli drove in the game-winner with a single. During the game, he collected five hits on a home run, two doubles and two singles in seven at-bats. The second contest ended in a 2–2 tie when called by darkness after six innings.

Rookie-of-the-Year Pete Reiser and Dolph Camilli shouldered the lumber and carried the Dodgers to the National League pennant in 1941.

Camilli won the National League Most Valuable Player Award in 1941. He led the league in home runs (23), RBIs (120) and hit .285 with an on-base percentage of .407.

SEPTEMBER 4   The idle Dodgers take first place when the Cardinals lose twice to the Cubs in a double-header in Chicago.

The Dodgers held on to the top spot for the remainder of the season, but didn't wrap up the pennant until the final weekend.

SEPTEMBER 7   The Dodgers win two from the Giants 13–1 and 4–3 in a double-header at Ebbets Field. Kirby Higbe won his 20th game of the season in the opener. In the nightcap, the Dodgers scored two in the ninth and one in the tenth for the victory. In the ninth, Joe Medwick delivered a two-out single to deadlock the contest. Pete Reiser drove in the game-winner with a single.

Medwick hit .318, scored 100 runs, and struck 18 homers in 1941.

SEPTEMBER 13   Whit Wyatt earns his 20th victory of the season with a 1–0 decision over the Cardinals in St. Louis. Mort Cooper no-hit the Dodgers until the eighth inning when Dixie Walker and Billy Herman hit back-to-back doubles to score the lone run of the contest. Wyatt pitched a three-hitter. The victory put the Dodgers two games up in the pennant race with 14 contests left on the schedule.

SEPTEMBER 15   With all of the scoring done in the 17th inning, the Dodgers defeat the Reds 5–1 at Crosley Field. The umpires considered calling the game because of darkness with the score 0–0 at the end of the 16th but let play continue. Pete Reiser led off the 17th with a home run. The rest of the game was somewhat of a farce because the Reds tried to stall to prevent the inning from being completed. By the time the contest ended, the outfielders were barely visible from the upper deck behind home plate. Johnny Allen pitched the first 15 innings for the Dodgers and allowed only six hits. Hugh Casey hurled the final two. Paul Derringer tossed 16 shutout innings before being relieved after surrendering Reiser's homer.

SEPTEMBER 17   Trailing 3–1, the Dodgers score five runs in the fifth inning and beat the Pirates 6–4 in Pittsburgh. Pete Reiser put Brooklyn into the lead with a two-run triple.

SEPTEMBER 18   The Dodgers score five runs in the eighth inning for a 5–4 lead, then allow two tallies in the bottom half for a 6–5 loss to the Pirates at Forbes Field. The tying run in the eighth scored on a balk committed by Hugh Casey. Infuriated with the call, Casey threw the next three pitches over the head of umpire George Magerkurth, who headed toward the mound to have a word with him. Durocher rushed out of the dugout to get between Magerkurth and Casey, and the Dodgers skipper was ejected. After the game, several Dodgers surrounded Magerkurth, threatening him with bodily harm before fellow umpire Bill Stewart broke up the gathering.

SEPTEMBER 24   The Dodgers take a 1¹/₂-game lead over the Cardinals in the NL pennant race with a 4–2 victory over the Braves at Braves Field. There were only three games left on the schedule. On his 31st birthday, Dixie Walker hit a three-run triple in the seventh inning, which erased a 2–0 Boston advantage.

In anticipation of the upcoming World Series, the Dodgers built a new press box at Ebbets Field, which hung from the roof of the upper deck.

SEPTEMBER 25   The Dodgers clinch their first pennant in 21 years with a 6–0 win over the Braves in Boston. Whit Wyatt pitched the shutout.

A crowd of some 10,000 fans gathered at Grand Central Terminal in Manhattan to greet the Dodgers when they got off the train.

SEPTEMBER 28   On the final day of the season, the Dodgers win their 100th game of 1941 with a 5–1 decision over the Phillies at Ebbets Field.

SEPTEMBER 29   A parade is held in the Dodgers' honor in Brooklyn. An estimated one million lined the streets on the 1¹/₂-mile trip from the Heroes Arch at Grand Army Plaza off Prospect Park to the reviewing stand at Borough Hall.

The Dodgers met the Yankees in the World Series. Managed by Joe McCarthy, the Yanks were 101–53 in 1941 and won the American League pennant by 17 games. It was the first time that the Dodgers and Yankees met in a World Series. There would be six more Brooklyn-New York Fall Classics in 1947, 1949, 1952, 1953, 1955 and 1956. After the Dodgers moved to Los Angeles, the two storied franchises met again in October in 1963, 1977, 1978 and 1981.

OCTOBER 1   In the opening game of the World Series, the Yankees edge the Dodgers 3–2 at Yankee Stadium. The Dodgers scored in the seventh inning to narrow the gap to a run, but failed to dent the plate again. Red Ruffing, who was 37-years-old, pitched the complete game for the Yanks. Curt Davis, also 37, lasted 5⅓ innings for Brooklyn. Pee Wee Reese collected three hits in the losing cause.

Leo Durocher tried to con the Yankees by warming up three pitchers before the game. The other two, besides Davis, were Kirby Higbe and Whit Wyatt.

OCTOBER 2   The Dodgers even the series with a 3–2 victory at Yankee Stadium. After the Yanks took a 2–0 lead, the Dodgers countered with two tallies in the fifth and one in the sixth. Dolph Camilli's single drove in the go-ahead run. Whit Wyatt, who celebrated his 34th birthday five days earlier, pitched the distance for the Dodgers.

OCTOBER 3   In another low-scoring, one-run contest, the Yankees win game three 2–1 before 33,100 at Ebbets Field. The game was scoreless through seven innings in a duel between 39-year-old Freddie Fitzsimmons of the Dodgers and Yankees hurler Marius Russo. On the third out of the seventh inning, Russo hit a liner up the middle that struck Fitzsimmons, who was forced to leave the game with a fractured kneecap. Hugh Casey relieved, and allowed two runs and four hits in the eighth. The Dodgers countered with one in their half, but it wasn't enough to avert the defeat.

OCTOBER 4   The Yankees move within one win of the world championship by scoring four runs in the ninth and beat the Dodgers 7–4 after catcher Mickey Owen fails to catch a third strike. Attendance at Ebbets Field was 33,813. The Yanks took a 3–0 lead before the Dodgers scored twice in the fourth, on a pinch-double by Jimmy Wasdell, and two more in the fifth on a home run from Pete Reiser. Brooklyn still led 4–3 heading into the ninth with Hugh Casey on the mound. He entered the game with two out in the fifth and had yet to allow a run. Casey retired the first two batters and had two strikes on Tommy Henrich but a called third strike glanced off Owen's glove and got away from him, allowing Henrich to reach first base. Casey then imploded, allowing the next five batters to reach base on a single, double, walk, another double, and a second walk before recording the third out.

OCTOBER 5   The Yankees wrap up the world title by beating the Dodgers 3–1 on a four-hitter by Tiny Bonham before 34,072 at Ebbets Field. After Tommy Henrich homered in the fifth inning, Whit Wyatt decked Joe DiMaggio, who flied out then went after the Dodgers pitcher. Both dugouts emptied before the umpires intervened.

DECEMBER 7   The Japanese attack Pearl Harbor. A day later, the United States declared war on Japan. On December 11, the U.S. also declared war on Germany. Over the next four years, World War II would alter every aspect of American life, and baseball was no exception (see January 15, 1942).

DECEMBER 10   The Dodgers sell Mace Brown to the Red Sox.

DECEMBER 12   The Dodgers trade Pete Coscarat, Babe Phelps, Luke Hamlin and Jimmy Wasdell to the Pirates for Arky Vaughan.

Vaughan might be the most underrated player in major league history. In 2000, Bill James ranked Vaughan as the second best shortstop ever to play the game, but few today would recognize his name. It wasn't until 1985 that Vaughan was elected to the Hall of Fame. He was 29-years-old when acquired by the Dodgers and was named to his ninth consecutive All-Star team in 1942 before leading the

NL in runs scored and stolen bases in 1943. Vaughan decided to retire, however, and spent the 1944, 1945 and 1946 seasons living on his ranch in California. He returned in 1947 to the Dodgers, and played in 64 regular season and three World Series games before calling it quits for good. Vaughan died in a drowning accident in 1952.

1942

Season in a Sentence

The Dodgers lead the National League for 148 days and take a 10-game advantage over the Cardinals in early August, but blow the advantage and finish second despite winning 104 games.

Finish • Won • Lost • Pct • GB

Second   104   50   .675   2.0

Manager

Leo Durocher

Stats

Stats	Dods	NL	Rank
Batting Avg:	.265	.249	2
On-Base Pct:	.338	.318	2
Slugging Pct:	.362	.343	2
Home Runs:	62		5
Stolen Bases:	81		1
ERA:	2.84	3.31	3
Fielding Avg:	.977	.973	2
Runs Scored:	742		2
Runs Allowed:	510		2

Starting Lineup

Mickey Owen, c
Dolph Camilli, 1b
Billy Herman, 2b
Arky Vaughan, 3b
Pee Wee Reese, ss
Joe Medwick, lf
Pete Reiser, cf
Dixie Walker, rf
Johnny Rizzo, rf
Augie Galan, cf-lf

Pitchers

Whit Wyatt, sp
Kirby Higbe, sp
Curt Davis, sp
Johnny Allen, sp-rp
Max Macon, sp-rp
Hugh Casey, rp
Larry French, rp-sp
Ed Head, rp-sp

Attendance

1,037,765 (first in NL)

Club Leaders

Batting Avg:	Pete Reiser	.310
On-Base Pct:	Pete Reiser	.375
Slugging Pct:	Dolph Camilli	.471
Home Runs:	Dolph Camilli	26
RBIs:	Dolph Camilli	109
Runs:	Dolph Camilli	89
	Pete Reiser	89
Stolen Bases:	Pete Reiser	20
Wins:	Whit Wyatt	19
Strikeouts:	Kirby Higbe	115
ERA:	Curt Davis	2.36
Saves:	Hugh Casey	13

JANUARY 15   President Franklin Roosevelt gives baseball commissioner Kenesaw Landis the go-ahead to play ball for the duration of World War II. In his statement, Roosevelt said that he believed the continuation of the sport would be beneficial to the country's morale.

There were 71 players who appeared in the majors in 1941 and were in the service at the start of the 1942 season, an average of 4.4 per team. Among those who enlisted or were drafted, Cookie Lavagetto was the most significant member of the Dodgers. Lavagetto had been the starting third baseman since 1937 and had made the All-Star team the previous four seasons. He enlisted the Navy. Other Brooklyn players in the service in 1942 were Herman Franks, Don Padgett, Joe Gallagher, Tommy Tatum and Joe Hatten.

FEBRUARY 19   The Dodgers announce that servicemen in uniform would be admitted to Ebbets Field for free for the duration of the war.

MARCH 23   The Dodgers purchase Frenchy Bordagaray from the Yankees.

APRIL 14   On Opening Day, the Dodgers win 7–5 over the Giants at the Polo Grounds. Brooklyn scored four runs in the first inning and took a 7–0 lead before New York countered with five tallies in the seventh off Curt Davis. Pee Wee Reese homered.

The contest was played five days after the fall of Bataan, one of the many shocking military defeats the United States suffered at the hands of Japan early in 1942. Before the game, there were appeals to the crowd to buy war bonds. Some 2,100 soldiers, sailors and marines were sprinkled through the crowd. And, after both clubs formed a giant "V" at the foot of the center field flagpole for flag-raising ceremonies, the public address system advised everyone in the ballpark of what to do in case of an air raid by following the green arrows to places of safety.

APRIL 17   The Dodgers win the home opener 7–1 over the Phillies before 15,430 at Ebbets Field. Dolph Camilli homered and Johnny Allen pitched a complete game.

During World War II, the "Star-Spangled Banner" was played before every game. Previously, the National Anthem was played only on special occasions. The practice of playing the anthem before sporting events continued after the war ended.

APRIL 21   Three days after Major General Doolittle's air raid on Tokyo, the Dodgers score six runs in the first inning and three in the second and maul the Braves 13–2 at Ebbets Field.

APRIL 22   A day after playing in Brooklyn, the Dodgers and Braves travel to Boston and play 11 innings. After ten scoreless innings, the Dodgers exploded for four runs in the 11th to win 4–0. Whit Wyatt (nine innings) and Hugh Casey (two innings) combined on the shutout. Jim Tobin went all the way for the Braves. Pee Wee Reese broke the 0–0 tie with a two-run single.

For the duration of World War II, balls hit into the stands at major league ballparks were returned by the fans and donated to the recreation departments of the Armed Forces.

APRIL 30   The Dodgers purchase Schoolboy Rowe from the Tigers.

MAY 5   Larry French pitches 11 innings and allows only four hits in beating the Cardinals 3–1 in St. Louis.

MAY 8   All of the proceeds from the Dodgers 7–6 victory over the Giants at Ebbets Field go to the Navy Relief Society, which was established to benefit the families of sailors slain during the war. There were 42,822 paid, which raised over $60,000. Everyone, including the owners, players, umpires, vendors and members of the media paid their way into the ballpark.

The game started at 6:00 p.m. because of "dimouts" ordered by the U.S. government in coastal areas as a result of the threat of enemy attack. Lights had to be extinguished throughout New York City one hour after sunset. Even the bright lights of Broadway were turned off. The blackout regulations prevented night baseball at Ebbets Field until they were lifted in 1944. The Dodgers started many "twilight" games at the dinner hour during the 1942 and 1943 seasons.

MAY 13   Curt Davis pitches a two-hitter to beat the Reds 1–0 at Ebbets Field. The only Cincinnati hits were singles by Frank McCormick in the first inning and Eddie Joost in the third.

The Dodgers led major league baseball in attendance for the second year in a row with a figure of 1,037,765. The Yankees were second by drawing 922,011 fans, and the Giants third with 779,621. It was also the second straight year that the three New York teams ranked one, two and three in attendance.

MAY 19   The Dodgers extend their winning streak to eight games with a 6–1 decision over the Cubs at Ebbets Field. The victory gave Brooklyn a 25–8 record and a seven-game lead over the second place Cardinals.

On the same day, the Dodgers purchased Babe Dahlgren from the Cubs.

MAY 25   Curt Davis pitches his second two-hitter in less than two weeks, defeating the Phillies 3–0 at Ebbets Field. The only Philadelphia hits were singles by Stan Benjamin in the fifth inning and Al Glossop in the eighth.

MAY 29   Ed Head allows only one hit in eight innings, but the Dodgers lose 3–1 in ten innings against the Giants at Ebbets Field. The only hit off Head was a single by Harry Danning in the eighth. Hugh Casey allowed two tenth-inning runs.

MAY 30   A two-run walk-off double by Pee Wee Reese in the ninth inning beats the Giants 7–6 in the first game of a double-header at Ebbets Field. New York won the second game 7–3.

MAY 31   Dixie Walker hits a grand slam off Johnny Sain in the fourth inning of a 10–2 win over the Braves in the first game of a double-header at Ebbets Field. Brooklyn also won game two 3–1. Pete Reiser collected six hits, including a homer, triple and double, in eight at-bats during the double-header.

JUNE 2   Pete Reiser garners five hits in five at-bats on a homer, three doubles and a single during a 17–2 thrashing of the Pirates in Pittsburgh. The Dodgers scored in every inning but the second and ninth.

In three consecutive games on May 31 and June 2, Reiser had 11 hits in 13 at-bats. The hits included two homers, a triple and four doubles.

JUNE 18   Twelve days after America's victory over Japan in the Battle of Midway, a fistfight erupts during a 5–2 win over the Cardinals at Ebbets Field. In the sixth inning, Joe Medwick tried to advance from first to second on a passed ball. St. Louis catcher Walker Cooper recovered in time to make the play at second, and Medwick went in with his spikes high at shortstop Marty Marion. As soon as Medwick was called out, Marion pounced on him, and as they were getting up, Cards second baseman

Creepy Crespi rushed up and knocked Medwick down. Both clubs rushed from the dugouts. It was nearly ten minutes before peace was restored. Medwick and Crespi were ejected. Dixie Walker had to leave the game because he twisted an ankle during the rumpus.

JUNE 23   Curt Davis retires the first 23 batters to face him and finishes with a two-hitter to defeat the Giants 6–0 in the first game of a double-header at Ebbets Field. The first New York base runner was Dick Bartell, who singled with two out in the eighth inning. The other hit was a single by Johnny Rucker in the ninth. The Dodgers completed the sweep with a 7–2 victory in the nightcap.

Between games, 1,040 WAVES (Women Accepted for Volunteer Emergency Service), a branch of the Navy, paraded on the field accompanied by a band.

JUNE 25   Joe Medwick extends his hitting streak to 27 games during a 4–0 win over the Reds at Ebbets Field. Medwick collected 43 hits in 107 at-bats during the streak, a batting average of .402.

JUNE 26   A squeeze bunt by Pee Wee Reese in the tenth inning scores Billy Herman from third base to defeat the Reds 4–3 at Ebbets Field.

The Dodgers installed an organ at Ebbets Field in 1942 with Gladys Goodding at the keyboard. The instrument caused some controversy in the Flatbush neighborhood, however. J. Reid Spencer, a 70-year-old retired college music teacher who lived three blocks away from the ballpark, filed a complaint in court because the music disturbed his afternoon nap. Spencer claimed the organ was a waste of money and was "subversive and disloyal at this time and had better be diverted to the purchase of war bonds." In September, a judge dismissed Spencer's petition to silence the organ. Goodding continued as the Ebbets Field organist until the last game was played at the ballpark in 1957. She also played the organ during Rangers and Knickerbockers games at Madison Square Garden.

JULY 4   The Dodgers rout the Phillies 14–0 and 5–4 in a holiday double-header in Philadelphia. All of the runs in the opener were scored in the first five innings.

JULY 6   Mickey Owen homers for the lone National League run in a 3–1 loss in the All-Star Game at the Polo Grounds in New York City. It was struck in the eighth inning off Al Benton. Owen also became the first Dodger batter to homer in an All-Star Game. Leo Durocher was the NL manager.

Owen didn't hit a single home run in 421 regular season at-bats in 1942, or in 365 at-bats in 1943. He struck only 14 homers in 3,649 big league at-bats over 13 seasons.

JULY 11   The Dodgers need 15 innings to defeat the Reds 3–2 in the second game of a double-header in Cincinnati. The 15th-inning run scored without a base hit. Pee Wee Reese walked, was sacrificed to second, and advanced two bases on a passed ball. The Dodgers also won the opener 5–0.

JULY 15   Angered over the taunts from the Dodgers players, Cubs pitcher Hi Bithorn fires a ball into the dugout during a 10–5 Brooklyn win at Ebbets Field. The ball narrowly missed hitting Leo Durocher.

JULY 19   Pete Reiser runs into the right field wall at Sportsman's Park in St. Louis during an 11-inning 7–6 loss. Reiser attempted to make a one-handed catch of a drive by Enos Slaughter in the 11th when Reiser's head struck the barrier. Slaughter circled the bases for a game-winning inside-the-park homer. The Cardinals also won the opener 8–5. In the third inning, Stan Musial had to be restrained from charging Les Webber after the Brooklyn hurler threw two pitches at Musial's head.

Reiser suffered a severe concussion from hitting the wall. He was batting .350 at the time of the injury. Reiser returned to the line-up four days later, but suffered from blurred vision and sporadic headaches and hit only .244 over the remainder of the season. He finished the campaign with a .310 average, ten homers, and a league-leading 20 stolen bases. Reiser spent the entire 1943, 1944 and 1945 seasons serving in the Army.

AUGUST 1   An umpire's reversal of a call helps the Dodgers defeat the Cubs 9–6 at Ebbets Field. With the Dodgers leading 6–2 in the eighth inning with two out, two runners on base and the count 2–2, Pete Reiser hit a foul tip into the mitt of Chicago catcher Clyde McCullough. Home plate Lee Ballanfant ruled it a strikeout, but after protests from the Dodgers, second base umpire Babe Pinelli overruled Ballanfant stating the ball struck the dirt before it was caught by McCullough. Reiser hit the next pitch for a three-run homer. The runs became important when the Cubs scored four times in the ninth.

The victory gave the Dodgers a 71–29 record at the 100-game point of the season.

AUGUST 3   A game at the Polo Grounds between the Dodgers and Giants ends in controversy. A crowd of 57,305 turned out with all of the proceeds going to the Army Relief Fund. The game began at 6:00 p.m. The Dodgers led 7–4 heading into the ninth. Dolph Camilli helped stake Brooklyn to the advantage with a grand slam off Van Lingle Mungo in the fifth inning. The first two Giants in the ninth reached base before umpire George Magerkurth called the game because of coastal dimout regulations, which required the lights to be turned off one hour after sunset (see May 8, 1942). At this point, all of the lights were turned off except for a spotlight on the American flag. A band played "The Star-Spangled Banner," but sustained booing by the crowd because of the way the game ended nearly drowned out the presentation of the National Anthem.

AUGUST 4   For the second straight night, a game at the Polo Grounds ends in controversy because of the dimout regulations. With the score 1–1 in the tenth, Pee Wee Reese hit an inside-the-park grand slam for an apparent 5–1 lead. Before the inning was completed, however, the lights had to be turned off because it was one hour after sunset. This wiped out the entire tenth inning and the score reverted back to the last completed inning. The contest went into the books as a 1–1 tie.

AUGUST 5   Max Macon pitches a two-hitter to defeat the Giants 4–0 at Ebbets Field. The only New York hits were a double by Mickey Witek in the sixth inning and a single by Dick Bartell with two out in the ninth.

The victory gave the Dodgers a 74–30 record and a ten-game lead over the Cardinals in the National League pennant race. Over the remainder of the season, the Dodgers were a respectable 30–20 for a then-club record of 104 victories, but the Cards were able to take the title by two games by winning 43 of their last 51 games.

AUGUST 8   The umpires have to step in to curtail bloodshed during a 2–0 loss to the Braves in Boston. In the seventh inning, Whit Wyatt brushed the uniform of Boston pitcher Manny Salvo with a pitch. Salvo retaliated by plunking Wyatt in the eighth and the Dodger hurler responded by heaving his bat toward the mound. The bat missed its mark and slid toward shortstop. Salvo moved in the direction of Wyatt with intent to inflict bodily harm, but was intercepted by teammates and the umpires.

Wyatt had a 19–7 record and a 2.73 ERA in 1942. Kirby Higbe had a 16–11 mark and an earned run average of 3.25.

AUGUST 12   Larry French pitches the Dodgers to a 1–0 win over the Phillies at Ebbets Field. The lone run scored in the ninth inning when Rube Melton walked Dolph Camilli with the bases loaded.

Camilli hit .252 with 26 homers and 109 RBIs in 1942.

AUGUST 14   The Dodgers sweep the Braves 10–0 and 7–3 at Ebbets Field.

AUGUST 15   The Dodgers capture a 5–4 win over the Braves on a two-out, two-run homer by Dolph Camilli in the ninth inning.

AUGUST 18   A 3–1 loss to the Phillies at Shibe Park is interrupted for 25 minutes by a blackout ordered by the government throughout the Philadelphia area to test the Civilian Defense System.

AUGUST 19   The Dodgers wallop the Braves 11–1 at Ebbets Field.

AUGUST 20   Whit Wyatt pitches a one-hitter to defeat the Giants 2–1 at Ebbets Field. The lone New York hit was a home run by Johnny Mize in the second inning.

AUGUST 23   After the Giants score two runs in the top of the tenth inning, Dolph Camilli hits a grand slam in the bottom half for a 6–4 win in the first game of a double-header at Ebbets Field. The Dodgers also won the second game, called after five innings by darkness.

AUGUST 26   A ten-inning, 2–1 loss to the Cardinals in St. Louis cuts the Dodgers lead in the NL pennant race to 4$\frac{1}{2}$ games.

AUGUST 30   The Dodgers purchase Bobo Newsom from the Senators.

Louis (Bobo) Newsom came to the majors as a 21-year-old rookie in 1929, but lasted only five games with the club. It began a long and colorful career full of ups and downs. Newsom won at least 20 games in a season three times, and lost 20 or more in three others. He was still pitching in the big leagues as late as 1953 and changed uniforms 15 times. Newsom's second tour of duty would end in controversy (see July 9, 1943).

SEPTEMBER 4   In his first game with the Dodgers, Bobo Newsom shuts out the Reds 2–0 in Cincinnati.

SEPTEMBER 12   The Cardinals defeat the Dodgers 2–1 at Ebbets Field. The loss dropped the Dodgers into a first-place tie with the Cards. Both clubs had a record of 94–46.

SEPTEMBER 13   The Dodgers lose a double-header by scores of 6–3 and 4–1 to the Reds at Ebbets Field to fall one game behind the Cardinals in the pennant race. St. Louis split a twin bill against the Phillies in Philadelphia.

SEPTEMBER 16   Several members of the Dodgers fight with fans prior to a 10–3 win over the Pirates at Ebbets Field. The fists started to fly about an hour before the game when four young men, ranging in age from 23 to 33, became embroiled in a heated argument with a couple of ushers behind the Dodgers dugout. Several players, led by Mickey Owen and Dixie Walker climbed into the stands and joined the fray. According to witnesses, the fans began beating the ushers and the ballplayers rushed to defend them. Two of the four fans suffered injuries that landed them in the hospital. The ushers filed assault charges against the four fans, who in turn filed similar charges against Owen, Walker and Leo Durocher. The charges and counter-charges were dropped on October 5.

SEPTEMBER 19   The Dodgers keep alive their faint hopes of winning a pennant when Si Johnson of the Phillies walks four batters in a row with two out in the 11th to enable Brooklyn to win 5–4 at Ebbets Field. Fans who brought scrap metal for the war effort were admitted for free.

SEPTEMBER 22   Dolph Camilli hits a walk-off homer in the 12th inning to defeat the Giants 9–8 at Ebbets Field. Despite the win, the Dodgers hopes for the pennant were also gone. The club was 2½ games out with five to play.

SEPTEMBER 23   Larry French pitches a one-hitter, allows only one base runner, and faces the minimum 27 batters in defeating the Phillies 6–0 at Ebbets Field. The lone Philadelphia hitter to reach base was Nick Etten, who singled in the second inning, then was erased on a double play. It was also the Dodgers 100th victory of the season.

> *After a 5–14 record with the Cubs and Dodgers in 1941, French bounced back in 1942 with a 15–4 mark and a 1.83 ERA at the age of 34. The September 23 one-hitter would prove to be his last big league game, however, closing out a career in which he won 197 games and lost 171. French joined the Navy after the 1942 season ended and became an officer. When the war ended, he decided against resuming his baseball career, remained in the service, and saw active duty again during the Korean War. French retired as a captain in the reserves in 1969. Also on September 23, 1942, Larry MacPhail announced he was resigning his position as president and general manager of the Dodgers to join the Army with the rank of lieutenant colonel. MacPhail was 52 years old and served in Washington as a special assistant to the secretary of war. In 1945, MacPhail bought a one-third interest in the Yankees and headed the organization as president and general manager before resigning at the end of the 1947 season.*

SEPTEMBER 27   On the last day of the season, the Dodgers extend their winning streak to eight games by beating the Phillies 4–3 in Philadelphia, but are eliminated from the pennant race.

Heading into the day, the Dodgers needed a win and two Cardinals losses in a double-header against the Cubs to end the regular season in a tie for first, which would have forced a playoff for the pennant. The Cards won twice, however.

OCTOBER 29   Branch Rickey is appointed president and general manager of the Dodgers, replacing Larry MacPhail, who resigned to join the Army on September 23.

One of the most complex, intelligent, influential, successful individuals in the long history of baseball, Rickey had been general manager of the Cardinals since 1917 and helped transform that franchise from doormats to the best franchise in the National League by building baseball's first extensive farm system. While he was in St. Louis, the Cards won the NL pennant in 1926, 1928, 1930, 1931, 1934 and 1942. The club would reach the World Series again in 1943, 1944 and 1946 with players largely acquired by Rickey. He was born in 1881, the son of a poor farmer in Lucasville, Ohio. Raised by strict Methodist parents who scrimped and saved for his education, Rickey attended Ohio Wesleyan University and graduated 1¹/₂ years ahead of schedule. He starred on semi-pro football and baseball teams and coached Ohio Wesleyan's baseball team. Rickey caught the attention of major league scouts and played 118 games as a catcher with the Browns and Yankees from 1905 through 1907. After his playing days ended, Rickey attended the University of Michigan Law School and earned a degree by squeezing a three-year course of study into two years while coaching the baseball team. He came to St. Louis as manager of the Browns, a job he held from 1913 through 1915 before moving on to the Cardinals. Despite more than two decades of sustained success, Rickey's working relationship with Cardinals owner Sam Breadon became strained over the years and by 1942 was no long workable. In Brooklyn, Rickey had much more freedom to operate the club by his own standards than he had in St. Louis. He began to buy stock in the Dodgers and by August 1945 had purchased a controlling interest in a partnership with Walter O'Malley. Two months later, Rickey announced the signing of Jackie Robinson, who integrated Organized Baseball when he played with Montreal in the International League in 1946 and the majors when debuting with the Dodgers in 1947. The Dodgers won the NL pennant in 1947 and 1949, but by the end of the 1950 season, Rickey and O'Malley were at odds over the direction of the club and Rickey sold his stock and left the club.

DECEMBER 12   The Dodgers trade Johnny Allen to the Phillies for Rube Melton.

1943

Season in a Sentence

With many star players in the military, a patched-up roster holds first place through early June, but a ten-game losing streak in July ends the pennant aspirations.

Finish • Won • Lost • Pct • GB

Third 81 72 .529 23.5

Manager

Leo Durocher

Stats

Stats	Dods	NL	Rank
Batting Avg:	.272	.258	2
On-Base Pct:	.346	.324	1
Slugging Pct:	.357	.347	3
Home Runs:	39		7 (tie)
Stolen Bases:	58		2
ERA:	3.88	3.38	7
Fielding Avg:	.972	.974	7
Runs Scored:	716		1
Runs Allowed:	674		6

Starting Lineup

Mickey Owen, c
Dolph Camilli, 1b
Billy Herman, 2b
Frenchy Bordagaray, 3b-lf-rf
Arky Vaughan, ss-3b
Dixie Walker, lf-rf
Augie Galan, cf
Paul Waner, rf
Luis Olmo, cf
Bobby Bragan, c
Al Glossop, ss-2b

Pitchers

Whit Wyatt, sp
Kirby Higbe, sp
Curt Davis, sp-rp
Bobo Newsom, sp-rp
Rube Melton, sp-rp
Les Webber, rp
Ed Head, rp-sp
Max Macon, rp-sp

Attendance

661,739 (first in NL)

Club Leaders

Batting Avg:	Billy Herman	.330
On-Base Pct:	Augie Galan	.412
Slugging Pct:	Bill Herman	.417
Home Runs:	Augie Galan	9
RBIs:	Billy Herman	100
Runs:	Arky Vaughan	112
Stolen Bases:	Arky Vaughan	20
Wins:	Whit Wyatt	14
Strikeouts:	irby Higbe	108
ERA:	Whit Wyatt	2.49
Saves:	Ed Head	10

JANUARY 21   A week after Franklin Roosevelt and Winston Churchill begin meetings in Casablanca, Morocco, to formulate strategy for the war in Europe, the Dodgers sign Johnny Cooney and Paul Waner as free agents.

MARCH 9   The Dodgers trade Babe Dahlgren to the Phillies for Lloyd Waner and Al Glossop.

Lloyd, who was Paul's younger brother, decided to retire rather than join the Dodgers. He sat out the 1943 season, then played in 15 games with the club in 1944. The Waner brothers were also teammates with the Pirates from 1927 through 1940 and with the Braves in 1941.

MARCH 14   The Dodgers open spring training camp at Bear Mountain, New York.

During World War II, teams had to train north of the Ohio River and east of the Mississippi to save on travel expenses. In 1943, 1944 and 1945, the Dodgers trained at Bear Mountain, New York, a ski resort about 50 miles north of New York City near the U.S. Military Academy. A diamond was laid out near the foot of the toboggan slide and ski jump. The club also had the use of the spacious field house at West Point. Between the 1942 and 1943 seasons,

Dodger players who entered military service included Pete Reiser, Pee Wee Reese, Larry French, Hugh Casey, Lew Riggs, Johnny Rizzo, Chet Kehn, Cliff Dapper, Stan Rojek, Carl Furillo, Bruce Edwards and Hank Behrman. During the season, Gene Hermanski, Boyd Bartley, and Ed Ankenman were either drafted or enlisted. With the war on, most big league clubs curtailed their scouting operations, believing it was fruitless to sign high school and college players who would soon be drafted and might be killed or seriously injured in combat. Branch Rickey took the opposite tactic, increasing his scouting budget and signing amateurs by the boatload. Once the war ended, the Dodgers had one of the best farm systems in baseball. In the eleven seasons beginning in 1946, the Dodgers won six pennants and lost three others on the final day of the season.

MARCH 24   The Dodgers sell Schoolboy Rowe to the Phillies.

APRIL 21   The scheduled opener between the Dodgers and Giants at Ebbets Field is postponed by inclement weather.

APRIL 22   The Dodgers open the season with a 5–2 win over the Giants before 16,775 at Ebbets Field. Ed Head pitched the complete game.

                On the same day, the Dodgers purchased Johnny Allen from the Phillies.

MAY 1   Bobo Newsom pitches a one-hitter to defeat the Giants 3–0 in the first game of a double-header at the Polo Grounds. The only New York hit was a single by Babe Barna in the sixth inning. The Dodgers also won the opener 9–2.

                Most of the games early in the 1943 season were low-scoring affairs because of an inferior batch of baseballs manufactured with different specifications due to wartime shortages. A more resilient ball was soon rushed into use.

MAY 5   The Dodgers collect 23 hits and overwhelm the Phillies 18–6 at Ebbets Field.

                The Dodgers attendance dropped from 1,037,765 in 1942 to 661,739 in 1943, but it was still good enough to lead the majors for the third straight year. The Yankees were second to the Dodgers with a figure of 618,330.

MAY 15   The Dodgers break a scoreless tie with 10 runs in the fourth inning and defeat the Cubs 13–6 at Ebbets Field. The 10 runs scored on five hits and five walks. The big blows were a two-run homer by Al Glossop and a three-run double from Billy Herman.

                Herman had a standout year in 1943 with a .330 batting average on 193 hits, 41 of which were doubles. He drove in 100 runs despite hitting only two homers.

MAY 17   Five days after Germany surrenders in North Africa, Rube Melton pitches the Dodgers to a 1–0 win over the Cardinals at Ebbets Field. The lone run scored in the second inning on a double by Dixie Walker and two infield outs.

                The victory gave the Dodgers a 17–7 record and a 3½-game lead in the NL pennant race.

MAY 26   Les Webber allows seven hits, nine walks, and 10 runs in 1²/₃ innings of relief during a 17–4 loss to the Pirates in Pittsburgh. Webber surrendered nine runs after two were out in the third inning and walked five batters with the bases loaded.

The Dodgers scored 716 runs in 1943 to lead the National League, but pitching was a problem all season. The club's earned run average of 3.88 ranked seventh.

MAY 31   The Dodgers beat the Cardinals 1–0 in the second game of a double-header at Sportsman's Park. Freddie Fitzsimmons (seven innings), Max Macon (one inning) and Curt Davis (one inning) combined on the shutout. The lone run scored in the eighth inning when Dixie Walker doubled, moved to third base on a sacrifice, and scored on Dee Moore's bunt. St. Louis won the opener 7–0 on a one-hitter by Mort Cooper.

Walker hit .302 with five homers in 1943.

JUNE 4   The Dodgers score seven runs in the first inning after the first two batters are retired and wallop the Cubs 18–5 in Chicago. There were 23 Brooklyn hits in the contest.

Connie Desmond joined Red Barber in the Dodgers radio booth in 1943. Desmond would announce Dodgers games until 1956.

JUNE 18   Leading 8–0, the Dodgers allow nine runs in the sixth inning and lose 10–8 to the Phillies at Ebbets Field.

JUNE 19   Dixie Walker collects two homers, a double and a single in four at-bats during a 7–5 triumph over the Phillies at Ebbets Field.

JULY 1   The Dodgers are knocked out of first place with a 12-inning, 10–9 loss to the Reds at Ebbets Field.

The Dodgers fell out of contention in a hurry as the Cardinals ran away with the pennant race. By August 14, Brooklyn was 17 games out of first place.

JULY 5   The Dodgers announce that any woman who brings one-half pound of kitchen fat to Ebbets Field would be admitted for free. The kitchen fat was used in the manufacture of explosives by the military.

JULY 6   The Dodgers sell Joe Medwick to the Giants.

JULY 9   After the Pirates score three runs in the top of the tenth inning, the Dodgers rally with four in their half to win 8–7 at Ebbets Field. The winning tally crossed the plate on a bunt by Billy Herman that brought in Arky Vaughan from third base.

In the third inning, Bobo Newsom berated rookie catcher Bobby Bragan for a passed ball that cost the Dodgers a run. After the game, Newsom and Leo Durocher had a heated argument and the Dodgers manager suspended Newsom.

JULY 10   On a weird afternoon at Ebbets Field, the Dodgers threaten to go on strike, then go on the field and clobber the Pirates 23–6. Players contemplated the strike because they were livid over the suspension of Bobo Newsom by Leo Durocher the previous day. Facing a forfeit, Durocher finally persuaded everyone to take the field except for Arky Vaughan, who sat in the stands in his street clothes next to Newsom. The Dodgers struck quickly with 10 runs in the first inning. After plating two runs in the third, the Dodgers erupted for 10 more tallies in the fourth. A run in the fifth made the score 23–4. Billy Herman led the attack with seven RBIs on a double and two singles. Newsom was traded to the Browns five days later.

JULY 13   Billy Herman collects two singles in five at-bats during a 5–3 National League loss at the All-Star Game at Shibe Park in Philadelphia.

JULY 15   The Dodgers trade Bobo Newsom to the Browns for Fritz Ostermueller and Archie McKain.

JULY 26   Arky Vaughan hits an inside-the-park grand slam with two out in the tenth inning to down the Pirates 10–6 in Pittsburgh. The blow off Ed Brandt was a liner to center field that rolled 425 feet to the center field wall.

Vaughan hit .305, smacked 39 doubles, and led the National League with 112 runs in 1943.

JULY 30   Johnny Allen allows two home runs on two consecutive pitches with one baseball during a 12–3 loss to the Cubs at Wrigley Field. In the sixth inning, Phil Cavarretta homered off the right field foul pole. The ball was retrieved, and Bill Nicholson hit the next pitch out of the park.

JULY 31   The Dodgers trade Dolph Camilli and Johnny Allen to the Giants for Bill Lohrman, Bill Sayles and Joe Orengo.

Camilli refused to report to the Giants and retired.

AUGUST 1   The Dodgers lose two to the Cardinals 7–1 and 5–4 in a double-header at Sportsman's Park. The opener was marred by a fight between opposing catchers Mickey Owen and Walker Cooper. The mix-up began when Cooper, thrown out on a close play at first, nearly spiked first baseman Augie Galan. Owen charged into Cooper, and the two began exchanging punches. Both were ejected.

Galan batted .287 and led the NL in walks with 103.

AUGUST 8   Six days after six die in a riot in the Harlem neighborhood of New York City, the Dodgers lose their tenth in a row, dropping a 5–4 decision to the Braves at Ebbets Field.

AUGUST 28   The Dodgers utilize 21 hits to clobber the Phillies 14–7 in Philadelphia.

SEPTEMBER 4   The day after the Allies invade the Italian mainland, the Dodgers outlast the Giants 4–3 in 17 innings at Ebbets Field. The Giants tied the contest 2–2 in the ninth on a two-out homer by Sid Gordon. Both teams scored in the 14th. A throwing error by second baseman Mickey Witek allowed Luis Olmo to score the winning run. Rookie Rex Barney pitched the first 14 innings and allowed two runs and seven hits. Ed Head hurled the last three frames. It was Brooklyn's eighth win in a row.

Olmo was the second individual born in Puerto Rico to reach the majors. The first was Hi Bithorn of the Cubs in 1942.

SEPTEMBER 6   The day after the Allies begin the invasion of the Italian mainland, the Dodgers score seven runs in the sixth inning to beat the Braves 7–3 in the first game of a double-header at Ebbets Field. It was the club's tenth victory in a row. The winning streak ended when Boston took the second tilt 3–2 in ten innings. The streak came less than a month after the Dodgers lost ten games in succession.

SEPTEMBER 8   Whit Wyatt pitches a one-hitter to beat the Braves 3–0 at Ebbets Field. He retired 22 batters in a row after Chuck Workman singled with two out in the first inning.

SEPTEMBER 9   With former President Herbert Hoover in attendance, the Dodgers defeat the Phillies 7–6 at Ebbets Field.

SEPTEMBER 23   Whit Wyatt wins his tenth consecutive decision by defeating the Cardinals 4–3 in St. Louis. He hurt his knee in the fourth inning and had a pronounced limp throughout the remainder of the game.

Wyatt had a 14–5 record in 1943. He pitched two more seasons in the majors with the Dodgers and Phillies and was 2–13 with a 6.07 ERA.

SEPTEMBER 29   Trailing 4–2, the Dodgers erupt for nine runs in the eighth inning and defeat the Pirates 14–7 in Pittsburgh.

OCTOBER 3   On the final day of the season, the Dodgers lose 6–1 to the Reds in Cincinnati. The game was notable for several reasons. Gil Hodges made his major league debut at the age of 19, played third base, and was hitless in two at-bats. He spent the next two seasons in the Marines and didn't play another big league game until 1947. Chris Haughey, on his 18th birthday, also played in his first game in the majors, and pitched seven innings allowing 10 walks, five hits and six runs, three of them earned. Haughey also entered military service soon afterward, but never played in another game in the major leagues. Also, the Reds fell one short of the National League record for double plays because of the chicanery of Leo Durocher. The Reds turned their 193rd double play of 1943 in the fourth inning. The record of 194 was set by the Reds in both 1928 and 1931. Durocher was the shortstop on the 1931 team and had no desire to see the record broken. For the remainder of the game, every Dodger who reached first base attempted to steal second on the next pitch.

1944

Season in a Sentence

With the war continuing to deplete the roster, the Dodgers experience a club-record 16-game losing streak in mid-season and finish in seventh place.

Finish • Won • Lost • Pct • GB

Seventh   63   91   .409   42.0

Manager

Leo Durocher

Stats

	Dods •	NL •	Rank
Batting Avg:	.269	.261	2
On-Base Pct:	.331	.326	3
Slugging Pct:	.366	.363	4
Home Runs:	56		6
Stolen Bases:	45		4
ERA:	4.66	3.61	8
Fielding Avg:	.966	.972	8
Runs Scored:	690		4
Runs Allowed:	832		8

Starting Lineup

Mickey Owen, c
Howie Schultz, 1b
Eddie Stanky, 2b
French Bordagaray, 3b
Bobby Bragan, ss-c
Augie Galan, lf
Luis Olmo, cf-3b-2b
Dixie Walker, rf
Goody Rosen, cf

Pitchers

Curt Davis, sp
Hal Gregg, sp
Rube Melton, sp-rp
Ben Chapman, sp
Cal McLish, sp-rp
Les Webber, rp

Attendance

605,905 (third in NL)

Club Leaders

Batting Avg:	Dixie Walker	.357
On-Base Pct:	Dixie Walker	.434
Slugging Pct:	Dixie Walker	.529
Home Runs:	Dixie Walker	13
RBIs:	Augie Galan	93
Runs:	Augie Galan	96
Stolen Bases:	Luis Olmo	10
Wins:	Curt Davis	10
Strikeouts:	Hal Gregg	92
ERA:	Curt Davis	3.34
Saves:	Curt Davis	4

APRIL 18   The Dodgers start the season with a 4–1 loss to the Phillies in Philadelphia. Hal Gregg, a 22-year-old rookie, was the losing pitcher. Gene Mauch, who was just five months past his 18th birthday, was Brooklyn's starting shortstop. Mauch played five games before entering the service.

Mauch never played again for the Dodgers after 1944, but lasted in the majors as a player until 1957 and was a manager for four teams from 1960 until 1987. Among the Dodgers who entered the military between the 1943 and 1944 seasons were Billy Herman, Kirby Higbe, Rex Barney, Gil Hodges, Dutch Dietz, Bill Sayles and Alex Campanis. Those who were drafted or enlisted in the service during the season were Jack Bolling, Roy Jarvis, Ed Head, Lou Rochelli and Mauch. There was an almost constant roster turnover because of the war. The Dodgers used 53 players during the 1944 season. Seven were teenagers and four were 40 or older.

APRIL 21   The Giants ruin the first game of the season at Ebbets Field by beating the Dodgers 3–2 before 11,861.

APRIL 25   The Dodgers break a 3–3 tie by erupting for eight runs in the ninth inning to defeat the Braves 11–3 in Boston.

Dixie Walker led the league in hitting in 1944 and was a fan favorite throughout much of the 1940s.

APRIL 27   Jim Tobin of the Braves pitches a no-hitter to beat the Dodgers 2–0 in Boston. Tobin also hit a home run in the eighth inning off Fritz Ostermueller. Dixie Walker ended the game by grounding out to second baseman Steve Shemo.

Walker had an outstanding season in 1944, winning the NL batting title with an average of .357 in addition to hitting 13 home runs.

APRIL 30   The Giants pummel the Dodgers 26–8 in the first game of a double-header at the Polo Grounds. Phil Weintraub led the way with eleven runs batted in on a homer, a triple and two doubles. Mel Ott tied a major league record by scoring six runs. Dodger pitchers Rube Melton, Les Webber, Chink Zachary, Fritz Ostermueller and Tommy Warren tied a National League mark by combining to walk 17 batters. To add to the strangeness of the day, Melton's brother Cliff was the starting pitcher for the Giants. The 26 are the most allowed by the Dodgers in either Brooklyn or Los Angeles since a 28–5 loss to the Cubs on August 25, 1891. The Dodgers rebounded to win the second tilt, called on account of darkness after seven innings, by a score of 5–4.

The game marked Zachary's big league debut. Roy Jarvis also played in his first game in the majors as a substitute catcher for Brooklyn during the 26–8 debacle at the age of 17 years, 308 days. He soon joined the service and never played again for the Dodgers. Jarvis later appeared in 19 contests with the Pirates in 1946 and 1947.

MAY 3   The Dodgers score three runs in the ninth inning to defeat the Braves 4–3 at Ebbets Field. Augie Galan tied the score with a two-run double. Lloyd Waner drove in the winning run with a squeeze bunt that scored Luis Olmo from third base.

Galan hit .318 with 43 doubles, 12 homers and a league-leading 101 walks in 1944.

MAY 4   Hal Gregg holds the Phillies hitless for 6⅓ innings and wins 10–1 with a four-hitter at Ebbets Field. The first Philadelphia hit was a single by Ted Cieslak with one out in the seventh inning.

MAY 15   The Dodgers score seven runs in the sixth inning and submerge the Cubs 14–3 in Chicago.

MAY 17   Howie Schultz hits a grand slam off Preacher Roe in the sixth inning, but the Dodgers lose 8–5 in a contest at Pittsburgh called after six innings by rain.

Schultz was a six-foot-six first baseman who played for the Dodgers from 1943 through 1947. He also played pro basketball for six seasons, including two (1951–52 and 1952–53) with the NBA champion Minneapolis Lakers.

MAY 23   The Dodgers score two runs in the ninth inning on a Giants error to win 3–2 at Ebbets Field. With Hal Gregg and Frenchy Bordagaray on base and two out, Lloyd Waner lifted a fly ball that was muffed by center fielder Johnny Rucker and allowed both runners to score. It was also the first night game at Ebbets Field since 1941 as blackout restrictions in New York City were lifted.

JUNE 2   Two days before Allied troops enter Rome, fans react to the ejection of Leo Durocher in the eighth inning of a 2–1 loss to the Cubs at Ebbets Field by throwing hundreds of bottles onto the field.

JUNE 6   All major league games are postponed in observance of D-Day. President Franklin Roosevelt urged Americans to spend the day in prayer at home or in church.

On the same day, the Dodgers traded Bob Chipman to the Cubs for Eddie Stanky. It proved to be one of the best short-term deals in Dodgers history. Branch Rickey once said that the hustling and combative Stanky "can't hit, he can't run, he can't field, he can't throw. All he can do is beat you." Stanky's ability to irritate opponents and teammates alike earned him the nickname "The Brat." Stanky was the starting second baseman from the day he arrived in Brooklyn until he was traded to the Braves at the end of the 1947 season to allow Jackie Robinson to move from first base to second. While with the Dodgers, Stanky led the NL in walks twice, on-base percentage once, and runs scored once.

JUNE 14   The Dodgers release Johnny Cooney and Lloyd Waner.

JUNE 15   Hal Gregg walks 11 batters in five innings during a 9–2 loss to the Giants in New York.

JUNE 17   The Dodgers score four runs in the ninth inning to defeat the Phillies 4–3 in
                 Philadelphia. Up until the ninth inning, Bill Lee had allowed the Dodgers only one
                 hit, a single to lead-off batter French Bordagaray in the first inning. In the ninth,
                 Bordagaray drove in the first run with a single. Augie Galan brought two across the
                 plate with a double. Mickey Owen drove in the winning run with a single. Eddie
                 Miksis made his major league debut at the age of 17 years, 280 days as a substitute
                 shortstop in the ninth inning.

                 *Although a utility player through most of his career, Miksis lasted in the majors
                 until 1958. He played for the Dodgers until 1951.*

JUNE 18   The Dodgers use three teenage pitchers during a 6–2 loss to the Phillies in the
                 second game of a double-header in Philadelphia. The trio consisted of 18-year-old
                 Cal McLish, 18-year-old Ralph Branca, 17-year-old Charlie Osgood. Brooklyn won
                 the first game 7–3.

                 *McLish's given name was Calvin Coolidge Julius Caesar Tuskahoma McLish.
                 He was 3–10 with the Dodgers in 1944 before serving in France with the Army
                 in 1945. McLish bounced around the majors and minors for more than a decade
                 before finding some success with the Indians during the late-1950s. He ended his
                 big league career in 1964 with a record of 92–92. Branca will always be known
                 for the fateful pitch he threw to Bobby Thomson (see October 3, 1951), but few
                 remember his record as a young phenom when he won 21 games as a 21-year-
                 old in 1947. The June 18, 1944, contest was the only one that Osgood played as
                 a major leaguer. He was 17 years and 208 days of age on that date.*

JUNE 23   Ed Head pitches a two-hitter to defeat the Phillies 2–0 at Ebbets Field. Both
                 Philadelphia hits were delivered Charlie Letchas with a single in the third inning
                 and a double in the eighth.

JUNE 25   The Dodgers sweep the Phillies 4–1 and 2–1. The second contest went ten innings.

                 *The twin victories represented the peak of the season. The Dodgers were 33–30,
                 but lost 30 of their next 34 games, including a club-record 16-game losing streak.*

JUNE 26   Over 50,000 turn out at the Polo Grounds to watch a three-cornered, nine-inning
                 exhibition game between the Dodgers, Giants and Yankees. The proceeds helped
                 raise money for wartime charities. Each team batted in six innings and took the field
                 in six others. The Dodgers scored five runs, the Yankees one, and the Giants none.

JULY 11   Dixie Walker collects two hits in four at-bats and Augie Galan drives in a run with a
                 single during the National League's 7–1 victory in the All-Star Game at Forbes Field
                 in Pittsburgh.

JULY 16   The Dodgers lose their 16th consecutive game by dropping an 8–4 decision to the
                 Braves in the first game of a double-header in Boston. The streak was shattered with
                 an 8–5 triumph in the nightcap.

JULY 24   Trailing 7–3, the Dodgers break loose with nine runs in the seventh inning to defeat the Pirates 12–7 in Pittsburgh.

JULY 30   Tommy Warren is both the winning and losing pitcher in a double-header against the Cardinals at Ebbets Field. Warren pitched a complete game in the opener, a 10–4 victory. In the second tilt, he hurled the last 2²/₃ innings in relief and allowed two runs in the 11th for a 9–7 defeat.

               Warren served in the Army during World War II. He was honorably discharged after being wounded in a battle in Casablanca, Morocco.

AUGUST 3   At the age of 16 years and 241 days, Tommy Brown becomes the youngest player in Dodgers history by starting at shortstop in both games of a double-header against the Cubs at Ebbets Field. Brown collected a double and single in eight at-bats. The Dodgers lost both games 6–2 and 7–1.

               Brown played for the Dodgers until 1951 and lasted in the majors until 1953. He played in his last big league game at the age of 25.

AUGUST 4   Ben Chapman returns to the majors as a pitcher and hurls a complete game to defeat the Braves 9–4 at Ebbets Field.

               Chapman was an outfielder with five different American League clubs from 1930 through 1941 and played in four All-Star Games. With the wartime manpower shortage, Chapman went back to the minors to become a pitcher. He was 8–6 with a 4.26 ERA in two seasons with the Dodgers.

AUGUST 6   The Braves score 10 runs in the seventh inning and beat the Dodgers 14–2 in the first game of a double-header at Ebbets Field. Boston also won the second tilt 8–7.

SEPTEMBER 1   A week after Allied troops liberate Paris, the Dodgers beat the Giants 8–1 at Ebbets Field, as New York's Joe Medwick is hit on the elbow and leaves the game for treatment. Leo Durocher allowed Medwick to re-enter the contest if the Dodger manager could pick the pinch-runner for Medwick. Durocher selected slow-footed, 38-year-old catcher Gus Mancuso, who was promptly erased on a double play.

               On the same day, the Dodgers released Paul Waner.

SEPTEMBER 2   Dixie Walker hits for the cycle during an 8–4 triumph over the Giants at Ebbets Field. Walker singled in the first inning and homered in the second off Bill Voiselle, and tripled in the fourth and doubled in the sixth facing Ace Adams.

SEPTEMBER 4   Frank Wurm, a 20-year-old Dodgers pitcher, has a rocky outing in what proves to be his only big league appearance. Given the starting assignment against the Braves in the second game of a double-header in Boston, Wurm walked five of the seven batters he faced and gave up a hit while retiring only one. The Dodgers rallied to win 6–4. Brooklyn also took the opener 4–1.

SEPTEMBER 15   The sun is shining in Boston, but the game between the Dodgers and Braves is postponed by a hurricane. The two clubs left Brooklyn when the storm struck the New York and Connecticut coasts. The train carrying the teams was stranded because the track was washed out between Mystic, Connecticut, and Westerly, Rhode Island. Store windows were shattered and the subways flooded in New York City.

SEPTEMBER 23   The Dodgers score seven runs in the fifth inning and defeat the Cubs 12–3 at Ebbets Field.

OCTOBER 21   Franklin Roosevelt stages a campaign rally at Ebbets Field before a crowd of 10,000. Two weeks later, Roosevelt won his fourth term as president by defeating Thomas Dewey.

NOVEMBER 1   Branch Rickey, Walter O'Malley and Andrew Schmitz combine their resources to purchase 25 percent of the Dodgers stock controlled by the estate of Ed McKeever, who died in 1944. The purchase price was estimated at $250,000. Rickey was hired by the club as president and general manager in October 1942. A native of Brooklyn, O'Malley was a 41-year-old attorney who had been employed to handle the legal affairs of the club. Schmitz was an insurance executive who grew up in Brooklyn and lived on Long Island. The estate of Charles Ebbets, who died in 1925, still controlled 50 percent of the club. Dearie Mulvey, McKeever's daughter, held the other 25 percent. Less than a year later, Rickey and O'Malley would increase their holdings (see August 13, 1945).

1945
LA

Season in a Sentence

With the best offense in the league, the Dodgers win 11 games in a row in May and hold a 4½-game lead in July before a second half nose-dive.

Finish • Won • Lost • Pct • GB

Third   87   67   .565   11.0

Manager

Leo Durocher

Stats

Stats	Dods	NL	Rank
Batting Avg:	.271	.265	3
On-Base Pct:	.349	.333	1
Slugging Pct:	.376	.364	3
Home Runs:	57		5 (tie)
Stolen Bases	75		3
ERA:	3.70	3.80	3
Fielding Avg:	.962	.971	7
Runs Scored:	795		1
Runs Allowed:	724		6

Starting Lineup

Mike Sandlock, c
Augie Galan, 1b-lf-3b
Eddie Stanky, 2b
Frenchy Bordagaray, 3b
Eddie Basinski, ss
Luis Olmo, lf
Goody Rosen, cf
Dixie Walker, rf
Ed Stevens, 1b

Pitchers

Hal Gregg, sp
Vic Lombardi, sp-rp
Curt Davis, sp
Tom Seats, sp-rp
Art Herring, sp-rp
Ralph Branca, sp
Clyde King, rp
Cy Buker, rp

Attendance

1,059,220 (first in NL)

Club Leaders

Batting Avg:	Goody Rosen	.325
On-Base Pct:	Augie Galan	.423
Slugging Pct:	Luis Olmo	.462
Home Runs:	Goody Rosen	12
RBIs:	Dixie Walker	124
Runs:	Goody Rosen	126
Stolen Bases:	Luis Olmo	15
Wins:	Hal Gregg	18
Strikeouts:	Hal Gregg	139
ERA:	Vic Lombardi	3.31
Saves:	Cy Buker	5

MARCH 28   The Dodgers sell Whit Wyatt to the Phillies.

APRIL 17   Five days after the death of Franklin Roosevelt, the Dodgers win 8–2 before an Opening Day crowd of 9,585 at Ebbets Field. Curt Davis, who was 41 years old, pitched a complete game and hit a two-run homer. Mike Sandlock contributed three RBIs. Playing in his first game since 1943, Leo Durocher started at second base and drove in two runs. Durocher appeared in only one more game before ending his playing career.

With Harry Truman succeeding Franklin Roosevelt as president, the war in Europe was winding to a close, but the conflict with Japan had no end in sight. The country was well into its fourth year of war, and everyone in the Ebbets Field grandstand could claim a loved one, friend, or neighbor who had been, or were currently, involved in fighting somewhere in the world. While the 1945 opener was taking place, U.S. forces were involved in a deadly struggle to capture Okinawa. Dodgers players who entered military service between the 1944 and 1945 seasons were Rube Melton, Cal McLish, Bobby Bragan and Eddie Miksis. Mickey Owen joined the service after the season began.

APRIL 19   Hal Gregg pitches a two-hitter to defeat the Phillies 3–1 at Ebbets Field. The only Philadelphia hits were singles by Rene Monteagudo and Jimmy Wasdell.

Gregg had a record of 18–13 and an ERA of 3.47 in 1945.

APRIL 21   Erv Palica makes his major league debut at the age of 17 years, 71 days as a pinch-runner during a 3–2 loss to the Giants in New York.

Palica played in two games in 1945, both as a pinch-runner. He was converted from an infielder to a pitcher in the minors in 1946, and played again for the Dodgers as a hurler from 1947 through 1954. Palica's given name was Ervin Pavliecivich.

APRIL 28   The Dodgers score three runs in the ninth inning and beat the Giants 4–3 at Ebbets Field. Four walks forced in one run and loaded the bases for Goody Rosen, who singled in the tying and winning runs.

Rosen hit .325 with 12 homers and 126 runs scored in 1945.

MAY 5   The Dodgers sweep the Phillies 10–1 and 12–8 at Shibe Park. Philadelphia made things interesting in the second tilt by scoring seven runs in the ninth inning. Dixie Walker collected six hits in seven at-bats, scored six runs, and drove in four during the twinbill.

Walker led the league in RBIs in 1945 with 124 despite hitting only eight homers. He also batted .300, scored 102 runs and collected 182 hits and 42 doubles.

MAY 6   The day before Germany surrenders to end the European phase of the war, the Dodgers sweep the Phillies for the second day in a row with 7–5 and 10–7 decisions in Philadelphia. Luis Olmo collected eight hits, including a homer and two doubles, in nine at-bats during the twinbill. He also drove in eight runs, six of them in the second tilt.

Olmo batted .313 with ten homers, 110 RBIs and a league-leading 13 triples in 1945.

MAY 16   The Dodgers extend their winning streak to 11 games with a 3–1 decision over the Pirates at Ebbets Field. Brooklyn's record was 16–6.

MAY 18   Luis Olmo drives in seven runs on a grand slam and a bases-loaded triple during a 15–12 win over the Cubs at Ebbets Field. The slam was struck in the first inning and the triple in the fifth. Ray Prim was the victim of both blows.

MAY 25   The Dodgers pitcher and catcher are both over 40 during a 9–7 loss to the Cardinals in St. Louis. Curt Davis, age 41, pitched 7^2/$_3$ innings of relief. Clyde Sukeforth, 43, caught the entire game.

MAY 26   Luis Olmo hits a grand slam off Blix Donnelly in the fourth inning of an 11–2 win over the Cardinals in St. Louis.

MAY 30   The Dodgers lose 13–5 and win 14–10 in a high-scoring Memorial Day double-header against the Pirates in Pittsburgh.

JUNE 5   A three-run homer by Goody Rosen in the 14th inning beats the Giants 6–3 in New York. A two-run pinch-single by Ben Chapman in the ninth inning sent the game into extra innings.

JUNE 7   The Dodgers commit eight errors and lose 10–5 to the Giants in New York.

JUNE 10   Leo Durocher is arrested after being accused of striking a fan following an 8–7 win over the Phillies at Ebbets Field.

The fan who filed the complaint was 21-year-old John Christian, a war veteran and Brooklyn resident. According to Christian, Durocher beat him in reaction to Christian's heckling during the game. The complaint claimed that John Moore, a 50-year-old special policeman working at the ballpark, requested that Christian go to the Dodgers clubhouse. Christian told police he was struck with a blunt instrument by both Moore and Durocher. Christian was treated at the hospital with a broken jaw and other injuries. Durocher was acquitted in a trial on April 25, 1946. The jury deliberated only 38 minutes before issuing the verdict of innocence. Eventually, Christian was paid $6,750 by the Dodgers for his injuries following a civil suit.

JUNE 15   The Dodgers trade Ben Chapman to the Phillies for Johnny Peacock.

JUNE 23   Two days after Japan surrenders Okinawa to U.S. Forces, the Dodgers outlast the Braves 14–12 at Ebbets Field. Brooklyn scored five runs in the seventh inning to take a 10–7 lead.

JUNE 24   The Dodgers extend their winning streak to eight games with a 9–6 decision over the Braves in the first game of a double-header at Ebbets Field. The Dodgers lost the second contest, highlighted by a fistfight, 3–1. The fight flared suddenly in the eighth inning. Covering the plate, Braves pitcher Ewald Pyle tried to trip Eddie Stanky as the Dodger second baseman was crossing the plate. Dixie Walker threw Pyle to the ground and began pummeling him with his fists. Walker and Pyle were both ejected.

JUNE 29   Three days after the signing of the United Nations charter, the Dodgers score three
           runs in the ninth inning to defeat the Cubs 5–4 in the first game of a double-header
           at Ebbets Field. The runs were driven in by singles from Goody Rosen, Dixie Walker
           and Luis Olmo. Chicago won game two 3–1.

JULY 1   The Dodgers take a 4½-game lead on the second-place Cardinals after splitting a
           double-header with the Pirates at Forbes Field. Pittsburgh won the first game 4–3 and
           Brooklyn the second 4–2.

           *The Dodgers record was 41–25. The club tumbled out of first place seven days
           later and limped to third place, 11 games behind by the end of the season.*

JULY 2   The Dodgers endure a harrowing plane trip following an exhibition game against a
           squad of Marines in Cherry Point, North Carolina. The Navy transport plane ran
           into a bad storm and the pilot lost radio contact. They finally landed in Norfolk,
           Virginia, when the plane had only 30 minutes of fuel remaining.

JULY 8   Dixie Walker hits a grand slam off Ken Burkhardt in the first inning, but the Dodgers
           lose 6–4 to the Cardinals in the second game of a double-header at Ebbets Field. The
           Cards won the opener by the same 6–4 score.

           *In the opener, Babe Herman played in his first major league game since 1937.
           He was 42 years old in 1945 when the Dodgers signed him after playing with
           the Hollywood Stars in the Pacific Coast League. Known for his legendary base
           running mistakes while a Dodger from 1926 through 1931, Herman didn't
           disappoint in the July 8 game against the Cardinals. First, he broke his bat fouling
           off his first pitch, and in throwing the bat away, endangered several fans when it
           glanced off the box seats. Then after hitting a single, Herman fell rounding first and
           had to crawl on all fours to get back to the bag safely. Playing almost exclusively as
           a pinch-hitter, Herman hit .265 in 34 at-bats in his wartime comeback.*

JULY 29   The day after the Empire State Building in New York City is accidentally struck by
           an Army B-25 bomber, killing 13, the Dodgers sweep the Braves 5–2 and 15–4 at
           Ebbets Field. In the second tilt, the Dodgers scored nine runs in the fourth inning.
           It was called after eight innings by darkness. Augie Galan drove in eight runs during
           the twin bill on a homer, double and three singles.

           Galan hit .307 with nine homers and 114 runs scored in 1945.

AUGUST 3   Hal Gregg pitches a one-hitter to defeat the Braves 5–1 in the first game of a double-
           header in Boston. The only hit off Gregg was a single by Joe Medwick in the eighth
           inning. The Braves won the second game 5–3.

           *Eddie Basinski was a wartime fill-in as a shortstop for the Dodgers while
           Pee We Reese was in the service. In the off-season, Basinki was a violinist
           with the Buffalo Philharmonic.*

AUGUST 8   Two days after an atom bomb is dropped on Hiroshima, Japan, Dixie Walker hits
           a homer off Vern Kennedy in the seventh inning for the lone run of a 1–0 win over
           the Reds at Ebbets Field. The drive barely cleared the right field screen. Hal Gregg
           pitched the shutout.

AUGUST 13   Branch Rickey, Walter O'Malley and John L. Smith join together to purchase
               50 percent of the stock in the Dodgers. Combined with the 25 percent share bought
               earlier (see November 1, 1944), Rickey and O'Malley had a controlling interest
               in the franchise. Smith was the president of a drug company that manufactured
               penicillin. The trio purchased the stock held by the estate of Charles Ebbets, who
               died in 1925, for $750,000. Smith later bought the small portion of stock owned
               by Andrew Schmidt. At the end of 1945, Rickey, O'Malley and Smith each held
               25 percent of the stock. The other 25 percent was in the hands of Dearie McKeever
               Mulvey, the daughter of the late Ed McKeever. Her husband, James Mulvey, was
               second on the club organization chart as vice-president.

AUGUST 15   The day after Japan surrenders, ending World War II, the Cubs wallop the Dodgers
               20–6 at Ebbets Field.

AUGUST 17   A controversial decision by umpire Tom Dunn at the end of a 4–3 loss to the Cubs
               results in a riot at Ebbets Field. Dunn called Dixie Walker out on a close play at first
               base to end a two-run Brooklyn rally. A barrage of bottles were thrown on the field,
               and Dunn soon found himself surrounded by hundreds of fans and a dozen Dodgers.
               It took several minutes for Dunn, with the help of police, to extricate himself from
               the situation.

AUGUST 20   At 17, Tommy Brown becomes the youngest player in major league history to hit a
               home run. It was struck off Preacher Roe of the Pirates and was the only Dodger run
               in an 11–1 loss at Ebbets Field.

AUGUST 25   The Dodgers sweep the Giants 8–6 and 13–3 at Ebbets Field.

SEPTEMBER 6   Ralph Branca walks 10 batters in six innings during a 5–4 loss to the Giants
               in New York.

SEPTEMBER 15   A two-run homer by Goody Rosen in the tenth inning beats the Pirates 5–3
               in Pittsburgh.

               *The Dodgers were involved in a train wreck on the way to Pittsburgh at
               6:30 a.m. Traveling from St. Louis, the train struck a gasoline truck. The
               explosion blanketed the entire train in a sheet of flame, with the intense heat
               shattering windows. The engineer was killed and the fireman badly burned.
               Other than a few bruises, no one in the Dodger entourage was hurt.*

SEPTEMBER 21   The Dodgers swamp the Phillies 1–0 and 11–5 in a double-header in Philadelphia.
               Ralph Branca (eight innings) and Cy Buker (one inning) combined on the shutout.
               The lone run scored in the ninth inning on a pinch-single by Frenchy Bordagaray,
               who was batting for Branca. Tommy Brown hit three triples in the twin bill, two of
               them in the second game.

               *The Dodgers defeated the Phillies in 15 consecutive games in 1945, and won 19
               and lost three overall. From 1939 through 1946, the Dodgers amassed a record
               of 139–36 against the Phils, a winning percentage of .794.*

SEPTEMBER 23   Hal Gregg pitches a one-hitter to defeat the Phillies 9–0 in the first game of a double-
               header at Shibe park. The only Philadelphia hit was a single by Rene Monteagudo

in the second inning. Eddie Stanky just missed the ball before it went into right field. The Dodgers lost the second contest 4–3.

> *Stanky hit only .258 in 1945, but had an on-base percentage of .417 and led the National League in walks (148) and runs scored (128). The walks figure is a club record. Stanky also has the second most base on balls in Dodgers history with 137 in 1946.*

SEPTEMBER 25   Goody Rosen hits a three-run homer in the ninth inning to defeat the Giants 7–4 in New York.

OCTOBER 23   Branch Rickey announces the signing of Jackie Robinson to become the first African-American in Organized Baseball in more than 50 years.

> *Until the signing of Robinson by the Dodgers, baseball, like much of American society, was rigidly segregated. There had been no African-Americans in the major or minor leagues since the 1880s. Some of the greatest players in baseball history competed in the Negro Leagues, but they were unable to break the cycle of racism that would permit them to test their skills against their Caucasian counterparts, except in exhibition games in which all-white teams were matched up against all-black teams. The Negro Leagues were virtually ignored by the mainstream press. Robinson had played second base and shortstop for the Kansas City Monarchs, one of the best clubs in the Negro Leagues, in 1945. Prior to that, he served in the Army as a lieutenant during World War II and excelled in baseball, football, basketball and track at UCLA. Born in Cairo, Georgia, and raised in Pasadena, California, Robinson was 26 years old at the time he was signed by the Dodgers. He was selected after a three-year search by Dodgers scouts to determine the individual who would be able to withstand the pressure of being the first African-American in the majors since 1884. Robinson was chosen not only because of his athletic ability, but as a result of his intelligence, college education, military background, family values and demeanor. He had also played on integrated teams as a youngster in California and in college. Robinson would have to endure the racist insults hurled his way from fans, opposing players, and even teammates, without reacting aggressively, either physically or verbally. At the same time, he had to exhibit a fierce competitiveness to excel on the field. In short, Robinson would have to bring new meaning to the phrase "turn the other cheek" with the nearly impossible task of walking a tightrope between assertiveness and acquiescence.*
> *If Robinson failed in any way, those who wanted to keep African-Americans out of Organized Baseball could claim their justifications for taking such actions were correct. Branch Rickey acknowledged the criticism he would face by undertaking the momentous step of breaking baseball's color barrier but was willing to take the risk and put his career on the line. For his part, Rickey foresaw the abuse Robinson would encounter and informed him in graphic detail what he was up against both on and off the field. "I have never meant to be a crusader," Rickey told the media after the signing of Robinson, "and I hope I won't be regarded as one. My purpose is to be fair to all people, and my selfish objective is to win baseball games." Robinson played with the Montreal Royals of the International League, a top Dodgers farm club, in 1946. After a year in Montreal, he joined the Dodgers in 1947.*

1946

Season in a Sentence

With the war over, the veterans return and the Dodgers squander a seven-game lead in July before losing a post-season series to the Cardinals to decide the NL champion.

Finish • Won • Lost • Pct • GB

Second   96   60   .615   2.0

Manager

Leo Durocher

Stats

Stats	Dods	NL	Rank
Batting Avg:	.260	.256	3
On-Base Pct:	.348	.329	1
Slugging Pct:	.361	.355	3
Home Runs:	55		7
Stolen Bases:	100		1
ERA:	3.05	3.41	2
Fielding Avg:	.972	.974	6
Runs Scored:	701		2
Runs Allowed:	570		2

Starting Lineup

Bruce Edwards, c
Ed Stevens, 1b
Eddie Stanky, 2b
Cookie Lavagetto, 3b
Pee Wee Reese, ss
Pete Reiser, lf
Carl Furillo, cf
Dixie Walker, rf
Augie Galan, lf
Dick Whitman, cf-lf
Howie Schultz, 1b

Pitchers

Kirby Higbe, sp-rp
Joe Hatten, sp
Vic Lombardi, sp-rp
Hal Gregg, sp-rp
Rube Melton, sp-rp
Hugh Casey, rp
Hank Behrman, rp
Art Herring, rp

Attendance

1,796,824 (first in NL)

Club Leaders

Batting Avg:	Dixie Walker	.319
On-Base Pct:	Eddie Stanky	.436
Slugging Pct:	Dixie Walker	.448
Home Runs:	Pete Reiser	11
RBIs:	Dixie Walker	116
Runs:	Eddie Stanky	98
Stolen Bases:	Pete Reiser	34
Wins:	Kirby Higbe	17
Strikeouts:	Kirby Higbe	134
ERA:	Joe Hatten	2.84
Saves:	Hugh Casey	5
	Art Herring	5

FEBRUARY 11   The Dodgers open training camp in Daytona Beach, Florida, the first held in peacetime in five years.

The 1946 major league training camps were unique as returning war veterans competed with wartime fill-ins for spots on the roster. The Dodgers spring training roster included 27 players who had spent all or most of the 1945 season in the service. Among those returning from military obligations were Pee Wee Reese, Pete Reiser, Kirby Higbe, Hugh Casey, Billy Herman and Cookie Lavagetto. They joined 1945 holdovers including Dixie Walker, Vic Lombardi, Hal Gregg and Augie Galan, along with rookies Carl Furillo, Bruce Edwards, Hank Behrman and Joe Hatten to form the nucleus of the 1946 squad.

FEBRUARY 18   Luis Olmo signs with the Mexican League.

The Mexican League was controlled by five Pasquel brothers who belonged to one of Mexico's richest and most powerful families. Jorge Pasquel was the one determined to upgrade Mexican baseball and create a third major league by attracting big leaguers with offers of much higher salaries than they were being paid in the States. In all, the brothers persuaded 18 players to take their offer. Besides Olmo, the Pasquels signed Mickey Owen, who was Brooklyn's starting catcher from 1941 through 1945. All of those who jumped to Mexico were suspended for five years by commissioner Happy Chandler. The Mexican League was a financial and artistic failure, however, and most of the players who went south of the border soon regretted the decision. Much of the promised money never materialized, and living and playing conditions were often primitive compared to major league standards. Chandler lifted the suspensions in 1949. Olmo returned to the Dodgers. With Roy Campanella firmly entrenched as the Dodgers catcher, Owen was sold to the Cubs.

MARCH 18   The Dodgers release French Bordagaray.

APRIL 16   The Dodgers open the first post-Word War II season with a 5–3 loss to the Braves in Boston. Billy Herman, in his first major league game since 1943, contributed four singles and drove in two runs. Carl Furillo made his major league debut. Playing center field, Furillo collected two singles in four at-bats. Hal Gregg was the starting and losing pitcher.

APRIL 18   The Dodgers win their home opener 8–1 against the Giants before 29,825 at Ebbets Field. Vic Lombardi pitched the complete game.

On the same day, Jackie Robinson made his debut in Organized Baseball. He collected a home run and three singles in four at-bats in leading Montreal to a 14–1 win over Jersey City just across the Hudson River from Brooklyn at Roosevelt Field. Two of the singles came on bunts. Robinson also stole two bases and scored four runs. In the fifth inning, Robinson singled, stole second, reached third on an infield out, and scored by coaxing the pitcher into a balk by dashing toward home plate and stopping halfway. Robinson's debut was covered by most of the major news organizations and publications. During the 1946 season, he arguably underwent more media scrutiny than any minor leaguer in history, with the possible exception of Michael Jordan in 1994. By the end of the season, Robinson led the International League in batting average (.349), on-base percentage (.468), and runs (113), and ranked second in walks (92), second in stolen bases (27) and fifth in hits (155). He also had the highest fielding percentage and the most double plays of any second baseman. Montreal had a record of 100–54 and won the International League pennant by 18½ games.

APRIL 22   The Dodgers score two runs in the ninth inning and one in the tenth to defeat the Braves 5–4 at Ebbets Field. The tying run in the ninth was scored by Otis Davis, who was making his only appearance in a big league game. Davis entered the contest as a pinch-runner for Eddie Stanky and crossed the plate on Pete Reiser's double. Billy Herman drove in the winning run with a single.

APRIL 23   In his first major league game since July 1944, Ed Head pitches a no-hitter to defeat the Braves 5–0 at Ebbets Field. Head served over a year in military service during World War II. He walked three and struck out two. Head started the ninth inning by walking Chuck Workman. Connie Ryan struck out, and Workman was retired on a quick throw from catcher Ferrell Anderson to first baseman Ed Stevens for a double play. The final out was recorded on a grounder by Johnny Hopp to second baseman Billy Herman.

The 1946 season was Head's last in the majors. He won only two more games following the no-hitter and finished the campaign with a 3–2 record and a 3.21 ERA. Head had a 27–23 record over five seasons in the majors.

APRIL 26   The Dodgers win their eighth game in a row with an 11–3 decision over the Giants in New York.

On the same day, the Dodgers sold Goody Rosen to the Giants.

MAY 1   The Dodgers release Curt Davis.

MAY 8   The Dodgers score four runs in the ninth inning and three in the tenth to stun the Reds 8–5 Crosley Field. With Cincinnati leading 5–2 with two out in the ninth, first baseman Bert Haas tripped over the bullpen mound and missed an easy foul fly by Eddie Stanky, who then walked to load the bases. Billy Herman's three-run double tied the score. In the tenth, pinch-hitter Don Padgett hit a three-run homer.

Stanky hit .273 and led the NL in walks (137) and on-base percentage (.436) in 1946.

MAY 11   Pete Reiser homers on the first pitch of the ninth inning to beat the Phillies 12–11 at Ebbets Field. At the end of the fourth inning, Philadelphia led 11–10. There was no more scoring until the Dodgers tied the contest in the eighth.

MAY 12   The Dodgers score seven runs in the second inning and whip the Phillies 13–4 at Ebbets Field.

MAY 15   A fight enlivens a 1–0 loss to the Cardinals at Ebbets Field. In the fifth inning, Enos Slaughter rolled a grounder down the first base line that was fielded by Dodgers pitcher Les Webber. The pair collided at the bag and came up swinging before players and umpires broke up the duel.

MAY 16   The Dodgers score seven runs in the sixth inning and clobber the Pirates 16–6 at Ebbets Field.

MAY 22   The Dodgers fight the Cubs and win 2–1 in 13 innings at Ebbets Field. Chicago's Lennie Merullo knocked down Eddie Stanky trying to break up a double play in the tenth. Stanky wrapped his legs around Merullo's neck in a scissors hold and both punched each other until the umpires and players intervened. During the brawl, Cubs pitcher Claude Passeau ripped the jersey of Leo Durocher.

MAY 23   This time, the Dodgers and Cubs fight before the game at Ebbets Field. During batting practice, Dixie Walker took exception to some remarks Lennie Merullo made to Pee Wee Reese. Walker wrestled Merullo to the ground. Phil Cavarretta came to the rescue and landed a few blows before a squad of police arrived and separated the players. Walker had one tooth knocked out and another one chipped. The Dodgers won the game 2–1 in 11 innings.

MAY 30   Bama Rowell of the Braves hits the clock above the scoreboard at Ebbets Field with a long drive during a 10–8 loss to the Braves in the second game of a double-header. The ball struck by Rowell shattered the glass on the clock, which rained down on right fielder Dixie Walker, and the ball stayed inside the clock. The play was ruled a double. An hour later, the clock stopped. The Dodgers won the opener 5–0.

The hit by Rowell was the inspiration of the scene in Brooklyn-native Bernard Malamud's 1952 book The Natural *and the 1984 movie version. The Bulova Company promised a free watch to anyone who hit the clock, but Rowell didn't receive his until 1985 in his hometown of Citronelle, Alabama.*

JUNE 2   The Dodgers win 1–0 in the second game of a double-header against the Reds in Cincinnati. Art Herring (five innings) and Hugh Casey (four innings) combined on the shutout. Herring had a no-hitter in progress when he left the game because his shoulder tightened. The lone run scored on a single by Dixie Walker in the first inning. The Dodgers also won the second game 2–1 in 11 innings.

Walker hit .319 with nine homers and 116 RBIs in 1946.

JUNE 6   The Dodgers break a 1–1 tie by scoring nine runs in the fifth inning and defeat the Pirates 13–8 in Pittsburgh.

JUNE 7   Claude Passeau of the Cubs not only shuts out the Dodgers, but hits a two-run, walk-off homer off Joe Hatten in the ninth inning for a 2–0 victory in Chicago.

JUNE 12   The Dodgers score four runs in the ninth inning to beat the Cardinals 10–7 in Sportsman's Park. Rex Barney had a no-hitter through six innings before St. Louis erupted for five runs in the seventh and took a 7–6 lead in the eighth. All four ninth-inning runs scored after two were out. Cookie Lavagetto drove in the tying run with a triple and scored on Pee Wee Reese's single.

Reese hit .284 with five home runs in 1946.

JUNE 15   The Dodgers trade Billy Herman to the Braves for Stew Hofferth.

JULY 2   The Dodgers win 3–2 over the Phillies at Ebbets Field to take a 7½-game lead over the Cardinals.

The win gave the Dodgers a 45–23 record. They lost 11 of the next 16 games, however, and the Cards tied them for the top spot in the National League on July 19. Brooklyn and St. Louis waged a neck-and-neck battle for the pennant from that point until the final day of the season.

JULY 5   Leo Durocher issues his famous quote on "nice guys" before a 7–6 loss to the Giants in New York.

After listening to a discourse from Durocher, Dodgers radio announcer Red Barber asked, "Why can't you be a nice guy?" Durocher responded, "Do you know a nicer guy in the world than (Giants manager) Mel Ott? Or any of the other Giants? Why they're the nicest guys in the world. And where are they? In last place." This quote morphed into the phrase "Nice guys finish last," which was the title of Durocher's 1975 autobiography.

JULY 21   The Dodgers sweep the Pirates 3–0 and 6–5 at Forbes Field. A fight in the seventh inning highlighted the second game. Pittsburgh third baseman Lee Handley and

Dodgers outfielder Dick Whitman threw punches and wrestled to the ground after Whitman was called out on a close play. Players from both teams swarmed onto the field. The umpires finally restored order after sending Handley and Whitman to the showers. Carl Furillo, who replaced Whitman, hit a two-run, inside-the-park homer in the ninth.

Nicknamed "The Reading Rifle" for his hometown in Pennsylvania and his strong throwing arm, Furillo spent 38 months in the service during World War II and fought the Japanese in bloody skirmishes in Guam and the Philippines. He was a Dodger during his entire major league career, which lasted from 1946 through 1960. Furillo played in six World Series, was named to two All-Star teams, and won a batting title. Among Dodgers, Furillo ranks eighth in games played (1,806), ninth in at-bats (6,378), fourth in runs batted in (1,056), fifth in doubles (324), seventh in home runs (192), seventh in hits (1,910), seventh in total bases (2,922) and eighth in runs (895).

AUGUST 1   While trying to catch a fly ball off the bat of Whitey Kurowski, Pete Reiser hits his head against the wall at Ebbets Field during a 3–1 win over the Cardinals at Ebbets Field. Reiser was knocked unconscious and carried off the field on a stretcher. He was back in action seven days later.

AUGUST 4   The Dodgers outlast the Reds 5–4 in 14 innings at Ebbets Field. The winning run came on a squeeze bunt by Pee Wee Reese that scored Howie Schultz from third base.

AUGUST 8   Pete Reiser hits a solo homer in the first inning and a two-run triple in the tenth to beat the Giants 3–1 in New York. It was Reiser's first game back since hitting the wall on August 1.

AUGUST 9   Kirby Higbe pitches the Dodgers to a 1–0 win over the Phillies in Philadelphia. Pete Reiser drove in the lone run with a single in the eighth inning.

Higbe was 17–8 with a 3.03 ERA in 1946.

AUGUST 10   The Dodgers win their 18th game in a row at Shibe Park by beating the Phillies 6–0. The victory gave the Dodgers a 2½-game lead in the pennant race. Brooklyn's last loss in Philadelphia was on September 10, 1944.

AUGUST 11   The Dodgers streak of 18 wins in a row in Philadelphia is shattered in a 7–6 and 6–4 double-header loss to the Phillies at Shibe Park. Leo Durocher and the entire Dodgers bench were ejected in the second game by umpire George Magerkurth. Philadelphia fans unleashed a bottle barrage in the ninth inning over a decision at home plate.

AUGUST 14   In the first separate-admission, day-night double-header at Ebbets Field, the Dodgers beat the Giants 8–4 and 2–1. Played on a Wednesday, the afternoon clash drew 26,970 and the night encounter 30,254.

AUGUST 15   Bruce Edwards ties a major league record for most assists by a catcher in an inning with three in the fourth during a 7–1 win over the Giants at Ebbets Field. Edwards threw out two batters on rollers in front of the plate and another on a dropped third strike.

AUGUST 28   The Dodgers drop out of first place with a 4–3 loss to the Cubs in Chicago.

AUGUST 31   A fight highlights a 2–1 loss to the Giants in New York. In the fifth, Goody Rosen of the Giants spiked second baseman Eddie Stanky sliding into the bag. Stanky pounced on Rosen and the two wallowed in the infield dirt for a full minute before umpires Jocko Conlan and Dusty Boggess, with the aid of practically the entire squads of both teams, were able to separate them. Stanky and Rosen were banished from the game.

The Dodgers were 56–22 at Ebbets Field in 1946 and 40–38 on the road.

SEPTEMBER 5   Vic Lombardi pitches the Dodgers to a 1–0 win over the Braves in Boston.

SEPTEMBER 7   Kirby Higbe hurls a one-hitter to defeat the Giants 4–1 at Ebbets Field. The only New York hit was a home run by Ernie Lombardi in the second inning which cleared the foul pole by only two feet.

SEPTEMBER 11   The Dodgers and Reds play a 19-inning scoreless tie at Ebbets Field, the longest 0–0 game in major league history. The contest was called by darkness before a decision could be reached. The game lasted four hours and 40 minutes. The Brooklyn pitchers were Hal Gregg (ten innings), Hugh Casey (five innings), Art Herring (three innings) and Hank Behrman (one inning). For Cincinnati, Johnny Vander Meer pitched the first 15 innings and fanned 14. Harry Gumbert hurled the final four frames for the Reds.

SEPTEMBER 12   The Dodgers lose 10–2 to the Cardinals at Ebbets Field to fall 2½ games back in the pennant race.

SEPTEMBER 14   Ralph Branca pitches a three-hit shutout to defeat the Cardinals 5–0 at Ebbets Field. Branca was supposed to be a "decoy." Leo Durocher planned to have Branca throw to only one batter, then leave for lefty Vic Lombardi to face the Cardinals predominately left-handed batting order. But impressed with Branca's stuff in retiring leadoff batter Red Schoendienst, Durocher decided against the plan and left Branca in the game.

The Dodgers drew a then-record 1,796,824 fans in 1946. The previous club high was 1,215,772 in 1941.

SEPTEMBER 15   The second game of a double-header against the Cubs is called when a swarm of gnats suddenly invade Ebbets Field in the top of the sixth inning with Brooklyn leading 2–0. Dodger hurler Kirby Higbe couldn't deliver a pitch because he was too busy slapping at the pesky insects. The umpires insisted that the game was called because of darkness, however, not because of the gnats. The Cubs won the first game 4–3 in ten innings.

SEPTEMBER 25   The Phillies score five runs in the ninth inning to stun the Dodgers 11–9 at Ebbets Field. Leo Durocher used eight pitchers in the contest. The loss left the Dodgers one game behind the Cardinals with three contests left on the schedule.

Before the game, Branch Rickey was presented with a cabin cruiser purchased with donations from players. The boat was driven through the center field gate on a truck trailer.

Leo Durocher and Branch Rickey clown during a happy moment in the 1940s, when the unlikely pair led the Dodgers to successful seasons.

SEPTEMBER 26   The Dodgers stay alive in the pennant race with an 8–2 win over the Phillies at Ebbets Field. The Dodgers tied a major league record by using four left fielders. Pete Reiser started but broke his ankle sliding back into first base. Dick Whitman, Joe Medwick and Augie Galan followed Reiser in left.

SEPTEMBER 27   The idle Dodgers tie for first place when the Cardinals lose 7–2 to the Cubs in St. Louis. Both Brooklyn and St. Louis had two games left to play.

SEPTEMBER 28   On the second-to-last day of the season, the Dodgers and Cardinals remain tied for first place after the Dodgers defeat the Braves 7–4 at Ebbets Field and the Cardinals win 4–1 over the Cubs in St. Louis.

SEPTEMBER 29   On the final day, the Dodgers and Cardinals both lose to remain tied for first place. The Dodgers fell 4–0 to the Braves at Ebbets Field. Mort Cooper pitched the shutout. The Cardinals dropped an 8–3 decision to the Cubs in St. Louis. The deadlock for first place forced a best-two-of-three playoff for a berth in the World Series. It was the first pennant playoff in major league history.

OCTOBER 1   The Dodgers lose the first game of the playoff series against the Cardinals by
              a 4–2 score in St. Louis. Ralph Branca was the starter and allowed three runs in
              2$^2/_3$ innings. Howie Schultz drove in both Brooklyn runs, one with a homer in
              the third.

OCTOBER 2   The Cardinals win the National League pennant by beating the Dodgers 8–4 before
              31,437 at Ebbets Field. The Dodgers took a 1–0 lead in the first inning, but St. Louis
              scored eight unanswered runs before the Dodgers added three tallies in the ninth.

              The Cardinals went on to defeat the Red Sox in seven games in the World Series.

NOVEMBER 7   The Dodgers announce that WCBS-TV will carry all of the club's home games on
              television in 1947. The first regular telecasts of Dodgers games were carried on
              WNBT-TV during the 1946 season. The policy of carrying all home games on TV
              continued until the Dodgers left Brooklyn following the 1957 season.

DECEMBER 4   The Dodgers trade Augie Galan to the Reds for Ed Heusser.

1947

L A

Season in a Sentence

In an eventful year, Jackie Robinson integrates baseball, Leo Durocher is suspended for the season, and the Dodgers lose a thrilling seven-game World Series to the Yankees.

Finish • Won • Lost • Pct • GB

First   94   60   .610   +5.0

World Series

The Dodgers lost to the New York Yankees four games to three.

Managers

Clyde Sukeforth (2–0) and Burt Shotton (92–60)

Stats

Stats	Dods	NL	Rank
Batting Avg:	.272	.265	2
On-Base Pct:	.364	.338	1
Slugging Pct:	.384	.390	5
Home Runs:	83		6
Stolen Bases:	88		1
ERA:	3.82	4.06	3
Fielding Avg:	.978	.976	2
Runs Scored:	774		3
Runs Allowed:	668		3

Starting Lineup

Bruce Edwards, c
Jackie Robinson, 1b
Eddie Stanky, 2b
Spider Jorgensen, 3b
Pee Wee Reese, ss
Pete Reiser, lf-cf
Carl Furillo, cf
Dixie Walker, rf

Pitchers

Ralph Branca, sp
Joe Hatten, sp
Vic Lombardi, sp-rp
Harry Taylor, sp-rp
Hugh Casey, rp
Hank Behrman, rp
Hal Gregg, rp-sp

Attendance

1,807,526 (first in NL)

Club Leaders

Batting Avg:	Dixie Walker	.306
On-Base Pct:	Dixie Walker	.415
Slugging Pct:	Carl Furillo	.437
Home Runs:	Jackie Robinson	12
	Pee Wee Reese	12
RBIs:	Dixie Walker	94
Runs:	Jackie Robinson	125
Stolen Bases:	Jackie Robinson	29
Wins:	Ralph Branca	21
Strikeouts:	Ralph Branca	148
ERA:	Ralph Branca	2.67
Saves:	Hugh Casey	18

JANUARY 21   Leo Durocher marries actress Larraine Day in El Paso, Texas. It was his third marriage and her second. The nuptials took place the day after Day was granted a divorce from airport executive J. Ray Hendricks. Day's decree prevented her from getting married in California for a year, so she got a divorce decreed in Juarez, Mexico. Durocher and Day then crossed the border for the wedding in El Paso. Angered over the union, the 125,000-member Catholic Youth Organization of Brooklyn ended his affiliation with the team's Knothole Club.

APRIL 9   Leo Durocher is suspended by Baseball Commissioner Happy Chandler for the entire 1947 season for "conduct detrimental to baseball."

The suspension was one of the most controversial ever delivered by any commissioner. The charges were vague and involved several incidents involving Durocher over the previous several years. Among them were his fight with

John Christian (see June 10, 1945), his marriage to Larraine Day (see January 21, 1947), and his friendship and association with individuals involved in illegal gambling activities. In a statement, Chandler said the suspension was due to an "accumulation of incidents" which were "construed as detrimental to baseball." The Dodgers named coach Clyde Sukeforth as interim manager to start the season.

APRIL 10   The Dodgers announce the purchase of Jackie Robinson from the Montreal Royals.

The promotion from the minors made Robinson the first African-American in the major leagues since 1884. The announcement came as no surprise. Both the Dodgers and Royals trained in Havana in 1947, with Robinson playing several games against the Dodgers as a first baseman. Robinson played shortstop in the Negro Leagues and second base at Montreal in 1946, but the Dodgers were well fortified at those positions with Pee Wee Reese and Eddie Stanky. The club had no established first baseman, hence the switch in positions. Several Dodgers players expressed dissatisfaction in having to play with Robinson, but Branch Rickey and Leo Durocher, prior to the latter's suspension, put down the rebellion by making it clear that Robinson would stay. Others were skeptical about Robinson's major league ability. Those concerns evaporated quickly. Robinson hit .297 with 12 homers in 1947, led the National League in stolen bases with 29 and ranked second in runs scored with 125.

APRIL 11   Jackie Robinson makes his debut in a Dodgers uniform during an exhibition game against the Yankees at Ebbets Field. Playing first base, Robinson was hitless in four at-bats during a 14–6 win.

Robinson was assigned uniform number 42. The only Dodger to previously wear the numeral was George Jeffcoat in 1939.

APRIL 15   Jackie Robinson makes his debut in a regular season major league game before an Opening Day crowd of 25,623 at Ebbets Field. Playing first base and batting second, Robinson was hitless in three at-bats during a 5–3 victory over the Braves before being lifted in the ninth inning for defensive purposes by

Jackie Robinson changed major league baseball forever by breaking the color barrier and went on to produce many great seasons for the Dodgers.

Howie Schultz. Facing Johnny Sain in his first plate appearance, Robinson received a rousing cheer from the crowd, then grounded out to third baseman Bob Elliott.

The National Football League was integrated for the first time in the modern era during the fall of 1946 when Kenny Washington and Woody Strode played for the Rams during the club's first season in Los Angeles. It would be 1950 before the National Basketball Association included African-Americans.

APRIL 17   Jackie Robinson collects his first hit, a bunt single in the fifth inning off Mort Cooper, during a 12–6 victory over the Braves at Ebbets Field. Spider Jorgensen drove in six runs on a homer and two doubles. Duke Snider made his big league debut in the contest, and collected a hit in two at-bats as a substitute left fielder.

Snider was 20-years-old in 1947 and spent much of the 1947 season in the minors. It would take until 1949 before he nailed down a starting job in the Brooklyn outfield.

APRIL 18   The Dodgers name 62-year-old Burt Shotton as manager to replace the suspended Leo Durocher (see April 9, 1947) and beat the Giants 10–4 in New York. Jackie Robinson hit his first major league homer, connecting off Dave Koslo.

A longtime confidante of Branch Rickey, Shotton played in the majors as an outfielder from 1909 through 1923. He previously managed the Phillies from 1928 through 1933. The Phils had only one winning season during his tenure, in 1932, but it was the only winning season for the franchise from 1918 through 1948. After leaving Philadelphia, Shotton managed in the minors and coached for the Indians from 1942 through 1945. At the time he was named manager of the Dodgers, Shotton was a scout for the club and supervised the minor league camp during spring training. His easygoing personality was a stark contrast to the hyperkinetic Durocher, but Shotton led the Dodgers to the World Series in 1947.

APRIL 22   Hal Gregg pitches a one-hitter to defeat the Phillies 1–0 at Ebbets Field. The only Philadelphia hit was a single by Del Ennis in the first inning. Gregg retired 20 in a row at one point. The lone run scored in the eighth inning when Jackie Robinson singled, stole second, and crossed the plate on a single by Dixie Walker.

During the series in Philadelphia, Jackie Robinson was subjected to a torrent of racially motivated insults and ethnic slurs from the Phillies, led by manager Ben Chapman. Commissioner Happy Chandler rebuked Chapman and told him to control his players and himself.

APRIL 27   A squeeze bunt by Eddie Stanky scores the winning run in the ninth inning to beat the Giants 9–8 at Ebbets Field.

APRIL 29   The Dodgers score seven runs in the eighth inning and defeat the Cubs 10–6 in Chicago.

MAY 3   The Dodgers send Kirby Higbe, Cal McLish, Gene Mauch, Hank Behrman and Dixie Howell to the Pirates for Al Gionfriddo and $100,000. The Dodgers brought Behrman back from Pittsburgh in an outright purchase on June 14.

MAY 8   The AP issues a story that claims the Cardinals threatened to strike over the prospect of playing against Jackie Robinson during a series in St. Louis, which began on May 6. According to the report, the strike was averted by the intervention of NL president Ford Frick and Cards owner Sam Breadon. Frick publicly threatened any player who refused to take the field with Robinson with an indefinite suspension. "I do not care if half the league strikes," said Frick. "Those who do will encounter swift retribution. All will be suspended. I don't care if it wrecks the National League for five years. This is the United States of America and one citizen has as much right to play as another." Breadon and Cards manager Eddie Dyer denied the report, however. A number of Cardinals insist to this day that there was never a strike threat. According to those on the club in 1947, there was grumbling about the integration of the sport among Cardinals players, but no more than any other club, including the Dodgers. Whether the threat of a strike was real, exaggerated, or non-existent, Frick's action was an important step because it gave Robinson the unequivocal support of baseball's hierarchy. Earlier, Commissioner Happy Chandler, a former governor of Kentucky, had made it clear that he would not tolerate any opposition to Robinson's presence on the Dodger roster.

MAY 17   After striking out during a 4–0 loss to the Pirates in Pittsburgh, Eddie Stanky throws his bat 80 feet. After the bat glanced off a box seat railing, Stanky was ejected by umpire Dusty Boggess.

             During the series in Pittsburgh, Jackie Robinson received some encouraging words from Pirates first baseman Hank Greenberg, who had himself been the target of bigots because of his Jewish heritage. "Stick in there," said Greenberg. "You're doing fine. Keep your chin up." Robinson afterward declared: "Class tells. It sticks out all over Mr. Greenberg."

MAY 28   Bruce Edwards drives in six runs on a homer, double and single during a 14–2 walloping of the Giants in New York.

             Standing five-foot-seven and weighing 185 pounds, Edwards hit .295 with eight home runs and made the All-Star team in 1947 in a season in which he turned 24 in July. It appeared as though he had a long career ahead of him, but during the following off-season he hurt his throwing arm while playing an exhibition game against inmates at Folsom Prison. In 1948, he lost his starting job to Roy Campanella and was a back-up for the remainder of his career.

JUNE 4   Pee Wee Reese hits a grand slam off Elmer Singleton in the second inning of a 9–4 win over the Pirates at Ebbets Field. The win was costly, however, because Pete Reiser hit his head against the wall while making a sensational catch of a drive off the bat of Culley Rikard. It was the third time that Reiser smacked his head against the outfield wall (see July 19, 1942 and August 1, 1946).

             Reese hit .284 with 12 homers and led the NL in walks with 104.

JUNE 5   Harry Taylor pitches a two-hitter to beat the Pirates 3–0 at Ebbets Field. Wally Westlake collected both Pittsburgh hits with a single and a triple.

             The Dodgers drew 1,807,526 fans, an increase over the 1946 record attendance of 1,796,824.

JUNE 15   The Dodgers fall three games behind in the NL pennant race with an 11–3 loss to the Cardinals at St. Louis. They were 27–25 and in fourth place.

JUNE 22   In the first game of a double-header in Cincinnati, the Dodgers break up Reds pitcher Ewell Blackwell's bid to pitch consecutive no-hitters. In his previous start on June 18, Blackwell no-hit the Braves. He held the Dodgers hitless until Eddie Stanky slashed a single up the middle with one out in the ninth. Blackwell missed fielding the grounder by inches. After retiring Al Gionfriddo, Blackwell allowed a single to Jackie Robinson before closing out a 4–0 win on a two-hitter. In the second tilt, Carl Furillo hit a grand slam in the fourth inning of a 9–8 Brooklyn victory.

JULY 2   The Dodgers break a scoreless tie with nine runs in the fourth inning and beat the Giants 11–3 at Ebbets Field.

JULY 3   The Giants pin a 19–2 loss on the Dodgers at Ebbets Field.

JULY 4   The Dodgers sweep the Giants 16–7 and 4–3 at Ebbets Field in a separate morning-afternoon double-header. The first contest began at 10:00 a.m. and was called by agreement at 1:06 p.m. at the end of the eighth inning to enable the crowd to leave the park and to permit holder of tickets for the second contest to enter. Jackie Robinson extended his hitting streak to 21 games in the opener and was hitless in four at-bats in the nightcap.

JULY 5   Larry Doby becomes the second African-African in the major leagues when he makes his debut with the Cleveland Indians.

           There were five African-American players in the majors in 1947. Besides Robinson and Doby, Willard Brown and Hank Thompson were signed by the St. Louis Browns later in July. Both were released by the Browns within a few weeks, however. The Dodgers added Dan Bankhead in August (see August 26, 1947).

JULY 6   The Dodgers take over first place with a 4–0 win over the Braves at Ebbets Field.

           The Dodgers remained in first for the rest of the 1947 season.

JULY 12   The Dodgers sweep the Cubs 7–2 and 6–5 at Ebbets Field. Brooklyn scored twice in the ninth inning to win the nightcap.

           Pee Wee Reese was tagged out on an unusual play during the twin bill. With Reese on first base, Dixie Walker missed a third strike and let the bat slip out of his hands. Reese stepped off the bag to retrieve the bat without calling time, and was retired on a throw from catcher Clyde McCullough to first baseman Eddie Waitkus.

JULY 18   Ralph Branca comes within six outs of a no-hitter and finishes with a one-hitter to win 7–0 over the Cardinals at Ebbets Field. The only St. Louis hit was a single by Enos Slaughter to start the eighth inning.

           Branca had a 21–12 record with a 2.67 earned run average and struck out 148 batters in 1947. He was only 21 in 1947 but never came close to reaching those numbers again as the 280 innings, 15 complete games and seven relief appearances in addition to a league-leading 36 starts may have caused too large of strain on him. He never won more than 14 games, made more than 28 starts, or pitched more than 215²/₃ innings in a season again, and had only 12 major league victories after celebrating his 26th birthday in 1952.

JULY 20   The Dodgers score three runs in the ninth inning to defeat the Cardinals 3–2 at Ebbets Field.

The game was later wiped off the books because of a protest by the Cardinals. In the ninth inning with two outs and two Cardinals on base, umpire Beans Reardon signaled that Ron Northey's long hit had gone into the stands for a home run, and the St. Louis outfielder slowed down to a jog on his trip around the bases. Northey arrived at the plate to find catcher Bruce Edwards waiting to tag him with ball in hand. The umpires conferred and ruled that the ball had struck the top of the wall and that Northey was out. After the game was over, the Cardinals filed a protest with NL president Ford Frick. After deliberation, Frick ruled the game should go into the books as a 3–3 tie and that Northey should be credited with a home run. The contest was replayed on August 18, with the Dodgers winning 12–3. The proceeds of the replayed game totaled $46,000 and went toward the erection of a memorial to World War II veterans in Brooklyn.

JULY 22   The Dodgers rout the Reds 12–1 in Cincinnati.

JULY 30   The Dodgers blow a ten-run lead, but beat the Cardinals 11–10 in ten innings in St. Louis. Brooklyn led 10–0 after four innings, and 10–4 heading into the ninth, when the Cardinals put together a furious six-run rally to send the contest into extra innings. In the tenth, Gene Hermanski doubled and Pee Wee Reese singled for the winning run. It was the Dodgers 12th win in a row.

JULY 31   The Dodgers extend their winning streak to 13 games with a 2–1 win over the Cardinals in St. Louis.

AUGUST 14   The Dodgers win 1–0 over the Braves at Ebbets Field. Carl Furillo drove in the lone run with a single in the eighth inning off Warren Spahn. Before the game, Furillo was presented with a new Buick convertible. Vic Lombardi pitched the shutout.

AUGUST 20   Ralph Branca holds the Cardinals hitless through seven innings and allows only one hit in 8²/₃, but the Dodgers lose 3–2 at Sportsman's Park. Branca was relieved by Hugh Casey with a runner on first base and two out in the ninth. Casey allowed two runs in the inning to allow St. Louis to tie the contest, then surrendered a walk-off homer in the 12th to Whitey Kurowski.

The game featured a controversial incident in which Enos Slaughter of the Cardinals spiked Jackie Robinson on a play at first base in the 11th inning. Brooklyn players believed that Slaughter spiked Robinson deliberately, and the accusations reached newspapers across the country the following day. As a result, Slaughter has been branded a racist by many historians. Slaughter and his teammates asserted that the spiking was accidental.

AUGUST 25   The Dodgers score seven runs in the second inning for a 7–0 lead and outlast the Pirates 11–10 at Ebbets Field. It was the Dodgers fifth in a row and gave the club a 6½-game lead in the NL race.

AUGUST 26   Dan Bankhead becomes the first African-American pitcher in major league history
             during a 16–3 loss to the Pirates at Ebbets Field. In his first plate appearance,
             Bankhead launched a home run, but was less than successful on the mound. In
             3⅓ innings of relief, he allowed eight runs and 10 hits.

             *Bankhead pitched in only four games in 1947, and after two seasons in the
             minors, returned to play for the Dodgers again in 1950 and 1951. His final big
             league record was 9–5, but his earned run average was 6.52 in 153⅓ innings.
             The home run he struck in his first plate appearance was his only one as a major
             leaguer in 45 at-bats.*

SEPTEMBER 11   Ralph Branca wins his 20th game of 1947 with a 4–3 decision over the Cardinals in
             St. Louis.

SEPTEMBER 14   The Dodgers sweep the Reds 13–2 and 6–3 in Cincinnati.

SEPTEMBER 18   The Dodgers win 7–6 over the Pirates in Pittsburgh to take a 10-game lead in the
             pennant race.

SEPTEMBER 22   The idle Dodgers clinch the NL pennant when the second-place Cardinals spilt a
             double-header against the Cubs in St. Louis.

             *The Dodgers met the Yankees in the World Series. Managed by Bucky Harris,
             the Yanks were 97–57 in 1947 and won the AL pennant by 12 games.*

SEPTEMBER 30   The Yankees open the 1947 World Series by defeating the Dodgers 5–3 before
             73,365 at Yankee Stadium. Ralph Branca retired the first 12 batters to face him, but
             allowed five runs in the fifth after the first five batters in the inning reached base on
             a single, a walk, a hit batsman, a double and another walk. The outburst gave New
             York a 5–1 lead. Playing first base and batting second, Jackie Robinson became the
             first African-American in World Series history. He was hitless in two official at-bats,
             drew two walks, and stole a base.

             *Starting pitching was a problem for the Dodgers during the seven-game 1947
             Fall Classic. Burt Shotton gave starting assignments to six different hurlers, who
             combined to last only 23⅓ innings and allowed 32 hits and 25 earned runs for
             an ERA of 9.94. The relievers kept the Dodgers in the Series, with an earned run
             average of 2.95. Hugh Casey led the way with one run allowed in 10⅓ innings
             over six games.*

OCTOBER 1   The Yankees win game two 10–3 at Yankee Stadium. After the Dodgers tied the
             score 2–2 in the top of the fourth inning, the Yankees scored eight unanswered runs
             by scoring in every inning from the fourth through the eighth. Dixie Walker homered
             in the losing cause.

             *The 1947 World Series was the first ever on television, but the microwave
             technology that transmitted the images from New York City was available to just
             four cities on the Eastern Seaboard. The only stations to telecast the Series were
             in New York, Philadelphia, Washington and Schenectady, New York. Only a
             small handful of individuals possessed televisions in their homes in 1947, as there
             were only 160,000 sets in operation nationwide. Most of those who watched*

the games on TV saw them in appliance stores selling the sets or in bars or lunch counters. The rights to the 1947 Series were sold for $65,000 to the Gillette Safety Razor Company and the Ford Motor Company. Liebmann Breweries offered $100,000 for the rights, but it was turned down by Commissioner Happy Chandler on the grounds that it wouldn't be good public relations for baseball to have the Series sponsored by an alcoholic beverage. By contrast, the radio rights went for $175,000.

OCTOBER 2   The Dodgers score six runs in the second inning for a 6–0 lead and outlast the Yankees 9–8 before 33,098 at Ebbets Field. Yogi Berra hit the first pinch-hit home run in World Series history in the seventh to cut the Brooklyn lead to a run, but Hugh Casey shut the door with 2⅔ innings of shutout relief.

OCTOBER 3   In one of the most thrilling games in World Series history, the Dodgers even the Series by taking game four 3–2 before 33,443 at Ebbets Field. Yankees pitcher Bill Bevens headed into the ninth inning with a no-hitter in progress and a 2–1 lead. The Dodgers scored in the fifth on two walks, a sacrifice and a fielder's choice. In the ninth, Carl Furillo walked with one out before Spider Jorgensen fouled out. Bevens was now one out from the first no-hitter in World Series history. Al Gionfriddo ran for Furillo and stole second. Pete Reiser was walked intentionally despite the fact that he represented the potential winning run. It was the tenth walk of the game for Bevens, which set a World Series record. Eddie Miksis ran for Reiser. Cookie Lavagetto pinch-hit for Eddie Stanky, and hit a double off the right field wall that scored Gionfriddo and Miksis with the tying and winning runs. With one pitch, Bevens lost his no-hitter and the game.

Bevens would make only one more appearance in a big league game, with 2⅔ innings of shutout relief in game seven. His near no-hitter followed a 1947 campaign in which he posted a 7–13 record. Bevens's final career record was 40–36. Likewise, Lavagetto would never play again after 1947. During the regular season, he hit .261 in 69 at-bats over 41 games. Lavagetto would later manage the Senators (1957–60) and Twins (1961–62). Gionffrido, who scored the tying run, also didn't play again after the 1947 Series. During the regular season, he played 37 games for the Dodgers and hit .177 in 62 at-bats. But he would have another big moment in the 1947 World Series two days later.

OCTOBER 4   The Yankees move within one game of a world championship by beating the Dodgers 2–1 before 34,379 at Ebbets Field. Spec Shea pitched a four-hitter for the Yanks. Pinch-hitter Cookie Lavagetto had a chance to be a hero for the second day in a row but struck out with a runner on first and two out in the ninth inning.

OCTOBER 5   The Dodgers force a seventh game by beating the Yankees 8–6 before 74,065 at Yankee Stadium. Brooklyn took a 4–0 lead in the top of the third inning, but the Yankees rebounded with four tallies in the bottom of the third and took a 5–4 advantage in the fourth. The Dodgers rebounded with four runs in the sixth. Pee Wee Reese broke the 6–6 tie with a two-run single. In the bottom of the sixth, the Yanks had two runners on base and two out when Joe DiMaggio slashed a drive to left field. Al Gionfriddo, who had just entered the game as a defensive replacement, took off with his back to the wall, twisted his glove out, and speared it just as he hit the bullpen fence 415 feet from home plate.

OCTOBER 6   The Yankees win the world championship by beating the Dodgers 5–2 at Yankee Stadium. New York took a 3–2 lead with two runs in the fourth inning. Joe Page prevented a Dodger comeback by pitching five innings of shutout relief in which he allowed only one hit.

DECEMBER 6   After being reinstated by commissioner Happy Chandler following his suspension (see April 9, 1947), Leo Durocher is hired as Dodgers manager for the 1948 season. Burt Shotton was retained by the Dodgers as a managerial consultant for the minor league system.

DECEMBER 8   The Dodgers trade Dixie Walker, Hal Gregg and Vince Lombardi to the Pirates for Preacher Roe, Billy Cox and Gene Mauch.

When Branch Rickey announced that Jackie Robinson would join the Dodgers, Walker challenged the decision by persuading other players to sign a petition stating they would refuse to play if Robinson was on the roster. An appeal by Leo Durocher quelled the revolt, but Walker asked to be traded. After playing with Robinson during the 1947 season, Walker regretted his action in opposing the integration of the club, and hit .306 in 148 games, but Rickey traded the outfielder anyway. It proved to be one of the greatest deals in Dodgers history. Despite the excellent season in 1947, Walker was 37 and near the end of the line. Roe and Cox were major contributors to the Dodgers success in the postwar decade. On Opening Day in 1948, Roe was a 33-year-old with a career record of 34–47. Developing a spitball helped turn around his career. In seven seasons with the Dodgers, Roe was 93–37. His winning percentage of .715 is the best in club history among pitchers with at least 100 decisions. Although a below average hitter, Cox was a brilliant defensive third baseman and played 742 games for the club over seven years from 1948 through 1954, although he played in more than 120 games in a single season only once. He had trouble staying healthy because of his slight frame (five-foot-ten and 150 pounds) and as a result of the after effects of his experiences as a solider in World War II while fighting in Sicily. Cox contracted malaria during the war and suffered from post-traumatic stress disorder.

1947

With the passage of time, it becomes more and more difficult for each succeeding generation to understand the impact of Jackie Robinson's entry into the major leagues, particularly in light of the election of Barack Obama as President of the United States. While racial issues were raised frequently during Obama's presidential campaign, America was a vastly different place when Robinson played his first season with the Dodgers. The following news items from 1947 help illustrate the rigid segregation and racism prevalent in the country at that time.

January 9
A basketball game between Duquense University and the University of Miami is canceled because of a law in Miami that prohibits whites and blacks from playing in the same athletic contest. Charles Cooper, an African-American, was a member of the Duquense team. Two weeks earlier, the University of Tennessee refused to meet Duquense in Knoxville after reaching the floor for a scheduled game because of Cooper's presence.

January 16
Clifford Adams, a member of the Cincinnati Lawyers Club, resigns in protest when the organization admits William McClain, an African-American. At the time, McClain was Cincinnati's assistant city solicitor.

February 17
Willie Earle, a 25-year-old African-American, is taken from the Pickens County jail in South Carolina and lynched by a mob. Earle died of knife and shotgun wounds. He had been arrested in connection with the murder of a 50-year-old cab driver. A total of 28 individuals were charged with either murder or conspiracy. All were acquitted in a jury trial in May.

February 28
The owner of a barbershop in Williamstown, Massachusetts, is fined $50 for charging an African-American student at Williams College three dollars for a one-dollar haircut. The barber said he charged the higher price because the student's hair was "unusually thick."

May 3
An all-night race riot at the Army disciplinary barracks in Ft. Leavenworth, Kansas, results in the death of one prisoner and injuries to six prisoners and five guards. The riot was the culmination of a long-smoldering resentment on the part of white men over being forced to eat in the same mess hall with African-American prisoners.

July 19
Elizabeth Ingalls is convicted of holding Dora Jones, her African-American maid, in slavery for 30 years in both Boston and San Diego. Ingalls was charged with keeping Jones in "harsh and unpaid servitude" as "atonement" for the maid's intimacy with Ingalls's first husband. Ingalls was given a suspended three-year sentence, placed on probation for five years, and ordered to pay Jones $6,000 in damages.

July 24
Harvey Jones, a 23-year-old African-American war veteran, is denied a new Cadillac won in a raffle conducted by the Ahoskie, North Carolina, Kiwanis Club on the grounds that blacks were not eligible. Jones was given a check for $3,200 instead.

August 11
A state law forbidding the marriage of individuals of different races is challenged before the California Supreme Court. The petition was filed after Sylvester S. Davis, Jr., an African-American, and Andrea Perez, who was white, were denied a marriage license in Los Angeles.

November 15
On a visit to Mobile, Alabama, James Routte, an African-American clergyman from New York City, reports he is treated like a "visiting dignitary" after donning a rented turban and speaking with a "slight Swedish accent." Routte had previously visited Mobile in 1943 and on that occasion had been "insulted and pushed around." The ruse of posing as a foreigner helped Routte receive service during his travels in the South, which was denied to every other person of his race born and raised in the United States. On the train, Routte was able to eat in dining cars reserved for whites. While in Mobile and Montgomery he ate in restaurants in which no African-Americans had ever been admitted. Routte asked the head waiter at one establishment what would happen if a black person came in to be served. Routte reported that the waiter told him that "no Negro would dare come in here to eat."

November 19
The Freedom Train is barred from Hattiesburg, Mississippi, unless racial segregation on the train is strictly enforced with whites and blacks occupying separate cars. The Freedom Train spent 18 months touring the country from 1947 through 1949 as a showcase for American democracy. It contained the original Declaration of Independence, the Constitution and the Bill of Rights.

November 28
The Lynn (Massachusetts) Classic High School football team is barred from playing a team from Miami in a game scheduled for Christmas Day at the Orange Bowl. The team had two African-American players and was prevented from playing at the event because of the racial strictures in Florida's largest city. "We don't play our boys against Negroes," said Orange Bowl director Robert Mulloy. "Lynn Classical has two so is definitely out."

1948

Season in a Sentence

The Dodgers stumble into last place in July, bring back Burt Shotton to replace Leo Durocher (who is immediately hired to manage the hated Giants), vault into first place in late-August, then fall back to third.

Finish • Won • Lost • Pct • GB

Third   84   70   .545   7.5

Managers

Leo Durocher (35–37), Ray Blades (1–0) and Burt Shotton (48–33)

Stats

Stats	Dods	NL	Rank
Batting Avg:	.261	.261	5
On-Base Pct:	.338	.333	3
Slugging Pct:	381	.383	4
Home Runs:	91		6 (tie)
Stolen Bases:	114		1
ERA:	3.75	3.95	2
Fielding Avg:	.973	.974	5
Runs Scored:	744		2
Runs Allowed:	667		3

Starting Lineup

Roy Campanella, c
Gil Hodges, 1b
Jackie Robinson, 2b
Billy Cox, 3b
Pee Wee Reese, ss
Marv Rackley, lf-cf
Carl Furillo, cf
Gene Hermanski, rf
Bruce Edwards, lf-c
Eddie Miksis, 3b

Pitchers

Rex Barney, sp
Ralph Branca, sp
Joe Hatten, sp
Preacher Roe, sp-rp
Hank Behrman, rp
Erv Palica, rp

Attendance

1,398,967 (fourth in NL)

Club Leaders

Batting Avg:	Jackie Robinson	.296
On-Base Pct:	Gene Hermanski	.391
Slugging Pct:	Gene Hermanski	.493
Home Runs:	Jackie Robinson	12
RBIs:	Jackie Robinson	85
Runs:	Jackie Robinson	108
Stolen Bases:	Pee Wee Reese	25
Wins:	Rex Barney	15
Strikeouts:	Rex Barney	138
ERA:	Preacher Roe	2.63
Saves:	Hank Behrman	7

JANUARY 6   The baseball Dodgers purchase the football Dodgers.

The football version of the Dodgers played in the NFL from 1930 through 1944 and in the All-American Football Conference beginning in 1946. Professional football had long been a losing proposition in Brooklyn, but Branch Rickey was convinced he could turn a profit. After a 2–12 season and meager crowds at Ebbets Field during the 1948 season, the football Dodgers disbanded.

MARCH 6   The Dodgers send Eddie Stanky to the Braves for Bama Rowell, Ray Sanders and $40,000.

Stanky was traded to allow Robinson to move from first base to second. Stanky was named to the All-Star team in 1948 and 1950 and played in the World Series for the Braves in 1948 and the Giants in 1951. Neither Sanders nor Rowell played a single game for the Dodgers.

MARCH 30   The Dodgers hold their first training session in Vero Beach, Florida. The club began spring training in 1948 in Ciudad Trujillo, Dominican Republic.

The Dodgers purchased an abandoned naval base in Vero Beach. The players slept in the barracks once used by World War II sailors. The site was acquired in part because of Jackie Robinson and the other African-Americans on the roster. The state of Florida was rigidly segregated, and by controlling the housing situation, the black and white players could stay at the same facility. Every other team training in Florida had to find separate quarters for their minority players until the early 1960s because players lived in private hotels that upheld the state's segregation statutes and traditions. Holman Stadium, where the Dodgers played their home spring training games in Vero Beach, was built in 1953. It was named for Bud Holman, a Vero Beach businessman and a Dodger stockholder. Holman Stadium was unique because it had no dugouts, just open-air benches. Until the early 1970s, there were no home run fences. Beyond the outfield were palm trees planted on a berm. The Vero Beach facility, which would become known as "Dodgertown," would be in use by the club until 2008. Beginning in 2009, the Dodgers trained in Glendale, Arizona.

APRIL 20   The Dodgers open the season with a 7–6 win over the Giants in New York. In his debut with the club, Billy Cox hit a two-run homer in the eighth to give the Dodgers the 7–6 lead. Rex Barney was the starting pitcher and went six innings. Gil Hodges was Brooklyn's starting catcher and was lifted for a pinch-hitter in the seventh inning. Roy Campanella, making his big league debut, caught the remainder of the game.

Soon afterward, Campanella was sent to the Dodgers minor league club in St. Paul in the American Association. He returned in July (see July 2, 1948) and Hodges moved to first base.

APRIL 23   The Dodgers lose the home opener 10–2 to the Phillies before 25,103 at Ebbets Field.

In part because of Pete Reiser's repeated collisions with fences, the Dodgers put rubber padding on the outfield walls at Ebbets Field in 1948.

APRIL 29   Six days after the Berlin airlift begins in Germany, the Dodgers collect 20 hits and clobber the Giants 17–7 at Ebbets Field. Preston Ward hit a grand slam off Thornton Lee in the second inning.

MAY 9   The Dodgers wallop the Pirates 14–2 in the first game of a double-header at Forbes Field. The Dodgers broke open a close game with five runs in the eighth inning and six in the ninth. Pee Wee Reese drove in six runs including a grand slam in the eighth. Pittsburgh won the second contest 10–8.

Reese hit .274, clubbed nine home runs, and scored 96 runs in 1948.

MAY 21   In his first game at Ebbets Field since his trade to the Pirates, Dixie Walker is presented with a new Ford prior to an 8–4 Pittsburgh victory. The automobile was paid for with donations from fans.

JUNE 4   Ralph Branca pitches the Dodgers to a 1–0 win over the Cardinals in St. Louis. Tommy Brown drove in the lone run with a sacrifice fly in the second inning.

JUNE 24   Jackie Robinson stars in a 6–2 and 8–6 sweep of the Pirates at Ebbets Field. In the first game, he broke a 2–2 deadlock with a walk-off grand slam in the ninth inning off Mel Queen. Robinson singled twice earlier in the contest. In game two, he collected four hits, two of them doubles, in a contest called after 7¹/₂ innings by darkness. All told, Robinson had seven hits in nine at-bats during the twin bill.

The grand slam was the first in major league history by an African-American. Robinson hit .296 with 12 homers and 108 runs scored in 1948. He was one of only four black players in the majors in 1948. The other three were Roy Campanella of the Dodgers and Larry Doby and Satchel Paige with the Indians. In 1947, there had been five African-American players in the majors.

JULY 2   Just a year after winning the National League pennant, the Dodgers fall into last place with a record of 27–35 following a 6–4 loss to the Giants at Ebbets Field. In his first game since being recalled from the minors, Roy Campanella collected three hits, including a double, in four at-bats.

JULY 4   The Dodgers score four runs in the ninth inning to defeat the Giants 13–12 at Ebbets Field. Gil Hodges singled and Roy Campanella homered to pull Brooklyn within a run. After Dick Whitman singled, Pee Wee Reese walked and Jackie Robinson delivered a bunt single to load the bases, Pete Reiser singled in the tying and winning runs. Campanella's ninth-inning homer was the second of his career. The first came earlier in the contest. In his first three games since being recalled from St. Paul in the American Association, Campanella garnered nine hits in 12 at-bats. The nine hits included two homers, a triple and a double.

Campanella was the first African-American catcher in baseball history, along with being one of the best of any race or nationality. He was born in Philadelphia in 1921 to an Italian father and African-American mother. Campanella began his professional playing career as a 15-year-old and barnstormed with Negro Leagues teams all over the United States, Canada, Mexico and the Caribbean before being signed by the Dodgers in 1946. He was named to eight consecutive All-Star teams beginning in 1949, won the National League Most Valuable Player in 1951, 1953 and 1955, and played in five World Series. His career ended tragically on January 28, 1958, when an auto accident left him a quadriplegic. He ranks fourth all-time among Dodgers in home runs (242), eighth in RBIs (756) and ninth in slugging percentage (.500). He was elected to the Hall of Fame in 1969.

JULY 6   A first-inning fistfight between Gene Hermanski and Philadelphia catcher Andy Seminick marks a 5–0 win over the Phillies at Shibe Park. The altercation started when Hermanki crashed into Seminick on a play at the plate. Players from both benches separated the combatants before they were banished to the clubhouse by the umpires.

JULY 10   Trailing 8–5, the Dodgers score seven runs in the seventh inning and beat the Giants 15–10 in New York. The big inning was highlighted by a three-run inside-the-park homer by Jackie Robinson.

JULY 13   Ralph Branca is the National League starting pitcher in the All-Star Game, and allows two runs in three innings in a 5–2 loss at Sportsman's Park in St. Louis. Leo Durocher managed the NL squad.

JULY 16   In a surprise move with a touch of the surreal, Leo Durocher is relieved of his duties as manager of the Dodgers and immediatcly becomes manager of the hated Giants. Burt Shotton, who had come out of semi-retirement to guide the Dodgers to the 1947 pennant during Durocher's suspension, returned to manage Brooklyn once more. Durocher succeeded Mel Ott in New York. Lee Allen, in his book *Giants and the Dodgers*, best summed up the enormity of the announcement that Durocher was changing uniforms. "Giants fans who had hated Leo simply because he managed Brooklyn now did not known what to think," wrote Allen. "Brooklyn rooters who idolized him were now required to despise him because he managed the Giants. Ambivalence spread through both boroughs, and the public was stunned."

Ott had been a longtime hero in New York. He played for the Giants from 1926 through 1947 and had managed the club since 1942. It was Ott who Durocher had denigrated with his famous quote about "nice guys" (see July 5, 1946). Ott departed even though he had a contract as manager through the end of the 1950 season. Durocher would remain the Giants manager through the end of the 1955 season. He won the NL pennant in 1951 when his Giants overcame a 13½-game Dodger lead in August. The Giants won the National league crown again in 1954, then swept the heavily favored Indians in the World Series. Shotton brought the Dodgers to the World Series again in 1949, then was fired after the 1950 season when the club lost a chance for the NL title on the final day of the season.

JULY 18   The first 17 Dodger batters reach base during a 13–4 win over the Cardinals in the second game of a double-header in St. Louis. Each of the three outs in the first inning were recorded on the base paths as the Dodgers scored five times. Brooklyn added eight tallies in the second. The 17 reached base on four doubles, five singles, six walks, and two force outs. The nine batters contributing to the streak were Pee Wee Reese, Jackie Robinson, Gene Hermanski, George Shuba, Carl Furillo, Tommy Brown, Roy Campanella, Gil Hodges and Hank Behrman. The Dodgers lost the opener 6–3 in 11 innings.

JULY 26   Leo Durocher returns to Ebbets Field for the first time as manager of the Giants and wins 13–4.

The Giants and Dodgers evenly split their 22 meetings in 1948. But teams managed by Durocher won 15 of the 22.

JULY 28   The Dodgers score eight runs in the fifth inning after two are out, and beat the Cardinals 12–4 at Ebbets Field. The first three runs scored on a bases-loaded triple by Gil Hodges.

AUGUST 5   Six days after President Harry Truman issues an executive order to integrate the American Armed Forces, three consecutive home runs by Gene Hermanski offsets six Dodger errors for a 6–4 win over the Cubs at Ebbets Field. Hermanski hit two-run homers off Ralph Hamner in the first and third inning, and after walking in the fifth, slammed a solo shot against Jess Dobernic in the eighth. The first two home runs cleared the right field screen and the third traveled into the left field seats. It was the first time that a Dodgers batter hit three homers in a game since Jack Fournier in 1926.

Hermanski hit 15 homers and batted .290 for the Dodgers in 1948.

AUGUST 8   Gil Hodges hits two homers and drives in five runs during a 10–2 win over the Reds
                at Ebbets Field. The Dodgers scored seven runs in the sixth inning.

                *Hodges was a catcher in the minor leagues and was the Dodgers Opening Day
                starter at the position in 1948. With the arrival of Roy Campanella in mid-season,
                Hodges was moved to first base, a position he had never played previously. It
                proved to be one of the best decisions in club history, as Hodges was not only one
                of the best first baseman of his generation offensively, but defensively as well. He
                played 16 seasons for the Dodgers, was named to eight All-Star teams and played
                in six World Series. Hodges never finished higher than seventh in the MVP voting,
                or led the league in a major hitting category, but his consistency was unmatched.
                He drove in over 100 runs in seven consecutive seasons beginning in 1949 and
                scored at least 100 runs three times. Among Dodgers, Hodges ranks fourth all-
                time in games played (2,006), sixth in at-bats (6,881), second in home runs (361),
                second in RBIs (1,254), third in total bases (3,357), third in walks (925), fifth
                in runs (1,088), eighth in doubles (294) and ninth in hits (1,884). His greatest
                achievement in baseball might be in managing the Mets to a world championship
                in 1969. Hodges died of a heart attack in 1973 two days before his 48th birthday.
                He has come closer to election to the Hall of Fame without being inducted than
                any other player. During his last year on the writer's ballot in 1983, Hodges
                received 63 per cent of the vote, just shy of the 75 per cent necessary for election.
                He has been a leading candidate for consideration by the Committee on Veterans
                for over 20 years, but has yet to receive a plaque at Cooperstown.*

AUGUST 18   Rex Barney pitches a one-hitter to defeat the Phillies 1–0 at Shibe Park in a duel
                with Robin Roberts. The only Philadelphia hit was a single by Putsy Caballero in
                the fifth inning.

AUGUST 22   The Dodgers steal a club record eight bases, including a triple steal in the fifth inning,
                but lose 4–3 to the Braves at Ebbets Field. The triple steal occurred in the fifth inning
                with Jackie Robinson swiping home, Gene Hermanski third and Pee Wee Reese
                second. The eight stolen bases were recorded by Hermanski (three), Reese (two),
                Robinson (one), Pete Reiser (one) and Marv Rackley (one).

AUGUST 24   Jackie Robinson is ejected for the first time during a 9–1 loss to the Pirates at
                Pittsburgh. He was tossed by umpire Butch Henline for arguing ball-and-strike calls.

                *When he reached the majors in 1947, Robinson was told by Dodgers management
                not to argue with umpires because of the sensitive situation surrounding his
                presence as the game's first African-American. The mental strain of keeping his
                emotions bottled up had, according to Robinson, made him "irritable, despondent
                and tense." He asked the club in 1948 to allow him to "let off steam" and to be
                himself and treated like every other player in professional baseball.*

AUGUST 25   At Forbes Field, the Dodgers fight with a photographer and have an apparent
                11–9 victory wiped out when the Pirates file a protest with NL president Ford Frick.
                In the seventh inning, Associated Press photographer Danny Jacino said that after he
                attempted to take pictures of Dodgers players next to the bench, he was dragged into
                the dugout by several players and pummeled. The game was held up for five minutes
                until order was restored. The Dodgers held an 11–6 lead heading into the ninth, but
                Hugh Casey was shelled for three runs before being relieved by Carl Erskine.

Eddie Bockman was the first batter to face Erskine, and with a 3–1 count, Erskine was relived by Hank Behrman, who retired Bockman. Pittsburgh manager Billy Meyer filed a protest because Erskine failed to pitch to one batter as required by the rules. Frick upheld the protest and ordered the game be replayed on September 21 from the point that Behrman relieved Erskine (see September 21, 1948).

AUGUST 29   The Dodgers take first place with a 12–7 and 6–4 sweep of the Cardinals in St. Louis. In the opener, Jackie Robinson hit for the cycle in five at-bats. The first hit was a homer off Harry Brecheen in the first inning. The second contest went ten innings.

AUGUST 30   The Dodgers sweep the Cardinals for the second day in a row with 6–5 and 6–1 decisions in a double-header in St. Louis. A thrilling four-run rally in the ninth inning won the opener. Gene Hermanski singled, followed by doubles from Duke Snider and Pete Reiser, an Arky Vaughan single, an intentional walk to Bruce Edwards, a sacrifice fly from Marv Rackley and George Shuba's single.

After dipping into last place on July 2, the Dodgers won 41 of 57 to gain the top spot. The club was 16–19 the rest of the way, however, to finish in third place, 7¹/₂ games behind.

AUGUST 31   Hank Borowy of the Cubs pitches a one-hitter to defeat the Dodgers in the first game of a double-header at Wrigley Field. The only Brooklyn base runner was Gene Hermanski, who singled in the second inning but was out on a stolen base attempt. Borowy faced the minimum 27 batters. The Cubs also won the second tilt 7–2. It was the third consecutive day in which the Dodgers played a double-header, a period that included travel between St. Louis and Chicago.

SEPTEMBER 5   The Dodgers score three runs in the 12th to defeat the Giants 4–3 at Ebbets Field. New York broke a 1–1 tie with two runs in the top half of the inning. The first Brooklyn run crossed the plate on a bases-loaded walk to Pee Wee Reese. With two out, George Shuba pinch-hit for Carl Furillo and delivered a two-run, walk-off double.

SEPTEMBER 9   Rex Barney pitches a no-hitter to defeat the Giants 2–0 at the Polo Grounds. Rain delayed the start by two hours and there were intermittent showers from the sixth inning through the end of the game. In the first inning, Barney loaded the bases with one out on two walks and his own error, but worked out of the jam with a double play. The two walks were the only ones he issued. Barney struck out four and retired the last 20 batters he faced. In the ninth, Barney struck out Joe Lafata. Lucky Lohrke popped out to first baseman Gil Hodges. The final out was recorded when Whitey Lockman lifted a foul pop to catcher Bruce Edwards.

Barney was 15–13 with a 3.10 ERA in 246²/₃ innings at the age of 23 in 1948. He lasted only two more seasons in the majors, however, as problems with control limited his progress. Barney became the public address announcer at Memorial Stadium in Baltimore in 1974 and was still on the job at Camden Yards when he died in 1997.

SEPTEMBER 21   The Pirates beat the Dodgers 12–11 at Forbes Field by scoring six runs in a ninth-inning rally that takes nearly a month to complete. The Pirates had scored the first three runs on August 25 before the Dodgers recorded the third out for an apparent 11–9 victory, but NL president Ford Frick ordered the game be replayed because of a rules violation (see August 25, 1948). Play resumed with Brooklyn holding a two-run lead, two Pittsburgh runners on base, Eddie Bockman at bat, and Carl Erskine on the mound. Bockman walked to load the bases and Erskine was replaced by Hank Behrman. Stan Rojek then cleared the bases with a double to give the Pirates a win. Pittsburgh also won the regularly scheduled game 6–3.

SEPTEMBER 28   Jackie Robinson leads off the 13th inning with a walk-off homer to defeat the Braves 9–8 at Ebbets Field. The blow was struck off Clyde Shoun, who had just entered the game as a reliever.

NOVEMBER 24   Three weeks after Harry Truman upsets Thomas Dewey in the Presidential election, the Dodgers draft Tommy Lasorda from the Phillies organization.

DECEMBER 15   The Dodgers trade Pete Reiser to the Braves for Mike McCormick.

1949   LA

Season in a Sentence

With the nucleus of the "Boys of Summer" in place, the Dodgers win a nail-biting pennant race by one game over the Cardinals, then lose their third World Series of the decade to the Yankees.

Finish • Won • Lost • Pct • GB

First   97   57   .630   +1.0

World Series

The Dodgers lost to the New York Yankees four games to one.

Manager

Burt Shotton

Stats

Stats	Dods	NL	Rank
Batting Avg:	.274	.262	2
On-Base Pct:	.354	.334	1
Slugging Pct:	.419	.389	1
Home Runs:	152		1
Stolen Bases:	117		1
ERA:	3.80	4.04	2
Fielding Avg:	.980	.975	1
Runs Scored:	879		1
Runs Allowed:	651		2

Starting Lineup

Roy Campanella, c
Gil Hodges, 1b
Jackie Robinson, 2b
Billy Cox, 3b
Pee Wee Reese, ss
Gene Hermanski, lf
Duke Snider, cf
Carl Furillo, rf

Pitchers

Don Newcombe, sp
Preacher Roe, sp-rp
Ralph Branca, sp
Joe Hatten, sp
Rex Barney, sp-rp
Erv Palica, rp
Jack Banta, rp
Carl Erskine, rp

Attendance

1,633,747 (first in NL)

Club Leaders

Batting Avg:	Jackie Robinson	.342
On-Base Pct:	Jackie Robinson	.432
Slugging Pct:	Jackie Robinson	.528
Home Runs:	Gil Hodges	23
	Duke Snider	23
RBIs:	Jackie Robinson	124
Runs:	Pee Wee Reese	132
Stolen Bases:	Jackie Robinson	37
Wins:	Don Newcombe	17
Strikeouts:	Don Newcombe	149
ERA:	Preacher Roe	2.79
Saves:	Erv Palica	6

FEBRUARY 26   The Dodgers sell Hank Behrman to the Giants.

APRIL 19   An Opening Day crowd of 34,530 watches the Dodgers trounce the Giants 10–3 at
                   Ebbets Field. Carl Furillo, Roy Campanella and Jackie Robinson homered. Robinson
                   also contributed two singles. Joe Hatten pitched a complete game. Among those in
                   attendance was Margaret Truman, daughter of President Harry Truman.

                   *Ernie Harwell joined Red Barber and Connie Desmond in the Dodgers radio
                   and TV booth in 1948 and 1949. The legendary Harwell lasted only two seasons
                   in Brooklyn before broadcasting for the Giants (1950–53), Orioles (1954–59)
                   and Tigers (1960–91, 1993–2002).*

APRIL 28   The Dodgers score eight runs before a batter is retired in the sixth inning and sweep
                   the Dodgers 15–2 in New York.

                   *The Dodgers wore satin uniforms at night during the 1949 season. The home
                   version included extra blue piping down the shoulders and on the sleeve ends.
                   The satin road suit was pale blue with white lettering and numbering. Dodger
                   management believed the reflective satin would add to the enjoyment of the
                   sport under the lights, but the outfits were almost impossible to clean and were
                   uncomfortable on hot, sticky summer evenings.*

MAY 6   Trailing 4–2, the Dodgers score seven runs in the fourth inning and defeat the Cubs
                   10–4 at Ebbets Field.

MAY 7   Down 7–2, the Dodgers score two runs in the sixth inning and four in the seventh to
                   win 8–7 against the Cardinals at Ebbets Field.

                   *Minor league systems vary widely in 1949. The Dodgers had more farm
                   clubs than any other team with 25, including three (Montreal, St. Paul and
                   Hollywood) at the Class AAA level. The Yankees had 21 farm teams and the
                   Cardinals 20. At the bottom end were the Senators (nine), Red Sox (nine) and
                   Reds (10). The Athletics had no minor league affiliates above the Class A level.*

MAY 14   Gil Hodges hits a grand slam off Bill Voiselle in the eighth inning, but the Dodgers
                   lose 7–6 in 12 innings in Boston.

                   *Through May 15, the Dodgers had a record of 12–13 and were four games out
                   of first.*

MAY 17   With the score 2–2, the Dodgers score six runs in the 11th inning, then withstand
                   a three-run Cub rally in the bottom half to win 8–5 in Chicago. During the six-run
                   rally, Jackie Robinson scored from second base on a bunt single from Gil Hodges.

                   *Robinson won the National League MVP award in 1949 with league-leading
                   figures in batting average (.342) and stolen bases (37), along with 38 doubles,
                   12 triples, 16 homers, 124 RBIs, 122 runs and 203 hits.*

MAY 18   The Dodgers rack up 20 hits and beat the Cubs 14–5 in Chicago. Every player in the
                   starting line-up collected at least two hits.

MAY 21   The Dodgers unleash an eight-run attack in the ninth inning for a 15–6 win over the
              Cardinals in St. Louis. Pee Wee Reese scored five runs during the game, reaching base
              on a double, three singles and an error. Jackie Robinson drove in six runs on two
              doubles and a single.

              Reese hit .279, drew 116 walks, and led the NL in runs with 132 in 1949.

MAY 22   Don Newcombe pitches a shutout in his first major league start, beating the Reds 3–0
              in the first game of a double-header at Crosley Field. Cincinnati won the second
              tilt 2–0.

              *Newcombe was 22-years-old at the time of his debut. By the end of the season,
              he led the National League in shutouts with five and posted a 17–8 record and
              a 3.17 ERA in 246²/₃ innings. Before his career ended, Newcombe had three
              seasons of 20 or more wins and another of 19 despite missing two prime seasons
              (1952 and 1953) while serving in the Army during the Korean War. His best
              season was in 1955, when he won 27. Overall, Newcombe was 123–66 as a
              Dodger. His .651 winning percentage ranks fifth in club history.*

MAY 30   Jackie Robinson homers in the 13th inning to beat the Giants 2–1 in the first game of
              a double-header at the Polo Grounds. New York took the second contest 7–4.

MAY 31   The Dodgers score twice in the 14th inning to defeat the Giants 6–4 in New York.
              Carl Furillo hit a solo homer to break the 4–4 tie before the Dodgers added an
              insurance run.

              Furillo hit .322 with 18 homers and 106 RBIs in 1949.

JUNE 10   The Dodgers break a 4–4 tie with six runs in the seventh inning and beat the
              Reds 10–5 at Ebbets Field.

JUNE 11   The Dodgers wallop the Reds 11–3 at Ebbets Field.

JUNE 12   The Dodgers reach double digits in runs for the third day in a row by overwhelming
              the Reds 20–7 at Ebbets FieldBrooklyn scored a run in the first inning, two in the
              second, one in the third, one in the fourth, ten in the fifth, four in the seventh and
              one in the eighth. The 20 runs came on only 13 hits, as the Dodgers benefited from
              11 walks. Gil Hodges drove in eight runs and Billy Cox six. Hodges hit a three-run
              homer and an RBI-single in the ten-run fifth, and a grand slam in the seventh. Cox
              also homered twice and hit a double.

JUNE 14   The Dodgers extend their winning streak to eight games with a 7–2 decision over the
              Cardinals in St. Louis.

              *Duke Snider became the Dodgers starting center fielder in 1949 and hit .292 with
              22 home runs. The following season he made the first of seven consecutive All-Star
              teams. During that period, he led the NL three times in runs, twice in slugging
              percentage, and once each in home runs, RBIs, walks and hits. Playing for the
              club from 1947 through 1962, Snider is the all-time Dodgers leader in home runs
              (389) andruns batted in (1,271). He also ranks seventh in games (1,923), seventh
              in at-bats (6,640), second in total bases (3,669), second in doubles (343), third in*

runs (1,199), fourth in slugging percentage (.553), fourth in walks (893), fourth in hits (1,995) and sixth in triples (82).

JUNE 24   Jack Banta pitches 6²/₃ innings of hitless relief, but the Dodgers lose 4–2 to the Pirates in Pittsburgh. Rex Barney allowed four runs in the first inning on three walks and a homer to Ralph Kiner.

JUNE 25   Gil Hodges hits for the cycle during a 17–10 win over the Pirates in Pittsburgh. The cycle included two home runs along with a triple, double and single in six at-bats. Hodges drove in four runs and scored four. The Dodgers scored nine runs in the third inning.

JUNE 26   The Dodgers break loose with a big inning for the second day in a row with ten runs in the seventh during a 15–3 defeat of the Pirates in Pittsburgh. The ten runs scored on nine hits and two errors. Carl Furillo collected five hits, including a homer and a triple, in five at-bats. He scored four and drove in four.

JULY 2   Trailing 8–4, the Dodgers score four runs in the sixth inning, one in the eighth, and four in the ninth to defeat the Giants 13–8 in New York. Gene Hermanski hit a grand slam off Andy Hansen in the sixth inning to tie the score 8–8.

           On the same day, the Dodgers sold Mickey Owen to the Cubs.

JULY 3   The Giants club the Dodgers 16–0 in New York.

Never the biggest name on the great Dodger teams, Gil Hodges supplied both a steady glove and bat. In 1949, he posted the first of seven straight seasons of more than 100 RBIs and the first of 11 straight seasons of more than 20 home runs.

JULY 8   An African-American pitcher faces an African-American batter for the first time in major league history during a 4–3 win over the Giants at Ebbets Field when Don Newcombe throws to Hank Thompson.

           Two years after Jackie Robinson's debut, there were still only nine black players on three teams in the majors in 1949. The nine were Robinson, Newcombe and Roy Campanella with the Dodgers, Thompson and Monte Irvin for the Giants, and Larry Doby, Satchel Paige, Luke Easter and Minnie Minoso on the Indians. Also in 1949, Robinson, Newcombe, Campanella and Doby became the first African-Americans in the All-Star Game, played at Ebbets Field.

JULY 12 — The All-Star Game is played at Ebbets Field, and the American League wins 11–7. The contest was played in an intermittent drizzle and drew 32,577. It was the only time the Midsummer Classic was ever played in Brooklyn. The AL scored four runs in the first inning, fell behind 5–4 in the third, and regained the advantage with two tallies in the fourth. Joe DiMaggio drove in three runs and Stan Musial collected three hits, one of them a home run. Ralph Kiner also homered.

Future Hall of Famers on the rosters of the two clubs included Yogi Berra, Roy Campanella, Joe DiMaggio, Larry Doby, George Kell, Bob Lemon, Ralph Kiner, Johnny Mize, Stan Musial, Pee Wee Reese, Jackie Robinson, Red Schoendienst, Enos Slaughter, Warren Spahn and Ted Williams.

JULY 14 — The Dodgers score two runs in the ninth inning and one in the tenth to beat the Reds 6–5 in Cincinnati. Billy Cox doubled in the winning run.

The Dodgers won 19 games in a row against the Reds in Cincinnati from 1947 through 1949 and were 65–23 at Crosley Field from 1947 through 1954. Part of the reason for the success may have been the Dodgers appeal with African-American fans throughout the South. Cincinnati was the closest National League city to the South during the 1940s and 1950s, and Union Terminal, the city's major train station, was only three blocks from Crosley Field. On Sundays, as many as 15,000 African-Americans were in the stands at the Cincinnati ballpark rooting for the Dodgers. Many traveled from as far as Atlanta and Birmingham.

JULY 17 — A walk-off homer by Luis Olmo in the ninth inning defeats the Cubs at Ebbets Field. The Dodgers scored three runs in the eighth inning, the last two on Roy Campanella's home run.

Campanella hit .287 with 22 home runs in 1949.

JULY 18 — Jackie Robinson testifies before Congress and steals home plate on the same day.

Robinson went to Washington after African-American singer and actor Paul Robeson declared that blacks would not fight against the Soviet Union if war broke out. Branch Rickey convinced Robinson to testify before the House Un-American Activities Committee. Robinson used the occasion to speak out against racial discrimination, but termed Robeson's assertions "silly." Robinson then traveled back to Brooklyn and stole home during a 3–0 win over the Cubs at Ebbets Field.

JULY 19 — The Dodgers take a 3½-game lead over the Cardinals in the NL pennant race with a 4–3 triumph over the Pirates at Ebbets Field.

The Dodgers had an extraordinary amount of young talent on the roster in 1949, which would sustain the club well into the 1950s. Duke Snider and Carl Erskine were 22, Don Newcombe and Ralph Branca 23, Gil Hodges 25, and Carl Furillo and Roy Campanella 27.

JULY 21 — The Dodgers score three runs in the ninth inning to defeat the Pirates 7–6 at Ebbets Field. Hank Edwards drove in the tying run and scored on Luis Olmo's single. Both Edwards and Olmo were inserted into the game as pinch-hitters.

JULY 24   The Dodgers drop out of first place with a 14–1 loss to the Cardinals at Ebbets Field. Stan Musial hit for the cycle.

During the 1948 and 1949 seasons, Musial played 22 games at Ebbets Field and had a .531 batting average on 43 hits, of which 11 were doubles, five were triples, and eight were homers. The nickname "Stan the Man" was coined by Brooklyn fans because of Musial's outstanding success against the Dodgers.

JULY 28   Gene Hermanski hits a grand slam off Bob Rush in the sixth inning of a 7–1 victory over the Cubs in Chicago.

AUGUST 6   The Reds score five runs in the eighth inning with the help of three errors by third baseman Billy Cox to beat the Dodgers 5–2 in Cincinnati. Cox threw high to first base on a grounder, misplayed a bunt, and dropped a throw, all in the span of five batters.

AUGUST 7   Hank Edwards hits a grand slam off Ken Raffensberger in the sixth inning of a 7–0 win over the Reds in the first game of a double-header in Cincinnati. The Dodgers completed the sweep with a 2–1 victory in game two.

AUGUST 19   Marv Rackley collects five hits, including a triple, in five at-bats during a 12-inning, 6–4 win over the Braves in Boston.

AUGUST 23   Don Newcombe pitches a shutout and collects a three-run double during a 6–0 win over the Cardinals at Ebbets Field.

AUGUST 28   The Dodgers score seven runs in the third inning and beat the Pirates 9–0 at Ebbets Field. Don Newcombe pitched the shutout.

AUGUST 30   A two-run walk-off homer by Gil Hodges in the ninth inning beats the Pirates 4–3 at Ebbets Field.

SEPTEMBER 2   Don Newcombe pitches his third consecutive shutout by beating the Giants 8–0 in New York.

Newcombe hurled 31 consecutive shutout innings over five starts.

SEPTEMBER 5   The Dodgers rout the Braves 7–2 and 13–2 in a separate admission morning-afternoon double-header at Ebbets Field.

SEPTEMBER 10   Erv Palica, in the game as a reliever, beats out a bunt in the ninth inning to drive in the winning run for a 5–4 triumph over the Giants at Ebbets Field.

SEPTEMBER 11   Carl Furillo hits a grand slam off Larry Jansen in the seventh inning of a 10–5 win over the Giants at Ebbets Field.

SEPTEMBER 13   The Dodgers score three runs in the tenth inning to defeat the Reds 6–3 in Cincinnati. Brooklyn was one out from defeat in the ninth inning when Gil Hodges and Carl Furillo hit back-to-back doubles.

SEPTEMBER 18   The Dodgers humiliate the Cubs 17–1 in Chicago, but are still 2½ games out of first place with two weeks left in the season.

SEPTEMBER 19	Rex Barney pitches a one-hitter to defeat the Cubs 4–0 at Wrigley Field. The only Chicago hit was a single by Phil Cavarretta in the eighth inning.
SEPTEMBER 20	The Dodgers lose 1–0 to the Cardinals in the first game of a crucial three-game series in St. Louis. The defeat left the Dodgers 2½ games out of first with ten contests left on the schedule. The Cards loaded the bases in the ninth with the score 0–0. At this point, play was interrupted for several minutes as Jackie Robinson resumed an argument with umpire Bill Stewart over a ball-and-strike decision on Robinson's last trip to the plate. Robinson was ejected, and Eddie Miksis replaced him at second base. Joe Garagiola subsequently singled off Miksis's glove to score the winning run.
SEPTEMBER 22	The Dodgers harass Cardinals pitching with 19 hits and 13 walks to win 19–6 at Sportsman's Park. Carl Furillo drove in seven runs on three doubles and two singles in six at-bats. Gene Hermanski drew five walks in seven plate appearances. The win put the Dodgers one-half game back of St. Louis in the pennant race.
SEPTEMBER 29	Six days after President Harry Truman reveals that the Soviet Union has tested an atom bomb, the Dodgers take first place with 9–2 and 8–0 wins over the Braves in Boston. The second game was called after five innings by darkness. The Cardinals lost 7–2 to the Pirates to fall one-half game behind the Dodgers.
SEPTEMBER 30	The idle Dodgers take a one-game lead when the Cardinals lose 6–5 to the Cubs in Chicago. Both the Dodgers and Cardinals had two games left to play.
	On the same day, the Dodgers sold Irv Noren to the Senators.
OCTOBER 1	On the second-to-last day of the season, the Dodgers lose 6–4 to the Phillies, but hang on to first place when the Cardinals lose 3–1 to the Cubs in Chicago.
OCTOBER 2	The Dodgers clinch the pennant on the final day of the season with a dramatic ten-inning, 9–7 win over the Phillies at Shibe Park. Brooklyn had leads of 5–0 after three innings and seized a 7–4 advantage with two runs in the top of the fifth, but allowed Philadelphia to knot the contest with a tally in the bottom of the fifth and two in the sixth. It was still 7–7 heading into extra innings. Pee Wee Reese opened the decisive tenth with a single and moved to second on a sacrifice by Eddie Miksis. Duke Snider singled home Reese, moved to second on the throw to home plate, and scored on Luis Olmo's single. Carl Furillo collected four hits. Jack Banta pitched 4⅓ innings of shutout relief. The Cardinals beat the Cubs 13–5 in Chicago to finish one game behind the Dodgers.
	The Dodgers met the Yankees in the World Series for the third time in nine years. The two New York clubs also clashed in a subway series in 1941 and 1947. Managed by Casey Stengel in his first season with the club, the Yankees were 97–57 and finished one game ahead of Boston by defeating the Red Sox twice on the final two days of the season.
OCTOBER 5	The Dodgers open the World Series with a 1–0 loss to the Yankees at Yankee Stadium. The lone run scored on a walk-off home run by Tommy Henrich off Don Newcombe, who allowed five hits and struck out 11. Allie Reynolds hurled a two-hitter for New York.

Those with televisions in their homes were still a distinct minority in 1949. The Fox Theater in Brooklyn, which seated 4,060, put the televised images on their screen and charged fans $1.20 to watch the action. Theaters owners expected a full house, but about a quarter of the seats were empty.

OCTOBER 6   Game two produces another 1–0 decision, but this time the Dodgers win at Yankee Stadium. Preacher Roe pitched the complete game shutout. The lone scored in the third inning on a double by Jackie Robinson and a single from Gil Hodges off Vic Raschi.

OCTOBER 7   The Yankees win game three 4–3 before 32,788 at Ebbets Field. The score was 1–1 after eight innings. Pee Wee Reese tied the score with a home run in the fourth. After 26 innings, the two teams had combined for only four runs. The ninth would set the stage for offensive fireworks of the remainder of the Series when the Yanks scored three times off Ralph Branca and the Dodgers countered with two in their half on solo homers by Luis Olmo with one out and Roy Campanella two batters later.

OCTOBER 8   The Yankees move within one win of the world championship with a 6–4 win over the Dodgers in front of a crowd of 33,934 at Ebbets Field. The Yanks scored three runs in the fourth inning and three more in the fifth for a 6–0 lead before the Dodgers responded with four tallies in the sixth. In relief, Allie Reynolds retired the last ten Brooklyn batters.

OCTOBER 9   The Yankees close out the Series with a 10–6 win over the Dodgers before 33,711 at Ebbets Field. New York led 10–1 in the sixth inning and withstood a futile Brooklyn rally. Gil Hodges delivered the final three Dodger runs in the seventh with a home run.

OCTOBER 14   The Dodgers sell Paul Minner and Preston Ward to the Cubs and Marv Rackley to the Reds.

DECEMBER 24 The Dodgers trade Luis Olmo to the Braves for Jim Russell and Ed Sauer.

THE STATE OF THE DODGERS

The Dodgers were at the center of history nearly every season during the 1950s. During the first two seasons of the decade, Brooklyn lost the NL pennant on the final day of the season. In 1951, the club blew a 13$\frac{1}{2}$-game lead and lost the pennant on Bobby Thomson's dramatic homer in the playoffs. In 1952 and 1953, with a team Roger Kahn dubbed "The Boys of Summer," the Dodgers lost the World Series to the Yankees. The 1953 defeat was the seventh in seven tries for the Dodgers in the Fall Classic, including five to the Yanks in a span of 13 years. In 1955, "next year" finally arrived for Brooklyn fans as the "Bums" won the Series in seven games against the Yankees. In 1956, the Dodgers lost a seven-game World Series to the Yankees, one of them on a perfect game by Don Larsen. In 1957, the Dodgers moved to Los Angeles in the most controversial franchise relocation in the history of American sports. In 1959, the Dodgers won the world championship again, defeating the White Sox in a Series which included three crowds in excess of 90,000 at Memorial Coliseum. Overall, the Dodgers were 913–630, a winning percentage of .592, which was second only to the Yankees in the majors. NL pennants won outside of Brooklyn or Los Angeles were taken by the Phillies (1950), Giants (1951 and 1954) and Braves (1957 and 1958).

THE BEST TEAM

The 1953 team posted a record of 105–49 and set a club record for victories in a season. The Dodgers lost the World Series in six games to the Yankees,

however. Counting the post-season, the 1955 outfit was the best. After a 98–55 regular-season record, the Dodgers polished off the Yankees in seven games in the Fall Classic.

THE WORST TEAM

The worst team was the first one in Los Angeles. The Dodgers were 71–83 and finished seventh in an eight-team league. It was the only losing season for the franchise between 1944 and 1964.

THE BEST MOMENT

The best and worst moments happened simultaneously on October 8, 1957, when it was officially announced that the Dodgers were moving west. It was the best moment for those in greater Los Angeles and the worst for Brooklyn residents. Exclusive of the franchise shift, the best moment took place on October 4, 1955, at Yankee Stadium when the Dodgers beat the Yanks in game seven of the World Series.

THE WORST MOMENT

The worst moment was on October 3, 1951, when Bobby Thomson's home run capped a pennant race in which the Dodgers blew a 13$\frac{1}{2}$-game lead.

THE ALL-DECADE TEAM • YEARS W/DODS

Roy Campanella, c	1948–57
Gil Hodges, 1b	1943, 1947–61
Jim Gilliam, 2b	1953–66
Billy Cox, 3b	1948–54
Pee Wee Reese, ss	1940–42, 1946–58
Jackie Robinson, lf	1947–56
Duke Snider, cf	1947–62
Carl Furillo, rf	1946–59
Don Newcombe, p	1949–51, 1954–57
Johnny Podres, p	1953–55, 1957–66
Carl Erskine, p	1948–59
Preacher Roe, p	1948–54

Reese and Robinson were also on the 1940s All-Decade Team. Robinson was the Dodgers' best player at three different positions (second base, third base and left field) during the 1950s. During his career, the versatile Robinson played 748 games at second base, 256 at third, 197 at first and 161 in left. He gets the nod here as a leftfielder because of a lack of viable alternatives. Despite winning five pennants, the club had a difficult time finding a consistent player at the position during the decade. No Dodger player appeared in at least 100 games in left field in consecutive seasons between Joe Medwick (1940–42) and Wally Moon (1959–61). Other outstanding Dodgers during the 1950s included second baseman Charlie Neal (1956–61) and pitchers Clem Labine (1950–60), Don Drysdale (1956–68) and Roger Craig (1955–61). Those four plus 10 of the 12 members of the 1950s All-Decade Team began their careers as Dodgers, a testament to the scouting and development staffs of the Dodgers. Cox and Roe were acquired in the same December 1947 trade with the Pirates. Campanella, Drysdale, Reese, Robinson and Snider are all in the Hall of Fame.

THE DECADE LEADERS

Batting Avg:	Jackie Robinson	.311
On-Base Pct:	Jackie Robinson	.416
Slugging Pct:	Duke Snider	.569
Home Runs:	Duke Snider	326
RBIs:	Duke Snider	1,031
Runs:	Duke Snider	970
Stolen Bases:	Jim Gilliam	132
Wins:	Carl Erskine	108
Strikeouts:	Carl Erskine	903
ERA:	Don Drysdale	3.33
Saves:	Clem Labine	82

THE HOME FIELD

Attendance at Ebbets Field peaked at 1,807,526 in 1947, but had fallen to 1,088,704 by 1952, then leveled off. In 1955, the club attracted 1,033,589 to rank seventh among 16 big-league clubs with a club that was in first place all year. The ballpark, built in 1913, was cramped and uncomfortable. The restrooms were outmoded, and the concessions overcrowded. The middle class was moving from the apartment buildings and row houses on the crowded streets of Brooklyn to detached suburban homes on Long Island. Ebbets Field was difficult to reach by car and parking lots in the vicinity were woefully insufficient. The lots could accommodate only 700 cars. The ballpark was built in Flatbush in part because of the neighborhood's excellent network of streetcars and subways, but by the 1950s, public transportation was in sharp decline. Walter O'Malley began looking for alternatives in Brooklyn, and focused on a downtown site at Atlantic and Flatbush Avenues. To emphasize his need for a new ballpark, O'Malley scheduled seven "home" games in both 1956 and 1957 in Jersey City, New Jersey.

When negotiations with New York City officials for a new stadium in Brooklyn failed to materialize, O'Malley moved the Dodgers to Los Angeles in October 1957. From 1958 through 1961, the Dodgers played at Memorial Coliseum. Built for football and track, the 105,000-seat coliseum had little to recommend it for baseball other than the huge seating capacity. The left-field line was only 251 feet long, topped by a 40-foot high screen. The Dodgers set a club attendance record in the first season in L.A. with 1,845,556, then drew 2,071,045 in 1959.

THE GAME YOU WISHED YOU HAD SEEN

Major league baseball came to Los Angeles on April 18, 1958. The Dodgers defeated the San Francisco Giants 6–5 before 78,672 at Memorial Coliseum.

THE MANAGEMENT

Branch Rickey became president and general manager in November 1942, began to buy stock in the club in 1944, and gained a majority stake in 1945 in a partnership with Walter O'Malley. The relationship between Rickey and O'Malley became strained during the late 1940s, however, and in 1950, O'Malley purchased Rickey's stock in the franchise. The O'Malley family would run the club until 1998. General managers were Rickey (1942–50) and Buzzie Bavasi (1950–68). Field managers were Burt Shotton (1947–50), Chuck Dressen (1951–53) and Walter Alston (1954–76).

THE BEST PLAYER MOVE

The best player move was the signing of Brooklyn native Sandy Koufax off the campus of the University of Cincinnati in 1955. The Dodgers scouting staff also signed Don Drysdale, Willie Davis and Jim Gilliam during the 1950s. The club didn't do as well in the trade market, as there were no deals with a long-term positive benefit.

THE WORST PLAYER MOVE

The worst move was the failure to retain Roberto Clemente on the 40-man roster in 1954, which allowed him to be drafted by the Pirates. The worst trade sent Don Elston to the Cubs in May 1957 for Jackie Collum and Vito Valentinetti.

1950
LA

Season in a Sentence

After falling nine games out of first place with 17 contests left on the schedule, the Dodgers rally and have a chance to tie for first place on the final day of the season only to lose to the Phillies.

Finish • Won • Lost • Pct • GB

Second   89   65   .578   2.0

Manager

Burt Shotton

Stats

Stats	Dods	NL	Rank
Batting Avg:	.272	.261	1
On-Base Pct:	.349	.336	1
Slugging Pct:	.444	.401	1
Home Runs:	194		1
Stolen Bases:	77		1
ERA:	4.28	4.14	6
Fielding Avg:	.979	.975	1
Runs Scored:	847		1
Runs Allowed:	724		4

Starting Lineup

Roy Campanella, c
Gil Hodges, 1b
Jackie Robinson, 2b
Billy Cox, 3b
Pee Wee Reese, ss
Gene Hermanski, lf
Duke Snider, cf
Carl Furillo, rf
Jim Russell, lf
Bobby Morgan, 3b

Pitchers

Don Newcombe, sp
Preacher Roe, sp
Carl Erskine, sp-rp
Erv Palica, rp-sp
Ralph Branca, rp-sp
Dan Bankhead, sp-rp

Attendance

1,185,896 (second in NL)

Club Leaders

Batting Avg:	Jackie Robinson	.328
On-Base Pct:	Jackie Robinson	.423
Slugging Pct:	Duke Snider	.553
Home Runs:	Gil Hodges	32
RBIs:	Gil Hodges	113
Runs:	Duke Snider	109
Stolen Bases:	Pee Wee Reese	17
Wins:	Don Newcombe	19
	Preacher Roe	19
Strikeouts:	Erv Palica	131
ERA:	Preacher Roe	3.30
Saves:	Ralph Branca	7

FEBRUARY 4   Jackie Robinson arrives in Hollywood for the filming of *The Jackie Robinson Story*. He was finished with the picture in time to report for spring training. Robinson starred as himself in the movie with Ruby Dee playing his wife Rachel. The idealistic, simple and direct biography is still valuable as a social history of the period. Interestingly, the fictional Negro League team in the movie is called the Black Panthers. Dee played Robinson's mother in the 1990 TV movie *The Court-Martial of Jackie Robinson*. Still acting at the age of 80, Dee was nominated for an Academy Award for her work in the 2007 movie *The Gangster*.

APRIL 18   The Dodgers open the season with a 9–1 win over the Phillies at Shibe Park. Robin Roberts hurled a complete game for Philadelphia. Don Newcombe was driven from the mound in the second inning. Roberts and Newcombe would face each other again on the final day of the season (October 1, 1950).

Vin Scully joined Red Barber and Connie Desmond in the Dodgers radio and TV booth in 1950. A native of Manhattan and a graduate of Fordham University, Scully was 22 years old. Barber was the sports director of CBS radio and hired Scully in the fall of 1949 to do the play-by-play for college football games. Barber was so impressed that he also hired Scully to announce Dodgers games.

All Dodger home games were telecast in 1950, but none on the road due to the high cost of transmitting the images from one city to another at the time. Jackie Robinson was also a radio personality in 1950. He had a 15-minute Sunday night program broadcast nationally on ABC which began at 10:30 p.m.

APRIL 21   The Dodgers win the home opener 8–1 over the Giants before 24,033 at Ebbets Field. Roy Campanella hit a grand slam off Dave Koslo in the third inning. Jim Russell homered in his Dodger debut.

              Campanella hit .281 with 31 homers in 1950.

APRIL 25   Joe Hatten retires 23 batters in a row between the second and ninth inning and beats the Braves 3–0 with a two-hitter at Braves Field. The only Boston hits were singles by Carden Gillenwater in the second inning and Sam Jethroe in the ninth.

              Jethroe, who played in the Dodgers minor-league system in 1948 and 1949, was the first African-American to play for the Braves. He was one of only nine black players in the majors in 1950. The others were Jackie Robinson, Roy Campanella, Don Newcombe and Dan Bankhead with the Dodgers, Monte Irvin and Hank Thompson of the Giants, and Larry Doby and Luke Easter for the Indians.

APRIL 26   A disputed play leads to the winning run in the tenth inning of a 5–4 victory over the Phillies at Ebbets Field. Roy Campanella lifted a fly to left field in which a fan reached over the railing and touched the ball. The Phillies argued that Campanella should be called out, claiming the fan interfered with left fielder Dick Sisler's ability to catch the drive. The umpires ruled it a double. Campanella scored on Pee Wee Reese's walk-off single.

APRIL 27   Burt Shotton calls on four pinch-hitters, and all four strike out during a 9–2 loss to the Phillies at Ebbets Field. The four were Cal Abrams, Wayne Belardi, Gene Hermanski and Jim Russell.

              Shotton was one of the last two individuals to manage a club in his street clothes. The other one was Connie Mack. Both Shotton and Mack managed for the last time in 1950.

MAY 18   Four errors by Cardinals third baseman Tommy Glaviano, three of them in the ninth inning struck by three consecutive batters, leads to a 9–8 Dodger win at Ebbets Field. St. Louis led 8–0 before Brooklyn scored four runs in the eighth inning. With rain falling on a cold night, the Dodgers renewed their assault in the ninth, scoring one run and filling the sacks with one out to set the stage for the Glaviano debacle. First, he threw wide to second trying for a force play on Roy Campanella's grounder, allowing a run to score and making the tally 8–6. Glaviano then pegged wide to the plate on Eddie Miksis's bounder to allow another run to cross the plate while leaving the bases full. When Glaviano let Pee Wee Reese's hopper go through his legs, the tying and winning runs scored.

MAY 20   Four Dodgers relievers combine to hold the Pirates hitless over the last 9⅔ innings of an 11-inning 4–3 win in the second game of a double-header at Ebbets Field. All four relievers had a last name which began with the letter B. Rex Barney went

3²/₃ innings without surrendering a hit, and Ralph Branca, Jack Banta and Dan Bankhead added two innings each. The Dodgers also won the opener 3–2.

MAY 30   Five days after the opening of the Brooklyn-Battery tunnel, the longest underwater vehicular tunnel in the North America, Duke Snider hits three consecutive solo homers during a 6–4 victory over the Phillies in the second game of a double-header at Ebbets Field. In the first and third innings, Snider homered over the right-field screen off Russ Meyer. In the fifth, Snider went deep on Blix Donnelly with a drive that landed in the left-field stands. Facing Bob Miller in the seventh, Snider nearly hit a record-tying fourth homer. The ball struck the right-field screen four feet from the top and fell for a single. The Dodgers also won the opener 7–6 in 10 innings.

Snider led the NL in hits with 199 in 1950 along with a .321 batting average, 31 doubles, 10 triples, 31 homers, 107 RBIs and 109 runs.

JUNE 4   A game between the Dodgers and Cardinals in St. Louis, rained out the previous day, is re-scheduled as part of a day-night double-header on July 16. It would have been the first Sunday night game in major league history, and was sold out within hours. Commissioner Happy Chandler canceled the contest, however, citing rules against the playing of games after dark on Sundays.

JUNE 5   The Dodgers wallop the Cubs 13–1 in Chicago. Preacher Roe pitched a three-hitter in which he faced only 28 batters.

Roe was 19–11 with a 3.30 ERA in 1950.

JUNE 11   Roy Campanella hits a grand slam off Willie Ramsdell in the eighth inning, but the Dodgers lose 8–5 against the Reds in the second game of a double-header in Cincinnati. The Dodgers won the opener 5–4.

JUNE 17   Roy Campanella sets a club record with a home run in his fifth consecutive game during a 10–2 win over the Cardinals at Ebbets Field. From June 11 through June 17, Campanella hit five homers and drove in 11 tallies in the five contests.

JUNE 20   Gil Hodges hits a grand slam off Frank Smith in the third inning of an 8–2 triumph over the Reds at Ebbets Field.

Hodges batted .283 with 32 homers and 113 runs-batted-in over the course of the 1950 season.

JUNE 23   The Dodgers score eight runs in the seventh inning and roll to a 15–3 rout of the Pirates at Ebbets Field.

The Dodgers were 19–3 against the Pirates in 1950.

JUNE 24   The game against the Pirates at Ebbets Field is suspended with the Dodgers leading 19–12 in the bottom of the eighth inning. The game was halted because of a state law prohibiting play after 11:59 p.m. on Saturday night. The Dodgers scored seven runs in the third inning to take an 8–5 lead and had already accounted for five runs in the eighth when play was stopped. Four of them scored on Jackie Robinson's grand slam off Vic Lombardi. The game resumed on August 1. On that day, Brooklyn added two more runs in the eighth for a 21–12 victory. The Dodgers collected 25 hits in all. Carl Furillo had four hits, including a double, in six at-bats and scored four runs.

JUNE 25   Ralph Kiner hits for the cycle and drives in eight runs to lead the Pirates to a 16–11 win over the Dodgers at Ebbets Field. The score was 5–5 before the two teams combined for 17 runs over the last three innings.

On the same day, North Korean forces attacked South Korea. The U.S. immediately became involved militarily. The Korean War lasted until 1953, and the military draft claimed such stars as Ted Williams and Willie Mays. Dodger players who missed time in the service during the war included Billy Loes (1951), Don Newcombe (1952–53) and Erv Palica (1952–53).

JULY 2   In the second game of a double-header in Philadelphia, the Dodgers and Phillies end a ten-inning affair in an 8–8 tie when the play is stopped because of the Sunday curfew law. According to Pennsylvania state statutes, games had to end at 6:00 p.m. on the Christian Sabbath. The Dodgers trailed 6–0 before scoring three runs in the seventh inning, three in the eighth and two in the ninth. The Phils won the opener 6–4.

JULY 11   Burt Shotton manages the National League to a 14-inning, 4–3 win in the All-Star Game at Comiskey Park in Chicago.

JULY 14   Erv Palica pitches the Dodgers to a 1–0 win over the Cubs in Chicago.

JULY 15   The Dodgers clout five home runs during a 13–5 pasting of the Cubs in Chicago. Roy Campanella and Carl Furillo struck two homers each, and Duke Snider one.

Furillo hit .305 with 18 homers and 106 RBIs in 1950.

JULY 16   Duke Snider collects five hits, including a triple and a homer, in five at-bats and also steals a base during a 10–2 win over the Cardinals in St. Louis.

JULY 22   The Dodgers score seven runs in the third inning and beat the Pirates 12–3 at Forbes Field. Brooklyn collected only three hits during the rally, benefiting from six Pittsburgh walks.

JULY 23   Jackie Robinson collects five hits, including a double and a homer, in six at-bats, during an 11–6 victory over the Pirates in Pittsburgh.

Robinson hit .328 with 19 doubles and 14 homers in 1950.

JULY 26   Jim Russell hits home runs from both sides of the plate during a 7–5 win over the Cardinals at Ebbets Field. Russell homered off lefty Harry Brecheen in the first inning and right-hander George Munger in the fifth.

After drawing 1,807,526 fans in 1947 and 1,633,747 in 1949, attendance plummeted to 1,185,596 in 1950. The home attendance paled in comparison to the 1,617,146 the club attracted on the road. Much of the problem had to with population shifts in post-war America. From 1940 through 1960, the population of Brooklyn dropped by 100,000. More importantly, the middle class was moving out of the borough farther out on Long Island, and they were being replaced by poorer residents. The three counties east of Brooklyn are Queens, Nassua and Suffolk. From 1940 through 1960, the population of Queens increased by 510,944, Nassau by 893,423 and Suffolk by 469,393. The populations of Nassau and Suffolk Counties more than tripled during those two decades. Many of those who filled the new suburban tracts on Long Island in the 1940s and 1950s were former Brooklyn residents. With Ebbets Field difficult to reach by car, only 700 parking spaces available, and every home game telecast, thousands who had regularly attended Dodger games simply chose to stay home and watch the club on TV.

AUGUST 11   Vern Bickford of the Braves beats the Dodgers 7–0 with a no-hitter in Boston. Bickford walked four and struck out three. The game ended on Duke Snider's double-play grounder.

AUGUST 12   The Dodgers commit seven errors during a 10–2 loss to the Braves in Boston.

Disgusted with the club's second-place standing, Branch Rickey charged the Dodgers with "complete satiety" and "complacency."

AUGUST 15   Preacher Roe beats the Giants 1–0 in New York.

AUGUST 24   Preacher Roe wins again 1–0 defeating the Reds in the first game of a double-header in Cincinnati. The lone run scored on a bases-loaded walk to Pee Wee Reese in the fifth inning. The Dodgers completed the sweep with a 7–3 victory in the second tilt to extend their winning streak to eight games.

AUGUST 26   Roy Campanella hits three home runs in three official at-bats during a 7–5 win over the Reds in Cincinnati. Each of the blows was struck off Ken Raffensberger with Gil Hodges on base. Two of them landed on the roof of the laundry building across the street from the left-field wall at Crosley Field. The other one struck the side of the edifice. It was the Dodgers tenth win in a row.

AUGUST 31   Gil Hodges ties a major league record with four home runs during a 19–3 thrashing of the Braves at Ebbets Field. In his six at-bats, Hodges also singled for 17 total bases, set a club record (since tied) with nine runs batted in, and scored five runs. Each of the homers was struck off of a different pitcher. Hodges went deep on Warren Spahn with a man on base in the second inning, a three-run shot against Norm Roy in a seven-run third, a two-run homer facing Bob Hall in the sixth and another two-run homer off Johnny Antonelli in the eighth. The first three homers went into the lower left-field stands, while the fourth landed in the upper deck. The single came off Antonelli in the seventh. Duke Snider also homered for Brooklyn. The Dodgers collected 21 hits, including four by pitcher Carl Erskine.

SEPTEMBER 6   Don Newcombe starts both games of a double-header against the Phillies in Philadelphia. He hurled a three-hit shutout in the opener, a 2–0 victory. Newcombe went seven innings in the nightcap and left with the Dodgers trailing 2–0. After collecting only one hit off Curt Simmons through the first eight frames, the Dodgers scored three times in the ninth for a 3–2 win. The bases were loaded and two were out when Gil Hodges tied the score with a two-run single. Jackie Robinson was caught in a rundown between third and home, but scored the winning run following a wild throw by Philadelphia catcher Andy Seminick.

Newcombe was 19–11 with a 3.70 ERA in 1950.

SEPTEMBER 7   The Dodgers win 4–3 over the Phillies in Philadelphia to pull with 4½ games of the first place.

The Dodgers lost seven of their next 10 games and it appeared as though the pennant race was over as the Phillies were firmly entrenched in first place. The Philadelphia club hadn't been to the World Series since 1915 and experienced 30 losing seasons in 31 years from 1918 through 1948. Managed by Eddie Sawyer, the young roster of the 1950 Phillies was dubbed "The Whiz Kids."

SEPTEMBER 10   The Dodgers sell Harry Taylor to the Red Sox.

SEPTEMBER 12   The Dodgers win 3–1 over the Reds at Ebbets Field with only one hit off Ewell Blackwell. The only Brooklyn hit was a run-scoring double by Gene Hermanski in the fourth inning. The Dodgers scored twice in the eighth on a hit batsman, an error by Blackwell, a wild pitch and an infield out. Carl Erskine pitched a three-hitter for Brooklyn.

SEPTEMBER 18   Batting lead-off and playing left field, Tommy Brown collects three homers, but the Dodgers lose 9–7 to the Cubs at Ebbets Field. Brown also singled and walked to reach base five times in five plate appearances. The homers were struck off Paul Minner with a runner on base in the third inning, a solo shot against Monk Dubiel in the fourth, and another facing Dubiel with a man on in the eighth.

Brown had only 86 at-bats in 1950 and hit eight home runs. He was playing on September 18 because the Dodgers were auditioning bench players with an eye toward 1951. Three days later, the Brooklyn starting pitcher was Jim Romano, who was making his major league debut. Rookie Steve Lembo was given three starts as a catcher ahead of Roy Campanella. Any chance for a pennant seemed impossible. The Dodgers were nine games out of first place with only 17 games left on the schedule over a period of 13 days. The fans appeared to have given up as well. Only 2,051 watched Brown's three-home run performance.

SEPTEMBER 19   The Dodgers mash the Pirates 14–3 and 3–2 in a double-header at Ebbets Field. In the opener, the Dodgers scored five runs in the first inning and five more in the second.

SEPTEMBER 20   Gil Hodges hits a grand slam off Bill Macdonald in the first inning of a 7–2 win over the Pirates before a "crowd" of 1,011 at Ebbets Field.

SEPTEMBER 24   Erv Palica pitches a two-hitter and hits a grand slam during an 11–0 win over the Phillies at Shibe Park. He struck the bases loaded homer off Bubba Church in the fifth inning. Palica held Philadelphia hitless until the eighth when Andy Seminick led off with a single and Del Ennis doubled with two out.

The win left the Dodgers five games behind with a week to play.

SEPTEMBER 29   The Dodgers come from behind to win twice over the Braves in a double-header at Ebbets Field. Trailing 5–2 in the opener, the Dodgers score five times in the eighth to win 7–5. Down 6–3 in the nightcap, Brooklyn scored three runs in the sixth and one in the seventh for a 7–6 victory.

With two games to play, the Dodgers were only two games behind the Phillies. Those two remaining contests were against the Phils at Ebbets Field in a showdown for the pennant. To reach the World Series, Brooklyn needed to win both games, then beat Philadelphia in a best-of-three pennant playoff. The Dodgers had cut a nine-game lead to two in 11 days by winning 12 of 15 while the Phillies lost eight of 11.

SEPTEMBER 30   The Dodgers pull within one game of first place with a 7–3 victory over the Phillies at Ebbets Field. Erv Palica was the winning pitcher.

OCTOBER 1   With a chance to tie for first place on the final day of the season, the Dodgers lose 4–1 in 10 innings to the Phillies before 35,073 at Ebbets Field. Don Newcombe and Robin Roberts were the starting pitchers. Both entered the contest with 19 victories. Roberts was making his third start in five days. The Phillies scored first in the top of the sixth inning. The Dodgers countered with one in the bottom half on a fluke home run by Pee Wee Reese on a drive which wedged between the screen and the top of the right-field fence. Cal Abrams walked to open the Brooklyn ninth and moved to second on Reese's single. Duke Snider followed with a single to second, but center fielder Richie Ashburn, playing shallow, made a peg to catcher Stan Lopata to nail Abrams at the plate by 15 feet to prevent the winning run from scoring. Abrams was tagged so far up the line he couldn't even go into his slide. After an intentional walk to Jackie Robinson, the Dodgers still had the bases loaded with one out, but Roberts pitched out of the jam. Roberts started the tenth inning rally with a single. After another single by Eddie Waitkus, Dick Sisler sliced a three-run homer into the left-field seats off Newcombe. The Dodgers went out in order in the bottom half. The Phillies were swept in four games by the Yankees in the World Series.

Milt Stock was the third-base coach who waved Abrams to the plate in the ninth inning. He was fired by the Dodgers the following week and never coached in the majors again. Sisler was the son of Hall of Fame first baseman George Sisler, who played in the majors from 1915 through 1930, mostly with the St. Louis Browns. In 1950, the elder Sisler was the chief scout for the Dodgers, experiencing a paradoxical moment by watching his son beat his own club with a pennant-clinching home run.

OCTOBER 10   The Dodgers send Dee Fondy and Chuck Connors to the Cubs for Hank Edwards.

Connors played only one game for the Dodgers before the trade, and only 66 as a major leaguer afterward, but had a long and fascinating life. Before reaching the big leagues in baseball, Connors played for the Boston Celtics from 1946 through 1948. Prior to the first game in Celtics history on November 5, 1946, the six-foot-five Connors shattered the glass backboard in pre-game warm-ups, delaying the contest for half an hour. While playing for the Pacific Coast League's Los Angeles Angels, a Cubs farm team, he caught the attention of a Hollywood producer and went into acting. Chuck's film debut was in the 1952 Spencer Tracy-Katherine Hepburn vehicle Pat and Mike. *Connors was Luke McCain, the lead character on the popular television series* The Rifleman *from 1957 through 1962. He appeared in numerous movies and television dramas until his death in 1992 and won critical acclaim in the role of a slave owner in the 1977 mini-series* Roots. *After the Dodgers relocated to Los Angeles, Connors was a frequent visitor to Dodger Stadium.*

OCTOBER 24   In a radical shake-up of the Dodgers hierarchy, Walter O'Malley becomes majority owner when he buys out Branch Rickey.

Rickey and O'Malley had developed an intense dislike for each other over the years, and by 1950 their differences were irreconcilable. Rickey had to sell because he was in debt. He had borrowed money to purchase his share of the Dodgers in 1945, and payment was due. Shortly before the season ended, Rickey revealed he had sold his 25 percent interest in the Dodgers to New York realtor William Zeckendorf. Under the terms of an agreement between Rickey, O'Malley and John L. Smith when the trio bought 75 percent of the stock in 1945, the other two partners were to have the right of first refusal. Smith died three months earlier, and his shares were held by his widow. Zeckendorf reportedly offered Rickey $1,025,000 for his 25 percent holdings. However, O'Malley and Smith's widow exercised their prior option and acquired Rickey's shares. O'Malley was livid over having to match Zeckendorf's offer, which was triple what he had paid for his share five years earlier, but had little choice if he wanted to gain control of the franchise. On October 28, the Dodgers announced that Rickey's contract as general manager would not be renewed. Within a few days, Rickey took a position as vice-president and general manager of the Pirates, a post he would hold until 1955. Buzzy Bavasi, who was 35 and had been general manager of the Dodgers farm club in Montreal, was promoted to succeed Rickey. Bavasi would be the Dodgers general manager until 1968, a period in which the club won eight NL pennants and four world championships. At the time he took over as majority owner of the Dodgers, the 47-year-old O'Malley wasn't well known in Brooklyn. Until then he had stayed behind the scenes, but once he started running the show everyone in the borough would know his name and would soon speak of it only with disdain. In less than seven years after taking over the Dodgers, O'Malley would move the franchise to Los Angeles.

NOVEMBER 16   The Cubs draft Turk Lown from the Dodgers organization.

NOVEMBER 28   The Dodgers fire Burt Shotton as manager and hire 52-year-old Chuck Dressen.

Shotton was blamed by many for the Dodgers' failure to repeat in 1950 and had close ties to the departed Branch Rickey, so it was no surprise he was fired. Dressen played in the majors as a third baseman from 1925 through 1933. He had previously managed the Reds from 1934 until 1937 to a record of 214–282 and coached in the majors with the Dodgers (1939–46) and Yankees (1947–48). In 1949 and 1950, Dressen was manager of the Oakland club in the Pacific Coast League and won the pennant in his second season. During his first year in Brooklyn, Dressen had the club 13 1/2 games ahead in August only to blow what seemed like a certain pennant to the Giants. The Dodgers recovered to reach the World Series in both 1952 and 1953, only to lose on both occasions to the Yankees. Dressen was fired at the end of the 1953 season when he asked for a multi-year contract.

1951

Season in a Sentence

After leading the Giants by 13½ games on August 11, the Dodgers squander the huge advantage and lose a pennant playoff to their New York rivals capped by Bobby Thomson's historic home run.

Finish • Won • Lost • Pct • GB

Second   97   60   .618   1.0

Manager

Chuck Dressen

Stats

Stats	Dods	NL	Rank
Batting Avg:	.275	.260	1
On-Base Pct:	.352	.331	1
Slugging Pct:	.434	.390	1
Home Runs:	184		1
Stolen Bases:	89		1
ERA:	3.88	3.96	5
Fielding Avg:	.979	.975	2
Runs Scored:	855		1
Runs Allowed:	672		6

Starting Lineup

Roy Campanella, c
Gil Hodges, 1b
Jackie Robinson, 2b
Billy Cox, 3b
Pee Wee Reese, ss
Andy Pafko, lf
Duke Snider, cf
Carl Furillo, rf

Pitchers

Preacher Roe, sp
Don Newcombe, sp
Ralph Branca, sp-rp
Carl Erskine, rp-sp
Clyde King, rp
Bud Podbielan, rp

Attendance

1,282,628 (first in NL)

Club Leaders

Batting Avg:	Jackie Robinson	.338
On-Base Pct:	Jackie Robinson	.429
Slugging Pct:	Roy Campanella	.590
Home Runs:	Gil Hodges	40
RBIs:	Roy Campanella	108
Runs:	Gil Hodges	118
Stolen Bases:	Jackie Robinson	25
Wins:	Preacher Roe	22
Strikeouts:	Don Newcombe	164
ERA:	Preacher Roe	3.04
Saves:	Clyde King	6

APRIL 17   Six days after President Harry Truman relieves General Douglas MacArthur from his command in Korea, the Dodgers lose the opener 5–2 to the Phillies before 19,217 at Ebbets Field. Robin Roberts, who defeated Brooklyn on Opening Day and in the season finale in 1950, pitched a complete game. Carl Erskine was the starter and loser.

APRIL 22   Hitless in his previous 18 at-bats, Carl Furillo homers in the tenth inning to beat the Giants 4–3 in New York. An RBI-single by Pee Wee Reese with two out in ninth sent the game into extra innings.

APRIL 23   Carl Furillo wins an extra-inning game for the second day in a row with a walk-off single in the 16th which beats the Braves 2–1 at Ebbets Field. Joe Hatten (11⅓ innings), Erv Palica (⅔ of an inning) and Clyde King (four innings) pitched for the Dodgers.

MAY 5   The Dodgers club five homers during a 12–8 win over the Reds at Ebbets Field. Gil Hodges hit two of the homers, and Roy Campanella, Cal Abrams and Billy Cox one each.

Campanella won the National league Most Valuable Player Award in 1951 by hitting .325 with 33 homers and 108 RBIs.

MAY 6 — Pee Wee Reese hits a grand slam off Cloyd Boyer in the seventh inning for a 7–5 lead, but the Cardinals rally for six runs in the eighth to defeat the Dodgers 11–7 at Ebbets Field.

Reese batted .286 with 10 home runs in 1951.

MAY 13 — Down 6–0, the Dodgers score two runs in the third inning, three in the fourth, four in the sixth and three in the eighth to defeat the Braves 12–6 in Boston. Carl Furillo's three-run homer in the sixth put Brooklyn into the lead.

MAY 15 — Duke Snider hits a grand slam off Cal McLish in the seventh inning of an 8–4 win over the Cubs in Chicago. Snider struck out in his previous three plate appearances.

MAY 20 — The Dodgers rout the Reds 10–3 and 14–4 in a double-header at Cincinnati. Brooklyn scored seven runs in the sixth inning of the second game.

MAY 22 — The Dodgers score seven runs in the seventh inning and power their way to a 17–8 win over the Pirates in Pittsburgh.

MAY 23 — The Dodgers reach double digits in runs scored for the fourth game in a row with a 11–4 victory over the Pirates in Pittsburgh. Billy Cox hit a grand slam off Bill Werle in the fifth inning.

MAY 31 — A rhubarb between Jackie Robinson and Phillies pitcher Russ Meyer develops in the eighth inning of a 4–3 win at Ebbets Field. Robinson was trapped off third when Carl Furillo missed the bunt on a squeeze attempt. As Robinson dashed home, Meyer, covering the plate, dropped the throw, but attempted to block Robinson off the plate by bumping him in the chest. After an angry exchange of words, players from both teams prevented blows from being struck. Meyer told Robinson to meet him under the stands after the game, but later cooled off and went to the Dodger clubhouse to apologize.

JUNE 3 — Don Newcombe strikes out 12 batters during an 8–3 win over the Cubs in the first game of a double-header at Ebbets Field. The Dodgers completed the sweep with a 3–2 victory in 10 innings in the nightcap.

JUNE 6 — Chuck Dressen is ejected three times from a 3–2 win over the Cardinals at Ebbets Field. Dressen was first given the thumb for objecting to the balls and strikes calls of umpire Art Gore in the fifth inning. Dressen was later spotted hiding in the dugout wearing a groundskeeper's cap and jacket and told to leave again. The Dodgers manager then dressed in his street clothes and tried to direct the club by giving signs from a box seat at the far end of the Brooklyn dugout until the umpires discovered the ruse.

JUNE 14 — Gil Hodges hits a two-run homer in the ninth inning to beat the Cardinals 2–1 in St. Louis. The Dodgers won despite surrendering 15 hits. In the fifth inning, five Cardinals reached base, but none scored because Roy Campanella picked two men off second base.

Hodges hit 20 home runs in the first 51 games of 1951, and finished with 40 to break the previous club record of 35 homers set by Babe Herman in 1930. Hodges also hit .268, scored 118 runs, and drove in 103.

JUNE 15   The Dodgers trade Gene Hermanski, Eddie Miksis, Bruce Edwards and Joe Hatten to the Cubs for Andy Pafko, Rube Walker, Wayne Terwilliger and Johnny Schmitz.

The Dodgers acquired Pafko, the best player on the Chicago roster, along with three others in exchange for four players who were sitting on the bench. The trade was seen as a steal for the Dodgers. The lineup was loaded with the exception of a capable left fielder, and Pafko filled that void. He never fully lived up to expectations in Brooklyn, but he was a solid starter until traded to the Braves in January 1953.

JUNE 17   Roy Campanella hits a two-run homer in the ninth inning which defeats the Cubs 3–2 in Chicago.

JUNE 21   Preacher Roe runs his record to 10–0 with a 6–4 victory over the Reds in Cincinnati.

JUNE 22   The start of the game between the Dodgers and Pirates in Pittsburgh is delayed for two hours and 10 minutes by a short circuit in the lighting system. There was another delay of 36 innings in the sixth inning by rain. The contest concluded at 1:56 a.m. with an 8–4 Dodger victory.

JUNE 23   Don Newcombe pitches a three hitter to defeat the Pirates 13–1 at Forbes Field. The only Pittsburgh hit was a single by Ralph Kiner in the first inning.

JUNE 30   The Dodgers score seven runs in the fourth inning and defeat the Phillies 14–8 at Ebbets Field.

JULY 1   The Dodgers collect only one hit off Russ Meyer, but defeat the Phillies 2–0 in Philadelphia. The two Brooklyn runs scored in the third on two walks and a triple by Pee Wee Reese. Don Newcombe pitched the shutout.

JULY 3   Hugh Casey, who played for the Dodgers from 1939 through 1948 and twice led the NL in saves, commits suicide at the age of 37.

JULY 4   The Dodgers win a thrilling 6–5 decision in 11 innings over the Giants in the first game of a double-header at Ebbets Field. Brooklyn trailed 4–0 before scoring three runs in the eighth inning and one in the ninth. New York took a 5–4 advantage in the top of the 11th on Bobby Thomson's home run, but the Dodgers rallied for two in their half. The winning run scored on a squeeze bunt by Preacher Roe which brought Jackie Robinson in from third base. Repeating his ploy of four weeks earlier, Chuck Dressen tried to manage the Dodgers from the box seats after being ejected until ordered from the park a second time (see June 6, 1951). The Dodgers also won the second contest 4–2.

After the Dodgers won again 8–4 over the Giants at Ebbets Field the following day, Dressen crowed, "We knocked them out. They'll never bother us again." At that point, the Dodgers had a lead of 9½ games.

Dodger hurlers take a pitching lesson, though in 1951 they didn't need one, dominating the league. Players are, from left to right, Preacher Roe, Don Newcombe, coach, pitcher, Carl Erskine and Ralph Branca.

JULY 8   A two-run homer by Jackie Robinson in the 10th inning beats the Phillies 6–4 in Philadelphia.

              Robinson batted .338 with 19 homers and 108 runs scored in 1951.

JULY 10   Jackie Robinson, Gil Hodges and Don Newcombe star in an 8–3 National League win in the All-Star Game at Briggs Stadium in Detroit. Robinson singled twice in four at-bats, scored a run and drove in one. Hodges collected two singles in plate at-bats, scored twice and accounted for two RBIs. Newcombe took the mound in the sixth and pitched three scoreless innings.

              Newcombe had a record of 20–9, a 3.28 ERA, and a league-leading 164 strikeouts in 272 innings in 1951.

JULY 13   The Dodgers extend their winning streak to eight games with an 8–6 decision over the Cubs at Ebbets Field.

JULY 16   Carl Erskine pitches a two-hitter to beat the Reds 11–2 at Ebbets Field. Erskine retired the first 21 batters to face him before the perfect-game bid ended when

Ted Kluszewski singled leading off the eighth. Virgil Stallcup followed with a two-run homer. Erskine pitched on only one day of rest. He lasted only three innings in a start against the Cubs on July 14.

Erskine's entire major league career, which lasted from 1948 through 1959, was spent with the Dodgers. His career highlights were no-hitters in 1952 and 1956 and a 14-strikeout performance in game three of the 1953 World Series. Erskine's final career record was 122–78.

JULY 18   Ralph Kiner hits three homers for the Pirates during a 13–12 win over the Dodgers at Ebbets Field. Brooklyn trailed 10–2 before scoring four runs in the fourth inning and six in the sixth for a 12–11 advantage, only to have the Pirates plate two runs in the eighth.

JULY 24   The Dodgers break a 2–2 tie with four runs in the 10th inning, three of them on Roy Campanella's home run, and beat the Cubs 6–3 in Chicago.

JULY 27   Trailing 9–3, the Dodgers score a run in the sixth inning, two in the seventh, three in the eighth and three in the ninth to win 12–9 over the Cardinals in St. Louis. Roy Campanclla's three-run homer in the ninth snapped the 9–9 tie.

JULY 29   Down 3–1, the Dodgers score seven runs in the seventh inning and beat the Cardinals 9–3 in St. Louis.

JULY 31   The Dodgers extend their winning strcak to 10 games with an 8–3 win over the Pirates in Pittsburgh.

AUGUST 5   The Dodgers sweep the Reds 9–8 and 2–0 at Crosley Field. Roy Campanella hit a grand slam off Ken Raffensberger in the sixth inning for a 9–3 lead before Cincinnati scored five times in the ninth. In the game two, Ralph Branca pitched the shutout and drove in both runs with singles in the third and eighth innings.

Campanella hit seven home runs in 10 games from August 5 through August 12.

AUGUST 9   The Dodgers defeat the Giants 6–5 at Ebbets Field despite walking 15 batters. Art Gore ejected the entire Dodgers bench because of the heckling of his decisions.

The win was the Dodgers' 12th in 15 games against the Giants and gave Brooklyn a 12½-game lead. Not content to let sleeping dogs lie, the Dodgers stood outside the Giants clubhouse after the game and taunted and ridiculed their New York rivals at length by letting them know their chances for the pennant were finished.

AUGUST 11   The Dodgers split a double-header with the Braves at Ebbets Field, winning 8–1 and losing 4–3. In between games of the double-header, the Dodgers had a lead of 13½ games over the second-place Giants, and were 16 games up in the loss column. The Dodgers possessed a record of 70–35 while the Giants were 59–51. The fact that the Giants were over .500 was remarkable. The club lost 11 games in a row in April.

Telecast by WCBS-TV, the two August 11 contests at Ebbets Field were also of historic significance as the first in baseball history to be shown in color.

It was conducted to test CBS monitors and equipment and wasn't available to the general public. CBS and RCA hoped to place color TV on the market within a few months, but the government put a stop to the plan because much of the material necessary to produce the sets were needed for war supplies. Color televisions weren't placed on the mass market until 1954, when a 12½-inch model sold for $1,000.

August 13   Those with musical instruments are admitted free on "Music Depreciation Night" at Ebbets Field. A total of 2,426 availed themselves of the opportunity, including a man with a piano, and watched the Dodgers beat the Braves 7–6. The promotion grew out of a controversy involving the Dodgers Sym-phony, a band of amateur musicians who had been playing at Ebbets Field since the 1930s. A month earlier, the band had to disband temporarily because the musicians' union objected to one of its members playing for free.

August 22   The Dodgers sweep the Cardinals 4–3 and 8–7 with a pair of 10-inning wins at Ebbets Field. A single by Gil Hodges drove in the winning run in the opener. In the second tilt, the Dodgers were down 7–2 before scoring one run in the fifth inning, one in the sixth, three in the ninth and one in the 10th. Jackie Robinson doubled in a run in the ninth and drove in the game-winner with a single. Robinson had seven hits, five of them in the second game, in 11 at-bats during the twin bill. Relief pitcher Clyde King was the winning pitcher in both games.

The Dodgers were 18–4 against the Cardinals in 1951, including one streak of 14 wins in a row.

August 24   Ralph Branca pitches the Dodgers to a 1–0 win over the Cubs at Ebbets Field. He retired the last 20 batters to face him. The lone run scored in the first inning on a bunt double by Jackie Robinson which rolled between first baseman Chuck Connors and second baseman Eddie Miksis.

August 26   A walk-off homer by Jackie Robinson beats the Pirates 4–3 in the second game of a double-header at Ebbets Field. Pittsburgh won the opener 12–11 after the Dodgers blew a 9–3, sixth-inning lead.

August 27   Ralph Branca pitches a two-hitter to defeat the Pirates 5–0 in the first game of a double-header at Ebbets Field. Branca had a no-hitter in progress after eight innings with the help of Carl Furillo, who picked up a grounder in right field and threw out Pittsburgh pitcher Mel Queen at first base in the third. In the ninth, Pete Castiglione and Catfish Metkovich singled with none out. It was Branca's third shutout during the month of August. Pittsburgh won the second contest 5–2.

On the same day, the Giants won their 16th game in a row with a sweep of the Cubs in a double-header in New York. The lead of 13½ games on August 11 had dwindled to just five.

August 29   Gil Hodges drives in seven runs with two homers and a double during a 13–1 lambasting of the Reds at Ebbets Field.

September 1   Don Mueller hits three homers for the Giants during an 8–1 win over the Dodgers in New York.

SEPTEMBER 2 — Don Mueller hits two more home runs for the Giants in an 11–2 win over the Dodgers at the Polo Grounds.

SEPTEMBER 3 — The Dodgers sweep the Braves with a pair of 7–2 wins at Ebbets Field. Roy Campanella collected six consecutive hits during the double-header, including two homers. One of them was a grand slam off Max Surkont in the third inning of the first game.

SEPTEMBER 5 — Gil Hodges breaks a 1–1 tie with a grand slam off Ken Johnson in the fifth inning of a 5–2 triumph over the Phillies at Ebbets Field.

SEPTEMBER 8 — Don Newcombe pitches a two-hitter to defeat the Giants 9–0 at Ebbets Field. The only New York hits were singles by Whitey Lockman and Bobby Thomson. The win gave the Dodgers a 6½ game lead. Afterward, Chuck Dressen said he was going to give his starting pitchers an extra day of rest and bench some of his regulars nursing nagging injuries in preparation for the World Series.

SEPTEMBER 14 — Preacher Roe earns his 20th win of the season with a 3–1 decision over the Pirates at Ebbets Field.

> *Roe had a record of 22–3 in 1951 with an ERA of 3.04. His winning percentage of .880 is the best in club history by a pitcher with at least 17 victories.*

SEPTEMBER 18 — The Dodgers' lead in the pennant race is whittled to three games with a 7–1 loss to the Cardinals in St. Louis.

SEPTEMBER 19 — In St. Louis, Preacher Roe is presented with a new Cadillac by friends in from southeastern Missouri and northeastern Arkansas, then pitches a shutout to beat the Cardinals 2–0.

SEPTEMBER 20 — The Dodgers defeat the Cardinals 4–3 in St. Louis to take a 4½-game lead in the pennant race. The Giants had seven games remaining and the Dodgers 10. Even if the Giants won all seven, the Dodgers needed to win only five of 10 to clinch the pennant.

SEPTEMBER 25 — The Dodgers lead by only one game over the Giants after losing 6–3 and 14–2 in a double-header against the Braves in Boston. The Dodgers had five games left to play, and the Giants three.

SEPTEMBER 26 — The Dodgers score seven runs in the eighth inning and crush the Braves 15–5 in Boston.

SEPTEMBER 27 — The Dodgers lose 4–3 to the Braves in Boston with the help of a controversial decision by umpire Frank Dascoli. With the score 3–3 in the Boston eighth, Bob Addis tried to score from first base on a grounder to Jackie Robinson, who fired plateward to Roy Campanella. Dascoli called Addis safe. Campanella slammed his mitt to the ground and was thumbed from the game. A few minutes later, Dascoli exiled the entire Dodgers bench to the clubhouse, leaving only Chuck Dressen and coach Jake Pitler. After the game, Dodger players splintered a panel in the door leading to the umpire's dressing room.

> *Among those ejected was Bill Sharman, a Dodger farmhand who was on the roster in September. Sharman never got into a big-league game, but later played on NBA championship teams with the Celtics in 1957, 1959, 1960 and 1961*

and coached the Lakers to the title in 1972, which helped him earn a berth in the Basketball Hall of Fame.

SEPTEMBER 28   The Dodgers fall into a first-place tie with a 4–3 loss to the Phillies in Philadelphia. Brooklyn had a 3–0 lead before the Phillies scored a run in the sixth, two in the eighth and one in the ninth for the win. Both the Dodgers and Giants had two games left to play.

SEPTEMBER 29   On the second-to-last day of the season, the Dodgers win 5–0 over the Phillies in Philadelphia. Don Newcombe pitched the shutout for his 20th victory of the season. The Giants stayed tied for the lead with a 3–0 victory over the Braves in Boston. For the third-straight season, and the fourth in six years, the Dodgers went into the final game of the season with the pennant still in doubt.

SEPTEMBER 30   On the final day of the regular season, the Dodgers and Giants both win to force a best-of-three playoff to decide the National League champion and a berth in the World Series against the Yankees. The Giants played the Braves in Boston and won 3–2. In Philadelphia, the Dodgers fell behind 6–1 in the third inning and were trailing 8–5 in the sixth when the Giants contest ended. The Dodgers scored three runs in the eighth to tie the score 8–8 to extend the contest into extra innings. With two out and Philadelphia runners on first and second in the 12th, Eddie Waitkus lashed a line drive which appeared to be headed toward the outfield. But second baseman Jackie Robinson made a sensational diving catch in which he hit the ground so hard that the wind was knocked out of him. After preventing the winning run from scoring, Robinson provided the winning tally with a homer in the 14th off Robin Roberts for a 9–8 Brooklyn victory. Don Newcombe, after shutting out the Phillies the day before, pitched 5^1/$_3$ innings of relief. Bud Podbielan, the seventh Dodger hurler, earned the victory by pitching the last 1^1/$_3$ innings.

After falling behind the Dodgers by 13^1/$_2$ games in August, the Giants went 37–7 to force the tie for first place. Over the same period, the Dodgers had a record of 26–23.

OCTOBER 1   The Giants open the playoff series with a 3–1 win before 30,707 at Ebbets Field. A home run by Andy Pafko put the Dodgers ahead 1–0 in the second inning. Bobby Thomson gave the Giants the advantage with a two-run homer off Ralph Branca in the fourth.

The first game of the 1951 playoff series was the first live sporting event televised from coast-to-coast. The cable equipment necessary to transmit televised images from the Atlantic to the Pacific coasts had just become available on September 4. The first game was televised by CBS, and games two and three by NBC. Chesterfield cigarettes was the sponsor.

OCTOBER 2   The Dodgers force a deciding third game by defeating the Giants 10–0 at the Polo Grounds. Clem Labine pitched the shutout. He was the starter because Preacher Roe had a sore arm and was unavailable. Home runs were struck by Jackie Robinson, Gil Hodges, Rube Walker and Andy Pafko. Walker was in the game as a catcher in place of the injured Roy Campanella.

A rookie for the Dodgers in 1951, Labine was brilliant down the stretch with a 5–1 record and a 2.20 ERA in 65^1/$_3$ innings. A reliever for most of his 13-year *career, Labine didn't pitch another complete game until 1955 and never threw another shutout in a regular season game, although he did record one during the 1956 World Series.*

OCTOBER 3   The Dodgers lose the pennant by dropping one of the most dramatic games in major league history. Brooklyn scored three runs in the eighth to take a 4–1 lead and carried the advantage into the ninth with Don Newcombe on the mound. Al Dark opened the New York ninth with a single and went to third on a one-base hit by Don Mueller. After Monte Irvin popped out, an announcement came over the public address system in the press box. "Attention press. World Series credentials for Ebbets Field can be picked up at 6 o'clock tonight at the Biltmore Hotel." Moments later, Whitey Lockman doubled, scoring Dark and sending Mueller to third. Mueller broke his ankle sliding into the bag, and was replaced by pinch-runner Clint Hartung. With the score 4–2, one out, and runners on first and third, Bobby Thomson was the next hitter. Chuck Dressen had Carl Erskine and Ralph Branca warming up in the bullpen and chose Branca, who had pitched eight innings two days earlier. Wearing uniform number 13, Branca got a called first strike past Thomson, but the next pitch sailed into the left-field seats for a three-run homer and a 5–4 Giants victory. As the Giants celebrated at home plate, the Dodgers trudged 500 feet across the field to the clubhouse behind the center field wall. Millions have probably claimed they were at the Polo Grounds for the historic game, but only 34,320 were in attendance, about 22,000 short of capacity even though two New York-based teams in one of the fiercest rivalries in history were playing to decide the National League pennant. Many of those left before the ninth-inning rally because they were convinced the game was over. The Giants also failed to sell out any of their three home World Series games even though the intra-city rival Yankees were the opponents. The Yanks won the Series in six games.

Chuck Dressen's decision to bring Branca into the game is still being second-guessed more than a half-century later, but Ralph had a 3.26 ERA in 1951 on a staff in which only four pitchers posted an earned-run average lower than 4.15. The other three were Newcombe (3.28), who was obviously weakening in the third playoff game; Clem Labine (2.20), who pitched nine innings the day before; and Preacher Roe (3.02), who had a sore arm and was a left-hander with three right-handed power hitters (Thomson, Willie Mays and Wes Westrum) up next for the Giants. The Dodgers had no closer in the present-day sense of the term. Branca had three saves in 1951. The only other pitchers with more were Carl Erskine (four saves and a 4.46 ERA) and Clyde King (six saves and a 4.15 ERA). There were also a myriad of reasons for leaving Branca on the bench. Counting the deciding playoff game, he had a 2–6 record and allowed 11 homers against the Giants in 1951, including three home runs to Thomson, one of them two days earlier when Branca pitched eight innings. Branca was also the losing pitcher in nine of Brooklyn's last 23 defeats. Entering the October 3 contest, he had allowed 21 runs in 21 innings in his previous six appearances. Newcombe wouldn't pitch another big-league game until 1954. He spent the 1952 and 1953 seasons in the Army.

OCTOBER 20   Ralph Branca marries Ann Mulvey at St. Francis of Assisi Church in Brooklyn. His bride was the daughter of James and Dearie Mulvey, who owned one-fourth of the Dodgers franchise. Ralph and Ann's daughter Mary would marry Bobby Valentine, who played for the Dodgers from 1970 through 1972 and later managed the Texas Rangers (1985–92) and Mets (1996–2002).

With All Deliberate Speed

Jackie Robinson changed baseball forever in 1947 by integrating the sport. He won the NL Rookie-of-the-Year award that season and was MVP in 1949. Despite his immediate success, and that of African-Americans and dark-skinned Latins over the next few years, including Larry Doby, Roy Campanella, Don Newcombe, Minnie Minoso and Willie Mays, most clubs were slow to accept minority players. By 1952, only six of the 16 clubs in the majors had integrated.

Even racial pioneers Branch Rickey and Bill Veeck were reluctant to add black players to their new clubs after they had moved out of Brooklyn and Cleveland. In 1949, Rickey's Dodgers and Veeck's Indians combined employed seven of the nine African-Americans in the majors that season. Rickey left the Dodgers for the Pirates at the end of the 1950 season, but Pittsburgh had no dark-skinned players until Carlos Bernier joined the club in 1953. The 1952 Pirates were notoriously inept, posting a record of 42–112 with an all-white roster. Veeck sold the Indians in 1949 and bought the St. Louis Browns in July 1951. From that time until Veeck sold the Browns in September 1953, the only African-American player on his St. Louis teams was Satchel Paige. The Browns finished in eighth place in 1951, seventh in 1952 and eighth in 1953 in an eight-team league.

The last team to integrate was the Red Sox in July 1959. They weren't the last all-Caucasian team, however. That honor goes to the Kansas City Athletics, which had no minorities on the roster during the entire 1960 season.

The American League was far slower to embrace integration than their National League counterpart. In 1959, there were 48 minority players in the NL, 18 in the AL and one who played in both circuits.

The following is a list of the number of minority players, including African-Americans and dark-skinned Latins, from 1947 through 1959.

Year	Teams	Minority Players
1947	3	5
1948	2	4
1949	3	9
1950	4	9
1951	6	19
1952	6	21
1953	9	25
1954	12	37
1955	13	44
1956	13	51
1957	14	52
1958	15	56
1959	16	67

1952

L A

Season in a Sentence

The Dodgers rebound from the 1951 debacle to hold off the Giants in the NL pennant race, then take a three-games-to-two lead in the World Series only to drop games six and seven to the Yankees.

Finish • Won • Lost • Pct • GB

First   96   57   .627   +4.5

World Series

The Dodgers lost to the New York Yankees four games to three.

Manager

Chuck Dressen

Stats

Stats	Dods	NL	Rank
Batting Avg:	.262	.253	3
On-Base Pct:	.348	.323	1
Slugging Pct:	.399	.374	2
Home Runs:	153		1
Stolen Bases:	90		1
ERA:	3.53	3.73	2
Fielding Avg:	.982	.976	1
Runs Scored:	775		1
Runs Allowed:	603		2

Starting Lineup

Roy Campanella, c
Gil Hodges, 1b
Jackie Robinson, 2b
Billy Cox, 3b
Pee Wee Reese, ss
Andy Pafko, lf
Duke Snider, cf
Carl Furillo, rf
George Shuba, lf
Bobby Morgan, 3b

Pitchers

Carl Erskine, sp
Billy Loes, sp-rp
Ben Wade, sp-rp
Preacher Roe, sp
Chris Van Cuyk, sp-rp
Johnny Rutherford, sp-rp
Joe Black, rp

Attendance

1,088,704 (first in NL)

Club Leaders

Batting Avg:	Jackie Robinson	.308
On-Base Pct:	Jackie Robinson	.440
Slugging Pct:	Gil Hodges	.500
Home Runs:	Gil Hodges	32
RBIs:	Gil Hodges	102
Runs:	Jackie Robinson	104
Stolen Bases:	Pee Wee Reese	30
Wins:	Carl Erskine	14
Strikeouts:	Carl Erskine	131
ERA:	Joe Black	2.15
Saves:	Joe Black	15

MARCH 5   Industrial designer Norman Bel Geddes reveals that Walter O'Malley has commissioned him to design a new stadium to eventually replace Ebbets Field. The new facility would include a retractable roof, 28-inch wide foam rubber seats to be heated in cold weather, a 7,000-car parking garage, automatic hot dog vending machines, a new lighting system without steel towers, and a synthetic substance to replace grass on the entire field which could be painted any color. A shopping center would be located underneath.

The futuristic design was revolutionary to say the least. The first domed stadium in baseball was the Astrodome in Houston, which opened in 1965, and was also the location of the first artificial turf a year later. The first retractable dome was Skydome in Toronto in 1989.

APRIL 15   The Dodgers open the season with a 3–2 win over the Braves in Boston as Preacher Roe outduels Warren Spahn. Roy Campanella collected three hits and drove in two runs.

Campanella hit .269 with 22 home runs in 1952.

APRIL 16   Duke Snider collects five hits in six at-bats during a 14–8 thrashing of the Braves in Boston. The Dodgers collected 20 hits in all.

Snider batted .303 with 21 home runs in 1952.

APRIL 18   The Dodgers win the home opener 7–6 in 12 innings over the Giants before 31,032 at Ebbets Field. The winning run scored on Andy Pafko's second home run of the game. Jackie Robinson also homered.

Robinson's on-base percentage of .440 led the National League in 1952. He also hit .308, clubbed 19 homers, and scored 108 runs.

APRIL 19   The Dodgers collect five homers during an 11–6 triumph over the Giants at Ebbets Field. In the seventh inning, Roy Campanella, Andy Pafko and Duke Snider hit consecutive homers. Pafko also homered in the second. Carl Furillo hit a grand slam off Max Lanier in the fourth. Ralph Branca, in his first appearance since game three of the 1951 playoff game (see October 3, 1951), pitched a complete game, but allowed four home runs. The victory gave the Dodgers a record of 5–0.

Branca seemed to take his pennant-losing pitch the previous October in stride. In February 1952, during the annual dinner of the New York chapter of the Baseball Writers' Association, he shared the stage with Bobby Thomson. Branca sang a song titled "Branca's Lament (Oh What He Did To Me)" to the tune of "Because of You." Branca switched from number 13 to number 12 hoping for better luck, but during spring training, he fell off a chair and onto a Coke bottle lying on the floor, injuring his back. Only 26 at the start of the 1952 season, he was 12–12 with a 4.69 ERA in four seasons over the remainder of his career. The Dodgers sold Branca to the Tigers in July 1953.

APRIL 29   A Dodgers-Cardinals game in St. Louis is delayed for 65 minutes because the bartenders go on strike and the electricians in charge of the lighting system refuse to cross the picket line. The Dodgers won the contest 4–1.

MAY 2   Held hitless by Turk Lown through eight innings, the Dodgers score three runs in the ninth to beat the Cubs 3–1 in Chicago. Billy Cox broke up the no-hit bid with a lead-off single, which was followed by a double from Jackie Robinson, Carl Furillo's single, and a sacrifice fly by Gil Hodges.

MAY 13   The Dodgers outslug the Cardinals 14–8 at Ebbets Field.

The Dodgers in 1952 became the first team in major league history to put numbers on the fronts of the uniforms. The numerals were in red, to contrast with the blue trim, and were placed on the front to aid television viewers. There were no numbers on the front of the road jerseys, because no away games were telecast that season. Numbers were added to the road grays in 1958. The red numerals have been a feature of Dodger uniforms ever since.

MAY 15	In his first major league start, Billy Loes pitches a shutout and defeats the Pirates 2–0 at Ebbets Field.
MAY 17	The Dodgers score nine runs in the second inning and defeat the Pirates 12–7 in Pittsburgh. Brooklyn pitcher Ben Wade struck out 11 batters, including six in a row in the first, second and third innings.
MAY 21	The Dodgers strike for 15 runs in the first inning, a modern National league record for runs in an inning, on the way to a 19–1 thrashing of the Reds at Ebbets Field. Things started innocently enough with a ground out by Billy Cox against starting pitcher Ewell Blackwell before the next 19 batters reached base on a home run, a double, eight singles, seven walks and two hit batsmen. The streak of 19 straight batters reaching base is a major league record. An even dozen of the 15 first-inning runs scored after two were out. Starting pitcher Chris Van Cuyk pitched his first career complete game and collected four hits.

> *After Cox grounded out to third baseman Bobby Adams, Pee Wee Reese walked on four pitches and Duke Snider homered on a 3–2 pitch to make the score 2–0. Jackie Robinson hit a bloop double over shortstop, Andy Pafko walked, and George Shuba contributed a single (3–0). Bud Byerly replaced Blackwell. Pafko was caught trying to steal third for the second out. After Gil Hodges was issued a walk, Rube Walker, Van Cuyk, Cox and Reese followed with four consecutive RBI-singles (7–0). Herm Wehemier replaced Byerly as the third Cincinnati pitcher of the inning. Snider walked on a full-count pitch to load the bases, and Robinson was hit by a pitch (8–0). Pafko brought two home with a single (10–0). Frank Smith came to the mound as the fourth Reds hurler and walked Shuba and Hodges (11–0), then gave up a two-run single to Walker, which took a bad hop over the head of second-baseman Grady Hatton (13–0). Van Cuyk singled in another run (14–0), and Cox was hit by a pitch to load the bases. Reese walked (15–0). The sacks were still full when Snider struck out looking to end the inning.*

MAY 23	Roy Campanella drives in all five Dodger runs in a 5–1 win over the Phillies in Philadelphia. Campanella hit a solo homer in the second inning and a grand slam in the third, both off Karl Drews.
MAY 24	The Dodgers extend their winning streak to eight games with a 5–0 decision over the Phillies in Philadelphia. Billy Loes pitched the shutout.
MAY 30	Gil Hodges drives in eight runs, five of them in the second game, during a double-header sweep of the Braves at Ebbets Field. The Dodgers won 5–4 and 11–2. In the two games, Hodges collected six hits, including a home run and a double, in seven at-bats. In the nightcap, Carl Erskine pitched seven innings of relief and allowed one run and one hit.

> *Hodges hit .254 with 32 homers and 102 runs batted in during the 1952 season.*

JUNE 5	The Dodgers strand 16 base runners, but beat the Pirates 2–0 at Forbes Field. Pittsburgh pitchers walked 15 batters.
JUNE 7	The Dodgers trounce the Reds 11–3 in Cincinnati. Carl Furillo drove in five runs.

JUNE 8   The Dodgers rout the Reds 11–7 and 10–4 in a double-header in Cincinnati. Trailing 4–2 in the second contest, the Dodgers exploded for seven runs in the eighth, four of them on a grand slam by Carl Furillo off Frank Smith.

JUNE 9   The Dodgers extend their winning streak to nine games with a 6–2 decision over the Cardinals in St. Louis. Brooklyn's record was 35–11.

JUNE 17   The Dodgers sign Tommy Holmes, most recently with the Braves, as a free agent.

JUNE 19   Carl Erskine pitches a no-hitter to defeat the Cubs 5–0 at Ebbets Field. The only Chicago base runner was opposing pitcher Willie Ramsdell, who walked on four pitches with two out in the third inning. Erskine struck out only one batter. In the ninth, Bob Ramazzotti bounced out to third baseman Bobby Morgan. Player-manager Phil Cavaretta inserted himself into the game as a pinch-hitter and lofted a fly ball to center fielder Duke Snider. The final out was recorded on a routine grounder by Eddie Miksis to shortstop Pee Wee Reese.

JUNE 20   A two-out, two-run, pinch-hit, walk-off homer by George Shuba beats the Pirates 5–4 at Ebbets Field.

JUNE 21   The Dodgers explode for nine runs in the eighth inning and beat the Pirates 14–4 at Ebbets Field.

JULY 6   Pitcher Ben Wade homers in consecutive plate appearances off Warren Spahn in the second and third inning of an 8–2 win over the Braves in Boston.

JULY 7   Baseball announces a worldwide tour termed "an important role in the United States truth crusade against Communism." It would involve the Dodgers and Cleveland Indians to start immediately after the 1952 World Series. The journey was scheduled to last 60 days and cover 35,000 miles, with 22 stops in Hawaii, the Philippines, Australia, Singapore, India, Israel, Greece, Italy, Spain, Portugal, Morocco, Bermuda, Puerto Rico, Venezuela, the Dominican Republic and Cuba. It was hoped that black players on both teams would "combat Communist propaganda that racial minorities are discriminated against and denied equal opportunity in the United States." In 1952, however, total equality was far from a reality in baseball as 10 of the 16 teams in the majors still fielded an all-white roster. Of the 21 black players in the majors, 11 were members of the Dodgers and Indians. The grandiose plan fell through because of a lack of financing and the reluctance of players to spend two months of the off-season traveling around the world.

JULY 10   Jackie Robinson homers off Vic Raschi in the first inning of the All-Star Game, played at Shibe Park in Philadelphia. The National League won 3–2 in a contest called after five innings by rain.

JULY 12   The Dodgers collect 22 hits and clout the Cubs 12–2 in Chicago. Pee Wee Reese had five hits, including two doubles, in five at-bats before being substituted in the eighth inning.

JULY 19   Pee Wee Reese hits a grand slam off Paul LaPalme in the eighth inning of a 9–1 victory over the Pirates in Pittsburgh.

Reese batted .272 and scored 94 runs in 1952.

JULY 22   After the Reds score two runs in the ninth inning and four in the 10th for a 6–2 lead, the Dodgers stage a dramatic rally with five tallies in the bottom of the 10th to win 7–6 at Ebbets Field. Pee Wee Reese doubled in the first run, and Andy Pafko the second with a single. Carl Furillo tied the contest, plating two runs with a bases-loaded single. After Gil Hodges walked to load the bases again, Rube Walker was hit by a pitch. It was Brooklyn's ninth win in a row and gave the club a 60–23 record.

JULY 24   A walk-off homer by Duke Snider in the 11th inning beats the Reds 2–1 in the second game of a double-header at Ebbets Field. Cincinnati won the opener 3–2.

                 The Dodgers beat up on the bottom three teams in the league in 1952. They were 19–3 against the Pirates, 18–3 against the Braves and 17–5 versus the Reds for a combined record of 54–11.

JULY 31   The Dodgers score three runs in the ninth inning and one in the 11th to beat the Pirates 7–6 in the first game of a double-header at Ebbets Field. Pittsburgh took a 6–0 lead with six runs in the top of the second, but the Dodgers rallied with two in their half and one in the third to set the stage for the late-inning heroics. In the ninth, the three runs scored on a homer by Gil Hodges, two walks, and singles from Jackie Robinson and Andy Pafko. In the 11th, the winning tally crossed the plate on a bases-loaded walk by Paul LaPalme to Rocky Bridges. The Dodgers completed the sweep with a 4–1 victory in the nightcap. Joe Landrum pitched a three-hitter in his first major league start.

                 The victory was Landrum's only one as a major leaguer. He was 1–3 with a 5.64 ERA in 44²/₃ innings during his career.

AUGUST 1   The Dodgers sell Johnny Schmitz to the Yankees.

AUGUST 5   Gil Hodges hits a grand slam off Jim Hearn in the sixth inning for a 4–0 lead, but the Dodgers lose 7–6 in 15 innings to the Giants at the Polo Grounds. Brooklyn scored in the top of both the 14th and 15th, but New York rallied in the bottom half each time.

AUGUST 7   Roy Campanella hits a grand slam off George Spencer in the first inning to pave the way for a 7–5 triumph over the Giants in the second inning at the Polo Grounds. New York won the opener 8–2.

AUGUST 8   A three-run homer by Andy Pafko in the 10th inning beats the Phillies 6–3 in Philadelphia.

AUGUST 13   King Faisal II, the 17-year-old ruler of Iraq, attends a double-header against the Giants at Ebbets Field. The Dodgers won 5–4 and lost 8–4.

                 King Faisal II was murdered during a military coup which eliminated the monarchy in 1958.

AUGUST 16   The Dodgers shell the Phillies 15–6 in a contest at Ebbets Field called after six innings by rain.

AUGUST 25   The Dodgers sweep the Cardinals 2–1 and 9–5 at Sportsman's Park. Johnny Rutherford pitched a two-hitter in the opener. The only St. Louis hits were a double by Red Schoendienst in the second inning and a single from Vern Benson in the fifth. The Dodgers scored five runs in the ninth to win the second tilt. Pee Wee Reese put Brooklyn into the lead with a two-run single.

AUGUST 26   The Dodgers take a 10½-game lead with a 4–3 win over the Cardinals in St. Louis. Brooklyn's record was 81–39.

AUGUST 31   Gil Hodges hits a grand slam off Jim Hearn in the third inning of a 9–1 win over the Giants at Ebbets Field.

SEPTEMBER 8 Joe Black pitches 7²/₃ innings of scoreless relief in a 10–2 win over the Giants in the first game of a double-header at the Polo Grounds. New York won game two 3–2.

A veteran of the Negro Leagues with a degree from Morgan State University, Black was a 28-year-old non-roster invitee to spring training in 1952. He made the club by Opening Day and soon became the Dodgers' best relief pitcher. By the end of the 1952 season, Black won the National League Rookie of the Year Award and finished third in the MVP voting with a 15–4 record, 15 saves and a 2.15 ERA in 142¹/₃ innings. He made 54 relief appearances before making his first start on the second-to-last Sunday of the season (see September 21, 1952) with the idea of making him the first-game starter in the World Series (see October 1, 1952). The Dodgers managed to win the pennant in 1952 without a true staff ace. The club used 14 different starting pitchers. Carl Erskine led the club in starts (26) and wins as a starter (13).

SEPTEMBER 11 Andy Pafko hits a grand slam off Bob Rush in the fifth inning, but it's too late to prevent an 11–7 loss to the Cubs at Ebbets Field.

In a situation eerily similar to 1951, the Dodgers saw their 10½-game lead over the Giants on August 26 slip to 3½ on September 11 by losing 12 of 19. During the meltdown, an article written under Chuck Dressen's byline in the September 13 issue of the Saturday Evening Post *hit the newsstand. It was titled "The Dodgers Won't Blow It Again."*

SEPTEMBER 14 Jim Greengrass of the Reds hits a grand slam off Johnny Rutherford in the third inning to account for all of the runs in a 4–0 win over the Dodgers at Ebbets Field.

SEPTEMBER 15 The Dodgers hit five home runs during an 11–5 win over the Reds at Ebbets Field. Jackie Robinson and Duke Snider each hit two homers, and Gil Hodges hit one.

SEPTEMBER 17 The Dodgers lead over the Giants shrinks to three games with a 4–1 loss to the Pirates at Ebbets Field. Each team had 10 contests left to play.

SEPTEMBER 20 Carl Erskine allows three hits in 10 innings and beats the Braves 1–0 in Boston. Jackie Robinson drove in the lone run with a single off Warren Spahn. The victory gave the Dodgers a five-game advantage over the Giants.

SEPTEMBER 21 Joe Black makes his first major league start and hurls a three-hitter to win 8–2 over the Braves in Boston.

The contest was the last National League game ever played in Boston. The Braves moved to Milwaukee in March 1953 in the first franchise shift in major league baseball since 1903.

SEPTEMBER 23   The Dodgers clinch the pennant with a 5–4 win in the first game of a double-header against the Phillies at Ebbets Field. The Dodgers lost the second tilt 1–0 in 12 innings.

The lack of crowds at Ebbets Field continued to alarm Walter O'Malley. The Dodgers had the best record in the majors in 1952, but were fifth in attendance and barely outdrew a couple of also-rans. The Dodgers drew 1,088,704, only 60,000 more than the Tigers, a team which posted a record of 50–104.

SEPTEMBER 27   Eddie Mathews hits three homers for the Braves during an 11–3 win over the Dodgers at Ebbets Field.

The Dodgers met the Yankees in the fourth subway series in a span of 12 years. The Dodgers lost the previous three in 1941, 1947 and 1949. Managed by Casey Stengel, the Yankees were 95–59 and won the AL pennant over the Indians by two games. Having beaten the Dodgers in 1949, the Phillies in 1950 and the Giants in 1951, the Yanks were gunning for a record-tying fourth consecutive world championship. The Yankees also won four in a row from 1936 through 1939.

OCTOBER 1   The gamble to start Joe Black in the opening game of the World Series pays off as he pitches a complete game to beat the Yankees 4–2 before 34,861 at Ebbets Field. Backing up Black's strong pitching were home runs by Jackie Robinson in the second inning, Duke Snider with a man on base in the sixth, and a solo shot from Pee Wee Reese in the eighth.

As television networks continued to expand their facilities to allow the transmission of live images across the country, residents of the future major league cities of Denver, Seattle, Phoenix, St. Petersburg and Miami saw the World Series for the first time in 1952.

OCTOBER 2   Vic Raschi pitches a three-hitter to lead the Yankees to a 7–1 win over the Dodgers in game two before 33,792 at Ebbets Field.

Gil Hodges suffered through an excruciating World Series. He was hitless in 21 at-bats.

OCTOBER 3   The Dodgers take a two-games-to-one lead in the World Series with a 5–3 win over the Yankees at Yankee Stadium. Leading 3–2 in the ninth inning, Jackie Robinson and Pee Wee Reese advanced to second and third on a double steal. Both scored on a passed ball by Yogi Berra, with Robinson advancing from second when Berra had trouble locating the ball. Preacher Roe pitched a complete game.

OCTOBER 4   Joe Black allows only a run and three hits in seven innings, but the Dodgers lose 2–0 to the Yankees at Yankee Stadium. Allie Reynolds pitched the shutout.

OCTOBER 5   The Dodgers take game five with an 11-inning 6–5 decision over the Yankees at Yankee Stadium. The Dodgers took a 4–0 lead with a three-run fifth inning, capped by a two-run homer from Duke Snider. After four shutout innings, Carl Erskine allowed five runs in the bottom of the fifth, the last three on a two-out home run by Johnny Mize. Erskine settled down quickly, however, and retired the final 19 hitters to face him. The Dodgers tied the contest in the seventh on an RBI-single by Snider. The winning run in the 11th scored on singles by Billy Cox and Pee Wee Reese and Snider's double.

With a three-games-to-two lead, all the Dodgers needed to take their first world championship was to win one of two games at Ebbets Field.

OCTOBER 6   The Yankees force a seventh game with a 3–2 win over the Dodgers before 30,037. Billy Loes, only 22 years old and a rookie, was the starting pitcher and entrusted with the task of winning Brooklyn's first World Series title. He took a 1–0 leading into the seventh before allowing two runs. Yogi Berra led off with a home run. Gene Woodling reached first on an infield single which glanced off Loes's leg, moved to second on a balk when Loes dropped the ball, and scored on Vic Raschi's single. The Yanks took a 3–1 edge in the eighth. Both Brooklyn runs scored on home runs by Duke Snider in the sixth and eighth. The blasts were his third and fourth homers of the 1952 Series.

After the game, the eccentric Loes claimed that he lost Woodling's ground ball "in the sun" and subsequently dropped the ball because it contained "too much spit." Loes had created controversy before the Series began. When asked who would win, Loes relied, "I'd like to pick the Dodgers, but I have to go along with the Yankees in six games." When Chuck Dressen confronted the pitcher and asked him if what he said was true, Loes contended he was misquoted and said he told a reporter the the Yankees would win in seven games. The pitcher's goofy reasoning surfaced again the following season when he advised against becoming a 20-game winner because "if you win 20 games they expect you to do it every year." He was 13–8 in his first full season in the majors, but his career high was 14 in 1953.

OCTOBER 7   The Yankees win game seven with a 4–2 decision over the Dodgers before 33,195 at Ebbets Field. Joe Black started his third game of the Series. The score was 2–2 when Mickey Mantle homered off Black in the sixth to break the deadlock. The Yanks added an insurance run against Preacher Roe in the seventh. The Dodgers had a golden opportunity in the bottom of the seventh with the bases loaded in the seventh and one out. Casey Stengel brought in Bob Kuzava to pitch, and Duke Snider popped out. On a full-count pitch, Jackie Robinson lifted another pop fly to the right side of the infield. First baseman Joe Collins lost the ball in the sun. With two runners already across the plate and another rounding third, it looked as though it might drop to the ground, but second baseman Billy Martin saved the day with a last-second sprint and caught the ball knee high. Kuzava retired the last six Brooklyn batters without incident.

DECEMBER 1   Four weeks after Dwight Eisenhower defeats Adlai Stevenson in the Presidential election, the Pirates draft Roy Face from the Dodgers organization.

Face was 24 years old at the time he was drafted by the Pirates and stood only five-foot-eight and weighed just 155 pounds. He had an ERA under 3.00 while pitching over 200 innings during 1950, 1951 and 1952 in the Dodger minor league system, but the club was concerned about his size. The Pirates converted Face into a reliever, and he became one of the best closers in the game. He led the NL in saves in 1958, 1961 and 1962 and set a major league record for relief wins in a season with an 18–1 record in 1959.

DECEMBER 2   The Dodgers draft Don Bessent from the Yankees organization.

1953

Season in a Sentence

The Dodgers win a club-record 105 games to cruise to the National League pennant, lose their fifth World Series to the Yankees in a span of 13 years, then fire Chuck Dressen as manager after he asks for a multi-year contract.

Finish • Won • Lost • Pct • GB

First   105   49   .682   +13.0

World Series

The Dodgers lost to the New York Yankees four games to two.

Manager

Chuck Dressen

Stats

Stats	Dods	NL	Rank
Batting Avg:	.285	.266	1
On-Base Pct:	.366	.335	1
Slugging Pct:	.474	.411	1
Home Runs:	208		1
Stolen Bases:	90		1
ERA:	4.10	4.29	3
Fielding Avg:	.980	.975	1
Runs Scored:	955		1
Runs Allowed:	689		3

Starting Lineup

Roy Campanella, c
Gil Hodges, 1b
Jim Gilliam, 2b
Billy Cox, 3b
Pee Wee Reese, ss
Jackie Robinson, lf-3b
Duke Snider, cf
Carl Furillo, rf
Bobby Morgan, 3b-ss

Pitchers

Carl Erskine, sp
Russ Meyer, sp
Billy Loes, sp
Preacher Roe, sp
Johnny Podres, sp-rp
Jim Hughes, rp
Clem Labine, rp
Bob Milliken, rp
Ben Wade, rp

Attendance

1,163,419 (second in NL)

Club Leaders

Batting Avg:	Carl Furillo	.344
On-Base Pct:	Duke Snider	.419
Slugging Pct:	Duke Snider	.627
Home Runs:	Duke Snider	42
RBIs:	Roy Campanella	142
Runs:	Duke Snider	132
Stolen Bases:	Pee Wee Reese	11

JANUARY 17   The Dodgers send Andy Pafko to the Braves for Roy Hartsfield and $50,000.

FEBRUARY 16   In a four-team trade, the Dodgers send Jim Pendleton to the Braves and Rocky Bridges to the Reds and receive Russ Meyer from the Phillies.

MARCH 11   The Dodgers play their first exhibition game at Holman Stadium in Vero Beach, and win 4–2 over the Philadelphia Athletics. Holman Stadium would serve as the Dodgers' spring home until 2008.

APRIL 14   The Dodgers win on Opening Day 8–5 over the Pirates before 12,433 at Ebbets Field in 40-degree weather. Pittsburgh scored four runs in the top of the fourth, and the Dodgers rebounded with four in their half and four more in the fifth. Roy Campanella hit a home run and collected two singles. Duke Snider also homered. Jim Gilliam made his major league debut and hit a single in five at-bats. Joe Black relieved Carl Erskine and pitched six innings, allowing only a run and two hits.

After his great season in 1952, Black was ineffective over the remainder of his career. From the start of the 1953 season until he was sold to the Reds in 1955, Black had a 5.40 ERA in 95 innings.

APRIL 19   The Dodgers defeat the Pirates 12–4 in Pittsburgh. The contest was interrupted by snow for 37 minutes in the third inning.

APRIL 25   In a game marked by an altercation between Carl Furillo and Giants pitcher Sal Maglie, the Dodgers lose 7–5 to their New York rivals at Ebbets Field. After being dusted by a pitch in the third inning, Furillo threw his bat at Maglie, causing both benches to empty. Plate umpire Larry Goetz and catcher Sal Yvars restrained Furillo before he could reach the mound.

A mainstay of the Dodger dynasty in the 1940s and '50s, right fielder Carl Furillo, put up his best season in 1953, leading the league in hitting.

After batting just .247 in 1952, Furillo won the NL batting title in 1953 with an average of .344, and hit 21 home runs. His season was cut short after another game with the Giants, however (see September 6, 1953).

MAY 9   A two-run walk-off homer by Roy Campanella off Robin Roberts in the ninth inning beats the Phillies 7–6 in the first game of a double-header at Ebbets Field. Philadelphia won the second contest 8–4.

Campanella won his second MVP award in 1953 with a league-leading 142 runs batted in along with 41 homers, 103 runs and a .312 batting average.

MAY 17   Carl Erskine pitches a one-hitter to beat the Reds 10–0 in the second game of a double-header at Crosley Field. Gus Bell beat out a bunt down the third-base line in the sixth inning for the only Cincinnati hit. A fly ball by Jim Greengrass in the second was the only ball hit out of the infield. In his previous start three days earlier, Erskine failed to retire a batter against the Cardinals. The Reds won the second game 13–5.

Erskine had the best season of his career in 1953 with a 20–6 record and a 3.54 ERA and 187 strikeouts in 246²/₃ innings.

MAY 18   The Dodgers leave 18 men on base and lose 2–1 in 10 innings to the Reds at Crosley Field. Cincinnati pitcher Bud Podbielan pitched a complete game, allowing 13 walks, a hit batsman and six hits.

MAY 19   The Dodgers play in Milwaukee for the first time and defeat the Braves 4–1 at County Stadium.

In their first season in Milwaukee, the Braves drew 1,826,397, breaking the National League record of 1,807,526 set by the 1947 Dodgers. Despite posting the best record in the majors with 105 victories, attendance at Ebbets Field in 1953 was 1,163,419, the fourth best in the majors behind the Braves, the Yankees and a third-place White Sox club. The Braves would draw over 2,000,000 each season from 1954 through 1957 while attendance in Brooklyn continued to stagnate. The figures at County Stadium, a ballpark surrounded by a parking lot capable of holding 10,000 cars, helped convince Walter O'Malley of the need for a new home for the Dodgers to replace Ebbets Field.

MAY 24   The Dodgers score 12 runs in the eighth inning before a batter is retired and beat the Phillies 16–2 in Philadelphia. Gil Hodges walked, Bill Cox singled and Duke Snider doubled for the first run. Carl Furillo was walked intentionally, filling the bases, and Billy Cox singled, scoring one. Jim Gilliam walked, forcing in another tally. Pee Wee Reese cleared the bases with a three-run triple. Reese scored on Jackie Robinson's single. After Roy Campanella walked, Hodges singled in Robinson for run number eight. Walks to Cox and Snider forced in the ninth tally of the inning. Furillo's bases-loaded triple brought across the 10th, 11th and 12th runs. Erskine recorded the first out by striking out. Furillo was thrown out trying to score on an infield grounder, and a strikeout by Reese ended the inning.

Dodgers pitcher Russ Meyer was ejected in the fourth inning after objecting to the calls of umpire Augie Donatelli. Nicknamed "The Mad Monk" for his explosive temper, Meyer then made obscene gestures which were caught on television. He was suspended for three days by National League president Ford Frick.

MAY 25   The Dodgers outslug the Phillies 11–9 in Philadelphia.

MAY 31   The Dodgers extend their winning streak to 10 games with a 4–3 and 4–1 sweep of the Pirates at Ebbets Field. The second game was called after 6¹/₂ innings by darkness because a National League rule prevented the use of lights for games played on a Sunday.

JUNE 6   A three-run homer by Gil Hodges in the ninth inning beats the Cardinals 5–4 at Ebbets Field.

After being hitless in 21 at-bats during the 1952 World Series, Hodges started the 1953 season in a slump with 15 hits, none for extra bases, in his first 83 at-bats, an average of .181. He recovered and finished the year hitting .302 with 31 homers, 122 RBIs and 101 runs in 1953.

JUNE 10	The Dodgers score seven runs in the eighth inning to defeat the Reds 13–3 in Cincinnati.
JUNE 19	Playing in 102-degree weather, the Dodgers lose 11–8 and win 7–1 against the Cubs in a double-header in Chicago.
JUNE 20	With the temperature reaching 104 degrees, the highest ever recorded in Chicago, the Dodgers beat the Cubs 5–3 at Wrigley Field.
JUNE 24	The Dodgers lose 7–4 to the Reds in Cincinnati to fall three games behind the first place Braves.

> *With the loss, the Dodgers had a record of 38–25. Brooklyn was 67–24 the rest of the way, including a streak of 46 wins in 57 games from the All-Star break through Labor Day and finished 13 games ahead of the Braves.*

JUNE 27	Pee Wee Reese homers in the 10th inning to beat the Braves 4–3 in Milwaukee.

> *Reese hit .271 with 13 homers and 108 runs scored in 1953.*

JUNE 29	The Dodgers take sole possession of first place with an 11–1 win over the Braves in Milwaukee.

> *The Dodgers scored 955 runs in 1953, the most in any season in franchise history since 1894. The club led the National League in runs five consecutive seasons from 1949 through 1953 with a remarkable blend of power and speed. Brooklyn topped the NL in home runs seven straight seasons from 1949 through 1955 and in stolen bases eight years in a row from 1946 through 1953.*

JULY 1	After the Phillies score in the top of the 10th inning, the Dodgers respond with two in their half on consecutive doubles by Carl Furillo, Roy Campanella and George Shuba off Robin Roberts to win 5–4 at Ebbets Field.

> *A few days later, Shuba had his car stolen. It was being stored at a gas station in Brooklyn while the Dodgers were on a road trip, and a bandit robbed the station and hopped in Shuba's vehicle to make his getaway.*

JULY 5	The Giants overwhelm the Dodgers 20–6 in New York.
JULY 6	The Dodgers wallop the Pirates 14–2 in Pittsburgh.
JULY 10	The Dodgers sell Ralph Branca to the Tigers.
JULY 14	Chuck Dressen manages the National League to a 5–1 win in the All-Star Game at Crosley Field in Cincinnati. Pee Wee Reese contributed a double and a single in four at-bats and drove in two runs.
JULY 16	Gil Hodges hits a grand slam off Stu Miller in the first inning of a 9–2 win over the Cardinals at Ebbets Field.

JULY 17   The Dodgers score seven runs in the first inning and clobber the Cardinals 14–0 in the first game of a double-header at Ebbets Field. Billy Cox hit a grand slam off Eddie Erautt in the fourth. The Dodgers also won the second tilt 7–4.

             The Dodgers were 11–0 against the Cardinals at Ebbets Field in 1953. Against all opposition, the Brooklyn club was 60–17 at home.

JULY 18   The Dodgers score nine runs in the fourth inning and beat the Cardinals 14–6 at Ebbets Field. Wayne Belardi walked as a pinch-hitter in the big inning, and, as the Dodgers batted around, stepped to the plate again and hit a grand slam off Cliff Chambers. It was the third consecutive game in which a Dodger cleared the bases with a homer.

JULY 19   Dodgers pitcher Glenn Mickens allows a homer to the first batter he faces in the majors, surrendering a blast to Ted Kluszewski in the ninth inning of a 4–1 loss to the Reds at Ebbets Field.

             Mickens pitched only four big-league games and had an 11.57 ERA in 6^1/$_3$ innings.

JULY 21   The Dodgers trounce the Cubs 15–4 at Ebbets Field.

JULY 22   The Dodgers swamp the Cubs 9–3 and 11–1 in a double-header at Ebbets Field.

JULY 28   The day after the armistice ending the Korean War, the Dodgers score seven runs in the second inning and romp to a 13–2 win over the Cubs in Chicago.

AUGUST 3   Roy Campanella takes exception to a couple of brushback pitches from Lew Burdette during the eighth inning of a 1–0 win against the Braves in Milwaukee. Campanella moved toward the mound with the bat still in his hands. Teammates wrestled the bat from Campanella, and along with the umpires, prevented any fisticuffs. The game was called in the bottom of the eighth by rain. Russ Meyer pitched the shutout and drove in the lone run with a single in the seventh.

AUGUST 9   Duke Snider hits a grand slam off Joe Nuxhall in the fourth inning of a 9–1 win over the Reds at Ebbets Field.

AUGUST 11   Carl Erskine pitches a two-hitter to beat the Giants 4–0 at the Polo Grounds. Hank Thompson collected both New York hits with singles in the fourth and seventh innings.

AUGUST 12   Down 5–0, the Dodgers score five runs in the seventh inning and one in the eighth to beat the Giants 6–5 in New York. Duke Snider tied the score with a grand slam off Ruben Gomez. It was Snider's second grand slam in four days.

             Snider led the NL in slugging percentage (.627) and runs (132) in 1953 in addition to batting .336 with 42 homers and 126 RBIs. He hit 15 home runs during the month of August.

AUGUST 13   The Dodgers erase a five-run New York advantage at the Polo Grounds for the second game in a row. Down 8–3, Brooklyn scored four runs in the seventh inning, one in the ninth and one in the 10th to beat the Giants 9–8. Roy Campanella hit home runs in the seventh and ninth. Carl Furillo drove in the game-winner with a homer in the 10th.

AUGUST 15   The Dodgers score three runs in each of the first four innings and defeat the Pirates 14–6 at Ebbets Field.

AUGUST 17   Duke Snider hits a two-run homer in the ninth inning to tie the score 2–2, and Gil Hodges belts a three-run, walk-off home run in the 11th to beat the Pirates 5–2 at Ebbets Field. It was the Dodgers 10th win in a row.

AUGUST 18   Gil Hodges drives in the winning run in extra innings for the second game in a row with a sacrifice fly in the 13th which defeats the Giants 4–3 at Ebbets Field. It was Brooklyn's 11th victory in a row.

AUGUST 19   St. Louis Browns owner Bill Veeck visits Los Angeles with the idea of moving his club to the West Coast. Veeck said that if the city purchased Wrigley Field from P. K. Wrigley, who owned both the Chicago Cubs and the Pacific Coast League's Los Angeles Angels, he would transfer the Browns. Los Angeles city officials were cool to the idea, however, and Wrigley refused to sell either his ball park or his Los Angeles franchise. In September 1953, the Browns moved to Baltimore and were renamed the Orioles (see August 24, 1953, and October 17, 1953).

AUGUST 20   The Dodgers extend their winning streak to 13 games with a 10–0 decision over the Giants at Ebbets Field.

AUGUST 21   The 13-game winning streak is snapped with a 7–1 loss to the Pirates at Forbes Field. The Dodgers also entered the contest with a 13-game winning streak over Pittsburgh, dating back to April.

After posting a 19–3 record against the Pirates in 1952, the Dodgers were 20–2 against the Pittsburgh club in 1953. Brooklyn had an incredible 51–8 record playing the Pirates from the start of the 1952 season through August 19, 1954.

AUGUST 24   At a meeting of major league owners, Walter O'Malley tells fellow owners that he has received a letter from a prominent Los Angeles resident "who is a leader in politics and is well fixed financially" inquiring about the Dodgers transferring to the West Coast. "The man whose name I cannot reveal," added O'Malley, "assured me that if the Brooklyn club were transferred to Los Angeles, a modern commodious stadium would be built for it."

AUGUST 30   The Dodgers erupt for 12 runs in the seventh inning and beat the Cardinals 20–4 at Ebbets Field. Strangely, all three outs in the 12-run inning were recorded on strikeouts. To score the dozen runs, the Dodgers collected a homer from Bobby Morgan, a double by Carl Furillo, two singles from Roy Campanella, and one each from Carl Erskine, Pee Wee Reese, Duke Snider along with two walks to Gil Hodges, and one apiece to Furillo, Morgan and Jim Gilliam.

Gilliam won the NL Rookie of the Year Award in 1953 with a .278 batting average, 125 runs and a league-leading 17 triples. He played his entire 14-year career as a Dodger, with five years in Brooklyn and nine in Los Angeles. As a major leaguer, Gilliam appeared in 1,048 games as a second baseman, 761 at third base and 222 in the outfield. He was a coach for the club from 1965 until 1978 when died of a brain hemorrhage just before the start of the World Series. Among Dodger players, Gilliam ranks fifth in games played (1,956), fifth in at-bats (7,119), second in walks (1,036), fourth in runs (1,163), seventh in doubles (304) and eighth in hits (1,889). As a player and coach, he was in a Dodger uniform in 10 World Series.

SEPTEMBER 1   Preacher Roe allows five homers, each with no one base, in pitching a complete game to beat the Cardinals 12–5 at Busch Stadium. Steve Bilko struck two of the St. Louis homers with Stan Musial, Rip Repulski and Harry Elliott accounting for the rest. None of the Dodgers homered during the contest.

With the emergence of Jim Gilliam as the Dodgers starting second baseman, Jackie Robinson played third base and left field over the remaining four years of his career. In 1953, Robinson hit .329 with 109 runs and 12 homers in 1953.

SEPTEMBER 4   Russ Meyer allows consecutive homers to Wes Westrum; opposing pitcher, Al Corwin; and Whitey Lockman in the fourth inning, but the Dodgers recover to win 8–6 against the Giants in New York.

SEPTEMBER 5   Roy Campanella hits two homers and drives in five runs during a 16–7 win over the Giants in New York.

SEPTEMBER 6   Carl Furillo fights Giants manager Leo Durocher during a 6–3 win in New York. Preacher Roe extended his winning streak to 10 games.

In the second inning, Furillo was struck on the wrist by a pitch from Ruben Gomez. After reaching first base, Furillo bolted for the dugout to grapple with Durocher. During the ensuing melee, Furillo's hand was stepped on, fracturing the fifth metacarpal bone and sidelining him for the rest of the regular season. He would return to play in the World Series.

SEPTEMBER 9   Pee Wee Reese hits a grand slam off Bud Podbielan in the fifth inning of a 6–0 win over the Reds in Cincinnati.

SEPTEMBER 12   The Dodgers clinch the pennant with a 5–2 win over the Braves in Milwaukee.

SEPTEMBER 13   Duke Snider extends his hitting streak to 27 games during a 3–2 loss to the Cubs in Chicago.

SEPTEMBER 17   The Dodgers win their 100th game of 1953 with a 4–3 decision over the Cardinals in St. Louis. It was also Carl Erskine's 20th victory of the season.

SEPTEMBER 27   On the final day of the season, the Dodgers win a club-record 105th game with an 8–2 decision over the Phillies in Philadelphia.

The Dodgers met the Yankees in the fifth subway series in 13 years. Brooklyn lost the previous four in 1941, 1947, 1949 and 1952. Managed by Casey Stengel, the Yankees were 99–52 and won the AL pennant by 8¹/₂ games. The Yanks were trying for a record-breaking fifth consecutive world championship. With 105 regular season wins, the Dodgers finally seemed to have a team which could beat the Yankees.

SEPTEMBER 30   The Dodgers open the World Series with a 9–5 loss to the Yankees at Yankee Stadium. Carl Erskine was the Brooklyn starting pitcher and was removed after allowing four runs in the first inning. The Dodgers rallied to tie the score 5–5 by the top of the seventh inning with the help of home runs from Jim Gilliam, Gil Hodges and George Shuba. The Yanks broke the deadlock with a tally in the bottom of the seventh and three more in the eighth.

The 1953 Fall Classic was the 50th between the champions of the National and American Leagues. Surviving members of the first Series (between the Red Sox and Pirates in 1903) threw out the ceremonial first pitch in each of the six games in 1953. Among those throwing out the ceremonial pitch were future Hall of Famers Cy Young, Honus Wagner and Fred Clarke.

OCTOBER 1   The Yankees take game two with a 4–2 win over the Dodgers at Yankee Stadium. A two-run double by Billy Cox in the fourth inning put Brooklyn into the lead, but New York rallied with a run in the seventh on Billy Martin's home run, and broke the tie with a two-run homer by Mickey Mantle in the eighth.

OCTOBER 2   Pitching on one day of rest after lasting only one inning in game one, Carl Erskine strikes out 14 batters and beats the Yankees 3–2 before 35,270 at Ebbets Field. Among those in the crowd were Humphrey Bogart and Lauren Bacall. Jackie Robinson scored in the fifth inning on a squeeze bunt by Billy Cox and drove in a run with a single in the sixth. Roy Campanella snapped a 2–2 tie with a home run in the eighth.

The 14 strikeouts by Erskine stood as the record for 10 years and is still the third highest in World Series history. Sandy Koufax struck out 15 for the Dodgers in 1963, and Bob Gibson fanned 17 for the Cardinals in 1968.

OCTOBER 3   The Dodgers even the Series with a 7–3 win over the Yankees before 36,775 at Ebbets Field. Duke Snider led the offensive attack with two doubles, a homer and four RBIs. Jim Gilliam collected three doubles.

OCTOBER 4   The Yankees move within one victory of the world championship by beating the Dodgers 11–7 before 36,775 at Ebbets Field. Mickey Mantle broke the game open with a grand slam off Russ Meyer in the third inning which put the Yankees up 6–1. Billy Cox and Jim Gilliam hit homers and Roy Campanella collected three hits in the losing cause.

OCTOBER 5   The Yankees become the first, and to date only, franchise in major league history to win five consecutive World Series by beating the Dodgers 4–3 in game six at Yankee Stadium. Trailing 3–1, the Dodgers tied the score 3–3 on a one-out, two-run homer by Carl Furillo. But with Clem Labine on the mound, the Yanks scored in the ninth on a walk, an infield single by Mickey Mantle and a game-winning single by Billy Martin.

OCTOBER 14   In a startling move, the Dodgers announce the dismissal of Chuck Dressen as manager after guiding the franchise to back-to-back pennant wins in 1952 and 1953. Dressen had demanded a three-year contract, while the club offered only a one-year renewal. O'Malley insisted the length of the contract was the only reason that Dressen would not be returning in 1954. Dressen refused to sign a one-year deal because other managers in baseball had the security of multi-year deals. Dressen later managed the Senators (1955–57), Braves (1960–61) and Tigers (1963–66), but never won another pennant. In between managerial assignments, O'Malley showed there were no hard feelings by twice re-hiring Dressen. Chuck was a coach with the Dodgers in 1958 and 1959 and a scout from 1961 through 1963. Dressen suffered a heart attack in May 1966 while at the helm of the Detroit club and died the following August at the age of 67. Dressen would be the last manager fired by the Dodgers until Bill Russell in 1998. The only two to manage the club in between Dressen and Russell were Walter Alston (1954–76) and Tommy Lasorda (1976–96). Both Alston and Lasorda left the Dodgers on their own accord, opting for retirement.

OCTOBER 17   P. K. Wrigley, owner of both the Chicago Cubs and Pacific Coast League's Los Angeles Angels, appoints Bill Veeck as special advisor "to spearhead the campaign to bring major league baseball to Los Angeles."

Veeck sold the St. Louis Browns three weeks earlier to a group which moved the club to Baltimore, where they were renamed the Orioles. Residents of Los Angeles were clamoring for a major league team. In 1953, big-league owners were debating over whether or not to expand the two eight-team leagues to 10, with L.A. as one of the expansion franchises, or create a third major league with eight teams located west of the Mississippi. "Bill would not only help Los Angeles get a major league club," said Wrigley, "his job also is to go out and organize the effort so that Los Angeles and possibly other Pacific Coast League cities get top-flight baseball in an orderly and sensible way as soon as it becomes physically possible." Veeck proposed that Los Angeles expand Wrigley Field, built in 1925 and located at Avalon Boulevard and East 42nd Street, from 22,000 seats to 55,000 in addition to tearing down the homes and businesses for blocks in each direction for parking. City officials rejected the notion of enlarging a 30-year-old ballpark and destroying the surrounding neighborhood for parking lots.

OCTOBER 28   Red Barber resigns as radio and TV announcer of the Dodgers following a salary dispute. He had been broadcasting Dodger games since 1939. Barber moved to the Yankees, joining Mel Allen. Vin Scully succeeded Barber as the Dodgers' lead announcer. Scully joined the club in 1950.

NOVEMBER 24   The Dodgers end six weeks of speculation as to the identity of the next manager of the club by hiring 42-year-old Walter Alston. At the time of his hiring, the quiet and uncharasmatic Alston was almost completely unknown in Brooklyn. The appointment was greeted with skepticism as fans and writers alike expected the Dodgers to hire a dynamic manager with a recognizable name. A native of rural Ohio, Alston's major league playing career consisted of one game with the Cardinals in 1936. He was a highly successful manager in the minors for 14 seasons. Alston was hired by Branch Rickey to manage in the Cardinals farm system in 1940, and moved to the Dodgers along with Rickey in 1942. Walter O'Malley refused to deviate from his policy of offering managers one-year contracts, but Alston signed 23 of them, managing the club until 1976. During that period, the Dodgers reached the World Series seven times and won four of them in 1955, 1959, 1963 and 1965. The 1955 Fall Classic was the only one the club won while in Brooklyn. During his first few years at the helm, Alston's authority was threatened by many veterans, including Jackie Robinson, who believed they shouldn't have to take orders from a man who played in only one big-league game. Alston was easygoing with a high-boiling point, but possessed a titanic temper when pushed too far. He left no doubt who was boss and wasn't averse to challenging his players, including Robinson, to a fight. As a late as 1976, when he was 64 years old, Alston physically threatened a much younger reporter. His adaptability and extraordinary patience may have been his greatest asset, however. Alston won with power-laden clubs during both the 1950s and 1970s and with teams that emphasized speed and pitching in the 1960s. He was also a winner during the conservative fifties and the free-spirited, swinging seventies. Overall, he had a 2,040–1,613 record as manager.

DECEMBER 10   Walter O'Malley reveals the Dodgers have definite plans to build a new stadium seating 52,000. Three sites in Brooklyn were being considered. "In any event I am certain," said O'Malley, "that we will have a new stadium within the next five years. The Dodgers will own it, but it will also be constructed to accommodate other events."

Los Angeles and the Pacific Coast League

Minor league baseball was played in Los Angeles in the Pacific Coast Lague from 1903 through 1957. The three franchises from Los Angeles which played in the league were the Los Angeles Angels (1903–57), Vernon Tigers (1909–25) and Hollywood Stars (1926–35 and 1938–57).

Los Angeles Angels
The Angels were one of six charter members of the Pacific Coast League, along with clubs from Oakland, Portland, Sacramento, San Francisco and Seattle. From 1903 through 1925, the Angels played at 15,000-seat Washington Park (also known as Chutes Park) at Hill and Eighth Streets in downtown Los Angeles.

The Los Angeles franchise was purchased in 1921 by chewing-gum magnate William Wrigley, Jr., who also owned the Chicago Cubs. Wrigley built the club a new ballpark at 42nd Place and Avalon Boulevard in what is now South Central Los Angeles. Known as Wrigley Field, it held 22,000 fans, opened in September 1925 and was modeled after Wrigley Field in Chicago.

The Los Angeles version of Wrigley Field was used by the Angels until 1957 when the franchise passed out of existence after the Dodgers moved to Los Angeles. Wrigley Field was a major league

venue for one season in 1961 when the American League expansion team, also called the Los Angeles Angels, was established. The ballpark was also the site of the 1959 television series *Home Run Derby* and served as the backdrop for several feature films over a 40-year period. Wrigley Field was demolished in 1966.

The Angels won the PCL regular season title in 1903, 1905, 1907, 1908, 1916, 1921, 1926, 1933, 1934, 1947 and 1956. Notable players included Steve Bilko, Chuck Connors, Gene Mauch, Jimmie Reese, Bill Sarni, Jigger Statz and Dixie Upright.

Vernon Tigers
The Vernon Tigers existed in the PCL from 1909 through 1925. Vernon was, and still is, a small town located about 13 miles southeast of downtown Los Angeles. A baseball franchise settled there because in 1909 it was one of only two communities in the county in which the sale of alcohol was legal. The other was Venice, where the Tigers played home games in 1913 and 1914.

Vernon is one of the most unusual municipalities in the United States. In 2000, it had a population of only 91, but some 46,000 were employed by businesses within its borders.

Vernon won the league pennant in 1919 and 1920 when the franchise was owned by Hollywood silent-film star Fatty Arbuckle. The beginning of the end came just before the title run of 1920 when the Prohibition amendment passed and barred the sale of alcohol nationwide. Few were willing to travel the distance to remote Vernon to watch baseball. The franchise transferred to San Francisco after the close of the 1925 season, where it became known as the Mission Reds.

Hollywood Stars

The first of two versions of the Hollywood Stars existed from 1926 through 1935. The franchise moved from Salt Lake City and filled the void left by the Vernon Tigers. The Stars played not in Hollywood, but at Wrigley Field as tenants of the Angels. Because of declining attendance, the Hollywood club moved to San Diego at the end of the 1935 season, but not before winning the PCL pennant in 1929 and 1930.

Los Angeles had only one PCL franchise in 1936 and 1937 while the San Francisco Bay area had three in the San Francisco Seals, the Mission Reds and the Oakland Oaks. In 1938, the Mission club, which was formerly the Vernon Tigers, moved to Hollywood. This time the club played near Hollywood on Beverly Boulevard in the Fairfax district of Los Angeles at 13,000-seat Gilmore Field. Today, the site is a parking lot at CBS Television City.

The principal owner of the Stars was Bob Cobb, who also owned the Brown Derby Restaurant and for whom the Cobb salad is named. He was married to actress Gail Patrick. Stock was sold to many Hollywood celebrities, including Gene Autry and William Frawley, and other movie and television stars regularly attended the games. The second version of the Stars won the PCL pennant in 1949 when it was a farm team of the Dodgers.

The road to major league status

The states of California, Oregon and Washington had 2.4 million people in 1900 which consisted of 3.2 percent of the U.S. population. By 1950, the population figure reached 15.2 million and comprised 10 percent of United States residents. That year, the 16 major league franchises were located in just 10 cities, none of them located west of St. Louis or south of Washington, D.C. From north to south, Pacific Coast League teams in 1950 were those of Seattle, Portland, Sacramento, San Francisco, Oakland, Hollywood, Los Angeles and San Diego.

PCL owners believed that the league had a sufficient population base in which to be considered a third major league. By 1946, they banded together as a group to request that status from the National and American Leagues. Either all of them or none of them would become big-league franchises.

The NL and AL repeatedly denied the PCL's request to became a third major league, believing that only Los Angeles and San Francisco had the population necessary to be considered as major league cities. There was also a concern that the talent level in the PCL was far below that of the NL and AL and that none of the ballparks on the Pacific Coast were up to major league standards.

Cracks in the coalition of PCL teams began to surface around 1953 when Los Angeles and San Francisco city officials desired to be included as part of the National and American Leagues. California's two largest cities wanted to test their mettle against clubs from New York and Chicago, not Sacramento and Portland. In 1957, the Dodgers transferred operations to Los Angeles and the Giants to San Francisco. The PCL franchises in Los Angeles, Hollywood, San Francisco and Oakland moved to Phoenix, Salt Lake City, Spokane and Vancouver.

1954

L A

Season in a Sentence

"Wait until next year" continues to be the battle cry of the Dodger fan as the club finishes second to the Giants in Walter Alston's first year as manager after winning the pennant the previous two seasons.

Finish • Won • Lost • Pct • GB

Second   92   62   .597   5.0

Manager

Walter Alston

Stats

Stats	Dods	NL	Rank
Batting Avg:	.270	.265	2
On-Base Pct:	.349	.335	2
Slugging Pct:	.444	.407	1
Home Runs:	186		1
Stolen Bases:	46		4 (tie)
ERA:	4.31	4.07	4
Fielding Avg:	.978	.976	2
Runs Scored:	778		2
Runs Allowed:	740		4

Starting Lineup

Roy Campanella, c
Gil Hodges, 1b
Jim Gilliam, 2b
Jackie Robinson, 3b-lf
Pee Wee Reese, ss
Sandy Amoros, lf
Duke Snider, cf
Carl Furillo, rf
Don Hoak, 3b
Billy Cox, 3b

Pitchers

Carl Erskine, sp
Billy Loes, sp
Russ Meyer, sp
Johnny Podres, sp
Don Newcombe, sp
Jim Hughes, rp
Clem Labine, rp

Attendance

1,020,531 (fourth in NL)

Club Leaders

Batting Avg:	Duke Snider	.341
On-Base Pct:	Duke Snider	.423
Slugging Pct:	Duke Snider	.647
Home Runs:	Gil Hodges	42
RBIs:	Gil Hodges	130
	Duke Snider	130
Runs:	Duke Snider	120
Stolen Bases:	Three tied with	8
Wins:	Carl Erskine	18
Strikeouts:	Carl Erskine	166
ERA:	Russ Meyer	3.99
Saves:	Jim Hughes	24

APRIL 13   The Dodgers lose the season opener 4–3 to the Giants in New York. Willie Mays, in his first game since his induction into the Army in May 1952, hit a home run off Carl Erskine. Roy Campanella hit two homers for the Dodgers.

APRIL 15   The Dodgers win the home opener 7–4 before 12,498 in 40-degree weather at Ebbets Field. Jackie Robinson, Jim Gilliam and Roy Campanella homered.

Despite the fine start, Campanella was hampered by a hand injury and suffered through an awful season in 1954. On May 4, he underwent an operation to remove bone chips, but the surgeon botched the procedure. Due to nerve damage, Campanella suffered temporary paralysis in his fingers. A year after hitting .312 with 41 homers in an MVP season in 1953, Campanella batted .207 and his home run production dropped to 19 in 1954.

APRIL 23   Jackie Robinson stars in a 13-inning, 6–5 win over the Pirates in Pittsburgh. In the sixth, Robinson stole second, third and home. The swipe of home came at the end of a triple steal also involving Gil Hodges and Sandy Amoros. Robinson doubled in the winning run in the 13th.

Robinson hit .311 with 15 homers in 1954.

APRIL 29
The Dodgers hit five homers in a 7–5 win over the Cubs in Chicago. Jim Gilliam swatted two home runs with Duke Snider, Pee Wee Reese and Dick Williams adding one each.

Snider had the best season of his career in 1954 with a .341 batting average, 39 doubles, 10 triples, 40 homers, 130 RBIs, 199 hits and a league-leading 120 runs.

MAY 12
A home run by Gil Hodges is the only Dodger hit off Lew Burdette during a 5–1 loss to the Braves at Ebbets Field.

Hodges hit .304 with 42 homers, 130 runs batted in and 106 runs scored in 1954.

MAY 15
Carl Erskine pitches a two-hitter to defeat the Cardinals 1–0 at Ebbets Field. The only St. Louis hits were a double by Stan Musial in the first inning and a single by Alex Grammas in the third. A single by Billy Cox in the second drove in the lone run.

Erskine was 18–15 with a 4.15 ERA and 166 strikeouts in 260$^1/_3$ innings in 1954.

MAY 16
A grand slam by Gil Hodges off Herm Wehmeier in the sixth inning drives in all of the Dodger runs in a 4–2 victory over the Reds in the first game of a double-header at Ebbets Field. Cincinnati won the second contest 7–2.

MAY 28
Eleven days after the Supreme Court rules in the *Brown vs. Board of Education of Topeka* that segregation of public schools is illegal, Ben Wade allows four home runs in the eighth inning of a 17–6 loss to the Giants in New York. The homers were struck by Davey Williams, Al Dark, Monte Irvin and Billy Gardner.

MAY 31
A home run by Gil Hodges in the top of the 12th inning lifts the Dodgers to a 5–4 win over the Phillies in Philadelphia. Duke Snider saved the victory in the bottom of the 12th with a leaping catch against the wall on a drive by Willie Jones with two out and two runners on base.

JUNE 2
The Dodgers score five runs in the fifth to take a 7–6 lead over the Braves in Milwaukee and win by that score when the contest is called by rain at the end of the inning.

In the fourth inning, umpire Lee Ballanfant cleared the entire Dodgers bench after the club objected to a ball four call to Johnny Logan which loaded the bases for Eddie Mathews, who hit a grand slam. An angry Jackie Robinson tossed his bat toward the dugout after being ejected. It slipped out of his hand on the rain-soaked night, however, and skidded along the dugout roof, where it hit a woman above the left eye and her husband on the forehead. The couple sued Robinson, and it was settled out of court three years later.

JUNE 7
The Dodgers extend their winning streak to 10 games with a 12-inning, 7–5 decision over the Cardinals in St. Louis. Roy Campanella homered in the seventh inning and stole home in the 12th.

The victory gave the Dodgers a 30–18 record and a two-game lead in the NL pennant race.

| June 11 | The Dodgers and Reds tie a major league record with five home runs in one inning during a 10–8 Brooklyn victory at Crosley Field. Cincinnati hit three home runs and the Dodgers two in the seventh. The Reds homers were struck by Harry Perkowski, Roy McMillan and Gus Bell, and Brooklyn's by Jim Gilliam and Duke Snider. |

June 13   The Dodgers rout the Reds 6–5 and 14–2 in Cincinnati.

June 16   The Dodgers club five home runs during an 8–4 win over the Braves at Ebbets Field. Going deep for Brooklyn were Duke Snider, Gil Hodges, Don Hoak, Roy Campanella and Pee Wee Reese.

Reese hit a career-high .309 in 1954 along with 10 home runs.

June 26   Trailing 6–0, the Dodgers score a run in the third inning, two in the fourth, one in the sixth, two in the ninth and one in the 11th to defeat the Cardinals 7–6 at Ebbets Field. Duke Snider's two-run homer in the ninth tied the contest. Jackie Robinson drove in the game-winner with a single.

July 9   The Dodgers score three runs in the ninth and two in the 10th to beat the Phillies 7–5 at Ebbets Field. Down 5–2 with two out in the ninth, Pee Wee Reese hit a bases loaded bloop double to score three. Roy Campanella struck for a two-run walk-off homer in the 10th.

July 11   Duke Snider extends his club-record streak of reaching base in consecutive games to 58 during a double-header against the Phillies at Ebbets Field. Brooklyn won 8–7 and lost 3–1.

July 13   Walter Alston manages the National League to an 11–9 loss in the All-Star Game at Municipal Stadium in Cleveland. Duke Snider contributed a double and two singles in four at-bats and scored two runs. Jackie Robinson doubled in two runs in the fourth.

July 14   Duke Snider's streak of reaching base in consecutive games ends at 58, but he drives in both Dodger runs with sacrifice flies in the first and 12th innings for a 2–1 win over the Braves in Milwaukee.

July 17   Minorities are a majority in a starting lineup for the first time in major league history as the Dodgers defeat the Braves 2–1 in 11 innings in Milwaukee. The five black players in the Brooklyn batting order were Jim Gilliam, Jackie Robinson, Sandy Amoros, Roy Campanella and Don Newcombe.

Amoros played in the outfield for the Dodgers from 1952 until 1960. He's best known for his game-saving catch in the seventh game of the 1955 World Series (see October 4, 1955). After his baseball career ended, Amoros became a prosperous rancher in his native Cuba, but the coming of Fidel Castro forced him to move to Miami in 1967. At that time, the Dodgers put Amoros on the active roster for seven days to give him the time necessary to qualify for baseball's pension plan. He lived in poverty and increasing ill health until his death in 1992.

July 21   Carl Erskine pitches a two-hitter to defeat the Reds 5–1 at Crosley Field. The only Cincinnati hits were a single by Roy McMillan in the first inning and a homer from Bob Borkowski in the second. Carl Furillo collected five hits, including a double, in five at-bats.

JULY 31 — Braves first baseman Joe Adcock clouts a record-tying four home runs off four Dodger pitchers to lead his club to a 15–7 win at Ebbets Field. Adcock also doubled. Adcock homered off Don Newcombe in the second inning, doubled off Erv Palica in the third, homered against Palica in the fifth, homered off Pete Wojey in the seventh and clubbed home run number four facing Johnny Podres in the ninth. Adcock drove in seven runs and scored five.

The 18 total bases by Adcock is the second highest in major league history, trailing only the 19 recorded by Shawn Green with the Dodgers on May 23, 2002.

AUGUST 1 — A day after hitting four home runs, Joe Adcock is struck in the temple by a pitch from Clem Labine in the fourth inning of a 14–6 Braves win at Ebbets Field. Previously, Adcock was brushed back by a pitch from Russ Meyer in the third. After Adcock was felled, the Braves poured out of their dugout, and Lew Burdette punched Labine. Fortunately, Adcock's batting helmet saved him from serious injury, and he was back in the lineup the following day.

AUGUST 2 — The Dodgers leave 20 men on base, but defeat the Braves 2–1 in 13 innings at Ebbets Field. Billy Cox drove in the winning run with a single.

AUGUST 8 — The Dodgers score 13 runs, 12 after two are out, in the eighth inning of a 20–7 win over the Reds at Ebbets Field. The Dodgers headed into the eighth with a 7–5 advantage. The scoring procession started with a triple from Gil Hodges, who crossed the plate on Carl Furillo's sacrifice fly. Jim Gilliam grounded out. The next 15 Brooklyn batters reached base. Roy Campanella, Clem Labine and Don Hoak walked to load the bases. Cincinnati third baseman Chuck Harmon bobbled Pee Wee Reese's grounder, and two runs scored. A walk to Duke Snider loaded the bases again, and was followed by a single from Jackie Robinson, a double by Hodges and Furillo's single. Gilliam was hit by a pitch, Campanella drove in a run with a single, and Labine walked to reload the bases. With Frank Smith on the mound, Hoak hit a grand slam. The Dodgers loaded the bases once more on a Reese walk, a Snider single and a walk to Sandy Amoros before Hodges was retired on a leaping catch by Gus Bell in center field.

On the same day, the Dodgers sold Ben Wade to the Cardinals.

AUGUST 14 — The Dodgers take a come-from-behind 6–5 decision over the Giants at Ebbets Field. With Brooklyn trailing 5–0, Carl Furillo hit a grand slam in the sixth off Ruben Gomez before two runs were added in the sixth.

AUGUST 25 — The Dodgers hit five home runs during a 13–2 mashing of the Reds in Cincinnati. Gil Hodges and Rube Walker each homered twice and Carl Furillo once.

AUGUST 27 — The Dodgers score two runs in the ninth inning and four in the 10th to defeat the Cardinals 8–4 in St. Louis. Walt Moryn provided the two ninth-inning runs with a pinch-home run.

AUGUST 29 — The Dodgers erupt for eight runs in the 11th inning to down the Braves 12–4 in the first game of a double-header in Milwaukee. The Dodgers completed the sweep with an 11–4 win in the nightcap.

The twin victories put the Dodgers 1½ games behind the first-place Giants, but Brooklyn lost eight of their next 10 games.

SEPTEMBER 2   The Dodgers score seven runs in the fourth inning and beat the Cubs 10–2 in Chicago.

SEPTEMBER 9   Duke Snider hits a freak home run during a 10–1 win over the Cardinals at Ebbets Field. The drive struck the lower half of the beveled right-field wall and caromed upwards into the lower center-field bleacher seats.

SEPTEMBER 12   The Dodgers win 4–2 and 4–3 over the Cubs in a double-header at Ebbets Field. The second tilt went 14 innings. With two out in the 14th inning, Carl Furillo lifted an easy foul fly, but third baseman Bobby Morgan and catcher Jim Fanning collided allowing the ball to drop. Furillo then singled in the winning run.

SEPTEMBER 15   The Dodgers are only three games behind the first-place Giants with nine contests left on the schedule following a 10–4 victory over the Reds at Ebbets Field.

SEPTEMBER 16   Even though the Dodgers enter the game only three games out of first, only 522 show up for a 9–3 loss to the Reds at Ebbets Field.

The Dodgers lost five of their last nine games to blow a chance for the pennant. The club both underachieved and overachieved in 1954. The club landed in second place with a 92–62 record after capturing the pennant the previous two years and winning 105 games in 1953. Walter Alston, in his first season as manager, drew considerable heat for his conservative and laid-back approach. But the Dodgers outscored the opposition by only 778–740 and had a 27–12 record in one-run games.

SEPTEMBER 22   Karl Spooner has a spectacular major league debut by pitching a three-hit shutout with 15 strikeouts for a 3–0 win over the Giants at Ebbets Field. Spooner walked three.

SEPTEMBER 24   Attendance is only 751 at Ebbets Field for a 6–5 win over the Pirates at Ebbets Field.

The Dodgers drew 1,020,531 fans in 1954, to rank fourth in the National League and ninth among 16 major league teams. The home attendance was in sharp contrast to the 1,616,586 the club attracted on the road. The Dodgers were outdrawn by a Cardinals team that was 72–82, the Tigers, who won only 68 games, and an Orioles club which lost 100 games during their first season in Baltimore.

SEPTEMBER 26   On the final day of the season, Karl Spooner pitches his second shutout in his second big-league game to defeat the Pirates 1–0 at Ebbets Field. He struck out 12, walked three, and allowed four hits. The lone run scored on a home run by Gil Hodges off Jake Thies in the seventh inning.

Spooner is one of only 14 pitchers in major league history with shutouts in his first two starts and the only Dodger to accomplish the feat. In those two games, Spooner struck out 27 batters and allowed only four hits. He was only 23, but Spooner's bright future was ruined by an arm injury suffered in spring training the following season. He was 8–6 with a 3.65 ERA in 1955 and made his last big-league appearance in that fall's World Series with a start that lasted only one-third of an inning.

NOVEMBER 22   The Pirates draft 21-year-old Roberto Clemente from the Dodgers organization.

The Dodgers signed Clemente out of his native Puerto Rico and assigned him to Montreal in the Class AAA International League in 1954, his first season as a professional. Clemente barely played and batted only .257 with two homers in 148 at-bats. The Dodgers left him off the 40-man roster, hoping the unimpressive season would escape the notice of the other major league clubs, but Pirates general manager Branch Rickey wasn't fooled. Clemente was Pittsburgh's starting right fielder as a rookie in 1955, and was named to 12 All-Star teams, played in two World Series, won four batting titles and collected an even 3,000 hits before his untimely death in 1972.

DECEMBER 13   The Dodgers send Billy Cox and Preacher Roe to the Orioles for John Janese, Harry Schwegeman and $50,000.

1955   LA

Season in a Sentence

"Next year" finally arrives as the Dodgers bolt out of the gate with 22 wins in their first 24 games, coast to the National League pennant, and finally break their World Series jinx by winning game seven at Yankee Stadium.

Finish • Won • Lost • Pct • GB

First   98   55   .641   +13.5

World Series

The Dodgers defeated the New York Yankees four games to three.

Stats

Stats	Dods	NL	Rank
Batting Avg:	.271	.259	1
On-Base Pct:	.356	.328	1
Slugging Pct:	.448	.407	1
Home Runs:	201		1
Stolen Bases:	79		1
ERA:	3.68	4.04	1
Fielding Avg:	.978	.976	2
Runs Scored:	857		1
Runs Allowed:	650		1

Starting Lineup

Roy Campanella, c
Gil Hodges, 1b
Jim Gilliam, 2b-lf
Jackie Robinson, 3b
Pee Wee Reese, ss
Sandy Amoros, lf
Duke Snider, cf
Carl Furillo, rf
Don Hoak, 3b
Don Zimmer, 2b

Pitchers

Don Newcombe, sp
Carl Erskine, sp
Johnny Podres, sp
Billy Loes, sp
Clem Labine, rp
Ed Roebuck, rp
Carl Spooner, rp-sp
Roger Craig, rp-sp

Attendance

1,033,589 (first in NL)

Club Leaders

Batting Avg:	Roy Campanella	.318
On-Base Pct:	Duke Snider	.418
Slugging Pct:	Duke Snider	.628
Home Runs:	Duke Snider	42
RBIs:	Duke Snider	136
Runs:	Duke Snider	126
Stolen Bases:	Jim Gilliam	15
Wins:	Don Newcombe	20
Strikeouts:	Don Newcombe	143
ERA:	Don Newcombe	3.20
Saves:	Ed Roebuck	12

MARCH 17   The Dodgers send Erv Palica to the Orioles for Frank Kellert and cash.

APRIL 12   The scheduled opener between the Dodgers and Pirates at Ebbets Field is postponed by rain and cold.

APRIL 13   The Dodgers open with a 6–1 win over the Pirates against the Pirates at Ebbets Field. The crowd was only 6,999 on a rainy and foggy day in which the temperature was 35 degrees. The Dodgers broke a 1–1 tie with five runs in the seventh inning. Carl Erskine pitched a complete game. Jim Gilliam and Carl Furillo homered.

                As they had in every season since 1947, the Dodgers telecast all 77 home games in 1955. For the first time, fans of the club could also watch road games in their homes with 25 shown on TV.

APRIL 14   Don Newcombe hits two homers during a 10–8 win over the Giants in New York.

APRIL 16   Russ Meyer pitches a two-hitter to defeat the Pirates 6–0 at Forbes Field. The only Pittsburgh hits were singles by Dick Groat in the third inning and Jack Shepard in the eighth.

APRIL 21   The Dodgers extend their season-opening winning streak to 10 games with a 14–4 decision over the Phillies before a crowd of only 3,874 at Ebbets Field. Seven of the 14 runs scored in the fourth inning.

                The 10–0 start is the best in Dodger history and is tied for the sixth best in the majors. The record is 13–0 by the 1982 Braves and the 1987 Brewers.

APRIL 22   The Dodgers lose for the first time in 1955, dropping a 5–4 decision to the Giants at Ebbets Field. The Dodgers led 3–0 before New York scored five times in the eighth.

APRIL 23   A bench-clearing incident mars a 3–1 win over the Giants at Ebbets Field. The trouble flared after Jackie Robinson was decked by a pitch from Sal Maglie. Robinson bunted along the first base line in the hopes of knocking Maglie over as the pitcher covered first base. Second baseman Davey Williams took the throw at first, however, and Robinson collided with Williams. Players from both teams rushed onto the field, but no blows were struck.

APRIL 24   The Dodgers lose 11–10 to the Giants at Ebbets Field in a contest in which 11 runs scored in the 10th inning. The Giants scored twice in the top of the ninth to tie the score 5–5, then added six runs in the 10th. The last of the six tallies was recorded when Carl Furillo caught a fly ball in right field, and believing it was the third out, trotted toward the infield while Al Dark scored from third base. The Dodgers plated five runs in a last-ditch rally which fell a run short.

APRIL 27   Billy Loes (seven innings) and Ed Roebuck (two innings) combine on a two-hitter to beat the Reds 7–2 at Ebbets Field. The only Cincinnati hits were singles by Ed Bailey in the sixth inning and Chuck Harmon in the ninth.

MAY 2   A two-run walk-off homer by Carl Furillo in the 12th inning are the only runs of a 2–0 win over the Braves at Ebbets Field. It was only the fourth hit off Gene Conley, who pitched a complete game for Milwaukee. Carl Erskine went all the way for Brooklyn, and surrendered six hits.

MAY 5   In his first major league start, Tommy Lasorda ties a major league record with three wild pitches in an inning before being relieved at the end of the first. The Dodgers won the game 4–3 against the Cardinals at Ebbets Field.

MAY 8   Duke Snider hits a grand slam off Bob Miller in the seventh inning of a 9–8 win over the Phillies in Philadelphia. It was the Dodgers 10th win in a row.

> *Snider had another terrific season in 1955, leading the league in runs (126) and RBIs (136). He also hit .309 with 42 home runs.*

MAY 10   The Dodgers extend their winning streak to 11 games with a 3–0 decision over the Cubs at Wrigley Field. Don Newcombe pitched a one-hitter. He faced the minimum 27 batters. The only Chicago base runner was Gene Baker, who singled in the fourth inning and was caught stealing. The one-hitter came only five days after Newcombe was suspended by Walter Alston for refusing to pitch batting practice. Newcombe apologized and was reinstated the following day.

> *The win gave the Dodgers a record of 22–2. The club already led the NL pennant race by 9½ games.*

MAY 14   The Dodgers score seven runs in the seventh inning and chalk up a 13–2 win over the Reds in Cincinnati. Carl Furillo hit a grand slam off Bob Hooper.

> *Furillo hit .314 with 26 home runs in 1955.*

MAY 17   Before a 3–0 loss to the Cardinals in St. Louis, Rube Walker and Cardinals catcher Del Rice stage a race. The foot race was the result of good-natured bantering about the identity of the "slowest man in baseball," and whether the dubious distinction belonged to Walker or Rice. In a 50-yard dash across the outfield, Rice won by about a foot. Commissioner Ford Frick was not amused because members of both clubs made wagers on the event, although the amount was only about $50.

MAY 26   The Dodgers break a 2–2 tie with four runs in the ninth inning to defeat the Pirates 6–2 in Pittsburgh. Don Newcombe drove in two runs with a triple, then stole home.

MAY 30   Don Newcombe hits two homers for the second time in 1955 during an 8–3 win over the Pirates in the second game of a double-header at Ebbets Field. The Dodgers also won the opener 8–4.

> *After winning 19 games in 1950 and 20 in 1951, Newcombe spent two years in the Army then struggled to a 9–8 record in 1954. He rebounded in a big way in 1955 with a 20–5 mark and a 3.20 ERA with 143 strikeouts in 23²/₃ innings. Newcombe was also highly effective with a bat in his hands. He hit .359 with a .632 slugging percentage and seven home runs in 117 at-bats in 1955.*

JUNE 1   Duke Snider hits three home runs and misses a fourth by only three feet during an 11–8 triumph over the Braves at Ebbets Field. Snider hit a solo shot off Gene Conley in the first inning, a three-run homer against Roberto Vargas in the fourth, and a two-run blast facing Ernie Johnson in the sixth. A double off Chet Nichols in the eighth hit the right-field screen three feet from the top. Pee Wee Reese, Jackie Robinson and Roy Campanella also homered for the Dodgers.

Roy Campanella and Duke Snider needed a lot of bats to power the Dodgers to a World Championship in 1955.

Campanella recovered from his awful season in 1954 (see April 15, 1954) to win his third MVP award. He hit .318 with 32 homers and 107 RBIs.

JUNE 2   The Dodgers score 10 runs in the eighth inning to defeat the Braves 13–3 at Ebbets Field. The 10-run rally consisted of nine hits and three walks, including a two-run triple by Jim Gilliam, a two-run double from Sandy Amoros and a two-run single by Carl Furillo.

JUNE 6   After failing in two attempts to sacrifice Gil Hodges to second base, Jackie Robinson smashes a two-run, walk-off homer to defeat the Cardinals 5–4 at Ebbets Field.

JUNE 8   Don Newcombe runs his record to 10–0 with a 3–1 win over the Reds at Ebbets Field.

JUNE 9   The Dodgers send Joe Black to the Reds for Bob Borkowski and cash.

JUNE 11   The Dodgers lead in the pennant race reaches 10½ games with a 4–3 victory over the Cubs at Ebbets Field. The club's record was 41–12. The lead remained in double digits for the rest of the year.

JUNE 17   Don Newcombe pitches a complete game and contributes a homer, double and a single to down the Cardinals 12–1 in St. Louis.

JUNE 24   Sandy Koufax makes his major league debut during an 8–2 loss to the Braves in Milwaukee. Koufax pitched the fifth and sixth innings and allowed no runs, a hit and a walk, and struck out two.

Koufax was only 18 years old and was on the club because of a rule in place between 1955 and 1957 which stipulated that any high school or college player given a bonus of $4,000 or more must remain on the active roster for two years without being sent to the minors. A native of Brooklyn, Koufax spent a year on the campus of the University of Cincinnati, where he attended on a basketball scholarship, before signing with the Dodgers. The bonus rule hampered the development of many players, including Koufax, who could have better used the time in the farm system. While showing flashes of brilliance, Koufax struggled during his first six seasons. At the end of the 1960 season, Koufax was nearly 25 years old and had a lifetime record of 36–40 with an earned run average of 4.10 and 683 strikeouts in 691²/₃ innings. Control was the major issue, as he also walked 405 batters during that span.

JUNE 30   After the Giants score two runs in the top of the 10th inning, the Dodgers respond with two in their half and one in the 11th to win 6–5 at Ebbets Field. In the 10th, Duke Snider tripled in a run and scored on Jackie Robinson's squeeze. George Shuba drove in the winner with a single.

JULY 6   Carl Erskine allows consecutive homers to Jerry Lynch, Frank Thomas and Dale Long in the sixth inning which ties the score 4–4, but the Dodgers go on to win 10–5 over the Pirates in the first game of a double-header at Forbes Field. Pittsburgh took game two 4–1.

JULY 8   Trailing 6–0, the Dodgers recover to win 12–8 over the Giants in New York. Brooklyn broke the 8–8 tie with a run in the eighth and added three more in the ninth.

JULY 16   Duke Snider's walk-off homer in the ninth inning beats the Reds 5–4 at Ebbets Field. It was his second home run of the game.

JULY 17   Two pitchers making their major league debuts start and win a double-header against the Reds at Ebbets Field. Roger Craig hurled a three-hit complete game in the opener for a 6–2 victory. Don Bessent went eight innings in the nightcap and won 8–5.

Craig and Bessent both pitched well during the stretch drive in 1955. Craig was 5–3 with a 2.78 ERA. Bessent had an 8–1 record and an earned run average of 2.70.

JULY 20   Don Newcombe pitches a two-hitter to defeat the Cubs 10–1 in the first game of a double-header at Ebbets Field. The only Chicago hits were singles by Clyde McCullough in the second inning and Dee Fondy in the eighth. Duke Snider and Don Zimmer both hit two homers and Gil Hodges added one. The Cubs won the second contest 5–3.

Hodges batted .289 with 27 homers and 102 RBIs in 1955.

JULY 22   Pee Wee Reese is given a night in his honor before a crowd of 33,033 at Ebbets Field. Seven cars of seven different makes were driven onto the field, and Reese's daughter Barbara picked one of seven keys out of a fishbowl. She chose a Chevrolet. In the fifth inning, the lights were turned off, fans lit matches, and sang "Happy Birthday." Reese contributed two doubles during an 8–4 win over the Braves in Milwaukee.

Turning 37 in 1955, Reese batted .282 with 10 home runs.

JULY 31   Don Newcombe runs his record to 18–1 with an 11–1 win over the Cardinals in St. Louis.

Plagued by a sore arm, Newcombe was only 2–4 over the remainder of the regular season, and lost his only World Series appearance.

AUGUST 3   Gil Hodges hits two homers and drives in six runs during a 9–6 win over the Braves in Milwaukee. He hit a grand slam in the first inning and a two-run shot in the fifth.

AUGUST 4   Trailing 9–6, the Dodgers erupt for five runs in the ninth inning and defeat the Braves 11–10 in Milwaukee. The five-run rally was climaxed by a three-run homer from Roy Campanella.

AUGUST 16   The Dodgers announce they will play seven home games at Roosevelt Field in Jersey City, New Jersey, in 1956. The ballpark held 25,000 and had parking for 4,000 cars. It was previously used by a minor league team in the Giants farm system from 1937 through 1950 and for stock car racing.

O'Malley continued to be disturbed by the attendance figures at Ebbets Field. The Dodgers were in first place all year in 1955, but drew 1,033,589 fans to rank eighth among 16 big-league clubs. It was fewer than any World Series participant between 1944 and 1971 and fewer than any National League pennant-winner between 1945 and the present day. The Dodgers and the Pirates were the only 1955 clubs to draw fewer fans than in the last pre-war season of 1941. The 1955 Pirates finished with the worst record in the NL for the fourth straight year. The Braves, a club never in serious contention for the pennant, had an attendance of 2,005,836 in 1955 which was nearly the figure in Brooklyn. O'Malley blamed the poor figures on the Brooklyn ballpark, which possessed too few seats, was relatively inaccessible by car or public transportation, had parking facilities for only 700 cars, and lacked modern facilities. Even if parking space could be found, traffic snarls around the ballpark were common. O'Malley shuddered to think of how he could bring fans into the ballpark if his club slipped out of contention and posted a losing record. The Dodgers drew 10,546 fans per victory in 1955, which ranked 12th in the majors ahead of only the Senators, Reds, Pirates and Giants, each clubs with losing records that season. The Senators and Giants would both relocate by 1960. O'Malley wanted to build a new stadium near the intersection of Flatbush and Atlantic Avenues in Brooklyn, then used by the Fort Greene Meat Market and the Long Island Railroad Terminal. The intersection was near downtown, and Atlantic and Flatbush were major traffic arteries to the south and eastern portions of the borough. O'Malley's idea would be to tear down the terminal, relocate the meat market, and clear enough of the surrounding property to make room for a new stadium, rail station, subway concourse and parking facilities. The rail station could bring fans to the new stadium by commuter rail from all over Long Island. Seven subway lines from nearly every point in New York City converged at Atlantic and Flatbush. O'Malley wanted the city to condemn the property and sell it to the Dodgers. He would then pay to build the stadium without public funds. It also would have been baseball's first downtown stadium. The Long Island Railroad was willing to go along with the plan, but O'Malley ran into stiff opposition from city officials. The move to Jersey City was meant to stir government action on the project and highlight the danger that the club might move out of the New York area. In addition, O'Malley unequivocally stated that the Dodgers would not play in Ebbets Field beyond 1957. The Giants also wanted the city to build them a stadium to replace the Polo Grounds, which faced many of the same problems as Ebbets Field. O'Malley warned mayor Robert Wagner "that it's unlikely only one team will move. You'll find that the two will move." Although Wagner was mayor, the real power broker in New York was city planner Robert Moses, who headed nearly every public works in the city, large and small, from the 1930s through the 1960s. Moses had a particular contempt for O'Malley and was opposed to the idea of building a new station for the railroad and a new ballpark for the Dodgers at the Atlantic and Flatbush location. Just the day before O'Malley's announcement of the move to Jersey City, Moses sent the Dodger owner a terse letter outlining his objections to the Atlantic-Flatbush site. The resentment between O'Malley and Moses grew over the next two years. Both were men who demanded complete control over their operations, possessed tremendous egos and didn't like to compromise. O'Malley refused to consider other sites in the New York area, including one Moses proposed in Queens, while Moses put one roadblock after another in the path of O'Malley's plans. The result was the loss of major league baseball in Brooklyn. Over the next two years, before the move became final in October 1957, O'Malley stated repeatedly that he intended to construct a new ballpark with his own capital, but that he needed government assistance to acquire the real estate at Atlantic and Flatbush. New York officials were unwilling to furnish him with the site he wanted while Los Angeles offered 300 acres in centrally located Chavez Ravine. As author Neil J. Sullivan stated in his book The Dodgers Move West, *"In the end it was more important to Los Angeles politicians to attract the Dodgers than it was for New York politicians to keep them."*

AUGUST 27   In his second major league start, Sandy Koufax pitches a two-hitter and strikes out 14 to defeat the Reds 7–0 at Ebbets Field. The only Cincinnati hits were a single by Ted Kluszewski in the first inning and a double by Sam Mele with two out in the ninth.

SEPTEMBER 2   In his third start, Sandy Koufax pitches his second shutout beating the Pirates 4–0 at Ebbets Field.

Koufax set a dubious major league record in 1955 by striking out in 12 consecutive plate appearances. The whiffs came in his first 12 career at-bats.

SEPTEMBER 5   Don Newcombe earns his 20th win off the 1955 season with an 11–4 decision over the Phillies in the first game of a double-header in Philadelphia. The Dodgers also won the second contest 8–4.

SEPTEMBER 8   The Dodgers clinch the National League pennant with a 10–2 win over the Braves in Milwaukee. At the time of the clinching, the club held a 17-game lead and had a record of 92–46.

SEPTEMBER 9   The Dodgers lose 11–4 and win 16–9 over the Cubs in Chicago. Don Zimmer hit a grand slam off Bill Tremel in the sixth inning of the second game. Clem Labine also homered for the Dodgers. The Cubs hit nine home runs during the twin bill.

Labine had an unusual season with a bat in his hand in 1955. He had only three hits in 31 at-bats, but all three hits were home runs. They were the only three homers of his career in 227 at-bats over 13 years. Labine's career batting average was .075. He was much more successful as a relief pitcher. Labine had a record of 13–5 with a 3.24 ERA in a league-leading 60 games during the 1955 campaign. He led the NL in saves in 1956 and 1957.

SEPTEMBER 11   Johnny Klippstein of the Reds comes within two outs of a no-hitter against the Dodgers in the first game of a double-header at Crosley Field. After Pee Wee Reese singled with one out in the ninth, Klippstein had to settle for a 9–0, one-hit victory. Cincinnati also won the second game 5–3.

The Dodgers entered the 1955 post-season with an 0–7 record in the era of the modern World Series. Brooklyn lost to the Red Sox in 1916, the Indians in 1920, and the Yankees in 1941, 1947, 1949, 1952 and 1953. The Yankees were the opponents again in 1955. Managed by Casey Stengel, New York was 96–58 and finished three games ahead of the defending AL champion Indians. The Dodgers had more regular season wins than the Yankees in 1955, but history had proven that was no guarantee of victory. The Dodgers also had the best record in the majors in 1916, 1952 and 1953 and were tied for the best in 1949.

SEPTEMBER 28   The Dodgers open the 1955 World Series with a 6–5 loss to the Yankees at Yankee Stadium. Carl Furillo started the scoring with a home run leading off the second inning. Both teams scored twice in the second and once in the third. The Yankees took a 4–3 lead with a run in the fourth inning and added two more in the fifth before a futile two-run Brooklyn rally in the eighth, one on Jackie Robinson's daring steal of home. Don Newcombe allowed all six New York runs in $5^2/_3$ innings. Suffering from a sore arm, the Dodger ace would not pitch again in 1955. In the first six games of the Series, the Dodgers used six different starting pitchers.

The 1955 World Series was the last ever played in the month of September. September 28 is the earliest date a Series game has ever been played, with the exception of 1918.

SEPTEMBER 29   The Dodgers fall behind two games to none with a 4–2 loss to the Yankees at Yankee Stadium. The Yanks scored all four of their runs in the fourth off Billy Loes.

Prior to 1955, no team had ever won a World Series after losing the first two games.

SEPTEMBER 30   The Dodgers break through with an 8–3 win over the Yankees before 34,209 at Ebbets Field. Johnny Podres, on his 23rd birthday, pitched a complete game. Roy Campanella put the Dodgers ahead 2–0 with a homer in the first. After the Yanks tied the score in the top of the second, Brooklyn responded with two in their half to take the lead for good.

The 1955 World Series was the first to be televised in color, although the transmission went to only a small fraction of the 180 stations in the United States and 20 in Canada that carried the games. Most stations had not yet acquired the equipment to transmit color images. It was probably just as well, as the process wasn't technologically sound in the mid-1950s. Jack Gould of the New York Times *reported that the "tinted version was far from impressive, because the outdoor pick-ups are not yet color's strong feature. [Yankee first baseman] Joe Collins appeared to be skipping around on an artist's palette."*

OCTOBER 1   The Dodgers even the Series with an 8–5 win over the Yankees before 36,242 at Ebbets Field. Carl Erskine was the Dodger starter, and left in the fourth with the club trailing 3–1. Brooklyn took the lead with three runs in the fourth inning on a solo homer from Roy Campanella and a two-run shot from Gil Hodges. A home run with two on base by Duke Snider in the fifth put the game away.

OCTOBER 2   The Dodgers move within one game of the world championship with a 5–3 triumph over the Yankees before 36,796 at Ebbets Field. Starter Roger Craig went six innings for the win. Duke Snider hit two homers and Sandy Amoros one for the Dodgers. The two by Snider gave him four home runs in the 1955 Series. He also hit four in 1952.

OCTOBER 3   With a chance to win Brooklyn's first world championship, the Dodgers lose game six 5–1 to the Yankees at Yankee Stadium. Karl Spooner was the Dodger starter and allowed five runs in one-third of an inning. Whitey Ford pitched a four-hitter for New York.

OCTOBER 4   The Dodgers finally win a World Series by beating the Yankees in game seven by a 2–0 score before 62,465 at Yankee Stadium, about 8,000 short of capacity. Johnny Podres pitched the eight-hit shutout. The first run scored in the fourth off Tommy Byrne on a double by Roy Campanella and a two-out single from Gil Hodges. In the fourth, Hodges delivered a bases loaded sacrifice fly. In the bottom of the sixth, Sandy Amoros replaced Jim Gilliam in left field. Gilliam moved to second base to succeed Don Zimmer, who had been lifted for a pinch-hitter in the top of the inning. Billy Martin walked and Gil McDougald singled to lead off the New York sixth. Yogi Berra, a left-handed pull hitter, sliced a long drive down the left-field line. Amoros, playing in left center, raced full speed to snag the ball by reaching out his gloved right hand. Amoros then whirled and threw out McDougald at first base to complete a double play. It was a play the right-handed Gilliam probably wouldn't have been able to make. In the ninth, Podres retired the side in order. The final out was recorded on a grounder by Elston Howard to shortstop Pee Wee Reese, who threw to Gil Hodges at first base.

Podres won his place in Dodgers lore with his seventh-game shutout in 1955. He was hardly a star at the time, however. During the regular season, Podres posted a mediocre 9–10 record with a 3.95 earned run average. He was 2–6 after July 1, and failed to complete any of his last 13 regular-season starts before throwing two in the World Series. Podres spent the 1956 season serving in the Navy, and returned in 1957 for a long career. He would pitch for the Dodgers until 1966.

With a 136–104 record for the club, Podres stands ninth in victories. Among franchise leaders, he is also seventh in strikeouts (1,331), eighth in games started (310) and 10th in shutouts (23).

Tommy Byrne of the Yankees and Johnny Podres of the Dodgers shake hands before pitching the seventh game of the 1955 World Series. Podres pitched a shutout for the victory.

DECEMBER 9   Eight days after Rosa Parks refuses to give up her seat on a bus, inspiring a boycott of the Montgomery, Alabama, public transportation system, the Dodgers trade Don Hoak, Walt Moryn and Russ Meyer to the Cubs for Randy Jackson and Don Elston.

Jackson was 29 years old and made the All-Star team in both 1954 and 1955. The Dodgers hoped he would solve their long-standing problem at third base, but Jackson proved to be a bust in Brooklyn. The Dodgers would have been much better off keeping Hoak, who was an All-Star third baseman with the Reds in 1957 and finished third in the MVP voting as a Pirate in 1960. Moryn was also a loss. He gave the Cubs three solid seasons and could have filled the Dodgers' need for a left fielder.

1956

L A

Season in a Sentence

The Dodgers win a thrilling pennant race by one game before losing a seven-game World Series to the Yankees.

Finish • Won • Lost • Pct • GB

First   93   61   .604   +1.0

World Series

The Dodgers lost to the New York Yankees four games to three.

Manager

Walter Alston

Stats	Dods	NL	Rank
Batting Avg:	.258	.256	4
On-Base Pct:	.342	.321	1
Slugging Pct:	.419	.401	3
Home Runs:	179		2
Stolen Bases:	65		2
ERA:	3.57	3.77	2
Fielding Avg:	.981	.977	1
Runs Scored:	720		2
Runs Allowed:	601		2

Starting Lineup

Roy Campanella, c
Gil Hodges, 1b
Jim Gilliam, 2b-lf
Jackie Robinson, 3b
Pee Wee Reese, ss
Sandy Amoros, lf
Duke Snider, cf
Carl Furillo, rf
Randy Jackson, 3b

Pitchers

Don Newcombe, sp
Sal Maglie, sp
Roger Craig, sp
Carl Erskine, sp
Clem Labine, rp
Don Bessent, rp
Ed Roebuck, rp
Don Drysdale, rp-sp

Attendance

1,213,562 (second in NL)

Club Leaders

Batting Avg:	Jim Gilliam	.300
On-Base Pct:	Jim Gilliam	.399
	Duke Snider	.399
Slugging Pct:	Duke Snider	.598
Home Runs:	Duke Snider	43
RBIs:	Duke Snider	101
Runs:	Duke Snider	112
Stolen Bases:	Jim Gilliam	21
Wins:	Don Newcombe	27
Strikeouts:	Don Newcombe	139
ERA:	Sal Maglie	2.87
Saves:	Clem Labine	19

MARCH 2   The Dodgers sell Tommy Lasorda to the Kansas City Athletics.

APRIL 17   The defending world-champion Dodgers open the 1956 season with an 8–6 loss to the Phillies before 24,236 at Ebbets Field. Don Newcombe was the starting pitcher, but lasted only 2⅓ innings. Jim Gilliam and Roy Campanella homered. Don Drysdale made his major league debut by pitching the ninth inning.

The opener was a rare bad outing for Newcombe. Following a 20–5 season in 1955, he was 27–7 in 1956 with a 3.06 ERA in 268 innings.

APRIL 19   The Dodgers play their first game at Roosevelt Field in Jersey City and beat the Phillies 2–1 in 10 innings (see August 16, 1955). The contest was scoreless through nine innings. After Philadelphia scored in the top of the 10th, Roy Campanella drove in the tying run in the bottom half with a double. The Dodgers loaded the bases on a sacrifice and two intentional walks before Rube Walker drove in the game-winner on a sacrifice fly. The tilt drew 12,214 on a Thursday afternoon.

The Dodgers drew 148,371 for the seven games at Jersey City, an average of 21,196. Each was played on a Monday, Tuesday, Wednesday and a Thursday. The club attracted 1,065,191 to Ebbets Field, an average of 15,217 a game.

APRIL 21   New York Governor Averill Harriman signs a bill authorizing a new ballpark for the Dodgers as part of a $30 million sports and civic center at the intersection of Atlantic and Flatbush Avenues, which includes plans to redevelop the Long Island Railroad Station (see August 16, 1955). The Dodgers stadium would include a sliding glass dome. On July 24, Mayor Robert Wagner created the Brooklyn Sports Authority to move the project forward. The plan ran into political opposition, however, and never came to fruition.

APRIL 23   Don Drysdale makes his first major league start and pitches a complete game to beat the Phillies 6–1 in 40-degree weather in Philadelphia. He struck out the side in the first inning and nine altogether.

Drysdale made the club as a 19-year-old non-roster invitee. He was used sparingly in 1956, pitching only 99 innings, but by 1957 was in the starting rotation and won 17 games. In 1958, Drysdale led the NL in hit batsmen for the first of four consecutive seasons and five in his career, thereby establishing his well-deserved reputation for headhunting. Plunking hitters with regularity wasn't the result of wildness. Drysdale walked only 2.24 batters per nine innings during his major league career. It was purely for intimidation purposes and proved to be an excellent strategy. He topped the league in strikeouts three times, innings twice, wins once, and the Cy Young Award voting in 1962, on the way to a 209–166 record and a berth in the Hall of Fame. Among Dodgers, Drysdale ranks second in wins, second in games pitched (518), second in games started (465), second in shutouts (49), second in innings pitched (3,432), second in strikeouts (2,486), fourth in walks (855), sixth in complete games (167) and eighth in ERA (2.95). In addition, Drysdale hit 29 career homers, the sixth most in major league history by a pitcher and a Dodger club record.

MAY 12   Carl Erskine pitches a no-hitter to defeat the Giants 3–0 at Ebbets Field. He struck out three and walked two and threw 102 pitches. In the ninth, pinch-hitter Ted Wilson fouled out. After a long foul fly to right field, Whitey Lockman hit a vicious bouncer up the middle which was fielded by Erskine. Al Dark followed with another grounder to Erskine, who threw to Gil Hodges at first for the final out. It was Erskine's second career no-hitter. He also threw one against the Cubs on June 19, 1952.

Jerry Doggett joined the Dodgers broadcasting team in 1956. He would remain with the club on both radio and TV for 32 years, the last 30 of them in Los Angeles, playing second banana to Vin Scully.

MAY 13   Duke Snider hits two homers, including a grand slam, during a 6–4 win over the Giants at Ebbets Field. His slam was struck off Jim Hearn in the third inning. Snider added a solo shot off Ramon Monzant in the fourth.

Snider led the NL in homers (43), on-base percentage (.399) and slugging percentage (.598) in addition to batting .292, 101 RBIs and 112 runs in 1956.

MAY 14   The Dodgers sell Billy Loes to the Orioles.

MAY 15   The Dodgers sell Jim Hughes to the Cubs and purchase Sal Maglie from the Indians.

> *Dodger fans were aghast at the sight of Maglie in a Brooklyn uniform. He had been a particularly hated member of the rival Giants throughout the first half of the 1950s. Maglie had a record of 81–33 for the New York club from 1950 through 1954, including a 22–6 mark against the Dodgers, and showed a proclivity for throwing at hitters, which earned him the nickname "The Barber." Maglie was sold by the Giants to the Indians late in the 1955 season. At the time he was purchased by the Dodgers, Maglie hadn't won a game in 10 months and was 39 years old. Even though the acquisition seemed to make little sense, the Dodgers couldn't have won the 1956 pennant without it. Maglie was 13–5 for Brooklyn over the remainder of the campaign along with a 2.87 ERA. He also threw a no-hitter.*

MAY 28   Pirates first baseman Dale Long sets a major league record (since tied) by hitting a home run in his eighth straight game during a 3–2 win over the Dodgers in Pittsburgh.

MAY 29   Don Newcombe halts Dale Long's streak of hitting home runs in eight consecutive games by holding the Pirate slugger hitless in four at-bats during a 10–1 Dodger win in Pittsburgh.

Roger Craig pitches a two-hitter to defeat the Braves 6–1 at County Stadium. The only Milwaukee hits were a home run by Eddie Mathews in the first inning and a single by Bill Bruton in the seventh.

JUNE 21   The Dodgers score four runs with two out in the ninth inning to stun the Cardinals 9–8 at Ebbets Field. The first two batters in the ninth were retired, then Carl Furillo and Jackie Robinson singled. Roy Campanella deadlocked the contest 8–8 with a three-run homer. It was his second three-run homer during the contest. Campanella's first was struck in the second. The Dodgers accounted for the

In 1956, Jim "Junior" Gilliam batted .300 for the only time in his career, but he gave the Dodgers many years of a steady glove and a steadying influence both on and off the field.

winning run on a walk to Sandy Amoros and singles by Jim Gilliam and Don Zimmer.

Gilliam hit a career high .300 and scored 102 runs in 1956.

JUNE 23   The Dodgers score three runs in the ninth inning to defeat the Reds 7–6 at Ebbets Field. Randy Jackson drove in two runs on a double and scored on Rocky Nelson's single.

Don Zimmer was struck by a pitch from Hal Jeffcoat during the game, resulting in a broken cheekbone. It was the second time that Zimmer was seriously injured by a pitch. In 1953 while with St. Paul in the American Association, he was plunked in the head by a fastball. Zimmer was unconscious and near death for two weeks, unable to speak for two months, and emerged 44 pounds lighter. Installed into his head were four screws. Zimmer recovered from both devastating setbacks and played in the majors until 1966. He managed in the majors with the Padres, Red Sox, Rangers and Cubs between 1972 and 1991, then served as Joe Torre's bench coach in five World Series with the Yankees. In 2008, Zimmer was still in uniform at the age of 77 as a coach with the Tampa Bay Rays.

JUNE 24   Ed Bailey hits three homers for the Reds during a 10–6 win over the Dodgers in the first game of a double-header at Ebbets Field. Cincinnati also won the second contest 2–1.

JUNE 25   The Dodgers sell Dick Williams to the Orioles.

JUNE 26   Rube Walker, subbing as catcher for the injured Roy Campanella, drives in six runs with a homer, triple and single during a 10–5 win over the Cubs at Ebbets Field.

The triple was Walker's first in the majors since 1950. He didn't hit another three-bagger before his career ended in 1958.

JUNE 29   Three consecutive homers with one out in the ninth inning produce four runs and a 6–5 win over the Phillies at Ebbets Field. Jim Gilliam walked before Duke Snider, Randy Jackson and Gil Hodges struck back-to-back-to-back home runs.

Jackson's given name was Ransom. He resembled actor Gregory Peck, earning Jackson the nickname of "Handsome Ransom." He was also a football star in college as a halfback at the University of Texas.

JULY 4   The Dodgers sweep the Giants 15–2 and 6–1 in New York. Brooklyn scored in nine consecutive innings from the second inning of the first game through the first inning of the nightcap.

JULY 10   Walter Alston manages the National League to a 4–3 loss in the All-Star Game at Griffith Stadium in Washington.

JULY 15   Carl Furillo hits two homers, one a grand slam, during a 10–8 win over the Cubs in Chicago. The bases-loaded homer was hit in the sixth inning off Warren Hacker.

Manager Walter Alston, owner Walter O'Malley and shortstop Pee Wee Reese celebrate the National League pennant.

JULY 18 Prior to a 6–3 win in Cincinnati, Sal Maglie throws balls at the scoreboard clock at Crosley Field until it stops ticking. Reds general manager Gabe Paul called the incident a "deliberate act of vandalism" and sent the Dodgers a bill for repairs.

JULY 21 Pee Wee Reese collects his 2,000th career hit during a 13–6 win over the Cubs in Chicago. Jim Gilliam tied a major league record for most assists by a second baseman with 12.

> *With the defeat, the Dodgers were 46–39 and in third place, six games behind the first place Braves.*

JULY 25 Duke Snider hits a walk-off homer in the ninth which beats the Reds 2–1 at Roosevelt Field at Jersey City.

JULY 29 The Dodgers extend their winning streak to eight games with a 1–0 decision over the Cubs in the first game of a double-header at Ebbets Field. Don Newcombe hurled the shutout. Pee Wee Reese drove in the winning run with a homer in the eighth inning off Jim Davis. Chicago won the second tilt 4–2.

> *On the same day, the Dodgers purchased Dale Mitchell from the Indians.*

AUGUST 2 Don Newcombe pitches his second consecutive shutout beating the Braves 3–0 at Ebbets Field.

AUGUST 4   Rookie shortstop Chico Fernandez hits a grand slam off Don Liddle in the seventh inning of a 12–4 win over the Cardinals at Ebbets Field.

                It was the first career homer for Fernandez and his only one in a Dodger uniform. He had only 66 at-bats in 34 games with Brooklyn before being traded to the Phillies in April 1957.

AUGUST 7   Don Newcombe pitches his third consecutive shutout, beating the Pirates 3–0 at Ebbets Field.

AUGUST 11   Don Newcombe's consecutive inning scoreless streak ends at 39, but he beats the Phillies 5–2 at Ebbets Field while allowing only two hits. Newcombe had a no-hitter in progress until the seventh inning when Marv Blaylock singled and Stan Lopata homered.

AUGUST 16   Duke Snider hits a walk-off homer in the 13th inning to beat the Giants 10–9 at Ebbets Field. The score was 9–9 at the end of the sixth inning.

AUGUST 23   Don Newcombe posts his 20th win of 1956 with a 6–5 decision over the Reds in Cincinnati.

SEPTEMBER 1   The Dodgers sweep the Giants 5–3 and 5–0 at the Polo Grounds. Sal Maglie (5$\frac{1}{3}$ innings) and Don Bessent (3$\frac{2}{3}$ innings) combined on a two-hitter in the nightcap. The only hit allowed by Maglie was a single by Jackie Brandt in the second inning. The Dodger pitcher was ejected for throwing his glove in the air in protest of umpire Art Gore's call of a ball. The second New York hit was a single by Red Schoendienst off Bessent in the sixth.

SEPTEMBER 7   A two-run, walk-off homer by Carl Furillo with two out in the 11th beats the Giants 3–1 in the second game of a double-header at Ebbets Field. New York won the opener 6–2.

SEPTEMBER 11   The Dodgers pull into a first place tie with a 4–2 win over the Braves at Ebbets Field. Sal Maglie was the winning pitcher in a duel with Bob Buhl, who had an 8–1 record against the Dodgers in 1956. Both Milwaukee and Brooklyn ended the day with 83–55 records.

SEPTEMBER 15   The Dodgers take undisputed possession of first place for the first time since April 28 with a 3–0 win over the Cubs at Ebbets Field. Don Newcombe pitched the shutout for his 24th victory of the season. At the end of the day, the Dodgers led by two percentage points over the Braves with a record of 85–66. The Reds were in third, two games back.

SEPTEMBER 17   A walk-off homer by Carl Furillo in the 10th inning beats the Reds 5–4 at Ebbets Field. Cincinnati scored three times with two out in the top of the ninth to tie the contest 4–4. The win gave the Dodgers a one-game lead over the Braves and virtually ended Cincinnati's hopes for a pennant.

SEPTEMBER 19   The Dodgers score eight runs in the fifth inning and overwhelm the Cardinals 17–2 at Ebbets Field. Don Newcombe pitched seven innings for his 25th victory of the season, and in addition, hit two homers. In only his second big-league at-bat, Don Demeter hit a home run. The win gave the Dodgers a lead of one-half game over Milwaukee.

Bob Aspromonte, an 18-year-old native of Brooklyn made his major league debut in the contest as a pinch-hitter and struck out. He didn't play in another big-league game until 1960.

SEPTEMBER 24   The Dodgers are knocked out of first place with a 6–5 loss to the Pirates in Pittsburgh.

SEPTEMBER 25   Sam Maglie keeps the Dodgers in the pennant race with a no-hitter to defeat the Phillies 5–0 at Ebbets Field. Maglie struck out two, walked three, and threw 118 pitches. Pinch-hitter Frank Baumholtz was the first Philadelphia batter in the ninth and lifted a high foul behind the plate. Roy Campanella made the catch with one foot in the dugout and several teammates holding him up. Harvey Haddix struck out on three pitches to put Maglie one out from his no-hitter, Richie Ashburn was hit by a pitch before Marv Blaylock was retired on a grounder from second baseman Jim Gilliam to first baseman Gil Hodges.

SEPTEMBER 28   The idle Dodgers move within one-half game of first place when the Braves lose 5–4 to the Cardinals in St. Louis. Milwaukee had two games remaining, and Brooklyn had three with two days left in the season.

SEPTEMBER 29   The Dodgers take a one-game lead in the pennant race with a sweep of the Pirates in a double-header at Ebbets Field while the Braves lose to the Cardinals in St. Louis. The Dodgers won 6–2 and 3–1. The second game was delayed for 10 minutes in the sixth inning when fans littered the field with debris following a call against the home team. The barrage ceased after the umpires threatened a forfeit to Pittsburgh. After the afternoon twin bill, Milwaukee lost a night game 2–1 to the Cards by a 2–1 score in 12 innings.

SEPTEMBER 30   On the final day of the season, the Dodgers clinch the pennant with an 8–6 victory over the Pirates at Ebbets Field. Duke Snider hit two homers and drove in four runs. Sandy Amoros also homered twice. Don Newcombe allowed six runs in 7$^{1}/_{3}$ innings, and nearly blew a 7–2 lead, but it was good enough for his 27th win of the season. Don Bessent earned the save with 1$^{2}/_{3}$ innings of relief. The Braves beat the Cardinals 4–2 in St. Louis to finish one game back. The Reds were third, two games behind.

The Dodgers were in first place only 17 days all season while the Braves held the top spot for 126 days. The 1956 World Series was the seventh Dodgers-Yankees match-up in 16 years, the sixth in 10, and the fourth in five. The Yanks defeated the Dodgers in 1941, 1947, 1949, 1952 and 1953, while Brooklyn claimed its first world championship in 1955. During the 1956 season, Casey Stengel's Yankees were 97–57 and won the AL race by eight games.

OCTOBER 3   The Dodgers open the 1956 World Series with a 6–3 win over the Yankees before 34,479 at Ebbets Field. Gil Hodges broke a 2–2 tie with a three-run homer in the third. Jackie Robinson also homered. After allowing two runs in the first, Sal Maglie settled down and pitched a complete game while fanning 10.

President Dwight Eisenhower attended the opening game of the 1956 Series. From a gate in left field, the presidential limousine drove hm onto the field and to his box. Before the contest, Ike shook hands with players from both the Dodgers and Yankees and threw out the first ball. It was a month before the presidential election, and Eisenhower was facing Adlai Stevenson for the second time. Stevenson went to game two of the 1956 Series. So as not to offend fans of either club, he wore a Dodgers cap and a Yankees cap simultaneously. It didn't help. As in 1952, Stevenson lost the 1956 election to Eisenhower.

OCTOBER 4   Rain postpones game two at Ebbets Field.

The postponement was the only day off during the 1956 World Series. There were no travel days scheduled because the two ballparks were only 10 miles apart. There has been two travel days in every World Series played after 1956, even when teams were located in the same geographic area, such as the Giants and Athletics in 1989 and the Yankees and Mets in 2000.

OCTOBER 5   The Dodgers take a two-games-to-none lead in the World Series by outslugging the Yankees 13–8 before 36,217 at Ebbets Field. New York took a 6–0 lead with five runs in the second inning off Don Newcombe, four on a grand slam by Yogi Berra. The Dodgers rebounded with six tallies in their half of the second, the last three on a homer by Duke Snider. Brooklyn broke a 7–7 deadlock on a two-run double by Gil Hodges in the fourth. The Dodgers scored their 13 runs on 12 hits. Seven Yankee hurlers combined to walk 11. Don Larsen was the New York starter and allowed four runs, a hit and four walks in 1²/₃ innings. Don Bessent pitched seven innings of relief for Brooklyn, and surrendered two runs.

On the same day, Washington Senators owner Calvin Griffith announced that he was "seriously considering" moving his team out of the nation's capital and mentioned Los Angeles as one of his choices. Griffith met with Los Angeles County supervisor Kenneth Hahn during game two at Ebbets Field. Walter O'Malley passed Hahn a note telling him not to strike a deal with Griffith until he talked to the Dodgers first.

OCTOBER 6   The Yankees win their first game of the Series with a 5–3 triumph over the Dodgers at Yankee Stadium. The New Yorkers took a 4–2 lead in the sixth on a three-run homer by Enos Slaughter off Roger Craig.

The Dodgers scored 19 runs in the first two games of the Series, but only six in the last five. After using six relief pitchers in game two, the Yankees received five consecutive complete games from pitchers Whitey Ford, Tom Sturdivant, Don Larsen, Bob Turley and Johnny Kucks in games three through seven.

OCTOBER 7   In game four, the Yankees even the Series with a 6–2 win over the Dodgers at Yankee Stadium.

OCTOBER 8   Yankee pitcher Don Larsen pitches a perfect game to beat the Dodgers 2–0 at Yankee Stadium. It is the only no-hitter of any description in post-season history. Larsen struck out seven and made 97 pitches. He was 27 years old with an 11–5 record in 1956 and a 30–40 mark during his career when he stepped to the mound in game five. Three days earlier, Larsen was relieved in the second inning in a start in game two. Sal Maglie retired the first 11 Yankees to face him before Mickey Mantle homered in the fourth. New York added another run in the sixth. In the

Brooklyn ninth, Carl Furillo led off with a fly ball to Hank Bauer to right field. Roy Campanella grounded out to second baseman Billy Martin. Dale Mitchell, pinch-hitting for Maglie, stood between Don Larsen and a perfect game. After a ball, two strikes, and a foul ball, Mitchell took strike three looking.

The at-bat was the second-to-last of Mitchell's 11-year career. He would pinch-hit again in game seven. Both Maglie and Mitchell began the season as members of the Cleveland Indians.

OCTOBER 9   The Dodgers force game seven with a 10-inning, 1–0 win over the Yankees before 33,225 at Ebbets Field. Walter Alston gambled by starting Clem Labine. During the regular season, Labine made only three starts among his 62 appearances while posting a 10–6 won-lost record and 19 saves. He rewarded his manager's confidence with a 10-inning shutout in which he allowed seven hits. Yankee starter Bob Turley entered the bottom of the 10th with a three-hit shutout of his own. He had struck out 11. Jim Gilliam walked with one out, and was sacrificed to second by Pee Wee Reese. Duke Snider was walked intentionally. Jackie Robinson drove in the winning run with a liner badly misplayed by left fielder Enos Slaughter.

OCTOBER 10   There is little suspense in game seven, as the Dodgers lose 9–0 to the Yankees before 33,782 at Ebbets Field. Johnny Kucks pitched the three-hit shutout. Don Newcombe allowed five runs in three innings, and Roger Craig surrendered a grand slam to Bill Skowron in the seventh. The last World Series game ever played at Ebbets Field ended on a Jackie Robinson strikeout. It would prove to be Robinson's final plate appearance (see December 13, 1956).

Newcombe had a record of 112–48 for the Dodgers during the regular season from 1949 through 1956, but struggled mightily in the World Series. He was 0–4 in five starts, with an ERA of 8.59 in 22 innings.

OCTOBER 11   The Dodgers leave Idlewild Airport in New York for a tour of Japan. After three games in Hawaii, the club played in Japan from October 19 through November 13 and posted a record of 14–4–1.

OCTOBER 12   On the way to Japan, Walter O'Malley stops in Los Angeles, and meets with Los Angeles County supervisor Kenneth Hahn. It was O'Malley's first visit to the city. He was shown, by helicopter, the site in Chavez Ravine that Hahn, and other Los Angeles officials, had touted for a new stadium. O'Malley called it "an ideal location," but there was considerable opposition by many government officials and private citizens over the viability of the area for a ballpark. On June 1, 1955, Los Angeles voters turned down a $4.5 million bond issue to build a 63,000-seat stadium in Chavez Ravine by a margin of 160,000 to 131,000.

A little over a mile from Los Angeles City Hall, Chavez Ravine in 1956 was at the vortex of the Harbor (I-110), Santa Ana (US 101) and Pasadena (CA 110) freeways. The Golden State (I-5) freeway was in the planning stages. At the time, the sprawling and inaccessible Chavez Ravine was hilly, undeveloped and unkempt. It was filled with rocks and cuts and consisted of rat-infested patches of weeds, tall grass, clumps of small gum trees, cactus, dirt dumped from the construction of freeways, and piles of garbage. In its remote spots, the ravine was a spot for clandestine trysts. Prior to 1949, Chavez Ravine was the home to a few *hundred Mexican-Americans living in small houses on steep, winding and mostly unpaved streets in three distinct neighborhoods. An elementary school was also located in the ravine. Photographs of the neighborhood taken during the 1940s are evocative of a remote rural mountain town. Yet, in sharp contrast, the busy Pasadena Freeway was on the base of a hill on the east side, and the downtown skyline was less than two miles distant. After World War II, city governments attempted to solve urban problems with a bulldozer by leveling "blighted" areas. Chavez Ravine was part of this movement. The federal government took over the ravine and used the power of eminent domain to force out most of the residents for a public housing project which was never built. The city of Los Angeles purchased the property from the federal government with the proviso that it be used for a "public purpose." The entire community was razed, but a few scattered residents still remained. The city government dismissed them as "squatters" and made every effort to have them removed. Despite the proximity to downtown, no one had built any large-scale developments on the site because of the expense. It would require moving millions of square feet of earth. The technology to move that much dirt wasn't available until World War II with the advent of the Seabees, which built airstrips in islands in the Pacific. City government tried to interest public groups in developing Chavez Ravine, but the only nibble came from a cemetery company desiring to use the site for burial plots. Los Angeles grew in all directions for miles around Chavez Ravine. In 1957, the 302-acre site took in only $8,000 in real estate taxes. (By contrast, in 1963, after Dodger Stadium was built, the Dodgers were assessed $750,000 for the property.) In an ironic twist, Chavez Ravine, once slated for public housing units, became home to the Dodgers. Ebbets Field was torn down in 1960, and public housing went up in its place.*

OCTOBER 30   The Dodgers sell Ebbets Field to real estate developer Marvin Kratter for a reported $3,000,000. The ballpark was then leased to the Dodgers through 1959 with an option for two more years.

DECEMBER 13   The Dodgers send Jackie Robinson to the Giants for Dick Littlefield and $35,000.

The trade was a shock not only because Robinson was forced to leave Brooklyn but was dealt to the crosstown Giants. Neither club was aware, however, that Robinson had already decided to retire. He sold a story to Look magazine for $50,000 in which he announced his intention to end his playing career. The issue was slated for publication in January 1957. The Giants tried to persuade Robinson to reconsider, but he was adamant in his decision. Once Robinson officially announced his retirement on January 5, the trade was voided.

DECEMBER 29   Growing impatient over the city's slow pace in approving a new stadium for the Dodgers, Walter O'Malley says there might be only a "short time" before an "irrevocable step" would have to be made to "commit the Dodgers elsewhere." Six weeks later O'Malley was more specific, warning New York officials that "unless something is done within six months, I will have to make other arrangements."

1957

Season in a Sentence

With an aging lineup in the club's last year in Brooklyn, the Dodgers finish in third place after winning the pennant four of the previous five years.

Finish • Won • Lost • Pct • GB

Third   84   70   .545   11.0

Manager

Walter Alston

Stats

Stats	Dods	NL	Rank
Batting Avg:	.253	.260	5
On-Base Pct:	.325	.322	4
Slugging Pct:	.387	.400	5
Home Runs:	147		4 (tie)
Stolen Bases:	60		2
ERA:	3.35	3.88	1
Fielding Avg:	.979	.977	3
Runs Scored:	690		4
Runs Allowed:	591		1

Starting Lineup

Roy Campanella, c
Gil Hodges, 1b
Jim Gilliam, 2b
Pee Wee Reese, 3b
Charlie Neal, ss
Gino Cimoli, lf-rf
Duke Snider, cf
Carl Furillo, rf
Don Zimmer, 3b-ss
Sandy Amoros, lf

Pitchers

Don Drysdale, sp
Johnny Podres, sp
Don Newcombe, sp
Danny McDevitt, sp
Sal Maglie, sp
Clem Labine, rp
Ed Roebuck, rp
Sandy Koufax, rp-sp
Roger Craig, rp-sp

Attendance

1,028,258 (fifth in NL)

Club Leaders

Batting Avg:	Gil Hodges	.299
On-Base Pct:	Duke Snider	.368
Slugging Pct:	Duke Snider	.587
Home Runs:	Duke Snider	40
RBIs:	Gil Hodges	98
Runs:	Gil Hodges	94
Stolen Bases:	Jim Gilliam	26
Wins:	Don Drysdale	17
Strikeouts:	Don Drysdale	148
ERA:	Johnny Podres	2.66
Saves:	Clem Labine	17

JANUARY 4   The Dodgers become the first team in major league history to own an airplane by purchasing a 44-passenger, two-engine craft to transport the club. The cost was $800,000.

JANUARY 28   The Dodgers hire famous clown and pantomime artist Emmett Kelly to perform during games at Ebbets Field. Dressed as a weary hobo, Kelly was a feature attraction of the Barmun and Bailey circus over the previous 15 seasons. Walter O'Malley told reporters the hiring of Kelly was made "to relieve the tension at Ebbets Field."

FEBRUARY 20   Walter O'Malley purchases the Los Angeles Angels franchise in the Pacific Coast League from P. K. Wrigley for a reported $3,250,000. Wrigley Field in Los Angeles was sold to the Dodgers as part of the deal. Most importantly, O'Malley also acquired baseball's rights to the Los Angeles territory. Previously, Wrigley owned those rights and no club could move to L.A. without Wrigley's approval. In addition to the cash, the Cubs received the Dodgers' Fort Worth franchise in the Texas League.

The Wrigley family had owned the Chicago Cubs since 1919 and the Los Angeles franchise since 1921. It was a good deal for both parties.

Wrigley wanted to be free of the Los Angeles situation. Many in the area accused him of being a roadblock to the city's ability to attract a major league club because of his ownership rights to the territory, and if the city were to build a new stadium, Wrigley Field would be worthless. Wrigley was able to sell it to O'Malley for millions. Attendance had also dropped dramatically at Angels games in previous years as fans clamored for the major league brand of baseball. Wrigley was also skeptical of the ability of the profitability and the ability of Los Angeles to support a major league franchise despite it's immense size. He thought the city was too spread out, too dependent on the automobile and wouldn't support a losing club. Most of baseball agreed with Wrigley. Others certainly had the opportunity to move to Los Angeles before 1957, but none took the plunge. Walter O'Malley was one of the few in baseball who foresaw Los Angeles as a potential gold mine, and the Dodgers were able to gain a foothold in the city by purchasing the territory from Wrigley. It was a last warning to New York City officials that they must build a new stadium in Brooklyn or lose the Dodgers. Publicly, O'Malley stated that he preferred remaining in Brooklyn. Privately, he had assured Los Angeles County supervisor Kenneth Hahn that the Dodgers would move at the end of the 1957 season.

MARCH 6   Walter O'Malley meets with Los Angeles mayor Norris Paulson and county supervisor Kenneth Hahn in Vero Beach concerning a possible move to the West Coast.

APRIL 5   The Dodgers send Chico Fernandez to the Phillies for Elmer Valo, Ron Negray, Tim Harkness and $75,000.

APRIL 16   The Dodgers win the opener 7–6 against the Phillies in Philadelphia on a 12th-inning homer by Gino Cimoli. It was his first big-league homer. Earlier in the contest, Cimoli singled twice. Gil Hodges and Don Zimmer also homered and Jim Gilliam collected three hits. Clem Labine pitched five shutout innings of relief.

APRIL 18   In the home opener, the Dodgers down the Pirates 6–1 before 11,202 at Ebbets Field. Gil Hodges and Duke Snider homered.

On the same day, New York Parks Commissioner Robert Moses announced a proposal to build a stadium for the Dodgers in Flushing Meadows in Queens on a 78-acre site used for the 1939–40 World's Fair. The site was bounded by Northern Boulevard, Roosevelt Avenue, Grand Central Parkway and 126th Street. O'Malley rejected the location. He stated that the Dodgers would lose their unique identity in Queens because the club would no longer be the Brooklyn Dodgers. O'Malley was still determined to build in downtown Brooklyn, but Moses would not approve the plan. The cost of building a stadium at the Atlantic and Flatbush intersection favored by O'Malley (see August 16, 1955) was estimated at $21 million. Moses said the city could build in Queens for $10 to 12 million. Shea Stadium would later be built on the Flushing Meadows location and open in 1964 as a home for both the Mets and Jets.

APRIL 19   In his first start since game seven of the 1955 World Series, Johnny Podres pitches a complete game to beat the Pirates 2–0 in Pittsburgh. He spent the 1956 season serving in the Navy. The two Brooklyn runs scored on back-to-back homers by Carl Furillo and Duke Snider in the fourth inning off Bob Friend.

Podres had a 12–9 record and a league-leading 2.66 earned run average in 194 innings in 1957.

APRIL 21   Don Newcombe allows consecutive homers to Frank Thomas, Paul Smith and Dick Groat in the third inning of a 6–3 loss to the Pirates at Ebbets Field.

APRIL 30   A walk-off homer by Don Zimmer in the 10th inning beats the Cubs 10–9 at Ebbets Field. It was his fifth hit of the game in six at-bats. The previous four were singles. The Dodgers hit five homers in all. Roy Campanella struck two and Gil Hodges and Sandy Amoros one each. Brooklyn blew a 6–0 lead, fell behind 9–8, then tied the contest on Amoros's pinch-homer in the ninth.

Hodges hit .299 with 27 homers and 98 RBIs in 1957.

MAY 4   A two-run, walk-off homer by Charlie Neal in the ninth inning beats the Cardinals 4–2 at Ebbets Field.

MAY 6   Gino Cimoli hits a walk-off homer in the 14th inning to beat the Braves 5–4 at Ebbets Field. It was his fifth hit in seven at-bats. Carl Furillo had four hits and drove in the first four Brooklyn runs on a three-run homer in the first inning and a run-scoring single in the 12th.

MAY 15   Don Zimmer homers in the 10th inning to defeat the Braves 3–2 at County Stadium. Don Drysdale (seven innings) and Clem Labine (three innings) combined on a two-hitter. The only Milwaukee hits were a single by Chuck Tanner in the fourth inning and a double from Frank Torre in the sixth.

MAY 16   Sandy Koufax strikes out 13 batters during a 3–2 win over the Cubs in Chicago.

MAY 19   The Dodgers snap a 3–3 tie with seven runs in the ninth inning to defeat the Cardinals 10–3 in St. Louis. Jim Gilliam hit two doubles in the inning.

MAY 23   The Dodgers trade Don Elston to the Cubs for Jackie Collum and Vito Valentinetti.

The Dodgers were taken in the deal as Elston became one of the better relievers in baseball over the next half-dozen seasons. Neither Collum nor Valentinetti panned out.

MAY 27   Don Drysdale pitches a two-hitter to defeat the Phillies 5–1 at Connie Mack Stadium. The only two Philadelphia hits were singles by Ed Bouchee and Joe Lonnett in the second inning.

Only 20 at the start of the season, Drysdale was 17–9 with a 2.69 ERA and 148 strikeouts in 221 innings in 1957.

MAY 28   The National League gives the Dodgers and Giants the green light to move to California "if and when" the two clubs "request such permission." The decision was made at a meeting of all NL owners which took place in Chicago. The formal vote was unanimous. In explaining the action, loop president Warren Giles declared that the Dodgers and Giants "now are free to carry on discussions and negotiations with the knowledge that they have the sanction of the league for such a shift."

Seven days later O'Malley and Giants owner Horace Stoneham met with New York mayor Robert Wagner, but no progress was made on providing a new stadium for either club.

MAY 29   Johnny Podres pitches the Dodgers to a 1–0 win over the Pirates in Pittsburgh. Gino Cimoli drove in the lone run with a single in the eighth inning.

JUNE 4   Sandy Koufax strikes out 12 batters in 7²/₃ innings during a 7–5 triumph over the Cubs at Ebbets Field.

> *In their last year in Brooklyn, the Dodgers drew 1,028,258 to rank fifth in the National League and 10th in the majors. The club led the NL in road attendance for the 12th consecutive year.*

JUNE 6   The Dodgers-Cubs game at Ebbets Field is postponed by fog. The umpires called time in the second inning when Chicago left fielder Bob Speake lost a fly ball, which fell for a double in the heavy pall. The umps waited one hour and 26 minutes for the atmosphere to clear before calling the game.

Lack of parking and lack of seating at Ebbets Field sparked the move from Brooklyn to Los Angeles after the 1957 season. But more than 50 years after the move, the field retains an iconic presence in baseball history.

JUNE 8   The Dodgers take first place with a 9–2 win over the Reds at Ebbets Field.

> *The Dodgers stayed on top only one day, but remained in the thick of the pennant race until mid-August.*

JUNE 12   The Dodgers take a 9–1 lead in the second inning and hang on to beat the Braves 11–9 at Ebbets Field.

JUNE 13   An 8–5 loss to the Braves at Ebbets Field is marred by a fight. The trouble started when Don Drysdale plunked Johnny Logan with a pitch in the second inning. After reaching first base, Logan rushed toward Drysdale, who dropped Logan with a clean punch to the face. Logan retaliated with a few blows of his own before being pulled away. Eddie Mathews then jumped Drysdale, knocked him down, and pummeled him as they rolled around on the mound. Gil Hodges grabbed Mathews by the ankle, and dragged him halfway to third base.

JUNE 14   Jim Gilliam steals home with two out in the 10th inning to beat the Cardinals 2–1 at Ebbets Field.

JUNE 18   Don Newcombe pitches a shutout and collects a homer, double and single to defeat the Reds 7–0 in Cincinnati.

JULY 9   Walter Alston manages the National League to a 6–5 loss in the All-Star Game at Busch Stadium in St. Louis.

JULY 11   The Dodgers and Reds brawl during a 5–4 win at Ebbets Field. The fight took place in the seventh inning after Jim Gilliam dropped a bunt down the first base line. Reds pitcher Raul Sanchez raced from the mound toward the ball and collided with Gilliam along the first base line. The two exchanged punches. Cincinnati third baseman Don Hoak rushed over to defend Sanchez, but was intercepted by a roundhouse right from Charlie Neal. Hoak was restrained before he could retaliate, although he publicly threatened revenge. A rematch never took place, however.

JULY 14   A two-run walk-off homer by Gil Hodges beats the Braves 3–2 at Ebbets Field.

JULY 15   The Dodgers hit five home runs and overwhelm the Braves 20–4 at Ebbets Field. Charlie Neal hit two homers, with Don Drysdale, Sandy Amoros and Duke Snider accounting for one each. Jim Gilliam scored four runs and collected four hits. The Dodgers scored a run in the first inning, one in the second, three in the third, four in the fourth, two in the seventh and nine in the eighth.

JULY 18   The Dodgers win a thrilling 10–9 decision in 11 innings over the Cardinals at Ebbets Field. The Dodgers led 4–2 before the Cardinals erupted for seven runs in the ninth. In an unbelievable rally, Brooklyn responded for five in their half of the ninth to tie 9–9, the last four on a grand slam off Vinegar Bend Mizell with one out. In the 11th, Duke Snider doubled and scored on an error.

        Snider hit 40 homers and batted .274 in 1957. It was his fifth consecutive season of 40 or more homers.

JULY 19   The Dodgers score four runs in the 10th inning to defeat the Cubs 6–3 in the first game of a double-header at Ebbets Field. After Chicago plated a run in the top of the 10th, Duke Snider tied the contest 3–3 with a home run. After two singles and a walk, Johnny Roseboro smacked a three-run walk-off homer. It was his first homer in the major leagues. The Dodgers completed the sweep with a 5–3 triumph in the second contest.

JULY 23	Johnny Podres pitches a shutout to defeat the Cardinals 1–0 in St. Louis. The lone run scored on a single by Rube Walker in the second inning.
JULY 27	Carl Furillo hits a grand slam off Brooks Lawrence in the fourth inning of a 7–2 win over the Reds in Cincinnati.
JULY 30	The Dodgers win 1–0 over the Cubs in the first game of a double-header at Wrigley Field. Sal Maglie (7⅓ innings) and Clem Labine (1⅔ innings) combined on the shutout. The lone run scored on a sacrifice fly by Carl Furillo in the fourth inning. Chicago won the second tilt 4–3.
JULY 31	Ed Roebuck wins twice in relief during a double-header in Chicago. He pitched two innings in the opener, a 3–2 victory. Roebuck hurled an inning in the nightcap, a 2–1 triumph. The Dodgers scored the winning run in the ninth inning of both games.
AUGUST 1	Gil Hodges hits a grand slam off Dick Littlefield in the fifth inning of a 12–3 win over the Cubs in Chicago.
AUGUST 13	The Dodgers lose 4–2 to the Giants in New York to fall 7½ games back in the pennant race and virtually end any hopes of a World Series in Brooklyn in 1957.
AUGUST 19	The Giants' board of directors vote 8–1 to move the franchise to San Francisco for the 1958 season.
AUGUST 20	A walk-off homer by Duke Snider in the 12th inning beats the Reds 6–5 in the second game of a double-header at Ebbets Field. The Dodgers also won the opener 11–5.
AUGUST 23	The Dodgers score three runs in the ninth inning to defeat the Braves 3–2 at Ebbets Field. The winning run scored on a two-out single by Gino Cimoli.
AUGUST 24	The Dodgers use eight pitchers during a 13–7 loss to the Braves at Ebbets Field.
SEPTEMBER 1	In the last game between the Dodgers and Giants at Ebbets Field, Brooklyn loses 7–5.
	On the same day, the Dodgers sold Sal Maglie to the Yankees.
SEPTEMBER 4	The Dodgers score seven runs in the eighth inning and beat the Phillies 12–3 in Philadelphia.
SEPTEMBER 8	In the last Dodgers-Giants game at the Polo Grounds, New York wins 3–2.
SEPTEMBER 24	On the day President Eisenhower sends federal troops to Little Rock, Arkansas, to integrate Central High School, the final game is played at Ebbets Field. Danny McDevitt pitched a shutout to defeat the Pirates 2–0. Dee Fondy made the last out on a grounder. The crowd numbered 6,702. Although no formal announcement had been made, it was almost certain that the Dodgers would leave Brooklyn at the end of the season. Organist Gladys Goodding started off every inning by playing "California Here We Come." Interspersed through the evening were "Don't Ask Me Why I'm Leaving" and "Say It Isn't So." As the crowd filed out, Goodding played "Auld Lang Syne."

SEPTEMBER 28   In his only big-league appearance, 17-year-old Rod Miller strikes out as a pinch-hitter for Randy Jackson in the ninth inning of an 8–4 win over the Phillies in Philadelphia.

SEPTEMBER 29   In the final game of the Brooklyn Dodgers franchise, the Phillies win 2–1 in Philadelphia.

OCTOBER 1   On his television variety program, Red Skelton performs a skit in which his "Freddie the Freeloader" character is faced with a problem because his shack is located on the site of the Dodgers' proposed ballpark in Chavez Ravine.

OCTOBER 7   Three days after the Soviet Union launches the earth satellite Sputnik, Los Angeles City Council votes 10–4 to approve the sale of Chavez Ravine to the Dodgers for $4.4 million. In turn, the city was to spend $2 million to grade the site and the county $2.7 million for connecting roads and freeways. The city would also buy Wrigley Field for $2.5 million. The Dodgers were required to spend $500,000 to develop 40 acres of the tract as a recreational area.

OCTOBER 8   The Dodgers formally announce the move from Brooklyn to Los Angeles at a press conference. Walter O'Malley didn't attend. Instead, he had assistant Arthur Patterson read a prepared statement.

The move was far from smooth. Almost immediately, the Chavez Ravine deal sparked opposition in Los Angeles. Many believed that the city gave away valuable and public property for a private enterprise, even though it had yet to be developed despite its prime location (see October 12, 1956). A group called the "Citizens Committee to Save Chavez Ravine for the People" obtained enough signatures to place the sale on the ballot in June 1958 (see June 3, 1958). Voters could void the contract at the ballot box. Walter O'Malley assumed he would be welcomed with open arms in Los Angeles and was stunned by the resistance. Completely ignorant of the peculiar, volatile and unpredictable nature of California politics, he was unaware that referendums existed. They didn't have them in New York. With the completion of a stadium at Chavez Ravine at least two years away, O'Malley also didn't have a deal in place with a venue for his club to play in 1958. None of the options in Los Angeles were appealing. Wrigley Field, with a capacity of less than 25,000 and parking for only 950 cars, was inadequate. The Rose Bowl and Memorial Coliseum were too large with over 100,000 seats and built for football and track. O'Malley favored the Rose Bowl because of superior parking facilities and a field which ran north and south, unlike the east-west configuration of the Coliseum, making the sun less of a problem. Opposition on the part of Pasadena residents developed, however, some even sporting "Go Home Dodgers" bumper stickers on their cars. After three months of heated negotiations, O'Malley finally struck a deal with the Coliseum (see January 17, 1958).

OCTOBER 23   With 1,000 spectators, invited dignitaries, 200 members of the news media and two bands on hand, Walter O'Malley and the Dodgers management team arrives at Los Angeles International Airport on the team plane with "Los Angeles Dodgers" emblazoned on it. As O'Malley stepped off the plane, he was served a summons which challenged the city's contract with the Dodgers (see October 7, 1958).

OCTOBER 29   The Dodgers hire Chuck Dressen as a coach. He managed the team from 1951 through 1953 to two World Series and a record of 298–166 before being fired for demanding a multi-year contract (see October 14, 1953). Dressen was a coach in Los Angeles for two years before taking a job as manager of the Braves.

NOVEMBER 5   New York City voters apparently harbor no ill will toward mayor Robert Wagner over the move of the Dodgers and Giants to California, as Wagner wins re-election by a nearly 3–1 margin, and plurality of nearly 1,000,000 votes. His opponent was Robert Christenberry. Wagner easily won all five of New York's boroughs, including Brooklyn.

1958   LA

Season in a Sentence

In the first season in Los Angeles, the Dodgers set a club attendance record, but flop on the field and tumble into seventh place.

Finish • Won • Lost • Pct • GB

Seventh   71   83   .461   21.0

Manager

Walter Alston

Stats	Dods	NL	Rank
Batting Avg:	.251	.262	8
On-Base Pct:	.317	.328	8
Slugging Pct:	.402	.405	6
Home Runs:	172		2
Stolen Bases:	73		1
ERA:	4.47	3.95	8
Fielding Avg:	.975	.977	5
Runs Scored:	668		5
Runs Allowed:	761		7

Starting Lineup

Johnny Roseboro, c
Gil Hodges, 1b
Charlie Neal, 2b
Dick Gray, 3b
Don Zimmer, ss
Jim Gilliam, lf-3b-2b
Duke Snider, cf
Carl Furillo, rf
Gino Cimoli, cf-lf
Norm Larker, lf-1b

Pitchers

Johnny Podres, sp
Don Drysdale, sp-rp
Sandy Koufax, sp-rp
Stan Williams, sp
Clem Labine, rp
Johnny Klippstein, rp
Fred Kipp, rp

Attendance

1,845,556 (second in NL)

Club Leaders

Batting Avg:	Carl Furillo	.290
On-Base Pct:	Jim Gilliam	.352
Slugging Pct:	Carl Furillo	.482
Home Runs:	Gil Hodges	22
	Charlie Neal	22
RBIs:	Carl Furillo	83
Runs:	Charlie Neal	87
Stolen Bases:	Jim Gilliam	18
Wins:	Johnny Podres	13
Strikeouts:	Johnny Podres	143
ERA:	Johnny Podres	3.72
Saves:	Clem Labine	14

JANUARY 17   The Dodgers complete arrangements to play at Memorial Coliseum until the club's new stadium at Chavez Ravine is built.

Memorial Coliseum was built in 1923 and had a capacity of 101,000. It was built for track and football and hosted the 1932 Olympic Games. In 1958, it was the home of the Los Angeles Rams, University of Southern California and UCLA football teams. Baseball had never been played at the facility. The conversion for use by the Dodgers, which had to take place in three short months before Opening Day, wasn't easy. A baseball press box, dugouts and a backstop had to be constructed. The two dugouts were closer together than most major league parks so they could be located near a service tunnel behind home plate. Since baseball had different lighting requirements than football, four light towers were added. The field needed to be regraded and flattened because it contained a hump in the middle for drainage. Otherwise, a player running to first base would be going uphill. Because of the oval configuration, the left-field foul line was only 251 feet long. A 40-foot high screen, 140 feet in length, was constructed in left to cut down on cheap home runs. The home-run distance down the line in right was just 300 feet, but veered dramatically so that the fence in right-center was 440 feet from home plate. (In 1959, that distance would be cut to a more reasonable 375 feet.) It was 425 feet from home to dead center. Seating capacity for Dodgers games was 94,600, making the Coliseum the largest venue in major league history. All of the seats were backless benches and fans broiled in the sun in the roofless stadium. On the plus side, none of them were obstructed by support posts. It was the only venue in the majors in 1958 with that distinction. The first ballpark built specifically for baseball without support posts was Candlestick Park in San Francisco, which opened in 1960.

JANUARY 28   Roy Campanella's career is ended by a car accident. The injuries left him a quadriplegic for the remainder of his life, which ended in 1993. The crash occurred at 3:30 a.m. Campanella was driving a rented 1957 Chevrolet because his station wagon was in the shop for repairs. Less than a mile from his Long Island home in Glen Cove, he failed to negotiate an "S" curve on an icy road, crashed into a telephone pole, bounced away, and turned over. Campanella suffered fractures of the fifth and sixth cervical vertebrae at the neck line.

MARCH 5   Duke Snider, Johnny Podres and Don Zimmer are hurt in a car accident in Vero Beach. The car was struck from behind. Snider, who was the driver, suffered a bruised knee. Podres needed seven stitches to close a cut in his forehead. Zimmer shattered the windshield with his head. All three recovered to play by Opening Day, but Snider had an off-year in large part because of problems with his knee. It was originally injured late in the 1957 season, and the accident set back an off-season of rehabilitation.

APRIL 15   The Giants and the Dodgers meet for the first time as California rivals before an Opening Day, sellout crowd of 23,448 at Seals Stadium in San Francisco. It was also the first major league game ever played west of Kansas City. The Giants won 8–0. Ruben Gomez pitched the complete-game shutout. The first batter to face Gomez leading off the first inning was Gino Cimoli, who struck out. Don Drysdale was the Dodgers starter, and allowed six runs in 3²/₃ innings.

APRIL 16   The Dodgers rebound from their shutout loss in the opener to thrash the Giants 13–1 in San Francisco. Third baseman Dick Gray became the first Los Angeles Dodger to homer with a shot in the second inning. It was Gray's first big-league home run. Duke Snider also homered. Johnny Podres was the winning pitcher.

At the start of the season, there was no television planned for Dodger games. Late in April, Walter O'Malley announced that the club would telecast the remaining eight games from San Francisco. The expense of line charges in 1958 made the televising of games from the Midwest and East cost prohibitive, a situation that would continue to exist until 1970 when Dodger contests played

*outside of Los Angeles were telecast for the first time. Dodger games on
Los Angeles TV were carried over KTTV. Vin Scully and Jerry Doggett were
the announcers on both television and radio over KMPC.*

APRIL 18   The Dodgers beat the Giants 6–5 in the first major league game ever played in
Los Angeles. The event, which took place on a Friday afternoon, drew 78,672 to
Memorial Coliseum and set a big-league record for a single game during the regular
season. The previous mark was 78,382 for an Indians-White Sox clash in Cleveland
in 1948. The attendance figure was nearly 2½ times the capacity of Ebbets Field. The
first pitch in L.A. was by Carl Erskine to Jim Davenport. Dick Gray, who hit the first
home run in the history of the Los Angeles Dodgers franchise two days earlier, also
hit the first major league home run by a Dodger in Los Angeles. Gray's homer was
struck in the seventh inning. Giants outfielder Hank Sauer holds the honor of hitting
the first major league homer in L.A. Sauer homered in the fourth, then hit another
one in the eighth. With the score 6–4 in the ninth inning, Davenport doubled off
the screen, but was called out on an appeal for failing to touch third base on Willie
Kirkland's triple. Kirkland scored on a single by Willie Mays before Clem Labine
nailed down the save.

*Among those in the crowd were many of Hollywood's elite including Jimmy
Stewart, Burt Lancaster, Jack Lemmon, Nat King Cole, Danny Thomas,
Gregory Peck, Edward G. Robinson, Tennessee Ernie Ford, Gene Autry,
Groucho Marx, Ray Bolger, Zsa Zsa Gabor and Brooklyn native Danny Kaye.
Earlier in the day was a 20-minute parade through the streets of downtown
Los Angeles. During the ceremonies, Walter O'Malley presented L.A. mayor
Norris Poulson with home plate from Ebbets Field.*

APRIL 22   In the first night game in Los Angeles, the Dodgers beat the Cubs 4–3 before 39,459
at Memorial Coliseum.

*The Dodgers finished the season with an attendance of 1,845,556, the second
highest in the majors that season, trailing only the Milwaukee Braves. The 1958
figure broke the previous Dodger club record of 1,807,526, set in 1947.*

APRIL 23   Gil Hodges hits his 300th career home run, and Pee Wee Reese plays in his 2,000th
career game during a 7–6 loss to the Cubs at Memorial Coliseum.

*Before the game, Duke Snider injured his arm trying to throw a ball out of the
Coliseum. He was docked a day's pay by Dodger management.*

APRIL 24   Lee Walls of the Cubs hits three homers over the left-field screen during a 15–2 win
over the Dodgers at Memorial Coliseum.

*There were 193 home runs hit at Memorial Coliseum in 1958 and 152 in Dodger
road games. Due to the odd dimensions of the playing field (see January 17,
1958), only 14 of the 193 homers were struck by left-handed batters, including
just six of the 101 hit by visiting players. There were eight home runs over the
right-field fence, three in center and 182 to left.*

MAY 2   Trailing 5–1, the Dodgers erupt for six runs in the fourth inning and beat the Pirates
9–5 at Memorial Coliseum.

According to the rules set down by the Memorial Coliseum Commission, no alcohol was sold at the stadium for Dodger games or any other event. The first time Los Angeles fans could buy a beer at a Dodger game was on Opening Day in 1962 at Dodger Stadium.

MAY 5   The Dodgers sweep the Phillies 8–7 and 15–2 in a double-header at Memorial Coliseum. Los Angeles scored seven runs in the fifth inning of the second game.

MAY 13   With an opposite field drive, Charlie Neal becomes the first player to hit a ball over the right-field fence at Memorial Coliseum during a 16–9 loss to the Giants. It was the 21st game at the facility.

MAY 18   Carl Erskine records the first Dodger shutout since the move to Los Angeles with a 4–0 victory over the Cardinals in the second game of a double-header at Busch Stadium. St. Louis won the opener 6–5.

The first game loss dropped the Dodgers record to 10–21. The club finished in seventh place with 71 wins and 83 defeats. It was the only losing season for the franchise between 1944 and 1964. Pitching was the main culprit. In 1957, the Dodgers led the NL in ERA with a mark of 3.35. In 1958, the club was dead last in the category at 4.47. Many Dodgers blamed Memorial Coliseum for their problems, but the club was 39–38 at home and an NL-worst 32–45 on the road.

MAY 20   Sandy Koufax pitches 11 innings and allows only two hits in beating the Braves 6–3 at County Stadium. Milwaukee scored three times in the first on a single by Johnny Logan, three walks, a wild pitch, an error and a sacrifice fly. Logan also collected the second hit off Koufax with a double in the eighth. Duke Snider drove in the tie-breaking run with a pinch-double.

Koufax led the NL in lowest opponent's batting average in 1958 with a mark of .220. It was the first of seven times in his career that he led the league in the category. The other six were consecutively from 1960 through 1965.

MAY 26   Carl Erskine pitches a two-hitter to defeat the Phillies 2–1 at Connie Mack Stadium. The only Philadelphia hits were singles by Chuck Essegian in the sixth inning and Willie Jones in the eighth.

MAY 30   Ex-Dodger Walt Moryn hits three homers for the Cubs, the third a ninth-inning, walk-off blast off Sandy Koufax, to defeat the Dodgers 10–8 in the second game of a double-header at Wrigley Field. In the opener, Chicago scored three runs in the ninth to win 3–2. Moryn drove in the tying run with a two-run double.

JUNE 1   Stan Williams pitches a two-hit shutout in his first major league start to defeat the Cubs 1–0 in 48-degree weather at Wrigley Field. The only Chicago hits were singles by Al Dark in the second inning and opposing pitcher Dick Drott in the third. The lone run crossed the plate in the fourth on a double by Carl Furillo and a single from Don Zimmer.

JUNE 3   A referendum on the Dodgers deal with the city of Los Angeles to build a stadium in Chavez Ravine (see October 7 and 8, 1957) passes by a margin of 345,435 to 321,142. The final count showed 62.3 percent of the electorate showed up at the polls, a record in a non-presidential year.

The fate of the measure was in doubt right up to Election Day. A few days earlier, Mayor Norris Poulson said that if voters failed to approve the Chavez Ravine agreement, the Dodgers "would have no alternative" other than to leave Los Angeles "and we'll be the laughingstock of the United States." An eight-hour telethon two days before the election helped sway voters in Walter O'Malley's favor. It featured such celebrities as Jack Benny, Dean Martin, Jerry Lewis, George Burns, Debbie Reynolds, Danny Thomas, Chuck Connors, Jeff Chandler, Joe E. Brown and Ronald Reagan (then an actor and television host and not yet a politician), each making their pitch for the Dodgers' new stadium. O'Malley hoped to break ground the following month and open the Chavez Ravine stadium in July 1959, but ran into new obstacles. Almost immediately after the referendum passed, a suit by two taxpayers was filed. In 1955, the land was transferred from the federal government to the city of Los Angeles with the stipulation that it be used for a "public purpose." On July 14, 1958, Judge Arnold Praeger of the Superior Court in Los Angeles ruled the contract between the city and the Dodgers invalid. Over the next 15 months, the case went to the State Court of Appeals, then to the California Supreme Court (see January 13, 1959) and finally the United States Supreme Court (see October 19, 1959).

JUNE 6
A walk-off homer by Don Zimmer in the ninth inning beats the Braves 4–3 in Los Angeles.

JUNE 13
A two-run, walk-off double by Pee Wee Reese with two out in the ninth inning beats the Pirates 5–4 at Memorial Coliseum.

John Ramsey was the Dodgers' public address announcer at Memorial Coliseum and Dodger Stadium from 1958 through 1982. Referred to as the voice of Los Angeles sports, Ramsey also did the games of the Angels, Lakers, Rams, Raiders, Kings and USC football.

JUNE 15
The Dodgers trade Don Newcombe to the Reds for Johnny Klippstein, Steve Bilko, Art Fowler and Charlie Rabe.

After winning 27 games in 1956, Newcombe was 11–12 and was 0–6 in 1958 at the time of the trade. He had a 13–8 record for the Reds in 1959, but 1960 would prove to be his last in the majors. In 1962, Newcombe became the first former major leaguer to play in Japan. He was named the Dodgers' director of community affairs in 1971, a job he still held in 2008. In that role, Newcombe has helped numerous people in their battles with substance abuse.

JUNE 18
Joe Pignatano's first major league home run creates controversy during a 3–0 win over the Phillies in Philadelphia. Facing Robin Roberts in the fifth inning, Pignatano's homer to left bounced back onto the playing field. Umpires ruled the drive cleared the fence and hit the seats. The Phils disagreed, contending the ball struck the wall. Irate fans stopped play by bombarding the field with beer cans. The can-throwing ceased when the arbiters threatened a forfeit.

JUNE 24
The Dodgers take two extra-inning games in Cincinnati, beating the Reds 13–10 in 10 innings and 7–2 in 11. In the opener, Gil Hodges and Joe Pignatano homered in the 10th. Los Angeles erupted for five runs in the 11th in the nightcap.

JULY 4   The Dodgers become the first team in major league history to be idle on the Fourth of July for reasons other than bad weather. The original schedule had the club playing the Cardinals, but the game had to be changed to a different date because a fireworks display had already been booked for Memorial Coliseum.

JULY 26   Gil Hodges collects four hits, including a double and homer and drives in five runs during a 10–4 win over the Phillies in Philadelphia.

AUGUST 4   The Dodgers sell Randy Jackson to the Indians.

AUGUST 23   Don Drysdale hits two homers, drives in four runs, and hurls a four-hit complete game to defeat the Braves 10–1 at Memorial Coliseum. Both homers were struck off Juan Pizarro. Gil Hodges hit a homer with the bases loaded off Bob Trowbridge in the eighth.

Drysdale hit seven home runs in 66 at-bats in 1958. On the mound, he had the worst season of his career with a 12–13 record and a 4.17 ERA. On September 27, the 22-year-old Drysdale married 18-year-old Ginger Dubberly, a former Tournament of Roses princess.

AUGUST 24   Johnny Roseboro and Reds second baseman Johnny Temple nearly come to blows during a 6–5 loss to the Reds at Memorial Coliseum after Roseboro took out shortstop Roy McMillan on a double play. Roseboro started the game in center field, the only time in his major league career he played the position.

Playing in his first full season in the majors, Roseboro hit .271 with 14 home runs and was named to the All-Star team in 1958. He was the Dodgers starting catcher until 1967 and played in two more All-Star Games and four World Series.

SEPTEMBER 3   A two-run walk-off homer by Duke Snider in the ninth inning beats the Giants 5–3 at Memorial Coliseum.

The Dodgers were 6–16 against the Giants in the first year of their California rivalry.

SEPTEMBER 5   The Dodgers collect only three hits off Vinegar Bend Mizell of the Cardinals, but the three are consecutive and result in two runs for a 2–1 victory in St. Louis. With one out in the second inning, Steve Bilko singled, Don Zimmer doubled and Charlie Neal singled.

A first baseman, Bilko stood six foot one and weighed between 230 and 260 pounds, depending upon the stage of his latest diet. He played in 266 games for the Cardinals and Cubs from 1949 through 1954 before becoming a minor league star in Los Angeles. With the Angels in the Pacific Coast League, Bilko hit .330 with 148 home runs. The popular television character Sgt. Bilko, played by Phil Silvers on The Phil Silvers Show, *was named after Steve Bilko because he was series-creator Nat Hiken's favorite player. As a Dodger, Bilko hit only .208 with seven homers in 101 at-bats. He would later play for the major league Angels in 1961 and 1962, the two first seasons of the American League franchise's existence, and hit 28 home runs in 458 at-bats.*

SEPTEMBER 7   The Dodgers hit five homers during a 7–5 win over the Cardinals in St. Louis. Gil Hodges hit two homers, with Don Zimmer, Johnny Roseboro and Charlie Neal accounting for one each.

Neal hit .254 with 22 home runs in 1958.

SEPTEMBER 9   A walk-off grand slam by Wally Post of the Phillies off Clem Labine beats the Dodgers 6–2 at Connie Mack Stadium. The game started on July 27 and was suspended with Philadelphia leading 2–1 in the sixth inning because of Pennsylvania's curfew law which stipulated that teams must stop playing at 6:00 p.m. on Sundays. The Phils also won the regularly scheduled game on September 9 by a 4–3 score.

The Dodgers had a 14–8 record against the first-place Braves in 1958, but were 10–12 when playing the last-place Phillies.

SEPTEMBER 10   Frank Howard hits a home run in the second at-bat of his major league debut during an 8–5 loss to the Phillies in Philadelphia. It was struck off Robin Roberts.

Standing six-foot-seven, Howard was a star in both basketball and baseball at Ohio State University. In 1957, he was a consensus second-team All-American in basketball. Howard's athletic ability earned him a contract with the Dodgers calling for a bonus of $108,000. He became the club's starting right fielder in 1960, a position he held for five seasons, but the Dodgers never fully appreciated his talents. Howard never accumulated more than 500 at-bats in a season before being traded to the Senators after the 1964 season.

SEPTEMBER 26   The Dodgers start a lineup which includes seven rookies in the first game of a double-header against the Cubs at Memorial Coliseum. The rookie starters in the 6–3 victory were Bob Lillis (SS), Johnny Roseboro (C), Ron Fairly (CF), Jim Gentile (1B), Don Demeter (RF), Frank Howard (LF) and Earl Robinson (3B). Joe Pignatano, another rookie, was the starting catcher in game two, a 2–1 loss. The starting pitchers in the twin bill were Don Drysdale and Sandy Koufax, a pair of 22-year-olds.

The Dodgers were at a crossroads in 1958. The nucleus of the club that went to the World Series in 1956 was either no longer with the club or near the end of their careers. Jackie Robinson was retired and Roy Campanella was paralyzed. Don Newcombe was traded in June. Pee Wee Reese was 39 and in the last season of his career. Gil Hodges, Duke Snider, Carl Furillo and Carl Erskine were no longer top flight players. The future of the Dodgers was in the hands of individuals such as Drysdale, Koufax, Fairly, Howard, Roseboro and 1958 farmhands like Maury Wills, Willie Davis and Tommy Davis.

DECEMBER 4   The Dodgers trade Gino Cimoli to the Cardinals for Wally Moon and Phil Paine.

The Dodgers made a great short-term deal as Moon gave the club three excellent seasons as a left fielder, batting .309 over that period. A left-handed batter, he developed a swing which propelled balls to the opposite field and exploited the short left-field fence at Memorial Coliseum. From 1959 through 1961, he hit 37 homers in Los Angeles and only 12 on the road. The home runs became known as "Moon Shots."

DECEMBER 23   The Dodgers trade Sparky Anderson to the Phillies for Rip Repulski, Gene Snyder and Jim Golden.

1959

Season in a Sentence

The Dodgers rebound from the seventh-place finish of the previous season to beat the Milwaukee Braves in a pennant playoff and the Chicago White Sox in the World Series.

Finish • Won • Lost • Pct • GB

First   88   68   .564   +2.0

World Series

The Dodgers defeated the Chicago White Sox four games to two.

Manager

Walter Alston

Stats

Stats	Dods	NL	Rank
Batting Avg:	.257	.260	6
On-Base Pct:	.334	.325	2
Slugging Pct:	.396	.400	6
Home Runs:	148		5
Stolen Bases:	84		1
ERA:	3.79	3.95	3
Fielding Avg:	.981	.977	1
Runs Scored:	705		3 (tie)
Runs Allowed:	670		3

Starting Lineup

Johnny Roseboro, c
Gil Hodges, 1b
Charlie Neal, 2b
Jim Gilliam, 3b
Don Zimmer, ss
Wally Moon, lf
Don Demeter, cf
Duke Snider, rf-cf
Norm Larker, 1b-lf
Ron Fairly, rf
Maury Wills, ss

Pitchers

Don Drysdale, sp
Johnny Podres, sp
Roger Craig, sp-rp
Danny McDevitt, sp-rp
Sandy Koufax, sp-rp
Clem Labine, rp
Stan Williams, rp-sp
Larry Sherry, rp-sp

Attendance

2,071,045

Club Leaders

Batting Avg:	Wally Moon	.302
On-Base Pct:	Wally Moon	.394
Slugging Pct:	Gil Hodges	.513
Home Runs:	Gil Hodges	25
RBIs:	Duke Snider	88
Runs:	Charlie Neal	103
Stolen Bases:	Jim Gilliam	23
Wins:	Don Drysdale	17
Strikeouts:	Don Drysdale	242
ERA:	Roger Craig	2.06
Saves:	Clem Labine	9

JANUARY 13   Ten days after Alaska is admitted as the 49th state in the Union, the California State Supreme Court unanimously votes to uphold the contract with the city and the Dodgers regarding the use of Chavez Ravine (see October 8, 1957). Opponents of the contract appealed the verdict (see October 19, 1959).

MARCH 20   The Dodgers play the first of two exhibition games against the Reds in Havana, Cuba. The Dodgers won 3–2 on March 20 and 4–3 on March 21.

The contests were played less than three months after Fidel Castro's takeover of the country. The Reds and Dodgers were the last major leagues teams to play in Cuba until the Orioles faced the Cuban national team during spring training in 1999.

APRIL 10   Snow postpones the scheduled opener against the Cubs in Chicago.

APRIL 11   The Dodgers open the season with a 6–1 loss to the Cubs in Chicago. The gametime temperature was 42 degrees. Don Drysdale was the starter and loser.

The Dodgers season would also end in Chicago (see October 8, 1959).

APRIL 14   The Dodgers lose 6–2 to the Cardinals in the home opener before 66,552 at Memorial Coliseum.

APRIL 20   Charlie Neal hits a walk-off homer in the ninth inning which beats the Giants 2–1 in Los Angeles. Don Drysdale pitched a three-hitter and struck out 11.

Neal hit .287, struck 19 homers, and scored 103 runs in 1959.

APRIL 21   Don Demeter hits three homers for the Dodgers, including a walk-off blast in the 11th inning, for a 9–7 win over the Giants at Memorial Coliseum. Each of his home runs came with a man on base. Demeter started the slugging outburst with an inside-the-park homer to right-center field off Dom Zanni. The second was struck when facing Mike McCormick in the fourth. The 11th-inning game-winner was against Al Worthington.

APRIL 26   The Dodgers collect 20 hits and outlast the Cardinals 17–11 in St. Louis. Los Angeles broke a 9–9 tie with four runs in the eighth inning. Charlie Neal collected five hits, including a triple and a double, in five at-bats.

MAY 7   A crowd of 93,103 attends an exhibition game against the Yankees on "Roy Campanella Night" at Memorial Coliseum. About 15,000 were turned away at the gate, and only quick intervention by police prevented a riot. It was the largest crowd in major league history, a record which stood for nearly 49 years (see March 29, 2008). Campanella was injured in an auto accident 15 months earlier (see January 28, 1958). He was pushed onto the field in his wheelchair by Pee Wee Reese for the pre-game ceremonies. At the end of the fifth inning, the lights were turned off and fans lit matches in honor of Campanella. The Dodgers had beaten the Giants in San Francisco earlier in the day 2–1 before flying to Los Angeles for the exhibition. The Yankees won 6–2. The Dodgers returned to San Francisco for a game the following day.

MAY 11   The Dodgers edge the Phillies 11–10 at Memorial Coliseum. The winning run scored on a perfectly executed squeeze bunt by Norm Larker with the bases loaded, bringing Don Demeter home from third base.

MAY 22   Don Drysdale pitches a 13-inning complete game and allows a run and six hits to beat the Giants 2–1 at Memorial Coliseum. San Francisco pitcher Johnny Antonelli went from the second through the 10th without allowing a hit. Gil Hodges drove in the winning run with a single.

Drysdale was 17–13 with a 3.46 ERA in 270²/₃ innings in 1959. He led the NL in strikeouts (242) and shutouts (four).

MAY 25   Johnny Podres pitches a two-hitter to defeat the Giants 8–0 in San Francisco. He had a no-hitter in progress until Daryl Spencer and Bob Schmidt delivered back-to-back singles with one out in the eighth inning.

MAY 26 — A walk-off grand slam by Leon Wagner of the Giants in the ninth inning beats the Dodgers 6–4 in San Francisco. It was struck on the second pitch delivered by Art Fowler, who had just entered the game in relief of Sandy Koufax.

In May 1959, the last remaining residents were removed from Chavez Ravine to make way for the Dodgers new stadium. Police forcibly evicted the Arechiga family, who had lived in the gulch for 36 years. The family received an outpouring of sympathy, particularly from those who were opposed to the construction of the club's new home. The Arechigas claimed they had no place to live and pitched a tent nearby. A few days later, newspapers revealed that Manuel Arechiga owned at least nine houses and a vacant lot which cost the remaining residents of the ravine much of the sympathy they had gained. It was later revealed that the Arechigas were actually a front for groups which filed taxpayers' suits against the construction of the ballpark and were looking for sympathy for their cause (see October 8, 1957). Nonetheless, the evictions strained relations between the Dodgers and the Latino community for decades. Many refused to come to games. It didn't help that the Dodgers had few Latins on their roster during their first 20 seasons in Los Angeles. During that period, the only Latin player to play in at least 100 games, or pitch in at least 50 games or 100 innings in a season was Manny Mota. The first Latin players developed in the farm system to play regularly for the Dodgers were Fernando Valenzuela and Pedro Guerrero in 1981.

MAY 30 — Home runs by Ron Fairly and Gil Hodges in the ninth inning beats the Cardinals 7–6 at Memorial Coliseum. St. Louis took a 6–5 advantage in the top of the ninth on a two-run, inside-the-park homer from Ken Boyer.

Fairly played for the Dodgers from 1958 through 1969 at the start of a 21-year big-league playing career.

JUNE 3 — Stan Williams pitches a two-hitter to defeat the Reds 5–1 at Crosley Field. The only Cincinnati hits were singles by Roy McMillan in the third inning and Frank Robinson in the fifth.

JUNE 6 — Maury Wills makes his major league debut during a 3–2 loss to the Braves in Milwaukee.

Wills had a long route to the majors before helping to change baseball forever with his base-stealing prowess. He was 26 years old when he played in his first big-league game. The Dodgers nearly lost Wills by sending him to the Tigers during the 1958–59 off-season. The Detroit club thought so little of his ability that they sent Wills back to the Dodgers. Beginning in 1960, he led the National League in stolen bases six consecutive seasons, including a then major league record 104 in 1962. Wills was named to five All-Star teams while a Dodger and played in four World Series. His 490 steals with the club is the career record. Wills also ranks 10th in runs with 876.

JUNE 11 — Johnny Podres pitches his second two-hitter in less than three weeks as the Dodgers overwhelm the Phillies 11–0 at Connie Mack Stadium. The only Philadelphia hits were singles by Richie Ashburn and Wally Post, both in the fourth inning.

JUNE 15   Don Drysdale strikes out 13 batters during a 4–0 win over the Braves at Memorial Coliseum.

Dodger pitchers incredibly led the National League in strikeouts 18 times in 19 seasons from 1945 through 1963, including 16 in a row beginning in 1948. At the end of the 1963 season, the Dodgers possessed the five largest single-season strikeouts totals by a team in big-league history with 1,077 in 1959, 1,122 in 1960, 1,105 in 1961, 1,104 in 1962 and 1,095 in 1963. Among those contributing to the streak were Drysdale, Sandy Koufax, Don Newcombe, Ralph Branca, Carl Erskine, Johnny Podres, Stan Williams, Rex Barney, Kirby Higbe and Hal Gregg.

JUNE 17   Danny McDevitt pitches a two-hitter to beat the Braves 4–0 in the second game of a double-header at Memorial Coliseum. Hank Aaron collected both Milwaukee hits with singles in the fourth and seventh innings.

JUNE 20   Don Drysdale hits a homer and a triple during a 9–2 win over the Reds at Memorial Coliseum.

JUNE 22   Sandy Koufax strikes out 16 batters during a 6–2 victory over the Phillies at Memorial Coliseum.

JUNE 30   A controversial infield single by Jim Gilliam is the only hit off Giants pitcher Sam Jones during a 2–0 loss at Memorial Coliseum. Gilliam bounced a grounder over Jones's head. Shortstop Andre Rodgers, charged the ball, picked it up and dropped it. The official scorer ruled that Gilliam would have beaten the throw even if Rodgers had made the play.

JULY 2   Charlie Neal ties a major league record for second basemen with 11 putouts during a 4–0 win over the Cardinals in St. Louis.

JULY 7   At Forbes Field in Pittsburgh, Don Drysdale starts the first of two All-Star Games played in 1959 and hurls three perfect innings, including four strikeouts. The National League won 5–4.

There were two All-Star Game played each season from 1959 through 1962.

JULY 9   Roger Craig pitches 11 innings of three-hit shutout relief during a 13-inning 4–3 win over the Braves in Milwaukee. The winning run scored on a double by Wally Moon and a single from Rip Repulski off Warren Spahn.

In his first season with the Dodgers, Moon hit .302 with 19 homers and a league-leading 11 triples.

JULY 15   Don Drysdale pitches a three-hit shutout and drives in two runs with a seventh-inning double to lead the Dodgers to a 3–0 triumph over the Pirates in Pittsburgh.

JULY 21   Charlie Neal hits a home run off Sam Jones in the ninth inning for the lone tally in a 1–0 victory over the Giants in San Francisco. Roger Craig pitched the shutout.

The game was delayed for eight minutes at the end of the first inning while groundskeepers watered down the infield because high winds created a dust storm.

JULY 31   Don Drysdale strikes out 14 batters and beats the Phillies 5–4 at Memorial Coliseum.

Don Drysdale solidified his role as the ace of the staff in 1959, leading the team to a World Championship.

AUGUST 3   The second of two All-Star Games in 1959 is played at Memorial Coliseum before a crowd of 55,105. The American League won 5–3. The contest started at 4:00 p.m. local time so that it could be telecast in prime-time in the East. (Prime-time telecasts of All-Star Games wouldn't become a regular feature until 1967.) The starting pitchers were Don Drysdale and 20-year-old Orioles rookie Jerry Walker. It was Drysdale's second All-Star start in 1959. He allowed three runs in three innings. Jim Gilliam thrilled the hometown crowd with a home run in the seventh off Billy O'Dell. Frank Robinson, Yogi Berra, Frank Malzone and Rocky Colavito also homered.

Future Hall of Famers on the rosters of the two clubs included Hank Aaron, Luis Aparicio, Ernie Banks, Yogi Berra, Orlando Cepeda, Don Drysdale, Nellie Fox, Al Kaline, Harmon Killebrew, Mickey Mantle, Eddie Mathews, Willie Mays, Bill Mazeroski, Stan Musial, Frank Robinson, Warren Spahn, Hoyt Wilhelm, Ted Williams, and Early Wynn

AUGUST 15   Larry Sherry pitches 8²/₃ innings of shutout relief and drives in three runs during a 4–3 victory over the Cardinals in St. Louis. Sherry singled in the fourth inning and clubbed a two-run homer in the fifth which tied the score 3–3. It was his first major league home run. Duke Snider's homer in the sixth broke the deadlock.

In 17 games between July 29 and August 17, Snider collected 26 hits, six of them home runs, in 50 at-bats.

AUGUST 24   Three days after Hawaii is admitted to the Union as the 50th state, Sandy Koufax fans 13 batters during a 6–2 win over the Phillies in Philadelphia.

AUGUST 31   Sandy Koufax strikes out 18 batters and Wally Moon hits a three-run homer in the ninth inning for a 5–2 win over the Giants at Memorial Coliseum. Koufax started the ninth-inning rally with a single. He fanned 15 in the last six innings, including three in the fifth, sixth and ninth. The 18-strikeout performance tied the existing major league record, set by Bob Feller in 1938. Combined with his 13 strikeouts seven days earlier, Koufax fanned 31 in consecutive starts.

The 18 strikeouts by Koufax was the modern major league record until 1969. It is still the Dodger team mark. Koufax struck out 18 again on April 24, 1962, and Ramon Martinez matched it on June 4, 1990.

SEPTEMBER 7   Johnny Podres strikes out 14 batters during a 7–1 win over the Cubs at Memorial Coliseum.

SEPTEMBER 9   Don Drysdale strikes out 11 and pitches a three-hitter to defeat the Phillies 1–0 in Philadelphia. In the sixth inning, Wally Moon singled and took second on a daring base-running gamble. Norm Larker, attempting to bunt, popped the ball into foul territory where catcher Carl Sawatski made a diving catch. Moon tagged up and went to second, then scored on a single by Gil Hodges.

SEPTEMBER 11   The Dodgers end the 22-game winning streak of Pirates reliever Roy Face with two runs in the ninth to win 5–4 in the first game of a double-header at Memorial Coliseum. Face won his last five decisions in 1958 and the first 17 in 1959. Chuck Churn was the winning pitcher. Jim Gilliam tripled in the tying runs and scored on Charlie Neal's single. The Dodgers also won the second game 4–0.

Churn finished his three-year career with a 3–2 record and a 5.10 ERA.

SEPTEMBER 15   After the Braves score in the top of the 10th, the Dodgers rally for two in their half to win 8–7 at Memorial Coliseum. Maury Wills started the rally with his fifth consecutive hit and scored on a single by Chuck Essegian and a sacrifice fly by Jim

Gilliam. After the Dodgers loaded the bases, Don McMahon walked in Ron Fairly with the winning run. The game featured a controversial double by Joe Adcock in the fifth inning. Adcock's drive cleared the screen in left field but did not land in the seats because it hit a steel girder and became caught in the mesh supporting the barrier. According to the ground rules, it should have been a home run, but the umpires gave Adcock a double after changing their minds twice. Adcock never scored. Shortly thereafter, a fan shook the screen, dislodging the ball, and it fell into the stands.

The incorrect decision by the umpires would have a significant effect on the NL pennant race in 1959. At the end of the September 15 game, the Dodgers and Braves were tied for second place, two games behind the Giants.

SEPTEMBER 17   Ground-breaking takes place for the Dodgers new stadium in Chavez Ravine. A crowd of 5,000 showed up even though the only access was a one-lane road. Most of the fans came with shovels and left with some dirt in boxes furnished by the Dodgers.

The construction of Dodger Stadium would require moving nearly eight million cubic yards of earth, including the leveling of an entire hill.

SEPTEMBER 19   The Dodgers move into a first-place tie with the Giants by virtue of a 4–1 and 5–3 sweep of the San Francisco club during a day-night double-header at Seals Stadium.

SEPTEMBER 20   The Dodgers take over first place with an 8–2 victory over the Giants in San Francisco. It was the last game ever played at Seals Stadium. The Giants moved into Candlestick Park in 1960.

With one week remaining in the season, the Dodgers were in first place in a tight three-way race. The Braves were one-half back and the Giants one game behind.

SEPTEMBER 22   The Dodgers fall into second place with an 11–10 loss to the Cardinals in St. Louis. Los Angeles set a major league record (since tied) by using nine pinch-hitters. The nine were Don Demeter, Carl Furillo, Joe Pignatano, Ron Fairly, Rip Repulski, Tommy Davis, Chuck Essegian, Sandy Amoros and Frank Howard. Three collected hits, including a homer by Howard, and one walked.

SEPTEMBER 23   The Dodgers move back into first place with the Braves by beating the Cardinals 3–0 in St. Louis. Roger Craig pitched the shutout.

SEPTEMBER 25   Gil Hodges hits a home run in the 11th inning to beat the Cubs 5–4 in Chicago. The win gave the Dodgers a one-game lead over the Braves.

SEPTEMBER 26   The Dodgers lose 12–2 to the Cubs while the Braves win 3–2 over the Phillies in Milwaukee. With one game remaining in the season, the Dodgers and Braves were tied for first game with 85–68 records.

SEPTEMBER 27   On the final day of the regular season, the Dodgers win 7–1 over the Cubs in Chicago while the Braves are victorious 5–2 against the Phillies in Milwaukee. Roger Craig pitched a complete game for the Dodgers, and Charlie Neal and Johnny Roseboro each homered. A best-of-three playoff would decide the pennant winner.

SEPTEMBER 28   The Dodgers win the first playoff game 3–2 before only 18,297 at County Stadium in Milwaukee. Johnny Roseboro broke a 2–2 tie with a home run in the sixth inning. Larry Sherry pitched 7²/₃ innings of shutout relief.

SEPTEMBER 29   The Dodgers clinch the National League pennant by scoring three runs in the ninth inning and one in the 12th to defeat the Braves 6–5 before 36,853 at Memorial Coliseum. Trailing 5–2, the Dodgers loaded the bases in the ninth on singles by Wally Moon, Duke Snider and Gil Hodges. Norm Larker drove in two runs with a single, and Carl Furillo tied the score with a sacrifice fly. In the 12th, Gil Hodges walked, moved to second on a single by Joe Pignatano and scored on a throwing error by shortstop Felix Mantilla.

The Dodgers met the Chicago White Sox in the World Series. Managed by Al Lopez, the Sox were 94–60 in 1959. It was the first post-season appearance for Chicago's American League franchise since 1919 and the last until 2005.

OCTOBER 1   The Dodgers open the 1959 World Series with an 11–0 loss to the White Sox at Comiskey Park in Chicago. It was over early, as the Sox scored all 11 of their runs in the first four innings. Ted Kluszewski hit two homers and drove in five runs. Early Wynn (seven innings) and Gerry Staley (two innings) combined on the shutout.

OCTOBER 2   The Dodgers even the Series with a 4–3 win over the White Sox in Chicago. With the Sox leading 2–0, Charlie Neal hit a solo homer in the fifth inning. In the seventh, Chuck Essegian tied the game with a pinch-homer. After Jim Gilliam walked, Neal hit his second homer of the contest to break the deadlock. Larry Sherry pitched three innings of relief for the save.

Neal's first homer brought about one of the most humorous incidents in World Series history. The drive landed in the first row of stands. A fan scrambling for the ball knocked a cup of beer off the top of the wall. Chicago left fielder Al Smith backed up to the wall for the catch and was looking straight up when the sudsy contents came tumbling down and splashed him in his face.

OCTOBER 4   The Dodgers win game three by a 3–1 score before 92,394 at Memorial Coliseum. The game was scoreless until Carl Furillo delivered a two-run, pinch-single in the seventh. Don Drysdale allowed 11 hits in seven innings, but survived for the win. Larry Sherry hurled the final two frames for the save.

The game was not only the first World Series game played on the West Coast, but the first west of St. Louis.

OCTOBER 5   The Dodgers move within one win of the world championship with a 5–4 win over the White Sox before 92,650 at Memorial Coliseum. The Dodgers scored four runs in the second inning off Early Wynn, but the Sox countered with four tallies in the seventh. Gil Hodges broke the tie with a homer in the eighth. Larry Sherry was the winning pitcher with two innings of relief.

OCTOBER 6   The Dodgers lose game five 1–0 to the White Sox before an all-time World Series-record crowd of 92,706 at Memorial Coliseum. The lone run scored in the fourth on two singles and a double play grounder. Sandy Koufax pitched well in the defeat, going seven innings. Bob Shaw (7¹/₃ innings) and Dick Donovan (1²/₃ innings) combined on the shutout.

OCTOBER 8   The Dodgers wrap up the world championship with a 9–3 win over the White Sox in Chicago. Duke Snider started the scoring with a two-run homer in the third inning. Six runs followed in the fourth. The key hits were a two-run double by Charlie Neal and a two-run homer from Wally Moon. Chuck Essegian added a pinch-homer in the ninth. Larry Sherry was the winning pitcher with $5^2/_3$ innings of shutout relief.

> *When the Series started, few expected Essegian and Sherry to play starring roles. Essegian was the first of two players to hit two pinch-homers in a single Series. He is also one of two athletes to play in both the Rose Bowl and the World Series. Essegian was a linebacker for Stanford in the Rose Bowl in 1952. Without Sherry, the Dodgers wouldn't have reached the World Series, much less won it. Summoned from the minors on July 2, Sherry was 7–2 with a 2.19 ERA during the regular season. During the Fall Classic, he became a national celebrity by winning two games and saving two others, allowing only one run in $12^1/_3$ innings. Sherry had only sporadic success over the remainder of his career, however, which ended in 1968 with a 53–45 record and a 3.67 earned run average. He was traded by the Dodgers to the Tigers in April 1964.*

OCTOBER 15   The Dodgers sell Jim Gentile to the Orioles.

> *A first baseman, Gentile was one of the top prospects in baseball but was stuck behind Gil Hodges on the Dodgers depth chart. The club would have been better off putting Gentile in the lineup ahead of Hodges in 1960. Gil went into a steep decline, while Gentile struck 152 homers over the next five seasons for Baltimore, including 46 in 1961.*

OCTOBER 19   The United States Supreme Court dismisses three appeals attacking plans by the city of Los Angeles to deed land in Chavez Ravine for a new stadium for the Dodgers. The action left standing a California Supreme Court decision upholding the city's plans. Los Angeles City Council had voted for the plan on October 7, 1957, but ran into more than two years of delays due to a referendum on the matter (see June 3, 1958) and lawsuits from taxpayers.

THE STATE OF THE DODGERS

The Dodgers won five NL pennants and two world championships during the 1950s, largely with offensive juggernauts playing in hitter's parks and backed by an adequate pitching staff. During the 1960s, the club won three National League titles and two more world championships with outstanding pitchers playing in a pitcher's park and back by an adequate batting attack built around speed. The Dodgers reached the World Series in 1963, 1965 and 1966, and won it in 1963 and 1965. Overall, the Dodgers were 878–729 during the decade, a winning percentage of .546, which was the third best in the NL, trailing only the Giants and Cardinals. NL pennants outside of Los Angeles were won by the Pirates (1960), Reds (1961), Giants (1962), Cardinals (1964, 1967 and 1968) and Mets (1969).

THE BEST TEAM

The 1963 Dodgers were 99–63 and swept the Yankees in the World Series. The 1962 club won the most games with a record of 103–62, but blew a golden opportunity to win a pennant and finished second.

THE WORST TEAM

The 1967 outfit was 73–89 to post the worst winning percentage of any Dodger club since 1944. It would be 1992 before another Dodger team won fewer than 73 times in a non-strike season.

THE BEST MOMENT

In a duel between Sandy Koufax and Whitey Ford, the Dodgers completed the sweep of the 1963 World Series with a 2–1 win on October 6 at Dodger Stadium.

THE WORST MOMENT

Holding a four-game lead in the 1962 National League pennant race with seven games remaining, the Dodgers wound up in a best-of-three playoff series against the Giants, then blew a two-run, ninth-inning lead in game three.

THE ALL-DECADE TEAM • YEARS W/DODS

Johnny Roseboro, c	1957–67
Wes Parker, 1b	1964–72
Jim Lefebvre, 2b	1965–72
Jim Gilliam, 3b	1953–66
Maury Wills, ss	1959–66, 1969–72
Tommy Davis, lf	1959–66
Willie Davis, cf	1960–73
Ron Fairly, rf	1958–69
Don Drysdale, p	1956–69
Sandy Koufax, p	1955–66
Claude Osteen, p	1965–73
Ron Perranoski, p	1961–67, 1972

Every member of the 1960s All-Decade Team made their major league debuts with the Dodgers with the exception of Osteen. Gilliam was also on the 1950s All-Decade Team. Koufax and Drysdale are in the Hall of Fame. Other outstanding Dodger players of the 1960s included left fielder Wally Moon (1959–64), right fielder Frank Howard (1958–64), catcher Tom Haller (1968–71) and pitchers Bill Singer (1964–72), Johnny Podres (1953–55, 1957–66) and Stan Williams (1958–62).

THE DECADE LEADERS

Batting Avg:	Tommy Davis	.304
On-Base Pct:	Wally Moon	.372
Slugging Pct:	Frank Howard	.498
Home Runs:	Frank Howard	121
RBIs:	Willie Davis	526
Runs:	Maury Wills	683
Stolen Bases:	Maury Wills	439
Wins:	Don Drysdale	158
Strikeouts:	Don Drysdale	1,910
ERA:	Sandy Koufax	2.36
Saves:	Ron Perranoski	101

THE HOME FIELD

The Dodgers played at misshapen Memorial Coliseum during their first four years in Los Angeles. The opening of Dodger Stadium took place on April 10, 1962. That season, the Dodgers set a major league at10dance record of 2,755,184, which stood until the club exceeded three million in 1978. The Dodgers led the major league in at10dance every season from 1959 through 1966.

THE GAME YOU WISHED YOU HAD SEEN

There were so many great moments at Dodger Stadium during the 1960s, it's nearly impossible to isolate just one. The best night to be at the ballpark may have been September 9, 1965, when Sandy Koufax pitched his perfect game. The Dodgers collected only one hit themselves, and beat the Cubs 1–0.

THE WAY THE GAME WAS PLAYED

Baseball was played in several new cities and ballparks during the 1960s. Candlestick Park, Dodger Stadium, Shea Stadium, the Astrodome, Atlanta-Fulton County Stadium and Busch Memorial Stadium were among the facilities to open. Expansion and franchise shifts brought National League baseball back to New York and major league ball to Houston, Atlanta, San Diego and Montreal. American League ball was played for the first time in Minnesota, Oakland, Anaheim and Seattle. Expansion to 12 teams in 1969 inaugurated divisional play and a playoff between the division champions to determine who would go on to the World Series. The Astrodome, opened in 1965, brought two more innovations: indoor baseball and artificial turf. In the wake of a strike zone expansion in 1963, offense declined in the 1960s until the owners lowered the mound for the 1969 season. The league ERA dipped to 2.99 in 1968, the first time since 1919 it had been below 3.00.

THE MANAGEMENT

Walter O'Malley became majority owner in 1950, a position he would hold until his death in 1979. Buzzie Bavasi was general manager from 1950 until 1968 when he took a post as president of the San Diego Padres. Fresco Thompson was named to succeed Bavasi, but died of cancer six months later. Al Campanis succeeded Thompson with the title of vice-president, player personnel and scouting. Walter Alston was the field manager from 1954 through 1976.

THE BEST PLAYER MOVE

The best player move was the signing of Don Sutton as an amateur free agent in September 1964. The best trade brought Ron Perranoski, two others and cash from the Cubs in April 1960 for Don Zimmer.

THE WORST PLAYER MOVE

The worst of the trades Bavasi made during the 1960s sent Ron Perranoski, Johnny Roseboro and Bob Miller packing to Minnesota on November 28, 1967, for Mudcat Grant and Zoilo Versalles.

1960

L A

Season in a Sentence

The Dodgers defend their world championship by continuing to replace aging stars who played in Brooklyn with rising young players, and finish fourth after a rough start.

Finish • Won • Lost • Pct • GB

Fourth 82 72 .532 13.0

Manager

Walter Alston

Stats

Stats	Dods	NL	Rank
Batting Avg:	.255	.255	3
On-Base Pct:	.324	.319	2
Slugging Pct:	.383	.388	6
Home Runs:	126		6
Stolen Bases:	95		1
ERA:	3.40	3.76	1
Fielding Avg:	.979	.977	1
Runs Scored:	662		4
Runs Allowed:	593		1

Starting Lineup

Johnny Roseboro, c
Norm Larker, 1b
Charlie Neal, 2b
Jim Gilliam, 3b
Maury Wills, ss
Wally Moon, lf
Tommy Davis, cf-lf
Frank Howard, rf
Duke Snider, cf-rf
Gil Hodges, 1b

Pitchers

Don Drysdale, sp
Johnny Podres, sp
Stan Williams, sp
Sandy Koufax, sp
Roger Craig, sp
Larry Sherry, rp
Ed Roebuck, rp

Attendance

2,253,887 (first in NL)

Club Leaders

Batting Avg:	Norm Larker	.323
On-Base Pct:	Wally Moon	.383
Slugging Pct:	Frank Howard	.464
Home Runs:	Frank Howard	23
RBIs:	Norm Larker	78
Runs:	Jim Gilliam	96
Stolen Bases:	Maury Wills	50
Wins:	Don Drysdale	15
Strikeouts:	Don Drysdale	246
ERA:	Don Drysdale	2.84
Saves:	Ed Roebuck	8

FEBRUARY 18   Nine days after Joanne Woodward becomes the first to be honored with a star on the Hollywood Walk of Fame, Walter O'Malley completes the purchase of property at Chavez Ravine to speed the grading process to construct the new stadium. Eleven landowners had refused offers sell their parcels to the city through eminent domain. Faced with the possibility of years of litigation, O'Malley paid the eleven individuals a total of $494,400 for property appraised at $92,850. The home and land of Francis Scott, with an appraised value of $9,000, sold for $150,000 because it was in a critical area used to fill dirt for the stadium project.

FEBRUARY 23   The demolition of Ebbets Field begins with a wrecking ball painted like a baseball, which smashes into the roof of one of the dugouts. Roy Campanella was on hand and given dirt from the area around home plate.

Walter O'Malley installed 1,500 Ebbets Field seats at Holman Stadium in Vero Beach. They formed the first few rows of box seats. The turnstiles were installed at Yankee Stadium. The light towers were put up at Downing Stadium, a 22,000-seat football stadium on Randall's Island. Downing Stadium was torn down in 2002 and replaced two years later by Icahn Stadium, but the light towers were left in place to illuminate the new field. The site of Ebbets Field was turned into a housing project called the Ebbets Field Apartments. The facility was renamed Jackie Robinson Apartments at Ebbets Field in 1972. Jackie Robinson School is located across the street.

APRIL 8   The Dodgers send Don Zimmer to the Cubs for Ron Perranoski, Johnny Goryl, Lee Handley and $25,000.

The Dodgers pulled off a brilliant deal in acquiring Perranoski. After a year in the minors, he joined the club in 1961 and became a mainstay in the bullpen for seven years. As a Dodger, he led the team in saves five times and played in three World Series. Overall, he was 54–41 with a 2.56 ERA in Los Angeles and ranks fourth in club history in games pitched (457) and fifth in saves (101).

APRIL 11   The Dodgers sell Johnny Klippstein to the Indians for $25,000.

The 1960 season was the first in which the Dodgers played a majority of its spring training home games in Vero Beach. From 1949 through 1958, the club played about 10 to 15 games each spring in Miami. In 1959, the Dodgers journeyed across the state to Sarasota for 12 contests.

APRIL 12   The Dodgers open with a dramatic 11-inning, 3–2 win over the Cubs before 67,550 at Memorial Coliseum. Among those in the crowd was California Governor Pat Brown. Chuck Essegian, who hit two pinch-hit homers in the 1959 World Series, won the 1960 opener with a walk-off, pinch-homer off Don Elston. Don Drysdale pitched a complete game and struck out 14.

Drysdale led the NL in strikeouts in 1960 with 246 in 269 innings along with a 15–14 record and a 2.84 ERA.

APRIL 14   The Dodgers score two runs in the ninth inning to beat the Cardinals 3–2 at Memorial Coliseum. Gil Hodges tripled in the tying run and scored on a wild pitch.

The Dodgers set a National League record for at10dance in 1960 with a figure of 2,253,887.

APRIL 19   The Dodgers play at Candlestick Park in San Francisco for the first time and win 4–0. Johnny Podres (8⅓ innings) and Ed Roebuck (two-thirds of an inning) combined on the shutout.

The Dodgers led the National League in ERA in 1960 despite the handicap of playing home games in an extreme hitter's park. The club allowed 334 runs and 97 homers in 77 games at Memorial Coliseum and 259 runs and 57 home runs on the road. The hitters scored 379 runs with 89 homers at home and 283 runs and just 37 home runs in contests outside of Los Angeles.

APRIL 22   In his major league debut, Dodgers pitcher Ed Rakow allows a home run to the first batter he faces during an 11–7 loss to the Cardinals in St. Louis. Rakow entered the contest in the eighth inning and immediately surrendered a homer to Daryl Spencer.

APRIL 23   Danny McDevitt gives up two homers with one baseball during a 9–5 loss to the Cardinals in St. Louis. Ken Boyer hit a home run into the right field pavilion that a spectator deflected back into play. Two batters later, Daryl Spencer launched the same ball against the scoreboard and into the bleachers.

APRIL 29   Johnny Roseboro hits a grand slam off Sam Jones in the fifth inning of a 10–2 win over the Giants at Memorial Coliseum.

MAY 6   Sandy Koufax strikes out 15 batters, but the performance is wasted when the Phillies score five runs in the 10th inning to win 6–1 at Memorial Coliseum. Koufax gave up four of the 10th-inning runs before being relieved with two out.

On the same day, the Dodgers sold Rip Repulski to the Red Sox.

MAY 7   The Sherry brothers star during a 3–2 win over the Phillies at Memorial Coliseum. Norm Sherry hit a walk-off homer in the 11th inning after entering the contest in the seventh as a pinch-hitter and remaining as a catcher. Younger brother Larry (by four years) pitched the final four innings for the victory.

On the same day, the Dodgers sell Sandy Amoros to the Tigers.

MAY 9   A three-run, walk-off homer by Charlie Neal in the ninth inning beats the Pirates 7–4 at Memorial Coliseum. Don Drysdale struck out 13 batters in 8⅓ innings, but received a no-decision after allowing the Pirates to tie the game with two runs in the top of the ninth.

MAY 14   Stan Williams pitches a two-hitter to win 2–1 over the Giants at Candlestick Park. The only San Francisco hits were a single by pitcher Billy O'Dell in the fifth inning and a homer from Willie Kirkland in the seventh. The Dodgers broke the 1–1 tie in the ninth inning on a single by Don Demeter that scored Maury Wills.

In his first full season in the majors, Wills led the National League in stolen bases with 50.

MAY 17   Trailing 4–1, the Dodgers score five runs in the eighth inning to win 6–4 over the Braves in Milwaukee. The last four crossed the plate on a 450-foot grand slam by Frank Howard off Bob Buhl.

On the same day, the Dodgers released Carl Furillo.

MAY 23   Sandy Koufax pitches a one-hitter for a 1–0 win over the Pirates at Forbes Field. The only Pittsburgh hit was a single by opposing pitcher Bennie Daniels in the second inning. The lone run scored in the seventh on doubles by Norm Larker and Tommy Davis.

Larker hit .323 for the Dodgers in 1960.

MAY 25   Frank Howard hits a home run estimated at 562 feet during a 5–1 win over the Pirates in Pittsburgh. It was struck off Jim Umbricht in the second inning, cleared the 12-foot left-field fence at Forbes Field 400 feet from home plate, rocketed over the trees, and slammed into the street just as Joe Tucker, the voice of the Pittsburgh Steelers, was parking his car. From the 400-mark at the fence, Tucker stepped off 54 paces to where the ball landed, a distance of 162 feet.

MAY 28

Sandy Koufax strikes out 15 batters, but is the losing pitcher in a 14-inning, 4–3 defeat at the hands of the Cubs in Chicago. Koufax had allowed only three hits through the first 13 innings. He started the 14th with two walks and was relieved by Ed Roebuck, who loaded the bases and allowed a game-winning single to Don Zimmer. Koufax threw an incredible 193 pitches during the contest. It was the second time during the month of May that Koufax fanned 15 batters and lost the game.

Koufax started the 1960 season with eight losses in his first nine decisions to drop his career record to 29–35. He finished the 1960 season with an 8–13 record.

MAY 31

Norm Sherry hits a grand slam off Ron Kline in the sixth inning of an 8–3 victory over the Cardinals at Memorial Stadium.

JUNE 4

An inside-the-park grand slam by Wally Moon highlights a 12–6 triumph over the Cubs at Memorial Coliseum. Facing Seth Morehead in the seventh inning, Moon hit a drive to center field which Richie Ashburn had in his glove, but the ball was knocked loose when he crashed into fence. Stunned by the impact, Ashburn couldn't retrieve the ball before Moon circled the bases.

Moon drove in 23 runs during a 12-game stretch in June. He finished the season with a .299 batting average, 13 home runs and 69 runs batted in.

JUNE 7

The Dodgers sign Irv Noren as a free agent following his release by the Cubs.

JUNE 15

The Dodgers wallop the Phillies 14–2 at Memorial Coliseum.

On the same day, the Dodgers sent Clem Labine to the Tigers for Ray Semproch and cash.

JUNE 27

The Dodgers play in New York for the first time since 1957 and beat the Yankees 4–3 in an exhibition game at Yankee Stadium. Most of the crowd of 53,492 rooted for the Dodgers. There were thunderous cheers for former Brooklyn heroes Duke Snider and Gil Hodges.

It was a year of bizarre injuries. Roger Craig covered a play at the plate, and wound up with a broken collarbone bone when Vada Pinson of the Reds crashed into him. Craig missed two months. Larry Sherry ran behind the plate to back up the catcher when an umpire tossed aside a discarded bat. Sherry turned his ankle on the bat and was out three weeks. Don Drysdale hurt his back slipping in the shower.

JULY 6

The Dodgers rout the Giants 10–0 at Memorial Coliseum.

The Dodgers had a 27–33 record on June 21 before winning 25 of their next 34 games to pull within four games of first place at the end of July. A 15–15 August, 14–14 September and 1–1 October doomed the defending world champions to fourth place.

JULY 11

At Municipal Stadium in Kansas City, Walter Alston manages the National League to a 5–3 win in the first of two All-Star Games played in 1960.

JULY 13   At Yankee Stadium, Johnny Podres and Stan Williams both pitch two shutout innings during a 6–0 National League win in the second of two All-Star Games played in 1960. Podres pitched the third and fourth innings and Stan Williams the fifth and sixth. Walter Alston was the NL manager.

JULY 15   On the day that John Kennedy receives the Democratic Party nomination for president at the convention in Los Angeles, the Dodgers beat the Giants 5–3 in a game in San Francisco delayed by fog for 24 minutes in the second inning. Play was halted after Willie McCovey's drive in the second inning fell for a triple and neither Wally Moon nor Duke Snider saw the ball before it thudded to the turf.

JULY 20   A two-run, walk-off homer by Tommy Davis in the 11th inning beats the Pirates 7–5 at Memorial Coliseum. Davis entered the game as a pinch-runner for Frank Howard and remained in the contest as a center fielder.

> *Davis attended Boys' High School in Brooklyn where he was a basketball teammate of future NBA star Lenny Wilkens.*

JULY 22   Don Drysdale strikes out 14 batters and pitches a four-hitter to beat the Phillies 2–0 at Memorial Coliseum.

JULY 23   Roger Craig pitches a three-hitter and shuts out the Phillies 2–0 at Memorial Coliseum.

JULY 24   Stan Williams records the Dodgers third consecutive shutout over the Phillies, winning 9–0 at Memorial Coliseum.

JULY 28   Frank Howard drives in six runs to lead the Dodgers to an 8–6 win over the Reds at Memorial Coliseum. Howard hits a grand slam in the first inning and a two-run single in the second, both off Jim O'Toole.

JULY 30   Tommy Davis hits a grand slam off Ron Piche in the seventh inning, but the Dodgers lose 8–7 in 11 innings to the Braves at Memorial Coliseum.

AUGUST 11   Sandy Koufax pitches a two-hitter and strikes out 13 batters to defeat the Reds 3–0 at Crosley Field. The only Cincinnati hits were singles by Frank Robinson in the first inning and Gordy Coleman in the second.

AUGUST 17   Ernie Banks hits a walk-off homer in the ninth inning off Don Drysdale to give the Cubs a 1–0 win over the Dodgers in Chicago. Bob Will preceded Banks to the plate, and hit a shot through the middle, which struck Drysdale in the right (pitching) hand. The ball caromed to first baseman Norm Larker, who caught it in the air for an out. Banks hit the next pitch over the fence.

AUGUST 18   Wally Moon hits a home run in the 13th inning to defeat the Cubs 4–3 in Chicago.

AUGUST 20   A two-run double by Gil Hodges in the ninth inning beats the Cardinals 2–1 in St. Louis. Tommy Davis extended his hitting streak to 20 games during the contest.

AUGUST 28   The Reds score nine runs in the top of the first inning, and beat the Dodgers 9–3 at Memorial Coliseum.

AUGUST 29   The Dodgers unveil a model of their new stadium in Chavez Ravine. It was displayed at the main office of the Bank of America in downtown Los Angeles.

SEPTEMBER 1   Don Drysdale strikes out 13 batters during an 11-inning complete game to down the Phillies 3–2 at Memorial Coliseum. Duke Snider drove in the winning run with a pinch-hit single.

SEPTEMBER 8   Willie Davis collects two hits in five at-bats during his major league debut, a 7–4 win over the Reds in Cincinnati.

Unrelated to teammate Tommy Davis, Willie played for the Dodgers until 1973 and was an important part of the 1963, 1965 and 1966 World Series teams, which won with a combination of pitching, speed and defense. A player who marched to a different beat, he became a Buddhist in 1971 and chanted prior to each game. Davis ranks sixth all-time among Dodgers in games played (1,952), third in at-bats (7,495), second in triples (110), third in hits (2,091), third in stolen bases (335), sixth in runs (1,004), sixth in doubles (321) and ninth in RBIs (849).

SEPTEMBER 11   Don Drysdale pitches a two-hitter to defeat the Braves 2–0 at County Stadium. The only Milwaukee hits were singles by Wes Covington in the fifth inning and Ed Mathews in the seventh. Norm Larker drove in both Los Angeles runs.

SEPTEMBER 14   Stan Williams strikes out 13 batters during a 5–2 win over the Pirates in Pittsburgh.

SEPTEMBER 26   Jim Gilliam scores four runs without a hit during a 13–9 loss to the Giants in San Francisco. Gilliam reached base four times on walks.

OCTOBER 1   On the last day of the season, Maury Wills and Bob Lillis both collect five hits during a 14-inning, 10–8 loss to the Cubs at Memorial Coliseum. Wills had five singles in eight at-bats, and Lillis was five-for-seven with four singles and a double.

The Coliseum was not only the home of the Dodgers in 1960, but four football teams. The Rams, Chargers, University of Southern California and UCLA all played their complete home schedule at the facility. The Chargers played in Los Angeles only one season before moving to San Diego in 1961.

OCTOBER 17   The National League votes to expand to 10 teams, adding New York and Houston. Both were to begin playing games in 1962.

OCTOBER 26   The American League votes to expand to 10 teams, including the addition of a franchise in Los Angeles to compete with the Dodgers. Unlike the National League, which gave their new clubs in New York and Houston until 1962 to compete in games, the AL decided its expansion teams would play in 1961. The Washington Senators were permitted to move to Minnesota and a new expansion team, also named the Senators, was installed in Washington.

The decision to invade Los Angeles drew criticism from Walter O'Malley. "We expected American League baseball eventually on the West Coast," said O'Malley, but "we had hoped to get our own problems in pioneering the territory and building our stadium behind us before the relatives moved in." Following a protest by O'Malley, Commissioner Ford Frick declared the

American League could not enter Los Angeles under existing major league rules. Baseball regulations provided that unanimous consent of all major league clubs was required for a team to enter a city already represented in the other league. This also placed the National League's expansion plans in New York in jeopardy. On December 6, the American League awarded its franchise in Los Angeles to Gene Autry. The team would be nicknamed the Angels, after the Pacific Coast League franchise, which existed from 1903 through 1957, and the Spanish to English translation of Los Angeles. A day later, O'Malley and Autry worked out an agreement to allow the AL to begin playing in L.A. in 1961. The Angels would play at Wrigley Field during their first season, then move into Dodger Stadium in 1962. The Angels signed a four-year lease to play at the new stadium with an option to renew for three more years. The Dodgers and Angels shared Dodger Stadium from 1962 through 1965. In 1966, the Angels moved south to Anaheim.

DECEMBER 22   Seven weeks after John Kennedy defeats Richard Nixon in the presidential election, the last obstacle to the construction of Dodger Stadium is removed when a tract map is approved by City Council. It came more than three years after council originally voted to grant Chavez Ravine to the Dodgers (see October 7, 1957).

1961   LA

Season in a Sentence

In the last season at Memorial Coliseum, the Dodgers hold a 2½-game lead on August 13 before a 10-game losing streak ends the club's World Series dreams.

Finish • Won • Lost • Pct • GB

Second   89   65   .578   4.0

Manager

Walter Alston

Stats

Stats	Dods	NL	Rank
Batting Avg:	.262	.262	5
On-Base Pct:	.338	.327	1
Slugging Pct:	.405	.405	6
Home Runs:	157		5
Stolen Bases:	86		1
ERA:	4.04	4.03	6
Fielding Avg:	.975	.976	5
Runs Scored:	735		2
Runs Allowed:	697		6

Starting Lineup

Johnny Roseboro, c
Gil Hodges, 1b
Charlie Neal, 2b
Jim Gilliam, 3b-2b
Maury Wills, ss
Wally Moon, lf
Willie Davis, cf
Tommy Davis, rf-lf-cf
Norm Larker, 1b
Frank Howard, rf-lf
Ron Fairly, rf
Duke Snider, rf-cf

Pitchers

Sandy Koufax, sp
Johnny Podres, sp
Stan Williams, sp
Don Drysdale, sp
Larry Sherry, rp
Ron Perranoski, rp
Dick Farrell, rp
Roger Craig, sp-rp

Attendance

1,804,250 (first in NL)

Club Leaders

Batting Avg:	Wally Moon	.328
On-Base Pct:	Wally Moon	.434
Slugging Pct:	Wally Moon	.505
Home Runs:	Johnny Roseboro	18
RBIs:	Wally Moon	88
Runs:	Maury Wills	105
Stolen Bases:	Maury Wills	35
Wins:	Sandy Koufax	18
Strikeouts:	Sandy Koufax	269
ERA:	Sandy Koufax	3.52
Saves:	Larry Sherry	15

JANUARY 9   The Dodgers sign Leo Durocher as a coach. After managing the Dodgers (1939–46, 1948) and Giants (1948–55), Durocher spent five years as a television commentator for NBC-TV. He was a coach for the Dodgers until he was fire at the end of the 1964 season.

APRIL 11   The Dodgers win the season opener 6–2 over the Phillies before 50,665 at Memorial Coliseum. Don Drysdale went seven innings for the win. Wally Moon homered.

             On the same day, the Angels played their first regular season game and won 7–2 over the Orioles in Baltimore.

APRIL 15   The Dodgers and Pirates tie a major league record by combining for nine double plays at Memorial Coliseum. The Dodgers turned five double plays, but lost 4–1.

             The Dodgers started the 1961 season with a 15-game home stand.

APRIL 16   On the day the United States launches the unsuccessful Bay of Pigs invasion in Cuba, the Dodgers blast their way to a 13–6 win over the Pirates at Memorial Coliseum.

             Dodger coach Leo Durocher was ejected from the game by umpire Jocko Conlan for his antics on the bench after a call against the Dodgers. Durocher charged at Conlan, and after an animated argument, the 55-year-old Durocher kicked the 61-year-old Conlan in the shins. The two kicked each other twice before being separated. Durocher was suspended for three days by NL President Warren Giles.

APRIL 17   Steve Bilko becomes the first individual to play for both the Dodgers and Angels during a 3–2 Angels loss to the Red Sox in Boston. Bilko was a Dodger in 1958 and also played for the Pacific Coast League version of the Los Angeles Angels from 1955 through 1957.

APRIL 22   Johnny Podres pitches the Dodgers to a 1–0 win over the Reds at Memorial Coliseum. The lone run scored in the first inning on a double by Jim Gilliam and a single from Wally Moon.

             Moon hit .328 with 17 homers and a league-leading .434 on-base percentage in 1961. Podres had an 18–5 record and a 3.74 ERA.

APRIL 27   The Angels play their first home game, and lose 4–2 to the Twins before 11,931 at Wrigley Field.

             The Dodgers attendance fell by over 400,000 to 1,804,250 in 1961, but it was still good enough to lead the major leagues for the third consecutive year. The Angels were able to attract only 603,510 fans to Wrigley Field.

APRIL 29   Frank Howard hits two homers and drives in six runs during a 9–4 drubbing of the Cubs in Chicago. Howard struck a two-run homer in the second inning and a grand slam in the fifth, both off Dick Ellsworth.

APRIL 30   A two-run homer by Tommy Davis in the ninth inning beats the Cubs 2–1 at Wrigley Field. Chicago won the second tilt 10–5.

MAY 2   Trailing 6–5, the Dodgers score six runs in the seventh inning and go on to defeat the Braves 11–9 in Milwaukee.

MAY 4   Joe Adcock hits a walk-off grand slam in the 10th inning off Jim Golden to lift the Braves to a 10–6 win over the Dodgers in Milwaukee.

             On the same day, the Dodgers traded Don Demeter and Charlie Smith to the Phillies for Dick Farrell and Joe Koppe. The deal turned out badly for the Dodgers. Farrell posted a 5.06 ERA for the Dodgers out of the bullpen in 1961, then went to Houston in the expansion draft. Los Angeles could have used Demeter in 1962 when he drove in 107 runs for the Phillies.

MAY 5   On the day Alan Shepard becomes the first American in space, the Dodgers thrash the Pirates 10–0 in Pittsburgh.

MAY 14   The Dodgers hit five home runs, but lose 10–8 in 11 innings to the Cubs at Memorial Coliseum. The homers were struck by Norm Larker, Charlie Neal, Tommy Davis, Ron Fairly and Don Drysdale.

MAY 17   Stan Williams pitches an 11-inning complete game in which he allows four hits, walks 12 and strikes out 11 to defeat the Braves 2–1 at Memorial Coliseum. The winning run scored on a bases-loaded walk to Bob Lillis by Seth Morehead.

MAY 25   Sandy Koufax pitches a three-hit shutout to defeat the Cardinals 1–0 in St. Louis. The lone run scored on a home run in the seventh inning by Tommy Davis off Bob Gibson.

MAY 29   Sandy Koufax pitches a three-hitter and strikes out 13 batters to defeat the Cardinals 2–1 at Memorial Coliseum.

             Koufax started the season as a 25-year-old with a 36–40 lifetime won-lost record and a 4.10 ERA. He struck out 683 batters in 691²/₃ innings, but walked 405. Koufax was often brilliant, with four games of 15 strikeouts or more, including one of 18 which tied the existing major league record. He also pitched a one-hitter and a two-hitter. But inconsistency plagued him, mainly because of control issues. Beginning in 1961, Koufax changed his pitching mechanics, which gave him greater control. The transformation was astounding. In 1961, Koufax was 18–13 with a 3.52 ERA and a league-leading 269 strikeouts in 255²/₃ innings. From 1962 through 1966, he had a record of 111–34 and led the NL in earned run average five straight years with marks of 2.54, 1.88, 1.74, 2.04 and 1.73. During that stretch Koufax also led the league in wins three times, going 25–5 in 1963, 26–8 in 1965 and 27–9 in 1966. He topped the NL in strikeouts four seasons, including the 1961 campaign, with a high of 382 in 1965. From 1963 through 1966, Koufax fired 31 shutouts, 11 of them in 1963. After his 27-win season in 1966, Sandy decided to retire at the age of 30 due to an arthritic condition in his elbow.

MAY 30   The Dodgers trade Daryl Spencer to the Cardinals for Bob Lillis and Carl Warwick.

JUNE 2   Tommy Davis hits a walk-off grand slam in the 10th inning off Eddie Fisher to beat the Giants 6–2 at Memorial Coliseum. A Willie Davis homer leading off the ninth tied the score.

There was a bizarre series of events after Willie Davis's homer in the ninth. Wally Moon walked, then was apparently thrown out at second base on a bunt by Tommy Davis. Moon strenuously objected to the call, and was ejected. Home plate umpire Stan Landes had called the

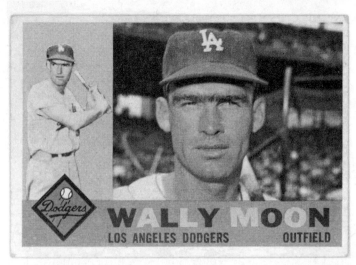

WALLY MOON
LOS ANGELES DODGERS   OUTFIELD

Wally Moon led the Dodgers in many offensive categories in 1961, his last good year in the majors. Hampered by injuries and struggling for playing time in the following seasons, he was released after the 1965 season.

bunt foul, however, which would have allowed Moon to return to first had he not been thrown out of the game. Bob Aspromonte ran for Moon. Davis bunted again, and was safe on an error by first baseman Willie McCovey. Aspromonte was trapped off second base, escaped the ensuing rundown, and was safe in returning to the bag. Davis, however, was already on second, having moved up during the rundown. Davis was tagged out. Before the inning ended, San Francisco manager Al Dark brought in Mike McCormick from the bullpen to issue an intentional walk to Norm Sherry, then replaced McCormick with Fisher.

JUNE 3   The Dodgers win on a walk-off homer for the second game in a row when Daryl Spencer tags a Juan Marichal pitch in the ninth inning for a 4–3 victory over the Giants at Memorial Coliseum. The blow came four days after Spencer was acquired from the Cardinals and was his first hit as a Dodger.

JUNE 10   Daryl Spencer hits another walk-off home run, this time with a man on base to defeat the Phillies 5–4 at Memorial Coliseum.

JUNE 15   A three-run, walk-off homer by Tommy Davis in the 12th inning defeats the Cubs 6–3 at Memorial Coliseum. The Dodgers scored twice in the ninth to tie the score 3–3.

JUNE 17   Stan Williams strikes out 12 batters to beat the Braves 3–0 at Memorial Coliseum.

JUNE 18   Don Drysdale allows consecutive homers to Hank Aaron, Joe Adcock and Frank Thomas in the third inning of a 10–2 loss to the Braves at Memorial Coliseum.

JUNE 20   Sandy Koufax pitches a two-hitter and strikes out 14 batters to defeat the Cubs 3–0 at Wrigley Field. The only Chicago hits were singles by Ernie Banks in the seventh inning and Don Zimmer in the ninth.

JUNE 24	The Dodgers club five home runs, two of them in a three-run ninth inning, to win 9–7 over the Reds in Cincinnati. In the ninth, Frank Howard hit a pinch-homer to deadlock the contest at 7–7. Maury Wills then collected his fifth single of the game before Jim Gilliam hit a game-winning homer. Earlier home runs were struck by Duke Snider, Charlie Neal and Tommy Davis.

Wills hit .282, scored 105 runs, and led the National League with 35 stolen bases in 1961.

JULY 4	The Dodgers score six runs in the first inning and make it stand up for a 6–5 win over the Braves in Milwaukee.
JULY 5	Bill White hits three homers to lead the Cardinals to a 9–1 win over the Dodgers at Memorial Coliseum.
JULY 15	The Dodgers fall six games behind the Reds n the pennant race with a 6–2 loss to the Phillies at Memorial Coliseum.
JULY 16	The Dodgers score two runs in the ninth inning and one in the 10th to edge the Pirates 12–11 at Memorial Coliseum. Los Angeles led 7–3 at the end of the fourth inning before falling behind 11–9. Johnny Roseboro homered in the ninth inning and drove in the winning run with a triple in the 10th.

The Dodgers had eight players with at least 10 home runs in 1961, but Roseboro was the club leader with 18. Six of the eight players to reach double digits in homers were outfielders (Wally Moon, Duke Snider, Tommy Davis, Frank Howard, Ron Fairly and Willie Davis).

JULY 22	Frank Howard's pinch-homer in the 11th inning beats the Cardinals 5–4 in St. Louis.
JULY 26	Norm Larker hits a grand slam off Frank Sullivan in the eighth inning of an 8–1 win over the Phillies in Philadelphia.
JULY 30	The Dodgers extend their winning streak to eight games with a 7–3 triumph over the Pirates in Pittsburgh.
JULY 31	Sandy Koufax pitches two shutout innings (the fifth and sixth) during the second of two All-Star Games played in 1961. The contest at Fenway Park in Boston ended after nine innings with the score tied 1–1 because of rain.
AUGUST 6	The Dodgers take first place with an 11–4 win over the Cubs at Memorial Coliseum.
AUGUST 9	Don Drysdale pitches a four-hitter and belts a grand slam off Don Nottebart in the second inning to lead the Dodgers to an 8–3 win over the Braves at Memorial Coliseum.
AUGUST 13	On the day construction of the Berlin Wall commences, the Dodgers take a 2½-game lead over the Reds in the National League pennant race with an 8–0 win over the Cardinals at Memorial Coliseum. Los Angeles had a record of 69–40.

AUGUST 16   The Dodgers drop out of first place with 6–0 and 8–0 losses to the Reds before a crowd of 72,140 at Memorial Coliseum. Bob Purkey and Jim O'Toole pitched the shutouts.

The two losses were the second and third of a losing streak that would reach 10 games on August 24. The Dodgers never regained first place in 1961.

AUGUST 29   Sandy Koufax pitches a two-hitter and strikes out 12 batters to defeat the Cubs 2–1 at Wrigley Field. The only Chicago hits were singles by Dick Bertell in the seventh inning and Ron Santo in the ninth.

AUGUST 30   Larry Sherry strikes out seven of the nine batters to face him during three perfect innings to close out a 5–2 win over the Cubs in Chicago.

SEPTEMBER 4   Don Drysdale pitches a two-hitter to beat the Giants 4–0 at Memorial Coliseum. The only San Francisco hits were singles by Felipe Alou in the fourth inning and Ed Bailey in the seventh.

SEPTEMBER 6   The Dodgers pull within one game of the first-place Reds with a 9–5 win over the Giants at Memorial Coliseum.

SEPTEMBER 11   Gordie Windhorn's first major league homer is a walk-off, pinch-hit blast in the 11th inning that beats the Phillies 6–5 at Memorial Coliseum. It was struck off Don Ferrarese, who entered the game in the fourth inning and pitched seven shutout innings before the game-winning homer. Before stepping to the plate, Windhorn confidently told teammates he would hit the ball over the fence.

Windhorn hit two homers in a three-year big league career spanning 95 games and 108 at-bats.

SEPTEMBER 12   The Dodgers fall 4½ games behind with a 19–10 loss to the Phillies at Memorial Coliseum, virtually eliminating any chance for a pennant in 1961.

SEPTEMBER 14   The Dodgers score four runs in the ninth inning, the last three on a walk-off homer by Duke Snider, to beat the Phillies 7–6 at Memorial Coliseum.

SEPTEMBER 17   Duke Snider hits a two-run, walk-off single in the 11th inning to beat the Braves 4–3 at Memorial Coliseum. Gil Hodges played in his 2,000th career game.

SEPTEMBER 20   Sandy Koufax strikes out 15 batters in a 13-inning complete game and beats the Cubs 3–2 at Memorial Coliseum. Ron Fairly drove in the winning run with a single. It was also the last regular season game ever played at the Coliseum and the final baseball game at the facility until an exhibition game against the Red Sox on March 29, 2008.

SEPTEMBER 28   The Dodgers rout the Phillies 10–0 in Philadelphia.

OCTOBER 10   In the expansion draft, the Dodgers lose Dick Farrell, Norm Larker and Jim Golden to Houston and Roger Craig and Gil Hodges to the Mets.

OCTOBER 24   The Lakers play their first regular season game in Los Angeles and beat the Knicks 111–101 at the Sports Arena.

DECEMBER 15   The Dodgers send Charlie Neal to the Mets for Lee Walls and $100,000.

1962   L·A

Season in a Sentence

Dodger Stadium opens and Maury Wills steals 104 bases, but the club squanders a four-game lead with seven games left on the schedule before blowing a two-run, ninth-inning lead in the deciding playoff game against the Giants.

Finish • Won • Lost • Pct • GB

Second   102   63   .618   1.0

Manager

Walter Alston

Stats

Stats	Dods	NL	Rank
Batting Avg:	.268	.261	4
On-Base Pct:	.337	.327	2
Slugging Pct:	.400	.393	4
Home Runs:	140		5
Stolen Bases:	198		1
ERA:	3.62	3.94	3
Fielding Avg:	.970	.975	9
Runs Scored:	842		2
Runs Allowed:	697		6

Starting Lineup

Johnny Roseboro, c
Ron Fairly, 1b
Larry Burright, 2b
Jim Gilliam, 3b-2b
Maury Wills, ss
Tommy Davis, lf
Willie Davis, cf
Frank Howard, rf
Wally Moon, lf-rf

Pitchers

Don Drysdale, sp
Johnny Podres, sp
Stan Williams, sp
Sandy Koufax, sp
Joe Moeller, sp
Ron Perranoski, rp
Ed Roebuck, rp
Larry Sherry, rp

Attendance

2,755,184 (first in NL)

Club Leaders

Batting Avg:	Tommy Davis	.346
On-Base Pct:	Ron Fairly	.379
Slugging Pct:	Frank Howard	.560
Home Runs:	Frank Howard	31
RBIs:	Frank Howard	119
Runs:	Maury Wills	130
Stolen Bases:	Maury Wills	104
Wins:	Don Drysdale	25
Strikeouts:	Don Drysdale	232
ERA:	Sandy Koufax	2.54
Saves:	Ron Perranoski	20

JANUARY 23   Jackie Robinson is elected to the Hall of Fame in his first year on the ballot.

MARCH 24   Five weeks after John Glenn becomes the first American to orbit the earth, the Dodgers trade Ramon Conde and Jim Koranda to the Phillies for Andy Carey.

APRIL 2   The Dodgers play the Angels for the first time and lose 6–5 before a sellout crowd of 5,181 at Palm Springs, California, that includes former President Dwight Eisenhower.

The Dodgers and Angels met in Los Angeles for the first time in 1963.

APRIL 9   A six-hour dedication ceremony takes place at Dodger Stadium. A total of 2,500 paid five dollars to attend. The day included a parade of uniformed players through the streets of downtown.

APRIL 10   The Dodgers play their first game at Dodger Stadium and lose 6–3 to the Reds before 52,564. The crowd was about 4,000 shy of capacity because of a ticket foul-up and a predicted traffic jam that never happened. Kay O'Malley, wife of Walter, threw out the ceremonial first pitch. The first pitch in game action was thrown by Johnny Podres to Eddie Kasko, who doubled. Cincinnati's Wally Post struck the first home run. It was hit off Podres in the seventh inning with two men on base and the score 2–2. Bob Purkey was the winning pitcher. Among those in attendance was Dodger stockholder Dearie Mulvey. She is the only individual to attend both the opening of Dodger Stadium and the first game at Ebbets Field in 1913. Stephen McKeever, her father, helped finance the construction of Ebbets Field (see January 2, 1912).

The only privately financed stadium built for baseball between 1923 and 2000, Dodger Stadium was unique for its time with 50,000 seats in four multi-colored tiers (yellow, light orange, turquoise and sky blue) with another 6,000 in the outfield pavilions. It was the first major league stadium with "dugout boxes" which put the fans on the same level as the players with a ground-level view of the game. The outfield scoreboards at 75 feet by 34 feet, were the largest anywhere in 1962. The most unique features of Dodger Stadium were the terraced parking lots, the only one of their kind, which allowed fans to park at the same level as their seats. The setting added to the experience of attending a game at Dodger Stadium, which was nestled in the tree-lined Elysian Park hills. Gardeners planted 183 trees and 30 varieties of shrubs. To the north were views of the San Gabriel Mountains, and to the south, the skyline of downtown Los Angeles. There was also the chance at spotting a Hollywood star or two.

APRIL 11   The Dodgers play their first night game at Dodger Stadium, and beat the Reds 6–2. Sandy Koufax pitched the complete game victory. Jim Gilliam hit the first Dodger homer at the new stadium.

In their first season at Dodger Stadium, the club set a major league attendance record by drawing 2,755,184 fans. The Dodgers drew over a million more fans than any team in either league in 1962. The Giants were second with 1,592,594.

APRIL 12   In a sensational major league debut, Dodger pitcher Pete Richert strikes out the first six batters he faces and seven in 3⅓ innings of perfect relief during an 11–7 win over the Reds at Dodger Stadium. He entered the game with two out in the first inning and fanned Vada Pinson. Richert tied a major league record in the third by striking out four. After Frank Robinson struck out, Gordy Coleman reached on a passed ball by Johnny Roseboro on a swinging third strike. Richert then fanned Wally Post and Johnny Edwards to close out the third and Tommy Harper starting the fourth. Richert also became the winning pitcher when the Dodgers erased a 4–0 deficit by scoring seven runs in the fifth.

Richert was 22 at the time of his major league debut and finished his rookie season with a 5–4 record and a 3.87 ERA in 81⅓ innings. After three seasons of bouncing between the majors and minors, he was traded by the Dodgers to the Senators in December 1964.

APRIL 16   The Angels play their first game at Dodger Stadium, and lose 5–3 to the Kansas City Athletics before a crowd of 18,416.

After drawing 603,510 at Wrigley Field in 1961, the first season of their existence, the Angels attracted 1,144,063 as tenants of the Dodgers at Dodger Stadium in 1962.

APRIL 24   Sandy Koufax equals his club record by striking out 18 batters during a 10–2 win over the Cubs in Chicago. He started the game by fanning Lou Brock, Ken Hubbs and Ron Santo on 10 pitches in the first inning. Koufax struck out two more in the second, three in the third, two in the fourth, two in the fifth, two in the seventh, one in the eighth and three in the ninth. He walked four and gave up six hits. Koufax also struck out 18 on August 31, 1959.

MAY 1   The Dodgers score two runs in the 15th inning and one in the 16th to defeat the Cubs 6–5 at Dodger Stadium. In the 15th, Chicago scored twice for a 5–3 lead, but Wally Moon delivered a two-run single in the bottom half to tie. Jim Gilliam was the third out in an attempted steal of home. Doug Camilli, who entered the contest as a catcher in the top of the 16th, drove in the winning run with a walk-off single.

Doug was the son of Dolph Camilli, who played for the Dodgers from 1938 through 1943.

MAY 7   The Dodgers play in Houston for the first time, and lose 9–6 to the Colts at Colt Stadium.

During the first three years of its existence, the Houston franchise was officially known as the Colt .45s, and informally as the Colts. The nickname was changed to Astros in 1965. The club played for three years at Colt Stadium, a temporary facility built in what would become the parking lot of the Astrodome, baseball's first indoor stadium, which opened in 1965.

MAY 12   The Dodgers tie a major league record by using four left fielders during a 15-inning, 6–5 loss to the Cardinals in St. Louis. Tommy Davis started the game in left, and was followed by Wally Moon, Jim Gilliam and Frank Howard.

MAY 15   The Houston Colts play at Dodger Stadium for the first time, and lose 10–7 to the Dodgers.

The original design for Dodger Stadium had a huge fountain in center field similar to the one at Kauffman Stadium in Kansas City. Oddly, during the first season at Dodger Stadium, fans couldn't get a drink of water because the ballpark had no water fountains.

MAY 17   The Dodgers come roaring from behind with four runs in the ninth inning and one in the 10th to beat the Colts 5–4 at Dodgers Stadium. Houston hurler Jim Golden, an ex-Dodger, allowed only two hits in the first eight innings. Wally Moon doubled in the first two runs and scored on a single by Tommy Davis, who stole second and crossed the plate on Ron Fairly's single. In the 10th, Moon delivered a bases-loaded single.

MAY 21   The Dodgers play the Giants for the first time at Dodger Stadium, and win 8–1.

When the foul poles were installed at Dodger Stadium in 1962, it was discovered that they had been positioned completely in foul territory. Special dispensation was received from the league to allow them to remain in place for one year, but before the next season, home plate had to be moved so the poles would be in fair territory.

MAY 24   The Dodgers play the Mets for the first time at Dodger Stadium and win 4–2.

MAY 25   With the help of six-run innings in the third and the sixth, the Dodgers wallop the Mets 17–8 at Dodger Stadium.

The Dodgers were 16–2 against the Mets in 1962. The expansion club posted a record of 40–120 that season to set a modern major league record for defeats in a season.

MAY 26   Sandy Koufax strikes out 16 batters to beat the Phillies 6–3 at Dodger Stadium.

Capacity at Dodger Stadium has been fixed at 56,000 since 1962. Every time seats have been added, an equal number has been removed in the outfield pavilions or the fourth deck because of the original permit for the park, which specifies a limit of 56,000 seats.

MAY 30   The Dodgers play the Mets for the first time in New York and win 13–6 and 6–5 at the Polo Grounds. It was the first regular season appearance by the Dodgers in New York City since 1957. The twin bill drew a crowd of 55,704, which rooted for the Mets but gave appreciative applause to former Brooklyn players still with the Dodgers, including Duke Snider, Jim Gilliam, Johnny Podres, Sandy Koufax, Ed Roebuck and Johnny Roseboro. The two victories extended the Dodgers winning streak to 10 games. In the opener, Maury Wills homered from both sides of the plate. Batting left-handed, Wills hit an inside-the-park homer off Dave Hillman in the fifth inning, then drove a pitch into the seats from the right side facing Vinegar Bend Mizell in the ninth. It was the only multi-homer game during Wills's 14-year career. He hit only 20 in 7,588 lifetime at-bats.

The Polo Grounds was the home of the Mets in 1962 and 1963 before the club moved into Shea Stadium.

JUNE 1   The Dodgers extend their winning streak to 13 games with 11–4 and 8–5 victories over the Phillies in a double-header in Philadelphia.

JUNE 4   Sandy Koufax strikes out 13 batters during a 6–3 win over the Phillies in Philadelphia.

JUNE 7   Larry Sherry enters the game against the Pirates in Pittsburgh with two men on base and the Dodgers leading 2–0, and promptly gives up a three-run homer to Dick Stuart, resulting in a 3–2 defeat.

JUNE 10   The Dodgers tie a major league record by using four right fielders during a 9–3 win in the first game of a double-header against the Colts in Houston. Wally Moon started, and was followed by Frank Howard, Ron Fairly and Lee Walls. The Dodgers also won game two 9–7.

JUNE 18   A walk-off homer by Tommy Davis off Bob Gibson in the ninth inning lifts the Dodgers to a 1–0 win over the Cardinals at Dodger Stadium. Sandy Koufax pitched the shutout.

It was obvious in the first year that Dodger Stadium was going to favor the pitchers. The original dimensions were 330 feet down each foul line, 380 feet to the power alleys, and 410 feet to center. In 1962, there were 698 runs scored by both clubs in 83 Dodgers home games, and 841 in 82 road contests.

JUNE 23   Tommy Davis drives in five runs on four hits, including a triple, during a 14–3 win over the Reds at Dodger Stadium.

JUNE 25   Tommy Davis collects five hits, including a double, in five at-bats during a 6–4 loss to the Braves at Dodgers Stadium.

Davis picked up 11 hits in 14 at-bats over three games from June 23 through June 25. In 1962, he had one of the best seasons in Dodger history by leading the National League in batting (.346), hits (230) and runs batted in (153) along with 27 homers and 120 runs scored. The RBI total is the all-time Dodger record. Roy Campanella is second with 142 in 1953. Since 1962, the closest anyone has come to Davis's RBI mark is Shawn Green, who had 125 in 2001. Tommy's 230 hits are second all-time to Babe Herman's 241 in 1930.

JUNE 26   Sandy Koufax strikes out 13 batters in eight innings, but the Dodgers lose 2–1 to the Braves at Dodger Stadium.

JUNE 29   Four Dodger pitchers combine to walk 16 batters, seven of them in the first inning, during a 10–4 loss to the Mets at Dodger Stadium. New York scored their 10 runs on only four hits. The walks were by Joe Moeller (four in one-third of an inning), Ron Perranoski (three in one-third of an inning), Phil Ortega (one in 3⅓ innings) and Stan Williams (eight in five innings).

Moeller is the youngest pitcher to start a game since the move to Los Angeles. He was only two months past his 19th birthday when the 1962 season began, and was hailed as the next Sandy Koufax. Those projections fell a bit shy of the mark, as Moeller was 26–36 during an eight-year big league career.

JUNE 30   Sandy Koufax pitches a no-hitter to beat the Mets 5–0 at Dodger Stadium. He walked five, struck out 13 and threw 138 pitches. Koufax began the game by fanning Richie Ashburn, Rod Kanehl and Frank Thomas in the first inning on nine pitches. Koufax started the ninth by walking Gene Woodling. Richie Ashburn bounced into a force play, which went from shortstop Maury Wills to second baseman Larry Burright. Rod Kanehl hit into another force, third baseman Jim Gilliam to Burright. Felix Mantilla became the third straight batter to hit into a force, grounding to Wills who flipped to Burright for the final out. It was the first of Koufax's four career no-hitters.

The no-hitter was the second at Dodger Stadium before the ballpark was three months old. The first was by Bo Belinsky for the Angels against the Orioles on May 5.

JULY 1   Don Drysdale strikes out 13 batters during a 5–1 win over the Mets at Dodger
               Stadium.

               *Drysdale won the Cy Young Award in 1962 by leading the NL in wins (with
               a 25–9 record), strikeouts (232), innings (314$\frac{1}{3}$) and games started (41) along
               with 19 complete games and a 2.83 ERA.*

JULY 2   Johnny Podres strikes out eight batters in a row, and 11 in all in 7$\frac{2}{3}$ innings, during
               a 5–1 triumph over the Phillies in the first game of a double-header in Philadelphia.
               From the fourth through the seventh, Podres fanned Ted Savage, Roy Sievers,
               Don Demeter, Tony Gonzalez, Bob Oldis, Jack Hamilton and Mel Roach.
               Willie Davis hit a grand slam off Hamilton in the fourth.

JULY 4   The Dodgers score seven runs in the fourth inning and clobber the Phillies 16–1
               in the first game of a double-header in Philadelphia. Despite the huge lead, Sandy
               Koufax pitched the complete game and made 150 pitches on three days' rest in his
               first start since his no-hitter. The Dodgers also took the second tilt 7–3.

JULY 8   The Dodgers take first place with a 2–0 win over the Giants in San Francisco.
               Sandy Koufax pitched the first 8$\frac{1}{3}$ innings, and Don Drysdale retired the final
               two hitters for the save.

               *The Dodgers retained sole possession of first place until the final day of the
               regular season.*

JULY 10   On the day Telstar is launched as the world's first communications satellite,
               Don Drysdale starts the first of two All-Star Games in 1962, and pitches three
               shutout innings with three strikeouts to lead the National League to a 3–1 win
               at D. C. Stadium in Washington.

JULY 14   The Dodgers score eight runs in the second inning and win 17–3 over the Mets in
               New York.

               *Before the game, the Mets staged an Old-Timers Game in which Ralph Branca
               faced Bobby Thomson for the first time since Thomson's pennant-winning home
               run 11 years earlier (see October 3, 1951). Thomson flied out to center field.*

JULY 17   Sandy Koufax is taken out of the game after one inning of a 7–5 loss to the Reds in
               Cincinnati because of numbness of his pitching hand.

               *The ailment was diagnosed as a circulatory problem and he was placed on the
               disabled list. At the time, he had a 14–5 record. Koufax was sidelined until late
               September and never won another game that season.*

JULY 18   The Dodgers score two runs in the ninth inning and three in the 11th for a 6–3 lead,
               then withstand a two-run Reds rally to win 6–5 in Cincinnati. Frank Howard hit a
               two-run homer in the ninth and a run-scoring single in the 11th.

               Howard hit 31 homers, drove in 119 runs, and hit .296 in 1962.

JULY 22 — The Dodgers win 13–6 over the Cubs in a contest in Chicago called after 6½ innings by rain.

JULY 30 — Johnny Podres starts the second of two All-Star Games played in 1962, and pitches two shutout innings, but the National League loses 9–4 at Wrigley Field in Chicago.

AUGUST 3 — Don Drysdale wins his 20th game of the season with an 8–3 decision over the Cubs at Dodgers Stadium.

AUGUST 5 — Tommy Davis hits a walk-off single in the 14th inning that beats the Cubs 4–3 in the first game of a double-header at Dodger Stadium. Chicago won the second tilt 4–2.

AUGUST 7 — The day after Marilyn Monroe is found dead at her home in Los Angeles, Don Drysdale extends his winning streak to 11 games and his won-lost record to 21–4 with a 7–5 decision over the Mets at Dodger Stadium.

AUGUST 9 — The Dodgers take a 5½-game lead over the Giants in the NL pennant race after beating the Phillies 8–3 at Dodger Stadium.

The win gave the Dodgers a 79–37 record. The club was swept by the Giants in three games in San Francisco from August 10 through 12 to reduce the margin to 2½ games. There was considerable controversy during the series at Candlestick Park as the Dodgers claimed the infield was intentionally soaked to handicap Maury Wills's base running. He was ejected from one of the contests after complaining about the conditions. Wills won the NL MVP award in 1962 by stealing a then-major league record 104 bases along with 130 runs, 208 hits, a .299 batting average, and a league-leading 10 triples. The 130 runs is a club record. The previous big league mark for steals in a season was 96 by Ty Cobb in 1915. As a team, the Dodgers stole 198 bases, the most by any club since the 1918 Pirates. During the 1950s, the stolen base was seldom used as an offensive weapon. In 1953, the 16 big league clubs combined for 668 steals, an average of 42 per club. From 1946 through 1961, only four teams stole as many as 104 bases in a season. From 1921 through 1961, no individual stole more than 61 bases in a single year. The stolen base record accomplished by Wills in 1962 helped transform baseball to a more speed-oriented game. By 1969, teams averaged 77 stolen bases. In 1976, that figure reached 127 and came two years after Lou Brock broke Wills's single season record by swiping 119. Rickey Henderson passed Brock with 130 in 1982.

AUGUST 19 — The Dodgers score five runs in the ninth inning to beat the Reds 5–1 in Cincinnati. Willie Davis hit a fluke inside-the-park homer during the rally. On a hit-and-run play, the ball bounced in front of first base, eluded Gordy Coleman, bounced off the railing in front of the right field bullpen, shot past Frank Robinson, and rolled to the bleacher fence.

AUGUST 20 — With the temperature in Cincinnati at 102 degrees, the Dodgers lose 7–3 to the Reds on a walk-off grand slam by Frank Robinson off Larry Sherry in the 10th inning.

AUGUST 24 — Dodger coach Leo Durocher suffers a near-fatal allergic reaction to a penicillin injection while in the clubhouse prior to a 6–3 loss to the Mets in New York.

An emergency intravenous injection of adrenaline saved his life. It was administered by a doctor summoned from the crowd after a public address announcement.

AUGUST 26   The Dodgers score seven runs in the sixth inning and beat the Mets 16–5 in New York.

AUGUST 29   The Dodgers score a run in the ninth inning and another in the 13th for a 2–1 win over the Reds at Dodger Stadium. With two out in the ninth, Frank Howard singled and Duke Snider smacked a triple. In the 13th, Johnny Roseboro delivered a game-winning single.

SEPTEMBER 7   Maury Wills steals four bases, but the Dodgers lose 10–1 to the Pirates at Dodger Stadium.

SEPTEMBER 10   Tommy Davis hits a grand slam off Dick Ellsworth in the third inning of an 8–1 win over the Cubs at Dodger Stadium.

SEPTEMBER 12   Frank Howard's home run off Ken Johnson in the fifth inning lifts the Dodgers to a 1–0 victory over the Colts in Houston. Pete Richert (three innings), Ed Roebuck (5⅓ innings) and Ron Perranoski (two-thirds of an inning) combined on the shutout. Ed Roebuck was the winning pitcher, giving him a 10–0 record on the season.

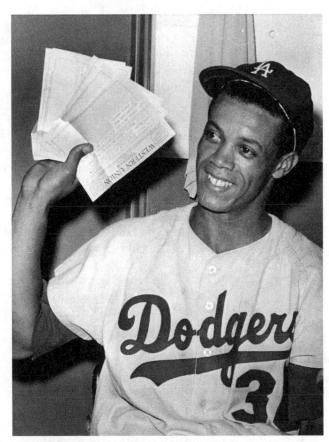

Maury Wills epitomizes the team's shift from power to speed, stealing an amazing 104 bases in 1962.

Roebuck finished the season with a 10–2 record after losing two key games during the final week, including the contest that decided the National League pennant (see October 3, 1962).

SEPTEMBER 14   The Dodgers score seven runs in the first inning and beat the Cubs 13–7 in Chicago.

SEPTEMBER 15   The Dodgers score two runs in the ninth inning to defeat 6–4 in Chicago. With the score 4–4 and two out, Tommy Davis stole home at the end of a triple steal. Tom Harkness took third base and Johnny Roseboro second on the play. Harkness then scored on pitcher Glen Hobbie's wild throw trying to nab Davis.

SEPTEMBER 19   Don Drysdale records his 25th victory with a 4–0 win over the Braves in Milwaukee.

SEPTEMBER 21   Sandy Koufax pitches his first game since July 17, but lasts only two-thirds of an inning and allows four runs in an 11–2 loss to the Cardinals in St. Louis. Koufax walked the bases loaded, then gave up a grand slam to Charlie James.

SEPTEMBER 22   The Dodgers defeat the Cardinals 4–1 in St. Louis. It was the club's 100th win of the season. The victory gave Los Angeles a four-game lead over the Giants with seven contests left on the schedule.

SEPTEMBER 23   Maury Wills ties and breaks Ty Cobb's record for stolen bases in a season by swiping his 96th and 97th but the Dodgers lost 12–2 to the Cardinals in St. Louis.

SEPTEMBER 26   The Dodgers wallop Houston 13–1 at Dodger Stadium. Maury Wills stole his 100th base of the 1962 season. The win gave the Dodgers a two-game lead with four games remaining.

SEPTEMBER 27   The Dodgers lose 8–6 to Houston at Dodger Stadium, but the Giants also lose. Los Angeles maintained a two-game lead with only three contests left to play.

SEPTEMBER 28   The Dodgers drop a 3–2 decision to the Cardinals in 10 innings at Dodger Stadium. The Giants game against Houston in San Francisco was postponed by rain. With two days left in the season, the Dodgers led by a game and a half.

SEPTEMBER 29   The Dodgers lose 2–0 to the Cardinals at Dodgers Stadium. Ernie Broglio hurled a two-hitter for St. Louis. The Giants split a double-header with Houston in San Francisco winning 11–5 and losing 4–2. The Dodgers led by one game heading into the final day of the regular season.

SEPTEMBER 30   The Dodgers and Giants end the regular season in a tie for first place, forcing a best-of-three playoff to decide the pennant. The Giants beat Houston 2–1 in San Francisco with Willie Mays breaking a 1–1 tie on a home run in the eighth inning. The slumping Dodgers lost 1–0 to the Cardinals at Dodger Stadium. The lone run scored on an eighth-inning homer by Gene Oliver off Johnny Podres. Curt Simmons pitched the shutout. St. Louis pitching held the Dodgers to two runs in the three-game series, including the back-to-back shutouts in the final two. The Dodgers squandered a four-game lead with seven games left on the schedule by losing six of the seven.

OCTOBER 1   The Dodgers open the playoff series with an 8–0 loss to the Giants before 32,652 at Candlestick Park in San Francisco. It was the third game in a row in which the Dodgers were held without a run. Billy Pierce hurled the shutout. Sandy Koufax was the starting pitcher, and was removed after facing two batters in the second inning with the Dodgers trailing 3–0. Willie Mays hit two homers.

OCTOBER 2   The Dodgers even the playoff series with an 8–7 win over the Giants before a disappointing crowd of only 25,321 at Dodger Stadium. The Giants scored four runs in the top of the sixth for a 5–0 lead before the Dodgers broke out of their batting slump in a big way with seven tallies in their half. Prior to the seven-run explosion, the Dodgers had been held scoreless for 35 consecutive innings. Pinch-hitter Lee Walls put Los Angeles into the lead with a three-run double. The Giants tied the score, however, with a two-run eighth. The game was won in the ninth on three walks and a sacrifice fly by Ron Fairly. The game lasted four hours and 18 minutes.

*Duke Snider and Willie Mays both played in the 1951 and 1962 playoffs
between the Dodgers and Giants. Leo Durocher managed the Giants in 1951
and was a coach for the Dodgers in 1962. Al Dark played for the Giants in 1951
and managed the club in 1962.*

OCTOBER 3   Three outs from a berth in the World Series, the Dodgers blow a two-run lead in the
ninth inning and lose the deciding third game of the playoff series 6–4 to the Giants
before 45,693 at Dodger Stadium. Johnny Podres started on two days' rest for the
first time in his career, and allowed two unearned runs in the third inning because of
three errors by his jittery teammates to give San Francisco a 2–0 lead. The Dodgers
responded with a run in the fourth, a two-run homer by Tommy Davis in the sixth
for a 3–2 lead, and another tally in the seventh. Ed Roebuck entered the game in relief
in the sixth inning with the bases loaded and none out, and induced a force out at
home plate and a double play. After a scoreless seventh and eighth, Roebuck was still
on the mound for the Dodgers at the start of the ninth. It was his sixth appearance in
the last seven games. Roebuck loaded the bases on a single and two walks with one
out. Willie Mays hit a rocket off Roebuck's hand for an infield hit, which scored a
run. Stan Williams came in from the bullpen and gave up a sacrifice fly to Orlando
Cepeda to tie the score. After a wild pitch put runners on second and third, Williams
walked Ed Bailey intentionally and Jim Davenport unintentionally to give the Giants
a 5–4 advantage. An insurance run crossed the plate on an error by second baseman
Larry Burright. Billy Pierce retired the Dodgers in order in the bottom of the ninth.
The Giants went on to lose the World Series in seven games to the Yankees.

*Alston was criticized heavily for sticking with Roebuck in the ninth and for
replacing him with Williams instead of Ron Perranoski or Don Drysdale.
Roebuck entered the ninth with a streak of 8^1/$_3$ consecutive scoreless innings over
four appearances, including three in the deciding playoff game. Perranoski was
the Dodgers top reliever, but was a left-hander and the meat of the Giants order
(Felipe Alou, Mays and Cepeda) was right-handed hitters. Drysdale pitched
5^1/$_3$ innings the day before on only two days' rest, and allowed five runs and
seven hits. There was considerable speculation that Leo Durocher would replace
Alston as manager because of the meltdown during the pennant race, but Walter
retained his job.*

NOVEMBER 26   A month after America's nerves are frazzled by the Cuban missile crisis, the Dodgers
trade Stan Williams to the Yankees for Bill Skowron.

*An All-Star five consecutive seasons from 1957 through 1961, Skowron was
supposed to fulfill the Dodgers need for a power-hitting first baseman, but he
completely flopped in Los Angeles with a .203 batting average and four homers
in 59 games in 1963 before being sold to the Senators. Williams was still an
effective pitcher in the majors as late as 1970.*

NOVEMBER 30   The Dodgers trade Larry Burright and Tim Harkness to the Mets for Bob Miller.

*Miller was 1–12 for the woeful Mets in 1962. Converted to a reliever, he played
on three NL champions in Los Angeles.*

1963

LA

Season in a Sentence

Sandy Koufax wins 25 games to lead the Dodgers to a National League title before sweeping the Yankees in the World Series to wipe out the horrible memories of 1962.

Finish • Won • Lost • Pct • GB

First   99   63   .611   +6.0

World Series

The Dodgers defeated the New York Yankees four games to none.

Manager

Walter Alston

Stats

Stats	Dods	NL	Rank
Batting Avg:	.251	.245	4
On-Base Pct:	.309	.306	5
Slugging Pct:	.357	.364	8
Home Runs:	110		7
Stolen Bases:	124		1
ERA:	2.85	3.29	1
Fielding Avg:	.975	.975	6
Runs Scored:	640		6
Runs Allowed:	550		1

Starting Lineup

Johnny Roseboro, c
Ron Fairly, 1b
Jim Gilliam, 2b-3b
Ken McMullen, 3b
Maury Wills, ss
Tommy Davis, lf
Willie Davis, cf
Frank Howard, rf
Wally Moon, rf-lf
Bill Skowron, 1b
Dick Tracewski, ss

Pitchers

Sandy Koufax, sp
Don Drysdale, sp
Johnny Podres, sp
Bob Miller, sp
Ron Perranoski, rp

Attendance

2,538,602 (first in NL)

Club Leaders

Batting Avg:	Tommy Davis	.326
On-Base Pct:	Tommy Davis	.359
Slugging Pct:	Frank Howard	.518
Home Runs:	Frank Howard	28
RBIs:	Tommy Davis	88
Runs:	Maury Wills	83
Stolen Bases:	Maury Wills	40
Wins:	Sandy Koufax	25
Strikeouts:	Sandy Koufax	306
ERA:	Sandy Koufax	2.88
Saves:	Ron Perranoski	21

JANUARY 24   The Dodgers trade Scott Breeden to the Reds for Don Zimmer.

APRIL 1   The Dodgers sell Duke Snider to the Mets.

                Snider played 16 seasons with the Dodgers and was 36 at the time he was sold to the Mets. He spent one season in New York and one with the Giants before retiring as a player.

APRIL 9   The Dodgers open the season with a 5–1 win over the Cubs in Chicago. Don Drysdale pitched the shutout.

APRIL 16   The Dodgers lose the home opener 2–1 in 12 innings to the Cubs before 33,758 at Dodger Stadium.

The Dodgers drew an attendance figure of 2,538,602 in 1963 to lead the majors. The Giants were second with 1,571,306.

APRIL 17   The Dodgers edge the Cubs in 10 innings at Dodger Stadium. Bill Skowron drove in the winning run with a single. Bob Miller (nine innings) and Ron Perranoski (one inning) combined on the three-hit shutout.

Miller pitched shutout ball over his first 21 innings as a member of the Dodgers.

APRIL 19   Sandy Koufax strikes out 14 batters and pitches a two-hitter to defeat Houston 2–0 at Dodger Stadium. The only hits off Koufax were singles by Johnny Temple in the first inning and Pete Runnels in the third. Frank Howard provided the offense with a two-run homer off Dick Farrell in the seventh inning. It was the first home run for the Dodgers in 1963. The club was homerless in the first eight games.

Koufax won both the MVP and Cy Young Awards in 1963. He led the NL in wins (with a 25–5 record), shutouts (11), ERA (1.88), strikeouts (306) and lowest opponent's batting average (.197) in addition to 311 innings, 20 complete games. The 11 shutouts comprise a Dodger club record.

MAY 2   A two-run homer by Ron Fairly in the ninth inning beats the Phillies 3–2 in Philadelphia.

MAY 6   The Dodgers lose 7–4 to the Pirates in Pittsburgh to drop the club's record to 12–15.

The players still held a lingering resentment of Walter Alston over the late-season collapse the previous season, and had frequently showed open disrespect toward their manager. On the way to the airport after the loss to the Pirates, several players griped about the condition of the bus. Alston told the driver to pull over and then challenged the whole team, stating emphatically that anyone who wanted to take a shot at him could "get off and come outside." Then Alston climbed down and waited. No one moved. The Dodgers had an 87–48 record over the remainder of the regular season before winning the World Series.

MAY 7   The Dodgers cruise to an 11–1 win over the Cardinals in St. Louis.

MAY 11   Sandy Koufax pitches his second career no-hitter, beating the Giants 8–0 at Dodger Stadium. He retired the first 22 batters he faced. With one down in the eighth, Koufax walked Ed Bailey before Jim Davenport grounded into a double play. In the San Francisco ninth, Koufax began by retiring Joe Amalfitano on a pop fly to first baseman Ron Fairly. Jose Pagan cracked a liner to deep center, caught by Willie Davis. After walking Willie McCovey on four pitches, Koufax faced Harvey Kuenn and recorded the final out on an easy tapper back to the mound. The two walks accompanied four strikeouts, an unusually low total for Koufax. During the 1963 season, he fanned 8.9 batters per nine innings. In all, Koufax made 112 pitches to catcher Johnny Roseboro, who also caught his 1962 no-hitter.

MAY 15   In his first start since his no-hitter, Sandy Koufax strikes out 12 batters in a 12-inning complete game to defeat the Phillies 3–2 at Dodger Stadium. Ron Fairly drove in the winning run with a single.

MAY 16 — A two-out, two-run single by Johnny Roseboro in the ninth inning beats the Pirates 1–0 at Dodger Stadium. Johnny Podres pitched the shutout.

MAY 19 — The Dodgers sweep the Mets 1–0 and 4–2 in a double-header against the Mets at Dodger Stadium. Sandy Koufax pitched a two-hitter in the opener, allowing only singles to Ron Hunt in the fourth inning and opposing pitcher Roger Craig in the sixth. The second game was won on a two-out, walk-off homer by Frank Howard in the 13th.

May 22 — The Dodgers extend their winning streak to eight games on a two-hitter by Don Drysdale, defeating the Mets 7–3 at Dodger Stadium. The only New York hits were home runs by former Dodgers Duke Snider in the second inning and Tim Harkness in the seventh.

MAY 29 — Heavy fog forces the umpires to call a Dodgers-Braves clash in Milwaukee with the score 3–3 in the bottom of the seventh.

JUNE 3 — Don Drysdale strikes out 13 batters in seven innings, but the Dodgers lose 2–1 to the Colts in Houston. The two runs off Drysdale scored in the fourth inning on Rusty Staub's first major league homer.

> *Drysdale had a 19–17 record with a 2.63 ERA and 251 strikeouts in 315$^{1}/_{3}$ innings in 1963.*

JUNE 9 — The Dodgers survive three homers by Ernie Banks to beat the Cubs 11–8 in Chicago.

JUNE 16 — Five days after the University of Alabama is integrated by federal troops over the objections of Governor George Wallace, Nick Willhite pitches a five-hit shutout in his major league debut to beat the Cubs 2–0 in the first game of a double-header at Dodger Stadium. Chicago won the opener 8–3.

> *Willhite pitched three seasons with the Dodgers and had a 6–9 record and a 4.29 ERA in 123$^{2}/_{3}$ innings. He never pitched another big league shutout before his career ended in 1967.*

JUNE 24 — The Dodgers sell Don Zimmer to the Senators.

JULY 1 — Johnny Podres strikes out 12 batters during a 2–1 victory over the Braves at Dodger Stadium. In the ninth inning, Maury Wills singled, stole second and crossed the plate on a single by Wally Moon.

> *After stealing 104 bases in 1962, Wills swiped 40 in 1963, but it was still good enough to lead the National League. He also batted .302.*

JULY 2 — The Dodgers take first place with a 1–0 win over the Cardinals at Dodger Stadium. Don Drysdale pitched the shutout. Ron Fairly drove in the lone run with a single in the seventh inning.

> *The Dodgers remained in first for the rest of the season.*

JULY 3	Sandy Koufax pitches a three-hit shutout to defeat the Cardinals 5–0 at Dodger Stadium.

Koufax pitched 22 consecutive scoreless innings from July 3 through July 16.

JULY 4   Trailing 4–2, the Dodgers score eight runs in the sixth inning and beat the Cardinals 10–7 at Dodger Stadium. Ken McMullen hit a grand slam off Ernie Broglio.

Despite spending most of the season in first place, the Dodgers had a revolving door at third with four players appearing in at least 30 games. McMullen played 71 contests at the hot corner, Jim Gilliam 55, Tommy Davis 40 and Maury Wills 33.

JULY 5   Johnny Podres pitches a two-hitter to beat the Reds 1–0 at Dodger Stadium. The only Cincinnati hits were singles by Tommy Harper in the fourth inning and Johnny Edwards in the sixth. The lone run scored on a home run by Frank Howard off Jim O'Toole in the seventh inning.

JULY 7   Sandy Koufax pitches his second straight shutout with a three-hitter to beat the Reds 4–0 in the first game of a double-header at Dodger Stadium. The Dodgers completed the sweep with the a 3–1 triumph in the second tilt.

JULY 9   At Municipal Stadium in Cleveland, Don Drysdale pitches shutout baseball in the eighth and ninth innings of the All-Star Game to save a 5–3 victory for the National League.

JULY 10   Johnny Podres pitches a three-hitter and strikes out 11 to defeat the Mets 1–0 in New York. The lone run scored on a home run by Johnny Roseboro off Carlton Willey. It was the second 1–0 victory won by Podres in consecutive starts with the winning run accounted for with a home run.

JULY 12   Sandy Koufax strikes out 13 batters and pitches a three-hitter to defeat the Mets 6–0 in New York. It was his third consecutive shutout and each was a three-hitter. Koufax recorded 33 consecutive scoreless innings from July 3 through July 16.

JULY 21   Ron Fairly hits a grand slam off Hank Fischer in the third inning, but the Dodgers lose 13–7 in the second game of a double-header against the Braves in Milwaukee. Los Angeles also lost the opener 7–5.

JULY 25   Sandy Koufax strikes out 12 batters in six innings, but allows four runs and the Dodgers lose 6–2 to the Pirates at Dodger Stadium.

JULY 30   Mets manager Casey Stengel is presented with a cake by Dodger management on his 73rd birthday. Then his club beats the home team 5–1. The win ended the Mets 22-game road losing streak, a modern major league record.

On the same day, the Dodgers traded Ed Roebuck to the Senators for Marv Breeding.

AUGUST 4 Johnny Podres narrowly misses a no-hitter during a 4–0 win over the Colts in Houston. The only hit off Podres was a single by Johnny Temple leading off the ninth inning. After hitting Bob Aspromonte with a pitch, Podres was relieved by Larry Sherry, who set down the last three hitters. It was also the first time in Dodger history that the club played a scheduled game on a Sunday night.

AUGUST 7   The Dodgers outlast the Cubs 3–1 in 11 innings in Chicago. Both teams scored in the 10th. Tommy Davis broke a 1–1 tie with a home run on the first pitch of the 11th before the Dodgers added an insurance run.

Davis won the National League batting title for the second consecutive season with an average of .326.

AUGUST 8   Frank Howard and Bill Skowron hit back-to-back pinch-hit home runs in the fifth, but the Dodgers lose 5–4 to the Cubs in 10 innings in Chicago.

AUGUST 10   Don Drysdale strikes out 13 batters during a 10–3 win over the Reds in Cincinnati.

AUGUST 18   The Dodgers play at the Polo Grounds for the last time, and win 7–0 and 3–2 over the Mets in a double-header.

The Mets moved into Shea Stadium in 1964.

AUGUST 21   The Dodgers take a 7½-game lead in the pennant race with a 2–1 triumph in 16 innings over the Cardinals at Dodger Stadium. Sandy Koufax (12 innings), Ron Perranoski (two innings) and Larry Sherry (two innings) pitched for the Dodgers. The winning run scored on a double by Ken McMullen and a single from Johnny Roseboro.

Perranoski had a 16–3 record, 21 saves and a 1.67 ERA in 69 relief appearances and 129 innings in 1963.

AUGUST 29   The day after Martin Luther King, Jr.'s "I Have a Dream" speech in Washington, Sandy Koufax wins his 20th game of the season with an 11–1 decision over the Giants at Dodger Stadium.

SEPTEMBER 2   Sandy Koufax strikes out 13 batters during a 7–3 win over Houston at Dodger Stadium.

SEPTEMBER 12   Johnny Roseboro drives in all five Los Angeles runs during a 5–3 win over the Pirates in Pittsburgh. The Dodger catcher hit a grand slam in the first inning and an RBI-single in the third, both off Bob Friend.

SEPTEMBER 15   The Dodgers lead over the Cardinals in the National League pennant race drops to one game after a 6–1 loss to the Phillies in Philadelphia.

The Cardinals closed the gap by winning 19 games in a 20-game span. The Dodgers and Cards met in a pennant-showdown series in St. Louis on September 16, 17 and 18.

SEPTEMBER 16   The Dodgers win the first game of the series against the Cardinals 3–1 in St. Louis. Los Angeles broke a 1–1 tie with two runs in the eighth. Johnny Podres pitched a three-hitter.

SEPTEMBER 17   The Dodgers extend their lead in the NL pennant race to three games with a 4–0 win over the Cardinals in St. Louis. Sandy Koufax pitched a four-hitter for his 11th shutout of the season.

SEPTEMBER 18   The Dodgers complete the sweep of the Cardinals with a 13-inning, 6–5 victory in St. Louis. The win gave Los Angeles a four-game lead. The Dodgers trailed 5–1 before scoring three runs in the eighth and one in the ninth. In the eighth, Tommy Davis drove in two runs with a single and Willie Davis put Los Angeles within a run with a sacrifice fly. With one out in the ninth inning, Dick Nen stepped to the plate in the second at-bat of his big league debut. He entered the contest in the eighth as a pinch-hitter and remained as a first baseman. Facing Ron Taylor, Nen ripped a home run to tie the score. In the 13th, Willie Davis singled, took third on an error, and scored on a Maury Wills ground out. Ron Perranoski pitched six shutout innings for his 16th victory of the season, all which were in relief.

In 1962 and 1963, few players in baseball could match Tommy Davis at the plate. He led the National League in hitting both years. Though he never reached that pinnacle again, he remained a dependable hitter throughout his 18-year career.

The day before, Nen played for the Dodgers Spokane farm club in Oklahoma City in the Pacific Coast League playoffs. The game-tying home run proved to be Nen's only hit in seven games and eight at-bats as a member of the Dodgers. After spending the entire 1964 season in the minors, Nen was traded to the Senators. He finished his big league career in 1970 with 21 homers and a .224 batting average in 367 games and 826 at-bats.

SEPTEMBER 21   A three-run walk-off homer in the ninth inning by Willie Davis beats the Pirates 5–3 at Dodger Stadium.

SEPTEMBER 24   After clinching the pennant during the afternoon when the Cardinals lose 6–3 to the Cubs in Chicago, the Dodgers polish off the Mets 4–1 in a night game at Dodger Stadium.

The Dodgers scored 640 runs in 1963, the sixth best in the National League. The club allowed 550 runs, the fewest in the NL. But Dodger Stadium, an extreme pitcher's park, caused the discrepancy between the success of the pitching staff and the mediocrity of the batting attack. In fact, away from Los Angeles, the hitters were better than the pitchers. In road games, in which the Dodgers posted a league-best 46–35 record, the club scored the second most runs in the league (344) and were sixth in runs allowed (302). At home the Dodgers were seventh in runs scored (296) and first in runs allowed (248).

SEPTEMBER 25   Sandy Koufax records his 25th win of the season with a 1–0 decision over the Mets at Dodger Stadium. In preparation for the World Series, he pitched only five innings. Bob Miller (three innings) and Ron Perranoski (one inning) completed the shutout.

The Dodgers met the Yankees in the World Series. Managed by Ralph Houk, the Yanks were 104–57 in 1963. It was the eighth Fall Classic between the Dodgers and Yankees, but the first that involved a coast-to-coast flight. The previous seven in 1941, 1947, 1949, 1952, 1953, 1955 and 1956, were played within the boroughs of New York City. It was also the first World Series to be played at Dodger Stadium.

OCTOBER 2   In the opening game of the 1963 World Series, Sandy Koufax strikes out 15 batters to beat the Yankees 5–2 in New York. Koufax fanned the first five batters he faced, setting down Tony Kubek, Bobby Richardson, Tom Tresh, Mickey Mantle and Roger Maris. He retired the first 14 batters to face him, 10 of them on strikeouts. Tresh hit a two-run homer in the eighth to prevent the shutout. The Dodgers scored three runs in the second inning. The inning started with a 460-foot double by Frank Howard off the left-center field fence in a portion of Yankee Stadium known as "Death Valley" for its deep dimensions. The scoring ended on a homer by Johnny Roseboro facing Whitey Ford, who had a 24–7 record in 1963. Tommy Davis collected three hits and stole a base.

The 15 strikeouts set the existing World Series record. It has been bettered only once since when Bob Gibson fanned 17 for the Cardinals against the Tigers in game one in 1968.

OCTOBER 3   The Dodgers win game two with a 4–1 decision over the Yankees in New York. Johnny Podres (8⅓ innings) and Ron Perranoski (two-thirds of an inning) pitched for Los Angeles. Willie Davis hit a two-run double in the first inning that was misplayed in right field by Roger Maris. Bill Skowron homered in the fourth.

Despite hitting only .203 with four homers and 19 RBIs in 237 at-bats in 1963, Skowron started all four games at first base in the World Series because of his post-season experience and his knowledge of the opposition. The move benched Ron Fairly, who batted .271 with 12 homers during the season. Skowron played in seven Fall Classics for the Yankees. During the 1963 Series, he hit .385 in 13 at-bats. Dick Tracewski was the starter at second base in each of the contests against the Yanks despite making only five regular season starts at the position. Jim Gilliam, the starter for most of the season at second, moved to third and Ken McMullen sat on the bench. Tracewski hit only .154 in the Series, but helped save game four with a stellar defensive play.

OCTOBER 5   The Dodgers move within one game of the world championship with a 1–0 win over the Yankees before 55,912 at Dodger Stadium. Don Drysdale pitched a three-hitter and struck out nine in a duel with Jim Bouton. The lone run scored in the first inning on a walk to Jim Gilliam, a wild pitch, and a single by Tommy Davis.

On NBC-TV, the announcers were broadcasting legends Mel Allen and Vin Scully. Allen was felled by laryngitis, however, and Scully did game four alone.

OCTOBER 6   The Dodgers complete the sweep of the Yankees with a 2–1 win before 55,912 at Dodger Stadium. Sandy Koufax and Whitey Ford were the starting pitchers in a rematch of game one. Ford allowed only two hits, both by Frank Howard with a single in the second inning and a homer in the fifth that landed in the eighth row second deck of the left field stands. It was the first homer hit into that sector since the ballpark opened the previous season. Mickey Mantle tied the contest with a homer in the seventh. In the bottom half of the seventh, Jim Gilliam grounded to third baseman Clete Boyer. First baseman Joe Pepitone lost Boyer's throw in the background of white shirts in the stands. The ball bounced off Pepitone's wrist and into right field. Gilliam reached third on the play and scored on a sacrifice fly by Willie Davis. The Yankees had runners on first and second when Koufax recorded the final out by inducing Hector Lopez to ground out to shortstop Maury Wills. The Dodger ace finished with a six-hitter and struck out eight.

The Yankees scored only four runs and batted .171 during the Series. Dodger starters pitched 35^1/$_3$ of the 36 innings. In all, the Dodgers used only 13 players during the four games.

OCTOBER 25   A 165-foot high ski jump is constructed at Dodger Stadium from the right side of the field to the left. It was erected for a trade show for manufacturers, retailers and area ski operators. Slalom racing, fashion shows and world-famous personalities highlighted the event.

DECEMBER 6   Two weeks after the assassination of President John Kennedy, the Dodgers sell Bill Skowron to the Senators.

DECEMBER 13 The Dodgers trade Dick Scott to the Cubs for Jim Brewer and Cuno Barragan.

Brewer came to the Dodgers as a 25-year-old with a 4–13 lifetime record and a 5.66 ERA in 163^2/$_3$ innings. He gave little indication he would develop into a solid major league pitcher, but he learned to throw a screwball and became one of the best relievers in baseball during his 12 seasons with the Dodgers. While in Los Angeles, he pitched 822^1/$_3$ innings with an earned run average of 2.62. Brewer ranks third all-time among Dodgers in games pitched (474) and fifth in saves (125).

1964   LA

Season in a Sentence

In a forgettable year filled with injuries to key players, the defending world champion Dodgers stumble to only their second losing season since 1944.

Finish • Won • Lost • Pct • GB

Sixth (tie) 80   82   .494 13.0

Manager

Walter Alston

Stats

	Dods	NL	Rank
Batting Avg:	.250	.254	6
On-Base Pct:	.305	.311	8
Slugging Pct:	.340	.374	9
Home Runs:	79		9
Stolen Bases:	141		1
ERA:	2.95	3.54	1
Fielding Avg:	.973	.975	8
Runs Scored:	614		8
Runs Allowed:	572		2

Starting Lineup

Johnny Roseboro, c
Ron Fairly, 1b
Nate Oliver, 2b
Jim Gilliam, 3b
Maury Wills, ss
Tommy Davis, lf
Willie Davis, cf
Frank Howard, rf
Dick Tracewski, 2b-3b
Derrell Griffith, 3b-rf
Wes Parker, rf-1b

Pitchers

Don Drysdale, sp
Sandy Koufax, sp
Phil Ortega, sp
Joe Moeller, sp
Ron Perranoski, rp
Bob Miller, rp
Jim Brewer, rp
Howie Reed, rp

Attendance

2,228,751 (first in NL)

Club Leaders

Batting Avg:	Willie Davis	.294
On-Base Pct:	Ron Fairly	.349
Slugging Pct:	Frank Howard	.432
Home Runs:	Frank Howard	24
RBIs:	Tommy Davis	86
Runs:	Willie Davis	91
Stolen Bases:	Maury Wills	53
Wins:	Sandy Koufax	19
Strikeouts:	Don Drysdale	237
ERA:	Sandy Koufax	1.74
Saves:	Ron Perranoski	14

February 2   A basketball double-header is played at Dodger Stadium. The Harlem Globetrotters played the Atlantic City Seagulls, while the 1963 world champion Dodgers squared off against the 1963 NFL champion Chicago Bears. The court was placed between home plate and third base.

April 9   Two months after the Beatles historic appearance on the "Ed Sullivan Show" which launches "Beatlemania," the Dodgers trade Larry Sherry to the Tigers for Lou Johnson.

April 14   In the season opener, the defending world champion Dodgers win 4–0 over the Cardinals before 50,451 at Dodger Stadium. Sandy Koufax pitched a six-hit shutout. Frank Howard hit a home run.

The Dodgers lost their next seven games and never recovered. The club stayed around the .500 mark for most of the season.

April 18   The Dodgers wreck a rare no-hit bid by two pitchers. Frank Howard accounted for the only Los Angeles hit on a two-strike single with two out in the ninth inning in a 3–0 loss to the Reds at Dodger Stadium. Jim Maloney started for Cincinnati and hurled six innings without allowing a hit before being forced to leave after pulling a muscle in his back. John Tsitouris relieved and kept the no-hitter alive for 2⅔ innings before Howard's single. In the third inning, Sandy Koufax struck out the side on nine pitches, fanning Leo Cardenas, Johnny Edwards and Maloney.

APRIL 26   Phil Ortega pitches the Dodgers to a 1–0 win over the Braves in Milwaukee. It was his first major league victory. Frank Howard drove in the lone run of the game with a sacrifice fly in the first inning.

MAY 4   Sandy Koufax strikes out 13 batters and allows only three hits in a 10-inning complete game to defeat the Cubs 2–1 at Dodger Stadium. Maury Wills drove in the winning run with a walk-off single.

Wills hit .275 in 1964 and led the NL in stolen bases with 53.

MAY 14   A two-run homer by Frank Howard in the 10th inning beats the Cubs 6–4 in the first game of a double-header in Chicago. The Dodgers also won the second contest 5–0.

MAY 28   The Dodgers play 17 innings to a 2–2 tie against the Reds in Cincinnati. The game was called because of a league rule stipulating that no inning could start after 12:50 a.m. The contest was scoreless through the first 11 innings. Both teams scored twice in the 12th.

JUNE 4   Sandy Koufax pitches his third career no-hitter to beat the Phillies 3–0 at Connie Mack Stadium. He made 97 pitches, walked one, struck out 12, and faced the minimum 27 batters. The only Philadelphia batter to reach base was Richie Allen, who walked in the fourth inning, then was caught stealing. The catcher was Doug Camilli.

Towering Frank Howard gave the Dodgers home run power in the early 1960s but his inability to make consistent contact allowed the Dodgers to trade him after the 1964 season, before he reached his prime.

All of the Dodger runs scored on a three-run homer by Frank Howard off Chris Short in the seventh inning. In the bottom of the ninth, Tony Taylor led off and struck out. Ruben Amaro hit a pop fly caught by first baseman Ron Fairly. The last out was recorded when pinch-hitter Bobby Wine struck out on four pitches.

Camilli hit .179 in 123 at-bats for the Dodgers in 1964 and scored only one run.

JUNE 5   The Dodgers play at Shea Stadium for the first time, and lose 8–0 to the Mets.

JUNE 24	The Dodgers break loose with a 15–4 win over the Braves in Milwaukee.

Bob Miller allowed only one run in 44 innings over 20 consecutive relief appearances in June and July.

JULY 7	Five days after President Lyndon Johnson signs a Civil Rights act banning discrimination in voting, jobs and public accommodations, Walter Alston manages the National League to a 7–4 victory in the All-Star Game at Shea Stadium. Don Drysdale was the starting pitcher, and allowed the American Leaguers a run in three innings. The NL scored four times in the ninth for the win, the last three on a walk-off homer by Phillies outfielder Johnny Callison.

JULY 11	The Dodgers outlast the Colts 11–9 in Houston. A two-run homer by Willie Davis in the sixth inning broke a 7–7 tie.

JULY 12	The Dodgers both win and lose on late rallies in a double-header against the Cubs at Wrigley Field. In the opener, Chicago scored four runs in the ninth to win 6–3. The contest ended on a three-run homer by Billy Williams. The Dodgers scored six runs in the ninth inning to win the second tilt 6–2. The rally consisted of six singles and three walks.

JULY 15	Ron Fairly hits two homers, drives in five runs, and scores four during a 13–3 rout of the Cardinals in St. Louis.

JULY 17	The Dodgers become the first team in major league history to use pay television. At the time, the only Dodger games shown on a commercial station were nine games against the Giants from San Francisco. Since moving to Los Angeles in 1958, the only regular season home game on television was the first at Dodger Stadium in 1962. The pay-TV outlet was Subscription Television Inc. Dodger games were available for $1.50, the price of a bleacher seat at Dodger Stadium. About 2,500 subscribed to the service.

Pay-TV was undone by a ballot initiative in November 1964 that banned subscription television companies from operating inside the state of California. It passed by a margin of 2–1.

JULY 22	Sandy Koufax strikes out 12 batters to beat Houston 1–0 at Dodger Stadium. The lone run scored in the third inning on doubles by Derrell Griffith and Ron Fairly.

JULY 23	The Dodgers score two runs in the eighth inning and three in the ninth to defeat Houston 5–4 at Dodger Stadium. Ron Fairly drove in the final two runs on a two-out single.

JULY 29	During a day off, the Dodgers take a tour of the World's Fair in New York.

AUGUST 4	The Dodgers score seven runs in the sixth inning and beat the Pirates 10–7 in the second game of a double-header in Pittsburgh. The Dodgers also won the opener 5–1.

AUGUST 8	The day after the Gulf of Tonkin resolution, authorizing the president to act militarily in Vietnam, the Angels announce a move from Los Angeles to Anaheim

beginning with the 1966 season. The city of Anaheim built a stadium for the Angels. In conjunction with the move, the club changed its name from the Los Angeles Angels to the California Angels in September 1965. The American League club continued to share Dodger Stadium with the Dodgers through the end of the 1965 season.

AUGUST 16   Sandy Koufax strikes out 13 batters and beats the Cardinals 3–0 in St. Louis.

The win was the 19th and last of the season for Koufax. Eight days earlier, he jammed his left elbow while diving into second base. The injury worsened and doctors ordered Koufax to sit out the rest of the season. He finished the season with a 19–5 win and a league-leading 1.74 ERA and 223 strikeouts in 223 innings.

AUGUST 23   On the day the Beatles appear at the Hollywood Bowl, Phil Ortega pitches the Dodgers to a 1–0 win over the Reds at Dodger Stadium. The lone run scored in the third inning on a double by Nate Oliver and a single from Dick Tracewski.

An accomplished singer, Oliver cut a record album and often sang the "Star-Spangled Banner" prior to games. His father played in the Negro Leagues.

AUGUST 31   Don Drysdale strikes out 12 batters during a 12–3 triumph over the Cardinals in St. Louis.

SEPTEMBER 9   Willie Davis hits a grand slam off Bob Hendley in the fifth inning of an 8–1 win over the Giants in San Francisco.

SEPTEMBER 12   Pete Richert pitches a two-hitter to beat the Mets 2–0 at Dodger Stadium. The only New York hits were a double by Joe Christopher in the fourth and a single by Jim Hickman in the eighth.

SEPTEMBER 16   Willie Crawford makes his major league debut only nine days after his 18th birthday during a 7–5 loss to the Phillies at Dodger Stadium. Crawford popped out as a pinch-hitter in the fifth inning.

A graduate of Fremont High School in Los Angeles, Crawford was one of the most sought after high school players in the country and signed with the Dodgers for $100,000. While never a star, Crawford had a 14-year career and was a semi-regular in the Dodger outfield from 1969 though 1975.

SEPTEMBER 19   Willie Davis steals home with two out in the 16th inning to give the Dodgers a 4–3 win over the Phillies at Dodger Stadium. Before dramatically scoring the winning run, Davis singled, stole second, and went to third on a wild pitch. Los Angeles had one-run leads in the first, third and seventh innings, but Philadelphia came back to tie each time. The Dodgers scored only four runs despite collecting 20 hits.

SEPTEMBER 27   On the day the Warren Commission releases a report concluding that Lee Harvey Oswald acted alone in assassinating President Kennedy, Don Drysdale allows only three hits in 10 shutout innings, but the Dodgers lose 1–0 to the Colts in 12 innings in Houston.

Drysdale was 18–16 with a 2.18 ERA in 1964. He struck out 237 batters in a league-leading 321⅓ innings.

SEPTEMBER 30   John Purdin makes his first major league start and pitches a two-hitter to defeat the Cubs 2–0 at Dodger Stadium. Dick Bertell accounted for both Chicago hits with singles in the third and fifth innings. The Dodgers started eight players 24 years of age or younger in the game. The eight were first baseman Wes Parker (24), center fielder Willie Davis (24), shortstop Bart Shirley (24), second baseman Nate Oliver (23), catcher Jeff Torborg (22), Purdin (22), left fielder Derrell Griffith (20) and right fielder Willie Crawford (18).

Purdin made only four more big league starts, and never pitched another shutout. He finished his career in 1969 with a 6–4 record and a 3.90 earned run average.

OCTOBER 3   Jim Brewer pitches a shutout and collects three hits to defeat Houston 7–0 at Dodger Stadium. It was the only shutout Brewer pitched during his 17 seasons in the majors.

OCTOBER 4   The Dodgers close out the season with an 11–1 win over Houston at Dodger Stadium.

At the end of only the second losing season by the franchise in 20 years, Walter Alston was retained, but the entire coaching staff was fired, including Leo Durocher. Jim Gilliam was one of the new coaches. He became only the third African-American coach in major league history. Buck O'Neill with the Cubs from 1962 through 1965 was the first. Gene Baker with the 1963 Pirates was the second. Gilliam coached for the Dodgers from 1965 until his death in 1978. He had retired as a player when named coach, but returned to the active roster in May 1965 and played in the 1965 and 1966 World Series.

DECEMBER 4   A month after Lyndon Johnson defeats Barry Goldwater in the presidential election, the Dodgers send Frank Howard, Ken McMullen, Pete Richert, Phil Ortega and Dick Nen to the Senators for Claude Osteen, John Kennedy and cash estimated at $100,000.

The Dodgers received a pitcher who was a valuable member of the starting rotation for nine years, but he wasn't worth the loss of the players involved. Osteen twice won 20 games for the Dodgers in addition to appearing in two World Series and two All-Star Games. Overall, he was 147–126 in Los Angeles, and ranks seventh all-time in franchise history in wins, third in games started (335), fifth in shutouts (34) and sixth in innings pitched (2,396⅔). But, it would have been a bad trade even if the Dodgers swapped Osteen for Howard even up. It was made worse by adding four other players in the deal. The Dodgers soured on Howard after he reported to spring training four weeks late in 1964 due to personal problems, then hit .226, although he accounted for 24 of the club's 79 home runs. The Dodgers decided to sacrifice their major power source for more pitching because of injuries that put Johnny Podres out for most of the 1964 season and Sandy Koufax for the final six weeks. It was uncertain that either would return in 1965. Howard was 28 at the time of the trade and found a home in Washington. From 1967 through 1970, he clubbed 172 home runs and twice led the American League in the category. In 1968, he hit 44 home runs.

The Dodgers team leader that season was Len Gabrielson with 10. Howard hit 10 homers during a single six-game stretch in May of 1968. McMullen was a starting third baseman for the Senators and Angels over the next eight years, and was a better player than most of the individuals the Dodgers played at the position during the same period. Richert pitched in the All-Star Game in 1965 and 1966, and in three World Series as an Oriole in 1969, 1970 and 1971.

1965

Season in a Sentence

After leading the National League race for most of the season, the Dodgers fall 4¹/₂ games behind in mid-September before winning the pennant with a 13-game winning streak and downing the Twins in the World Series.

Finish • Won • Lost • Pct • GB

First   97   65   .599   +2.0

World Series

The Dodgers defeated the Minnesota Twins four games to three.

Manager

Walter Alston

Stats

Stats	Dods	NL	Rank
Batting Avg:	.245	.249	7
On-Base Pct:	.314	.311	6
Slugging Pct:	.335	.374	9
Home Runs:	78		10
Stolen Bases:	172		1
ERA:	2.81	3.54	1
Fielding Avg:	.979	.977	3
Runs Scored:	608		8
Runs Allowed:	521		1

Starting Lineup

Johnny Roseboro, c
Wes Parker, 1b
Jim Lefebvre, 2b
Jim Gilliam, 3b
Maury Wills, ss
Lou Johnson, lf
Willie Davis, cf
Ron Fairly, rf
John Kennedy, 3b

Pitchers

Sandy Koufax, sp
Don Drysdale, sp
Claude Osteen, sp
Johnny Podres, sp
Ron Perranoski, rp
Bob Miller, rp

Attendance

2,553,577 (first in NL)

Club Leaders

Batting Avg:	Maury Wills	.286
On-Base Pct:	Ron Fairly	.361
Slugging Pct:	Lou Johnson	.391
Home Runs:	Jim Lefebvre	12
	Lou Johnson	12
RBIs:	Ron Fairly	70
Runs:	Maury Wills	92
Stolen Bases:	Maury Wills	94
Wins:	Sandy Koufax	26
Strikeouts:	Sandy Koufax	382
ERA:	Sandy Koufax	2.04
Saves:	Ron Perranoski	17

APRIL 12   The Dodgers open the season with a 6–1 win over the Mets in New York. Willie Davis contributed a home run, a double and a single in three at-bats. Don Drysdale pitched a four-hit complete game and hit a home run. It was his second Opening Day homer. He also hit one in 1959.

APRIL 14   In his Dodger debut, Claude Osteen pitches a two-hitter to defeat the Pirates 3–1 at Forbes Field. The only Pittsburgh hits were a double by Jim Pagliaroni in the fifth inning and a homer from Bob Bailey with two out in the ninth.

APRIL 17   Don Drysdale strikes out four batters during the second inning of a 3–2 loss to the Phillies in Philadelphia. Wes Covington led off the second by swinging and missing a third strike, but reached first when Drysdale's wild pitch sailed past catcher Johnny Roseboro. Drysdale then fanned Tony Gonzalez, Dick Stuart and Clay Dalrymple.

APRIL 20   In the home opener, the Dodgers lose 3–2 to the Mets before 36,161 at Dodger Stadium.

MAY 1   Tommy Davis fractures and dislocates his ankle sliding into second base in the fourth inning of a 4–2 win over the Giants at Dodger Stadium.

> With the exception of one at-bat in the last game of the season, Davis never played again in 1965. Fortunately, the Dodgers received some unexpected help from Lou Johnson, who filled the void in left field. Johnson was called up from the Spokane farm club after Davis went on the disabled list. At the time he was 30 years old, had only 185 big league at-bats with the Cubs, Angels and Braves and hit .254 with two home runs. Johnson hadn't played in the majors since 1962. He was acquired by the Dodgers in April 1964, but remained in the minors. Johnson wasn't even on the 40-man roster during spring training in 1965. Los Angeles would be his 19th stop in a professional career that began in 1953 and included 15 minor league cities from the state of Washington to the Canadian province of Quebec. Johnson was a pleasant surprise for the Dodgers in 1965, and became a fan favorite by hitting .259 and tying for the club lead in home runs with 12. Louis Brown Johnson put together his surprise season while another Johnson with the initials "LBJ" resided in the White House. Dodger fans adopted Lyndon Johnson's 1964 Presidential campaign slogan "All the Way with LBJ." When Davis returned in 1966, Johnson retained his spot in the Dodgers starting outfield.

MAY 13   Sandy Koufax strikes out 13 batters and pitches a three-hitter without a walk to beat the Astros 3–0 at Dodger Stadium.

> Koufax won his second Cy Young Award in 1965 and finished second in the MVP voting with another outstanding season. He set the existing record for strikeouts in a season with 382 in a league-leading 335²/₃ innings. Koufax also led the NL in wins (with a 26–8 record), winning percentage (.765), complete games (27) and earned average (2.04). Opponents had only a .179 batting average and .227 on-base percentage against Koufax. He also recorded eight shutouts. The 382 strikeouts broke the previous record of 349 set by Rube Waddell of the Athletics in 1904 and still ranks second all-time. Nolan Ryan beat Koufax by one with 383 with the Angels in 1973.

MAY 15   Al Ferrara's three-run homer is the only Dodger hit in a 3–1 win over the Cubs at Dodger Stadium. Dick Ellsworth held Los Angeles without a run or a hit through the first seven innings. In the eighth, Jeff Torborg reached first base on an error. Dick Tracewski bunted and Ellsworth threw too late to second base to retire Willie Crawford, who ran for Torborg. Pinch-hitting for pitcher Bob Miller, Ferrara followed by hammering his home run.

> *The homer was the second in Ferrara's career, his first since 1963, and the only one he struck in 1965. He played five seasons for the Dodgers and hit .256 with 25 homers in 594 at-bats. A colorful character who was a native of Brooklyn, Ferrara performed as a solo pianist at Carnegie Hall at the age of 12. During a brief acting career, he played a villain named "Mr. Trap Door" in several episodes of the TV series* Batman.

MAY 16   With the score 2–2 in the ninth inning, Don Drysdale doubles and scores the winning run on Wes Parker's single to beat the Cubs 3–2 in the second game of a double-header at Dodger Stadium. Chicago won the opener 5–3 in 10 innings.

> *Drysdale had a 10–3 record on June 3, and finished 23–12 with a 2.77 ERA in a league-leading 308$^{1/3}$ innings. In addition to his pitching prowess, Drysdale hit .300 with seven home runs in 130 at-bats. It was the fourth consecutive season that Drysdale topped the 300-inning mark. In addition to his 1965 figure, Drysdale threw 314$^{1/3}$ innings in 1962, 315$^{1/3}$ in 1963, and 321$^{1/3}$ in 1964. He started at least 40 games in five straight seasons with 41 in 1962, 42 in 1963, 40 in 1964 and 42 in 1965 and 40 in 1966. The workload would catch up with him. He had 156 career wins on his 29th birthday, more than Greg Maddux (131) or Roger Clemens (128) at the same age. But while Maddux and Clemens would win well over 350 career games, and over 200 of them after turning 29, Drysdale's career ended at the age of 32 with 209 victories. In fact, both Clemens and Maddux won more games after their 29th birthday than Drysdale did in his entire career. Sandy Koufax, who exceeded the 300-inning mark in 1963, 1965 and 1966, had 165 wins on his 31st birthday, but that workload led to a premature retirement (see November 18, 1966). Clemens had 161 wins at 31 and Maddux accumulated 166. Neither Maddux nor Clemens ever pitched 300 innings in a season. Clemens's career high was 281$^{2/3}$ and Maddux topped out at 268 innings.*

MAY 17   The Dodgers play at the Astrodome, baseball's first indoor stadium, for the first time, and win 5–3 over the Astros in 11 innings. The score was 1–1 when the Dodgers exploded for four runs in the 11th. Sandy Koufax started the rally with a single. He was relieved when Houston scored twice in the bottom half, but not before recording his 13th strikeout.

MAY 18   Before making his major league debut, Dodgers rookie pitcher Mike Kekich is ejected for jockeying from the bench during a 4–1 loss to the Astros in Houston.

> *Kekich pitched in five games for the club in 1965, and after two seasons in the minors, was 2–10 in 1968 before a trade with the Yankees. Kekich received notoriety while in New York in 1973 when he and teammate Fritz Peterson traded wives.*

MAY 19   Ron Fairly hits a two-run homer in the 14th inning to lead the Dodgers to a 4–2 win over the Astros in Houston.

MAY 22   Sandy Koufax strikes out 12 batters during a 3–1 win over the Cubs in Chicago.

MAY 25   Don Drysdale pitches a brilliant one-hitter to beat the Cardinals 2–0 at Dodger Stadium. Curt Flood led off the first inning with a single. Drysdale retired the next 14 batters, and after an error, set down the final 13. The two Los Angeles runs scored on a two-run double by Ron Fairly off Bob Gibson, who came into the game with a record of 8–0.

On the same day, the Dodgers activated Jim Gilliam, who had retired as a player at the end of the 1964 season to become a coach with the club. It was intended that Gilliam be used only as a pinch-hitter, but he soon became the starting third baseman. He hit .280 in 372 at-bats.

MAY 29   Don Drysdale strikes out 12 batters during a 5–3 win over the Braves at Dodger Stadium.

MAY 30   Sandy Koufax strikes out 13 batters during a 12–5 victory over the Reds at Dodger Stadium.

MAY 31   The Dodgers start a line-up of four switch-hitting infielders for a 6–1 loss to the Reds in the second game of a double-header at Dodger Stadium. The infielders were first baseman Wes Parker, second baseman Jim Lefebvre, shortstop Maury Wills and third baseman Jim Gilliam. The Dodgers won the opener 4–3.

Lefebvre won the National League Rookie of the Year Award in 1965 with a .250 batting average and 12 home runs. He spent his entire eight-year career with the Dodgers. His good looks helped him win acting jobs on television shows such as Gilligan's Island, Batman, M*A*S*H, Alice, *and* St. Elsewhere. *He later managed the Mariners, Cubs and Brewers. In 2006, Lefebvre managed China's national baseball team in the World Baseball Classic.*

JUNE 3   The Dodgers out-last the Cardinals 11–10 in St. Louis. Los Angeles took the lead with three runs in the eighth inning.

With the victory, the Dodgers had a record of 31–17 and a five-game lead in the pennant race. The lead didn't last long. Heading into September, the Dodgers were one of five clubs NL clubs with a shot at finishing in first place. The others were the Giants, Pirates, Reds and Braves.

JUNE 7   The Dodgers score seven runs in the fourth inning and rout the Phillies 14–3 in Philadelphia. Sandy Koufax struck out 13 batters.

JUNE 8   In the first amateur draft in major league history, the Dodgers select shortstop John Wyatt from Bakersfield High School in Bakersfield, California.

The Dodgers got off to a poor start in the first draft, as Wyatt never got higher than Class A ball. The only players drafted and signed by the club in 1965 to reach the majors were Alan Foster (second round), Leon Everett

(15th round) and Gary Moore (26th round). The Dodgers drafted Tom Seaver in the 10th round, but didn't offer him a contract. The Braves drafted Seaver in the secondary draft in January 1966, but he wound up with the Mets when the Braves offered him an illegal contract.

JUNE 17   Claude Osteen pitches a one-hitter to beat the Giants 3–0 at Dodger Stadium. The only San Francisco hit was a single by Jack Hiatt in the second inning.

In his first season with the Dodgers, Osteen was 15–15 with a 2.87 ERA in 287 innings. He was nicknamed "Gomer" because of his resemblance to Jim Nabors, who created the popular TV character Gomer Pyle.

JUNE 20   Sandy Koufax hurls a one-hitter and strikes out 12 to defeat the Mets 2–1 in the first game of a double-header at Dodger Stadium. The lone New York hit was a home run by Jim Hickman in the fifth inning. Ron Fairly's two-run double in the sixth drove in the Los Angeles runs. The Mets won the second contest 3–2.

JUNE 21   In his first start since a one-hitter four days earlier, Claude Osteen two-hits the Mets, but loses 1–0 at Dodger Stadium. Osteen had a no-hitter until Joe Christopher singled in the seventh. Billy Cowan won the game with a home run in the ninth. The Dodgers collected only three hits off Al Jackson.

Don Drysdale (42), Sandy Koufax (41) and Osteen (40) combined to start 123 of the Dodgers 162 regular season games in 1965. Only two others pitchers in baseball (Jim Kaat of the Twins and Chris Short of the Phillies) made at least 40 starts that season.

JUNE 24   Willie Stargell hits three home runs for the Pirates during a 13–3 win over the Dodgers at Dodger Stadium. He just missed a fourth homer with a double off the wall.

Dodger players hit only 26 homers in 81 home games in 1965. The only two players with more than the three that Stargell struck in a single game were Lou Johnson (six) and Willie Davis (five). Overall, Los Angeles finished last in the NL in home runs with 78 but first in stolen bases, swiping 172. Maury Wills led the way with 94 thefts in addition to a .286 batting average.

JUNE 25   Sandy Koufax strikes out 12 batters during a 4–1 win over the Pirates at Dodger Stadium.

JUNE 28   Don Drysdale strikes out 12 batters in eight innings, but loses 5–0 to the Giants in San Francisco.

JULY 18   The Dodgers score two runs in the ninth inning and one in the 11th to defeat the Cubs 4–3 at Dodger Stadium. Jim Lefebvre drove in the last three Los Angeles runs. He tied the score on a two-run single and provided the game-winning tally with an RBI-double.

JULY 20   Sandy Koufax wins his 11th game in a row and delivers a walk-off single in the ninth inning to beat the Astros 3–2 at Dodger Stadium. Despite an .097 career batting average, Koufax was allowed to hit with a runner on second base and two out. The win gave him a record of 17–3.

JULY 23 — Maury Wills collects five hits, including a double, in six at-bats, but the Dodgers lose 4–3 in 12 innings to the Cardinals at Dodger Stadium.

JULY 27 — Maury Wills extends his hitting streak to 20 games during a 9–7 win over the Reds at Dodger Stadium.

AUGUST 5 — Sandy Koufax strikes out 12 batters during a 6–3 triumph over the Braves in Milwaukee.

AUGUST 8 — In the worst shutout defeat in club history, the Dodgers lose 18–0 to the Reds in Cincinnati.

AUGUST 10 — Sandy Koufax records his 20th win of the season with a 4–3 decision over the Mets at Dodger Stadium. He struck out 14.

> *Koufax had a 17–2 lifetime record against the Mets.*

AUGUST 11 — Don Drysdale pitches the Dodgers to a 1–0 win over the Mets at Dodger Stadium. Jim Gilliam drove in the lone run with a single in the seventh inning.

> *On the same day, riots began in the Watts section of Los Angeles. The riots would last six days and result in 34 deaths.*

AUGUST 14 — Sandy Koufax strikes out 12 batters, pitches a 10-inning shutout, and scores the lone run in a 1–0 win over the Pirates at Dodger Stadium. With two out in the 10th, Don Cardwell walked Koufax and Wes Parker. Koufax scored on an error by right fielder Roberto Clemente.

AUGUST 19 — The Dodgers score three runs in the 15th inning to beat the Giants 8–5 in San Francisco. Lou Johnson broke the 5–5 tie with a two-run homer.

> *Before the game, the Candlestick Park groundskeeper spread several inches of loose peat moss around home plate to slow the Dodger runners. The umpires ordered it removed.*

AUGUST 20 — During a 5–1 loss to the Giants at Candlestick Park, Maury Wills is accused of intentionally hitting the mitt of San Francisco catcher Tom Haller with his bat. Giants outfielder Matty Alou then hit Johnny Roseboro's mask with his bat, and the Dodger catcher buzzed Alou's head with a throw to the mound.

AUGUST 21 — A two-run homer by Wes Parker in the 11th beats the Giants 6–4 in San Francisco.

> *The Dodgers headed to San Francisco concerned over the safety of their families due to the Watts Riots (see August 11, 1965). Johnny Roseboro lived near the epicenter. Giants players Juan Marichal and Matty Alou were natives of the Dominican Republic, where a bloody civil war was escalating. Those elements plus a heated rivalry between the two clubs, fueled by a close pennant race, two extra-inning games, the Giants creative groundskeeping (see August 19, 1965), the incidents in the August 20 contest, and an exchange of beanballs in games earlier in the season set the stage for a combustible situation in the fourth game of the series.*

AUGUST 22   Giants pitcher Juan Marichal strikes Johnny Roseboro in the head with a bat during a 4–3 Dodger defeat at Candlestick Park. The game began with Marichal dusting Maury Wills and Ron Fairly. Sandy Koufax threw a pitch over the head of Willie Mays. When Marichal came to bat in the third inning with the Dodgers leading 2–1, Koufax threw two inside pitches and Roseboro came close to Marichal's head with the return throw. Marichal claimed his ear was nicked with the ball. After an exchange of words, Marichal raised his bat and pounded Roseboro at least twice in the head. Koufax tried to separate them and disarm Marichal, before a 14-minute brawl broke out. Dodger coach Danny Ozark attacked Marichal after the Giants pitcher taunted Roseboro, who was bleeding profusely from a large gash over his eye. Lou Johnson had to be restrained several times from going after Marichal. Giants infielder Tito Fuentes, who had been in the on-deck circle wielded a bat during the fight, fortunately didn't use it as a weapon. Acting as peacemaker, Mays led Roseboro into the dugout and mopped the blood from his brow while umpire Shag Crawford dragged Marichal away. Before the inning ended, Koufax walked two batters and Mays hit a three-run homer. After the game, Mays went to the Dodger clubhouse to express concern to Roseboro over his condition.

> *Terming the vicious attack "unprovoked and obnoxious," National League president Warren Giles slapped Marichal with a $1,750 fine and a nine-day suspension. Later Giles also barred Marichal from accompanying the Giants on their final two-day visit to Los Angeles on September 6 and 7, although Marichal wouldn't have played anyway because he made a start against the Cubs on September 5. The Giants ace pitcher, who had a 22–13 record in 1965, missed only one start, with another delayed by only a day. Although it was one of the stiffest penalties ever handed to a player up that time, most believed the incident warranted a stiffer punishment. The fact that the Giants were in the pennant race and that Roseboro instigated the fight by buzzing Marichal's head influenced the leniency of Giles. The Dodger catcher filed a civil suit against Marichal for $110,000. It was settled for $7,500 in 1970.*

SEPTEMBER 3   Jim Lefebvre has a hand in all three runs of a 3–0 win over the Astros in Houston. He singled in a run in the second inning. In the ninth, Lefebvre contributed an RBI-triple and crossed the plate on a squeeze bunt. Nick Willhite (5$\frac{1}{3}$ innings), Howie Reed (2$\frac{1}{3}$ innings) and Ron Perranoski (1$\frac{1}{3}$ innings) combined on the shutout.

SEPTEMBER 7   The Giants knock the Dodgers out of first place with a 3–1 win at Dodger Stadium.

SEPTEMBER 9   Sandy Koufax pitches a perfect game, and Bob Hendley of the Cubs allows only one hit in a 1–0 Dodger win at Dodger Stadium. It is the only major league game of nine innings or more in history in which two teams combined for only one hit. Lou Johnson was the only batter for either team to reach base, collecting a walk and a double. Koufax struck out 14 batters and made 113 pitches. The Dodger catcher was Jeff Torborg. Hendley had a perfect game until the fifth inning when the Dodgers scored a run without a hit. Johnson walked, was sacrificed to second by Ron Fairly, stole third, and continued home on catcher Chris Krug's high throw. Johnson collected the only hit of the game with a double in the seventh. Koufax struck out the last six men he faced, fanning Ron Santo, Ernie Banks, Byron Browne in the eighth, and Krug, Joe Amalfitano and pinch-hitter Harvey Kuenn in the ninth.

The Reds and Cubs played a game on May 1, 1917, in which there were no hits through the first nine innings. The pitchers were Hippo Vaughn of Chicago and Fred Toney of Cincinnati. The Reds collected two hits in the 10th off Vaughn to win 1–0. The September 9, 1965, contest was the fourth of four career no-hitters for Koufax. His perfect game is the only one in Dodger history. The Cubs starting line-up included Byron Browne and Don Young, both making their major league debuts. Kuenn also made the final out in Koufax's no-hitter against the Giants on May 11, 1963. Amalfitano also played for San Francisco in that game.

SEPTEMBER 15   The Dodgers fall into third place, 4½ games behind the Giants, after an 8–6 loss to the Cubs in Chicago. There were 16 games left on the schedule. The Giants were in the midst of a 14-game winning streak, which ended on September 17.

SEPTEMBER 17   Don Drysdale records his 20th win of the season with a 3–2 decision over the Cardinals in St. Louis.

SEPTEMBER 18   Sandy Koufax pitches the Dodgers to a 1–0 win over the Cardinals in St. Louis. The lone run scored in the sixth inning on a walk to Don LeJohn, a sacrifice by Koufax, and a single from Wes Parker.

SEPTEMBER 19   The Dodgers play at the original Busch Stadium in St. Louis for the last time, and win 5–0.

SEPTEMBER 22   In the Braves last home game in Milwaukee, the Dodgers win 7–6 in 11 innings. On the same day, the Angels played their last home game at Dodger Stadium and swept the Red Sox 10–1 and 6–5.

In 1966, the Braves moved to Atlanta and the Angels to Anaheim. The Angels drew only 566,727 fans to Dodger Stadium in 1965, nearly two million fewer than the Dodgers figure of 2,553,577, which led the majors. The second highest attendance total that season was 1,546,075 by the Giants. The Angels' move to Anaheim affected the Dodgers in two ways. Walter O'Malley would no longer be collecting rent from the American League club, and the Angels would find new fans in Orange County, attracting 1,400,321 into Anaheim Stadium in 1966, which led the AL that season.

SEPTEMBER 25   Sandy Koufax strikes out 14 batters during a 2–0 victory over the Cardinals at Dodger Stadium. It was the Dodgers eighth win in a row. The 14 strikeouts gave Koufax a season total of 358, breaking the previous modern day record of 349 by Rube Waddell of the Philadelphia Athletics in 1904.

Koufax and Don Drysdale had a combined record of 49–20 in 1965. The rest of the staff was 48–45.

SEPTEMBER 26   The Dodgers move into a tie for first place with the Giants after beating the Cardinals 1–0 at Dodger Stadium. Don Drysdale pitched the shutout. Maury Wills led off the first inning with a single. Trapped off the bag, Wills reached second safely after a rundown, took third on a wild pitch, and scored on a single by Jim Gilliam. It was the Dodgers ninth win in a row.

SEPTEMBER 28   The Dodgers take sole possession of first place with a 12-inning, 2–1 win over the Reds at Dodger Stadium. The game was won on a walk-off homer by Lou Johnson. The victory extended the Los Angeles winning streak to 11 games.

SEPTEMBER 29   The Dodgers increase their lead over the Giants to two games and their winning streak to 12 with a 5–0 win over the Reds at Dodger Stadium. Sandy Koufax pitched a two-hitter and struck out 13. The only Cincinnati hits were singles by Vada Pinson in the fourth inning and Deron Johnson in the seventh.

SEPTEMBER 30   The Dodgers stretch their winning streak to 13 games with a 4–0 triumph over the Braves at Dodger Stadium. Don Drysdale pitched a three-hit shutout for his 23rd win. The win gave the Dodgers a two-game lead over the Giants. Both teams had three games to play.

OCTOBER 1   The 13-game winning streak comes to an end with a 2–0 loss to the Braves at Dodger Stadium, but the Dodgers maintain their two-game lead when the Giants lose 17–2 to the Reds in San Francisco.

OCTOBER 2   The Dodgers clinch the pennant with a 3–1 win over the Braves at Dodger Stadium. Sandy Koufax struck out 13 for his 26th win of the season. The Dodgers won despite collecting only two hits. Both were singles by Jim Lefebvre.

OCTOBER 3   With the team preparing for the World Series, the Dodgers use six pitchers who combine on a shutout to defeat the Braves 3–0 at Dodger Stadium. The six were Howie Reed (two innings), Bob Miller (one inning), Mike Kekich (two innings), John Purdin (two innings), Bill Singer (one inning) and Nick Willhite (one inning).

The Dodgers played the Minnesota Twins in 1965. Managed by Sam Mele, the Twins were 102–60 that season. It was the first World Series appearance for the franchise since 1933, when it was located in Washington and known as the Senators. The club moved to Minnesota between the 1960 and 1961 seasons.

OCTOBER 6   The Dodgers open the 1965 World Series with an 8–2 loss to the Twins at Metropolitan Stadium in Bloomington, Minnesota. Sandy Koufax sat out the game because it fell on Yom Kippur, a Jewish holiday. Don Drysdale started and was hammered for seven runs in 2²/₃ innings. Mudcat Grant pitched a complete game for Minnesota.

Hubert Humphrey, vice-president of the United States and a former mayor of Minneapolis, threw out the ceremonial first pitch.

OCTOBER 7   With Sandy Koufax on the mound, the Dodgers lose game two by a 5–1 score in Minnesota. Koufax allowed two runs, one earned in six innings before Don Drysdale pinch-hit for him in the top of the seventh. Ron Perranoski gave up three runs in the seventh and eighth. Jim Kaat pitched a complete game for the Twins.

Due to heavy rain during the previous night and morning, the Metropolitan Stadium grounds crew used helicopters and flame throwers to dry the field.

OCTOBER 9   The Dodgers win their first game of the Series with a 4–0 win over the Twins before 55,934 at Dodger Stadium. After losing the first two games with Don Drysdale and Sandy Koufax pitching, Claude Osteen spun a five-hit shutout.

Just a month past his 19th birthday, Willie Crawford made two pinch-hit appearances for the Dodgers in the 1965 Series, and collected a hit. He also played for Los Angeles in the 1974 Fall Classic.

OCTOBER 10   The Dodgers even the Series with a 7–2 win over the Twins before 55,920 at Dodger Stadium. Don Drysdale pitched a complete game and struck out 11. Ron Fairly drove in three runs and Lou Johnson and Wes Parker hit solo homers.

Fans remember the great Dodger starting pitchers of the 1960s, but ace reliever Ron Perranoski was one of the great closers of the era.

OCTOBER 11   The Dodgers win their third consecutive game and move within one victory of the world championship with a 7–0 decision over the Twins before 55,801 at Dodger Stadium. Sandy Koufax pitched a five-hit shutout and struck out 10 batters. Maury Wills collected four hits, two of them doubles, and stole a base. Willie Davis swiped three bases to tie a World Series record, and Ron Fairly picked up two singles and a double.

OCTOBER 13   With a chance to wrap up the World Series, the Dodgers lose 5–1 to the Twins in Minnesota. Claude Osteen was the starter and loser. Mudcat Grant pitched a complete game for Minnesota and walloped a three-run homer in the sixth inning.

Each team had won three of the first six games, but none of them were competitive. The smallest margin of victory was four runs. The home team won each of the six contests. For game seven, Walter Alston had a choice between pitching Don Drysdale on his normal three days' rest, or Sandy Koufax on two. He went with Koufax. Twins pitcher Jim Kaat also went on two days of rest.

OCTOBER 14   Behind another brilliant performance by Sandy Koufax, the Dodgers claim the world championship with a 2–0 win over the Twins in Minnesota. He pitched a three-hitter and struck out 10. Both Los Angeles runs scored in the fourth inning. Lou Johnson led off with a home run that struck the left field foul pole to break the scoreless deadlock. Ron Fairly doubled and Wes Parker singled for the second run. The only Twins threat came in the fifth inning when they placed runners on first and second with one out. Zoilo Versalles hit a smash down the left field line, but Jim Gilliam made a diving catch of the ball, turning in a force play at third. With a runner on first base, Koufax fanned Bob Allison for the final out of the game.

Koufax pitched 24 innings in the 1965 World Series and allowed 13 hits and one earned run for an ERA of 0.38.

DECEMBER 15   The Dodgers trade Dick Tracewski to the Tigers for Phil Regan.

At the time of the trade, Regan was 28 years old and had a 42–44 lifetime record with a 4.49 ERA, mostly as a starting pitcher. Converted to a full-time reliever, Regan suddenly blossomed as a Dodger. In 1966, pitched 65 games and 116²/₃ innings and compiled a 14–1 win with 21 saves and a 1.62 ERA. After a decent season in 1967, the Dodgers traded Regan to the Cubs in 1968.

Sandy's Perfect Game

Sandy Koufax pitched the only perfect game in Dodger history on September 9, 1965. The 27 outs were recorded as follows:

First Inning
Don Young popped out to second baseman Jim Lefebvre. Glenn Beckert struck out swinging. Billy Williams struck out looking.

Second Inning
Ron Santo fouled out to catcher Johnny Roseboro. Ernie Banks struck out swinging. Byron Browne lined out to center fielder Willie Davis.

Third Inning
Chris Krug flied out to Davis. Don Kessinger flied out to right fielder Ron Fairly. Bob Hendley struck out looking.

Fourth Inning
Young fouled out to first baseman Wes Parker. Beckert flied to Fairly. Williams struck out looking.

Fifth Inning
Santo flied to left fielder Lou Johnson. Banks struck out swinging. Browne grounded out, Lefebvre to Parker.

Sixth Inning
Krug grounded out Lefebvre to Parker. Kessinger grounded out third baseman Jim Gilliam to Parker. Hendley struck out swinging.

Seventh Inning
Young struck out swinging. Beckert flied to Fairly. Williams flied to Johnson.

Eighth Inning
Santo struck out looking. Banks struck out swinging. Browne struck out swinging.

Ninth Inning
Krug struck out swinging. Joe Amalfitano, batting for Kessinger, struck out swinging. Harvey Kuenn, batting for Hendley, struck out swinging.

1966

LA

Season in a Sentence

Behind another stellar pitching staff led by Sandy Koufax, the Dodgers use a hot September to leap past the Giants and Pirates and win the pennant before succumbing to a World Series sweep at the hands of the Orioles.

Finish • Won • Lost • Pct • GB

First   95   67   .586 +1.5

World Series

The Dodgers lost to the Baltimore Orioles four games to none.

Manager

Walter Alston

Stats

Stats	Dods •	NL •	Rank
Batting Avg:	.256	.256	5
On-Base Pct:	.314	.313	5
Slugging Pct:	.362	.284	9
Home Runs:	108		8 (tie)
Stolen Bases:	94		2
ERA:	2.62	3.61	1
Fielding Avg:	.979	.977	3
Runs Scored:	606		8
Runs Allowed:	490		1

Starting Lineup

Johnny Roseboro, c
Wes Parker, 1b
Jim Lefebvre, 2b
John Kennedy, 3b
Maury Wills, ss
Lou Johnson, lf
Willie Davis, cf
Ron Fairly, rf
Tommy Davis, lf
Jim Gilliam, 3b

Pitchers

Sandy Koufax, sp
Claude Osteen, sp
Don Drysdale, sp
Don Sutton, sp
Phil Regan, rp
Ron Perranoski, rp
Bob Miller, rp

Attendance

2,617,029 (first in NL)

Club Leaders

Batting Avg:	Willie Davis	.284
On-Base Pct:	Wes Parker	.351
Slugging Pct:	Jim Lefebvre	.460
Home Runs:	Jim Lefebvre	24
RBIs:	Jim Lefebvre	74
Runs:	Willie Davis	74
Stolen Bases:	Maury Wills	38
Wins:	Sandy Koufax	27
Strikeouts:	Sandy Koufax	317
ERA:	Sandy Koufax	1.73
Saves:	Phil Regan	21

FEBRUARY 28   Sandy Koufax and Don Drysdale announce they are staging a joint holdout and that neither will sign unless granted a three-year deal for a total of $1 million, to be split evenly. It would have made them the highest paid players in baseball history up to that time. In 1965, Koufax earned $85,000 and Drysdale $80,000. The two also hired an attorney to handle the negotiations. Baseball precedent was broken in two ways. Not only were two players joining together in bargaining with management on a contract, but were hiring an agent as well. Until 1966, players handled their own contract negotiations.

MARCH 5   The Major League Players Association hires Marvin Miller as the new executive director of the organization. Miller formally took office on July 1. Under Miller's leadership, the association would take actions that led to a revolution in player-owner relations, including free agency beginning in 1976.

MARCH 17 Sandy Koufax and Don Drysdale, still sitting out spring training while negotiating a new contract, sign movie contracts. Both were to appear in the film *Warning Shot* starring David Janssen.

MARCH 19 The Dodgers play in the first game in baseball history played on artificial turf during an exhibition game against the Astros in the Astrodome. The two clubs flew from their Florida training base to Houston for a two-game series. The Dodgers won both games, 8–3 on March 19 and 4–1 on March 20.

The Astrodome opened in 1965 with a conventional grass field, but fielders lost fly balls in the glare of the glass panels in the roof. The glass had to be painted, which killed the grass. The artificial surface, manufactured by Monsanto and named Astroturf, was the solution.

Sandy Koufax stunned the baseball world—and made National League hitters very happy—when he announced his retirement at the age of 32 after completing perhaps the finest year of his career.

MARCH 30 Sandy Koufax and Don Drysdale end their holdouts (see February 28, 1966) and sign individual one-year contracts. Dismissing their agent, each negotiated his own deal. Koufax signed for $120,000 and Drysdale for $100,000. "I have never discussed a player contract with an agent," said Walter O'Malley, "and I like to think I never will."

APRIL 3 In his first at-bat against Juan Marichal since their confrontation the previous season (see August 22, 1965), Johnny Roseboro hits a three-run inside-the-park homer to help the Dodgers to an 8–4 win over the Giants in an exhibition game in Phoenix.

APRIL 12 On Opening Day, the Dodgers win 3–2 over the Astros before a crowd of 34,520 at Dodger Stadium. Claude Osteen drew the start, and pitched a complete game.

APRIL 14 Don Sutton makes his major league debut, and allows three runs and seven hits in seven innings of a 4–2 loss to the Astros at Dodger Stadium.

Sutton would pitch 15 consecutive seasons for the Dodgers from 1966 through 1980, and never won fewer than 11 games during that span. He had 15 or more wins in eight years, with a high of 21 in 1976, and pitched in four All-Star Games and three World Series. As a Dodger, he had a record of 233–181 to become the club's all-time leader in victories. He is also the record holder in games pitched (550), games started (533), shutouts (52), innings pitched (3,816⅓), and strikeouts (2,696) in addition to ranking second in walks (996) and eighth in complete games (156). Sutton finished his sojourn in the majors in 1988 with a one-year return to the Dodgers. He won 324 games as a big leaguer and was elected to the Hall of Fame in 1988.

APRIL 18   At the Astrodome, the Dodgers defeat the Astros 6–3 in the first regular season game in major league history on artificial turf.

MAY 7   The Dodgers mash five homers and overwhelm the Reds 14–2 in Cincinnati. Jim Lefebvre hit two homers, and Don Drysdale, Lou Johnson and Al Ferrara one each. The switch-hitting Lefebvre homered from both sides of the plate, connecting off right-hander Sammy Ellis in the first inning and lefty Gerry Arrigo in the fourth.

            A 24-year-old in his second year in the majors, Lefebvre had the best season of his career in 1966 with 24 homers and a .274 batting average.

MAY 10   The Dodgers sell Johnny Podres to the Tigers. Podres had been a member of the Dodgers since 1953.

MAY 11   Don Sutton pitches a complete game and collects three hits in beating the Phillies 5–0 in Philadelphia.

            On May 13, the Dodgers had a record of 15–14 and were seven games behind the first place Giants.

MAY 17   The Dodgers win 2–1 in 13 innings against the Giants at Dodger Stadium. Juan Marichal made his first appearance in Los Angeles since the incident with Johnny Roseboro (see August 22, 1965) and was booed every time he stepped to the plate. Marichal collected two hits in four at-bats and pitched 10 innings, allowing just one run.

MAY 21   Don Drysdale strikes out 13 batters in eight innings and Ron Perranoski fans another four in four frames of relief as the Dodgers take a 12-inning, 5–4 decision from the Pirates at Dodger Stadium. Maury Wills drove in the game-winner with a single.

            Drysdale suffered thorough a shaky season in 1966 with a 13–16 record and a 3.42 ERA.

MAY 23   Johnny Roseboro crosses the plate with the winning run in the ninth, advancing two bases on an infield single that beats the Pirates 3–2 at Dodger Stadium. Derrell Griffith topped a roller down the first base line. Pittsburgh pitcher Pete Mikkelsen fielded the ball, and Griffith beat the throw to first base. Roseboro rounded third and scored when catcher Jerry May failed to cover the plate.

MAY 25   A two-out, two-run walk-off single by Wes Parker beats the Phillies 2–1 at Dodger Stadium.

MAY 28   The Dodgers sign Wes Covington following his release by the Cubs.

MAY 30   The Dodgers play in Atlanta for the first time, and beat the Braves 10–6 at Atlanta-Fulton County Stadium. Maury Wills led off the first inning with a home run. It was his first homer since 1964.

JUNE 1   Sandy Koufax pitches the Dodgers to a 1–0 win over the Cardinals in St. Louis. The lone run scored in the seventh inning when Willie Davis tripled and crossed the plate on an error. It was also the first time the Dodgers played in the second of three facilities in St. Louis named Busch Stadium, which served as the home of the Cardinals from 1966 through 2005.

In what would prove to be his last season in the majors, Koufax won his third Cy Young Award with a career-high 27 victories, posting a 27–9 record. He led the NL in wins, earned run average (a career low 1.73), games started (a career-high 41), complete games (a career-high 27), shutouts (five), strikeouts (317) and innings pitched (323).

JUNE 5   The Dodgers score seven runs in the seventh inning of a 16–3 romp past the Mets in the first game of a double-header at Shea Stadium. Tommy Davis collected five hits, including a triple, in five at-bats. Switch-hitter Wes Parker collected homers from both sides of the plate. He went deep on right-hander Jack Hamilton in the seventh inning and lefty Gordon Richardson in the ninth. New York won the second tilt 3–2.

JUNE 7   Jim Lefebvre and Al Ferrara homer in the 10th inning to defeat the Cubs 8–6 at Wrigley Field. Ferrara's home run was inside-the-park when Chicago shortstop Don Kessinger and left fielder Byron Browne collided trying to catch the towering fly ball. Ferrara hit another homer over the fence earlier in the game.

On the same day, the Dodges selected pitcher Larry Hutton form Greenfield High School in Greenfield, Indiana, in the first round of the amateur draft. Hutton never got past Class AA ball and the first seven players of the regular phase played a grand total of 13 big league games, but the Dodgers made some excellent picks in the later rounds. Future major leaguers drafted and signed by the Dodgers in 1966 were John Gamble (second round), Charlie Hough (eighth), Bill Russell (ninth), Bill Grabarkewitz (12th), Ted Sizemore (15th), Ray Lamb (40th), Jim Hibbs (third round of the secondary phase in January) and Bob Stinson (first round of the secondary phase in June). Russell, who played 18 years with the Dodgers from 1969 through 1986, was the best of the bench. Hough had a 25-year big league career and was still active in 1994. Sizemore played 12 years in the majors. Grabarkewitz was an All-Star as a 24-year-old in 1970 before injuries wrecked a promising career. Stinson, chosen first in the secondary phase, which consisted of previously drafted players who didn't sign a professional contract, lasted 12 seasons in the big leagues.

JUNE 24   All four runs of a 4–0 win over the Braves in Atlanta are scored in the eighth inning.

JULY 5   Sandy Koufax beats the Reds 1–0 at Dodger Stadium. The lone run scored on a single by John Kennedy in the second inning.

On the same day, the Dodgers signed Dick Stuart following his release by the Mets.

JULY 6

Claude Osteen gives the Dodgers their second straight 1–0 victory by beating the Reds at Dodger Stadium. Osteen not only pitched the shutout but drove in the lone run with a single in the eighth inning following John Kennedy's double.

Osteen had a 17–14 record and a 2.85 ERA in 1966.

JULY 12

Walter Alston manages the National League to a 10-inning, 2–1 win in the All-Star Game at Busch Stadium in St. Louis. On a day in which the temperature reached 105 degrees, Sandy Koufax was the NL starter and allowed a run in three innings. Maury Wills won the game with a walk-off single off Pete Richert.

JULY 21

Pirates pitcher Pete Mikkelsen hits John Kennedy with a pitch with the bases loaded in the 10th inning to force in the winning run for a 4–3 win at Dodger Stadium.

John Kennedy played for the Washington Senators in 1962 and 1963 when another John Kennedy was President of the United States.

JULY 24

The Dodgers sweep the Mets with shutouts during a double-header at Dodger Stadium. Don Drysdale won the opener 5–0. In the nightcap, Joe Moeller (seven innings) and Phil Regan (two innings) combined for a 6–0 victory.

JULY 27

Sandy Koufax strikes out 16 batters and allows four hits in 11 innings, but gets a no decision as the Dodgers win 2–1 in 12 innings over the Phillies at Dodger Stadium. In the 12th, Lou Johnson twice failed to get a bunt down before delivering a game-winning single. Jim Bunning started for the Phillies and fanned 12 in 11 innings while surrendering six hits.

Koufax (41), Don Drysdale (40), Claude Osteen (38) and Don Sutton (35) combined to start 154 of the Dodgers 162 games in 1966. Joe Moeller was the starter in the other eight contests, five of them in double-headers. The only two pitchers besides Koufax and Drysdale to start 40 games in 1966 were Jim Kaat of the Twins (41) and Jim Bunning of the Phillies (40). From 1962 through 1966, there were 16 pitchers with at least 40 starts in a season and 10 of them were Dodgers. Drysdale did it in all five seasons, Koufax in three, and Johnny Podres and Claude Osteen once each. The others were Kaat twice and Bunning, Juan Marichal, Chris Short and Jack Sanford once each.

AUGUST 5

The Dodgers breeze past the Astros 12–1 in Houston.

AUGUST 7

The Dodgers collect 20 hits and thrash the Astros 14–3 in Houston. The win put the Dodgers one percentage point ahead of the Pirates in a virtual three-way tie for first place. The Giants were in third place two percentage points back.

The Dodgers drew 2,617,029 fans at home and 2,141,212 on the road to become the first team in history to draw at least two million at home and away in the same season.

AUGUST 9

Sandy Koufax gives up a lead-off homer to Felipe Alou in the first inning and a walk-off homer to Eddie Mathews in the ninth to lose 2–1 to the Braves in Atlanta.

AUGUST 14	In a double-header against the Cubs at Dodger Stadium, the Dodgers win 4–3 in 14 innings and lose 12–10 in 10 innings. In the opener, Chicago scored in the top of the 14th to go ahead 3–2, but the Dodgers loaded the bases for Wes Covington, who delivered a two-run walk-off single with two out.
AUGUST 16	Don Sutton pitches a two-hitter to defeat the Reds 2–0 at Dodger Stadium. The only Cincinnati hits were a single by Johnny Edwards in the sixth inning and a double from Leo Cardenas in the eighth. The two Los Angeles runs scored in the first inning on a triple by Willie Davis, a walk to Jim Gilliam, and a two-run single by Tommy Davis in which Gilliam scored all the way from first base.
AUGUST 21	Sandy Koufax wins his 20th game of the season with a 4–1 decision over the Cardinals at Dodger Stadium.
AUGUST 23	The Dodgers score three runs in the ninth inning to defeat the Braves 8–7 at Dodger Stadium. The tying and winning runs crossed the plate on a two-out, two-run single by Willie Davis.
AUGUST 28	The Beatles play a concert at Dodger Stadium during their last American tour.

> *The Beatles were the first rock band to play at Dodger Stadium. The group played their final concert at Candlestick Park in San Francisco the following day. Later acts at Dodger Stadium included Elton John, the Rolling Stones, Simon and Garfunkel, KISS, Michael Jackson, The Bee Gees, David Bowie, Eric Clapton, Genesis, Bruce Springsteen, U-2, the Dave Matthews Band and the Police.*

SEPTEMBER 10	The Dodgers outlast the Astros 1–0 in 10 innings at Dodger Stadium. In the 10th, Maury Wills, singled, advanced to second base on a sacrifice, to third on an infield out, and home on a two-out single from Al Ferrara. Don Drysdale (8⅓ innings) and Phil Regan (1⅔ innings) combined on the shutout. It was Regan's 12th win in a row.
SEPTEMBER 11	The Dodgers take first place with a pair of shutout victories in a double-header against the Astros at Dodger Stadium. In the opener, Sandy Koufax pitched a complete game for a 4–0 win. The second tilt was won 1–0, the third straight shutout by Los Angeles pitchers over two days. Joe Moeller (five innings), Bob Miller (two innings) and Phil Regan (two innings) combined to hold Houston scoreless. The lone run scored on a pinch-single in the seventh inning by Johnny Roseboro.

> *At the end of the day, the Dodgers had a record of 83–59. The Pirates were a game back at 83–61 and the Giants two behind with an 82–62 won-lost ledger. The Dodgers held onto first place for the remainder of the season, but wouldn't clinch the pennant until the final day.*

SEPTEMBER 12	Ron Perranoski strikes out the first six batters he faces, and seven in four innings of relief, during a 3–2 win over the Mets at Dodger Stadium. He entered the contest in the fifth inning.
SEPTEMBER 16	The Dodgers extend their winning streak to eight games with a 5–1 decision over the Pirates at Dodger Stadium. The victory also extended the Dodgers lead in the pennant race to 3½ games.

SEPTEMBER 20   Sandy Koufax earns his 25th win of the season with an 11–1 rout of the Phillies at
                Dodger Stadium.

SEPTEMBER 23   Phil Regan wins his 13th game in a row, all in relief, and runs his won-lost record
                to 14–1 with a 4–2 victory over the Cubs in the second game of a double-header in
                Chicago. The Dodgers also won the opener 4–0.

SEPTEMBER 25   Ken Holtzmann of the Cubs carries a no-hitter into the ninth inning and emerges
                with a two-hitter and a 2–1 win over Sandy Koufax and the Dodgers in Chicago.
                Dick Schofield spoiled the no-hit bid on a single with none out in the ninth and later
                scored on a single by Maury Wills.

SEPTEMBER 27   Don Drysdale pitches the Dodgers to a 2–0 win over the Cardinals at Dodger
                Stadium. The win gave the Dodgers a three-game lead over the Pirates with five
                games left on the schedule. The Giants were four games back and appeared to be out
                of contention, but won their last six games while the Dodgers lost three of the next
                four, to stay in the race until the final day.

SEPTEMBER 28   Larry Jaster of the Cardinals shuts out the Dodgers for the fifth time in 1966 with a
                2–0 win in St. Louis.

                *In the five shutouts against the Dodgers, Jaster allowed 24 hits, all singles, in
                45 innings. Jaster is the only pitcher since 1916 to record five shutouts over one
                team in a season, and is the only one since 1900 to shutout an opposing club in
                five straight appearances. There were many oddities to Jaster's accomplishment,
                which is one of the strangest on the books. The five shutouts against the Dodgers
                in 1966 were his only five that season, the first five of his career, and came in
                his first five career starts against Los Angeles. He had an 11–5 record in 1966.
                Against the other eight teams in the NL, Jaster pitched 106²/₃ innings and had an
                ERA of 4.64. His ineffectiveness led to a trip to the minors for six weeks, during
                which he missed a June series against the Dodgers. After 1966, Jaster was 19–28
                as a major leaguer, including a 4–5 record against Los Angeles.*

SEPTEMBER 29   Sandy Koufax strikes out 13 batters during a 2–1 win over the Cardinals in St. Louis.

OCTOBER 1   On the second-to-last day of the regular season, the Dodgers are rained out against
                the Phillies in Philadelphia, forcing a double-header the following afternoon.
                Meanwhile in Pittsburgh, the Giants moved with 1¹/₂ games of first place by
                sweeping the Pirates 5–4 and 2–0 in a double-header. To clinch the pennant, the
                Dodgers needed to win one of the two games on October 2, or have the Giants lose
                to the Pirates.

OCTOBER 2   Playing a double-header against the Phillies at Connie Mack Stadium on the final
                day of the season, the Dodgers clinch the pennant, but not without difficulty. The
                Dodgers lost the opener 4–3 while the Giants kept their championship hopes by
                winning 7–3 in 11 innings over the Pirates in Pittsburgh. Needing a win to wrap up
                the pennant, Walter Alston pitched Sandy Koufax on two days' rest in the second
                game. Koufax responded with a 6–3 complete game win for his 27th victory of the
                season.

                *The Dodgers played the Baltimore Orioles in the World Series. Managed by
                Hank Bauer, the Orioles were 97–63 in 1966. It was the first World Series*

for the franchise since 1944 when it was known as the St. Louis Browns. The Browns moved to Baltimore between the 1953 and 1954 seasons, and were renamed the Orioles.

OCTOBER 5   The Dodgers open the 1966 World Series with a 5–2 loss to the Orioles before 55,941 at Dodger Stadium. Because Sandy Koufax pitched in the last game of the regular season three days earlier, Don Drysdale started for Los Angeles and allowed four runs in two innings. Jim Lefebvre homered leading off the second inning, but the Dodgers collected only two more hits. Moe Drabowsky was the unexpected star of the game. He relieved Dave McNally in the third and pitched 6²/₃ shutout innings, surrendering only one hit and striking out 11. Drabowsky fanned six batters in a row in the fourth and fifth, setting down Jim Barbieri, Maury Wills, Willie Davis, Lou Johnson, Tommy Davis and Lefebvre.

Barbieri played in the Little League World Series in 1954 on a team from Schenectady, New York, which won the championship. On the way to the title, Barbieri's team beat one from Lakeland, Florida, which featured Boog Powell, the starting first baseman on the 1966 Orioles.

OCTOBER 6   With Jim Palmer pitching the shutout, the Orioles beat the Dodgers 6–0 in game two before 55,947 at Dodger Stadium. Baltimore broke a scoreless tie in the fifth inning by scoring three runs with the help of three errors by center fielder Willie Davis. Boog Powell was the runner on first base when Paul Blair lifted a fly to center. Davis lost the ball in the sun and dropped it for an error. The next hitter was Andy Etchebarren, who lofted another fly to center. Davis again lost the ball, then dropped it as Powell scored and Blair headed toward third. Davis threw to third in an attempt to retire Blair, but the throw was wild and Blair scored. Davis was charged with two errors on the play, giving him three miscues in a span of two batters. The next inning, Davis caught a ball during warm-ups and was given a standing ovation. Altogether, the Dodgers made six errors to tie a Series record. Sandy Koufax started for the Dodgers and allowed four runs, one earned, in six innings.

The game would prove to be the last of Koufax's career. In World Series play, Koufax had a 4–3 record, but his ERA was 0.95 and he struck out 61 batters in 57 innings.

OCTOBER 8   The Dodgers are shutout again, losing 1–0 to the Orioles at Memorial Stadium in Baltimore to fall behind three games to none. Wally Bunker pitched the shutout. The lone run scored on a home run by Paul Blair off Claude Osteen in the fifth inning.

OCTOBER 9   In Baltimore, the Orioles complete the sweep of the Dodgers with their third straight shutout and second consecutive 1–0 victory. Dave McNally pitched the shutout. The lone run scored on a home run by Frank Robinson off Don Drysdale in the fourth inning. The time of the game was one hour and 45 minutes. It is the last contest completed in less than two hours in World Series history.

The three Baltimore shutouts were pitched by 23-year-old Dave McNally, 21-year-old Wally Bunker and 20-year-old Jim Palmer. Bunker didn't hurl a shutout during the 1966 regular season. Palmer is the youngest pitcher to pitch a shutout in World Series history. The Dodgers set World Series records for the fewest runs scored (two), the most consecutive innings without scoring a run (the last 33 innings of the Series), the lowest batting average (.142), the lowest slugging percentage (.192), and the fewest singles (13). The Orioles were hardly an offensive juggernaut, with 13 runs and a .200 batting average.

OCTOBER 22   The Dodgers open a tour of Japan with a 16–5 win over the Yomiyuri Giants in Tokyo.

The Dodgers played 18 games in Japan through November 16 and had a record of 9–8–1. Many star players stayed home, among them Sandy Koufax, Don Drysdale, Don Sutton, Wes Parker and Jim Gilliam. In addition, Maury Wills left the club on November 4, claiming his injured right knee required treatment in the United States.

NOVEMBER 18   After a season in which he compiles a record of 27–9 and a 1.74 ERA, Sandy Koufax announces his retirement at the age of 30. Speaking at a press conference in Los Angeles, Koufax cited his arthritic left elbow and concerns about a permanent and crippling disability. "I've had too many shots and taken too many pills because of my arm trouble," said Koufax. "I don't want to take a chance of disabling myself. I don't regret for one minute the 12 years I spent in baseball, but I could regret one season too many."

NOVEMBER 29   The Dodgers trade Tommy Davis and Derrell Griffith to the Mets for Ron Hunt and Jim Hickman.

After eight seasons with the Dodgers, Davis played for eight different franchises and changed teams 11 times between November 1966 and the end of his career in 1976.

DECEMBER 1   The Dodgers trade Maury Wills to the Pirates for Bob Bailey and Gene Michael.

Wills was dealt following his departure during the post-season trip to Japan. He hit .302 for the Pirates in 1967 and .278 in 1968. Wills would return to the Dodgers in 1969 after a trade with the Montreal Expos. Bailey was a native of Long Beach, California, who received a then-record signing bonus of $175,000 after graduating from high school in 1961. He hit only .227 in back-to-back seasons for the Dodgers before being sold to Montreal in October 1968.

1967

L A

Season in a Sentence

Suffering a hangover following the retirements of Sandy Koufax and Jim Gilliam and the trade of Maury Wills, the revamped Dodgers follow back-to-back World Series appearances with an eighth-place finish.

Finish • Won • Lost • Pct • GB

Eighth   73   89   .451   28.5

Manager

Walter Alston

Stats

Stats	Dods	NL	Rank
Batting Avg:	.236	.249	10
On-Base Pct:	.301	.310	8
Slugging Pct:	.332	.363	9
Home Runs:	82		10
Stolen Bases:	56		8
ERA:	3.21	3.38	5
Fielding Avg:	.975	.978	8
Runs Scored:	519		9
Runs Allowed:	595		5

Starting Lineup

Johnny Roseboro, c
Wes Parker, 1b
Ron Hunt, 2b
Jim Lefebvre, 3b
Gene Michael, ss
Lou Johnson, lf
Willie Davis, cf
Ron Fairly, rf-1b
Al Ferrara, rf
Bob Bailey, 3b
Len Gabrielson, lf-rf
Nate Oliver, 2b-ss
Dick Schofield, ss

Pitchers

Claude Osteen, sp
Don Drysdale, sp
Don Sutton, sp
Bill Singer, sp
Ron Perranoski, rp
Phil Regan, rp
Bob Miller, sp
Jim Brewer, rp-sp

Attendance

1,664,362 (second in NL)

Club Leaders

Batting Avg:	Jim Lefebvre	.261
On-Base Pct:	Wes Parker	.358
Slugging Pct:	Willie Davis	.367
Home Runs:	Al Ferrara	16
RBIs:	Ron Fairly	55
Runs:	Willie Davis	65
Stolen Bases:	Willie Davis	20
Wins:	Claude Osteen	17
Strikeouts:	Don Drysdale	196
ERA:	Bill Singer	2.64
Saves:	Ron Perranoski	18

JANUARY 15   Los Angeles hosts the first Super Bowl, although only 61,948 attend at Memorial Coliseum. There were 30,000 empty seats despite ticket prices ranging from $6 to $10. The Green Bay Packers defeated the Kansas City Chiefs 35–10.

APRIL 10   The Dodgers lose the season opener 7–1 to the Reds in Cincinnati. In his first start since 1965, Bob Miller only went four innings.

Miller had started only three games, and 178 made relief appearances, over the previous three seasons. After four starting assignments in 1967, he returned to the bullpen.

APRIL 14   After shutting out the Dodgers five times in 1966, Cardinals pitcher Larry Jaster faces Los Angeles for the first time in 1967. Jaster didn't allow a run for the first six innings and emerged with an 8–4 win in St. Louis.

APRIL 18   Coming into the game with an 0–4 record in 1967, the Dodgers win 7–2 over the Reds in the home opener before only 17,947 on a rainy night at Dodger Stadium.

The slow start and drop from first place in 1966 to eighth in 1967 brought about a severe decline in fan patronage in Los Angeles. After drawing 2,617,029 in 1966 to lead the majors in attendance for the eight straight years, the Dodgers attracted 1,664,362 in 1967. The figure was still good enough, however, to rank second in the National League and third in the majors, trailing only the pennant-winning Cardinals and Red Sox.

APRIL 21   Scheduled to play the Cardinals, the Dodgers are rained out at home for the first time since moving to Los Angeles in 1958.

APRIL 25   Playing third base, Jim Lefebvre makes four errors, including three in the fourth inning, during a 7–1 loss to the Braves at Dodger Stadium.

MAY 3   Leading the Pirates 5–0 in Pittsburgh, the Dodgers give up five runs in the ninth inning and one in the 15th to lose 6–5. The five ninth-inning runs were given up by Don Sutton and Phil Regan.

MAY 20   The Cubs maul the Dodgers 20–3 in Chicago. The pitchers who absorbed the pounding were Claude Osteen, Joe Moeller, Dick Egan and Bill Lee. In the Dodger dugout, Don Drysdale waved a white handkerchief signifying surrender.

MAY 27   The Dodgers defeat the Giants 10–5 in San Francisco. It was the only time the anemic Los Angeles batting attack reached double digits in runs all year.

MAY 31   After being held scoreless through the first 10 innings by Don Drysdale, the Phillies explode for six runs in the 11th to beat the Dodgers 6–0 at Dodger Stadium. Drysdale gave up four of the runs and Phil Regan two.

JUNE 6   In the first round of the amateur draft, the Dodgers select third baseman Don Denbow from Southern Methodist University.

            Denbow was a complete bust and never advanced past Class A. It was the third straight year that the first pick by the Dodgers in the draft failed to reach the majors. Future major leaguers drafted and signed by the Dodgers in 1967 were Steve Yeager (fourth round), Bruce Ellingsen (63rd round) and Larry Burchart (third round of the secondary phase). Yeager played 14 years with the Dodgers from 1972 through 1985.

JUNE 19   In the third inning, Dick Schofield hits his first home run in two years and adds a walk-off single in the ninth to beat the Braves 3–2 at Dodger Stadium.

JUNE 20   The Dodgers outlast the Braves 3–2 in 15 innings at Dodger Stadium. The winning run scored on a bases-loaded walk to Johnny Roseboro by Claude Raymond. Bill Singer pitched the first 14 innings and struck out 14 batters.

JUNE 23   Outfielder-first baseman Jim Hickman pitches the final two innings of a 7–1 loss to the Giants at Dodger Stadium. Hickman allowed a run and two hits.

JUNE 27   Don Sutton pitches a two-hitter and strikes out 11 batters to beat the Reds 9–0 at Crosley Field. The only Cincinnati hits were singles by Floyd Robinson in the first inning and Tommy Helms in the fifth.

JUNE 28   Down 5–0, the Dodgers score two runs in the seventh inning, three in the eighth, and two in the ninth to win 7–5 in Cincinnati.

JULY 11   Walter Alston manages the National League to a 15-inning, 2–1 win in the All-Star Game at Anaheim Stadium. Don Drysdale pitched the 13th and 14th innings without allowing a run.

JULY 19   The Dodgers score twice in the 10th inning on bases-loaded walks by Chris Short of the Phillies to Jeff Torborg and Ron Fairly to win 3–1 in Philadelphia.

JULY 30   Seven days after the start of week-long riots in Detroit that result in 43 deaths, Lou Johnson homers in the seventh inning off Chris Short for the only run in a 1–0 triumph over the Phillies at Dodger Stadium. Don Sutton pitched the shutout.

AUGUST 21   Bill Singer strikes out 12 batters during a 2–0 win over the Braves at Dodger Stadium.

AUGUST 24   The Dodgers score three runs in the ninth inning and one in the 10th to defeat the Reds 4–3 at Dodger Stadium. Bob Bailey drove in the game-winner with a single.

SEPTEMBER 15   The Dodgers win a pair of 1–0 victory against the Phillies in Philadelphia. Bill Singer threw the shutout in the opener. Johnny Roseboro accounted for the lone run with a homer in the fourth inning off Jim Bunning. Don Drysdale pitched a complete game in the nightcap. Wes Parker drove in the winning run with a single in the ninth.

SEPTEMBER 16   Rick Joseph of the Phillies hits a walk-off grand slam in the 11th inning off Ron Perranoski to beat the Dodgers 8–4 in Philadelphia. It was Joseph's first major league homer.

SEPTEMBER 28   Claude Osteen stars with his bat and arm in a 3–0 win over the Mets at Dodger Stadium. In addition to the complete game, he hit a two-run triple off Tom Seaver in the seventh inning, then scored on Willie Davis's single.

OCTOBER 1   In the final game of the season, Alan Foster (seven innings) and Phil Regan (two innings) combine on a two-hitter to beat the Mets 2–1 at Dodger Stadium. The only New York hits were singles by Ron Swoboda and Don Bosch in the second inning.

NOVEMBER 28   The Dodgers trade Johnny Roseboro, Ron Perranoski, and Bob Miller to the Twins for Zoilo Versalles and Mudcat Grant.

               The deal with Minnesota backfired, as Perranoski led the AL in saves in 1969 (31) and 1970 (34) with earned run averages of 2.11 and 2.43. A shortstop, Versalles won the Most Valuable Player Award in 1965 before slumping to a batting average of .200 in 1967. The Dodgers hoped for a recovery, but Versalles hit just .196 in his only season with the club. Grant, a 21-game winner on the 1965 Minnesota team that played the Dodgers in the World Series, was likewise a bust and played only one year in Los Angeles. The trade of Roseboro left Don Drysdale as the only remaining Dodger who had played for the club in Brooklyn.

NOVEMBER 30   Nine days before the Queen Mary docks in Long Beach, the Dodgers trade Lou Johnson to the Cubs for Paul Popovich and Jim Williams.

1968

Season in a Sentence

Six consecutive shutouts by Don Drysdale highlights a second straight losing season as attendance plummets to the lowest figure since the move to Los Angeles.

Finish • Won • Lost • Pct • GB

Seventh   76   86   .469   21.0
(tie)

Manager

Walter Alston

Stats

Stats	Dods	NL	Rank
Batting Avg:	.230	.243	9
On-Base Pct:	.289	.300	9
Slugging Pct:	.319	.341	8
Home Runs:	67		9
Stolen Bases:	57		7
ERA:	2.69	2.99	2
Fielding Avg:	.977	.978	8
Runs Scored:	470		10
Runs Allowed:	509		3

Starting Lineup

Tom Haller, c
Wes Parker, 1b
Paul Popovich, 2b-ss
Bob Bailey, 3b
Zoilo Versalles, ss
Len Gabrielson, lf-rf
Willie Davis, cf
Ron Fairly, rf
Jim Lefebvre, 2b
Ken Boyer, 3b

Pitchers

Don Drysdale, sp
Bill Singer, sp
Claude Osteen, sp
Don Sutton, sp
Mike Kekich, sp
Jim Brewer, rp
Jack Billingham, rp
Mudcat Grant, rp

Attendance

1,581,093 (third in NL)

Club Leaders

Batting Avg:	Tom Haller	.285
On-Base Pct:	Tom Haller	.345
Slugging Pct:	Tom Haller	.388
Home Runs:	Len Gabrielson	10
RBIs:	Tom Haller	53
Runs:	Willie Davis	86
Stolen Bases:	Willie Davis	36
Wins:	Don Drysdale	14
Strikeouts:	Don Drysdale	227
ERA:	Don Drysdale	2.15
Saves:	Jim Brewer	14

FEBRUARY 13   The Dodgers trade Ron Hunt and Nate Oliver to the Giants for Tom Haller and Frank Kasheta.

The trade was the first between the Giants and Dodgers since the Jackie Robinson trade of December 13, 1956, which was subsequently canceled. The last one prior to that was in 1946. Haller proved to be an excellent acquisition, serving as the Dodgers starting catcher for three seasons. He hit .285 and made the All-Star team in his first season in Los Angeles.

MARCH 24   The Dodgers defeat the Pirates 4–0 in the second of two exhibition games in Nassau, Bahamas.

MARCH 26   The Dodgers purchase Rocky Colavito from the White Sox.

APRIL 7   Phillies general manager John Quinn says his club will risk a fine and forfeit rather than play the scheduled opener against the Dodgers in Los Angeles on April 9. The funeral of Dr. Martin Luther King Jr., who was murdered on April 4, was to take place that day. Every other game slated for either April 8 or 9 had been postponed, but the Dodgers refused to call off the contest versus Philadelphia. National League president Warren Giles said, "It is strictly up to Los Angeles as to whether the game is played." Giles confirmed that the Philadelphia club would forfeit if it wasn't on the field by the scheduled start of the game. Under enormous public criticism, the Dodgers finally postponed the game the following day on April 8.

APRIL 10   The Dodgers lose the re-scheduled opener 2–0 to the Phillies before 28,138 at Dodger Stadium. Chris Short pitched a four-hit shutout. Claude Osteen was the Dodgers starter and loser.

APRIL 11   The Dodgers are shutout in the second game of the season as well, losing 4–0 to Jerry Koosman and the Mets at Dodger Stadium. It was Koosman's first big league victory.

APRIL 13   Ron Fairly's home run in the second inning off Don Cardwell is the lone run in a 1–0 victory over the Mets at Dodger Stadium. Don Drysdale pitched the shutout.

The next day, the Dodgers were shut out again, losing 3–0 to Jim Bunning and the Pirates at Dodger Stadium. Fairly's homer on April 13 accounted for the lone Los Angeles run in the first four games of the 1968 campaign. The season was historic because of the low offensive output throughout baseball. National League and American League clubs both averaged 3.4 runs per game in 1968, the lowest figure since 1908. Everyone had trouble scoring runs, but the Dodgers took it to an extreme. As a team, the club had a .230 batting average, .289 on-base percentage and a .319 slugging percentage and scored just 470 runs, the fewest in the NL, an average of 2.9 per game. At Dodger Stadium, the club scored 212 runs, an average of 2.6 per game.

APRIL 20   Bill Singer strikes out 12 batters and allows only two hits in seven innings, but loses 3–2 to the Mets in New York. In the sixth inning, Singer allowed a single to Bud Harrelson, a walk, and a three-run homer to Ron Swoboda.

APRIL 21   Phil Regan wins both games as a reliever during a double-header against the Mets in New York. In the opener, he allowed a run in the eighth inning to put the Dodgers behind 6–5, but his teammates rallied with two tallies in the ninth on a two-out, two-run double by Zoilo Versalles to win 7–6. Jack Billingham earned the save. In the second tilt, Regan pitched 4¹⁄₃ innings for a 3–2 victory.

Two days later, Regan was traded to the Cubs.

APRIL 22   The Dodgers score three runs with two out in the ninth inning to win 5–3 over the Pirates in Pittsburgh. Wes Parker tied the score with a double, and Zoilo Versalles broke it by hitting a two-run triple.

APRIL 23   The Dodgers trade Phil Regan and Jim Hickman to the Cubs for Ted Savage and Jim Ellis.

The deal with the Cubs proved to be a large roadblock in the Dodgers rebuilding plans. In the spring of 1968, Regan experienced an odd swelling in his joints and could barely lift a coffee cup. A physician diagnosed him as having rheumatoid arthritis. Fortunately, after a month, the symptoms subsided. The Dodgers, concerned that Regan wouldn't fully recover, practically gave him away to the Cubs. Ellis never played a game in a Los Angeles uniform, and Savage hit .206 for the club in 61 games. Regan, on the other hand, had a 12–5 record,

25 saves and a 2.27 ERA over the remainder of the 1968 seasons, and delivered another strong performance in 1969. Hickman hit only .163 in 65 games and 98 at-bats as a Dodger. Although it was the only good season of his career, he was an All-Star with the Cubs in 1970, hitting 32 homers with 115 RBIs.

APRIL 26	The Dodgers score four runs in the ninth inning to defeat the Giants 4–1 in San Francisco. Luis Alcaraz shattered the 1–1 tie with a three-run homer. It was his first home run as a big leaguer.
MAY 7	The Dodgers win a 17-inning marathon against the Braves at Dodger Stadium. Bob Bailey drove in both runs with singles in the sixth and 17th innings. Atlanta scored in the ninth to send the contest into extra innings. Claude Osteen (10 innings), Jack Billingham (three innings), John Purdin (three innings) and Mudcat Grant (one inning).
MAY 11	The Dodgers sign Ken Boyer following his release by the White Sox.
MAY 12	The Dodgers win 1–0 in 12 innings over the Braves at Dodger Stadium. The winning run scored on a triple by Willie Davis and an infield hit by Zoilo Versalles. Don Sutton (nine innings), Jack Billingham (two innings), John Purdin (two-thirds of an inning) and Mudcat Grant (one-third of an inning) combined on the shutout.
MAY 14	Don Drysdale pitches a two-hitter to defeat the Cubs 1–0 at Dodger Stadium. The only Chicago hits were singles by Don Kessinger in the fourth inning and Ferguson Jenkins in the fifth.
MAY 17	Bill Singer pitches a two-hitter and drives in two runs during a 6–0 victory over the Astros at Dodger Stadium. The only Houston hits were singles by Doug Rader in the fifth inning and Bob Aspromonte in the ninth.
MAY 18	Don Drysdale pitches his second consecutive shutout, beating the Astros by a 1–0 score at Dodger Stadium. It was also Drysdale's second straight 1–0 victory.
MAY 22	Don Drysdale pitches his third consecutive shutout, downing the Cardinals 2–0 in St. Louis. Bob Gibson pitched the first eight innings for St. Louis and allowed only one run and one hit.
MAY 24	The Dodgers score five runs in the 10th inning to take a 9–4 lead, then survive a Houston rally in the bottom half to win 9–7 at the Astrodome. The Astros scored twice in the ninth to force extra innings. Bob Bailey smashed the 4–4 deadlock with a three-run homer before the Dodgers added two more.
MAY 26	Don Drysdale pitches his fourth consecutive shutout, beating the Astros 5–0 in Houston. He allowed four batters to reach base in the ninth inning, but the Astros couldn't dent the scoreboard. After Denis Menke and Rusty Staub singled, Lee Thomas hit into a double play. Jim Wynn walked and Drysdale hit Bob Aspromonte with a pitch to load the bases. Dave Adlesh ended the game by grounding out.
MAY 27	The National League votes to expand from 10 teams to 12 with the addition of franchises in San Diego and Montreal. The San Diego franchise was the fifth to be located in California. There were none in the state as recently as 1957.

Buzzie Bavasi, executive vice-president and general manager of the Dodgers, headed a group that owned 50 percent of the San Diego franchise. Bavasi had been general manager since October 1950. During his tenure, the Dodgers won eight NL championships and four World Series. He inherited a winning team built by Branch Rickey, and it can be argued that Rickey should be given the lion's share of the credit for the pennants of 1952, 1953, 1955 and 1956. But by the time the stars of those teams had retired, Bavasi had replacements waiting. He put together a scouting and player development system that was second to none and the title teams of 1959, 1963, 1965 and 1966 won largely with home grown talent. Bavasi also should be given much of the credit for the World Series teams of 1974, 1977, 1978 and 1981, because the core group of players on those clubs were scouted, signed or drafted while Bavasi was running the front office. By the same token, Buzzie made few trades that benefited the club. Fortunately he made relatively few transactions with other clubs, because most of them turned out badly. Bavasi was unable to transfer his success with the Dodgers to San Diego. During the Padres first seven years of existence, the club averaged 100 losses per seasons. Bavasi resigned as president in 1977. Fresco Thompson succeeded Bavasi as general manager of the Dodgers. An infielder in the majors from 1925 through 1934, Thompson had been Bavasi's top assistant since 1950. Just weeks after earning his promotion, Thompson was diagnosed with cancer and died on November 20, 1968 at the age of 66. Al Campanis followed Thompson as general manager. Campanis was 52 years old in 1968 and had been a part of the Dodger family for more than 25 years. He played seven games with the Dodgers in 1943, and although he hit .100 in 20 at-bats, gained the distinction of being the only player in big league history to be born in Greece. His birthplace was Kos, in the Dodecanese Islands off the coast of Greece. Campanis was director of scouting when elevated to the post of general manager, although his official title was vice-president, player personnel and scouting. He was the club's general manager for nearly two decades and continued the success of the franchise fostered by Larry MacPhail, Rickey and Bavasi before being fired for making racist remarks on national television (see April 6, 1987).

MAY 31   Don Drysdale ties a major league record by pitching his fifth consecutive shutout, defeating the Giants 3–0 at Dodger Stadium. The mark was set by Doc White of the White Sox in 1904. Drysdale's fifth straight whitewash was not without controversy. He was saved by an umpire's call. In the ninth inning, Drysdale issued a walk to Willie McCovey, a single to Jim Ray Hart and a walk to Dave Marshall to load the bases with none out. Dick Dietz worked the count to 2–2 and was struck on the arm by a pitch to apparently force in a run. However, home plate umpire Harry Wendlestedt refused to allow Dietz to take first base, ruling he made no effort to avoid the pitch. On the next pitch, Dietz flied out. Ty Cline grounded into a force play at the plate and Jack Hiatt popped up to end the game.

JUNE 1   The Dodgers score two runs in the ninth inning to defeat the Giants 4–3 at Dodger Stadium. The runs were accounted for on a double by Willie Davis, a triple from Jim Fairey, two intentional walks, and Bob Bailey's single.

JUNE 4   Don Drysdale sets a major league record with his sixth consecutive shutout, beating the Pirates 5–0 at Dodger Stadium. He allowed three hits. The shutout extended Drysdale's scoreless streak to 54 innings, which broke the National League record of 46 set by Carl Hubbell of the Giants in 1933. At the time, the major league record was 56 innings, established by Walter Johnson of the Senators in 1913.

About two hours after the end of the game, Robert Kennedy was shot at the Ambassador Hotel in Los Angeles while celebrating victories in the California Democratic Party primary. Moments before the shooting, Kennedy publicly congratulated the Dodger ace on his record-breaking performance. "I wish to express my high regard for Don Drysdale, who pitched his sixth straight shutout tonight," said Kennedy, "and I hope we have his good fortune in this campaign." Kennedy died 25 hours later at 1:44 a.m. on June 6.

JUNE 5   Bill Singer strikes out 12 batters in 10 innings for a 2–1 win over the Pirates at Dodger Stadium. Zoilo Versalles scored the winning run on two errors. As he headed from first to third on a single by Wes Parker, third baseman Maury Wills let the throw from center fielder Matty Alou get past him and Versalles headed toward the plate. Pitcher Al McBean, backing up the play, threw home to catcher Jerry May, who dropped the ball.

JUNE 7   With the fifth overall pick in the first round of the amateur draft, the Dodgers select outfielder Bobby Valentine from Rippowam High School in Stamford, Connecticut.

Valentine had a 10-year career in the majors, but fell shy of projections largely because of injuries. Nonetheless, the Dodgers arguably had the greatest draft year of any team in major league history. In the secondary phase in January, the club chose Dave Lopes (second round) and Geoff Zahn (fifth). In the regular phase of the June draft, future major leaguers drafted and signed were Bill Buckner (second round), Mike Pazik (fourth), Tom Paciorek (fifth), Joe Ferguson (eighth), Doyle Alexander (ninth), Bob Gallagher (17th). In the secondary phase in June, Steve Garvey was drafted in the first round followed by Sandy Vance (second) and Ron Cey (third). Garvey, Lopes, Cey, Buckner and Ferguson played on multiple World Series teams for the Dodgers. Garvey, Lopes, Cey, Buckner, Paciorek and Alexander would all be named to All-Star teams. Ferguson and Zahn both had long and productive careers.

JUNE 8   On the day of Robert Kennedy's funeral, Don Drysdale breaks Walter Johnson's record for consecutive scoreless innings, but falls short of achieving his seventh consecutive shutout in a 5–3 loss to the Phillies at Dodger Stadium. Drysdale held Philadelphia scoreless through the first four innings to extend his scoreless streak to 58 innings, breaking the mark of 56 set by Walter Johnson in 1913. Drysdale was distracted in both the third and fourth innings when Phillie manager Gene Mauch instructed the umpires to search Drysdale, suspecting the Dodger pitcher of using a foreign substance on the ball. The umps found nothing suspicious, but told Drysdale not to touch his head. In the fifth, Tony Taylor singled, went to third on a single by Clay Dalrymple, and scored on a sacrifice fly by pinch-hitter Howie Bedell. Drysdale later surrendered runs in the sixth and seventh.

The RBI by Bedell that ended Drysdale's streak was the third and last of his big league career. Bedell played in 58 games for the Braves in 1962 and drove in just two runs in 138 at-bats. After spending five full seasons and part of a sixth in the minors, Bedell was called up by the Phillies in June 1968. The plate appearance against Drysdale was only the second of nine that Bedell made in 1968, his last big league season.

JUNE 9   The Dodgers score two runs in the ninth inning to win 4–3 over the Phillies at Dodger Stadium. A homer by Paul Popovich, his first in the majors, tied the score

3–3. The winning run scored on a walk, a single and a sacrifice fly by Willie Davis.

June 9 represented the high point of the season. The Dodgers were 32–26 and in second place, two games behind. The club hit a long rough patch, however, with 48 losses in the next 70 games. As a result, the team experienced consecutive losing seasons for the first time since 1937 and 1938. It wouldn't happen again until 1986 and 1987.

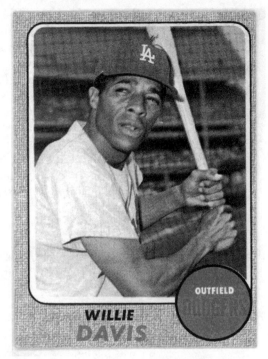

JUNE 20   Jim Fairey hits a pinch-homer in the 10th inning that beats the Pirates 3–2 in the second game of a double-header at Forbes Field. Pittsburgh won the first game 7–3.

During his 14 years with the team, Willie Davis embodied the Dodger focus on speed, defense and hustle.

JUNE 26   Don Drysdale loses a chance at a no-hitter in the eighth inning but wins his 200th career game with a two-hitter and a 2–1 decision over the Giants at Candlestick Park. With two out in the San Francisco eighth, Jack Hiatt walked, reached second on Drysdale's error, and scored on a single by Dave Marshall to end both the no-hit bid and the shutout. Jim Ray Hart added a single with two out in the ninth for the second Giants hit.

JUNE 27   Zoilo Versalles homers in the 11th inning off Juan Marichal to defeat the Giants 6–5 in San Francisco.

JULY 1   Heading into a game against the Dodgers at Dodger Stadium, Cardinals ace Bob Gibson has pitched five consecutive shutouts, one shy of the record set by Don Drysdale less than a month earlier. Ironically, Gibson's mound opponent in the July 1 contest was Drysdale. Gibson's bid for a sixth straight shutout ended in the first inning, but he still won 5–1. The lone Los Angeles run scored with two out when Len Gabrielson and Tom Haller singled and Gabrielson crossed the plate on a wild pitch.

           After surrendering the run, Gibson pitched 23 consecutive scoreless innings over three starts. Were it not for the first-inning run he allowed in the July 1 contest, Gibson would have pitched seven consecutive shutouts and 71 consecutive scoreless innings.

JULY 9   Don Drysdale is the starting pitcher in the All-Star Game at the Astrodome in Houston and pitches three scoreless innings to spark the National league to a 1–0 victory.

           Drysdale started five All-Star Games, a record he shares with Lefty Gomez and Robin Roberts. Overall, he pitched in eight games and allowed only three earned runs in $19^{1}/_{3}$ innings. He struck out 19 batters.

JULY 10   The National League votes to divide into two divisions in 1969 because of the addition of expansion teams in Montreal and San Diego. The Dodgers were placed in the Western Division with Atlanta, Cincinnati, Houston, San Diego and San Francisco.

               The rivalry between the Dodgers and Reds during the 1970s was created because of the shortsightedness of Mets chairman of the board M. Donald Grant. In 1968, the three biggest road draws were the Dodgers, Giants and Cardinals. Grant insisted that the Mets be placed in a division with at least one of the three. Being the easternmost of the three teams, St. Louis thus moved into the Eastern Division, but the Cardinals would agree only if long-standing rival Chicago were included. That put Atlanta and Cincinnati, two cities east of St. Louis and Chicago, into the west in defiance of geographic logic. Shortly after division play began, the Cardinals declined from their perch as one of the NL's best teams, while the Reds became one of the top attractions in baseball.

JULY 16   Ron Fairly hits a grand slam off Jim Maloney in the fifth inning of a 9–2 win over the Reds in Cincinnati. It was the first grand slam by a Dodger player since September 9, 1964.

AUGUST 4   Mike Kekich pitches a one-hitter and strikes out 11 batters for a 2–0 win over the Mets in the second game of a double-header at Dodger Stadium. The only New York hit was a single by Ron Swoboda with two out in the seventh inning. Willie Davis scored both Los Angeles runs. The Mets won the opener 8–4.

AUGUST 5   A single by Zoilo Versalles, his fourth hit of the game, drives in the lone run of a 1–0 win over the Pirates at Dodger Stadium. Jack Billingham (eight innings) and Jim Brewer (two innings) combined on the shutout.

               Billingham made 49 relief appearances and this lone start as a rookie with the Dodgers in 1968. Two months later, he went to the Expos in the expansion draft. By 1972 he landed in Cincinnati, and twice won 19 games as a starter with the Reds.

AUGUST 10   The Dodgers edge the Phillies 3–2 in 14 innings at Dodger Stadium. A single by Ken Boyer drove in the winning run.

               The Dodgers drew 1,581,093 fans in 1968, the lowest figure since the move to Los Angeles. The figure ranked fifth in the majors that season behind the Tigers, Cardinals, Red Sox and Mets.

AUGUST 11   Don Drysdale not only pitches a shutout, he drives in the lone run with a single in the fourth inning for a 1–0 victory over the Phillies at Dodger Stadium.

               The shutout was Drysdale's eighth of the season. He finished the 1968 campaign with a 14–12 record and a 2.15 ERA in 239 innings.

SEPTEMBER 3   Four days after the end of the Democratic National Convention in Chicago, marred by violent confrontations between antiwar demonstrators and police, the Dodgers trail 7–2 in the eighth inning before rallying to defeat the Phillies 10–9 in Philadelphia. Five Los Angeles runs in the eighth tied the score, and after a Philadelphia tally in the bottom half, three runs in the ninth put the Dodgers in the lead. A two-run double by Len Gabrielson broke the 8–8 tie. It was the first time that the Dodgers scored at least 10 runs in a game since May 27, 1967.

SEPTEMBER 4   Don Sutton strikes out 12 batters and allows only three hits to defeat the Phillies 3–0 in Philadelphia.

SEPTEMBER 9   The Dodgers score eight runs in the second inning and beat the Cardinals 10–1 in St. Louis. Bill Sudakis, in only his seventh big league game, hit a grand slam off Jim Hughes in the second inning.

SEPTEMBER 25   After allowing only one hit through eight innings, Bill Singer takes a 1–0 lead into the ninth inning, but loses 4–1 to the Cubs in Chicago on a walk-off grand slam by Ernie Banks.

OCTOBER 14   In the expansion draft, the Dodgers lose Jack Billingham, Mudcat Grant and Jim Fairey to the Expos and Zoilo Versalles, Al Ferrara and Jim Williams to the Padres.

OCTOBER 21   The Dodgers sell Bob Bailey to the Expos.

DECEMBER 15   Six weeks after Richard Nixon defeats Hubert Humphrey in the presidental election, general manager Jim Campanis trades his son Jim for two minor leaguers.

A catcher, Jim Campanis played in 113 big league games over six seasons with the Dodgers, Royals and Pirates, and hit only .147 with just four home runs in 217 at-bats.

Six in a Row

Don Drysdale set a major league record in 1968 with six consecutive shutouts. Given the strict pitch counts in today's game it is a mark that is unlikely to be matched. The last major league pitcher with at least six shutouts in an entire season was Tim Belcher, who had eight for the Dodgers in 1989. The six shutouts were accomplished as follows:

Date	Opponent	IP	H	R	BB	SO	Score
May 14	Cubs at Los Angeles	9	2	0	3	7	1–0
May 18	Astros at Los Angeles	9	5	0	2	6	1–0
May 22	Cardinals at St. Louis	9	5	0	0	8	2–0
May 26	Astros at Houston	9	6	0	2	6	5–0
May 31	Giants at Los Angeles	9	6	0	2	7	3–0
June 4	Pirates at Los Angeles	9	3	0	0	8	5–0
		54	27	0	9	42	

The streak ended on June 8 with a 5–3 win over the Phillies, but not before breaking the existing major league record for consecutive scoreless innings with 58. Despite the incredible feat and fact that he was 31 years old, Drysdale was near the end of his career. Following the June 8 victory, he won only 11 more games, while losing 13 and posting a 3.38 ERA before a torn rotator cuff ended his career. Orel Hershiser would break Drysdale's scoreless innings streak with 59 in 1988.

1969

LA

Season in a Sentence

With a young club dubbed "The Mod Squad," the Dodgers compete for the NL West pennant race well into September in the first year of divisional play before an eight-game losing streak drops the club into fourth place.

Finish • Won • Lost • Pct • GB

Fourth 85 77 .525 8.0

Manager

Walter Alston

Stats

Stats	Dods	NL	Rank
Batting Avg:	.254	.250	5
On-Base Pct:	.315	.319	8
Slugging Pct:	.359	.369	8
Home Runs	97		11
Stolen Bases:	80		3
ERA:	3.08	3.59	3
Fielding Avg:	.980	.977	3
Runs Scored:	645		8
Runs Allowed:	561		3

Starting Lineup

Tom Haller, c
Wes Parker, 1b
Ted Sizemore, 2b
Bill Sudakis, 3b
Maury Wills, ss
Willie Crawford, lf-rf
Willie Davis, cf
Andy Kosco, rf-lf
Manny Mota, lf
Jim Lefebvre, 3b
Bill Russell, ss

Pitchers

Claude Osteen, sp
Bill Singer, sp
Don Sutton, sp
Alan Foster, sp-rp
Jim Brewer, rp
Pete Mikkelsen, rp

Attendance

1,784,527 (second in NL)

Club Leaders

Batting Avg:	Willie Davis	.311
On-Base Pct:	Willie Davis	.356
Slugging Pct:	Willie Davis	.456
Home Runs:	Andy Kosco	19
RBIs:	Andy Kosco	74
Runs:	Wes Parker	76
Stolen Bases:	Maury Wills	25
Wins:	Claude Osteen	20
	Bill Singer	20
Strikeouts:	Bill Singer	247
ERA:	Bill Singer	2.34
Saves:	Jim Brewer	20

JANUARY 21   Roy Campanella is elected to the Hall of Fame.

FEBRUARY 4   Bowie Kuhn is appointed commissioner to replace the fired General William Eckert.

APRIL 3   The Dodgers play at Anaheim Stadium for the first time and win 4–2 over the Angels in an exhibition game.

APRIL 7   The Dodgers open the regular season with a 3–2 win over the Reds at Crosley Field. Things didn't go well for Don Drysdale at the beginning of the game. Both Pete Rose and Bobby Tolan, the first two hitters in the Cincinnati line-up, homered to start the first inning. There were no more runs scored off Los Angeles pitching the remainder of the contest, however. Drysdale hurled six innings and Bill Singer three. Ron Fairly put the Dodgers into the lead with a two-run homer in the third inning. Bill Russell made his major league debut as a substitute in right field and hit a single.

APRIL 11   In his first major league start, Bill Russell collects a homer, triple and a single in five at-bats during a 9–3 win over the Astros in Houston.

Russell played his entire 18-year major league career as a Dodger. He was an outfielder when he reached the majors as a 20-year-old in 1969. Russell was converted into a shortstop in 1972, and was the club's starter at the position until 1983. During that period he appeared in four World Series and three All-Star Games. By the time his career ended in 1986, Russell had played in 2,181 games to rank second all-time in club history to Zack Wheat, who last donned Dodger togs in 1926. Russell is also fourth in at-bats (7,318), sixth in hits (1,926) and 10th in doubles (293). In 1996, Russell succeeded Tommy Lasorda as manager of the Dodgers and held the position until 1998.

APRIL 15   The Dodgers win their home opener 14–0 over the Padres before 22,200 at Dodger Stadium. It was the first time that the Dodgers played their Southern California rivals from San Diego. In addition, it was the first time the Dodgers scored more than 10 runs in a game since September 20, 1966. Andy Kosco hit the first grand slam in Los Angeles by a Dodger player since 1964 when he connected off Johnny Podres in a six-run, fifth inning that snapped a scoreless tie. Kosco later added a two-run double to give him six RBIs on the night. Tom Haller also homered. Claude Osteen pitched a three-hit shutout.

APRIL 17   The Dodgers trade Tommy Dean and Leon Everett to the Padres for Al McBean.

APRIL 18   The Dodgers score three runs in the ninth inning to defeat the Astros 5–4 at Dodger Stadium. Doubles by Tom Haller and Bill Sudakis produced the first run. The last two scored on a pair of two-out walks by Dooley Womack to Bill Russell and Wes Parker.

APRIL 19   The Dodgers come from behind in the ninth inning for the second game in a row to defeat the Astros 5–4 at Dodger Stadium. A single by Tom Haller provided the winning run.

The Dodgers brought in the fences in 1969. The power alleys were shortened from 380 feet to 370 and center field from 410 feet to 400.

APRIL 27   The Dodgers rough up the Braves 10–0 in Atlanta.

APRIL 28   The Dodgers play in San Diego for the first time, and beat the Padres 4–3 with two runs in the ninth. The runs scored on hits by three pinch-hitters: a single by Bill Russell, a triple by Willie Crawford, and a single by Ken Boyer.

The Dodgers increased the number of televised games in 1969 from nine to 18. In addition to the nine games from San Francisco, KTTV telecast nine contests from San Diego.

MAY 1   Don Sutton pitches a one-hitter to defeat the Giants 5–0 in San Francisco. The no-hit bid was wrecked on a double by Jim Davenport with two out in the eighth inning.

Sutton pitched 27 consecutive scoreless innings from April 23 through May 16.

MAY 6   The Dodgers start five rookies, including the entire infield, during a 7–1 loss to the Cubs in Chicago. The five were John Miller (1b), Ted Sizemore (2b), Bill Grabarkewitz (ss), Bill Sudakis (3b) and Bill Russell (rf).

The young Dodgers were known collectively as "The Mod Squad" after a popular television program that aired from 1968 through 1973. Sizemore won the NL Rookie of the Year Award in 1969 with a .271 batting average in 159 games. He was a catcher during his first season in the minors in 1967 before being converted into a second baseman.

MAY 7   Willie Davis breaks a 1–1 tie with a three-run homer in the 12th inning, and the Dodgers win 4–2 over the Cubs in Chicago.

A rookie in 1960, Willie Davis frustrated the Dodgers for years with his erratic play and reluctance to hit the ball on the ground to best utilize his blazing speed. He was arguably the fastest player in the game during the 1960s. But he fancied himself a home run hitter, despite his warning-track power, particularly at spacious Dodger Stadium. He turned 29 just after Opening Day in 1969 and entered the season with a .266 lifetime batting average in 1,218 games, with a career-high of .294 in 1964, and he homered once every 51 at-bats. Davis was hospitalized three times during spring training and the early part of the 1969 season after being struck by pitches, once with a fractured cheekbone. As a result, he changed his batting approach and batted .311 with 11 homers in 498 at-bats in 1969. It was the first of three consecutive seasons in which he batted .300 or better.

MAY 9   The Dodgers score nine runs in the second inning and beat the Pirates 13–3 in Pittsburgh. Andy Kosco hit two homers and drove in five runs.

MAY 16   After the Pirates score three runs in the ninth inning for a 3–2 lead, Willie Crawford clubs a two-run walk-off homer in the bottom half for a 4–3 victory at Dodger Stadium.

MAY 18   For the second time in three days, the Dodgers score two runs against the Pirates in the ninth inning at Dodger Stadium, this time winning 6–5. Len Gabrielson tied the score with a home run. Wes Parker's single drove in the winning run.

MAY 27   The Dodgers play a regular season game outside of the United States for the first time, and beat the Expos 5–3 at Jarry Park in Montreal.

JUNE 1   The Dodgers score seven runs in the second inning and defeat the Phillies 12–4 in Philadelphia.

JUNE 4   The Dodgers allow only four hits, but lose 1–0 in 15 innings to the Mets in New York. Bill Singer (nine innings), Jim Brewer (two innings) and Al McBean (three innings) pitched shutout ball through the first 14 innings. In the 15th, Pete Mikkelsen the lone run of the game when Tommie Agee scored from first base on a single by Wayne Garrett and an error.

JUNE 5   In the first round of the amateur draft, the Dodgers select catcher Terry McDermott from St. Agnes High School in West Hempstead, New York.

McDermott's big league career consisted of nine games in which he hit .130 without an extra base hit. The best pick made by the Dodgers in 1969 was Lee Lacy in the second round of the secondary draft in February. Lacy played

16 years in the majors, seven of them with the Dodgers beginning in 1972. Others future major leaguers drafted and signed by the Dodgers that year were Stan Wall (sixth round), Royle Stillman (22nd round), Bob Randall (second round of the secondary phase in June) and Bob O'Brien (fourth round of the secondary phase in February).

JUNE 6   The Expos play in Los Angeles for the first time, and lose 4–2 to the Dodgers at Dodger Stadium.

JUNE 11   The Dodgers trade Ron Fairly and Paul Popovich to the Expos for Maury Wills and Manny Mota.

Wills was named to five All-Star teams, played in four World Series, and led the NL in stolen bases six times for the Dodgers in eight seasons from 1959 through 1966, He was then unceremoniously traded to the Pirates in December 1966 after being accused of "disloyalty" for leaving the team during a post-season tour of Japan. Although he was 36 years old when he returned to Los Angeles, Wills was an effective starting shortstop through the end of the 1971 season. Mota has been in a Dodger uniform ever since the June 11, 1969, trade. He was a player with the club from 1969 through 1980, and again in 1982, and has been a coach since 1969. Mota never accumulated more than 417 at-bats in a season as a player over a 20-year career but was a valuable player off the bench. His batting average of .315 as a Dodger ranks sixth all-time among players with at least 2,000 plate appearances. Mota's 150 career pinch-hits ranks third all-time behind Lenny Harris and Mark Sweeney. Mota was the record-holder in pinch-hits from 1980 until Harris passed him in 2001. The 2008 season was Mota's 29th as a club's coach, the second most in history with one club. The only individual with a longer tenure was Nick Altrock, who coached 42 years with the Senators from 1912 through 1953.

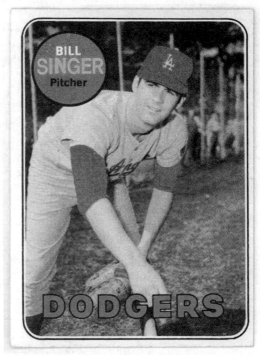

JUNE 12   Bill Singer strikes out 12 batters, but loses 1–0 to the Phillies at Dodger Stadium. The lone run scored in the first inning when leadoff batter Johnny Briggs hit the second pitch of the game for a home run.

In his third full year with the Dodgers, tall and lanky Bill Singer won 20 games as part of the team's youth movement. He also led the team in strikeouts.

JUNE 13   Alan Foster pitches the Dodgers to a 1–0 win over the Mets at Dodger Stadium. The lone run scored on a single in the second inning by Jim Lefebvre.

June 28   In the most lopsided shutout win in club history, the Dodgers overwhelm the Padres 19–0 in San Diego. It is also the largest winning margin by the Dodgers since 1892. Ten runs crossed the plate in the third inning on six singles, six walks and four wild pitches. The batting attack was spread throughout the line-up, as no one drove in more than two runs. Ten different players scored. Don Drysdale pitched what would prove to be the last of 49 career shutouts.

July 4   The famous nickname "The Big Red Machine" is used for the first time, as the Reds defeat the Dodgers 4–1 at Dodger Stadium. The name was placed in print by *Los Angeles Herald-Examiner* reporter Bob Hunter, who in his account of the game which appeared in the July 5 edition wrote, "...Bristol, the boy manager of the Big Red Machine, took (Tony Cloninger) out with two on and one down in the ninth." Given the rivalry that would develop between the Dodgers and Reds during the 1970s, it's ironic that the Big Red Machine nickname would be first used by a Los Angeles sportswriter.

July 8   Manny Mota collects eight hits in 10 at-bats during a double-header sweep of the Braves at Dodger Stadium. He was four-for-five in each game on seven singles and a double. The Dodgers won the opener 5–3. Mota capped the big day with a walk-off single in the ninth inning of game two, a 4–3 Los Angeles victory.

July 12   The Dodgers outlast the Giants 3–2 in 14 innings at Dodger Stadium.

July 16   The Dodgers take a 1½-game lead in the NL West with a 3–2 triumph over the Astros in Houston.

July 17   The Dodgers score seven runs in the seventh inning to take a 13–11 lead, only to lose 14–13 to the Giants in San Francisco.

July 23   Three days after Neil Armstrong becomes the first person to set foot on the moon, Bill Singer retires all six batters he faces in the fifth and sixth innings of the National League's 9–3 victory in the All-Star Game at RFK Stadium in Washington.

July 24   The Cubs defeat Don Sutton and the Dodgers 5–3 at Wrigley Field. The loss gave Sutton an 0–13 lifetime record against the Cubs. At the time, he was 46–40 against the rest of the league. He finished his career with an 18–20 mark versus Chicago.

July 27   Don Drysdale earns the last of his 209 career victories with a 6–2 win over the Cubs in Chicago.

                Drysdale announced his retirement in August because of a shoulder injury later diagnosed as a torn rotator cuff.

August 5   Willie Stargell hits a home run estimated at 506 feet during an 11–3 Pirates win over the Dodgers at Dodger Stadium. The blast off Alan Foster cleared the right field pavilion and is still the longest ever recorded at Dodger Stadium.

August 8   Bill Singer pitches a two-hitter to defeat the Cubs 5–0 at Dodger Stadium. The only Chicago hits were singles by Don Kessinger in the sixth inning and Jimmy Qualls in the eighth.

AUGUST 15   On the first day of the Woodstock Music Festival in Bethel, New York, the Dodgers send Chuck Goggin, Ron Mitchell and cash to the Pirates for Jim Bunning.

A future Hall of Famer, Bunning was near the end of the line when he arrived in Los Angeles. He pitched nine games for the Dodgers and had a 3–1 record before being released at the end of the season. Bunning was elected a U.S. Senator representing Kentucky in 1998 and won a second term in 2004.

AUGUST 16   Maury Wills hits the only grand slam of his career with a drive off Larry Jaster in the fifth inning of a 9–3 win over the Expos in Montreal.

AUGUST 17   Trailing 3–2, the Dodgers explode for seven runs in the ninth inning to win 9–3 over the Expos in Montreal.

AUGUST 24   The Dodgers are knocked out of first place with a 7–4 loss to the Mets in New York.

SEPTEMBER 1   Steve Garvey makes his major league debut during a 10–6 win over the Mets at Dodger Stadium. He struck out as a pinch-hitter in the seventh inning.

SEPTEMBER 3   Willie Davis runs his hitting streak to 31 games during a 5–4 win over the Mets at Dodger Stadium. He was hitless in his first four at-bats before coming to bat in the ninth inning with the score 4–4 and Maury Wills on second base. Davis delivered a run-scoring double.

The streak ended the next day when he was hitless during a 3–0 loss to the Padres in San Diego. The 31-game streak is the longest in Dodger history. It broke the record of 29 set by Zack Wheat in 1916.

SEPTEMBER 8   Ted Sizemore hits a two-run homer in the third inning for the only runs of a 2–0 win over the Braves in Atlanta. Bill Singer (eight innings) and Jim Brewer (one inning) combined on an 11-hit shutout. The Braves left 12 men on base.

SEPTEMBER 11   Claude Osteen pitches the Dodgers to a 1–0 win over the Astros in Houston. The lone run scored on back-to-back doubles by Maury Wills and Manny Mota leading off the first inning off Don Wilson.

SEPTEMBER 16   Jim Brewer wins two games in relief during a double-header against the Reds at Dodger Stadium. He pitched one inning in the opener as the Dodgers scored two runs in the ninth inning for a 2–1 win. Brewer hurled four innings during a 12-inning, 3–2 victory in the nightcap. Wes Parker ended the contest with a bases-loaded single.

Ray Lamb in 1969 is the only Dodger ever to wear number 42 during a regular season game since Jackie Robinson's retirement following the 1956 season. Lamb was re-assigned number 34 in 1970. The Dodgers retired number 42 in 1972. It was retired throughout major league baseball in 1997.

SEPTEMBER 18   The Dodgers are only one-half game out of first place after a 5–2 win over the Braves at Dodger Stadium.

The next day, the Dodgers began an eight-game losing streak, four of them to the lowly Padres, to fall out of contention.

SEPTEMBER 23   In what proves to be his last major league at-bat, John Miller hits a home run during a 6–3 loss to the Reds in the first game of a double-header at Crosley Field. Cincinnati also won the second tilt 5–2.

Miller hit only two major league home runs. The first was on September 11, 1966, as a Yankee in his first plate appearance in the majors. In between, Miller had 58 at-bats and spent the entire 1967 and 1968 seasons in the minors. His career batting average was .164.

OCTOBER 1   Claude Osteen earns his 20th victory of the decision with a 5–2 decision over the Astros at Dodger Stadium.

Osteen finished the season with a 20–15 record and a 2.66 ERA in 321 innings.

OCTOBER 2   On the last day of the season, Bill Singer picks up his 20th win of the season with a 5–4 decision over the Astros at Dodger Stadium.

Earning the nickname "The Singer Throwing Machine," Singer ended the season with a 20–12 record and a 2.34 earned run average and 247 strikeouts in $315^2/_3$ innings. The Dodgers apparently hadn't learned from overworking Don Drysdale and Sandy Koufax earlier in the decade. Claude Osteen (41), Don Sutton (41) and Singer (40) combined to start 122 games and pitch 930 innings in 1969. Singer was 25 years old in 1969 and Sutton was 24.

THE STATE OF THE DODGERS

The Dodgers reached the World Series three times during the 1970s, although the club lost on all three occasions to the Athletics in 1974 and the Yankees in 1977 and 1978. The only losing season during the 1970s was in 1979. In the NL West, the Dodgers were first three times, second in five seasons and third twice. Overall, the franchise had a record of 910–701, a winning percentage of .559 which was the third best in the NL behind only the Reds and Pirates. Four NL clubs reached the World Series during the decade. The Reds accomplished the feat in 1970, 1972, 1975 and 1976, the Mets in 1973 and the Pirates in 1971 and 1979. NL West champions outside of Los Angeles were the Reds (1970, 1972, 1975, 1976 and 1979) and the Giants (1971).

THE BEST TEAM

The 1974 Dodgers were 102–60 to post the best regular winning percentage (.630) and any team since 1955 before losing the World Series to Oakland in five games.

THE WORST TEAM

The 1979 Dodgers were 79–83, the only losing season between 1968 and 1984.

THE BEST MOMENT

The Dodgers scored three runs in the ninth inning of game three of the 1977 NLCS to beat the Phillies 6–5 and move one victory from the World Series.

THE WORST MOMENT

Steve Garvey and Don Sutton demonstrated that all was not harmonious in the Dodger clubhouse with a fight on August 20, 1978.

THE ALL-DECADE TEAM • YEARS W/DODS

Steve Yeager, c	1972–85
Steve Garvey, 1b	1969–82
Davey Lopes, 2b	1972–81
Ron Cey, 3b	1971–82
Bill Russell, ss	1969–86
Bill Buckner, lf	1969–76
Willie Davis, cf	1960–73
Reggie Smith, rf	1976–81
Don Sutton, p	1966–80, 1988
Burt Hooton, p	1975–84
Tommy John, p	1972–74, 1976–78
Jim Brewer, p	1964–75

Davis was also on the 1960s All-Decade Team. Sutton is in the Hall of Fame. Garvey, Lopes, Russell and Cey formed one of the best infields in baseball history. Other outstanding Dodgers during the 1970s included catcher Joe Ferguson (1970–76, 1978–81), right fielder Willie Crawford (1964–75), first baseman Wes Parker (1964–72), outfielders Manny Mota (1969–80, 1982), Dusty Baker (1976–83) and Jimmy Wynn (1974–75), and pitchers Doug Rau (1972–79), Andy Messersmith (1973–75), Claude Osteen (1965–73) and Charlie Hough (1970–80).

THE DECADE LEADERS

Batting Avg:	Steve Garvey	.304
On-Base Pct:	Reggie Smith	.388
Slugging Pct:	Reggie Smith	.537
Home Runs:	Steve Garvey	159
RBIs:	Steve Garvey	736
Runs:	Steve Garvey	645
	Davey Lopes	645
Stolen Bases:	Davey Lopes	375
Wins:	Don Sutton	166
Strikeouts:	Don Sutton	1,767
ERA:	Burt Hooton	2.95
Saves:	Jim Brewer	92

THE HOME FIELD

Opened in 1962, Dodger Stadium was the third oldest among the 12 NL ballparks by 1971. The Dodgers became the first team in major league history to draw over 3,000,000 fans with a figure of 3,347,845 in 1978. The club led the majors in attendance in 1973, 1974, 1975, 1977, 1978 and 1979.

THE GAME YOU WISHED YOU HAD SEEN

The Dodgers took a two-game lead in the 1978 World Series with a 4–3 win over the Yankees capped by a dramatic showdown between Bob Welch and Reggie Jackson.

THE WAY THE GAME WAS PLAYED

During the 1970s, speed and defense ruled, in part because of new stadiums with more distant fences and artificial turf. Opening in the NL during the decade were Riverfront Stadium in Cincinnati, Three Rivers Stadium in Pittsburgh, Veterans Stadium in Philadelphia and Olympic Stadium in Montreal. The average number of stolen bases per team rose from 87 in 1970 to 124 in 1979, while home runs declined from 140 to 119. The increased importance of relief pitching was underscored in 1970 when for the first time in major league history there were more saves recorded than complete games.

THE MANAGEMENT

Peter O'Malley succeeded his father as president of the Dodgers in March 1970 and ran the day-to-day operation of the club. Walter O'Malley became chairman of the board upon his son's appointment, and held the post in semi-retirement until his death in 1979. Al Campanis became general manager in 1968 and held the job throughout the 1970s. Walter Alston was field manager from 1954 until his retirement in 1976. Tommy Lasorda took over for Alston during the final week of the 1976 season and would continue as manager until 1996.

THE BEST PLAYER MOVE

The best move was a trade in April 1974 which brought Pedro Guerrero from the Indians for Bruce Ellingsen.

THE WORST PLAYER MOVE

The worst trade sent Bill Buckner, Ivan DeJesus and Jeff Albert to the Cubs for Rick Monday and Mike Garman in January 1977.

1970

Season in a Sentence

The Dodgers lose their first five games in 1970, hit the fewest home runs of any major league team, steal the most bases, and finish a distant second to the Reds in the NL West.

Finish • Won • Lost • Pct • GB

Second   87   74   .540   14.5

Manager

Walter Alston

Stats

Stats	Dods	NL	Rank
Batting Avg:	.270	.258	2
On-Base Pct:	.334	.329	3
Slugging Pct:	.382	.392	8
Home Runs:	87		12
Stolen Bases:	138		1
ERA:	3.82	4.05	5
Fielding Avg:	.978	.977	4
Runs Scored:	749		4
Runs Allowed:	684		5

Starting Lineup

Tom Haller, c
Wes Parker, 1b
Ted Sizemore, 2b
Billy Grabarkewitz, 3b-ss
Maury Wills, ss
Manny Mota, lf
Willie Davis, cf
Willie Crawford, rf-lf
Jim Lefebvre, 2b
Bill Russell, rf
Bill Sudakis, c-3b

Pitchers

Claude Osteen, sp
Don Sutton, sp
Alan Foster, sp
Joe Moeller, sp-rp
Bill Singer, sp
Sandy Vance, sp
Jim Brewer, rp

Attendance

1,697,142 (third in NL)

Club Leaders

Batting Avg:	Wes Parker	.319
On-Base Pct:	Billy Grabarkewitz	.399
Slugging Pct:	Wes Parker	.458
Home Runs:	Billy Grabarkewitz	17
RBIs:	Wes Parker	111
Runs:	Billy Grabarkewitz	92
	Willie Davis	92
Stolen Bases:	Willie Davis	38
Wins:	Claude Osteen	16
Strikeouts:	Don Sutton	201
ERA:	Claude Osteen	3.83
Saves:	Jim Brewer	24

MARCH 16   Peter O'Malley becomes president of the Dodgers, replacing his father as the head of the club's day-to-day operations. Walter O'Malley was named chairman of the board and went into semi-retirement.

APRIL 7   The Dodgers open the season with a 4–0 loss to the Reds before 30,457 at Dodger Stadium. Gary Nolan pitched a two-hitter for Cincinnati. Claude Osteen was the starting and losing pitcher.

The Dodgers started the 1970 season with five consecutive losses in which the club scored only four runs. Los Angeles finished the season 14 1/2 games behind Cincinnati. The Dodgers and Reds combined for nine of the 10 NL West titles during the 1970s and established a tremendous rivalry. The Reds won six division titles during the decade and finished second three times. The Dodgers finished first three times and second in five seasons.

APRIL 13   Don Sutton pitches a two-hitter to defeat the Astros 2–0 at the Astrodome. The only Houston hits were a double by Denis Menke in the second inning and a single by Norm Miller in the sixth.

On the same day, the Dodgers signed Camilo Pascual following his release by the Reds.

APRIL 24   The Dodgers win 1–0 in a 15-inning encounter against the Mets at Dodger Stadium. Tom Haller drove in the winning run with a single. Alan Foster (nine innings), Jim Brewer (four innings) and Ray Lamb (two innings) combined on the shutout.

The Dodgers added an organ to the Dodger Stadium experience in 1970. Helen Dell was at the keyboards from that season until 1987.

APRIL 25   The Dodgers beat the Mets 1–0 for the second day in a row at Dodger Stadium, this time in the conventional nine innings. The Dodgers won with only two hits off Nolan Ryan. The lone run scored on a single by Maury Wills in the third inning. Claude Osteen pitched the shutout.

MAY 3   The Dodgers pummel the Expos 15–1 at Dodger Stadium.

MAY 7   Three days after Ohio National Guardsmen shoot and kill four students at Kent State University, Wes Parker hits for the cycle during a 10-inning, 7–4 win over the Mets in New York. Parker doubled in the second inning and hit a homer in the seventh batting from the right side of the plate against Ray Sadecki. Hitting left-handed, Parker collected a single off Cal Koonce in the ninth inning and a triple facing Jim McAndrew in the 10th. Parker is the only Dodger since 1949 to hit for the cycle.

For the first time, fans in Los Angeles were able to watch Dodger regular season games played outside of the state of California on local television. KTTV telecast all nine games from San Francisco and every road game played on a Sunday.

MAY 8   The Dodgers explode for four runs in the 12th inning to defeat the Phillies 8–4 in Philadelphia.

MAY 9   The Dodgers win in extra innings for the third day in a row with a five-run eruption in the 14th to down the Phillies 9–4 in Philadelphia. The Dodgers scored 12 extra inning runs in the three contests.

MAY 16   During a 5–4 loss to the Giants at Dodger Stadium, 13-year-old Alan Fish is struck in the head while sitting in the stands by a line drive off the bat of Manny Mota.

The youngster said he was fine, but after the game became disoriented and began walking in circles. Fish was hospitalized and died four days later. His parents brought a lawsuit against the Dodgers and the doctor attending the first aid station. The legal action was settled in favor of the team and the physician in 1973. The teenager is the only known fatality from being hit by a foul ball in a major league game.

MAY 26   Billy Grabarkewitz scores five runs during a 19–3 thrashing of the Giants in San Francisco. The Dodgers collected 20 hits in the contest, four of them by Claude Osteen. The Dodger pitcher also drove in four runs with his homer, double and two singles. Battery mate Tom Haller, batting eighth, also picked up four hits. The fifth through ninth spots in the lineup accounted for 15 runs, 15 hits and 13 RBIs.

MAY 31   Trailing 6–1, the Dodgers score five runs in the seventh inning and two in the 11th to defeat the Cardinals 8–6 in St. Louis. Billy Grabarkewitz drove in four runs with a two-run single in the seventh inning and a two-run homer in the 11th.

Playing third base and shortstop, Grabarkewitz was a 24-year-old sensation in 1970 with a .289 batting average, 17 home runs, and an appearance in the All-Star Game. A succession of injuries wrecked a promising career. Outside of the 1970 season, Grabarkewitz had 632 career at-bats with five different teams and hit just .191. His career ended in 1975.

JUNE 4   In the first round of the amateur draft, the Dodgers select pitcher Jim Haller from Creighton Prep High School in Omaha, Nebraska.

Haller never reached the majors. Doug Rau, the first pick in the secondary phase, had an 80–58 record with the Dodgers from 1972 through 1979 and was in the starting rotation on three clubs which reached the World Series. Other future major leaguers drafted and signed by the Dodgers in 1970 were Lance Rautzhan (third round of the regular phase) and Greg Shanahan (33rd round). The Dodgers picked Mike Garrett, who won the Heisman Trophy as a running back with USC in 1965 and played in the 1970 Super Bowl with the Kansas City Chiefs, was drafted at the age of 26 in the 35th round. He said he was playing out his option with the Chiefs and would turn to baseball. Garrett decided he was better off playing football and never signed with the Dodgers.

JUNE 7   The Dodgers play at Forbes Field for the last time and lose 3–1 to the Pirates.

JUNE 14   A two-out, two-run, walk-off, pinch-homer by Bill Sudakis in the ninth inning beats the Cubs 5–4 at Dodger Stadium.

JUNE 16   A home run by Billy Grabarkewitz off Bob Veale in the fourth inning is the only run of a 1–0 win over the Pirates at Dodger Stadium. Don Sutton pitched the shutout.

JUNE 21   The Dodgers play at Crosley Field for the last time and split a double-header with the Reds. Both games ended with a 9–3 score.

JUNE 23   Bill Singer (7²/₃ innings) and Pete Mikkelsen (1²/₃ innings) combine on a two-hitter to defeat the Braves 8–0 in Atlanta. Singer, still recuperating from an attack of hepatitis which sidelined him for seven weeks, pitched no-hit ball until Clete Boyer singled with two out in the eighth inning. Singer was immediately relieved by Mikkelsen, who surrendered a single to Gil Garrido in the ninth.

Singer and Mikkelsen were both hospitalized with hepatitis. Singer spent 54 days on the disabled list with the disease, and Mikkelsen 53.

JULY 5   Bill Singer pitches a two-hitter to defeat the Giants 4–0 at Candlestick Park. The only San Francisco hits were singles by Bob Heise in the third inning and Willie McCovey in the fourth.

JULY 6   The Dodgers score five runs in the 10th inning, then withstand a three-run Astros rally in the bottom half to win 10–8 in Houston.

Outfielder Andy Kosco drew only one walk and struck out 40 times in 228 plate appearances in 1970.

JULY 8   Trailing 4–1, the Dodgers score five runs in the ninth inning and beat the Astros 6–5 in Houston. Out of the starting lineup because of a foot injury, Maury Wills put the Dodgers into the lead with a two-run pinch-double.

The Dodgers were outhomered 164–87 in 1970.

JULY 10   The Padres score five runs in the ninth inning on four home runs, but the Dodgers survive to win 9–7 in San Diego. Bill Singer gave up homers to Ivan Murrell, Ed Spezio and Dave Campbell before being relieved. Jose Pena surrendered a blast to Cito Gaston before closing out the victory.

JULY 14   Billy Grabarkewitz participates in the game-winning rally in the All-Star Game at Riverfront Stadium in Cincinnati. With the score 4–4 and two out in the NL 12th, Pete Rose singled and moved to second on a single by Grabarkewitz. Rose scored by slamming into Indians catcher Ray Fosse at the plate following a one-base hit by Jim Hickman. Claude Osteen, a Cincinnati native, pitched a scoreless 10th, 11th and 12th.

JULY 17   Don Sutton strikes out 12 batters and pitches a 10-inning shutout to defeat the Mets 1–0 at Dodger Stadium. A single by Wes Parker off Tom Seaver drove in the winning run.

Parker had the best season of his career in 1970 with a .319 batting average, 10 home runs, 111 RBIs, 196 hits and a league-leading 47 doubles.

JULY 20   Bill Singer pitches a no-hitter to defeat the Phillies 5–0 at Dodger Stadium. He struck out 10 without issuing a walk. The game was played at 4 p.m. to accommodate national television, although NBC later decided not to telecast the game. The only two Philadelphia base runners were Oscar Gamble, who was hit by a pitch in the first inning, and Don Money, who reached on an error in the seventh. Terry Harmon led off the top of the ninth grounding to first baseman Wes Parker with Singer taking the throw and making the putout at first. Denny Doyle lined to center field where Willie Davis made the catch after a long run. The last out was recorded on a foul pop up by Byron Browne to catcher Jeff Torborg.

Singer would lose his next seven decisions at Dodger Stadium. He didn't win again in Los Angeles until May 29, 1971.

JULY 22   Trailing 10–4, the Dodgers explode for eight runs in the seventh inning to win 12–10 over the Expos at Dodger Stadium. Tom Haller hit a pinch-hit grand slam off Claude Raymond which gave the Dodgers an 11–10 lead. Von Joshua pinch-hit in the big inning, then stepped to the plate after the Dodgers batted around and delivered a home run.

JULY 28   The Dodgers play at Connie Mack Stadium in Philadelphia for the last time and beat the Phillies 6–2.

AUGUST 2	The Dodgers score five runs in the ninth inning to win 6–3 over the Expos in Montreal. Back-to-back homers by Tom Haller and Bill Sudakis tied the score 3–3. Willie Davis broke the deadlock with a two-run double.
AUGUST 5	Willie Davis hits a grand slam off Don Cardwell in the fifth inning of a 12–2 win over the Braves at Dodger Stadium.
AUGUST 9	The Dodgers sweep the Reds 7–3 and 13–3 at Dodger Stadium, Ted Sizemore collected seven hits, including a double, and drove in six runs in nine at-bats.
AUGUST 11	The Dodgers play at Three Rivers Stadium in Pittsburgh for the first time and beat the Pirates 5–4.
AUGUST 12	Leading 4–2, the Dodgers break open a close game with seven runs in the ninth inning and win 11–4 over the Pirates in Pittsburgh.
AUGUST 14	After the Cubs take a 5–0 lead in the first inning, the Dodgers come up slugging and win 13–9 in Chicago. Maury Wills collected five hits, including a double, in five at-bats.
AUGUST 22	Roberto Clemente collects five hits in seven at-bats to lead the Pirates to a 16-inning, 2–1 win over the Dodgers at Dodger Stadium.
AUGUST 23	Roberto Clemente garners five hits in six at-bats during an 11–0 Pirate win over the Dodgers at Dodger Stadium.
	Clemente is the only major leaguer since 1876 to collect five hits in consecutive games.
SEPTEMBER 13	Tom Haller hits a three-run homer during a four-run Dodger ninth inning, and the Dodgers win 5–3 over the Giants in San Francisco.
	Steve Garvey and Tom Paciorek, teammates with the Dodgers from 1970 through 1975, played each other in a college football game on September 23, 1967 in East Lansing, Michigan. Paciorek's University of Houston team beat Garvey's Michigan State squad 37-7. Both were defensive backs. Paciorek was drafted in the ninth round by the Miami Dolphins, but declined to play football professionally.
SEPTEMBER 20	Trailing 6–5 in the 14th inning, Billy Grabarkewitz triples in a run and scored on Manny Mota's single to down the Astros 7–6 at Dodger Stadium.
SEPTEMBER 22	Alan Foster not only pitches a three-hit shutout, but draws a bases loaded walk in the second inning off Ron Bryant for the lone run of a 1–0 win over the Giants at Dodger Stadium. Foster had no official at-bats in the game with two walks and a sacrifice in three plate appearances.
SEPTEMBER 24	The Dodgers blow an eight-run lead and lose 14–10 in 10 innings to the Giants at Dodger Stadium. Trailing 8–0, the Giants took a 9–8 advantage with a nine-run eruption in the seventh inning. The Dodgers battled back to tie the contest only to have the Giants score four times in the 10th.
SEPTEMBER 25	The Dodgers play at Riverfront Stadium in Cincinnati for the first time and win 9–3 over the Reds.

SEPTEMBER 28   The Dodgers sell Fred Norman to the Cardinals.

OCTOBER 5   The Dodgers trade Ted Sizemore and Bob Stinson to the Cardinals for Richie Allen.

After finishing last in the major leagues in home runs in 1970, the Dodgers were in desperate need of a power hitter. Allen was 29 when he came to the Dodgers with a .297 career batting average and 211 home runs over the previous seven seasons, an average of 30 per year. The only Dodger with at least 30 home runs in a season since the move to Los Angeles in 1958 was Frank Howard, who clouted 31 in 1962. No Dodger had collected as many as 20 home runs since 1966. Allen came with a reputation for frequent drinking escapades, playing the horses, and divisiveness in the clubhouse, however. In addition, first base was the only position Allen could handle adequately, but the Dodgers already had Wes Parker, who was coming off a season in which he hit .319 and drove in 111 runs. Allen played third base and left field for the Dodgers, where he fielded abysmally. At bat, he posted a .295 average and 23 homers before being traded to the White Sox in December 1971.

DECEMBER 11   The Dodgers trade Alan Foster and Ray Lamb to the Indians for Duke Sims.

1971   LA

Season in a Sentence

The Dodgers cut the Giants lead in the NL West from eight games to one in nine days in September, but can pull no closer.

Finish • Won • Lost • Pct • GB

Second   89   73   .549   1.0

Manager

Walter Alston

Stats

	Dods • NL • Rank		
Batting Avg:	.266	.252	3
On-Base Pct:	.325	.316	4
Slugging Pct:	.370	.366	6
Home Runs:	95		9 (tie)
Stolen Bases:	76		5
ERA:	3.23	3.47	4
Fielding Avg:	.979	.979	6
Runs Scored:	663		4
Runs Allowed:	587		4

Starting Lineup

Duke Sims, c
Wes Parker, 1b
Jim Lefebvre, 2b
Richie Allen, 3b-lf
Maury Wills, ss
Willie Crawford, lf-rf
Willie Davis, cf
Bill Buckner, rf
Bobby Valentine, ss
Manny Mota, lf
Steve Garvey, 3b

Pitchers

Al Downing, sp
Don Sutton, sp
Claude Osteen, sp
Bill Singer, sp
Doyle Alexander, sp
Jim Brewer, rp
Pete Mikkelsen, rp

Attendance

2,064,594 (second in NL)

Club Leaders

Batting Avg:	Willie Davis	.309
On-Base Pct:	Richie Allen	.395
Slugging Pct:	Richie Allen	.468
Home Runs:	Richie Allen	23
RBIs:	Richie Allen	90
Runs:	Richie Allen	82
Wins:	Al Downing	20
Strikeouts:	Don Sutton	194
ERA:	Don Sutton	2.54
Saves:	Jim Brewer	22

FEBRUARY 10   On the day after an earthquake strikes Los Angeles, resulting in the death of 51 people, the Dodgers trade Andy Kosco to the Brewers for Al Downing.

Downing had a 5–13 record with the Athletics and Brewers in 1970 and had never won more than 14 games in a season during his first 10 years in the big leagues. In a tremendous comeback, he posted a 20–9 record, five shutouts, and a 2.68 earned run average for the Dodgers in 1971. Downing proved to be a one-year wonder, however, and never won more than nine games in a season before his career ended in 1977. He's best known for giving up Hank Aaron's record-breaking 715th home run on April 8, 1974.

MARCH 13   The Dodgers sell Jeff Torborg to the Angels.

MARCH 25   Running at full speed, Richie Allen crashes into a palm tree while shagging fly balls prior to an exhibition game against the Reds in Vero Beach. Allen was knocked unconscious and suffered a mild concussion and severe contusions of the head, right shoulder and wrist. Fortunately, he recovered from his injuries in time for Opening Day. At the time, Holman Stadium had no outfield fences. There were 12 palm trees planted on a berm, all of which were in play. Allen ran into the one nearest to the left-field foul line. By the time spring training started the following season, a fence had been erected in front of the trees.

APRIL 5   On Opening Day, the Dodgers lose 5–2 to the Astros in Houston. Bill Russell, playing second base, collected three hits. Bill Singer was the starting and losing pitcher.

The Dodgers wore double-knit uniforms for the first time in 1971. The newly-designed road jerseys had "Dodgers" written across the front instead of "Los Angeles," which had been the case from 1958 through 1970. The road uniforms had piping down the shoulders to the sleeve ends. The shoulder stripe on the road uniforms disappeared by the 1974 season.

APRIL 6   A two-run homer by Bill Buckner, his first in the majors, are the only runs of a 2–0 victory over the Astros in Houston. Claude Osteen pitched the shutout.

APRIL 9   In the home opener, the Dodgers lose 6–3 to the Padres before 31,413 at Dodger Stadium.

APRIL 21   Willie Davis collects five hits, including a triple, in five at-bats during a 10–2 win over the Padres in San Diego.

MAY 15   Bill Singer (seven innings) and Jim Brewer (one inning) combine on a two-hitter but the Dodgers lose 1–0 to the Giants in San Francisco. A double by Willie Mays drove in the lone run.

MAY 23   The Dodgers score two runs in the ninth inning off Ferguson Jenkins on a triple by Duke Sims and a homer from Jim Lefebvre to defeat the Cubs 4–3 in Chicago.

The Dodgers were 11½ games behind the first place Giants on May 26 with a record of 21–24.

MAY 26   Maury Wills collects his 2,000th career hit with a single off Gaylord Perry in the fifth inning of a 6–4 loss to the Giants at Dodger Stadium.

JUNE 2   Willie Davis runs his hitting streak to 25 games during a 7–1 win over the Expos at Dodger Stadium.

JUNE 6   Batting clean-up as a last-minute replacement for Richie Allen, Bill Russell collects a triple, double and single during a 4–3 win over the Mets at Dodger Stadium. Allen was in the hallway of the clubhouse while a pre-game Old-Timers' Game was in progress and didn't return to the field in time for the start of the game. Maury Wills played in both the Old-Timers' Game and the regular game.

JUNE 8   The Dodgers play at Veterans Stadium in Philadelphia for the first time, and defeat the Phillies 4–2.

> *On the same day the Dodgers selected pitcher Rick Rhoden from Atlantic High School in Boynton Beach, Florida in the first round of the amateur draft. Rhoden pitched the first five years of a 16-season career as a Dodger. In Los Angeles, he was 42–24 from 1974 through 1978. Other future major leaguers drafted and signed by the Dodgers in 1971 were Rex Hudson (fifth round), John Hale (14th round) and Kevin Pasley (29th round).*

JUNE 9   Bill Russell strikes out five consecutive times during a 9–4 loss to the Phillies in Philadelphia.

JUNE 11   The Dodgers score eight runs in the second inning of a 12–1 triumph over the Expos in Montreal.

JUNE 15   A two-run single by Maury Wills off Nolan Ryan in the fifth inning accounts for the only two runs of a 2–0 win over the Mets in New York. Al Downing pitched the shutout.

JUNE 19   Don Sutton pitches a one-hitter to win 4–0 over the Astros in Houston. The hit off Sutton was a double by Jimmy Wynn in the sixth inning. All four Los Angeles runs scored in the sixth.

> *Sutton had a 17–12 record with a 2.54 ERA with 194 strikeouts in $265^1/_3$ innings.*

JUNE 21   In his first major league start, Bob O'Brien pitches a shutout, defeating the Cardinals 4–0 at Dodger Stadium.

> *O'Brien made nine prior relief appearances before the June 21. After the shutout, he made only three more big-league starts and never won another game. He finished his career with a 2–2 record and a 3.00 ERA.*

JUNE 24   The Dodgers score eight runs in the second inning and defeat the Cardinals 11–4 at Dodger Stadium.

JUNE 26   Richie Allen hits a walk-off homer in the 13th inning to defeat the Padres 4–3 in the second game of a double-header at Dodger Stadium. The Dodgers also won the opener 4–2.

JULY 3   Al Downing pitches the Dodgers to a 1–0 win over the Padres in San Diego. The lone run scored in the ninth inning on a double by Willie Davis.

JULY 4   Trailing 4–3, the Dodgers explode for 10 runs in the eighth inning and beat the Giants 14–4 in San Francisco. The runs scored on two homers (by Richie Allen and Jim Lefebvre), a double, five singles, two walks, two errors and a wild pitch.

JULY 10   The Dodgers sign 47-year-old Hoyt Wilhelm following his release by the Braves.

              Wilhelm pitched the last 25 games of his Hall of Fame career with the Dodgers, and had a 3.14 ERA in 43 innings.

JULY 18   Joe Ferguson's home run leading off the ninth inning is the only Los Angeles hit, robbing Luke Walker of the Pirates of a no-hitter. It was Ferguson's first major league homer. The Dodgers lost 7–1 in the second game of a double-header at Three Rivers Stadium. Pittsburgh also won the opener 3–2.

              Ferguson was the first Dodger since ill-fated Ralph Branca in 1953 to wear uniform number 13. Like many Dodgers of the 1970s, Ferguson began his professional career at one position before becoming a regular at another. He was an outfielder in the minors in 1968 before making a switch to catcher.

JULY 27   Down 5–1, the Dodgers score six runs in the seventh inning and beat the Pirates 8–5 at Dodger Stadium. Bill Buckner put the Dodgers into the lead with a grand slam off Mudcat Grant.

AUGUST 1   After the Reds take a 4–3 lead in the top of the 11th, the Dodgers score twice in their half in bizarre fashion to win 5–4 at Dodger Stadium. First, Bill Buckner was hit by a Joe Gibbon pitch with the bases loaded to force in the tying run. With the sacks still full, Manny Mota tried to steal home and was tagged out by Cincinnati catcher Johnny Bench. However, home plate umpire Harry Wendelstedt ruled catcher's interference on Bench because he stepped in front of hitter Willie Crawford, in addition to a balk on Gibbon. Either penalty allowed Mota to score the winning run.

AUGUST 2   A three-run homer by Steve Garvey in the ninth inning beats the Giants 5–4 in San Francisco.

              Garvey was born in Tampa, and during spring training, his father often drove the Dodger team bus when the club played on Florida's west coast. Steve sometimes came along for the ride. He played football and baseball at Michigan State before being drafted by the Dodgers in 1968. Garvey broke in as a third baseman, and initially struggled both offensively and defensively. He didn't become a regular until the middle of the 1973 season when he was moved across the diamond to first base. Once in the lineup, Garvey refused to leave and played in 1,207 consecutive games with the Dodgers and Padres from 1975 through 1983. During his career, Garvey won an MVP award in 1974, and appeared in five World Series, four as a Dodger, and 10 All-Star Games, eight of them in a Los Angeles uniform. He collected 200 or more hits in six seasons and batted over .300 seven times. On the all-time club lists, Garvey ranks ninth in games played (1,727), eighth in at-bats (6,543), third in doubles (333), fifth in hits (1,968), fifth in runs batted in (992) and sixth in homers (211).

August 7	Matty Alou of the cardinals beats out a bunt and scores in the 10th inning for the deciding run in a 3–2 win over the Dodgers in St. Louis. After Alou reached first, second baseman Jim Lefebvre huddled with pitcher Pete Mikkelsen halfway between the mound and second base, but they failed to call time. Alou suddenly took off for second, and Mikkelsen threw high to Lefebvre, who had backtracked to the bag. Alou continued on to third. Lefebvre charged the ball but had difficulty picking it up in short-center, and Alou raced home ahead of Lefebvre's hurried throw.
August 24	Willie Davis collects five hits, including a bases-loaded triple, in five at-bats during a 6–4 victory over the Expos in Montreal.
September 1	The Dodgers score eight runs in the second inning and defeat the Astros 9–1 in Houston. Don Sutton struck out 12 batters.
September 2	Cesar Cedeno of the Astros hits a fluke grand slam which helps beat the Dodgers 9–3 in Houston. The ball fell between second baseman Jim Lefebvre and right fielder Bill Buckner near the foul line and rolled into the corner. Lefebvre got his glove on the ball, but he dropped it as he tried to leap out of the way of the onrushing Buckner. Both fielders performed acrobatics to avoid a head-on collision.
September 3	The Dodgers score four runs in the ninth inning and beat the Reds 6–5 at Dodger Stadium. Los Angeles loaded the bases on two walks and a single. In his first major league plate appearance, Ron Cey stepped to the plate and struck out, but Maury Wills drove in a run with a single and Manny Mota stroked a three-run triple for the victory.
September 4	Woody Woodward of the Reds is almost hit by a 10-pound sack of flour which drops from an airplane passing over Dodger Stadium. The sack hit the ground and exploded just 15 feet from where Woodward was standing at his shortstop position during the ninth inning of a 2–1 Dodger win.
September 5	The Dodgers fall eight games behind the Giants with a 7–5 loss to the Reds at Dodger Stadium.
September 13	The streaking Dodgers win their seventh consecutive game and pull within two games of first place with a 5–4 win over the Giants in San Francisco. The contest was marred by a beanball battle. Bill Singer hit Willie Mays with a pitch in the first inning and Chris Speier with another in the fourth. In the fifth, Juan Marichal knocked down Singer twice, then plunked Bill Buckner with a pitch. Ominously, Buckner headed toward the mound with a bat in his hands. The home plate umpire was Shag Crawford, who was also behind the plate during the infamous confrontation between Marichal and Johnny Roseboro six years earlier (see August 22, 1965). About 10 feet shy of the mound, Crawford and Giant catcher Russ Gibson stopped Buckner. Crawford ejected both Marichal and Buckner. Giants pitcher Jerry Johnson was also tossed for shoving Crawford.
September 14	A three-run, pinch-double by Matty Mota in the ninth inning defeats the Giants 6–5 at Candlestick Park. It was the Dodgers eighth win in a row and put the club one game behind San Francisco. Los Angeles made up seven games in a span of nine games.

SEPTEMBER 19   The Dodgers sweep the Braves 12–0 and 4–0 at Dodger Stadium behind shutouts from Al Downing and Don Sutton.

SEPTEMBER 24   Al Downing earns his 20th win of the season with a 2–0 decision over the Braves in Atlanta. Willie Davis scored both Dodger runs, one of them on a home run in the fourth inning.

SEPTEMBER 25   The Dodgers are one game behind the first place Giants after a 5–4 victory over the Braves in Atlanta.

SEPTEMBER 29   In the second-to-last game of the season, the Dodgers have a chance to move into a tie for first place, but lose 11–0 to the Astros at Dodger Stadium.

SEPTEMBER 30   On the final day of the season, the Dodgers beat the Astros 2–1, but the Giants clinch the NL West pennant by defeating the Padres 5–1 in San Diego.

OCTOBER 21   The Dodgers trade Tommy Hutton to the Phillies for Larry Hisle.

DECEMBER 2   On a busy day, the Dodgers trade Doyle Alexander, Bob O'Brien, Sergio Robles and Royle Stillman to the Orioles for Frank Robinson and Pete Richert. In a second deal, Richie Allen went to the White Sox for Tommy John and Steve Huntz. In a third transaction, Tom Haller was sent to the Tigers for Bernie Beckman and cash.

Robinson came to the Dodgers as an 11-time All-Star and had twice won the MVP award. He played in both the All-Star Game and the World Series in each of the previous three seasons. Robinson had an off-year with the Dodgers in 1972, however, and went to the Angles in a trade in December 1972 which netted Andy Messersmith. Alexander was still active in 1989 and won 188 games after leaving the Dodgers, but none of the other three players who went to Baltimore were missed. Allen won the American League Most Valuable Player Award in 1972, his first season in Chicago. He provided the Sox with two more excellent seasons before going into a steep decline. At the time of the trade, John had a lifetime record of 84–91. He was 40–18 with the Dodgers from 1972 through 1974 before undergoing innovative surgery (see July 17, 1974). After missing the entire 1975 campaign in rehabilitation, John had a record of 47–27 as a Dodger from 1976 through 1978 before moving to the Yankees as a free agent. John's winning percentage of .674 with the club is the third best all-time and the best of any pitcher since the move to Los Angeles.

1972

Season in a Sentence

After an off-season of bold trades and the introduction of several promising rookies, the Dodgers continue to tread water with a winning percentage nearly identical to that of each of the previous three seasons.

Finish • Won • Lost • Pct • GB

Third   85   70   .548   10.5

Manager

Walter Alston

Stats

Stats	Dods	NL	Rank
Batting Avg:	.256	.248	6
On-Base Pct:	.319	.315	6
Slugging Pct:	.360	.365	7
Home Runs:	98		9 (tie)
Stolen Bases:	82		5
ERA:	2.78	3.45	1
Runs Scored:	584		7
Runs Allowed:	527		2

Starting Lineup

Chris Cannizzaro, c
Wes Parker, 1b
Bobby Valentine, 2b-3b
Steve Garvey, 3b
Bill Russell, ss
Manny Mota. lf
Willie Davis, cf
Bill Buckner, rf-1b
Frank Robinson, rf
Willie Crawford, lf-rf
Lee Lacy, 2b

Pitchers

Claude Osteen, sp
Don Sutton, sp
Tommy John, sp
Al Downing, sp
Bill Singer, sp
Jim Brewer, rp

Attendance

1,860,858 (second in NL)

Club Leaders

Batting Avg:	Willie Davis	.289
On-Base Pct:	Wes Parker	.367
Slugging Pct:	Willie Davis	.441
Home Runs:	Willie Davis	19
	Frank Robinson	19
RBIs:	Willie Davis	79
Runs:	Willie Davis	81
Wins:	Claude Osteen	20
Strikeouts:	Don Sutton	207
ERA:	Don Sutton	2.08
Saves:	Jim Brewer	17

JANUARY 19		Sandy Koufax is elected to the Hall of Fame in his first time on the ballot. At 36, Koufax is the youngest individual ever inducted.
MARCH 27		The Dodgers sell Bill Sudakis to the Mets.
APRIL 7		The Dodgers scheduled opener against the Reds in Los Angeles is canceled by baseball's first player strike. The Dodgers first seven games were eliminated by the labor action, which began on April 1 and ended on April 13.
APRIL 14		The Dodgers purchased Dick Dietz from the Giants.
APRIL 15		The Dodgers open the strike-delayed season with a 3–1 win over the Reds in Cincinnati. Don Sutton (seven innings) and Jim Brewer (two innings) combined on a three-hitter. Duke Sims homered.

The Dodgers were an odd mix of veterans and youngsters in 1972, with few players in their prime. Of the 12 players who played in 71 games or more, none were between the ages of 25 and 32. The 12 were Maury Wills (39), Frank Robinson (36), Manny Mota (34), Chris Cannizzaro (34),

*Wes Parker (32), Willie Davis (32), Willie Crawford (25), Lee Lacy (24),
Bill Russell (23), Steve Garvey (23), Bobby Valentine (22) and Bill Buckner (22).
Wills hit only .129 in 132 at-bats. The pitching staff was among the oldest in
baseball.*

APRIL 19   Don Sutton pitches a two-hitter to defeat the Braves 4–0 in Atlanta. The only hits off Sutton were a double by Rico Carty in the second inning and a single from Marty Perez in the third.

Sutton led the National league with nine shutouts in 1972, the second highest in club history behind the 11 thrown by Sandy Koufax in 1963. Overall, Sutton was 19–9 with a 2.08 ERA and 207 strikeouts in 272²/₃ innings. He had a streak of 27 consecutive scoreless innings from April 30 through May 12, and another streak of 35 scoreless innings from September 10 through October 3.

APRIL 20   The Dodgers score six runs in the second inning to take an 11–1 win over the Braves in Atlanta.

APRIL 21   The Dodgers win the first home game of the season with a 12–2 decision over the Padres before 30,320 at Dodger Stadium.

APRIL 22   A home run by Jim Lefebvre off Fred Norman in the seventh inning is the only run of a 1–0 victory over the Padres at Dodger Stadium. Bill Singer pitched the shutout.

APRIL 26   The two-out, two-run homer by Willie Crawford in the ninth inning off Bill Stoneman beats the Expos 2–0 at Dodger Stadium. Claude Osteen pitched the shutout.

APRIL 29   The Dodgers score four runs in the first inning to spark an 11–1 triumph over the Mets at Dodger Stadium.

MAY 7   On the day the Lakers end years of frustration by winning their first NBA championship since moving to Los Angeles, the Dodgers waste a brilliant pitching performance in a 13-inning, 1–0 loss to the Expos in Montreal. Don Sutton pitched the first 10 innings and allowed only one hit, a single by Bob Bailey in the seventh inning. Jim Brewer followed Sutton with two hitless innings of relief. In the 13th, with Pete Richert on the mound, the Expos used two singles and a walk to load the bases. Richert then booted a bouncer back to the mound by Mike Jorgensen. The Dodgers outhit the Expos 10–3.

MAY 20   Al Downing pitches a two-hitter to defeat the Astros 3–0 at Dodger Stadium. Bobby Valentine hit the first pitch of the game from Dave Roberts for a home run. The only Houston hits were singles from Roger Metzger in the third inning and Jay Alou in the eighth.

MAY 28   The Dodgers score two runs in the ninth inning and one in the 11th to defeat the Astros 6–5 in Houston.

JUNE 3   Don Sutton pitches the Dodgers to a 1–0 win over the Cardinals at Dodger Stadium. Duke Sims drove in the only run of the game with a single in the fifth inning.

JUNE 4 — In ceremonies before a 4–0 loss to the Cardinals at Dodger Stadium, the Dodgers retire uniform numbers for the first time. Those honored were Sandy Koufax (32), Roy Campanella (39) and Jackie Robinson (42). In 1997, baseball permanently retired Robinson's number 42.

JUNE 6 — The Dodgers take a 1½-game lead with a 5–0 win over the Cubs at Dodger Stadium. The win gave Los Angeles a record of 29–18, but the club lost 22 of their next 33 games to slide out of the pennant race.

On the same day, the Dodgers selected shortstop John Harbin from Newbury College in the first round of the amateur draft. Harbin never advanced beyond Class A. The only players drafted and signed by the Dodgers in 1972 were Bob Detherage (third round), Glenn Burke (17th round) and Dennis Lewallyn (eighth round of the secondary draft in January).

JUNE 28 — Eleven days after the break-in of Democratic Party National Committee offices at the Watergate complex in Washington, D.C., Don Sutton pitches a two-hitter to defeat the Astros 5–0 at Dodger Stadium. The only Houston hits were singles by Bob Watson in the fourth inning and Tommy Helms in the eighth.

JULY 9 — Lee Lacy has a hand in both runs of a 2–0 win over Tom Seaver and the Mets in New York. Lacy scored after leading off the first inning with a single and drove in a run with another single in the ninth. Claude Osteen pitched the shutout.

JULY 18 — Frank Robinson hits a walk-off homer in the 10th inning to beat the Mets 2–1 at Dodger Stadium.

JULY 21 — The Dodgers release Hoyt Wilhelm two days after his 49th birthday.

JULY 25 — Don Sutton pitches two shutout innings (the fourth and fifth) during the National League's 10-inning 4–3 win in the All-Star Game at Atlanta-Fulton County Stadium.

AUGUST 2 — A two-out, walk-off homer by Bill Russell in the ninth inning beats the Giants 12–11 at Dodger Stadium.

AUGUST 4 — The Dodgers sell Duke Sims to the Tigers.

AUGUST 5 — The Dodgers edge the Padres 1–0 at Dodger Stadium. Bobby Valentine drove in the lone run with a single in the eighth inning. Claude Osteen (eight innings) and Jim Brewer (one inning) combined on the shutout.

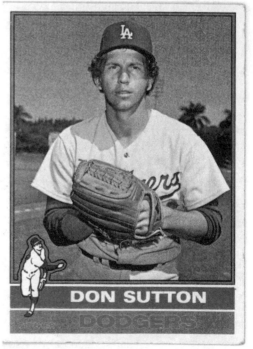

A cornerstone of the Dodgers rotation for many years, Hall-of-Famer Don Sutton posted a 2.08 ERA in 1972.

AUGUST 7	The Dodgers sign Ron Perranoski following his release by the Tigers.
AUGUST 8	Dodger pitchers strike out a club record 22 batters, but the Reds win a 19-inning marathon in Cincinnati 2–1. The strikeouts were recorded by Tommy John (13 in nine innings), Jim Brewer (six in three innings), Pete Richert (one in two innings), Ron Perranoski (two in three innings) and Pete Mikkelsen (none in an inning). Mikkelsen allowed the 19th inning run without retiring a batter. Joe Hague drove in the winning run with a single.
AUGUST 22	Al Downing pitches the Dodgers to a 1–0 win over the Cardinals at Dodger Stadium. The lone run scored in the first inning on a single by Willie Davis.
SEPTEMBER 2	In his major league debut, Doug Rau pitches a three-hitter to defeat the Cardinals 5–1 in St. Louis.
SEPTEMBER 4	The Dodgers make seven errors during an 8–4 loss to the Reds in the second game of a double-header at Dodger Stadium. Three of the errors were committed by third basemen with Bobby Valentine accounting for two and Steve Garvey one. Shortstop Bill Russell had two errors and second baseman Billy Grabarkewitz and catcher Chris Cannizzaro one each. The Dodgers won the opener 6–5.

Six different players appeared in games at third base for the Dodgers in 1972, and they combined for 53 errors. Garvey played only 85 games at third in 1972, but managed to lead the major leagues in errors at the position with 28. A year later, he was moved to first base, where he would win four consecutive Gold Glove Awards from 1974 through 1977. Shortstops made 40 errors in 1972, with a league-leading 34 made by Bill Russell.

SEPTEMBER 16	The Dodgers clobber the Astros 10–0 in Houston.
SEPTEMBER 18	The Dodgers use four walks in the 10th inning to beat the Padres 3–2 in San Diego. Steve Simpson loaded the bases by issuing walks to Maury Wills, Wes Parker and Frank Robinson. Gary Ross forced in the winning run by walking Willie Crawford with two out.
SEPTEMBER 22	Wes Parker is hit by a Jim Willoughby pitch with the bases loaded in the 11th inning for the lone run of a 1–0 win over the Giants at Dodger Stadium. Don Sutton pitched a complete game shutout, allowing only three hits and striking out 12. Davey Lopes made his major league debut. Playing second base and batting lead-off, Lopes was hitless in five at-bats.
SEPTEMBER 27	A two-run double by Joe Ferguson in the second inning are the only runs of a 2–0 win over the Padres at Dodger Stadium. Don Sutton pitched the shutout.
SEPTEMBER 30	Claude Osteen drives in three of the four runs during a 4–2 win over the Reds in Cincinnati. Osteen's single in the eighth inning tied the score 2–2. In the 10th, he smacked a two-run double which gave him his 19th victory of the season.
OCTOBER 4	On the final day of the season, Claude Osteen wins his 20th game of 1972 with a 4–1 decision over the Braves in Atlanta.

Osteen finished the season with a 20–11 record and a 2.64 ERA.

OCTOBER 24   Jackie Robinson dies at the age of 53 following a heart attack. Nine days earlier, in honor of the 25th anniversary of his becoming the first African-American in the major leagues, Robinson threw out the first pitch of the World Series between the Reds and Athletics in Cincinnati.

OCTOBER 26   The Dodgers trade Larry Hisle to the Cardinals for Rudy Arroyo and Greg Millikan.

NOVEMBER 21   Wes Parker retires at the age of 33. He would have a relatively successful acting career and appeared in several television programs and movies during the 1970s and 1980s.

NOVEMBER 28   Three weeks after Richard Nixon defeats George McGovern in the Presidential election, the Dodgers trade Frank Robinson, Bill Singer, Bill Grabarkewitz, Bobby Valentine and Mike Strahler to the Angels for Andy Messersmith and Ken McMullen.

> *Wielding a devastating change-up, Messersmith gave the Dodgers three terrific seasons with a record of 53–30 before leaving the club as one of baseball's first two free agents (see December 23, 1975). After posting a 17–33 record for the Dodgers in 1971 and 1972, Singer was 20–14 for the Angels in 1973, but accomplished little afterward. Robinson was named the first African-American manager in the majors when hired by the Indians just after the end of the 1974 season. Only 22 when traded, Valentine was considered to be one of the top prospects in baseball but failed to develop with the Dodgers largely because of a series of injuries. The problem continued with the Angels when he broke his leg in two places in 1973 running into the outfield wall at Anaheim Stadium, then separated his shoulder in 1974. Valentine finished his career in 1979 with a .260 average and only 12 homers in 1,698 at-bats.*

1973

Season in a Sentence

The Dodgers win 51 of their first 76 games before blowing an 8½-game lead to fail to reach the World Series for the seventh consecutive year for the first time since the 1930s.

Finish • Won • Lost • Pct • GB

Second   95   66   .590   3.5

Manager

Walter Alston

Stats

Stats	Dods •	NL •	Rank
Batting Avg:	.263	.254	2
On-Base Pct:	.323	.322	6
Slugging Pct:	.371	.376	7
Home Runs:	110		10
Stolen Bases:	109		3
ERA:	3.00	3.66	1
Fielding Avg:	.981	.977	3
Runs Scored:	675		6
Runs Allowed:	565		1

Starting Lineup

Joe Ferguson, c
Bill Buckner, 1b-lf
Davey Lopes, 2b
Ron Cey, 3b
Bill Russell, ss
Manny Mota, lf
Willie Davis, cf
Willie Crawford, rf
Steve Garvey, 1b

Pitchers

Don Sutton, sp
Claude Osteen, sp
Tommy John, sp
Andy Messersmith, sp
Al Downing, sp
Jim Brewer, rp

Attendance

2,136,192 (first in NL)

Club Leaders

Batting Avg:	Willie Crawford	.295
On-Base Pct:	Willie Crawford	.396
Slugging Pct:	Joe Ferguson	.470
Home Runs:	Joe Ferguson	25
RBIs:	Joe Ferguson	88
Runs:	Joe Ferguson	84
Stolen Bases:	Davey Lopes	36
Wins:	Don Sutton	18
Strikeouts:	Don Sutton	200
ERA:	Don Sutton	2.42
Saves:	Jim Brewer	20

MARCH 27   Two months after the United States ends its military involvement in Vietnam, the Dodgers sell Dick Dietz to the Brewers.

APRIL 6   The Dodgers lose the opening game of the season 4–2 to the Padres in San Diego. Don Sutton was the starting and losing pitcher. Joe Ferguson homered.

   Sutton went 18–10 with a 2.42 ERA and 200 strikeouts in 256⅓ innings.

APRIL 11   The Dodgers lose their home opener 4–1 to the Reds before 24,755 at Dodger Stadium.

   After a highly successful career as a manager in the minor leagues, Tommy Lasorda joined the Dodgers as a coach in 1973.

APRIL 16   After striking out four times and hitting into a double play in his first five plate appearances, Lee Lacy delivers a walk-off single in the 13th inning to beat the Astros 2–1 at Dodger Stadium. Don Sutton pitched 10 shutout innings and allowed only three hits.

Lacy began the season as the Dodgers starting second baseman, but soon lost his job to Davey Lopes, who held the position for until 1981. Lopes was an outfielder during his first three seasons in the minors and was moved to second base in 1971. He played in four World Series and four All-Star Games as a Dodger in addition to leading the NL in stolen bases twice, with a high of 77 in 1975. Lopes's 418 steals with the club ranks second all-time to the 490 accumulated by Maury Wills.

APRIL 19   Willie Davis hits two homers and drives in five runs, but the Dodgers lose 8–6 to the Giants at Dodger Stadium.

APRIL 21   Don Sutton shuts out the Dodgers 1–0 at Dodger Stadium.

The Dodgers lost six of their first seven games in 1973 and were 7–11 on April 24. The club rebounded from the rough start and posted a 44–16 record from April 25 through June 30.

APRIL 29   The Dodgers sweep the Pirates 9–8 in 13 innings and 2–1 in nine during a double-header in Pittsburgh. Tom Paciorek drove in the winning run in game one with a double. He entered the contest as a right fielder in a double switch in the 10th inning. Manny Mota collected five hits in seven at-bats in the opener, but was benched in the nightcap.

MAY 4   Down 5–0, the Dodgers score one run in the fifth inning, three in the sixth, one in the ninth and one in the 10th to defeat the Cardinals 6–5 at Dodger Stadium. The winning run scored on a double by Bill Russell and a single by Davey Lopes.

During the 1972 season, Oakland Athletics owner Charlie Finley paid his players to grow mustaches, becoming the first major leaguers since the turn of the century to sport facial hair. Several Dodgers grew mustaches in 1973, including Lopes, Ron Cey, Bill Buckner, Joe Ferguson, Ken McMullen, Chris Cannizzaro and Doug Rau.

MAY 6   Al Downing pitches a two-hitter to beat the Cardinals 3–0 at Dodger Stadium. The only two St. Louis hits were a single by opposing pitcher Alan Foster in the sixth inning and a double from Ray Busse in the eighth.

MAY 8   Willie Stargell clears the right-field pavilion at Dodger Stadium with a 470-foot home run off Andy Messersmith during a 7–4 Dodger win over the Pirates. It was the second time that Stargell cleared the pavilion (see August 5, 1969). Over the first 35 years of the ballpark's existence, Stargell was the only individual to hit a ball out of Dodger Stadium.

MAY 13   The Dodgers score nine runs in the fourth inning and demolish the Giants 15–3 in San Francisco. The Dodgers collected 20 hits during the contest. Ron Cey picked up four hits and drove in five runs. Willie Davis had two hits, including two doubles, and scored four runs.

Ken McMullen began the 1973 season as the Dodgers starting third baseman, but after injuring his back, yielded to Ron Cey. Nicknamed "The Penguin" for his oddly-proportioned stocky build and waddling gait, Cey held the starting third base job until 1982 and played in four World Series and six All-Star Games as a Dodger. He ended a revolving door at third base. The last player prior to Cey to play in more than 100 Dodger games at the position in at least three consecutive seasons was Cookie Lavagetto from 1938 through 1941. Cey ranks fifth among franchise leaders in home runs (228), fifth in walks (765) and 10th in runs batted in (842).

MAY 16 Consecutive homers by Joe Ferguson and Ron Cey in the 11th inning beats the Reds 8–6 in Cincinnati.

Ferguson hit .263 and clubbed 25 homers in 1973.

MAY 24 Willie Davis collects six hits in nine at-bats, but the Dodgers lose 7–3 to the Mets in a 19-inning marathon at Dodger Stadium. The Dodgers didn't score after the third inning and crossed the plate only three times despite 18 hits, in part because of five Met double plays. New York scored four times in the 19th off Doug Rau. Each of the eight Dodger position players played all 19 innings. The contest lasted five hours and 42 minutes and ended at 1:45 a.m. Los Angeles time.

MAY 25 Down 3–0, Willie Crawford hits a grand slam off Jon Matlack in the fifth inning to spark a 6–4 win over the Mets at Dodger Stadium.

In his 10th season in the majors, Crawford finally nailed down a job as a regular in 1973 and hit .295.

MAY 28 Andy Messersmith strikes out the first six batters he faces and 12 in all during a 5–1 win at Dodger Stadium. The half-dozen who Messersmith fanned in succession were Cesar Tovar, Del Unser, Willie Montanez, Greg Luzinski, Bill Robinson and Mike Schmidt.

JUNE 2 Davey Lopes commits three errors in the first inning of a 6–3 loss to the Expos at Dodger Stadium. Lopes bobbled two grounders and made a wild throw.

JUNE 5 In the first round of the amateur draft, the Dodgers select catcher Ted Farr from Shadle Park High School in Spokane, Washington.

The 1973 draft was largely a wasted exercise. Farr never reached the majors. The only future big leaguers drafted and signed by the Dodgers that year were Joe Simpson (third round) and Mike Dimmel (sixth).

JUNE 13 The famous infield of first baseman Steve Garvey, second baseman Davey Lopes, shortstop Bill Russell and third baseman Ron Cey plays together for the first time during a 16–3 loss to the Phillies in Philadelphia. Garvey didn't start, coming into the game at first in place of Tom Paciorek, who was playing in place of the injured Bill Buckner (see June 23, 1973).

JUNE 17 The Dodgers take over first place with a 12-inning, 3–2 win over the Expos in Montreal. The club would remain in first in the NL West until September 4.

JUNE 18 Bill Russell collects four hits and drives in five runs during a 13–3 trouncing of the Braves at Dodger Stadium.

Russell played in all 162 games in 1973 and missed only one inning all year.

JUNE 19

Willie Davis records the 2,000th hit of his career with a two-run homer off Phil Niekro in the sixth inning of a 3–0 victory over the Braves at Dodger Stadium.

JUNE 20

The Dodgers take a 12-inning, come from behind win over the Braves by a 6–5 score at Dodger Stadium. Atlanta scored twice in the top of the 11th but the Dodgers tied the contest on a two-run homer by Willie Davis.

The Dodgers had a 15–2 record against the Braves in 1973.

JUNE 23

The infield of Steve Garvey, Davey Lopes, Bill Russell and Ron Cey start together for the first time, and the Dodgers win 5–1 over the Reds in the second game of a double-header at Dodger Stadium. Cincinnati won the opener 4–1.

The final piece of the puzzle came when Garvey was made the everyday first baseman and Bill Buckner moved from first to left field. At the time, Lopes was the oldest of the four infielders at 28. Cey was 25, Russell 24 and Garvey 23. The quartet comprised the Los Angeles starting infield through the end of the 1981 season. During that period, the Dodgers played in four World Series and Garvey appeared in eight All-Star Games, Cey in six, Lopes in four and Russell in three. The four infielders were not the only young players with a bright future in 1973. Joe Ferguson was 26, Charlie Hough and Lee Lacy 25, Steve Yeager and Doug Rau 24 and Bill Buckner 23.

JUNE 26

Don Sutton pitches a two-hitter to defeat the Padres 7–0 in San Diego. The only hits off Sutton were singles by Dwain Anderson in the fifth inning and John Grubb in the sixth.

JUNE 29

The Dodgers score three runs in the 12th inning to defeat the Braves 12–9 in Atlanta.

JUNE 30

The Dodgers overcome a 5–1 deficit to defeat the Reds 8–7 in 13 innings at Riverfront Stadium in the first game of an unusual four-game, Saturday through Monday series.

Cincinnati's pennant hopes looked hopeless. The defending National League champion Reds were 39–37, in fourth place, and 11 games behind the Dodgers.

JULY 1

Leading 3–1, Don Sutton is one strike from putting the Reds 12 games out of first place when third-string catcher Hal King hits a stunning three-run, pinch-hit, walk-off homer to give Cincinnati a 4–3 win in the first game of a double-header at Riverfront Stadium. The Reds also won the nightcap 3–2 in 10 innings with Tony Perez driving in the winning run with a double off Charlie Hough.

The King home run turned Cincinnati's season around. The Reds were 60–26 from July 1 through the end of the season. Over the same period, the Dodgers had a record of 44–39.

JULY 2

The Dodgers lose on a walk-off hit for the third game in a row when Tony Perez hits a two-run homer in the ninth inning off Jim Brewer for a 4–2 Reds win in Cincinnati.

JULY 8

Willie Davis hits a walk-off homer in the 12th inning to down the Pirates 3–2 at Dodger Stadium.

JULY 11   Don Sutton strikes out 12 batters during a 3–1 triumph over the Cardinals at Dodger Stadium.

JULY 14   Al Downing strikes out seven batters in a row during a 7–3 win over the Cubs at Dodger Stadium. Downing started the first inning by loading the bases on two walks and by hitting a batter, then threw a wild pitch to score a run. He worked out of the jam by fanning Jose Cardenal, Ron Santo and Carmen Fanzone. In the second, Downing struck out Randy Hundley, Paul Popovich and Burt Hooton. The seventh straight strikeout victim was Rick Monday leading off the third. Downing fanned nine in all in seven innings.

JULY 16   A home run by Willie Crawford off Nelson Briles accounts for the lone run of a 1–0 win over the Pirates in Pittsburgh. Don Sutton pitches the shutout.

JULY 17   The Dodgers take an 8½-game lead over the second place Reds with an 8–4 win over the Pirates in Pittsburgh. Los Angeles had a record of 61–34.

JULY 20   The Dodgers edge the Cardinals 4–3 in 15 innings in St. Louis. The Dodgers scored three runs in the first inning before 13 consecutive scoreless innings. The winning run scored on a double by Steve Garvey.

JULY 24   In the All-Star Game at Royals Stadium in Kansas City, Claude Osteen pitches shutout ball in the third and fourth innings and Don Sutton a perfect fifth to help the National League to a 7–1 victory.

AUGUST 4   Dodger coach Tommy Lasorda trades punches with Giants manager Charlie Fox prior to a 3–2 loss in San Francisco. The incident occurred while the Giants were taking batting practice. "Lasorda was riding our players and I told him to cut it out," said Fox. Lasorda landed a blow to Fox's stomach and the San Francisco skipper retaliated with a punch to Lasorda's head before players intervened.

AUGUST 9   On his 34th birthday, Claude Osteen pitches the Dodgers to a 1–0 win over the Mets at Dodger Stadium. The lone run scored in the eighth inning on a triple by Davey Lopes and Manny Mota's single.

AUGUST 14   A two-out, two-run, pinch-hit, walk-off homer by Ken McMullen beats the Expos 4–3 at Dodger Stadium.

AUGUST 19   A two-out, two-run homer by Joe Ferguson defeats the Cubs 2–1 at Wrigley Field. Chicago pitcher Rick Reuschel struck out 13 batters and didn't allow a hit until the eighth inning.

SEPTEMBER 3   Nine outs from victory, the Dodgers blow a seven-run lead and lose 11–8 to the Giants at Candlestick Park. San Francisco narrowed the gap to 8–7 with six runs in the seventh inning. With Pete Richert on the mound in the ninth, the Giants loaded the bases on a walk and two bunts in which the Dodgers threw too late to second base to force the runner. Alston brought in Jim Brewer to face Bobby Bonds, who smacked a grand slam to end the game. The defeat dropped the Dodgers into a tie for first place with the Reds.

SEPTEMBER 4   Collecting only one hit off Ron Bryant and Elias Sosa, the Dodgers lose 3–1 to the Giants in San Francisco and drop out of first place.

SEPTEMBER 9   The Dodgers end a nine-game losing streak with a 5–3 win over the Padres at Dodger Stadium.

SEPTEMBER 11   In the second game of a pennant showdown series against the Reds in Cincinnati, the Dodgers lose 7–3 to the Reds. It was the 11th loss in a span of 12 games and dropped the Dodgers five games behind Cincinnati with 16 contests left on the schedule.

SEPTEMBER 14   The Dodgers bury the Astros 13–1 in Houston.

SEPTEMBER 20   A two-run, walk-off homer by Davey Lopes beats the Braves 5–3 at Dodger Stadium.

SEPTEMBER 26   Two weeks before the resignation of U.S. vice-president Spiro Agnew due to financial improprieties, the Dodgers score three runs in the ninth inning to beat the Braves 9–8 in Atlanta. Ken McMullen broke the tie with a pinch-double.

DECEMBER 3   James Mulvey, vice-president of the Dodgers since 1937, dies at the age of 74. Mulvey and his wife Dearie owned 25 per cent of the Dodgers stock. Dearie's father bought the stock in 1912 (see January 2, 1912). Walter O'Malley bought out the Mulvey family in 1975, which gave him 100 percent ownership of the franchise.

DECEMBER 5   The Dodgers trade Willie Davis to the Expos for Mike Marshall and send Pete Richert to the Cardinals for Tommie Agee.

                   At 33, Davis was at the end of the productive phase of his career, while Marshall became the first reliever to win the Cy Young Award in 1974 with an historic season. Entering the 1972 campaign, Marshall was 29 years old and had a 12–29 record and a 4.01 ERA with four clubs. A graduate of Michigan State University, he became obsessed with kinesiology, the study of the principle of mechanics and anatomy as they relate to human movement, and by 1978 earned his doctorate in the subject. His dissertation was titled A Comparison of an Estimate of Skeletal Age With Chronological Age When Classifying Adolescent Males for Motor Proficiency Norms. *Marshall developed his own theories of pitching and believed he pitched his best when he worked four or five times a week. He didn't wear a sweatshirt even on the coldest of days. Arrogant and conceited, Marshall looked down most everyone else in baseball considering them to be below his intellectual level. His unique views extended beyond pitching. Marshall refused to sign autographs, arguing they were meaningless. Learning to throw a screwball, he blossomed in Montreal in 1972 with a 1.78 ERA in 65 games and 116 innings. In 1973, Marshall pitched in 92 games, 179 innings, all in relief, and had a 2.66 ERA with a 14–11 record and 31 saves. His workload increased to record-breaking levels with the Dodgers in 1974. Marshall set still standing major league records for games pitched (106) and relief innings (208⅓). He was on the mound at the conclusion of 83 of the Dodgers 162 regular season games and had a 15–12 record, 21 saves, and a 2.42 earned run average. Marshall also pitched in seven of the nine Dodger post-season games, allowing only one run in 12 innings. Knee, ribcage and back injuries limited his effectiveness after 1974, however, and Marshall would be traded to the Braves in 1976.*

DECEMBER 6   The Dodgers trade Claude Osteen and Dave Culpepper to the Astros for Jim Wynn.

The Dodgers pulled off two tremendous trades on consecutive days which helped the club reach the World Series in 1974. After the trade, Osteen went into a steep decline, and was 16–27 over the next two seasons before retiring. Wynn was nicknamed "The Toy Cannon" because of the power he generated despite standing five-foot-nine and weighing 170 pounds. He made the All-Star team in each of his two seasons in Los Angeles. In 1974, Wynn hit six homers and drove in 17 runs in his first 12 games as a Dodger and finished the campaign with 32 home runs, the most of any Dodger since 1957, along with 108 RBIs and 104 runs.

DECEMBER 27   The Dodgers announce that night games in 1974 will start 30 minutes earlier at 7:30 p.m. and Saturday night contests at 7:00 p.m. In addition, all Saturday games in April and May would be played in the afternoon. The moves were made because of the energy crisis.

1974

Season in a Sentence

Fully committed to a youth movement, the Dodgers win 42 of their first 58 games and hold off the Reds to reach the World Series, before losing to the Athletics.

Finish • Won • Lost • Pct • GB

First   102   60   .630   +4.0

National League Championship Series

The Dodgers defeated the Pittsburgh Pirates three games to one.

World Series

The Dodgers lost to the Oakland Athletics four games to one.

Manager

Walter Alston

Stats

Stats	Dods	NL	Rank
Batting Avg:	.272	.255	2
On-Base Pct:	.342	.326	2
Slugging Pct:	.401	.367	1
Home Runs:	139		1
Stolen Bases:	149		2
ERA:	2.97	3.62	1
Fielding Avg:	.975	.976	8
Runs Scored:	798		1
Runs Allowed:	561		1

Starting Lineup

Joe Ferguson, c
Steve Garvey, 1b
Davey Lopes, 2b
Ron Cey, 3b
Bill Russell, ss
Bill Buckner, lf
Jim Wynn, cf
Willie Crawford, rf
Steve Yeager, c

Pitchers

Andy Messersmith, sp
Don Sutton, sp
Doug Rau, sp
Tommy John, sp
Al Downing, sp
Mike Marshall, rp
Charlie Hough, rp

Attendance

2,632,474 (first in NL)

Club Leaders

Batting Avg:	Bill Buckner	.314
On-Base Pct:	Jimmy Wynn	.387
Slugging Pct:	Jimmy Wynn	.497
Home Runs:	Jimmy Wynn	32
RBIs:	Steve Garvey	111
Runs:	Jimmy Wynn	104
Stolen Bases:	Davey Lopes	59
Wins:	Andy Messersmith	20
Strikeouts:	Andy Messersmith	221
ERA:	Andy Messersmith	2.59
Saves:	Mike Marshall	21

APRIL 3   Two months after the kidnapping of Patty Hearst, the Dodgers trade Bruce Ellingsen to the Indians for Pedro Guerrero.

Although it would turn into one of the best trades ever made by the Dodgers, the deal for Guerrero barely received a mention in the Los Angeles papers. Ellingsen was a 24-year-old pitcher who had yet to make his big-league debut. Guerrero was merely 17. His professional career consisted of 44 games at the Rookie level in which he hit .255 with just two home runs. Guerrero reached the majors in 1978, although it would be 1981 before he nailed down a job as a regular. That season he would make the first of five career All-Star selections and was co-MVP of the World Series in which the Dodgers defeated the Yankees in six games. Although a bonafide star with a bat in his hands, Guerrero was slowed by frequent injuries and was frequently moved around on defense because of his deficiencies with the glove. During his big-league career, he played 573 games at first base, 541 in right field, and 373 at third. Guerrero's days as a Dodger would end during the world championship season of 1988 with a trade to the Cardinals. On the all-time club statistical lists, Guerrero is ninth in home runs with 171. Among players with at least 4,000 plate appearances as a Dodger, he is second in slugging percentage (.512) and fourth in batting average (.309). All of this production came in exchange for Ellingsen, who pitched in only 16 games in the majors.

APRIL 5   The Dodgers open with an 8–0 victory over the Padres before 31,566 at Dodger Stadium. Don Sutton pitched the shutout. In his Dodger debut, Jim Wynn hit a home run and two singles and drove in three runs. Ron Cey also contributed three runs batted in. Willie Crawford rapped three hits.

The see-through windows in the bullpen fences were added in 1974.

APRIL 6   In the second game of the season, the Dodgers win again 8–0 over the Padres at Dodger Stadium. Tommy John pitched the shutout. Jimmy Wynn homered and drove in three runs for the second day in a row.

On the same day, Bobbie McMullen, the wife of Dodger third baseman Ken McMullen, died from cancer at the age of 30. The death came only four months after the birth of the couple's third child. The cancer was detected during the pregnancy, and Bobbie delayed radiation treatments until after the birth because of fear the procedure would harm the child. The Dodgers donned black arm bands in her honor, which are visible on the often-repeated video of Hank Aaron's record-breaking 715th career home run, which took place two days later.

APRIL 7   Jimmy Wynn homers for the third game in a row during a 9–2 win over the Padres at Dodger Stadium.

In the opening game of the series of the season, the Dodgers outscored the Padres 25–2. Over the course of the 1974 campaign, Los Angeles had a 16–2 record against San Diego and outscored their Southern California rivals 124–45.

APRIL 8   Hank Aaron hits the 715th career home run to break the existing record set by Babe Ruth. The blow was struck off Dodger hurler Al Downing during a 7–4 Braves win in Atlanta. Aaron tied the record four days earlier with a blow off Jack

Billingham of the Reds in Cincinnati during Aaron's first at-bat on Opening Day. Facing Downing in the second inning, Aaron walked and came around to score the 2,063rd run of his career, which broke the National League record set by Willie Mays. In the fourth, Aaron smacked a 1–0 pitch over the left-center-field fence to pass Ruth. Left fielder Bill Buckner futilely tried to climb the fence in an attempt to catch the ball.

Aaron finished his career in 1976 with 755 home runs. His home run record was broken by Barry Bonds in 2007.

APRIL 17   The Dodgers wallop the Reds 14–1 in Cincinnati. Los Angeles broke open a close game with four runs in the seventh inning, four in the eighth and four in the ninth.

APRIL 19   The Dodgers hold the Giants to two hits, but lose 5–4 at Dodger Stadium. Bobby Bonds homered in the sixth inning for the first San Francisco hit. The Giants scored four times in the seventh on an error, three walks by Don Sutton, a two-run single by Chris Speier off Mike Marshall, and a run-producing infield out.

APRIL 23   A three-run, walk-off, pinch-homer by Tom Paciorek beats the Phillies 5–3 at Dodger Stadium.

APRIL 25   Tommy John pitches the Dodgers to a 1–0 win over the Phillies at Dodger Stadium. The lone run crossed the plate in the first inning on a sacrifice fly by Jimmy Wynn. It was John's 10th win in a row over two seasons. He won his last five decisions in 1973 and the first five in 1974.

MAY 1   The Dodgers edge the Mets 2–1 in 14 innings at Dodger Stadium. The winning run scored on a double by Willie Crawford and a single from Steve Garvey. Tom Seaver pitched the first 12 innings for New York and struck out 16 while allowing only three hits. Garvey also provided the first Los Angeles run with a homer in the fifth inning.

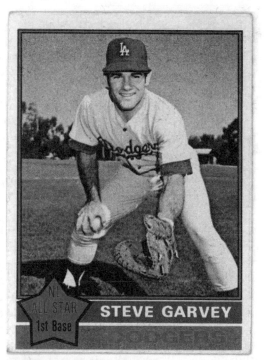

The National League MVP in 1974, Steve Garvey was seen as the face of the Dodger organization throughout the 1970s.

At the start of the season, Garvey was 25, had yet to accumulate more than 349 at-bats in a season, and had a career batting average of .272 with 25 homers in 964 at-bats. He wasn't even on the All-Star ballot, but won a spot as the National League's starting first baseman after being elected in a write-in campaign. He not only won the MVP Award at the All-Star Game (see July 23, 1974), but captured the National League MVP Award with a .312 batting average, 200 hits, 21 homers and 112 runs batted in.

MAY 9 — Don Sutton pitches a one-hitter and beats the Padres 1–0 in San Diego. The lone hit off Sutton was a single by John Grubb in the second inning.

> *Sutton was 19–9 in 1974 with a 3.23 ERA in 276 innings despite a long slump in which he failed to win a game from May 14 until July 25. From July 25 through the end of the regular season, Sutton was 13–1, then had a 3–0 record in the post-season.*

MAY 11 — Jimmy Wynn hits three homers during a 9–6 win over the Padres in San Diego. Wynn hit solo homers off Mike Corkins in the first inning, against Rich Troedson in the fifth, and facing Gary Ross in the seventh. Wynn also drove in two runs with a single in the second to give him five runs batted in.

MAY 12 — The Dodgers blow a seven-run lead, but win 15–9 against the Padres in San Diego. Los Angeles had a 9–2 advantage before allowing a run in the sixth inning and six in the seventh. The Dodgers exploded for six runs in the 13th inning and collected 23 hits in the contest.

MAY 14 — Don Sutton pitches a shutout and drives in the lone run of a 1–0 win over the Astros at Dodger Stadium with a single off Larry Dierker in the second inning.

MAY 15 — The Dodgers sweep the Astros 11–7 and 10–2 in a double-header at Dodger Stadium to extend their winning streak to nine games. In the opener, the Dodgers trailed before scoring seven runs in the fifth inning. Joe Ferguson homered twice and drove in five runs in the second tilt. The two wins gave Los Angeles a record of 27–9.

MAY 18 — Breaking up a scoreless duel, Steve Garvey's single drives in the lone run of a 1–0 triumph over the Braves at Dodger Stadium. Andy Messersmith (10 innings), Mike Marshall (two innings) and Charlie Hough (one inning) combined on the five-hit shutout.

> *Messersmith had a 20–6 record with a 2.59 ERA and 221 strikeouts in 292$\frac{1}{3}$ innings in 1974.*

MAY 28 — The Dodgers collect 20 hits and defeat the Cardinals 11–5 in St. Louis.

JUNE 1 — Ron Cey drives in seven runs during a 10–0 win over the Cubs in Chicago. Twenty members of his family were in attendance, including his wife Fran. Cey hit a three-run homer in the first inning, a two-run single in the third and a two-run homer in the fourth. Miked for the Saturday afternoon national telecast by NBC-TV, third base coach Tommy Lasorda predicted the first of Cey's two homers.

JUNE 5 — A walk-off homer in the ninth inning by Steve Garvey beats the Pirates 3–2 at Dodger Stadium. Dou Rau held the Pirates hitless for the first 7$\frac{1}{3}$ innings. A single by Richie Hebner broke up the no-hit bid. Rau surrendered three hits in 8$\frac{1}{3}$ innings.

> *On the same day, the Dodgers selected pitcher Rick Sutcliffe from Van Horn High School in Kansas City, Missouri. Sutcliffe was the National League Rookie of the Year with a 17–10 record in 1979, but after two years of injuries, was dealt to the Indians in an ill-advised trade in December 1981. The only other future major leaguer drafted and signed in 1974 was Steve Shirley in the second round.*

JUNE 7   A walk-off homer by Jimmy Wynn in the ninth inning defeats the Cubs 6–5 at Dodger Stadium.

Through June 7, the Dodgers had a record of 24–0 when Steve Yeager was the starting catcher. The club won 28 in a row with Yeager as the starting backstop dating back to 1973. In 1974, Yeager started 92 games and Joe Ferguson 70. A year later, Yeager did the bulk of the catching, with Ferguson playing both behind the plate and in the outfield.

JUNE 8   A walk-off single by Von Joshua in the ninth inning downs the Cubs 4–3 at Dodgers Stadium. It was the third walk-off hit by the Dodgers in a span of four games.

JUNE 19   The Dodgers score a run on a bizarre play in the first inning of a 7–3 loss to the Pirates at Three Rivers Stadium. With the bases loaded and two out, Joe Ferguson took a 3–2 pitch on what Pittsburgh catcher Manny Sanguillen thought was a called third strike. Sanguillen rolled the ball to the mound, but umpire Satch Davidson had called ball four.

Lee Lacy, the Dodger runner on third, thought the inning was over and started for the dugout, but Jimmy Wynn, alert to the situation, raced for home from second base and was tagged out on a throw from pitcher Jerry Reuss to Sanguillen. Lacy came back and was also tagged out on a play at the plate. After consultation, the umpires ruled Wynn out for passing Lacy on the base paths, but held that Lacy was immune to the tag and entitled to score because of the bases loaded walk to Ferguson.

JUNE 21   Bill Buckner hits a walk-off homer in the 10th inning, his fourth hit of the game, to beat the Giants 4–3 at Dodger Stadium. Mike Marshall pitched three innings of hitless relief for the win.

JUNE 22   Jimmy Wynn's homer in the ninth inning ties the score 2–2, and Joe Ferguson's walk-off home run in the 10th defeats the Giants 3–2 at Dodger Stadium. Mike Marshall picked up the win with two scoreless innings of relief. It was the second game in a row won by a walk-off homer in the 10th and the second win in succession for Marshall.

JUNE 23   A walk-off single by Ken McMullen in the ninth inning downs the Giants 4–3 at Dodger Stadium. Mike Marshall picked up the victory with two scoreless innings of relief. The Dodgers swept the Giants in the three-game series with three straight walk-off hits and three victories in a row by Marshall.

JUNE 25   The Dodgers score two runs in the ninth inning to defeat the Braves 2–1 at Dodger Stadium. Mike Marshall was the winning pitcher for the fourth time in a span of five games.

JUNE 26   The Dodgers strike in their final at-bat again with two runs in the ninth inning to defeat the Braves 5–4 at Dodger Stadium. Joe Ferguson tied the score with a homer. Davey Lopes singled, stole second, and scored on a single by Manny Mota. It was the fifth walk-off hit by the Dodgers in six games. In addition, Mike Marshall was the winning pitcher for the fifth time in six contests.

During the game, three gunmen robbed an armored truck carrying ticket receipts in the parking lot at Dodger Stadium and escaped with $5,000 after firing one shot. No one was hurt.

JULY 3   Mike Marshall sets a major league record (since tied) by pitching in his 13th consecutive game during a 4–1 win over the Reds in the first game of a double-header against the Reds in Cincinnati. Marshall didn't pitch in the second tilt, a 2–1 loss.

The 13 consecutive games came in a period of 16 days and Marshall pitched $26\frac{2}{3}$ innings. The only other pitcher to hurl 13 games in a row was Dale Mohoric of the Rangers, who went 14 innings in 15 days in 1986.

JULY 4   The Dodgers score two runs in the ninth inning to win 3–2 over the Reds in Cincinnati. The game-winning rally consisted of doubles by Steve Garvey and Willie Crawford and a single from Bill Russell.

JULY 9   The Dodgers take a $10\frac{1}{2}$-game lead over the Reds with an 8–4 lead over the Phillies in Philadelphia. Los Angeles had a record of 60–27.

JULY 14   The New Orleans Saints begin their training camp at Dodgertown in Vero Beach, Florida. The Saints trained at Dodgertown until 1984.

JULY 17   Tommy John leaves a 5–4 loss to the Expos at Dodger Stadium because of pain in his left elbow.

At the time of the injury, John was 31 years old and had a 13–3 record and a 2.59 ERA in 153 innings in 1974. Doctors determined John had ruptured a ligament which would require a transplant from his right wrist. A ligament transplant had never been done on a pitcher, and orthopedist Dr. Frank Jobe estimated the odds of John returning to the mound at 100–1. The surgery was done on September 25. Two weeks later he threw out the first ceremonial pitch, right-handed, before game three of the NLCS at Dodger Stadium. John required a second operation in December to repair nerve damage because his left hand had gone numb and contracted into a fist. After missing the entire 1975 season, John made a comeback in 1976 and posted a 10–10 record. A year later he won 20 games for the first of three times during his major league career. John continued to pitch until 1989 and won 164 big-league games after being given a 100–1 shot at ever playing again. Today, "Tommy John surgery" is routine and hundreds of players have been given a second chance because of the procedure.

JULY 18   The Dodgers score seven runs in the seventh inning for all of the runs of a 7–5 win over the Expos at Dodger Stadium.

JULY 23   Elected as the National League's starting first baseman as a write-in candidate, Steve Garvey collects a double and a single and drives in a run in four at-bats to win the Most Valuable Player Award. The NL won the game 7–2 at Three Rivers Stadium in Pittsburgh. Ron Cey contributed a two-run double. Andy Messersmith was the starting pitcher, and allowed two runs in three innings.

JULY 31   Ron Cey drives in eight runs during a 15–4 win over the Padres in San Diego. Cey hit a two-run single in the third inning and three-run homers in the eighth and ninth.

AUGUST 4   Davey Lopes steals four bases during a 2–1 win over the Astros at Dodger Stadium.

AUGUST 5   A grand slam by Steve Yeager off Don Gullett in the seventh inning breaks a 2–2 tie and helps the Dodgers defeat the Reds 6–3 at Dodger Stadium. It was the club's eighth win in a row.

The NBC nationally televised game was interrupted in the eighth inning for eight minutes when 19-year-old Alex Stein, a college student from Ohio, and his tiny Whippet named Ashley invaded the playing field. Stein threw a Frisbee and the dog astonished the crowd by running 35 miles per hour and leaping nine feet in the air to catch the disc. The act was so novel for its time that Joe Garagiola did the play-by-play on TV. Stein was arrested. He later worked with two others to create the Frisbee Dog World Championship. Stein is credited for inventing the sport and is still involved in events to this day.

AUGUST 7   A brawl erupts during a 2–0 loss to the Reds at Dodger Stadium. Bill Buckner slid high into Cincinnati second baseman Joe Morgan trying to break a double play. Buckner struck Morgan in the chest with his spikes. Morgan immediately leaped on Buckner and the two were rolling on the ground, prompting players to pour out of both dugouts. Pete Rose shoved Rick Auerbach to the ground and a wave of about 10 Dodgers swept Rose to the mound before he was rescued by his teammates. Reds reliever Pedro Borbon punched a fan who leaped into the bullpen.

AUGUST 19   Eleven days after Richard Nixon resigns as President, Mike Marshall pitches six innings of relief and scores the winning run of a 12-inning, 8–7 victory over the Cubs in Chicago. In the 12th, Marshall singled and scored from first base. The play began with Rick Auerbach hitting a roller down the first base line which was fielded by catcher Steve Swisher. Neither pitcher Oscar Zamora nor third baseman Bill Madlock backed up the plate, allowing Marshall to advance three bases.

AUGUST 20   Davey Lopes hits three homers, doubles and singles during an 18–8 rout of the Cubs in Chicago. Heading into the contest, Lopes hit three homers in 378 at-bats during the 1974 season. Lopes began the day with homers off Tom Dettore in the first and second innings. Facing Dave LaRoche, Lopes doubled in the third. In the fourth, Lopes was sent sprawling by a LaRoche pitch and moved slowly toward the mound. Both benches emptied, but umpire Paul Pryor prevented bloodshed. Lopes gained revenge by hitting a single, then homered off LaRoche in the sixth. The Dodger second baseman batted again in the seventh inning and grounded out. Jimmy Wynn, Steve Garvey and Willie Crawford also hit home runs for Los Angeles. Crawford's homer was inside-the-park in the role of pinch-hitter when the Dodgers scored seven times for an 18–4 lead. The Dodgers collected 24 hits and set a club record with 48 total bases.

AUGUST 24   Davey Lopes sets a Dodger club record with five stolen bases during a 5–0 win over the Cardinals at Dodger Stadium. Lopes stole third base in the first inning, second base in the third, second and third base in the fifth inning and second base in the sixth. The major league record for stolen bases in a game is six. Lopes twice tried to get a share of the mark, but was thrown out trying to steal third in the sixth inning and second base in the eighth. The Dodgers set a club record with eight stolen bases. Bill Russell added two to Lopes's total and Jimmy Wynn one.

SEPTEMBER 4   A three-run, walk-off homer by Jimmy Wynn in the 11th inning beats the Giants 6–3 at Dodger Stadium. Joe Ferguson tied the score with a home run in the ninth.

SEPTEMBER 10   Two days after President Gerald Ford pardons Richard Nixon, Don Sutton pitches the Dodgers to a 1–0 win over the Braves in Atlanta. Ron Cey drove in the lone run with a single in the second inning.

SEPTEMBER 12   Making his first start since August 13, Al Downing pitches a two-hitter to defeat the Giants 11–0 at Candlestick Park. The only San Francisco hits were singles by Dave Rader in the third inning and Bobby Bonds in the fourth.

SEPTEMBER 14   The Dodgers lead over the Reds shrinks to 1½ games after a 4–2 loss to Cincinnati at Dodger Stadium.

The Dodgers had a 10½-game lead over the Reds on July 9. It looked as though 1974 might be a repeat of 1973, when the Dodgers led the Reds by 11½ games on June 30, and wound up finishing the year in second place.

SEPTEMBER 15   Jimmy Wynn hits a grand slam off Pedro Borbon in the seventh inning of a 7–1 win over the Reds at Dodger Stadium. The victory gave the Dodgers a 2½-game lead.

SEPTEMBER 22   The Dodgers extend their lead in the NL West to 4½ games with a 6–5 victory over the Padres at Dodger Stadium.

SEPTEMBER 28   Andy Messersmith wins his 20th game of the season with a 5–2 decision over the Padres in San Diego. It was also the Dodgers' 100th victory of 1974.

OCTOBER 1   The Dodgers clinch the NL West pennant during an 8–5 win over the Astros in Houston. The club wrapped up the title when the Reds lost 7–1 in Atlanta. News of the Cincinnati defeat arrived in the fifth inning of the Dodgers-Astros clash, and the game was interrupted for five minutes while Los Angeles players celebrated.

The Dodgers played in the National League Championship Series for the first time. The Pirates were the opponent. Managed by Danny Murtaugh, Pittsburgh was 88–74 in 1974 and won the NL East by a game-and-a-half over the Phillies. The Dodgers were 4–8 against the Pirates during the regular season and lost all six games played in Pittsburgh.

OCTOBER 5   The Dodgers open the best-of-five series against the Pirates with a 3–0 win at Three Rivers Stadium in Pittsburgh. Don Sutton pitched the four-hit shutout.

OCTOBER 6   The Dodgers take game two with a 5–2 victory over the Pirates in Pittsburgh. The Pirates scored twice in the seventh to tie the contest 2–2, but Los Angeles responded with three tallies in the eighth. Ron Cey was the batting star with a homer, two doubles and a single in five at-bats.

OCTOBER 8   The Pirates avoid the sweep by beating the Dodgers 7–0 before 55,953 at Dodger Stadium. Doug Rau was bombed for five runs in the first inning. Bruce Kison (6⅔ innings) and Ramon Hernandez (2⅓ innings) combined on the shutout.

OCTOBER 9   The Dodgers win the National League pennant by thumping the Pirates 12–1 before 54,424 at Dodger Stadium. Don Sutton (eight innings) and Mike Marshall (one inning) pitched for Los Angeles. The Dodgers scored in six of the eight turns at bat. Steve Garvey hit two homers, two singles, drove in four runs and scored four. Bill Russell drove in three runs and Jimmy Wynn scored three.

The Dodgers played the Oakland Athletics in the World Series. The A's won the world championship in 1972 by defeating the Reds and in 1973 against the Mets. Both of those series went seven games. Oakland was gunning to become the first team to win at three consecutive World Series since the Yankees won five in succession from 1949 through 1953. Dick Williams managed both the 1972 and 1973 clubs, but resigned due to disagreements with owner Charlie Finley. Al Dark was the Oakland manager in 1974 and led the club to a 90–72 record. The Athletics managed to win despite disharmony in the clubhouse and a genuine dislike of Finley. It contrast to the dysfunctional A's, the Dodgers were united and went about their business in a quiet and restrained manner. The 1974 Series was the first between two California teams, but the cities, like the teams, couldn't have been more different. It was blue collar Oakland against the glitz of Los Angeles.

OCTOBER 12   The Athletics defeat the Dodgers 3–2 in the first game of the World Series before 55,974 at Dodger Stadium. Jimmy Wynn homered with two out in the ninth to close the gap to a run, but in a reversal of their usual roles, Catfish Hunter relieved Rollie Fingers and closed out the win. Hunter didn't make a single relief appearance during the regular season.

OCTOBER 13   The Dodgers even the Series with a 3–2 win over the Athletics before 55,989 at Dodger Stadium. Joe Ferguson's two-run homer in the sixth inning gave Los Angeles a 3–0 lead. Don Sutton pitched eight innings of shutout ball. In the ninth, he hit Sal Bando with a pitch and gave up a double to Reggie Jackson. Mike Marshall relieved and gave up a two-run single to Joe Rudi. Marshall got out of the inning by striking out two batters and by picking Herb Washington, who ran for Rudi, off first base. Washington was an experiment of A's owner Charlie Finley. Used only as a pinch-runner, Washington played in 92 games in 1974, and 105 in his career, without a single plate appearance. Washington was a track star at Michigan State when Marshall taught at the school while working on his doctorate.

OCTOBER 15   In the third consecutive game settled by a 3–2 score, the Athletics win in Oakland. The A's took a 3–0 lead off starter Al Downing with two runs in the third inning and one in the fourth. The Dodger runs came on solo homers by Bill Buckner in the eighth and Willie Crawford in the ninth.

OCTOBER 16   The Athletics move within one win of the world championship by beating the Dodgers 5–2 in Oakland. A's pitcher Ken Holtzman homered off Andy Messersmith in the third inning for a 1–0 lead, but the Dodgers responded with two tallies in the fourth. Oakland won the contest with four runs in the sixth.

OCTOBER 17   The Athletics win the World Series with a 3–2 win over the Dodgers in Oakland. It was the fourth time in five games the final score was 3–2. The Dodgers tied the game 2–2 with two runs in the sixth inning. In the seventh, fans delayed the game for six minutes by throwing debris onto the field. The target was Bill Buckner, who had made some derogatory comments about the A's. Buckner was hit on the head by a whiskey bottle during the barrage. After order was restored and the game resumed, Joe Rudi hit the first pitch from Mike Marshall for a home run. It was the only run Marshall allowed in 12 post-season innings.

Despite playing in a pitcher's park, the Dodgers led the National League in runs scored in 1974 with 798. The club scored 443 runs in 81 regular season road contests, an average of 5.5 per game. The batting attack was the equal of the great lineups of the 1950s, but was shut down by the Athletics in the World Series. The Dodgers scored only 11 runs in five games.

1975

Season in a Sentence

The Dodgers take a 5½-game lead in May but the batting attack is weakened under the weight of injuries and the club finishes a distant second.

Finish • Won • Lost • Pct • GB

Second   88   74   .543   20.0

Manager

Walter Alston

Stats

	Dods	NL	Rank
Batting Avg:	.248	.257	9
On-Base Pct:	.325	.327	6
Slugging Pct:	.365	.369	7
Home Runs:	118		4
Stolen Bases:	138		2
ERA:	2.92	3.62	1
Fielding Avg:	.979	.976	2
Runs Scored:	648		8
Runs Allowed:	534		1

Starting Lineup

Steve Yeager, c
Steve Garvey, 1b
Davey Lopes, 2b
Ron Cey, 3b
Bill Russell, ss
Bill Buckner, lf
Jimmy Wynn, cf
Willie Crawford, rf
Lee Lacy, 2b-lf
John Hale, rf-cf
Joe Ferguson, c-rf

Pitchers

Andy Messersmith, sp
Burt Hooton, sp
Don Sutton, sp
Doug Rau, sp
Mike Marshall, rp
Rick Rhoden, rp-sp

Attendance

2,539,349 (first in NL)

Club Leaders

Batting Avg:	Steve Garvey	.319
On-Base Pct:	Jimmy Wynn	.403
Slugging Pct:	Steve Garvey	.476
Home Runs:	Ron Cey	25
RBIs:	Ron Cey	101
Runs:	Davey Lopes	108
Stolen Bases:	Davey Lopes	77
Wins:	Andy Messersmith	19
Strikeouts:	Andy Messersmith	213
ERA:	Andy Messersmith	2.29
Saves:	Mike Marshall	13

MARCH 15   The Dodgers sign Juan Marichal as a free agent.

Dodger fans weren't happy with the signing of Marichal, who had won 238 games for the hated Giants and was public enemy number one in Los Angeles for many years for striking Johnny Roseboro with a bat (see August 22, 1965). The Dodgers soon discovered Marichal had nothing left in the tank. He pitched in only two games for the club, both starts, and had a 13.50 ERA in six innings before being released.

APRIL 7   The Dodgers open the season with a 14-inning, 2–1 loss to the Reds in Cincinnati. The winning run scored on George Foster's infield single.

The Dodgers held a lead in each of the three games of the opening series against the Reds, but would up losing all three by one run.

APRIL 14   In the home opener, the Dodgers defeat the Reds 5–2 before 45,502 at Dodger Stadium. Ron Cey and Jimmy Wynn hit homers.

Francis Friedman, a devoted Dodger fan, threw out the ceremonial first pitch from the left-field pavilion.

APRIL 15   Don Sutton pitches a one-hitter to beat the Reds 3–1 at Dodger Stadium. The lone Cincinnati hit was a homer by Johnny Bench in the seventh inning.

APRIL 16   A walk-off single by Steve Garvey in the ninth inning beats the Reds 7–6 at Dodger Stadium. Jimmy Wynn tied the score 6–6 with a grand slam off Pat Darcy in the seventh inning.

APRIL 17   The Dodgers score runs in the ninth and 11th innings to beat the Reds 5–4 and complete a sweep of the four-game series at Dodger Stadium. Steve Garvey collected five hits, including a double, in six at-bats.

Garvey hit .319 with 18 homers and 210 hits in 1975. Many on the club resented Garvey's All-American image and his role as the face of the franchise, however, creating dissension in the clubhouse. His detractors believed the persona was more part of a public relations campaign than genuine. The leadership of the club, marked by a contrast between 63-year-old manager Walter Alston and 48-year-old coach Tommy Lasorda was also a problem. Some on the team lined up behind the rah-rah approach of Lasorda, who had managed the most of the younger players in the minors. Others remained loyal to stoic Walter Alston, who was in his 22nd season as manager of the club.

APRIL 19   Don Sutton wins his 15th straight game, counting the 1974 post-season, with a 3–2 decision over the Giants at Dodger Stadium. Sutton won his last nine regular games in 1974, all three in the post-season, and the first three regular season contests in 1975.

APRIL 24   Ken McMullen hits a pinch-hit grand slam off Danny Frisella in the sixth inning of an 11–6 win over the Padres in San Diego.

APRIL 25   Andy Messersmith ties a major league record for doubles by a pitcher in a game with three during a 6–5 victory over the Giants in San Francisco. The three doubles also tied a club record.

Messersmith had a record of 19–14 in 1975 with a 2.29 earned run average. He struck out 213 batters and led the league in innings (321²/₃), games started (40) and complete games (19).

MAY 2   The Dodgers extend their winning streak to eight games with a 3–0 decision over the Padres at Dodger Stadium.

On the same day, the Dodgers traded Burt Hooton to the Cubs for Geoff Zahn and Eddie Solomon. The trade worked out so well for the Dodgers it became known as the "Great Arm Robbery." Hooton had shown flashes of brilliance in Chicago, including a no-hitter, but posted a 34–44 record with the Cubs. The club believed he would never develop into a winning pitcher, but made a huge miscalculation. Perfecting a knuckle curve, Hooton was 18–7 over the remainder of the 1975 season, including a 12-game winning streak. As a Dodger from 1975 through 1981, he was 96–63 and pitched in three World Series. Neither Zahn nor Solomon won a game for the Cubs, although Zahn later went on to pitch several fine seasons in the starting rotations of the Twins and Angels.

MAY 5   Doug Rau pitches a two-hitter to defeat the Astros 2–0 at Dodger Stadium. The only Houston hits were singles by Doug Rader in the second inning and opposing pitcher Larry Dierker in the third.

MAY 13   Burt Hooton pitches a two-hitter to defeat the Cardinals 5–0 at Busch Memorial Stadium. It was Hooton's first win as a Dodger. The only St. Louis hits were a double by Ted Sizemore in the fourth inning and a single from Luis Melendez in the ninth.

MAY 16   Don Sutton retires the first 22 batters to face him, but winds up losing 3–2 to the Pirates at Dodger Stadium. He entered the contest with a record of 23–2 since July 25, 1974, counting a 3–0 ledger in the post-season. The no-hit bid was broken up on consecutive singles by Richie Zisk, Dave Parker, and Manny Sanguillen with one out in the eighth inning which tied the score 1–1. Al Oliver clubbed a two-run homer in the ninth.

MAY 21   The Dodgers rout the Cubs 10–0 at Dodger Stadium. Andy Messersmith pitched the shutout for his 11th consecutive regular season victory over two seasons. He won his last four decisions in 1974 and the first seven in 1975.

MAY 22   The Dodgers take a 5½-game lead with an 8–3 win over the Cubs at Dodger Stadium.

The win gave the Dodgers a record of 27–15, but the club was 61–59 the rest of the way. The Reds overcome an 18–19 start to win 108 games and run away with the NL West title.

JUNE 3   In the first round of the amateur draft, the Dodgers select shortstop Mark Bradley from Elizabethtown High School in Elizabethtown, Kentucky.

Converted into an outfielder, Bradley played in only 90 big-league games and hit just .204 with three homers. Other future major leaguers drafted and signed by the Dodgers in 1975 were Myron White (second round), Dave Stewart (16th) and Brad Gulden (17th). Only Stewart would become a big-league regular. He won 20 or more games four seasons in a row beginning in 1987. Unfortunately, Stewart accomplished the feat in Oakland because the Dodgers traded him away in 1983.

JUNE 4   The Dodgers score three runs in the fifth inning without a hit off Expos pitcher Dennis Blair to win 3–0 in Montreal. The runs scored on two walks, an error, a hit batsman, two wild pitches and a sacrifice fly. The only two Los Angeles hits in the game were singles by Willie Crawford and Ron Cey in the eighth inning off Don DeMola.

Offense was a problem all year. The Dodgers led the majors in runs in 1974 with 798, but slipped to 648 in 1975, to rank eighth in the National League.

JUNE 8	The Dodgers fall out of first place with a 4–2 loss to the Phillies in Philadelphia.

JUNE 18   Ron Cey's grand slam in the first inning off Tom Griffin accounts for all of the runs in a 4–0 triumph over the Astros at Dodger Stadium.

Cey hit .283 with 25 homers and 101 RBIs in 1975.

JUNE 24   Davey Lopes steals four bases during an 8–3 win over the Astros in Houston.

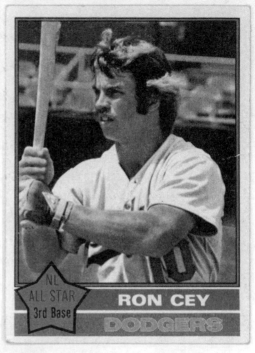

Ron Cey handled the hot corner for the Dodgers during the great years of the 1970s, collecting 25 homers and 101 RBIs in 1975.

JULY 1   Joe Ferguson's breaks his right wrist in a brawl during a 10–1 loss to the Padres at Dodger Stadium. The Dodgers were livid because they believed the Padres were trying to rub the win in their faces. The Padres were angry because they had lost 24 of their previous 30 decisions against the Dodgers, dating back to 1973. San Diego held the nine-run margin with two out in the eighth inning when Dave Winfield tried to bunt for a hit with a runner on third base. Charlie Hough's next pitch hit Winfield on the wrist and a brawl was narrowly averted. John Grubb then tried to steal home and was out on a hard tag by Ferguson. Willie Crawford led off the ninth, was brushed back by a pitch from Bill Grief and the fight was on. Ferguson rushed from the bench to get at Grief, and fractured the wrist during the melee.

Ferguson didn't play again for the remainder of the season. With Ferguson out of action, Steve Yeager was the starting catcher in 81 of the Dodgers last 82 games.

JULY 2   Steve Garvey's walk-off single with two out in the 14th beats the Padres 6–5 at Dodger Stadium.

JULY 12   To display their resentment over the failure of Walter Alston to select Al Hrabosky for the National League All-Star team, the Cardinals hold "Hrabosky Hbanner Hday." The club encouraged fans to show their support for the colorful reliever by bringing banners to the Dodgers-Cardinals clash televised nationally by NBC on a Saturday afternoon. The Cards won 2–1 by scoring a run in the ninth and another in the 10th. Hrabosky was the winning pitcher with two innings of scoreless relief.

JULY 13   Al Hrabosky is the winning pitcher for the second game in a row as the Cardinals beat the Dodgers 2–1 in St. Louis.

JULY 15   Walter Alston manages the National League to a 6–3 win in the All-Star Game at County Stadium in Milwaukee. Steve Garvey and Jimmy Wynn hit back-to-back homers off Vida Blue in the second inning. Don Sutton pitched the fourth and fifth innings and didn't allow a run.

On the same day, the Dodgers sold Jim Brewer to the Angels. Brewer had pitched for the Dodgers since 1964.

JULY 20   A two-run, walk-off homer by John Hale in the 12th inning beats the Cubs 5–3 at Dodger Stadium.

JULY 23   After a walk to John Hale, Willie Crawford and Lee Lack hit back-to-back pinch-homers with two out in the ninth inning, but it's too late to prevent a 5–4 loss to the Cardinals at Dodger Stadium.

Called up in September 1974, Hale collected hits in each of his four plate appearances that season for a batting average of 1.000, but finished his career in 1979 with a .201 average in 681 at-bats. He played for the Dodgers from 1974 through 1977.

JULY 31   The Braves score six runs in the ninth inning off Rick Rhoden and Mike Marshall to stun the Dodgers 11–10 in Atlanta. The game ended on a three-run homer by Rowland Office.

AUGUST 1   A two-run, walk-off homer by Ron Cey in the 10th inning beats the Reds 5–3 at Dodger Stadium.

AUGUST 9   Davey Lopes scores both runs of a 2–0 win over the Mets in New York.

AUGUST 12   Steve Yeager hits a three-run homer in the top of the 10th inning before the Phillies counter with two in their half for a 7–6 win in Philadelphia.

AUGUST 19   Don Sutton (six innings) and Mike Marshall (three innings) combine on a two-hitter to beat the Cubs 2–1 at Wrigley Field. Sutton was lifted for a pinch-hitter. The only Chicago hits were a triple by Bill Madlock in the fourth inning and a single from Jerry Morales in the seventh.

AUGUST 24   Davey Lopes steals three bases to extend his streak to 38 consecutive successful attempts before being caught stealing during a 14-inning, 5–3 loss to the Expos at Dodger Stadium. Bill Buckner had appeared to give the Dodgers a 3–2 lead in the sixth inning with a pinch-single, but was called out for using an illegal bat. The bat was heavily grooved. Buckner claimed he grabbed one of his practice bats by mistake.

Montreal catcher Gary Carter threw out Lopes to end the successful stolen base streak of the Dodger second baseman. Carter was also the last catcher to throw out Lopes prior to August 24. That happened on June 10. At the time, the 38 consecutive stolen bases by Lopes was a major league record. It stood until Vince Coleman swiped 50 in a row for the Cardinals in 1989. In 1975, Lopes led the NL with 77 steals along with 108 runs scored and a .262 batting average.

AUGUST 27   The Dodgers score seven runs in the sixth inning and win 10–0 over the Phillies at Dodger Stadium.

SEPTEMBER 3   After missing two games with the flu, Steve Garvey returns to the lineup for a 13–2 loss to the Reds in Cincinnati.

Garvey had played in 138 consecutive games before missing the two contests due to illness. The September 3, 1975 tilt started a streak of 1,207 consecutive games played that still ranks as the fourth longest of all-time behind only Cal Ripken, Jr. (2,632), Lou Gehrig (2,130) and Everett Scott (1,307). Garvey played in 1,107 of the 1,207 games as a Dodger and 100 with San Diego.

SEPTEMBER 15   Burt Hooton strikes out 12 batters and beats the Giants 5–4 at Dodger Stadium. The Dodgers scored four runs in the eighth inning, the last three on a pinch-homer by Willie Crawford, to lift Hooton to his 11th straight win.

SEPTEMBER 24   Steve Garvey drives in six runs on a homer, double and two singles during a 14–0 trouncing of the Padres in San Diego.

SEPTEMBER 26   Burt Hooton wins his 12th game in a row when Steve Garvey mashes a two-run, walk-off homer in the ninth inning to defeat the Astros 3–2 at Dodger Stadium.

SEPTEMBER 27   Steve Yeager hits a grand slam off Ken Forsch in the third inning of a 5–1 victory over the Astros at Dodger Stadium.

Yeager is a nephew of famed test pilot Chuck Yeager.

OCTOBER 25   Wearing a sequined Dodgers uniform complete with an "LA" cap, Elton John performs before a sellout crowd at Dodger Stadium.

NOVEMBER 17   The Dodgers trade Jimmy Wynn, Tom Paciorek, Lee Lacy and Jerry Royster to the Braves for Dusty Baker and Ed Goodson.

After struggling through 1976 with the worst season of his career, Baker went on to be a regular in the Dodger outfield for eight seasons. He played in three World Series and two All-Star Games.

DECEMBER 23   In a 61-page decision, arbitrator Pete Seitz rules that Andy Messersmith and Expos pitcher Dave McNally are free agents and now may play for the highest bidder. The case would dramatically alter the structure of baseball and bring about an end to the reserve clause and the beginning of free agency for all players, starting with the 1976–77 off-season.

Messersmith joined the Dodgers in December 1972 with a trade from the Angels. After the 1974 season, he asked the Dodgers for a no-trade clause in his contract. The Dodgers refused, and Messersmith played the 1975 campaign under a renewed contract which called for a $25,000 increase over his 1974 salary of $90,000. Messersmith was aware the Players Association did not believe a renewed contract was valid for more than one year, but the owners contended that each renewal carried an additional one-year renewal clause in perpetuity, effectively binding a player to his team for life. The situation, known as the reserve clause, had been in effect since 1880. On the advice of Marvin Miller, the executive director of the Players Association, Messersmith, and McNally decided to test the reserve clause in arbitration. The two players won their case in the hearing before Seitz. In 1976, players and owners worked out an agreement *in which a player could declare himself a free agent if his contract with a club had expired and he had at least six years of service in the majors. Messersmith posted a combined 39–20 record for the Dodgers in 1974 and 1975, and there was a large demand for his services. On April 10, 1976, he signed a three-year deal with the Braves worth $1 million. There were concerns over the soundness of Messersmith's arm, however, and those proved to be well-founded. He had pitched 634²/₃ regular and post-season innings in 1974 and 1975. After becoming a free agent, he pitched only four more seasons and had a record of 18–22.*

1976

Season in a Sentence

The Dodgers lose Andy Messersmith to free agency after he wins a challenge against the reserve clause, and Walter Alston retires following a second place finish.

Finish • Won • Lost • Pct • GB

Finish	Won	Lost	Pct	GB
First	92	70	.568	10.0

Managers

Walter Alston (90–68) and Tommy Lasorda (2–2)

Stats

Stats	Dods	NL	Rank
Batting Avg:	.251	.255	7
On-Base Pct:	.313	.320	9
Slugging Pct:	.349	.361	7
Home Runs:	91		7
Stolen Bases:	144		3
ERA:	3.02	3.50	2
Fielding Avg:	.980	.977	3
Runs Scored:	608		8
Runs Allowed:	543		2

Starting Lineup

Steve Yeager, c
Steve Garvey, 1b
Davey Lopes, 2b
Ron Cey, 3b
Bill Russell, ss
Bill Buckner, lf
Dusty Baker, cf
Reggie Smith, rf
Ted Sizemore, 2b

Pitchers

Don Sutton, sp
Doug Rau, sp
Burt Hooton, sp
Rick Rhoden, sp
Tommy John, sp
Charlie Hough, rp

Attendance

2,396,301 (third in NL)

Club Leaders

Batting Avg:	Steve Garvey	.317
On-Base Pct:	Steve Garvey	.363
Slugging Pct:	Ron Cey	.462
Home Runs:	Ron Cey	23
RBIs:	Ron Cey	80
	Steve Garvey	80
Runs:	Steve Garvey	85
Stolen Bases:	Davey Lopes	63
Wins:	Don Sutton	21
Strikeouts:	Don Sutton	161
ERA:	Doug Rau	2.57
Saves:	Charlie Hough	18

FEBRUARY 1   East Lansing, Michigan police arrest Mike Marshall for trespassing and criminal damaging. The Michigan State University police had ordered Marshall not to take batting practice for fear he would hit the ball too far and injure students on an adjacent tennis court. Marshall used a hacksaw to break his way into the batting cage. The Dodger pitcher filed a lawsuit against the school.

MARCH 2   The Dodgers trade Willie Crawford to the Cardinals for Ted Sizemore.

APRIL 9   The Dodgers lose 4–2 on Opening Day against the Giants in San Francisco.
                 Don Sutton went six innings and took the loss. Dusty Baker hit a home run
                 in his first at-bat as a Dodger.

                 *Hampered by a knee injury, Baker didn't hit another home run until June
                 and finished the season with only four and hit just .242. Following off-season
                 surgery, he would recover, and hit 30 home runs in 1977 and 144 in eight
                 seasons in Los Angeles.*

APRIL 10   Andy Messersmith signs with the Braves as a free agent (see December 23, 1975).

APRIL 12   The scheduled home opener against the Padres is rained out. It was only the
                 second time a Dodger home game was postponed by the weather since the move
                 to Los Angeles. The first was on April 21, 1967.

                 *After having only one game called during their first 18 seasons in Los Angeles,
                 the Dodgers would have three postponements by rain at Dodger Stadium in
                 1976. The other two were on consecutive days on September 10 and 11 in
                 contests scheduled against the Braves.*

APRIL 13   In the re-scheduled home opener, the Padres defeat the Dodgers 8–5 before 52,703
                 at Dodger Stadium. Burt Hooton pitched shutout ball through the first six innings
                 before allowing five of the seven San Diego runs in the fifth inning. It was Hooton's
                 first loss since July 10, 1975, ending a 12-game winning streak.

                 *Vendor Roger Owens threw out the ceremonial first pitch from the loge level.
                 The ball traveled 150 feet and was a perfect strike to Steve Yeager, standing
                 at home plate. Known as "The Peanut Man," Owens had astounded fans for
                 years by accurately throwing $1^1/_2$-ounce bags of peanuts. He easily hit the hands
                 of fans by tosses overhand, underhand, behind his back and between his legs.
                 Owens is likely the only ballpark vendor to have a biography written about him.
                 It was published in 2004.*

APRIL 16   Tommy John makes his first appearance in 21 months and loses 3–1 to the Braves in
                 Atlanta. He missed the entire 1975 season due to elbow surgery (see July 17, 1974).

                 *The loss dropped the Dodgers record to 0–5. The club would fall to 1–7 before
                 reversing course with 23 wins in 27 games from April 24 through May 23.*

APRIL 21   The Dodgers lose 1–0 in 16 innings to the Astros in Houston. A single by Jose Cruz
                 drove in the winning run. The Dodgers wasted a tremendous pitching performance
                 from Tommy John (seven innings), Charlie Hough (four innings) and Stan Wall
                 ($4^2/_3$ innings).

                 *Hough developed a knuckleball while in the minors and debuted with the
                 Dodgers in 1970. He pitched for the club until 1980, and made 401 appearances,
                 which still ranks sixth in club history, and is fourth in Dodger history in relief
                 appearances with 385. The Rangers converted Hough into a starting pitcher in
                 1982, and he enjoyed a second career. He was still pitching in 1994 at the age of
                 46 and ended his 25 seasons in the majors with a 216–216 record in 858 games.
                 Hough made 417 of his 440 career starts after his 34th birthday.*

APRIL 25   Cubs outfielder Rick Monday rescues the American flag during a 10-inning, 5–4 Dodger win at Dodger Stadium.

Playing center field, Monday noticed two fans climb out of the stands and run to left-center in the fourth inning. One of them was holding something under his arm. As the man unfurled his bundle and spread it on the field, Monday recognized it was the American flag. As he later recalled, "I saw they had a can of something and were pouring it over the flag. That's when I started to move." Before the men could set the flag on fire, Monday swept in, snatched it away, and carried it to the bullpen. As he ran off, security personnel moved in and arrested the intruders. The crowd gave Monday a standing ovation, and burst out with "God Bless America." Overnight, Monday became a hero in the year of the nation's bicentennial, and received more recognition for the flag incident than anything else he did during his 19-year playing career. The Illinois legislature proclaimed a statewide "Rick Monday Day," and he was named marshal of the Flag Day parade in Chicago. The flag that Monday rescued was presented to him by Dodger vice-president Al Campanis in pre-game ceremonies at Wrigley Field on May 4. The pair who attempted to burn the flag were William Thomas of Eldon, Missouri and his 11-year-old son, who were protesting the treatment of Native Americans. They were charged with trespassing. Nine months later, Monday would become a member of the Dodgers (see January 11, 1977).

APRIL 26   Tommy John wins his first game since 1974 with a 7–1 decision over the Pirates at Dodger Stadium.

APRIL 28   A walk-off homer by Ron Cey in the ninth inning beats the Pirates 2–1 at Dodger Stadium.

Cey hit .277 with 23 homers in 1976.

MAY 1   After the Cardinals score in the top of the 10th inning, the Dodgers rally with two in their half to win 4–3 at Dodger Stadium. Steve Garvey doubled in the first run and scored on Manny Mota's single. It was the Dodgers eighth win in a row.

MAY 2   Doug Rau wins his 10th game in succession over two seasons with a 3–1 decision over the Cardinals at Dodger Stadium. Rau won his last six games in 1975 and the first four in 1976.

Rau was 16–12 with an earned run average of 2.57 in 1976.

MAY 5   With the aid of a 31-mile-per-hour wind, the Dodgers set a club record with seven homers and extend their winning streak to 11 games by outslugging the Cubs 14–12 in Chicago. Henry Cruz hit two homers, with Ed Goodson, Bill Buckner, Ron Cey, Bill Russell and Steve Yeager rapping one each. Going into the game, the Dodgers hit 11 homers in the first 22 contests of the season. The club didn't hit more than three homers in any other game in 1976.

MAY 7   The Dodgers extend their winning streak to 12 games with a 10–8 decision over the Phillies in Philadelphia. Ron Cey collected four hits, one of them a homer, and drove in five runs. Steve Yeager and Bill Russell, the seventh and eighth hitters in the batting order, also had four hits each.

MAY 10	A two-out, two-run homer by Ron Cey in the ninth inning defeats the Cardinals 4–3 in St. Louis.
MAY 22	A walk-off sacrifice fly by pinch-hitter Manny Mota in the 13th inning beats the Astros 6–5 at Dodger Stadium.
MAY 23	Manny Mota drives in the winning run as a pinch-hitter in extra innings for the second game in a row at Dodger Stadium. After the Astros scored in the top of the 10th, the Dodgers rallied for two runs in their half, capped by Mota's walk-off single, to win 6–5.

> *The win represented the high point of the season. The Dodgers were 26–13 and led the NL West by 2½ games.*

MAY 30	Ron Cey collects five hits, including a club record three doubles, in five at-bats during a 6–5 win over the Reds in the first game of a double-header against the Reds at Riverfront Stadium. Cincinnati won the second tilt 7–2.

> *The Dodgers regained first place with the opening game win, then dropped back to second with the defeat. The Dodgers wouldn't recapture the top spot in the NL West for the rest of the season and finished 10 games behind the Reds. Los Angeles was ninth in the NL in runs and was outscored 857–608 by Cincinnati.*

JUNE 4	Dave Kingman hits three homers for the Mets during an 11–0 win over the Dodgers at Dodger Stadium.
JUNE 7	Ron Cey hits a grand slam off Ron Reed in the first inning, but the Dodgers lose 8–6 to the Phillies at Dodger Stadium.
JUNE 8	In the first round of the amateur draft, the Dodgers select catcher Mike Scioscia from Springfield High School in Morton, Pennsylvania.

> *Scioscia reached the majors in 1980 and played his entire 13-year career with the Dodgers, appearing in 1,441 games, two All-Star contests and two World Series. Other future major leaguers drafted and signed by the Dodgers in 1976 were Max Venable (third round), Mike Howard (sixth), Keith MacWhorter (15th), Jack Perconte (16th) and Daryl Patterson (second round of the secondary phase in January).*

JUNE 12	Steve Yeager marries Gloria Gaione on the steps of Los Angeles City Hall with Mayor Thomas Bradley serving as the Dodger catcher's best man. Yeager wanted to be married at home plate at Dodger Stadium, but Peter O'Malley denied the request.
JUNE 15	The Dodgers trade Joe Ferguson, Bobby Detherage and Freddie Tisdale to the Cardinals for Reggie Smith.

> *Smith was 31 at the time of the trade and a five-time All-Star. He was off to a rough start with the Cardinals in 1976, hitting only .218 in 47 games, but proved to be a steal for the Dodgers. Smith played in three more All-Star Games in a Los Angeles uniform. He hit .297 as a Dodger and his .528 slugging*

percentage ranks sixth in franchise history among players with at least 2,000 plate appearances.

JUNE 17 — Dave Kingman of the Mets hits a walk-off homer off Charlie Hough in the 14th inning to beat the Dodgers 1–0 in New York.

JUNE 23 — Rick Rhoden pitches a three-hit shutout and scores the lone run of a 1–0 win over the Astros in Houston. Rhoden singled in the sixth inning and scored on a double by Bill Buckner and a sacrifice fly from Ted Sizemore.

> *On the same day, the Dodgers trade Mike Marshall to the Braves for Elias Sosa and Lee Lacy. Marshall struggled after his record-setting season in 1974. He sealed his fate in Los Angeles with his arrest (February 1, 1976) and attributing his problems to fielding deficiencies of the Dodger infield which he called "four cigar store Indians." Marshall would have a brief revival in 1978 and 1979 with the Twins before the end of his career in 1981.*

JUNE 27 — The Dodgers outlast the Giants 12–8 at Dodger Stadium. Los Angeles broke a 6–6 tie with two runs in the sixth inning.

JULY 4 — On the day of the nation's bicentennial, the Dodgers lose 5–2 to the Padres at Dodger Stadium.

JULY 5 — Burt Hooton pitches a two-hitter to defeat the Phillies 6–0 at Veterans Stadium. Garry Maddox collected both Philadelphia hits with a single in the third inning and a double in the eighth.

JULY 11 — Trailing 5–1, the Dodgers explode for seven runs in the seventh inning to win 9–6 over the Cardinals in St. Louis. During the big inning, the Dodgers were rewarded with three consecutive pinch-singles from Ted Sizemore, Ed Goodson and Lee Lacy and a three-run homer from Reggie Smith. As the Dodgers batted around, Sizemore stepped to the plate a second time and delivered another single.

> *Smith was a true Renaissance Man. He played seven different musical instruments, scuba dived, flew airplanes, trained quarter horses, cooked, played tennis, dabbled in real estate, and was even a lab assistant in a morgue.*

JULY 13 — Steve Garvey drives in a run in the first inning with a triple, sparking the National League to a 7–1 win in the All-Star Game at Veterans Stadium in Philadelphia.

JULY 17 — Walter Alston wins his 2,000th game as manager with a 5–4 decision over the Cubs at Dodger Stadium. Rick Rhoden was the winning pitcher to run his record in 1976 to 9–0.

> *Future managers who played for Alston between 1954 and 1976 were Dusty Baker, Ken Boyer, Roger Craig, Gil Hodges, Frank Howard, Tommy Lasorda, Jim Lefebvre, Davey Lopes, Gene Michael, Frank Robinson, Bill Russell, Jeff Torborg, Bobby Valentine, Dick Williams, Maury Wills and Don Zimmer. Even with all of his success, Alston never had the luxury of hiring his own coaches. Dodger management believed that coaches should be instructors and not cronies of the manager. Many had ambitions beyond coaching the Dodgers. Alston*

coaches who were later major league managers include Bobby Bragan, Charlie Dressen, Leo Durocher, Preston Gomez, Roy Hartsfield, Tommy Lasorda, Danny Ozark and Lefty Phillips.

JULY 25   Doug Rau pitches the Dodgers to a 1–0 win over the Padres in San Diego. The Dodgers scored their run in the seventh inning when Bill Russell singled, stole second, and crossed the plate on a double from Lee Lacy.

JULY 26   Don Sutton records his 2,000th career strikeout during a 6–2 win over the Braves at Dodger Stadium by fanning Carl Morton in the second inning.

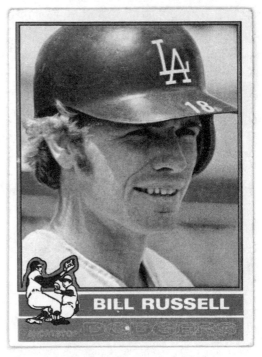

AUGUST 1   Bill Buckner collects seven hits in nine at-bats during a double-header sweep of the Giants in San Francisco. The Dodgers won 4–1 and 4–3, with the second contest going 10 innings. Buckner garnered six singles and a double.

A key part of the great Dodger infield of the 1970s, Bill Russell provided consistent defense and leadership throughout his career.

AUGUST 2   Dusty Baker hits a two-out, walk-off homer in the 11th inning which beats the Astros 5–4 at Dodger Stadium. Baker was scratched from the starting lineup because earlier he was fitted for contact lenses, which affected his vision. Once his sight was restored to a normal level, Baker entered the contest as a defensive replacement in center field in the 10th inning.

AUGUST 3   Bill Buckner drives in Davey Lopes with both runs of a 2–0 win over the Astros at Dodger Stadium with singles in the fourth and seventh innings. Burt Hooton pitched a two-hitter. The only Houston hits were singles by Greg Gross and Cesar Cedeno in the first inning.

In his next start on August 8, Hooton held the Reds without a hit for the first four innings, giving him 12 consecutive scoreless innings. He ended up as the losing pitcher in a 3–2 decision at Dodger Stadium.

AUGUST 9   John Candelaria of the Pirates pitches a no-hitter to defeat the Dodgers 2–0 at Three Rivers Stadium. He struck out seven and walked one. Candelaria needed only three pitches to retire Davey Lopes, Ted Sizemore and Bill Russell in the ninth.

The no-hitter was the first by a Pirate in Pittsburgh since 1907. It was also the first against the Dodgers since Don Larsen's perfect game in 1956 and the first no-hitter during the regular season since Vern Bickford of the Braves accomplished the feat in 1950.

AUGUST 13   The Dodgers score three runs in the ninth inning to beat the Cubs 8–7 in the second game of a double-header at Wrigley Field. Los Angeles trailed 7–2 before narrowing the gap with three tallies in the seventh. In the ninth, Jim Lyttle doubled, Bill Buckner and Steve Garvey contributed singles, and Bill Russell smacked a two-out, two-run triple. Chicago won the opener 3–2 in 15 innings.

Garvey hit .317 with 200 hits and 13 home runs in 1976. It was his third consecutive season with 200 or more hits.

AUGUST 19   The Dodgers explode for four runs in the ninth inning without a batter being retired and beat the Mets 6–5 at Dodger Stadium. Ted Sizemore and Bill Buckner opened the inning with singles, followed by a three-run homer from Steve Garvey off Skip Lockwood. After Bob Apodaca relieved Lockwood, Ron Cey clubbed a walk-off-homer.

AUGUST 21   Don Sutton pitches a two-hitter to defeat the Pirates 5–1 at Dodger Stadium. He retired the first 22 batters to face him. The perfect game bid was broken up by a Dave Parker homer with one out in the eighth inning. Manny Sanguillen doubled in the ninth for the second Pittsburgh hit.

SEPTEMBER 2   The Dodgers play at Jarry Park in Montreal for the last time, and sweep the Expos 2–1 and 5–3.

The following season, the Expos began playing at Olympic Stadium.

SEPTEMBER 6   Steve Yeager is injured in a freak accident during a 4–1 win over the Padres in San Diego. Yeager was in the on-deck circle when Bill Russell's bat shattered on a ground out to third base. The heavy end of the bat slammed into Yeager's neck, and he went down as if shot. Nine splinters were removed during a delicate 90-minute operation which also repaired a punctured esophagus. One doctor commented that the Dodger catcher was lucky to be alive.

The next season, Yeager wore a protective neck flap designed by Dodger trainer Bill Buhler. The device soon became universal gear for catchers.

SEPTEMBER 22   Don Sutton wins his 20th game of the season with a 3–1 decision over the Giants in San Francisco.

Sutton finished the year with a 21–10 record and a 3.06 ERA in $267^{2}/_{3}$ innings.

SEPTEMBER 24   A two-run single by Ron Cey in the ninth inning beats the Reds 7–6 at Dodger Stadium.

SEPTEMBER 27   Near the end of his 23rd year as manager of the Dodgers, Walter Alston announces his retirement. He exited with a record of 2,040–1,613, a winning percentage of .558, along with seven National League pennants and four world championships. The only individuals to manage one club for a longer period of time was Connie Mack with the Philadelphia Athletics (1901–50) and John McGraw with the New York Giants (1902–32). Alston returned to his native Ohio in retirement. He was elected to the Hall of Fame in 1983, and died a year later at the age of 72.

Two days after Alston's retirement, the Dodgers hired 49-year-old Tommy Lasorda as manager. The appointment of Lasorda was no surprise, as he had been groomed as Alston's successor for years. A native of Norristown, Pennsylvania, Lasorda had an unsuccessful major league career as a pitcher, compiling a record of 0–4 and a 6.48 ERA with the Dodgers and Athletics from 1954 through 1956. After receiving a taste of the big leagues, it took Lasorda nearly two decades to make his way back. After being released as a player while in the minors in 1960, he was a scout for the Dodgers from 1961 through 1964 and managed in the minors from 1965 through 1972. Five of Lasorda's eight clubs won pennants while advancing from the Rookie level to Class AAA. In 1973, he donned a major league uniform for the first time in 17 years as a coach with the Dodgers, and served four years under Alston while managing in the winter league in the Dominican Republic during the off-season. During that period, Lasorda had several offers to manage other big-league clubs, but remained in Los Angeles. "I bleed Dodger blue," the loquacious Lasorda was fond of saying, "and when I die, I'm going to the Big Dodger in the sky." He would buck conventional managerial wisdom with his unrestrained optimism and by openly fraternizing and making friends with his players, a policy that most believed would undermine team discipline. Lasorda would manage the club until retiring in 1996, then remain in the organization in various capacities. The Dodgers won National League pennants in the first two years under his leadership, took the World Series in 1981 and 1988, and managed nine players who won the NL Rookie of the Year Award. In contrast to the taciturn Alston, Lasorda wore his emotions on his sleeve and motivated his troops with his boundless enthusiasm, and was more cheerleader that tactician. Tommy loved the spotlight, the show-biz atmosphere of Los Angeles, and mugging for the camera. He became close friends with Frank Sinatra and Don Rickles. The wall of Lasorda's office was lined with autographed photos of Hollywood celebrities. The press loved him because he was always quotable with original one-liners. The fans in Los Angeles turned out in record numbers because his teams usually won. The front office brought him back year after year because of the championships and his tireless promotion of the franchise. But while promoting the Dodgers, Lasorda was also promoting himself. His extroverted personality and fame-seeking antics grated on many, including some of his own players, who were less enamored with Lasorda. He loved Italian cuisine but his detractors thought he was full of baloney. Joe Garagiola once said, "You can plant 2,000 rows of corn with the fertilizer Lasorda spreads around." Many had to resist the temptation to test the theory that Lasorda actually bled "Dodger blue."

SEPTEMBER 29   The Dodgers edge the Astros 1–0 at Dodger Stadium. Steve Garvey drove in the lone run with a single in the seventh inning. Starter Rick Sutcliffe pitched five innings in his major league debut. Stan Wall (three innings) and Charlie Hough (one inning) completed the shutout.

The Dodgers finished second to the Reds in the NL West for the fourth time in seven seasons. The others were in 1970, 1973 and 1975.

DECEMBER 20   Six weeks after Jimmy Carter defeats Gerald Ford in the Presidential election, the Dodgers trade Ted Sizemore to the Phillies for Johnny Oates and Quency Hill.

1977

Season in a Sentence

In Tommy Lasorda's first season, the Dodgers use a 22–4 start and a revived offense to reach the World Series before losing to the Yankees.

Finish • Won • Lost • Pct • GB

First   98   64   .605 +10.0

National League Championship Series

The Dodgers defeated the Philadelphia Phillies three games to one.

World Series

The Dodgers lost to the New York Yankees four games to two.

Stats	Dods	NL	Rank
Batting Avg:	.266	.262	6
On-Base Pct:	.336	.328	3
Slugging Pct:	.418	.396	3
Home Runs:	191		1
Stolen Bases:	114		7
ERA:	3.22	3.91	1
Fielding Avg:	.981	.977	3
Runs Scored:	769		3
Runs Allowed:	582		1

Starting Lineup

Steve Yeager, c
Steve Garvey, 1b
Davey Lopes, 2b
Ron Cey, 3b
Bill Russell, ss
Dusty Baker, lf
Rick Monday, cf
Reggie Smith, rf

Pitchers

Tommy John, sp
Rick Rhoden, sp
Don Sutton, sp
Doug Rau, sp
Burt Hooton, sp
Charlie Hough, rp
Mike Garman, rp
Elias Sosa, rp

Attendance

2,955,087 (first in NL)

Club Leaders

Batting Avg:	Reggie Smith	.307
On-Base Pct:	Reggie Smith	.427
Slugging Pct:	Reggie Smith	.576
Home Runs:	Steve Garvey	33
RBIs:	Steve Garvey	115
Runs:	Reggie Smith	104
Stolen Bases:	Davey Lopes	47
Wins:	Tommy John	20
Strikeouts:	Burt Hooton	153
ERA:	Burt Hooton	2.62
Saves:	Charlie Hough	22

JANUARY 11   The Dodgers trade Bill Buckner, Ivan DeJesus and Jeff Albert to the Cubs for Rick Monday and Mike Garman.

Already popular in Los Angeles for rescuing the American flag at Dodger Stadium (see April 25, 1976), Monday was 31 at the time of the trade and was expected to be the Dodgers starting center fielder. He played for eight seasons in Los Angeles, but hit only .254 with 72 homers in 1,526 at-bats. A back injury limited Monday's effectiveness, and he was never able to play everyday after the trade. Monday became a Dodger broadcaster in 1993. Buckner played another 14 seasons in the majors after leaving the Dodgers and won a batting title and played in an All-Star Game before his regrettable error with the Red Sox in the 1986 World Series.

APRIL 5   Two months after Americans were transfixed by the television miniseries *Roots*, the Dodgers sign Boog Powell as a free agent following his release by the Indians.

APRIL 7   After giving up a home run to Gary Thomasson on the first pitch on Opening Day, Don Sutton allows no more runs and only three more hits to beat the Giants 5–1 before 51,022 at Dodger Stadium. The ball struck by Thomasson went into the Hall of Fame as the first major league home run with a Rawlings baseball.

Ross Porter joined Vin Scully and Jerry Doggett in the Dodger broadcast booth in 1977. Porter would continue to announce Dodger games until 2004.

APRIL 12   The Dodgers score six runs in both the first and fifth innings and defeat the Braves 14–10 at Dodger Stadium. Rick Rhoden was the winning pitcher despite allowing eight runs in five innings.

Rhoden pitched for the Dodgers from 1974 through 1978. He overcame long odds to reach the majors at the age of 21. When he was eight-years-old, Rhoden accidentally fell on a pair of rusty scissors. He was stricken with osteomyelitis, wore a brace on his right leg for three years, and needed a cane for some time afterward.

APRIL 25   The Dodgers score seven runs in the eighth inning and wallop the Braves 16–6 at Dodger Stadium. Nine different players homered during the game. Charlie Hough, Lee Lacy, Dusty Baker, Steve Garvey and Ron Cey went deep for the Dodgers. Gary Matthews, Jerry Royster, Jeff Burroughs and Willie Montanez each clouted home runs for Atlanta. Cey's blast was a grand slam off Rick Camp in the eighth. The homer by Hough was his only one in 226 career at-bats over 25 seasons.

Cey finished April with 29 runs batted in, which at the time was a record for the month. He finished the season with a batting average of only .241, but hit 30 homers and drove in 110 runs.

APRIL 30   The Dodgers win their eighth game in a row with a 6–4 decision over the Expos at Dodger Stadium.

MAY 5   The Dodgers score seven runs in the fifth inning off Tom Seaver for all of the tallies in a 7–2 victory over the Mets at Dodger Stadium. Ron Cey hit a grand slam.

The Dodgers hit 191 home runs in 1977, exactly 100 more than the 91 the club struck in 1976.

MAY 6   The Dodgers run their record to 22–4 with a 9–3 win over the Phillies at Dodger Stadium. The club's lead in the NL West was already 11 games.

The Dodgers set an all-time major league attendance record in 1977 by drawing 2,955,087 in 1977. It broke the previous mark of 2,755,184 set by the Dodgers in 1962.

MAY 10   In the first Dodger game at Olympic Stadium in Montreal, Rick Monday is injured in a bizarre play during a 4–3 loss. A long drive by Warren Cromartie caromed off the wall, struck Monday on the forehead and bounded over the barrier for a ground rule double.

MAY 15
John Hale drives in the winning run with a single in the 12th inning to beat the Mets 4–3 in New York. Ron Cey hit a two-run homer in the top of the 10th, but the Mets scored two in their half, the second coming on Cey's error.

MAY 21
The Dodgers extend their won-lost record to 30–9 with a 4–3 triumph over the Pirates in Pittsburgh.

JUNE 3
The Dodgers collect only two hits in 11 innings and lose 1–0 to the Padres at Dodger Stadium on Dave Winfield's homer off Charlie Hough. With two out in the bottom of the 11th, Winfield leaped above the fence to rob Ed Goodson of a homer.

JUNE 5
The Dodgers retire Walter Alston's number 24 in ceremonies before a 4–2 victory over the Padres at Dodger Stadium. Doug Rau was the winning pitcher.

Rau had an 11–1 record before the All-Star break in 1977, but was only 3–7 afterward.

JUNE 7
In the first round of the amateur draft, the Dodgers select pitcher Bob Welch Eastern Michigan University.

Welch reached the majors a year later and played for the Dodgers until 1987 and was 115–87. He pitched in two World Series and an All-Star Game as a Dodger. Welch finished his career in the majors with a record of 211–146. Other future major leaguers drafted and signed by the Dodgers in 1977 were Joe Beckwith (second round), Mickey Hatcher (fifth), Bobby Mitchell (seventh), Mitch Webster (23rd), Tom Niedenfuer (36th) and Ron Roenicke (first round of the secondary phase). Webster was traded by the Dodgers before making his major league debut with the Blue Jays in 1983. He played in Los Angeles from 1992 through 1995, the final four seasons of a 13-year career. Niedenfuer was the 761st player drafted out of 762 in 1977. Niedenfuer and Hatcher both won world championship rings with the Dodgers.

JUNE 10
The Dodgers overcome a 6–0 deficit after five innings to take a 7–6 lead, only to lose 8–7 in 12 innings to the Cardinals in St. Louis.

JUNE 11
Reggie Smith charges Cardinals pitcher John Denny after being hit by a pitch in the second inning, sparking a bench-clearing fight during a 9–8 win in St. Louis. Denny was ejected along with Dodger pitcher Elias Sosa.

JUNE 15
The Dodgers score seven runs in the sixth inning to defeat the Pirates 10–1 at Dodger Stadium. Steve Garvey extended his streak of hitting home runs in consecutive games to four.

JUNE 19
Reggie Smith charges the mound for the second time in nine days sparking a benches-clearing brawl during a 3–1 win over the Cubs at Dodger Stadium. In the third inning, Smith rushed toward Chicago pitcher Rick Reuschel after being hit in the ankle with a pitch. Both Smith and Reuschel were ejected along with Cubs player George Mitterwald and manager Herman Franks.

JUNE 22
A grand slam by Steve Garvey in the fourth inning off Clay Carroll highlights a 12–1 win over the Cardinals at Dodger Stadium. Garvey finished the contest with four hits and five runs batted in.

June 29   Steve Garvey collects four hits, two of them homers, in four at-bats during a 13–7 win over the Braves at Dodger Stadium.

Garvey had at least 200 hits and hit over .300 in the three seasons prior to 1977 and in each of the three years afterward. During the 1977 campaign, he fell short of those benchmarks with a .297 average and 192 hits, but hit career highs in home runs (33) and runs batted in (115). Garvey also had a junior high school in Lindsay, California named after him in 1977. Lindsay is a town of about 10,000 residents some 160 miles north of Los Angeles at approximately the midpoint between Bakersfield and Fresno.

July 3   Ron Cey collects five hits, including two doubles, in five at-bats and drives in four runs during a 10–7 win over the Giants in San Francisco. Combined with a single in his last at-bat the night before, a 10–3 victory over the Giants at Candlestick Park, Cey had six hits in a row.

July 4   During a 4–0 triumph over the Dodgers in San Francisco, Ron Cey picks up three hits, all singles, in his first three official at-bats to give him nine in succession over three games. The streak ended with a strikeout in the ninth inning. The nine hits, collected in the contests of July 2, 3 and 4, were seven singles and two doubles. He was also hit by a pitch to reach base 10 straight times.

July 9   Don Sutton strikes out 12 batters in nine innings, but the Dodgers garner only two hits off Dan Freisleben and Rollie Fingers of the Padres during a 2–1 loss in San Diego.

July 16   After Bob Owchinko of the Padres retires the first 22 batters to face him, the Dodgers put together three singles in the eighth inning to win 1–0 in San Diego. The perfect game bid was stopped when Steve Garvey beat out a bunt. Glenn Burke and Steve Yeager followed with two-out singles. Tommy John, after missing his two previous starts with the flu, pitched the shutout.

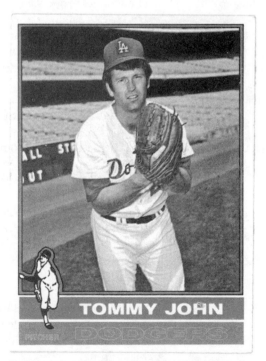

TOMMY JOHN

Tommy John posted a 20–7 record in 1977 and a 2.78 ERA. Bothered by arm trouble early in his career, John was known for his durability after having the surgery that is now named for him.

At the age of 34 and following reconstructive elbow surgery, John was a 20-game winner for the first time in his career in 1977. He finished the year with a 20–7 record and a 2.78 ERA.

July 19   Don Sutton starts the All-Star Game at Yankee Stadium and pitches three shutout innings to help the National League to a 7–5 victory. The performance earned Sutton the game's MVP award. Steve Garvey contributed a home run in the third inning off Jim Palmer.

JULY 24   Given a second life when Mets right fielder Bruce Bosclair drops a foul fly, Davey Lopes crashes a three-run, walk-off homer for a 5–3 win at Dodger Stadium.

                 Lopes hit .283 with 11 homers and 47 stolen bases in 1977.

JULY 31   The Dodgers erupt for six runs in the 10th inning to beat the Expos 8–2 in Montreal. Reggie Smith hit a two-run homer during the rally.

                 Smith hit .307 with 32 homers and 104 runs scored in 1977.

AUGUST 8   Tommy John pitches a two-hitter and hit a home run to beat the Reds 4–0 at Dodger Stadium. It was John's first homer since 1968. The only Cincinnati hits were a single by George Foster in the second inning and a double from Ken Griffey, Sr. in the third.

AUGUST 9   The Dodgers avoid a no-hitter on a close call at first base during a 4–0 loss to the Reds at Dodger Stadium. The only Los Angeles hit was an infield single off Doug Capilla in the seventh inning. Cey's one-hopper glanced off Capilla's glove to shortstop Dave Concepcion, whose throw to first was an eyelash too late.

AUGUST 10   Rick Rhoden pitches a two-hitter to defeat the Reds 1–0 at Dodger Stadium. Dave Concepcion collected both Cincinnati hits with singles in the fifth and eighth innings. Reggie Smith drove in the lone run with a single in the third inning.

AUGUST 13   The Dodgers rout the Braves 10–0 at Dodger Stadium.

AUGUST 14   The Dodgers edge the Braves 1–0 at Dodger Stadium. Doug Rau pitched the shutout. Teddy Martinez drove in the lone run with a single in the fourth inning. Martinez subbed at third base for Ron Cey, who was given the day off.

AUGUST 17   On the day after Elvis Presley dies in Memphis, the Dodgers purchase Vic Davalillo from Aguascalientes of the Mexican League.

AUGUST 18   After being four outs from a no-hitter, Don Sutton settles for a one-hitter and a 7–0 win over the Giants at Dodger Stadium. The lone hit was a single by Marc Hill with two out in the eighth inning.

                 During his career, Sutton won 324 games, pitched 58 shutouts, and hurled five one-hitters. Despite those accomplishments, he never recorded a no-hitter.

AUGUST 21   Rick Rhoden collects three hits, including a homer, and beat the Cubs 5–1 in Chicago.

AUGUST 22   The Cardinals stun the Dodgers with seven runs in the ninth inning to win 8–6 in St. Louis. The game ended on a three-run homer by Roger Freed off Charlie Hough with two out. Steve Yeager hit a grand slam for Los Angeles off John Denny in the third inning.

AUGUST 24   Reggie Smith drives in both runs of a 10-inning, 2–1 win over the Pirates in Pittsburgh. Smith homered in the third inning and drove in the winning run with a single in the 10th.

AUGUST 28   In a fantastic hitting performance, Steve Garvey ties a major league record with five extra base hits during an 11–0 win over the Cardinals at Dodger Stadium. He hit two homers and three doubles. Garvey also tied a club record with five runs scored, and drove in five runs. Facing starter Bob Forsch, Garvey hit doubles in the second and fourth innings and a homer in the fifth. Steve finished the day by hitting a grand slam off Clay Carroll in the seventh and added a double against Tom Underwood in the eighth. Don Sutton pitched the shutout.

During the 1977 season, Garvey co-hosted a weekly show on local television in Los Angeles with Regis Philbin. At the same time, Steve's wife Cyndy co-hosted a daily morning show on KABC-TV with Philbin called "A.M. Los Angeles." The program was a forerunner of the popular show Philbin currently co-hosts with Kelly Ripa.

SEPTEMBER 12   A two-out, two-run, walk-off homer by Ron Cey in the 10th inning beats the Padres 7–6 at Dodger Stadium. Dusty Baker hit a grand slam off Dave Freisleben in the fifth inning.

Baker rebounded from an awful year in 1976 to hit 30 homers with a .291 average in 1977 (see October 2, 1977).

SEPTEMBER 13   The Dodgers score 10 runs in the second inning and take an 18–1 lead after five innings to breeze to an 18–4 trouncing of the Padres at Dodger Stadium. Dusty Baker drove in five runs in the big inning with a two-run double and a three-run homer. The 10 runs were accomplished with seven hits, four walks and two stolen bases.

SEPTEMBER 20   The Dodgers clinch the NL West pennant with a 3–1 win over the Giants in San Francisco.

SEPTEMBER 24   Burt Hooton pitches a two-hitter to down the Astros 1–0 at the Astrodome. The only Houston hits were a double by Bob Watson in the second inning and a single from Ed Herrmann in the fourth.

SEPTEMBER 25   Tommy John wins his 20th game of the season with a 5–4 decision over the Dodgers in Houston.

SEPTEMBER 30   The Dodgers edge the Astros 6–5 in 14 innings at Dodger Stadium. Steve Garvey drove in the winning run with a single.

OCTOBER 2   During a 6–3 loss to the Astros at Dodger Stadium on the final day of the season, Dusty Baker homers in his final at-bat. It was his 30th homer of the year, making the Dodgers the first team in major league history with four players to hit at least 30 homers in a season. Steve Garvey had 33, Reggie Smith 32 and Ron Cey 30. Glenn Burke is credited with inventing the high-five when he congratulated Baker with the gesture on his way back to the bench. Burke was standing at the plate. The next Dodger hitter, Burke hit his first major league homer. When Burke arrived in the dugout, Baker returned the high five.

The Dodgers played the Phillies in the National League Championship. Philadelphia reached the NLCS in 1976, but was swept by the Reds. Managed by former Dodger coach Danny Ozark, the Phils were 101–61 in 1977.

OCTOBER 4   The Dodgers open the best-of-five NLCS with a 7–5 loss to the Phillies before 55,968 at Dodger Stadium. Two errors by shortstop Bill Russell helped put Los Angeles in a 5–1 hole. With Steve Carlton on the mound in the seventh, the Dodgers loaded on walks to Jerry Grote and Reggie Smith sandwiched around a single from Davey Lopes. After fouling off three full count pitches, Ron Cey hit a grand slam to tie the score. The Phillies won the contest, however, with two tallies in the ninth off Elias Sosa.

OCTOBER 5   The Dodgers even the series with a 7–1 win over the Phillies before 55,973 at Dodger Stadium. Dusty Baker broke a 1–1 deadlock with a grand slam off Jim Lonborg in the fourth inning. Don Sutton pitched a complete game.

After splitting two games in Los Angeles, the Dodgers moved to Veterans Stadium in Philadelphia, where the Phillies were 60–21 during the 1977 regular season.

OCTOBER 7   In game three, the Dodgers score three runs in the ninth inning to defeat the Phillies 6–5 in Philadelphia. Los Angeles scored two runs in the top of the second, but the Phils responded with three tallies in their half off Burt Hooton and took a 5–3 advantage into the ninth. Philadelphia reliever Gene Garber came into the contest in the seventh inning and retired the first eight batters he faced, including the first two in the ninth. Two aging pinch-hitters started the game-winning rally. Vic Davalillo, who was 41-years-old, hit for Steve Yeager and beat out a drag bunt. Manny Mota, who was 39 and hit .395 in 38 at-bats during the regular season, followed Davalillo and hit a two-strike pitch to deep left field. Greg Luzinski got his glove on the ball but could not hang on as he hit the wall. Mota went to second with a double that scored Davalillo. Mota advanced to third on a botched relay throw. Davey Lopes hit a shot off the glove of third baseman Mike Schmidt which glanced to shortstop Larry Bowa, who threw to first. Umpire Bruce Froemming called Lopes safe on a close play hotly disputed by the Phillies, and Mota scored the tying run. Lopes moved to second on Garber's errant pick-off attempt and scored on a single by Bill Russell. Mike Garman pitched the ninth for the save.

OCTOBER 8   The Dodgers win the National League pennant with a 4–1 victory over the Phillies in Philadelphia. The contest was played almost entirely in a steady downpour of rain. Tommy John pitched the complete game. Dusty Baker's two-run homer off Steve Carlton in the second inning put the Dodgers in the lead.

The Dodgers played the Yankees in the World Series. Managed by Billy Martin, the Yankees ended a controversy-filled regular season with a 100–62 record. The season was marked by almost continuous bickering, highlighted by a dugout confrontation between Martin and Reggie Jackson in June. The incident was captured on national television. In the deciding fifth game of the ALCS, the Yanks trailed the Royals 3–1 in Kansas City before scoring a run in the eighth inning and three in the ninth to win 5–3 to win their second straight AL pennant. In 1976, the Yanks were swept by the Reds in the World Series. The 1977 match-up was the eighth between the Yankees and Dodgers in the Fall Classic, but the first since 1963.

OCTOBER 11   The Dodgers open the 1977 World Series with a 12-inning, 4–3 loss to the Yankees in New York. Los Angeles took a 2–0 lead in the first inning off Don Gullett, but the Yanks took a 3–2 advantage with single runs in the first, fifth and the eighth against Don Sutton. In the ninth, Dusty Baker singled, moved to second on a walk to Steve Yeager and scored on a pinch-single by Lee Lacy. After allowing the hit to Lacy, Sparky Lyle retired 11 Dodger batters in a row. In the 12th, Willie Randolph doubled off Rick Rhoden and crossed the plate on a single from Paul Blair.

OCTOBER 12   The Dodgers even the Series with a 6–1 win over the Yankees in New York. Los Angeles scored five runs in the first three innings off Catfish Hunter. Ron Cey hit a two-run homer in the first inning, Steve Yeager a solo shot in the second, and Reggie Smith belted a home run with a man on base in the third. Steve Garvey clouted the fourth L.A. homer in the ninth. Burt Hooton pitched a five-hit complete game.

The crowd at Yankee Stadium became an issue in the ninth. Someone tossed a smoke bomb onto the field and Reggie Jackson scooped it up with his glove and threw it back in the stands. Reggie Smith was knocked to his knees after a heavy object from the stands hit him in the back of the head. He had to be fitted with a cervical collar, but was back in the lineup for game three.

OCTOBER 14   In the third game of the Series, the Dodgers lose 5–3 to the Yankees before 55,992 at Dodger Stadium. The Yankees scored three runs in the first inning off Tommy John and Dusty Baker responded with a three-run homer in the third facing Mike Torrez. John allowed runs in the fourth and fifth for the loss.

OCTOBER 15   The Dodgers fall behind three games to one with a 4–2 loss before 55,995 at Dodger Stadium. Doug Rau allowed three Yankee runs in the second inning. Davey Lopes hit a two-run homer in the third off Ron Guidry, but the Dodgers couldn't score again.

OCTOBER 16   The Dodgers stay alive with a 10–4 win over the Yankees before 55,955 at Dodger Stadium. Los Angeles held a 10–0 lead after six innings with the help of home runs from Reggie Smith and Steve Yeager. Dusty Baker contributed three hits. Don Sutton pitched a complete game. The last two New York runs were scored on a home run by Reggie Jackson in the eighth.

OCTOBER 18   The Yankees win the world championship with an 8–4 decision over the Dodgers in New York behind one of the greatest hitting demonstrations in post-season history. Steve Garvey gave the Dodgers a 2–0 lead, but the Yankees tied the score in the second when Reggie Jackson walked on four pitches and Chris Chambliss homered off Burt Hooton. Reggie Smith broke the deadlock with a solo homer in the third. In the New York fourth, Thurman Munson singled and Jackson homered on Hooton's first pitch to put the Dodgers behind 4–3. Jackson next stepped to the plate in the fifth with Elias Sosa on the mound, and again clubbed a first-pitch homer. In the eighth, Jackson faced Charlie Hough and hit his third first-pitch home run. It traveled about 450 feet into the center field bleachers. Counting his home run in his last at-bat the previous game, Jackson incredibly hit home runs on four straight swings off four different pitchers. The only other player with three homers in a World Series game is Babe Ruth, who accomplished the feat twice in 1926 and 1928. Jackson is the only one to do it in three consecutive plate appearances. Jackson also set a record with five total home runs in the 1977 Series.

NOVEMBER 21   The Dodgers sign Terry Forster, most recently with the Pirates, as a free agent.

Following an agreement between players and owners, players with at least six years in the majors and whose contracts had expired can declare themselves free agents at the end of the 1976 season. Forster was the first player signed by the Dodgers under the new system. He gave the club an excellent season out of the bullpen in 1978 with 22 saves and a 1.93 ERA in 47 games, but had trouble staying healthy. Forster lasted only four seasons in Los Angeles.

1978   LA

Season in a Sentence

The Dodgers become the first team to draw over 3,000,000 fans and win the NL West before a post-season with the identical result of the previous season.

Finish • Won • Lost • Pct • GB

First   95   67   .586   +2.5

National League Championship Series

The Dodgers defeated the Philadelphia Phillies three games to one.

World Series

The Dodgers lost to the New York Yankees four games to two.

Manager

Tommy Lasorda

Stats

Stats	Dods	NL	Rank
Batting Avg:	.264	.254	2
On-Base Pct:	.338	.320	1
Slugging Pct:	.402	.372	1
Home Runs:	149		1
Stolen Bases:	137		4 (tie)
ERA:	3.12	3.58	1
Fielding Avg:	.978	.978	8
Runs Scored:	727		1
Runs Allowed:	573		1

Starting Lineup

Steve Yeager, c
Steve Garvey, 1b
Davey Lopes, 2b
Ron Cey, 3b
Bill Russell, ss
Dusty Baker, lf
Rick Monday, cf
Reggie Smith, rf
Billy North, cf
Lee Lacy, rf-2b-lf

Pitchers

Burt Hooton, sp
Tommy John, sp
Don Sutton, sp
Doug Rau, sp
Rick Rhoden, sp
Bob Welch, sp-rp
Terry Forster, rp
Charlie Hough, rp
Lance Rautzhan, rp

Attendance

3,347,845 (first in NL)

Club Leaders

Batting Avg:	Steve Garvey	.316
On-Base Pct:	Reggie Smith	.382
Slugging Pct:	Reggie Smith	.559
Home Runs:	Reggie Smith	29
RBIs:	Steve Garvey	113
Runs:	Davey Lopes	93
Stolen Bases:	Davey Lopes	45
Wins:	Burt Hooton	19
Strikeouts:	Don Sutton	154
ERA:	Burt Hooton	2.71
Saves:	Terry Forster	22

JANUARY 31   The Dodgers sell Elias Sosa to the Pirates.

APRIL 7   The Dodgers open the season with a 13–4 win over the Braves in Atlanta. Davey Lopes and Rick Monday each homered and drove in four runs. Monday also contributed a double and two singles and scored three runs. Steve Yeager collected three hits. Don Sutton was the starting pitcher and went seven innings. It was his seventh straight start on Opening Day. The contest was also noteworthy because it marked the managerial debut of Bobby Cox.

APRIL 10   The Dodgers run their record to 4–0 with a 5–2 victory over the Astros in Houston.

APRIL 14   In the home opener, the Dodgers win 5–1 over the Braves before 38,397 at Dodger Stadium. Rick Monday homered.

APRIL 26   The Dodgers score seven runs in the ninth inning to cap a 14–4 win over the Reds in Cincinnati. Dusty Baker collected five hits, including three doubles, in five at-bats.

Baker has worn number 12 throughout his career as both a player and manager because his boyhood hero was Tommy Davis, who also wore number 12 as a Dodger.

MAY 2   Steve Garvey extends his hitting streak to 21 games, but the Dodgers lose 5–4 in 10 innings to the Cubs in Chicago.

Garvey finished the season with 21 homers, 113 RBIs, 202 hits, and a .316 batting average.

MAY 14   Dave Kingman hits three homers and drives in eight runs to lead the Cubs to a 15-inning, 10–7 win over the Dodgers at Dodger Stadium. His third home run was a three-run shot in the 15th off Rick Rhoden which won the game. Kingman also hit three home runs at Dodger Stadium on June 4, 1976 while playing for the Mets.

MAY 17   Lee Lacy ties a major league record by homering in the third consecutive pinch at-bat. It came during a 10–1 pasting of the Pirates at Dodger Stadium. Lacy previously homered as a pinch-hitter on May 2 and May 6. He finished the season with a .394 batting average and five homers in 33 at-bats as a pinch-hitter.

On the same day, the Dodgers traded Glenn Burke to the Athletics for Billy North. Burke's big-league career ended in 1979 with a .237 batting average and two homers in 523 at-bats. In addition to being credited with inventing the high-five (see October 2, 1977), Burke became the first athlete in a team sport to publicly declare he was gay. He made the announcement in 1982. Burke died in 1995 after contracting AIDS.

MAY 19   Rick Monday drives in six runs on a pair of three-run homers in the second and sixth innings, but the Dodgers lose 10–7 to the Giants at Dodger Stadium.

MAY 20   Coming into the game in the ninth inning with the score tied and the bases loaded, Giants reliever Randy Moffitt hits Bill Russell with his first pitch to force in the winning run of a 3–2 Dodger win at Dodger Stadium.

MAY 22   The Dodgers break a 1–1 tie with seven runs in the eighth inning and win 8–1 over the Padres in San Diego. The highlight was a three-run double by pinch-hitter Manny Mota.

MAY 26   The Dodgers lose 6–1 to the Giants on a wild night in San Francisco. One fan received an ovation for burning a Dodger flag. Late in the game, so many beer cans, rocks and tomatoes rained on the Dodgers that the umpires threatened a forfeit. After the final out, Reggie Smith climbed into the stands after a fan who had been hurling racial epithets at him. Fortunately, teammates and security personnel prevented Smith from reaching the fan.

MAY 27   Burt Hooton (6²/₃ innings) and Terry Forster (2¹/₃ innings) combine on a two-hitter to defeat the Giants 3–1 at Candlestick Park. The only San Francisco hits were singles by Darrell Evans in the fourth inning and Jack Clark in the seventh. Forster retired all seven batters he faced.

JUNE 6   The Dodgers draft, and later sign, four future major leaguers. The early round picks in the regular phase were busts, but the club chose Mike Marshall in the sixth round, Steve Sax in the ninth and Gary Weiss in the 16th. In the secondary phase, Dann Bilardello was picked in the first round. Sax played 14 years in the majors, eight with the Dodgers, and Marshall 11 years overall, nine of which were spent in Los Angeles. Both were starters on the 1988 world championship club.

JUNE 8   A home run by Reggie Smith in the first inning is the only Dodger hit off Steve Rogers during a 4–1 loss to the Expos in Montreal.

          The Dodgers had a record of 28–27 on June 9, then went 63–31 over their next 94 games to clinch the NL West pennant.

JUNE 11   The Dodgers collect 21 hits and win 11–4 over the Expos in Montreal.

JUNE 12   A grand slam by Dusty Baker off Jim Lonborg in the sixth inning gives the Dodgers a 5–2 lead in a 6–5 victory over the Phillies at Dodger Stadium.

JUNE 18   Davey Lopes steals four bases during a 4–0 win over the Expos at Dodger Stadium.

          Lopes stole 45 bases in 49 attempts in 1978 along with 17 homers and a .278 batting average.

JUNE 24   Reggie Smith is involved in a frightening incident while attempting to leave Dodger Stadium after a 4–3 win over the Reds. One man stepped in front of Smith's car and shattered the windshield by punching it. Smith got out of his vehicle and pursued him, but another individual hit Smith over the head with a beer bottle. The two assailants were booked on a charge of assault with a deadly weapon.

          Smith finished the season with 29 homers and a .295 batting average.

JUNE 23   A home run by Steve Garvey in the sixth inning is the only run of a 1–0 win over the Reds at Dodger Stadium. It was struck off Fred Norman. Burt Hooton pitched a three-hit shutout.

          Hooton was 19–10 with a 2.71 ERA in 1978.

JUNE 26   The Dodgers fall six games behind the first place Giants with a 5–2 loss to the Braves in Atlanta.

JUNE 27   A three-run homer by Ron Cey off Dave Campbell provides the only runs of a 3–0 win over the Braves in Atlanta. Doug Rau pitched the shutout.

JUNE 28   For the second day in a row, a three-run homer by Ron Cey accounts for all of the Los Angeles runs. Cey connected off Phil Niekro for a 3–2 victory in Atlanta. The Dodgers collected only three hits.

               Cey hit .270 with 23 homers in 1978.

JULY 1   Steve Garvey homers off Tom Seaver in the seventh inning and singles during a rally in the ninth to lead the Dodgers to a 2–0 win over the Reds in Cincinnati. Rick Rhoden pitched the shutout.

               On the same day, the Dodgers traded Jeffrey Leonard and Rafael Landestoy to the Astros for Joe Ferguson.

JULY 5   The Braves score six runs in the ninth inning off Lance Rautzhan and Charlie Hough to defeat the Dodgers 9–8 at Dodger Stadium.

JULY 6   A walk-off grand slam by Davey Lopes in the 11th inning beats the Braves 5–1 at Dodger Stadium. The Dodgers scored in the ninth on Dusty Baker's single to force extra innings.

JULY 8   Steve Garvey takes a throw on the chin from Bob Welch during a 9–5 win in the second game of a double-header against the Astros in Houston.

               The blow caused a cut which required 20 stitches to close. Nonetheless, Garvey was in the starting lineup the next day to extend his playing streak to 434 games.

JULY 11   With a large bandage on his chin from a 20-stitch cut suffered three days earlier, Steve Garvey wins the Most Valuable Player Award in the All-Star Game, a 7–3 National League victory in San Diego. Garvey singled and tripled in three at-bats. It was his second All-Star MVP trophy. He first won it in 1974. Davey Lopes also drove in a run. Tommy Lasorda was the manager of the NL squad.

JULY 14   Don Sutton is ejected from a 4–1 loss to the Cardinals in St. Louis for "pitching a defaced baseball" in a controversial decision by umpire Doug Harvey. Sutton was tossed after Harvey found suspicious scuff marks on the balls. "I was three-fourths sure Sutton was doing it," said Harvey.

               The National League declined to take disciplinary action, but warned Sutton that "defacing" balls in the future would lead to suspension. Sutton in response threatened to sue the league. When asked by a reporter if he used foreign substances on the ball, Sutton answered, "Vaseline is made right here in the USA."

JULY 18   In his first start since being ejected for "defacing" baseballs, Don Sutton earns his 200th career victory with a 7–2 decision over the Pirates in Pittsburgh.

JULY 22   Reggie Smith extends his streak of hitting home runs to four consecutive games during a 4–3 win over the Cardinals at Dodger Stadium.

> *Beginning with the two he struck during a 4–3 win over the Cubs in Chicago on July 17, Smith hit six home runs in a span of six games.*

JULY 26   Steve Garvey hits a grand slam off Dave Roberts in the third inning of an 8–2 win over the Cubs at Dodger Stadium.

JULY 29   Don Sutton pitches a two-hitter to defeat the Pirates 2–1 at Dodger Stadium. The only Pittsburgh hits were a single by opposing pitcher Don Robinson in the third inning and a homer from Willie Stargell in the seventh which tied the contest 1–1. Dusty Baker drove in the winning run in the eighth with a single.

AUGUST 3   At Candlestick Park, Lee Lacy ties the score 4–4 in the ninth inning on a controversial inside-the-park homer, but the Dodgers lose 5–4 when the Giants score in the bottom of the ninth. Right fielder Jack Clark and center fielder Larry Herndon collided charging Lacy's fly ball, and Lacy circled the bases as the two lay stunned on the turf. San Francisco manager Joe Altobelli was ejected after a long argument with the umpires. Altobelli contended that Herndon caught the ball before Clark crashed into him.

AUGUST 5   Bill Russell singles in a run and scores on Ron Cey's one-base hit for the only two runs of a 2–0 win over the Giants in San Francisco. Bob Welch, a 21-year-old rookie, pitched the shutout, retiring the last two hitters with two runners on base. The win ended the Dodgers six-game losing streak.

> *The Giants came into the four-game series in San Francisco with a 2$\frac{1}{2}$-game lead over the Dodgers. The Giants won the first two games, and the Dodgers the last two. Fans at Candlestick Park were menacing. They showered apples, bananas, oranges, beer, ice, bottles, cups, coins, golf balls and firecrackers on Dodger outfielders. At one point, Dodger players armed themselves with bats to defend their dugout should the fans storm the field. During the August 5 game, which was played on national television, a Giant fan tried to dump beer on Reggie Smith as he chased a fly ball down the right-field line. The beer missed Smith, but the distraction caused Smith to miss the ball.*

AUGUST 10   Reggie Smith collects four hits, including a homer, and drives in five runs during a 12–2 thrashing of the Giants at Dodger Stadium.

AUGUST 16   The Dodgers take sole possession of first place with a 5–2 win over the Phillies in Philadelphia. Reggie Smith hit a grand slam off Jim Kaat in the third inning.

> *The Dodgers remained in first for the rest of the season.*

AUGUST 20   Steve Garvey and Don Sutton fight in the clubhouse before a 5–4 win over the Mets in New York. The incident left both with facial scratches and Garvey with a blood-red eye caused by a poke of Sutton's finger. Despite being bloodied, Garvey collected two hits in four at-bats during the victory.

The confrontation belied Tommy Lasorda's contention that the Dodgers were one big happy family. Over the years, Garvey had become increasingly isolated from his teammates, who considered him selfish and egotistical and resented his All-American image, believing it was phony. In August 1978, Sutton brought the dissension of the team into the open. "All you hear about on our team is Steve Garvey," Sutton told a reporter. "Well, the best person on this team for the last two years, and we all know it, is Reggie Smith. Reggie Smith doesn't go out and publicize himself. Reggie's not a facade or a Madison Avenue image. He's a real person." Garvey, with a copy of the article in his hand, approached Sutton in front of his locker. Sutton said it was true and added a gratuitous remark about Steve's wife Cyndy, who was also a local celebrity as a television personality. Garvey poked a finger in Sutton's chest and Sutton responded by leaping at Garvey and shoved him into a row of lockers. They went down on the floor clawing and scratching at each other trying to get in blows. It took two minutes to separate them. Four days later, Sutton tearfully apologized in a statement to the media. The fight didn't affect the Dodgers on the field. The club was 19–7 over the next 26 games following the Garvey-Sutton scrap. The Dodgers were 30–11 from August 5 through September 16. The battle with Sutton was the beginning of the end for Garvey's squeaky-clean image, however. In 1978, he openly talked of running for the U.S. Senate when his playing career ended. In 1983, he divorced Cyndy and she responded by writing a tell-all book detailing his numerous affairs. In 1987, two different women filed paternity suits against Garvey which tarnished his image irreparably.

AUGUST 28   Two-run homers by Davey Lopes in the seventh inning and Lee Lacy in the ninth beats the Expos 4–0 at Dodger Stadium. Burt Hooton pitched the shutout.

SEPTEMBER 10   Steve Garvey collects five hits, including a double, in five at-bats during an 11–5 victory over the Braves in Atlanta.

The victory was the start of a seven-game winning streak which sealed the NL West title. The Dodgers increased their lead from three games to nine in a period of seven days. During the last six games of the winning streak, the Dodgers allowed only three runs. Included were four shutouts by Burt Hooton, Bob Welch and Don Sutton and the combined efforts of Dog Rau and Terry Forster.

SEPTEMBER 15   The Dodgers become the first team to draw 3,000,000 fans during the regular season when 47,188 attend a 5–0 win over the Braves at Dodger Stadium. The final attendance figure was 3,347,845.

Despite reaching the attendance milestone, it was a tragic day in Dodger history because Jim Gilliam suffered a brain hemorrhage. He was rushed to Daniel Freeman Hospital, and after seven hours of surgery, lapsed into a coma. Gilliam had been with the Dodgers since 1953 as a player and coach. He died on October 8 at the age of 49.

SEPTEMBER 16   Joe Ferguson hits a two-run single in the sixth inning to account for the only runs of a 2–0 victory over the Braves at Dodger Stadium.

SEPTEMBER 22   In his major league debut, Pedro Guerrero hits a pinch-single during a 12–3 loss to the Padres at Dodger Stadium.

SEPTEMBER 24   The Dodgers clinch the pennant with a 4–0 win over the Padres at Dodger Stadium. Bob Welch pitched the shutout.

In his first season in the majors, Welch was 7–4 with a 2.02 ERA in 111⅓ innings. In his first 11 big-league innings, Welch didn't allow a run and struck out 13. He threw three shutouts in 13 starts.

SEPTEMBER 28   The Reds score six runs in the ninth inning off Lance Rautzhan to stun the Dodgers 8–7 in Cincinnati.

SEPTEMBER 29   Trying for his 20th win of the season, Burt Hooton loses 3–1 to the Padres in San Diego.

SEPTEMBER 30   Steve Garvey extends his hitting streak to 20 games during a 7–0 win over the Padres in San Diego.

OCTOBER 1   On the final day of the season, Gaylord Perry records his 3,000th career strikeout during an 11-inning, 4–3 Padre win over the Dodgers in San Diego. The victim of the milestone strikeout was Joe Simpson in the eighth inning. Two innings later, Perry recorded strikeout 3,001 by fanning Simpson.

The Dodgers played the Phillies in the National League Championship Series for the second year in a row. Managed by Danny Ozark, the Phillies were 90–72 in 1978 and won the NL East by 1½ games over the Pirates. It was the third straight division title for Philadelphia. The club lost to the Reds in 1976 and the Dodgers in 1977.

OCTOBER 4   The Dodgers open the NLCS with a 9–5 win over the Phillies at Veterans Stadium in Philadelphia. Los Angeles took a 4–1 lead with four runs in the third inning. Steve Garvey led the attack with two homers and a triple in five at-bats. He drove in four runs and scored three.

OCTOBER 5   Tommy John pitches a four-hit shutout to defeat the Phillies 4–0 in Philadelphia. Davey Lopes drove in three of the four Los Angeles runs with a homer, a triple and a single.

OCTOBER 6   The Phillies avoid a sweep in the best-of-five series by defeating the Dodgers 9–4 before 55,043 at Dodger Stadium. Steve Carlton hit a home run and pitched a complete game for the Phils. Steve Garvey homered for the Dodgers in the losing cause.

OCTOBER 7   The Dodgers win the National League pennant by beating the Phillies 4–3 in 10 innings before 55,124 at Dodger Stadium. Greg Luzinski gave the Phils a 2–1 lead with a homer off Doug Rau in the third inning. Ron Cey countered with a game-tying home run in the fourth. Steve Garvey put Los Angeles ahead 3–2 with a home run in the sixth, but Bake McBride deadlocked the contest with a home run off Rick Rhoden in the seventh. With two out in the 10th, Tug McGraw walked Ron Cey on four pitches and Dusty Baker followed with a liner that center fielder Garry Maddox caught, then dropped for an error. Bill Russell singled in Cey for the pennant-clinching run. The victory gave Tommy Lasorda two National League pennants in his first two seasons as manager.

The result of the 1978 NLCS was the same as 1977 with the Dodgers winning three games to one. The Dodgers played the Yankees in the World Series. On July 19, the Yanks trailed the Red Sox by 14 games, then put on a furious rush to win the pennant in a playoff game at Fenway Park. The key blow in the 5–4 victory was a seventh-inning home run by Bucky Dent. In the ALCS, the Yankees defeated the Royals three games to one. New York was managed by Bob Lemon, who replaced Billy Martin on July 17. Lemon and Tommy Lasorda both shared September 22 as a birthday. Lemon, at 58, was seven years older.

OCTOBER 10   The Dodgers defeat the Yankees 11–5 in game one of the 1978 World Series before 55,997 at Dodger Stadium. Dusty Baker started the scoring onslaught with a home run in the second inning. Davey Lopes added a two-run homer later in the second and a three-run shot in the fourth for a total of five runs batted in. Reggie Jackson homered for the Yankees.

The Dodgers wore black armbands during the Series in honor of Jim Gilliam, who died two days earlier (see September 15, 1978). Gilliam played in seven World Series with the club and was a coach in two others.

OCTOBER 11   The Dodgers take a two-games-to-none lead in the Fall Classic with a 4–3 win over the Yankees before 55,982 at Dodger Stadium. The Yankees scored twice in the third for a 2–0 lead. Ron Cey drove in a run in the fourth with a single, then belted a three-run homer in the sixth off Catfish Hunter. The Yankees scored in the seventh to narrow the gap to 4–3, then threatened in the ninth. Bob Welch relieved Terry Forster with runners on first and second with one out. Thurman Munson flied out which brought Reggie Jackson to the plate. Jackson hit five home runs in the 1977 World Series, added another one in game one in 1978, and drove all three Yankee runs in game two. In a dramatic confrontation with Bob Welch in which Jackson fouled off four pitches, went sprawling into the dirt on an inside pitch, and the count went to 3–2, Reggie struck out swinging to end the game. The nine-pitch at-bat lasted seven minutes. The 21-year-old rookie, who made his major league debut only four months previously, won the showdown against the veteran who was nicknamed "Mr. October" for his post-season heroics.

Don Sutton was on the roster of five World Series teams, but never won a world championship. He played for the losing Dodgers in 1966, 1974, 1977 and 1978 and the Brewers in 1982.

OCTOBER 13   The Yankees defeat the Dodgers 5–1 at Yankee Stadium in game three. Ron Guidry, who had a 25–3 record during the winning season, pitched a complete game. Third baseman Graig Nettles robbed the Dodgers of base hits four times with sparkling plays.

OCTOBER 14   The Yankees even the Series with a 10-inning, 4–3 win over the Dodgers in New York. Reggie Smith gave the Dodgers a 3–0 lead in the fifth inning with a three-run homer off Ed Figueroa. The Yankees scored twice in the sixth with the help of a controversial play. With one out, a runner on first and second and the score 3–1, Lou Piniella hit a drive right at shortstop Bill Russell, who dropped it, perhaps intentionally, and stepped on second to force Jackson. Russell's throw to first struck Jackson, who was standing in the base path, and caromed toward right-field scoring Munson. The Dodgers vehemently disputed the play, contending that Jackson deliberately stuck his hip in the way and demanded he be called out for interference. The umpires were not swayed by the argument, although television replays made it clear that Jackson swiveled his hip into the path of the ball. The Yankees tied the score in the eighth inning and won in the 10th. With two out in the New York 10th and one out, Bob Welch faced Reggie Jackson in rematch of their classic confrontation three days earlier in game two. This time Jackson singled. Lou Piniella drove in the winning run with a walk-off single.

Russell collected 11 hits in 26 at-bats during the 1978 Series.

OCTOBER 15   The Yankees win their third game in a row by pummeling the Dodgers 12–2 at Yankee Stadium. Jim Beattie pitched all nine innings for New York for his first major league complete game.

OCTOBER 17   The Yankees claim the World Series over the Dodgers for the second year in a row with a 7–2 victory before 55,985 at Dodger Stadium. Davey Lopes led off the first inning with a homer off Catfish Hunter, but the Yanks scored three times in the second for a lead the club never relinquished. Reggie Jackson homered in the seventh.

The loss in game four seemed to take something out of the Dodgers, who were outscored 19–4 in the final two contests. Los Angeles lost both the 1977 and 1978 Series in six games.

NOVEMBER 14   The Dodgers sign Derrel Thomas, most recently with the Padres as a free agent.

NOVEMBER 22   The Yankees sign Tommy John as a free agent.

The Dodgers made a big mistake in not signing John to a contract. Not only did they lose one of their top starting pitchers, but John went to the Yankees, a club which beat the Dodgers twice in the World Series over the previous 13 months. Although he turned 36 during 1979, he posted a 21–9 record that season and followed with a 22–9 mark in 1980. John pitched his last major league game in 1989 at the age of 46.

1979

Season in a Sentence

After two consecutive World Series appearances, the Dodgers are 36–57 at the All-Star break due to a sharp decline in the effectiveness of the pitching staff, and finish with their first losing record in 11 years.

Finish • Won • Lost • Pct • GB

| Third | 79 | 83 | .488 | 11.5 |

Manager

Tommy Lasorda

Stats

Stats	Dods	NL	Rank
Batting Avg:	.263	.261	7
On-Base Pct:	.331	.325	3
Slugging Pct:	.412	.385	2
Home Runs:	183		1
Stolen Bases:	106		8
ERA:	3.83	3.73	7
Fielding Avg:	.981	.978	2
Runs Scored:	739		2
Runs Allowed:	717		9

Starting Lineup

Steve Yeager, c
Steve Garvey, 1b
Davey Lopes, 2b
Ron Cey, 3b
Bill Russell, ss
Dusty Baker, lf
Derrel Thomas, cf
Joe Ferguson, rf-c
Gary Thomasson, cf-rf
Reggie Smith, rf

Pitchers

Rick Sutcliffe, sp
Don Sutton, sp
Burt Hooton, sp
Jerry Reuss, sp
Charlie Hough, rp
Bob Welch, sp-rp

Attendance

2,860,954 (first in NL)

Club Leaders

Batting Avg:	Steve Garvey	.315
On-Base Pct:	Ron Cey	.389
Slugging Pct:	Ron Cey	.499
Home Runs:	Ron Cey	28
	Steve Garvey	28
	Davey Lopes	28
RBIs:	Steve Garvey	110
Runs:	Davey Lopes	109
Stolen Bases:	Davey Lopes	44
Wins:	Rick Sutcliffe	17
Strikeouts:	Don Sutton	146
ERA:	Burt Hooton	2.97
Saves:	Dave Patterson	6

JANUARY 22   Lee Lacy signs a contract with the Pirates as a free agent.

FEBRUARY 7   The Dodgers sign Andy Messersmith, most recently with the Braves, as a free agent.

Messersmith was 53–30 as a Dodger from 1973 through 1975 before becoming a free agent (see December 23, 1975), then went into a rapid decline. He didn't find his fastball during his return engagement with the Dodgers. Messersmith was 2–4 with a 4.91 ERA in 1979, his last year as a major leaguer.

MARCH 10   Billy North signs a contract with the Giants as a free agent.

APRIL 5   Five days after the nuclear disaster at Three Mile Island, the Padres score two runs in the ninth inning to beat the Dodgers 4–3 before an Opening Day crowd of 46,536 at Dodger Stadium. Burt Hooton took a 3–2 lead into the ninth and gave up the first run. Lance Rautzhan surrendered the winning tally by throwing a wild pitch. Ron Cey hit a two-run homer in the seventh.

Cey hit .281 with 28 home runs in 1979.

APRIL 6	Joe Ferguson hits a grand slam off Randy Jones in the first inning to propel the Dodgers to a 10–1 win over the Padres at Dodger Stadium.

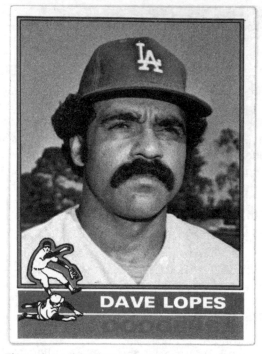

DAVE LOPES

APRIL 7	The Dodgers trade Rick Rhoden to the Pirates for Jerry Reuss.

The Dodgers came out ahead in a swap of starting pitchers. An outspoken free spirit, Reuss struggled in his first season in Los Angeles, but was 46–21 from 1980 through 1982. He pitched a no-hitter and appeared in the All-Star Game in 1980 and won a game in the World Series in 1981.

APRIL 8	A walk-off homer by Davey Lopes in the 12th inning beats the Padres 6–5 at Dodger Stadium.

Lopes had the best season of his career in 1979 with 28 homers, 109 runs scored, 44 stolen bases in 48 attempts, and a .265 batting average.

Throughout the 1970s, second baseman Dave Lopes provided speed on the base paths. In 1979, he completed his sixth straight season of stealing more than 40 bases.

APRIL 14	Trailing 1–0, the Dodgers explode for six runs in the sixth inning and then withstand two-run rallies by the Braves in the eighth and ninth to win 6–5 at Dodger Stadium. Joe Ferguson drove in three runs with a bases-loaded double.
APRIL 22	The Dodgers score seven runs in the fourth inning of a 9–2 triumph over the Giants in San Francisco. Don Sutton struck out 12 batters without walking a batter.
MAY 9	Don Sutton retires the last 20 batters to face him during a 7–2 win over the Mets at Dodger Stadium. Sutton allowed three hits.
MAY 10	The Dodgers rout the Mets 14–1 at Dodger Stadium.
MAY 11	Doug Rau is four outs from a no-hitter before settling for a one-hit, 7–0 triumph over the Expos at Dodger Stadium. The only Montreal hit was a single by Chris Speier with two out in the eighth inning.

The one-hitter proved to be Rau's only victory of the 1979 season. He finished with a 1–5 record and a 5.30 ERA and didn't pitch after June 3. It was also Rau's last win as a member of the Dodgers and the second-to-last of his career. His next notch in the win column after the May 11, 1979 one-hitter was on May 21, 1981 while playing for the Angels.

MAY 12   The Dodgers come from behind to beat the Expos 4–3 in 11 innings at Dodger Stadium. Los Angeles tied the score three times on solo homers by Joe Ferguson in the fifth inning, Steve Garvey in the ninth and Davey Lopes in the 11th. After Lopes's homer, the Dodgers loaded the bases before Dusty Baker singled in the winning run.

              Garvey hit .315 with 28 homers, 110 RBIs and 2–4 hits in 1979.

MAY 15   Dusty Baker's homer in the 10th inning lifts the Dodgers to a 5–4 win over the Braves in Atlanta.

              The May 15 victory was the eighth in a row. It gave the Dodgers a 19–18 record and seemed to right the ship. The club lost 38 of its next 55 games, however, to fall to 36–57 at the All-Star break. The Dodgers were 43–26 after the break, but couldn't get back over the .500 mark. It was the only losing season between 1968 and 1984. In spite of the miserable performance following back-to-back National League pennants, the Dodgers led the majors in attendance with a figure of 2,860,954.

MAY 20   Don Sutton becomes the winningest pitcher in Dodgers' history with a 6–4 decision over the Reds in Cincinnati. It was Sutton's 210th career victory to put him past Don Drysdale.

MAY 25   The Dodgers club seven homers during a 17–6 win over the Reds at Dodger Stadium. The seven homers were struck by seven different players. The seven were Dusty Baker, Rick Sutcliffe, Steve Garvey, Gary Thomasson, Joe Ferguson, Derrell Thomas and Davey Lopes. The game was marred by a bench-clearing incident, as the Reds accused the Dodgers of running up the score. The seventh homer came off a 3–0 pitch to Lopes with the Dodgers leading 14–2 in the sixth inning. The next time Lopes stepped to the plate, Dave Tomlin threw four straight pitches at the head of the Los Angeles second baseman.

MAY 29   A three-run outburst in the ninth inning beats the Giants 6–5 at Dodger Stadium. A single by Reggie Smith drove in the first tally. With the bases loaded, Steve Yeager surprised San Francisco by beating out a bunt to score on Russell. Dusty Baker delivered the game-winner with a single.

MAY 30   The Dodgers score seven runs in the fourth inning and outlast the Giants 12–10 at Dodger Stadium.

JUNE 5   In the first round of the amateur draft, the Dodgers select pitchers Steve Howe and Steve Perry. Both Steves were teammates at the University of Michigan.

              The Dodgers had two first-round draft choices due to free agent compensation. Perry never reached the majors. Howe made it in 1980 and was an immediate sensation as a rookie, but his career was derailed by a drug addition he never conquered. Other players drafted and signed by the Dodgers in 1979 were Don Crow (third round), Greg Brock (13th), Orel Hershiser (17th) and Morris Madden (24th). Hershiser was one of the best late round bargains in major league history. Brock played 10 seasons in the majors, five of them with the Dodgers.

JUNE 11

The Dodgers sign Ken Brett following his release by the Twins.

The brother of George, who spent his entire 21-year career in Kansas City, Ken was a pitcher who played for 10 teams. The Dodgers were club number nine. After his career ended, Ken did a Miller Lite commercial in which he had trouble determining what town he was in.

JUNE 13

Leading 9–1, the Dodgers barely stave off a seven-run Cardinals uprising in the ninth inning to win 9–8 at Dodger Stadium.

JULY 2

A three-run homer by Steve Yeager in the 12th inning beats the Padres 6–3 in San Diego.

JULY 6

The Dodgers purchase 18-year-old pitcher Fernando Valenzuela from Yucatan in the Mexican League.

JULY 15

In Philadelphia, several Dodgers anonymously point the finger at Reggie Smith for the club's losing ways, accusing him of "quitting on us." One player said, "They should get rid of him even if they have to buy him off."

Smith reacted angrily and called a team meeting the following day. Tommy Lasorda termed it "one of the best meetings this club has ever had." But Smith injured his leg five days later and didn't start a game for the rest of the season.

JULY 17

Tommy Lasorda manages the National League to a 7–6 win in the All-Star Game at the Kingdome in Seattle.

JULY 20

The Dodgers win a thrilling 6–5 decision in 11 innings against the Expos at Dodger Stadium. Montreal scored twice in the top of the 10th before Steve Garvey countered with a two-run homer in the bottom half to tie the contest 4–4. The Expos scored again in the 11th, but Bill Russell settled the issue with a two-run walk-off homer

JULY 24

The Dodgers utilize a 22-hit attack to defeat the Phillies 15–3 at Dodger Stadium. Dusty Baker hit a grand slam in the sixth inning off Warren Brusstar.

JULY 25

The offense erupts for the second day in a row to defeat the Phillies 16–8 at Dodger Stadium. The Dodgers scored six runs in the third inning to take an 8–4 lead and never looked back.

JULY 28

A benches-clearing brawl mars a 5–2 loss to the Astros in Houston. Tempers were heated after a collision at home plate between Cesar Cedeno and Steve Yeager. Cedeno came in high and spiked the Dodger catcher in the thigh. Moments later, Teddy Martinez threw a foul ball onto the field, and Cedeno fired the ball back into the Los Angeles dugout, narrowly missing Reggie Smith. The final straw came in the ninth inning when Dodger reliever Ken Brett struck Enos Cabell in the thigh with a pitch. It took 20 minutes to clear the field.

AUGUST 7

Trailing 8–4, the Dodgers score six runs in the eighth inning and beat the Astros 10–8 at Dodger Stadium. The rally was highlighted by a three-run homer from Steve Yeager, his second of the game.

In shows taped during August and September, Yeager and his family won several thousand dollars during a six-day run on the television game show Family Feud. *Yeager was joined by his wife Gloria, his sister-in-law, and a niece and a nephew.*

AUGUST 9   Walter O'Malley dies at the age of 75. O'Malley had battled cancer for several years, but his death was attributed to heart failure. His wife Kay, a childhood sweetheart, passed away on July 13. Control of the Dodger franchise passed to Walter and Kay's son Peter.

AUGUST 10   Derrell Thomas hits a grand slam off Bob Knepper in the second inning of a 9–0 win over the Giants in San Francisco. Don Sutton pitched the shutout, the 50th of his career.

A Los Angeles native, Thomas wore the number 30 of his boyhood idol Maury Wills. Thomas was the first Dodger player to don number 30 since Wills's retirement in 1972.

AUGUST 14   Burt Hooton pitches a two-hitter to defeat the Cardinals 9–0 at Busch Stadium. The only St. Louis hits were singles by opposing pitcher John Denny in the sixth inning and Ken Reitz in the eighth.

AUGUST 16   A two-run single by Steve Garvey in the 15th inning beats the Cardinals 4–2 in St. Louis.

AUGUST 27   A three-run, walk-off homer by Dusty Baker with two out in the ninth inning defeats the Pirates 4–3 at Dodger Stadium.

SEPTEMBER 2   The Dodgers score five runs off Bruce Sutter in the ninth inning to beat the Cubs 6–2 at Dodger Stadium. Gary Thomasson singled in the first run. After a one-base hit from Steve Yeager loaded the bases, Davey Lopes delivered a walk-off grand slam.

SEPTEMBER 3   Jerry Reuss pitches a two-hitter to defeat the Astros 1–0 in the Astrodome. Only two balls were hit out of the infield. The only Houston hits were singles by Jeffrey Leonard and Jose Cruz in the fifth inning.

SEPTEMBER 14   Rick Sutcliffe pitches a three-hitter to beat the Reds 2–0 at Dodger Stadium. He held Cincinnati hitless until George Foster singled with one out in the seventh inning.

Sutcliffe won the Rookie-of-Year Award in 1979 with a record of 17–10 and a 3.36 ERA. He was one of the few bright spots on an injury-riddled pitching staff. The Dodgers allowed 573 runs in 1978 and 717 in 1979.

SEPTEMBER 25   The Dodgers score eight runs in the second inning of an 11–2 win over the Giants in San Francisco. Ron Cey hits a grand slam off Ed Halicki.

SEPTEMBER 28   Trailing 5–1, the Dodgers scored five runs in the eighth inning, the last four on a grand slam off Vern Ruhle, and defeat the Astros 6–5 at Dodger Stadium.

NOVEMBER 14   Ten days after Iranian militants seize the U.S. Embassy in Teheran, taking 52 hostages, the Dodgers sign Dave Goltz, most recently with the Twins, as a free agent.

Goltz won at least 14 games in each of the previous five seasons in Minnesota, with a high of 20 in 1977. The Dodgers signed him to a six-year deal, but Goltz posted an abysmal record of 9–19 over three seasons.

NOVEMBER 17   The Dodgers sign Don Stanhouse, most recently with the Orioles, as a free agent.

Stanhouse made the AL All-Star team and pitched in the World Series in 1979. He signed a five-year contract with the Dodgers and was expected to be the club's closer, but like Goltz, was an expensive flop. Hampered by back trouble, Stanhouse lasted only one year in Los Angeles and compiled a 5.04 ERA just in 21 games.

DECEMBER 4   The Dodgers sign Jay Johnstone, most recently with the Padres, as a free agent.

THE STATE OF THE DODGERS

In an age of parity, 12 different teams won the 13 World Series played from 1978 through 1990. The Dodgers were the only one to win a world championship twice during that period, taking the title in 1981 and 1988. The franchise also reached the post-season in 1983 and 1985 after winning the NL West. The club's winning percentage of .527 during the 1980s, based on a record of 825–741, was the second-best in the National League, trailing only the .529 mark posted by the Cardinals. Nonetheless, the Dodgers were less successful during the 1980s than in the 1940s (.581 winning percentage), 1950s (.592), 1960s (.546) or 1970s (.565). NL pennant-winners outside of Los Angeles during the 1980s were the Phillies (1980 and 1983), Cardinals (1982, 1985 and 1987), Padres (1984), Mets (1986) and Giants (1989). NL West champions other than the Dodgers were the Astros (1980 and 1986), Braves (1982), Padres (1984) and Giants (1987 and 1989).

THE BEST TEAM

The 1988 club was 94–67 during the regular season before defeating the Mets and Athletics in the post-season.

THE WORST TEAM

A year after winning the NL West title, the 1986 Dodgers were 73–89 and finished 23 games out of first place.

THE BEST MOMENT

Winning a World Series is the pinnacle of success, and it's nearly impossible to separate the two won during the 1980s. The Dodgers came into the 1981 Fall Classic at the end of a season stopped for seven weeks by a strike. The club had lost its last four attempts at winning the Series in 1966, 1974, 1977 and 1978, the latter two to the Yankees. Facing the Yanks again, the Dodgers won in six games. In 1988, Los Angeles was given little chance of winning the World Series, but it polished off the heavily-favored Oakland Athletics in five games with the help of Kirk Gibson's dramatic Game One homer.

THE WORST MOMENT

Speaking on national television about Jackie Robinson in April 1987, general manager Al Campanis made a series of comments comparing blacks and whites that led to his dismissal after spending more than four decades in the Dodger organization.

THE ALL-DECADE TEAM • YEARS W/DODS

Mike Scioscia, c	1980–92
Steve Garvey, 1b	1969–82
Steve Sax, 2b	1981–88
Pedro Guerrero, 3b	1978–88
Bill Russell, ss	1969–86
Dusty Baker, lf	1976–83
Ken Landreaux, cf	1981–87
Mike Marshall, rf	1981–89
Orel Hershiser, p	1983–94
Fernando Valenzuela, p	1980–90
Bob Welch, p	1978–87
Jerry Reuss, p	1979–87

Garvey and Russell were on the 1970s All-Decade Team. Other outstanding Dodgers during the decade include pitchers Alejandro Pena (1981–89), Jay Howell (1988–92) and Tom Niedenfuer (1981–87), third baseman Ron Cey (1971–82) and left fielder Kirk Gibson (1988–90).

THE ALL-DECADE LEADERS

Batting Avg:	Pedro Guerrero	.309
On-Base Pct:	Pedro Guerrero	.382
Slugging Pct:	Pedro Guerrero	.513
Home Runs:	Pedro Guerrero	169
RBIs:	Pedro Guerrero	575
Runs:	Steve Sax	574
Stolen Bases:	Steve Sax	290
Wins:	Fernando Valenzuela	128
Strikeouts:	Fernando Valenzuela	1,644
ERA:	Orel Hershiser	2.69
Saves:	Tom Niedenfuer	64

THE HOME FIELD

The Dodgers unveiled a new video scoreboard in 1980. There were few other changes to the stadium, which opened in 1962. The club led the major leagues in attendance every season from 1977 through 1986, with a high of 3,608,881 in 1982.

THE GAME YOU WISHED YOU HAD SEEN

The best day to be at Dodger Stadium from the day it opened to the present was on October 15, 1988, when Kirk Gibson capped Game One of the World Series by limping to the plate and delivering a walk-off home run against Dennis Eckersley to defeat the Athletics 5–4.

THE WAY THE GAME WAS PLAYED

The 1980s had a little something for everyone. Trends that surfaced during the 1970s continued, with teams emphasizing speed over power. Earned run averages hovered around 3.60. But 1987 combined the speed numbers of the dead-ball era with the power numbers of the 1950s. NL teams averaged more than 150 steals and 150 homers, the only time that has ever occurred. But the offensive bubble burst sharply afterward, and in 1988 and 1989, the NL experienced its lowest batting averages in nearly 20 years.

THE MANAGEMENT

Continuity was the watchword of the Dodgers throughout most of the second half of the 20th century. Walter O'Malley, who purchased a controlling interest in the Dodgers in 1950, passed away in 1979. His son Peter ran the club from that point until 1996. Al Campanis was general manager from 1968 until his dismissal in 1987. He was succeeded by Fred Claire, who held the post from 1987 through 1998. Tommy Lasorda was field manager from 1976 through 1996.

THE BEST PLAYER MOVE

The best move was the selection of Mike Piazza in the 62nd round of the 1988 amateur draft. There were no outstanding trades.

THE WORST PLAYER MOVE

The Dodgers made several puzzling moves during the 1980s, most of them involving pitchers. The worst of them occurred on May 9, 1983, when the club sent John Franco to the Reds for Rafael Landestoy. Other players dealt too soon in their careers included Dave Stewart, Charlie Hough, Rick Sutcliffe, Sid Fernandez, Juan Guzman, Bob Welch, Ted Power and Sid Bream.

1980

Season in a Sentence

Trailing the Astros by three games with three contests left on the schedule, the Dodgers beat Houston three in a row in thrilling fashion, only to lose the pennant playoff game.

Finish • Won • Lost • Pct • GB

Second   92   71   .564   1.0

Manager

Tommy Lasorda

Stats

Stats	Dods	NL	Rank
Batting Avg:	.263	.259	4
On-Base Pct:	.323	.320	7
Slugging Pct:	.388	.374	3
Home Runs:	148		1
Stolen Bases:	123		8
ERA:	3.25	3.60	2
Fielding Avg:	.981	.978	3
Runs Scored:	663		6
Runs Allowed:	591		2

Starting Lineup

Steve Yeager, c
Steve Garvey, 1b
Davey Lopes, 2b
Ron Cey, 3b
Bill Russell, ss
Dusty Baker, lf
Rudy Law, cf
Reggie Smith, rf
Derrell Thomas, ss-cf
Jay Johnstone, rf

Pitchers

Jerry Reuss, sp
Bob Welch, sp
Burt Hooton, sp
Don Sutton, sp
Dave Goltz, sp
Steve Howe, rp
Bobby Castillo, rp
Rick Sutcliffe, rp

Attendance

3,249,287 (first in NL)

Club Leaders

Batting Avg:	Steve Garvey	.304
On-Base Pct:	Ron Cey	.342
Slugging Pct:	Dusty Baker	.503
Home Runs:	Dusty Baker	29
RBIs:	Steve Garvey	106
Runs:	Ron Cey	81
Stolen Bases:	Rudy Law	40
Wins:	Jerry Reuss	18
Strikeouts:	Bob Welch	141
ERA:	Don Sutton	2.20
Saves:	Steve Howe	17

FEBRUARY 17   A month after the Los Angeles Rams lose 31–19 to the Pittsburgh Steelers in the Super Bowl in Pasadena, and five days before the U.S. Olympic hockey team upsets the Russians, 52-year-old Tommy Lasorda fights 37-year-old Jim Lefebvre in a television studio.

> *Lefebvre was a coach with the Dodgers in 1978 and 1979 before being fired by Lasorda. Lefebvre then signed a deal as a coach with the Giants for the 1980 season. Both were at the KNBC studios in Burbank for separate interviews when the altercation took place. Lefebvre wanted to discuss his termination face-to-face, which soon developed into a screaming match. Lefebvre decked Lasorda with one punch, leaving the Dodger manager with a fat lip.*

APRIL 10   At the Astrodome, the Astros defeat the Dodgers 3–2 in the season opener. Starter Burt Hooton lasted only two innings and gave up the three Houston runs. J. R. Richard struck out 13 Los Angeles batters.

APRIL 12   A two-out single by Mickey Hatcher in the 17th inning scores Dusty Baker for a 6–5 win over the Astros in Houston. The Dodgers scored in the ninth to tie the score 5–5. Houston was held without a run over the last 12 innings by relievers

Bobby Castillo (two innings), Charlie Hough (one inning), Don Stanhouse (three innings), Steve Howe (five innings) and Burt Hooton (one inning). It was Hooton's only relief outing between 1977 and 1983. Tommy Lasorda used 23 players, including pitchers Rick Sutcliffe and Hooton as pinch-hitters. Sutcliffe singled and Hooton laid down a perfect sacrifice bunt. Bob Welch, another hurler, was utilized as a pinch-runner.

APRIL 16   Because of injuries, Derrell Thomas is used as a starting catcher during a 10–4 win over the Padres in San Diego.

The versatile Thomas played eight positions during his five seasons with the Dodgers from 1979 through 1983. He appeared in 229 games as a center fielder, 95 at shortstop, 80 at second base, 54 in right field, 53 at third base, 28 in left field, five as a catcher and one at first base.

APRIL 17   The Dodgers win the home opener 6–4 over the Astros before 45,476 at Dodger Stadium. Ron Cey broke the 4–4 tie with two runs in the eighth inning.

The Dodgers started the season with a 3–7 record and then won 27 of their next 39 games.

APRIL 24   Dusty Baker hits a three-run walk-off homer in the 10th inning to beat the Giants 5–2 at Dodger Stadium.

Baker batted .294 with 29 homers and 97 RBIs in 1980.

MAY 4   The Dodgers blow a 9–0 lead, but they prevail 12–10 over the Phillies at Veterans Stadium. Philadelphia scored four runs in the sixth inning, three in the seventh and two in the eighth to tie the game at 9–9. The Dodgers broke the deadlock with three tallies in the ninth.

MAY 12   Rudy Law steals four bases during a 2–1 win over the Cubs at Dodger Stadium.

Law swiped 40 bases as a rookie center fielder in 1980, but he struggled at the plate and spent the entire 1981 season in the minors before a March 1982 trade to the White Sox.

MAY 29   Eleven days after the eruption of Mount St. Helens in Washington and 13 days after the Lakers defeat the Philadelphia 76ers to win the NBA championship, Bob Welch allows only one base runner and faces the minimum 27 batters during a 3–0 win over the Braves at Dodger Stadium. The perfect-game bid was ruined by a single from Larvell Blanks in the fourth inning. Blanks was erased by a double play.

The 1980 Dodgers had six pitchers who finished their career with at least 170 wins. They were Don Sutton (324), Jerry Reuss (220), Charlie Hough (216), Bob Welch (211), Fernando Valenzuela (173) and Rick Sutcliffe (171).

JUNE 3   A 5–1 win over the Reds at Dodger Stadium gives the Dodgers a three-game lead in the NL West with a record of 30–19.

On the same day, the Dodgers selected shortstop Ross Jones from the University of Miami in Florida. Jones lasted only 67 games as a major leaguer and hit just .221 without a home run. The only other future major leaguer drafted and signed by the Dodgers in 1980 was Tom Klawitter in the 19th round.

JUNE 6 — Jerry Reuss pitches a three-hitter to defeat the Braves 5–0 in Atlanta. Reuss carried a no-hitter into the seventh inning before Jeff Burroughs doubled with two out.

JUNE 12 — A gaffe by Ron Cey and Steve Garvey contributes to a 6–5 loss to the Mets at Shea Stadium. In the seventh inning, Cey was at bat with Garvey the runner on first base. Cey took a ball on a 2–2 count and, believing it was ball four, headed toward first. Garvey then sauntered toward second and was thrown out easily by New York catcher John Stearns for the third out of the inning.

JUNE 15 — Bob Welch pitches a three-hitter to defeat the Expos 1–0 in Montreal. Dusty Baker drove in the lone run with a single in the sixth inning.

After a 7–4 record, a 2.03 ERA and a celebrated World Series duel with Reggie Jackson as a rookie in 1978, Welch sank to 5–6 in 1979 while battling alcoholism. After off-season treatment, he was 9–3 at the All-Star break and finished with a 14–9 record in 1980. Welch went public with his problem and recounted his struggles in the book Five O'clock Comes Early.

JUNE 18 — Trailing 7–2, the Dodgers erupt for six runs in the seventh inning and beat the Expos 8–7 at Dodger Stadium. Bill Russell started the rally with a three-run homer. Steve Garvey drove in the go-ahead run with a single.

Garvey led the NL in hits in 1980 with 200 along with a .304 batting average, 26 homers and 106 RBIs. His squeaky-clean image took a major hit during the season, however, when Inside Sports *magazine ran an article detailing the troubled marriage of Steve and Cyndy Garvey. The couple denied the allegations and sued the publication for $11.2 million, but they divorced in 1983 amid much public acrimony. Cyndy called Steve a "sociopath" and "in need of therapy."*

JUNE 19 — Joe Ferguson hits a two-run homer in the 10th inning to defeat the Expos 5–3 at Dodger Stadium. The Dodgers tied the score in the ninth inning on Dusty Baker's sacrifice fly.

The Dodgers unveiled baseball's first DiamondVision color scoreboard in 1980. It was 20 feet by 28 feet and showed replays, close-up features and highlights of other events.

JUNE 27 — Jerry Reuss pitches a no-hitter to defeat the Giants 8–0 at Candlestick Park. The only San Francisco base runner was Jack Clark, who reached on a throwing error by shortstop Bill Russell with two out in the first inning. Reuss retired the next 25 batters. He struck out only two batters. In the ninth, Reuss retired Mike Sadek on a grounder to third baseman Ron Cey and Rennie Stennett on a bouncer to Russell. The final out was recorded on Bill North's feeble tapper back to Reuss, who threw to Steve Garvey at first base.

In 1979, his first season with the Dodgers, Reuss had a record of 7–14 and started the 1980 campaign in the bullpen. He was put into the starting rotation in May and finished the year with an 18–6 record, a 2.51 ERA and six shutouts.

JULY 6

The Dodgers retire Duke Snider's number 4 in ceremonies prior to a 10-inning, 7–4 loss to the Giants at Dodger Stadium.

JULY 8

The All-Star Game is played at Dodger Stadium before a crowd of 56,088, with the National League winning 4–2. Bob Welch gave up a two-run homer to Fred Lynn in the fifth inning to put the AL ahead 2–0. In the bottom half, Ken Griffey Sr. homered off Tommy John to spark the NL comeback. Two runs were added in the sixth and another in the seventh. Jerry Reuss pitched the sixth inning and struck out all three batters he faced.

The contest was the second All-Star Game played in Los Angeles. The first was at Memorial Coliseum in 1959. Future Hall of Famers on the rosters of the two clubs were Johnny Bench, George Brett, Rod Carew, Steve Carlton, Gary Carter, Carlton Fisk, Rich Gossage, Reggie Jackson, Paul Molitor, Mike Schmidt, Bruce Sutter, Dave Winfield and Robin Yount. Other prominent players included Dave Concepcion, Steve Garvey, Rickey Henderson, Keith Hernandez, Tommy John, Graig Nettles, Dave Parker, Jim Rice and Pete Rose.

JULY 27

The Dodgers defeat the Cubs 3–2 in 12 innings at Dodger Stadium in the longest game without a walk in National League history. The pitchers were Don Sutton (seven innings), Don Stanhouse (two innings) and Steve Howe (three innings) of the Dodgers and Rick Reuschel (eight innings), Dick Tidrow (three innings) and Bill Caudill (two-thirds of an inning) for Chicago.

Howe won the Rookie of the Year Award in 1980 with a 7–9 record, 17 saves and a 2.66 ERA in 59 relief appearances covering 84²/₃ innings. After being drafted out of the University of Michigan, Howe pitched in only 13 minor league games, all at the Class AA level, before reaching the majors.

AUGUST 1

The Dodgers defeat the Cardinals 2–1 at Dodger Stadium on home runs by Jay Johnstone in the ninth inning and Joe Ferguson in the 10th.

The Dodgers' road to the pennant in 1980 was hampered by injuries to Reggie Smith, who hit .322 in 92 games. One of them was self-inflicted. Smith needed 60 stitches in his wrist after hitting a water cooler during a fight with Derrell Thomas.

AUGUST 7

The Dodgers erupt for seven runs in the second inning and beat the Reds 9–4 at Dodger Stadium.

AUGUST 21

A home run by Steve Garvey in the 10th inning beats the Expos in Montreal.

AUGUST 29

The Dodgers sign coach Manny Mota to a contract as an active player.

Mota helped the Dodgers during the pennant stretch drive with three hits in seven pinch-hit at-bats at the age of 42.

AUGUST 31   Davey Lopes scores both runs of a 2–0 win over the Expos in the first game of a
                 double-header at Dodger Stadium. Lopes crossed the plate in the first and sixth
                 innings. Jerry Reuss tossed the shutout. In the second tilt, Ron Cey, Rick Monday
                 and Joe Ferguson hit consecutive homers in the second inning of a 7–2 victory.
                 Ferguson hit another homer later in the game.

                 *The Dodgers had an 11–1 record vs. the Expos, a club which posted a 90–72
                 record in 1980.*

SEPTEMBER 5   A home run by Ron Cey off Steve Carlton in the second inning is the lone run of a
                 1–0 win over the Phillies at Dodger Stadium. Don Sutton (eight innings) and Don
                 Stanhouse (one inning) combined on the shutout.

SEPTEMBER 13   Derrell Thomas, subbing for the injured Bill Russell at shortstop, triples in the tying
                 run with two out in the ninth inning and then scores on a balk by Mario Soto for a
                 3–2 win over the Dodgers in Cincinnati.

SEPTEMBER 21   A five-run 11th inning by the Reds beats the Dodgers 7–2 at Dodger Stadium. The
                 defeat knocked the Dodgers out of first place with two weeks remaining in the
                 season. The Astros were in first in the NL West.

SEPTEMBER 24   A walk-off pinch-single by Manny Mota in the 12th inning beats the Giants 5–4 at
                 Dodger Stadium. The victory put Los Angeles into a tie with Houston for first place.

SEPTEMBER 30   A three-run homer by Pedro Guerrero in the 10th inning beats the Giants 6–3 in
                 San Francisco. Fernando Valenzuela earned his first major league victory.

                 *Only 19 years old, Valenzuela made his major league debut on September 15,
                 1980. The teenager was invaluable down the stretch. In 10 appearances, all in
                 relief, Valenzuela had a 2–0 record in pitching $17^2/_3$ innings. He allowed eight
                 hits, walked five, struck out 16 and surrendered two runs, both unearned, for a
                 perfect ERA of 0.00. It was only a warm-up to the excitement Valenzuela would
                 provide Dodger fans the following season (see April 9, 1981).*

OCTOBER 2   The Dodgers lose 3–2 to the Giants in San Francisco to fall three games behind the
                 Astros in the pennant race with three contests left on the schedule.

                 *The final three games remaining were all against the Astros in Los Angeles.
                 In order to win the NL West crown, the Dodgers needed to defeat Houston
                 four games in a row, including a one-game pennant playoff game.*

OCTOBER 3   One out from being eliminated from the pennant race, the Dodgers score a run in
                 the ninth inning and one in the 10th to defeat the Astros 3–2 at Dodger Stadium.
                 A two-out single by Ron Cey drove in the tying run. Joe Ferguson won the game on a
                 walk-off homer on the first pitch of the 10th from Ken Forsch. Fernando Valenzuela
                 pitched the final two innings for his second big-league win.

OCTOBER 4   The Dodgers edge the Astros 2–1 to pull within a game of first place. Steve Garvey's
                 homer off Nolan Ryan in the fourth inning snapped the 1–1 tie. Jerry Reuss pitched
                 the complete game.

OCTOBER 5   Trailing 3–0, the Dodgers score a run in the fifth inning, another in the seventh and two in the eighth to beat the Astros 4–3 at Dodger Stadium and pull into a tie for first place. A two-run homer by Ron Cey in the eighth inning drove in the go-ahead run. Don Sutton, making his only relief appearance of the year, recorded the final out in the ninth with runners on first and third. The Los Angeles victory, the third in a row by one run, forced a one-game playoff to decide the NL West champion.

Normally laid-back Los Angeles fans roared themselves hoarse during the three thrilling wins over Houston. Business in the city came to a virtual stop for the afternoon playoff game the following day.

OCTOBER 6   The Dodgers lose an anticlimactic one-game playoff against the Astros 7–1 before 51,127 at Dodger Stadium. After Mayor Tom Bradley threw out the ceremonial first pitch and Toni Tenille sang the national anthem, Los Angeles starter Dave Goltz lasted only three innings. The contest ended on a sour note when the players in the Houston bullpen had to move to the dugout to escape debris thrown by fans. The Astros went on to lose the NLCS to the Phillies three games to two.

The Dodgers were 55–27 at home in 1980 and 37–44 on the road.

DECEMBER 4   A month after Ronald Reagan defeats Jimmy Carter in the presidential election, Don Sutton signs a contract as a free agent with the Astros.

Sutton had played 15 seasons for the Dodgers before leaving for Houston. In his last season in Los Angeles, Sutton had a 13–5 record and his 2.20 ERA led the National League. He produced earned run averages below the league average for six more years, although he did it with four different teams (the Astros, Brewers, Athletics and Angels). Sutton pitched in the 1982 World Series with Milwaukee. He returned to the Dodgers in 1988, his final big-league season.

1981

L A

Season in a Sentence

Dodger fans experience Fernandomania, a seven-week strike, a National League pennant-winning home run by Rick Monday and a World Series win over the Yankees.

Finish • Won • Lost • Pct • GB

*   63   47   .573   *
* Because of the strike, the season was split into two halves. In the first half of the season, the Dodgers were 36–21 and finished in first place, one-half game ahead. In the second half, the Dodgers were 27–26 and finished in fourth place, six games behind.

Manager

Tommy Lasorda

National League Division Series

The Dodgers defeated the Houston Astros three games to two.

National League Championship Series

The Dodgers defeated the Montreal Expos three games to two.

World Series

The Dodgers defeated the New York Yankees four games to two.

Stats	Dods	NL	Rank
Batting Avg:	.262	.255	4
On-Base Pct:	.323	.319	4
Slugging Pct:	.374	.364	4
Home Runs:	82		1
Stolen Bases:	73		10
ERA:	3.01	3.49	2
Fielding Avg:	.980	.978	4
Runs Scored:	450		4
Runs Allowed:	356		2

Starting Lineup

Mike Scioscia, c
Steve Garvey, 1b
Davey Lopes, 2b
Ron Cey, 3b
Bill Russell, ss
Dusty Baker, lf
Ken Landreaux, cf
Pedro Guerrero, rf
Derrell Thomas, 2b-ss-cf
Rick Monday, rf

Pitchers

Fernando Valenzuela, sp
Burt Hooton, sp
Jerry Reuss, sp
Bob Welch, sp
Steve Howe, rp
Bobby Castillo, rp
Dave Stewart, rp
Dave Goltz, rp-sp

Attendance

2,381,292 (first in NL)

Club Leaders

Batting Avg:	Dusty Baker	.320
On-Base Pct:	Ron Cey	.372
Slugging Pct:	Ron Cey	.474
Home Runs:	Ron Cey	13
RBIs:	Steve Garvey	64
Runs:	Steve Garvey	63
Stolen Bases:	Davey Lopes	20
Wins:	Fernando Valenzuela	13
Strikeouts:	Fernando Valenzuela	180
ERA:	Burt Hooton	2.28
Saves:	Steve Howe	8

MARCH 30   Two months after 52 American hostages are released after 444 days of captivity in Iran, and on the day that President Ronald Reagan is shot in John Hinckley's assassination attempt, the Dodgers trade Mickey Hatcher, Kelly Snider and Matt Reeves to the Twins for Ken Landreaux.

APRIL 9   Pressed into the starting assignment on Opening Day when Jerry Reuss pulls a calf muscle, Fernando Valenzuela makes his first major league start and hurls a five-hit shutout to defeat the Astros 2–0 before 50,511 at Dodger Stadium. The losing pitcher was Joe Niekro, who defeated the Dodgers in the final pennant-deciding game the previous season.

Valenzuela became an international sensation with his pitching in the early part of the 1981 season in what became known as "Fernandomania." A native of Sonora, Mexico, he was the last of 12 children born to a farming family. Valenzuela was purchased by the Dodgers from Yucatan of the Mexican League as an 18-year-old in 1979. He learned to throw a screwball from Dodger pitcher Bobby Castillo and moved quickly through the Dodger minor league system. Valenzuela was promoted to the Dodgers late in the 1980 season and didn't allow an earned run in 17^2/$_3$ innings over 10 relief appearances (see September 30, 1980). After his sensational beginning during the 1981 season, which included five shutouts in his first seven starts, each appearance by Valenzuela turned into a festive occasion. The Dodgers had trouble drawing Hispanic fans through their first two decades in Los Angeles, in large part because of the controversy over acquiring the land in Chavez Ravine for Dodger Stadium and the absence of prominent Latin players on the roster. Fernando changed all of that as Mexican-Americans streamed to Dodger Stadium whenever he pitched. Outside the park, vendors sold an array of Fernando T-shirts, phonograph records and other memorabilia. Back in his native Mexico, most of his starts were carried live on national television. As author Eric Enders put it, Valenzuela was a storybook character who "could have been the invention of a pulp novelist's overactive imagination." With poise, pitching acumen and facial features that made him seem much older than his 20 years, Valenzuela's short and pudgy physique and unconventional pitching style added to his allure. He lifted his leg high, spun around almost backward, stuck out his tongue and gazed skyward before delivering the pitch to the plate. Even though Valenzuela didn't speak English, the press loved him. Speaking through an interpreter, Fernando was glib, funny and completely at ease with his sudden fame. Nothing seemed to faze him. After winning his first eight starts, which ran his career record to 10–0, Valenzuela ended the strike-torn season with a 13–7 record, a 2.48 ERA, league-leading figures in games started (25), complete games (11), shutouts (eight), innings pitched (192^1/$_3$) and strikeouts (180). He also made appearances in the All-Star Game and the World Series and won the Rookie of the Year and Cy Young awards. Valenzuela pitched for the Dodgers until 1990. On the all-time club lists he ranks eighth in wins (141), sixth in games started (320), seventh in shutouts (29), ninth in innings pitched (2,348^2/$_3$), third in walks (915) and fifth in strikeouts (1,759).

APRIL 11   After 15 seasons with the Dodgers, Sutton makes his first appearance with the Astros and allows six runs in four innings. Los Angeles won 7–4 at Dodger Stadium.

APRIL 14   In his second start, Fernando Valenzuela beats the Giants 7–1 at Candlestick Park. The lone San Francisco run scored in the eighth inning. It was the first earned run allowed by Valenzuela in his big-league career after 34^1/$_3$ innings.

The number of scheduled telecasts on KTTV increased from 24 in 1980 to 50 in 1981, although that number was cut considerably by the strike. No home games were carried on local TV.

APRIL 18   Fernando Valenzuela pitches his second shutout in three starts, defeating the Padres 2–0 in San Diego. The Dodger runs scored on homers by Mike Scioscia in the seventh inning and Dusty Baker in the eighth.

Baker hit .320 and played in his first All-Star Game in 1981.

APRIL 22   Fernando Valenzuela pitches his third shutout in four starts, defeating the Astros 1–0 in Houston. He also drove in the lone run with a single in the fifth inning and struck out 11 batters.

APRIL 27   Fernando Valenzuela pitches his fourth shutout in five starts, and his third in a row, beating the Giants 5–0 at Dodger Stadium. He also collected three hits to run his batting average to .438. In his first five 1981 starts, Valenzuela had a 5–0 record and a 0.20 ERA in 45 innings. The Dodger team record was 14–3.

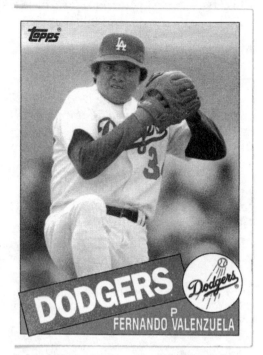

Fernando Valenzuela stunned the baseball world in 1981, winning both the Cy Young and Rookie of the Year awards. He remained a superb pitcher through most of the 1980s.

MAY 3   The Dodgers score five runs in the 10th inning to win 6–1 over the Expos at Olympic Stadium. Coming into the contest with three consecutive shutouts, Fernando Valenzuela pitched the first nine innings to run his record season record to 6–0. His scoreless streak was snapped at 35 innings when Montreal scored in the eighth.

MAY 8   Fernando Valenzuela runs his 1981 season record to 7–0 with a 1–0 triumph over the Mets in New York. It was his fifth shutout in seven starts. Valenzuela struck out 11. The lone run scored in the first inning on a single by Dusty Baker.

MAY 13   The Dodgers score four runs in the ninth inning to defeat the Expos 8–6 at Dodger Stadium. Steve Garvey tied the score with a two-out, two-run single. Ron Cey won the game with a walk-off homer.

Cey batted .288 with 13 homers in 1981. The top Dodger hitter was Pedro Guerrero in his first year as an everyday player. He batted an even .300 with 12 homers. Guerrero would continue to be the centerpiece of the Dodger offense until he was traded to the Cardinals in 1988. He seemed to be headed for the Hall of Fame, but injuries prevented him from attaining that goal. Guerrero played in at least 150 games only four times during his career. On the all-time club career lists, he ranks eighth in home runs (171), sixth in slugging percentage (.512) and 11th in batting average (.309).

MAY 14   The Dodgers win with a walk-off homer for the second day in a row as Pedro Guerrero goes deep in the ninth inning for a 3–2 win over the Expos at Dodger Stadium.

Fernando Valenzuela was the winning pitcher, giving him a record of 8–0 in 1981 with an 0.50 ERA in 72 innings. His career record was 10–0 with an 0.40 earned run average in 92²/3 innings.

MAY 18   Fernando Valenzuela takes the first loss of his career with a 4–0 decision at the hands of the Phillies at Dodger Stadium.

MAY 20   A walk-off, pinch-hit homer by Rick Monday in the 10th inning beats the Phillies 3–2 at Dodger Stadium.

              The Dodgers led the National League in home runs five consecutive seasons from 1977 through 1981.

MAY 22   A bases-loaded single by Dusty Baker in the 12th inning scores two runs to defeat the Reds 4–2 in Cincinnati.

MAY 23   The Dodgers win their third consecutive extra-inning game, downing the Reds 9–6 in 10 innings in Cincinnati.

MAY 31   Trailing 4–0, the Dodgers explode with a seven-run barrage in the fourth inning and blast the Reds 16–4 at Dodger Stadium.

JUNE 8   In the first round of the amateur draft, the Dodgers select shortstop Dave Anderson from Memphis State University.

              Anderson played 10 seasons in the majors, eight of them with the Dodgers, as a utility infielder. Other future major leaguers drafted and signed with the Dodgers in 1981 were Sid Bream and Lemmie Miller (both in the second round), Sid Fernandez (third round), John Franco (fifth round), Stu Pederson (ninth round) and Ralph Bryant (first round of the secondary phase). Bream, Fernandez and Franco had long and effective major league careers, but the Dodgers traded each of them while they were still prospects.

JUNE 9   As a guest of President Ronald Reagan, Fernando Valenzuela attends a White House luncheon in honor of President Jose Lopez Portillo of Mexico.

JUNE 11   With a midnight strike deadline looming, the Dodgers lose 2–1 to the Cardinals in St. Louis. Despite the defeat, the Dodgers maintained a one-half game lead over the Reds in the NL West pennant race with a record of 36–21.

JUNE 12   The major league players begin a strike that lasts 50 days and wipes out nearly two months of the 1981 baseball season. The strike reduced the Dodgers schedule to 110 games.

JULY 31   Just two days after Prince Charles marries Lady Diana Spencer in London, the players and owners hammer out an agreement that ends the strike.

AUGUST 6   The owners vote to split the 1981 pennant race, with the winners of the two halves of the season competing in an extra round of playoffs for the division title. The standings when the strike was called comprised the first half. This had major implications for the Dodgers, because as the first-half champion, Los Angeles had clinched a spot in the post-season.

AUGUST 10   In the first regular season game following the strike, the Dodgers defeat the Reds 4–0 at Dodger Stadium. Jerry Reuss (six innings) and Steve Howe (three innings) combined on the shutout.

AUGUST 19   The Dodgers end a 4–3 loss to the Cubs at Wrigley Field on a bizarre play. The
                 Dodgers had the bases loaded with one out in the ninth. Reggie Smith grounded
                 sharply to Chicago second baseman Mike Tyson, who threw to shortstop Ivan
                 DeJesus for the force of Pedro Guerrero. Guerrero ran out of the base path waving
                 his arms to distract DeJesus, and the return throw to first was wild. The tying
                 run was nullified, however, because umpire Jim Quick called Guerrero out for
                 interference.

AUGUST 22   Fernando Valenzuela strikes out 12 batters in $8^2/_3$ innings during a 3–2 win over the
                 Cardinals in St. Louis.

AUGUST 26   The Dodgers score seven runs in the second inning and wallop the Pirates 16–6 in
                 Pittsburgh.

SEPTEMBER 7   In his first major league at-bat, Dodger outfielder Mike Marshall hits a disputed
                 double during the third inning of a 5–1 win over the Giants at Dodger Stadium.
                 It appeared to be a home run, but the umpires ruled the drive a two-bagger.
                 San Francisco right fielder Jack Clark later admitted the ball went into the
                 stands and bounced out.

SEPTEMBER 8   Two-run homers by Dusty Baker and Ron Cey off Doyle Alexander in the sixth
                 inning defeat the Giants 4–0 in San Francisco. Burt Hooton (six innings), Alejandro
                 Pena ($2^1/_3$ innings) and Dave Stewart (two-thirds of an inning) combined on the
                 shutout.

SEPTEMBER 17   Fernando Valenzuela sets a National League record for shutouts by a rookie with his
                 eighth of the 1981 campaign by defeating the Braves 2–0 at Dodger Stadium.

SEPTEMBER 24   Reggie Smith attacks a fan during the sixth inning of a 7–3 win over the Giants in
                 San Francisco. While in the dugout, Smith was grazed in the leg by a batting helmet
                 thrown from the stands. Smith suddenly jumped into the seats and began pounding
                 the fan. Smith tried to pull him out of the first row onto the playing field, and the fan
                 was hanging half over the railing while Smith continued to flail at him. Other fans
                 joined in the fracas while the Dodger players attempted to pull Smith back into the
                 dugout. When the five-minute disturbance ended, eight fans were taken into custody.
                 Smith was ejected and later suspended five days by the National League.

SEPTEMBER 26   Nolan Ryan pitches a no-hitter for the Astros in defeating the Dodgers 5–0 in
                 Houston. The contest was nationally televised on NBC. Dusty Baker accounted for
                 the final out with a grounder to third baseman Art Howe.

OCTOBER 2   Squaring around to bunt, Astros pitcher Don Sutton suffers a fractured kneecap
                 when struck by a pitch from Jerry Reuss in the third inning of a 6–1 Dodger win in
                 Houston. The injury put Sutton out of action for the upcoming post-season series
                 between the Dodgers and Astros. Sutton was 7–1 with a 1.46 ERA in games played
                 following the strike.

                 *After playing the Astros over the final three games of the regular season, the
                 Dodgers met Houston in the National League Division Series. Managed by Bill
                 Virdon, the Astros won the NL West pennant over second half of the 1981 season.*

OCTOBER 6   The Dodgers lose the first game of the Division Series 3–1 to the Astros in Houston. Fernando Valenzuela pitched the first eight innings and allowed only one run before being lifted for a pinch-hitter. The Astros won on a two-run walk-off homer by Alan Ashby off Dave Stewart with two out in the ninth. Ten days after pitching a no-hitter against Los Angeles, Nolan Ryan allowed only two hits.

OCTOBER 7   The Astros take a two-games-to-none lead in the best-of-five series with a 1–0 win over the Dodgers in 11 innings in Houston. The winning run scored on a walk-off single by pinch-hitter Denny Walling off Tom Niedenfuer. Starter Jerry Reuss pitched nine shutout innings.

OCTOBER 9   The Dodgers avoid elimination by beating the Astros 6–1 before 46,820 at Dodger Stadium. Burt Hooton (seven innings), Steve Howe (one inning) and Bob Welch (one inning) combined on a three-hitter. Steve Garvey homered in the first inning.

OCTOBER 10   The Dodgers even the series by beating the Astros 2–1 before 55,983 at Dodger Stadium. Neither Fernando Valenzuela nor Houston starter Vern Ruhle allowed a base runner during the first four innings. Pedro Guerrero broke the deadlock with a homer in the fifth. Valenzuela pitched the complete game and allowed four hits.

OCTOBER 11   After being down two games to none, the Dodgers win their third straight game to take the Division Series with a 4–0 decision over the Astros before 55,979 at Dodger Stadium. It was the eighth consecutive game between the two clubs and the 11th in a span of 17 days. The contest was scoreless until Los Angeles scored three runs in the sixth off Nolan Ryan. Jerry Reuss pitched the shutout.

The Dodgers played the Expos in the best-of-five National League Championship Series. The club was managed by Jim Fanning. It was Montreal's only appearance in the post-season during the 36-year history of the Expos, which lasted from 1969 through 2004. The Dodgers had won 18 of their previous 19 meetings against the Expos in Los Angeles dating back to 1978.

OCTOBER 13   The Dodgers open the NLCS by defeating the Expos 5–1 before 51,273 at Dodger Stadium. Pedro Guerrero and Mike Scioscia homered. Starter Burt Hooton pitched 7¹/₃ shutout innings.

OCTOBER 14   The Expos even the series by defeating the Dodgers 3–0 before 53,463 at Dodger Stadium. Ray Burris pitched the five-hit shutout.

OCTOBER 16   The Expos move within one victory of a World Series berth by defeating the Dodgers 4–1 at Olympic Stadium in Montreal. Steve Rogers pitched a complete game for the Expos.

OCTOBER 17   The Dodgers even the NLCS by downing the Expos 7–1 in Montreal. Los Angeles broke open a 1–1 tie with two runs in the eighth inning and four in the ninth. Burt Hooton was the winning pitcher, going 7¹/₃ innings. Steve Garvey homered. Dusty Baker collected three hits, including a double, and drove in three runs.

OCTOBER 18   Rain postpones the deciding fifth game of the NLCS by one day.

OCTOBER 19 — The Dodgers win the National League pennant with a 2–1 win over the Expos in Montreal on a ninth-inning homer by Rick Monday. The temperature was 40 degrees. The Expos took a 1–0 lead in the first inning off Fernando Valenzuela, but they couldn't score again. The Dodgers tied the score 1–1 in the fifth. Monday started the rally with a single and eventually scored on Valenzuela's ground out. Ray Burris hurled the first eight innings for Montreal before being lifted for a pinch-hitter. Steve Rogers pitched the ninth in his first relief appearances in three years. Monday's game-winning drive came with two out and cleared the center-field wall. Valenzuela went 8²/₃ innings and allowed only three hits before Bob Welch record the final out.

The Dodgers met the Yankees in the World Series. The New York club was managed by Bob Lemon. Los Angeles was thirsting for a championship after losing its four previous World Series attempts, to the Orioles in 1966, the Athletics in 1974 and the Yanks in 1977 and 1978. It was the 11th Dodger-Yankee matchup in the World Series since 1941.

OCTOBER 20 — The Yankees win the opener, defeating the Dodgers 5–3 at Yankee Stadium. New York had a 5–0 lead after four innings before a futile Los Angeles rally. Steve Yeager homered in the losing cause.

OCTOBER 21 — The Yankees win Game Two with a 3–0 decision over the Dodgers in New York. Tommy John (seven innings) and Goose Gossage (two innings) combined on the shutout.

OCTOBER 23 — The Dodgers win their first game of the 1981 World Series with a 5–4 victory over the Yankees before 56,236 at Dodger Stadium. The starting pitchers were rookies Fernando Valenzuela and Dave Righetti. The Dodgers took a 3–0 lead in the first inning on a home run by Ron Cey with two on base, but the Yanks rallied to take a 4–3 lead with two in the second and two more in the third. The Dodgers took the lead back with two runs in the fifth off George Frazier. Pedro Guerrero drove in the first run with a double. The winning run scored on a double-play grounder with the bases loaded. Valenzuela pitched shutout ball over the last six innings. The 20-year-old threw 146 pitches during the three hour and four minute night game.

OCTOBER 24 — The Dodgers even the Series by overcoming a four-run deficit to defeat the Yankees 8–7 before 56,242 at Dodger Stadium. The Yanks took a 4–0 lead in the third and were still ahead 6–3 heading into the bottom of the sixth. The Dodgers scored three times in the sixth to tie the contest. Jay Johnstone pulled the Dodgers within a run with a two-run pinch-homer off George Frazier. Lopes then reached second on a two-base error by right fielder Reggie Jackson, stole third and scored on a single by Bill Russell. The Dodgers added two tallies in the seventh to take the lead off George Frazier before the Yanks scored in the eighth. A sacrifice fly by Steve Yeager broke the 6–6 tie. Steve Garvey was one of the stars of the comeback with a double and two singles.

OCTOBER 25 — The Dodgers move within one win of the world championship with a 2–1 triumph over the Yankees before 56,115 at Dodger Stadium. The Yanks took a 1–0 lead with a run in the second. The advantage stood until the seventh when Pedro Guerrero and Steve Yeager hit back-to-back homers off Ron Guidry. Jerry Reuss pitched a complete-game five-hitter.

A frightening incident took place in the eighth when Ron Cey was hit in the helmet by a Goose Gossage fastball. After several minutes, Cey left the field under his own power and played in Game Six two days later. After the game, George Steinbrenner got into a brawl with two fans in a hotel elevator, then left for New York with his hand in a cast.

OCTOBER 28   The Dodgers win the world championship with a 9–2 trouncing of the Yankees in New York. The contest was close until Los Angeles broke a 1–1 tie with three runs in the fifth off George Frazier. The rally resulted in Frazier's third defeat of the 1981 Series. Pedro Guerrero led the attack with a home run, a triple and a single and drove in five runs. Steve Howe pitched 3²/₃ innings of shutout relief. The final out was recorded on a fly ball by Bob Watson to center fielder Ken Landreaux.

The Dodgers overcame deficits in all three post-season series in 1981, compiling a record of 1–5 in games one and two, and 9–1 in games three, four, five and six.

DECEMBER 9   The Dodgers trade Rick Sutcliffe and Jack Perconte to the Indians for Jorge Orta, Jack Fimple and Larry White.

After winning the Rookie of the Year Award in 1979, Sutcliffe was a combined 5–11 with a 5.10 ERA during his injury-plagued 1980 and 1981 seasons. He turned his career around, and from 1982 through 1984 was 51–25 with the Indians and Cubs. Sutcliffe won a total of 149 big-league games after leaving Los Angeles. He was named to the All-Star team in 1983, 1987 and 1989 and won the NL Cy Young Award in 1984. The Dodgers received virtually nothing in the exchange. Orta was a complete flop, hitting only .217 in 86 games as a Dodger. Fimple played in 92 games in the majors; White played in 11.

DECEMBER 11   The Dodgers sign Mark Belanger, most recently with the Orioles, as a free agent.

1982

L A

Season in a Sentence

Trailing the Braves by 10½ games on July 30, the Dodgers put together a tremendous surge to take a four-game lead on August 18, but they are unable to sustain the momentum and lose the pennant on the final day of the season.

Finish • Won • Lost • Pct • GB

Second   88   74   .543   1.0

Manager

Tommy Lasorda

Stats

Stats	Dods	NL	Rank
Batting Avg:	.264	.258	3
On-Base Pct:	.327	.319	2
Slugging Pct:	.388	.373	3
Home Runs:	138		2
Stolen Bases:	151		5 (tie)
ERA:	3.26	3.60	1
Fielding Avg:	.979	.978	6
Runs Scored:	691		4
Runs Allowed:	612		2

Starting Lineup

Mike Scioscia, c
Steve Garvey, 1b
Steve Sax, 2b
Ron Cey, 3b
Bill Russell, ss
Dusty Baker, lf
Ken Landreaux, cf
Pedro Guerrero, rf
Rick Monday, rf-lf

Pitchers

Fernando Valenzuela, sp
Jerry Reuss, sp
Bob Welch, sp
Burt Hooton, sp
Steve Howe, rp
Terry Forster, rp
Tom Niedenfuer, rp
Dave Stewart, rp-sp

Attendance

3,608,881 (first in NL)

Club Leaders

Batting Avg:	Pedro Guerrero	.304
On-Base Pct:	Pedro Guerrero	.378
Slugging Pct:	Pedro Guerrero	.536
Home Runs:	Pedro Guerrero	32
RBIs:	Pedro Guerrero	100
Runs:	Steve Sax	88
Stolen Bases:	Steve Sax	49
Wins:	Fernando Valenzuela	19
Strikeouts:	Fernando Valenzuela	199
ERA:	Fernando Valenzuela	2.87
Saves:	Steve Howe	13

FEBRUARY 8   The Dodgers trade Davey Lopes to the Athletics for Lance Hudson.

The trade broke up the starting infield of Steve Garvey, Lopes, Ron Cey and Bill Russell, which had been together since June 1973. Lopes was 36 at the time of the trade and was coming off a 1981 season in which he batted only .206 and made six errors in six games during the 1981 World Series. Lopes was adequately replaced at second by Steve Sax, but the Dodgers received nothing in the trade. Hudson never played a major league game.

MARCH 23   Fernando Valenzuela ends his holdout. He had earned $42,500 while winning the Cy Young Award and filling Dodger Stadium almost every time he pitched. Fernando asked for $1 million in 1982 before settling for $500,000.

APRIL 5   Reggie Smith signs a contract with the Giants as a free agent.

APRIL 6   The defending world champion Dodgers win 4–3 over the Giants with a run in the ninth inning before an Opening Day crowd of 49,662 at Dodger Stadium.

The winning tally scored on a double by Bill Russell and singles from Steve Sax and Dusty Baker. Steve Yeager homered earlier in the contest. Terry Forster was the winning pitcher. It was his first victory since 1979 after recovering from two elbow operations.

From 1982 through 1985, Tommy Lasorda appeared as the "Baseball Wizard" on the syndicated television program "The Baseball Bunch." The show was hosted by Johnny Bench.

APRIL 21   Jerry Reuss fires a one-hitter to defeat the Astros 6–0 at Dodger Stadium. The only Houston hit was a double by Art Howe with two out in the first inning.

Reuss was 18–11 with a 3.11 ERA in 254²/₃ innings in 1982.

APRIL 24   The Dodgers score two runs in the ninth inning to defeat the Giants 7–6 at Candlestick Park. The Dodgers took a 5–0 lead before San Francisco scored six times in the seventh inning. Rick Monday drove in the winning run with a single.

APRIL 29   Burt Hooton pitches a one-hitter to defeat the Phillies 4–0 at Dodger Stadium. The lone Philadelphia hit was a single by Ivan DeJesus in the fourth inning.

From 1980 through 1982, the Dodgers had a record of 55–15 in shutout games.

MAY 8   The day after the Raiders win a lawsuit against the NFL that allows the franchise to move from Oakland to Los Angeles, Dusty Baker collects five hits in six at-bats and drives in five runs during a 10–8 triumph over the Expos in Montreal. Baker garnered two home runs and three singles.

MAY 18   Pedro Guerrero hits a walk-off homer in the ninth inning to beat the Cubs 2–1 at Dodger Stadium.

Guerrero batted .304 with 32 homers and 100 RBIs in 1982.

JUNE 6   The Dodgers score three runs in the ninth inning to defeat the Cardinals 5–3 in St. Louis. Steve Sax drove in two runs with a triple and scored on a sacrifice fly from Ken Landreaux.

Sax become the fourth consecutive Dodger to win the Rookie of the Year Award, hitting .282 with 49 stolen bases. Sax followed Rick Sutcliffe (1979), Steve Howe (1980) and Fernando Valenzuela (1981).

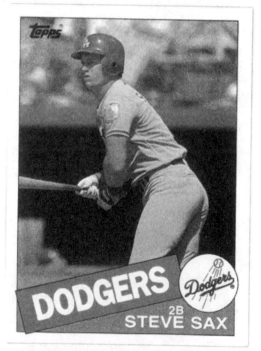

The 1982 Rookie of the Year, Steve Sax was a fan favorite throughout his years with the Dodgers, a heady, hustling player who brought a new level of excitement to the team.

JUNE 7   Steve Garvey extends his playing streak to 1,000 games with his appearance in a 4–3 loss to the Braves in Atlanta.

On the same day, the Dodgers selected first baseman Franklin Stubbs from Virginia Tech University in the first round of the amateur draft. Stubbs played 10 years in the majors, six of them with the Dodgers, but hit only .232 during his career with 104 homers in 945 games. Other future major leaguers drafted and signed by the Dodgers in 1982 were Ken Howell (third round), Reggie Williams (13th) and Jeff Hamilton (29th).

JUNE 9   On the day after the Lakers defeat the Philadelphia 76ers to win the NBA championship, Vin Scully is honored with a star on the Hollywood Walk of Fame. It's located at 6675 Hollywood Boulevard.

JUNE 11   After allowing a double to leadoff batter Eddie Milner in the first inning, Jerry Reuss retires 27 batters in a row to defeat the Reds 11–1 at Dodger Stadium. Milner scored on two ground outs. Reuss struck out seven.

The Dodgers entered the game with a record of 27–31. The club was 61–43 the rest of the way.

JUNE 14   Dusty Baker homers in the 11th inning to defeat the Padres 4–3 in San Diego.

JUNE 28   Steve Garvey is taken out of a 4–3 loss to the Cubs in Chicago because of a pulled hamstring.

Garvey created some controversy because he played a full nine innings only once over the next 13 games while nursing the injury and used some subterfuge to keep his streak of consecutive games played intact. In four starts over that span Garvey was in the starting lineup but played two innings or less. Twice, he batted in the top of the first but didn't play defensively because he was taken out of the game in the bottom half. In three others, Garvey was used only as a pinch-hitter.

JUNE 30   Dusty Baker breaks open a scoreless game with a grand slam off Juan Eichelberger in the fifth inning to spark the Dodgers to a 5–1 win over the Padres in the first game of a double-header at Dodger Stadium. San Diego won the contentious second tilt 6–4. In the ninth inning, Tom Niedenfuer hit Padres outfielder Joe Lefebvre in the head with a pitch. Kurt Bevacqua rushed out of the dugout toward the Dodger reliever, but he was stopped by umpire Joe West. Bevacqua was thumbed from the game.

JULY 13   Tommy Lasorda manages the National League to a 4–1 win in the All-Star Game at Olympic Stadium in Montreal.

JULY 17   The Dodgers score four runs in the ninth inning to stun the Mets 6–5 at Dodger Stadium. Dusty Baker drove in the first two runs in the ninth with a bases-loaded single. After the Dodgers reloaded the sacks, Ron Cey delivered a two-run walk-off single for the victory.

Baker hit .300 with 23 homers in 1982.

JULY 29 | The idle Dodgers fall 10½ games behind the Braves when the Atlanta club defeats the Padres 6–2 at Atlanta-Fulton County Stadium.

JULY 30 | Trailing 8–3, the Dodgers score two runs in the sixth inning and five in the seventh to defeat the Braves 10–9 in the first game of a double-header in Atlanta. Ron Roenicke's two-run pinch-single broke the 8–8 tie. The Dodgers also won the second tilt 8–2.

The wins were the first two of a four-game sweep of the Braves.

AUGUST 5 | A walk-off sacrifice fly by Ron Cey in the 10th inning defeats the Braves 3–2 at Dodger Stadium.

AUGUST 6 | After the Braves take a 4–3 lead in the 10th, the Dodgers score two runs in the bottom of the inning to win 5–4 at Dodger Stadium. Los Angeles tied a dubious major league record in the fifth when three runners were caught stealing. Atlanta catcher Bruce Benedict threw out Ken Landreaux, Pedro Guerrero and Dusty Baker, each attempting to swipe second.

AUGUST 7 | The Dodgers win in extra innings over the Braves for the third game in a row, taking a 7–6 decision in 11 innings. Pinch-hitter Mike Marshall drove in the winning run with a single.

AUGUST 8 | The Dodgers complete a four-game sweep of the Braves at Dodger Stadium with a 2–0 victory. Bob Welch (eight innings) and Tom Niedenfuer (one inning) combined on the shutout.

The Dodgers were 8–0 against the first-place Braves over a 10-day period from July 20 through August 8. The wins helped cut Atlanta's lead from 10 games to 1½.

AUGUST 9 | The Dodgers win their fourth extra-inning game in five days by downing the Reds 3–2 in 13 innings at Dodger Stadium. The winning run scored on a walk-off homer by Pedro Guerrero. Dave Stewart pitched six inning of hitless relief. He retired 18 batters in a row after walking the first batter he faced.

AUGUST 10 | The Dodgers take over first place with an 11–3 win over the Reds at Dodger Stadium. It was the club's eighth win in a row and the 12th during a span of 13 games.

The Dodgers went from 10½ games behind to one-half game ahead in an amazing stretch of 12 days.

AUGUST 17 | The game against the Cubs in Chicago is suspended by darkness at the end of the 17th inning with the score 1–1 because of darkness. It was completed the following day prior to a regularly-scheduled contest.

AUGUST 18 | Picking up the previous day's suspended game in the top of the 18th inning, the Dodgers win 2–1 over the Cubs in 21 innings at Wrigley Field. The total time consumed to play the two-day marathon was six hours and 10 minutes. The Cubs scored in the first inning and the Dodgers in the second. Over the next 18 innings, neither team could dent the plate. The winning run scored on a double by Steve Sax, a wild pitch and a sacrifice fly by Dusty Baker. Tommy Lasorda used all 25 players in the game. The pitchers were Burt Hooton (six innings), Tom Niedenfuer (two innings), Steve Howe (two innings), Dave Stewart (two innings), Terry Forster (one inning), Joe Beckwith (3²/₃ innings), Ricky Wright (one-third of an inning) and Jerry Reuss (four innings). In addition, Fernando Valenzuela and Bob Welch each played one inning in the outfield. They played left field against left-handed batters and right field when right-handers were at the plate. The pitchers alternated with Dusty Baker. Reuss also started the regularly scheduled game and went five innings for his second win of the day as the Dodgers emerged with a 7–4 triumph.

The two wins gave the Dodgers a four-game lead over the Braves. Los Angeles gained 14¹/₂ games on Atlanta in a span of 20 days. During that period the Dodgers were 16–4 and the Braves 2–19.

AUGUST 20   Fernando Valenzuela pitches a two-hitter to defeat the Pirates 1–0 at Three Rivers Stadium. The lone run scored on a home run in the second inning by Ron Cey off Larry McWilliams. The only Pittsburgh hits were singles by Dale Berra in the first inning and Johnny Ray in the fifth.

At the age of 21, in his second full season in the majors, Valenzuela had a 19–13 record and a 2.87 ERA in 287 innings. He completed 18 of his 37 starts. Fernando won his 19th game on September 19 before earning a defeat and two no-decisions in his last three starts.

AUGUST 27   A record-tying two pinch-hit home runs highlight a 9–4 win over the Cubs at Dodger Stadium. Mike Marshall hit a solo blast in the fifth inning and Rick Monday added another pinch-homer in the eighth with two on base.

AUGUST 29   The Dodgers drop out of first place with a 7–2 loss to the Cubs at Dodger Stadium.

SEPTEMBER 1   The Dodgers use a record nine pinch-hitters during a 13-inning, 6–5 loss to the Cardinals at Dodger Stadium. The nine were Ron Roenicke, Manny Mota, Greg Brock, Rick Monday, Dave Sax, Jorge Orta, Jose Morales, Mike Marshall and Candy Maldonado. It was the last big-league appearance for Mota, who was 44-years-old. It was also the first game in the majors for both Sax and Brock.

Steve Yeager created controversy late in the 1982 season by posing for nude photos that appeared in the October 1982 issue of Playgirl *magazine.*

SEPTEMBER 13   A walk-off homer in the 16th inning by Steve Garvey defeats the Padres 4–3 at Dodger Stadium. The marathon victory put the Dodgers back into first place ahead of the Braves.

SEPTEMBER 14   Fernando Valenzuela pitches the Dodgers to a 1–0 win over the Padres at Dodger Stadium. The lone run scored in the first inning on doubles by Ken Landreaux and Pedro Guerrero.

The Dodgers set a major league record of 3,608,881 in 1982. It stood until the Toronto Blue Jays attracted 3,885,284 in 1990. The 1982 figure stood as the club record until 2006.

SEPTEMBER 19   A two-out, two-run, walk-off double by Pedro Guerrero in the 10th inning beats the Astros 5–4 at Dodger Stadium.

SEPTEMBER 20   The idle Dodgers take a three-game lead in the NL West race when the Braves lose 4–3 to the Astros in Houston. There were 12 games left on the schedule.

SEPTEMBER 21   The Dodgers lose 3–0 to the Padres in San Diego.

The defeat was the start of an excruciating eight-game losing streak that knocked the Dodgers out of first place. Six of the eight losses were by one run, and three came in extra innings.

SEPTEMBER 27   The Dodgers fall into a tie for first place with the Braves after a 6–1 loss to the Reds at Dodger Stadium. The Giants were in third place, just one game back of the leaders.

SEPTEMBER 28   The Dodgers fall out of first place with a 4–3 loss to the Reds in 10 innings at Dodger Stadium. The Dodgers had the bases loaded with none out in the 10th, but they failed to score.

SEPTEMBER 29   With a chance to move into a tie for first place, the Dodgers lose 4–3 to the Braves in 12 innings at Dodger Stadium. It was the club's eighth defeat in a row.

SEPTEMBER 30   The Dodgers pull back within a game of first place with a 10–3 thrashing of the Braves at Dodger Stadium. There were three games left on the schedule.

OCTOBER 1   Rick Monday hits a grand slam off Fred Breining in the eighth inning for the only runs of a 4–0 win over the Giants in San Francisco. Jerry Reuss pitched the shutout.

OCTOBER 2   The Dodgers stay alive in the pennant race with a 15–2 rout of the Giants in San Francisco. The defeat eliminated the Giants from the pennant race. Los Angeles headed into the final day of the regular season one game behind the Braves.

OCTOBER 3   On the final day of the season, the Dodgers blow a chance at the NL West title with a 5–3 loss to the Giants in San Francisco. In a controversial decision, Fernando Valenzuela, gunning for his 20th win of the season, was lifted for pinch-hitter Jorge Orta in the seventh. In the bottom half, Tom Niedenfuer put two men on base and Joe Morgan snapped a 2–2 tie with a three-run homer off Terry Forster. The Dodgers had a chance to move into a tie for first place because the Braves lost 5–1 to the Padres in San Diego. It was the last game for Steve Garvey and Ron Cey as members of the Dodgers.

OCTOBER 15   The Dodgers sell Ted Power to the Reds.

Power was 27 at the time of the sale and had a 5.63 ERA in 48 big-league innings. His departure didn't seem to be any great loss, but Power proved to be a capable pitcher for many years and pitched 13 seasons in the majors with eight clubs. In 1985, Power saved 27 games for Cincinnati.

DECEMBER 1   Terry Forster signs a contract as a free agent with the Braves.

Forster gave Atlanta three effective seasons out of the bullpen while battling issues with his weight. He gained some notoriety in 1985 when Dave Letterman called Forster a "fat tub of goo" on his late-night television program.

DECEMBER 21   Steve Garvey signs a contract as a free agent with the Padres.

Garvey had been a member of the Dodgers since 1969 and the club's starting first baseman since 1973. He was 33 at the time of his departure, and with youngsters Mike Marshall and Greg Brock waiting in the wings, the Dodgers didn't believe Garvey was worth the risk of a long-term contract. Garvey was in the decline phase of his career, but he gave San Diego four seasons as a starter, including one that led to the team's appearance in the 1984 World Series.

DECEMBER 28   The Dodgers trade Jorge Orta to the Mets for Pat Zachry.

1983   LA

Season in a Sentence

The Dodgers win the NL West in the midst of a youth movement before losing the NLCS to the Phillies.

Finish • Won • Lost • Pct • GB

First   91   71   .562   +3.0

Manager

Tommy Lasorda

National League Championship Series

The Dodgers lost three games to one to the Philadelphia Phillies.

Stats

Stats	Dods	NL	Rank
Batting Avg:	.250	.255	8
On-Base Pct:	.318	.322	9
Slugging Pct:	.379	.376	6
Home Runs:	146		1
Stolen Bases:	166		3
ERA:	3.10	3.63	1
Fielding Avg:	.974	.978	11
Runs Scored:	654		8
Runs Allowed:	609		1

Starting Lineup

Steve Yeager, c
Greg Brock, 1b
Steve Sax, 2b
Pedro Guerrero, 3b
Bill Russell, ss
Dusty Baker, lf
Ken Landreaux, cf
Mike Marshall, rf
Derrell Thomas, cf-rf

Pitchers

Fernando Valenzuela, sp
Bob Welch, sp
Jerry Reuss, sp
Alejandro Pena, sp
Burt Hooton, sp
Steve Howe, rp
Tom Niedenfuer, rp
Dave Stewart, rp
Joe Beckwith, rp

Attendance

3,510,313 (first in NL)

Club Leaders

Batting Avg:	Pedro Guerrero	.298
On-Base Pct:	Pedro Guerrero	.373
Slugging Pct:	Pedro Guerrero	.531
Home Runs:	Pedro Guerrero	32
RBIs:	Pedro Guerrero	103
Runs:	Steve Sax	94
Stolen Bases:	Steve Sax	56
Wins:	Fernando Valenzuela	15
	Bob Welch	15
Strikeouts:	Fernando Valenzuela	189
ERA:	Bob Welch	2.65
Saves:	Steve Howe	18

JANUARY 19   The Dodgers trade Ron Cey to the Cubs for Vance Lovelace and Dan Cataline.

With the trade of Cey, only Bill Russell was left from the infield that started for the Dodgers from 1973 through 1981. The move was made to create a place for prospect Mike Marshall in the outfield. Pedro Guerrero was moved from the outfield to third base. Cey still had three years ahead of him as a regular third baseman. Neither Lovelace nor Cataline ever played a game for the Dodgers.

MARCH 4   Steve Howe publicly acknowledges his addiction to cocaine at a press conference at Dodgertown in Vero Beach, Florida. Howe admitted that he became dependent daily on alcohol and cocaine during the final month of the 1982 season. He said he used drugs during games. The previous November, Howe entered The Meadows drug rehabilitation center in Wickenburg, Arizona, for five weeks of treatment. It was also revealed that Ken Landreaux spent part of the winter in a drug clinic. While there were no indications of a relapse on Landreaux's part, Howe wound up being suspended three times in 1983 for drug-related incidents (see May 28, 1983).

MARCH 10   Walter Alston is elected to the Hall of Fame by the Committee on Veterans.

MARCH 24   The Executive Board of the International Olympic Committee agrees to stage a six-team exhibition baseball tournament as part of the 1984 Summer Olympics in Los Angeles. Dodger Stadium was later selected as the venue. It was the first time baseball was played at the Olympics since 1936.

APRIL 5   The Dodgers open the season with a 16–7 pasting of the Astros in Houston. Fernando Valenzuela was the starting pitcher and allowed six runs in 2⅔ innings. The Dodgers broke a 6–6 tie with six runs in the sixth inning. Ken Landreaux was the batting star with six runs batted in on a double and two singles. Pedro Guerrero homered, tripled and singled while driving in five runs.

APRIL 8   The Dodgers lose the home opener 8–3 to the Expos before 45,369 at Dodgers Stadium. Walter Alston threw out the ceremonial first pitch. Ken Landreaux homered in the losing cause.

APRIL 13   Steve Yeager hits a two-run, walk-off homer in the 14th inning to beat the Astros 5–3 at Dodger Stadium.

APRIL 16   Playing for the Padres against the Dodgers at Dodger Stadium, Steve Garvey breaks the all-time National League record for consecutive games played with 1,118. He broke the mark set by Billy Williams with the Cubs from 1963 through 1970. Williams was at the game, won by the Dodgers 8–5.

MAY 4   Pedro Guerrero wallops a walk-off home run in the ninth inning to defeat the Pirates 3–2 at Dodger Stadium.

Guerrero hit .298 with 32 homers and 103 RBIs during the 1983 season.

MAY 6   The Dodgers squander a 6–0 lead but bounce back to defeat the Cardinals 16–10 at Dodger Stadium. St. Louis tied the game 9–9 with three runs in the fifth inning. The Dodgers broke the deadlock with three tallies in the sixth.

MAY 9   Ken Landreaux ties the score 3–3 with a solo homer in the sixth inning, then beats
                 out an infield single with two out in the ninth to score the winning run for a 4–3
                 victory over the Cubs at Dodger Stadium.

                 *On the same day, the Dodgers traded John Franco and Brett Wise to the Reds
                 for Rafael Landestoy. The deal with Cincinnati proved to be one of the worst
                 in club history. Franco was only 22 at the time of the transaction and wouldn't
                 make his big-league debut until April 1984, but it proved to be the first of 1,119
                 big-league appearances, all in relief. Franco played 21 seasons in the majors,
                 was named to four All-Star teams and recorded 424 saves. He led the NL in that
                 category in 1988 with the Reds and 1990 and 1994 as a Met. Landestoy hit just
                 .178 in 118 at-bats with the Dodgers over two seasons.*

MAY 17   Greg Brock draws five walks in seven plate appearances, but the Dodgers lose 3–2 to
                 the Expos in 15 innings in Montreal.

MAY 18   Greg Brock drives in six runs during a 13–3 triumph over the Expos in Montreal.
                 Brock hit a grand slam off Bill Gullickson in the fifth inning and a two-run homer
                 against Chris Welsh in the eighth.

                 *Brock was given the impossible task of replacing Steve Garvey at first base, as
                 press notices billed him as "the best power hitting prospect the Dodgers have
                 had since Duke Snider." Brock hit 44 home runs at Albuquerque in 1982, but he
                 proved to be one of many Dodger prospects who were overrated after putting up
                 big batting numbers in the thin mountain air of New Mexico. Brock spent five
                 mediocre seasons in Los Angeles before being traded to Milwaukee.*

MAY 22   Bob Welch pitches a two-hitter to defeat the Mets 5–0 at Shea Stadium. The only
                 New York hits were singles by Tom Seaver in the fifth inning and Danny Heep in
                 the ninth.

MAY 23   Fernando Valenzuela pitches a four-hit shutout to down the Phillies 2–0 in
                 Philadelphia.

MAY 24   The Dodgers record their third consecutive shutout as Alejandro Pena four-hits the
                 Phillies to win 3–0 in Philadelphia.

                 Over five games, Dodger pitchers threw 35 consecutive scoreless innings.

MAY 28   Fernando Valenzuela pitches a two-hitter to defeat the Giants 5–0 at Dodger
                 Stadium. The only San Francisco hits were doubles by Johnnie LeMaster in the
                 first inning and opposing pitcher Renie Martin in the third.

                 *Steve Howe failed to report for the game, citing "car trouble." He was
                 suspended by the club the following day and was admitted to the CareUnit in
                 Orange, California, a drug rehabilitation center. At the time, Howe had pitched
                 in 14 games and 22$\frac{1}{3}$ innings during the 1983 season and had a perfect ERA
                 of 0.00. Howe returned to the club on June 29, was fined $54,000, and placed
                 on three-year probation. Part of Howe's probation involved periodic testing
                 (see September 22, 1983).*

June 1   The day after the Lakers defeat the Philadelphia 76ers to win the NBA championship, Bob Welch pitches a one-hitter to defeat the Phillies 1–0 at Dodger Stadium. The only Philadelphia hit was a single by Von Hayes in the fourth inning. The lone run scored in the fourth inning when Steve Sax singled, stole second and crossed the plate on a single by Pedro Guerrero.

June 2   A two-run, walk-off, pinch-single from Candy Maldonado in the 14th inning beats the Mets 5–4 at Dodger Stadium.

The victory boosted the Dodgers record to 34–14. The club was only 57–57 the rest of the way, but it managed to win the Western Division by three games over the Braves. The final 91–71 record was also the best in the National League.

June 3   The Sax brothers both start against the Mets at Dodger Stadium. Steve started at second base and Dave as a catcher. Both were hitless in four at-bats during the 5–2 loss.

June 6   In the first round of the amateur draft, the Dodgers select pitcher Eric Sonberg from Wichita State University.

Sonberg never reached the majors. In a largely unproductive draft, the only future major leaguers signed by the Dodgers were Luis Lopez (second round), Scott May (sixth) and Wayne Kirby (13th).

June 11   A two-out, two-run homer by Bill Russell in the ninth inning beats the Reds 3–2 in Cincinnati.

June 17   Bob Welch not only pitches a shutout but accounts for the only run of a 1–0 win over the Reds at Dodger Stadium by smacking a home run in the sixth inning off Mario Soto. It was the first of two homers Welch hit in 582 career at-bats. The other one was struck in 1986.

June 25   A bases-loaded squeeze bunt by Ron Roenicke in the 11th inning scores Pedro Guerrero from third base for the winning run in a 2–1 decision over the Astros at Dodger Stadium.

June 28   The Dodgers erupt for eight runs in the fourth inning and defeat the Padres 9–5 in San Diego. Pedro Guerrero hit a grand slam off Elias Sosa.

July 1   A three-run double by Dusty Baker in the 10th inning beats the Astros 5–2 in Houston.

July 6   Steve Sax collects an RBI-single in the All-Star Game, but the National League loses 13–3 at Comiskey Park in Chicago.

Sax went through an erratic streak in mid-season in which he had trouble making the simplest of throws to first base due to an unexplained mental block. He made 30 errors, 13 more than any other National League second baseman, but only two of Sax's numerous errors came after August 5 as he seemed to conquer his problems. They would resurface periodically over the next few years, however (see August 19, 1985).

JULY 11	The Dodgers score three runs in the ninth inning to defeat the Cardinals 7–6 at Dodger Stadium. Steve Sax started the rally with a single and scored on Ken Landreaux's double. Dusty Baker finished off St. Louis with a two-run homer. He ended the game with two homers and two singles.
JULY 12	Dusty Baker drives in all three runs of a 3–1 win over the Cardinals at Dodger Stadium.
JULY 20	Ken Landreaux collects five hits, including a double, in five at-bats but the Dodgers lose 7–3 to the Pirates in Pittsburgh.
JULY 23	The Dodgers break a 3–3 tie with seven runs in the eighth inning and defeat the Cardinals 10–5 in St. Louis. Ken Landreaux hit a grand slam off Bruce Sutter.
AUGUST 10	The Dodgers lose 9–2 to the Reds in Cincinnati. *Afterward, Tommy Lasorda delivered a paint-blistering oration on the club's lack of effort. From June 19 through August 10, the Dodgers were 18–29. Beginning on August 11, Los Angeles won 30 of its next 49 games to take the NL West title. One of the reasons cited for the turnaround was the awarding of a Mr. Potato doll to the team MVP after each victory. The silly ritual was credited for uniting the team.*
AUGUST 13	The Braves score two runs in the ninth inning on a walk-off homer by Bob Watson to defeat the Dodgers 8–7 in Atlanta. The loss dropped the Dodgers 6½ games behind the first-place Braves with a record of 64–50.
AUGUST 19	The Dodgers trade Dave Stewart and Ricky Wright for Rick Honeycutt. *At the time of the trade, Honeycutt was a 29-year-old veteran who had a 14–8 record for Texas and was leading the AL in ERA with a mark of 2.42. He had a 42–65 career record, however, and the strong early showing in 1983 proved to be an aberration. Signed to a long-term contract after the trade, Honeycutt pitched with the Dodgers until 1987 and compiled a record of 33–45. Stewart was 25 and had shown flashes of brilliance with the Dodgers, but little consistency. He struggled until 1987, when he suddenly blossomed into one of the best, and most intimidating, starting pitchers in the game. From 1987 through 1990, Stewart was 84–45 with the Athletics and pitched in three World Series. He won at least 20 games in each of those four seasons.*
AUGUST 21	In his Dodger debut, Rick Honeycutt hurls seven shutout innings during a 6–0 win over the Phillies at Dodger Stadium. Tom Niedenfuer pitched the eighth and ninth.
AUGUST 24	The Dodgers extend their winning streak to eight games with a 3–2 decision over the Expos at Dodger Stadium.
AUGUST 29	The Dodgers take first place with a 6–1 and 7–3 sweep over the Mets in New York.
SEPTEMBER 7	Six days after the Soviets shoot down a South Korean passenger plane, resulting in the deaths of 269 people, including 61 Americans, the Dodgers defeat the Reds 7–3 on a walk-off grand slam by Mike Marshall off Ben Hayes in the 10th inning.

Marshall was only 23 when he won a job in the Dodger outfield. He was the Minor League Player of the Year in 1981 by hitting .373 with 34 homers and 137 runs batted in at Albuquerque, but a string of injuries wrecked his chance at stardom at the big-league level. His maladies included a beaning by Jeff Reardon in 1983, separate surgeries on a foot and kneecap in 1984, an appendectomy in 1985 and back strain and astigmatism in 1986. During the 1987 campaign, Marshall's problems included a wart removal, food poisoning and back, wrist and ankle injuries. Many teammates questioned his dedication to the game. Marshall also received considerable attention for dating Belinda Carlisle of the rock band The Go-Gos.

SEPTEMBER 11   On a 101-degree day in Los Angeles, the Dodgers score four runs in the ninth inning to defeat the Braves 7–6 at Dodger Stadium. The winning run scored on a squeeze bunt by R. J. Reynolds that brought Pedro Guerrero home from third base. The win stretched the Dodgers lead over Atlanta to three games.

SEPTEMBER 15   The Dodgers widen their lead to 4½ games with a 6–0 win over the Astros in Houston. Alejandro Pena pitched the shutout.

SEPTEMBER 22   Steve Howe is suspended again by the Dodgers for missing the team's charter flight to Atlanta. Upon arriving later that night, Howe refused to undergo urinalysis. He didn't pitch again until 1985. Howe had a 1.44 ERA and 18 saves in 46 games and 68⅔ innings during the 1983 season while battling his addiction (see December 15, 1983).

SEPTEMBER 26   The Dodgers score three runs in the ninth inning and four in the 10th to beat the Reds 12–9 in Cincinnati. Pedro Guerrero drove in the first two runs in the 10th with a double.

SEPTEMBER 30   The Dodgers clinch the NL West with a 4–3 win over the Giants at Dodger Stadium.

The Dodgers played the Phillies in the National League Championship Series. The Phils were 90–72 in 1983 and won the NL East by six games. The team was managed by Paul Owens, who took over in July after Pat Corrales was fired. The Dodgers dominated Philadelphia during the regular season, winning 11 of 12 meetings.

OCTOBER 4   The Dodgers open the NLCS with a 1–0 loss to the Phillies before 49,963 at Dodger Stadium. Mike Schmidt's first-inning home run off Jerry Reuss was all the offense that Philadelphia needed. Steve Carlton (7⅔ innings) and Al Holland (1⅓ innings) combined on the shutout. Steve Sax collected three of the seven Los Angeles hits.

OCTOBER 5   The Dodgers even the series with a 4–1 win over the Phillies before 55,967 at Dodger Stadium. Pedro Guerrero broke a 1–1 tie with a two-run triple in the fifth. Fernando Valenzuela (eight innings) and Tom Niedenfuer (one inning) pitched for Los Angeles.

OCTOBER 7   The Phillies take a two-games-to-one lead in the best-of-five NLCS with a 7–2 victory over the Dodgers at Veterans Stadium in Philadelphia. Mike Marshall drove in both Los Angeles runs with a fourth-inning homer that made the score 3–2.

OCTOBER 8   The Phillies win the National League pennant with their second straight 7–2 win over the Dodgers in Philadelphia. Dusty Baker homered in the losing cause.

The Phillies went on to lose the World Series to the Orioles in five games.

DECEMBER 8   Seven weeks after a bomb rips through a Marine compound in Beirut, killing 241, and six weeks after the U.S. invasion of Grenada, the Dodgers trade Sid Fernandez and Ross Jones to the Mets for Carlos Diaz and Bob Bailor.

During a 24-month span, the Dodgers traded away future All-Star pitchers Rick Sutcliffe (December 1981), John Franco (May 1983), Dave Stewart (August 1983) and Fernandez for little or nothing. A native of Honolulu, Fernandez pitched in the All-Star Game for the Mets in 1986 and 1987. Diaz was also born in Honolulu, but he proved to be a disappointment as a left-handed reliever.

DECEMBER 15   Commissioner Bowie Kuhn suspends Steve Howe for one year for the use of illegal drugs.

1984   LA

Season in a Sentence

Scoring the fewest runs of any major league team, the Dodgers tumble to only their second losing record since 1968.

Finish • Won • Lost • Pct • GB

Fourth   79   83   .488   13.0

Manager

Tommy Lasorda

Stats

Stats	Dods	NL	Rank
Batting Avg:	.244	.255	12
On-Base Pct:	.306	.319	12
Slugging Pct:	.348	.369	12
Home Runs:	102		8
Stolen Bases:	109		10
ERA:	3.17	3.59	2
Fielding Avg:	.975	.978	10
Runs Scored:	580		12
Runs Allowed:	600		3

Starting Lineup

Mike Scioscia, c
Greg Brock, 1b
Steve Sax, 2b
Pedro Guerrero, 3b-rf-cf
Dave Anderson, ss
Mike Marshall, lf
Ken Landreaux, cf
Candy Maldonado, rf-cf
Bill Russell, ss
R. J. Reynolds, lf-rf-cf
German Rivera, 3b
Franklin Stubbs, 1b

Pitchers

Fernando Valenzuela, sp
Alejandro Pena, sp
Bob Welch, sp
Rick Honeycutt, sp
Jerry Reuss, sp-rp
Pat Zachry, rp
Burt Hooton, rp
Orel Hershiser, rp-sp

Attendance

3,134,824 (first in NL)

Club Leaders

Batting Avg:	Pedro Guerrero	.303
On-Base Pct:	Pedro Guerrero	.358
Slugging Pct:	Pedro Guerrero	.462
Home Runs:	Mike Marshall	21
RBIs:	Pedro Guerrero	72
Runs:	Pedro Guerrero	85
Stolen Bases:	Steve Sax	34
Wins:	Bob Welch	13
Strikeouts:	Fernando Valenzuela	240
ERA:	Alejandro Pena	2.48
Saves:	Tom Niedenfuer	11

JANUARY 10   Don Drysdale is elected to the Hall of Fame.

FEBRUARY 2   Eleven days after the Los Angeles Raiders defeat the Washington Redskins 38–9 in
                 the Super Bowl in Tampa, Florida, Derrell Thomas signs a contract with the Expos
                 as a free agent.

APRIL 1   Dusty Baker signs a contract as a free agent with the Giants.

APRIL 3   The Dodgers open the season with an 11–7 loss to the Cardinals before 50,103 at
                 Dodger Stadium. Fernando Valenzuela was the starting pitcher and allowed six runs
                 in three innings. Mike Marshall contributed a double, two singles and drove in three
                 runs. Terry Whitfield hit a three-run pinch-homer in his first plate appearance with
                 the Dodgers. It was also Whitfield's first game in the majors since 1980. He spent the
                 previous three seasons playing for the Seibu Lions in Japan.

                 *After decades of offering managers one-year contracts, the Dodgers broke
                 tradition and gave Tommy Lasorda a three-year deal beginning with the
                 1984 campaign.*

APRIL 5   A three-run, walk-off homer by Mike Marshall in the 12th inning beats the Cardinals
                 5–2 at Dodger Stadium.

                 *A portion of the Dodgers games were carried over ON-TV a subscription
                 television service, in 1984. Al Downing announced the games.*

APRIL 13   Steve Sax singles and doubles and
                 scores both runs during a 2–0 win
                 over the Giants at Dodger Stadium.
                 Bob Welch (seven innings) and Tom
                 Niedenfuer (two innings) combined
                 on the shutout.

APRIL 16   A two-out, two-run double by Mike
                 Marshall in the ninth inning beats the
                 Astros 5–4 in Houston.

APRIL 17   Rick Honeycutt pitches the Dodgers
                 to a 1–0 victory over the Astros in
                 Houston.

APRIL 22   Mike Marshall drives in six runs
                 during a 15–7 win over the Padres
                 at Dodger Stadium. He collected five
                 hits on two homers, a double and
                 two singles in six at-bats. Greg Brock
                 homered in his fourth consecutive
                 game. The Dodgers scored all of
                 their runs in the first four innings,
                 beginning with a six-run rally in
                 the first.

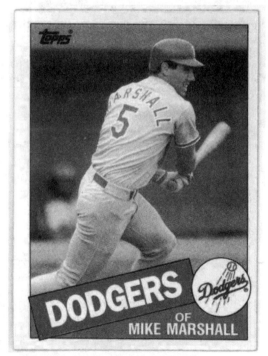

Though never quite the power source Dodger
fans hoped he would be, Mike Marshall provided
a strong, consistent bat during his years in Los
Angeles.

APRIL 27	Rick Honeycutt pitches a rain-shortened one-hitter to defeat the Padres 1–0 in San Diego. The contest was called with two out in the top of the seventh. Steve Yeager drove in the only run with a homer in the second inning off Tim Lollar.
APRIL 30	Fernando Valenzuela beats the Giants 1–0 in San Francisco. The lone run scored in the second inning when Greg Brock singled, stole second base and scored on Mike Scioscia's single.

The Dodgers had a record of 18–8 on May 1 before going into a steady decline. The club was 45–64 from May 2 through August 31. Injuries took a toll and contributed to a losing season in between division titles in 1983 and 1985. Fifteen Dodgers were placed on the disabled list in 1984, and Steve Howe was suspended for the entire season because of drug use. Some of the injuries were on the bizarre side. Rick Honeycutt hurt his shoulder when he tripped in the Dodger Stadium parking lot, and Tom Niedenfuer swallowed his tongue while passing a kidney stone.

MAY 23	Fernando Valenzuela strikes out 15 batters and drives in the lone run of a 1–0 victory over the Phillies at Veterans Stadium. In the fifth inning, Mike Scioscia doubled, moved to third base on a wild pitch and scored on Valenzuela's ground out. Philadelphia came into the contest on a 10-game winning streak.
JUNE 4	In the first round of the amateur draft, the Dodgers select pitcher Dennis Livingston from Oklahoma State University.

Livingston never played at the major league level. Future major leaguers drafted and signed by the Dodgers in 1984 were Tim Scott (second round), Tracy Woodson (third round), Darren Holmes (16th round) and Jeff Nelson (22nd round). Only Nelson would have a long and productive big-league career, but he was drafted by the Mariners from the Dodger organization before reaching the majors.

JUNE 6	A walk-off single by Mike Marshall in the 14th inning beats the Reds 3–2 at Dodger Stadium.
JUNE 12	Pedro Guerrero collects five hits in five at-bats during an 8–7 win over the Giants at Dodger Stadium. The fifth hit was a homer in the eighth inning that broke a 7–7 tie.

Guerrero hit .303 with 16 home runs in 1984.

JUNE 13	Mike Marshall hits a grand slam of Scott Garrelts in the third inning, but the Dodgers lose 10–5 to the Giants at Dodger Stadium.
JUNE 21	A pinch-hit grand slam off Bob Owchinko highlights a five-run seventh that gives the Dodgers the lead in a 9–7 victory over the Reds in Cincinnati. The win ended a seven-game losing streak.
JULY 1	The Dodgers retire number 53 in honor of Don Drysdale in ceremonies prior to a 4–3 loss to the Cubs at Dodger Stadium.

JULY 4   Orel Hershiser strikes out 11 batters during a 9–0 triumph over the Pirates at Dodger Stadium.

A rookie in 1984, Orel Leonard Quinton Hershiser IV looked more like an accountant than an athlete, with a name to match. Undrafted out of high school in Cherry Hill, New Jersey, Hershiser attended college at Bowling Green and was picked by the Dodgers in the 17th round of the amateur draft in 1979. He began the 1984 season in long relief and was moved into the starting rotation in late June. From 1984 through 1989, he compiled a record of 98–64 with an ERA of 2.68. During that span, he led the NL in innings pitched three times, shutouts twice and complete games, wins and winning percentage once each. Orel won the Cy Young Award in 1988 after setting a major league record with 59 consecutive scoreless innings. His innocent, boyish looks were in sharp contrast to his toughness. Hershiser was nicknamed "Bulldog" by Tommy Lasorda because of his tenacious demeanor on the mound. Injuries caught up with Hershiser in 1990 when he tore his rotator cuff, and he struggled during his last five seasons in Los Angeles before moving to the Indians as a free agent. On the all-time club lists, he ranks 10th in wins (135), ninth in games started (309), ninth in shutouts (24) and sixth in strikeouts (1,454).

JULY 10   Fernando Valenzuela pitches two scoreless innings (the third and fourth) during a 3–1 National League victory in the All-Star Game at Candlestick Park in San Francisco.

JULY 14   Orel Hershiser pitches a two-hitter to defeat the Cubs 8–0 at Wrigley Field. It was his second consecutive shutout. The only Chicago hits were singles by Jay Johnstone in the first inning and Bob Dernier in the third.

JULY 19   Orel Hershiser pitches his second consecutive two-hitter and third straight shutout and defeats the Cardinals 10–0 at Busch Stadium. The only St. Louis hits were a single by Lonnie Smith in the first inning and a double from Terry Pendleton in the second.

Hershiser pitched 32 consecutive scoreless innings from June 29 through July 24. He pitched four shutouts in July, which were the first four of his career. They were also his only four in 1984, but it was enough to lead the National League in the category.

JULY 28   The opening ceremonies of the Olympic Games takes place at Memorial Coliseum. The Olympics concluded on August 12. Baseball, an exhibition sport in 1984, was played at Dodger Stadium. The U.S. won the silver medal. Among those on the U.S. team were Mark McGwire, Barry Larkin, Will Clark, Scott Bankhead, Oddibe McDowell, Bobby Witt, B. J. Surhoff, Cory Snyder and Chris Gwynn.

JULY 29   Bob Welch pitches a two-hitter to beat the Reds 1–0 at Dodger Stadium. The only Cincinnati hits were singles by Gary Redus in the first and ninth innings. The lone run crossed the plate on a sacrifice fly by Mike Marshall in the sixth inning.

JULY 30   Orel Hershiser pitches a two-hitter to defeat the Reds 1–0. It was his third two-hitter in a span of 16 days and the team's second straight 1–0 victory. Hershiser retired the first 23 batters before Nick Esasky broke up the no-hit bid with a single with two out in the eighth inning. Gary Redus added a single in the ninth. The lone run scored in the fourth inning on a single by right fielder Ed Amelung. It was his first career base hit.

Both of the runs in the back-to-back 1–0 wins over the Reds were unearned. The feeble Dodger offense went 53 consecutive innings without scoring an earned run from July 26 through July 31.

AUGUST 4   A home run by Greg Brock in the 11th inning breaks a 3–3 tie and the Dodgers win 5–3 over the Reds in Cincinnati after adding an insurance tally.

AUGUST 9   Greg Brock's home run off Rick Camp in the fourth inning beats the Braves 1–0 in Atlanta. Orel Hershiser (8$\frac{1}{3}$ innings), Ken Howell (one-third of an inning) and Jerry Reuss (one-third of an inning) combined on the shutout. It was the only save recorded by Reuss between 1980 and 1989.

AUGUST 12   A home run by Mike Marshall in the 10th inning downs the Giants 5–4 in San Francisco.

SEPTEMBER 6 The Dodgers lose 3–2 in an 18-inning marathon against the Braves at Dodger Stadium. The winning run scored on a home run by Randall Johnson off Larry White. Atlanta tied the game with two runs in the eighth. There was no scoring from the ninth through the 17th.

The decision was the only one of White's brief two-year career. He had an 0–1 record in 11 games, all in relief.

SEPTEMBER 26 Fernando Valenzuela strikes out 12 batters, but he loses 3–1 to the Astros at Dodger Stadium.

SEPTEMBER 30 In the last game of the season, the Dodgers win 7–2 over the Giants at Dodger Stadium. In what proved to be his last major league at-bat, right fielder Tony Brewer hit a home run.

The homer was the only one of Brewer's career, which spanned 24 games and 37 at-bats. He collected only four hits for a lifetime average of .108.

DECEMBER 20   Six weeks after Ronald Reagan wins re-election as president in a race against Walter Mondale, Burt Hooton signs a contract as a free agent with the Rangers.

1985

Season in a Sentence

With a rejuvenated batting attack, the Dodgers win 59 of their last 92 games to win the NL West before losing to the Cardinals in the NLCS, four games to two.

Finish • Won • Lost • Pct • GB

First   95   67   .586   +5.5

Manager

Tommy Lasorda

Stats

Stats	Dods	NL	Rank
Batting Avg:	.261	.255	3
On-Base Pct:	.328	.319	2
Slugging Pct:	.382	.374	5
Home Runs:	129		4
Stolen Bases:	136		5
ERA:	2.96	3.59	1
Fielding Avg:	.974	.979	12
Runs Scored:	682		5
Runs Allowed:	579		3

Starting Lineup

Mike Scioscia, c
Greg Brock, 1b
Steve Sax, 2b
Dave Anderson, 3b
Mariano Duncan, ss
Pedro Guerrero, lf-3b
Ken Landreaux, cf
Mike Marshall, rf
Candy Maldonado, cf-rf

Pitchers

Orel Hershiser, sp
Fernando Valenzuela, sp
Jerry Reuss, sp
Bob Welch, sp
Rick Honeycutt, sp
Tom Niedenfuer, rp
Ken Howell, rp
Carlos Diaz, rp

Attendance

3,264,593 (first in NL)

Club Leaders

Batting Avg:	Pedro Guerrero	.320
On-Base Pct:	Pedro Guerrero	.422
Slugging Pct:	Pedro Guerrero	.577
Home Runs:	Pedro Guerrero	33
RBIs:	Mike Marshall	95
Runs:	Pedro Guerrero	99
Stolen Bases:	Mariano Duncan	38
Wins:	Orel Hershiser	19
Strikeouts:	Fernando Valenzuela	202
ERA:	Orel Hershiser	2.03
Saves:	Tom Niedenfuer	19

FEBRUARY 4   The Dodgers trade Pat Zachry to the Phillies for Al Oliver.

Oliver was in the last season of an 18-year career in which he collected 2,743 hits. He was traded to the Blue Jays in July. Oliver holds the distinction of being the only individual in Dodger history to wear uniform number 0.

FEBRUARY 20   The Dodgers sign Jay Johnstone, most recently with the Cubs, as a free agent.

APRIL 9   The Dodgers open the season with a 2–1 loss to the Astros in Houston. Fernando Valenzuela was the winning pitcher and gave up two unearned runs in the seventh inning.

APRIL 12   The Dodgers lose their season opener 4–1 to the Giants before 46,910 at Dodger Stadium.

APRIL 13   Candy Maldonado homers off Mark Davis in the eighth inning for the only run of a 1–0 win over the Giants at Dodger Stadium. Fernando Valenzuela pitched the shutout.

APRIL 17	The Dodgers win 1–0 in 11 innings over the Astros at Dodger Stadium. Mike Marshall drove in the winning run with a single. Rick Honeycutt (eight innings) and Orel Hershiser (three innings) combined on the shutout.
APRIL 21	Orel Hershiser pitches a two-hitter to defeat the Padres 2–0 at Jack Murphy Stadium. The only San Diego hits were a double by Tony Gwynn in the seventh inning and a single from Carmelo Martinez in the eighth. The runs scored on solo homers by Candy Maldonado in the seventh inning and Mariano Duncan in the eighth.
APRIL 24	Ken Howell strikes out eight batters in 3²/₃ innings of relief to close out a 4–2 win over the Giants in San Francisco.

APRIL 26 — In his first start since pitching a two-hitter against the Padres, Orel Hershiser one-hits San Diego to win 2–0 at Dodger Stadium. Tony Gwynn spoiled the no-hit bid with a single in the fourth inning. Pedro Guerrero drove in both runs with a double in the third inning.

Hershiser led the NL in winning percentage with a 19–3 record and his 2.03 earned run average ranked third in 1985. He pitched 239²/₃ innings.

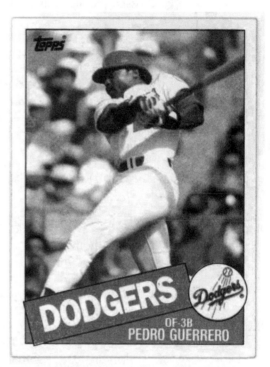

One of the most feared sluggers of the 1980s, Pedro Guerrero posted big numbers again in 1985, finishing among the league leaders in many offensive categories.

APRIL 28 — Fernando Valenzuela pitches a two-hitter but loses 1–0 to the Padres at Dodger Stadium. The lone run scored on a home run by Tony Gwynn in the ninth inning.

Gwynn's home run was the first earned run allowed by Valenzuela in 1985. At the conclusion of the contest, he had a 0.21 ERA in 42 innings, but he had only a 2–3 record to show for it because of a lack of batting support. Fernando finished the regular season with a 17–10 record, a 2.45 earned run average and 208 strikeouts in 272¹/₃ innings.

MAY 3	Bill Russell makes three errors at shortstop during a 16–2 loss to the Pirates in Pittsburgh.
MAY 10	The Dodgers defeat the Pirates 1–0 at Dodger Stadium. The lone run scored on a single by Greg Brock. Jerry Reuss (8²/₃ innings) and Steve Howe (one-third of an inning) combined on the shutout.
MAY 12	Greg Brock drives in both runs of a 2–0 victory over the Pirates at Dodger Stadium. He struck a solo home run in the second inning and drove in a run with a single in

the sixth. Bobby Castillo ($6^{1}/_{3}$ innings) and Tom Niedenfuer ($2^{2}/_{3}$ innings) combined on the shutout.

MAY 21   The Dodgers record falls to 18–21 with a 6–1 loss to the Expos in Montreal.

MAY 25   Greg Brock hits two homers and drive in five runs during a 6–2 win over the Mets in New York.

JUNE 3   The Dodgers score two runs in the ninth inning and one in the 12th to defeat the Mets 5–4 at Dodger Stadium. The runs in the ninth scored on an RBI-double by R. J. Reynolds and a run-scoring single from Pedro Guerrero. The winning run crossed the plate on an error by shortstop Rafael Santana.

On the same day, the Dodgers selected outfielder Chris Gwynn from San Diego State University in the first round of the amateur draft. The younger brother of Tony (by four years), Chris was considered the better prospect coming out of college. Chris was the 10th overall pick in the first round, while Tony wasn't selected until round three. Tony finished his career with 3,141 hits and eight batting titles. Chris Gwynn was far less successful, playing 10 seasons in the majors, six of them with the Dodgers, and batting .261 with 17 home runs in 599 games. Other future major leaguers drafted and signed by the Dodgers in 1985 were Mike Devereaux (fifth round), Jack Savage (eighth round) and Mike Huff (16th round). During the secondary phase in January, the Dodgers picked John Wetteland in the second round and Greg Briley in the third.

JUNE 16   Seven days after the Lakers defeat the Celtics to win the NBA championship, Pedro Guerrero homers in his fourth consecutive game as the Dodgers defeat the Astros 9–0 in Houston.

In late May, the Dodgers moved Guerrero from third base, where he had struggled defensively, to left field. After hitting just four home runs in 168 at-bats through May 31, he responded with one of the best months in club history. Guerrero hit seven home runs in seven games from June 7 through 16 and eight in nine games beginning on June 4. By the end of June, he had tied the Dodger record for most home runs in a month with 15 (see June 30, 1985). The mark was set by Duke Snider in August 1953. Guerrero also drove in 28 runs in June 1985 and batted .344. During June and July combined, he batted a scorching .391 in 156 at-bats with 19 home runs Guerrero finished the season with a .320 average and 33 home runs while leading the NL in on-base percentage (.422) and slugging percentage (.577).

JUNE 22   Fernando Valenzuela strikes out 14 batters during a 6–3 win over the Astros at Dodger Stadium.

JUNE 23   Steve Howe shows up three hours late for a game against the Astros at Dodger Stadium. Howe explained that his wife took the car keys and that he had to take a taxicab to the ballpark. The Dodgers fined him $300.

JUNE 29   Steve Howe fails to show for an appearance at a Boy Scout dinner for which he was chairman. The next day, the Dodgers placed Howe on the restricted list after he missed a game against the Braves at Dodger Stadium.

JUNE 30	On his last at-bat of the month, Pedro Guerrero ties the club record for most home runs in a month (15) with a blast off Bruce Sutter during a 4–3 win over the Braves at Dodger Stadium.
JULY 3	The Dodgers release Steve Howe.

Five weeks later, Howe was signed by the Twins, but Minnesota released him after a relapse. He later pitched for the Rangers in 1987 and, after a three-year absence from the majors, with the Yankees from 1991 through 1996. While with the Yanks, Howe was suspended for life by baseball for trying to purchase cocaine, but he successfully appealed the suspension. He was arrested in 1996 for trying to take a loaded weapon onto an airplane. Howe died in 2006 when his pickup truck rolled over on a highway in Coachella, California. Toxicology reports indicated he had an undisclosed amount of methamphetimine in his system.

JULY 9	The Dodgers trade Al Oliver to the Blue Jays for Len Matuszek.
JULY 10	The Dodgers trade German Rivera and Rafael Montalvo to the Astros for Enos Cabell.
JULY 13	The Dodgers take first place with a 9–1 win over the Cubs in Chicago. Los Angeles remained in first for the rest of the year.
JULY 23	Orel Hershiser pitches a one-hitter to defeat the Pirates 6–0 at Dodger Stadium. The lone Pittsburgh hit was a single by Jason Thompson in the second inning.
JULY 24	Greg Brock hits a grand slam off Al Holland in the fifth inning of a 9–1 win over the Pirates at Dodger Stadium.

Pedro Guerrero set a club record by reaching base 14 consecutive times over four games against the Pirates and Cubs from July 23 through July 26. He reached on two home runs, three doubles, two singles, six walks and one hit by pitch.

JULY 26	Mike Marshall hits a grand slam off Warren Brusstar in the sixth inning of a 10–0 win over the Cubs at Dodger Stadium.

Marshall had the best season of his career in 1985: a .293 batting average and 28 home runs.

JULY 29	The Dodgers score three runs in the ninth inning to beat the Giants 4–2 at Dodger Stadium. The rally climaxed with a two-out, two-run, walk-off home run by Steve Sax. It was his only homer of the season.
AUGUST 3	Bob Welch pitches a two-hitter to defeat the Reds 2–0 at Dodger Stadium. The only Cincinnati hits were a single by Dave Concepcion in the fifth inning and a double from Eddie Milner in the sixth. The runs scored on solo homers by Mike Scioscia in the third inning and Pedro Guerrero in the ninth.

Scioscia hit .296 with seven home runs in 1985.

AUGUST 6 The Dodgers game against the Reds in Cincinnati is postponed by a players strike. The August 7 game between the two clubs was also called off. The strike ended on August 8, and both games were made up with double-headers.

AUGUST 15 The Dodgers take a nine-game lead in the NL West pennant race with a 5–4 victory over the Braves at Dodger Stadium.

AUGUST 16 The Dodgers extend their winning streak to eight games with a 5–1 win over the Giants in San Francisco.

AUGUST 19 After the throwing problems of Steve Sax resurface, Tommy Lasorda tries levity to fix the problem. In a practical joke inspired by *The Godfather*, Sax found a pig's head in his hotel bed in Philadelphia with a note demanding better defensive play. He led NL second baseman in errors in 1985 for the second time in three seasons.

AUGUST 21 Candy Maldonado collects five hits, including a homer and a double, in six at-bats during a 15–6 thrashing of the Phillies in Philadelphia. Mike Marshall drove in five runs with four hits, including a grand slam off Jerry Koosman in the first inning. The Dodgers had 22 hits as a team.

AUGUST 23 Pedro Guerrero and Mariano Duncan both hit grand slams to account for all eight runs in an 8–4 win over the Expos in Montreal. With the Dodgers trailing 3–0, Guerrero connected off Tom Burke in the sixth inning. In the seventh, Duncan cleared the bases with a homer off of Gary Lucas. Both Guerrero and Duncan hailed from San Pedro de Macoris in the Dominican Republic.

AUGUST 31 The Dodgers trade Sid Bream, Cecil Espy and R. J. Reynolds to the Pirates for Bill Madlock.

> *A four-time batting champion, Madlock was 34 at the time of the trade and had a batting average of only .251 with the Pirates in 1985. He hit .360 in 34 games for the Dodgers that season, however, and proved to be a clubhouse leader during the pennant drive. But he contributed little in 1986 and 1987 before being traded to the Tigers.*

SEPTEMBER 1 In his first start with the Dodgers, Bill Madlock collects three hits, including a double, in five at-bats, although the club loses 4–1 to the Phillies at Dodger Stadium.

SEPTEMBER 2 Jay Johnstone hits a pinch-hit, walk-off single in the 11th inning that beats the Expos 5–4 at Dodger Stadium.

> *Johnstone wrote a book in 1985 titled* Temporary Insanity *detailing his 20-year career in the majors with seven clubs, mostly as a utility outfielder. He collected at least 500 at-bats in a season only once, with the Angels in 1969. Johnstone's book was banned from Dodger Stadium concession stands, however, because it contained too much profanity for the tastes of club management. Johnstone played for the Dodgers from 1980 through 1982 and again in 1985.*

SEPTEMBER 8 The Dodgers use nine pinch-hitters during a 14-inning, 4–3 loss to the Mets at Dodger Stadium. The nine were Terry Whitfield, Ken Landreaux, Franklin Stubbs, Stu Pederson, Len Matuszek, Jay Johnstone, Ralph Bryant, Greg Brock and Mike Scioscia.

SEPTEMBER 9   In a bizarre sequence, Dodger reliever Brian Holton wins his major league debut without retiring a batter. He entered the game against the Braves in Atlanta in the seventh inning. The only batter he faced was Brian Harper, who hit a two-run double to give the Braves a 6–3 lead. Harper was out attempting to steal. With Holton still the pitcher of record, the Dodgers scored five runs in the top of the eighth and won 9–7.

SEPTEMBER 10   The Dodgers sweep the Braves 10–1 and 10–4 during a double-header in Atlanta. Greg Brock hit a grand slam off Steve Shields in the seventh inning of game two.

SEPTEMBER 11   The Dodgers reach double digits in runs scored for the third straight game in beating the Braves 12–3 in Atlanta.

SEPTEMBER 21   The Dodgers score seven runs in the fifth inning and down the Giants 11–2 in San Francisco.

OCTOBER 2   The Dodgers clinch the NL West crown with a 9–3 triumph over the Braves at Dodger Stadium. Orel Hershiser won his 11th game in a row to run his season record to 19–3.

The Dodgers played the St. Louis Cardinals in the National League Championship Series. Managed by Whitey Herzog, the Cards were 101–61 in 1985 and won the NL East by three games over the Mets. The NLCS had been a best-of-five affair from 1969 through 1984. Beginning in 1985, four wins were needed to advance to the World Series.

OCTOBER 9   The Dodgers open the NLCS with a 4–1 win over the Cardinals before 55,270 at Dodgers Stadium. Fernando Valenzuela (6⅓ innings) and Tom Niedenfuer (2⅔ innings) combined for the victory. The Dodgers scored a run in the fourth inning and three in the seventh. The offense was a team effort as four different players drove in the four runs.

OCTOBER 10   The Dodgers take a two-games-to-none lead with an 8–2 triumph over the Cardinals before 55,222 at Dodger Stadium. Orel Hershiser pitched a complete game. Greg Brock homered with a man in base in the fourth inning to give Los Angeles a 5–1 lead. Ken Landreaux collected two doubles and a single and scored three times. Bill Madlock also had three hits.

Hershiser had a 12–0 record at Dodger Stadium in 1985, including the playoff victory.

OCTOBER 12   The Cardinals bounce back to beat the Dodgers 4–2 at Busch Stadium in St. Louis in game three. Bob Welch gave up two runs in the first inning and two in the second.

OCTOBER 13   The Cardinals even the series by routing the Dodgers 12–2 in St. Louis. The Cards put the game away with a nine-run second inning off Jerry Reuss and Rick Honeycutt. Bill Madlock homered during the losing cause.

Before the game, Cardinals outfielder Vince Coleman was injured in a bizarre accident as the fastest man in baseball was disabled by Busch Stadium's slow-moving automatic tarpaulin. While doing stretching exercises, the tarp, which weighed nearly a ton, rolled over Coleman's left leg up to his thigh. He was trapped for 30 seconds. Coleman was removed from the field on a stretcher and was diagnosed with a bone chip near his left knee.

OCTOBER 14   The Cardinals win their third straight over the Dodgers on a ninth-inning, walk-off home run by Ozzie Smith. The Cards scored two runs in the first inning and the Dodgers deadlocked the contest in the fourth on a two-run homer by Bill Madlock. Tommy Lasorda pulled left-hander Fernando Valenzuela after eight innings and 132 pitches and right-hander Tom Niedenfuer started the ninth. Smith shocked the nationwide television audience and those at the ballpark by drilling a one-out, 1–2 pitch down the right field line for a home run.

Entering the game, Smith had 13 career homers in 4,225 regular season at-bats and 50 post-season at-bats. The switch-hitter had never hit a homer from the left side of the plate in more than 3,000 at-bats. He would bat 1,114 times in 1986 and 1987 without hitting a single home run.

OCTOBER 16   The Cardinals win the National League pennant by beating the Dodgers 7–5 with three runs in the ninth inning before a game six crowd of 55,208 at Dodger Stadium. The Dodgers held a 4–1 lead after six innings with the help of a triple, double and single from Mariano Duncan. Bill Madlock also contributed with a home run, his third of the series. The Cards scored three runs in the seventh to tie the game 4–4. The third tally scored on a triple by Ozzie Smith off Tom Niedenfuer, who had just come into the game in relief of Orel Hershiser. Mike Marshall put Los Angeles ahead 5–4 with a home run in the eighth. Niedenfuer was still on the mound in the ninth. Willie McGee singled with one out, Ozzie Smith walked, and the pair advanced to second and third on a ground out. Tommy Lasorda elected to pitch to Jack Clark rather than issue an intentional walk. That decision, and the one to leave Niedenfuer in the game, proved to be disastrous as Clark hit a three-run homer. Trailing 7–5, the Dodgers went down in order in the ninth facing Ken Dayley.

A Dodger since 1981, Niedenfuer was never fully forgiven by Los Angeles fans for giving up home runs in the ninth inning of game five and six in the 1985 NLCS. He was booed frequently at Dodger Stadium until he was traded to the Orioles in 1987.

DECEMBER 11   The Dodgers trade Candy Maldonado to the Giants for Alex Trevino and Steve Yeager to the Mariners for Ed Vande Berg.

1986

LA

Season in a Sentence

A spring training knee injury to Pedro Guerrero puts a hole in the lineup that can't be adequately filled and sets the stage for a long and painful season.

Finish • Won • Lost • Pct • GB

Fifth 73 89 .451 23.0

Manager

Tommy Lasorda

Stats

Stats	Dods	NL	Rank
Batting Avg:	.251	.253	9
On-Base Pct:	.313	.322	11
Slugging Pct:	.370	.380	11
Home Runs:	130		7
Stolen Bases:	155		5
ERA:	3.76	3.72	5
Fielding Avg:	.971	.978	12
Runs Scored:	638		9
Runs Allowed:	679		5

Starting Lineup

Mike Scioscia, c
Greg Brock, 1b
Steve Sax, 2b
Bill Madlock, 3b
Mariano Duncan, ss
Franklin Stubbs, lf
Reggie Williams, cf
Mike Marshall, rf
Ken Landreaux, cf
Enos Cabell, 1b
Bill Russell, rf-lf-ss
Dave Anderson, 3b-ss
Alex Trevino, c

Pitchers

Fernando Valenzuela, sp
Orel Hershiser, sp
Rick Honeycutt, sp
Bob Welch, sp
Ken Howell, rp
Tom Niedenfuer, rp
Ed Vande Berg, rp

Attendance

3,023.208 (first in NL)

Club Leaders

Batting Avg:	Steve Sax	.332
On-Base Pct:	Steve Sax	.390
Slugging Pct:	Steve Sax	.441
Home Runs:	Franklin Stubbs	23
RBIs:	Bill Madlock	60
Runs:	Steve Sax	91
Stolen Bases:	Mariano Duncan	48
Wins:	Fernando Valenzuela	21
Strikeouts:	Fernando Valenzuela	242
ERA:	Fernando Valenzuela	3.14
Saves:	Ken Howell	12

APRIL 3   A little over two months after the space shuttle Challenger explodes, killing six astronauts and teacher Christa McAuliffe, Pedro Guerrero severely injures his knee during an exhibition game against the Braves in Vero Beach, Florida. He started his slide into third base but had a change of mind and caught his spikes in the dirt, then tumbled over the bag. Guerrero had only 61 at-bats in 1986 and hit just .246 with five homers.

APRIL 7   The Dodgers open the season with a 2–1 win over the Padres at Dodger Stadium. Fernando Valenzuela pitched a complete game while scattering 10 hits. Mike Marshall homered in the seventh inning to put the Dodgers up 2–0.

APRIL 9   The Dodgers edge the Padres 1–0 at Dodger Stadium. Bob Welch pitched the shutout. Mike Marshall singled in the lone run in the fourth inning.

APRIL 10   The Dodgers sign Cesar Cedeno, most recently with the Cardinals, as a free agent.

Cedeno played in his fifth All-Star Game in 1976 at the age of 25, but he never appeared in another one. The 1986 season was his last in the majors and he batted only .231 in 76 at-bats as a Dodger.

APRIL 11   The Dodgers rally from an 8–1 deficit with four runs in the seventh inning and three in the ninth to tie the game, but they lose 9–8 when the Giants score in the 12th at Dodger Stadium.

APRIL 15   The Dodgers lose for the fourth time in five games in extra innings, dropping a 12-inning, 2–1 decision to the Padres in San Diego.

APRIL 16   On the day the U.S. bombs Libya in response to terrorist attacks, the Dodgers play their 10th consecutive one-run game at the start of the 1986 season and lose 2–1 to the Padres in San Diego. The Dodgers were 3–7 in the 10 games. Over the course of the season, the Dodgers were 28–38 in one-run contests.

APRIL 23   Fernando Valenzuela throws 163 pitches during a 6–4 victory over the Giants in San Francisco.

MAY 7   Steve Sax hits a grand slam off Jay Baller to break a 4–4 tie in the seventh inning and lead to an 8–4 win over the Cubs in Chicago.

            Sax had by far the best year of his career in 1986, hitting .332 with six home runs.

MAY 13   Mike Marshall rips a two-run homer in the 11th inning to give the Dodgers a 6–4 lead in a 6–5 win over the Cardinals in St. Louis.

MAY 20   Fernando Valenzuela pitches a two-hitter to defeat the Expos 4–0 at Dodger Stadium. The only Montreal hits were singles by Mitch Webster in the seventh inning and Jim Wohlford in the eighth.

MAY 24   Fernando Valenzuela strikes out 11 batters and pitches his second consecutive two-hitter to defeat the Phillies 6–0 at Dodger Stadium. Von Hayes collected both Philadelphia hits with a single in the first inning and a double in the sixth.

MAY 27   A brawl erupts in the sixth inning of an 8–1 loss to the Mets in New York. After a grand slam by George Foster, Tom Niedenfuer hit Ray Knight in the left elbow with a pitch. Knight charged the mound and was tackled by Niedenfuer. Both benches emptied, but no one was ejected.

JUNE 2   In the first round of the amateur draft, the Dodgers select outfielder Mike White from Loudon High School in Loudon, Tennessee.

            White peaked in Class AAA. Future major leaguers drafted and signed by the Dodgers in 1986 were Dave Hansen (second round), Wade Taylor (also in the second round), Mike Munoz (third round), Kevin Campbell (fifth round) and Paul Quantrill (26th round).

JUNE 5   Rick Honeycutt (eight innings) and Ken Howell (one inning) combine on a two-hitter to defeat the Astros 1–0 at Dodger Stadium. The only Houston hits were singles by Kevin Bass in the fifth inning and Phil Garner in the eighth.

JUNE 9   Mariano Duncan hits an inside-the-park homer in the fifth inning to tie the Reds 5–5 and an RBI-single in the seventh to lift the Dodgers to a 6–5 win at Dodger Stadium.

JUNE 10   Mariano Duncan advances two bases on a fielder's choice in the ninth inning to beat the Reds 1–0 at Dodger Stadium. The play started with Duncan as the base runner on second base and Enos Cabell on first. Bill Madlock grounded to third baseman Buddy Bell, who threw to second baseman Ron Oester for the force out, but Oester's throw to first baseman Tony Perez was too late to complete the double play. Duncan kept running on the play and slid under the tag of catcher Bo Diaz. Rick Honeycutt (eight innings) and Tom Niedenfuer (one inning) combined on the shutout.

JUNE 22   Craig Shipley becomes only the second major leaguer born in Australia, and the first in over 80 years, when he makes his major league debut as the Dodgers starting shortstop in a 5–4 loss to the Padres at Dodger Stadium.

> *The first Australian major leaguer was Joe Quinn, who played from 1884 through 1901. Shipley was born in Parramatta, New South Wales. He came to the U.S. in 1982 and played three years at the University of Alabama before signing with the Dodgers. Shipley spent two seasons with the Dodgers at the start of an 11-year big-league career.*

JUNE 23   The Braves leave 18 men on base, but they still beat the Dodgers 6–5 at Dodger Stadium.

JULY 7   Four pitchers combine on a two-hitter to defeat the Cardinals 1–0 at Dodger Stadium. The quartet consisted of Alejandro Pena (five innings), Carlos Diaz (one inning), Tom Niedenfuer (two innings) and Ken Howell (one inning). The St. Louis hits were singles by Andy Van Slyke in the second inning and Tommy Herr in the fourth.

JULY 13   A two-out, two-run double by Alex Trevino off Lee Smith in the ninth inning beats the Cubs 4–3 at Dodger Stadium.

JULY 15   In the All-Star Game at the Astrodome in Houston, Fernando Valenzuela pitches three shutout innings (the fourth through the sixth) but the National League loses 3–2.

JULY 22   A two-run homer by Reggie Williams climaxes a three-run rally in the ninth inning that beats the Pirates 4–3 in Pittsburgh.

JULY 27   The Dodgers outlast the Cubs 13–11 at Wrigley Field. Los Angeles scored four runs in the eighth inning for a 9–8 lead, but Chicago responded with three in their half to move ahead 11–9. The Dodgers scored four times in the ninth for the victory. Mike Scioscia drove in two of the runs in the ninth with Jeff Hamilton and Greg Brock accounting for the others.

AUGUST 1   Greg Brock's grand slam in the first inning off Mario Soto sparks a 9–5 win over the Reds at Dodger Stadium.

AUGUST 2   A grand slam by Enos Cabell off John Franco highlights a six-run eighth inning that beats the Reds 7–1 at Dodger Stadium. Alejandro Pena (seven innings) and Tom Niedenfuer (two innings) combined on a one-hitter. The only Cincinnati hit was a home run by Eddie Milner in the sixth inning.

AUGUST 4   The Dodgers extend their winning streak to eight games with a 7–3 win over the Astros at Dodger Stadium.

                  The win gave the Dodgers a 53–52 record, but the club lost 37 of its final 57 games.

AUGUST 18   Mariano Duncan breaks a toe on a freak play in the fifth inning of a 5–4 loss to the Mets at Dodger Stadium. Duncan was hurt running across the plate when he was struck by a throw from center fielder Lenny Dykstra.

SEPTEMBER 2   Vance Law of the Expos hits a walk-off homer off Bob Welch in the ninth inning to defeat the Dodgers 1–0 in Montreal.

SEPTEMBER 6   Fernando Valenzuela strikes out 14 batters to defeat the Phillies 3–2 in Philadelphia.

                  Steve Sax had a streak of nine hits in 10 consecutive at-bats over three games from September 3 through September 6.

SEPTEMBER 11   The Dodgers rout the Astros 14–6 at Dodger Stadium.

SEPTEMBER 19   The Dodgers score three runs in the ninth inning, two of them on a home run by Steve Sax, to beat the Reds 9–7 in Cincinnati. The victory ended a six-game losing streak.

SEPTEMBER 22   Fernando Valenzuela pitches a two-hitter for his 20th win of the season, beating the Astros 9–2 in Houston. It was Tommy Lasorda's 59th birthday. The only hits off Valenzuela were a single by Davey Lopes in the first inning and a triple by Phil Garner in the ninth. Right fielder Ralph Bryant had an interesting evening. He homered in the fourth inning, then made a four-base error in the seventh when he lost track of a fly ball from Kevin Bass in the Astrodome roof. Bass circled the bases before Bryant could recover the ball.

                  Valenzuela was 25 in 1986 and compiled a 21–11 record with a 3.14 ERA and 242 strikeouts in 269$^{1}/_{3}$ innings. He completed 20 of his 34 starts. Valenzuela finished in the top five in the NL in innings pitched seven consecutive seasons from 1981 through 1987 and pitched at least 250 innings in six straight years beginning with 1982. Pitch counts weren't kept for every game during his career, but there are several documented cases in which Valenzuela threw at least 160 pitches in a game. The workload took a toll. Fernando had a record of 99–68 through 1986, but was only 74–85 afterward in a career which lasted until 1997. He never pitched more than 204 innings in any year after 1987 and didn't post a winning season between 1986 and 1995. Valenzuela's last year with the Dodgers was 1990.

SEPTEMBER 23   Astros pitcher Jim Deshaies sets a major league record by striking out the first eight Dodger batters and wins 4–0 in Houston. Deshaies fanned Steve Sax, Reggie Williams, Enos Cabell, Pedro Guerrero, Alex Trevino, Jeff Hamilton, Dave Anderson and Jose Gonzalez.

                  Despite the losing season, the Dodgers drew over three million fans for the seventh time. Through the 1986 season, the Dodgers were the only team ever with an attendance of over three million. The first team outside of Los Angeles to reach that figure was the Mets in 1987.

SEPTEMBER 25   Jeff Hamilton hits a walk-off homer in the 10th inning that beats the Padres 4–3 in the first game of a double-header at Dodger Stadium. San Diego scored three runs in the top of the ninth to tie the contest. The Padres won game two 7–6 with a two-run rally in the ninth.

SEPTEMBER 28   The 25-game hitting streak of Steve Sax comes to an end when he is hitless in seven at-bats during a 16-inning, 6–5 loss to the Giants in San Francisco. The Dodgers used 27 players in the marathon and the Giants used 25.

SEPTEMBER 29   The Dodgers rout the Padres 10–0 in San Diego. Orel Hershiser twirled the shutout.

DECEMBER 9   Jeff Nelson is drafted by the Mariners organization.

Nelson didn't reach the majors until 1992, but he had a 15-year career in which he pitched in 798 games as a highly effective reliever, mostly as a set-up man. He pitched in four World Series with the Yankees and on a 2001 Seattle team that won 116 games.

DECEMBER 10   The Dodgers trade Greg Brock to the Brewers for Tim Leary and Tim Crews and swap Dennis Powell and Matt Walters to the Mariners for Matt Young.

1987

L
A

Season in a Sentence

The comments by Al Campanis on "Nightline" set the stage for a miserable year as the Dodgers follow a losing season with another one for the first time since 1968.

Finish • Won • Lost • Pct • GB

Fourth   73   89   .451   17.0

Manager

Tommy Lasorda

Stats

Stats	Dods	NL	Rank
Batting Avg:	.252	.261	12
On-Base Pct:	.309	.328	12
Slugging Pct:	.371	.404	12
Home Runs:	125		8
Stolen Bases:	128		9
ERA:	3.72	4.08	2
Fielding Avg:	.975	.979	12
Runs Scored:	635		12
Runs Allowed:	675		2

Starting Lineup

Mike Scioscia, c
Franklin Stubbs, 1b
Steve Sax, 2b
Mickey Hatcher, 3b
Dave Anderson, ss
Pedro Guerrero, lf
John Shelby, cf
Mike Marshall, rf
Mariano Duncan, ss

Pitchers

Orel Hershiser, sp
Bob Welch, sp
Fernando Valenzuela, sp
Rick Honeycutt, sp
Matt Young, rp
Brian Holton, rp
Tim Leary, rp-sp
Alejandro Pena, rp

Attendance

2,979,409 (third in NL)

Club Leaders

Batting Avg:	Pedro Guerrero	.338
On-Base Pct:	Pedro Guerrero	.416
Slugging Pct:	Pedro Guerrero	.539
Home Runs:	Pedro Guerrero	27
RBIs:	Pedro Guerrero	89
Runs:	Pedro Guerrero	89
Stolen Bases:	Steve Sax	37
Wins:	Orel Hershiser	16
Strikeouts:	Bob Welch	196
ERA:	Orel Hershiser	3.06
Saves:	Matt Young	11
	Alejandro Pena	11

APRIL 6   The Dodgers open the season with a 4–3 loss to the Astros in Houston. The Astros scored the winning run in the seventh inning off Orel Hershiser. Franklin Stubbs led the offense with three hits.

Following the game, general manager Al Campanis made racially insensitive remarks on the ABC-TV program "Nightline." Campanis said that blacks may lack "some of the necessities to be a field manager or a general manager." Faced with a storm of public criticism, the Dodgers fired Campanis two days later. Fred Claire took over as general manager. He was 51 and had been Campanis's top assistant. Claire joined the Dodgers in 1969 in the public relations department after covering the club for a number of newspapers. He helped the Dodgers win a world championship in 1988, but he was far less successful afterward. Claire was relieved of his duties in 1998.

APRIL 9   In the first home game of the season, the Dodgers lose 8–1 to the Giants before 46,289 at Dodger Stadium.

APRIL 10   The Dodgers record drops to 0–5 with an 11-inning, 5–4 loss to the Giants at Dodger Stadium.

Al Campanis

Major League Baseball planned a series of commemorations in honor of the 40th anniversary of Jackie Robinson's debut in the major leagues in 1987. Robinson's former uniform number (42) was emblazoned on second base in all 26 major league parks for the season opener. Many clubs staged tributes and numerous private groups observed the occasion in various ways. In Montreal, a monument to Robinson was unveiled May 16 at the site where Robinson first played Organized Baseball in 1946 with the Montreal Royals, then a Dodger farm team in the International League. The Baseball Writers' Association of America joined the celebration by voting to name the annual rookie of the year award after Robinson.

Just hours after the Dodgers season opener against the Astros in Houston, the Robinson tribute took an unexpected turn that sent shockwaves throughout baseball and created a nationwide furor. It came about when ABC-TV dedicated a segment of its "Nightline" show to Jackie's memory. Host Ted Koppel had arranged to have Don Newcombe and Roger Kahn, who were both closely associated with Robinson, as guests on the program.

Unfortunately, Newcombe, director of community relations for the Dodgers, missed plane connections and was unable to reach New York on time. To replace him, Koppel contacted Dodger vice president and general manager Al Campanis, who played shortstop alongside Robinson with Montreal and was his roommate. The two had been close and Campanis was known as a supportive friend of Robinson, who died in 1972. Campanis had been general manager since 1968 and part of the organization for more than 40 years.

While the "Nightline" show was intended to be a memorial to Robinson, it turned out to be something else entirely. During his nearly 20 years as general manager, Campanis rarely appeared on camera. The interview took place at around midnight in a nearly empty Astrodome. Koppel was in his New York studio with Kahn. Early in the program, Campanis recalled some of his 1946 experiences with Jackie that he had been telling for years. "I was his enforcer," Campanis explained.

"He took a lot of guff. He couldn't fight. Mr. Rickey wouldn't let him. But I could." Later the discussion veered to the subject of African-Americans in baseball in 1987 and some of Koppel's questions elicited comments from Campanis that were blatant racial slurs.

When Koppel asked why there were no black managers or general managers in the major leagues at that time, the 70-year-old Campanis commented: "I can't answer that question directly. The only thing I can say is you have to pay your dues to become a manager. Generally you have to go to the minor leagues. There's not a lot of pay involved, and some of the better-known black players have been able to get into other fields and make a pretty good living that way."

Characterizing the reply as "a lot of baloney," Koppel probed deeper and asked: "Is there still that much prejudice in baseball today?" "No, I don't believe it's prejudice," Campanis responded. "It's just that they (African-Americans) may not have some of the necessities to be, let's say, a field manager or a general manager." The comments shocked Koppel, who gave Campanis a chance to clarify his remarks and proceeded to ask whether he really believed that. "Well, I don't say all of them, but they certainly are short," Campanis answered. "How many black quarterbacks do you have? How many pitchers are black?" Koppel responded by saying: "That sounds like the same garbage we were hearing 40 years ago about players." Campanis responded angrily and dug himself deeper. "It's not garbage," he said. "Why are black people not good swimmers? Because they don't have the buoyancy."

The inflammatory comments, in which Campanis inferred that African-Americans were mentally inferior to whites, quickly stirred an outcry of protest. Many who had known Campanis for all of his long career as a Dodger official came to his defense, said they had never heard him previously express such beliefs and absolved him of bigotry. Before the television commentary, Campanis had been considered to be one of baseball's more enlightened executives concerning race relations. Some felt that, either because of his age or the glare of national television, his thoughts became sidetracked and he just had a "bad day."

Peter O'Malley viewed a tape of the program the following morning and, when the media asked him if Campanis's job was in jeopardy, the Dodger owner declared: "Absolutely not." Later that day, both O'Malley and Campanis issued apologies for the controversial remarks. "I apologize to the American people, particularly to all black Americans, for my statements and in my inability under the circumstances to express accurately my beliefs," Campanis said. He attempted to say he was referring to a lack of experience by African-Americans rather than any innate abilities. Campanis also said he was "wiped out" at the end of a long day and therefore not himself.

But in the end, no type of apology could excuse what Campanis said and the damage it had done to the Dodger franchise. On April 8, two days after the Campanis remarks, O'Malley announced he had asked for his resignation. "The comments Al made were so removed, so distant from what I believe the organization believes, that it was impossible for Al to continue the responsibilities he had with us," said the Dodger owner. He immediately appointed Fred Claire to assume Campanis's duties. Claire was already second in command in his position as executive vice president.

The uproar created by Campanis brought the teams in all professional sports under close scrutiny. In the 40 years since Jackie Robinson's debut, the only African-Americans to serve as field managers were Frank Robinson, Larry Doby and Maury Wills, and the only general manager was Bill Lucas. None were at those posts at the start of the 1987 season, although 20 percent of the players were black. Partly because of the furor caused by Campanis, baseball stepped up its minority hiring practices.

On the same day, the Dodgers signed Mickey Hatcher, most recently with the Twins, as a free agent and released Jerry Reuss. A utility man who played five positions for the Dodgers, Hatcher previously played in Los Angeles in 1979 and 1980. He became a fan favorite with his unbridled enthusiasm and hustle. A clubhouse comic, Hatcher sometimes sat in the dugout wearing a batting helmet with a propeller attached. Subbing for the injured Kirk Gibson, Hatcher was also a hero of the 1988 post-season with his play both offensively and defensively.

APRIL 11   The Dodgers finally win their first game of the 1987 season with a 5–1 decision over the Giants at Dodger Stadium.

APRIL 19   Mike Marshall hits two homers and drives in five runs during a 9–1 triumph over the Padres in San Diego.

APRIL 21   Mike Marshall hits a three-run homer in the 10th inning to defeat the Giants 11–8 at Candlestick Park. The Dodgers also scored three runs in the ninth to take an 8–7 lead, only to have San Francisco tie the contest in the bottom half. Franklin Stubbs contributed two homers and five runs batted in.

Marshall's homer followed an intentional walk to Pedro Guerrero. As he rounded the bases, Marshall pumped his fists and made a gesture toward Giants manager Roger Craig. Scott Garrelts threw the next pitch at the head of Alex Trevino and both benches emptied. Guerrero and San Francisco's Chris Brown had to be physically restrained during the 15-minute melee. On the way back to the dugout, the Dodgers were showered with debris. About 75 fans were ejected and several were arrested.

APRIL 22   The Dodgers score three runs in the ninth inning to defeat the Giants 5–3 in San Francisco. Alex Trevino put Los Angeles into the lead with a two-run double. Fernando Valenzuela struck out 12 batters in eight innings.

Alejandro Pena missed two starts early in the season when he contracted chicken pox.

MAY 10   The Dodgers defeat the Cardinals 7–6 at Dodger Stadium.

The victory represented the high point of the season. After losing the first five games of 1987, the Dodgers had an 18–14 record on May 10. The club was 12–24 from May 11 through June 21, however, and never reached the .500 level again.

MAY 22   The Dodgers trade Tom Niedenfuer to the Orioles for John Shelby and Brad Havens.

MAY 26   The Dodgers release Bill Madlock.

JUNE 2   In the first round of the amateur draft, the Dodgers select pitcher Dan Opperman from Valley High School in Las Vegas, Nevada.

Opperman was a freshman at Valley High when Greg Maddux was a senior, but all similarities ended there. Opperman never reached the majors. Future major leaguers drafted and signed by the Dodgers in 1987 included Chris Nichting (third round), Darrin Fletcher (sixth), Tony Barron (seventh), Rafael Bournigal (19th), Jose Munoz (20th), Dennis Springer (21st), Zak Shinall (29th) and Mike James (43rd). None would have a significant impact on the fortunes of the Dodger franchise, however.

JUNE 7   The Dodgers score in seven of nine innings, including the first six, and defeat the Reds 13–7 in Cincinnati. Mike Marshall had a huge day with four hits, including two homers, in five at-bats. He drove in five runs and scored four.

JUNE 19   Five days after the Lakers defeat the Celtics to win the NBA championship, Orel Hershiser strikes out 14 batters in 10 innings, but he winds up with a no-decision as the Dodgers lose 3–2 to the Astros in 11 innings in Houston.

On the same day, the Dodgers traded Jeff Edwards to the Astros for Phil Garner.

JUNE 23   A three-run homer by Franklin Stubbs in the second inning accounts for all of the runs in a 3–2 win over the Braves at Dodger Stadium.

JULY 8   The Dodgers lose a double-header for the second day in a row against the Cardinals in St. Louis. Three of the defeats were by one run and two in extra innings. On July 7, the Dodgers lost 5–4 twice, with the second game going 10 innings. On July 8, Los Angeles dropped 6–3 and 8–7 decisions, with the second tilt again taking 10 innings to complete.

JULY 12   The Dodgers clobber the Cubs 12–0 in Chicago. The even dozen runs scored on 11 hits. The Dodgers put the game away with consecutive four-run innings in the fifth and sixth. Bob Welch pitched the shutout.

JULY 14	Orel Hershiser pitches two shutout innings (the fifth and sixth) during the All-Star Game in Oakland, won by the National League 2–0 in 13 innings.
JULY 22	Don McMahon dies of a heart attack while pitching batting practice to the Dodgers prior to a 3–1 loss at Dodger Stadium. At the time, he was an instructional coach and a scout with the club. McMahon was 57 and had heart bypass surgery 3½ years prior to his death. He pitched in the majors with seven clubs from 1957 through 1974.
JULY 27	A walk-off homer by Franklin Stubbs in the 12th inning defeats the Giants 6–5 at Dodger Stadium.
AUGUST 3	Mike Marshall hits a grand slam off Ted Power in the third inning of a 7–2 win over the Reds in Cincinnati.
AUGUST 12	The Dodgers edge the Reds 1–0 at Dodger Stadium. Tim Leary (seven innings), Tim Crews (one inning) and Matt Young (one inning) combined on the shutout. Leary also drove in the lone run of the game with a single in the seventh inning.
AUGUST 14	Left fielder Chris Gwynn collects three hits in four at-bats in his major league debut to help the Dodgers defeat the Giants 4–3 in San Francisco.
AUGUST 19	Trailing 7–1 after three innings, the Dodgers rally to win 10–9 over the Expos in Montreal. Los Angeles took the lead with five runs in the eighth inning. Craig Shipley's two-run single gave the Dodgers the advantage. It was a team effort, as eight different players scored runs and six contributed runs batted in.
AUGUST 25	Fernando Valenzuela fans 13 batters during a 3–1 win over the Mets in New York. He walked eight and threw 160 pitches.
AUGUST 26	The Dodgers use five pitchers in the eighth inning of a 3–2 loss to the Mets in New York. The five were Tim Leary, Rick Honeycutt, Tim Crews, Matt Young and Brian Holton. Young didn't pitch to a complete batter. He left the contest with an injury after throwing three pitches to Keith Hernandez.
AUGUST 29	The Dodgers trade Rick Honeycutt to the Athletics for Tim Belcher.
	The Dodgers lost Honeycutt's last 14 starts prior to the trade. The pitcher was charged with the loss in 11 of them, giving him a record of 2–12. Honeycutt became a successful set-up man for Dennis Eckersley in Oakland and pitched in three World Series. Belcher was an above-average starter with the Dodgers until 1991 and posted a 50–38 record with the club.
SEPTEMBER 2	Mike Marshall and Phil Garner fight before a 6–2 loss to the Phillies at Dodgers Stadium. During batting practice, Garner ordered Marshall to shag balls in the outfield. Marshall, who was 27, stood six-foot-five and weighed 218 pounds, took exception and was soon grappling with Garner, who was 38 years old, five-foot-eight and weighed in at 177 pounds. Garner came out of the scuffle with an inch-long scratch on his cheek and several welts on his face.

SEPTEMBER 6   The Dodgers end a nine-game losing streak by defeating the Mets 3–2 at Dodgers Stadium. New York tied the game with a run in the ninth. Mike Devereaux drove in the winning run with a single. Tim Belcher was the winning pitcher with two innings of scoreless relief in his major league debut. The Dodgers used 24 players. Only pitchers were left on the bench at the conclusion of the contest.

SEPTEMBER 13   The Dodgers score single runs in six different innings (the first, fourth, fifth, sixth, eighth and ninth) to defeat the Braves 6–2 in Atlanta.

SEPTEMBER 16   Pope John Paul II celebrates Mass before 60,000 at Dodger Stadium.

SEPTEMBER 28   The Dodgers announce that Don Drysdale will return to the organization as a broadcaster beginning with the 1988 season. He replaced Jerry Doggett, who retired after 32 seasons. Drysdale previously did games on television and radio for the Expos (1970–71), Rangers (1972), Angels (1973–81) and White Sox (1982–87) as well as ABC-TV (1982–86). He served as a play-by-play man and analyst on Dodgers games until his death in 1993.

OCTOBER 1   Bob Welch pitches a one-hitter to down the Giants 1–0 at Dodger Stadium. Mike Aldrete delivered the only San Francisco hit with a single in the sixth inning. It proved to be Welch's last game with the Dodgers (see December 11, 1987).

OCTOBER 2   Pedro Guerrero sprains his wrist when he tries to save a television set in his home from being smashed during an earthquake in the Los Angeles area.

After missing most of the 1986 season with a knee injury, Guerrero bounced back in 1987 with a .338 batting average and 27 home runs.

OCTOBER 23   Tommy Lasorda is honored by the National Italian-American Foundation in Washington. Vice President George Bush attended the event.

DECEMBER 11   Three weeks after the end of the six-month Congressional hearings investigating the Iran-Contra scandal, the Dodgers participate in a three-team trade, dealing Bob Welch to the Athletics and Matt Young and Jack Savage to the Mets and receiving Alfredo Griffin and Jay Howell from the A's and Jesse Orosco from New York.

Over the next three years, Welch was 61–23 for three World Series teams in Oakland, including a 27–6 record in 1990. Fortunately, the Dodgers received some compensation in the deal. Howell came to the Dodgers as an unheralded 32-year-old reliever with a 4.17 ERA in 434$\frac{1}{3}$ big-league innings. He proved to be a pleasant surprise and was a closer for most of his five years in Los Angeles, in which he had a 2.07 ERA in 308$\frac{1}{3}$ innings with the club. Orosco set a major league record by pitching in 1,252 games, all in relief, with nine teams from 1979 through 2003. He appeared in 55 games with the Dodgers in 1988 and 91 more in 2001 and 2002.

DECEMBER 15   The Dodgers sign Mike Davis, most recently with the Athletics, as a free agent.

Davis had some excellent years in Oakland and was expected to nail down a job as a starting outfielder with the Dodgers. He was an extreme disappointment in Los Angeles, however, and over two seasons he hit just .216 with seven home runs in 454 at-bats.

1988

L A

Season in a Sentence

Following losing seasons in 1986 and 1987, the inspirational leadership of Kirk Gibson and pitching of Orel Hershiser results in an NL West pennant and post-season upsets of the Mets and Athletics to win the world championship.

Finish • Won • Lost • Pct • GB

First   94   67   .584   +7.0

Manager

Tommy Lasorda

National League Championship Series

The Dodgers defeated the New York Mets four games to three.

World Series

The Dodgers defeated the Oakland Athletics four games to one.

Stats

Stats	Dods	NL	Rank
Batting Avg:	.248	.248	6
On-Base Pct:	.305	.310	11
Slugging Pct:	.352	.363	8
Home Runs:	99		8
Stolen Bases:	131		6
ERA:	2.96	3.45	2
Fielding Avg:	.977	.979	10
Runs Scored:	628		7
Runs Allowed:	544		2

Starting Lineup

Mike Scioscia, c
Franklin Stubbs, 1b
Steve Sax, 2b
Jeff Hamilton, 3b
Alfredo Griffin, ss
Kirk Gibson, lf
John Shelby, cf
Mike Marshall, rf
Dave Anderson, ss
Mike Davis, rf
Pedro Guerrero, 3b

Pitchers

Orel Hershiser, sp
Tim Leary, sp
Tim Belcher, sp
Fernando Valenzuela, sp
Don Sutton, sp
Jay Howell, rp
Alejandro Pena, rp
Jesse Orosco, rp
Brian Holton, rp
Tim Crews, rp

Attendance

2,980,262 (second in NL)

Club Leaders

Batting Avg:	Kirk Gibson	.290
On-Base Pct:	Kirk Gibson	.377
Slugging Pct:	Kirk Gibson	.483
Home Runs:	Kirk Gibson	25
RBIs:	Mike Marshall	82
Runs:	Kirk Gibson	106
Stolen Bases:	Steve Sax	42
Wins:	Orel Hershiser	23
Strikeouts:	Tim Leary	180
ERA:	Orel Hershiser	2.26
Saves:	Jay Howell	21

JANUARY 5   The Dodgers sign Don Sutton, most recently with the Angels, as a free agent.

Sutton previously played for the Dodgers from 1966 through 1980. He was 43 years old in 1988 and about finished. After a 3–6 record and a 3.92 ERA in 16 starts, Sutton was released in August.

JANUARY 29   The Dodgers sign Kirk Gibson, most recently with the Tigers, as a free agent.

The signing of Gibson was part of an uncharacteristic spending spree by the Dodgers during the 1987–88 off-season. The club hadn't signed a front-line free agent since being burned by the Dave Goltz and Don Stanhouse deals (see November 14, 1979 and November 17, 1979). Gibson was a Michigan native who was an All-American wide receiver at Michigan State, but he signed to play baseball with the Tigers. Known for his ferocious determination, Gibson played nine seasons in Detroit and was an instrumental figure in Detroit's 1984 world championship season. But he was frequently beset with injuries and, prior to

1988, had played in at least 130 games only twice in his career. The 1988 regular season was relatively injury-free, and he appeared in 150 games for the Dodgers, winning the NL MVP Award with a .290 batting average, 25 homers, 76 RBIs, 31 stolen bases and 106 runs scored. His batting numbers paled in comparison to most outfielders who have won the honor, but Gibson's leadership in the clubhouse was cited by many writers who participated in the voting. A severely pulled hamstring and a strained left knee left Gibson on the bench for much of the post-season, however. He made only one plate appearance during the 1988 World Series against the Athletics, but he won Game One by limping off the bench to hit a pinch-hit, walk-off homer against Dennis Eckersley. A panel of local sports experts later declared Gibson's homer as the greatest moment in Los Angeles sports history. Injuries again weakened Gibson in 1989 and 1990, his last two seasons with the Dodgers. Those two seasons combined, he batted .239 with 17 homers in 568 at-bats, but his golden season of 1988 will never be forgotten.

MARCH 3   Kirk Gibson sets the tone for the 1988 Cinderella season prior to the Dodgers exhibition game against the Chunichi Dragons in Vero Beach. Taking off his hat to wipe sweat from his head during pre-game warm-ups in the outfield, Gibson noticed people laughing. He soon realized that someone had greased the inside of his cap with eye black and he had unknowingly wiped it all over himself. Gibson immediately took off for the clubhouse, ordering Tommy Lasorda to "Find out who did this because I'm going to take his head off." Lasorda tried to smooth things over and culprit Jesse Orosco eventually tried to apologize to no avail. Gibson called his teammates clowns and made it clear he was there to win games and would not participate in any clubhouse frivolity. "I told Tommy Lasorda that I can now understand why the Dodgers finished fifth the last two years." Gibson said. "They have their priorities wrong." His no-nonsense approach eventually rubbed off on the rest of the team.

MARCH 30   The Dodgers sign Rick Dempsey, most recently with the Indians, as a free agent.

APRIL 4   The Dodgers open the 1988 season with a 5–1 loss to the Giants before 48,484 at Dodger Stadium. Steve Sax led off the first inning with a first-pitch homer off Dave Dravecky, but the Dodgers didn't score again. Fernando Valenzuela was the starting and losing pitcher.

Hampered by shoulder problems, Valenzuela was only 5–8 with a 4.24 ERA in 1988. He ended his streak of 255 consecutive starts in July.

APRIL 21   The Dodgers suffer through their third consecutive postponement at Dodger Stadium. All three contests were scheduled against the Padres. The last of the three was only the 15th rainout in the history of the ballpark, which opened in 1962. Six of the 15 were against San Diego.

APRIL 23   Mike Marshall hits a grand slam off Don Robinson in the ninth inning to cap a 10–3 win over the Giants in San Francisco.

MAY 3   The Dodgers pummel the Pirates 14–6 at Dodger Stadium.

MAY 8   The Dodgers score seven runs in the fourth inning and defeat the Cardinals 12–6 in St. Louis.

MAY 10   Kirk Gibson's homer in the 14th inning beats the Cubs 6–5 at Wrigley Field. Chicago scored a run in the ninth to tie the contest.

MAY 15   The Dodgers score seven runs in the fourth inning and win 9–2 over the Phillies at Dodger Stadium.

MAY 21   Playing the Mets at Dodger Stadium, Alfredo Griffin has his hand broken by a pitch from Dwight Gooden in the fifth inning. Howard Johnson was the first New York batter in the sixth and was struck by an offering from Brian Holton in retaliation. The Dodgers lost 4–0. Griffin was out of action for two months.

MAY 22   Tensions from the previous day spill over during a 5–2 loss to the Mets at Dodger Stadium. Pedro Guerrero was hit by a David Cone pitch in the sixth inning. The ball glanced off Guerrero's shoulder and struck him in the head. Guerrero threw his bat with both hands in the direction of Cone. The bat landed near shortstop Kevin Elster. As Guerrero walked toward the mound, he was tackled by catcher Barry Lyons. Both benches emptied, but no punches were thrown. Guerrero was suspended for four days, which most observers believed was far too lenient.

MAY 25   Tim Leary pitches a one-hitter to defeat the Phillies 4–0 at Veterans Stadium. The lone Philadelphia hit was a single by Darren Daulton in the third inning. The Dodger runs scored on two-run homers by Mike Scioscia in the fourth inning and Jeff Hamilton in the seventh.

          After a 3–11 record in 1987, his first year with the Dodgers, Leary was 17–11 with a 2.91 ERA in 1988. It was the only season during his 13-year career in which he won more than 12 games.

MAY 26   The Dodgers score three runs in the ninth inning to defeat the Phillies 10–8 in Philadelphia. The tying run scored on doubles by Kirk Gibson and John Shelby. Pinch-hitter Mickey Hatcher drove in the go-head tally with a single.

          The win put the Dodgers into sole possession of first place. The club remained there for the rest of the season.

MAY 29   The Dodgers defeat the Expos 2–1 in Montreal with solo homers from Kirk Gibson in the fourth inning and John Shelby in the seventh.

JUNE 1   In the first round of the amateur draft, the Dodgers select pitcher Bill Bene from Cal State Los Angeles.

          Bene never reached the majors, but it proved to be a highly successful draft for the Dodgers as the club drafted and signed eight future major leaguers, including Billy Ashley (third round), Eric Karros (sixth), Jim Poole (ninth), Eddie Pye (10th), Jerry Brooks (12th), Brian Traxler (16th), Hector Ortiz (35th) and Mike Piazza (62nd). Over the next few weeks, the Dodgers also signed Pedro Martinez and Raul Mondesi as free agents. Karros was the Dodgers starting first baseman for 11 seasons beginning in 1992. Piazza also arrived in 1992 and proved himself to be the greatest hitting catcher in major league history. He lasted until the 62nd round because almost no one considered him to be a prospect while in high school in Norristown, Pennsylvania, or at Miami-Dade North Community College.

Piazza was selected only as a favor to a family friend. Mike's father, Vince, was a close friend of Tommy Lasorda.

JUNE 3   The Dodgers unleash a 22-hit barrage to upend the Reds 13–7 at Dodger Stadium. Steve Sax and Mickey Hatcher both collected five singles in six at-bats. The Reds used Dave Concepcion to pitch the final 1¹/₃ innings.

JUNE 6   The Dodgers score in six of eight turns at bat and defeat the Astros 11–1 at Dodger Stadium.

JUNE 9   John Shelby extends his hitting streak to 24 games during a 4–2 win over the Astros at Dodger Stadium.

JUNE 19   The Dodgers sweep the Padres 12–2 and 5–4 in 11 innings during a double-header at Dodger Stadium.

JUNE 26   Five days after the Lakers defeat the Pistons in game seven of the NBA finals, the Dodgers score four runs in the ninth inning to beat the Reds 9–6 in Cincinnati. Steve Sax broke the 6–6 tie with a three-run double.

JUNE 29   Orel Hershiser pitches a two-hitter to defeat the Astros 2–0 at the Astrodome. The only Houston hits were singles by Craig Biggio in the third inning and Mickey Hatcher in the fifth. Mike Marshall drove in both Los Angeles runs off Nolan Ryan. Marshall was hit by a pitch with the bases loaded in the third inning and singled in the eighth.

JULY 6   Trailing 3–0, the Dodgers erupt for seven runs in the eighth inning to defeat the Cardinals 7–3 at Dodger Stadium. Franklin Stubbs broke the 3–3 tie with a grand slam off Todd Worrell.

JULY 12   Orel Hershiser pitches a perfect eighth inning in the All-Star Game, but the National League loses 2–1 at Riverfront Stadium in Cincinnati.

JULY 14   The Dodgers sweep the Cubs 1–0 and 6–3 in Chicago. Tim Leary not only pitched seven innings in the opener, but he drove in the lone run with a single in the second inning. Alejandro Pena pitched the final two innings.

JULY 18   Tim Leary pitches his second consecutive 1–0 victory, beating the Cardinals in St. Louis. The lone run of the game scored on a home run by Mike Marshall in the ninth inning off Todd Worrell.

Orel Hershiser dominated hitters in 1988, winning the Cy Young Award with a 23–8 record and winning two games in the World Series.

JULY 26 — The Dodgers take a seven-game lead with 7–3 and 6–5 wins against the Giants during a double-header in San Francisco. The second contest went 11 innings. The winning run scored when Scott Garrelts balked in John Shelby from third base.

JULY 30 — Outfielder Danny Heep pitches the eighth and ninth innings of a 14–6 loss to the Astros at Dodger Stadium. Heep allowed two runs and two hits in the two innings.

AUGUST 2 — In the first inning, Kirk Gibson doubles in a run and scores on Pedro Guerrero's single for the only two runs of a 2–0 victory over the Reds at Dodger Stadium. Tim Leary pitched the shutout.

AUGUST 9 — The Dodgers lead over the second-place Astros shrinks to one-half game with a 6–0 loss to the Reds in Cincinnati.

The Dodgers lost 6¹/₂ games off their lead in a span of 14 days. The club won 10 of its next 12 to right the ship.

AUGUST 10 — The Dodgers release Don Sutton, ending his playing career after 23 seasons in the majors.

AUGUST 13 — The Dodgers win a dramatic 2–1 decision over the Giants at Dodger Stadium. With the score 1–1, Pedro Guerrero started off the 11th inning with a fly ball that outfielder Candy Maldonado lost in the lights. A passed ball moved Guerrero to second. But both Tommy Lasorda and Guerrero were ejected after arguing that Joe Price should be charged with a balk. Because of this, Franklin Stubbs had to pinch-run for Guerrero, leaving Los Angeles with no position players on the bench. Pitcher Tim Leary pinch-hit for Alejandro Pena and delivered a walk-off single for the victory.

Beginning in 1988, Tommy Lasorda appeared in televisions ads for the Slim Fast diet shakes with the slogan "If I can do it, you can do it." The ads ran for years.

AUGUST 15 — The Dodgers edge the Giants 1–0 at Dodger Stadium. The lone run scored on a sacrifice fly by Franklin Stubbs in the fourth inning. Tim Belcher (7¹/₃ innings) and Jesse Orosco (1²/₃ innings) combined on the shutout.

AUGUST 16 — The Dodgers trade Pedro Guerrero for John Tudor.

Guerrero had played in only 59 games in 1988 prior to the trade because of a pinched nerve in his neck. Tudor was 6–5, but his 2.29 ERA was leading the National League. He was 4–3 with a 2.41 earned run average down the stretch of the 1988 pennant race, but injuries limited him to six games as a Dodger afterward. Guerrero gave the Cardinals an All-Star season in 1989, but he then went into a rapid decline before his career ended in 1992.

AUGUST 19 — Mike Marshall hits a two-run homer off Dennis Martinez in the fourth inning to account for the only runs of a 2–0 win over the Expos at Dodger Stadium.

AUGUST 20 — Kirk Gibson scores from second base on a wild pitch by Joe Hesketh in the ninth inning to beat the Expos 4–3 at Dodger Stadium. Los Angeles trailed 3–2 heading into the ninth. Gibson drove in the tying run with a single, and then stole second with two out before his spectacular dash to the plate with the winning run. Gibson later admitted that he knew Hesketh was recovering from a broken leg and wouldn't be aggressive in covering the plate.

AUGUST 21   Tim Leary strikes out 12 batters during a 4–0 win over the Expos at Dodger Stadium.

AUGUST 27   Tommy Lasorda wins his 1,000th game as manager with a 4–2 decision over the Phillies in Philadelphia and fights the Phillie Phanatic.

After the Phillie Phanatic stomped numerous times on a stuffed doll dressed in a Dodger uniform with the name "Lasorda" on the back, the Dodger manager wrestled it away from the mascot. The 60-year-old Lasorda then hit the Phanatic in the face with the doll, pinned him to the ground, and threw a few punches. "What he did wasn't entertainment," explained Lasorda. "I love the Dodgers and it wasn't right for him to stomp on the doll with the uniform. There's a lot of kids there, and he's showing them violence. He didn't need to do that."

AUGUST 30   Orel Hershiser beats the Expos 4–2 in Montreal. He didn't allow a run over the last four innings, which started his record-breaking streak of 59 consecutive scoreless innings.

SEPTEMBER 5   Orel Hershiser pitches a four-hit shutout to defeat the Braves 3–0 in Atlanta.

SEPTEMBER 10   Orel Hershiser twirls his second consecutive shutout, defeating the Reds 5–0 at Dodger Stadium on seven hits.

The win gave the Dodgers a five-game lead with 22 contests remaining. The club was never seriously challenged for the NL West crown again.

SEPTEMBER 11   A three-run, walk-off homer by Jeff Hamilton off John Franco in the ninth inning beats the Reds 5–3 at Dodger Stadium.

SEPTEMBER 13   John Tudor (five innings), Ramon Martinez (two innings) and Ken Howell (two innings) combine on a two-hitter to defeat the Braves 2–0 at Dodger Stadium. The only Atlanta hits were singles by Ron Gant in the first inning and Andres Thomas in the fourth. Mike Scioscia's two-run homer off John Smoltz in the fifth inning accounted for the only runs of the game.

SEPTEMBER 14   Orel Hershiser pitches his third consecutive shutout, defeating the Braves 1–0 at Dodger Stadium. The lone run scored on a walk-off double by Mike Marshall in the ninth inning.

SEPTEMBER 16   Tom Browning of the Reds pitches a perfect game to defeat the Dodgers 1–0 at Riverfront Stadium. The game didn't start until 10:02 p.m. Cincinnati time because of a two hour and 27 minute rain delay. Browning threw 102 pitches and fanned seven. In the ninth inning, he retired Rick Dempsey on a deep fly ball to the warning track to right fielder Paul O'Neill. Steve Sax hit a first-pitch grounder to shortstop Barry Larkin, and Browning completed the masterpiece by fanning pinch-hitter Tracy Woodson. Dodger hurler Tim Belcher allowed only three hits and carried a no-hitter into the sixth inning. The only run of the game scored in the sixth on Belcher's throwing error.

Combined with his previous start against the Dodgers on September 11 at Dodger Stadium, Browning retired 38 Los Angeles batters in a row.

SEPTEMBER 19   Orel Hershiser pitches his fourth consecutive shutout for his second straight 1–0 win, defeating the Astros in Houston. The lone run scored in the seventh inning on a home run by John Shelby off Danny Darwin. The victory came three days after Hershiser's wife, Jamie, gave birth to a daughter the couple named Jordan.

SEPTEMBER 20   Tim Belcher pitches the Dodgers third consecutive shutout, downing the Astros 6–0 in Houston.

SEPTEMBER 23   Orel Hershiser pitches his fifth consecutive shutout in defeating the Giants 3–0 at Candlestick Park. The five shutouts put him one short of Don Drysdale's six in a row in 1968. Hershiser also extended his streak of scoreless innings to 49, nine shy of Drysdale's 58 that same season. It was also Orel's 23rd win of the season. The streak nearly ended in the third inning. With men on first and third and one out, Ernest Riles hit a double-play ball, but shortstop Alfredo Griffin's throw went wild and Jose Uribe crossed the plate. But umpire Paul Runge ruled that Brett Butler had slid out of the baseline and gave the Dodgers the double play, wiping the run off the board. Mickey Hatcher accounted for all three runs with a home run in the eighth inning off Atlee Hammaker. It was Hatcher's only homer of the regular season.

SEPTEMBER 26   The Dodgers clinch the NL West pennant with a 3–2 win over the Padres in San Diego.

The unexpected NL West title couldn't have been won without the contributions of a group of utility players known collectively as "The Stunt Men" for their ability to fill multiple position and roles. The key contributors off the bench were Mickey Hatcher, Dave Anderson, Tracy Woodson, Rick Dempsey, Danny Heep and Mike Sharperson.

SEPTEMBER 28   Squaring off against the Padres in San Diego in his last start of the regular season, Orel Hershiser breaks the all-time record for consecutive scoreless innings by extending his streak to 59, but he fails to achieve a record-tying sixth consecutive shutout when his teammates fail to score. Hershiser came into the contest with 49 scoreless innings, nine short of Don Drysdale's 58 in 1968. Drysdale was in the Dodger broadcast booth. At the end of nine innings, the score was 0–0 and Hershiser tied the consecutive innings mark. He had thrown just 98 pitches, but he asked to leave the game. Hershiser wanted to break the record in Los Angeles in a brief relief appearance or just leave the record tied. Tommy Lasorda wouldn't hear of it and ordered Hershiser to pitch the 10th. In that inning, runners were on first and third when Hershiser retired Keith Moreland on a fly ball to right field for the third out. The Dodgers pitcher allowed only four hits. Hershiser left the game at that point. At the end of 15 innings, the score was still 0–0. The Dodgers scored in the top of the 16th, but the Padres won the game in the bottom half on a two-run, walk-off homer by Mark Parent off Ricky Horton, who had just come into the game in relief of Ken Howell.

During the 59-inning scoreless streak, Hershiser allowed 31 hits and walked 11 while striking out 38. He won the Cy Young Award by leading the NL in wins (with a 23–8 record), complete games (15), shutouts (eight) and innings pitched (267). Hershiser's ERA was 2.26. He carried the streak into the NLCS against the New York Mets. Managed by Davey Johnson, the Mets were 100–60 in 1988. The Dodgers were 1–10 against the Mets during the regular season.

OCTOBER 4   The Mets score three runs in the ninth inning to defeat the Dodgers 3–2 in game one of the NLCS before 55,582 at Dodger Stadium. Orel Hershiser was the Dodger starter, coming into the game without allowing a run over his last 59 regular season innings. He continued his mastery by shutting down the Mets over the first eight innings. Los Angeles held a 2–0 lead with single runs in the first and seventh off Dwight Gooden. Gregg Jefferies led off the New York ninth with a single to center and went to second on a ground out. Darryl Strawberry doubled in Jefferies ending Hershiser's scoreless streak at 67 innings. Jay Howell replaced Hershiser, and after a walk and a strikeout, Gary Carter lifted an 0–2 pitch into center field where John Shelby dived but could not make the catch. Strawberry scored easily on the play and Kevin McReynolds tallied the winning run when he collided with Mike Scioscia on a close play at the plate.

Post-season statistics don't count in the record books, so Hershiser's record of consecutive scoreless innings is still listed at 59. Mets pitcher David Cone enraged the Dodgers for comments he made in a column he wrote in the New York Daily News. *Cone said that Howell reminded him of a "high school pitcher" and that Hershiser was lucky to shut out the Mets for eight innings. Cone was the starter in game two and was riding an* eight-game winning streak.

OCTOBER 5   The Dodgers even the NLCS by beating the Mets 6–3 before 55,780 at Dodger Stadium. Los Angeles hitters made quick work of David Cone with a run in the first inning and four in the second. "We wanted to make sure that Cone had time to meet his deadlines," scoffed Steve Sax. Mike Marshall was the batting leader with three hits. Tim Belcher struck out 10 batters.

Game two was moved from 12:07 p.m. Los Angeles time to 7:08 p.m. so as not to conflict with the vice presidential debate between Lloyd Bentsen and Dan Quayle. The following day Cone apologized to Howell for his remarks and wrote no more newspaper columns.

OCTOBER 7   Game three is postponed by a heavy rainfall in New York City.

OCTOBER 8   Jay Howell is ejected for using pine tar and the Dodgers lose game three 8–4 to the Mets at Shea Stadium. Howell came into the contest in relief of Orel Hershiser with the Dodgers leading 4–3 in the eighth. The Mets complained to umpire Joe West that Howell had a foreign substance on his glove. Crew chief Harry Wendelstedt checked the glove and ejected Howell. Three Dodger relievers combined to allow five runs, resulting in the Los Angeles defeat.

National League President Bart Giamatti suspended Howell for three games.

OCTOBER 9   On the brink of trailing the NLCS three games to one, the Dodgers stage a comeback by scoring two runs in the ninth inning and one in the 12th to win 5–4 over the Mets in New York. Trailing 4–2, Mike Scioscia hit a two-run homer in the ninth off Dwight Gooden to tie the game at 4–4. Kirk Gibson belted a solo home run in the 12th facing Roger McDowell for the victory. After pitching seven innings the day before, Orel Hershiser was the seventh Dodger hurler and recorded the final out in the New York 12th to earn a save.

Hershiser had only five regular-season saves during his career: one in 1983, two in 1984 and one in 1988.

OCTOBER 10   The Dodgers move within one win of a World Series berth by defeating the Mets 7–4 in New York. The Dodgers scored three runs in the fourth for a 3–0 advantage. Kirk Gibson gave the Dodgers a 6–0 lead with a three-run homer in the fifth. Tim Belcher was the winning pitcher.

OCTOBER 11   The Mets even the NLCS by defeating the Dodgers 5–1 before 55.885 at Dodger Stadium. Booed heavily by the crowd for his controversial comments in the newspaper after game one, David Cone walked the first two batters to face him, then settled down and pitched a complete-game five-hitter.

OCTOBER 12   The Dodgers win the National League pennant with a 6–0 triumph over the Mets before 55,693 at Dodger Stadium. Orel Hershiser continued his remarkable streak of pitching with a five-hit shutout. Los Angeles pummeled Ron Darling with a run in the first inning and five in the second. Steve Sax led the attack with three hits.

The Dodgers met the Oakland Athletics in the World Series. Managed by Tony LaRussa, the A's came into the Series heavily favored following a 104–58 record during the regular season. It was Oakland's first World Series appearance since 1974, when they defeated the Dodgers.

OCTOBER 15   In one of the most dramatic moments in World Series history, the Dodgers take Game One with a 5–4 win over the Athletics on a pinch-hit home run in the ninth inning by Kirk Gibson, who was sidelined by a leg injury. Mickey Hatcher started in left field in place of Gibson and started the scoring with a two-run homer in the first off Dave Stewart. During the regular season, Hatcher hit only one homer in 191 at-bats. The A's countered with four runs in the second on a grand slam by Jose Canseco off Tim Belcher. The Dodgers plated a run in the sixth to make the score 4–3. Dennis Eckersley replaced Stewart and started the ninth. Tommy Lasorda sent Mike Davis up to pinch-hit for Alfredo Griffin. Davis drew a walk. Gibson had been taking swings in the batting cage under the stands and let Lasorda know he would be available to pinch-hit in an emergency. The prospects weren't encouraging. Gibson was in obvious pain, hobbling from the dugout to the plate, and was swinging with only one leg firmly planted. He was facing one of the best relievers in baseball history. Gibson had 58 career pinch-hits with 11 hits and no homers up to that point. Wincing in pain with each swing, Gibson fouled off four pitches, three with two strikes, before sending a breaking ball over the right-field fence. In an image worthy of a Hollywood feature, Gibson limped and grimaced around the bases while pumping his fist in triumph.

Gibson never played in another post-season game over the rest of the career, which ended in 1995. Hatcher continued his stellar play throughout the remainder of the 1988 Series with seven hits, two of them homers, in 19 at-bats. He also made two spectacular defensive plays in the outfield.

OCTOBER 16   Orel Hershiser pitches a three-hitter to defeat the Athletics 6–0 in Game Two before 56,051 at Dodger Stadium. Hershiser also collected three hits, two of them doubles, in three at-bats. Mike Marshall belted a three-run homer in the third inning.

Hershiser was the first pitcher to collect three hits in a game since 1924. Orel is also the only individual to pitch a shutout and gather three hits in a World Series game.

OCTOBER 18   The Athletics defeat the Dodgers 2–1 in Oakland on a walk-off home run in the ninth by Mark McGwire off Jay Howell. It was Howell's first appearance in the post-season since being ejected from game three of the NLCS. John Tudor started for the Dodgers but left after 1⅓ innings due to an injury.

The Dodgers held Jose Canseco and Mark McGwire to a combined two hits in 36 at-bats during the 1988 Fall Classic.

OCTOBER 19   The Dodgers move within one victory of the world championship with a 4–3 win over the Athletics in Oakland. The Dodgers scored twice in the first inning and maintained the lead throughout the game, although victory was never secure until the final out. Jay Howell relieved Tim Belcher, who was celebrating his 27th birthday, with two out in the seventh, the bases loaded and Los Angeles still clinging to a 4–3 lead. Howell induced Mark McGwire to pop up, then pitched shutout ball in the eighth and ninth.

In addition to losing Gibson, Mike Marshall failed to start Game Four because of an injury. NBC's Bob Costas proclaimed the Los Angeles starting lineup in Game Four to be probably the weakest ever to appear in a World Series game. The Dodgers watched the pre-game show in their clubhouse and angrily chanted: "Kill Costas! Kill Costas!"

OCTOBER 20   The Dodgers win an improbable world championship with a 5–2 victory over the Athletics in Oakland. Orel Hershiser pitched a four-hit complete game. The Dodgers bolted into the lead with two runs in the first inning on a home run by Mickey Hatcher. Unused to home run trots, Hatcher sprinted around the bases. Mike Davis, who batted only .196 with two homers during the regular season, hit a two-run homer in the fourth on a 3–0 pitch. Hershiser recorded the final out by striking out Tony Phillips.

In his final 101⅔ innings of 1988, including the post-season, Hershiser allowed only five earned runs for an ERA of 0.44.

NOVEMBER 23   Two weeks after George Bush defeats Michael Dukakis in the presidential election, Steve Sax signs with the Yankees as a free agent.

DECEMBER 3   Jesse Orosco signs with the Indians as a free agent.

DECEMBER 4   The Dodgers trade Ken Howell, Brian Holton and Juan Bell to the Orioles for Eddie Murray.

A future Hall of Famer who closed his career in 1997 with 504 home runs and 3,255 hits, Murray was a Los Angeles native who played in seven All-Star

Games with the Orioles. He gave his hometown Dodgers one great season in three by hitting .330 in 1990.

DECEMBER 10   The Dodgers sign Willie Randolph, most recently with the Yankees, as a free agent.

The signings of Sax (see November 23, 1988) and Randolph were essentially a trade of second baseman between the Dodgers and Yankees. Both were All-Stars in 1989, but they contributed little to their new clubs afterward.

1989

Season in a Sentence

The Dodgers allow the fewest runs in the majors, but a punch-less offense also scores the fewest runs, and the memorable world championship season is followed with a forgettable 77–83 record.

Finish • Won • Lost • Pct • GB

Fourth   77   83   .481   14.0

Manager

Tommy Lasorda

Stats

Stats	Dods	NL	Rank
Batting Avg:	.240	.246	11
On-Base Pct:	.306	.312	12
Slugging Pct:	.339	.365	12
Home Runs:	89		11
Stolen Bases:	81		12
ERA:	2.95	3.50	1
Fielding Avg:	.981	.978	3
Runs Scored:	554		12
Runs Allowed:	536		12

Starting Lineup

Mike Scioscia, c
Eddie Murray, 1b
Willie Randolph, 2b
Jeff Hamilton, 3b
Alfredo Griffin, ss
Kirk Gibson, lf
John Shelby, cf
Mike Marshall, rf
Jose Gonzalez, cf-rf
Mickey Hatcher, lf

Pitchers

Orel Hershiser, sp
Tim Belcher, sp
Fernando Valenzuela, sp
Tim Leary, sp
Ramon Martinez, sp
Jay Howell, rp
Alejandro Pena, rp
Tim Crews, rp
Ray Searage, rp
Mike Morgan, rp-sp
John Wetteland, rp-sp

Attendance

2,944,653 (second in NL)

Club Leaders

Batting Avg:	Willie Randolph	.282
On-Base Pct:	Willie Randolph	.366
Slugging Pct:	Eddie Murray	.401
Home Runs:	Eddie Murray	20
RBIs:	Eddie Murray	88
Runs:	Eddie Murray	66
Stolen Bases:	Kirk Gibson	12
Wins:	Orel Hershiser	15
	Tim Belcher	15
Strikeouts:	Tim Belcher	200
ERA:	Orel Hershiser	2.31
Saves:	Jay Howell	28

MARCH 12   The Dodgers trade Mike Devereaux to the Orioles for Mike Morgan.

Morgan came to the Dodgers as a 29-year-old with a lifetime record of 34–68. He was 33–36 in three seasons in Los Angeles. The Dodgers were the sixth of 12 teams that Morgan played for during his major league career, which began in 1978 and ended in 2002. He also appeared in games with the Athletics, Yankees, Blue Jays, Mariners, Orioles, Cubs, Cardinals, Reds, Twins, Rangers and Diamondbacks.

APRIL 3
Ten days after the Exxon Valdez spills oil into Alaska's Prince William Sound, the defending world champion Dodgers open the 1989 season with a 6–4 loss to the Reds in Cincinnati. Kirk Gibson, in his first plate appearance since his dramatic game-winning home run in Game One of the 1988 World Series, hit a two-run homer in the first inning. Tim Belcher started in place of Orel Hershiser, who was suffering from the flu, but Belcher allowed six runs in 2^1/$_3$ innings.

Suffering through knee and hamstring problems, Gibson batted only .213 in 71 games and 253 at-bats in 1989. He went on the disabled list on July 23 and underwent season-ending knee surgery in August.

APRIL 5
In his first appearance of the season, Orel Hershiser allows a run in the first inning of a 4–3 loss to the Reds on a chilly night in Cincinnati, ending his regular season streak of scoreless innings at 59 dating back to August 30, 1988. The run scored on a two-out, RBI-single by Todd Benzinger. The run was set up by Hershiser's throwing error on a wild pick-off attempt at first base. He ended the contest allowing four runs, two earned, in seven innings. Tom Browning was the winning pitcher in his first game against the Dodgers since his perfect game on September 16, 1988.

Hershiser's ERA rose only slightly from 2.26 in 1988 to 2.31 in 1989, but due to a lack of offensive support, his won-lost record fell from 23–8 to 15–15. Hershiser pitched 256^2/$_3$ innings in 1989, which marked the third consecutive season he led the NL in that category.

APRIL 10
Trailing 3–2, the Dodgers score five runs in the ninth inning and defeat the Giants 7–4 in San Francisco. Eddie Murray capped the rally with a grand slam off Mike LaCoss. It was Murray's first homer as a Dodger.

APRIL 13
The Dodgers lose their home opener 4–2 in 15 innings to the Astros before 47,136 at Dodger Stadium.

MAY 1
The Dodgers down the Pirates 1–0 at Dodger Stadium on a pinch-hit, walk-off, bases-loaded sacrifice fly by Mickey Hatcher in the ninth inning. Mike Morgan (eight innings) and Jay Howell (one inning) combined on the shutout.

MAY 4
Mickey Hatcher pitches the eighth inning of a 12–0 loss to the Cardinals at Dodger Stadium. Hatcher didn't allow a hit, but he walked three and surrendered a run.

MAY 14
Orel Hershiser pitches a two-hitter to defeat the Phillies 9–0 at Veterans Stadium. The only Philadelphia hits were a single by Ricky Jordan in the first inning and a double from Steve Jeltz in the eighth. Eddie Murray contributed two homers and five runs batted in.

MAY 17
An unorthodox move by New York manager Davey Johnson helps the Dodgers defeat the Mets 4–3 in 10 innings at Shea Stadium. With two out in the 10th, Johnson ordered an intentional walk to Eddie Murray with runners on first and third. Rick Aguilera then proceeded to walk Rick Dempsey to force in the winning run.

MAY 19
Jeff Hamilton hits a grand slam off Kevin Gross in the seventh inning of an 8–0 win over the Expos in Montreal.

MAY 25   The Dodgers score seven runs in the first inning for a 7–0 lead, then hold on to beat the Phillies 7–6 at Dodger Stadium. The big blow was a three-run double by Eddie Murray.

MAY 28   Dave Anderson scores from third base in the 12th inning on a balk by Roger McDowell to provide the winning run of a 4–3 victory over the Mets at Dodger Stadium.

MAY 31   Trailing 3–1, the Dodgers score seven runs in the seventh inning and beat the Expos 9–4 at Dodger Stadium.

A brawl erupted in the seventh inning. The sparking point was a fastball by Montreal pitcher Pascual Perez that struck Mike Scioscia in the helmet. Scioscia flipped his bat away and headed straight for the mound, but was cut off by Expo third baseman Tim Wallach. Kirk Gibson tried repeatedly to get at Perez, but he was wrestled to the ground by three Montreal players.

JUNE 3   The Dodgers lose a 22-inning marathon to the Astros 5–4 at the Astrodome. The Dodgers held a 4–1 lead before Houston scored three times in the sixth off Tim Leary and Ricky Horton. There was no scoring by either team from the seventh through the 21st. While the score was tied 4–4, the Dodgers threw out two Houston runners at the plate. For Los Angeles, Tim Crews and John Wetteland pitched the seventh, Jay Howell the eighth and ninth, and Alejandro Pena the 10th and 11th. Mike Morgan, two days after making a start, hurled the 12th and 13th. Orel Hershiser, three days after a starting assignment, entered the fray in the 14th and pitched seven shutout innings without allowing a run. After Hershiser went as far as he could, Tommy Lasorda had to resort to some ingenuity. The only two players left on the bench were pitchers Fernando Valenzuela and Tim Belcher. Valenzuela started the previous day, and Belcher was the scheduled starter the following day. Lasorda moved Jeff Hamilton from third base to the mound, Valenzuela to first base and Eddie Murray from first base to third. It was the only time Hamilton ever pitched, Valenzuela's initial appearance at first and Murray's first game at third since 1978. Hamilton retired the Astros in order in the 21st, but in the 22nd, he gave up a single, a walk and a two-out, game-winning single by Rafael Ramirez that glanced off the glove of Valenzuela at first. John Shelby, in the midst of a season in which he hit .183 in 345 at-bats, went 0-for-10 during the long night. The game lasted seven hours and 14 minutes and ended at 2:50 a.m. Houston time.

JUNE 4   The Dodgers lose another long game against the Astros at Houston, dropping a 7–6 decision in 13 innings. Mike Scioscia hit a grand slam in the first inning and the Dodgers led 6–0 in the fifth inning, but they couldn't hold the advantage. The winning run scored on a sacrifice fly by pitcher Mike Scott. The contest started at 1:35 p.m. Houston time, less than 11 hours after the end of the previous night's marathon. In a little more than 22 hours, the Dodgers played 35 innings involving 11 hours and 31 minutes of playing time, but they lost twice.

JUNE 5   With three picks in the first round of the amateur draft, the Dodgers select pitcher Kiki Jones from Hillsborough High School in Tampa, Florida, outfielder Tom Goodwin from Fresno State University and pitcher Jamie McAndrew from the University of Florida.

Jones never reached the majors. Goodwin spent 14 seasons in the big leagues, mostly as a run-of-the-mill spare outfielder. McAndrew's career at baseball's highest level lasted only 15 games. Other future major leaguers drafted and signed by the Dodgers in 1989 were Matt Howard (34th round), Eric Young (43rd) and Garey Ingram (44th). Despite his late-round status, Young proved to be the best of the bunch. He had a 15-year career and played for the Dodgers in 1992 and again from 1997 through 1999.

JUNE 14   Kirk Gibson drives in all three runs of a 3–0 win over the Astros at Dodger Stadium with a bases-loaded ground ball in the fifth inning and a two-run homer in the seventh off Bob Knepper. Orel Hershiser pitched the shutout.

JUNE 15   Mariano Duncan hits a walk-off single in the 11th inning to beat the Astros 2–1 at Dodger Stadium.

The victory represented the high point of the season as the Dodgers attained a record of 33–31. The club wouldn't rise above the .500 level after June 27, however.

JULY 1   A walk-off single by Jose Gonzalez in the ninth inning beats the Pirates 1–0 at Dodger Stadium. Tim Leary (eight innings) and Tim Belcher (one inning) combined on the shutout.

Belcher had an unusual season in 1989. He started his first 15 games, then after a few bad starts in a row, he made nine relief appearances before making 15 more starts in succession. He pitched 10 complete games, and eight of them were shutouts. Counting the July 1 game, he was the winning pitcher in nine Los Angeles shutouts. Belcher finished the year with a 15–12 record and a 2.82 ERA in 230 innings. His 200 strikeouts were one shy of league leader Jose DeLeon.

JULY 11   Tommy Lasorda manages the National League to a 5–3 loss in the All-Star Game in Anaheim.

JULY 18   The Dodgers trade Tim Leary and Mariano Duncan to the Reds for Kal Daniels and Lenny Harris.

Daniels came to the Dodgers at the age of 25 with a .301 lifetime batting average, .406 on-base percentage and .524 slugging percentage, but also with severe knee problems. He played in only 11 games in 1988 with the Dodgers before undergoing surgery. Daniels recovered in 1990 to hit .296 with 27 home runs for the Dodgers but missed 32 games due to injuries. Daniels faded rapidly afterward, and he played in his last big-league game in 1992. He had six knee operations during his seven-year career, in addition to being treated for an irregular heartbeat and a collapsed lung after hitting the wall at Candlestick Park while chasing a fly ball.

JULY 27   A three-run homer by Eddie Murray in the ninth inning defeats the Astros 7–5 in Houston. The Dodgers trailed 5–1 after six innings before mounting the comeback.

AUGUST 8   Mike Scioscia hits a grand slam off John Smoltz in the second inning of a 10–2 win over the Braves at Dodger Stadium.

AUGUST 12   Fernando Valenzuela pitches a two-hitter to defeat the Giants 5–1 at Candlestick Park. The only San Francisco hits were a single by Kurt Manwaring in the fifth inning and a double from Matt Williams in the sixth.

AUGUST 20   Trailing 3–1, the Dodgers score four runs in the ninth inning and defeat the Mets 5–4 in New York. A three-run homer by Willie Randolph gave the Dodgers a 4–3 advantage. It was the first of only two homers that Randolph hit in 1989. Los Angeles added an insurance run on a double by Mike Marshall and a single from Jeff Hamilton. It was necessary when the Mets scored in the bottom of the ninth.

AUGUST 23   On the day before Pete Rose is banned from baseball for life for gambling activities, Rick Dempsey hits a home run in the 22nd inning to defeat the Expos 1–0 in Montreal. Dempsey's home run is the latest in major league history to settle a 1–0 contest. The only longer 1–0 game in history was a 24-inning affair in which the Astros defeated the Mets on April 15, 1968. The Dodgers-Expos clash at Olympic Stadium lasted six hours and 14 minutes. The Los Angeles pitchers who twirled the 22-inning shutout were Orel Hershiser (seven innings), Jay Howell (two innings), Alejandro Pena (four innings), Tim Crews (three innings) and John Wetteland (six innings). The five combined allowed 13 hits, walked six and struck out 18. The game almost ended in the 16th when Larry Walker appeared to score on a sacrifice fly. The Dodgers appealed, claiming Walker left third base too soon, and umpire Bob Davidson concurred. Dempsey's homer was the 20th Los Angeles hit, but only the second for extra bases. It was struck leading off the 22nd against Dennis Martinez, who was making his only relief appearance between 1986 and 1993. The marathon ended when Rex Hudler was caught attempting to steal second base. Dodger second baseman Lenny Harris collected five hits in nine at-bats. The 1989 Dodgers are the only team in baseball history to play at least two contests of 21 innings or more in the same season (see June 3, 1989).

After complaints by Tommy Lasorda, Youppi!, the Montreal mascot, was ejected by the umpires in the 11th inning for dancing on top of the Dodger dugout. Youppi! was permitted to return if confined to the Expos dugout. The mascot put on pajamas in the 13th and pretended to go to sleep on the roof of the dugout.

SEPTEMBER 6   Facing the first batter of his major league career, Mike Munoz allows a home run to Jeff Richardson in the eighth inning of a 9–5 loss to the Reds in Cincinnati.

SEPTEMBER 10   The Dodgers score in five of the first six innings and rout the Padres 14–8 in San Diego. It was the only time all year that the Dodgers scored more than 10 runs in a game.

The Dodgers were last in the NL in runs scored (554) while leading the circuit in runners left on base (1,171).

SEPTEMBER 12   A two-run, walk-off double by Mike Marshall in the ninth inning beats the Reds 5–4 at Dodger Stadium.

SEPTEMBER 15   Ramon Martinez strikes out 12 batters during a 5–0 triumph over the Braves at Dodger Stadium.

SEPTEMBER 16   A run in the ninth inning beats the Braves 1–0 at Dodger Stadium. Lenny Harris led off with a pinch-hit double and went to third on a ground out. Two intentional walks were followed by an unintentional walk by Mike Stanton to Mike Sharperson on four pitches. Tim Belcher pitched a three-hit shutout.

SEPTEMBER 20   The Giants score five runs in the ninth inning to stun the Dodgers 8–7 in San Francisco. Jay Howell, Mike Hartley and John Tudor allowed seven consecutive hits, including a homer and two doubles, without retiring a batter.

SEPTEMBER 27   Tim Belcher shuts out the Giants and fans 11 for a 1–0 win over the Giants at Dodger Stadium. It was his eighth shutout of the season.

Belcher had surgery the following day to remove a bone spur and cartilage chips from his pitching hand.

NOVEMBER 28   Six weeks after the San Francisco Bay area earthquake, which interrupts the World Series, Dave Anderson signs with the Giants as a free agent.

DECEMBER 7   The Dodgers sign Jim Gott, most recently with the Pirates, as a free agent.

DECEMBER 20   The Dodgers trade Mike Marshall and Alejandro Pena to the Mets for Juan Samuel.

DECEMBER 21   The Dodgers sign Hubie Brooks, most recently with the Expos, as a free agent.

THE STATE OF THE DODGERS

The Dodgers failed to reach the World Series for the first time in any decade since the 1930s. The franchise reached the post-season as a division champion in 1995 and as a wild card in 1996, but were swept in the Division Series each time. Overall, the Dodgers were 797–757, a winning percentage of .513 which ranked fourth in the National League behind the Braves, Astros and Reds. National League pennant winners were the Reds (1990), Braves (1991, 1992, 1993, 1995, 1996 and 1999), Marlins (1997) and Padres (1998). NL West title holders outside of Los Angeles were the Reds (1990), Braves (1991, 1992 and 1993), Padres (1996 and 1998), Giants (1997) and Diamondbacks (1999).

THE BEST TEAM

The best team was the 1991 edition, which compiled a record of 93–69 and finished second in the NL West, one game behind the Braves.

THE WORST TEAM

The worst team was the 1992 Dodgers, who finished 63–99. The 99 defeats are the most of any club in franchise history from 1908 to the present. The .389 winning percentage is the lowest since 1912. The dismal year also marked the only time since 1905 that the Dodgers had the worst record in the National League.

THE BEST MOMENT

Fernandomania had all but faded by 1990, but Fernando Valenzuela revived those memories with a no-hitter against the Cardinals at Dodger Stadium on June 29, 1990.

THE WORST MOMENT

In a span of eight days in June and July of 1993, Dodger greats Roy Campanella and Don Drysdale both died. The passing of Campanella and Drysdale came three months after ex-Dodger Tim Crews was killed in a boating accident.

THE ALL-DECADE TEAM • YEARS W/DODS

Mike Piazza, c	1992–98
Eric Karros, 1b	1991–2002
Delino DeShields, 2b	1994–96
Tim Wallach, 3b	1993–96
Jose Offerman, ss	1990–95
Todd Hollandsworth, lf	1995–2000
Brett Butler, cf	1991–97
Raul Mondesi, rf	1993–99
Ramon Martinez, p	1988–98
Hideo Nomo, p	1995–98, 2002–04
Chan Ho Park, p	1994–2001
Ismael Valdez, p	1994–2000

The Dodgers had a rotating group of disappointments at second base, third base, shortstop and left field throughout most of the 1990s. DeShields, Offerman, Wallach and Hollandsworth are on the All-Decade Team as the best of a bad lot. Other prominent Dodgers included pitchers Tom Candiotti (1992–97) and Pedro Astacio (1992–97).

THE DECADE LEADERS

Batting Avg:	Mike Piazza	.331
On-Base Pct:	Mike Piazza	.394
Slugging Pct:	Mike Piazza	.572
Home Runs:	Eric Karros	211
RBIs:	Eric Karros	734
Runs:	Eric Karros	574
Stolen Bases:	Brett Butler	179
Wins:	Ramon Martinez	116
Strikeouts:	Ramon Martinez	1,202
ERA:	Ramon Martinez	3.46
Saves:	Todd Worrell	127

THE HOME FIELD

The only significant change to Dodger Stadium during the 1990s was the addition of Prescription Athletic Turf during the 1995–96 off-season. The Dodgers drew over 3,000,000 fans in seven of the10seasons, missing only in 1992, when the club lost 99 games, and in the strike-shortened seasons of 1994 and 1995. The franchise led the NL in attendance in 1990 and 1991.

THE GAME YOU WISHED YOU HAD SEEN

In a dominating performance, Ramon Martinez struck 18 batters against the Braves at Dodger Stadium on June 4, 1990.

THE WAY THE GAME WAS PLAYED

Baseball experienced one of its pivotal transitions during the 1990s, as offensive numbers soared to new heights. Fueled by expansion to 30 teams, newer ballparks with fences closer to home plate, and the use by some players of performance-enhancing substances, the average number of home runs in the NL increased from 114 per team in 1989 to 181 in 1999. The average number of runs per game increased from 7.9 in 1989 to 10.0 in 1999. The trend of the 1970s and 1980s toward artificial turf ended as every new ballpark that opened or was on the drawing board featured a grass field. Most of the new parks, beginning with Camden Yards in Baltimore in 1992, had "retro" features that tried to emulate the older, classic venues. Four new teams were added in Miami, Denver, St. Petersburg and Phoenix. Beginning in 1994, there were three divisions in each league, adding a new tier of playoffs. Inter-league play started in 1997, giving the Dodgers a chance to settle their rivalry with the Angels on the field.

THE MANAGEMENT

Walter O'Malley bought a 25 percent interest in the Dodgers in 1944 and became principal owner in 1950. He passed the day-to-day operation of the club over to his son Peter in 1970. Walter died in 1979. Peter owned the club until 1998 when the sale of the franchise to the Fox Group, an affiliate of Rupert Murdoch's New Corporation, became official. Bob Graziano succeeded O'Malley as president and CEO. Graziano was replaced as CEO by Robert Daly in October 1999. Daly remained in that position until 2004. General managers were Fred Claire (1987–98)

and Kevin Malone (1998–2001). In between the firing of Claire and the hiring of Malone, Tommy Lasorda served as interim general manager for three months. Lasorda was named the field manager of the Dodgers during the last week of the 1976 season and continued in the role until retiring during the 1996 season. He was followed by Bill Russell (1996–98), Glenn Hoffman (1998) and Davey Johnson (1999–2000).

THE BEST PLAYER MOVE

The best trade brought Shawn Green from the Blue Jays for Raul Mondesi in November 1999.

THE WORST PLAYER MOVE

The worst trade in Dodger history was perpetrated on November 19, 1993, when the club dealt Pedro Martinez to the Expos for Delino DeShields.

1990

Season in a Sentence

A revived batting attack helps the Dodgers win nine more games than the previous season, but unexpected pitching problems prevent the club from capturing the NL West title.

Finish • Won • Lost • Pct • GB

Second   86   76   .531   5.0

Manager

Tommy Lasorda

Stats

Stats	Dods	NL	Rank
Batting Avg:	.262	.256	4
On-Base Pct:	.328	.321	2
Slugging Pct:	.382	.383	7
Home Runs:	129		6
Stolen Bases:	141		6
Fielding Avg:	.979	.980	7
ERA:	3.72	3.79	7
Runs Scored:	728		3
Runs Allowed:	685		7

Starting Lineup

Mike Scioscia, c
Eddie Murray, 1b
Juan Samuel, 2b
Lenny Harris, 3b-2b
Alfredo Griffin, ss
Kal Daniels, lf
Kirk Gibson, cf
Hubie Brooks, rf
Mike Sharperson, 3b
Stan Javier, cf

Pitchers

Ramon Martinez, sp
Fernando Valenzuela, sp
Mike Morgan, sp
Tim Belcher, sp
Jay Howell, rp
Tim Crews, rp
Jim Gott, rp

Attendance

3,002,396 (first in NL)

Club Leaders

Batting Avg:	Eddie Murray	.330
On-Base Pct:	Eddie Murray	.414
Slugging Pct:	Eddie Murray	.520
Home Runs:	Kal Daniels	27
RBIs:	Eddie Murray	95
Runs:	Eddie Murray	96
Stolen Bases:	Juan Samuel	38
Wins:	Ramon Martinez	20
Strikeouts:	Ramon Martinez	223
ERA:	Ramon Martinez	2.92
Saves:	Jay Howell	16

FEBRUARY 15   The owners lock the players out of spring training because of a lack of progress during negotiations for a new basic agreement.

FEBRUARY 20   The Dodgers sign Don Aase, most recently with the Mets, as a free agent.

MARCH 18   The labor dispute between the players and owners is resolved.

> *Spring training camps opened on March 20. The season, scheduled to open on April 1, was delayed a week, with missed games made up with double-headers and by extending the close of the campaign by three days. The Dodgers started on April 9 with an unusual four-games series against the Padres in which the first game was played in Los Angeles and the last three in San Diego.*

APRIL 1   The Dodgers trade Franklin Stubbs to the Astros for Terry Wells.

APRIL 9   The Dodgers win the season opener 4–2 over the Padres before a crowd of 48,686 at Dodger Stadium. San Diego pitcher Bruce Hurst kept Los Angeles hitless until the seventh inning when Hubie Brooks, who was making his Dodger debut, hit a single. An inning later, Brooks clubbed a three-run homer to give the Dodgers the lead. Orel Hershiser was the starting pitcher and allowed a run in six innings.

Brooks often had trouble holding onto his bat during swings. During one 1990 game in San Diego, his bat traveled 140 feet and landed in the lap of general manager Fred Claire, who was sitting in the stands.

APRIL 10   Tim Belcher pitches a three-hit shutout to defeat the Padres 1–0 in San Diego. The lone run scored on a homer by Juan Samuel off Eric Show in the fifth inning. It was Samuel's first home run as a member of the Dodgers.

APRIL 18   Eddie Murray homers from both sides of the plate during a 6–2 win over the Giants in San Francisco. Murray homered against lefty Eric Gunderson in the third inning and right-hander Randy O'Neal in the seventh.

At the age of 34, Murray had a tremendous year in 1990 with a .330 batting average, and 26 home runs. The .330 mark was a career high. Murray also had the unique distinction of leading the majors in batting average without winning a batting title. It came about because of the trade of Willie McGee from the Cardinals to the Athletics on August 29. McGee hit .335 in 125 games with the Cardinals before the trade. Counting his stats with the A's, he batted .324, but his average in St. Louis was enough to beat out Murray for the National League batting crown. George Brett led the American League with a .329 average.

APRIL 22   Lenny Harris drives in both runs of a 2–0 win over the Astros at Dodger Stadium with singles in the third and fifth innings. Ramon Martinez pitched the shutout.

APRIL 27   Orel Hershiser undergoes season-ending surgery to repair a rotator cuff.

Hershiser hadn't missed a start since 1984. He returned in 1991, but struggled with a 35–37 record from that season through 1994 with the Dodgers before leaving the club as a free agent.

APRIL 29   The Dodgers play a regularly scheduled Sunday night game at Dodger Stadium for the first time and lose 4–0 to the Cubs. The game was part of ESPN's Sunday night baseball package.

APRIL 30   During a three-inning relief appearance, Mike Hartley strikes out six batters, including five in a row, but the Dodgers lose 8–4 to the Giants at Dodger Stadium.

Though just 22 years old in 1990, Ramon Martinez won 20 games for the Dodgers and finished second in the Cy Young Award balloting. While never reaching such lofty heights again, he remained a vital arm in the rotation during the 1990s, twice winning 17 games.

MAY 5   Back-to-back homers in the second inning provide all of the runs in a 3–0 win over the Phillies in Philadelphia. A two-run homer from Hubie Brooks was followed by a solo blast from Mike Scioscia, both off Ken Howell. Mike Morgan pitched the shutout.

            Scioscia hit .264 with a career-high 12 homers in 1990.

MAY 13   The Dodgers trade Willie Randolph to the Athletics for Stan Javier.

MAY 14   Both starting pitchers homer during the third inning of a 3–1 victory over the Expos at Dodger Stadium. Kevin Gross homered for Montreal in the top of the third off Fernando Valenzuela, and Fernando returned the favor facing Gross in the bottom half.

MAY 16   A one-out, walk-off homer by Hubie Brooks in the ninth inning beats the Expos 3–2 at Dodger Stadium. Brooks was given second life when Montreal catcher Mike Fitzgerald dropped a foul pop-up. The victory completed a three-game sweep in which the Dodgers won each contest by a 3–2 score.

MAY 19   Kal Daniels hits a grand slam off Don Carman in the fourth inning to give the Dodgers an 8–5 lead, but the Phillies wind up winning 15–12 in 11 innings at Dodger Stadium.

MAY 24   The Dodgers collect 20 hits and beat the Cubs 15–6 in Chicago.

MAY 27   The Dodgers explode for nine runs in the first inning and win 14–7 over the Cardinals in St. Louis. There were 10 Los Angeles hits in the inning on nine singles and a double. Stan Javier, Lenny Harris, Chris Gwynn and Eddie Murray each had two hits in the opening inning. Seven different players drove in the nine tallies.

MAY 28   The Pirates score five runs in the ninth inning to shock the Dodgers 6–5 in Pittsburgh. Tim Belcher allowed only one hit in eight innings, but Tommy Lasorda elected to go to the bullpen. Pat Perry and Jay Howell blew the four-run lead. The game ended on a two-out, bases-loaded single by Jose Lind that scored three runs.

MAY 31   A walk-off homer by Kal Daniels in the 10th inning beats the Reds 2–1 at Dodger Stadium.

JUNE 4   Ramon Martinez ties a club record set by Sandy Koufax with 18 strikeouts during a 6–0 win over the Braves at Dodger Stadium. Koufax fanned 18 on August 31, 1959, and again on April 24, 1962. Martinez walked only one, surrendered just three hits, and had two strikes on six other hitters. He retired 18 batters in a row from the first through the seventh innings, 14 of them on strikeouts. He started the game by striking out six of the seven batters he faced in the first and second innings, added a strikeout in the third inning, three in the fourth, two in the fifth and two in the sixth. He added two more two strikeouts in the seventh and the first two to face him in the eighth. At that point, Martinez had struck out 18 of 25 batters, tied Koufax's club record, and was two short of the major league record of 20 with four outs to go. He would record no more strikeouts, however. Prior to June 4, 1990, his career-high in strikeouts in a single game was 12.

On the same day, the Dodgers selected pitcher Ron Walden from Blanchard High School in Blanchard, Oklahoma, in the first round of the amateur draft. Walden never reached the majors. Those drafted and signed by the Dodgers in 1990 who did have a big league career were Mike Busch (fourth round), Steve Mintz (seventh round), Mike Mimbs (24th round) and Todd Williams (54th round).

JUNE 9   Eddie Murray hits home runs from both sides of the plate during an 11-inning, 5–4 win over the Padres in San Diego. He homered off lefty Bruce Hurst in the second inning, then struck the game-winner in the 11th facing Eric Show. It was the second time in 1990 that Murray hit switch homers in the same game.

JUNE 15   The Dodgers fall to a 28–33 won-lost record with a 13-inning, 3–1 loss to the Padres at Dodger Stadium.

JUNE 29   Fernando Valenzuela pitches his only career no-hitter, defeating the Cardinals 6–0 at Dodger Stadium. He threw 119 pitches, walked three, and struck out seven. Valenzuela nearly lost his no-hitter in the first inning when lead-off batter Vince Coleman grounded deep to shortstop and was barely beaten by Alfredo Griffin's throw. In the ninth, Coleman led off again and struck out looking. Willie McGee walked. Pedro Guerrero hit a bouncer up the middle that deflected off Valenzuela's glove to second baseman Juan Samuel, who stepped on second for the force of McGee and threw to first baseman Eddie Murray to complete the double play.

            Dave Stewart of the Athletics pitched a no-hitter on the same night, defeating the Blue Jays 5–0 in Toronto. It is the only time since 1898 that two no-hitters were throw on the same day.

JULY 3   Trailing 6–3, the Dodgers erupt for four runs in the ninth inning to defeat the Cubs 7–6 at Dodger Stadium. The rally started with a walk to Mike Scioscia and a home run by Juan Samuel, followed by a walk to Alfredo Griffin, a single from Mike Sharperson, a sacrifice by Lenny Harris that advanced both runners, and a two-run, walk-off single from Kirk Gibson.

JULY 14   Kal Daniels drives in six runs during a 7–0 win over the Cubs in Chicago. He hit a pair of three-run homers in the first and eighth innings. Mike Morgan pitched the shutout.

JULY 21   Tim Belcher pitches a one-hitter to defeat the Pirates 6–0 at Three Rivers Stadium. He faced the minimum 27 batters. The only two Pittsburgh base runners were Jay Bell on a single in the fourth inning and Mike LaValliere on a walk in the sixth. Bell was out attempting to steal and LaValliere was erased on a double play. Juan Samuel hit a home runs just hours after being arrested.

            Samuel was arrested for assault along with Alfredo Griffin in the early morning hours following an altercation with a bartender at a Pittsburgh nightclub. The bartender told police that Griffin grabbed a man by the arm, turned him around, and pushed him against the bar for intervening in a domestic dispute. According to police, the bartender grabbed Griffin and was punched by Samuel. Griffin had to be treated at the hospital for a cut near his left eye, and was out of action for a week. The assault charges were later dropped in an out-of-court settlement a month later.

JULY 22   The Dodgers fall 13½ games behind at 45–47 with an 11–6 loss to the Pirates in Pittsburgh.

JULY 23   The Dodgers score three runs in the first inning and six in the second and cruise to an 11–1 win over the Padres at Dodger Stadium.

JULY 24   Ramon Martinez pitches a two-hitter to defeat the Giants 9–2 at Dodgers Stadium. The only San Francisco hits were singles by Brett Butler leading off the first inning and Kevin Mitchell with one out in the ninth. The Giants scored twice in the eighth without a hit.

JULY 27   The Dodgers leave 25 men on base, but beat the Braves 5–4 in 12 innings at Dodger Stadium. The Dodgers collected 14 hits and drew 15 walks from Atlanta pitchers. Los Angeles batters were 2-for-17 with runners in scoring position. The winning run scored on a single by Mike Sharperson.

JULY 28   Trailing 7–4, the Dodgers explode for four runs in the ninth inning to win 8–7 at Dodger Stadium. With two out and a runner on first base, the Dodgers still trailed by three runs. Six straight batters then reached base for the victory. Kirk Gibson and Kal Daniels singled for the first run. Eddie Murray walked and Hubie Brooks delivered a two-run single to tie the score 7–7. After an intentional walk to Mike Scioscia, Juan Samuel singled in the winning tally.

JULY 30   A two-hitter by Mike Morgan beats the Reds 4–1 at Dodger Stadium. Morgan had a no-hitter in progress until Barry Larkin and Paul O'Neill singled in the seventh inning.

AUGUST 5   Three days after Iraq invades Kuwait and two days before Operation Desert Storm troops leave for Saudi Arabia, Eddie Murray and Kirk Gibson both star in a 12–6 triumph over the Giants in San Francisco. Murray drove in six runs on a pair of three-run homers in the first and fourth innings. Gibson also homered twice, along with a single, four RBIs and four runs.

AUGUST 7   Dodger rookie Jim Neidlinger allows only two hits in 7⅔ innings, but loses 1–0 to the Reds in Cincinnati. Paul O'Neill had both hits with singles in the fourth and sixth, but neither figured in the scoring. The lone run crossed the plate in the eighth on two walks and two wild pitches. It was Neidlinger's second big league game.

               Neidlinger's career in the majors lasted 12 games. He had a 5–3 record and a 3.28 ERA.

AUGUST 11   A two-run homer by Kal Daniels in the 10th inning beats the Braves 6–4 in Atlanta.

AUGUST 14   In his first major league start, Mike Hartley pitches six shutout innings allowing only two hits and the Dodgers win 2–1 over the Mets in the second game of a double-header at Shea Stadium. New York won the opener 9–8.

AUGUST 19   Leading off the first inning in the first plate appearance of his major league debut, shortstop Jose Offerman homers on an 0–2 pitch from Dennis Martinez for a home run. It accounted for the only run of a 2–1 loss to the Expos at Dodger Stadium. Later in the contest, Offerman hit two singles, stole a base, and made an over-the-shoulder catch in short left field. He was the first Dodger to homer in his first at-bat since Dan Bankhead in 1947.

Oddly, Offerman didn't hit a home run in 454 at-bats at Albuquerque in 1990 before being called up to the Dodgers. He didn't hit another major league home run until 1992. Offerman finished a 15-year career in 2005 with 57 home runs in 5,681 at-bats.

AUGUST 20   A walk-off homer by Mike Sharperson in the ninth inning beats the Phillies 2–1 at Dodger Stadium.

In the seventh inning, Lenny Dykstra of the Phillies complained to home plate umpire Ron Barnes about balls and strikes calls. Dykstra accused Rick Dempsey of "brown-nosing" the umpire, then dropped his bat and took a step toward the Dodger catcher. The 40-year-old Dempsey responded by popping Dykstra in the face with his glove then delivered a hard right. The two tangled and fell to the ground as benches cleared. Dempsey ended up with a big welt on the side of his face. Dempsey and Dykstra were ejected, and Dempsey was suspended for one day.

AUGUST 21   In the most improbable defeat in club history, the Dodgers blow an 11–1 lead by allowing two runs in the eighth and nine in the ninth to lose 12–11 to the Phillies at Dodger Stadium. The Dodgers erupted for eight runs in the fifth inning for the 11–1 advantage and were still ahead 11–3 heading into the ninth. Dave Walsh, Tim Crews and Jay Howell combined to allow the nine runs, all before the second out was recorded, during the Philadelphia ninth. The three pitchers surrendered eight hits and three walks. Five of the runs were unearned with the aid of two errors. John Kruk tied the score 11–11 with a three-run homer. The winning tally crossed the plate on a single by Rod Booker and a double from Carmelo Martinez.

AUGUST 25   A walk-off homer by Jose Gonzalez in the 14th inning beats the Mets 3–2 at Dodger Stadium. Gonzalez entered the contest in the eighth inning as a pinch-runner for Hubie Brooks and remained in the lineup in right field.

AUGUST 29   The Dodgers score eight runs in the sixth inning to beat the Phillies 12–2 in Philadelphia. Chris Gwynn contributed two homers and five runs batted in, including a grand slam off Darrel Akerfelds. It was only the third start in two months for Gwynn, who was playing left field in place of the injured Kal Daniels.

SEPTEMBER 4   Kal Daniels hits two homers and drives in six runs to help the Dodgers to a 7–0 lead, but Los Angeles loses 10–8 to the Astros at Dodger Stadium. Daniels hit a two-run homer in the first inning and a grand slam in the second, both off Mark Portugal.

SEPTEMBER 13   The Dodgers trade Darrin Fletcher to the Phillies for Dennis Cook.

SEPTEMBER 14   Trailing 2–1, the Dodgers explode for eight runs in the sixth inning to defeat the Reds 10–4 in Cincinnati. Kal Daniels hit a grand slam off Tim Layana. It was Kal's third grand slam of 1990.

SEPTEMBER 20   The Dodgers defeat the Padres 7–2 at Dodger Stadium to pull within 3½ games of the first place Reds with 12 contests left on the schedule.

The Dodgers split their last 12 games and finished five games behind Cincinnati.

SEPTEMBER 21   The Dodgers collect 20 hits and bury the Giants 16–3 at Dodger Stadium. With a big lead, Tommy Lasorda emptied the bench. None of the nine players in the starting lineup finished the game.

SEPTEMBER 25   A two-run homer by Hubie Brooks in the 11th inning beats the Astros 3–1 in Houston.

OCTOBER 1   Ramon Martinez wins his 20th game of 1990 with a 2–1 decision over the Padres at Dodger Stadium.

The older brother of Pedro Martinez (by 3½ years), Ramon was only 22 years old in 1990 and finished the season with a 20–6 record, a 2.92 ERA and 223 strikeouts in 234⅓ innings. He also led the NL in complete games with 12 in 33 starts. During one five-start stretch from June 16 through July 5, Martinez threw 617 pitches. He looked like a star for years to come, but the strain on his young right arm during the 1990 season took a toll. Martinez was an above average pitcher for most of the 1990s, but never reached the heights expected of him as he often battled arm miseries. In 11 seasons with the Dodgers (1988–98), Martinez was 123–77. He ranks eighth on the all-time club list in strikeouts with 1,314 and 10th in winning percentage (.615).

OCTOBER 2   The Dodgers come-from-behind to win 8–7 in 10 innings over the Padres at Dodger Stadium. Trailing 6–2, the Dodgers scored five runs in the eighth inning for a 7–6 lead, only to have San Diego tie the game in the ninth. The winning run scored on a bases-loaded single by Juan Samuel.

NOVEMBER 8   The Dodgers sign Darryl Strawberry, most recently with the Mets, as a free agent.

Strawberry was the top draft pick in the country when selected by the Mets out of Crenshaw High School in Los Angeles in 1980. He reached the majors in 1983 and made an immediate impact with 26 home runs and the Rookie of the Year Award. In eight seasons with the Mets, Strawberry played in seven All-Star Games, five as a starter. Along the way, he hit a franchise-record 252 home runs, topped the 100-RBI mark three times, scored 100 runs twice and was the runner-up in the MVP balloting in 1988. Strawberry signed a five-year deal with his hometown Dodgers. It seemed like a perfect match. "His best years are ahead of him," said general manager Fred Claire. "He's a premier player who can lead the Dodgers into the 1990s." There were warning signs, however, that Strawberry could cause a problem as a long-term investment. He was treated for alcoholism in February 1990, and there were rumors of drug use and domestic violence along with well-publicized battles with teammates and manager Davey Johnson. The Mets made no attempt to sign him. "We're a better franchise without him," said team president Frank Cashen. The Dodgers usually avoided troubled players like Strawberry, but believed they needed a star offensive attraction to make the club a contender. It was hoped that coming home to Los Angeles would help Strawberry avoid his previous problems. It didn't work. During his first year with the club, Strawberry missed 23 games with injuries, and hit .265 with 28 home runs, then played in only 75 contests in 1992 and 1993 due to back problems. He started the 1994 season at the Betty Ford Clinic with a drug problem and was released by the Dodgers.

DECEMBER 1   Kirk Gibson signs a contract as a free agent with the Royals.

Gibson never fully recovered from his leg injuries, and played five more seasons in the majors, the last three with the Tigers.

DECEMBER 3   The Dodgers sign Kevin Gross, most recently with the Expos, as a free agent.

DECEMBER 14   The Dodgers sign Brett Butler, most recently with the Giants, as a free agent. On the same day, the Dodgers dealt Jose Vizcaino to the Cubs for Greg Smith.

Butler was born in Los Angeles and always dreamed of playing for the Dodgers. He was an All-Star in 1991 and was the club's starting center fielder for four seasons, batting .303 during that period. He went to the Mets as a free agent in 1995, but returned to the Dodgers in a trade later that season and played with the club until the end of his career in 1997. Butler won the hearts of Dodger fans in 1996 during a courageous battle with cancer.

DECEMBER 15   The Dodgers trade Hubie Brooks to the Mets for Bob Ojeda and Greg Hansell.

1991   LA

Season in a Sentence

The Dodgers allow fewer runs than any other team in the major leagues and hold first place for 132 days, but lose three of their last four games to finish one game behind the Braves.

Finish • Won • Lost • Pct • GB

Second   93   69   .574   1.0

Manager

Tommy Lasorda

Stats

Stats	Dods	NL	Rank
Batting Avg:	.253	.250	6
On-Base Pct:	.326	.317	3
Slugging Pct:	.359	.373	8
Home Runs:	108		9
Stolen Bases:	126		5
ERA:	3.06	3.69	1
Fielding Avg:	.980	.980	7
Runs Scored:	665		5
Runs Allowed:	565		1

Starting Lineup

Mike Scioscia, c
Eddie Murray, 1b
Juan Samuel, 2b
Lenny Harris, 3b
Alfredo Griffin, ss
Kal Daniels, lf
Brett Butler, cf
Darryl Strawberry, rf
Gary Carter, c
Mike Sharperson, 3b

Pitchers

Ramon Martinez, sp
Mike Morgan, sp
Tim Belcher, sp
Bobby Ojeda, sp
Orel Hershiser, sp
Jay Howell, rp
Tim Crews, rp
John Candelaria, rp
Jim Gott, rp
Kevin Gross, rp

Attendance

3,348,170 (first in NL)

Club Leaders

Batting Avg:	Brett Butler	.296
On-Base Pct:	Brett Butler	.401
Slugging Pct:	Darryl Strawberry	.491
Home Runs:	Darryl Strawberry	28
RBIs:	Darryl Strawberry	99
Runs:	Brett Butler	112
Stolen Bases:	Brett Butler	38
Wins:	Ramon Martinez	17
Strikeouts:	Tim Belcher	156
ERA:	Tim Belcher	2.62
Saves:	Jay Howell	16

JANUARY 15   Rick Dempsey signs a contract as a free agent with the Brewers.

JANUARY 22   Five days after the U.S. and its allies attack Iraq to start the Persian Gulf War, Dodger broadcaster Don Drysdale is arrested on a charge of drunken driving stemming from a traffic accident in which a 24-year-old woman is injured. Drysdale's vehicle collided with the woman's car. He was fined $2,350, ordered to attend a 90-day alcohol education program, and perform 200 hours of community service.

MARCH 25   Four weeks after President George Bush orders a ceasefire to end the Persian Gulf War against Iraq, the Dodgers sign John Candelaria, most recently with the Blue Jays, as a free agent.

MARCH 26   The Dodgers sign Gary Carter, most recently with the Giants, as a free agent.

              Carter spent the 18th season of his 19-year Hall of Fame career as a Dodger. He hit .246 with six homers in 101 games and 246 at-bats.

MARCH 28   The Dodgers release Fernando Valenzuela.

              After winning 21 games in 1986, Valenzuela was 42–48 from 1987 through 1990. He was hit hard during spring training in 1991, leading to his release. Valenzuela signed with the Angels, but was released again after pitching in only two games. He spent the 1992 season in the Mexican League, before pitching for the Orioles, Phillies, Padres and Cardinals from 1993 until the end of the career in 1997, and compiled a record of 32–35 after leaving the Dodgers. Valenzuela's final record was 173 wins and 153 losses.

APRIL 10   The Dodgers open the season with a 6–4 win over the Braves in Atlanta. Tim Belcher went 7⅓ innings for the win. Mike Scioscia led the offense with three hits, including a double.

              In addition to telecasts on KTTV, Dodger games were carried on the cable outlet SportsChannel Los Angeles in 1990. The announcers were Joel Meyers and Ron Cey.

APRIL 12   The Dodgers lose the home opener 4–2 to the Padres before 49,676 at Dodger Stadium.

APRIL 24   Kal Daniels drives in six runs during an 8–4 win over the Braves at Dodger Stadium. Daniels drove in two runs with a single in the first inning off John Smoltz and four on a grand slam facing Doug Sisk in the fifth.

APRIL 25   Kal Daniels drives in four runs on a ground out and a three-run homer to lead the Dodgers to a 7–1 victory over the Giants at Dodger Stadium. The outburst gave Daniels 10 RBIs within consecutive games.

APRIL 26   Brett Butler collects five hits, including a double, in five at-bats during a 9–0 win over the Giants at Dodger Stadium.

              At the age of 34, Butler led the NL in runs (112) and walks (108) in 1991 in addition to batting .296. Only 20 of his 182 hits went for extra bases. Butler also earned an All-Star berth for the only time during his 17-year career.

APRIL 30   Mike Morgan holds the Expos to two hits, but the second one is a walk-off home run by Delino DeShields leading off the ninth inning, beating the Dodgers 1–0 at Olympic Stadium. The first Montreal hit was a single by Tim Wallach in the first inning.

> *Morgan entered the season with a 53–94 lifetime record and had never had a winning season in his first 11 in the majors. He finally shed that albatross with a 14–10 mark in 1991.*

MAY 1   Darryl Strawberry ties a major league record by striking out five times in five plate appearances during a 9–3 loss to the Expos in Montreal. Strawberry also committed a three-base error by dropping a fly ball in the first inning. "I really can't figure it out," said Strawberry after the game. "I felt good up there."

MAY 7   In his first game against the Mets since leaving the club as a free agent, Darryl Strawberry hits a home run during a 6–5 Dodger loss in New York. Strawberry was booed relentlessly by the Shea Stadium crowd all night long.

MAY 18   The Dodgers take first place with a 4–3 win over the Mets at Dodger Stadium. Los Angeles held first until August 28.

MAY 23   Lenny Harris drives in both runs of a 2–0 win over the Astros in Houston with run-scoring singles in the fourth and sixth innings. Tim Belcher (7$^1\!/_3$ innings), John Candelaria (one-third of an inning) and Jay Howell (one inning) combined on the shutout.

MAY 29   Orel Hershiser pitches his first game since April 25, 1990, and allows four runs in four innings of an 8–2 loss to the Astros at Dodger Stadium.

> *Hershiser had missed 13 months while recovering from surgery to repair a torn rotator cuff. He made 21 starts in 1991, and had a 7–2 record and a 3.46 ERA in 112 innings.*

JUNE 3   In the amateur draft, the Dodgers select future major leaguers Todd Hollandsworth (third round), Chris Latham (11th), Chad Zerbe (17th), Rick Gorecki (19th) and Ken Huckaby (22nd). The club had no picks in the first and second rounds due to free agent compensation for signing Darryl Strawberry and Brett Butler.

> *On the same day, Tommy Lasorda, Jr., the 33-year-old son of the Dodger manager, died. Some newspapers reports cited pneumonia as the reason from the death, while others reported that Tommy, Jr. passed away from complications from AIDS. Father and son had been estranged for several years until just before the tragic death.*

JUNE 6   The Dodgers edge the Cardinals 1–0 in St. Louis. Chris Gwynn drove in the lone run with a sacrifice fly in the first inning. Bob Ojeda (7$^1\!/_3$ innings), John Candelaria (one-third of an inning) and Tim Crews (1$^1\!/_3$ innings) combined on the shutout.

> *Often called upon to get one out against a left-handed batter, Candelaria pitched in 109 games in 1991 and 1992, but only 59 innings.*

JUNE 10   Lenny Harris hits a grand slam off Chuck McElroy in the fourth inning of a 13–5 win over the Cubs in Chicago.

JUNE 13   The Dodgers beat the Pirates 3–2 at Three Rivers Stadium with the help of the reversal of an umpire's call. With the score 2–2 in the ninth inning, Lenny Harris tried to avoid a high-and-tight pitch from Randy Tomlin, was struck on the right hand and dropped to the ground in pain. Home plate umpire Ed Rapuano initially ruled the pitch hit the bat but changed his mind after he saw that Harris was hurt. Pittsburgh manager Jim Leyland and second baseman Curtis Wilkerson were ejected arguing the decision of Rapuano. Harris eventually scored the winning run on Alfredo Griffin's single.

JUNE 18   At Dodger Stadium, the Dodgers come from behind twice in extra innings before defeating the Cubs 6–5 in the 13th. The Cubs scored in the top of the 11th and 12th, but the Dodgers responded with a run each time with two-out hits. Chris Gwynn drove in the tying run in the 11th and Stan Javier in the 12th. Eddie Murray's walk-off single in the 13th was the game-winner.

JUNE 19   The Dodgers win with a walk-off hit for the second game in a row as Mike Scioscia singles in the ninth for the winning run of a 9–8 triumph over the Cubs at Dodger Stadium.

The Dodgers were 54–27 at home in 1991, and 39–42 on the road.

JULY 3   The Dodgers trade Jose Gonzalez to the Pirates for Mitch Webster. At the time of the trade, Gonzalez was hitless in 28 at-bats during the 1991 season.

JULY 5   Gary Carter collects his 2,000th career hit during a 4–1 loss to the Braves at Dodger Stadium.

JULY 9   In the All-Star Game at Toronto's SkyDome, Mike Morgan pitches a perfect eighth inning, but the National League loses 4–2.

JULY 12   Brett Butler runs his hitting streak to 23 games during a 6–5 loss to the Expos in Montreal.

JULY 23   Mitch Webster leads off the ninth inning with a home run to tie the score 5–5, then hits a walk-off single in the 10th to defeat the Phillies 6–5 at Dodger Stadium.

JULY 24   The Dodgers win with a walk-off hit in the ninth inning for the second

Speedster Brett Butler was 34 years old when he arrived in Los Angeles, but he remained a sparkplug for the offense, a rangy centerfielder and a fan favorite for years.

game in a row to down the Phillies 2–1 at Dodger Stadium. In the ninth, Kal Daniels doubled, went to second on a ground out, and scored on a sacrifice fly from Mike Scioscia.

JULY 25   The Dodgers score all five runs of a 5–0 win over the Cardinals in the eighth inning. Ramon Martinez pitched the shutout.

JULY 26   After being held hitless by Mike Gardner of the Expos for the first nine innings, the Dodgers collect three consecutive hits in the 10th without a batter being retired to win 1–0 at Dodger Stadium. Montreal garnered only two hits. Orel Hershiser went six innings and surrendered only a single to Tim Wallach in the second. Kevin Gross pitched three innings, and allowed a single to Marquis Grissom with two out in the ninth. Jay Howell set down the Expos in order in the 10th. A Los Angeles native, Gardner started the 10th with his no-hitter still intact. It ended when Lenny Harris led off with an infield single. Eddie Murray followed with another single, and Gardner was relieved by Jeff Fassero. Darryl Strawberry singled in Harris with the winning run.

JULY 27   Bob Ojeda pitches the Dodgers third straight shutout, defeating the Expos 7–0 at Dodger Stadium.

The Dodgers held the opposition without a run in 38 consecutive innings over four games from July 24 through July 28.

JULY 28   Dennis Martinez of the Expos pitches a perfect game to defeat the Dodgers 2–0 at Dodger Stadium. Mike Morgan pitched for the Dodgers and had a perfect game through five innings. Between them, Martinez and Morgan retired the first 30 batters of the game. The first of four Montreal hits was a single by Ron Hassey leading off the sixth. The two runs scored in the seventh. In the ninth, Martinez retired Mike Scioscia on a fly ball to left fielder Ivan Calderon for the first out. Stan Javier pinch-hit for Alfredo Griffin and struck out swinging. Chris Gwynn hit for Morgan, and ended the game with a long fly ball to center fielder Marquis Grissom.

It was the second time in three days the Dodgers were the victims of a no-hitter through nine innings. It was the second perfect game against Los Angeles in less than three years. Tom Browning pitched one for the Reds on September 16, 1988. The gem by Martinez was the first complete game no-hitter against the Dodgers at home since Johnny Vander Meer of the Reds accomplished the feat at Ebbets Field on June 15, 1938.

JULY 31   The Dodgers trade Mike Hartley and Braulio Castillo to the Phillies for Roger McDowell.

AUGUST 2   Trailing 7–0 after three innings, the Dodgers rally to take an 8–7 lead with two runs in the top of the ninth, only to have the Astros score twice in the bottom half to win 9–8 in Houston.

AUGUST 7   Mike Sharperson triples in a run and scores on a sacrifice fly by Kal Daniels to account for the only two tallies of a 2–0 win over the Reds in Cincinnati. Bob Ojeda (six innings), Kevin Gross (two innings) and Roger McDowell (one inning) combined on the shutout.

AUGUST 8   The Dodgers take a six-game lead in the NL West with a 6–4 win over the Reds in Cincinnati. The club's record was 61–46.

AUGUST 16   A three-run, walk-off homer by Darryl Strawberry in the 13th inning beats the Astros 4–1 at Dodger Stadium. Strawberry tied the game 1–1 with a sacrifice fly in the eighth.

AUGUST 17   The Dodgers win with a walk-off hit in extra innings for the second game in a row as Eddie Murray's single in the 10th defeats the Astros 8–7 at Dodger Stadium.

AUGUST 21   Darryl Strawberry drives in seven runs during a 9–5 win over the Padres at Dodger Stadium. Strawberry hit a grand slam off Ricky Bones in the fifth inning and a three-run homer against Rich Rodriguez in the seventh.

AUGUST 26   Trailing 3–0, the Dodgers erupt for four runs in the ninth inning to defeat the Cubs 4–3 in Chicago. Mitch Webster singled in the first run, followed by Brett Butler's RBI-double. Both crossed the plate on Juan Samuel's two-bagger.

AUGUST 28   The Dodgers drop out of first place for the first time since May 18 with a 6–4 loss to the Pirates at Dodger Stadium.

                No more than two games separated the Braves and Dodgers in the battle for first place in the NL West from August 11 through the end of the season.

SEPTEMBER 12   A three-run homer by Darryl Strawberry and a solo shot from Kal Daniels in the 10th beats the Astros 6–2 in Houston.

SEPTEMBER 16   After the Reds score two runs in the top of the 12th, the Dodgers rally with three in their half to win 6–5 at Dodger Stadium. The first run in the 12th crossed the plate on Eddie Murray's only triple of the season. He scored on a double by Eric Karros, his first major league hit. Jeff Hamilton drove in the winning run with a walk-off single. Boneheaded base running nearly cost the Dodgers the win in the 11th. Jose Offerman was on third base and Brett Butler on first when Lenny Harris hit a ground ball. Offerman tried to score but failed to touch home plate and was tagged out on the throw. Harris was called out for passing Butler on the base paths after Butler inexplicably stood watching the play between first and second. The Dodgers used 27 players including nine pitchers. The nine who took the mound were Orel Hershiser, Jim Gott, John Candelaria, Roger McDowell, Steve Wilson, Kevin Gross, Tim Crews, Dennis Cook and John Wetteland. Ten players hit in the seventh spot in the batting order, including starting second baseman Juan Samuel, seven pitchers, and two pinch-hitters.

SEPTEMBER 21   The Dodgers score runs in the eighth and ninth innings to defeat the Braves 2–1 at Dodger Stadium and take over first place in the NL West. Juan Samuel's triple drove in the winning run.

SEPTEMBER 26   The Dodgers take a two-game lead with eight contests left on the schedule after beating the Giants 6–2 at Dodger Stadium.

SEPTEMBER 29   The Dodgers score a run in the eighth inning and two in the ninth to defeat the Giants 3–2 at Dodger Stadium. A single by Darryl Strawberry drove in the winning run. There were six games left to play and the Dodgers led the Braves by one game.

OCTOBER 1	The Dodgers maintain their tenuous one-game lead in the NL West with four contests left to play by defeating the Padres 3–1 at Dodger Stadium. It was the club's 23rd win in the last 31 games.

OCTOBER 2   The Dodgers drop into a tie with the Braves for first place after losing 9–4 to the Padres at Dodger Stadium. San Diego broke a 3–3 tie with six runs in the eighth inning. During the six-run rally, the Padres collected five hits that never left the infield.

OCTOBER 4   The Dodgers drop a game behind the Braves with two contests left to play by losing 4–1 to the Giants in San Francisco. The crowd at Candlestick Park chanted "Beat L.A.!" in unison all night long and greeted the Dodgers with Atlanta's "Tomahawk Chop."

OCTOBER 5   The Dodgers lose their third game in a row and are eliminated from the pennant race by losing 2–0 to the Giants in San Francisco. Trevor Wilson held Los Angeles batters to two hits.

After finishing in last place in 1990, the Braves took the NL West pennant by winning 53 of their last 81 games. Atlanta went to the World Series, and lost to the Twins in seven games. With the exception of the strike-shortened season of 1994, the Braves finished first every year from 1991 through 2005.

OCTOBER 6   On the last day of the season, Chris Gwynn scores both runs of a 2–0 win over the Giants in San Francisco. Dennis Cook ($5^2/3$ innings), Tom Crews (one-third of an inning), Steve Wilson (one inning), Mike Christopher (one inning) and Jay Howell (one inning) combined on the shutout.

NOVEMBER 15   Gary Carter signs a contract as a free agent with the Expos.

NOVEMBER 27   Eddie Murray signs a contract as a free agent with the Mets. On the same day, the Dodgers traded Tim Belcher and John Wetteland to the Reds for Eric Davis and Kip Gross.

A native of Los Angeles and a graduate of Fremont High School, Davis made the All-Star team in 1987 and 1989 and was one of the top talents in baseball when healthy. His health was a big issue, however. Davis was 29 when acquired by the Dodgers and had never played in more than 139 games in a season. He was a childhood friend of Darryl Strawberry and it was hoped that the reunion of the two would form a formidable duo in the center of the Dodger batting order. The plan completely backfired, as they were extreme disappointments in 1992 and 1993. Davis's injury history continued, while Strawberry battled alcohol and drug abuse and his own problems with injuries. During his two seasons with the Dodgers, Davis hit .232 with 19 home runs in 643 at-bats. Belcher was a capable starting pitcher for several clubs over the remainder of the 1990s. After the Reds dealt Wetteland to the Expos, he became one of the top relief pitchers in baseball.

DECEMBER 3   The Dodgers sign Tom Candiotti, most recently with the Blue Jays, as a free agent. On the same day, Mike Morgan signed a contract as a free agent with the Cubs.

1992

L
A

Season in a Sentence

With the second highest payroll in baseball, the Dodgers lose 99 games and finish in last place for the first time since 1905.

Finish • Won • Lost • Pct • GB

Sixth   63   99   .389   35.0

Manager

Tommy Lasorda

Stats	Dods •	NL •	Rank
Batting Avg:	.248	.252	9
On-Base Pct:	.313	.315	7
Slugging Pct:	.339	.368	12
Home Runs:	72		12
Stolen Bases:	142		3
ERA:	3.41	3.50	6
Fielding Avg:	.972	.981	12
Runs Scored:	548		12
Runs Allowed:	636		7 (tie)

Starting Lineup

Mike Scioscia, c
Eric Karros, 1b
Lenny Harris, 2b
Dave Hansen, 3b
Jose Offerman, ss
Eric Davis, lf
Brett Butler, cf
Mitch Webster, rf-lf
Mike Sharperson, 3b-2b
Todd Benzinger, 1b-rf-lf
Darryl Strawberry, rf

Pitchers

Tom Candiotti, sp
Orel Hershiser, sp
Kevin Gross, sp
Bob Ojeda, sp
Ramon Martinez, sp
Pedro Astacio, sp
Roger McDowell, rp
Jim Gott, rp
Steve Wilson, rp
John Candelaria, rp
Tim Crews, rp
Jay Howell, rp

Attendance

2,473,266 (second in NL)

Club Leaders

Batting Avg:	Brett Butler	.309
On-Base Pct:	Brett Butler	.413
Slugging Pct:	Eric Karros	.426
Home Runs:	Eric Karros	20
RBIs:	Eric Karros	88
Runs:	Brett Butler	86
Stolen Bases:	Brett Butler	41
Wins:	Tom Candiotti	11
Strikeouts:	Kevin Gross	158
ERA:	Tom Candiotti	3.00
Saves:	Roger McDowell	14

FEBRUARY 12   An episode of the TV series *Seinfeld* airs with a cameo role by Dodger reliever Roger McDowell. The show starred McDowell's ex-Met teammate Keith Hernandez and featured McDowell as a grassy knoll-type figure spitting on Kramer and Newman during a Zapruder film parody after Kramer and Newman insulted Hernandez.

MARCH 25   Alfredo Griffin signs a contract as a free agent with the Blue Jays.

APRIL 6   The Dodgers open the season with an 8–1 loss to the Giants before 49,018 at Dodger Stadium. Ramon Martinez was the starting and losing pitcher.

> *Dodger telecasts were carried over KTTV-TV for the first last season in 1992. The station had handled the over-the-air telecasts from the Dodgers for 35 seasons beginning with the first year in Los Angeles in 1958. KTLA-TV took over the telecasts in 1993.*

APRIL 12   Down 4–0 in San Diego, the Dodgers score four runs in the top of the ninth inning with a pair of two-run, pinch-singles from Juan Samuel and Mitch Webster to tie the score, but wind up losing 5–4 when the Padres score in the bottom half of the innings.

The Dodgers were 17–40 in one-run games in 1992.

APRIL 17   Darryl Strawberry hits a two-run, walk-off homer in the ninth inning to defeat the Braves 7–5 at Dodger Stadium.

APRIL 20   In his first game against his former Reds teammates, Eric Davis collects three hits in three at-bats during a 6–0 win at Dodger Stadium.

Davis and Darryl Strawberry were expected to carry the Dodger offense, but were troubled with injuries all year. Combined, the pair had only 423 at-bats and hit .232 with 10 home runs and 57 RBIs.

APRIL 29   The Dodgers lose 7–3 to the Phillies at Dodger Stadium as riots break out in Los Angeles.

Racial tensions exploded into violence soon after a jury, which included no black members, acquitted four white policemen of savagely beating African-American motorist Rodney King. At the end of two days of rioting, 52 were dead and thousands injured. The Dodgers postponed games against the Phillies on April 30 and the Expos on May 1, 2 and 3. Michael Strawberry, a Los Angeles patrolman and brother of Dodger outfielder Darryl Strawberry, was wounded on May 1 in the South-Central section of Los Angeles when his patrol car was strafed by fire from an AK-47 assault rifle.

MAY 5   Playing for the first time in six days, the Dodgers lose 6–2 to the Phillies in Philadelphia.

MAY 12   A two-run homer by Darryl Strawberry off Chris Haney provides the only runs of a 2–0 win over the Expos in Montreal. Kevin Gross pitched a three-hit shutout and struck out 13 batters without issuing a walk.

MAY 18   Kevin Gross strikes out 12 batters in seven innings and allows only a run and three hits, but the Dodgers lose 3–0 to the Cubs at Dodger Stadium.

MAY 23   Trailing 4–1, the Dodgers erupt for four runs in the ninth inning to stun the Pirates 5–4 at Dodger Stadium. Mike Scioscia drove in the first run with a single. The game ended on a three-run homer by Eric Karros with one out.

Scioscia ended his career in 1992 with 1,395 games as a catcher, the most of any individual in Dodger history.

MAY 27   Todd Benzinger hits a grand slam off Jose DeLeon in the third inning of a 9–2 win over the Cardinals in St. Louis.

MAY 29   A double by Eric Karros in the ninth inning drives in the only run of a 1–0 win over the Cubs in Chicago. Ramon Martinez pitched a complete game three-hitter.

Karros won the NL Rookie of the Year Award with a .257 batting average, 20 home runs and 88 RBIs. No one else on the power-starved Dodgers hit more than six home runs. The runs batted in figure by Karros was more than any other two Dodgers combined. Brett Butler was second in the category with 39. Butler also hit .309 with 95 walks. Eleven of his 28 extra base hits were triples. He had 67 infield singles, 43 of them on bunts.

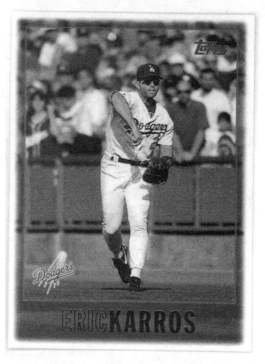

Eric Karros won the Rookie of the Year Award in 1992 and brought a new power to the lineup. During his years with the Dodgers he had five seasons with more than 30 home runs and a hundred RBIs.

JUNE 1   With their two choices in the first round of the amateur draft, the Dodgers select catcher Ryan Luzinski of Holy Cross High School in Medford, New Jersey, and outfielder Michael Moore from UCLA. The 1992 draft was the worst in club history. The only future big leaguer chosen by the Dodgers was Keith Johnson in the fourth round. Johnson's major league career lasted only six games with the 2000 Angels.

The Dodgers were 23–23 on June 1 and only 2½ games out of first place. Over the remainder of the season, the club was 40–76. Attendance fell to 2,473,266, the lowest of any non-strike year between 1977 and the present.

JUNE 7   Tom Candiotti pitches the Dodgers to a 1–0 win over the Reds at Dodger Stadium. The lone run scored in the fifth inning. Jose Offerman reached on an error, went from first to third on Candiotti's bunt, and crossed the plate on Brett Butler's single.

Candiotti won only six big league games before his 28th birthday and 145 afterward. His career took off with the Indians in 1986 when he learned to throw a knuckleball from Phil Niekro. Candiotti spent six seasons (1992–97) with the Dodgers.

JUNE 16   Trailing 7–3 in Atlanta, the Dodgers erupt for five runs in the ninth inning to take an 8–7 lead, only to have the Braves score two in their half to win 9–8.

Tommy Lasorda was so upset over the defeat, he refused to take the team bus and attempted to walk the four miles from the stadium to the team hotel. Along the way, his big toe caused him considerable pain because it had been hit by a line drive while pitching batting practice. An ambulance cruised by and recognized the limping Lasorda and offered him a ride. After declining, the Dodger manager reconsidered, hopped in and arrived at the hotel at 12:45 a.m.

JUNE 21	The Dodgers extend their losing streak to 10 games with a 2–0 defeat at the hands of the Astros in Houston.

During the 10-game losing streak, the Dodgers were shut out three times and were held to just one run in four other games.

JUNE 27	The Dodgers trade Kal Daniels to the Cubs for Michael Sodders.

Daniels hit .250 in 108 at-bats and was released after the season, ending his major league career. Sodders never made a major league appearance.

JUNE 29	The Dodgers win a thrilling 6–5 decision in 11 innings over the Padres at Dodger Stadium. San Diego scored in the top of the 10th, and the Dodgers tied the contest again in the bottom half. The Padres scored twice in the 11th, and this time the Dodgers responded with three runs and the victory. A two-run single by Todd Benzinger tied the score. Mike Sharperson drove in the winner with a two-out single.

Sharperson made the All-Star team, but started only 24 games after the break as Tommy Lasorda looked at other options at third and second base. Sharperson finished the season hitting .300 in 317 at-bats. He died in an auto accident in 1996 at the age of 34 while playing for Las Vegas in the Pacific Coast League.

JULY 2	Trailing 4–0, the Dodgers explode for eight runs in the fifth inning and beat the Phillies 9–4 at Dodger Stadium.

On the same day, the Dodgers traded Stan Javier to the Phillies for Steve Searcy and Julio Peguero.

JULY 3	In his major league debut, Pedro Astacio pitches a three-hit shutout to defeat the Phillies 2–0 in the second game of a double-header at Dodger Stadium. He struck out 10 batters and threw 144 pitches. The Dodgers won the opener 5–1.

The 22-year-old Astacio was called up from the minors because the Dodgers had to play four double-headers in six days to make up for games lost during the riots two months earlier (see April 29, 1992). The Dodgers played twin bills against the Philadelphia on July 3 and Montreal on July 6, 7 and 8. After making a start on July 8, Astacio returned to the minors, but was recalled in August. He was 5–5 in 1992, but four of his 11 starts were shutouts and he had an ERA of 1.98. Astacio pitched five seasons with the Dodgers and had a record of 41–38.

JULY 8	Playing a double-header against the Expos at Dodger Stadium for the third day in a row, the Dodgers win 1–0 in 11 innings and lose 4–1. Bob Ojeda (6⅓ innings), John Candelaria (one-third of an inning), Roger McDowell (three innings) and Tom Candiotti (one inning) combined on the opening game shutout. The winning run scored on a two-out single by Dave Hansen.
JULY 30	Darryl Strawberry's season ends with back surgery to repair a herniated disk.
AUGUST 13	The Dodgers commit six errors and collect only four hits, but manage to defeat the Reds 4–3 in Cincinnati. Shortstop Jose Offerman and second baseman Eric Young each made two errors, and pitcher Pedro Astacio and right fielder Henry Rodriguez one each.

AUGUST 17   Kevin Gross pitches a no-hitter to defeat the Giants 2–0 at Dodger Stadium. Gross made 99 pitches, walked two, hit a batter, and struck out six. He retired 19 batters in a row between the second and eighth innings. In the ninth inning, Mark Leonard led off and was hit by a pitch. Greg Litton bounced into a force play from shortstop Jose Offerman to second baseman Eric Young. Mike Felder hit a fly ball to left fielder Mitch Webster for the second out. Gross completed his no-hitter by inducing Willie McGee to hit another fly ball to Webster.

Gross was 8–13 with a 3.17 ERA with the Dodgers in 1992. He was 35–39 in four seasons with the Dodgers (1991–94) and 142–158 over the course of a career, which lasted from 1983 through 1997.

AUGUST 31   Tom Candiotti pitches a two-hitter, but loses 2–0 to the Cubs at Wrigley Field. The only Chicago hits were singles by Steve Buechele and Dwight Smith in the seventh, an inning in which the Cubs scored their two runs.

The Dodgers scored only two runs and were shut out four times during a five-game span from August 26 through August 31.

SEPTEMBER 1   Mike Piazza makes his major league debut and reaches base four times in four plate appearances during a 13-inning, 5–4 win over the Cubs in Chicago. Piazza collected a double, two singles and a walk before being lifted for a pinch-runner in the eighth.

In his next game, on September 4, Piazza singled in his first plate appearance giving him four hits in his first four at-bats. Recognized by many as the best hitting catcher in baseball history, Piazza seldom let up until his career ended in 2007. Chosen in the 62nd round, Piazza was the last player chosen in the 1988 amateur draft and the 1,389th overall. The selection was largely a favor to Mike's father, Vince, a childhood friend and distant cousin of Tommy Lasorda in Norristown, Pennsylvania. Vince Piazza became a multi-millionaire running used car dealerships. He built a batting cage in his basement for his son and even arranged a meeting with Ted Williams. Nonetheless, Piazza was undrafted out of high school and went to Miami-Dade North Community College as a first baseman. After being drafted by the Dodgers, Lasorda insisted Mike become a catcher. Piazza rocketed through the Dodger farm system and reached the majors three days before his 24th birthday. He was an All-Star in each of his five full seasons in a Los Angeles uniform. On the all-time club lists among players with at least 2,000 plate appearances, Piazza ranks second in slugging percentage (.572), fourth in batting average (.331), sixth in on-base percentage (.394) and eighth in home runs (177). The batting average is the best among Dodgers with 2,000 plate appearances since 1930.

SEPTEMBER 4   Todd Benzinger hits a pinch-hit grand slam off Bob Patterson in the ninth inning that gives the Dodgers a 5–3 lead, but the Pirates score three times in their half to win 6–5 at Pittsburgh. Benzinger also homered in his previous pinch-hit appearance on September 2.

SEPTEMBER 10   In the seventh inning of a 3–1 loss to the Padres at Dodger Stadium, rookie catcher Mike Piazza neglects to call time when he goes to the mound, and San Diego's Jerald Clark scores from third base.

SEPTEMBER 11   The Dodgers commit seven errors during a 7–3 loss to the Giants at Dodger Stadium. Shortstop Jose Offerman made three of them. The others were by left fielder Henry Rodriguez, center fielder Mitch Webster, right fielder Bill Ashley and second baseman Lenny Harris.

As a team, the Dodgers 174 errors led, by far, the National League. The Phillies finished second with 131. Offerman led the majors in errors with 42 at shortstop. In all, Los Angeles shortstops committed 53 errors.

SEPTEMBER 18   The Dodgers beat the Giants 11–4 in San Francisco. It was the only time all year that the Dodgers reached double digits in runs in a single game.

SEPTEMBER 24   Pedro Martinez makes his major league debut with two scoreless innings of relief in which he allows two hits and a walk during an 8–4 loss to the Reds at Dodger Stadium.

NOVEMBER 17   Two weeks after Bill Clinton defeats George Bush in the presidential election, the Dodgers lose Eric Young and Roberto Mejia to the Colorado Rockies and Jamie McAndrew to the Florida Marlins in the expansion draft. On the same day, the Dodgers traded Rudy Seanez to the Rockies for Jody Reed.

DECEMBER 5   The Dodgers sign Cory Snyder, most recently with the Giants, as a free agent.

DECEMBER 8   Bob Ojeda signs a contract as a free agent with the Indians (see January 22, 1993).

DECEMBER 9   The Dodgers sign Todd Worrell, most recently with the Cardinals, as a free agent.

DECEMBER 16   John Candelaria signs a contract as a free agent with the Pirates.

DECEMBER 24   The Dodgers trade Tim Barker to the Expos for Tim Wallach.

1993

Season in a Sentence

After a 93–69 record in 1991 and a 63–99 mark in 1992, the Dodgers settle in the middle and win 81 while losing 81 in 1993.

Finish • Won • Lost • Pct • GB

Fourth   81   81   .500   23.0

Manager

Tommy Lasorda

Stats	Dods	NL	Rank
Batting Avg:	.261	.264	10
On-Base Pct:	.321	.327	11
Slugging Pct:	.383	.399	13
Home Runs:	130		10
Stolen Bases:	126		5
ERA:	3.50	4.04	3
Fielding Avg:	.979	.978	4
Runs Scored:	675		12
Runs Allowed:	662		4

Starting Lineup

Mike Piazza, c
Eric Karros, 1b
Jody Reed, 2b
Tim Wallach, 3b
Jose Offerman, ss
Eric Davis, lf
Brett Butler, cf
Cory Snyder, rf

Pitchers

Pedro Astacio, sp
Kevin Gross, Sp
Orel Hershiser, sp
Ramon Martinez, sp
Tom Candiotti, sp
Jim Gott, rp
Pedro Martinez, rp
Roger McDowell, rp
Omar Daal, rp
Ricky Trlicek, rp

Attendance

3,170,392 (third in NL)

Club Leaders

Batting Avg:	Mike Piazza	.318
On-Base Pct:	Brett Butler	.387
Slugging Pct:	Mike Piazza	.561
Home Runs:	Mike Piazza	35
RBIs:	Mike Piazza	112
Runs:	Mike Piazza	81
Stolen Bases:	Brett Butler	39
Wins:	Pedro Astacio	14
Strikeouts:	Tom Candiotti	155
ERA:	Tom Candiotti	3.12
Saves:	Jim Gott	25

JANUARY 14   Dave Anderson signs a contract as a free agent with the Giants.

JANUARY 22   Jay Howell and Tim Crews sign contracts as free agents. Howell went to the Braves and Crews to the Indians. Crews played for the Dodgers from 1987 through 1992.

> *On March 22, Crews and Cleveland teammate Steve Olin were killed in a boating accident on Little Lake Nellie in Clermont, Florida, on a day off during the Indians training camp schedule. Bob Ojeda, who played for the Dodgers in 1991 and 1992 was seriously injured. Just after dark, the three were riding in an aluminum 18-foot, open-air fishing boat piloted by Crews when it slammed into the side of a pier. Olin was killed instantly and Crews died the next morning. Ojeda underwent surgery for severe damage to his scalp, which had to be surgically re-attached.*

APRIL 5   Six weeks after a bomb explodes in a parking garage beneath the World Trade Center, killing six people, the Dodgers participate in the first regular season game in Florida Marlins history. The Marlins won 6–3 at Dolphin Stadium in Miami. The winning pitcher was 45-year-old Charlie Hough, who played for the Dodgers from 1970 though 1980. Orel Hershiser was the Los Angeles starter, and took the loss by allowing five runs in five innings. Tim Wallach homered in his Dodger debut.

APRIL 13	The Dodgers lose their home opener 9–7 to the Cardinals before 53,529 at Dodger Stadium. Los Angeles fell behind 5–0 in the second inning and rallied to take a 7–5 lead in the sixth, only to lose.
APRIL 27	Eight days after the raid on the Branch Davidian compound in Waco, Texas, the Dodgers collect only two hits but win 4–1 over the Mets at Shea Stadium. Mike Piazza hit a solo homer off Dwight Gooden in the second inning. The Dodgers scored three times in the eighth with one hit, a single by Orel Hershiser, along with two walks, a sacrifice bunt, and two New York errors.

Piazza won the NL Rookie of the Year Award with one of the best rookie campaigns in big league history. He hit .318 with 35 homers and 112 runs batted in.

MAY 8	The Dodgers score three runs in the 12th inning, the last two on a home run by Mitch Webster, to defeat the Giants 5–2 in San Francisco.
MAY 12	Trailing 3–2, the Dodgers score seven runs in the eighth inning and win 9–3 over the Cubs in Chicago.
MAY 17	The Dodgers score three runs in the ninth inning and one in the 10th to defeat the Reds 5–4 at Dodger Stadium. In the ninth, Dave Hansen put the Dodgers within a run by stroking a two-run single. Brett Butler tied the contest with a sacrifice fly. In the 10th, Cory Snyder won the game with a walk-off single.
MAY 18	Eric Davis hits a grand slam off John Smiley in the fifth inning of a 5–1 win over the Reds at Dodger Stadium.
MAY 19	The Dodgers beat the Reds 5–2 at Dodger Stadium in the first major league game ever broadcast in Mandarin Chinese. It was carried over Los Angeles radio station KZAN-AM. The contest was also broadcast in English on KABC-AM, Spanish on KWKW-AM, and Korean over KBLA-AM.
MAY 21	The Dodgers play the Rockies for the first time and win 8–0 at Dodger Stadium.
MAY 29	The Dodgers run their winning streak to 11 games with a 6–1 decision over the Pirates in Pittsburgh. It was the club's longest winning streak since 1976.

The Dodgers started the season 14–22, then won 35 of their next 55 games. The club was 32–39 over the final 71 contests to settle at the .500 mark.

JUNE 3	In the first round of the amateur draft, the Dodgers select pitcher Darren Dreifort from Wichita State University.

Dreifort was the second overall pick in the draft behind Alex Rodriguez. Dreifort pitched nine seasons with the Dodgers and never lived up to expectations, in large part because of a long history of injuries. He missed the entire 1995 and 2002 season with Tommy John surgery. Those were just two of the eight operations that Dreifort endured during a career in which he posted a record of 48–60. The only other future major leaguers drafted and signed by the Dodgers in 1993 were Nate Bland (fourth round) and Paul LoDuca (25th round). It took LoDuca until 2001 to become a regular in the Dodger lineup, but he proved to be the best player drafted by the Dodgers in 1993.

JUNE 7   The Marlins play at Dodger Stadium for the first time and score three runs in the ninth inning to defeat the Dodgers 5–3.

JUNE 10   A fight breaks out in the sixth inning of a 14–2 loss to the Padres in San Diego. Garry Sheffield charged the mound after Dodger reliever Ricky Trlicek hit him in the back with a pitch. Sheffield plowed into Trlicek and threw a punch that grazed the pitcher's head. The two wrestled to the ground as both benches emptied. Sheffield and Trlicek were pulled apart quickly and ejected.

JUNE 11   The Padres score five runs in the ninth inning to stun the Dodgers 5–4 in San Diego. Kevin Gross pitched eight innings of three-hit shutout ball and was relieved after throwing 116 pitches. Pedro Martinez, Jim Gott and Omar Daal blew the lead.

           The game was a rare lapse for Martinez, who started the season as a 21-year-old rookie and a teammate of his older brother Ramon. Pedro was a starter in the minors, but the Dodgers used him as a relief pitcher in 1993. He appeared in 65 games and compiled a 2.61 ERA and struck out 119 batters in 107 innings. Unfortunately, the Dodgers traded Martinez at the end of the season (see November 19, 1993).

JUNE 14   The Dodgers play in Denver for the first time and beat the Rockies 9–4 at Mile High Stadium.

JUNE 15   The Dodgers score three runs in the eighth inning and seven in the ninth to defeat the Rockies 12–4 in Denver. Mike Piazza hit two homers, two singles, and drove in five runs.

           The game was marked by two fights. With the Dodgers trailing 3–2 in the bottom of the seventh, Rockies first baseman Andres Galarraga was brushed back by Ramon Martinez, then hit a single for his eighth consecutive hit against Los Angeles pitching over two games. While on first base, Galarraga was hit by an errant pick-off throw, then was out trying to steal second, and kicked second baseman Jody Reed as he slid behind the throw. On the next pitch, Martinez drilled Charlie Hayes in the chest. Hayes charged the mound to touch off the first fight. The scuffle lasted three minutes and Martinez and Hayes were both ejected. An inning later, Piazza hit his second homer, which put the Dodgers ahead 5–3. Cory Snyder was next at bat and was hit by a pitch from Keith Shepherd. Snyder glared at the Colorado pitcher, who made a motion toward Snyder to come to the mound and fight. The Dodgers poured out of the dugout, led by Darryl Strawberry, who was held back by Rockies catcher Joe Girardi before Strawberry could reach Shepherd. Jim Gott used his judo skills on Shepherd and Roger McDowell landed a couple of punches, bloodying Shepherd's nose.

JUNE 21   Ramon Martinez pitches a two-hitter to defeat the Astros 7–0 at Dodger Stadium. The only Houston hits were a single by Craig Biggio in the first inning and a double from Luis Gonzalez in the second.

JUNE 26   Roy Campanella dies from heart failure at the age of 71 in his home in the Woodland Hills suburb of Los Angeles. Campanella had been paralyzed by an auto accident since 1958 and served as an inspiration and a symbol of courage for the handicapped. He was employed by the Dodgers as a spring training instructor and as a member of the club's community service division.

JUNE 28   A walk-off grand slam by Dave Hansen off Mike Jackson in the ninth inning accounts for all four runs of a 4–0 win over the Giants at Dodger Stadium. Hansen's slam was preceded by a walk to Mike Piazza, a single by Eric Karros, a sacrifice from Cory Snyder advancing both runners, and an intentional walk to Eric Davis.

JULY 3   Dodger broadcaster Don Drysdale dies of a heart attack at the age of 56. He was found dead in his Montreal hotel room. Drysdale left his wife—Ann Meyers Drysdale, an All-American basketball player at UCLA and a television commentator—and three children ranging from six years to four months of age. Rick Monday replaced Drysdale on the Dodger broadcast team.

JULY 4   The Dodgers outlast the Expos 1–0 in 11 innings in Montreal. The lone runs scored on a single by Cory Snyder, two errors by shortstop Mike Lansing, and a passed ball by catcher Tim Laker. Tom Candiotti (seven innings), Pedro Martinez (1 1/3 innings), Omar Daal (one-third of an inning), Jim Gott (one inning) and Roger McDowell (one inning) combined on the shutout.

JULY 7   The Dodgers lose 7–6 to the Phillies in a 20-inning marathon at Veterans Stadium. The contest lasted six hours and 10 minutes and ended at 1:47 a.m. The Dodgers scored two runs in the ninth to tie the game 5–5. After 10 consecutive scoreless innings, L.A. scored again in the top of the 20th, only to have Philadelphia cross the plate twice in their half. The contest ended on Lenny Dykstra's two-run double off Rod Nichols.

JULY 8   The day after a 20-inning game in Philadelphia, the Dodgers play a double-header in New York. The Dodgers won the first game 11–8 and lost the second 6–3 in 10 innings. The nightcap ended on a three-run homer by Bobby Bonilla off Rod Nichols.

Nichols pitched only four games as a Dodger, but two of them ended on walk-off hits in extra innings on back-to-back days.

JULY 24   Vince Coleman of the Mets is arrested for throwing an M-80 firecracker out of a car window into a crowd of fans waiting for autographs in the Dodger Stadium parking lot. The car was driven by Dodger outfielder Eric Davis. The explosion injured three people, including two-year-old Amanda Santos. Coleman was given a one-year suspended sentence, put on probation for three years, fined $1,000, and required to perform 200 hours of community service.

JULY 26   The day after being shutout by the Mets at Dodger Stadium, the Dodgers wallop the Giants 15–1 in San Francisco.

JULY 31   The Dodgers erupt for five runs in the 13th inning to win 7–2 over the Cubs in Chicago. Raul Mondesi capped the rally with his first major league home run.

AUGUST 6   A two-run walk-off homer by Eric Karros in the ninth inning defeats the Reds 3–2 at Dodger Stadium.

AUGUST 20   The Dodgers score three runs in the ninth inning to defeat the Cardinals 3–2 in St. Louis. Brett Butler started the rally with a triple. Henry Rodriguez and Tim Wallch drove in the tying and winning runs with a pair of two-out singles off Lee Smith.

AUGUST 24   Eric Karros drives in six runs with a pair of three-run homers in the third and eighth innings to lead the Dodgers to a 13–4 triumph over the Pirates at Dodger Stadium.

AUGUST 31   The Dodgers trade Eric Davis to the Tigers for John DeSilva.

               Plagued be a series of injuries, Davis never proved to be the offensive weapon the Dodgers expected when he came aboard.

SEPTEMBER 12   Pedro Astacio pitches the Dodgers to a 1–0 win over the Marlins at Dodger Stadium. Cory Snyder drove in the lone run with a single in the sixth inning.

               The TV series The X-Files *began its ten-year run in September 1993. The character of Dana Scully, played by Gillian Anderson, was named as a tribute to longtime Dodger broadcaster Vin Scully.*

SEPTEMBER 14   Major League Baseball announces its three-division alignment, plus an extra round of playoffs, including a wild card team, to be put into effect for the 1994 season. The Dodgers were placed in a four-team Western Division with the Colorado Rockies, San Diego Padres and San Francisco Giants. The Arizona Diamondbacks were added in 1998.

SEPTEMBER 17   Darryl Strawberry is arrested for hitting his girlfriend, Charisse Simon, who is three months pregnant. Witnesses reported she had been hitting him with a bat near where he had back surgery. The incident came at the end of an awful season in which Strawberry hit .140 in just 100 at-bats. Simon later refused to press charges. In October, Strawberry divorced his wife Lisa and married Simon in December. They later had three children together.

OCTOBER 3   On the last day of the season, the Dodgers knock the Giants out of the pennant race with a 12–1 win at Dodger Stadium. San Francisco won 103 games in 1993, but finished one game behind the Braves in the NL West.

OCTOBER 29   As part of a post-season tour of Asia, the Dodgers become the first major league team to play in Taiwan. The Dodgers won 4–2 against a combined team of the Dragons and Bears, two of Taiwan's six pro teams.

NOVEMBER 19   The Dodgers trade Pedro Martinez to the Expos for Delino DeShields.

               This trade has risen to the top of the list as the worst ever made by the Dodgers. Martinez had just turned 22, but Tommy Lasorda believed he was too skinny to survive the rigors of big league ball. Martinez disproved that theory by posting a record of 187–78 with the Expos, Red Sox and Mets from 1994 through 2005. During that span, he won three Cy Young Awards, led his league in ERA five times, strikeouts in three seasons, winning percentage twice, and wins, complete games and shutouts once each. Through the 2008 season, Martinez has been named to eight All-Star teams. DeShields was 24 in 1993, and had four years as a starting second baseman under his belt with a batting average of .277 and 187 stolen bases. It looked as though he was going to be star for years to come. DeShields was a bust with the Dodgers, however, and batted only .241 in three seasons in Los Angeles.

NOVEMBER 24   Lenny Harris signs a contract as a free agent with the Reds.

1994   LA

Season in a Sentence

When the players go on strike in August, the Dodgers were two games over .500 with a 3½-game lead in the NL West.

Finish • Won • Lost • Pct • GB

First   58   56   .509   +3.5

Manager

Tommy Lasorda

Stats

Stats	Dods	NL	Rank
Batting Avg:	.270	.267	6
On-Base Pct:	.333	.333	7
Slugging Pct:	.414	.415	6
Home Runs:	115		7
Stolen Bases:	74		8
ERA:	4.17	4.21	9
Fielding Avg:	.980	.980	9
Runs Scored:	532		7
Runs Allowed:	509		7

Starting Lineup

Mike Piazza, c
Eric Karros, 1b
Delino DeShields, 2b
Tim Wallach, 3b
Jose Offerman, ss
Henry Rodriguez, lf
Brett Butler, cf
Raul Mondesi, rf
Cory Snyder, lf

Pitchers

Ramon Martinez, sp
Kevin Gross, sp
Tom Candiotti, sp
Pedro Astacio, sp
Orel Hershiser, sp
Todd Worrell, rp
Jim Gott, rp
Roger McDowell, rp

Attendance

2,279,355 (fourth in NL)

Club Leaders

Batting Avg:	Mike Piazza	.319
On-Base Pct:	Brett Butler	.411
Slugging Pct:	Mike Piazza	.541
Home Runs:	Mike Piazza	24
RBIs:	Mike Piazza	92
Runs:	Brett Butler	79
Stolen Bases:	Brett Butler	27
	Delino DeShields	27
Wins:	Ramon Martinez	12
Strikeouts:	Kevin Gross	124
ERA:	Kevin Gross	3.60
Saves:	Todd Worrell	11

JANUARY 17   A predawn earthquake in the Los Angeles area claims 61 lives and causes widespread devastation. The quake centered in the Northridge suburb in the San Fernando Valley.

JANUARY 20   Michael Scully, the 33-year-old son of Dodger broadcaster Vin Scully, dies in a helicopter crash. Michael was working as an engineering supervisor inspecting an oil pipeline for earthquake damage.

FEBRUARY 3   Jody Reed signs a contract as a free agent with the Brewers.

MARCH 2   Delino DeShields suffers a small fracture of the bone below his right eye when a bat accidentally slips out of a teammate's hands during batting practice in Vero Beach, Florida.

APRIL 3   Darryl Strawberry fails to show for an exhibition game against the Angels.

Five days later, Strawberry entered a drug treatment facility. He was released by the Dodgers on May 25 and signed by the Giants in June. Strawberry played for the Yankees from 1995 through 1999, but was never a regular again and often found himself embroiled in legal and health problems. He was indicted for tax evasion in 1994, started the 1995 season with a 60-day drug suspension, missed most of the 1997 season with a knee injury, underwent a successful recovery from colon cancer in 1998 and 1999, and was suspended for one year in 2000 for drug use, which ended his playing career.

APRIL 5   The Dodgers open the season with a 4–3 win over the Marlins in front of a crowd of 53,761 at Dodger Stadium. The Dodgers trailed 3–2 before scoring runs in the seventh and eighth. Pinch-hitter Jeff Treadway drove in the go-ahead tally with a sacrifice fly.

APRIL 8   Kent Mercker of the Braves pitches a no-hitter to defeat the Dodgers 6–0 at Dodger Stadium. He walked four and struck out ten. The last out was recorded on a ground out by Eric Karros to Mercker, who threw to first baseman Fred McGriff. Chan Ho Park pitched the ninth for Los Angeles to become the first player born in Korea to appear in a major league game.

APRIL 17   Cory Snyder hits three homers during a 19–2 pasting of the Pirates in Pittsburgh. He drove in seven runs and scored four. Snyder clubbed a pair of two-run homers off Steve Cooke in the second and fifth inning. The Dodger outfielder batted twice in the nine-run seventh. Snyder walked and scored in his first plate appearance, then smacked a three-run homer off Jeff Ballard. Raul Mondesi contributed four hits, including a homer and a triple, and scored four runs.

Mondesi won the NL Rookie of the Year Award in 1994 with a .306 batting average and 16 home runs.

APRIL 19   Down 7–2, the Dodgers score a run in the seventh inning, four in the eighth and one in the ninth to win 8–7 over the Phillies in Philadelphia. Mitch Webster's single broke the 7–7 tie.

APRIL 20   Brett Butler's fifth hit of the game is a walk-off single in the 11th that beats the Mets at Dodger Stadium. Butler collected three singles, a double and a triple in six at-bats.

Butler batted .314 with a league-leading nine triples in 1994.

APRIL 21   The Dodgers wallop the Mets 13–3 at Dodger Stadium. The contest was stopped in the fourth inning when fans threw baseballs onto the field. The balls had been given away as part of a promotional gimmick.

APRIL 30   Down 10–5, the Dodgers score six runs in the eighth inning and one in the ninth to win 12–10 over the Mets in New York. The six eighth-inning runs scored on three two-out home runs. Chris Gwynn hit a two-run homer, Mike Piazza a three-run blast, and Tim Wallach a solo shot.

Piazza batted .319 with 24 home runs in 1994.

MAY 9 — Trailing 8–2, the Dodgers stun the Astros with three runs in the eighth inning and four in the ninth to win 9–8 at Dodger Stadium. Los Angeles still trailed 8–5 with two out in the ninth inning when Mike Piazza hit a two-run single and Tim Wallach a two-run, walk-off homer.

MAY 11 — The Dodgers collect only two hits, but defeat the Astros 1–0 at Dodger Stadium. The lone run scored on a homer by Raul Mondesi off Shane Reynolds leading off the sixth inning. Reynolds retired the first 15 Los Angeles batters. Pedro Astacio pitched a four-hit shutout.

MAY 15 — Brett Butler collects his 2,000th career hit with a single off A. J. Sager in the first inning of a 7–1 win over the Padres at Dodger Stadium.

MAY 19 — In his first major league at-bat, Garey Ingram hits a pinch-home run in the eighth inning of an 8–2 victory over the Rockies in Denver.

Ingram finished his three-year career with three homers in 142 at-bats.

MAY 20 — After Reds owner Marge Schott is quoted as saying "only fruits wear earrings," Dodger reliever Roger McDowell, a Cincinnati native, buys earrings for the whole team. The Dodgers wore them in the clubhouse at Riverfront Stadium, but Tommy Lasorda wouldn't allow the players to wear them on the field. The Reds won 3–2.

MAY 27 — After the Pirates score four runs in the ninth inning and one in the 10th for a 5–4 lead, the Dodgers rally for two runs in the bottom of the 10th to win 6–5. The two tallies in the 10th scored on RBI-singles by Mitch Webster and Darren Dreifort. A pitcher, Dreifort was sent to the plate as a pinch-hitter. It was also his first major league at-bat.

JUNE 2 — In the first round of the amateur draft, the Dodgers select catcher Paul Konerko from Chaparral High School in Scottsdale, Arizona.

The Dodgers converted Konerko into a first baseman during his third year in the minors. He reached the majors in 1997, but the Dodgers traded him a year later. In 2008, he was in his 10th season as a starting first baseman with the White Sox. Other future big leaguers drafted and signed by the Dodgers in 1994 were Gary Rath (second round), Mike Metcalfe (third round), Ricky Stone (fourth round), Eric DuBose (sixth round), Eddie Oropesa (14th round) and Adam Riggs (22nd round).

JUNE 6 — Mike Piazza hits a grand slam off Mark Gardner in the second inning, but the Dodgers lose 11–10 to the Marlins in Miami. The drive traveled an estimated 477 feet.

JUNE 19 — Two days after 95 million Americans tune in to the eight-hour police chase of O. J. Simpson in his Ford Bronco through the highways of Greater Los Angeles, Mike Piazza hits a grand slam off Kent Bottenfield in the seventh inning during a 7–3 triumph over the Rockies at Dodger Stadium.

JUNE 24 — Jeff Bagwell hits three home runs, two of them in the sixth inning, to lead the Astros to a 16–4 win over the Dodgers in Houston.

JUNE 30 — A three-run, walk-off double by Delino DeShields beats the Phillies 4–3 at Dodger Stadium.

JULY 3 — Pitching for the Phillies, Fernando Valenzuela makes his first appearance at Dodger Stadium in an opposing team's uniform and allows two runs in six innings during a 3–1 Dodger victory.

> *After starting the season 3–8, the Dodgers took a 5½-game lead in the NL West on July 3 with a 43–38 record. On July 27, the Dodgers were 49–52, but still held first place by one-half game. When the strike was called on August 12, Los Angeles was 58–56 and led by 3½ games.*

JULY 5 — Pedro Astacio (eight innings) and Ismael Valdez (two innings) combine on a two-hitter to defeat the Expos 2–1 in 10 innings at Dodger Stadium. The only Montreal hits were a homer by Lenny Webster and a single from Mike Lansing, both in the fifth innings. The winning run scored on a walk-off homer by Raul Mondesi.

JULY 12 — Mike Piazza drives in a run with a single in the third inning during an 8–7 National League win in the All-Star Game at Three Rivers Stadium in Pittsburgh.

JULY 16 — Jose Carreras, Placido Domingo and Luciano Pavarotti, known collectively as The Three Tenors, perform at Dodger Stadium. The atmosphere was provided by two four-story waterfalls producing 600 gallons of water a minute. A 440-foot backdrop, covered with 2,500 cans of paint, created a rain-forest paradise. Twenty fake classical pillars were imported from Hungary. A total of 56,000 attended the event, with the top ticket price going for $1,000. An estimated 1.3 billion watched on television around the world. The concert was held on the eve of the World Cup soccer championship game between Brazil and Italy at the Rose Bowl in Pasadena.

JULY 17 — Trailing 9–0, the Dodgers make things interesting by scoring seven runs in the ninth inning before losing 9–7 to the Phillies at Veterans Stadium. Fernando Valenzuela pitched eight shutout innings for Philadelphia before allowing three of the seven ninth-inning runs.

JULY 24 — Rondell White drives in all seven Expos runs during a 7–4 win over the Dodgers in Montreal.

JULY 29 — A two-out, three-run walk-off homer by Delino DeShields in the ninth inning beats the Astros 7–5 at Dodger Stadium.

AUGUST 3 — Brett Butler records his 500th career stolen base during a 4–2 loss to the Padres at Dodger Stadium.

AUGUST 4 — Mike Piazza homers in the fourth inning off Andy Benes for the only run of a 1–0 win over the Padres at Dodger Stadium. Kevin Gross (eight innings) and Todd Worrell (one inning) combined on the shutout.

AUGUST 11   With the midnight strike deadline looming, the Dodgers beat the Reds 2–0 in Cincinnati.

AUGUST 12   With about 70 percent of the season completed, the major league players go on strike.

The strike, baseball's eighth interruption since 1972, had been anticipated all season. The owners wanted to put a lid on escalating payrolls by capping salaries and revising, if not eliminating, salary arbitration procedures. The players, who were obviously not interested in these reforms, had only one weapon once talks broke down: a strike.

SEPTEMBER 14   The owners of the 28 major league clubs vote 26–2 to cancel the remainder of the season, including the playoffs and the World Series.

DECEMBER 13   Kevin Gross signs a contract as a free agent with the Rangers.

1995

Season in a Sentence

In a season shortened to 144 games by the strike, the Dodgers win nine of their last 13 games to nail down the NL West by one game over the Rockies before being swept by the Reds in the Division Series.

Finish • Won • Lost • Pct • GB

First   78   66   .542   +1.0

National League Division Series

The Dodgers lose to the Cincinnati Reds three games to none.

Manager

Tommy Lasorda

Stats

Stats	Dods	NL	Rank
Batting Avg:	.264	.263	7
On-Base Pct:	.329	.331	9
Slugging Pct:	.400	.408	8
Home Runs:	140		7
Stolen Bases:	127		6
ERA:	3.66	4.18	2
Fielding Avg:	.976	.980	14
Runs Scored:	634		10
Runs Allowed:	609		2

Starting Lineup

Mike Piazza, c
Eric Karros, 1b
Delino DeShields, 2b
Tim Wallach, 3b
Jose Offerman, ss
Billy Ashley, lf
Robert Kelly, cf-lf
Raul Mondesi, rf
Chad Fonville, ss-2b
Dave Hansen, 3b

Pitchers

Ramon Martinez, sp
Hideo Nomo, sp
Ismael Valdez, sp
Tom Candiotti, sp
Todd Worrell, rp
Pedro Astacio, rp

Attendance

2,766,251 (second in NL)

Club Leaders

Batting Avg:	Mike Piazza	.346
On-Base Pct:	Mike Piazza	.400
Slugging Pct:	Mike Piazza	.606
Home Runs:	Mike Piazza	32
	Eric Karros	32
RBIs:	Eric Karros	105
Runs:	Raul Mondesi	91
Wins:	Ramon Martinez	17
Strikeouts:	Hideo Nomo	236
ERA:	Hideo Nomo	2.54
Saves:	Todd Worrell	32

JANUARY 13   Major league owners vote to use replacement players during the 1995 season if the strike, which began on August 12, 1994, is not settled.

The Dodgers opened training camp in February at Vero Beach, Florida, with replacement players and used them until the strike came to an end on April 2.

FEBRUARY 8   The Dodgers sign Hideo Nomo, most recently with the Kinetsu Buffaloes of the Japanese League, as a free agent.

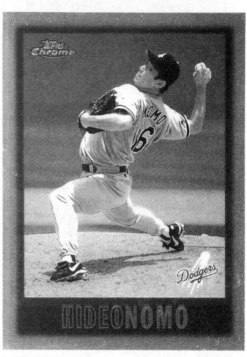

In 1995, Hideo Nomo won the Rookie of the Year Award, was selected for the All-Star team, and led the National League in strikeouts and shutouts. His success sparked interest among major league teams in bringing Asian pitchers to America.

Nomo was one of the best pitchers in Japan, but after the 1994 season became embroiled in a contract dispute with team management. The Buffaloes rejected Nomo's demands to have an agent negotiate his contract and a multi-year deal. Unable to work things out with the Buffaloes, Nomo and his agent exploited a loophole in the agreement between Japanese baseball and the major leagues. If a player retired, he was free to play for whomever he wished. This allowed the Dodgers to sign Nomo. He became only the second Japanese player to appear in a major league game. The first was Masonori Murikami with the Giants in 1964 and 1965. Previously, cultural differences, particularly the importance of loyalty in Japanese society, had discouraged Japanese players from going to the United States. No one in the Dodger organization had seen Nomo pitch in more than a year, with the exception of a two-minute highlight video. There was considerable uncertainty over whether or not success in Japan would translate to the States. The Dodgers were intrigued by the idea of opening up markets to the club and attracting Japanese-Americans to Dodger Stadium. The gamble to sign Nomo paid off. With his whirling delivery, he baffled American hitters as a rookie in 1995 with a 13–6 record. Nomo led the league in strikeouts (236) and shutouts (three) in addition to a 2.54 ERA in 191 1/3 innings. He was the National League starter in the All-Star Game and won the Rookie of the Year Award. Nomo was also a huge box office draw, as attendance increased whenever he pitched. In addition, he was a hero in his home country. The games that Nomo pitched were carried on live television in Japan, and Japanese reporters came to the United States to interview him. Nomo's arrival couldn't have come at a better time, because baseball needed attractions to bring fans back to the ballpark following the 234-day strike. The remainder of his career following his splash as a rookie was plagued with inconsistency and injuries, and he was unable to stick with a team for long, though he did turn in several good seasons and amass a 123–109 record in 12 seasons. He was 45–36 as a Dodger from 1995 through 1998, and after pitching for the Mets, Brewers, Tigers and Red Sox, played in Los Angeles again from 2002 through 2004. His second tour with the Dodgers produced a record of 36–30. Nomo's success inspired other Japanese players to play in the United States, including Ichiro Suzuki and Hideki Matsui.

APRIL 2   The 234-day strike comes to an end.

The opening of the season, originally scheduled to begin on April 3, was pushed back to April 26 with each team playing 144 games. The replacement players were either released or sent to the minors.

APRIL 7   Jim Gott signs a contract with the Pirates as a free agent.

APRIL 8   Orel Hershiser signs a contract with the Indians as a free agent.

With the best offense in baseball backing him, Hershiser gave the Indians three excellent seasons with a record of 16–6 in 1995, 15–9 in 1995 and 14–6 in 1997.

APRIL 10   Roger McDowell signs with the Orioles as a free agent.

APRIL 11   The day before the Los Angeles Rams officially announce their move to St. Louis, Brett Butler signs with the Mets as a free agent.

The Dodgers failed to pursue Butler after he was granted free agency, in part because he was an outspoken advocate of the players during the strike. The club soon realized their mistake, however, and traded for Butler in August. A few weeks later, the Dodgers called up Mike Busch, a replacement player during the strike, from the minors. Butler led an unsuccessful clubhouse insurrection to have Busch removed from the roster. With little sympathy for the strike, fans at Dodger Stadium cheered Busch and booed Butler.

APRIL 25   Six days after the bombing of a federal office building in Oklahoma City, resulting in the deaths of 168 people, the Dodgers open the season with an 8–7 win over the Marlins in Miami. It was the only game scheduled on April 25, and therefore was the first major league game since August 11, 1994. The Dodgers led 8–2 before Florida scored a run in the eighth inning and four in the ninth. Raul Mondesi hit two homers and drove in four runs. Jose Offerman contributed three hits and drove in three runs. Ramon Martinez was the starting and winning pitcher. He also doubled in the top of the fifth and raced to catch a foul ball at a critical juncture in the bottom half.

Martinez was 17–7 with a 3.66 ERA in 1995.

APRIL 28   The Dodgers win 9–1 over the Braves in the home opener before 51,181 at Dodger Stadium. Bill Ashley homered, doubled and drove in five runs.

Ashley was touted as star in the making, but was never able to nail down a job as a regular because he found it impossible to make contact consistently. He had 594 at-bats with the Dodgers over six seasons and hit 25 home runs, but batted only .231 and struck out an astonishing 225 times.

MAY 2   After 14 scoreless innings, the Dodgers score three runs in the top of the 15th, only to have the Giants score four in their half to win 4–3 in San Francisco. Making his major league debut, Hideo Nomo pitched the first five innings and was the first of nine Los Angeles pitchers. Nomo, Antonio Osuna, Ismael Valdez, Todd Worrell, Rudy Seanez, Omar Daal and Todd Williams combined for 14 shutout innings, allowing only five hits while striking out 15. Ron Murphy and Greg Hansell surrendered the four runs in the 15th.

MAY 3   The Dodgers score four runs in the top of the ninth for a 7–4 lead, then survive a two-run Giants rally in the bottom half to win 7–6 in San Francisco. The ninth-inning runs scored on a two-run single by Chris Gwynn and a two-run triple from Jose Offerman.

MAY 5   The Dodgers play at Coors Field in Denver for the first time, and beat the Rockies 6–4.

MAY 6   The Dodgers collect 21 hits and outlast the Rockies 17–11 in Denver. The Dodgers led 14–3 after five innings and let Colorado creep to within three runs at 14–11 before scoring three in the ninth. There were a record-tying three pinch-hit homers in the game by Mitch Webster of the Dodgers and Mike Kingery and John Vander Wal of the Rockies.

MAY 7   Mike Piazza hits two homers, a double and a single and drives in six runs, including a grand slam in the third inning off Bill Swift, to lead the Dodgers to a 12–10 win over the Rockies in Denver.

Piazza hit .346 with 32 homers and 95 RBIs in 1995.

MAY 9   Jose Offerman makes three errors in the fourth inning of a 9–2 loss to the Padres in San Diego. On three consecutive plays, Offerman made two errant throws and booted a ground ball.

MAY 12   The Dodgers and Cardinals combine for 12 errors during an 8–4 Los Angeles win in St. Louis. The Cards made seven errors and the Dodgers five, three of them by third baseman Garey Ingram.

MAY 15   Ramon Martinez (seven innings), Rudy Seanez (one inning) and Todd Worrell (one inning) combine on a one-hitter to defeat the Pirates 4–0 at Dodger Stadium. The only Pittsburgh hit was a single by Jeff King in the seventh inning, which just slipped past the glove of third baseman Dave Hansen.

Worrell struggled in 1993 and 1994, his first two seasons with the Dodgers, but was brilliant in 1995 with 32 saves and a 2.02 ERA in 59 games and 62$\frac{1}{3}$ innings.

MAY 17   Hideo Nomo strikes out 14 batters in seven innings while allowing two hits and no runs, but the Dodgers lose 3–2 to the Pirates in Pittsburgh as the bullpen fails to hold a two-run lead.

MAY 24   The Dodgers trade Henry Rodriguez and Jeff Treadway to the Expos for Roberto Kelly and Joey Eischen.

MAY 31   The Dodgers score three runs in the 10th inning, two on a home run by Eric Karros, to defeat the Phillies 4–1 in Philadelphia.

> *Karros had the best year of his career in 1995 with 32 homers, 105 RBIs and a .298 batting average.*

JUNE 1   In the first round of the amateur draft, the Dodgers select pitcher David Yocum from Florida State University.

> *Yocum never reached the majors. The only future big leaguers drafted and signed by the Dodgers in 1995 were Onon Masaoka (third round) and Pedro Feliciano (31st round), neither of whom ever had to worry about being besieged by autograph seekers. The Dodgers salvaged something from their scouting budget by signing Eric Gagne as an undrafted free agent in July.*

JUNE 2   Hideo Nomo (eight innings) and Todd Worrell (one inning) combine on a two-hitter to defeat the Mets 2–1 at Dodger Stadium. Bobby Bonilla collected both New York hits with a home run in the second inning and a single in the sixth.

JUNE 14   Hideo Nomo strikes out 16 batters in eight innings during an 8–5 win over the Pirates in Pittsburgh.

JUNE 17   The Dodgers club five home runs during a 12–5 win over the Cubs in Chicago. Billy Ashley hit two of them, with Mike Piazza, Eric Karros and Raul Mondesi adding the rest.

JUNE 21   The Dodgers score seven runs in the second inning of a 10–1 win over the Cardinals in St. Louis. Delino DeShields hit a grand slam off Vince Palacios.

JUNE 24   Hideo Nomo pitches a two-hitter and strikes out 13 to defeat the Giants 7–0 at Dodger Stadium. Darren Lewis collected both San Francisco hits with singles in the first and ninth innings. Nomo retired 22 batters in a row from the first through the eighth.

JUNE 26   A three-run walk-off homer by Mike Piazza beats the Padres 8–5 at Dodger Stadium.

JUNE 29   Hideo Nomo strikes out 13 batters in a 3–0 win over the Rockies at Dodger Stadium.

> *During the month of June, Nomo had a 6–0 record an ERA of 0.89.*

JULY 8   The Dodgers rout the Reds 12–2 in Cincinnati.

JULY 11   Hideo Nomo is the starting pitcher in the All-Star Game and pitches two shutout innings to help the National League to a 3–2 win in Arlington, Texas. Mike Piazza tied the score 2–2 with a home run off Kenny Rogers in the seventh inning.

JULY 14   Ramon Martinez pitches a no-hitter to defeat the Marlins 7–0 at Dodger Stadium. He threw 114 pitches, walked one and struck out eight. He retired the first 23 batters before a walk to Tommy Gregg with two out in the eighth inning. Gregg was the only Florida base runner. In the ninth, Charles Johnson struck out swinging,

Jerry Browne grounded out from second baseman Delino DeShields to first baseman Eric Karros, and Quilvio Veras hit a fly ball to Roberto Kelly in left.

A month earlier, on June 3, Ramon's brother Pedro pitched a near perfect game for the Expos against the Padres in San Diego. Pedro Martinez retired the first 27 batters to face him, but had to go to extra innings because his teammates failed to score. After Montreal scored a run in the top of the 10th, Pedro allowed a leadoff double to Bip Roberts. He was immediately relieved by Mel Rojas, who closed out the 1–0 victory.

JULY 18   With a 13–4 loss to the Astros at Dodger Stadium, the Dodgers drop five games behind the first-place Rockies in the NL West race with a record of 36–39.

JULY 26   Ismael Valdez (eight innings) and Todd Worrell (one inning) combine on a shutout to beat the Braves 1–0 at Dodger Stadium.

JULY 31   The Dodgers trade Ron Coomer, Greg Hansell, Jose Parra and Chris Latham to the Twins for Kevin Tapani and Mark Guthrie.

AUGUST 1   Raul Mondesi hits two homers and a single and drives in six runs during a 9–6 victory over the Rockies in Denver.

AUGUST 5   The day after the Giants wallop the Dodgers 15–1, Hideo Nomo strikes out 11 and pitches a one-hitter against San Francisco for a 3–0 victory at Candlestick Park. The only hit off Nomo was a single by Royce Clayton in the seventh inning.

AUGUST 7   A two-run homer by Eric Karros in the 12th inning defeats the Giants 3–1 in San Francisco.

AUGUST 10   The Dodgers are forced to forfeit a game to the Cardinals at Dodger Stadium.

With one out in the bottom of the ninth and the Cardinals leading 2–1, the umpires stopped the game after some in the raucous crowd of 53,361 on Ball Night littered the field with baseballs for the third time. The contest was delayed six minutes in the top of the seventh, and again in the ninth after Raul Mondesi and Tommy Lasorda were ejected after Mondesi struck out. The umpires ordered the Cardinals to leave the field while the balls were picked up. After another delay of five minutes, the Cards went back on the field and a few more balls were thrown. One just missed St. Louis center fielder Brian Jordan's head. At that point, the umpires called the game. It was the first forfeit in the major leagues since 1979 and the first in the National League since 1974.

AUGUST 12   After the Pirates score three runs in the top of the 10th inning, the Dodgers rally for three tallies in their half and one in the 11th to win 11–10 at Dodger Stadium.

In the 10th, Mike Piazza doubled in two runs and crossed the plate on a single from Eric Karros. The run in the 11th scored on an odd play. With the potential winning run at third base, Mitch Webster swung at and missed a pitch in the dirt. Pittsburgh catcher Angelo Encarnacion casually picked up the ball with his mask. Tommy Lasorda appealed, citing a rule that awards a runner two bases if a fielder uses his mask on a thrown ball. The umpires agreed and allowed the run to score.

AUGUST 13   Todd Worrell strikes out three batters on nine pitches in the ninth inning to close out a 4–1 win over the Pirates at Dodger Stadium. Worrell fanned Mark Johnson, Angelo Encarnacion and Steve Pegues.

AUGUST 15   Raul Mondesi hits a grand slam off Steve Trachsel in the fourth inning to give the Dodgers a 4–3 lead, but the Cubs rally to win 7–5 at Dodger Stadium.

AUGUST 18   The Dodgers trade Dwight Maness and Scott Hunter to the Mets for Brett Butler.

AUGUST 20   Hideo Nomo strikes out 13 batters in seven innings, but gives up five runs and the Dodgers lose 5–3 in New York.

AUGUST 27   Mike Piazza hits two homers and two doubles and drives in seven runs during a 9–1 win over the Phillies in Philadelphia. Piazza doubled in a run in the third inning, doubled in the fifth and hit a grand slam in the sixth, all off Tommy Greene. Facing Paul Fletcher in the eighth, Piazza smacked a two-run homer.

AUGUST 31   Leading 5–0, the Dodgers allow the Mets to score five runs in the ninth inning, but a run in the Los Angeles half of the ninth results in a 6–5 victory. The winning run scored on a line drive by Eric Karros that was dropped by Ryan Thompson for an error with the bases loaded.

SEPTEMBER 17   Ismael Valdez pitches a two-hitter to defeat the Cardinals 8–0 at Busch Stadium. The only St. Louis hits were a single by Scott Howard in the third inning and Bernard Gilkey in the sixth.

SEPTEMBER 21   The Dodgers fall 1½ games behind the first-place Rockies with a 5–1 defeat at the hands of the Padres in San Diego. The Dodgers led the wild card race by one-half game over the Astros.

SEPTEMBER 23   A two-run, pinch-hit, walk-off home run by Chris Gwynn in the ninth inning beats the Padres 4–2 at Dodger Stadium.

SEPTEMBER 25   Raul Mondesi ties a National League record for right fielders with 10 putouts during a 4–3 win over the Rockies at Dodger Stadium.

SEPTEMBER 27   The Dodgers take over first place with a 7–4 victory over the Rockies at Dodger Stadium.

SEPTEMBER 30   On the second to last day of the regular season, the Dodgers clinch the NL West title with a 7–2 triumph over the Padres in San Diego.

The Dodgers played the NL Central champion Cincinnati Reds in the National League Division Series. Managed by Davey Johnson, the Reds were 85–59 in 1995.

OCTOBER 3   In the first game of the Division Series, the Dodgers lose 7–2 to the Reds before 44,199 at Dodger Stadium, which was over 10,000 short of capacity. Cincinnati scored four runs in the first inning off Ramon Martinez and never trailed. Mike Piazza homered in the losing cause.

OCTOBER 4   The Dodgers out-hit the Reds 14–6, but lose game two of the Division Series 5–4 before 46,051 at Dodger Stadium. The Dodgers stranded 11 base runners. Eric Karros drove in all four Los Angeles runs with two homers and a double. His two-run homer in the ninth cut the Cincinnati margin to one run, but the Dodgers couldn't dent the plate again. Shortstop Chad Fonville collected four hits in four at-bats. Brett Butler picked up three hits. Raul Mondesi was ejected in the seventh inning for objecting to a call by home plate umpire Bob Davidson.

OCTOBER 6   The Reds complete the sweep of the Dodgers with a 10–1 win at Riverfront Stadium in Cincinnati. Hideo Nomo was the starter and allowed five runs before being removed with no one out in the sixth inning. With the score 3–1 in the sixth, pinch-hitter Mark Lewis hit a grand slam off Mark Guthrie.

NOVEMBER 30   The Dodgers sign Greg Gagne, most recently with the Royals, as a free agent.

DECEMBER 5   Tim Wallach signs a contract with the Angels as a free agent.

DECEMBER 17   The Dodgers trade Jose Offerman to the Royals for Billy Brewer.

Offerman had an odd year in 1995. He was named to the All-Star team, but was so unpopular in Los Angeles that the announcement of the selection was booed at Dodger Stadium. During the second half of the season, Offerman lost his starting shortstop job to Chad Fonville. After leaving the Dodgers, Offerman played 10 more seasons in the majors as a second baseman and first baseman with six different clubs.

1996

LA

Season in a Sentence

Tommy Lasorda retires, Bill Russell takes over as manager, the Dodgers blow a 2½-game lead in the NL West by losing their last four games, still make the playoffs as a wild card, and are swept by the Braves in the Division Series.

Finish • Won • Lost • Pct • GB

Second   90   72   .556   1.0
The Dodgers won the wild card race by two games.

National League Division Series

The Dodgers lost to the Atlanta Braves three games to one.

Managers

Tommy Lasorda (41–35) and Bill Russell (49–37)

Stats

Stats	Dods	NL	Rank
Batting Avg:	.252	.262	13
On-Base Pct:	.316	.330	14
Slugging Pct:	.384	.408	14
Home Runs:	150		6 (tie)
Stolen Bases:	124		6
ERA:	3.46	4.21	1
Fielding Avg:	.980	.979	7
Runs Scored:	703		12
Runs Allowed:	652		2

Starting Lineup

Mike Piazza, c
Eric Karros, 1b
Delino DeShields, 2b
Mike Blowers, 3b
Greg Gagne, ss
Todd Hollandsworth, lf
Roger Cedeno, cf
Raul Mondesi, rf

Pitchers

Hideo Nomo, sp
Ismael Valdez, sp
Ramon Martinez, sp
Pedro Astacio, sp
Tom Candiotti, sp
Todd Worrell, rp
Antonio Osuna, rp
Mark Guthrie, rp
Scott Radinsky, rp
Chan Ho Park, rp

Attendance

3,188,454 (second in NL)

Club Leaders

Batting Avg:	Mike Piazza	.336
On-Base Pct:	Mike Piazza	.422
Slugging Pct:	Mike Piazza	.563
Home Runs:	Mike Piazza	36
RBIs:	Mike Piazza	105
Runs:	Raul Mondesi	98
Stolen Bases:	Delino DeShields	48
Wins:	Hideo Nomo	16
Strikeouts:	Hideo Nomo	234
ERA:	Hideo Nomo	3.19
Saves:	Todd Worrell	44

JANUARY 29   Roberto Kelly signs a contract with the Twins as a free agent.

FEBRUARY 3   Kevin Tapani signs a contract with the White Sox as a free agent.

APRIL 1   The Dodgers open the season with a 4–3 win over the Astros in Houston. All four Los Angeles runs scored in the fifth inning, the last three on a bases-loaded double by Todd Hollandsworth. Ramon Martinez was the starting pitcher, and gave up three runs in six innings. Relievers Darren Hall (two innings) and Todd Worrell (one inning) did not allow a batter to reach base.

Hollandsworth became the fifth Dodger in a row to win the Rookie of the Year Award by hitting .291 with 12 home runs. The previous winners were Eric Karros (1992), Mike Piazza (1993), Raul Mondesi (1994) and Hideo Nomo (1995).

APRIL 4   The day after "Unabomber" Ted Kacynski is arrested in Montana, the Cubs beat snow, sleet, rain, wind, bitterly cold weather and the Dodgers to win 9–4 on a day in Chicago unfit for man or beast, much less baseball. Game-time temperature was 34 degrees with a 19-mile-per-hour northerly gale that dropped the wind chill to 12 above zero. The Wrigley Field aisles were salted to keep people from slipping on the ice.

APRIL 6   Chan Ho Park becomes the first pitcher born in Korea to win a major league game with a 3–1 decision over the Cubs in Chicago. Park pitched four scoreless innings of relief and struck out seven.

The Dodgers staff was known as the International House of Pitchers in 1996 because of the presence of Park (from Korea), Hideo Nomo (Japan), Ramon Martinez and Pedro Astacio (Dominican Republic) and Ismael Valdez and Antonio Osuna (Mexico). The roster also included players from Venezuela, Mexico and Puerto Rico. The diverse backgrounds of the players often led to disharmony and disunity in the clubhouse, however, and led to many cultural misunderstandings (see June 19, 1996). Over the next few years, the team fractured into cliques and factions. It didn't help that few players seemed to stay with the team for long due to free agency and frequent trades.

APRIL 8   The Dodgers win the home opener 1–0 over the Braves before 53,180 at Dodger Stadium. Hideo Nomo pitched a three-hit shutout. The lone run crossed the plate in the third inning on a single by Raul Mondesi.

APRIL 13   Hideo Nomo strikes out 17 batters, one short of the club record, during a 3–1 triumph over the Marlins at Dodger Stadium. From the fifth through eighth innings, Nomo had a stretch in which he fanned nine of the 12 batters to face him. He had a chance to break the club record after fanning the leadoff batter in the ninth for strikeout number 17, but the final two outs were recorded on a ground out and a line out.

Nomo was 16–11 with a 3.19 ERA and 234 strikeouts in 228$^{1}/_{3}$ innings in 1996.

APRIL 17   The Dodgers score seven runs in the fourth inning and defeat the Giants 11–2 in San Francisco. Delino DeShields led off the game with a home run, and doubled and singled during the seven-run fourth.

APRIL 24   A home run by Delino DeShields off Steve Trachsel accounts for the only run of a 1–0 victory over the Cubs at Dodger Stadium. Pedro Astacio (eight innings) and Todd Worrell (one inning) combined on the shutout.

Worrell recorded 44 saves in 1996 and had a 3.03 ERA in 72 games and 65$^{1}/_{3}$ innings.

MAY 3   The Dodgers break open a close game by erupting for eight runs in the ninth inning to defeat the Pirates 10–1 in Pittsburgh. Seven runs scored after two were out. Eric Karros hit a three-run homer during the rally.

MAY 6   Brett Butler is diagnosed with cancer, caused by his longtime use of smokeless tobacco. A tumor the size of a plum was discovered while Butler had a tonsillectomy. The diagnosis came nine months after Butler's mother died of brain cancer. The first of two surgeries was completed on May 21 to remove the lymph nodes. Butler then had to undergo radiation treatments five times a week for six weeks. Survival rates for that type of cancer were 70 percent. Doctors told Butler he wouldn't be able to play again in 1996, and the outfielder promptly announced his retirement. After a remarkable recovery, he returned to playing status four months later, however (see September 6, 1996).

MAY 10 Raul Mondesi scores from second base on an error in the 12th inning to defeat the Cardinals 3–2 at Busch Stadium. Mondesi raced across the plate when St. Louis first baseman Pat Borders mishandled a grounder off the bat of Eric Karros. Normally a catcher, Borders was playing first base for the only time during his 17-year major league career.

MAY 26 Trailing 1–0, the Dodgers score four runs in the ninth inning and hang on for a 4–3 victory over the Expos in Montreal. Mike Blowers hit a three-run double, took third on a throw to the plate, and scored on a ground out.

MAY 31 Roger Cedeno collects five hits in five at-bats during a 10–3 win over the Mets in New York.

JUNE 2 The Dodgers edge the Mets 1–0 in New York. Ismael Valdez (eight innings), Scott Radinsky (one-third of an inning) and Todd Worrell (two-thirds of an inning) combined on the shutout. The lone run scored on a single by Todd Hollandsworth in the sixth inning.

> *From 1993 through 1996, the Dodgers set a major league record by going four consecutive seasons without a single left-hander making a start. The right-handed starting pitchers during that period were Pedro Astacio, Tom Candiotti, Kevin Gross, Orel Hershiser, Pedro Martinez, Ramon Martinez, Hideo Nomo, Chan Ho Park, Kevin Tapani and Ismael Valdez.*

JUNE 4 In the first round of the amateur draft, the Dodgers select third baseman Damian Rolls from Schlagel High School in Kansas City, Kansas.

> *Rolls was drafted by the Royals and sold to the Devil Rays before making the majors. He played five seasons in Tampa Bay, and hit .248 with nine home runs in 819 at-bats as a utility player. Other future major leaguers drafted and signed by the Dodgers in 1997 were Alex Cora (third round), Peter Bergeron (fourth round), Ted Lilly (23rd round), Wayne Franklin (36th round) and Jeff Kubenka (38th round).*

JUNE 15 The Dodgers complete their first triple play since 1949 in the first inning of a 6–2 win over the Braves in Atlanta. Marquis Grissom was the base runner on second with Mark Lemke on first. The two took off with the crack of the bat when Chipper Jones lofted a fly ball into short left field, where shortstop Juan Castro made a running catch with his back to the plate. Castro relayed the ball to second baseman Delino DeShields, who in turn threw to first baseman Eric Karros to nab both Grissom and Lemke.

JUNE 19 Chan Ho Park draws a two-out, bases-loaded walk in the 13th inning that forces in the winning run of a 4–3 victory over the Cubs in Chicago. Park, who had one career base hit in 13 at-bats when he stepped to the plate, batted for himself because the

Dodgers were out of positions players to pinch-hit. Park also threw three shutout innings.

Park had problems with his teammates in June. As part of a rookie hazing prank, his clothes were cut to shreds and a disco outfit was placed in his locker to wear through the airport on the way back to Los Angeles. Park threw a fit over the incident, and threw chairs all over the clubhouse because the suit was a gift from his mother and had great sentimental value. Park later apologized, but not before Mike Piazza criticized him in the media.

JUNE 23   A walk-off homer by Mike Piazza in the ninth inning defeats the Astros 4–3 at Dodger Stadium. The Dodgers scored twice in the eighth inning to tie the contest.

Piazza hit .336 with 36 homers and 105 RBIs in 1996.

JUNE 26   Tommy Lasorda suffers a mild heart attack. He had been hospitalized for a stomach ulcer when additional tests revealed a heart problem and the blockage of the distal right coronary artery. Coach Bill Russell took over as interim manager.

JUNE 27   Rockies first baseman Andres Galarraga drives in eight runs during a 13–1 win over the Dodgers in Denver.

JUNE 28   The Dodgers allow an unlucky 13 runs for the second day in a row, and lose 13–4 to the Rockies in Denver.

JUNE 29   The Dodgers outlast the Rockies 13–10 in Denver. The two teams combined for 14 runs in the eighth inning. Los Angeles took a 13–0 lead with six runs in the top of the eighth, only to have the Rockies score eight in their half and two more in the ninth. Mike Piazza led the way with three home runs and six RBIs. He hit a solo homer in the fourth inning and a grand slam in the fifth, both off Bryan Rekar. Piazza's third home run was a solo blast off Lance Painter in the eighth. The Dodgers had six homers and 20 hits in all. Billy Ashley, Eric Karros and Greg Gagne accounted for the other three home runs.

JUNE 30   The Dodgers engage in another slugfest with the Rockies at Coors Field and lose 16–15 in a contest that lasts four hours and 20 minutes. There were seven lead changes, two of them in the ninth inning. The Dodgers scored three times in the top of the ninth inning for a 15–14 advantage, but Colorado responded with two tallies in their half for the win. The Dodgers hit six home runs. Eric Karros and Raul Mondesi each hit two, with Todd Hollandsworth and Mike Piazza accounting for the others. It was the second consecutive game in which the Dodgers hit six home runs. In the third, Piazza, Karros and Mondesi hit three consecutive homers on three consecutive pitches from Mark Thompson. Mondesi also tripled and single and drove in six runs. For the Rockies, Eric Young tied a major league record by stealing six bases, including second base, third base and home plate in succession in the third inning. Colorado stole 10 bases in all, nine of them off Hideo Nomo in five innings.

Despite allowing 52 runs in four games in Denver, the Dodgers finished the season with a 3.46 ERA, the lowest in the National League. Los Angeles scored 703 runs during the season, to rank 12th among 14 NL clubs.

JULY 1   The Dodgers reach double figures in runs scored for the third consecutive game in defeating the Padres 10–2 in San Diego. Todd Hollandsworth collected five hits, including a homer and a triple, in five at-bats. Mike Piazza and Eric Karros also homered.

> *Combined with the six homers the Dodgers struck in both the June 29 and June 30 games, the club established a National League record (since tied) with 15 home runs in three consecutive games. The 15 homers were accounted for by Piazza (five), Karros (four), Hollandsworth (two), Raul Mondesi (two), Greg Gagne (one) and Billy Ashley (one).*

JULY 4   The Dodgers score eight runs in the second inning and best the Rockies 9–4 at Dodger Stadium.

> *After allowing the Rockies 52 runs in four games at Coors Field from June 27 through June 30, the Dodgers surrendered just 10 runs to Colorado in a four-game set at Dodger Stadium from July 4 through July 7.*

JULY 9   Mike Piazza is the All-Star Game MVP after the National League wins 6–0 at Veterans Stadium in Philadelphia. He homered leading off the second inning against Charles Nagy and doubled in a run in the third. Piazza also homered in the 1995 All-Star Game. He was born in nearby Norristown, Pennsylvania, and was once the visiting team batboy at Veterans Stadium.

JULY 15   A walk-off single by Dave Hansen in the 10th inning beats the Giants 1–0 at Dodger Stadium. Pedro Astacio (8$^1/_3$ innings) and Mark Guthrie (1$^2/_3$ innings) combined on the shutout.

> *Tommy Lasorda made his first appearance at Dodger Stadium since his heart attack on June 26. He was given a standing ovation when introduced to the crowd before the game.*

JULY 18   Third baseman Mike Busch hits a grand slam off Mark Dewey in the seventh inning of an 8–3 win over the Giants in San Francisco. Busch was called up from the minors earlier in the day after Mike Blowers went on the disabled list with a torn ligament in his knee.

JULY 25   The Dodgers sign Tim Wallach, most recently with the Angels, as a free agent.

JULY 27   On the day a bomb explodes in an Atlanta park filled with people attending the Olympics, the Dodgers score three runs in the ninth inning and one in the 10th to beat the Astros 6–5 in Houston. Billy Ashley tied the score in the ninth with a three-run pinch-homer. Eric Karros drove in the game-winner with a single.

> *Ashley hit five pinch-hit home runs in 1996.*

JULY 29   Tommy Lasorda announces his retirement as manager of the Dodgers.

> *Lasorda made the decision in the wake of his heart attack on June 26. "as excitable as I am, I could not go down there and not be the way I've always been," explained Lasorda, "and I have decided it was best for me and best*

for the organization to step down." He was 68 years old and had managed the Dodgers since 1976. Overall, he had a 1,599–1,439 record and won four National League pennants and two world championships. Walter Alston and Lasorda combined to manage the Dodgers for 42 seasons and part of a 43rd from 1954 through 1996. Lasorda was given a front office job as a vice-president. Bill Russell, who was 47 year old and took over as interim manager after Lasorda's heart attack, was given the position on a permanent basis. Russell played for the Dodgers from 1969 through 1986 and ranks second all-time on the franchise lists in games played with 2,181. He was a coach with the club from 1987 through 1991, and after two years managing in the minors at Albuquerque, was a coach again in 1994 until his appointment as manager. Stoic and calm, Russell presented a sharp contrast to the excitable Lasorda, who was accused of losing touch with the young players on the Dodger roster and for giving preferential treatment to the stars on the club. Russell would manage the Dodgers 74 games into the 1998 season. He had an overall record of 173–149.

AUGUST 3   The Dodgers lose 5–3 in 18 innings to the Braves at Dodger Stadium. The marathon lasted five hours and five minutes. The Dodgers tied the score 3–3 with a run in the ninth on Wayne Kirby's two-out single. The two teams combined for eight consecutive scoreless innings before Atlanta crossed the plate twice in the 18th. From the eighth inning through the 15th, the Braves were held without a hit by the combined efforts of Ismael Valdez, Jim Bruske, Antonio Osuna, Scott Radinsky, Todd Worrell and Ramon Martinez. Martinez pitched the final four innings after the bullpen was depleted. It was his only relief appearance between his rookie season in 1988 and the end of his career in 2001.

AUGUST 7   Ramon Martinez is struck in the face by a batted ball in the first inning of a 12–2 loss to the Pirates in Pittsburgh. The Dodger pitcher was felled by a liner off the bat of Jeff King, which hit him in the left cheek. Martinez was motionless for several minutes before slowly getting to his feet. After a few warm-up tosses, he stayed in the game, and on the first pitch, allowed a home run to Mark Johnson. Martinez lasted five innings before being relieved.

AUGUST 11   The Dodgers break a 5–5 tie with five runs in the ninth inning to defeat the Reds 10–5 in Cincinnati. The last four crossed the plate on a grand slam by Tim Wallach off Hector Carrasco. It was Wallach's first game with the club since being re-acquired on July 25.

AUGUST 29   The Martinez brothers face each other for the first time, and Ramon and the Dodgers defeat Pedro and the Expos 2–1 in Montreal. Ramon allowed a run and three hits in eight innings. Todd Worrell worked the ninth. Pedro surrendered two runs and six hits in a complete game. The Los Angeles runs scored on back-to-back homers by Mike Piazza and Eric Karros in the fourth inning.

AUGUST 31   The Dodgers score eight runs in the fourth inning for an 11–0 lead and hang on to defeat the Phillies 11–7 in Philadelphia.

SEPTEMBER 6   Brett Butler returns for his first game since being diagnosed with cancer on May 6. Batting leadoff and playing center field, Butler hit a single in three at-bats and stole a base during a 2–1 win over the Pirates at Dodgers Stadium.

Butler lost about 20 pounds while taking radiation therapy. Upon his return to the game, his saliva glands were still malfunctioning and there were sores on the roof of his mouth from his treatment. As a result, he received special permission from the National League to take a water bottle with him to center field.

SEPTEMBER 10   Four days after his return from cancer, Brett Butler breaks his hand when struck by a pitch from Giovanni Carrara while bunting in the fourth inning of a 5–4 win over the Reds at Dodger Stadium. The injury ended Butler's season.

Butler returned to the Dodgers in 1997, the last season of his career.

SEPTEMBER 12   Hideo Nomo (eight innings) and Antonio Osuna (one inning) combine on a two-hitter to defeat the Cardinals 4–1 at Dodger Stadium. The only St. Louis hits were a home run by Ron Gant in the fourth inning and a single from Dmitri Young in the eighth.

SEPTEMBER 17   At Coors Field in Denver, Hideo Nomo pitches a no-hitter in one of the best hitter's parks in major league history and a location where the Dodgers allowed 52 runs during a four-game series in June. The Dodgers won 9–0 over the Rockies. Nomo made 110 pitches, walked four and struck out eight. In the ninth inning, Eric Young and Quinton McCracken both grounded out to second baseman Delino DeShields. The last out was recorded on a swinging strikeout by Ellis Burks.

With about seven weeks left in the presidential campaign, Bob Dole trailed Bill Clinton in the polls amid accusations that he was out of touch with the present state of the nation. The day after Nomo's no-hitter, Dole made matters worse at a rally. "The Brooklyn Dodgers had a no-hitter last night last night," said Dole, "and I'm going to follow what Nomo did. And we're going to wipe them out between now and November 5." At the time, the Brooklyn Dodgers hadn't existed for 39 years.

SEPTEMBER 19   Ramon Martinez strikes out 12 batters and beats the Padres 7–0 in San Diego.

SEPTEMBER 21   The Dodgers score seven runs in the fifth inning and defeat the Padres 9–2 in San Diego.

SEPTEMBER 24   Ramon Martinez (seven innings), Antonio Osuna (one innings) and Todd Worrell (one inning) combine on a two-hitter to defeat the Giants 6–2 at Dodger Stadium. The only San Francisco hits were singles in the fifth inning by Desi Wilson and opposing pitcher Allen Watson.

SEPTEMBER 25   The Dodgers take a 2¹/₂-game lead over the second place Padres with a 7–5 victory over the Giants at Dodger Stadium.

The Dodgers had four games remaining and the Padres three. The two NL West contenders were scheduled to meet in a season-concluding, three-game series at Dodger Stadium.

SEPTEMBER 26   With a chance to clinch the NL West pennant, the Dodgers lose 6–1 to the Giants in San Francisco.

SEPTEMBER 27   In the first of a three-game pennant showdown series against the Padres at Dodger Stadium, the Dodgers lose 5–2 in ten innings. The defeat cut the first-place margin to one game. The Dodgers did clinch a playoff spot with no worse than a wild card berth, however, when the Expos lost 6–4 to the Braves.

SEPTEMBER 28   The Padres tie the Dodgers for first place with a 4–2 win at Dodger Stadium.

SEPTEMBER 29   On the final day of the season, the Dodgers and Padres meet to decide the NL West champion, and the Padres win 2–0 in 11 innings. Ex-Dodger Chris Gwynn drove in both runs with a double off Chan Ho Park.

The Dodgers needed only one victory in their last four games to win the NL West crown, but lost all four while scoring only six runs. A wild card berth provided some consolation. Los Angeles met the Atlanta Braves in the National League Division Series. Managed by Bobby Cox, the Braves were 96–66 in 1996.

OCTOBER 2   A 10th-inning home run by Braves catcher Javy Lopez off Antonio Osuna beats the Dodgers 2–1 in the first game of the Division Series before 47,428 at Dodger Stadium. The lone Los Angeles run scored in the fifth on doubles by Greg Gagne and Todd Hollandsworth which tied the score 1–1. Ramon Martinez pitched eight innings and allowed a run and three hits.

OCTOBER 3   In game two of the Division Series, the Braves win 3–2 over the Dodgers before 51,916 at Dodger Stadium. Atlanta scored their three runs on solo homers off Ismael Valdez. Ryan Klesko tied the game 1–1 with a home run in the second inning, and after the Dodgers took a 2–1 lead in the fourth, Fred McGriff and Jermaine Dye hit home runs in the seventh.

OCTOBER 5   The Braves complete their sweep of the Dodgers in the Division Series with a 5–2 win in Atlanta. All five runs scored off Hideo Nomo in 3²/₃ innings.

The contest marked the last time that the Dodgers played at Atlanta-Fulton County Stadium. Counting the post-season, the Dodgers lost their last seven games in 1996 and scored only 11 runs.

NOVEMBER 20   Two weeks after Bill Clinton wins re-election as president by defeating Bob Dole, Delino DeShields signs a contract as a free agent with the Cardinals.

DECEMBER 8   The Dodgers sign Todd Zeile, most recently with the Orioles, as a free agent.

Zeile played for 11 teams during his 16-year big league career and hit at least five home runs for each one of them. The Dodgers were club number five, and he hit a career-high 31 homers in 1997. The other 10 teams were the Cardinals, Cubs, Phillies, Orioles, Marlins, Rangers, Mets, Angels, Yankees and Expos. He also married Julianne McNamara, the first American gymnast to earn a perfect 10.0 in the Olympics. She accomplished the feat in 1984.

1997

Season in a Sentence

For the second year in a row, the Dodgers drop out of first place and blow a chance to win the NL West in late-September.

Finish • Won • Lost • Pct • GB

Second   88   74   .543   2.0

In the wild card race, the Dodgers finished tied for second place four games behind.

Manager

Bill Russell

Stats

Stats	Dods	NL	Rank
Batting Avg:	.268	.263	4
On-Base Pct:	.330	.333	8
Slugging Pct:	.418	.410	4
Home Runs:	174		2 (tie)
Stolen Bases:	131		7
ERA:	3.62	4.20	2
Fielding Avg:	.981	.981	8
Runs Scored:	742		7
Runs Allowed:	645		2

Starting Lineup

Mike Piazza, c
Eric Karros, 1b
Wilton Guerrero, 2b
Todd Zeile, 3b
Greg Gagne, ss
Todd Hollandsworth, lf
Brett Butler, cf-lf
Raul Mondesi, rf

Pitchers

Hideo Nomo, sp
Chan Ho Park, sp
Ismael Valdez, sp
Ramon Martinez, sp
Tom Candiotti, sp
Pedro Astacio, sp
Todd Worrell, rp
Scott Radinsky, rp
Darren Hall, rp
Mark Guthrie, rp
Darren Dreifort, rp
Antonio Osuna, rp

Attendance

3,319,504 (third in NL)

Club Leaders

Batting Avg:	Mike Piazza	.362
On-Base Pct:	Mike Piazza	.431
Slugging Pct:	Mike Piazza	.631
Home Runs:	Mike Piazza	40
RBIs:	Mike Piazza	124
Runs:	Mike Piazza	104
Stolen Bases:	Raul Mondesi	32
Wins:	Hideo Nomo	14
	Chan Ho Park	14
Strikeouts:	Hideo Nomo	233
ERA:	Ismael	
	Valdez	2.65
Saves:	Todd Worrell	35

JANUARY 6   Peter O'Malley announces his intention to sell the Dodgers, the last family-run franchise in the major leagues. Peter and his sister Terry Seidler cited the need for estate tax planning as the reason for the sale. He was also disenchanted with the city's rejection of his plan to build a football stadium adjacent to Dodger Stadium to field an NFL team. Walter O'Malley, Peter's father, first bought a 25 percent share in the club in 1944 and became the majority shareholder in 1950. In May 1997, Peter announced he was negotiating with the Fox Group, an affiliate of Rupert Murdoch's News Corporation, with a deal in place three months later (see September 21, 1997).

> At the time Walter O'Malley bought the Dodgers in 1950, families dominated the sport. They included such individuals as P. K. Wrigley (Cubs), Horace Stoneham (Giants), Lou Perini (Braves), Bob Carpenter (Phillies), Powel Crosley (Reds), Tom Yawkey (Red Sox), Clark Griffith (Senators), Connie Mack (Athletics), the Comiskeys (White Sox), and Walter Briggs (Tigers). By the 1990s, it was nearly impossible for a family to operate a franchise because of escalating costs.

MARCH 5   Tommy Lasorda is elected to the Hall of Fame by the Committee on Veterans.

APRIL 1   The Dodgers lose the season opener 3–0 to the Phillies before 53,079 at Dodger Stadium. Los Angeles batters collected only two hits off Curt Schilling (eight innings) and Ricky Bottalico (one inning). Ramon Martinez was the starting and losing pitcher.

APRIL 7   The Dodgers outlast the Mets 3–2 in 15 innings at Dodger Stadium. Hideo Nomo, Tom Candiotti, Scott Radinsky, Darren Hall, Mark Guthrie and Pedro Astacio combined to allow only seven hits. Tom Prince singled in the winning run. He replaced Mike Piazza at catcher in the 11th inning during a double switch.

APRIL 9   The Dodgers defeat the Mets in extra innings for the second time in three days, this time in 14 innings at Dodger Stadium. The winning run was driven in on a single by Mike Piazza.

A 62nd round draft choice, catcher Mike Piazza became one of the great catchers of his era, mostly through his hitting prowess. In 1997, his last full season as a Dodger, he posted some of the best numbers of his career.

Piazza had the best offensive season of any catcher in major league history in 1997. He hit .362 with 104 runs, 201 hits, 40 home runs and 124 runs batted in. That he accomplished the feat in pitcher-friendly Dodger Stadium is all the more remarkable.

APRIL 13   The Dodgers score nine runs in the third inning and defeat the Pirates 14–5 in Pittsburgh. The rally was capped by a three-run homer from Todd Hollandsworth.

After winning the Rookie of the Year Award in 1996, Hollandsworth slumped early in the season and spent two weeks in the minors in June getting himself untracked. He hit only .247 with four home runs.

APRIL 15   On the 50th anniversary of his first game in the major leagues, Jackie Robinson is honored during a 5–0 Dodger loss to the Mets at Shea Stadium. Play was stopped for 35 minutes at the end of the fifth inning for the ceremonies.

President Bill Clinton attended the event, walking with the help of two canes because of an injured knee. Robinson's widow, Rachel, and daughter Sharon made remarks to the sellout crowd and grandson Jesse Robinson Simms threw out the ceremonial first pitch. Other dignitaries included former teammates Ralph Branca and Joe Black. Commissioner Bud Selig spoke first, and announced that Robinson's number 42 would be retired throughout baseball. The tribute took place just a few miles from Ebbets Field, where Robinson made his debut. It didn't escape notice, however, that the Dodgers opened the

1997 season with Wayne Kirby, a seldom-used outfielder, as the only American-born black player in the roster. Later in the year, the club would add African-Americans Otis Nixon, Eric Young, Darren Lewis and Eddie Murray.

APRIL 16   Pedro Astacio (seven innings), Mark Guthrie (one inning) and Todd Worrell (one inning) combine on a one-hitter to defeat the Mets 5–2 at Shea Stadium. The only New York hit was a double by Carlos Baerga off Astacio leading off the eighth inning. Brett Butler had four more hits than the entire Met team with five singles in five at-bats.

Worrell had 35 saves in 1997, but they came with an earned run average of 5.28 in 65 games and 59¹/₃ innings. At the end of the season he opted for retirement. Worrell's 127 saves as a Dodger ranks third on the all-time club list.

APRIL 28   The Dodgers play at Turner Field in Atlanta for the first time and lose 14–0 to the Braves.

MAY 22   Tony Gwynn collects three hits in four at-bats against Hideo Nomo during a 4–1 loss to the Padres in San Diego. A week earlier, Nomo sued Gwynn's wife, Alicia, for using Nomo's likeness on a jigsaw puzzle she was marketing.

JUNE 1   Mike Piazza, Eric Karros and Todd Zeile hit consecutive home runs during a span of nine pitches from Alan Benes in the fourth inning of a 6–1 win over the Cardinals in St. Louis.

Dodger second baseman Wilton Guerrero was ejected in the first inning for using a corked bat. The ruse was discovered when his bat shattered. The National League suspended Guerrero for eight days and fined him $1,000. Wilton is the older brother (by 16 months) of Vladimir Guerrero.

JUNE 3   In the first round of the amateur draft, the Dodgers select first baseman Glenn Davis from Vanderbilt University.

Davis never reached the majors. The only future big leaguer drafted and signed by the Dodgers in 1997 was second rounder Steve Colyer, whose career lasted only two seasons. The club also drafted Long Beach native Chase Utley, but he refused to sign a contract, deciding instead to attend UCLA. Utley was drafted by the Phillies in 2000.

JUNE 11   Raul Mondesi hits two homers and drives in five runs during a 10–5 win over the Astros at Dodger Stadium.

Mondesi hit .310 with 42 doubles and 30 home runs and won his second Gold Glove Award in 1997.

JUNE 12   The Dodgers play a regular season game against an American League opponent for the first time and lose 5–4 to the Athletics in Oakland.

JUNE 14   The Dodgers play a regular season game against the Mariners for the first time, and lose 9–8 at the Kingdome in Seattle.

JUNE 17   The Dodgers play the Angels during the regular season for the first time, and win 4–3 at Dodger Stadium with a run in the eighth inning and two in the ninth. It was also the first time that the Dodgers played a regular season game against an AL opponent at home. Todd Zeile was the hero of the contest. He homered leading off the eighth inning and delivered a walk-off homer in the ninth with two out and the score deadlocked at 3–3.

JUNE 18   Two Japanese pitchers face each other for the first time in a major league game during a 7–5 Dodger win over the Angels at Dodger Stadium. Hideo Nomo started for the Dodgers, and pitched $6^{1}/_{3}$ innings. Shigetoshi Hasegawa hurled $1^{1}/_{3}$ innings for Anaheim during the six and seventh.

              Nomo struck out 233 batters in $207^{1}/_{3}$ innings during a season in which he compiled a record of 14–12 and an ERA of 4.25.

JUNE 21   The Dodgers wallop the Giants 11–0 in San Francisco.

JUNE 25   A two-run homer by Mike Piazza off John Burke in the first inning accounts for all of the scoring in a 2–0 win over the Rockies at Dodger Stadium. Ismael Valdez ($8^{1}/_{3}$ innings), Scott Radinsky (one-third of an inning) and Darren Hall (one-third of an inning) combined on the shutout.

              Valdez had embarrassing and ugly confrontations with Bill Russell and Eric Karros during the 1997 season, both of whom accused the pitcher of lacking the guts to pitch out of tough situations. Valdez argued with Russell in the Dodger dugout in plain view of the fans, and fought with Karros in the clubhouse shower following a team meeting designed to promote unity. Russell also nearly got into an altercation with Pedro Astacio, who had to be physically restrained from going after the Dodger manager during a game against the Giants on June 5. Astacio was traded to the Rockies in August. Karros commented, "You could spend every last dime on every world-class psychologist, and they couldn't figure this team out."

JUNE 30   The Dodgers play the Rangers for the first time during the regular season and lose 3–2 at Dodger Stadium.

              The defeat represented the low point of the season. The Dodgers were 39–42 and eight games out of first place. The club righted itself with a 39–17 record from July 1 through August 30.

JULY 2   The Dodgers play a regular season game in Anaheim for the first time and beat the Angels 5–4.

              The Dodgers were 4–0 against the Angels in 1997.

JULY 10   The Dodgers clobber the Giants 11–0 for the second time in less than a month, this time at Dodger Stadium.

JULY 11   The Dodgers extend their winning streak to eight games with a 6–2 decision over the Giants at Dodger Stadium.

JULY 13	Dennys Reyes becomes the first left-handed starting pitcher for the Dodgers since 1992 and is the winner in a 9–3 decision over the Giants at Dodger Stadium. The last southpaw prior to Reyes to start for the Dodgers was Bob Ojeda. The streak of right-handers spanned 681 games. *Left-handers still started only six games for the Dodgers in 1997. Reyes was the starter in five of them and Rick Gorecki in one. No lefty started as many as 20 games for the Dodgers in any season between Ojeda in 1992 and Carlos Perez in 2000.*
JULY 14	The Dodgers collect 22 hits and beat the Rockies 14–12 in 10 innings in Denver. Eric Karros broke an 11–11 tie with a two-run homer.
AUGUST 1	The Dodgers collect 20 hits and down the Cubs 13–9 in Chicago.
AUGUST 5	A home run by Mike Piazza in the 10th inning beats the Expos 5–4 in Montreal.
AUGUST 12	The Dodgers trade Bobby Cripps to the Blue Jays for Otis Nixon.
AUGUST 14	Mike Piazza's home run off Pedro Martinez in the third inning is the only run of a 1–0 win over the Expos at Dodger Stadium. Ismael Valdez (8⅓ innings) and Scott Radinsky (two-thirds of an inning) combined on the shutout. Playing in only his second game with the Dodgers, Otis Nixon twice robbed Montreal's David Segui of home runs by leaping above the fence in the second and fourth innings.
AUGUST 15	The Dodgers retire Tommy Lasorda's number 2 in ceremonies prior to a 5–3 loss to the Reds at Dodger Stadium.
AUGUST 16	At Dodger Stadium, the Dodgers score all five of their runs and collect three of their four hits of a 5–3 win over the Reds during the third inning.
AUGUST 19	The Dodgers trade Pedro Astacio to the Rockies for Eric Young.
AUGUST 20	The Dodgers sign Eddie Murray, most recently with the Angels, as a free agent. *Murray closed out his career with the Dodgers, playing nine games, all as a pinch-hitter, over the remainder of the 1997 season.*
AUGUST 22	The Dodgers score four runs in the ninth inning to beat the Phillies 5–3 in Philadelphia. The last three runs scored on a three-run double by Greg Gagne. *On the same day, the Dodgers traded Chad Fonville to the White Sox for Darren Lewis.*
AUGUST 24	The Dodgers take sole possession of first place with a 5–1 win over the Phillies at Philadelphia.
AUGUST 27	Mike Piazza hits two homers and a single and drives in six runs during a 9–5 victory over the Pirates at Dodger Stadium. Otis Nixon collected five hits and a stolen base in six at-bats.

AUGUST 28   The Dodgers play the Athletics at Dodger Stadium for the first time during the regular season, and win 7–1.

AUGUST 29   A two-run, walk-off single by Otis Nixon in the 10th inning defeats the Athletics 5–4 at Dodger Stadium.

AUGUST 30   The Dodgers play the Mariners at Dodger Stadium for the first time, and win 11–2.

The victory gave the Dodgers a 2¹/₂-game lead in the NL West race.

SEPTEMBER 2   In the first Dodger game ever played in Arlington, Texas, the Rangers score six runs in the ninth inning to win 13–12. Rusty Greer started and finished the rally with singles. The Los Angeles relievers who gave up the six runs during the ninth were Scott Radinsky, Todd Worrell and Darren Dreifort.

SEPTEMBER 7   Todd Zeile hits a grand slam off Tony Saunders in the first inning of a 9–5 win over the Marlins at Dodger Stadium.

SEPTEMBER 13   Tom Candiotti ties a major league record by hitting three batters in an inning and four in a game during a 5–1 loss to the Astros in Houston. Losing control of his knuckleball, Candiotti hit Derek Bell, Tony Eusebio and Darryl Kile in the first inning and Bell again leading off the second.

SEPTEMBER 15   The Dodgers outlast the Cardinals 7–6 in 15 innings in St. Louis. Los Angeles scored three times in the top of the 15th inning before the Cards countered with a pair in their half. Wayne Kirby drove in the first run with a pinch-single and scored on a two-run single by Tom Prince.

SEPTEMBER 16   Trailing 6–3, the Dodgers score four runs in the ninth inning to beat the Cardinals 7–6 in St. Louis. The ninth-inning runs were driven in by Raul Mondesi, Todd Hollandsworth, Todd Zeile and Eric Young.

The win gave the Dodgers a two-game lead in the NL West with 11 contests left on the schedule. The club lost their next five games, however, to drop out of first behind the Giants. At the end of the season, the Dodgers trailed San Francisco by two games. Bad luck contributed to the second-place finish. The Dodgers outscored the opposition by 97 runs (742–645). The Giants were outscored 793–784, yet somehow posted a 90–72 record.

SEPTEMBER 18   With a chance to take a two-game lead in the NL West race, the Dodgers lose 6–5 to the Giants in 12 innings in San Francisco. The game ended on a home run by Brian Johnson. The Dodgers had the bases loaded with none out in the 10th inning, but couldn't score. At the end of the day, the Dodgers and Giants were tied for first place with nine games remaining.

SEPTEMBER 19   The Dodgers drop out of first place with a 6–4 loss to the Rockies at Dodger Stadium.

SEPTEMBER 21   Mike Piazza hits a 478-foot homer over the left field pavilion, the longest ever by a Dodger at Dodger Stadium, during a 10–5 loss to the Rockies.

On the same day, Pete O'Malley agreed in principle to sell the Dodgers to the Fox Group, bringing one of baseball's most prestigious and successful franchises under the umbrella of Rupert Murdoch's global business empire. Fox already had a deal in place to telecast major league games. Fox Sports West carried Dodger games over cable. The sale was pending, needing the approval of major league owners (see March 19, 1998).

SEPTEMBER 24   The Dodgers lose 4–1 to the Padres at Dodger Stadium to fall 2½ games out of first with four contests remaining.

NOVEMBER 18   In the expansion draft, the Dodgers lose Karim Garcia to the Arizona Diamondbacks and Rick Gorecki to the Tampa Bay Devil Rays.

DECEMBER 8   The Dodgers sign Jose Vizcaino, most recently with the Giants, as a free agent.

DECEMBER 9   Tom Candiotti signs a contract with the Athletics as a free agent.

DECEMBER 11   Otis Nixon signs a contract as a free agent with the Twins.

DECEMBER 23   Darren Lewis signs a contract as a free agent with the Red Sox.

1998

Season in a Sentence

In the first year under new ownership, the Dodgers franchise, once a model of stability, undergoes a tumultuous year in which two managers and a general manager are fired and Mike Piazza is traded.

Finish • Won • Lost • Pct • GB

Third   83   79   .512 15.0
In the wild card race, the Dodgers finished tied for fourth place, seven games behind

Managers

Bill Russell (36–38) and Glenn Hoffman (47–41)

Stats

Stats	Dods	NL	Rank
Batting Avg:	.252	.262	13
On-Base Pct:	.310	.331	15
Slugging Pct:	.387	.410	15
Home Runs:	159		8 (tie)
Stolen Bases:	137		3
ERA:	3.81	4.23	5
Fielding Avg:	.978	.981	13
Runs Scored:	669		12
Runs Allowed:	678		5

Starting Lineup

Charles Johnson, c
Eric Karros, 1b
Eric Young, 2b
Bobby Bonilla, 3b
Jose Vizcaino, ss
Roger Cedeno, lf-cf
Raul Mondesi, cf-rf
Gary Sheffield, rf
Matt Luke, lf
Trenidad Hubbard, cf-rf
Juan Castro, ss-2b

Pitchers

Chan Ho Park, sp
Ismael Valdez, sp
Darren Dreifort, sp
Dave Mlicki, sp
Ramon Martinez, sp
Brian Bohanon, sp
Jeff Shaw, rp
Scott Radinsky, rp
Antonio Osuna, rp
Mark Guthrie, rp

Attendance

3,089,201 (fifth in NL)

Club Leaders

Batting Avg:	Eric Karros	.296
On-Base Pct:	Eric Karros	.355
Slugging Pct:	Raul Mondesi	.497
Home Runs:	Raul Mondesi	30
RBIs:	Raul Mondesi	90
Runs:	Raul Mondesi	85
Stolen Bases:	Eric Young	42
Wins:	Chan Ho Park	15
Strikeouts:	Chan Ho Park	191
ERA:	Chan Ho Park	3.71
Saves:	Jeff Shaw	25

JANUARY 16   The Dodgers sign Mike Devereaux, most recently with the Rangers, as a free agent.

MARCH 19   The sale of the Dodgers by the O'Malley family to the Fox Group, an affiliate of Rupert Murdoch's News Corporation, is approved by major league owners. The sale, reported to be $311 million, included Dodger Stadium and its 300 surrounding acres, the spring training headquarters in Vero Beach, Florida, and other facilities in the Dominican Republic. The price was the largest ever paid for a sports franchise up to that time. The Australian-born Murdoch had little do with the day-to-day operation of the club, assigning corporate executives to the task. He tended to be involved in projects only when a crisis arose, or large amounts of money were involved. Bob Graziano became the president and chief operating officer. The Fox Group would run the Dodgers during a turbulent six-year period until Frank McCourt purchased the franchise in 2004. The Dodgers were the picture of stability under the O'Malley family, rarely changing managers or general managers. During the period the

O'Malleys ran the Dodgers (1950–97), the club won 13 National League pennants and six world championships. Under Murdoch, the club changed management personnel frequently, made wholesale roster shifts, and spent lavishly, yet never reached the post-season.

MARCH 31   In their first ever regular season game in March, the Dodgers open with a 6–0 loss to the Cardinals in St. Louis. Cardinal starter Todd Stottlemyre and four relievers held Los Angeles to three hits. Mark McGwire hit a grand slam off Ramon Martinez. It was the first of a record 70 home runs that McGwire would hit in 1998.

The Dodgers lost their first four games in 1998. Over the course of the season, the club was never more than five games above the .500 mark, or more than four games below.

APRIL 5   Ramon Martinez (eight innings) and Scott Radinsky (one inning) combine on a two-hitter to defeat the Reds 1–0 in Cincinnati. Martinez retired the first 20 batters to face him before walking Willie Greene with two out in the seventh inning. The no-hit bid ended when Eddie Taubensee singled with one out in the eighth. The second Cincinnati hit was a single by Chris Stynes off Radinsky in the ninth. Raul Mondesi provided the only run of the game with a home run off Mike Remlinger in the seventh.

The 1998 season was the last of 11 that Martinez would pitch with the Dodgers. He was 7–3 with a 2.82 ERA before surgery in June for a torn rotator cuff.

APRIL 7   The Dodgers win their home opener 9–1 before 52,424 at Dodger Stadium. It was also the Dodgers first game against Arizona. Todd Hollandsworth and Thomas Howard hit home runs.

APRIL 9   Mike Piazza hits two homers and drives in six runs during a 7–2 win over the Diamondbacks at Dodger Stadium. Piazza hit a two-run homer in the first inning and a grand slam in the third, both off Jeff Suppan.

APRIL 10   Mike Piazza hits a grand slam for the second game in a row, helping the Dodgers to a 7–2 win over the Astros at Dodger Stadium. The slam was struck in the eighth inning off Mark Magnante.

Piazza is the only player in Dodger history to hit grand slams in consecutive games. He hit another bases-loaded homer on April 24 to tie a major league record for most grand slams in a month.

APRIL 12   Late-inning heroics lead to a 10-inning, 7–6 win over the Astros at Dodger Stadium. A two-out single by Mike Devereaux in the ninth inning tied the game 5–5. After Houston scored in the top of the 10th, Raul Mondesi struck a two-out, two-run, walk-off homer in the bottom half for the victory.

APRIL 21   The Dodgers play the Brewers for the first time and lose 5–2 at County Stadium.

The Brewers moved to the National League in 1998. The Dodgers previously played at County Stadium when the Braves resided in Milwaukee from 1953 through 1965.

APRIL 22   Trailing 6–0, the Dodgers score a run in the fourth inning, five in the fifth and three in the ninth to win 9–6 over the Brewers in Milwaukee. Mike Piazza snapped the 6–6 deadlock with a three-run homer.

APRIL 24   The Dodgers score nine runs in the third inning and down the Cubs 12–4 at Dodger Stadium. Mike Piazza hit a grand slam off Kerry Wood.

APRIL 27   The Brewers play at Dodger Stadium for the first time, and beat the Dodgers 3–2 in 12 innings.

APRIL 30   The Dodgers break open a close game with four runs in the eighth inning and five in the ninth to defeat the Pirates 14–6 in Pittsburgh.

MAY 4   The Dodgers become the first team to have an office in Asia with the opening of their headquarters in Japan.

MAY 8   Todd Zeile hits a grand slam off Jesus Sanchez in the first inning, but the Dodgers lose 12–6 to the Marlins in Miami.

MAY 14   The Dodgers trade Mike Piazza and Todd Zeile to the Marlins for Gary Sheffield, Bobby Bonilla, Charles Johnson, Jim Eisenreich and Manuel Barrios.

Due to become a free agent at the end of the 1998 season, Piazza was dealt because the Dodgers refused his demand of a six-year deal worth $100 million. Piazza had turned down an $80 million offer from the club. After five games with the Marlins, Piazza was traded to the Mets, where he played until 2005. He kept up his high level of play in New York, and was named to seven more All-Star teams and hit 250 home runs after being dealt by the Dodgers. In retrospect, the club should have paid Piazza the money he wanted and kept him in Los Angeles for at least six more years, but didn't come out of the trade with Florida completely empty-handed. Sheffield played for the Dodgers until 2001 and appeared in three All-Star games with the team. Among players with at least 2,000 plate appearances as a Dodger, Sheffield is first in on-base percentage (.424) and slugging percentage (.573) and is eighth in batting average (.312). He hit 129 home runs and drove in 367 runs in 526 games. The four players acquired with Sheffield flopped in Los Angeles, however, and were gone by the start of the 1999 season.

MAY 16   The Dodgers score eight runs in the sixth inning and beat the Expos 9–4 at Dodger Stadium.

MAY 22   The Dodgers play a regular season game in Phoenix for the first time, and defeat the Diamondbacks 5–0.

MAY 23   Ramon Martinez pitches a two-hitter to beat the Diamondbacks 7–1 in Phoenix. The only Arizona hits were singles by Andy Fox leading off the first inning and Brent Brede leading off the ninth. In between the two hits, Martinez retired 24 batters in a row.

MAY 25   Gary Sheffield homers in the 10th inning to defeat the Astros 4–3 in Houston.

MAY 31   Raul Mondesi hits a grand slam off Mike Remlinger in the first inning, but the Dodgers lose 6–5 to the Reds in Cincinnati.

JUNE 2   In the first round of the amateur draft, the Dodgers select outfielder Bubba Crosby from Rice University.

Like most of the drafts during the 1990s, the Dodgers selected poorly. Crosby has been a bust at the major league level. The only other future major leaguers drafted and signed by the Dodgers in 1998 have been Scott Proctor (third round) and David Ross (seventh round).

JUNE 4   The Dodgers trade Hideo Nomo and Brad Clontz to the Mets for Dave Mlicki and Greg McMichael.

Nomo struggled early in the 1998 season and had a 2–6 record at the time of the trade. He would play for the Dodgers again from 2002 through 2004. McMichael went back to the Mets in another trade five weeks later.

JUNE 8   The Dodgers sell Matt Luke to the Indians.

Eleven days later, the Dodgers inexplicably bought Luke back from the Cleveland club. He played two games with the Indians.

JUNE 10   Ismael Valdez pitches a two-hitter to defeat the Athletics 1–0 at Dodger Stadium. The only Oakland hits were singles by Matt Stairs with two out in the seventh inning and Mike Macfarlane in the eighth. The lone run of the contest crossed the plate on a single by Raul Mondesi in the third.

JUNE 18   Eric Karros drives in all five runs of a 5–0 win over the Rockies in Denver. Karros hit a three-run homer in the first inning and a two-run double in the fifth. Dave Mlicki pitched the shutout.

The shutout was the only one that Mlicki recorded as a member of the Dodgers and the second of two he pitched during his big league career.

JUNE 19   Eric Karros homers in the 10th inning to defeat the Rockies 4–3 in Denver.

JUNE 22   The Dodgers fire general manager Fred Claire and manager Bill Russell. Tommy Lasorda became the interim general manager and Glenn Hoffman interim manager.

The club had a record of 36–38 at the time of the changes. Claire had been general manager since 1987. After capturing a world championship in 1988, the Dodgers didn't win another post-season game under his leadership (see September 11, 1998). Russell was the first manager fired by the Dodgers since Chuck Dressen in 1953. Walter Alston (1954–76) and Lasorda (1976–96), Dressen's two successors, both retired on the job. Russell never managed another big league team. Hoffman, the older brother of longtime Padres closer Trevor Hoffman, was a utility infielder in the majors with three clubs, mainly the Red Sox, from 1980 through 1989. He played in 40 games with the Dodgers in 1987. At the time of his appointment as interim manager, Hoffman had been managing the Dodgers Class AAA affiliate in Albuquerque. He finished the season, and guided the Dodgers to a record of 47–41 (see September 30, 1998). Lasorda was on the job as interim general manager for only three months, but it was enough time to make a couple of damaging trades.

JUNE 24   Third baseman Adrian Beltre makes his major league debut at the age of 19, and singles and doubles in five at-bats during an 11-inning, 6–5 victory over the Angels at Dodger Stadium.

JUNE 27   Ismael Valdez pitches a one-hitter to defeat the Pirates 2–0 at Dodger Stadium. The no-hit bid was ruined by a leadoff single in the eighth inning from Kevin Young. Raul Mondesi drove in both runs with a two-run single in the sixth inning.

JUNE 28   Gary Sheffield and Pirates catcher Jason Kendall fight in the sixth inning of a 6–4 loss at Dodger Stadium. As Sheffield crossed the plate he swatted Kendall's helmet off his head. The two exchanged words and were soon wrestling each other to the ground as both benches emptied. At one point, Sheffield tried to pick up Kendall, but instead got hit in the face with the catcher's shin guard, opening a cut near Sheffield's eye. Both were ejected and later suspended. The two were teammates at the All-Star Game nine days later, but Sheffield refused to speak to Kendall.

JULY 1   The Dodgers score three runs in the ninth inning to win 7–5 over the Rangers in Arlington. Gary Sheffield drove in the first run with a single, and scored on a two-run double by Eric Karros.

JULY 4   The Dodgers trade Paul Konerko and Dennys Reyes to the Reds for Jeff Shaw.

The deal was made three days before the All-Star Game, and Shaw had already been selected to the team. In an unusual situation, Shaw made his first appearance in a Dodger uniform in the All-Star Game and pitched one inning in a 13–8 National League loss at Coors Field in Denver. In the short run, the Dodgers made a successful trade, as Shaw was a solid closer through the end of the 1999 season. He recorded 129 saves with the club, which ranks second all-time to Eric Gagne. In the long run, the transaction with Cincinnati has been a disaster, however. First all, interim general manger Tommy Lasorda was unaware that Shaw's contract gave him the right to demand a trade at the end of the season. This caused the Dodgers to overpay for his services in signing him to a new deal, which carries through the 2001 season. Konerko, who was only 22 at the time of the trade, was stuck behind Eric Karros on the Dodger depth chart. The Reds dealt Konerko to the White Sox at the end of the 1998 season, and he has been the club's starting first baseman ever since. Konerko was an All-Star in 2002, 2005 and 2006.

JULY 8   Tommy Lasorda speaks before the United States Senate as an advocate of a Constitutional amendment to ban flag burning. During his testimony, Lasorda related the story of Rick Monday rescuing the flag during a game at Dodger Stadium (see April 25, 1976).

JULY 10   The Dodgers trade Greg McMichael back to the Mets for Brian Bohannon.

JULY 12   Ken Caminiti hits three homers for the Padres during a 6–3 win over the Dodgers at Dodger Stadium.

JULY 18   Trailing 8–3, the Dodgers score two runs in the sixth inning, one in the seventh and two in the eighth to defeat the Cardinals 10–8 in St. Louis. The four eighth-inning runs scored on a pair of two-run homers by Gary Sheffield and Matt Luke.

JULY 20   Darren Dreifort (eight innings) and Jeff Shaw (one inning) combine on a one-hitter to defeat the Reds 2–0 at Dodger Stadium. The only Cincinnati hit was a double by Willie Greene in the second inning.

JULY 23   The Dodgers score six runs in the first inning for a 6–0 lead, but wind up losing 8–6 in 10 innings to the Astros at Dodger Stadium.

JULY 30   Chan Ho Park (eight innings) and Jeff Shaw (one inning) combine on a two-hitter to defeat the Phillies 3–1 at Veterans Stadium. The only Philadelphia hits were singles by Doug Glanville in the first inning and Gregg Jefferies in the fourth.

JULY 31   The Dodgers score three runs in the ninth inning to win 4–3 over the Mets in New York. Roger Cedeno drove in the first run with a two-out triple and scored on a wild pitch. A single by Tom Prince and a double from Eric Young accounted for the winning tally.

> *On the same day, the Dodgers traded Wilton Guerrero, Ted Lilly, Peter Bergeron and Jonathan Tucker to the Expos for Carlos Perez, Mark Grudzielanek and Hiram Bocachica. Perez was preceded to the majors by older brothers Pascual and Melido, both of whom were pitchers. The Dodgers gave Carlos a two-year contract worth $15.6 million, which proved to be a monumental waste of money. On the field, he was 7–18 with a 6.26 ERA in 233²/₃ innings over the season. Off the field, he caused the club nothing but trouble. After one poor performance, he spent several minutes methodically destroying the dugout water cooler with a bat. Perez was later arrested for drunk driving. The final straw came during the 2000 season when he was accused of assaulting a 45-year-old flight attendant. During the flight, Perez became angry when he was told to buckle his seat belt and turn off his cell phone. He grabbed the flight attendant by the hair and shook her, causing neck and back injuries that required three surgeries. Both Perez and the Dodgers were sued, and the case was settled out of court.*

AUGUST 7   Brian Bohannon (7¹/₃ innings), Antonio Osuna (two-thirds of an inning) and Jeff Shaw (one inning) combine on a two-hitter to defeat the Pirates 3–1 at Dodger Stadium. The only Pittsburgh hits were back-to-back doubles by Manny Martinez and Kevin Young in the fourth inning.

AUGUST 14 Don Sutton's number 20 is retired in ceremonies prior to a 5–2 loss to the Braves at Dodger Stadium. Sutton was elected to baseball's Hall of Fame in January 1998.

AUGUST 16 Darren Dreifort (seven innings), Scott Radinsky (one inning) and Jeff Shaw (one inning) combine on a two-hitter to defeat the Braves 1–0 at Dodger Stadium. The Atlanta hits were a single by Javy Lopez and a double from Andres Galarraga in the eighth. The lone run scored on a home run by Eric Young off Denny Neagle in the eighth.

AUGUST 22   Darren Dreifort and Andres Galarraga fight in the second inning of a 7–5 loss to the Braves in Atlanta. Dreifort hit Galarraga with a pitch for the second time in a week. Galarraga charged the mound and swung wildly at the Los Angeles pitcher, who ducked and grabbed his attacker's legs. The two wrestled to the ground causing both dugouts and bullpens to empty. Galarraga was ejected. Dreifort was forced to leave because of cuts on his pitching elbow.

AUGUST 23   Eric Karros hits two homers and drives in five runs off Greg Maddux, but the Dodgers lose 12–7 to the Braves in Los Angeles.

AUGUST 27   After leading 9–1 at the end fourth inning, the Dodgers barely eke out a 10–9 victory over the Expos at Dodger Stadium.

SEPTEMBER 2   Carlos Perez pitches a two-hitter to defeat the Phillies 6–0 at Dodger Stadium. The only Philadelphia hits were singles by Mark Lewis in the second inning and Kevin Sefcik in the sixth.

SEPTEMBER 10   After the first 18 batters are retired by Padres pitcher Kevin Brown, the Dodgers erupt for four runs in the seventh inning and win 4–3 at San Diego.

SEPTEMBER 11   Kevin Malone is named general manager of the Dodgers. He was 41 years old. Malone beat out other leading candidates, which included Jim Bowden, Bob Watson, Dave Dombrowski and Omar Minaya. Malone had previously been general manager of the Expos in 1994 and 1995, but resigned because the club had the lowest payroll in baseball and he wanted an opportunity to build a club with a reasonable expectation of winning. From 1995 through 1998, he was the assistant general manager of the Orioles. When hired, Malone said, "There's new sheriff in town, and the Dodgers will be back." He later wanted to be nicknamed "Dodger Boy." He was the Dodger general manager until 2001, a period marred by underachieving teams, ill-fated signings and trades, almost constant turmoil, and a failure to reach the post-season. Malone was unprepared for the media scrutiny of a large market like Los Angeles and a prominent team like the Dodgers, which was unlike his previous stops in Montreal and Baltimore. He constantly put his foot in his mouth. One writer described his acquisitions as "has-beens, retreads, headcases and flameouts, all paid like future Hall of Famers." The roster changed so frequently, it was difficult for the most loyal of fans to identify with the club.

SEPTEMBER 19   The Giants wallop the Dodgers 18–4 at Candlestick Park. Bill Mueller and Jeff Kent both hit grand slams for San Francisco. Mueller connected off Ismael Valdez in the third inning and Kent against Mike Judd in the fourth.

SEPTEMBER 20   The day after an 18–4 loss, the Dodgers collect only two hits but defeat the Giants 1–0 in San Francisco. The lone run scored on a home run by Trenidad Hubbard off Shawn Estes with one out in the first inning. Carlos Perez pitched the shutout.

SEPTEMBER 30   The Dodgers announce that Glenn Hoffman will not return as manager in 1999, but would be retained by the organization as a coach under the new manager. Hoffman was a coach with the club until 2005 under both Davey Johnson and Jim Tracy.

OCTOBER 23   The Dodgers hire 55-year-old Davey Johnson as manager.

Johnson was at least the second option for the Dodgers as manager. Felipe Alou was the first choice, but Alou chose to remain with the Expos. Nonetheless, Johnson had impressive credentials. He played in the majors as a second baseman for 13 years, and with the Orioles, was named to four All-Star teams and appeared in four World Series. He had previously managed the Mets (1984–90), Reds (1993–95) and Orioles (1996–97). None of the 10 teams he managed a full season ever had a losing record or finished lower than second place. With Johnson at the controls, the Mets had the best season in history with 108 wins and a world championship in 1986. The Reds in 1995 had the best winning percentage of any team from 1981 through the present. The Orioles of 1997 won more games than any other Oriole team between 1983 and the present. He had a reputation for being arrogant, however, and often had problems with management. Johnson resigned after a 98–64 season with the Orioles in 1997 because he couldn't get along with owner Pete Angelos. The Dodgers were expected to approach the 98-win mark under Johnson in 1999. Johnson even said that with the talent the club possessed "they could hire the village idiot and win." The Dodgers limped to a 77–85 finish, however. Johnson was fired after an 86–76 record in 2000.

NOVEMBER 9   The Dodgers sign Devon White, most recently with the Diamondbacks, as a free agent.

NOVEMBER 11   The Dodgers trade Bobby Bonilla to the Mets for Mel Rojas.

DECEMBER 1   The Dodgers trade Charles Johnson and Roger Cedeno to the Mets for Todd Hundley and Arnold Gooch.

DECEMBER 12   The Dodgers sign Kevin Brown, most recently with the Padres, as a free agent.

One of the most highly coveted free agents on the market, Brown signed a contract worth $105 million over seven years. He was the first player in history to ink a deal worth over $100 million. Brown also got a hotel suite on road trips and 12 charter round trips for his family each year from Macon, Georgia, to wherever he was pitching. At the time he was acquired by the Dodgers, Brown had a 139–99 lifetime record and was a four-time All-Star. Other owners were shocked and angry over the contract because it set a new pay standard for number one starting pitchers. The contract to Brown was almost $40 million more than the next highest offer by another big league team. It was also much higher than the one that Randy Johnson, a superior pitcher, signed with the Diamondbacks 12 days earlier. Johnson spurned an offer from the Dodgers before agreeing to the Arizona deal. There was also the issue of a seven-year deal to someone of Brown's age. He turned 34 in March 1999. Brown lasted five seasons in Los Angeles and was highly effective when healthy, but in the end fell well short of living up to the enormous contract. He was on the disabled list in four of his five seasons in Los Angeles and missed most of the 2001 and 2002 seasons. Brown was also prickly with teammates, fans and the media and added to the widespread belief that the Dodgers were a team of mercenaries and not a cohesive unit. In five years as a Dodger, he had a 2.83 ERA in 872²/₃ innings with a won-lost record of 58–32. Brown spent the last two years of his seven-year contract (2004 and 2005) pitching for the Yankees following a trade.

1999

LA

Season in a Sentence

Expectations are high under new manager Davey Johnson, but the Dodgers compile their first losing season since 1992 with a roster full of underachieving and overpriced players on long-term contracts.

Finish • Won • Lost • Pct • GB

Third   77   85   .475   23.0

Manager

Davey Johnson
In the wild card race, the Dodgers were tied for fifth place, 19$^1/_2$ games behind.

Stats

Stats	Dods	NL	Rank
Batting Avg:	.266	.268	10
On-Base Pct:	.339	.342	10
Slugging Pct:	.420	.429	12
Home Runs:	187		8
Stolen Bases:	167		2
ERA:	4.45	4.56	7
Fielding Avg:	.978	.980	13
Runs Scored:	793		10
Runs Allowed:	787		8

Starting Lineup

Todd Hundley, c
Eric Karros, 1b
Eric Young, 2b
Adrian Beltre, 3b
Mark Grudzielanek, ss
Gary Sheffield, lf
Devon White, cf
Raul Mondesi, rf
Jose Vizcaino, ss-2b
Todd Hollandsworth, cf-lf
Dave Hansen, 1b-3b

Pitchers

Kevin Brown, sp
Chan Ho Park, sp
Darren Dreifort, sp
Ismael Valdez, sp
Carlos Perez, sp
Jeff Shaw, rp
Pedro Borbon, Jr., rp
Alan Mills, rp
Onon Masaoka, rp
Mike Maddux, rp

Attendance

3,095,346 (fourth in NL)

Club Leaders

Batting Avg:	Mark Grudzielanek	.326
On-Base Pct:	Gary Sheffield	.407
Slugging Pct:	Eric Karros	.550
Home Runs:	Eric Karros	34
	Gary Sheffield	34
RBIs:	Eric Karros	112
Runs:	Gary Sheffield	103
Stolen Bases:	Eric Young	51
Wins:	Kevin Brown	18
Strikeouts:	Kevin Brown	221
ERA:	Kevin Brown	3.00
Saves:	Jeff Shaw	34

MARCH 11   A month after Bill Clinton is acquitted following his impeachment trial in the House of Representatives, Ramon Martinez signs a contract as a free agent with the Red Sox, where he joins his brother Pedro.

MARCH 13   Angered after a teammate flushes a toilet while he is taking a shower in the clubhouse at Vero Beach, Kevin Brown picks up a bat and smashes the toilet to smithereens.

APRIL 5   On Opening Day, Raul Mondesi leads a tremendous comeback to defeat the Diamondbacks 8–6 in 11 innings at Dodgers Stadium before a crowd of 53,109. Mondesi started the scoring with an RBI-single in the first inning, but the Dodgers trailed 6–3 heading into the ninth. With two out, Mondesi hit a three-run homer on a 3–0 pitch to tie the score. With two away in the 11th, Mondesi clubbed a two-run, walk-off home run to give the Dodgers an 8–6 victory in Davey Johnson's debut as the team's manager. Kevin Brown, in his first game with the Dodgers, was the starting pitcher and allowed five runs in 5$^2/_3$ innings.

In his first season in Los Angeles, Brown led the NL in starts (35) and had a record of 18–9 with an earned run average of 3.00 and 221 strikeouts in 252 1/3 innings.

APRIL 6 — In the second game of the season, the Dodgers win with a walk-off homer in extra innings for the second time when Gary Sheffield clears the left field wall with a drive in the 10th inning that beats the Diamondbacks 3–2 at Dodger Stadium.

APRIL 10 — Solo homers by Raul Mondesi and Eric Karros off Darryl Kile in the seventh inning beats the Rockies 2–0 at Dodger Stadium. Kevin Brown (eight innings) and Jeff Shaw (one inning) combined on the shutout.

APRIL 11 — The Dodgers-Rockies game at Dodger Stadium is postponed by rain. It was the first rainout at the ballpark since April 19, 20 and 21, 1988, when three games in a row were postponed.

APRIL 15 — Darren Dreifort (seven innings) and Pedro Borbon, Jr. (two innings) combine on a two-hitter to defeat the Diamondbacks 8–1 in Phoenix. The only Arizona hits were a triple by Luis Gonzalez in the fourth inning and a single from Damian Miller in the fifth.

APRIL 16 — The Dodgers trade Dave Mlicki and Mel Rojas to the Tigers for Robinson Checo, Aposto Garcia and Richard Roberts.

APRIL 21 — The Braves erupt for seven runs in the 12th inning to beat the Dodgers 11–4 at Dodger Stadium.

APRIL 23 — Cardinals third baseman Fernando Tatis becomes the only player in major league history to hit two grand slams in a single inning during a 12–5 St. Louis win over the Dodgers at Dodger Stadium. Tatis also set a major league record for most RBIs in an inning with eight. The blows were struck during an 11-run third. Chan Ho Park gave up both grand slams and all 11 runs. The first slam by Tatis came with the Dodgers leading 2–0 and no out. Tatis faced Park a second time as the Cards batted around, and delivered on a 3–2 pitch with two out. The only other pitcher in baseball history to give up two grand slams in an inning was Bill Phillips of the Pirates 109 years earlier in 1890.

MAY 14 — The Dodgers win 7–3 over the Cardinals in St. Louis.

The win represented the high point of the season. The Dodgers were 20–15 and one-half game out of first place. Over the remainder of the 1999 season, the club was 57–70.

MAY 22 — During a 5–4 Cardinals victory, Mark McGwire becomes only the third player to hit a ball out of Dodger Stadium. The drive, off Jamie Arnold, bounced off the roof of the left field pavilion and was estimated to have traveled 484 feet. The only other two players to hit a home run out of the Los Angeles ballpark were Willie Stargell in both 1969 and 1973 and Mike Piazza in 1997.

MAY 23 — An 8–3 loss to the Cardinals at Dodger Stadium is marred by a fight. In the ninth inning, Dodger pitcher Terry Arnold hit Shawon Dunston in the back with a fastball.

Dunston, the third Cardinal to be hit in the game, and the second in the inning, rushed the mound and tackled Arnold before they were engulfed by players from both benches and bullpens.

MAY 25   Kevin Brown strikes out 12 batters in eight innings, but loses 3–2 to the Reds in Cincinnati.

JUNE 2   In the first round of the amateur draft, the Dodgers select outfielder Jason Repko from Hanford High School in West Richland, Washington.

> *Repko reached the majors in 2005, but has yet to live up to his first round billing. Other future major leaguers drafted and signed by the Dodgers in 1999 have been Joe Thurston (fourth round), Shane Victorino (sixth), Eric Junge (11th) and Reggie Abercrombie (23rd). Victorino has been the best of the bunch, but he was drafted out of the Dodger organization by the Phillies before reaching the majors.*

JUNE 5   With the Dodgers trailing 4–1 in the sixth inning, Devon White hits a grand slam off Tim Belcher to lead to a 7–4 victory over the Angels at Dodger Stadium.

> *A fight broke out in the fifth inning with the Angels leading 4–0. Chan Ho Park bunted up the first base line and was tagged hard in the chest by Belcher. Park took a few steps back and karate-kicked Belcher in the midsection. Belcher proceeded to throw Park to the ground and pummel him. Park was suspended for seven days and fined $3,000 by the National League.*

JUNE 11   Miguel Tejada hits three homers for the Athletics during a 12–6 win over the Dodgers in Oakland.

JUNE 15   The Dodgers trade Ryan Moskau to the Marlins for Craig Counsell.

JUNE 26   Todd Hundley hits a three-run homer in the ninth inning to defeat the Giants 7–6 in San Francisco. Hundley also hit a two-run homer in the third.

JULY 11   The Dodgers score in each of the first six innings and rout the Mariners 14–3 at Dodger Stadium.

> *An inside pitch by Frankie Rodriguez to Mark Grudzielanek in the sixth inning with the Dodgers leading 12–3 sparked a 15-minute brawl. Rodriguez challenged Grudzielanek to fight causing both benches to empty. There was little more than some perfunctory grabbing and gesturing until Jose Paniagua sucker punched a Dodger player. Suddenly fights broke out all over the field including those between Raul Mondesi and David Segui, Angel Pena and Butch Huskey, David Hansen and Jose Mesa, Devon White and Paniagua, Pedro Borbon, Jr. and Jay Buhner, and Todd Hundley and Damaso Marte. When it appeared the melee had finally ended, Segui challenged the entire Dodger bench. Seven were ejected, including four Dodgers. The ejections left Los Angeles without a catcher, and outfielder Trenidad Hubbard had to play the position for the final three innings. It was the only time he donned catcher's gear during his big league career. Coach Rick Dempsey was suspended for 17 days by the National League for his role in the brawl.*

JULY 17   Eric Karros hits two homers and drives in five runs during a 13–3 thrashing of the Angels in Anaheim.

JULY 19   Todd Hundley hits a grand slam off Jose Silva in the third inning of a 12–7 win over the Pirates in Pittsburgh.

JULY 22   Mark Grudzielanek collects five hits and scores four runs, but the Dodgers lose 12–11 to the Rockies in the second game of a double-header in Denver. Colorado also won the opener 4–1.

                 Grudzielanek batted .326 with seven home runs in 1999.

AUGUST 8   Raul Mondesi hits two homers and drives in five runs during a 14–3 walloping of the Mets in New York.

AUGUST 11   Trailing 6–0, the Dodgers score six runs in the seventh inning and three in the eighth and win 9–7 over the Phillies in Philadelphia. Eric Karros led the comeback with six runs batted in on a grand slam in the seventh inning off Anthony Telford and a two-run single in the eighth.

                 Karros had a stellar season in 1999 with 40 doubles, 34 home runs, 112 runs batted in and a .304 average.

AUGUST 22   Gary Sheffield drives in six runs to lead the Dodgers to a 9–7 win over the Expos in Montreal. Sheffield collected a two-run single in the first inning off Anthony Schumaker and a grand slam in the eighth against Steve Montgomery.

                 Sheffield hit .301 with 34 homers, 101 RBIs and 103 runs scored in 1999.

SEPTEMBER 4   Kevin Brown pitches a two-hitter to defeat the Cubs 6–0 at Wrigley Field. Both Chicago hits were singles by Jeff Reed in the second and fifth innings.

SEPTEMBER 17   The Dodgers lose an 18–10 slugfest to the Rockies in Denver.

SEPTEMBER 28   The Dodgers fire president and CEO Bob Graziano after the club with the highest payroll in baseball stumbles to a losing record. Graziano had been employed by the Dodgers since 1986 and succeeded Peter O'Malley as president and CEO after the Fox Group bought the Dodgers in March 1998 (see October 28, 1999).

SEPTEMBER 30   The Dodgers participate in the last game played at Candlestick Park, and win 9–4 over the Giants.

OCTOBER 3   The Dodgers participate in the last regular season played at the Astrodome, and lose 9–4 to the Astros.

OCTOBER 28   Eleven days after the Staples Center opens with a concert by Bruce Springsteen and the E Street Band, Robert Daly is named chairman, CEO and managing partner of the Dodgers, replacing Bob Graziano at the top of the Dodger organizational chart. The 62-year-old Daly also purchased 10 percent of the stock in the club for about $30 million. Daly had run the Warner Brothers Studios for the previous 19 years. With the new position, Daly was placed in charge of the day-to-day operation of the Dodgers on behalf of the Fox group. He was born in Brooklyn, and grew up as a Dodger fan. Just a month after being fired as president and CEO of the franchise, Graziano was hired by Daly to be the number two man in the organization. Graziano's new title was president and chief operating officer.

NOVEMBER 8   The Dodgers trade Raul Mondesi and Pedro Borbon, Jr. to the Blue Jays for Shawn Green and Jorge Nunez.

The Dodger got rid of the disgruntled Mondesi for Green, who was in the Dodger starting lineup for five years. Green hit a team record 49 homers in 2001 and 42 more in 2002. Mondesi's fate was sealed three months earlier on August 11 when he unleashed a profanity-laced attack against Kevin Malone and Davey Johnson. Mondesi believed he was being unfairly singled out for the team's losing season. He would later play for six different teams in a four-year span from 2002 through 2005.

DECEMBER 12   The Dodgers trade Eric Young and Ismael Valdez to the Cubs for Terry Adams, Chad Ricketts and Brian Stephenson.

DECEMBER 17   The Dodgers sign Orel Hershiser, most recently with the Mets, as a free agent.

Hershiser signed a one-year deal worth $2 million after winning 13 games for the Mets in 1999. The 2000 season proved to be Hershiser's last in the majors. He had a 1–5 record and an astonishing ERA of 13.14 in 24²/₃ innings.

DECEMBER 21   The Dodgers are fined $50,000 and banned from scouting in the Dominican Republic for one year as a penalty for signing Adrian Beltre as a 15-year-old in 1994. According to major league rules, a Latin American player must be at least 16 before signing.

THE STATE OF THE DODGERS

The tradition-laden Dodgers have experienced a myriad of changes since the dawn of the new millennium without experiencing a great deal of success. From the beginning of the 1954 season through Opening Day in 1996, the club had four general managers and just two field managers. The O'Malley family ran the franchise during that entire period. Since the start of the 1996 campaign, the Dodgers have had seven general managers, seven field managers and three owners. This has also led numerous roster changes on an almost yearly basis, and the phrase, "Once a Dodger, always a Dodger," no longer seems to apply. Since winning the 1988 World Series, the Dodgers have a record of 1–12 in the post-season and haven't reached the National League Championship Series since that historic 1988 season. From 2000 through 2008, the Dodgers have a record of 767–691, a winning percentage of .526. National League champions during the 2000s have been the Mets (2000), Diamondbacks (2001), Giants (2002), Marlins (2003), Cardinals (2004 and 2006), Astros (2005), Rockies (2007) and Phillies (2008). NL West champs were the Giants (2000 and 2003), Diamondbacks (2001, 2002 and 2007), Giants (2003), Dodgers (2004 and 2008), and Padres (2005 and 2006).

THE BEST TEAM

The 2004 Dodgers won the NL West with a record of 93–69. The 2008 club was 84–78, but became the first Dodger club to win a postseason series since 1988.

THE WORST TEAM

The Dodgers sank to a 71–91 record in 2005 leading to the dismissal of general manager Paul DePodesto and manager Bill Russell.

THE BEST MOMENT

Shawn Green had the best offensive day of any player in major league history on May 23, 2002, against the Brewers in Milwaukee. He hit four home runs, a double and a single in six at-bats, scored six runs and drove in seven.

THE WORST MOMENT

The Dodgers fought with fans at Wrigley Field on May 16, 2000, resulting in numerous fines and suspensions.

THE ALL-DECADE TEAM • YEARS W/DODS

Paul LoDuca, c	1998–2004
Eric Karros, 1b	1991–2002
Jeff Kent, 2b	2005–08
Adrian Beltre, 3b	1998–2004
Rafael Furcal, ss	2006–08
Gary Sheffield, lf	1998–2001
Dave Roberts, cf	2002–04
Shawn Green, rf	2000–04
Eric Gagne, p	1999–2006
Kevin Brown, p	1999–2003
Derek Lowe, p	2005–08
Brad Penny, p	2004–08

Karros was also on the 1990s All-Decade Team. Before the decade is completed, James Loney will likely be considered the number one first baseman. Finding a capable center fielder has been a problem since the early 1990s when Brett Butler manned the position. Other outstanding Dodgers during the 2000s have been second baseman Mark Grudzielanek (1999–2002) and catcher Russell Martin (2006–08).

THE DECADE LEADERS

Batting Avg:	Jeff Kent	.291
On-Base Pct:	Jeff Kent	.367
Slugging Pct:	Shawn Green	.510
Home Runs:	Shawn Green	162
RBIs:	Shawn Green	509
Runs:	Shawn Green	505
Stolen Bases:	Dave Roberts	118
Wins:	Derek Lowe	54
Strikeouts:	Kevin Brown	563
	Derek Lowe	563
ERA:	Kevin Brown	2.76
Saves:	Eric Gagne	161

THE HOME FIELD

The Dodgers have inaugurated several new features to Dodger Stadium since the beginning of the new century. In 2000, the club added the Dugout Club, 30 new luxury boxes, a revamped sound system and a synthetic warning track as part of a $100 million upgrade. Beginning in 2004, new owner Frank McCourt began the transformation of the ballpark, built in 1962 and once known as "The Taj Mahal of Baseball." The entire concrete structure was repaired and improved. All of the seats were replaced and returned to the original color scheme (yellow, light orange, turquoise and sky blue). Two new LED scoreboards were added along with an LED ribbon board. A new terrace was added outside the Loge level seating entrance. Some 1600 seats were added along the base lines. The changes had a positive effect on fans as the club led the NL in attendance four straight years beginning in 2004. In 2008, owner Frank McCourt announced a $500 million renovation to take place by 2012 (see April 24, 2008). In 2009, Dodger Stadium will be the third oldest ballpark in the majors, behind only Fenway Park (1912) and Wrigley Field (1914). Angel Stadium in Anaheim (1966) will be the fourth oldest.

THE GAME YOU WISHED YOU HAD SEEN

Trailing the Padres 9–5 in the ninth inning on September 18, 2006, the Dodgers hit four home runs in succession to tie the score 9–9. After San Diego plated a run in the top of the tenth, Nomar Garciaparra hit a two-run, walk-off homer in the bottom half for an 11–10 victory.

THE WAY THE GAME WAS PLAYED

The offensive explosion experienced during the last half of the 1990s continued into the 2000s, as did the trend toward new baseball-only ballparks with grass fields. About mid-decade, allegations of the use of performance-enhancing drugs became a hot topic, and Major League Baseball instituted much harsher penalties for players caught using the substances.

THE MANAGEMENT

Rupert Murdoch's Fox Group bought the Dodgers from the O'Malley family in 1998. The franchise was sold to Frank McCourt, Jr. in 2004. General managers have been Kevin Malone (1998–2001), Dave Wallace (interim 2001), Dan Evans (2001–04), Paul DePodesta (2004–05) and Ned Colletti (2005-present). Field managers have been Davey Johnson (1999–2000), Jim Tracy (2001–05), Grady Little (2006–07) and Joe Torre (2008).

THE BEST PLAYER MOVE

Thus far, the best move has been the signing of Jeff Kent to a free agent deal between the 2004 and 2005 seasons.

THE WORST PLAYER MOVE

The worst move was signing injury-prone Darren Dreifort to a five-year, $55 million contract at the end of the 2000 season. Dreifort pitched only $205 2/3$ innings and had a record of 9–14 over the course of the deal.

2000

Season in a Sentence

The Dodgers win 86 games, nine more than the previous season, but are out of contention for a post-season berth by Labor Day and Davey Johnson is dismissed as manager.

Finish • Won • Lost • Pct • GB

Second 86 76 .531 10.0
In the wild-card race, the Dodgers were second place, eight games behind.

Manager

Davey Johnson

Stats

Stats	Dods	NL	Rank
Batting Avg:	.257	.266	12
On-Base Pct:	.341	.342	8
Slugging Pct:	.431	.432	7
Home Runs:	211		4
Stolen Bases:	95		9
ERA:	4.10	4.63	2
Fielding Avg:	.978	.981	14
Runs Scored:	798		8
Runs Allowed:	729		2

Starting Lineup

Todd Hundley, c
Eric Karros, 1b
Mark Grudzielanek, 2b
Adrian Beltre, 3b
Alex Cora, ss
Gary Sheffield, lf
Todd Hollandsworth, cf
Shawn Green, rf
Kevin Elster, ss
Chad Kreuter, c
Dave Hansen, 1b-3b

Pitchers

Chan Ho Park, sp
Kevin Brown, sp
Darren Dreifort, sp
Carlos Perez, sp
Eric Gagne, sp
Jeff Shaw, rp
Terry Adams, rp
Matt Herges, rp
Mike Fetters, rp
Antonio Osuna, rp

Attendance

3,010,819 (sixth in NL)

Club Leaders

Batting Avg:	Gary Sheffield	.325
On-Base Pct:	Gary Sheffield	.438
Slugging Pct:	Gary Sheffield	.643
Home Runs:	Gary Sheffield	43
RBIs:	Gary Sheffield	109
Runs:	Gary Sheffield	105
Stolen Bases:	Shawn Green	24
Wins:	Chan Ho Park	18
Strikeouts:	Chan Ho Park	217
ERA:	Kevin Brown	2.58
Saves:	Jeff Shaw	27

JANUARY 10   Nine days after the dawn of the new millennium and the end of worries about the Y2K problem, the Dodgers sign Gregg Olson, most recently with the Diamondbacks, as a free agent.

JANUARY 14   The Dodgers sign Kevin Elster, most recently with the Rangers, as a free agent.

APRIL 3   The Dodgers open with a 10–4 win over the Expos in Montreal. Eric Karros hit a grand slam off Scott Strickland in the seventh inning. Todd Hundley contributed a homer and two singles. Kevin Brown was the starting and winning pitcher.

   Brown was 13–6 in 2000, but his 2.58 ERA in 230 innings led the National League.

APRIL 4   In the second game of the season, the Dodgers win 10–4 over the Expos in Montreal for the second time. Los Angeles broke the game open with seven runs in the third inning.

APRIL 7   Darren Dreifort allows only two hits in five innings but walks eight and winds up losing 2–1 to the Mets in New York.

APRIL 8   Trailing 5–1, the Dodgers score four runs in the ninth inning and one in the 10th to defeat the Mets 6–5 in New York. Eric Karros led off the ninth with a home run. Five batters later, Devon White smacked a two-out, three run homer to tie the score. Karros struck another home run in the 10th to win the game.

APRIL 9   The Dodgers-Mets game in New York is postponed by snow.

APRIL 11   In the first regular season game at Pacific Bell Park in San Francisco, Kevin Elster hits three homers to lead the Dodgers to a 6–5 victory. Elster hit a solo homer in the third inning, a two-run shot in the fifth, both off Kurt Rueter, and another solo blast in the eighth against Felix Rodriguez. The third-inning homer by Elster was also the first at the new ballpark. Devon White was the first batter, facing Rueter.

Elster sat out the 1999 season, then earned a spot as the club's starting shortstop as a 35-year-old non-roster player in spring training. The three-homer game was accomplished in only the fifth regular season contest following his return. Elster hit .227 with 14 homers in 220 at-bats in 2000, his last year in the majors.

APRIL 14   The Dodgers win the home opener 8–1 over the Reds before 53,223. Garry Sheffield homered.

There were several changes at Dodger Stadium in 2000. The most prominent was the construction of the Dugout Club, a nine-row 565-seat area which brought fans 25 feet closer to home plate. There were also upgrades to the press box and Stadium Club and the addition of 30 new luxury boxes. The sound system was completely revamped. A hard synthetic warning track was also installed and caused problems for defensive players. Many stumbled when stepping from the grass to the rock-hard track, and anyone who dared to slide on it never did so again. It was put in place to protect the irrigation system that helped keep the grass green and soft during the dry summer months.

APRIL 19   Orel Hershiser tied a modern major league record by hitting four batters and the Dodgers tie another mark with five hits batsmen during a 10–3 loss to the Astros in Houston. Hershiser struck Richard Hidalgo and Shane Reynolds in the first inning and Jeff Bagwell and Hidalgo in the second. In the seventh, Hidalgo tied a major league record by being struck by a pitch a third time, this time from Matt Herges.

The Dodgers had starting pitchers from six different countries in 2000. They were Luke Prokepec (Australia), Ismael Valdez (Mexico), Carlos Perez (Dominican Republic), Eric Gagne (Canada), Chan Ho Park (Korea), and Kevin Brown, Darren Dreifort, Mike Judd, Herges and Hershiser (United States).

APRIL 21   Kevin Elster hits a grand slam off Norm Charlton in the ninth inning of a 9–2 win over the Reds in Cincinnati.

The start of the game was delayed 27 minutes because the umpire's equipment was mistakenly sent from Montreal to New York, instead of to Cincinnati. The Reds clubhouse manager found a sporting goods store open, running up a bill of *more than $600, but became embroiled in bumper-to-bumper traffic on the way back to the stadium before receiving a police escort.*

APRIL 22   The Dodgers rout the Reds 16–2 in Cincinnati. Todd Hollandsworth led off the first inning with a home run.

APRIL 23   The Dodgers score eight runs in the sixth inning and defeat the Reds 11–3 in Cincinnati.

APRIL 24   After scoring 36 runs in three games in Cincinnati, the Dodgers lose 1–0 to the Mets at Shea Stadium on a ninth-inning walk-off single by Matt Franco. The Dodgers played only one game on the trip to New York to make-up for the contest postponed by snow on April 9.

APRIL 25   The Dodgers lose 1–0 for the second game in a row, this time to the Braves in Atlanta.

APRIL 29   The Dodgers blow an eight-run lead, but win 13–12 over the Marlins at Dodger Stadium. The Dodgers held a 10–2 advantage at the end of the fourth inning, but allowed Florida to battle their way back to a 12–12 tie, beginning with a seven-run rally in the fifth. The winning run scored on a walk-off single by Eric Karros. Gary Sheffield contributed two homers and five runs batted in.

Sheffield was outstanding in 2000 with 43 homers, 109 RBIs, 105 runs scored, 101 walks and a .326 batting average.

MAY 5   Tommy Lasorda is named manager of the United States Olympic team, which will compete in September in Sydney, Australia. Lasorda guided the team to a gold medal.

MAY 6   Todd Hundley hits a grand slam off Octavio Dotel in the third inning of a 9–6 win over the Astros at Dodger Stadium.

The Dodgers set a team records for total home runs (211) and grand slams (nine) in 2000.

MAY 7   The Astros score seven runs in the 10th inning and defeat the Dodgers 14–8 at Dodger Stadium.

MAY 9   After the Dodgers score in the top of the tenth, the Diamondbacks counter with five runs, all off Orel Hershiser, in the bottom half to win 11–7. The final blow was a walk-off grand slam by Damian Miller.

MAY 12   Darren Dreifort pitches a two-hitter to defeat the Cardinals 13–0 at Busch Stadium. The only St. Louis hits were a double by Eric Davis in the first inning and a single from Fernando Vina in the sixth.

MAY 16   A fan punches Dodger catcher Chad Kreuter, then steals his cap, causing a melee between the Dodgers and fans at Wrigley Field during the ninth inning of a 6–5 win over the Cubs. Krueter was sitting on the bullpen bench when he was hit on the head, and entered the stands to try and stop the assailant. Other members of the

Dodgers bullpen crew followed Kreuter before the rest of the team raced over from the dugout. With beer flying and players fighting fans, it took nine minutes to quell the disturbance. Four fans were arrested.

A total of 19 Dodger players and coaches were suspended for a total of 84 days as a result of the incident. The suspensions were given to Krueter and coaches Rick Dempsey, John Shelby and Glenn Hoffman (eight days each), Carlos Perez, F. P. Santangelo and Gary Sheffield (five days), Mike Fetters (four days) and Eric Gagne, Terry Adams, Darren Dreifort, Onon Masaoka, Alan Mills, Antonio Osuna, Chan Ho Park, Todd Hundley, Eric Karros, Geronimo Berroa, and Shawn Green (three days). Fines were also levied on each of them in addition to the suspensions. After appeal, most of the suspensions were overturned. Only Krueter, Dempsey, Shelby, Sheffield, Perez and Santangelo had their suspensions upheld. The suspension to Fetters was reduced to one game.

MAY 20   Gary Sheffield hits a grand slam off Joe Strong in the seventh inning of a 12–6 win over the Marlins in Miami.

MAY 21   Shawn Green and Adrian Beltre both hits grand slams during a 12–6 win over the Marlins in Miami. Beltre struck first with a slam off Jesus Sanchez in the fifth. Green connected of Antonio Alfonseca during a seven-run ninth.

This was the third time that the Dodgers hit two grand slams in a game. The others were on September 23, 1901 and August 23, 1985.

MAY 22   The Dodgers outlast the Reds 4–3 in 14 innings at Dodger Stadium.

The victory over Cincinnati represented the high point of the season in terms of games above .500. The Dodgers were 25–17 and 1½ games out of first. The club still harbored hopes of a pennant into late summer. The Dodgers were 57–50 and two games out of first on August 2, but were out of contention by the end of the month. A nasty viral bug that spread through the Dodger clubhouse was a contributing factor. Mark Grudzielanek and Gary Sheffield both missed more than a week with the ailment.

MAY 29   Shawn Green hits a grand slam off Al Leiter in the sixth inning to account for all four runs of a 4–1 win over the Mets at Dodger Stadium.

Green reached base in 53 consecutive games during the 2000 season, the second longest streak in club history. The record is 58 by Duke Snider in 1954.

JUNE 5   In the first round of the amateur draft, the Dodgers select pitcher Ben Diggins from the University of Arizona.

Thus far, future major leaguers drafted and signed by the Dodgers in 2000 have included Diggins, Joel Hanrahan (second round), Koyie Hill (fourth round), Shane Nance (11th round) and Victor Diaz (37th round).

JUNE 20   The day after the Lakers win the NBA title in a six-game series against the Indiana Pacers, the Dodgers score four runs in the 10th inning, the last three on a homer by

Gary Sheffield, and defeat the Astros 9–6 in Houston. It was also the first time that the Dodgers played at Minute Maid Park.

On the same day, the Dodgers traded Jose Vizcaino to the Yankees for Jim Leyritz.

JUNE 21   Gary Sheffield collects two homers and two singles and scores four runs during a 7–6 win over the Astros in Houston.

JUNE 27   The Dodgers release Orel Hershiser. A week later, he announced his retirement.

JULY 6   Eight days after Elian Gonzalez returns to Cuba following a bitter legal battle, Kevin Brown strikes out 12 batters during a 9–3 win over the Padres in San Diego.

JULY 7   Eric Karros homers in the 11th inning to defeat the Mariners 3–2 in Seattle. It was also the first time that the Dodgers played at Safeco Field.

JULY 19   Kevin Brown (eight innings) and Mike Fetters (one inning) combine on a one-hitter to beat the Rockies 9–1 at Dodger Stadium. The only Colorado hit was a single by Larry Walker in the first inning.

JULY 23   Darren Dreifort (seven innings), Terry Adams (1²/₃ innings) and Jeff Shaw (one-third of an inning) combine on a two-hitter to defeat the Giants 5–0 at Dodger Stadium. The only San Francisco hits were a single by Barry Bonds in the fourth inning and a double from Bobby Estalella in the fifth.

JULY 24   Gary Sheffield leads the way in a 4–1 win over the Rockies at Dodger Stadium. In his first three at-bats, he homered, tripled and doubled. A single away from the cycle, Sheffield walked and was hit by a pitch in his final two plate appearances.

JULY 27   The Dodgers win a 16–11 slugfest against the Rockies in Denver. Adrian Beltre belted a grand slam off Kevin Jarvis in the third inning and added a two-run single in the eighth for a total of six runs batted in.

JULY 28   Darren Dreifort (seven innings), Mike Fetters (one inning) and Jeff Shaw (one inning) combine on a two-hitter to defeat the Phillies 2–0 at Veterans Stadium. The only Philadelphia hits were a double by Mickey Morandini in the sixth inning and a single from Scott Rolen in the seventh.

JULY 31   The Dodgers trade Todd Hollandsworth, Kevin Gibbs and Randey Gorame to the Rockies for Tom Goodwin and cash.

AUGUST 2   The Dodgers play at Three Rivers Stadium in Pittsburgh for the last time and win 11–5 over the Pirates.

AUGUST 4   Kevin Brown strikes out 12 batters in 7²/₃ innings during a 2–1 win over the Brewers at Dodger Stadium.

AUGUST 8   The Dodgers hit four homers in an inning and five in the game during a 7–5 win over the Cubs at Dodger Stadium. The four homers were struck in the fourth off Phil Norton, who was pitching in his second big league game. Kevin Elster and pitcher

Darren Dreifort led off with back-to-back homers. Later, Gary Sheffield hit a solo shot with two out, and Eric Karros followed with a round-tripper with a man on base. Dreifort hit another home run in the sixth against Todd Van Poppel.

The eruption in the fourth marked the first time the Dodgers hit four homers in an inning. It happened a second time on September 18, 2006, when the club hit four in succession.

AUGUST 16   Trailing 4–3, the Dodgers score seven runs in the eighth inning to win 10–4 over the Marlins in Miami.

AUGUST 22   The Dodgers clout six home runs, including two by Eric Karros in a single inning, during a 14–6 win over the Expos at Dodger Stadium. Karros homered off Julio Santana and Anthony Telford in the sixth. The others were struck by Jim Leyritz, Todd Hundley, Devon White and pitcher Ismael Valdez. It was the only home run by Valdez in 399 career at-bats.

Karros is the only player in Dodger history to hit two home runs in a single inning.

AUGUST 26   The Fox television network shows how baseball production has changed since the first televised game in 1939 (see August 26, 1939) during the telecast of the Dodgers 6–4 loss to the Cubs at Wrigley Field. The era changed with each half-inning as the scratchy black-and-white gradually turned to muddy color and became crystal clear by the end of the game. Graphics, at first non-existent, grew more sophisticated as the game progressed. There were no replays until about one-third of the way through the contest when the broadcast emulated the way baseball looked on TV during the early 1960s.

AUGUST 29   Chan Ho Park (eight innings) and Mike Fetters (one inning) combine on a one-hitter to defeat the Brewers 7–2 at Dodger Stadium. Park retired the first 17 batters to face him before walking Mark Sweeney and surrendering a home run to James Mouton with two out in the sixth. Park struck out 14 batters.

Park had the best season of his career in 2000 with an 18–10 record and a 3.26 ERA and 217 strikeouts in 226 innings.

Between 1997 and 2001, few pitchers in the league were more electrifying than Chan Ho Park, who won a career-high 18 games in 2000. After stints with three other teams, he returned to the Dodgers in 2008.

AUGUST 31   The Dodgers play at County Stadium for the last time, and lose 8–2 to the Brewers.

SEPTEMBER 2   A double by Jeff Branson and a single from Tom Goodwin in the 10th inning provides the only run of a 1–0 triumph over the Phillies at Dodger Stadium. Kevin Brown (seven innings), Antonio Osuna (one inning), Jeff Shaw (one inning) and Matt Herges (one inning) combined on the shutout.

SEPTEMBER 10   The Dodgers wallop the Rockies 12–1 in Denver.

SEPTEMBER 12   Dave Hansen sets a major league record by hitting his seventh pinch-hit home run of the season during a 5–4 loss to the Diamondbacks in Phoenix.

                Hansen broke the record of six pinch-homers, set by Johnny Frederick of the Dodgers in 1932. Craig Wilson of the Pirates tied Hansen's mark with seven in 2001. During the 2000 season, Hansen had 65 pinch-hit plate appearances and hit his seven home runs in 55 official at-bats. Overall, he had eight home runs in 121 at-bats. Hansen hit 15 career pinch-hit home runs, five short of the all-time record of 20 set by Cliff Johnson. Hansen had a total of 35 lifetime home runs in 1,793 at-bats over 15 seasons. He played for the Dodgers from 1990 through 1996 and again from 1999 through 2002. The only season in his time in the majors that Hansen had more than 200 at-bats was in 1992, when he accumulated 341.

SEPTEMBER 15   A walk-off homer by Mark Grudzielanek in the 10th inning defeats the Rockies 4–3 at Dodger Stadium.

SEPTEMBER 17   The Dodgers hit five home runs during a 12–6 victory over the Rockies at Dodger Stadium. Adrian Beltre clubbed two of them, with Chris Donnels, Chad Kreuter and Alex Cora adding the remainder.

SEPTEMBER 18   A walk-off homer by Kevin Elster with two-out in the ninth inning beats the Diamondbacks 2–1 at Dodger Stadium.

SEPTEMBER 19   The Dodgers edge the Diamondbacks 1–0 at Dodger Stadium. Chan Ho Park (eight innings) and Jeff Shaw (one inning) combined on the shutout.

SEPTEMBER 20   The Dodgers beat the Diamondbacks 1–0 for the second day in a row at Dodger Stadium. The game was won on a walk-off homer in the ninth inning by Eric Karros off Byung-Hyun Kim, who had just entered the contest in relief. Darren Dreifort (7²/₃ innings), Terry Adams (one-third of an inning) and Matt Herges (one inning) combined on the shutout.

                Herges had a record of 11–3 in 2000. He was 11–0 as a relief pitcher and 0–3 as a starter. The three defeats came in four starting assignments in August. They are the only four starts of Herges's career, which was in its 10th season in 2008.

SEPTEMBER 23   Kevin Brown pitches a two-hitter and strikes out 13 batters to defeat the Padres 2–1 at Dodger Stadium. The only San Diego hits were a single by Ryan Klesko in the fourth inning and a double from Damian Jackson in the ninth.

SEPTEMBER 24   Chan Ho Park (eight innings) and Jeff Shaw (one inning) combine on a two-hitter to beat the Padres 1–0 at Dodger Stadium. The only San Diego hits were a single by John Mabry in the fourth inning and a triple from Ruben Rivera in the fifth.

The Dodgers collected only three hits in the contest. Shawn Green scored the lone run in the fourth inning on a wild pitch by Matt Clement.

SEPTEMBER 26   Darren Dreifort (seven innings), Mike Fetters (one inning) and Terry Adams (one inning) combine on a two-hitter to beat the Giants 9–0 at Dodger Stadium. The only San Francisco hits were singles by Barry Bonds in the first inning and Ellis Burks in the fourth. It was the third consecutive game in which Los Angeles pitchers held the opposition to exactly two hits.

SEPTEMBER 29   Chan Ho Park pitches a two-hitter and strikes out 13 batters to beat the Padres 3–0 in San Diego. The only hits off Park were singles by Phil Nevin in the fourth inning and Greg LaRocca in the fifth. It was the fourth two-hitter by Los Angeles pitchers in a span of six games.

Park closed the 2000 season with 25 consecutive scoreless innings.

SEPTEMBER 30   Todd Hundley hits a grand slam off Matt Clement in the first inning to spark a 10–2 win over the Padres in San Diego.

OCTOBER 6   The Dodgers fire Davey Johnson as manager.

Given clubs with payrolls among the highest in baseball, Johnson was 77–85 in 1999 and 86–76 in 2000 before being dismissed. He never managed another big league club.

NOVEMBER 1   The Dodgers hire 44-year-old Jim Tracy as manager.

The Dodgers had two managers (Walter Alston and Tommy Lasorda) in 42 years and seven months from November 1953 through June 1996, then had four (Bill Russell, Glenn Hoffman, Davey Johnson and Tracy) in four years and five months from June 1996 through November 2000. Tracy's big league playing career lasted only 87 games as an outfielder with the Cubs in 1980 and 1981. After managing more than 1,000 games in the minors, Tracy was a coach with the Expos from 1995 through 1998 and with the Dodgers in 1999 and 2000. He managed the Dodgers for five full seasons to a record of 427–383, including a division title in 2004.

DECEMBER 6   The Dodgers sign Andy Ashby, most recently with the Braves, as a free agent.

Signed to a hefty three-year contract, Ashby was injured often and pitched poorly when healthy while in Los Angeles. He had only a 14–23 record with the club.

DECEMBER 13   The day after the U.S. Supreme Court declares George Bush the winner over Al Gore in the disputed 2000 presidential election, Todd Hundley signs with the Cubs as a free agent.

2001

Season in a Sentence

In his first year as manager, Jim Tracy keeps the Dodgers in contention deep into September amid continued front office turmoil and lack of direction.

Finish • Won • Lost • Pct • GB

Third   86   76   .531   6.0
In the wild-card race, the Dodgers finished tied for fourth place, seven games behind.

Manager

Jim Tracy

Stats

Stats	Dods	NL	Rank
Batting Avg:	.255	.261	11
On-Base Pct:	.323	.331	12
Slugging Pct:	.425	.425	8
Home Runs:	206		6
Stolen Bases:	89		8 (tie)
ERA:	4.25	4.36	8
Fielding Avg:	.981	.982	11
Runs Scored:	758		8
Runs Allowed:	744		8 (tie)

Starting Lineup

Paul LoDuca, c
Eric Karros, 1b
Mark Grudzielanek, 2b
Adrian Beltre, 3b
Alex Cora, ss
Gary Sheffield, lf
Marquis Grissom, cf
Shawn Green, rf
Tom Goodwin, cf
Jeff Reboulet, ss
Dave Hansen, 1b

Pitchers

Chan Ho Park, sp
Terry Adams, sp-rp
Kevin Brown, sp
Luke Prokopec, sp
Eric Gagne, sp
Darren Dreifort, sp
Jeff Shaw, rp
Matt Herges, rp
Giovanni Carrara, rp

Attendance

3,017,502 (fourth in NL)

Club Leaders

Batting Avg:	Paul LoDuca	.326
On-Base Pct:	Gary Sheffield	.417
Slugging Pct:	Shawn Green	.598
Home Runs:	Shawn Green	49
RBIs:	Shawn Green	125
Runs:	Shawn Green	121
Stolen Bases:	Tom Goodwin	22
Wins:	Chan Ho Park	15
Strikeouts:	Chan Ho Park	218
ERA:	Chan Ho Park	3.50
Saves:	Jeff Shaw	43

JANUARY 4   Ismael Valdez signs a contract with the Angels as a free agent.

FEBRUARY 2   The Dodgers establish a working agreement with a baseball team in Parma, Italy. Under the agreement, the Dodgers were to assist Parma with instruction and worked with the Italian team's coaches in the United States.

FEBRUARY 8   The Dodgers sign Jesse Orosco, most recently with the Cardinals, as a free agent.

Orosco previously pitched for the Dodgers in 1987. He turned 44 shortly after Opening Day in 2001. He appeared in 91 games for the club in 2001 and 2002, but was primarily a situational lefty, and pitched only 43 innings in those 91 contests.

FEBRUARY 24   The Dodgers trade Devon White to the Brewers for Marquis Grissom and Ruddy Lugo.

MARCH 17   The Dodgers trade Antonio Osuna and Carlos Ortega to the White Sox for Gary Majewski, Andre Simpson and Orlando Rodriguez.

Adrian Beltre had a burst appendix in January 2001 and underwent an emergency operation in the Dominican Republic. He reported to spring training in Vero Beach, but soon had an oozing hole in his abdomen because the surgery was botched. He endured another operation to repair a damaged intestine. He lost 24 pounds during the ordeal and was on the disabled list until mid-May.

APRIL 2   The Dodgers open the season with a 1–0 win over the Brewers before 53,154 at Dodger Stadium. The lone run scored on a homer by Gary Sheffield off Jamey Wright in the sixth inning. Sheffield reached base four times in four plate appearances. He also singled and walked twice. Chan Ho Park (seven innings), Mike Fetters (one inning) and Jeff Shaw (one inning) combined on the shutout.

Sheffield spent much of spring training complaining about his contract and demanding a trade. Although he apologized for his remarks, Sheffield was booed heavily by the Opening Day crowd at Dodger Stadium. He finished the season with a .311 batting average and 36 home runs.

APRIL 5   Tom Goodwin and Mark Grudzielanek lead off the first inning with back-to-back homers off Brian Anderson to spark a 7–5 win over the Diamondbacks at Dodger Stadium. It is the only time in Dodger history that the first and second hitters have started the first inning with home runs.

APRIL 6   The Dodgers clout five home runs during a 10–1 victory over the Giants at Dodger Stadium. Mark Grudzielanek hit two home runs with Marquis Grissom, Eric Karros and Paul LoDuca accounting for the rest.

LoDuca was 29 years old before he finally nailed down a starting job as the Dodgers catcher, and made the most of it by hitting .320 with 25 home runs in 2001. He was also the rare catcher who was used as a leadoff hitter. LoDuca batted first in the lineup 44 times in 2001.

APRIL 7   The Dodgers hit five home runs for the second game in a row while defeating the Giants 10–4 at Dodger Stadium. Shawn Green walloped two of them, with Mark Grudzielanek, Eric Karros and Chris Donnels adding the rest.

Green set a club record for home runs in a season with 49 in 2001. He also collected 84 extra bases hits, 370 total bases, 125 RBIs, 121 runs scored and a .297 batting average. Thirty of his 49 home runs were hit on the road.

APRIL 8   Mark Grudzielanek homers for his fifth consecutive game during an 8–3 loss to the Giants at Dodger Stadium. He hit five home runs in the four games.

APRIL 14   General manager Kevin Malone challenges Padres fan Jim Esterbrook to a fight during a 5–4 loss to the Padres in San Diego.

Malone took exception to Esterbrook's heckling Gary Sheffield, which led to the confrontation. Five days later Malone resigned his position. "Throughout my career, I've played with passion both on the field and in the front office," explained Malone. "That passion, I'm sure, has annoyed some, been misunderstood by others, but respected by those who know me best." Dave Wallace was named interim general manager (see October 3, 2001).

APRIL 17 Barry Bonds hits his 500th career homer during a 3–2 Giant win over the Dodgers in San Francisco. It was struck off Terry Adams in the eighth inning.

APRIL 21 The Dodger Stadium press box is named in Vin Scully's honor prior to a 4–2 win over the Padres in San Diego.

MAY 2 The Dodgers hit five home runs during a 7–3 win over the Reds in Cincinnati. Marquis Grissom hit two of the home runs. The first one was struck on the first pitch of the game from Pete Harnisch. The others were hit by Gary Sheffield, Eric Karros and pitcher Kevin Brown.

MAY 5 The Cubs pummel the Dodgers 20–1 at Wrigley Field. Chicago scored eight runs in the seventh inning and eight more in the eighth. Oddly, Dodger pitchers fanned 13 batters in eight innings despite the drubbing. Terry Adams pitched to seven batters in the seventh, retired no one, and allowed seven runs, all earned. Jose Nunez went 1²/₃ innings for Los Angeles, and surrendered nine runs (five earned), six hits and five walks. All five of the outs he recorded were on strikeouts. Chris Donnels pitched to the last batter of the eighth.

MAY 7 Kevin Brown (eight innings) and Jeff Shaw (one inning) combine on a two-hitter to beat the Marlins 1–0 at Dodger Stadium. The only Florida hits were singles by Luis Castillo in the sixth inning and Alex Gonzalez in the eighth. Gary Sheffield provided the lone run with a homer off A. J. Burnett in the sixth inning.

MAY 12 Gary Sheffield's walk-off home run off Matt Whiteside in the ninth inning is the lone run of a 1–0 win over the Braves at Dodger Stadium. Sheffield became the first batter in major league history to win three 1–0 games in a season with a home run. He also accomplished the feat on April 2 and May 7. Kevin Brown (eight innings) and Jeff Shaw (one inning) combined on the shutout.

MAY 26 Marquis Grissom hits two homers and drives in five runs during a 7–2 win over the Astros at Dodger Stadium.

MAY 27 After the Astros score twice in the top of the 12th, the Dodgers rebound with three in their half to win 5–4 at Dodger Stadium. Adrian Beltre singled in the first run. The game ended on a two-run single by Marquis Grissom.

MAY 28 Paul LoDuca ties a team record with six hits in six at-bats during an 11-inning, 11–10 win over the Rockies at Dodger Stadium. LoDuca had a home run and five singles, drove in four runs and scored three. His sixth hit was a single leading off the 11th. He went to third on a walk and a single and crossed the plate with the winning run on Shawn Green's one-base hit.

JUNE 1 Mark Grudzielanek hits a grand slam off Nelson Cruz in the seventh inning of a 9–8 loss to the Astros in Houston.

JUNE 3 Trailing 8–3, the Dodgers score two runs in the fifth inning, two in the seventh, one in the eighth and one in the 10th to down the Astros 9–8 in Houston. The run in the 10th scored on a pinch-hit home run by Tim Bogar. Tom Goodwin collected five hits, including a double, in five at-bats.

JUNE 4 — Five players hit five homers during an 8–4 win over the Diamondbacks in Phoenix. The five were Paul LoDuca, Tom Goodwin, Shawn Green, Marquis Grissom and Adrian Beltre.

JUNE 5 — In the second round of the amateur draft, the Dodgers select pitcher Brian Pilkington from Santiago High School in Garden Grove, California. The club had no first round choice due to free agent compensation. Through 2008, the only major leaguer drafted and signed by the Dodgers in 2001 is sixth-rounder Edwin Jackson.

JUNE 12 — Pitcher Darren Dreifort steals home in the second inning of an 8–4 win over the Rangers at Dodger Stadium. It was accomplished on the back end of the double steal with Tom Goodwin swiping second.

JUNE 20 — Five days after the Lakers wrap up their second straight NBA title in a five-game series against the Sixers, Eric Karros is hit by a pitch from Erik Sabel with the bases loaded in the ninth inning to force in the winning run of a 4–3 win over the Diamondbacks at Dodger Stadium.

JUNE 26 — Trailing 8–5, the Dodgers score five runs in the seventh inning and four in the ninth to win 14–8 over the Giants in San Francisco. Paul LoDuca led the way with six runs batted in on a home run, two double and a single.

The Dodgers came into the contest with a record of 38–37, in third place, and 7$\frac{1}{2}$ games behind the first-place Diamondbacks.

JULY 4 — The Dodgers extend their winning streak to nine games with a 4–3 decision over the Giants at Dodger Stadium. Marquis Grissom was ejected for arguing balls and strikes with umpire Marvin Hudson. Grissom was later suspended for six games because he bumped the umpire during the discussion.

JULY 7 — A walk-off homer by Adrian Beltre in the ninth inning beats the Mariners 2–1 at Dodger Stadium. All three runs in the contest scored on solo homers. The other two were by John Olerud and Gary Sheffield in the fourth.

JULY 10 — Tommy Lasorda is felled by a bat during the All-Star Game at Safeco Field in Seattle.

Lasorda was named honorary National League manager, and was given the opportunity to coach third base during the sixth inning. On a pitch from Mike Stanton, Vladimir Guerrero's bat splintered with the barrel end nailing the 73-year-old Lasorda. Tommy tumbled backward, head over heels, then got up quickly. When it was apparent that Lasorda was unhurt, Barry Bonds ran out the NL dugout and tried to put a chest protector on the former Dodger skipper.

JULY 13 — Shawn Green hits a grand slam off Tim Hudson in the sixth inning, but the Dodgers lose 11–7 to the Athletics in Oakland.

JULY 14 — The Dodgers score two runs in the 15th inning on bases-loaded walks to Chad Krueter and Paul LoDuca and win 5–3 over the Athletics in Oakland. Both teams scored in the 14th, with the Dodger tally coming on a home run by LoDuca.

JULY 15 — The Dodgers play at PNC Park in Pittsburgh for the first time, and win 4–2 over the Pirates.

JULY 18	Chan Ho Park pitches a two-hitter to defeat the Brewers 5–0 at Dodger Stadium. The only Milwaukee hits were singles by Mark Loretta in the third inning and Richie Sexson in the fourth.
JULY 21	The Dodgers trounce the Rockies 22–7 in Denver. Through 2008, it is the only time since moving to Los Angeles in 1958 that the Dodgers have scored at least 20 runs in a game. It was also the most by any Dodger club in a game since plating 23 on July 10, 1943. The Dodgers belted Colorado pitching with five runs in the first inning, one in the fifth, six in the sixth, nine in the eighth and one in the ninth. Gary Sheffield led the way with two homers, four runs scored, and four runs driven home.
JULY 23	The Dodgers play at Miller Park in Milwaukee for the first time, and win 3–1 over the Brewers.
JULY 26	In his first game with the Dodgers after being acquired in a trade with the Brewers, Tyler Houston stars in an 11–6 win over the Giants in San Francisco. Playing first base, he collected four hits, including a triple, along with four runs batted in and three runs scored.

Houston played only 34 more games with the Dodgers in which he collected just nine hits in 61 at-bats for an average of .148.

JULY 27	The Dodgers take first place with a 4–2 victory over the Rockies at Dodger Stadium.
JULY 31	The Dodgers trade Mike Fetters and Adrian Burnside to the Pirates for Terry Mulholland. The Dodgers also dealt Kris Foster and Geronimo Gil to the Orioles for Mike Trombley.
AUGUST 8	The Dodgers take a 1½-game lead in the NL West with a 9–4 triumph over the Pirates in Pittsburgh.

The Dodgers had a 65–49 record on August 8 and had won 27 of their last 39 games. The club was 21–27 the rest of the way, however, to drop out of first place and eventually out of post-season contention altogether.

AUGUST 15	Shawn Green hits three home runs and drives in seven during a 13–1 thrashing of the Expos at Dodger Stadium. Green hit a three-run homer in the second inning and a two-run blast in the fourth, both off Carl Pavano. The final blow was a home run with a man on base facing Masato Yoshii.
AUGUST 21	Gary Sheffield homers for the fourth consecutive game during a 5–4 triumph over the Marlins in Miami. Previously, Sheffield hit home runs in each of three games against the Mets at Dodger Stadium on August 17, 18 and 19.
SEPTEMBER 5	Trailing 2–0, the Dodgers erupt for seven runs in the ninth inning and win 7–2 over the Rockies in Denver.
SEPTEMBER 7	Shawn Green collects two home runs and two singles in five at-bats during a 7–1 win over the Cardinals in St. Louis.

SEPTEMBER 11   Two hijacked commercial airliners strike and destroy the twin towers of the World Trade Center in New York in the worst terrorist attack ever on American soil. A third hijacked plane destroyed a portion of the Pentagon in Northern Virginia just outside Washington D. C., and a fourth crashed in rural Pennsylvania. Some 3,000 were killed, including about 2,800 at the World Trade Center.

Almost immediately, commissioner Bud Selig canceled the slate of games scheduled for that day, including the Dodgers-Padres match-up in San Diego. Later in the week, Selig announced that all games through Sunday, September 16, would be postponed. The contests were made up by extending the regular season by a week. When play resumed, an air of heightened security and patriotism imbued every game. Fans endured close scrutiny by stadium personnel. "God Bless America" replaced "Take Me Out to the Ball Game" as the song of choice during the seventh-inning stretch.

SEPTEMBER 17   In the first game following the September 11 terrorist attacks, the Dodgers lose 6–4 to the Padres at Dodger Stadium.

SEPTEMBER 20   A walk-off homer by Shawn Green with two out in the 13th inning beats the Diamondbacks 3–2 at Dodger Stadium.

SEPTEMBER 22   The Dodgers win a thrilling 11-inning, 6–5 decision over the Diamondbacks at Dodger Stadium. Los Angeles scored twice in the ninth on a home run by Paul LoDuca to tie the score 3–3. After Arizona added two runs in the top of the 12th, the Dodgers responded with three in their half for the victory. The first scored on a bases-loaded walk to Eric Karros. Adrian Beltre ended the contest with a two-run single.

The Dodgers still had an outside shot at the division title with the September 22 win. The club was three games out of first place with 13 left to play, but went 6–7 over those 13 contests.

SEPTEMBER 25   The Dodgers score seven runs in the sixth inning and win 9–5 over the Giants at Dodger Stadium.

SEPTEMBER 26   Shawn Green's streak of playing in 414 consecutive games comes to an end when he sits out on Yom Kippur. The Dodgers lost 6–4 to the Giants at Dodger Stadium.

OCTOBER 3   The Dodgers name 41-year-old Dan Evans as general manager.

Evans had been a senior advisor with the club. The Dodgers improved in each of the two seasons he served as general manager, but Evans was fired in February 2004 when Frank McCourt, Jr. purchased the franchise. Early indications are that Evans's legacy will last awhile despite his short tenure, because the two drafts that he presided over have been fruitful.

OCTOBER 4   Rickey Henderson breaks Ty Cobb's career record for runs scored during the Padres 6–3 win over the Dodgers in San Diego. Henderson broke the record, which stood at 2,246, by hitting a home run off Luke Prokopec.

OCTOBER 5   Barry Bonds hits his 71st and 72nd homers of the season during an 11–10 Dodgers win over the Giants in San Francisco. The first homer broke Mark McGwire's record of 70, set in 1998. Both of Bonds's homers on October 5 were struck off Chan Ho Park, in the first and third innings.

OCTOBER 7   On the last day of the season, and on the day the United States launches a sustained air campaign in Afghanistan against al-Qaeda, Barry Bonds hits his 73rd homer of the season during a 2–1 Giants win over the Dodgers in San Francisco. It was struck off Dennis Springer in the first inning.

The October 7 contest was the fourth of five that Springer pitched as a member of the Dodgers, and was his last big league start. He finished his career with a record of 24–48.

DECEMBER 5   The Dodgers hire Kim Ng as assistant general manager. She became only the second female in major league history to hold that post.

DECEMBER 13   The Dodgers trade Luke Prokopec and Chad Ricketts to the Blue Jays for Paul Quantrill and Cesar Izturis.

DECEMBER 21   Hideo Nomo returns to the Dodgers after signing a contract as a free agent. He pitched for the Red Sox in 2001.

Nomo started the 2002 season with a 2–5 record, then went 14–1 the rest of the way to finish at 16–6 with a 3.38 ERA.

DECEMBER 22   Chan Ho Park signs a contract with the Rangers as a free agent.

2002

L A

Season in a Sentence

Saddled with a roster of high-salaried and declining veterans, Jim Tracy keeps the Dodgers in contention for a wild-card berth into the last half of September.

Finish • Won • Lost • Pct • GB

Third   92   70   .568   6.0
In the wild-card race, the Dodgers finished in second place, 3½ games behind.

Manager

Jim Tracy

Stats

Stats	Dods	NL	Rank
Batting Avg:	.264	.259	5
On-Base Pct:	.320	.331	15
Slugging Pct:	.409	.410	10
Home Runs:	155		11
Stolen Bases:	96		6
ERA:	3.69	4.11	3
Fielding Avg:	.985	.982	3
Runs Scored:	713		7
Runs Allowed:	643		3

Starting Lineup

Paul LoDuca, c
Eric Karros, 1b
Mark Grudzielanek, 2b
Adrian Beltre, 3b
Cesar Izturis, ss
Brian Jordan, lf
Dave Roberts, cf
Shawn Green, rf
Marquis Grissom, cf-lf
Alex Cora, ss-2b
Dave Hansen, 1b

Pitchers

Hideo Nomo, sp
Odalis Perez, sp
Kazuhisa Ishii, sp
Omar Daal, sp
Andy Ashby, sp
Eric Gagne, rp
Paul Quantrill, rp
Giovanni Carrara, rp
Jesse Orosco, rp
Guillermo Mota, rp

Attendance

3,131,077 (third in NL)

Club Leaders

Batting Avg:	Brian Jordan	.285
On Base Pct:	Shawn Green	.385
Slugging Pct:	Shawn Green	.558
Home Runs:	Shawn Green	42
RBIs:	Shawn Green	114
Runs:	Shawn Green	110
Stolen Bases:	Dave Roberts	45
Wins:	Hideo Nomo	16
Strikeouts:	Hideo Nomo	193
ERA:	Odalis Perez	3.00
Saves:	Eric Gagne	52

JANUARY 15   The Dodgers trade Gary Sheffield to the Braves for Brian Jordan, Odalis Perez and Andrew Brown.

> Sheffield demanded a trade after the Dodgers refused his request for a contract extension. With some justification, he publicly bashed the front office for making a series of long-term deals with other players that worked out badly. After leaving the Dodgers, Sheffield continued to be a highly productive player who wore out his welcome quickly. In 2008, he played for the Tigers, his seventh big league team. Jordan was 35 when he arrived in Los Angeles, and was worn down by injuries. A former pro football player who played defensive back for the Atlanta Falcons from 1989 through 1991, Jordan appeared in only 194 games for the Dodgers in two seasons. Perez gave the Dodgers one good season with a 15–10 record and a selection to the All-Star team in 2002 before fading.

MARCH 28   Angry over being hit by a pitch in the seventh inning of an exhibition game, Mets catcher Mike Piazza confronts Dodger pitcher Guillermo Mota. A few moments later, Mota walked off the field when Piazza approached him. Piazza then grabbed

Mota by the collar with both hands before eventually letting go and walking away (see March 12, 2003).

APRIL 2   The Dodgers open the season with a 9–2 loss to the Giants before 53,336 at Dodgers Stadium. Kevin Brown was the starting pitcher, and allowed seven runs in four innings. A year after hitting a record 73 home runs (see October 5 and 7, 2001), Barry Bonds clubbed two home runs, connecting off Brown and Omar Daal.

APRIL 3   In the second game of the season, Barry Bonds hits two more home runs during a 10–0 Giants victory over the Dodgers at Dodger Stadium. Bonds connected against Hideo Nomo and Terry Mulholland.

The Giants outscored the Dodgers 22–2 in the opening three-game series.

APRIL 5   Andy Ashby (seven innings) and Omar Daal (two innings) combine on a one-hitter to defeat the Rockies 9–0 at Dodger Stadium. The lone Colorado hit was a single by Todd Zeile in the fifth inning.

APRIL 6   In his major league debut, Kazuhisa Ishii pitches $5^{2}/_{3}$ innings, allowing no runs and two hits while striking out ten, leading the Dodgers to a 9–2 victory over the Rockies at Dodger Stadium. Kevin Jordan hit a grand slam off Todd Jones in the seventh inning.

Ishii was 28 years old and was acquired as a free agent after leaving his native Japan. He previously pitched for the Yakult Swallows. Ishii won his first six major league starts, all before the end of April, and was 10–1 on June 8. The league caught up with him, however, and Ishii finished the 2002 season with a 14–10 record and a 4.27 ERA in 154 innings (see September 8, 2002).

APRIL 7   Eric Gagne records his first major league save by pitching the ninth inning of a 6–4 triumph over the Rockies at Dodger Stadium.

Gagne was born in Montreal and spoke only French when he started attending classes at Seminole Junior College in Seminole, Oklahoma, in 1994. He was signed by the Dodgers as an undrafted free agent a year later, and made his big league debut in 1999. During his first three seasons, Gagne struggled as a starter with an 11–14 record and a 4.61 ERA. Converted to relief in 2002, he found his niche and could be categorized as the biggest surprise in baseball that season. He also created an aura about him with his bushy goatee, prescription goggles (worn to protect an injury suffered while playing youth hockey) and rumpled uniform. His entrance into games at normally staid Dodger Stadium created a fervor and was accompanied by "Welcome to the Jungle" blaring on the ballpark sound system. During the 2002 season, he had a 1.97 earned run average, a 4–1 record and 52 saves in 77 games and $82^{1}/_{3}$ innings. Gagne struck out 114 batters and walked only 16. It was the first of three seasons in which Gagne was virtually unhittable until arm troubles developed. His 161 saves as a member of the Dodgers is the all-time club record.

APRIL 12   Kazuhisa Ishii (six innings), Giovanni Carrara (two innings) and Eric Gagne (one inning) combine on a two-hitter to down the Padres 3–0 at Qualcomm Stadium. The only San Diego hits were a double by Deivi Cruz in the second inning and a single from Phil Nevin in the sixth.

APRIL 26   Odalis Perez just misses a perfect game by allowing only one base runner during a 10–0 win over the Cubs at Wrigley Field. Perez retired the first 18 batters to face him. Corey Patterson led off the Chicago seventh and hit a grounder up the middle that went behind the bag and came up high for shortstop Cesar Izturis, whose throw to first base was not in time. After Patterson's infield single, Perez set down the last nine Cub batters.

MAY 2   The Dodgers outlast the Reds 3–2 in 14 innings at Dodger Stadium. Adrian Beltre drove in the winning run with a walk-off single. Odalis Perez (eight innings), Eric Gagne (one inning), Paul Quantrill (one inning), Omar Daal (three innings) and Giovanni Carrara (one inning) combined to allow only five hits, none after the seventh inning.

Quantrill pitched in 86 games for the Dodgers in 2002 and 89 more in 2003.

MAY 5   The Dodgers win 6–5 during a 16-inning marathon against the Braves in Atlanta. Brian Jordan hit two homers and two singles in seven at-bats. In the 16th, Marquis Grissom singled, stole second, went to third on an error, and scored on a ground out by Paul LoDuca.

MAY 11   A three-run double by Mark Grudzielanek in the fourth inning are the only runs of a 3–0 win over the Marlins in Miami. Kevin Brown (seven innings), Paul Quantrill (one inning) and Eric Gagne (one inning) combined on the shutout.

MAY 22   The Dodgers edge the Brewers 1–0 in Milwaukee. Hideo Nomo (six innings), Omar Daal ($1\frac{1}{3}$ innings), Paul Quantrill (two-thirds of an inning) and Eric Gagne (one inning) combined on the shutout.
The lone run scored on a triple by Shawn Green.

MAY 23   Shawn Green has the best offensive game of any player in major league history during a 16–3 win over the Brewers in Milwaukee. He collected six hits on four home runs, a double and a single in six at-bats. Green also scored six runs and drove in seven. In the first inning, he had a run-scoring double off Glendon Rusch. Green hit a three-run homer off Rusch in the second. Facing Brian Mallette, Green led off the fourth with a home run, then hit another solo homer off Mallette in the fifth. In the eighth, Green singled against Jose Cabrera. Green collected his sixth hit and fourth home run in the ninth with Cabrera still on the mound. The Dodgers set a team record with a total of eight home runs. The others were struck by Adrian Beltre, Dave Hansen, Brian Jordan and Hiram Bocachica.

In 2001 and 2002, Shawn Green powered the Dodger offense as one of the team's most popular players.

In the ninth, Beltre, Green and Hansen hit consecutive homers in a span of nine pitches against Cabrera.

MAY 24   Shawn Green ties a major league record with five home runs in consecutive games with a solo homer off Curt Schilling in the first inning of a 14–3 loss to the Diamondbacks in Phoenix.

MAY 25   Shawn Green sets another major league record by hitting two home runs during a 10–5 win over the Diamondbacks in Phoenix. With the outburst, Green became the first player in big league history to hit seven home runs in three consecutive games. He smacked a three-run homer in the fifth inning, a sacrifice fly in the sixth, and a two-run home run in the ninth for a total of six runs batted in.

In a three-game span from May 23 through 25, Green collected 11 hits for 33 total bases in 13 at-bats. He had seven home runs and a double among his 11 hits, scored 10 runs, and drove in 14. Over a five-game span from May 21 through May 25, Green hit nine home runs and had 14 hits and 44 total bases in 21 at-bats. He entered the May 21 contest with only three homers in the first 44 games of the season.

Green's Day

No one in major league history has had a day like Shawn Green on May 23, 2002. During a 16–3 drubbing of the Brewers at Miller Park, He was six-for-six, had four homers, five extra base hits, 19 total bases, and scored six runs in re-writing the record books.

Home Runs
The four home runs tied both a major league and Dodger record. Through 2008, only 15 players in major league history have struck four homers in a game. The only other Dodger to accomplish the feat was Gil Hodges on August 31, 1950.

Extra Base Hits
In addition to the four home runs, Green also doubled giving him five extra base hits, which tied another record. Through 2008, just eight players have collected five extra base hits in a game. The only other Dodger to do it was Steve Garvey with three doubles and two homers on August 28, 1977.

Hits
Green tied a Dodger record with six hits. It was accomplished previously by George Cutshaw (1915), Jack Fournier (1923), Hank DeBerry (1929),

Wally Gilbert (1931), Cookie Lavagetto (1939), Willie Davis (1973) and Paul LoDuca (2001). Green is the only player in major league history with six hits and four home runs in the same game. The only players with six hits and three homers in the same contest are Ty Cobb of the Tigers in 1925, Jimmie Foxx of the Athletics in 1932 (in an 18-inning game) and Edgardo Alfonso of the Mets in 1999.

Total Bases
Green's 19 total bases on four homers, a double and a single set a major league record. The previous mark was 18 by Joe Adcock of the Braves against the Dodgers on July 31, 1954.

Runs
Green's six runs tied a modern (since 1900) major league record. Only seven players since 1900 have scored six times in a game. Green is the only Dodger to do it. Green is the only player in the majors to combine six runs and four homers in the same game. The only other players with six runs and six hits in six at-bats in the same game are Ginger Beaumont of the Pirates in 1899 and Edgardo Alfonso of the Mets exactly 100 years later in 1999.

JUNE 1   The Dodgers defeat the Diamondbacks 2–0 at Dodger Stadium with just two hits. Both were collected off Brian Anderson in the fourth inning on a single from Cesar Izturis and a two-out, two-run homer by Brian Jordan.

JUNE 3   Trailing 4–2, the Dodgers score four runs in the eighth inning and five in the ninth to win 11–5 over the Rockies in Denver.

JUNE 4   The Dodgers break a 4–4 tie with six runs in the ninth inning to defeat the Rockies 10–4 in Denver. Adrian Beltre hit a three-run homer in the ninth for the second day in a row. Several Los Angeles players got into a heated argument with fans behind their dugout in the sixth. One player threw water over the dugout and another tossed his gum at a fan, who responded by throwing food over the dugout. Two fans were escorted from their seats.

On the same day, the Dodgers had two selections in the first round of the amateur draft and chose first baseman James Loney from Elkins High School in Missouri City, Texas, and pitcher Greg Miller from Esperanza High School in Yorba Linda, California. Through 2008, future major leaguers drafted and signed by the Dodgers in 2002 include Loney, Jonathon Broxton (second round), Delwyn Young (fourth round), Eric Stilts (15th round) and Russell Martin (17th round). The excellent draft could prove to be one of the most successful in club history depending upon the continued development of Loney, Martin, Broxton and Young.

JUNE 7   The Dodgers play a regular season game against the Orioles for the first time, and lose 4–2 in Baltimore.

JUNE 10   The Dodgers play the Devil Rays for the first time during the regular season, and win 10–5 in St. Petersburg.

JUNE 14   Two days after the Lakers sweep the New Jersey Nets to win their third straight NBA title, Shawn Green homers in his final two at-bats during an 8–4 loss to the Angels at Dodger Stadium. Both were struck off Ramon Ortiz, in the sixth and ninth innings.

JUNE 15   Shawn Green extends his streak of consecutive homers to a major league record-tying four during a 10–5 victory over the Angels at Dodger Stadium. Green homered in his first two at-bats off Scott Schoeneweis in the first and second innings.

Green is the only batter in Dodger history to homer in four consecutive at-bats. He accomplished the feat less than a month after he hit four home runs in a game against the Brewers on May 23. Green hit 23 home runs in a 41-game span during May, June and July. He finished the season with 42 homers, 114 RBIs, 110 runs scored and a batting average of .285.

JUNE 18   The Dodgers play the Blue Jays for the first time during the regular season, and lose 2–1 at Dodger Stadium.

JUNE 21   The Dodgers play the Red Sox for the first time during the regular season, and win 3–2 at Dodger Stadium.

JUNE 23	The Dodgers take sole possession of first place with a 9–6 win over the Red Sox at Dodger Stadium.
JUNE 25	Odalis Perez pitches his second one-hitter of 2002, beating the Rockies 4–0 at Dodger Stadium. The only Colorado hit was a single by Bobby Estalella leading off the sixth inning.

> *Dave Roberts stole 45 of the Dodgers 96 bases in 2002. No other player had more than eight. In 2003, Roberts swiped 40 bases, exactly half of the team total of 80. No one else had more than ten.*

JUNE 28	The Dodgers take a 3½-game lead in the NL West race with a 7–5 win over the Angels in Anaheim.
JULY 16	The Dodgers fall out of first place with a 9–2 loss to the Cardinals at Dodger Stadium.

> *The Dodgers didn't regain first place for the rest of the season, but weren't eliminated from the wild-card spot until the final weekend of the season.*

JULY 28	The Dodgers trade Terry Mulholland, Ricardo Rodriguez and Francisco Cruceta to the Dodgers for Paul Shuey.
AUGUST 1	The Dodgers play at Cinergy Field in Cincinnati for the last time, and lose 6–4 to the Reds in 13 innings.
AUGUST 3	Shawn Green clubs two homers, a double and a single in six at-bats during a 6–4 triumph over the Phillies in Philadelphia.
AUGUST 10	The Dodgers survive three homers from Mike Lieberthal of the Phillies to win 10–8 at Dodger Stadium.
AUGUST 15	The Dodgers edge the Expos 1–0 in Montreal. Omar Daal (seven innings), Paul Quantrill (two-thirds of an inning), Jesse Orosco (one-third of an inning) and Eric Gagne (one inning) combined on the shutout.
AUGUST 23	Paul LoDuca is hit by a pitch from Kevin Gryboski in the ninth inning to force in the winning run of a 4–3 win over the Braves at Dodger Stadium.
AUGUST 28	Odalis Perry wins his own game with a homer in the fifth inning off Rick Heiling to beat the Diamondbacks 1–0 at Dodger Stadium. Perez pitched the first eight innings, with Eric Gagne hurling the ninth.

> *The homer is the only one of Perez's career in over 300 at-bats through the 2002 season.*

SEPTEMBER 2	The Dodgers collect 24 hits and beat the Diamondbacks 19–1 in Phoenix. Los Angeles scored eight runs in the seventh inning. A total of 13 different players garnered hits, 13 scored runs, and 10 contributed at least one RBI. Homers were struck by David Ross, Adrian Beltre, Shawn Green, Brian Jordan and Mike Kinkade. The homer by Ross was the first of his career and came off Mark Grace, who took the mound in the ninth inning to relieve the beleaguered Arizona pitching staff.

It was the only time in Grace's 16-year career that he appeared in a game as a pitcher.

SEPTEMBER 8   Kazuhisa Ishii is struck in the face in the fourth inning of a 6–2 loss to the Astros at Dodger Stadium.

The drive off the bat of Brian Hunter struck Ishii on the left side of the forehead with such force that it bounced all the way to the backstop for a run-scoring double. Ishii left the field in an ambulance. The blow caused multiple fractures to his cranium and nasal cavity.

SEPTEMBER 14   The Dodgers trounce the Rockies 16–3 in Denver. Chin-Feng Chen became the first player born in Taiwan to play in a major league game when he walked as a pinch-hitter in the sixth inning. Chen was one of a major league record-tying six pinch-hitters utilized by the Dodgers in the inning as Jim Tracy emptied the bench in the wake of the rout. The others were Chad Krueter, Wilkin Ruan, Jolbert Cabrera, Jeff Reboulet and Luke Allen.

Cabrera was shot in the right buttock during a carjacking in his native Colombia on December 21, 2001. The bullet was removed on Christmas morning.

SEPTEMBER 16   Brian Jordan hits a grand slam off Jason Schmidt in the third inning of a 7–6 win over the Giants at Dodger Stadium.

SEPTEMBER 19   The Dodgers move within one game of the Giants in the wild-card race with a 6–3 victory over San Francisco at Dodger Stadium. Shawn Green scored a run for the 11th consecutive game, tying a Dodger team record. Davey Lopes also had 11 in 1979.

SEPTEMBER 26   The Dodgers score two runs in the ninth inning to defeat the Rockies 3–2 at Dodger Stadium. Marquis Grissom doubled in the first run and scored on Shawn Green's single.

SEPTEMBER 27   The Dodgers keep their slim hopes for a wild-card berth alive with a 10-inning, 1–0 win over the Padres at Dodger Stadium. Paul LoDuca won the game with a walk-off homer. Omar Daal (eight innings) and Eric Gagne (two innings) combined on a three-hitter.

SEPTEMBER 28   On the second-to-last day of the season, the Dodgers win 14–2 over the Padres at Dodger Stadium, but are eliminated from the wild-card race when the Giants also win.

After pulling one game behind the Giants on September 19, the Dodgers won six of their remaining nine games, but San Francisco won eight in a row over the same period to advance to the playoffs, and eventually to the World Series. The Giants lost the Fall Classic to the Angels in seven games.

SEPTEMBER 29   In his first major league start, second baseman Joe Thurston collects four singles in five at-bats during a 2–0 loss to the Padres at Dodger Stadium.

NOVEMBER 20   Jesse Orosco signs a contract as a free agent with the Padres.

DECEMBER 4   The Dodgers trade Eric Karros and Mark Grudzielanek to the Cubs for Todd Hundley and Chad Hermansen.

Karros ended his days with the Dodgers ranking third on the all-time club lists in home runs (270), fifth in extra base hits (582), sixth in RBIs (976), eighth in doubles (302), eighth in total bases (2,740) and 10th in games played (1,601).

DECEMBER 7   Marquis Grissom signs a contract as a free agent with the Giants.

DECEMBER 10   Dave Hansen signs a contract as a free agent with the Padres.

DECEMBER 20   The Dodgers sign Fred McGriff, most recently with the Cubs, as a free agent.

McGriff came to the Dodgers at 39 years old with 478 lifetime home runs. He was coming off a season in which he hit 30 home runs and drove in 103 runs for the Cubs. He had hopes of hitting his 500th career homer in a Los Angeles uniform, but aged quickly and had only 297 at-bats as a Dodger with 13 homers and a .249 average. McGriff finished his career in 2004 with 493 home runs.

2003

Season in a Sentence

The Dodgers allow fewer runs than any other team in the majors, but also score the fewest and finish the year out of contention for a post-season berth.

Finish • Won • Lost • Pct • GB

Second   85   77   .525 15.5
In the wild-card race, the Dodgers finished tied for fourth place, six games behind.

Manager

Jim Tracy

Stats

Stats	Dods	NL	Rank
Batting Avg:	.243	.262	16
On-Base Pct:	.303	.332	16
Slugging Pct:	.368	.417	16
Home Runs:	124		15 (tie)
Stolen Bases:	80		6 (tie)
ERA:	3.16	4.28	1
Fielding Avg:	.981	.983	12
Runs Scored:	574		16
Runs Allowed:	556		1

Starting Lineup

Paul LoDuca, c
Fred McGriff, 1b
Alex Cora, 2b
Adrian Beltre, 3b
Cesar Izturis, ss
Brian Jordan, lf
Dave Roberts, cf
Shawn Green, rf
Jolbert Cabrera, cf-2b
Jeromy Burnitz, lf
Mike Kinkade, lf

Pitchers

Hideo Nomo, sp
Kevin Brown, sp
Odalis Perez, sp
Kazuhisa Ishii, sp
Wilson Alvarez, sp
Eric Gagne, rp
Paul Quantrill, rp
Tom Martin, rp
Guillermo Mota, rp
Paul Shuey, rp

Attendance

3,138,626 (second in NL)

Club Leaders

Batting Avg:	Shawn Green	.280
On-Base Pct:	Shawn Green	.355
Slugging Pct:	Shawn Green	.460
Home Runs:	Adrian Beltre	23
RBIs:	Shawn Green	85
Runs:	Shawn Green	84
Stolen Bases:	Dave Roberts	40
Wins:	Hideo Nomo	16
Strikeouts:	Kevin Brown	185
ERA:	Kevin Brown	2.39
Saves:	Eric Gagne	55

JANUARY 21   The Dodgers sign Wilson Alvarez, most recently with the Devil Rays, as a free agent.

MARCH 12   Mike Piazza and Guillermo Mota battle again during a 13–6 exhibition game win over the Mets in Port St. Lucie, Florida. The pair had a previous confrontation during spring training a year earlier (see March 28, 2002). Round two started when Mota nailed Piazza with a pitch in the sixth inning. The Met catcher charged the mound with his fist clenched. Mota threw his glove at Piazza's head and backpedaled away. As Piazza gave chase, the Dodger pitcher ran into the outfield. Piazza was intercepted and tackled by to the ground by Brian Jordan, Adrian Beltre and Larry Barnes. As Piazza tried to struggle free, Jeromy Burnitz took up the chase of Mota, who ran into the dugout and escaped to the locker room. Piazza got into his car, drove to the other side of the ballpark, and entered the Dodger clubhouse. He searched every nook and cranny looking for Mota, who had left about 10 minutes earlier. Both Piazza and Mota were suspended for the first four regular season games.

MARCH 31   Twelve days after the United States launches the Iraq War, Hideo Nomo pitches an Opening Day complete game shutout to defeat the Diamondbacks 8–0 in Phoenix. He allowed four hits. Brian Jordan hit a home run off Randy Johnson.

APRIL 7   The Dodgers lose the home opener 6–4 in 12 innings to the Diamondbacks before 53,819 at Dodger Stadium. Adrian Beltre and Fred McGriff homered.

Fernando Valenzuela became part of the Spanish language broadcasts of Dodger games as an analyst in 2003.

APRIL 17   The Dodgers score four runs with two out in the eighth inning, the last three on a pinch-homer by Todd Hundley, to defeat the Padres 4–3 at Dodger Stadium.

The 2003 season marked the first time that two teams located within 35 miles of one another both drew at least three million fans. The Dodgers attracted 3,138,626 and the Angels 3,061,090. The 2008 season was the sixth in a row in which the Dodgers and Angels both exceeded the three million mark. The only other geographic area to match it is New York. The Mets and Yankees drew three million or more in 2006, 2007 and 2008.

APRIL 20   The Dodgers score eight runs in the seventh inning and trounce the Giants 16–4 at Dodger Stadium.

APRIL 22   The Dodgers play at Great American Ball Park in Cincinnati for the first time, and win 2–1 over the Reds.

APRIL 25   The Dodgers score five runs in the ninth inning to defeat the Pirates 5–2 in Pittsburgh. Five different players drove in runs on doubles by Fred McGriff, Paul LoDuca, Adrian Beltre and Alex Cora and a single from Todd Hundley.

MAY 20   Eric Gagne closes out a 3–1 win over the Rockies at Dodger Stadium by striking out all three batters he faces on 12 pitches.

Gagne saved six consecutive games from May 16 through May 22. It was part of a season in which Gagne was placed into 55 save situations and converted them all. His eye-popping numbers included a 1.20 ERA in 77 games and 82 1/3 innings. He allowed only 37 hits as batters compiled a measly .133 average against him, the lowest in major league history for anyone with at least 75 innings pitched. Gagne struck out 137 batters of the 306 batters he faced (44.8 percent) while walking only 20. He averaged 15.0 strikeouts per nine innings. The performance earned Gagne a Cy Young Award.

MAY 22   Five Dodger pitchers combine on a two-hitter and strike out 16 batters to defeat the Rockies 4–3 at Dodger Stadium. Darren Dreifort struck out seven batters in the first two innings and a total of 12 in six innings. He fanned four in the second with the help of Aaron Cook, who swung at and missed a wild pitch with two strikes and reached first base. The other strikeout victims that inning were Bobby Estalella, Brent Butler and Greg Norton. Mark Sweeney had both Colorado hits with doubles in the first and third. Los Angeles relievers were Paul Shuey (one inning), Tom Martin (two-thirds of an inning), Paul Quantrill (one-third of an inning) and Eric Gagne (one inning).

MAY 24   Hideo Nomo pitches a two-hitter to defeat the Brewers 6–0 in Milwaukee. Nomo had a no-hitter in progress until John Vander Wal and Wes Helms hit back-to-back singles with one out in the seventh inning. Fred McGriff hit a grand slam off Matt Kinney in the seventh. The victory was the club's ninth in succession.

MAY 25   The Dodgers extend their winning streak to 10 games with a 5–0 decision over the
                  Brewers in Milwaukee. The runs scored on a two-run homer by Fred McGriff in
                  the sixth inning and a three-run blast from Paul LoDuca in the eighth. Kevin Brown
                  (eight innings) and Tom Martin (one inning) combined on the shutout.

                  *The victory gave the Dodgers a 30–20 record and put the club one-half game out
                  of first. During the 10-game winning streak, starting pitchers were 10–0 and had
                  an earned run average of 1.62. Over the course of the season, the Dodgers had
                  an ERA of 3.16, which was 0.57 better than the next closest staff (the Giants),
                  tying the 1907 Cubs for the largest differential in NL history. On the flip side,
                  Los Angeles scored only 574 runs, which was 68 fewer than the next worst team
                  (the Mets).*

JUNE 3   The Dodgers play the Royals for the first time and win 4–3 at Dodger Stadium. The
                  winning run scored on a bases-loaded walk by D. J. Carrasco to Adrian Beltre with
                  two out in the ninth.

                  *On the same day, the Dodgers selected pitcher Chad Billingsley from Defiance
                  High School in Defiance, Ohio, in the first round of the amateur draft. Among
                  the 2003 draftees, Billingsley, Matt Kemp (sixth round) and Adam LaRoche
                  (39th round) were in the majors by 2008. Billingsley and Kemp were regulars
                  on the 2008 club. The successful drafts in the early part of the decade led to the
                  team's later success.*

JUNE 6   The Dodgers play the White Sox for the first time during the regular season and win
                  2–1 at Dodger Stadium.

JUNE 10   The Dodgers play the Tigers for the first time during the regular season and win 3–1
                  in 12 innings at Comerica Park in Detroit.

JUNE 13   The Dodgers play the Indians for the first time in the regular season, and win 4–3 in
                  10 innings at Jacobs Field in Cleveland.

JUNE 14   A 5–2 win over the Indians at Jacobs Field features some trash talk between Paul
                  LoDuca and Cleveland outfielder Milton Bradley, who were wired with microphones
                  for TV. After connecting for a home run in the fourth inning, Bradley loosened the
                  straps on his batting gloves as he ran toward first base, an act of showboating that
                  rankled the Dodgers. An inning later, Bradley struck out and argued with umpire
                  Mark Carlson about the call. LoDuca, normally the Los Angeles catcher but playing
                  first base on this day, yelled "Take your batting gloves off for that one," toward
                  Bradley. On his way out to the field, Bradley ripped off the microphone he was
                  wearing. In the seventh, Bradley threw out LoDuca, who was trying to advance from
                  second to third on a fly ball. Bradley waved in the direction of LoDuca, and the two
                  continued their running argument.

                  *A year later, Bradley was a member of the Dodgers, and he and LoDuca were
                  teammates.*

JUNE 18   The Dodgers beat the Giants 8–2 at Dodger Stadium to pull into a tie for first place.
                  It was the club's eighth win in a row. Paul LoDuca extended his hitting streak to
                  25 games.

The Dodgers were tied for first place four of five days from June 18 through June 22. But a streak of 12 losses in 14 games June 22 through July 8 eliminated any chance of winning the NL West title. The club was in contention for a wild-card berth until mid-September, however.

JULY 5   Mike Kinkade has a hand in both runs of a 2–0 victory over the Diamondbacks at Dodger Stadium. In the fourth inning, Kinkade singled in a run and scored on Alex Cora's double. Odalis Perez (eight innings) and Eric Gagne (one inning) combined on the shutout.

JULY 10   Shawn Green collects four hits, including two doubles, and scores four runs during a 9–4 win over the Cardinals in St. Louis.

Green hit 49 doubles in 2003, the most of any Dodger since Johnny Frederick's 52 in 1929. Green's home run total dropped dramatically, however, from 49 in 2001 and 42 in 2002 to just 19 in 2003.

JULY 14   The Dodgers sign Rickey Henderson as a free agent. He had been playing for the Newark Bears in an independent minor league.

Henderson was already 44 years old and baseball's all-time leader in career runs scored and stolen bases when he played for the Dodgers in 2003, his 25th, and last, season in the majors. The Dodgers were his 10th big league club, which included four stops with the Athletics and two with the Padres. Henderson played 30 games for the Dodgers and hit .208 in 72 at-bats.

JULY 15   In a year in which he converts all 55 regular-season save opportunities, Eric Gagne blows one in the All-Star Game at U.S. Cellular Field in Chicago. He entered the contest in the eighth inning with the National League leading 6–4 and gave up three runs, the last two on a two-out homer by Hank Blalock, which resulted in a 7–6 AL victory. Since the All-Star Game doesn't count in the official statistics, Gagne's streak of converting consecutive save chances remained intact (see September 2, 2003).

JULY 23   Kazuhisa Ishii ties a major league record by hitting three batters in an inning during an 8–3 loss to the Rockies at Dodgers Stadium. In the fourth, Ishii plunked Larry Walker, Mark Bellhorn and Rafael Belliard in a span of 16 pitches.

JULY 24   A walk-off single by Shawn Green in the 11th inning is the lone run of a 2–0 win over the Rockies at Dodger Stadium. Kevin Brown (eight innings), Eric Gagne (one inning), Paul Quantrill (one inning), Tom Martin (two-thirds of an inning) and Paul Shuey (one-third of an inning) combined on the shutout.

After missing most of the 2001 and 2002 seasons with an assortment of injuries, Brown had a streak of 11 starts early in the 2003 campaign in which he went 9–0 with a 1.38 ERA, but was sidelined for a couple of weeks with an abdominal strain. He finished the season at 14–9 with an earned run average of 2.39 in 211 innings.

JULY 27   The Dodgers win 1–0 over the Diamondbacks in Phoenix. In a rare start, first baseman Larry Barnes doubled off Curt Schilling in the second inning to drive across the lone run. Hideo Nomo ($7\frac{2}{3}$ innings) and Eric Gagne ($1\frac{1}{3}$ innings) combined on the shutout.

In eight games from July 24 through August 1, the Dodgers scored only eight runs in 79 innings.

JULY 31   The Dodgers play at Veterans Stadium in Philadelphia for the last time and lose 7–3 to the Phillies.

On the same day, the Dodgers traded Bubba Crosby and Scott Proctor to the Yankees for Robin Ventura.

AUGUST 12   A walk-off homer by Ruben Castro of the Marlins off Paul Shuey in the 13th inning beats the Dodgers 4–3 in Miami.

AUGUST 13   The Dodgers are the victims of an extra-inning, walk-off homer by the Marlins in Miami for the second day in a row. Mike Mordecai cleared the wall with a drive off Wilson Alvarez in the 11th inning for a 2–1 Florida victory.

AUGUST 20   A three-run homer in the 10th inning by Adrian Beltre beats the Expos 4–1 at Dodger Stadium.

SEPTEMBER 2   Eric Gagne breaks the all-time record for consecutive saves by converting his 55th in a row in a 4–1 win over the Astros at Dodger Stadium. The record was set over two seasons. The old mark was 54, established by Tom Gordon of the Red Sox in 1997 and 1998. Gagne's streak would eventually reach 84 (see July 3 and July 5, 2004).

SEPTEMBER 8   Cesar Izturis collects five hits, including a homer and a triple, in five at-bats, during a 10–3 triumph over the Diamondbacks in Phoenix. Shawn Green hit a grand slam off Stephen Randolph in the ninth.

SEPTEMBER 9   With a 4–1 win over the Diamondbacks in Phoenix, the Dodgers pull within two games of the wild-card lead shared by the Marlins and Phillies.

SEPTEMBER 10   The Diamondbacks score five runs with two out in the eighth inning to beat the Dodgers 5–4 in Phoenix. In a controversial move, Jim Tracy brought in Paul Quantrill instead of Eric Gagne to face Steve Finley with two on base and the Dodgers leading 4–2. Finley was 7-for-9 in his career against Quantrill, and proceeded to hit a three-run homer.

Beginning with the September 10 defeat, the Dodgers lost 11 of the last 19 games to squash any post-season dreams.

SEPTEMBER 19   A fan is murdered in the parking of Dodger Stadium during the eighth inning of a 6–4 loss to the Giants.

Mark Antenorcruz, a 25-year-old Dodger fan from Covina, California, got into an argument with three Giants fans, one of whom shot him twice in the chest. Pete Marron, age 20, was convicted and sentenced to 50 years in prison for the crime.

SEPTEMBER 21   Robin Ventura, Adrian Beltre and Jeromy Burnitz combine to hit three homers in a row in a span of 10 pitches off Kevin Correia in the fourth inning of a 7–5 win over the Giants at Dodger Stadium. The homers tied the score 5–5.

SEPTEMBER 23   The Dodgers play at Qualcomm Stadium in San Diego for the last time and lose 6–1 to the Padres.

SEPTEMBER 27   Edwin Jackson (six innings), Guillermo Mota (one inning), Tom Martin (one-third of an inning), Paul Quantrill (two-thirds of an inning) and Eric Gagne (one inning) combine on a two-hitter to defeat the Giants 5–0 in the day game of a day-night double-header in San Francisco. In his third major league start just 18 days after celebrating his 20th birthday, Jackson allowed only a double by Jeffrey Hammonds in the third inning and a single by Benito Santiago in the sixth, but he walked eight batters.

Jackson was born in Neu-Ulm, West Germany.

OCTOBER 10   Three days after Arnold Schwarzenegger is elected governor of California, Boston real estate mogul Frank McCourt purchases the Dodgers from the Fox Group, which had bought control the club in 1998. The sale to McCourt was formally approved by Major League Baseball on January 29, 2004. The price was $430 million. The Fox Group paid $311 million for the franchise in 1998.

McCourt unsuccessfully tried to purchase the Red Sox before putting in his bid for the Dodgers. His grandfather was a part owner of the Boston Braves during the 1940s and 1950s. Since taking over the team, McCourt has invested heavily in renovating Dodger Stadium. His efforts to return the Dodgers to its glory days of the 1940s through the 1980s, when the franchise won 16 National League pennants and six world championships, have yet to reap their reward, though the success at the end of 2008 bodes well for the team.

NOVEMBER 18   Ex-Dodger pitcher Bill Singer is fired by the Mets only 12 days after being hired as assistant to general manager Jim Duquette. Singer was dismissed after making racially insensitive remarks to Dodger assistant general manager Kim Ng regarding her Chinese-American heritage. Singer blamed his diet and state of inebriation for his actions. Ironically, Singer was hired in 2006 by the Nationals to head scouting operations in Asia.

DECEMBER 10   The city of Brooklyn announces plans for a $4.2 billion project in the area surrounding the corner of Atlantic and Flatbush Avenues. This was the intersection where Walter O'Malley wanted to build a ballpark for the Dodgers (see August 16, 1955). The project will include offices, residences and a shopping complex as well as a 19,000-seat arena for the New Jersey Nets that will be named the Barclays Center. The arena is scheduled to open for the 2009–10 season, and the team will likely be redubbed the Brooklyn Nets.

DECEMBER 13   The Dodgers trade Kevin Brown to the Yankees for Jeff Weaver, Yhency Brazoban, Brandon Weeden and cash.

The Dodgers were happy to find someone who would take the last two years of the injury-prone Brown's contract. He was 14–13 in two seasons with the Yankees.

DECEMBER 20   Jeromy Burnitz signs a contract with the Rockies as a free agent.

DECEMBER 22   Paul Quantrill signs a contract with the Yankees as a free agent.

DECEMBER 26   Brian Jordan signs a contract with the Rangers as a free agent.

2 0 0 4   L A

Season in a Sentence

In Frank McCourt's first season as owner, the Dodgers made their first playoff appearance since 1996, capture their first division title since 1995 and win their first post-season game since 1988.

Finish • Won • Lost • Pct • GB

First   93   69   .574   +2.0

National League Division Series

The Dodgers lost to the St. Louis Cardinals three games to one.

Manager

Jim Tracy

Stats	Dods	NL	Rank
Batting Avg:	.262	.263	10
On-Base Pct:	.332	.333	8
Slugging Pct:	.423	.423	8
Home Runs:	203		4
Stolen Bases:	102		5
ERA:	4.01	4.30	4
Fielding Avg:	.988	.983	1
Runs Scored:	761		9
Runs Allowed:	684		4

Starting Lineup

Paul LoDuca, c
Shawn Green, 1b-rf
Alex Cora, 2b
Adrian Beltre, 3b
Cesar Izturis, ss
Jayson Werth, lf
Milton Bradley, cf
Juan Encarncion, rf
Dave Roberts, lf
Steve Finley, cf
Jose Hernandez, 2b
Jason Grabowski, lf
Robin Ventura, 1b

Pitchers

Jeff Weaver, sp
Kazuhisa Ishii, sp
Jose Lima, sp
Odalis Perez, sp
Hideo Nomo, sp
Eric Gagne, rp
Duaner Sanchez, rp
Darren Dreifort, rp
Tom Martin, rp
Giovanni Carrara, rp
Wilson Alvarez, rp-sp

Attendance

3,488,283 (first in NL)

Club Leaders

Batting Avg:	Adrian Beltre	.334
On-Base Pct:	Adrian Beltre	.388
Slugging Pct:	Adrian Beltre	.629
Home Runs:	Adrian Beltre	48
RBIs:	Adrian Beltre	124
Runs:	Adrian Beltre	104
Stolen Bases:	Dave Roberts	33
Wins:	Three tied with	13
Strikeouts:	Jeff Weaver	153
ERA:	Odalis Perez	3.25
Saves:	Eric Gagne	45

JANUARY 28   The Dodgers sign Jose Lima, most recently with the Royals, as a free agent.

FEBRUARY 4   Three days after Janet Jackson's "wardrobe malfunction" at the Super Bowl, the Dodgers sign Jose Hernandez, most recently with the Pirates, as a free agent.

FEBRUARY 10   Fred McGriff signs a contract with the Devil Rays as a free agent.

FEBRUARY 16   The Dodgers hire Paul DePodesta as general manager replacing Dan Evans.

DePodesta had been an executive with the Oakland A's, a club noted for winning pennants on a limited budget under general manager Billy Beane. A cum laude economics graduate from Harvard, DePodesta was only 31 at the time of his hiring. With the help of some mid-season trades, the Dodgers won the NL West in 2004, but DePodesta was fired following a 71–91 record in 2005.

APRIL 3   The Dodgers trade Franklin Gutierrez and Andrew Brown to the Indians for Milton Bradley.

The Dodgers acquired a starting outfielder for two minor leaguers, but Bradley had anger issues throughout his career and came with enormous risks. He was arrested in February 2004 and jailed three days for driving away from the police after being stopped for speeding. When the trade was completed, Bradley was under suspension by the Indians for failing to run out a ground ball during an exhibition game and for arguing with manager Eric Wedge. Bradley's problems controlling his temper continued in Los Angeles (see June 1, 2004 and September 28, 2004).

APRIL 5   The Dodgers lose the season opener 8–2 to the Padres before 53,530 at Dodger Stadium. The Dodgers scored only two runs despite collecting 15 hits. Fifteen runners were left on base. Shawn Green hit a home run. In his Dodger debut, Juan Encarnacion had three hits, two of them doubles. Paul LoDuca also garnered three hits. Hideo Nomo was the starting and losing pitcher.

The Dodgers won 93 games without a single pitcher with more than 13 victories. The team leaders were Jose Lima (13–5), Kazuhisa Ishii (13–8) and Jeff Weaver (13–13). Nomo had a rough year with a 4–11 record and an 8.25 ERA in 84 innings. It was the highest ERA ever recorded by a pitcher with at least 15 decisions.

APRIL 9   Dave Roberts steals four bases during a 5–1 win over the Rockies at Dodger Stadium. He reached base four times in four plate appearances on a single and three walks. He stole second base on each occasion.

Roberts led the Dodgers in steals in 2004 with 33 in 34 attempts despite playing in only 68 games with the club before a July 31 trade to the Red Sox. In the fall, he played on the first Red Sox team to win a World Series since 1918.

APRIL 13   The Dodgers play at Petco Park in San Diego for the first time and lose 8–3 to the Padres.

APRIL 14   Shawn Green collects four hits, including two doubles, and scores four runs during an 11–4 win over the Padres in San Diego.

APRIL 16   Milton Bradley drives in three runs without a base hit and Dave Roberts scores three to account for all of the runs in a 3–2 victory over the Giants in San Francisco. Bradley scored Roberts from third base on groundouts in the first, sixth and ninth innings. Roberts reached base on a single and two walks.

APRIL 18   Adrian Beltre, Juan Encarnacion and David Ross hit consecutive homers in the fifth inning of a 7–6 win over the Giants in San Francisco. They were struck during a span of five pitches from Brett Tomko. Beltre's homer came with two men on base.

Through the 2003 season, Beltre had frustrated the Dodgers with his lack of progress. He was considered the best prospect in baseball when he made his major league debut at the age of 19 in 1998. After hitting .240 in 2003, Beltre had a lifetime batting average of .262 and 99 home runs in 2,864 at-bats. He had a breakout year in 2004 with 48 home runs, 121 runs batted in, 104 runs scored and a .334 batting average. Beltre's slugging percentage of .629 is the fifth best in Dodger history. His 376 total bases are the most by a Dodger batter since 1954 and the third most in the history of the franchise. The 48 home runs were one shy of Shawn Green's team record. Beltre also became the first Dodger to lead the National League in home runs since Tim Jordan, who hit 12 in 1908. In addition, the 48 home runs tied the major league record for home runs in a season by a third baseman, which was set by Mike Schmidt in 1980. (The mark was broken by Alex Rodriguez in 2007, but Beltre and Schmidt still share the National League record.) Beltre cashed in after the season by signing a lucrative deal with the Mariners as a free agent. Thus far, he has disappointed Seattle fans by failing to come anywhere close to his 2004 batting numbers.

APRIL 30   The Dodgers wallop the Expos 13–4 at Dodger Stadium.

MAY 2   The Expos play at Dodger Stadium for the last time and win 6–4 over the Dodgers.

MAY 7   Wilson Alvarez (seven innings) and Guillermo Mota (two innings) combine on a one-hitter to defeat the Pirates 4–0 at PNC Park. The only Pittsburgh hit was a single by Chris Stynes in the sixth inning.

MAY 9   A two-run pinch-hit home run by Olmedo Saenz in the 14th inning beats the Pirates 9–7 in Pittsburgh. It was his first home run as a member of the Dodgers. The Pirates scored five runs in the eighth to tie the score 7–7 with the help of five consecutive walks by four Los Angeles relievers, four with the bases loaded. Five straight Pittsburgh batters reached base in the inning off five pitchers. Jose Lima walked the first two batters, and was replaced by Darren Dreifort, who walked Tom Martin and Abraham Nunez. Duaner Sanchez succeeded Nunez to the mound, and surrendered a run-scoring single.

MAY 12   Alex Cora hits a remarkable home run during a 4–0 win over the Cubs at Dodger Stadium. Facing Matt Clement in the seventh inning, Cora worked the count to 2–1, then fouled off 14 straight pitches before delivering the home run. The 18 pitches in the plate appearance is the most ever documented in major league history.

            The win gave the Dodgers a 22–10 record and a three-game lead in the NL West race, but the club dropped out of the top spot with an eight-game losing streak that began on May 13.

MAY 13   Jose Lima sings the National Anthem before the game and "God Bless America" in the seventh inning and pitches $5^2/_3$ innings of shutout relief, but the Dodgers lose 7–3 to the Cubs at Dodger Stadium.

MAY 18   The Dodgers play at Citizens Bank Park in Philadelphia for the first time and lose 8–7 to the Phillies.

MAY 29   The Dodgers rout the Diamondbacks 10–0 at Dodger Stadium. Jose Lima (eight innings) and Eric Gagne (one inning) combined on a three-hit shutout.

Gagne pitched exactly 82$\frac{1}{3}$ innings in 2002, 2003 and 2004.

MAY 31   The Dodgers score two runs in the ninth inning and one in the 10th to beat the Brewers 3–2 at Dodger Stadium. The runs in the ninth scored on RBI-singles from Juan Encarnacion and Joe Grabowski. Cesar Izturis drove in the game-winner with a one-base hit in the tenth.

JUNE 1   Milton Bradley is ejected by umpire Terry Craft for arguing balls and strikes in the sixth inning of a 4–1 loss to the Brewers at Dodger Stadium. On the way to the clubhouse, Bradley heaved a ball bag that sprayed some six dozen baseballs onto the field. As the ballboys picked them up, Bradley fired one deep into left field.

Bradley was suspended for four days because of the incident.

JUNE 7   With two selections in the first round of the amateur draft, the Dodgers choose pitcher Scott Elbert from Seneca High School in Seneca, Missouri, and Blake DeWitt from Sikeston High School in Sikeston, Missouri. DeWitt reached the majors in 2008 and became the Dodgers starting third baseman.

JUNE 8   The Dodgers play in Toronto for the first time and lose 7–1 to the Blue Jays at SkyDome.

JUNE 11   The Dodgers play at Fenway Park for the first time, and lose 2–1 to the Red Sox.

JUNE 12   The Dodgers score seven runs in the fifth inning and defeat the Red Sox 14–5 in Boston.

JUNE 15   The Orioles play at Dodger Stadium for the first time since the 1966 World Series and lose 5–1 to the Dodgers.

JUNE 18   After meeting 11 times in the World Series, the Dodgers and Yankees square off during the regular season for the first time, and the Dodgers win 6–3 at Dodger Stadium.

JUNE 25   The Dodgers lose 13–0 to the Angels at Dodger Stadium. Robin Ventura pitched the ninth inning and didn't allow a run. It was the only time that Ventura took the mound during his 16-year career.

JUNE 27   The Dodgers score seven runs in the fourth inning and beat the Angels 10–5 at Dodger Stadium. Adrian Beltre hit two homers and drove in five runs.

JULY 3   Eric Gagne coverts his 84th consecutive save, accomplished over three seasons, by closing out an 8–5 win over the Angels in Anaheim.

JULY 5   Eric Gagne's streak of consecutive saves ends at 84, although the Dodgers recover to win 6–5 in 10 innings over the Diamondbacks at Dodger Stadium. He entered the game in the ninth with a 5–3 lead, but Arizona scored twice to tie the score 5–5. Nonetheless, Gagne was accorded standing ovations after allowing the second run and again at the end of the inning. The 10th-inning run scored on a sacrifice fly by Shawn Green.

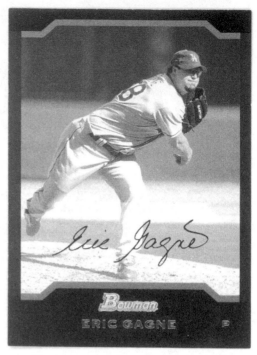

The last blown save by Gagne prior to July 5, 2004, was on August 26, 2002. He finished the season with 45 saves in 47 chances, a 7–3 record, a 2.19 ERA in 70 games and 82 1/3 innings. Gagne struck out 114 batters and walked 22. He saved 152 games from 2002 through 2004, the most by any reliever over a three-year period in major league history. The second most is 142 by Dennis Eckersley with the Athletics from 1990 through 1992. During those three prime seasons, Gagne had a 14–7 record in addition to the 152 saves, and had an earned run average of 1.80 in 245 innings. He allowed only 145 hits, walked 58 and struck out 365, an average of 13.4 per nine innings. Opponents

Arguably the most dominating pitcher in the game in the mid 2000s, Eric Gagne filled the role of closer as few pitchers have ever done.

batted only .168 against him. Because of his success, Gagne signed a two-year deal worth $19 million for the 2005 and 2006 seasons to avoid an arbitration hearing. Unfortunately, Gagne was limited two just 13 1/3 innings in 2005 and only two in 2006 due to an assortment of injuries to his knee, back and elbow. He pitched for the Rangers and Red Sox in 2007 and the Brewers in 2008 and has yet to replicate his role as a dominant closer.

JULY 7   Kazuhisa Ishii pitches a one-hitter to defeat the Diamondbacks 11–0 at Dodger Stadium. The only Arizona hit was a single by Shea Hillenbrand in the fifth inning.

JULY 8   The Dodgers take sole possession of first place with a 7–2 win over the Astros at Dodger Stadium.

The Dodgers held onto first place until the end of the season, but didn't clinch the division title until the second-to-last day.

JULY 11   Paul LoDuca hits a grand slam off David Weathers in the eighth inning of a 7–4 win over the Astros at Dodger Stadium.

JULY 17   The Dodgers score three runs in the ninth inning to beat the Diamondbacks 7–6 in Phoenix. Adrian Beltre doubled in the first run and scored on Robin Ventura's homer. The Dodgers tied a major league record by using four first basemen in the game. Olmedo Saenz started the contest, and was followed by Jason Grabowski, Jose Hernandez and Ventura.

JULY 24   Adrian Beltre hits a grand slam off Ismael Valdez in the fourth inning of a 12–2 triumph over the Padres at Dodger Stadium.

JULY 30   The Dodgers score seven runs in the fourth inning and win 12–3 over the Padres in San Diego.

On the same day, the Dodgers traded Paul LoDuca, Juan Encarnacion and Guillermo Mota to the Marlins for Brad Penny, Hee Seop Choi and Bill Murphy. The Dodgers hoped to flip the three players they acquired in the trade to the Diamondbacks for Randy Johnson, but a deal couldn't be worked out. Fans were livid because LoDuca was one of the most popular players on the club. Thus far, the controversial trade has worked out well, as Penny became a staff ace and Russell Martin has put up better numbers than LoDuca at the catching position over the last three years through 2008.

JULY 31   The Dodgers trade Dave Roberts to the Red Sox for Henri Stanley and deal Koyie Hill, Bill Murphy and Reggie Abercrombie to the Diamondbacks for Steve Finley and Brent Mayne.

Although 39, Finley was brilliant for the Dodgers down the stretch with 13 homers and 46 RBIs in 58 games. He had several key hits, including a grand slam on October 2 that clinched the division championship.

AUGUST 1   Robin Ventura homers in the 12th inning to beat the Padres 2–1 in San Diego.

AUGUST 3   In his first start with the Dodgers, Brad Penny pitches eight shutout innings and allows only two hits while facing the Pirates at Dodger Stadium. Eric Gagne allowed two runs in the ninth, but the Dodgers hung on for a 3–2 win.

AUGUST 5   The Dodgers hit five home runs, including three in a row, to defeat the Pirates 8–3 at Dodger Stadium. Cesar Izturis led off the first with a walk that was followed by back-to-back-to-back homers from Jayson Werth, Milton Bradley and Adrian Beltre in a span of nine pitches off Sean Burnett. Bradley hit another home run in the fifth and Jose Hernandez added one more in the seventh.

AUGUST 8   In his second start with the Dodgers, Brad Penny is pulled in the first inning of a 4–1 loss to the Phillies at Dodger Stadium with a biceps injury. He missed the next six weeks.

AUGUST 10   Adam Dunn hits a home run estimated to have traveled 535 feet during a 5–2 Dodger win over the Reds at Great American Ball Park. It was struck off Jose Lima in the fourth inning. The drive cleared the 35-foot-high batter's eye in right-center field, bounced onto a street behind the ballpark, and ended up in the Ohio River. Since the entirety of the Ohio River is officially located in the state of Kentucky, it is the only home run in major league history to travel across state lines.

AUGUST 11   The Dodgers take a 7½-game lead in the NL West race by defeating the Reds 11–1 in Cincinnati. It was the club's 27th win in the last 35 games.

AUGUST 20 Adrian Beltre drives in all three runs in an 11-inning, 3–2 win over the Braves at Dodger Stadium. Beltre hit a run-scoring double in the fourth inning, a leadoff home run in the ninth, and a walk-off homer in the 11th with one out.

AUGUST 21 Shawn Green hits a grand slam off Mike Hampton in the first inning of a 7–4 win over the Braves at Dodger Stadium. Green added a solo homer off Hampton in the third. Jeff Weaver tied a major league record in the first inning by hitting three batters in succession. Weaver plunked J. D. Drew, Chipper Jones and Johnny Estrada in a span of six pitches, but got out of the inning without a run being scored.

AUGUST 24 The Dodgers score eight runs in the fifth inning and win 10–2 over the Expos in Montreal. Adrian Beltre hit a grand slam off Rocky Biddle.

AUGUST 26 The Dodgers break a 3–3 tie with seven runs in the sixth inning and win 10–3 at Olympic Stadium. It was also the last time the Dodgers played in Montreal.

AUGUST 28 Adrian Beltre collects five hits, including a home run, during a 4–2 win over the Mets in New York.

AUGUST 29 Robin Ventura hits a grand slam off Kris Benson in the fifth inning of a 10–2 win over the Mets in New York.

AUGUST 31 A three-run double by Steve Finley in the 13th inning beats the Diamondbacks 4–1 in Phoenix.

SEPTEMBER 4 The Cardinals score five runs on only two hits and defeat the Dodgers 5–1 in St. Louis.

SEPTEMBER 7 Robin Ventura hits a grand slam off Chad Durbin in the seventh inning of an 8–2 triumph over the Diamondbacks at Dodger Stadium.

SEPTEMBER 8 Olmedo Saenz hits a pinch-hit grand slam off Casey Fossum in the fifth inning of a 6–5 win over the Diamondbacks at Dodger Stadium.

SEPTEMBER 12 The Dodgers take a six-game lead in the NL West race after beating the Cardinals 6–5 at Dodger Stadium. There were 21 contests left on the schedule.

SEPTEMBER 17 Trailing 6–1, the Dodgers score three runs in the fourth inning, two in the fifth and two in the 10th to defeat the Rockies 8–6 in Denver.

SEPTEMBER 19 A two-out, two-run homer by Shawn Green in the ninth inning beats the Rockies 7–6 in Denver.

SEPTEMBER 22 The Dodgers lead over the Giants shrinks to one-half game after losing 4–0 to the Padres in San Diego. The Dodgers had led by six games just 11 days earlier. There were 11 games left on the schedule, six of them against the Giants.

SEPTEMBER 26 The Dodgers win 7–4 over the Giants in San Francisco to take a 2½-game lead with seven games remaining.

SEPTEMBER 27   Adrian Beltre hits a grand slam off Shawn Estes in the second inning of an 8–7 victory over the Rockies at Dodger Stadium.

SEPTEMBER 28   The Dodgers score five runs in the ninth inning to stun the Rockies 5–4 at Dodger Stadium. Four straight walks, the last one to Cesar Izturis, produced the first run. Jayson Werth doubled in two. Steve Finley ended the game with a two-run single. The tremendous comeback victory gave the Dodgers a three-game lead over the Giants with five left to play.

Milton Bradley wasn't around in the ninth, having been ejected in the eighth. Bradley dropped a fly ball in right field that inning leading to two Rockies runs and a 3–0 Dodger deficit. One fan threw a plastic beer bottle in his direction. Bradley picked up the bottle, menacingly approached the stands and slammed the bottle into a group of fans. The umpires ejected him. As Bradley walked toward the dugout, he ripped off his uniform. He was suspended for the final five games in the midst of a pennant race.

SEPTEMBER 30   A two-run, walk-off homer by David Ross in the 11th inning beats the Rockies 4–2 at Dodger Stadium.

The win gave the Dodgers a three-game lead over San Francisco with three games left to play. The three were against the Giants at Dodger Stadium.

OCTOBER 1   With a chance to clinch the division title, the Dodgers lose 4–2 to the Giants at Dodger Stadium.

OCTOBER 2   On the second-to-last day of the regular season, the Dodgers clinch the division title in dramatic fashion by scoring seven runs in the ninth inning to defeat the Giants 7–3 at Dodger Stadium. The Dodgers trailed 3–0 heading into the ninth and it appeared as though the Giants would close the gap to one game heading into the final day of the regular season. The first run in the ninth scored on a bases-loaded walk to Hee Seop Choi and the second on an error. Jayson Werth drove in the tying run with a single. The bases were loaded with one out when Steve Finley hit a game-ending grand slam off Wayne Franklin.

The Dodgers played the Cardinals in the National League Division Series. Managed by Tony LaRussa, the Cards were 105–57 in 2004.

OCTOBER 5   The Dodgers open the Division Series with an 8–3 loss to the Cardinals at Busch Stadium. The Cards broke the game open with five runs in the third inning off Odalis Perez. There were five St. Louis home runs. Larry Walker hit two with Albert Pujols, Jim Edmonds and Mike Matheny accounting for the others. Los Angeles back-up catcher Tom Wilson homered in the ninth.

In 12 regular season at-bats, Wilson had only two hits, both singles. The home run came on his last plate appearance in a major league game.

OCTOBER 6   The Cardinals win game two by the same score as game one with an 8–3 decision in St. Louis. The Cards broke a 3–3 tie with three tallies in the fifth inning off Jeff Weaver. The three Dodger runs came on solo homers by Jayson Werth in the first inning and Shawn Green and Milton Bradley back-to-back in the fourth.

OCTOBER 9   The Dodgers win game three 4–0 over the Cardinals before 55,992 at Dodger
                   Stadium. Jose Lima pitched a complete game shutout, allowing five hits. Shawn
                   Green hit home runs in the fourth and sixth inning off Matt Morris.

                   *The win was the first by the Dodgers in the post-season since the 1988 World
                   Series.*

OCTOBER 10   The Cardinals win the Division Series three games to one by defeating the Dodgers
                   6–2 before 56,268 at Dodger Stadium. The Cards snapped a 2–2 tie with three
                   runs in the fourth inning against Wilson Alvarez. Jayson Werth homered in the
                   losing cause.

                   *The two teams shook hands on the field after the game, an unusual sight in
                   baseball. Many in the Los Angeles media criticized Jim Tracy for the sportsman
                   like gesture.*

DECEMBER 6   Five weeks after George Bush wins re-election as president by defeating John Kerry,
                   Steve Finley signs a contract as a free agent with the Angels.

DECEMBER 14   Jose Hernandez signs a contract as a free agent with the Indians.

DECEMBER 15   The Dodgers sign Jeff Kent, most recently with the Astros, as a free agent.

                   *Kent was 37 on Opening Day in 2005 but has proven to be well worth the
                   investment by putting up better batting numbers than any Dodger second
                   baseman since Jackie Robinson.*

DECEMBER 17   Adrian Beltre signs a contract as a free agent with the Mariners.

DECEMBER 21   The Dodgers sign Jose Valentin, most recently with the White Sox, as a free agent.

DECEMBER 23   The Dodgers sign J. D. Drew, most recently with the Braves, as a free agent.

DECEMBER 25   Jose Lima signs a contract as a free agent with the Royals.

2005

Season in a Sentence

Coming into the season with a rosy outlook following the division title of 2004, the Dodgers win 12 of their first 14 games but wind up losing 91 times leading to the firing of Paul DePodesta and Jim Tracy.

Finish • Won • Lost • Pct • GB

Fourth   71   91   .438   11.0
In the wild-card race, the Dodgers finished in 11th place, 18 games behind.

Manager

Jim Tracy

Stats

Stats	Dods	NL	Rank
Batting Avg:	.253	.262	15
On-Base Pct:	.326	.330	11
Slugging Pct:	.395	.414	14
Home Runs:	149		12
Stolen Bases:	58		15
ERA:	4.38	4.22	12
Fielding Avg:	.983	.983	10
Runs Scored:	685		12
Runs Allowed:	755		12

Starting Lineup

Jason Phillips, c
Hee Seop Choi, 1b
Jeff Kent, 2b
Oscar Robles, 3b-ss
Cesar Izturis, ss
Jayson Werth, lf-rf-cf
Milton Bradley, cf
J. D. Drew, rf-cf
Olmedo Saenz, 1b
Jason Repko, cf-rf
Ricky Ledee, lf
Antonio Perez, 3b-2b
Mike Edwards, 3b

Pitchers

Jeff Weaver, sp
Derek Lowe, sp
Brad Penny, sp
D. J. Houlton, sp
Odalis Perez, sp
Yhency Brazoban, rp
Duaner Sanchez, rp
Giovanni Carrara, rp
Steve Schmoll, rp
Kelly Wunsch, rp

Attendance

3,603,646 (first in NL)

Club Leaders

Batting Avg:	Jeff Kent	.289
On-Base Pct:	Jeff Kent	.377
Slugging Pct:	Jeff Kent	.512
Home Runs:	Jeff Kent	29
RBIs:	Jeff Kent	105
Runs:	Jeff Kent	100
Stolen Bases:	Jayson Werth	11
	Antonio Perez	11
Wins:	Jeff Weaver	14
Strikeouts:	Jeff Weaver	157
ERA:	Derek Lowe	3.61
Saves:	Yhency Brazoban	21

JANUARY 3   The Anaheim Angels change their name to the Los Angeles Angels of Anaheim in an effort to increase the club's "marketability through this metropolitan area and beyond."

The Dodgers were livid over the Angels using the name Los Angeles, but were powerless do to anything about it. For a time, Frank McCourt jokingly referred to his club as the "Los Angeles Dodgers of Los Angeles." The ballpark of the American League club was located 30 miles from downtown L.A. The Angels hadn't had a direct connection to Los Angeles since playing at Wrigley Field as an expansion team in 1961 and at Dodger Stadium from 1962 through 1965. The Angels moved to Anaheim in 1966.

JANUARY 11   The Dodgers sign Derek Lowe, most recently with the Red Sox, as a free agent, and trade Shawn Green to the Diamondbacks for Dioner Navarro, Danny Muegge, Beltran Perez and William Juarez.

JANUARY 25 Hideo Nomo signs a contract as a free agent with the Devil Rays.

JANUARY 31 The Dodgers sign Scott Erickson, most recently with the Rangers, as a free agent.

MARCH 20 The Dodgers trade Kazuhisa Ishii to the Mets for Jason Phillips.

APRIL 5 The Dodgers open the season with a 4–2 loss to the Giants in San Francisco. Leading off the first inning, Cesar Izturis hit the third pitch of the game off Jason Schmidt for a home run, but the Dodgers scored only once more. In his debut in a Los Angeles uniform, Derek Lowe was the starter and loser.

> *In 2005, Charley Steiner, Steve Lyons and Al Downing joined Vin Scully and Rick Monday in the Dodger broadcast booth. Jerry Reuss replaced Downing in 2006.*

APRIL 8 The Dodgers score four runs with two out in the ninth inning and defeat the Diamondbacks 8–7 in Phoenix. Ricky Ledee doubled in the first run and scored on a single by Cesar Izturis to make the score 7–6. Jose Valentin gave the Dodgers the lead with a two-run, pinch-hit home run. The Dodgers held a 4–1 advantage in the sixth inning before letting Arizona take a three-run lead heading into the ninth.

> *The homer was the first of only two that Valentin would hit in 147 at-bats with the Dodgers along with a .170 batting average. It was the first time he failed to reach double figures in home runs since 1993. The previous season Valentin belted 30 homers for the White Sox.*

APRIL 9 The Dodgers score four runs in the top of the 11th and withstand a two-run Diamondback rally in the bottom half to win 12–10 in Phoenix. Jeff Kent broke the 8–8 tie with a three-run double in the 11th.

> *In his first season with the Dodgers, Kent hit .289 with 29 homers and 105 RBIs.*

APRIL 12 In the first game of the season at Dodger Stadium, the Dodgers strike again with late-inning lightning to score four times with two out in the ninth inning to defeat the Giants 9–8 before a crowd of 55,892. Jeff Kent drove in the first run with a Bases loaded walk. Milton Bradley cleared the sacks with a three-run single.

APRIL 18 Switch-hitter Milton Bradley hits home runs from both sides of the plate during a 7–3 win over the Brewers in Milwaukee. Bradley hit a solo homer off lefty Chris Capuano in the third inning, and a three-run shot against Ricky Bottalico in the ninth.

APRIL 19 Trailing 6–0, the Dodgers score a run in the sixth inning, four in the seventh, one in the ninth and two in the 10th to defeat the Brewers 8–6 in Milwaukee. Cesar Izturis tied the score in the ninth with a two-out, RBI-single. Milton Bradley won the game with a two-run homer in the 10th. The Dodgers also tied a record by using four first basemen in the contest. In addition, the team set a record by utilizing first baseman from four different countries. Hee Seop Choi (South Korea) started, and was followed by Jason Grabowski (United States), Olemdo Saenz (Panama) and Norihiro Nakamura (Japan).

APRIL 20 The Dodgers win 3–1 over the Padres in 10 innings in San Diego.

The victory gave the Dodgers a 12–2 record, matching the 1940 and 1955 clubs for the best 14-game start in franchise history. The 1940 team finished 88–65 in second place. The 1955 club was 98–55 and won the first world championship in Dodger history. The 2005 team went 59–89 the rest of the way to wind up at 71–91. Injuries played a large role in the collapse with closer Eric Gagne comprising the biggest loss. Jeff Kent was the only player with at least 500 plate appearances. Despite the poor record, the Dodgers led the National League in attendance with a figure of 3,603,646. The team record up to the 2005 season was 3,608,881 in 1982.

APRIL 24   Four Dodger batters are hit by pitches from three Colorado hurlers during an 8–6 win over the Rockies in Denver. Jason Repko was struck twice and J. D. Drew and Jeff Kent once.

The Dodgers had a three-year run in which no one played more than 53 games in a season at third base. In 2005, Oscar Robles led the Dodgers in games played (40) and games started (33) at the position. Wilson Betimet led in games at third in 2006 with 49 and again in 2007 with 53. Altogether, the Dodgers used 18 players at third from 2005 through 2007.

APRIL 29   Hee Seop Choi hits a grand slam off Jason Jennings in the fifth inning of a 6–3 win over the Rockies at Dodger Stadium.

MAY 2   The Dodgers play the Washington Nationals for the first time, and lose 6–2 at Dodger Stadium.

MAY 6   The Dodgers score 10 runs in the first inning of a 13–6 win over the Reds in Cincinnati. The first eight Los Angeles batters reached base off Paul Wilson on two homers, two doubles, a single, two hit batsmen and a walk. Jeff Kent tied a team record with five runs batted in during the inning on a two-run homer and a two-run double. Brad Penny pitched seven shutout innings and allowed one hit. Reliever D. J. Houlton allowed all six Reds runs in the eighth.

MAY 8   Jason Phillips hits a grand slam off Eric Milton in the sixth inning of a 9–3 win over the Reds in Cincinnati.

MAY 12   The Dodgers play for the last time in the second of three St. Louis ballparks named Busch Stadium, and lose 10–3 to the Cardinals.

The second Busch Stadium was the home of the Cardinals from 1966 through 2005.

MAY 13   With the Dodgers trailing 4–3 in the eighth inning, Milton Bradley hits a grand slam off Chris Reitsma for a 7–4 win over the Braves at Dodger Stadium. Bradley also clubbed a solo shot off Horacio Ramirez in the fourth. The two homers were struck from opposite sides of the plate. It was the second time in less than a month that Bradley hit switch homers in the same game.

MAY 15   The Dodgers drop out of first place with a 5–2 loss to the Braves at Dodger Stadium.

MAY 17   The Dodgers clobber the Marlins 15–4 at Dodger Stadium.

MAY 20   Following the name change by the Angels (see January 3, 2005), the first Los Angeles vs. Los Angeles match-up takes place during the regular season. The Dodgers defeated the Angels 9–0 at Dodger Stadium.

MAY 27   Jeff Kent hits a grand slam off Shawn Estes in the third inning of a 7–4 win over the Diamondbacks in Phoenix.

MAY 28   The Dodgers lose an unusual 5–4 decision to the Diamondbacks in Phoenix. Facing Duaner Sanchez in the seventh inning with the Dodgers leading 4–2, Luis Terrero hit a bounder high over the head of Sanchez, who threw his glove at the ball, knocking it down. Sanchez picked up the ball and threw too late to retire Terrero at first, but baseball rules call for a player to be credited with a triple when a fielder throws his glove at a batted ball. Terrero scored from third on a grounder to cut the Dodgers lead to 4–3. Arizona pitcher Javier Vazquez followed with his first major league homer to tie the score 4–4. Vazquez was relieved before throwing another pitch. The Diamondbacks won the game with a run in the ninth on a bases-loaded walk to Kelly Stinnett by Giovanni Carrara.

          In 2008, Vasquez was in his 11th big league season and has yet to hit another home run.

JUNE 4   Back-to-back homers by J. D. Drew and Jeff Kent in the fourth inning account for the only runs of a 2–1 win over the Brewers at Dodger Stadium.

JUNE 6   The Dodgers play the Tigers at Dodger Stadium for the first time and win 5–3.

JUNE 7   In the first round of the amateur draft, the Dodgers select pitcher Luke Hochevar from the University of Tennessee. Hochevar didn't sign with the Dodgers. He was also drafted by the Dodgers out of high school in the 39th round in 2002, but elected to attend college instead of signing a professional contract. The Royals made Hochevar the first overall pick in the 2006 draft. He reached the majors in 2007. The first player drafted and signed by the Dodgers in 2005 to become a big leaguer was fifth-rounder Jon Meloan.

JUNE 10   The Dodgers play the Twins for the first time during the regular season, and win 6–5 at Dodger Stadium. The winning run scored on a walk-off homer by Hee Seop Choi on the first pitch of the ninth inning by Terry Mulholland.

JUNE 12   Hee Seop Choi hits three consecutive homers during a 4–3 win over the Twins at Dodger Stadium. All four Los Angeles runs scored on solo homer off Brad Radke. Choi homered in the first, fourth and sixth innings. J. D. Drew also homered in the fourth.

JUNE 14   The Dodgers play the Royals in Kansas City for the first time, and lose 3–2. Hee Seop Choi hit his seventh home run over a span of four games from June 10 through June 14.

JUNE 17   The Dodgers play the White Sox in Chicago during the regular season for the first time, and lose 6–0.

JULY 4   Oscar Robles collects five hits, including a double, in six at-bats during an 11-inning, 4–3 win over the Rockies in Denver.

JULY 8	Jeff Kent collects his 2,000th career hit during a 3–2 loss to the Astros in Houston.
JULY 16	The Dodgers score two runs with two out in the ninth inning to defeat the Giants 5–4 at Dodger Stadium. The runs were driven in on a double by Cesar Izturis and a single from Jason Phillips.
JULY 20	The Dodgers break a scoreless tie with nine runs in the fifth inning and defeat the Phillies 10–2 in Philadelphia.
JULY 21	The Dodgers edge the Phillies 1–0 in Philadelphia. The lone run scored in the first inning on doubles by Oscar Robles and Jeff Kent. Odalis Perez (seven innings), Steve Schmoll (one-third of an inning), Wilson Alvarez (two-thirds of an inning) and Yhency Brazoban (one inning) combined on the shutout.
JULY 25	Derek Lowe allows only one hit in eight innings in beating the Reds 4–0 at Dodger Stadium. The only Cincinnati hit was a single by Rich Aurilia.
AUGUST 2	The Dodgers play the Nationals in Washington for the first time and win 5–4 at RFK Stadium. It was the first time the Dodgers played in Washington during the regular season since 1899.
AUGUST 5	Olmedo Saenz drives in six runs during a 12–6 win over the Pirates in Pittsburgh. He hit a three-run homer in the fourth inning, an RBI-single in the seventh, and a two-run double in the ninth.
AUGUST 9	The Dodgers purchase Jose Cruz, Jr. from the Red Sox.
AUGUST 12	Dioner Navarro hits a walk-off homer in the 10th inning to beat the Mets 7–6 at Dodger Stadium. It was his first major league homer.
AUGUST 14	Despite being out-hit 10–2, the Dodgers defeat the Mets 2–1 at Dodger Stadium. Pedro Martinez held the Dodgers hitless until there were one out in the eighth inning. Antonio Perez broke up the no-hit bid with a triple and Jayson Werth followed with a home run.
AUGUST 16	The Dodgers score three runs in the ninth inning to win 6–4 over the Diamondbacks in Phoenix. Olmedo Saenz put the Dodgers into the lead with a two-run pinch-hit single.
AUGUST 20	Jeff Kent confronts Milton Bradley about Bradley's lack of hustle during an 11–6 win over the Marlins in Miami. A yelling match ensued with Bradley throwing a chair. Three days later, Bradley accused Kent of not knowing "how to deal with African-American people."
AUGUST 28	A single by Oscar Robles in the eighth inning drives in the only run of a 1–0 win over the Astros at Dodger Stadium. Jeff Weaver (eight innings) and Duaner Sanchez (one inning) combined on the shutout.
AUGUST 31	Two days after Hurricane Katrina strikes the Gulf Coast causing widespread devastation, including the flooding of New Orleans, Derek Lowe pitches a one-hitter to defeat the Cubs 9–0 at Wrigley Field. A single by Jerry Hairston, Jr. leading off the first inning was the only Chicago hit. Lowe walked two and struck out seven.

SEPTEMBER 4   Jeff Kent hits a grand slam off David Cortes in the seventh inning, but the Dodgers lose 7–6 in 10 innings to the Rockies in Denver.

SEPTEMBER 6   A two-run, walk-off homer by Jeff Kent in the 10th inning beats the Giants 4–2 at Dodger Stadium.

SEPTEMBER 7   A three-run rally in the ninth inning defeats the Giants 9–8 at Dodger Stadium. Oscar Robles tied the score with a two-out, two-run homer. Mike Edwards drove in the winner with a walk-of single.

OCTOBER 3   A day after the Dodgers end the season with a record of 71–91, Jim Tracy resigns as manager after five years on the job. He had one year remaining on his contract. Tracy managed the Pirates in 2006 and 2007 to a record of 133–189.

OCTOBER 29   Paul DePodesto is fired as general manager less than two years into a five-year contract. Owner Frank McCourt cited the team's lack of success for the move.

NOVEMBER 15   The Dodgers hire 50-year-old Ned Colletti as general manager. He had been the assistant general manager with the Giants for the previous nine seasons. Kim Ng, the Dodger assistant general manager, was among those seriously considered for the position. She would have been the first female general manager in baseball history.

DECEMBER 6   The Dodgers hire Grady Little as manager. Little had previously been manager of the Red Sox for two seasons and had records of 93–59 in 2002 and 95–67 in 2003. He was fired amid accusations that he left Pedro Martinez in game seven of the 2003 ALCS against the Yankees too long, resulting in a loss. Little also managed the Dodgers two years and was 88–74 in 2006 and 82–80 in 2007.

DECEMBER 13   The Dodgers sign Sandy Alomar Jr., most recently with the Rangers, as a free agent, and trade Milton Bradley and Antonio Perez to the Athletics for Andre Ethier.

DECEMBER 15   The Dodgers sign Bill Mueller, most recently with the Red Sox, as a free agent.

Mueller signed a two-year deal and was expected to take over as the starting third baseman, but retired with a knee injury after playing only 30 games with the Dodgers.

DECEMBER 19   The Dodgers sign Rafael Furcal, most recently with the Braves, and Nomar Garciaparra, most recently with the Cubs, as free agents.

DECEMBER 20   The Dodgers sign Kenny Lofton, most recently with the Phillies, as a free agent.

The signings of Alomar, Mueller, Garciaparra and Lofton were designed to give the Dodgers a veteran presence until youngsters such as Russell Martin, Chad Billingsley, James Loney, Andy LaRoche, Matt Kemp, Andre Ethier and Blake DeWitt were ready for the majors. Furcal, only 28 in 2006, was obtained as a long-term solution at the shortstop position. With a roster consisting mostly of players well past 30, plus Furcal and Brad Penny in their prime, and rookies like Martin and Ethier, the Dodgers made the post-season in 2006 as a wild card.

2006

L A

Season in a Sentence

After a massive turnover of the roster following the debacle of 2005, the Dodgers win the wild card before being swept by the Mets in the playoffs.

Finish • Won • Lost • Pct • GB

First (tie)   88   74   .543   0.0
The Padres were declared the division champion and the Dodgers the wild card because the Padres won the season series between the two clubs 13–5. The Dodgers won the wild-card race by three games.

National League Division Series

The Dodgers lost to the New York Mets three games to none.

Manager

Grady Little

Stats

Stats	Dods	NL	Rank
Batting Avg:	.276	.265	1
On-Base Pct:	.348	.334	1
Slugging Pct:	.432	.427	6
Home Runs:	153		16
Stolen Bases:	128		2
ERA:	4.23	4.49	4
Fielding Avg:	.982	.983	13
Runs Scored:	820		4
Runs Allowed:	686		4

Starting Lineup

Russell Martin, c
Nomar Garciaparra, 1b
Jeff Kent, 2b
Wilson Betimet, 3b
Rafael Furcal, ss
Andre Ethier, lf
Kenny Lofton, cf
J. D. Drew, rf
Jose Cruz, Jr., lf-rf
Olmedo Saenz, 1b-3b

Pitchers

Derek Lowe, sp
Brad Penny, sp
Aaron Sele, sp
Chad Billingsley, sp
Takashi Saito, rp
Jonathan Broxton, rp
Joe Beimel, rp
Danys Baez, rp
Brett Tomko, rp-sp

Attendance

3,758,545 (first in NL)

Club Leaders

Batting Avg:	Nomar Garciaparra	.303
On-Base Pct:	J. D. Drew	.393
Slugging Pct:	Nomar Garciaparra	.505
Home Runs:	Nomar Garciaparra	20
	J. D. Drew	20
RBIs:	J. D. Drew	100
Runs:	Rafael Furcal	113
Stolen Bases:	Rafael Furcal	37
Wins:	Derek Lowe	16
	Brad Penny	16
Strikeouts:	Brad Penny	148
ERA:	Derek Lowe	3.63
Saves:	Takashi Saito	24

JANUARY 3   The Dodgers sign Brett Tomko, most recently with the Giants, as a free agent.

FEBRUARY 7   The Dodgers sign Takashi Saito as a free agent.

Saito was 36 when signed after playing 14 seasons with the Yokohama BayStars in the Japanese Central League. He started the 2006 season in the minors, but was called up after Eric Gagne went down with an elbow injury. Saito soon became the closer, and had 24 saves, a 2.07 ERA and 107 strikeouts in 78$^1/_3$ innings.

FEBRUARY 15   Jeff Weaver signs a contract as a free agent with the Angels.

APRIL 3   The Dodgers open the season with an 11–10 loss to the Braves before 56,000 at Dodger Stadium. Los Angeles trailed 11–5 before scoring three times in the eighth inning and twice in the ninth. Derek Lowe was the starter and loser. Jose Cruz, Jr. collected four hits, including a double, and scored three runs. Rafael Furcal, in his Dodger debut, had three hits and three runs. Jeff Kent drove in four.

In his first season with the Dodgers, Furcal hit an even .300 with 15 homers.

APRIL 11   Bill Mueller collects four hits, two of them home runs, in four at-bats, but the Dodgers lose 7–6 to the Pirates in Pittsburgh.

The Dodgers were first in the National League in batting average (.276) and on-base percentage (.348), but last in home runs (153) in 2006. The trend continued in 2007 when the club was third in batting average (.275), but last in homers (129).

APRIL 13   Right fielder Cody Ross puts together an unexpected batting display by driving in seven runs during a 13–5 win over the Pirates in Pittsburgh. Ross hit a grand slam off Oliver Perez in the fifth inning and a three-run shot off Damaso Marte in the sixth.

Ross entered the game with one career home run, which was struck while playing with the Tigers in 2003. That one was also a grand slam. The seven RBIs he collected on April 13, 2006, represented 70 percent of his total while playing for the Dodgers. He played in 22 games with the club over two seasons and had 10 runs batted in 39 at-bats. The two home runs on April 13 were his only two in a Los Angeles uniform. The game was also his only start with the Dodgers in 2006. He was playing to give J. D. Drew a day off. Ross made four starts as a Dodger in 2005. He was traded to the Reds eleven days after his seven-RBI outburst on April 24. After two games in Cincinnati, Ross was dealt to the Marlins on May 26. He had another seven-RBI game with Florida in September, and finished the year with a total of 46 runs batted in.

APRIL 18   J. D. Drew drives in both runs of a 2–1 win over the Cubs at Dodger Stadium. Drew drove in a run with a double in the fifth and had a walk-off single in the ninth.

The Dodgers drew a club record 3,758,545 fans in 2006, breaking the previous mark of 3,608,881 set in 1982. The attendance mark would last only one year. The Dodgers attracted 3,857,036 in 2007.

APRIL 24   The Dodgers score five runs in the ninth inning and beat the Astros 6–2 in Houston. The first four runs of the inning scored on a grand slam by Nomar Garciaparra off Brad Lidge.

APRIL 28   Jae Seo (six innings), Tim Hamulack (one inning), Takashi Saito (one inning) and Danys Baez (one inning) combine on a two-hitter to beat the Padres 3–0 at Petco Park. The only San Diego hits were a single by Adrian Gonzalez and a double by Khalil Greene, both in the second inning.

APRIL 30   The Dodgers blow a five-run lead against the Padres in San Diego by allowing five runs in the ninth inning and one in the 10th to lose 6–5. The advantage was blown by relievers Lance Carter, Danys Baez and Tim Hamulack.

The Dodgers were a streaky team all year under Grady Little. The club was 12–17 on May 4, and after reeling off 18 wins in 23 games, soared to 30–22 on May 30. From July 13 through July 26, the Dodgers lost 13 of 14, to drop to 47–55, 7¹/₂ games out of first place. The team reversed course with 17 victories in 18 games, including an 11-game winning streak, from July 28 through August 15 to take first place with a 3¹/₂-game lead. The Dodgers dropped in and out of first place throughout September, and put on a rush at the end of the season, winning nine of their last 10 to make the playoffs. Altogether, the Dodgers were 41–19 over the last 60 games.

MAY 5   Nomar Garciaparra hits a walk-off single in the ninth inning to beat the Brewers 4–3 at Dodger Stadium.

MAY 6   Nomar Garciaparra delivers a walk-off single in the ninth inning for the second day in a row to defeat the Brewers 5–4 at Dodger Stadium.

Garciaparra was 32 at the start of the 2006 season. A five-time All-Star and two-time batting champion as a shortstop with the Red Sox, Garciaparra became the Dodgers starting first baseman in 2006. He had never played the position previously and responded with a .303 batting average and 20 homers in 122 games. Nomar moved to third base during the second half of the 2007 season to make room for James Loney. Garciaparra married Mia Hamm, a World Cup soccer champion, in 2003. Both are Olympians. Garciaparra played on the U.S. baseball team in 1992 and Hamm was in the Olympics in 1996, 2000 and 2004.

MAY 19   The Dodgers collect 25 hits and rout the Angels 16–3 at Dodger Stadium. The Dodgers scored nine of their runs in the sixth inning. Andre Ethier contributed five hits, including a home run, in five at-bats. Nine different players had at least two hits.

MAY 22   For the first time in major league history, two Korean-born pitchers face each other. Joe Seo and the Dodgers defeated Byung-Hyun Kim and the Rockies 6–1 at Dodger Stadium.

JUNE 1   Matt Kemp homers in the second at-bat of his second big league start to help the Dodgers beat the Phillies 7–2 at Dodger Stadium.

Kemp hit seven homers in his first 15 games in the majors, but hit no more for the Dodgers in 2006. He was optioned back to Class AAA Las Vegas on July 14 and returned on September 1.

JUNE 3   Brad Penny (six innings), Tim Hamulack (1²/₃ innings) and Jonathan Broxton (1¹/₃ innings) combine on a two-hitter to defeat the Phillies 8–2 at Dodger Stadium. The only Philadelphia hits were doubles by Aaron Rowand in the fourth inning and Bobby Abreu in the eighth.

It was an odd year in the National League in which six pitchers tied for the lead in wins with 16. Two were Dodgers. Derek Lowe had a record of 16–8 and Brad Penny was 16–9. It was the first time since 1988 that the club had two pitchers with at least 16 wins in a season.

JUNE 6   On 6/6/06, Eric Gagne and Russell Martin form the first French-Canadian battery in major league history during an 8–5 win over the Mets at Dodger Stadium. Gagne was born in Montreal and Martin in East York, Ontario. Martin lived in Paris, France, between the ages of eight and ten.

The amateur draft took place on the same day. With three picks in the first round, the Dodgers selected pitcher Clayton Kershaw from Highland Park High School in Highland Park, Texas, pitcher Avery Morris from Motlow Community College in Tennessee, and Preston Mattingly from Evansville Central High School in Evansville, Indiana. Preston is the son of former Yankee star Don Mattingly.

JUNE 11   The Dodgers score two runs in the ninth inning to defeat the Rockies 6–5 in Denver. Russell Martin drove in the first run with a double, and scored on a pinch-single from Sandy Alomar, Jr.

JUNE 17   The Dodgers lose 5–4 in 17 innings to the Athletics in Oakland. Rafael Furcal tied the score 4–4 with a two-out triple in the ninth. The winning run scored on a Bases loaded walk by Jae Seo to Bubba Crosby.

JUNE 26   The Dodgers play at the Metrodome for the first time, and lose 8–2 to the Twins.

JULY 3   Nomar Garciaparra ties a major league record when he is hit three times by pitches from three different pitchers during a 10–4 win over the Diamondbacks at Dodger Stadium. Garciaparra was nailed by Juan Cruz, Edgar Gonzalez and Randy Choate.

JULY 11   At PNC Park in Pittsburgh, Brad Penny is the NL starter in the All-Star Game and allows a run in two innings. The AL won 3–2 with two runs in the ninth.

JULY 13   Nomar Garciaparra extends his hitting streak to 22 games during a 14-inning, 3–2 loss to the Cardinals in St. Louis. It was the also the first time that the Dodgers played at the new Busch Stadium.

JULY 23   The Dodgers trade Sandy Alomar, Jr. to the White Sox for B. J. LaMura.

JULY 25   The Dodgers trade Odalis Perez, Blake Johnson, Julio Pimentel and cash to the Royals for Elmer Dessens.

JULY 28   J. D. Drew hits a grand slam off Roy Corcoran in the fourth inning of a 13–1 thrashing of the Nationals at Dodger Stadium.

JULY 31   The Dodgers trade Cesar Izturis to the Cubs for Greg Maddux.

Maddux had 327 career wins when acquired by the Dodgers. Over the remainder of the 2006 season, he was 6–3 with a 3.30 ERA.

AUGUST 3   In his debut with the Dodgers, Greg Maddux pitches six no-hit innings and is the winning pitcher in a 3–0 decision over the Reds in Cincinnati. He left the game following a 46-minute rain delay. Through the 2008 season, his 23rd in the majors, Maddux has never pitched a no-hitter. Joe Beimel, Jonathan Broxton and Takashi Saito pitched the last three innings of relief and allowed two hits.

AUGUST 8	The Dodgers extend their winning streak to 11 games with a 4–2 decision over the Rockies at Dodger Stadium.
AUGUST 13	Russell Martin hits a walk-off homer on the second pitch of the 10th inning for the only run of a 1–0 victory over the Giants at Dodger Stadium. Greg Maddux (eight innings), Brett Tomko (one inning) and Takashi Saito (one inning) combined on the shutout. Maddux retired the last 22 batters to face him.
AUGUST 15	The Dodgers take a 3½-game lead in the NL West race with a 4–0 triumph over the Marlins at Dodger Stadium. It was the club's 17th win in the last 18 games.
AUGUST 19	The Dodgers score seven runs in the second inning for a 10–0 lead and defeat the Giants 14–7 in San Francisco. Greg Maddux retired the first 10 batters to face him. Combined with his previous start against the Giants on August 13, Maddux retired 32 batters in a row.
AUGUST 29	A walk-off homer by Ramon Martinez in the 16th inning beats the Reds 6–5 at Dodger Stadium. He entered the game as a pinch-hitter in the 11th and remained in the lineup at third base. Tim Hamulack (two innings), Takashi Saito (one inning), Joe Beimel (two innings), Elmer Dessens (two innings) and Derek Lowe (three innings) combined to shut out the Reds over the last 10 innings. It was Lowe's first regular season relief appearance since 2001. *Martinez hit only two home runs in 305 at-bats over two seasons with the Dodgers.*
AUGUST 31	The Dodgers trade Jhonny Nunez to the Nationals for Marlon Anderson. *Little was expected of Anderson. The Dodgers were his sixth team in five years, but Anderson was invaluable in September with 24 hits, seven of them home runs, in 64 at-bats for a batting average of .375.*
SEPTEMBER 2	Nomar Garciaparra drives in six runs during a 14–5 rout of the Rockies at Dodger Stadium. He hit a three-run homer in the third inning and a three-run double in the sixth. *The win gave the Dodgers a record of 73–62 and a four-game lead in the NL West.*
SEPTEMBER 8	Taiwan native Hong-Chih Kuo makes his first major league start on Taiwanese Heritage Night at Shea Stadium, and pitched six scoreless innings for a 5–0 win over the Mets and his first big league victory.
SEPTEMBER 15	Greg Maddux (seven innings), Jonathan Broxton (one inning) and Takashi Saito (one inning) combine on a two-hitter to defeat the Padres 3–1 at Dodger Stadium. Maddux had a no-hitter in progress until Brian Giles singled in the seventh. The other San Diego hit was a single by Geoff Blum off Broxton in the eighth.
SEPTEMBER 18	In one of the most thrilling victories in club history, the Dodgers use five homers, including four in a row, in the ninth and 10th innings to beat the Padres 11–10 at Dodger Stadium. The incredible comeback also put the Dodgers into first place one-half game ahead of the Padres. San Diego scored three runs in the top of the ninth for

a 9–5 lead, causing a mass exodus from the ballpark. Jon Adkins was the Padre hurler at the start of the Dodger half of the ninth. Jeff Kent led off, and hit the second pitch for a home run over the center field wall. Four pitches later, J. D. Drew clubbed a homer three-quarters of the way up the left field bleachers. Trevor Hoffman relieved Adkins. On Hoffman's first pitch Russell Martin, hit a third straight home run, this one clearing the left field barrier. On Hoffman's second pitch, Marlon Anderson delivered the Dodgers fourth straight home run to tie the score 9–9. The next three batters were retired, but Rafael Furcal narrowly missed a fifth home run on a fly ball to the wall for the final out. During the inning, a massive traffic tie-up was created in the parking lot as fans listening on the radio tried to return to the stadium. It appeared as though the rally would go for naught, however, when the Padres scored in the top of the 10th for a 10–9 lead. But the Dodger heroics weren't over. Rudy Seanez relieved Hoffman, and issued a walk to Kenny Lofton and a two-run homer to Nomar Garciaparra for the 11–10 victory.

The Dodgers are one of five major league teams to hit four consecutive home runs. The others are the 1961 Braves, 1963 Indians, 1964 Twins and 2007 Red Sox. J. D. Drew also participated in the four-home run onslaught by the Sox.

SEPTEMBER 19   The Dodgers drop back out of first place with a 10–6 loss to the Pirates at Dodger Stadium.

SEPTEMBER 23   Brad Penny strikes out four batters during the second inning to tie a major league record, but also gives up three runs contributing to a 9–3 loss to the Diamondbacks at Dodger Stadium. Chad Tracy reached on first base on a passed ball after swinging at a third strike and later scored. Penny tied the major league record for strikeouts in an inning by also fanning Stephen Drew, Miguel Batista and Eric Byrnes.

SEPTEMBER 24   A walk-off grand slam by Nomar Garciaparra off Luis Vizcaino with two out in the ninth inning beats the Diamondbacks 5–1 at Dodger Stadium.

With six games to go, the Dodgers were 1½ games behind the Padres in the NL West, and a half-game behind the Phillies in the wild-card chase.

SEPTEMBER 26   The Dodgers take a one-game lead in the wild-card race with an 11–4 win over the Rockies in Denver.

SEPTEMBER 28   Rookie first baseman James Loney drives in nine runs during a 19–11 victory over the Rockies in Denver. The outburst tied the club record for RBIs in a game set by Gil Hodges on August 31, 1950. Loney hit a grand slam of Byung-Hyun Kim in the second inning, a two-run double in the third, an RBI-single in the fifth and a two-run double in the sixth. The Dodgers broke a 10–10 tie with seven runs in the sixth inning.

Loney was in the lineup in place of the injured Nomar Garciaparra. Loney entered the game with one career home run and only eight runs batted in 93 at-bats.

SEPTEMBER 29   The Dodgers score two runs in the ninth inning to beat the Giants 4–3 in San Francisco. The win gave Los Angeles a two-game lead in the wild-card race with two games left on the schedule and put the club into a tie with the Padres for first place in the NL West.

SEPTEMBER 30   The Dodgers clinch at least a wild-card berth in the playoffs and remain tied for first place in the NL West race with a 4–2 victory over the Giants in San Francisco.

> *After clinching a spot in the playoffs, Grady Little had to make a difficult decision as to the starting pitcher in the final game of the season. To win the division title, and home field advantage in the playoffs, the Dodgers needed a victory and a Padres loss. If the two clubs were tied for first at the end of the regular season, San Diego would be the division champion based on a better record in head-to-head games against the Dodgers (13–5). Little elected to save his best pitchers for the playoffs. The starting pitcher for the final game was rookie Eric Stults, who had made only one previous big league start.*

OCTOBER 1   The Dodgers close out the regular season with a 4–3 win over the Giants in San Francisco. The Padres also won to wrap-up the division title.

> *The Dodgers played the New York Mets in the National League Division Series. Managed by Willie Randolph, the Mets were 97–65 in 2006 to post the best record in the National League.*

OCTOBER 3   On the eve of the playoffs, Joe Beimel cuts his hand severely on a broken glass in a New York bar at 2:30 a.m., rendering him unavailable to pitch against the Mets.

OCTOBER 4   The Dodgers open the National League Division Series with a 6–5 loss to the Mets at Shea Stadium. A potential rally was wiped out in the second inning on some miserable base running in which two Dodgers were tagged out at the plate on one play. Jeff Kent was on second base and J. D. Drew on first when Russell Martin lashed a drive into right field. Shawn Green played the ball off the wall and relayed to second baseman Jose Valentin, who threw home to catcher Paul LoDuca. Kent got a terrible read on the ball, started late, and was tagged out at the plate. Drew, running right behind Kent, was also tagged out. To add to the bizarre nature of the play, Green, Valentin and LoDuca all played for the Dodgers in 2004. Derek Lowe was the starting pitcher and exited in the sixth with the Dodgers trailing 4–1. Three Los Angeles runs in the seventh tied the score. Brad Penny relieved in the bottom of the seventh and surrendered two runs to put the Dodgers behind 6–4. The Dodgers scored a run in the ninth to pull within a run on doubles by Wilson Betemit and Ramon Martinez.

OCTOBER 5   The Mets win game two 4–1 over the Dodgers in New York. Grady Little made a controversial selection of a starting pitcher, electing to go with lefty Hong-Chih Kuo, a native of Taiwan, over right-hander Greg Maddux. Maddux had a lifetime record of 333–203, while Kuo, with only five big league starts, was 1–6. But Little believed that a left-hander was a better choice against the Met lineup, and Kuo pitched six shutout innings against the New Yorkers on September 8 for his only big league victory. Kuo allowed two runs in $4^2/3$ innings in the game two defeat.

OCTOBER 7   The Mets complete the sweep of the Dodgers with a 9–5 win before 56,293 at Dodger Stadium. Greg Maddux was the starting and losing pitcher. Jeff Kent collected four hits, including a homer and a double, in five at-bats. James Loney had three hits and three runs batted in.

DECEMBER 5   J. D. Drew signs a contract as a free agent with the Red Sox.

DECEMBER 6   The Dodgers sign Mike Lieberthal, most recently with the Phillies, as a free agent.

DECEMBER 8   The Dodgers sign Luis Gonzalez, most recently with the Diamondbacks, and Jason Schmidt, most recently with the Giants, as free agents.

DECEMBER 12   Eric Gagne and Kenny Lofton both sign contracts as a free agents with the Rangers.

DECEMBER 13   Greg Maddux signs a contract as a free agent with the Padres.

DECEMBER 19   Jayson Werth signs a contract with the Phillies as a free agent.

2 0 0 7

Season in a Sentence

A disappointing season ends with 11 losses in the last 14 games, clubhouse dissension, the resignation of Grady Little, and the hiring of Joe Torre.

Finish • Won • Lost • Pct • GB

Fourth   82   80   .506   8.0
In the wild-card race, the Dodgers finished in sixth place, 7½ games behind.

Manager

Grady Little

Stats

Stats	Dods	NL	Rank
Batting Avg:	.275	.266	3
On-Base Pct:	.337	.334	6
Slugging Pct:	.406	.423	14
Home Runs:	129		16
Stolen Bases:	137		3
ERA:	4.20	4.43	4
Fielding Avg:	.981	.983	13
Runs Scored:	735		10
Runs Allowed:	727		4

Starting Lineup

Russell Martin, c
James Loney, 1b
Jeff Kent, 2b
Nomar Garciaparra, 3b-1b
Rafael Furcal, ss
Luis Gonzalez, lf
Juan Pierre, cf
Andre Ethier, rf-lf
Matt Kemp, rf

Pitchers

Brad Penny, sp
Derek Lowe, sp
Randy Wolf, sp
Takashi Saito, rp
Joe Beimel, rp
Jonathan Broxton, rp
Rudy Seanez, rp
Chad Billingsley, rp-sp
Brett Tomko, rp-sp
Mark Hendrickson, rp-sp

Attendance

3,857,036 (first in NL)

Club Leaders

Batting Avg:	Russell Martin	.293
	Juan Pierre	.293
On-Base Pct:	Jeff Kent	.375
Slugging Pct:	Jeff Kent	.500
Home Runs:	Jeff Kent	20
RBIs:	Russell Martin	87
Runs:	Juan Pierre	96
Stolen Bases:	Juan Pierre	64
Wins:	Brad Penny	16
Strikeouts:	Derek Lowe	147
ERA:	Brad Penny	3.03
Saves:	Takashi Saito	39

APRIL 2   The Dodgers lose the season opener 7–1 to the Brewers in Milwaukee. Derek Lowe was the starting and losing pitcher. Jeff Kent homered in the second inning for the lone Los Angeles run.

Kent finished the season with a .302 batting average and 20 home runs.

APRIL 8   Luis Gonzalez hits his first two home runs as a member of the Dodgers during a 10–4 win over the Giants in San Francisco.

APRIL 9   In the home opener, the Dodgers lose 6–3 to the Rockies before 56,000 at Dodger Stadium. Jason Schmidt hit a home run, but allowed four runs in four innings.

APRIL 11   Brad Penny (6⅓ innings), Jonathan Broxton (1⅔ innings) and Takashi Saito (one inning) combine on a two-hitter to defeat the Rockies 3–0 at Dodger Stadium. The only Colorado hits were singles by Chris Iannetta in the second inning and Garrett Adkins in the third.

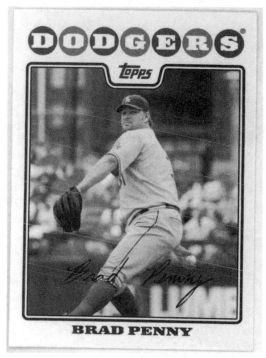

Brad Penny came to Los Angeles in an unpopular trade in 2004, but he has proven to be an excellent addition, winning 16 games in 2006 and 2007.

APRIL 15   On the 60th anniversary of his first game in the majors, Jackie Robinson is honored in ceremonies prior to a 9–3 win over the Padres at Dodger Stadium. Robinson's widow Rachel was in attendance. Both Hank Aaron and Frank Robinson threw out ceremonial first pitches. Each of the Dodgers in uniform wore number 42.

APRIL 21   Five days after 32 die in a shooting on the campus of Virginia Tech University, a walk-off grand slam by Russell Martin off Shawn Chacon in the 10th inning beats the Pirates 7–3 at Dodger Stadium. The Dodgers scored a run in the ninth to tie the contest.

APRIL 27   Trailing 4–2, the Dodgers score four runs in the ninth inning and beat the Padres 6–5 at San Diego. The runs in the ninth scored on a pair of two-run doubles by Nomar Garciaparra and Russell Martin.

Martin batted .293 with 19 home runs in 2007.

APRIL 29   The Dodgers win 5–4 in a 17-inning marathon over the Padres in San Diego. Brady Clark drove in the winning run with a two-out double. Relievers Joe Beimel (one inning), Jonathan Broxton (1⅔ innings), Chin-hui Tsao (two innings), Rudy Seanez (two innings), Takashi Saito (two innings) and Chad Billingsley (two innings) combined to allow no runs and only one hit over the last 10⅔ innings.

The uniform number 97 worn by Joe Beimel is the highest ever issued by the Dodgers.

MAY 7   Brad Penny strikes out 14 batters without issuing a walk in seven innings of pitching during a 6–1 triumph over the Marlins in Miami.

MAY 10   A three-run, walk-off homer by Josh Willingham off Derek Lowe in the ninth inning accounts for the only runs of a 3–0 loss to the Marlins in Miami.

MAY 11   A two-run single by Russell Martin in the first inning accounts for the only runs of a 2–0 win over the Reds at Dodger Stadium. Randy Wolf (seven innings), Jonathan Broxton (one inning) and Takashi Saito (one inning) combined on the shutout. Nomar Garciaparra become the first Dodger first baseman in club history to go through a game of nine innings or more without a fielding chance.

Beimel and Broxton both pitched in 83 games for the Dodgers in 2008.

MAY 13   Rafael Furcal collects four hits, including two doubles, in four at-bats during a 10–5 win over the Reds at Dodger Stadium. He also stole two bases.

MAY 14   For the second game in a row, Rafael Furcal has four hits, but the Dodgers lose 8–4 to the Cardinals at Dodger Stadium. All four hits were singles over five at-bats

MAY 15   Rafael Furcal has his third four-hit game in a row with three singles and a triple in five at-bats during a 9–7 victory over the Cardinals at Dodger Stadium.

Over five games from May 12 through May 16, Furcal had 14 hits in a stretch of 16 at-bats. The 14 hits included three doubles and a triple.

MAY 16   The Dodgers take a three-game lead in the NL West race with a record of 25–16 after beating the Cardinals 5–4 at Dodger Stadium.

MAY 27   Juan Pierre is hit by a pitch from Carlos Marmol with the bases loaded in the 11th to force in the winning run of a 2–1 decision over the Cubs at Dodger Stadium.

MAY 29   Juan Pierre collects four extra base hits with three doubles and a triple during a 10–0 rout of the Nationals in Washington.

JUNE 7   The Padres score five runs off Jonathan Broxton in the ninth inning to stun the Dodgers 6–5 in San Diego. The winning run scored on a bases loaded walk to Russell Branyan.

JUNE 8   After the Padres score in the top of the 10th inning, Olmedo Saenz hits a two-run, pinch-hit, walk-off homer in the bottom half for a 4–3 Dodger victory at Dodger Stadium.

JUNE 12   The seven, eight and nine hitters in the Dodger lineup hit consecutive homers on three straight pitches from John Maine in the second inning of a 4–1 win over the Mets at Dodger Stadium. The back-to-back-to-back homers were hit by Wilson Betimet, Matt Kemp and pitcher Hong-Chih Kuo. The homer by Kuo was the first ever in the majors by a player born in Taiwan.

JUNE 26   A pinch-hit homer by Tony Abreu in the 10th inning beats the Diamondbacks 6–5 in Phoenix. It was the first home run of his career.

Abreu was angry when the Dodgers tried to send him to the minors a few weeks later. He claimed he had an abdominal strain and should be placed on the

disabled list. General manager Ned Colletti publicly questioned the veracity of the injury. Off-season surgery confirmed that Abreu had suffered a sports hernia.

JULY 6   The Dodgers sign Roberto Hernandez, most recently with the Indians, as a free agent.

JULY 10   In the All-Star Game at AT&T Park in San Francisco, Brad Penny sets down the AL in order in the second inning and Takashi Saito does the same in the seventh, but the NL loses 5–4.

JULY 17   The Phillies clobber five Dodger pitchers for 26 hits in a 15–3 win at Dodger Stadium.

JULY 26   Brad Penny runs his record to 13–1 with a 5–4 decision over the Rockies in Denver.

Penny finished the season with a 16–4 record and an ERA of 3.03.

JULY 31   The Dodgers drop out of first place with a 3–1 loss to the Giants at Dodger Stadium.

AUGUST 9   A home run by Rafael Furcal in the 11th inning beats the Reds 5–4 in Cincinnati. The Dodgers were shut out in each of the three previous games.

AUGUST 22   The Dodgers trounce the Phillies 15–3 in Philadelphia.

AUGUST 24   The Dodgers sign David Wells following his release by the Padres.

At the age of 44, Wells was 4–1 with a 5.12 ERA with the Dodgers in 2007, the last of his 21 seasons in the majors.

AUGUST 27   The Dodgers purchase Esteban Loaiza from the Athletics.

AUGUST 29   After trailing 8–3 in the sixth inning, the Dodgers rally to win 10–9 in 12 innings against the Nationals at Dodger Stadium. The winning run scored on a sacrifice fly by Shea Hillenbrand.

SEPTEMBER 6   The Dodgers score four runs in the ninth inning, the first three on a home run by Andre Ethier, to beat the Cubs 7–4 in Chicago.

SEPTEMBER 12   James Loney hits his fifth home run in a span of six games during a 6–1 win over the Padres at Dodger Stadium.

SEPTEMBER 15   Rafael Furcal steals four bases during a 6–2 win over the Diamondbacks at Dodger Stadium.

The win put the Dodgers 3½ games back of Arizona in the NL West and 1½ games behind San Diego in the wild-card chase. The Dodgers lost 11 of their last 14 games, however, to wreck any chance for a post-season berth.

OCTOBER 30   Grady Little resigns as manager of the Dodgers.

Little resigned amid rumors that Joe Torre was about to be hired as manager of the club. Two weeks earlier, Torre declined an offer to manage the Yankees in 2008 at a reduced salary. Little had a year remaining on his contract and called his departure a "mutual resignation." Later, he said it was his choice to leave for "personal reasons." Dodger general manager Ned Coletti insisted he wanted Little to return in 2008. Little had come under fire after the Dodgers dropped 11 of their last 14 games in 2007 to fade out of contention and finish the season at 82–80. Clubhouse acrimony had surfaced between veterans and young players during the last two weeks. Jeff Kent publicly questioned the professionalism of some of the team's younger players. James Loney and Matt Kemp shot back with verbal volleys at Kent.

NOVEMBER 5   The Dodgers formally introduce 67-year-old Joe Torre as manager at a press conference.

Torre signed a three-year contract. He managed the Yankees to 12 post-season berths in 12 seasons, including World Series appearances in 1996, 1998, 1999, 2000 and 2001, and world championships in 1996, 1998, 1999 and 2000. Torre played in the majors as a catcher, third baseman and first baseman from 1960 through 1977 with the Braves, Cardinals and Mets. He was named to nine All-Star teams and won the MVP award in St. Louis in 1971. Before joining the Yankees, Torre managed the Mets (1977–81), Braves (1982–84) and Cardinals (1991–95). None of the clubs on which he played or managed had ever reached the World Series until he managed the Yankees to the world championship in his first season at the helm in 1996.

DECEMBER 3   Walter O'Malley, majority owner of the Dodgers from 1950 until his death in 1979, is elected to the Hall of Fame in Cooperstown.

DECEMBER 12   The Dodgers sign Andruw Jones, most recently with the Braves, as a free agent.

2008

Season in a Sentence

After falling five games below .500 in late August, the Dodgers put together a streak of 18 wins in 23 games to win the NL West and reach the Championship Series for the first time since 1988.

Finish • Won • Lost • Pct • GB

First   84   78   .519   2.0

National League Division Series

The Dodgers defeated the Chicago Cubs three games to none.

National League Championship Series

The Dodgers lost to the Philadelphia Phillies four games to one.

Manager

Joe Torre

Stats

Stats	Dods	NL	Rank
Batting Avg:	.264	.260	5
On-Base Pct:	.333	.331	6
Slugging Pct:	.399	.413	13
Home Runs:	137		13
Stolen Bases:	126		4
ERA:	3.68	4.30	1
Fielding Avg:	.984	.983	8
Runs Scored:	700		13
Runs Allowed:	648		1

Starting Lineup

Russell Martin, c
James Loney, 1b
Jeff Kent, 2b
Blake DeWitt, 3b
Angel Berroa, ss
Juan Pierre, lf
Matt Kemp, cf-rf
Andre Ethier, rf
Casey Blake, 3b
Manny Ramirez, lf
Rafael Furcal, ss

Pitchers

Chad Billingsley, sp
Derek Lowe, sp
Hiroki Kuroda, sp
Clayton Kershaw, sp
Brad Penny, sp
Takashi Saito, rp
Jonathan Broxton, rp
Joe Beimel, rp
Cory Wade, rp
Chan Ho Park, rp
Hong Chih-Kuo, rp

Attendance

3,730,553 (second in NL)

Club Leaders

Batting Avg:	Andre Ethier	.305
On-Base Pct:	Russell Martin	.385
Slugging Pct:	Andre Ethier	.510
Home Runs:	Andre Ethier	20
RBIs:	James Loney	90
Runs:	Matt Kemp	93
Stolen Bases:	Juan Pierre	40
Wins:	Chad Billingsley	16
Strikeouts:	Chad Billingsley	201
ERA:	Chad Billingsley	3.14
Saves:	Takashi Saito	18

JANUARY 1   The Dodgers place a float in the Tournament of Roses Parade for the first time. It was done in honor of the 50th anniversary of the move to Los Angeles. The float featured a 35-foot tall Dodger player and was adorned with peanuts and popcorn. Among those riding the float were Tommy Lasorda, Vin Scully, Carl Erskine, Don Newcombe, Wes Parker, Steve Garvey, Nomar Garciaparra, James Loney, Fernando Valenzuela and stadium vendor Roger Owens. Nancy Bea Hefley, the Dodger Stadium organist, played "Take Me Out to the Ballgame" and other familiar tunes.

JANUARY 20   The Dodgers sign Chan Ho Park, most recently with the Mets, as a free agent.

MARCH 15   The Dodgers participate in the first game ever played in China and tie the Padres
                3–3 before 12,224 at Wukesong Stadium in Beijing. The facility was also the venue
                for baseball games during the 2008 Olympics the following August. The two clubs
                played again the following day, with the Dodgers winning 6–3.

                *Because of a recent security crackdown by the Chinese government due to an
                outbreak of violence in Tibet, all pregame activities were canceled, including live
                performances of the Chinese and American national anthems. Former Dodger
                Jim Lefebvre was head of the Chinese national team during the Olympic Games.*

MARCH 17   The Dodgers play their last game at Vero Beach, the club's spring training home
                since 1948, and lose 12–10 to the Astros before a sellout crowd of 7,327 at Holman
                Field. Tommy Lasorda, at the age of 80, managed the team in the absence of Joe
                Torre, who was on his way back from China. Lasorda's first appearance in Vero
                Beach was as a 20-year-old pitcher in 1948.

                *Carl Erskine, who played for the Dodgers from 1948 through 1959, played the
                National Anthem on his harmonica before the game. Erskine was the pitcher
                during the Dodgers' first game at Holman Stadium in 1953. The Dodgers moved
                to Glendale, Arizona, in 2009 to be closer to Los Angeles.*

MARCH 28   The Red Sox defeat the Dodgers 7–4 before 115,300 in an exhibition game at
                Memorial Coliseum. It was the first time the Dodgers played at the facility since
                1961 and was part of the celebration of the club's 50th anniversary in Los Angeles.
                The crowd was the largest in major league history, surpassing the 93,103 for Roy
                Campanella Night at Memorial Coliseum on May 7, 1959.

                *The Dodgers originally placed 90,000 seats on sale at a price ranging from $10
                to $25, with the proceeds going to cancer research. The game sold out in a few
                hours, prompting the club to put 25,000 standing-room tickets on sale. When
                the club played at Memorial Coliseum from 1958 through 1961, the left-field
                foul line was only 251 feet long, topped by a 40-foot fence. After 1961, rows
                of seats 50 feet deep were added at field level. As a result, the configuration for
                the 2008 exhibition was even stranger with a 201-foot left-field foul line and
                a 60-foot fence. The Dodgers played the game with a five-man infield and
                two-man outfield. Andruw Jones was positioned behind second base.
                Kevin Youkilis of Boston was the only player to clear the left-field
                fence with a home run.*

MARCH 31   Joe Torre wins his first game as Dodger manager with a 5–0 decision over the
                Dodgers before 56,000 at Dodger Stadium. Brad Penny (6²/₃ innings), Scott Proctor
                (one-third of an inning), Joe Beimel (one inning) and Takashi Saito (one inning)
                combined on the shutout. Jeff Kent hit a two-run homer.

                *In celebration of the 50th anniversary of the Dodgers' move from Brooklyn
                to Los Angeles, Duke Snider, Carl Erskine, Don Newcombe, Sandy Koufax,
                Maury Wills, Steve Garvey, Bill Russell, Ron Cey, Fernando Valenzuela and
                Tom Lasorda were among those introduced to the crowd. Most wore the
                uniforms of their era.*

APRIL 1   Third base coach Larry Bowa is suspended for three days by the commissioner's office because of "inappropriate and aggressive conduct" following his ejection during a 3–2 win over the Giants at Dodgers Stadium. Umpire Ed Montague tossed Bowa for his failing to stay within the boundaries of the coaching box, a rule new to baseball in 2008.

APRIL 24   Chad Billingsley strikes out 12 batters in six innings, but the Dodgers lose 6–4 to the Diamondbacks at Dodger Stadium.

On the same day, the Dodgers unveiled a four-year upgrade plan for Dodger Stadium. Frank McCourt said the renovations amounted to a new home for the team built around the nearly 50-year-old core of the old. The total cost was estimated at $500 million and is expected to be completed by Opening Day in 2012, the 50th anniversary of the opening of Dodger Stadium. The plan includes a three-lined entrance to a landscaped grand plaza beyond center field that will connect a promenade of restaurants, shops and a Dodger museum. Acres of parking around the stadium will be turned into a perimeter walkway, which the team is calling a "green necklace," allowing fans to move outdoors around the ballpark while inside the gates. One plaza will have views encompassing downtown, the Pacific Ocean and the mountains. "We're creating a new stadium without tearing down the old," said McCourt in a statement. "That may take more effort and more resources, but we're talking about Dodger Stadium."

APRIL 25   Russell Martin caps a four-for-four day with a walk-off sacrifice fly in the 13th inning to defeat the Rockies 8–7. Martin also played a position other than catcher for the first time in his career. In the ninth inning after Nomar Garciaparra strained his abdomen, Martin moved to third with Gary Bennett installed as the catcher. On the next pitch, Bennett committed a passed ball which scored a run, tying the score at 7–7 and forced extra innings.

APRIL 26   The Dodgers score 10 runs in the first inning and defeat the Rockies 11–3 at Dodger Stadium. Shawn Kemp hit a sacrifice fly during his first at-bat in the inning, then hit a grand slam to cap the rally. Colorado starter Mark Redman gave up all 10 runs in the first, then remained on the mound and pitched five scoreless innings before being relieved.

There was a near tragedy when umpire Kerwin Danley, a Los Angeles native, was struck in the head by a 96-mile-per-hour pitch from Brad Penny. Danley lay motionless on the field for several minutes before being transported by ambulance through a gate in the center-field fence. The contest was delayed for 18 minutes. Danley was released from the hospital a few days later.

APRIL 30   Rafael Furcal collects five hits, including a double, in six at-bats during a 13–1 thrashing of the Marlins in Miami.

MAY 2   Trailing 3–0, the Dodgers score seven runs in the sixth inning and beat the Rockies 11–6 in Denver. Rafael Furcal struck a three-run homer during the rally.

MAY 3   James Loney drives in six runs during a 12–7 win over the Rockies in Denver. Loney hit a three-run double in the first inning and a three-run homer in the fifth.

MAY 11   Hiroki Kuroda allows only one hit, a run-scoring single by Hunter Pence with two
            out in the seventh inning, while pitching 6²/₃ innings, but the Dodgers lose 8–5 to
            the Astros at Dodger Stadium. With the Dodgers leading 2–1, Kuroda was relieved
            before Houston erupted with six runs in the eighth.

            *Mired in a deep slump after signing a $36-million contract over two years,
            Andruw Jones was booed during the game when he appeared on the big screen
            in left field to wish everyone a happy Mother's Day. Jones had a season so awful
            it defied belief. He batted .158 with three home runs and 76 strikeouts in 209
            at-bats over 73 games.*

JUNE 1   The Dodgers play at Shea Stadium for the last time and lose 6–1 to the Mets.

JUNE 3   A fight erupts during a 3–0 loss to the Rockies at Dodger Stadium. In the eighth
            inning Matt Kemp swung and missed a third strike, but Colorado catcher Yorvit
            Torrealba dropped the ball. Kemp headed for first base and became tangled with
            Torrealba, who tagged Kemp in the neck with the ball. Torrealba took Kemp down,
            and the two grappled in the dirt before being separated.

            Kemp was suspended for four days as a result of the incident.

JUNE 5   In the first round of the amateur draft, the Dodgers select pitcher-third baseman
            Ethan Martin from Stephens County High School in Georgia.

JUNE 6   Hiroki Kuroda pitches a complete game shutout and strikes out 11 without a walk to
            beat the Cubs 3–0 at Dodger Stadium.

            *Kuroda was a 33-year-old rookie in 2008. He pitched 11 seasons for the
            Hiroshima Toyo Carp in Japan.*

JUNE 20   The Dodgers play the Indians at Dodger Stadium for the first time, and lose 6–4 in
            10 innings.

            *On the same day, the Dodgers received a star on the Hollywood Walk of Fame.
            Frank McCourt accepted the honor. Tommy Lasorda, Joe Torre, Vin Scully and
            Jaime Jarrin also participated in the ceremony.*

JUNE 29   The Dodgers win 1–0 over the Angels at Dodger Stadium without collecting a hit off
            Jered Weaver (six innings) and Jose Arredondo (two innings). The Dodgers scored
            the lone run of the game in the fifth. Matt Kemp reached base when Weaver couldn't
            handle a twisting roller between the mound and the first base line. At first, it was
            ruled a hit, then changed to an error. On a stolen base attempt, Kemp moved from
            first to third when the throw from catcher Jeff Mathis sailed into center field. Kemp
            scored on a sacrifice fly by Blake DeWitt. Weaver was lifted for a pinch-hitter in the
            seventh. Chad Billingsley (seven innings), Jonathan Broxton (one inning) and Takashi
            Saito (one inning) combined on the five-hit shutout.

            *The Dodgers were the fifth team in major league history to win a game without
            a base hit. The others were the 1964 Reds against Houston (with Ken Johnson
            pitching), the 1967 Tigers playing the Orioles (with Steve Barber and Stu Miller
            combining on the no-hitter), the 1990 White Sox versus the Yankees and*

Andy Hawkins, and the 1992 Indians facing the Red Sox and Matt Young. The Reds and Tigers were the only two of the five to bat nine times. The White Sox, Indians and Dodgers batted eight times as the winning team at home.

JULY 1   Jeff Kent homers in the 11th inning to defeat the Astros 7–6 in Houston.

JULY 7   Hiroki Kuroda narrowly misses a perfect game by allowing only one base runner during a 3–0 win over the Braves at Dodger Stadium. Kuroda retired the first 21 batters to face him before Mark Texeira led off the eighth inning with a double. Kuroda then retired the last six hitters to seal the victory.

JULY 12   Andruw Jones strikes out five times in five plate appearances during an 11-inning, 5–3 loss to the Marlins at Dodger Stadium.

JULY 13   Chad Billingsley strikes out 13 batters in seven innings without walking a batter during a 9–1 win over the Marlins in Miami. The Dodgers scored six runs in the first inning.

              Billingsley headed a pitching staff which led the National League in earned run average. He was 16–10 with a 3.14 ERA and 201 strikeouts in 200²/₃ innings.

JULY 18   James Loney's home run in the 11th inning beats the Diamondbacks 8–7 in Phoenix.

JULY 20   Trailing 4–1, the Dodgers score five times in the ninth inning and defeat the Diamondbacks 6–5 in Phoenix. Five different players drove in the five runs, four of them after two were out. The runs batted in were collected by Andruw Jones (on a ground out), Adam LaRoche (single), Matt Kemp (double), Andre Ethier (triple) and Russell Martin (single).

JULY 21   The Dodgers score eight runs in the first inning and beat the Rockies 16–10 in Denver. The Dodgers built a 16–3 lead after five innings without hitting a home run.

JULY 26   Derek Lowe pitches eight innings and allows only one hit during a 6–0 triumph over the Nationals at Dodger Stadium. The only hit off Lowe was a single by Ron Belliard in the fourth inning. On the same day, the Dodgers traded Carlos Santana and Jonathan Meloan to the Indians for Casey Blake.

              From July 26 through July 30, the Dodgers shut out the opposition four times in five games. In addition to the 6–0 victory on July 26, the club won 2–0 over Washington on July 27, 2–0 against the Giants at Dodger Stadium on July 29 and 4–0 versus San Francisco in Los Angeles on July 30.

JULY 31   As part of a three-team deal, the Dodgers send Andy LaRoche and Bryan Morris to the Pirates and receive Manny Ramirez from the Red Sox.

              Ramirez was unhappy in Boston and demanded a trade. At the time of the transaction, he was 36 years old and had 510 career homers along with a .312 batting average. It's doubtful that the Dodgers could have reached the postseason without Ramirez. In 53 games and 187 regular-season at-bats, he hit .396 with an on-base percentage of .489 and a slugging percentage of .743. Manny belted 17 homers and drove in 53 runs. In eight postseason games, he batted .520 (13-for-25) with four homers, 10 RBIs and 11 walks.

AUGUST 1 — Manny Ramirez plays in his first game with the Dodgers and collects two singles in four at-bats during a 2–1 loss to the Diamondbacks at Dodger Stadium. The club sold 11,000 tickets for the game in the 24 hours between the time the trade was announced and the first pitch. Ramirez received a tremendous ovation just for grounding out in his first at-bat. The crowd of 55,239 was the fifth largest of the regular season, topped only by Opening Day and three September games against the Giants.

Ramirez wore number 24 throughout his major league career with the Indians and Red Sox, but that number was retired by the Dodgers in honor of Walter Alston. Ramirez was assigned number 99.

AUGUST 12 — Andre Ethier hits a walk-off single in the ninth inning to defeat the Phillies 4–3 at Dodger Stadium.

Ethier hit .378 with nine homers and 31 RBIs in 164 at-bats from August 5 through the end of the season.

AUGUST 13 — A walk-off homer by Nomar Garciaparra in the ninth inning beats the Phillies 7–6 at Dodger Stadium. A two-run double by Jeff Kent in the eighth tied the game 6–6.

AUGUST 14 — Hiroki Kuroda (seven innings) and Hong-Chih Kuo (two innings) combine on a two-hitter to defeat the Phillies 2–1 at Dodger Stadium. The only Philadelphia hits were doubles by Chase Utley in the fourth inning and Jayson Werth in the seventh.

AUGUST 17 — Andre Ethier hits a two-run walk-off homer in the ninth inning to beat the Brewers 7–5 at Dodger Stadium. It was Ethier's second home run of the game.

The win put the Dodgers into a tie for first place, a record of 64–60, but the club lost 10 of their next 11 games to fall 4½ games behind Arizona. The Dodgers rebounded, however, to win 18 of 23 games from August 30 through September 24 to clinch the NL West title.

AUGUST 19 — The Dodgers send two players to be named later to the Padres for Greg Maddux. Maddux previously pitched 12 games for the Dodgers in 2006 in another transaction designed to bolster the pitching staff for a run at a postseason berth.

AUGUST 25 — The Dodgers collect 13 hits and draw three walks from three Philadelphia pitchers, but lose 5–0 to the Phillies at Citizens Bank Park. The Dodgers left 14 runners on base.

AUGUST 26 — The Dodgers play for the first time at Nationals Park in Washington, and lose 2–1 to the Nationals.

SEPTEMBER 1 — Greg Maddux wins his 354th career game to tie Roger Clemens for eighth place all-time with a 5–2 decision over the Padres at Dodger Stadium.

SEPTEMBER 5 — Andre Ethier collects five hits, including a homer and two doubles, and drives in five runs in five at-bats during a 7–0 triumph over the Diamondbacks at Dodger Stadium. Derek Lowe (eight innings) and Chan Ho Park (one inning) combined on a two-hitter. The only Arizona hits were singles by Conor Jackson in the fourth inning and Chris Young in the fifth.

SEPTEMBER 6   The Dodgers take over first place with their seventh win in a row, defeating the Diamondbacks 7–2 at Dodger Stadium.

SEPTEMBER 7   The Dodgers extend their winning streak to eight games and close out a three-game sweep of the Diamondbacks with a 5–3 decision at Dodger Stadium.

SEPTEMBER 13   With their 12th win in a span of 13 games, the Dodgers take a 4½-game lead in the NL West by defeating the Rockies 5–1 in Denver.

SEPTEMBER 20   Manny Ramirez drives in five runs on two homers and a single during a 10–7 win over the Giants at Dodger Stadium.

SEPTEMBER 24   The Dodgers clinch a tie for the division title with a 12–4 victory over the Padres at Dodger Stadium.

SEPTEMBER 25   The Dodgers clinch the NL West championship during the afternoon when the Diamondbacks lose 12–4 to the Cardinals in St. Louis. In the evening, the Dodgers celebrated the title after a 7–5 loss to the Padres at Dodger Stadium.

SEPTEMBER 27   Greg Maddux wins his 355th career game to pass Roger Clemens into eighth place all-time. Among pitchers since 1920, Maddux ranks second behind Warren Spahn's 363.

The Dodgers met the Chicago Cubs in the National League Division Series. Managed by Lou Piniella, the Cubs were 97–64 to post the best record in the NL in 2008.

OCTOBER 1   The Dodgers open the Division Series with a 7–2 win over the Cubs at Wrigley Field. The Cubs took a 2–0 lead in the second inning on a two-run homer by Mark DeRosa off Derek Lowe. Los Angeles responded with four in the fifth on a grand slam by James Loney off Ryan Dempster. Later, Manny Ramirez and Russell Martin added solo homers.

OCTOBER 2   The Dodgers score five runs in the second inning, the last three on a bases-loaded double by Russell Martin and beat the Cubs 10–3 in game two of the Division Series in Chicago. Rafael Furcal collected three hits and Manny Ramirez hit a two-run homer. The Cubs helped the Dodgers by making four errors, one from each of the infielders.

OCTOBER 4   The Dodgers complete a sweep of the Cubs in the Division Series with a 3–1 victory before 56,000 at Dodgers Stadium. James Loney drove in two runs with a double in the first inning. Starting pitcher Hiroki Kuroda contributed 6⅓ innings of shutout baseball.

The triumph over the Cubs was the Dodgers' first in a postseason series since the 1988 World Series. The opponent in the National League Championship Series was the Philadelphia Phillies. Managed by Charlie Manuel, the Phillies were 92–70 in 2008 and won the NL East. The Phils beat the Brewers in four games in the Division Series.

OCTOBER 9   The Phillies defeat the Dodgers 3–2 at Citizens Bank Park in the first game of the Championship Series. Derek Lowe took a 2–0 lead into the sixth inning before allowing a two-run homer to Chase Utley and a solo shot to Pat Burrell.

OCTOBER 10   The Dodgers drop game two against the Phillies in Philadelphia by an 8–5 score. The Phils took an 8–2 lead after three innings. Manny Ramirez belted a three-run homer in the fifth, but the Dodgers could pull no closer. Phillies pitcher Brett Myers, an .069 hitter in 58 at-bats during the regular season, went 3-for-3. The game was played just hours after the death of the mother of Philadelphia manager Charlie Manuel.

OCTOBER 12   The Dodgers score five runs in the first inning and beat the Phillies 7–2 before 56,000 at Dodger Stadium. The big hits were a bases-loaded triple by Blake DeWitt in the first and a home run from Rafael Furcal in the second. Hiroki Kuroda went six innings for the win. After a series of brushback pitches in game two and early in game three, benches cleared in the third when Kuroda fired the ball over the head of Shane Victorino. Words were exchanged, mostly notably between Manny Ramirez and an unidentified Phillie and between coaches Mariano Duncan of the Dodgers and Davey Lopes of the Phillies, but no punches were thrown.

OCTOBER 13   The Dodgers are one game from elimination after losing 7–5 to the Phillies before 56,000 at Dodger Stadium. Casey Blake broke a 3–3 tie with a homer in the sixth, and the Dodgers added another run before the inning was over. But Philadelphia scored four times in the eighth on a pair of two-run homers by Shane Victorino and Matt Stairs.

OCTOBER 15   The Dodgers are eliminated from the playoffs with a 5–1 defeat at the hands of the Phillies before 56,000 at Dodger Stadium. Jimmy Rollins led off the first inning with a homer off Chad Billingsley. Shortstop Rafael Furcal made three errors, two of them on one play in the fifth inning. First, he booted a grounder and made a wild throw on a ball hit by Pat Burrell. Three batters later, Furcal made another errant throw. Manny Ramirez accounted for the only Los Angeles run with a homer in the sixth.

LA By the Numbers

Dodgers All-Time Batting Leaders 1884–2008

Batting Average

(minimum 2,000 plate appearances)

1	Willie Keeler	.352
2	Babe Herman	.339
3	Jack Fournier	.337
4	Mike Piazza	.331
5	Zack Wheat	.317
6	Manny Mota	.315
7	Fielder Jones	.313
8	Gary Sheffield	.312
9	Jackie Robinson	.311
10	Dixie Walker	.311
11	Pedro Guerrero	.309
12	Johnny Frederick	.308
13	Pete Reiser	.306
14	Mike Griffin	.305
15	Del Bissonette	.305
16	Jake Daubert	.305
17	Tommy Davis	.304
18	Steve Garvey	.301
19	Augie Galan	.301
20	Duke Snider	.300

Home Runs

1	Duke Snider	389
2	Gil Hodges	361
3	Eric Karros	270
4	Roy Campanella	242
5	Ron Cey	228
6	Steve Garvey	211
7	Carl Furillo	192
8	Mike Piazza	177
9	Pedro Guerrero	171
10	Raul Mondesi	163
11	Shawn Green	162
12	Willie Davis	154
13	Adrian Beltre	147
14	Dusty Baker	144
15	Dolph Camilli	139
16	Jackie Robinson	137
	Mike Marshall	137
18	Zack Wheat	131
19	Gary Sheffield	129
20	Pee Wee Reese	126

Runs Batted In

1	Duke Snider	1,271
2	Gil Hodges	1,254
3	Zack Wheat	1,210
4	Carl Furillo	1,058
5	Steve Garvey	992
6	Eric Karros	976
7	Pee Wee Reese	895
8	Roy Campanella	856
9	Willie Davis	849
10	Ron Cey	842
11	Jackie Robinson	734
12	Dixie Walker	725
13	Bill Russell	627
14	Tom Daly	614
15	Oyster Burns	606
16	Babe Herman	594
17	Dusty Baker	586
18	Pedro Guerrero	585
19	Dolph Camilli	572
20	Mike Piazza	563

Runs

1	Pee Wee Reese	1,338
2	Zack Wheat	1,255
3	Duke Snider	1,199
4	Jim Gilliam	1,163
5	Gil Hodges	1,088
6	Willie Davis	1,004
7	Jackie Robinson	947
8	Carl Furillo	895
9	Mike Griffin	881
10	Maury Wills	876
11	Steve Garvey	852
12	Bill Russell	796
13	Tom Daly	787
14	George Pinckney	761
15	Davey Lopes	759
16	Eric Karros	752
17	Jimmy Johnston	727
18	Ron Cey	715
19	Dixie Walker	666
20	Jake Daubert	648

Hits

1	Zack Wheat	2,804
2	Pee Wee Reese	2,170
3	Willie Davis	2,091
4	Duke Snider	1,995
5	Steve Garvey	1,968
6	Bill Russell	1,926
7	Carl Furillo	1,910
8	Jim Gilliam	1,889
9	Gil Hodges	1,884
10	Maury Wills	1,732
11	Eric Karros	1,608
12	Jackie Robinson	1,518
13	Jimmy Johnston	1,440
14	Dixie Walker	1,395
15	Jake Daubert	1,387
16	Ron Cey	1,378
17	Hi Myers	1,253
18	Steve Sax	1,218
19	Davey Lopes	1,204
20	Tom Daly	1,181

Doubles

1	Zack Wheat	464
2	Duke Snider	343
3	Steve Garvey	333
4	Pee Wee Reese	330
5	Carl Furillo	324
6	Willie Davis	321
7	Jim Gilliam	304
8	Eric Karros	302
9	Gil Hodges	294
10	Bill Russell	293
11	Dixie Walker	274
12	Jackie Robinson	273
13	Babe Herman	232
14	Ron Cey	223
15	Mike Griffin	210
16	Johnny Frederick	200
17	Mike Scioscia	198
18	Wes Parker	194
19	Tom Daly	190
	Raul Mondesi	190

Triples

1	Zack Wheat	171
2	Willie Davis	110
3	Hi Myers	91
4	Jake Daubert	87
5	Oyster Burns	85
6	John Hummel	82
	Duke Snider	82
8	Pee Wee Reese	80
9	Tom Daly	76
	Jimmy Sheckard	76
11	Jimmy Johnston	73
12	Jim Gilliam	71
13	Harry Lumley	66
	Babe Herman	66
15	Dave Foutz	65
16	Mike Griffin	64
17	John Anderson	57
	Bill Russell	57
19	Three tied at	56

Games

1	Zack Wheat	2,322
2	Bill Russell	2,181
3	Pee Wee Reese	2,166
4	Gil Hodges	2,006
5	Jim Gilliam	1,956
6	Willie Davis	1,952
7	Duke Snider	1,923
8	Carl Furillo	1,806
9	Steve Garvey	1,727
10	Eric Karros	1,601
11	Maury Wills	1,593
12	Ron Cey	1,481
13	Mike Scioscia	1,441
14	Jackie Robinson	1,382
15	Ron Fairly	1,306
16	John Roseboro1	1,289
17	Wes Parker	1,288
18	Jimmy Johnston	1,266
19	Steve Yeager	1,219
20	Roy Campanella	1,215

At-Bats

1	Zack Wheat	8,859
2	Pee Wee Reese	8,058
3	Willie Davis	7,495
4	Bill Russell	7,318
5	Jim Gilliam	7,119
6	Gil Hodges	6,881
7	Duke Snider	6,640
8	Steve Garvey	6,543
9	Carl Furillo	6,378
10	Maury Wills	6,156
11	Eric Karros	6,002
12	Ron Cey	5,216
13	Jackie Robinson	4,877
14	Jimmy Johnston	4,841
15	Davey Lopes	4,590
16	Jake Daubert	4,552
17	Dixie Walker	4,492
18	Hi Myers	4,448
19	Mike Scioscia	4,373
20	Steve Sax	4,212

Walks

1	Pee Wee Reese	1,210
2	Duke Snider	1,036
3	Gil Hodges	925
4	Duke Snider	893
5	Ron Cey	765
6	Jackie Robinson	740
7	Zack Wheat	632
8	Davey Lopes	603
9	Dolph Camilli	584
10	Mike Scioscia	567
11	Mike Griffin	544
12	Dixie Walker	539
13	Roy Campanella	533
14	Wes Parker	532
15	Tom Daly	526
16	Ron Fairly	522
17	Eric Karros	517
18	Carl Furillo	514
19	Bill Russell	483
20	Maury Wills	456

Stolen Bases

1	Maury Wills	490
2	Davey Lopes	418
3	Willie Davis	335
4	Tom Daly	298
5	Steve Sax	290
6	George Pinckney	280
7	Darby O'Brien	272
8	Mike Griffin	264
9	Dave Foutz	241
10	Pee Wee Reese	232
11	Jimmy Sheckard	212
12	Zack Wheat	203
	Jim Gilliam	203
14	Jackie Robinson	197
15	Hub Collins	195
16	Jake Daubert	187
17	Brett Butler	179
18	Oyster Burns	172
19	Bill Russell	167
20	George Cutshaw	166

Slugging Percentage

(minimum 2,000 plate appearances)

1	Gary Sheffield	.573
2	Mike Piazza	.572
3	Babe Herman	.557
4	Duke Snider	.553
5	Jack Fournier	.552
5	Reggie Smith	.528
6	Pedro Guerrero	.512
7	Shawn Green	.510
8	Raul Mondesi	.504
9	Roy Campanella	.500
10	Dolph Camilli	.497
11	Frank Howard	.495
12	Gil Hodges	.488
13	Del Bissonette	.486
14	Jeff Kent	.479
15	Johnny Frederick	.477
16	Jackie Robinson	.474
17	Adrian Beltre	.463
18	Pete Reiser	.460
19	Steve Garvey	.459
20	Carl Furillo	.458

DODGERS ALL-TIME PITCHING LEADERS 1884–2008

	Wins			Losses			Winning Percentage	
							(minimum 100 decisions)	
1	Don Sutton	233	1	Don Sutton	181	1	Preacher Roe	.715
2	Don Drysdale	209	2	Don Drysdale	166	2	Bob Caruthers	.683
3	Dazzy Vance	190	3	Brickyard Kennedy	149	3	Tommy John	.674
4	Brickyard Kennedy	177	4	Adonis Terry	139	4	Sandy Koufax	.655
5	Sandy Koufax	165	5	Nap Rucker	134	5	Don Newcombe	.651
6	Burleigh Grimes	158	6	Dazzy Vance	131	6	Kirby Higbe	.648
7	Claude Osteen	147	7	Claude Osteen	126	7	Whit Wyatt	.640
8	Fernando Valenzuela	141	8	Burleigh Grimes	121	8	Hugh Casey	.631
9	Johnny Podres	136	9	Fernando Valenzuela	116	9	Tom Lovett	.619
10	Orel Hershiser	135	10	Orel Hershiser	107	10	Ramon Martinez	.615
11	Nap Rucker	134	11	Johnny Podres	104	11	Carl Erskine	.610
12	Adonis Terry	127	12	Van Lingle Mungo	99	12	Dazzy Vance	.592
13	Don Newcombe	123	13	Harry McIntyre	98		Chan Ho Park	.592
	Ramon Martinez	123	14	Watty Clark	88	14	Jeff Pfeffer	.585
15	Carl Erskine	122	15	Sandy Koufax	87	15	Ralph Branca	.580
16	Bob Welch	115	16	Bob Welch	86		Doug Rau	.580
17	Jeff Pfeffer	113	17	Burt Hooton	84		Ed Stein	.580
18	Burt Hooton	112	18	Jeff Pfeffer	80	18	Clem Labine	.574
19	Bob Caruthers	110	19	George Bell	79	19	Bob Welch	.572
20	Watty Clark	106	20	Carl Erskine	78	20	Burt Hooton	.571

	ERA			Games			Games Started	
	(minimum 1,000 innings)		1	Don Sutton	550	1	Don Sutton	533
1	Jeff Pfeffer	2.31	2	Don Drysdale	518	2	Don Drysdale	465
2	Nap Rucker	2.42	3	Jim Brewer	474	3	Claude Osteen	335
3	Sandy Koufax	2.76	4	Ron Perranoski	457	4	Brickyard Kennedy	332
4	George Bell	2.85	5	Clem Labine	425	5	Dazzy Vance	326
5	Whit Wyatt	2.86	6	Charlie Hough	401	6	Fernando Valenzuela	320
6	Sherry Smith	2.91	7	Sandy Koufax	397	7	Sandy Koufax	314
7	Bob Caruthers	2.92	8	Brickyard Kennedy	381	8	Johnny Podres	310
8	Don Drysdale	2.95	9	Dazzy Vance	378	9	Orel Hershiser	309
9	Doc Scanlan	2.95	10	Johnny Podres	366	10	Burleigh Grimes	285
10	Tommy John	2.97	11	Orel Hershiser	353	11	Adonis Terry	276
11	Bill Singer	3.03	12	Claude Osteen	339	12	Nap Rucker	272
12	Claude Osteen	3.09	13	Nap Rucker	336	13	Bob Welch	267
13	Don Sutton	3.09	14	Carl Erskine	335	14	Burt Hooton	265
14	Harry McIntyre	3.11	15	Fernando Valenzuela	331	15	Ramon Martinez	262
	Leon Cadore	3.11	16	Watty Clark	322	16	Don Newcombe	230
	Jerry Reuss	3.11		Ed Roebuck	322	17	Carl Erskine	216
17	Orel Hershiser	3.12		Burt Hooton	322	18	Van Lingle Mungo	215
18	Burt Hooton	3.14	19	Burleigh Grimes	318	19	Jerry Reuss	201
19	Bob Welch	3.14	20	Tom Niedenfuer	310	20	Jeff Pfeffer	200
20	Dazzy Vance	3.17						